THE SEVEN NAMES OF LAMAŠTU

The Seven Names of

Lamaštu

A Journey through Mesopotamian Magick and Beyond

Jan Fries

Published by Avalonia
www.avaloniabooks.co.uk

Published by Avalonia

BM Avalonia, London, WC1N 3XX, England, UK

www.avaloniabooks.co.uk

THE SEVEN NAMES OF LAMAŠTU

First Published by Avalonia, March 2017

ISBN 978-1-910191-04-0

Typeset and designed by Satori

Cover image: Astrid Bauer (digital artwork) and Jan Fries

Illustrations by Jan Fries

British Library Cataloguing in Publication Data. A catalogue record for this book is available from the British Library.

In every generation of gods there is a Chosen One,
who is sent to earth by her relations to do the dirty work for them.
She alone will stand against the mad Asakku,
the paralysing Alû and the mindless greed of mankind.
She is the Slayer.

Dedication

This book is dedicated, with much love and admiration, to several brilliant artists. One way or another, all of you were and are an inspiration. In particular, I would like to thank Joss Whedon, Neil Gaiman, Chuck Lorre, Carrie Vaughn, Kumi Koda, the 12 Girls Group and Dengue Fever.

Please turn this book into a musical.

Abbreviations:

AfÖ: Archiv für Orientkunde

ANET: Pritchard, James (ed.): *Ancient Near Eastern Texts Relating to the Old Testament*, Princeton University Press, 1969

CDA: *Concise Dictionary of Akkadian* by Black, George and Postgate, Harrassowitz Verlag, Wiesbaden, 2000

EE: *Enûma Eliš, the Babylonian Epic of Creation*

LS: *Lamaštu Series*

RlA: *Reallexikon der Assyriologie*

SAHG: Falkenstein, A, & von Soden, W.: *Sumerische und akkadische Hymnen und Gebete*, Artemis Verlag, Zürich, 1953

SEAL: *Sources of Akkadian Literature* (online).

TUAT: *Texte aus der Umwelt des Alten Testaments*

Table of Contents

Part One: Child of Heaven

INTRODUCTION **15**

TIME AND SPACE **20**

Swampland Mysteries 20
Marvels of Irrigation 25
City People 30
Inventing Cuneiform 33
Early Sumerian Religion: Fertility Cults, Dying Gods, Sacred Marriage or What? 38
God Lists 52
Theodiversity 55
The Nature of the Gods 56
Religious specialists 59
A fast journey through Mesopotamian History 66
Prehistoric Period *66*
The Uruk Period *67*
The Early Dynastic Period *68*
The Akkadian Period *74*
Ur III *76*
The Isin-Larsa Period *77*
The Old Babylonian Period *78*
Occupation by Kassites and Hurrians *81*
The Second Dynasty of Isin and the Assyrian Revival *83*
Assyrian Supremacy *85*
Neo-Babylonian rule and its successors *89*

Part Two: Watchful One of the Gods of the Streets

THE LAMAŠTU SERIES **92**

This Compilation: Sources, Scholars and the Problem of Evil 97
Face Values and Hidden Meanings 108

FIRST PART OF THE LAMAŠTU SERIES **114**

SECOND PART OF THE LAMAŠTU SERIES **207**

THIRD PART OF THE LAMAŠTU SERIES **248**

Supplement to LS III, 105*:* 267

Part Three: Decapitator

LAMAŠTU: ORIGINS **270**

DIM.ME: What's in her name? 272
A cluster of Dimme's 273
Lamaštu: Iconography 275
Pigs and Dogs 277
Anu's Daughter 279
Lamaštu and Sorcery 279

Part Four: Fire-Starter

Diagnosis by Bubbles, Flames and Dreams 288
Medical Textbooks 290
Diagnosis and Treatment 293
Placebo Medicine 295
Meet the Conjurers 296
The Training of a Conjurer 298
Lamaštu Diseases 299
Heat and Shuddering: a Magical Interpretation 302
The Hands of the Gods 302
Inseminating Yourself 304
Waters from Eridu 308
Knot Magic 310
Maths, Star-Gazing, and Sacred Numerology 311
God Numbers 315
A Sacred Calendar 325
Sacred Music 327

Part Five: Wild Countenance

LAMAŠTU: DIASPORA 340

In the Wake of the Winds 340
Inventing a Goddess 343
The Making of a Myth 344
Appeal for Ištar 348
Goddesses, with and without Feathers. 350
In the Hands of Ereškigal 353
Close Cousins 359
Living in a Tree 360
Riders of the Gale 364
Lilû Diseases 369
Holidays in Edom 370
The Amulet of Arslan Tash 371
Lilith in *Talmud* and *Midrash* 375
Incantation Bowls from Nippur 375
Lilith Reloaded 384
Lilith the Seducer 387
Sisters of Lilith 389
Child Slayer 390
Family Affairs 391
Our Lady of Crisis 396
Names of Lilith 398
Ḳarīna 400
From Lamaštu to Lamia 402
Medusa 406
Tiger Goddesses of China 415
Albasti and Āl: Across Asia 420
Indian Mothers 425
The Lion-faced Goddess 434

PART SIX: THE TRUSTED

PART SEVEN: OATHBOUND, FREE TO FLY

Rites of Thanksgiving

Books are always a joint venture. Like it or not, there are few original thoughts on Planet Earth. We all carry our luggage with us. When we are lucky, the ideas in our heads come from many times and cultures, and permit creative insights that appear new. We can try to be original and arrive at something rather normal. Or we explore the normal and find it amazingly different to what we expected. All of this is only possible in an environment that encourages research, practical experience and years of whole-hearted creative passion.

In many ways, this book is more bibliographical than my other works. In the early eighties, I had my first spiritual break-through experiences with deities like Medusa, Kālī, Lilith and Xiwangmu. They made me embark on a quest that has been going on for ages, and will do so, life after life, whenever we meet again. My thanks go to them, first of all, for waking me up and keeping me awake. Much later, I realised which goddess inspired them. Here's to Lamaštu!

Where it comes to human beings, I wish to thank my parents for their patience and support. I know, they could have had an easier kid. My friends supported me in many ways, and ensured a healthy return into magickal normality when I was happily going over the top or suffered from fits of crisis and desperation. Magick is no easy way, and plenty of fireworks and upheavals are built in. That's why the dark gods, the frightening deities and the beings of chaos and madness are so important. Sanity can only be attained by those who face their demons and integrate them. But sanity is overestimated. The modern industrial world gets along without much need of it. So do the truly vibrant spiritual traditions, like Tantra and Daoism. When you wish to understand Lamaštu and her colourful relations, you only have to use it now and then. Learning to design your emotions is much better.

In writing this book, many people were supportive, or at least interested in what I was doing. I shared a deep interest in Mesopotamian magick with Julia and Volkert for more than 35 years. Thank you for listening, for agreeing and disagreeing, for your insights and enthusiastic support for many forest walks and rituals. Others who were caught up by the vortex contributed their share. I am deeply grateful to the late Kenneth Grant and to Maggie (Nema) of the Horus Maat Lodge. Astrid and Gavin were always fascinated by the strange material fermenting in my head, and supplied their share of encouragement, laughter and confusion. Astrid is the creator of the gorgeous picture which graces the cover of this book. It turned out much better than I had hoped. Look at the bright star in the centre, left of the Andromeda nebula. This is Lamaštu's star, Mirach, the *Devouring Snake/Dragon-Mouth*.

During the last years, I enjoyed meeting and corresponding with Asenath Mason. One of her favourites is the mysteries of Tiāmat, a topic which we discussed many times. We shared a Lilith ritual that remains a happy memory.

Magick appears wherever people are really good at something, no matter whether they are interested in science, occult studies or simply doing what is natural to them. While I wrote this book, I became increasingly obsessed by scholarly issues and found it hard to disentangle myself from the world of academic thought. It can be a great relief to be reminded of the wonders and joys of 'everyday' reality.

Over the years, friendship with Jing and Xinyue reminded me of the simple joys of life. I gave a book of cardboard animal masks to Xinyue (then almost four years old) and she decided to spend much of her time, at home and outside, wearing the mask of a lion. 'Look Mum', she went, 'see, it's only me. Don't be afraid'. And she continued romping all over the flat. That too is Lamaštu. One day she told me that she would grow up to be a magician, a princess, and Ponyo's mother (Guanyin). I am sure she will.

Over the years I had many discussions about Egyptian magic with Mogg Morgan. He is a brilliant enthusiast and has published much on that exciting topic. It made me realise how rarely Mesopotamian magick is appreciated. Thank you for reminding me!

Holger and Christiane, my German publishers, and their incomparable daughter Silvana showed much interest in this book. I am deeply thankful for your laughter, your simple, natural way of being, and of course for getting on with the job in a happy mood.

Luci, Axel and Victor invited me to Berlin. I felt right at home in your place, the greatest Halloween exhibition in history. Thank you for everything.

Sorita d'Este and Lokabandhu encouraged me to get my thoughts sorted out and to keep this book a small and simple introduction to a huge and multi-leveled subject. Your intelligent, gentle editing and your enthusiastic encouragement are true blessings.

Finally, I wish to thank my in-laws in Kurdistan who, back in the 1980's made me feel at home with them. Thanks to you I saw the Euphrates leisurely flowing through palm plantations and the Tigris thundering down mountain gorges, great cities like Diyarbakir and Malatya, the stony deserts where, ten thousand years ago, agriculture was invented, camels, blue roller birds, golden eagles and more stars than I had assumed possible.

I feel deeply grateful to the many dedicated scientists, linguists, historians, archaeologists and ethnologists whose research has made this book possible. Your work added life and truth to this venture. Thank you for your patient effort, thank you for many different interpretations, thank you for your courageous originality. Your work allowed me to write this book. I apologise for not always agreeing with your estimates. I am sure this book contains plenty of mistakes, but they are all mine.

Last, let me thank you.

Disclaimer: If life appears more difficult than it should, and especially while reading this book and exploring the rituals and meditations, be sure to carry a spindle, a comb, a bit of multicolour string, a piece of cloth, sandals that don't wear out in all eternity, travelling boots, perfumed oil, assorted jewellery, a pin to close the blouse, food, water and plenty of beer. Snakes, scorpions, wild asses, wild boar piglets and dog-, wolf- or hyena puppies will also be appreciated. Just in case you meet you-know-who and want to make her feel welcome.

This book is basically a bird's eye view of Mesopotamian magick and religion and some of the developments thereof. In case you wonder, the bird happens to be a vulture. Think of the happy bearded vulture, for instance, a carefree and optimistic character with a huge wing span and a long beak that comes to the point. Bearded vultures are patient. They rise on hot air currents and circle around until they see something that stopped moving a long time ago. Then they glide lower, come closer, and cautiously make a landing. The table is set. The yummy bits are long gone. Scavengers have had their fill, flies and maggots swarmed, and bacteria devoured the rest. Bare shiny bones remain. They are quite a treat. Unlike other animals, the bearded vulture can digest bones. It cracks them into a convenient size (18cm length is the maximum) and swallows them. Just imagine the gastric juices you need to dissolve bone! The bearded vulture, as you guessed, is the holy guardian mascot of everybody who explores the past for something crunchy, chewy and ultimately nourishing. It gains fresh energy, builds new cells and breeds baby vultures from things that are so dead no other animal will touch them. The past is its future, and good things go around. Now it's your turn. Join the feast. Welcome to prehistory.

Part One:
Child of Heaven

Figure 1 - Stalker of the Steppe

Introduction

The punctuation of time creates its own beginnings, usually, when something radically new is discovered. In southern Germany, in the Schwäbisch Alb, near Asselfingen, a cluster of caves was excavated. Imagine hillside country, where large pillars of pale chalky stone rise from thickly wooded slopes. Nearby, the Danube flows steadily. The Palaeolithic migrants went there from time to time. They did not live in the caves (so-called 'Cave Men' rarely inhabited caves, as they were usually following the migration of the animals) but they certainly used them as temporary campsites and for rituals.

Like so much stone-age magic, these rituals and sorceries are long forgotten. Nowadays, scholars are trying to interpret surviving evidence, and arriving at widely different conclusions. When we look into the studies that try to untangle these mysteries, we face, first of all, the dreams, hopes and prejudices of scholars. It's much easier to study the scholars than our Stone Age ancestors! But whatever it may have been, some people who came to the Schwäbisch Alb made little statuettes. The migrants usually made small objects. When you spent your life dragging a tent around, meaning a mammoth hide and mammoth tusks to set it up, and have to migrate across boggy ground to keep close to the herds of reindeer, wild horse and mammoth, you try to keep your luggage light. Remarkable tiny animal images appeared in the Vogelherd Höhle, and were, for a while, classed as the earliest pieces of human art. Most of them are damaged, but what remains of them is breathtakingly beautiful. The collection came in one package with a skull. Some experts assumed it may have been the artist, but recent studies indicate that the head is younger than the ivory animals. The statuettes and images made around 32,000 BCE are small. You see tiny mammoth, rhino, horse and the head of a cave lion/ess. Note that the dating is uncertain. C-14 tests get increasingly uncertain the older an item is, and the experts wouldn't dream of trusting them unless other evidence supports the date. Most remarkable is a figurine showing a **lion-human hybrid**. The figurine was discovered in the cave Hohlenstein-Stadel ('*Hollow-Stone-Barn*'). It's not much of a cave. The entrance is large and the cavity extends over maybe fifty metres. Maybe the statuette was made, deposited, lost or even buried there. It is two or three times bigger than the usual figurines of the period, or at least those we chance to know about. For whether we like it or not, we know hardly anything. The piece was carefully carved out of mammoth ivory and is, at almost 30cm height, much larger than the usual figurines. In all likeliness, the statuette is the earliest known piece of art showing a human-animal mixed creature. It could have portrayed a shaman or shamaness with an animal mask. Or it might represent an ancestor or a deity. Statuettes of what may or may not be deities have caused a lot of controversy. Everyone has seen the so-called Venus-statuettes, and many scholars have declared that Palaeolithic migrants happily worshipped fat, fertile women without faces. That, as it turned out, was far too simple. However, it said something about the scholars. Most so-called Venus statuettes came from a narrow time-range of the Gravettien between 25,000 and 21,000 BCE. That's much later than the period we are discussing. The fat ones survived the millennia much better than the thin ones, which easily broke to pieces. And for one complete item there are several dozen human images which only survived in tiny fragments. I discussed this topic at length in *Helrunar*. It turns out that there are the remnants of more than a hundred human statuettes, and most of them are neither fat nor can their gender be identified. When all you have is a bit of leg or buttocks, it becomes somewhat hard to determine the rest. We could think of these pieces as deities. Or we could assume that they represent ancestors, or absent relations, lost children or even images of the worshippers. Maybe they even personified enemies! Or they were lucky objects. Or toys. As most of these human statuettes lack their heads, there may have been further human-animal hybrids among them. We simply don't know. Plenty of people all over the world use and used statuettes, and most of them did not worship them. It leaves us in nowhere land where anything is possible. The assumption that Palaeolithic migrants worshipped fat fertility goddesses went down the drain when ethnographic studies proved that in a hunter-gatherer group of, say, fifteen to thirty people, fertility is just as much a threat as it is a blessing. Our Stone Age migrants lacked the resources to feed loads of children. To survive, they had to migrate continuously. They understood that each group has limits, and that too much fertility is a curse. These people knew ecology from the hard side of life. They understood the limits. And, like many hunter-gatherer cultures of our time, they went to some lengths to keep the population down. Some used contraceptive herbs, some aborted pregnancies and some killed babies. It wasn't easy and it will never be. Our migrants were just as human as you and me. They responded to the laugh of a child; they wanted to keep a family, and everybody happy. But they also knew everything about starvation and misery. More than you and I, with any luck, will ever know.

The dating of the lion-human statuette was and is controversial. Some rather enthusiastic scholars proposed an age of 40,000-35,000 BCE. Others are conservative and prefer the time around 32,000 BCE. By 37,000 the Aurignacian period had begun in southern Germany, and it was bloody cold. Around 32000 BCE, the temperature rose a little, and trees began to grow in the tundra. These trees were hardly higher than shrubs. People may have felt optimistic. Not that there were many around; according to the estimates of some experts, only some 50,000 people may have lived in Central Europe. Most of them never met.

Our artist did something incredible. She or he carefully smoothed a piece of mammoth ivory. After much carving with various flint tools, it became a figurine of a human being with the head of a cave lioness or lion. We don't know whether the figure is male or female. The body is a mess; the whole item was put together by generations of scholars as more and more fragments were excavated. For its present shape, computer simulation was required. The figure wears a parka, the standard costume of a cold period. It's a hard, stiff long tube-like mantle of animal skin with its hair turned inside. Maybe it was made of reindeer skin. Reindeer hair is hollow; it insulates perfectly but it breaks easily. Wherever you are, whatever you do, you leave a trail of broken hair. It gets anywhere. I used to sit on a reindeer skin. The hair appeared in my clothes, my bed, my underwear and in my teacup, and finally I was glad to get rid of it. That's perfect insulation but it doesn't really make you very sexy. The last Ice-Age was going strongly, in winter temperatures could drop to minus 40°C or worse, and people wore what kept them alive. Male and female costume was decidedly practical and did not allow for fashionable extras. There seems to have been ornamentation, however. On the left arm of the figure are seven deep, parallel gouges. The right arm is too damaged to be sure. It's the first time the number seven appears on a religious object.

The figure has the head of a cave lion/ess. That species died out several thousand years ago. Cave lions were roughly a third larger than African lions, and much bigger than their Indian cousins. The figurine seems to have the head of a lioness: there is no evidence for a mane. This may or may not be relevant. After all, the huge mane of the African lion is not a must. Indeed, it causes problems: when something the size of a haystack is sneaking through the savannah, even stupid zebras will notice. Among African lions, the male is seriously handicapped, and will usually hunt after sunset, by attacking large game like elephants. The male also goes extremely hot in his head when having sex, and can suffer a heat stroke, but that shouldn't bother us here. Most of the time, the real threat is a team of lionesses. Male Indian lions, nowadays a badly endangered species, have a much smaller mane. Only two thousand years ago, they lived all over

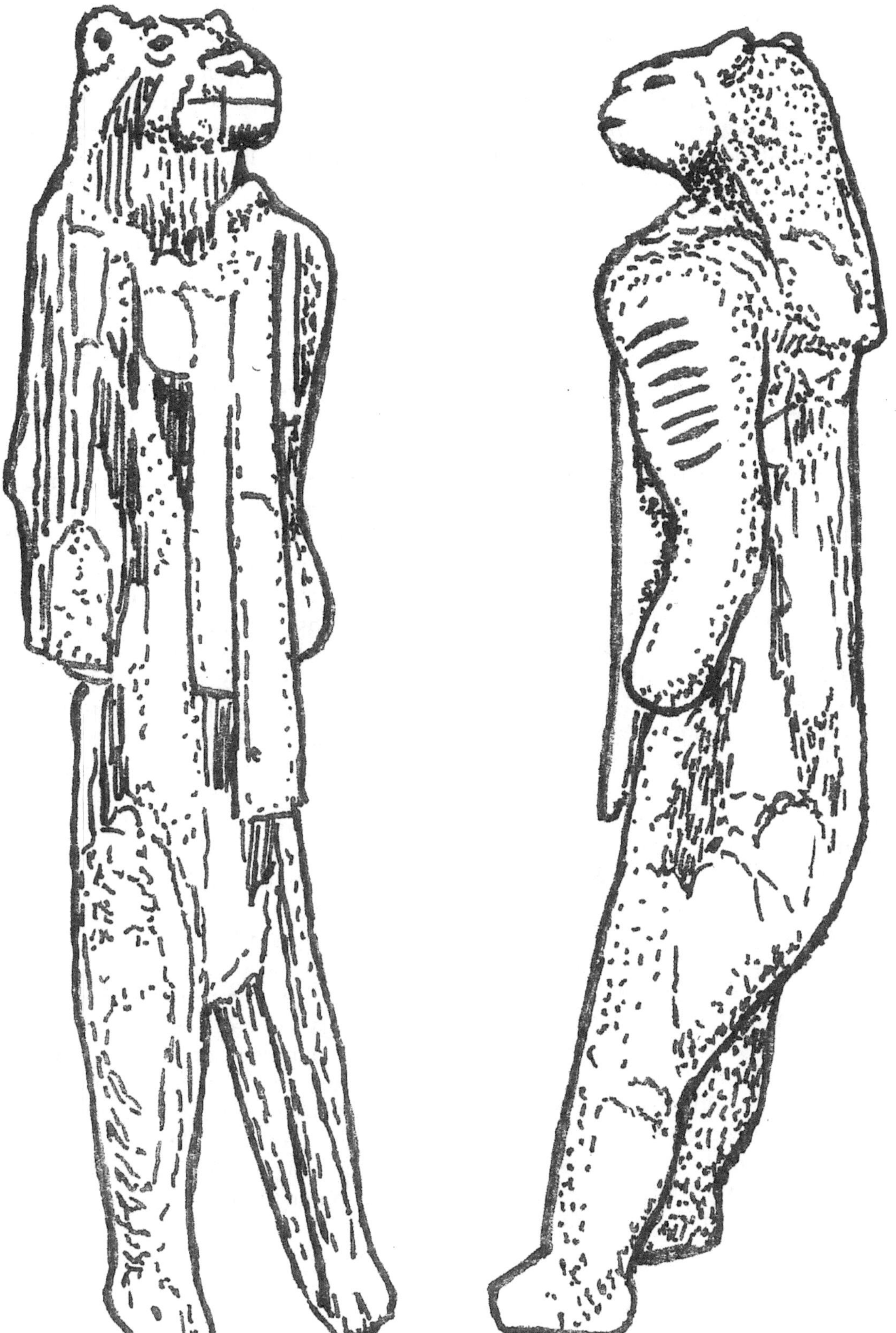

Figure 2 Lion-Human figure, Hohlenstein-Stadel cave

the Near and Middle East. They were even common in Greece and the Balkans, and their territory extended all the way to the southern edge of the Alps. But how did the cave lion look? The evidence is tricky. In the early days of Palaeolithic study, hardly any cave lion images were known. Scholars argued that the Stone Age migrants didn't like carnivores; hence, they are extremely rare in cave art. Then, one bonny day in 1994, Grotte Chauvet was discovered near Vallon-Ponz-d'Arc. As a cult place, the cave is ancient and its art is many thousand years older than that of, say Lascaux or Altamira. Dating the pictures is difficult, but it seems that artists made their contributions mainly between 30,000 and 23,000 BCE. It contains images of dozens of predators; most of them cave lions, plus a large cave hyena, a few bears, an owl and a small leopard. Apart from them, there are rhinos, horses, bovines, buffalos, a buffalo-human and an extraordinary mammoth-human hybrid. This singular cave changed everything. Before its discovery, many researchers had assumed that Stone Age artists only painted animals which they liked to hunt and eat. Stone Age art, so it was assumed, was for hunting magic and fertility. Lions, hyenas and leopards were a terrible danger. Why should our Stone Age artist want them to breed, thrive and multiply? Just due to the Stockholm syndrome, i.e. the tendency of the victim to identify with its persecutor? Most Stone Age people were scared of cave lions, and for good reasons. The people of Grotte Chauvet loved them. Who could generalise about Palaeolithic religion? There were plenty of different ones. We may guess about a few but should recall there were thousands of faiths before agriculture was invented. Grotte Chauvet contains more terrifying predators than any cave discovered before. It turned all statistics and theories upside down.

One remarkable fact is that none of the lions shows a mane. Two interpretations are possible. Either the male cave lion had no mane, or such a tiny mane that the artists didn't bother painting it. In this case, the gender of the lion in our statue remains unknown. Or Stone Age artists only painted lionesses. It may have had religious reasons: the lioness is a better hunter than the lion, and our ancestors probably had more trouble with them. A religious taboo is possible. And we are still thinking in terms of real animals. If the images represented deities, myths, heroes or clans, entirely different interpretations are likely. Whatever it may be, we arrive at an enigma. The gender of the lion-human statuette cannot be determined.

More important is the fact that we are dealing with a mixed creature. Several really early pieces of Stone Age art show people with animal aspects. Usually, the gender cannot be identified. That's a fascinating detail. Quite a few people assume that Stone Age people were obsessed with sex. This is definitely not the case: the cave walls are quite unlike what you see in contemporary gent's toilets. Our Stone Age artists were fascinated by a different phenomenon. The mixed creatures might represent gods, shamans, shape-shifters, ghosts, ancestors or witches. It's the earliest trace of religion. A lion-human being was important enough to inspire one of the first works of human art. Perhaps it was venerated. Maybe it was placated. It may have had myths and meanings we can't imagine. But whatever it may be, it was the archetype for a cluster of deities that appear in many cultures. When you encounter the lion-human deity, you are facing at least 34,000 years of human religion. The evidence doesn't get much older than that.

Figure 3 Home in the Reeds: Eurasian bittern

Time and Space

Swampland Mysteries

How do we understand an ancient text? In the good old days when serious scholars knew what everything was all about, and did their work by candlelight, sipping wine to keep the grey matter buzzing, life was a little easier than today. 'It's simple' many presumed, 'a piece of writing has a specific content. When we can isolate the meaning, and eliminate all errors, we know what it's all about'. Courageous fellows. They struggled and fought and made sense, of sorts. They distilled the gold nuggets of truth from the jumble of possibilities, put on their nightcaps and went into their feather beds proud of a tough job well done. Those were the days when scholars were paid for being right. Then, in the middle of the night, the bad fairy godmother came around and changed the gold to oak leaves, spiderwebs and moonshine. Some faded away by daybreak; other bits disappeared when the next generation of scholars moved in. Hardly any is left today. Life can be tough when you are living on the edge. If you are lucky, you'll learn that the world is not a safe place, unless you are a tough bad fairy godmother, and that of a million babes of thought a bare handful is fitted to survive.

Ancient texts are bastards. If you are lucky, you understand a line or two. You make sense of it, as it makes sense of you. Most of the sense is not in the text but in your head.

Or it resides in a vague but utterly convincing way, in the heads of your colleagues, your community, culture, or in that terrible realm of dull-minded common sense where eldritch errors roam. When you take too much for granted, no matter how attractive it may seem, your head won't be open for new insights. Then you've had it. Time for the nightcap and the bad fairy godmother!

The text is not the message. No matter how deeply you explore a given statement: the message is a lot bigger than the text. The real meaning, if ever there is one, is not in the text but in its relationship to everything else.

Try this spell.

Incantation.

Pure reed, clean reed, growing in the heart of the reed-thicket!

Above you sparkle, below you sparkle,

above (and) below you are filled with sparks;

above, you bring the justice of Utu,

below, you bring to perfection the handwashing (ceremony) of Enki.

With bathed head, for the releasing [...],

A man with bathed head speaks (thus) to you:

you cleanse, you purify the mouth of humans,

may the evil tongue stand aside.

(*Šurpu Series*, IX, 17-22, translation Reiner)

This is magic. Real magic. And it contains more than we will ever understand.

Let's have some fun. Explore these lines. Read them aloud a couple of times. Try different tonalities until you find one that really touches you. Good spells should raise strong emotions. Make notes of what they might mean. And wonder. What visions do they conjure? Watch the beautiful reeds, as they sway gently under a wide azure sky. It's a vision of tranquillity. Oops! Sorry! I mentioned the sky. The sky is not inside the text; it came out of my mind. I imagined a blue sky, and there is some reason for it. The thick marshland, the extensive swamps of southern Mesopotamia had very little rain. I visualised a huge, soggy realm, with ducks and herons, with bitterns calling from the thickets, grey fishes moving through the muddy water, and clouds of mosquito males showing off before the wily females hiding under leaves, awaiting the twilight and the time to suck and swell. Perfect. But it could also be a vision of the night: the sparkle above could be the stars, twinkling in diamond-bright grandeur, filling the Book of Heaven with all the signs, words and images of the universe. Another mistake. I'm guessing. I'm making things up. I'm remembering my first outdoor rituals, which happened at night in enchanting swampland scenery. Or I borrowed them from Mesopotamian poetry. The sky in our spell is unspecified. The sparkle could be stars, glow-worms, fireflies or entirely in the mind. The next line introduces Utu/Šamaš, the sun god, judge of the living and dead. How do the reeds relate to him? Why should the sun bring justice? And how come his opposite in this spell is Enki/Ea, the god of deep water, magic, science and music, teaching the sacred art of handwashing, a mighty spell that eluded the doctors of backwards Europe almost into the twentieth century? You read that a head is bathed. Whose head would it be? Is it yours or mine? Is it the conjurer, or the conjuress, or the patient? How does the head look? Should we imagine the hair long, short, braided, plaited, a wig or completely shaved? Whose mouth is purified? How is it cleansed? Will a simple mouthful of water do? Will it be perfumed, aromatised, disinfected or blessed with a spell? Or is this all about pure speech, about keeping silence and words in a perfect balance as you wade through the swamp of life?

Where does the evil tongue come in? Whose evil tongue is it? Yours, mine, or that of the people in the flat next to you? Or is the evil tongue an abstract being, a spirit or a deity? It's quite a possibility. The Tibetans imagine Gossip as a dangerous, blood-drinking goddess, and have spells and sorceries to scare her away (Kapstein in Lopez, 2007:389-399). In our verse, the evil tongue appears at the end, but it is not an extra. Our spell is a short section of a longer ritual. The other verses banish the evil tongue by the lone tamarisk, by the purification plant that rises from the watery abyss, by the horn-like soap plant, by pure salt, full of life, by the tall cedar of the mountain, by the juniper growing from a sprout and by the water of the sea. How come there are six plants, plus salt and sea water in this spell? Eight ingredients: what is the meaning of the number eight? Should we assume that these things did the banishment or do they represent a magical environment? Or is each a reference to a state of mind, a mood, a feeling, or a deity? How did the Mesopotamian conjurers understand these lines? The spell mentions mountains and the open sea. What did the conjurers know about these habitats? Most of them were living inland, in wealthy cities surrounded by orchards, gardens, plantations, fields, a network of canals and further out, the swamps, grasslands, steppes and deserts. Their neighbourhood was mostly flat: mountains and the open sea were far away.

And who made use of this spell? Was it recited to stop nasty rumours, evil gossip, negative thinking? Or was it spoken by the conjurer to keep him- or herself from saying bad things? Are we banishing an evil influence from a client or performing a purification ritual for ourselves? Is the conjurer banishing her or his own evil tongue?

Agreed. This is enough. We've had our share of question marks for now. The world is a complicated place. We can't even think about a few words without messing them up with preconceptions. To listen or read is to make sense. Much of it happens subconsciously. We have to hallucinate to fill in the gaps. When we slow down, we can catch ourselves inventing things that were never there. Human beings are story-telling animals. We make up meanings, relationships and explanations as we go along. We like our simple interpretations, even if they are predictably untrue. For whatever the spell may really mean, it interacts with the entire luggage we bear between our ears. If we are lucky, our hallucinations come from genuine Mesopotamian sources, or similar cultural groups. If we are not, they come from anywhere.

To understand anything, we have to contextualise it. Think of a reed. See the stalk, the slim, lancet-like leaves, and maybe the soft filaments at the top. Imagine it in full detail. Now consider the rest. You can't think of a reed without placing it in a context. Things have to be somewhere. What background did you invent? A scenery, a colour, a brightness or darkness, a time, a place, a memory? You made up a reed, but it came in a package. Ideas are always surrounded by something. Most people do not notice. Some writers give the impression that we can present a cultural phenomenon, like art, philosophy, religion or magic, and talk about it without considering the setting. What good is it to explore the deities of a culture when you ignore their context? In general, deities don't fall from the sky, unless they are kicked out of heaven for no reason at all or maybe because they want to pounce on you. Deities and ritualists always evolve in a context. Whatever it may be: the divine transforms human experience; humans transform the divine. Religion is not as conservative as used to be assumed: when people change, their understanding changes. When understanding changes, people change. Gods adapt as people adapt. We may perform a ritual that developed four thousand years ago, but, whether we like it or not, we do it with a different mindset. People and their gods (or ideals) evolve together. They interact; they support, transform and develop each other. They are shaped by environment, climate, ecology, society, economy, history, education, desires and taboos; by the dream of what happened before and the hope of what will happen next.

You just met Utu/Šamaš. He is a solar god, sure enough. It sounds deceptively simple. But how do we imagine a sungod? Look at the sun. There's this huge burning star in the middle of our solar system and all life depends on its warmth. Some early scholars assumed that in the primitive old days, the simple crusties who worshipped the sun personified a force of nature. They saw a blindingly bright ball of light and imagined it to have a human shape. That's as far as many thinkers went. They assume that 'primitive' or 'early' cultures deified any force. If it was strong, it must be divine. And they presume that when we enjoy the sun we understand what our ancestors thought. It's wrong. The term 'solar deity' lacks a context. When you are living in a cold country, where the sun lurks behind clouds, rain, sleet, snow and winterish gloom for several dreary months of the year, you will naturally associate it with abundance, with warmth, brightness, joy and all sorts of happy feelings. It's no surprise the Germanic people experienced the sun, Lady Sol or Sunna, as a generous and friendly goddess. When you go to arid Mesopotamia, everything is different.

In the very south, where the mighty rivers meet the sea, you encounter extensive marshes and swamps. Swaying reeds emerge from mudbanks and tiny islets form which may well be gone when the next flood rushes in. The air is damp and hot, and the maze of rivulets and islands is often hidden in thick fog. Fishes dart between the rushes, a heron stands like a statue on a half-submerged willow and great flocks of ducks are winging through the sky. Slowly, a turtle raises its head above the murky water and disappears into the deep again. The reeds are everywhere. Imagine that you row upstream on a boat made of woven reeds. The sealand of the south gives way to a belt of stronger vegetation. You meet poplars and willows at the water's edge, and many palms. The soil gets firmer and the rivers try to stay in their beds. You can leave your boat and proceed on foot. The land is flat. You are walking on the rich alluvial clay that has been swept along by mighty rivers. It has travelled for more than two thousand kilometres. The level ground continues endlessly. It will do so for a long, long time. From the Persian Gulf to the north of Sumer, the ground only rises a few dozen metres. In many places, the water table is close to the surface. But as you travel, you will notice that fertility is confined to the edges of rivers and rivulets. You will see palm trees, tamarisks and poplars. They rim the riverside and provide shelter and shade. But further out, the world becomes a hostile place. The great rivers Euphrates and Tigris, which gave Mesopotamia its Greek name *'Land of Two Rivers'* emerge from the high mountains of Armenia and Turkish Kurdistan. On their way, they wash salt out of the rocks, and as they stream to the Persian Gulf, they deposit minerals at the water's edge. Only trees that tolerate saline water or have exceptionally deep roots thrive at the riverside. Beyond the river's edges, the ground grows hard and dusty. In Sumer, the southern Sea-Land of Mesopotamia, hardly any rain falls. For months and months, through the whole scorching summer, the land lies parched and dry under a merciless blue sky. The annual rainfall is insufficient to permit farming. The earth is crunchy dry and brittle clay. It produces grasses, thistles, shrubs and thorns. You encounter grasslands, if you are lucky. In other places, you might imagine that it has snowed, as the salt is pushed up by the watertable.

Is this the Garden of Eden, the cradle of civilisation, the richest land of the entire Near East?

The local settlers, and the Proto-Sumerians who entered this country around the fifth millennium BCE, developed their magnificent culture by turning hostile nature into a man-made environment. The great cities, the vast fields, pasturelands and gardens were only possible thanks to massive irrigation. It transformed Sumer into a wealthy country and one of the first high civilisations. In such a setting, the sun is not gentle and friendly but fierce and stern. Utu/Šamaš, fierce and unforgiving, travels over the land and observes everything. People remain indoors or rest in the shade during the oppressive noontime heat when terrible spirits stalk the streets. Utu/Šamaš is not a generous giver of life and fertility but a terrifying judge, a custodian of the law, an observer of mankind, who protects the just and punishes evildoers. Everybody was glad when the sun set and the short twilight gave way to evening and cooler temperatures. Sun god Utu/Šamaš cudgelled the land with heat waves; he was feared and dreaded, and exorcists invoked him to enforce justice. By contrast, his father Nanna/Suen/Sîn, the god of the moon, was loved for his peaceful and friendly character. Where the day is suffocating hot, the night is kind and gentle.

What people of the 'moderate' climatic zones consider the 'dead season' of winter equals summer in Mesopotamia, when the heat is at its worst and the vegetation, unless it is carefully watered, droops, withers, shrivels and dies. The Near East in summer is stunning. You might enjoy a belt of gorgeous, lavish green, willows and poplars, rimming a tiny watercourse. Orange-rosy hoopoes flutter through the branches, the water gurgles, leaves dance and everything is teeming with life. A few dozen metres away the fun comes to a sudden end. Further on, there are parched thistles; dust from sandstorms, the sad remnants of spring flowers, and beyond them you walk on dusty earth, cracked, blasted and scorched, in sand-desert, stone-desert, a desert of uni-sized boulders, naked rocks or sunburned, cracked mud. Very few animals can survive under such conditions. Those who can, come out at night. Moths fly, spiders creep, centipedes hunt, scorpions raise their stings and go dancing. And when the full moon shines, the barren wasteland is pale flesh and bleached bones under a sky so over-full with stars that you can hardly tell one constellation from the other.

In the Deep South, where the heat comes down like a blanket, smothering and suffocating, the land is a flat and dusty plain. A few hillocks rise; here and there a canal is set above the general level of the land. The Sumerians had three natural resources: terrifying rivers, rich, nourishing clay and plenty of reeds. Almost everything else had to be imported or worked for. It wasn't much. The earliest-known civilisation of mankind had to struggle to survive. Such conditions have much bearing on cosmology. To the Sumerians, the north wind was benevolent, as it brought coolness and made life a little more bearable. The south wind was a tempestuous fury, a raging goddess with spiralling legs who brought wet heat and typhoons from the Persian Gulf. In the Sumerian mindset, the earth was not fruitful or supportive at all: unless it was carefully watered, it only produced thistles and thorny shrubs.

Figure 4 Sumerian worshippers. Such figures were popular in third millennium BCE religion. They were set up in the temple to represent their donor.

Left: Man holding a cup (missing), Abu temple, Ešnunna (Tell Asmar), c.2600 BCE, chalk, Bagdad Museum.

Right: female worshipper, southern Mesopotamia, c.2900-2650 BCE, alabaster, Berlin Museum.

Marvels of Irrigation

Sometime around the fifth millennium BCE the Proto-Sumerians arrived at the shores of the Persian Gulf. The land was marshy and, further inland, a formidable swamp. Salt water was pushed inland by the tides, sweet water streamed seawards and carried huge amounts of rich fertile mud from the distant highlands of what is nowadays Kurdistan. The Proto-Sumerians liked what they saw and settled. In all likeliness, they were not the first people to do so. Swamps have many advantages, if you like an easy life and plenty of fish and waterfowls, though, given the many diseases; it was not necessarily a long one. But who are we talking about? Frankly, at the present time, nobody has the faintest idea. We don't know who lived in the marshes, and we don't know where the Proto-Sumerians came from. Sumerian is only related to Elamite, the language of a culture in the nearby highlands of Iran. Both languages stand pretty much alone: they are not related to any other known languages on earth. If mankind ever needs a beautiful international language without political or ethnic connotations, Sumerian would be a much better choice than Esperanto.

The Proto-Sumerians brought along the basic know-how of agriculture and kept the classical domestic animals: cattle, sheep, goats, pigs and dogs. You might ask where they came from. So have many scholars. One option is Central Asia. Another option is the Fertile Crescent, where agriculture developed around ten thousand BCE. Or maybe they came via the highlands and rugged mountains of south-west Iran. The Sumerians had a passionate love-hate relationship with their Iranian neighbours. In many ways, they resembled the Elamites. Both cultures shared major gods, developed writing and monumental architecture, built the largest cities in the Near East and created what we might call civilisation. Over the millennia they had trade and alliances, but they also raided each other or engaged in extensive warfare. Much of the time, Elam and Mesopotamia were enemies. It is a distinct possibility that the Proto-Sumerians migrated to the shores of the Persian Gulf via the high mountains of Elam. A major Sumerian god is Enlil, praised as the *High Mountain,* whose temple is the Ekur, the *House of the Mountain.* Sumer has no mountains; the Proto-Sumerians may have picked up the cult of Enlil when they migrated through Iran. Another option would be a journey by sea. Neither can be proved. However it may have been, the Proto-Sumerians came from somewhere, saw the swampland, realised that the wet earth was immensely fertile and decided to stay. They merged with the locals and all sorts of migrating neighbours, thus forming the mixed culture we call Sumerian.

Living in the swamp has advantages. You can catch more fish than you can eat, make almost everything you need out of reeds and enjoy a fresh water supply, a natural waste disposal system and protection from enemies. Less pleasing are reed fires, floods, parasites and diseases. Between the reed beds and along the water's edge, thick clouds of mosquitoes dance. In the soft, soggy mud along the shoreline, worms are waiting for intruders. Stagnant pools are full of microbes. For all its perks, life in the swampland could be short. Naturally, some people began to fancy the drier land a little beyond the swamps and marshes. Here, some pioneering farmers made their first efforts of cultivating grains. It turned out to be a success, and food resources increased. The downside of agriculture soon appeared. More food means that more people survive, and they breed further people who need larger fields. Each dream of progress has limits.

Let's consider early agriculture. The **Neolithic Revolution** has been celebrated as a major achievement, usually by people who never worked their hands to blisters during harvest time. Farming revolutionised human development, but it came at a very heavy price. When you examine the skeletons of early farmers in the Fertile Crescent, you will notice that they are characteristically smaller (by an average 10cm!) than their free-roaming hunter-gatherer contemporaries. Many of them show signs of malnutrition. Their bones are brittle and weak, and their teeth eroded. The early farmers survived on a monotonous diet lacking in proteins and fat. Hunger and malnutrition were common. It wasn't that they stopped hunting. But when a population increases beyond a very small margin, it requires so much game that the ecosystem cannot fulfil the demand. That's the reason why hunter-gatherers live in tiny groups, need large hunting grounds and are almost continuously on the move. The pioneers of farming hunted as much as they could, and before long they had exhausted their resources and forced their wild hunter-gatherer contemporaries to move elsewhere or to take up farming too.

Farming is horribly hard work when your technology consists of a digging stick, a hoe, a shovel made from a shoulder blade or a deer's antler and a few stone tools. Neolithic farmers suffered from back pains, aching joints and developed bad posture at a young age. The gravel of the stone churns went into the flour and ground their teeth away. Their year involved several periods of bitter hunger, and when a harvest failed, the entire community, too numerous to survive by living off the land, faced starvation, hostility and war. Human life has always involved violence. It took the Neolithic Revolution to turn the odd killing into organised warfare. Hunter-gatherers own very little, everyone has pretty much the same, and can only keep as much as can be carried. Farmers, by contrast, store food and make nice targets for raids. Some people invented war and others invented defences. Before long, the status of young men was measured by their fighting skills. But there are further disadvantages of stationary communities. When people live together in a single place, each new disease infects lots of folk. The community produces waste and lives in it. The early farmers had a poorer, harder and shorter life than the hunter-gatherers. But what could they do? They had become so numerous that a return to small mobile hunter-gatherer communities was impossible. Their environment changed with them. The bright forest around the settlements was burned to the ground to clear space for fields. Edible grasses were cultivated. They did not produce as much food as the modern types and were much harder to digest. However, some plants, like wheat and poppy, contained opiates. It may have made life a little easier. When you cultivate plants something amazing happens. We have selected and bred plants that suited our taste and digestion, but meanwhile, the plants have used us to conquer the planet. Domestication happened in both directions: people bred useful plants and plants permitted the survival of those who cared for them. Wheat, rice and corn made us transform most of the planet. These plants have created the landscapes we find 'natural' and the way of life which goes with it. It was a long and painful process. Animal husbandry and fertilisation were yet to be invented. Most groups of early farmers subsisted on only one or two edible grains. They cut down the ancient forest to create tiny fields. Monoculture attracts pests. The more successful a field, the more insects and animals came to feed. The early farmers had to keep their fields at a healthy distance from each other. And they had to guard their fields against birds, beasts and marauders. Ploughing tore open the ground, killing the microbes, the nematodes, the countless tiny animals and fungi that make the humus vibrate with life. Wind and rain carried the fertile topsoil away. Fields were fertilised with manure until the ground was worn out. Agriculture is a killer. When fields were exhausted, the early farmers moved on. The major difference between the first farmers in the 'fertile crescent' (around 10,000 BCE) and the first farmers in Central Europe (around 5,000 BCE) is that the latter had much better soil. When the last Ice Age ended, the thawing glaciers released an enormous amount of finely ground dust. It was carried by the winds and collected in valleys and along rivers, where it turned into amazingly fertile loess ground. The first Central European farmers could cultivate their fields for much longer than their Near Eastern colleagues. They enjoyed a steady, balanced climate with few interruptions by extreme drought or flooding. Wherever loess was available, settlements rose, usually halfway up the slope between the river or brook and the top of the hillside. Neglected fields were reclaimed by grasses, shrubs, birches and eventually overgrown by forest. In the Near East, this rarely happened. When the forest was gone, it rarely returned. With a bit of luck, grasses covered the wounded soil, but the forest would never recover its fecundity (Küster, 1996:71-75). But there were locations that brought better harvests. Along the great rivers, a fresh helping of nourishing mud appeared each year. Living close to the great waterways was risky, but profitable. Only in places with a natural supply of fertiliser could lasting cultures develop.

And here we arrive in old Sumer. The early Sumerian farmers transformed their environment. In a flat country, flooding is an overwhelming problem. The settlers minimised the risk by erecting dykes, **canals** and elevated living spaces. They created artificial basins to permit flood drainage. They dug canals to increase the range of arable land. It seems so easy and obvious to us, but canal engineering is a science. You have to calculate the amount of annual flooding, the height and strength of the dykes, the wind (a canal in wind direction received fresher water), the sub-canals and their network of tiny outlets. The canals were connected by a network of sluices, they were fortified with bricks and waterproofed with bitumen, and in places where the land rose, equipped with systems of levers and lifting machines that allowed the transportation of water from lower to higher levels. When the first archaeologists excavated in Mesopotamia, they thought that the country around the cities must have been a maze of canals and sub-canals. Most canals were fed from the river Euphrates, which is fairly gentle and tends to meander peacefully through a level countryside. The Tigris is a fierce river that cuts its way through deep gorges in the Kurdish mountains. It moves faster than the Euphrates and produces swift and devastating floods. Consequently, most of the Mesopotamian canals were connected with the easy-going Euphrates. Each spring, the annual flood supplied fresh mud from the mountains of the north. That was the good news. The bad news was canal maintenance. Each year, sediment had to be shovelled out. It was dumped along the canal edges. Within a few decades, every canal acquired an elevated waterfront, and as the centuries passed, the major canals rose several metres above the scenery. In this setting, the water supply came from above the fields, which were located below the canal banks. When a sudden flood or bad maintenance broke a dyke, the fields were submerged. In consequence, the farmers erected dykes around their fields. Keeping a section of the canal embankment in bad condition was a major crime. People who purposely damaged the system or flooded a neighbour were heavily punished. It also happened in war: clogging canals and flooding fertile countryside were common strategies.

Consider the destruction of Babylon during the reign of the Neo-Assyrian king Sennaḫerib (see Brinkman in Sasson, 1983:35-42). It's a pretty story, and it even has a moral. As Sennaḫerib's son Asarḫaddon recorded, the people of Babylon had been living in sin. They neglected temple worship; they allied themselves with the enemy land Elam, and before long the god Marduk was fed up with them. Evil omens appeared. Marduk created a terrible flood that devastated Babylon and brought its citizens to submission. The gods left their shrines and flew away. The city was left in ruins, poplars and reeds grew in the streets, birds and fishes sported where humans used to walk. Many citizens left for foreign parts, others concealed themselves or were taken as slaves. Duly humbled, the few remaining Babylonians reconsidered, swore to follow a life of virtue and the gods returned. The story has a happy ending: the friendly Neo-Assyrian king Asarḫaddon did much to rebuild the city and life was good again. Or so his historians recorded. They failed to mention a few details. In plain fact, the Babylonians had allied themselves with the Elamites against Sennaḫerib's Assyrian armies. Sennaḫerib spent years campaigning against Babylonian and Elamite troops and lost a son to them. Finally, he surrounded the city of Babylon and blocked the major canals: the flood was his making. The gods did not really flee: their statues were abducted by the Assyrians. For a decade, Sennaḫerib left Babylon in shambles. He simply loathed the place and wanted it to remain a lifeless ruin. But life has its happy moments. Sennaḫerib was assassinated by a son. Another son, Asarḫaddon became king and killed the murderer. Asarḫaddon was one of the sanest kings that Mesopotamia ever saw. He did much to rebuild Babylon, an act his father would not have approved of. Nor did his contemporaries: they had been with Sennaḫerib and hated the Babylonians. So the scribes did their job and eliminated the conquest from the history books: it was fate, the gods and Babylonian vices that had brought on a supernatural disaster. Asarḫaddon was not a disobedient son but a benevolent reformer, who did much to make the priesthood happy. And of course it was not his own choice. The gods ordered him to rebuild the city. Plenty of his countrymen hated him for it. However, when the gods decree something, a good king has to obey their commands. That's Mesopotamian history for you: it may not be accurate, but it worked.

Canals were the life and soul of southern Mesopotamia. Roads frequently followed major canals, boats made their way, bearing goods, travellers and soldiers, and in the evening cool, the embankment was a nice place for a leisurely walk. From the bank, you had slopes leading to the fields below. These slopes were planted with different layers of vegetation. Near the water, the farmers grew poplars, palms, willows, fruit trees and raised vegetables in their shade. On the slopes, they occasionally grew evergreens, such as pines, which were much needed for building and tools, provided the climate and the salty soil allowed it. Further down, they sowed grains. Life could have been fruitful and happy, but it wasn't. The Mesopotamians had to deal with severe ecological problems. Each year, a layer of fresh mountain salt ended up in the canals. The silting was worst where canals were far from the river, out of the wind, and full of stagnant water. When you clean such a canal, the salty debris ends up near the waterfront on top of the dyke. Before long, this strip of land will only support salt-water vegetation, and tough, salt-resistant trees like the Euphrates poplar and the tamarisk with its remarkably deep roots, and after a while, nothing useful will grow nearby. By then, it becomes vital to dig a new canal. That, essentially, is how the Mesopotamians came to have so many canals. They were not in use simultaneously, but accumulated over many centuries. Much of Mesopotamian history is related to territorial fights between city-states as vast ranges of land became useless for cultivation.

Canal making may have been the first proper 'science'. Enki/Ea, the god of water and fertility, is also the deity of magic, music and science. By creating canals, the Sumerians developed their maths by practical experiment. They learned to calculate gradients and water flow, measured time to prepare for the annual drought and the springtime deluge, invented geometry to assess and allot fields and to re-measure them when a flood had covered all boundary markers under thick, heavy mud. Canal repairs required plenty of logistics. You had to estimate how many bricks and how much bitumen you would need for each section, the size of the workforce, the food supply of the workers, the strength of the embankments and so on. Such skills were part of the education of the scribes. Some tablets relate how property was measured and calculated for its value, under consideration of water supply, location, fertility and accessibility. The canals were amazingly influential on the development of urban society. On this topic, the experts disagree. It used to be fashionable to call the canals the major reason why Mesopotamian civilisation developed. When villages have to work in cooperation, larger economic units develop. These turn into towns, and before long we say hello to cities. Contemporary scholars are more cautious, as so far, single reasons have never adequately explained anything. Nevertheless, the canals were a powerfully unifying influence. The larger they grew, the more farmland could be cultivated. With it came flourishing communities, villages, towns and finally great urban centres. Anything that happened to a canal ceased to be a local problem: when a whole string of farms, villages and towns depended on a major waterway, all of them had a real interest in keeping it functional.

In consequence, the Mesopotamians invented the first (known) police force in history. In Sumerian, they were called GAL_5LA. The pronunciation is uncertain. In Akkadian, they were called the gugallû, or gallû. Think of them as canal inspectors, policemen or as a bunch of uncouth public servants. It isn't easy to generalise about them. In some periods and places, especially during wars and migrations, the gallû were a local force that supervised a small range of canals. In other periods, when peace prevailed and the large city-states controlled much of the countryside around them, the gallû were a centralised task force that operated independently of the local communities. Either way, a gallû was not a popular person. The gallû's task was to control the maintenance of the canals, dykes, ditches, sluices and field walls. They ensured that people did not pollute the water supply and left the boundary markers where they ought to be. They also conscripted people to work on communal projects, whether they liked it or not.

So far, irrigation and canals may appear as an easy road to fertility, wealth and civilisation. Sadly, life wasn't that kind. For a bit of contrast, let us take a look at ancient Egypt. Egyptian economy depended on the annual deluge of the Nile. The rains in Africa made the river swell, which could be counted on to flood around August. For several weeks, the fields were submerged. When the water level sank in early autumn, the fields were covered by a thick layer of fertile sediment and all property boundaries could be re-measured. The damp, fertile soil was excellent to plant crops and the timing was perfect. The deluge of the Nile, though almost catastrophic, was a much-desired event that could be easily predicted and that happened almost without failure at exactly the right time of the year. It influenced Egyptian thought: the river ensured fertility, as it always had and always would. When you look into Egyptian religion you find an emphasis on Ma'at, who is a charming, cheerful goddess with a remarkable vulture head-dress, but also the principle of justice, rightness, truth and tradition. To live in accordance with Ma'at, as all people, the kings and even the gods had to, it was necessary to *return to the place of yesterday*, and to repeat what had been good and true in the past. Much of Egyptian religion is self-confidently conservative. New things and sudden changes were distinctly unpleasant and almost always dangerous. Whenever a regent introduced changes, these were carefully disguised as old traditions. Though Egyptian culture underwent a steady development over the millennia, the scribes pretended that what had been would always be. The flooding of the Nile, the growing of cereals, the harvest and the next flood were a gift of the gods in accordance with Ma'at: they functioned like a clockwork and brought blessings and abundance to everyone. The literate upper class was basically optimistic and pleased with the world, while the peasant population had one hell of a life.

In Mesopotamia, things didn't work as punctually. When the Sumerian farmers wanted to plant their grain in autumn, they had to flood their little fields first. It made the hard earth soft and allowed for ploughing and planting. Sadly, when this season came, the water level of the great rivers was at a low point and fresh water was in very short supply. Wealthy farms close to the great canals, many of them owned by temples and aristocrats had a better supply than the poorer peasants struggling to survive on the minor branches and ditches of the water network. In bad years, water was so valuable that it had to be reserved for the grains while vegetables, with their much greater need for moisture, went to waste. Many farmers became desperate, especially those who had borrowed from rich people and temple organisations. Now imagine the gallû, the canal inspectors, as they controlled the water supply and rationed the water to the farmers. The word 'corruption' comes to mind. Some farmers made it. Others went bankrupt, and ended up in loan slavery for several years. Yes, the gallû were thoroughly unpopular. Their name became an insult, a byword for cruelty, and finally the name of a deadly shape-changing spirit.

And as if this wasn't bad enough, the springtime floods came at the worst possible moment: when the grains were almost ripe for harvesting, and a broken embankment could destroy the livelihood of an entire community. Mesopotamian farmers had a very unpleasant life. Things were still fairly simple in the Sumerian period, when the temples owned almost everything. After the fall of Ur III, the last Sumerian period, around 2000 BCE, private property became the norm. Farmers owned fields, but so did the temples, the palace and the employees of the king. Ḫammurapi (1792-1750 BCE), the king who turned the small city-state Babylon into an empire consisting of Sumer, Akkad and parts of Assyria, set a trend by acquiring as much land as he could. It allowed him to pay his employees in property grants. Scribes, officers, administrators, agents, representatives, artists and musicians ended up 'owning' land they would not work personally. They rented their land to farmers. For barley, the interest was usually 33.3%. The farmers paid their dues and had to take most of the risk. When they became indebted, they had to borrow money from aristocrats, merchants, the palace or the wealthy temples. As a typical condition of such loans, the farmer was obliged to harvest for his benefactor before he could see to his own fields. It ensured that the rich got their grains safely stowed away before the farmer reaped a single grain. And when the personal harvest failed, and the debt couldn't be repaid, the farmers were obliged to sell their property, their family members and themselves. Debt slavery usually lasted for three years. Many farmers were so burdened by debts that they ended up tilling their family land, which had shifted into the property of an aristocrat or a temple, for a minimal wage. The next step was inevitable. Impoverished farmers and their families tended to abandon their homes and migrated to the big cities, where, they were sure, everyone was rich, and life would be easy. It didn't work then, nor does it work in our days. The fringes of the cities were full of poor and homeless people desperate to make a living. When the problem became too large, the kings built new canals or waged war to gain arable ground, graciously annulled debts, granted new property and relocated the farmers on small patches of low-quality land in the country. It started the cycle anew. Generally, a few bad harvests were enough to make the farmers lose their land again. Over the millennia, Mesopotamian cities witnessed a regular inflow and outflow of poor farmers.

City People

Mesopotamian boasted the first large cities in known history. These cities grew out of towns, and one of the reasons was war. We are badly informed about the fifth millennium BCE, when several major cities, like Eridu and Nippur, were founded. Between them were vast stretches of uncultivated land and a lot of small towns and villages. Nor do we know much about the early and central fourth millennium BCE. During this period, the Sumerian high culture was happily progressing, but most of the details of this process are lost to us. Here we encounter a phenomenon which palaeontologists like to call **Deep Time**: the inability of people to comprehend long periods. When we imagine time, we tend to make models. These models usually show time as a line, or a series of lines. We think in terms of space to process time, and fill the space with details. When we have hardly any evidence for a period, except for some ceramic vessels, stone tools, building sites, tombs and rubbish pits, we tend to imagine that very little happened. This impression is misleading. After all, we are trying to evaluate a model in our heads, not the living reality of a people we know hardly anything about. When we think of the many innovations that characterise our lifetimes, we get lost in a tangle of details. It creates the impression that we are experiencing more changes than the people of other periods. It can be totally in error. Modern people waste so much time with electronic toys, smartphones, tablets, internet platforms, 'social' media, games, and TV, that arguably their emotional life and intellectual sensibility is much poorer than that of earlier generations. To understand how the first cities developed, let's do a thought experiment. Imagine that large settlements are growing together and that a vast amount of peasants and migrants from several ethnic groups move in. You are witnessing the development of the first large cities in human history. Everything is fresh and new and you have no earlier models to rely on. How do you invent a metropolis? How do you handle the problems that come up when people of many cultures, religions and languages crowd into one place? How would you standardise law and custom? How do you regulate water supply, trash disposal, religious diversity, traffic, the flow of goods, raw materials, edibles and defence? Which marriage customs will be the norm? How will you shape a system of administration? By what system will administrators be selected and trained? How will you prevent anyone from building as she or he feels like it? How can prices, public works, agriculture and prices be regulated? How do you avoid violence, poverty, unemployment, crime, fires, hunger, rebellion and plague? And how will you explain to granddad, who has been herding sheep in the open steppe for all of his life, that in a city the rules apply to everyone? Who decides the rules, who maintains them and who can change them? What will granddad say when he sees his lazy grandson loitering on the street and his granddaughter going out at night to dance with her girlfriends? And that's just the beginning. The Sumerians had to recognise their new problems and find ways of dealing with them. No doubt they made plenty of mistakes. But they did succeed in developing a high culture from scratch. Anyone who imagines that hardly anything changed during the fifth and fourth millennium BCE should reconsider now. The changes were enormous. It's just that we know far too little.

Writing was developed between 3500 and 3200 BCE. It was the first truly functional script of mankind. Records from this time are rare and mostly limited to inventory lists and accounts. The main purpose of writing was economic. The first scribes were busy keeping the huge temples organised. We learn about goods, economy, transactions, but next to nothing about the people and what they believed. However, as a real blessing, extensive word lists were compiled. They were used for training, allowing the students who copied them to acquire a large and varied vocabulary. By 2900 BCE legal documents, like contracts, appear. Longer texts, royal inscriptions, and the first literary, magical and religious texts were being recorded by 2700. Sadly, the documentation is full of gaps. Commonly, inscriptions survived from places and periods which enjoyed peace and prosperity. When the economy disintegrated, wars escalated or foreign invaders came plundering, the documentation could end, possibly for centuries.

Around the start of the third millennium BCE the cities had grown so much that territorial conflicts were becoming the norm. We might consider this period 'early', as it provides the earliest written documentation, but Sumerian culture was not. Several cities and city-states already had a history of more than a thousand years. Sumer suffered from overpopulation, wide stretches of formerly fertile land were barren, and new, fertile ground was desperately needed. During the third millennium BCE the settlements kept growing, and so did the armies that defended them.

By the start of the third millennium BCE, the cities began to fortify themselves, erecting bigger and bigger walls. One reason was the risk of flooding. Many Mesopotamian cities had walls waterproofed with bitumen to survive the occasional deluge. They also ensured protection against rain. While rainfall was and is rare in southern Mesopotamia, it can be catastrophic. City walls, made of bricks (most of them sun-dried) were vulnerable. But the city-states were also, and for much better reasons, preparing for war. Here, the prime example is Uruk, a city that emerged in the second half of the fourth millennium BCE, when two sizeable settlements merged. At this time it had already become a formidable influence, attracting trade and migrants and controlling wide stretches of the surrounding land. As myths claim, it was fortified by Gilgameš, a regent who was one-third human and two-thirds divine, and who turned into a god of the underworld after his demise. His memorable building project created walls that were five metres wide. The legends say that chariots could race on them, and turn at full speed. At its greatest extension, the city wall was 9 km long. The *Gilgameš Epic* boasts that the bricks were baked, a major achievement in a country lacking forests, and probably an enormous strain on the environment. One-third of the city consisted of buildings, one-third of gardens and fields while the rest was dedicated to clay pits and the vast premises of the Inanna/Ištar temple. Outside of the city wall another major settlement of cheaper buildings rose and in all likeliness plenty of people lived in tents and huts that cannot be traced today. Uruk was so amazing that it was said that the Seven Sages of prehistory had founded the metropolis. It remained the largest city in the world until Rome was ruled by the Caesars. Gilgameš was well aware how violent life was becoming. To achieve this monumental project, much of the population toiled incessantly. The king had good reasons to keep everybody busy. According to a Sumerian legend, Uruk was almost conquered. When the enemy, King Aga/Aka of Kiš approached, Gilgameš ordered the mobilisation of the army, but the congress, divided into two houses of old and young men, couldn't agree. The young men called for war, the old men for negotiations. Before they could arrive at a decision, the army of Kiš had surrounded Uruk. Gilgameš had to put on a fake smile and swear eternal loyalty and friendship to Aga (Kramer, 1981:30-35). This embarrassing episode was not included in the grandiose *Gilgameš Epic*. Similar building projects occurred in other cities. The cities attracted people from the neighbourhood. Each major settlement was surrounded by fields, orchards and plantations. In the fourth millennium, there had still been villages and farms on the periphery of the city. By the third millennium, farmers had got used to city lives. Each morning, they had to walk or take a boat to reach their fields. For a few miles, the city could protect the neighbouring canals, fields, gardens and plantations. Further out, life became risky, and fertile land turned into steppe and desert.

To organise their swiftly growing cities, the Sumerians came up with something new. They invented a theocratic form of government. The gods, or really their representatives, became the largest landowners.

It used to be thought that the growing Sumerian cities were mainly the property of their major deities, and that every person, animal or piece of land was owned by the temple and its subdivisions. Several scholars (especially in Russia) proposed that Sumer had an early sort of communism. That civilisation arose from communism sounded like great propaganda. That 'communism', however, was of a theocratic nature. Saggs, (1966:338) wrote that: *In the Sumerian period each city-state had its own god, or rather, to look at things from the Sumerian point-of-view, each god had a farm which took the form of a city-state, or (in some cases where neighbouring villages had grown together into a city) of a section of a city-state.* Farms. Let's consider his metaphor. Just as people kept animals, the gods kept people. Who cares for individuals? As long as humans did their duty, providing sacrifices, worship and entertainment, the gods were content. They even favoured some people, just like people favour their pets. Early researchers attributed a single god or a divine family to each city and left the matter there: easy to understand, well-organised and misleading. Nowadays, scholars have become more cautious. Yes, there were a few cities which were controlled pretty much in the name of one or two deities or a divine family. However, there were also shrines and buildings for different gods around. Their importance could change, depending on popular support. Some gods were represented in several cities. Most cities left us no records; in fact, our knowledge of the early city-states is desperately patchy. Plenty of important cities provide no documentation at all. The evidence for a monolithic form of divine ownership comes from few places and periods and was not necessarily the rule. There has been plenty of speculation on this topic. It used to be assumed that private land-ownership was a development that eventually cost the temples much of their influence while it strengthened the power of the king and the aristocracy. This assumption is based on a rather modern idea: that religion and state are separate entities. The temples seem to be antagonistic to the palace. However, the Sumerians did not think like that. A secular government was unthinkable. The royal family was part of the religious environment. Kings had religious duties and so had their family members. Often enough, they must have had the same interests as the priesthood. In fact, high-ranking priests and priestesses were often members of the royal family.

And how did ownership function? When we read that the temples owned most of the land, do we imagine an organised workforce, marching to the communal ground in early daylight, singing 'God Enlil made the hoe'? Or did the farmers rent a piece of land and cultivate it according to their likes and needs, grumbling all the time about their lazy good-for-nothing sons and daughters? Or were the farmers busy on common temple land on some days and rented some fields for their own needs? All of this is too simple.

Another hypothesis claimed that the Sumerians preferred major temple-ownership while the intruding Semites promoted private property. It's impossible to verify. The Semitic intrusion into southern Mesopotamia started much earlier than used to be assumed, and cities that were thought to be Sumerian also housed pre-Sumerian natives and Semitic migrants. Just look at the names of the early Sumerian cities: they are not in Sumerian but derive from an earlier language. Some Semites may have been around before the Proto-Sumerians appeared. At the time of writing, few scholars imagine a purely Sumerian population anywhere. Each city-state was populated by a unique mixture of ethnic groups, had its own rules and regulations, and we don't know enough to generalise about anything.

Inventing Cuneiform

Writing is magic. It creates an external record that is independent of a specific person. It allows people to record vast amounts of information and to consult them, if need be, many years or generations later. Writing improved the organisation of temples, the palace, the army; it permitted clear accounts of taxes, obligations, and wealth. The ability to record ideas on a slab of clay created a revolution of thought. Let's take a look at this. Here is real magic: it changed the way we perceive the world. Symbols which can be understood as the prototypes of writing were scratched into clay discs around 3,500 BCE. This stage is called 'archaic documents'. Most of them are indecipherable. They served as property markers and mnemonic devices, i.e. they recorded things. Strictly speaking, they continued a tradition of book-keeping and administration that used differently formed tokens and markers to calculate and record things. In earlier times, number-tokens were sealed in small clay vessels to commemorate payments, transactions and debts. The vessels served as documents. You could break them, in the presence of witnesses, to prove how many sheep someone owed you. The use of a tablet and stylus simply replaced these objects with symbols. Between 3,500 and 3,200 BCE, a primitive script had developed, but documents were extremely simple. They tended to show what looks like numbers next to images that represented goods and marks that indicated names. Imagine a list going: number, bovine, name. As a mnemonic device, this document worked perfectly well. Whoever wrote it was sure to remember what it meant. So did the people who used the same customary shorthand. For the modern researcher, the text is tantalisingly incomplete. It simply records a relationship but does not tell us what it means. Was it 'Person x (gave) six bovines'? Did person x receive them? Did he owe them? Or own them? The crucial point is missing. That's the trouble with pictographic writing: it is so brief that only the initiated can make sense of it.

Over the centuries the inscriptions gained detail.

Here is a tablet from Uruk, dating around the end of the fourth millennium BCE (Brunke in *Uruk*, 2013:174). It is divided into four columns and five horizontal rows. The text of the first row reads: *(length) 290 ninda* (one nindan = c. 6m*), name of an administrator, (width) 100 ninda, (total space) 16 bur* (one bur = 3 eše, each 6,48 hectares) *plus 2 extra eše* (one eše = 6,48 ha). As Brunke notes, the result is 30,000 SAR but should be 29,000. A calculation error? Underneath, we read the measurements of four more fields. Each names another administrator. We don't know if they measured, owned or rented these fields.

Here is a Sumerian document composed around maybe 2850, (after Falkenstein 1936 in Ifrah 1993:219). Front side: *15 bags of barley, 30 bags of wheat, 60 bags of X, 40 bags of X, 15 birds.* Reverse: *145 bags of varied contents, 15 birds* and finally what looks like a signature. The tablet was a delivery note, the front giving a detailed account and the reverse a summary. Most early documents are like that. They refer to names, dates, numbers and objects.

The Sumerians started with pictures. They were dealing with things, and things can be symbolised. Symbols can be simplified. Instead of a cow, you can simply draw its head. And when you know that a cow's head is meant, you can make it even simpler. A downward pointing triangle and two curvy lines for the horns will do. Signs for abstract ideas were rarely needed. The first scribes may have had grandiose ideas, but they devoted their writing to accounts and book-keeping. It took centuries before someone realised that there might be more to writing than administration. To become a fully functional script, the Sumerian scribes needed the ability to express abstract ideas.

Our early scribes were clever. They realised that a picture has several uses: a bull can mean an animal, but it can also mean a quality (like the bull-like vigour of gods, kings, temples and cities) and, best of all, it can signify a sound. When you use a picture for its sound, instead of its imagery, you transcend the realm of material objects. It was a major advance in human history: story telling with pictures turned into a true script. Pictographic signs are limited: they can only show things that exist, or indicate simple relationships between things. But how do you make a picture signifying 'hope', 'idea' or 'understanding'? Pictures have limits. Phonetic writing is superior. A spoken word can be recorded as a series of syllables. For the syllables, you can use pictures that convey the proper sound. You could draw an eye for 'I', a bee for to 'be' and so on. It proved to be an enormous breakthrough, as it allowed the scribes to record ideas, abstracts, concepts, feelings and anything that happens to be inexpressible in pictures. Over a very few centuries, the Sumerians developed a script that could be used to record anything. Phonetic writing could have been the way of the future. Had they been more radical, they might have abolished the pictures entirely. But as they were proud of their achievement and liked the old symbolic images, they used pictures and phonetic values simultaneously. As their script had begun with images of things, and there are lots and lots of things, they had more pictures than sounds. Sumerian is composed of simple syllables, and many words could be written with different pictures of the same sound. Some syllables were simply sounds, like 'u' which could mean, depending on which signs you used to write it, *food; and, also; sleep; day; storm; mother-sheep; o woe.* Please consider: to write the sound 'u' you could use any of these pictures/words/symbols. On the other hand, and this is one of the reasons Assyriologists need special training to avoid nervous breakdowns, many pictures can be pronounced in several different ways. Imagine a picture of a wavy line. In the English language, you could use it to write 'river', 'stream', 'watercourse', 'canal' or 'tributary'. A given Sumerogram can be pronounced in several ways; a given syllable can be written with several Sumerograms. In between we meet Sumerograms that were used in the traditional way, as pictures of the things they represent. As a result, Sumerian texts cannot be read fluently. They have to be carefully worked out. Luckily, word lists occasionally indicate how Sumerograms ought to be pronounced. Large amounts of Sumerian words were integrated into Akkadian and its daughter languages, Babylonian and Assyrian. When you read a Sumerian word in ordinary script, you can be fairly sure it was pronounced more or less like it looks. At least in the opinion of the scholar who transcribed it. When it appears in capital letters, the pronunciation is uncertain. It might be pronounced that way, or in an entirely different one. In some contexts, the sign ^{d}MUŠ$_3$ was pronounced 'Inanna'. The name usually written with the Sumerograms ^{d}GIŠ.GIN.MAŠ was pronounced '(Deity) Gilgameš'. As a result, writing was a high art requiring experience, patience and deduction. Some scribes used phonetic signs with little consideration for the pictures they represented. Others tried to make the spelling pretty and meaningful, and chose characters that supplied an extra symbolism to the phonetic information.

Another important change happened thanks to the **writing material**. Long before good paper was developed, the Sumerians used clay tablets. It was a brilliant idea. Clay was everywhere. Sumer was practically built on it. It was cleaned, smoothed and inscribed with a reed stylus, another cheap and easily available item. In the process, a popular deity of grains, vegetation, grasses and reeds, Nidaba/Nisaba, became the goddess of scribes, scholars and scientists: she measures the universe and records everything. Thanks to her, contracts were made, history recorded, hymns were composed and royal deeds commemorated. Her former interest in grains and other cereals shifted to other goods: reeds were enough to turn her into an all-time favourite.

Drawing little pictures on clay is not as easy as you think. You get uneven, serrated edges and the surface of the tablet looks scarred and worn. Curves are especially difficult. It was much easier to press the stylus into the clay, creating what is known as cuneiform (wedge-shaped) signs. In the process, edges and angles replaced curves and circles. It was the start of abstraction: in a very short time, the pictographs did not look like images anymore. The scribes still knew what they signified, but they had all the freedom in the world to simplify them.

The result is confusing. A given sentence in Sumerian may include phonetic passages and symbolic pictograms. To make things a little easier, the scribes invented **determinatives**. These special signs indicate the class of objects or ideas a given word belongs to. Determinatives were (probably) not pronounced. Here are some of the most common. Imagine a star. In the earliest period, that star had many rays. By phase IV it had been simplified to eight rays. By phase VIII you could write it with three impressions of the reed, and it didn't look like a star any longer. The star symbolised An/Anu, heaven, the father of many gods, the divine in general. As a determinative, in modern transcription, this star appears as a small d before a word indicates 'dingir', a Sumerian word meaning deity or divine. A reader of Akkadian would read the same sign as 'ilu' or 'iltu(m)', i.e. god or goddess. Determinatives are helpful, but they were not a must. Many but not all scribes bothered about the divine determinative; hence, lack of it is not always an indication that a name is not a deity. In modern transcription, a small 'e' means 'house' in Sumerian and can refer to a building, house, temple or shrine. 'Giš' (Sumerian for wood) tends to appear before wooden objects of all sorts. Sumerian giš GU.ZA is pronounced kussûm and means throne. The Sumerian determinative 'id' indicates a river in general, but the sign, when not in use as a determinative, can also refer to a river goddess. 'Itu' signifies that the name of a month follows. 'Kur', a term meaning: land, country, mountains, foreign realms, foreigners and the realm of chaos, death, danger and the underworld, appears in front of country and state names. 'Kuš'

(Sumerian: leather) signifies objects made of or with leather. 'Lu' (Sumerian: man) is common before the names of professions. 'Mi' (Sumerian: woman) appears before the names of female professions. 'Tug' signifies articles of clothing; 'u' is common before plant names, and 'uru' (Sumerian: city) signifies large settlements. Determinatives also appear behind words; an example is 'meš', indicating a plural; 'sar' (Sumerian: plot) signifying a garden plant, or 'ki' (Sumerian: place, earth) meaning some location. Thanks to determinatives, modern scholars may deduce the sort of category an unknown word belongs to. It makes life a little easier in this uncertain world.

Writing had a formidable influence on society. The Sumerians had the first **schools** in known history, some of them associated with temples, like Eanna, the House (e) of Heaven (anna), the temple of Inanna and An/Anu in Uruk. But learning was not a monopoly of the priesthood; there were also schools run by the palace and by private individuals. In these institutions the sons of wealthy and influential people received their education. Literate women and female scribes also existed. They were a minority, and whether they were trained in schools is unknown. However, we can be sure that many aristocratic ladies and priestesses were literate. The first author in history who dared to sign a composition by name was a woman, the high priestess Enḫeduanna, daughter of Sargon I, whose hymns influenced Mesopotamian literature for centuries. Several queens were busy in administrative functions, or corresponded with other queens. Like their husbands, they did not really have to be literate. However, there is evidence that at least some of them were. An example is Šērūaētirat, wife of Asarḫaddon, who reprimanded her daughter-in-law, Libbālišarrat, wife of Aššurbanipal, for not practising tablet writing and schoolwork (Melville in Chavalas, 2014:215).

Schooling was tough: much of it consisted of writing practice. For this purpose, the students copied documents, letters, business records, contracts and similar practical things. As some of them would make a temple career, religious texts, hymns, rituals, spells and similar materials were copied, plus literary works, myths, proverbs, sayings, poetry and so on. Maths was an important subject; there are hundreds of tablets providing multiplication tables, logarithms, numerical progressions, geometric designs and, above all, practical exercises. Lazy students were frequently beaten. Luckily, there were ways of reducing punishment. A Sumerian practice tablet dating around 2000 BCE (Kramer, 1981:10-13) relates the story of a young man who was incessantly punished for his sloth, lack of discipline and writing errors. His father knew the solution. He invited the teacher for a lavish meal, had him sit in the place of honour and his son served him. After the meal, the teacher received new clothes, a gift and a ring. The teacher, delighted by the bribes, immediately blessed his student: *'Young man, because you did not neglect my word, did not forsake it, may you reach the pinnacle of the scribal art, may you achieve it completely...Of your brothers may you be their leader, of your friends may you be their chief, may you rank the highest of schoolboys... you have carried out well the school's activities, you have become a man of learning.'* The text, as Kramer notes, is quite common. Countless schoolmasters let their students copy it to improve their income.

One of the most astonishing inventions of the Sumerians is the **list**. We could compare its importance to the invention of the wheel. Does that sound exaggerated? Please stop for a moment and consider. A list allows you to record and contemplate a cluster or series of different thoughts, ideas, objects and events. It can contain more ideas than your conscious mind can handle. Do you use a shopping list? Do you make plans on paper? And where would your computer be if it couldn't list anything? Lists are fantastic tools. They allow you to collect ideas, to detail or summarise them and to sort them in various ways. They permit a way of thinking that was impossible before the advent of writing. Without lists, large-scale or long-term projects are difficult. To draw up lists gave a tremendous lead to the

Sumerians. Imagine there will be war. Who has the advantage: the culture that can list troops, equipment, chains of command, distances to locations and schedules of supply, or the culture that simply sends a call for people to turn up with as many relations and stuff as they can, sometime around the next full moon? Lists allowed the scribes to organise things, and to turn communities into states. I would like to propose that the invention of the list was the first step towards science. To make a list is to order the world. You can use a list to break up big ideas into smaller sections, or to contain smaller ideas in bigger ones. One way is specification, the other generalisation. You can zoom in and explore details: it turns the world into a bigger place. Or you can step back and observe the whole picture. It makes the world smaller, and easier to handle. Both of them are magic: they create ways to experience, organise and manipulate the environment, and the way you think about it. If you want a high culture you need lists, book-keeping, accounts and histories: they are the basic tools to organise the world.

To teach their students vocabulary, the Sumerian scholars drew up lists on many topics. It began quite early: the first lists date around 3200, to the very beginning of the written record.

The scribes did not approach list-making systematically. Some tried to order words in a meaningful way; others simply went along by association or recorded words as they came into their minds. They listed countries, place names, personal names, royal genealogies, the names of rivers, stars, animals, plants, trees, stones, tools, professions and so on. It gave the students a large vocabulary and ensured that difficult signs remained in use. While wave after wave of Semitic migrants entered the country, bilingual word-lists developed: the first language dictionaries of history. The scribes also composed lists of gods and temples. You might consider them a teaching device, but they also structured religion. Sumerian religion had not emerged from a single source. Each city-state, each ethnic group, had its own preferences and introduced its own deities. Places had their gods, and so had villages and towns. When towns merged, their deities came together. Some gods formed families; others were identified with each other, exchanging symbols, insignia and divine powers. Conquest introduced powerful new gods: Sumerian religion was chaotic and overwhelmingly complicated. The scribes drew up a whole series of god-lists, sorted according to priorities, such as family ties, geography, or general popularity. Each of them is different, and each provides a glimpse into the way the Sumerian scholars experienced reality.

Within a few centuries, writing transformed from pictographic notes to proper records. It proved to be a winner. During the Uruk period, there were trade contacts between Mesopotamia and Egypt, and the Egyptians recognised that something amazing was happening. They borrowed the know-how of writing, including the breakthrough invention of phonetic writing, but they made up their own imagery. Egyptian writing is beautifully suited to the Egyptian language and to the art and symbolism of the Old Kingdom. It does include a few peculiarities. Unlike the Sumerians, the Egyptians did not write vowels. A special element of Semitic languages are the **word-roots**. Usually, they consist of three consonants. By filling in the spaces between them with various vowels, you get different grammatical forms. Or you get entirely different ideas. An example. The Akkadian root dmq appears as damqu(m) (good, kind, lucky, pleasing) and can turn into damāqu(m) (to be good), idmiq (became good), idammiq (will be good), damqat (she is good) or damiq (he is good). Related are damqiš (well, kindly), dumuqqû (sign of gratitude), dumuqtu(m) (good deed, favour), dummuqu(m) (good quality of metal; very good) and dumāqū (jewellery). Without the vowels, these words look very similar. This is Akkadian: the Akkadians based their writing system on the Sumerian, and wrote vowels. We can be truly grateful for it. The Egyptians and the West Semites did not. It produced lots of different words that look exactly alike and makes translations of Egyptian far more uncertain than translations of

Mesopotamian literature. Thanks to the Sumerian inspiration, Egyptian writing emerged almost ready-made. It did not undergo the long and tortuous process that turned pictures into phonetics and into a fully developed system of recording information. Cuneiform became a major influence on the entire Near East. Around the end of the third millennium BCE, the Akkadians adapted it to their language. The Akkadians spoke a Semitic language unrelated to Sumerian, and had to introduce changes to make the system work. They assimilated many Sumerian terms into their language, and as the Sumerian script was based on syllables, and syllables include vowels, we are much better informed about Akkadian, and its later developments, Babylonian and Assyrian, than about Egyptian. It did not stop at this point. The Hittites, the Syrians and many of their neighbours picked up cuneiform writing and adapted it to their languages. It is only in regard to Elam that uncertainty abounds. The Elamites left us few written records, and used their own script. Some scholars propose that it antedates Sumerian writing.

Early Sumerian Religion: Fertility Cults, Dying Gods, Sacred Marriage or What?

How did Sumerian religion start? And where do we start from? Several traditionally-minded writers proposed that 'primitive man', no matter when and where he lived, was obsessed with fertility. It seemed so obvious. 'Primitive man' was a messy creature. He squatted in the squalor of his earth-hole, tent or mud-hut. He lacked soccer, TV and a university degree. To make up for them, he spent his time thinking about sex until 'primitive woman' came home.

'Primitive Man' had simple desires. A full belly, an empty head, yes, he is alive today and spends his days on social networks. All he ever wanted is fertility. Fertile animals, fertile fields and loads of kids which were raised by 'primitive woman' while he went to see his 'primitive mates' at the 'primitive pub'.

Many respectable experts of the nineteenth century thought along these lines. It made them feel civilised. 'Primitive man' was a fact of life. The colonies were full of them. So were the countryside and the factories. Scholars who spent their lives in libraries had a clear idea what they were missing. Between 1860 and 1880 Wilhelm Mannhardt composed the first systematic study of peasant customs. It was a pioneering achievement, as, before him, nobody had bothered to study the subject. Mannhardt focussed mainly on harvest rituals of Prussia and came to the conclusion that peasants are totally obsessed with fertility rites. These ceremonies and festivities, he assumed, were so odd that they must have been invented in pagan prehistory. Had he studied other aspects of rural life, like births, baptisms, funerals, topping-out ceremonies, hunting traditions, prayers, superstitions, healing rituals and the exorcism of evil spirits, his study would have been more balanced. But as it was, 'fertility' became the heart and soul of peasant traditions. Behind them, he was certain, lurked the memories of ancient vegetation cults. Mannhardt's speculations were welcomed by many European scholars, who fancied that any custom, the cruder the better, must derive from ancient prehistory. That people are creative and that new customs are invented all of the time did not cross their minds. To support their assumption, they proposed that religion is always conservative and that the peasants never had a new idea while everywhere else, mankind changed and transformed. The scholars discovered fertility cults all over the world and made very little difference between, say, hunter-gatherers, nomads, small peasant communities and people living in large cities like the Sumerians. Yes, the Sumerians of the extremely badly documented fourth and early third millennium BCE were assumed to be into fertility cults. One prime piece of evidence was the famous Uruk vase, dating from the middle of the fourth millennium, hence, from a period when writing was still unknown. The vase shows nude men carrying foodstuffs and sheep to a woman, who might be a priestess, queen or goddess, standing near the top. Next to her is the roll of reeds which is Inanna's symbol. The woman, it was assumed, is the goddess, or at least a representative of hers. However, we can't be sure. Inanna assimilated much from other goddesses. The bundle of reeds, her symbol in the literate period, may have been the emblem of another goddess in the preliterate period. It seemed so simple: victuals, a goddess of the storehouse and every farmer, herdsman, shepherd and city dweller busy ensuring the food supply. Food and sex. That's what fertility is all about. However, the vase does not show an everyday event. We see an offering; in real life, people would not have walked around nude. It raises questions. Who made the vase? Who commissioned it? What was it used for? What does it represent? Is it simply fruitfulness? Or is it wealth and power, a celebration of the mighty temple complex that demands, hoards and controls the food? Are we talking food or power? Does the scene show the 'bridal offerings for the sacred marriage', as some assumed? Or is it a commemoration of donations to the cult, coming in from the countryside? Is the Uruk vase a useful representation of early Sumerian religion? Or is it just a chance item that has influenced scholarly opinion for decades?

We might start simple, but I'm sure you wouldn't like it. Let's try 'sophisticated' for a change. When you examine the term 'fertility' you'll notice that it means very little. Fertility is well and good when you identify it with wealth, prosperity and happiness. The term describes what people like (instead of what they need) and, to be sure, owning stuff, eating lots and having kids are major aims of human prayers, no matter which cult, religion or period. In the years of early Assyriology, plenty of researchers subscribed to the idea that the Sumerian gods were simply personifications of nature, and that 'primitive man' stood in powerless awe before them. He looked up to the magnificence of the powers of the gods and tried to keep his bladder under control. Heaven, yea, that's huge. And thunder, wow, scary! Unlike clever folk like us, he was too dumb to understand what was going on. The general opinion of sophisticated, educated people who happened to rather well-off, proposed that early mankind consisted of simple crusties with simple gods and simple desires. Anything that happened between the 'wow' and the 'scary' was basically divine.

It's such a simple picture. It could be totally wrong. In a preliterate society composed of dozens of differing cultural groups pretty much anything may have been worshipped. People were not stupid. In fact, people were never 'primitive'. It takes lots of brains to survive in a society lacking science, education, medical services and old age pensions. And what gives us the idea the Sumerians were 'primitive'? Farmers cultivated the soil for many thousands of years before they even reached Sumer. And they had built amazing settlements, cemeteries and cult places requiring major effort, planning and organisation for millennia. Just look at Göbekli Tepe, Jericho, Çatal Höyük, Nevalı Çori, Çayönu Qermez Dere, Nemrik and Jarmo. People in Anatolia began to experiment with metal in the ninth millennium BCE (Aşıklı Höyük and Çayönü). Sumerian 'primitive man' did not simply stand there, scratching his balls, muttering 'I wonder where babies come from?'

Let us take a look at some of the most exciting, bedazzling and misleading fantasies of early Sumerology. As usual, when stories are meant to be successful, they have to involve love, sex and death. Our pioneers of Assyriology had a thing about sex, sacred or not, and were, like everybody else, strongly influenced by Sir James Frazer's beautifully written and nowadays badly outdated *The Golden Bough, A Study in Magic and Religion.* We are talking about a massive work that extended, in its third edition, over twelve fat volumes. Frazer (1854-1941) was innovative, brilliant and convincing. Think of him as an unsung philosopher of the twentieth century. He was a shy armchair anthropologist who spent decades haunting libraries. He also questioned scholars, travellers, military men and bought drinks for sailors to learn about the customs of the primitives in the British colonies. To understand Frazer you have to consider his personal agenda. Sir James was a passionate atheist. He wanted to prove that Christianity was a normal, run-of-the-mill Near Eastern fertility cult and that the crucifixion of Christ was based, on a symbolic level, on the death and rebirth of vegetation deities. Frazer loved Mannhardt's study and was ready to discover vegetation cults all over the world. Christianity, he assumed, was just as primitive and superstitious as the cults of Adonis, Attis, Tammuz, Dumuzi and Osiris. Also, Near Eastern cults were sure to have a debasing, corrupting influence on society. In Frazer's opinion, the introduction of Near Eastern religions was a major reason for the fall of the Roman Empire. Christianity, he knew, was having the same sort of influence on civilised Europe. It did not stop him from going to church each Sunday.

Frazer, writing in gloriously poetic prose, influenced generations of philosophers, artists and novelists. It was magic on a grand scale: his fancies shaped the mindset of the early twentieth century. In his literary masterpiece, Frazer elaborated on several topics which he assumed to be basic to human religion, in particular to the 'primitive' phases. Some of his insights were highly valuable. The principles of sympathetic magic, taboos, the scape-goat and his observations on tree cults are still worth considering. Not so his major fancies. Let's start with the **death of the king**. Primitive kings, Frazer assumed, represented the power, virility and fertility of their kingdoms, hence, when their hair went white, their teeth fell out, and their erections wouldn't last, the kingdom was sure to go downhill. Frazer imagined that these regents were ritually killed when they began to age. He thought that all sorts of 'primitive' people disposed of their kings when they showed signs of wear and tear. Some of his ideas could be traced to myths. Imagine that the king represents fertility and potency. He might be the personified wealth of agriculture, the procreation of domesticated animals, the well-being of the realm. Each economy, no matter whether it focuses on farming or animal husbandry, is fundamentally based on plants. In short, the king had much in common with vegetation deities. And here we come to a fascinating mindset. Several vegetation deities undergo death and rebirth to keep mankind alive. Dying is part of the pattern. Some are sacrificed, others sacrifice themselves. The Egyptian grain and vegetation god Osiris, for instance, is killed by Seth, chopped into small pieces and scattered all over Egypt. It turned him into a dark god of the underworlds. Luckily, Isis collects the bits and pieces, revives them, and Osiris is reborn when the new seeds start to sprout. It turned Osiris, as far as Frazer was concerned, into a perfect vegetation deity, and a model for the 'death of the king'. Mind you, there is a vast amount of lore and symbolism connected with Osiris which does not fit the pattern. Frazer simply ignored it. He and several enthusiasts began to collect 'dying gods'. They found so many that they assumed they had discovered a universal formula, a specific stage in the development of religions worldwide. In Mesopotamia, Inanna's husband Dumuzi is killed and departs for the Underworld: after the harvest is gathered, summer begins and the vegetation withers and dies. In autumn, the temperature cools, the fields are flooded and ploughed and Dumuzi, the reborn vegetation, rises again. Life and death and rebirth. That's what divine harmony is all about. For a proper dying god cult, you need deities who are killed and reborn every year. If I may put this extremely simply (unlike Frazer, who devoted many volumes to the subject): when the regent is an incarnation of a vegetation deity, the harvest necessitates the death of the king. Luckily, after the grains are cut, their seeds can be used to plant a new harvest: life reappears, the king is dead, long lives the king! Frazer explored world mythology and encountered the death of the corn king all over the place.

Dying gods appeared to be a universal formula of religious experience. It turned out to be wrong.

Figure 5 God Struck. Inspired by a Third Millennium BCE figurine

Frazer had the bad luck of writing at a time when research was badly wanting. Many of his sources were highly questionable, if not totally off the mark. Dying gods and sacrificed kings did exist, mainly in myths and gossip, but they were certainly not a universal custom. Nor was it really sensible to identify Christ's crucifixion as the ritual death of the corn king. The Roman soldiers who nailed him to the cross were not celebrating a fertility rite but getting rid of a fanatic troublemaker. Frazer started a fashionable new trend. Soon enough, any dying Mesopotamian god was identified as a vegetation deity. Sumer seemed to be full of dying gods. Inanna/Ištar travels into the underworld, where she dies and is revived. The same thing happens in the sky: ever so often, Inanna/Ištar's planet Venus disappears. Sun and moon sink into the deep every day, and reappear the next morning. King Gilgameš dies and is deified. Ningišzida dies and remains in the deep. As it turns out, most of those 'dying gods' did not really fit the pattern. Quite a lot were not reborn like the grains each year; others, like sun and moon, travelled into the deep and returned without dying. It happened every day (you watch it!) and had nothing to do with the farmer's year. Many 'dying gods' were not related to plants, nor to the fate of kings. Even Dumuzi is not a perfect representation of the type. Originally, Dumuzi/Tammuz was a human being, a king who governed the city Badtibira. He became the husband of Inanna/Ištar and of course he was related to 'fertility'. At least, there is a gorgeous collection of enchanting Sumerian love poetry describing how the two met, flirted, married and went to bed. As life is tragic, their happy union did not last. For a number of reasons, Dumuzi was hunted and killed by a bunch of evil gallûs, henchmen of the goddess of the deep, who dragged him to the underworld. Luckily, after remaining dormant for six months he is allowed to return for half the year. In his stead, his sister Geštianna, the goddess of the vine harvest, has to die and descend into the deep. It's a lovely description of the farmer's year. Dumuzi is the grain harvest, and when he dies, summer begins, the heat becomes unbearable and the vegetation withers and dies. When autumn comes, the new seeds are planted, but meanwhile, the grapes have to be cut and 'die' until the next spring. The farmers identified Dumuzi with the vegetation. That's one opinion, and there were others. The herders and shepherds believed in a Dumuzi who breeds livestock. Sure enough, sheep are born, live and die. In between, they have plenty of lambs. The conception of new sheep is not related to the death of the elder generation. When Dumuzi was identified with Amaušumgalanna, he became a warrior god and a god of the date harvest. Warrior deities are a long way from vegetation gods. Date palms don't fit the dying god pattern at all: they prosper for many years, and the fruit can be stored for long periods. His identification with Damu, the divine child, made things even more complicated. Damu is a healer and maybe a warrior and her/his activity is not related to death and rebirth. In the end, it turns out that only a few aspects of Dumuzi correspond to Frazer's 'dying god' pattern. To turn Dumuzi into a simple 'dying vegetation god' you have to ignore a lot of conflicting evidence. As it turned out, ignoring details and ripping facts out of their proper contexts were two major talents of James Frazer. What made him so enchanting was his amazing knowledge and his beautiful literary style. Even today, many years after his death, the *Golden Bough* is bedazzling. Frazer's dramatic visions influenced Wittgenstein, Campbell, Freud, Jung and their followers. Freud's Oedipus complex is soundly rooted in Frazer's pipedreams. The pioneers of the pagan movements, of Thelema, Wicca and mystic feminism were enchanted and spellbound. Margaret Murray, Robert Graves, W.B. Yeats, Aleister Crowley, Dion Fortune, Gerald Gardner and Alex Sanders built their religious fantasies on Frazer's myths. Frazer influenced Ernest Hemmingway, Ezra Pound, H.P. Lovecraft, D.H. Lawrence, T.S. Eliot, E.M. Forster, Edith Sitwell, James Joyce, John Synge, Wyndham Lewis, John Buchan, Joseph Conrad and Evangeline Walton, plus a wide range of fantasy writers. We also meet Frazer in

Pasolini's *Medea* and in music by the Doors and Rainbow. I am sure you noticed that none of these enthusiasts had any training in ethnology. Among scholars, Frazer's studies were a great deal less popular. For good reasons, his contemporaries criticised Frazer for mixing myths and speculations in a thoroughly unscientific way. He used too little reliable evidence, did not distinguish between facts, fables and unsupported gossip, ignored conflicting evidence and was obviously motivated by missionary zeal. Frazer replied by trying hard to prove the ritual death of the king, but only came up with a single certain example from the Congo. For an almost universal custom, it was not enough. Instead, he supplied perfect proof that good studies are impossible when you work without reliable data, clear contextualization, love for detail and critical examination. By the time the third edition of the *Golden Bough* appeared, Frazer had to admit that his identification of Christ with the dying vegetation god was a little farfetched. Only a very few scholars tried to support Frazer's amazing assumptions, among them Carlo Ginzburg and Arne Runeberg. They did not get far; indeed, most anthropologists had learned their lesson. Like a vegetation deity, Frazer was ritually killed by the academics of his time. He keeps on being reborn in the works of occultists, pagans, feminists, psychologists and artists.

Another bee in Frazer's bonnet, which he shared with plenty of academics (such as Sir Edward Taylor), was the idea that 'primitive man' preferred rough action to abstract symbolism. Countless thinkers, impressed, inspired and excited by Frazer's voluminous work, imagined that early religion revolved around messy, bloody and wicked things, like human sacrifice and ritual copulation.

Welcome to the term **'sacred marriage'**. It sounds like fun. It appears in plenty of books. It looked like one of the few attestable rituals of the Mesopotamian 'fertility cults'.

The expression 'sacred marriage' was borrowed from the Greek: *Hieros gamos.* Several Greek authors used it for the annual ritual celebrating the marriage of Zeus and Hera. Shy Assyriologists lifted the name from its Greek context and applied it to a range of Mesopotamian customs, many of them quite different from what the Greeks were thinking about. Whatever the Mesopotamian 'sacred marriage' may have been, we don't know what the Mesopotamians called it, if they had a name for it at all. The 'sacred marriage' as Frazer believed, came in three variations: a) as the symbolic marriage of trees, b) as crude sexual rites to promote fertility (like lovemaking in the fields) and c) divine nuptials: the union of gods. The latter category included the lovemaking of deities and/or their representatives; it could be enacted in a symbolic or physical way. These ideas were picked up by numerous thinkers. They influenced many modern faiths, such as Wicca, the Pagan Movement, New Age thought, mystical feminism, Crowley's cult of Thelema and silly ersatz religions like Freudian and Jungian Psychoanalysis.

As the Sumerians are the first traceable culture on record, they were assumed to be cruder than the cultures that followed them. Like all early religions, so Frazer's followers assumed, the Sumerians of the illiterate period worshipped fertility.

True enough: the hymns to the Sumerian gods contain plenty of references to growth, abundance and productiveness. However, they also praise a lot of other things, such as large-scale warfare, the execution of huge building projects and public festivals in major cities. They eulogised law, order, and civilisation. And they were anything but early. When the first Sumerian hymns were recorded around 2700 BCE, their civilisation was over a thousand years old, and 'primitive man' had become a suave city dweller!

Just because a given text is early does not mean that it is 'primitive'. People had come a long way before they began to write. What about the 'fertility rites' then? What about lovemaking in the fields to encourage the peas to grow? Some venerable scholars would have been disappointed. Religious sex is very hard to trace. There are no ritual handbooks for the 'Sacred Marriage', in fact, the

Figure 6 Adorants. Inspired by figurines of worshippers from Ur, Ešnunna, Mari etc.

textual evidence is small, hard to translate and comes from specific regions and a short period. Let's tackle the problems one after the other. There are plenty. And do remember to breathe.

The concept of the 'Sacred Marriage' was developed by scholars who fused two distinct literary sources. One of them is a group of songs describing the courtship of the herder- or farmer god Dumuzi with young and bedazzling Inanna. Their meeting, courtship, marriage, and happy union is described in detail. The Sumerians were not prudish and had a healthy respect for natural pleasures. Inanna, in particular, knows what life was all about, and is famous for enjoying her vulva. In Sumerian society, most forms of sex were acceptable, except for incest, paedophilia and congress with animals. Inanna is a happy girl. She laughs and rejoices with her girlfriend Bau/Baba while she prepares the bridal bed and goes to have a bath. Her breasts have risen; her pubic triangle is covered by hair. Soon, her newly wedded husband will *go to the holy loins of Inanna*, he will kiss and bed her; he will *sprout vigorously like lettuce*. Inanna calls for the royal bed, the queenly bed, the *bed for the sweetening of the loins*. At last, her *garden* will be watered; her fertile *field* will be ploughed. She can hardly wait. This is what lovemaking can be like: beautiful, innocent and charming. Our protagonists seem to be human; the fact that they are deities is rarely stated. However, we are talking myth here: the songs do not tell us 'This is a ritual schedule. Do it in your temple once a year!' Our pioneering Assyriologists simply guessed that goddess and god were role models for ritualists who actually did what the songs hinted at.

The other source of 'sacred marriage' literature is a collection of enchanting love songs dealing with the amorous encounter of a goddess with a few specific kings. The evidence is clear: the king represents Dumuzi or Amaušumgalanna. He goes to the sacred lap of the goddess, or rather, a woman who represents her, the two have a happy night together and in the morning, the king and his kingdom are blessed by the divine. Several scholars assumed that this was the earliest and most essential part of Sumerian religion. They even dated the custom to the preliterate fourth century BCE, which is imaginative, to say the least. In real life, things are less glamorous. Sadly, most of our 'sacred marriage' songs come from the Isin-Larsa period and were written for King Šusîn. In the popular books, the goddess is generally and conveniently identified as Inanna, while her mate, the king, is supposed to represent her husband Dumuzi. She is the eternal goddess; he is the god/king who dies and is reborn like the vegetation every year. It fitted Frazer's visions perfectly. But life isn't as simple as that. Several songs of the 'sacred marriage' genre are not dedicated to Inanna but to the goddess Bau/Baba. The latter was a leading goddess of Isin, and a major competitor of Inanna. If politics had turned out differently, we would think of Bau/Baba as the major goddess of Mesopotamia. Though Dumuzi dies, he is not only a vegetation deity. He may appear as a farmer's god or as a nomadic sheepherder's god; when he is called Amaušumgalanna, he is a god of the fig/date harvest and a fierce warrior. There are even songs identifying him with a deity called Damu, the child. These gods came from different ethnic and cultural groups, each of them with their own preferences regarding the husband of the goddess. Only the farmers had this thing about the dying and reborn vegetation. Sorry, Mr. Frazer, things are a lot more complicated than you assumed.

How common was the 'primitive' ritual? Some early scholars made it the sum and summit of old Sumerian religion. But there is no evidence for the 'sacred marriage' in most city-states and periods. More so, only a few songs actually hint at real, physical congress. Usually, we don't know how the 'sacred marriage' was celebrated, and whether it was a bodily event or just a symbolic gesture. The ceremony happened in private, and for good reasons Assyriologists with their clipboards and stop-watches were not invited to watch, take notes, and argue about it. In third millennium BCE literature, the bulk of evidence comes from city Uruk, and the dynasty of Urnammu, which started in Uruk but made Ur their capital. It could have been a local tradition. As J. Renger remarks (RlA: *'Heilige Hochzeit*), the gods of Eridu and Nippur show no connection to the 'sacred marriage' tradition. It means a lot: these cities were the major spiritual centres of old Sumer.

And just how old is the custom? There are mythical texts that hint at a 'sacred marriage' involving prehistoric heroes like Enmerkar, Lugalbanda and Gilgameš. Sadly, their tales are far from what we would call 'history'. Nor do they supply any reliable details.

Several respectable scholars tried to find evidence. It was a tough job and we should respect their efforts. There are figurines and clay images showing people making love. You see a man mounting a woman from behind. She is drinking beer from a vessel through a long tube. Or you see a couple embracing in bed. Both types are common. Both were identified, at one time or another, as images of the 'sacred marriage'. We could just as well consider them erotica, or pornography, or maybe they were supposed to bring good luck and plenty of kids. There is no evidence that connects them with any ritual or hints at a religious background.

What about literature? The 'sacred marriage' songs contain plenty of sexual allusions. However, they are also extremely difficult, and it is hard to generalise from them. Samuel Kramer published the best-known translation of the assorted pieces in *The Sacred Marriage Rite*. In the first publication, Kramer noted with disarming honesty that *unfortunately the text contains many ambiguities and obscure passages, and the interpretation here presented may turn out completely erroneous* (quoted by Henshaw, 1994:241). Sadly, this disclaimer is missing in Kramer's popular works and in the selection published in *ANET*.

The most detailed description of the 'Sacred Marriage' is a text celebrating a New-Year ritual procession of musicians and drummers, dancers, and selected cultic personnel who are extremely hard to identify. In the parade walked sag-ur-sag ritualists who combed their hair and graced the right side of their dress with men's clothing and the left with women's; there were šugia maidens, and kurgarrûs carrying swords. It would be wonderful to say more about them. However the translations vary substantially and the nature of these cultic persons has been interpreted in many different ways. Please allow me to shut up and watch the parade in silence. Our ritualists passed by, and above them, the NU.GIG shone from the evening sky. Usually the NU.GIG is a high-ranking priestess; in our text, she is planet Venus and the goddess of the ritual. There were games with hoops and rope-jumping, communal worship and purification of citizens, animals and plants. The song culminates in a short passage indicating that a bed was set up. Here are the crucial lines, after SAHG 1953:97, trans. JF:

That her heart may delight in the [...] dress, and enjoy the bed,

the lady is bathed for the sacred lap,

is bathed for the lap of the king,

is bathed for the lap of (king) Iddindagan,

is holy Inanna bathed,

and the ground is perfumed with cedar resin.

The king approaches the sacred lap with his head held high,

Walks with proudly lifted head to the lap of Inanna,

Amaušumgalanna lies with her,

delights in her beautiful body.

That's it. Sorry. In the next verses, the union is over. Day has come, king and 'Inanna' are seated in the throne chamber. The 'goddess' commands that the incense is ignited, food is served, and music is played. She embraces the king and sits at his side. It's a day of celebration for everyone. The 'sacred' gives way to the 'profane', and both are having a wonderful time.

Our king was Iddindagan of the Isin-Larsa period. He was an Amorite, not a Sumerian king. An Amorite? Oh damn it! I thought we were discussing ancient Sumerian fertility rites! It's a beautiful and elaborate piece of poetry that exists in several widely different translations.

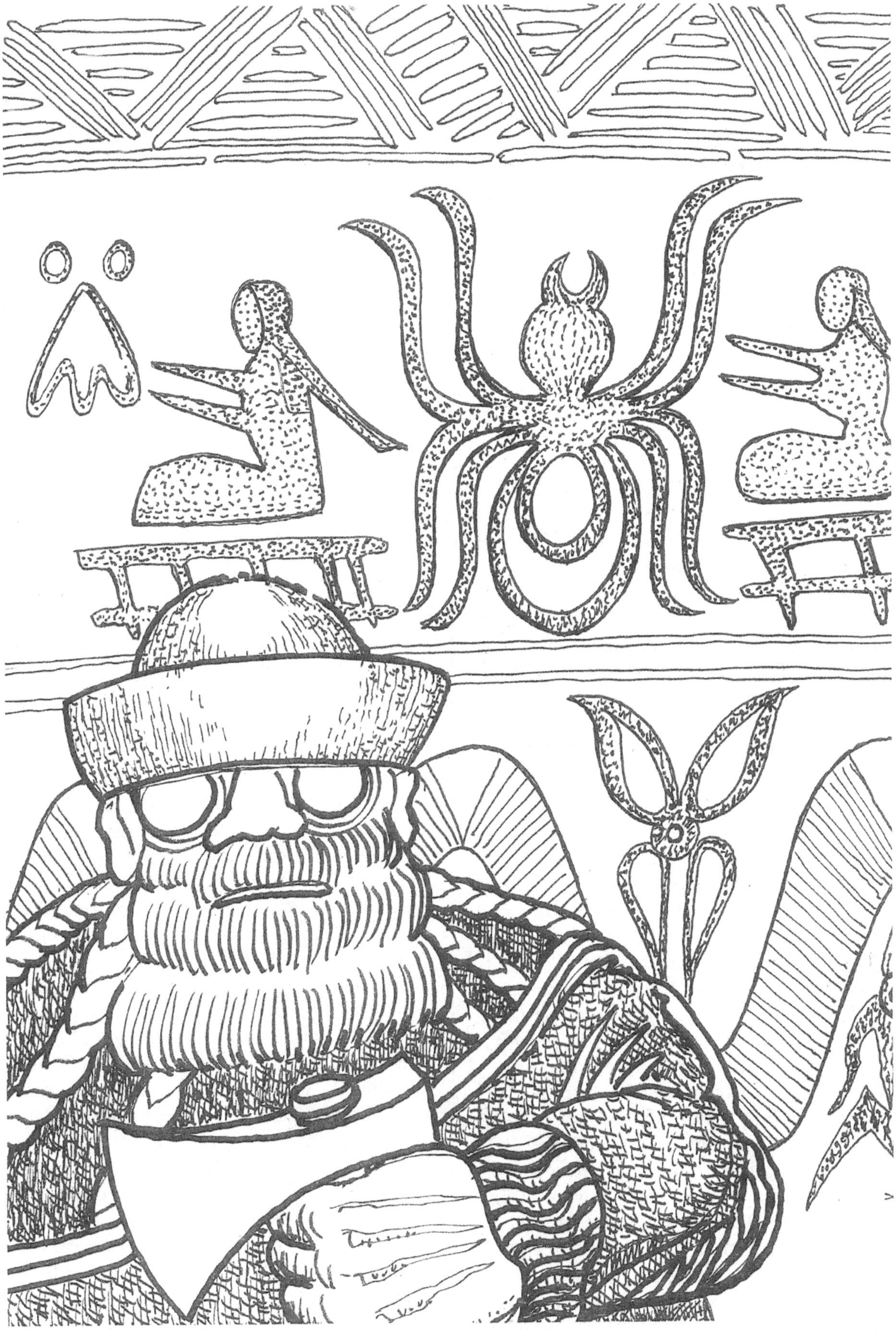

Figure 7 Bearded Person (priest?) with Axe. Inspired by a figurine from Tellō, c.2040-1870 BCE. Background based on roll seals from the Ur- and Jemdet-Nasr period.

Two songs supply a few extra details. The woman who represented the goddess enjoyed a bath before congress with the king, and the two shared a meal after the lovemaking. Finally, the incarnate goddess confirmed (or blessed) the king's fate by a prediction of success, prosperity and well-being.

In another so-called 'sacred marriage' song we read how King Šulgi of Ur III was invested. He went to the ritual wearing a long robe and a wig, and received throne, crown, robes, weapons, sceptre and sandals from the goddess, plus the assurance that he would now be worthy of kingship.

The songs seem to describe different rituals. In the first, we are facing an annual event: it's a New Year ritual. In the second, a young king gains the legitimization to rule: this sort of thing happens only once. Nor was it the only ritual a king required to rise to his office. The very kings of the Ur III and Isin-Larsa periods who are firmly associated with the 'sacred marriage' frequently recorded that they received their kingship from Enlil or from the Great Gods. A 'sacred marriage' may have been part of the ordination, but not necessarily the only or most important one.

Now for the timing. Our evidence comes from a short period between the end of the third millennium BCE and the start of the second. Narāmsîn (c.2291 BCE) is the first king on record who claimed to have participated in the ritual. Note that he was a descendant of Sargon I, an Akkadian and not a Sumerian king. He was also the first king who deified himself. There is, so far, very little evidence for 'sacred marriage' rites at the start of the Ur III period. As far as we know, King Urnammu did not bother to have himself deified, nor did he participate in 'sacred marriage' rites. He is famous for the first known law-code in human history. Only a fragment survives. His son Šulgi boasted that his mother was an entu(m) (*a woman who is a goddess*), but this does not indicate that his parents performed a 'sacred marriage' ceremony. However, Šulgi said he participated in something similar. And he certainly deified himself: being the summit of royal perfection was not enough for him. Most of the so-called 'sacred marriage' songs come from the Amorite kings of the Isin-Larsa period (c.2000-1800 BCE). Tough luck that the Isin-Larsa period is not representative for the fourth or third millennium: it is precisely the time when Sumerian culture fell apart. The Amorite kings were foreign invaders. They did their best to continue Sumerian traditions. But they also introduced new ideas. Under their rule, the power of the temples waned disastrously, while the influence of the kings increased. How come the foreign Amorites wrote much more about the topic than the people before and after them? And why did the 'sacred marriage' gradually disappeared with the advent of the Old Babylonian period?

Next, let us take a look at the way the ritual allegedly happened. As usual, Frazer's mind-blowing flying circus is lurking in the background.

In popular books, a woman called entu(m) represents the goddess, and granted abundance and blessings to the regent and country, while the king remained a divine but mortal being, just as Dumuzi was. Dumuzi appears as a mythical pre-flood king in the *Sumerian Kings Lists*: he governed Badtibira for 36,000 years. That's amazingly long lived. However, according to Sumerian belief, the pre-flood kings governed for extremely long periods. That's one way of looking at it. As Dumuzi's regency is far from certain, he can just as easily be understood as a deity, and even, in some aspects as a vegetation god. Inanna, however, has many characteristics which do not make her a 'fertility goddess', let alone a 'mother goddess'. There is just one minor local tradition from the city-state Umma claiming that she had a son (who turned out to be a devoted hairdresser). Inanna was anything but a mother goddess; she was not interested in pregnancy and birth. Instead, we meet her leading armies to war. And what function did the ceremony have? Kramer assumed that the 'Sacred Marriage' granted fertility to the kingdom. Falkenstein believed that the ritual ensured the deification of the kings of Ur III and the Isin-Larsa period. Jacobsen considered it primarily 'a woman's cult', whatever that may mean.

Let's approach things from another angle. In the late nineteenth century, many scholars assumed that fertility is a natural attribute of women. It seemed so obvious. In their age, men went to work, explored the world and waged war while women stayed at home and raised the kids. Provided they came from good families with some income. Naturally, the same ought to apply to the realm of the gods. It was a charming idea that suited the romantic concept of 'Mother Nature', though it did not always accord with reality. According to the opinion of many scholars of the early twentieth century, the allegedly 'matriarchal' early societies were based on a single, monotheistic great goddess who was basically in charge of 'fertility'. Indeed, there are cultures where happy motherly goddesses grant abundance to everyone. However, it is by no means the norm. Nor are they monotheistic, or related to such a vague construct as a 'matriarchal' society. In Sumer, many goddesses represent principles of social order, like Ninisina and Bau/Baba, of writing and science like Nidaba/Nisaba, of truth like Kittu, of magic like Ningirima and healing like Gula. Abundance, fertility and wealth were often attributed to male gods like An, Enki, Enlil, and farmer gods like Adad, Ninurta and Ningirsu. Guys like them were praised for making rain fall, rivers swell, fishes swim, trade thrive, grains sprout and flocks multiply. Inanna may grant a blessing to the king and his realm, or authenticate his right to govern. These are political activities. Where does she act as a 'fertility goddess'? Her functions are amazingly numerous, but they emphasise love, sex, struggle, war and conquest. Inanna keeps the principles of civilisation in her city Uruk. She was not invoked for childbirth and we do not see her raising kids. Except for her lonely son in provincial Umma, she does not even have a family. Her husband is away half of the year! Several of her lovers were kicked out, cursed, transformed or came to a messy end. And while she spends lots of time making love she obviously doesn't get pregnant. So how about widening our horizon? If we have to drag the tired old concept 'fertility' into the ritual, what if the UNION of goddess and the god-king grant abundance to the state?

Let me introduce two common and complicated concepts. The title **en** means a regent, a king or, as Jacobsen details, a miraculously successful manager. The term is Sumerian and was commonly used for male and female leaders or directors, or managing priests if you like. Several early regents had themselves praised as en. The en could hold a high religious rank or that of a superior administrator: what it really entailed is far from certain. In different periods and places, the title had different meanings. Maybe a note of caution is due. The title en was not always related to the extreme upper class. It was also used for the heads of organisations. There was an en running each manufactory, each group of shepherds, the bakers, cooks and the cleaning staff. Some were male, some female, and in many contexts it is helpful to think about them simply as administrators. To understand the 'sacred marriage' we have to focus our attention on a small range of badly documented high-level ens, and ignore a lot of minor ens who had very little to do with statecraft and religion.

Related to them are the ensis; an **ensi** is a city governor.

The other word is **entu(m).** It is not the female counterpart of the en, but an entirely different type of religious specialist: entu(m) means a *woman who is a goddess.* What this implies remains a mystery. Was she a special priestess, or the queen, or maybe both? Maybe the entu(m) was deified, maybe she impersonated a goddess or maybe she was obsessed by a deity on special occasions: we simply don't know. For the 'sacred marriage' the en, in this case a man, had some sort of union with the local goddess, who was represented by the entu(m). She conferred blessings on him and the land, but this couldn't have been a one-sided affair. The loins of the king, as you just read, were just as sacred as the loins of the goddess. In early times and as far as is

Figure 8 An, God of Heaven, Fecund Breed Bull of the Sky. Inspired by the bull-ornament of a harp, early third millennium BCE and a head from Tellō, late third millennium BCE.

known, some en were married to a major goddess and some entu(m)s to a major god. This is an important point: en and entu(m) related to these deities as partners. It does not, however, entail that all ens and entu(m)s were involved in 'sacred marriage' rites. To be married to a deity does not imply that there is a human being around who represents the deity in bed. Nor were the ens always kings. A few kings called themselves en around the end of the third millennium and during the Isin-Larsa period. Most kings did not. The office of en was separated from kingship during the Old Babylonian period. By the time the historical record improves, the en is not a king and the entu(m) does not confer kingship: the entire 'sacred marriage' seems to have gone out of fashion. It seems to have disappeared during the Old Babylonian period.

If the king acted the part of the en, perhaps his queen personified the city goddess, as Jacobsen assumed. Or maybe it was a leading priestess. Kramer believed that it was performed with a 'hierodule'. That's another slick Greek term. It means 'sacred slave', refers to a woman 'owned' by a deity or temple, a 'nun' dedicated to the cult or to a 'sacred prostitute'. The word is rather useless when we discuss Mesopotamian religion. Several prominent scholars (and I'm being nice when I won't mention names) seem to have assumed that Mesopotamia was simply crawling with overheated, sweaty priestesses raising cash for their temples by spreading their jittery legs. Nowadays the evidence for them is so weak that we should better forget the topic.

If we have to guess which priestesses acted as the goddess, one group of candidates were the NU.GIG (Akkadian: qadištu). We'll discuss them at length later on (commentary to LS II, 159): Lamaštu is a qadištu for or among the gods, her brothers. Some qadištu were associated with the cult of Inanna but most of them were not. Or maybe we should think of the LUKUR (Akkadian: nadītu), who were high-ranking, often aristocratic priestesses. Other possible candidates are medium rank priestesses, a maid of the high priestess, a maid of the queen and of course all sorts of 'sacred prostitutes'. Twenty years ago the books were full of them; nowadays, due to lack of reliable evidence, they are disappearing at an alarming rate. It turns out that the 'sacred prostitution' of Mesopotamia is a popular myth. Whatever it may have been, the evidence is very patchy.

A detailed ritual schedule of the extensive Babylonian New Year ritual survives (*ANET*, 1992:331-334). It does not mention a 'sacred marriage'. Sadly, the tablets come from the Seleucid period. Now that is awfully late. At the time, Mesopotamia was governed by the descendants of Alexander! Most scholars assume that this Babylonian New Year ritual goes back to earlier times, but just how early is difficult to say. Worse, the account only covers four or five days, and the rest is missing. Some scholars insist that a 'sacred marriage' must have taken place on the tablets that have not been found. Others claim the custom had long disappeared.

Whatever the 'sacred marriage' may have been, it faded into oblivion during the Old Babylonian period. Middle Babylonian kings seem to have done without sacred sex. Neither were 'sacred marriages' required by the Assyrians and Neo-Assyrians; the kings represented divine success with or without female blessings. Many of them were on good terms with Inanna's Semitic counterpart Ištar, whom they worshipped as a goddess of love, war and oracular revelation, but they did not attempt to go to bed with her.

And now for something completely different. In the late first millennium BCE we encounter a few 'sacred marriages' that were not enacted between kings, queens or members of a priesthood but between deities: processions carried the figures of the major god and goddess to a temple bedroom. The statues were placed on a bed and the audience departed so the deities could enjoy their lovemaking in private. Afterwards, the statues were treated to a lavish meal. The ritual was just as symbolic as the daily feeding and dressing of statues, as putting them to sleep and waking them in the morning. The kings prayed while the divine couple made love. They beseeched their favourite goddess, such as Tašmētu(m), Zarpānītu(m), Antu(m), Bau/Baba and Aya to have a good word for them with their respective husbands Marduk, Nabû, An, Ningirsu and Šamaš. This marriage of the gods was an occasion for public festivity. Whether it had much to do with the earlier versions is open to debate.

What happened in the Neo-Babylonian period is even harder to understand. Once the Assyrian empire had collapsed, the Neo-Babylonian kings made serious efforts to revive the customs of antiquity, as far as they knew them. Maybe they were simply inventing things. King Nabûšumaiškum dressed up as Marduk and proposed marriage to the goddess Tašmētum. His contemporaries derided him for sacrilege. Antiochus IV, a regent of the Greek Seleucid period, formally married the goddess Nanay of Susa. He had other things than sacredness in mind: his new status allowed him to waste her temple treasure.

Where does it leave us? The 'sacred marriage' turns out to be an artificial and misleading term. It creates the illusion that there was a single, well-established ritual ensuring fertility, royal success and divine blessings, allegedly characteristic for the so-called 'fertility' cults of the fourth millennium BCE and earlier. Far from being a typical expression of Sumerian fertility ritual in the fourth millennium BCE, it was a ritual practised, in several different and badly documented ways, in a few city-states, like Uruk, Ur and Isin, between the end of the third and the early centuries of the second millennium BCE. Before and after this brief period, characterised by the disintegration of Sumerian culture, occupation by the foreign Amorites and the dawn of the Old Babylonian period, there is very little evidence for it. And even in this brief time-span, the 'sacred marriage' may have been a local phenomenon. During some ritual, maybe the New Year celebration or maybe the inauguration of a new king, some ritualists made love, in a real or symbolic way, in a few city-states. For the majority of states, the evidence is missing. Apart from this, there is verification for similar rites enacted in a thoroughly symbolic fashion during the first millennium BCE, when statues of deities were assumed to make love. As the evidence for the 'sacred marriage' is very weak, limited to a short period and small geographical districts, we had better keep our minds open. It will take plenty of excavation to bring some clarity to the situation. At the present time, we are simply happy to know that for a small group of people, based around the cities Uruk and Ur, and later around the state of Isin, during a period of fewer than five hundred years, the lovemaking, real or symbolic, of a few ritualists, ensured a blessing to the state. It's a splendid idea, which may or may not have influenced the much later tantric rituals of sacred lovemaking in India.

God Lists

The scribes of the third millennium worried about religious diversity. In Fāra and Tell Abû Ṣalābīkh, they tried to get some order into the local deities by listing them for the local scribal schools. Maybe they were not the first, but their records are the oldest in evidence. The *Fāra list* names c.560 deities. That's a lot when you consider that the scribes were only acquainted with the deities in their immediate neighbourhood. The list begins with An, Enlil, Inanna, Enki, Nanna and Utu: all of them major deities with a great future. The scribes started their list by ordering the gods according to their importance. Or maybe they were promoting these deities. A list is not necessarily a record: it could be an advertisement or a legitimisation. It might have legitimised political decisions. After all, behind the gods were mighty temple organisations, some of them rich, influential and rather unscrupulous. As ever, it's all about money. Further down things become confusing. It was an impossible task to sort so many local gods by precedence. Provided the order was based on priorities at all: most of the deities have Sumerian names and are completely unknown. We just don't know how important they were. Apart from the major players in the first lines, it is impossible to discern the organising structure of the Fāra list.

Figure 9 Goddess Bau/Baba. Fragment of a Gudea Stele, c.2200 BCE, Tellō

Here's another tricky issue. Long before the Proto-Sumerians migrated to lower Mesopotamia, the country had a mixed population consisting of unknown aboriginal groups, some of them of Semitic origin. Migrants were streaming into Sumer all the time. Of the 560 deities on the Fāra list, only three (!) have Akkadian names. Bottéro proposed that the Semitic people may have had fewer gods than the Sumerians, but it's just as possible that the Sumerian scribes didn't give a damn for them. The Fāra list is, at best, a selection. Similar objections can be raised regarding other god lists.

During the Ur III period, the *Weidner list* was composed. It contained over 200 names and was popular as a practice text for scribes. Most of it lacks any reasonable structure: it only ensured that students were familiar with the names of deities. Aššurbanipal's librarians did not bother to keep copies; the king did not collect exercise texts. By the Old Babylonian period, a whole range of god lists had been drawn up. The *Nippur list* is known in two versions, one containing sixty extra names. The organising structure begins by sorting gods according to their importance and changes to lexical entries towards the end. The list was a local affair: fragments have only been found in the Nippur region.

Proto-Diri (?) is a god list of a hundred names. Next, the *Genouillac list* was drawn up. It starts with Enlil's theogony, demonstrating his importance, followed by his celestial parents and their ancestors. Then the scribe returns to Enlil's family and court. A total of 473 gods appear.

The greatest list, a product of the Middle Babylonian period, is *An=Anu(m)*. It is a much-expanded version of the *Genouillac list* consisting of c.1970 deities, plus a few explanatory comments. The scribes tried to impose order on chaos: a sure way of making a perfect mess. The pattern goes: first a major god in all of his aspects, followed by his spouse in all her forms, their children, and finally the members of the household. Then we can turn to the next deity. It's a neat idea that didn't work. The Enki/Ea section starts with Enki, continues with Enki's wife, and then Enki's sons follow. One of them is Marduk, who was becoming a major player at the time, so before we learn about the staff of Enki's temple we have to digest an extensive account of everybody belonging to the Marduk circle. It's a major interruption. Several versions of this list survive; late ones include the *Fifty Names of Marduk*. Another major criterion was popularity and political power: Lamaštu, who ought to be close to her father An and her mother Antu(m) right at the top, finds herself dumped unceremoniously near the bottom. The next list is considerably shorter. *An=Anu=ša ameli* lists 157 gods and goddesses and identifies them as 24 major deities. It was written around the Kassite period or later: Marduk takes priority over his father Ea. Further lists show their own agenda. A list from Aššur starts, predictably, with Aššur. In Sultanepe a small list of 200 deities appeared which did not become popular anywhere else. Another list from Aššurbanipal's library tried to cover new ground and introduced lots of unknown gods. Finally, a god list was composed in the Emesal dialect of Sumerian, traditionally a language (or dialect) used by well-educated women and special ritual singers. The list contained 115 deities and was created by selecting material from *An=Anu(m)*. Whoever wrote it was good at language studies but ignorant about deities: some of them appear in the wrong place, with Enki and Ninki ancestors of Enlil, and even a god whose name, spelt in two variations, appears as two deities. There are fragments of other god lists showing that plenty of scribes and theologians were worried about the abundance of gods, and tried to enforce their own vision of spiritual reality (Lambert in RlA *'Götterlisten'*, Bottéro 2004:45-55).

There was never a single, well-organised order to the gods.

An example: In south Sumerian Eridu cosmology, Enki is the son of Nammu, the primal creative goddess of water. In central Sumerian myths, based around Nippur, he is a son of An and Antu(m). When Enlil rose to power and became king of the gods, Enki appears as his son, and An's grandson. It's not as if there was a single true tradition. Different people had different beliefs and arranged their vision of the divine according to their needs and preferences. Sumerian religion was full of surprising characters, but the mythical record is a mess. The deeper you get into Mesopotamian religion the more you will be amazed by local and temporal theodiversity. By, say, 1500 BCE several thousand deities had been catalogued. That's an enormous number. Old Mesopotamia was not a large country. In the process, many god names had become titles of more successful deities. Deimel, in 1914 narrowed them down to 3300; of these Tallquist only accepted 2400 as distinct divinities (Bottéro, 2004:45). And that just goes for the gods that attracted the attention (instead of the indifference or scorn) of the scribes.

Theodiversity

Cities and the states that surrounded them were not simply owned by a single god. In real life, gods were rarely single. The Sumerians, like so many other people of the Near East, liked to organise their deities in family structures. A successful god was assumed to be married, and in many cases, the couple had children, who were minor deities of the neighbourhood. In practice, this did not always work out. Some gods were equipped with a whole range of partners. It does not mean that they lived in a harem, but simply indicated that various population groups wanted to relate their favourite deity to a famous one. Nor was city ownership a permanent institution: when gods lost popularity, they disappeared into the background, while a new divine family took over. Usually, dozens of gods were worshipped in each city-state, and each wave of migrants brought along their own favourites. Some of those new gods remained as they were; others were identified with existing ones, which equipped them with new functions, myths and symbols.

Just like modern researchers, some scribes (and regents) were unhappy about so much diversity. They tried to narrow down the scope by identifying deities as 'aspects' or 'names' of other gods. Maybe they were right. It made things easier to organise. And when you think about it, how many distinct god types does a community need? A few dozen should cover most functions. The scribes may have had good intentions. But they certainly destroyed a lot of fascinating cultural variety. Some contemporary scholars argue that there was only a small group of major deities who were worshipped under a wide range of different names and titles. Just as possibly it was the other way around. Small population groups discovered or invented deities, and when small groups became large groups, plenty of independent deities had rather similar functions. Consider the birth goddesses: people wouldn't need so many different ones if they were satisfied with a single great mother goddess. For this reason, a lot of titles and offices were shared. The hymns are full of repetitions. Who was the one and only creator of the world? Nammu, An, Antu(m), Enki, Enlil, Mami, Aruru, Ninḫursag. The singular Creator of mankind? An, Antu(m), Enki, Marduk, Mami and a host of birth goddesses. The supreme warrior? Try Enlil, Ninurta, Ningirsu, Erra, Nergal, Ninazu, Zababa, Amaušumgalanna, Marduk and, for the fun of it, Inanna/Ištar/Irnina. There must have been more: thousands of gods remain unknown. Each goddess was the queen of everything, the ruler of mankind, the victorious lady governing all other ladies. Pretty much every deity was eulogised as all-powerful, as regent of the lands, as supreme, majestic, exalted, perfect, unsurpassable. Almost every god is praised for fertile fields, for abundant herds, for carps in spring and blissful rain. Few gods were specialists. Most deities were in charge of lots of things.

Unlike some of the Greek and Roman gods, most of the Mesopotamian deities were not limited to a single job or function. When a god was praised as the summit of divine authority, it simply tells us that this was and is true, for some people in specific places and periods. That one god is supreme never implies that the others are not. It was simply good form to celebrate many deities as the supreme ones. You encounter the same thing in the conglomerate of religions that are so easily classed as 'Hinduism': to each worshipper the personal deity is the greatest of them all. It does not mean that everybody subscribes to the same view, nor does anybody try to enforce this choice. In a truly polytheistic mindset, gods may appear and act like people, natural phenomena or abstract principles, but they are not confined to these or any other specific forms. The divine keeps changing and so do the forms that reveal its essence. People live and die, but gods merge, change, shift into one another. For them, name, personality, gender and job definition are temporary conveniences. In this respect they are much like us.

It takes us into a world where many gods can be narrowed down to several gods and a few gods expand to many gods. The divine can be one, two, several, many and all players in the game: it can be you, me, all or none of us. It depends on your point of view. When you search for similarity you discover a few dozen deities in a lot of variations. When you explore difference, you discover thousands of unique gods with their own special history and background. We can widen and narrow the scope as we like. But no matter whether you search for similarity or difference, you are not discovering what is really going one. You merely get a chance to watch your mind making a selection that appears to be 'real'. Maybe a bit of pragmatism can help. Why limit yourself? Why insist on one choice over the other? Why bother to be right, to convert your acquaintances or to enforce the one true creed? Each cult is embedded in a cycle of expansion and contraction, interrupted by foreign influences and major shifts in power and wealth. Consider sudden changes in the religious world when charismatic seers preach a new and fashionable creed. Reflect on stubborn people clinging to traditions that may be long out of date. Imagine students copying texts and getting errors into them. The world is a remarkable place. All of these things happen all the time.

The major influences in streamlining so many local religions were inspiration, economics and politics. First you have a handful of visionaries and enthusiasts. They introduce something which touches hearts and blows minds, and when it turns out popular, politics, influence, war and wealth decide the success of a given god. The mystics can step back: the bankers and warlords have taken control.

One thing that deeply influenced religion was the growth of settlements into city-states. Early Sumerian gods are basically village folk, members of a divine clan. In early hymns, the gods are family people. They live like local strong-men, farmers, herders, fishers, simple folk, just like most of the population. It did not stay that way. During the third millennium BCE, while the cities were growing and struggling for fertile land, the pantheon was increasingly modelled on the organisation of a large and powerful state. The gods transformed from family members to regents and ministers. The divine world began to reflect sophisticated city life. Major gods suddenly ran a little court and employed minor deities as their officials, scribes, advisors, bakers, cooks, slaughterers, brewers, priests, magicians, musicians, hairdressers, fighters and guards. The divine world mirrored a social world that was becoming more complex the bigger the states became. By the end of the third millennium two major things had happened. Sargon I had proved that an empire can be won and governed. Šulgi had demonstrated that bureaucracy is fun. Both lessons had immense effects. The pantheon was imagined as a divine empire and its members had their places in a hierarchy. But as there was never a single church or dogma in Mesopotamia, various people in different periods invented their own hierarchies and functions for the gods.

The Nature of the Gods

How did the people get along with the deities? It depends on which people we are talking about. Jean Bottéro (2004:40) expressed an opinion commonly found in the studies of his generation: '*The gods were above all "lords and masters" (bēlu) who might show kindness but always remained enveloped in majesty, distant and fearsome, isolated in their own sphere, inaccessible to everything but their own kind (...) Reverence, admiration, and self-effacement with respect to the gods dominate the texts. I know of no text that represents another side of religious sentiment: the tendency to get closer to the divine, to seek it out as a positive source of happiness, a strictly "mystical" attitude. Anything that might get close to this "mystical" sense – and there are hardly any instances of it – is open to contextual interpretation that leads it back to fear and to the "sentiment of distance" maintained constantly between humans and the gods. Furthermore, no document reveals a sense of the presence of the divinity within a person.'*

This passage, I'm happy to say, is based on an essay composed in 1948. It reflects the academic horizon of the time: commonplace topics of our age, like Voodoo, Tantra, Daoism and shamanism were largely unexplored or misrepresented. So, with all due respect, I disagree.

It used to seem so simple. Small, helpless humans are facing almighty gods. People are on one side: mortal, frail and given to error and sin. Gods are on the other: powerful, everlasting, incomprehensible and utterly overwhelming. Between them appears a gap that could only be crossed by a very few heroic individuals, most of whom happened to be kings. The Sumerians, so we read too frequently, imagined that mankind and the divine were separate. The gods made everything, owned everything and were everything, while mankind was there to serve, to sacrifice, to work and suffer for the divine. But did this go for all people and all gods?

Special rules applied to the very ritualists who interacted with the gods on an everyday basis. On closer examination, we encounter highly unusual relationships. Let us begin with the basics: the Mesopotamians were never a monotheistic culture. To them, the divine was inherent in the world: you encounter the gods in the powers of nature, in the howling storms, the much-desired rains, in the flashes of lightning, the sprouting of plants, the flicker of the hearth fire and the stars in the night sky. Here we talk nature, but I would not want to give the impression that the Mesopotamians simply deified the scenery. Their religion was more sophisticated. A god of fire was fire, to be sure, and provided warmth, light, protection and a digestible meal. He was also abstract enough to banish evil, mete out punishment, protect justice and keep the family together: qualities that are not self-evident from the nature of fire. Water brought fertility, but it also taught learning, maths, science, engineering, magic and music; it provided physical hygiene and spiritual purification. To say that Enki/Ea is a water god is to miss a lot. The Mesopotamians experienced the divine in nature, but they also perceived it in daily life, in social affairs, in the pattern of society. Far from being 'primitive' nature gods, the deities also represented highly abstract concepts, like power, authority, wisdom, truth, reliability, attraction, justice, knowledge, hospitality and so on.

Unlike YHVH of the *Old Testament* the Mesopotamian gods are very close. Christianity is a transcendental religion: it emphasises that god created the world, but he is not the world. To reach god, a mystic had to give up the world, the body and all attachments. Plants and animals were created for mankind: they were god's creatures, but man was encouraged to abuse them any way he liked. Plants were not even acknowledged as living beings; I'm sure you noticed that Noah didn't take any into the ark. How they survived the flood remains a mystery.

The Mesopotamian gods are creators, but they are also inherent in their creation: we are dealing with deities who are transcendent, immanent and both. They are beyond the world, they are in the world, and they are the world. In such a worldview, the divine is not far away, nor is it necessary to make an extra effort to get in touch with it.

Religion is a complex and multi-layered phenomena. Belief in a deity differs, depending on whether we question an illiterate farmer, a well-educated priest, a healer/conjurer or a member of the royal house. The first probably believes themselves to be far from the divine, and is likely to be awed by it, and by the majesty of the temple cult that goes with it. The priest is much better informed, and will be aware of theological contradictions. However, in most cases, a dualist worldview and a safe distance to the divine were cultivated. Look at the Catholic clergy: unless a priest was trained by Jesuits and explored Loyola's remarkable exercises, he is not supposed to feel just what Jesus experienced, or to witness the major events of the *Bible* as a participant. Many early Assyriologists took the Christian clergy of their time as a model: intellectual, respectable, well-educated persons who interacted with the divine without being part of it. Maybe Mesopotamian priests and priestesses acted and thought in a similar way. Their training demanded that they feared and respected the gods, and if they were spiritually competent they retained a sense of humility.

Things are different when we look into the daily business of the conjurer/ healer/ exorcist/ magicians: the mašmaššu, the āšipu and the (rare) female āšiptu. We will discuss their activities in another chapter. For now, it should suffice that a conjurer had to face his or her fears every day. Patients exhibited horrible diseases, they were frequently impure, cursed, haunted by malignant spirits or doomed by a disapproving deity. All of these influences (just like diseases) were dangerous and contagious. Luckily, the risk could be reduced. The conjurers used magic and meditation to remain happy and well. They bathed and washed and cultivated a form of positive thinking (or self-hypnosis) to overcome their fears. They bolstered their courage by carrying sacred plants, by wearing talismans and special clothing. More important was the meditative side: several spells reveal that the conjurers improved their health and mood with visualisations. They reduced the risk of pollution by imagining how sacred fluids washed through their bodies, providing healing, vitality and purification. Furthermore, they moved within a cluster of protective deities. When you have to face evil spirits and contagious diseases, it is sound reasoning to have several major gods on your side.

In Mesopotamian thought, every person was accompanied by at least one personal deity. Documents of the third millennium BCE mention them. Kings claimed that they were born and raised by specific goddesses; that major gods were their parents or that some deities were their brothers, sisters and friends. Some were married to deities. Whether it was just aristocrats who thought like that remains open to speculation: nobody bothered to record the beliefs of common people. For most worshippers, the personal gods were parent figures. Unless your parents were horrible, incompetent or absent the relationship was based on mutual sympathy and caring. It is not what I would call *'distant'* or *'based on fear'*. For kings and queens, the relationship was even closer. The regents had to represent the divine on earth, and many of them felt close to the gods or even pretended to be divine. Several kings claimed that a deity *'loves'* them, and that's as close as it gets. The so-called 'sacred marriage' rites give good evidence that some people represented the divine in ritual and lovemaking. For conjurers, having a pair of personal deities was not sufficient. Usually, they surrounded themselves with a whole group of gods before they entered the sickroom. It was a professional relationship: the conjurer did the work of the gods, and the gods supported her or him. Some conjurers literally became deities. An example appears in the bilingual *Compendium* from Aššurbanipal's library (Consecration of the êru wand, Schramm 2008:81, after the German by JF). The setting is simple: a priest in the sickroom conjures a series of destructive spirits and banishes them in the name of Enki/Ea, the god of water, magic and healing. The Sumerian version of the ritual states:

I, the high priest call to you, (I), the wise of Enki, the high priest call to him:

The Akkadian version of the text shows a remarkable difference:

I, the high priest call herewith, (I), the wise Ea, the high priest call herewith...

In the Sumerian version, the conjurer acts in Enki's name, and in the younger Akkadian version he is Ea. It's an enormous difference. Under special conditions, a person can be divine. Call it identification, playacting, or obsession: our conjurer is Ea, and acts like Ea, as he or she shares a common nature with the god. Personally, I find this a very obvious insight: the divine and you enjoy a common substratum of consciousness that simply wants to come out.

Our conjurer is by no means the only example. Several ritualists in old Mesopotamia did not belong to the respectably well-behaved churchy type. In some cults male and female priests went into wild, ecstatic trances, were obsessed by the gods and channelled prophecy. We will discuss some of them in the comments to LS II, 1. Obsession is a useful practice that unites you with your deities. It may not look nice and occasionally it can take your personality apart, but it's as close to your gods as you can get. And that, for the time being, eliminates the alleged 'distance' between gods and devotees. For the Mesopotamians, as for so many other polytheistic cultures all around the world, the gods were as close as the devotee chose to approach them. Normal people could remain at a safe distance and special people, like ritualists, mediums and aristocrats could cross the imaginary divide, embrace the gods and remember their shared selfhood. It's one of those experiences that make life worth living.

Religious specialists

Each Sumerian temple employed many people. We might call them priesthood. It would be wrong. What is a priest or a priestess? We might imagine a professional religious specialist who mediates between mankind and the deities and spirits. Such a distinction makes sense in a secular society that admits to a division between state and church, between human and the divine, body and soul, however vague that distinction may be. In the ancient Near East, such a division was not only lacking; it was unthinkable. When we consider each city as the property of a few major deities (plus a range of smaller ones), the main temples appear as large organisations that incorporate all sorts of 'secular' functions simply to keep things running. Provided such terms like 'secular' make sense. The same goes for the government. The temple was a religious organisation but so was the royal palace. In Sumer and Akkad, kings governed thanks to divine permission. The later Babylonians thought pretty much the same, though they had different rituals to keep it so. My favourite was recorded rather late, during in the Seleucid period, when Mesopotamia was governed by the descendants of Alexander. During the long New Year festival in Babylon, the king had his hands washed. Then he was accompanied to the Esagila temple. When the king had arrived in the presence of Bēl (here: Marduk), the urigallu priest emerged from the sanctuary. He stripped the king of his sceptre, circle and sword. He took him into the temple and made him sit on a chair. Then he hit the king's cheek. He took the king into the presence of the god, dragged him by the ear and forced him to bow down to the ground. The king uttered a negative confession: *I did [not] sin, lord of the countries, I was not neglectful of your godship. [I did not] destroy Babylon, I did not command its overthrow, [I did not] [...] the temple Esagil, I did not forget its rites. [I did not] rain blows on the cheek of a subordinate [...] I did [not] humiliate them. [I watched out] for Babylon; I did not smash its walls...*the next lines are illegible. It would be great to know if these lines are a new invention, adapted to a foreign king, or based on an elder formula. That being done, the urigallu priest reassured the king of the god's friendship. Indeed Bēl was listening, would magnify the king, was sure to raise and bless him forever, and destroy all enemies. The priest announced that the royal insignia would be returned to the king. Then he struck the king's cheeks again. Our ritual text tells us that it was excellent luck when tears ran down the king's face, as this indicated the friendship of Bēl. If no tears appeared, an enemy was sure to arise and bring the king's downfall. (ANET, 1992:334). Painful blows? I am sure the king simply asked for it! Afterwards, he was allowed to become king again. The ritual continued. It's one of those traditions that ought to be revived.

When we come to several Akkadian rulers, to the Assyrians and the Neo-

Assyrians, we encounter kings who happened to be more or less divine, and who still retained their function as the major 'priests' of state. However, they were also human beings, prone to err and make a mess out of everything. Can frail, damnstupid human beings be divine? In a Christian worldview, they cannot. In the mind of the Mesopotamians they could. We might call this paradox, but to the people of the ancient Near East, it made sense. Also, nobody would want to disagree with an Assyrian king.

When we wish to understand the religious specialists we have two major difficulties. Call them space and time. Culture and civilisation developed in many city-states at once. While little can be said about the preliterate fourth millennium BCE, we observe plenty of violence between the cities in the third. They form alliances, betray each other, make friends and new enemies, and, in between, barbarian invasion livened up the day. Large states came together under successful leaders and fell apart under inefficient ones. Whenever a royal house went down the drain, a lot of people proposed independence. In the meantime we encounter usurpers and a lot of rebellion. The result is a bundle of divergent traditions, ensuring that some religious ranks, titles and functions varied, depending on the temple and its relationship to other city-states. So much for the general idea. In prosaic reality, our knowledge is wanting. We are lucky to have some data regarding a few temples in some periods. For most temples and periods this information is lacking. To generalise from a deficient database is tempting but pretty certain to mislead. I'll try it nevertheless, and ask your forgiveness.

In early Mesopotamia, many religious specialists were directly employed by the temples. Others were only employed on occasion; some did their job in the palace, and a lot worked in society or out in the countryside. It brings us our first generalisation: temple personnel were employed in a sacred context, but did not necessarily participate in ritual. To begin with, the major temples were not simply buildings or complexes of buildings but major landowners. The temple of Bau/Baba in Lagaš provides an impressive example: at the time of Gudea (c.2143-2124 BCE), it owned roughly 11,000 acres, i.e. 44.53 km² of fertile land. During the Neo-Babylonian period, King Kurigalzu I presented 525 km² to the Eanna temple of Inanna/Ištar and An/Anu of Uruk. As Renger remarks (RlA *'Großgrundbesitz'*), this amazing grant of property would have surrounded the city of Uruk by 25 km. It raises the question what happened to the property of the major city Larsa, which was only 20 km from Uruk. Renger cited the property of several temples and calculated their probable income regarding the people who could be supported. Given an average income of 8 gur barley per person per year, the Bau/Baba temple in Girsu could have provided food for 21,240 persons. The temple Guabba during period Ur III would have fed 27,982 people. The Eanna temple of Uruk in the Neo-Babylonian period may have fed 62,000 people, which is a record. All of these numbers should be considered with care; they do not incorporate extra deductions like interest. Each temple needed a wide range of professionals doing very ordinary things. The temple grounds were cultivated: there were farmers, gardeners, herdsmen in temple employ. The food was stored in huge granaries and storehouses. Shepherds, herdsmen, hunters, fowlers and fishers were working to provide food for the employees and offerings for the gods. Bakers made bread and cakes, butchers slaughtered sacrificial animals, and cooks prepared the food of the gods. Large temples employed beer makers. Some had a department of fumigation, which looked after the incense burners. There were door guards, carpenters, potters and metalworkers. Others were employed to spin, weave, sew, stitch and clean garments. Administrators, secretaries and librarians kept accounts, did the planning, the logistics, and saw to it that the organisation ran smoothly. Often enough, large temple organisations had so much wealth that they could finance traders and grant loans. Large temples functioned like a city within a city, and many of those who had access to the sacred spaces wore clean robes and shaved their heads. In many temples, though not necessarily all of them, hair may have threatened ritual purity. Or maybe it didn't. Maybe people simply didn't want to be pestered by lice and fleas. Hair is a tricky subject. Images of priestesses show long hair, or wigs, and the same may apply to a few types of priests and musicians. Kings did enter the inner sanctum, and their portraits usually show perfect coiffure and beards. But can we trust such works of art? Images of kings were often standardised. What looks like hair may be fake beards and wigs. Some people wore special costume. Others did not.

Large temples employed thousands of people. Many of them never entered the inner spaces. Some temple buildings were huge. Much of the space was needed for storage, administration and manufacture. Think of them as multi-purpose buildings.

Temple employees were religious specialists as their office followed religious regulations and served religious ends, but they were not what we might call a 'priesthood' in the modern sense. Every person attached to a temple gained the right to enter some spaces and had to undergo basic purification. Most of these rituals and customs are unknown.

What about spiritual training and **initiation** rites? Our knowledge is extremely wanting. A young Babylonian ritual text regarding the dedication of a 'priest' to the cult of Enlil and Ninlil gives a few insights. First, the candidate was carefully examined by some experts (unmânu), a priest (nêšaku), a higher-ranking priest (aḫu rabû) and a barber (šuginakku). The body of the candidate had to be without blemishes, and had to look like *an image of gold.* Attitude mattered. Candidates had to show *fear and humility.* An aspirant who took her or his duties lightly, who lacked respect for the temple and its deities was unacceptable. He (or she) also needed a good reputation: criminals were not admitted. Having passed the basic examination, the initiate had to serve for a trial period. He was not permitted to enter the inner spaces yet, received special training and had to qualify as *one who knows but does not talk.* After a trial period, he could undergo ritual purification, and learned the duties of his office. Later, for initiation, the candidate underwent a ceremonial bath with water and soap, was shaved and had his fingernails cut, which qualified him to enter the temple. The candidate of our text was by no means a priest yet. During a ceremony, he received a special, sanctified linen head-cloth and was dressed in white clothes. He had to renounce numerous misdeeds and sins, recite sacred texts and perform a ritual to wash his mouth out. After this ceremony, he was wrapped in a white blanket, just like the cult statues during their consecration. Only after these ceremonies was he fit to perform a religious office.

I am sure that the text, as we have it, is incomplete. To become a ritual specialist was a highly desirable job, ensuring a lifetime of good meals, income and status. Many of those who were attracted to wealth, comfort, food and power were spiritually unqualified. I wonder what ordeals, trials and scary episodes a candidate had to undergo before being admitted to the higher ranks. In any case, each religious specialist had to be confirmed by an oracle. As far as we know, a diviner (bārû) made a sacrifice and examined the liver of a sacrificial animal. If the signs were good and supported by other portents, the diviner received a symbolic gift and the training of the candidate continued.

Though this young Babylonian account is helpful, it does not say much regarding the initiations during the three thousand years that preceded it. An old Babylonian text (Farber 2003) offers at least six Sumerian conjurations to purify a person for the rather minor office of a gudu priest. The procedure involved frequent baths in sacred water and a ceremony for the rising sun. Similar rituals were performed on a daily basis: the priesthood had the duty to maintain physical, mental and spiritual purity. Considering how many misdeeds, accidents and events could pollute a person, it was a major undertaking.

The same applied to the haruspex diviners (**bārû**): they were only entitled to do their job after lengthy purification rituals. To become a diviner, i.e. a person fit to communicate the will of a deity, one had to undergo an extensive education including literature and science. Numerous omen catalogues were memorised. The diviner had to be 'sanctified' (quddušu), had to bathe in sacred water, salve his body with oil and aromatic perfumes, clean himself with sacred plants, put on fresh clothes, chew on cedar foliage, eat barley, and wash his hands and mouth with sacred water. If the diviner happened to touch something polluting or tabooed, make mistakes in handling the sacrifices and divination gear, was clumsy, forgot sections of the sacred texts or did a sloppy job; if he suffered from bad dreams in the night before or ignored the finer details of the ritual, the divination was worthless.

Similar rules applied to female diviners and indeed to any officiating 'priest', 'priestess' or any other sort of ritualist. To some extent they affected ordinary temple personnel and laypeople who wanted to pray, make a sacrifice or perform a simple everyday ritual. To the Mesopotamians, **contamination** was a constant threat. To touch or see a corpse, to handle something dirty, to talk with a polluted person, to go out of the house on an unlucky day or to encounter a bad omen could suffice to make a person ritually impure. To point a finger, show lack of generosity, cause a quarrel in the family, speak badly about one's city, fight the neighbours, cheat business partners, swear false oaths, use fake weights, shift boundary stones, give bad advice, lie, exploit, slander, abuse... all of these could make the personal deities depart. And that was just the beginning. The *Šurpu Series* lists hundreds of forbidden acts. Most of them can be understood as breaches of moral, social and religious obligations. Some show a good practical understanding of hygiene: it is bad luck to eat the food of a cursed (=polluted or sick) man, or to stay in his house. Nor is it recommended to urinate or vomit into a river. Then there were taboos connected with animals and plants. It was polluting to destroy reeds in the marsh and tear out grasses on the plain, to damage sacred trees, to strike animals on the cheek and to throw fertile earth into water. Religious misdeeds were just as common. The gods did not approve of people who promised offerings and did not make them, who stole offerings, threw (sacred) salt and cress into the fire, and went to worship in a state of pollution.

So much for taboos which we understand. It just covers a small range. Many taboos mentioned by the *Šurpu Series* are not even explained. There were taboos of the ford and quay, of harbour, boat and ferry, of tamarisk and date palm, of cup and table, bellows and stove, of bed and couch, of mountains, ravines, canals, rivers, sources, rams, owls, frogs, of shovels, pitchforks, cymbals, harps, of fire, lamps and so on. We have no idea what they entailed. It made life exceedingly complicated but ensured plenty of excitement.

I am sure you would like to know how complicated Neo-Assyrian lovemaking could be. A tablet from the end of the second millennium gives detailed instructions. We are at the beginning of the Neo-Assyrian period, and the relatively easygoing sexuality of the Sumerians has long been forgotten. Life was hard; people were aggressive, and women had fewer rights than before. Here comes trouble: coitus with a woman on top weakens the man, invigorates the woman, and can scare his personal deity away for an entire month. It must have been an exciting month, as a man without a personal deity is liable to be attacked by any passing spirit. People who had made love were not permitted to worship, pray or sacrifice on the next day. If a man made love and ejaculated later in the night, he was sure to be facing great expenses. Ejaculation while dreaming ensured wealth. A man who raped a woman at the street crossing (i.e. a prostitute) faced bad luck: either the hand of a god or the hand of the king would seize him. If a man masturbated without ejaculation, he was sure to encounter disaster on the same day. If a man talked with a woman in bed, got up (left?) and masturbated he won joy and good luck. Wherever he walked, everyone agreed with him, and he always reached his goals. Excessive sex and frequent ejaculations ensured an early death. Making love with a house-slave caused trouble. If a man asked a woman to touch his penis, his personal deity was sure to ignore his prayers. If a man stared at the vulva of a woman continuously, he was bound to gain things which did not belong to him, and his health would be excellent. If the woman used the opportunity to stare back at his penis, anything the man might find would not be safe in his house. Sexual congress with an assinnu freed a man from worries; with a girseqû employee of a temple or the palace ensured good luck for an entire year (Haas, 1999:19-21).

With regard to the initiation of **priestesses,** we have little reliable material. Most of it comes from the Sumerian and Old Babylonian period. In general, a priestess had to be confirmed by oracle and underwent a similar process of purification as her male colleagues. The main difference was that her initiation could resemble a marriage ritual: some women were wedded to a deity. This process is best known from the late Sumerian and early Akkadian period (late third millennium BCE), when a selected, educated and high-ranking princess was married to a special god. It did not hinder her from worshipping other gods but nominated her as a custodian of a major temple, and its spiritual and political authority. The first steps of this initiation could happen early in life: meet the **nadītu** (*Barren Ones*). Most nadītu women came from aristocratic or rich families and were dedicated to their future office in childhood. The girl received a sacred name and had to undergo a period of training and purification. When she succeeded at her tasks, she underwent a three-day ceremony that allowed her to become a member of the cloister buildings, to meet, for the first time, the divine couple who were to become her patrons and to participate in a ritual feast that confirmed her entrance into the temple of her deity. Family and temple exchanged gifts, just as we would expect in a marriage. The nadītu women spent most of their lives in the confinement of a large and luxurious cloister complex including gardens and fields. Some cloisters were like small cities. Usually, nadītu were not allowed to have children, but they could adopt children. Those who lived in the cloister of Sippar were dedicated to the cult of sun god Utu/Šamaš and his wife Aya, the goddess of dawn. They led a childless life. Elsewhere and later on, nadītus were dedicated to Marduk, and permitted to marry. Ḫammurapi protected their rights, in case their husbands divorced them. They received their dowry and half of their husband's property, and were allowed to raise their sons. When these had grown up, the nadītu could choose to marry another husband, if she liked. If a married nadītu did not have sons, she could provide her husband with a slave woman or he could marry a šugītum priestess as a second wife. However, no matter how many sons these bore, they remained inferior to the nadītu. Those nadītus who lived in the cloisters were wealthy and of high rank: we encounter their names in business documents and contracts. They seem to have spent much of their time praying for the well-being of their families and investing money in business ventures. From the seclusion of the cloisters they ran their private enterprises, speculating in goods, financing voyages, buying and renting land and slaves. When they died most of their wealth returned to their families.

Each temple had its own tradition and customs. Sadly, the evidence is limited to singular cases and events. We read of a high-ranking priestess dedicated to the weather, storm and oracle god Adad. She underwent ritual baths in sacred water, was anointed from the *bowl of the city god*, shaved, re-anointed, purified and sanctified (quddušu). The word implies more than becoming sacred; it also designates a person who is *set apart* from the world. The next day she was settled in her future office. The goddess NIN.KUR (an image?) was sent to her family, while the priestess underwent the final consecrations at the temple. She was seated on a throne, adorned with special earrings (a gift from her family) and the ring of Adad on her right hand, and received a red head-cloth as a sign of her office. The elders of the city paid their respects to her. Afterwards, the priestess returned to her family in full regalia, where she remained for the night. The next day she formally left her family and moved to the temple of Adad, where she was installed into her office with sacrifices and a great feast, and received fresh ceremonial clothes plus ritual furniture indicating her status as the bride of the god: a bed, a chair and a bench. Another part of the ceremony, practised by at least some of the en-priestesses of Sumer and some of the nadītu in the Old Babylonian period, was a special sacrifice for the women who had preceded them in their office (Sallaberger & Vulliet, RlA '*Priester*').

One of the problems in understanding Mesopotamian religions is the lack of a clear terminology. There were so many priestly ranks. Some of the terms appeared in several cities and states, but they did not have the same status, function or significance.

Consider the **gala** priests, who usually functioned as experts in song, music, literature, language, history, hymns and lamentation. In some places, they acted as the heads of temples. A few had such a high status that they could act as formal witnesses to contracts between kings. Others, obviously of a much lower rank, gained a bit of extra income by accompanying doctors and exorcists to visit patients.

Another example. In many places, the **sagga** or **sanga** (Akkadian: **šangu**) was the head of the temple. A few were powerful like the governors of cities. Several sanga performed rituals with the kings. But there were also tiny temples, little better than huts, where a lonely sanga performed without employees. He would make offerings, clean the altar, sweep the floor, and lead a life of dedicated poverty.

Sadly, this book is not the place to discuss the priestly ranks and offices. Please read Henshaw's brilliant study. For a little extra information, I have listed a few priestly types in the glossary.

Let me end this section by pointing out that in many families, priesthood was inherited. It could mean that one or several children embarked on a spiritual life.

Maybe one daughter was dedicated to become a nadītu and the other to become a qadištu. Their rank and function could differ, but we don't understand how, as these terms meant different things in different places and periods. Maybe a conjurer passed his office and personal library to a gifted son or daughter. Or it could mean that someone wealthy and important gained an honorary priestly rank, or even bought one. Religion was business. Such priests were not required to do their job in the temple every day. Many only came round from time to time, to perform a little service for the gods and have a lavish meal. Kings often boasted of their priestly ranks, but were usually too busy to spend their days worshipping in a dark temple hall. Indeed, some 'priests' hardly ever participated in the temple duties. Instead, they rented their duties and privileges to people who were keen to enter the temple, win the favour of the gods, and feed on the delicious offerings.

Figure 10 Top: Roll seal showing Utu/Šamaš, third millennium BCE, London. The sun god is flanked by the mountains to the east (Iran) and west (Lebanon). Note the sun rays rising from his shoulders.

Bottom: Mythical scene. The bird-man is probably the Zu bird. He stole the tablets of destiny and is now being lead to Enki/Ea for judgement. Note that the sacred rivers Euphrates and Tigris are pouring out of Enki's shoulders. The figure holding Zu might be Ningirsu/Ninurta. BM 103317.

A fast journey through Mesopotamian History

We are discussing the religion and magick of a comparatively small country. The Greek term Mesopotamia means Land of Two Streams. That's a useful notion which should not be taken too seriously. The mighty rivers Euphrates and Tigris extend over thousands of kilometres, and there were many ethnic groups living along their meandering routes which did not belong to the Sumerians, Akkadians, Babylonians or Assyrians. Assyriologists tend to use the word Mesopotamia mainly for the cultures that lived in the fertile alluvial plain extending south towards the Persian Gulf. Old Mesopotamia had pretty much the same size as modern Iraq, but the cultures that developed there made up much smaller sections. Sumer near the Persian Gulf was traditionally known as the Sea-Land. North of it was the land of irrigation: grasslands, fields and pastures surrounding cities, with desert and steppe in between. Call it the 'Cradle of Civilisation' if you like, but remember that the country was tiny. Its size was limited to a few hundred kilometres of fertile land along the major rivers and canals. The fertile alluvial plain was barely 200 km wide. Sumer rarely covered more than 120 km from east to west and had a basic length of maybe 200 km. Only parts of it were inhabited. Upstream, Akkad had a similar size. Beyond Akkad, the grasslands and hills of Assyria began. What we call Mesopotamia was mainly the belt of inhabitable land along the major watercourses. Mesopotamian history is nightmarishly complicated. It is far harder to comprehend than, say, the history of Egypt. The main reason is accessibility: unlike Egypt, Mesopotamia was open in several directions. Traders and armies had access to many routes, leading to the Mediterranean, the Kurdish mountains, the highlands of Elam. On the other hand, the great city cultures were always threatened by outsiders: the Elamites, Gutians and people of the Iranian highlands, the cultures of the north, the nomads who invaded from the Syrian and Arabian deserts. Lots of people were attracted by the comparative wealth and lure of urban life. It turned Mesopotamian history into a chaotic merry-go-round.

Let me take you on a swift guided tour through a few thousand years. Please hold on tight to your brain and remember to breathe.

Prehistoric Period

Agriculture started around 12,000-10,000 BCE in the 'fertile crescent', a range of land extending from Palestine and Syria at the coast of the Mediterranean across southern Turkey, Iraq and ending in the highlands of Iran. Systematic farming spread from the mountains of southern Kurdistan along the rivers Euphrates and Tigris. Settlers and small-scale irrigation appear in the north of Mesopotamia around 8000 BCE. They did not get very far. The land south of Turkey has rainfall and can be cultivated with some ease. But when we reach the centre of Mesopotamia, the temperature rises and rainfall becomes a rarity. The country was hot and bleak. No doubt there were some settlers in these ranges, and shepherds moving with their flocks. Here and there a bit of irrigation allowed small farmers to survive. The major impulse of cultivation probably came from the south. At the time of writing, we can be sure that people lived in southern Mesopotamia since at least the sixth millennium BCE. We simply don't know who they were. At some point, possibly around the fifth millennium BCE, the Proto-Sumerians entered the country. We don't know who they were or where they came from. Wherever it may have been, the Sumerians did not remain in contact with their ancient homelands. Their migration may have been a fast or slow process, but after they had arrived in the alluvial plain, they remained.

One myth that may be pertinent is the story of the Seven Sages, the ABGAL/Apkallu, Abgallu, who arrived, at Enki's request, from overseas, or from under the sea, or from Dilmun. The seven are a set of strange culture heroes who like to walk around in fish costume. Occasionally they wear the heads of birds of prey. They allegedly invented advanced agriculture, the domestication of animals, city administration and rituals. There are usually seven named ABGAL: Adapa, Bandura, Enmeduga, Enmegalama, Enmebuluga, Anenlilda and Utuabzu. Each of them was a councillor of one of the kings who governed before the flood. For some reason they angered Enki and he forced them to return into the Abzu. In exorcist ceremonies they fight evil spirits. The seven sages brought civilisation to Mesopotamia. So did the Proto-Sumerians. They introduced farming, technology and an amazing ambition to turn the hostile country into a fertile and wealthy land. They merged with the locals and other migrants and became the Sumerian culture, perhaps the earliest high civilisation of this planet. At this point of proto-history, the fate of the Sumerians was already rather certain. Sure, they were an amazingly inventive and adaptable people, who impressed the entire Near East with their cultural achievements. Their ideas and insights are with us today: we owe them myths, maths, musical scales, organisation, bureaucracy, technology and the first functional script in history. But as their population group was limited, while other ethnic groups kept migrating into Mesopotamia, it was just a matter of time before the Sumerians, as an ethnic group, disappeared. Their culture survived.

The Uruk Period

The Uruk Period is a general term for the prehistoric period between c.4000–3200 BCE. In this time, Sumerian culture reached its first traceable flowering. It is named after the city Uruk (Sumerian: Unug, the biblical Erech), the largest and most impressive city of its time. In the late Uruk period it measured c.100 ha. Only a few centuries later, in the Early Dynastic period, the inhabited space had grown to c.400 ha. and was surrounded by a city wall 9 km in length. For the ancient world, this is immense. Some enthusiasts suggested that Uruk and its neighbourhood might have housed almost a million people. Others, more cautious, guessed at 50,000. Population estimates vary from 50 people per ha to 200 for towns. At the present time, many scholars guess that a hundred people lived on each hectare of city space (Liverani in RlA '*Stadt*'). We will never know whether it is true. The foundations of houses do not tell us how many people lived in them. Were the Urukians dwelling in crowded rooms or was it small families with plenty of individual space? How many servants or slaves were attached to the average family? And what was the size of the family? How many children died in their first years, how many old people were there? And just what means 'old' in the first known civilisation of this planet? Age-estimates are extremely uncertain. Most of the citizens of Mesopotamia did not receive the sort of funeral that makes the archaeologist happy. And while we are at it, how high were the buildings? Was there a second storey, or a third? How crowded were the streets near the city wall, where homeless people sought their shelter? At some point, extra settlements were built outside of the city, which may have housed another 30,000-60,000 people. And that only covers those living in real buildings. How many poor people lived outside the city, in simple huts, shelters or tents that escape the attention of the excavator? Such questions complicate population estimates.

Several myths recorded in the early second millennium BCE can be traced to the Uruk period, though, of course, we have to allow for differences and plenty of local development. By the middle of the Uruk period the essentials of civilisation were well developed. There were large cities in southern Sumer, some of them more than a thousand years old, set within states that were exceptionally well organised. Music had reached an astonishing degree of refinement; witness the wide range of lyres, harps, lutes, wind instruments and drums that appear in art. Mighty temple buildings prove an impressive knowledge of architecture and mathematics. The builders made bricks in standardised moulds, they imported and cut limestone blocks, and they started to erect the first ziggurat temple towers. Ziggurats were usually parts of large temple complexes. Today, the eroded remains of several can be admired. Their use and symbolism are still unclear. We do not know what rituals or customs inspired them. Even their appearance raises questions: were plants and trees planted on the many layers, so that the ziggurats appeared like green mountains, towering over the alluvial plain? There were platforms of pounded earth rising above a landscape threatened by annual floods, extensive cities with impressively large walls and drainage systems, plus a refined system of canals, sluices, dams and wharves. In arts and crafts, consider the invention of the potter's wheel and the first workshops for copper.

At the end of the Uruk period and the start of the Jemdet Nasr Period two major innovations changed life. First, around 3500 BCE we encounter a fashion for cylinder seals. Important people, officials, priests, representatives and aristocrats used beautifully carved seals to mark property, and later contracts, documents and the like. Some seals were carried as signs of office; others may have functioned much like talismans. The seals could be rolled over large clay surfaces, which made them eminently practical. Before long, people all over the Near East used similar seals, from the highlands of Iran to Cyprus, Turkey and Crete. The only exception were the Egyptians: cylinder seals don't work on papyrus, but stamp seals (another Mesopotamian invention) proved superior. The seals provide us with a great insight into the art, thought and symbolism of a people who were largely Sumerian, partly Semitic, and partly descended from the natives, whoever they may have been. The imagery is original, courageous and largely incomprehensible. Generations of scholars have tried to associate Sumerian myths with specific seal images, which usually did not work. In museums, visitors tend to stream past the seals. They seem so small and insignificant. Their imagery wasn't. There is good evidence that the motifs which you find on seals were also painted, much larger, as wall decorations. So when you study seals, imagine their images huge and colourful.

The other great innovation was writing. You read about it earlier.

The Uruk period was either followed by the **Jemdet Nasr** period, or simply extended into it. In this brief time span, the use of cylinder seals and writing began to get around. While during the Uruk period, civilisation was mostly confined to the cities of southern Sumer, by the beginning of the Jemdet Nasr period, the cities of northern Sumer, Kiš, Nippur and Ešnunna began to expand, to build larger temples, to dig better canals, and use the new technology for their own ends. Simultaneously, Sumerian ideas began to influence the Egyptians, the Elamites, and roll seals began to appear in Troy and near the Black Sea. Traces of typical Uruk culture appear in a wide range of places hundreds of kilometres from Uruk. Such evidence raises questions. Did Urukian traders found colonies or outposts in, say, Susa (modern Iran) or in Arslantepe near Malatya (Turkish Kurdistan)? What about Aruda, Habuba, Qraya, and Ramadi, in what is today Syria? Trade goods, roll seals, buildings and temple architecture show typical Uruk characteristics. Should we imagine trading colonies, coexisting with the natives, and military establishments enforcing access to the trade routes? So far, these questions cannot be answered. In all likeliness, relations to the locals kept changing and such outposts of Sumerian culture should not be viewed as singular evidence of a sudden expansion. Trade had been going on for millennia before the Urukians began to carve roll seals.

The Early Dynastic Period

This is a general term for the period between c.3000 BCE and 2350 BCE when Sargon I founded the Akkadian dynasty. The ED. is divided into three periods: c.3000–2750 BCE is ED. I; 2750–2600 BCE is ED. II and 2600–2350 BCE is ED. III. The first of these is the least known. A functional form of writing existed in E. I, but as far as we know, it was confined to basic matters like administrative documents, land sale contracts and lexical lists. These were largely focused on practical, administrative matters. Maybe our evidence is misleading. Many early documents came from administrative buildings. Simultaneously, the scribes began to compose word-lists. As literature, hymns and royal inscriptions only became popular around 2700 BCE, our knowledge of Early Dynastic Period I is distinctly limited. The best evidence for the importance of the approximately thirty city-states is provided by a number of early temple hymns, collections of city seals indicating alliances, and ***Sumerian King Lists***, a range of disagreeing documents composed between the late third and early second millennium BCE. The *King Lists* are an amazing effort to create a streamlined history reaching from the very beginnings to the prime of civilisation. As Mesopotamian historians were myth-makers and propaganda specialists, they included several massive innovations. The accounts start with the beginning of kingship. Let's quote the first lines:

When kingship came down from heaven, the kingship was in Eridu. In Eridu Alulim became king and reigned 28,800 years. Alalgar reigned 36,000 years. Two kings: they reigned 64,800 years. Eridu was cast down (=abandoned); its kingship was carried to Badtibira. In Badtibira, Enmeluana reigned for 43,200 years, Enmegalana for 28,800 years, Dumuzi the Shepherd for 36,000 years. Three kings: their years were 108,000. Then Badtibira was cast down and kingship moved to Larak. Ensipazianna reigned for 28,800 years. One king: these years amount to 28,800. Larak was cast down and the kingship was carried to Sippar...

(Ebeling in Gressmann, 1970/1926:147-149, Saggs, 1966:35, Michalowsky in Chavalas, 2007:81-85).

Clearly, the beginning of civilisation was a magnificent event. The office of kingship descended thanks to the grace of An, the god of Heaven, and the first regents were wonderfully long-lived people. While the descent from heaven may be questioned, the reference to Eridu in the marshland near the Persian Gulf is an excellent idea. What became the elaborate temple of Enki was started around 4900 BCE, so maybe the city Eridu is truly the first city in Mesopotamian history. According to the *Sumerian King Lists*, the government moved from Eridu to Badtibira, then to Larak, Sippar and Šurupak. These five cities, governed by a mere eight rulers, controlled the south of Mesopotamia for an amazing 241,200 years. I dearly hope you don't take these numbers seriously. They do not reflect history but sacred numerology. The Sumerians and their descendants had a hexagesimal system for religious calculations, meaning the number 60 and its multiples were sacred.

Their dominance ended when the **flood** swept over the land. You might think of a disaster, a terrible change in world climate, a massive tsunami, or maybe the great rivers shifted. In an exceedingly flat country, the result would have been devastating. The flood hit southern Sumer, but did not extend to the north of Mesopotamia, as the scribes were well aware. You could think of it as a cataclysm, but the flood was also a spiritual event.

Let's have a simplified summary. I base my remarks on the *Atraḫasīs Epic*, on several versions of the *Gilgemeš Epic* and on the much earlier Sumerian fragments of the flood-myth. As the *Atraḫasīs Epic* explains, the flood did not occur by chance. Mankind had become so numerous and loud that the *Land was roaring like a bull.* The gods, deeply upset by the clamour, did their best to keep the human population within sensible limits. First they stopped the rains and made people starve. The priesthood appealed to the storm god Iškur/Adad and offered rich sacrifices. It shamed the deity, who felt obliged to let the rains return. As people don't learn much that goes against their personal instincts, they bred like rabbits. When the noise became too much, the gods tried population control by sending a plague. Again, an appeal to the relevant god eliminated the threat and life continued much as ever. People lived and bred and before long, Enlil/Ellil was totally fed up with the racket. He conferred with An and oath-bound the assembly of the gods to exterminate mankind. Total secrecy, Enlil demanded, was a must. To settle the matter, a terrible flood was released. But Enki/Ea, cunning and less impulsive than his elder brother, had secretly informed King Atraḫasīs of Šuruppak that a huge boat might be a brilliant idea. The king loaded his family and plenty of animals, and when the flood drowned the country, the royal family stayed alive. After seven days of tempest and sea-sickness, they landed and made an offering. By that time, the gods had realised that the flood had been a stupid idea. For one thing, it killed the very beings on whose offerings the gods depended. For another, the act was so overwhelmingly cruel that many deities felt deeply ashamed. When the first sacrifices were made, the gods descended on them like a swarm of flies. Since then, global cataclysms were not on the agenda any longer. However, as the Sumerians knew (and even modern people are starting to realise), overpopulation and limited resources are a terrible combination. So the divine assembly introduced a few changes. For one thing, they instituted death after old age. Before the flood, everybody had lived for an enormously long time. After the deluge, most people (some kings are an exception) grew old after a couple of centuries and died of natural causes. It was a start, and to make life more bearable, the gods ordered that the number of births should be regulated. They created a goddess, or entrusted her with the task of slaying selected infants. This goddess appears as Pašittu in the *Atraḫasīs epic*; elsewhere she is known as DIM.ME and Lamaštu. Finally, the gods decided that not all women should have children. They created a range of priestesses who were supposed to have no children. Some could only bear children generated on holy occasions like the 'sacred marriage'. Having no children does not imply abstention from sex. We read of babies placed in small vessels, drifting down the river, like the future emperor Sargon I, and an omen text mentions an entu(m) (*woman who is a goddess*) who favoured anal sex to avoid conception. The author of that omen text was offended by her behaviour, as she should have reserved herself to an en, instead of taking a lover. The people who populated earth after the flood were a new breed with a different and significantly shorter outlook on life.

The *Sumerian King Lists* make allowance for the major change. The new regents are semi-historical figures; they fight wars and do mighty deeds, but they are not as long-lived as their ancestors. We meet mythical kings who only live for a few hundred years, and eventually the regencies sink to a level that may be called genuine history, if there was ever such a thing.

After the flood had destroyed everything, kingship descended from heaven and belonged to the city Kiš. And here we are right within the Early Dynastic Period: the Kiš Dynasty had 23 kings and extended over c.900 years. The *Sumerian King Lists* have kept many Sumerologists upset and sleepless in the middle of the night. Their very composition is such a bizarre blend of myth and facts that they should belong in a genre all of their own. Did the scribes really believe in kings who ruled for thousands of years? Or were the numbers chosen for numerological reasons, or simply to represent people who were far superior to modern man? How do you distil 'real history' from a series of disagreeing documents that start within the realm of fiction? Some of the regents on the *Sumerian King Lists* can be traced. Many others seem like inventions. *Sumerian Kings Lists* were composed and recomposed by generations of scholars. Most of them were not interested in the sort of history we consider factual. In their opinion, history was supposed to confirm the status of the present rulers. As a result, new king lists were made up whenever a king thought a bit of respectable legitimisation would do him good. Nobody argues with a good pedigree. In the scribal schools, *Sumerian King Lists* were copied by beginners, as they were good writing practice. And we observe astonishing omissions. The *Sumerian King Lists* focus on major regents of central Sumer and ignore the equally powerful dynasties in the very south of Sumer, the kings of Girsu in the city-state Lagaš, who had much wealth and influence thanks to their thriving sea trade. If we only had the *Sumerian King Lists*, we wouldn't even know about their existences. A similar problem appears as a result of the neat sequences in the *Sumerian King Lists*. They create the illusion that there was always a single, dominant city-state, and that one regency followed after the other in a divinely ordained sequence. It's very close to the Chinese Zhou period model: that the 'Mandate of Heaven' is granted to specific dynasties until their virtue runs out. In plain reality, some of those dynasties existed at the same time. The Old Babylonian students who copied the *Sumerian King Lists* gained the impression that history is a neat and linear event, and that the present era, with its short-lived kings, was hardly comparable to the glorious past.

Many major city-states existed at the beginning of the Early Dynastic period, forming an intricate network of religious, political, economic and strategic alliances that shifted repeatedly. These cities interacted and shared a unifying idea, calling themselves Kalam (*the Land*), but they did not have a unified religion, nor were they inclined to interfere in the internal affairs of each other. There were plenty of local differences with regard to customs, traditions, organisations, mythology and the way society was structured. The city-states thought locally. They had their own cults and religious preferences. However, and this is a major characteristic that can be observed all the way through Mesopotamian history: they did not assume that the deities of other states or ethnic groups were wrong, false or demonic. Gods were universal. Some of the major ones were worshipped in several states: Inanna, Enlil, An, Enki, Ninḫursag and their relations were there for anyone. Others were local, but could become major players. And there were great gods who faded into oblivion. Gods were gods and it was not the job of humans to limit their sphere of interest. When an intruding ethnic group had different deities, these were identified with the local gods or the new cults were assimilated.

One astonishing indication of cultural diversity are the so-called **'royal graves'** excavated by C.L. Woolley at Ur. The First Dynasty of Ur ruled sometime around 2700-2500 BCE, but these dates are rather uncertain. The cemetery had at least two thousand graves, which is a ridiculously small number, considering the size of the city next to it. Of these, sixteen were classed as 'royal' as they were so elaborate. Whether their inhabitants were really kings remains unknown. Several 'royal tombs' were surrounded by stone walls or a solid brick casing; some had up to four rooms. Within these tombs, the excavators uncovered rich treasures and an astonishing amount of corpses. One particularly elaborate tomb contained the corpses of six soldiers, four ladies with lyres and sixty-four elaborately costumed women lying in an orderly row. 28 of them wore gold in their hair; the rest wore silver. Woolley gives an almost poetic description: *It must have been a very gaily dressed crowd that assembled in the open mat-lined pit for the royal obsequies, a blaze of colour with the crimson coats, the silver, and the gold; clearly these people were not wretched slaves killed as oxen might be killed, but persons held in honour, wearing their robes of office, and coming, one hopes, voluntarily to a rite which would in their belief be but a passing from one world to another...* (1950:32).

Woolley was amazed that the women and men who accompanied the main burial had such a tranquil attitude. These people died of poison, and went into death without a struggle. We don't know if it was a human sacrifice or a voluntary mass–suicide. They had everything you need for a happy afterlife: rich clothes, costly ornaments, food, drink, vessels, art, games, several gorgeous harps, plus ceremonial carts and the oxen and donkeys to pull them. These burials, and indeed human sacrifices, are an exception. The regents and priests before and after this period did not take other people to the Underworld and they made do with few grave goods. All in all, it seems as if the so-called 'kings' of Ur I were unique, represented a different religion, and maybe came from an unknown culture.

The last years of the Early Dynastic saw the emergence of increasingly strong city-states. There was plenty of warfare, but only a few conflicts can be traced with any sort of certainty. Best documented is the frontier conflict between the states Umma and Lagaš in the south of Sumer, not far from the shores of the Persian Gulf. One king of Lagaš, Urnanše, celebrated himself as a builder of temples and canals. It was a common custom: kings showed their devotion to the gods by building and repairing temples. Urnanše fought the states Ur and Umma, and carefully listed the enemy generals, regents and chief merchants whom he executed after the victory. Not much later, Eanatum governed Lagaš. The regent of Umma had occupied a fertile section of his frontier land. Eanatum protested, as the land belonged to Ningirsu, a leading god of Lagaš. In the battle, Eanatum was struck by an arrow but survived. He forced the king of Umma to pay dues for the amount of grain reaped on the abducted land. A peace treaty was made, and a remarkable ritual occurred. Eanatum had the king of Umma swear on the hunting net of Enlil that he would respect the boundary stones and the irrigation canals, and that the land would henceforth be considered loaned. Eanatum prepared pigeons. Kohl was smeared around their eyes, cedar (perfume) was put on their heads, and then the doves were released to carry the message to the major temples of Sumer: to Enlil in Nippur, to Ninḫursag in Keš, Enki in Eridu, Suen in Ur, Utu in Larsa and to Ninki, the *Lady of the Earth*, who is a wife of Enki and/or a goddess of the Underworld. The doves asked the gods that if the king of Umma dared to break his oath, they should cast their battle nets on him and Ninki was petitioned to make serpents rise from the deep to bite the feet of intruders. It must have been a beautiful ceremony. After Eanatum, his son Enanatum ruled, and when his son Enmetena had grown up, Umma broke the treaty. It may have been due to the outstanding debt. They owed 4,478,976,000,000 litres of barley to Lagaš, calculated at 33.3% interest over a span of approximately fifty years, and simply couldn't raise that much. Umma recruited an army of foreign mercenaries, destroyed the boundary stones and canals, torched the shrines of the gods and invaded Lagaš. Old Enanatum seems to have died during the war, but Enmetena triumphed.

What really ruined Lagaš was corruption. The population was exploited by swarms of inspectors and officials, who demanded charges for pretty much anything, and kept most of the profit to themselves. Injustice and bribes were a matter of course. The last king of Lagaš, UruKAgina, started his reign by introducing much-needed reforms. He gained popular support by eliminating most of these officials, by introducing tax cuts, fixing prices and freeing debt-slaves. He proudly announced his success in protecting the weak from the strong and the widows from the clutch of the wealthy. The property of the queen was turned to the temple of the goddess Bau/Baba. It appeared like the start of a perfect reign. Or maybe it didn't: contemporary scholars are arguing whether these reforms were actually enforced. Whatever it may have been, it didn't last. While Lagaš was breathing a sigh of relief, a newcomer usurped kingship in Umma. It was Lugalzagesi, an upstart with a shady background but a sound head for strategy. Lugalzagesi destroyed UruKAgina of Lagaš, and conquered the city-states of southern Sumer: Uruk, Ur, Larsa, Zabalam, Kidingir. If we can trust the self-laudatory hymns of Lugalzagesi, his influence extended from the Persian Gulf to the Mediterranean Sea. Lugalzagesi proudly offered water and food to Enlil in the Ekur, the major temple of Nippur, and received the blessing of the deity. He praised himself as the King of the Land, the išib priest of An, the lumaḫ priest of Nisaba, the favourite of An, the ensigal priest of Enlil, the one to whom Enki had granted wisdom, the one named by Utu, the grand vizier of Suen, the commander of Utu, the provider of Inanna, the son of Nisaba, the one reared on the milk of Ninḫursag, the man of Messangaunug, the one raised by Ningirima, Lady of Uruk, and the chief steward of all gods. And while the king was wallowing in megalomania, and all the land was rejoicing and making merry, his fate was settled in the north.

Figure 11 Top: Roll seal showing a worshipper who faces goddess Ninkarrag/Gula and her dog. Above them is the half moon, representing the moon god Sîn. The goat and the tree are a popular motif that defies interpretation. Note the hand position of the worshipper: she (or he?) has raised the hands in prayer. Late Assyrian period. BM 89846

Bottom: Roll seal showing a lady with a sceptre worshipping the goddess Ištar. The date palm might represent kingship, the goats are enigmatic. Neo-Assyrian period, c.7-6th century BCE. BM 89769.

The Akkadian Period

The Akkadian Period started when Sargon I conquered southern and central Mesopotamia around 2350 BCE. The date is much disputed; it could have happened a hundred years later, depending on which chronology you favour. Sargon came from a realm called Akkad, maybe close to modern Baghdad, just north of Sumer. Sargon was an upstart. His chosen name Šarrukenu means *the King is Legitimate*; good evidence that he wasn't. His pedigree is doubtful. One legend claims that he was an illegitimate son of an aristocratic lady or high priestess, who put the baby in a basket coated with bitumen (to waterproof it) and sent it drifting on the Euphrates. Allegedly, he was raised by an anonymous, high-ranking gardener (i.e. a person managing palm plantations), and gained the favour of King Urzababa as the goddess Inanna/Ištar liked him. Another tradition equips him with a proper father called La'ibum. Whatever it may have been, Sargon won the goodwill of King Urzababa of Kiš, who was devoted to Inanna, and became the cup-bearer of his lord. It was a high-status job, as cup-bearers poured offerings in temples, witnessed the intimate conferences of their lord, and acted as royal representatives. One legend says that Urzababa was sick. He dribbled urine, and there was blood in it. He sent Sargon to the temple to have a true dream. Sargon prayed, performed an offering, fell asleep and met the goddess Inanna.

The vision was nightmarish. Sargon yelled and gnawed the ground. The king heard the screams and sent for him. Sargon told his lord:

There was a single young woman, she was high as the heavens, she was broad as the earth. She was firmly set as the base of the wall. For me, she drowned you in a great river, a river of blood.

(Cooper and Heimpel, in Sasson, 1983: 67-82)

King Urzababa paled, chewed on his lips and was desperately afraid. How could his divine sister, the pure Inanna, greatest goddess of Kiš and Uruk, send such a terrifying omen? Would this cupbearer be his doom? As legend hints, he set traps to have Sargon killed, who evaded them all. What happened next is mysterious. Maybe Sargon killed his liege. Maybe he fled the country, and his lord found his death without Sargon's initiative. Some texts claim that after Urzababa, other kings ruled. Whatever it may have been, at some point, Sargon usurped the throne and made the goddess Inanna/Ištar his special favourite. Meanwhile, in the south, Lugalzagesi had brought all city-states under control. Lugalzagesi governed happily, and was supported by fifty minor kings. It must have been a weak and quarrelsome assembly, and their cooperation left much to be desired. Sargon gathered an army, marched to the south, crushed Lugalzagesi and conquered all of Sumer. He eliminated the fifty kings and made Lugalzagesi, chained in a neckstock, march to Nippur. In front of Enlil's temple, the former king was exhibited like a trophy: a clear example that Enlil had withdrawn his support. It was a major achievement and not even half of what Sargon was hoping for.

Unlike Lugalzagesi and Urzababa, Sargon was not a Sumerian but a Semitic king. His native language was Akkadian. The city Agade, in central Mesopotamia, became the capital and Akkadian the official language. Sargon united his realm Akkad with the Sumerian south. For the Sumerians, the conquest was traumatic. All of a sudden a Semitic king was ruling their venerable old civilisation! Luckily, Sargon admired the ancient Sumerian ways. As a gesture of respect, he appointed his daughter Enḫeduanna as the high priestess of Ur and Uruk, two major centres of traditional Sumerian culture. Enḫeduanna was married to the moon god Nanna/Suen/Sîn. She composed a famous collection of temple hymns celebrating the most important cities, temples and deities of Sumer and Akkad. These hymns were a gesture of benevolence: they assured the Sumerians that their rights and customs would not be injured. She also wrote long and fascinating hymns for Inanna/Ištar, whom she celebrated as a fierce and devastating goddess, delighting to grind enemy countries and rebellious states into the dust. It seems that everybody got the message. The new regent allowed things to continue as before. Sargon was not interested in oppressing his freshly conquered southern subjects. He led his armies to the east, where they broke into the mountains of Elam, to the north, where they invaded Turkey, and to the west, until they reached the Mediterranean Sea. Standing in the waves, Sargon washed his weapons. He was deeply grateful. Inanna/Ištar had turned his kingdom into a vast state, the first (known) empire of human history. There was just one problem: it was simply too big. Sargon did not have the means to keep everything under control. He installed his family members in new territories and tried hard to make the legislation work. The new terrain was not really controllable, but his administrators kept the trade routes functional. From all over the Middle East, foreign goods came to Agade: an unheard of wealth that bedazzled his contemporaries. Sargon and his family introduced major religious changes. They promoted their family god Ilaba, who returned to ignominy after the Akkadian period, and the Semitic goddess Ištar, by identifying her with the Sumerian Inanna and the foreign mountain goddess Irnina. It transformed these three goddesses into raging war deities. Inanna/Ištar/Irnina turned Sargon's campaigns into a success story. Thanks to imperial preferences, several major Sumerian goddesses, who had been competitors of Inanna, faded into the background. One of them was Bau/Baba, who was allowed to remain in a subservient role as Inanna's girlfriend. Another was Ningirima, the goddess of Magic, who lost her status as the leading goddess of megacity Uruk. Her cult survived, on a much-reduced scale, in the town Muru/m. Thanks to Sargon's family, Inanna became the *Queen of Heaven* and was identified with Antu(m) and several other wives of celestial An. After Sargon I (probably) came his son Rimuš (c.2315 BCE) who struggled against the revolts of the Sumerian kings of Ur, Lagaš, Zabala, Adab and Umma. He was possibly murdered by another son, Maništušu (c.2306 BCE). The sequence is under discussion: it is not clear whether Rimuš or Maništušu succeeded Sargon I. Sargon's grandson Naramsîn (c.2291 BCE) was the first Akkadian king to claim divinity, after he had fought nine kings in a single year. Under his reign, *the four corners of the world rebelled* but the uprisings were violently put down. Last we have Šarkališari (c.2254 BCE), who governed for maybe 25 years and retained a certain prosperity, even though he lost most of the territory outside of Mesopotamia. His reign ended around 2230 BCE. Maybe one or two other regents followed, who simply did not make it. The proud state Akkad shrank until it consisted of a narrow strip of land, extending for 125 km. Elamites, Lullubaeans and Hurrites came invading. The Akkadian period finished with a whimper. The records simply evaporate. Documents and letters fade away, royal influence disappears, and finally Akkad is lost. The Gutians, a primitive people from the Zagros region of Iran, devastated Assyria, Akkad and parts of Sumer. To the Akkadians, they appeared as *Dragons of the Mountains*: savage, illiterate and ruthless. The Sumerians and Akkadians were shocked. Unlike a good many neighbouring states, the Gutians did not care about writing, science and civilisation. They governed and quarrelled with each other, but the names of their kings and how they got along remain uncertain. According to various sources, 21 Gutian kings governed for 124 or 125 years, or 23 kings over 99 years. As an extra, there were probably five years when no king governed and the army ruled. Life under the Gutian kings may have been difficult. The documentation is tiny and questionable; we cannot be sure that it actually comes from the period. Apparently some trade in grains, oils, timber, textiles, copper and silver continued. The Gutian influence, however, did not extend all over Sumer. In the south, the former city-states held out. Gudea of Lagaš, famous for his rebuilding of the temple of Ningirsu, a religious visionary, poet and perhaps a hobby architect, managed to keep a cautious peace with them, and his country prospered.

Ur III

This period received its name as, according to the *Sumerian Kings Lists*, it was the third time that Ur was the major power of Sumer. The period started when Utuḫegal, king of Ur, defeated the last Gutian regent, Tirigan. Or maybe it was Urnammu, or both of them together. Of course, neither was really proud of the achievement. A century ago, Enlil had ordered the Gutians to conquer the land. Now Enlil was tired of them and ordered the South Sumerians to expel them. Everybody gave a sigh of relief: it was time to rebuild civilisation along traditional lines. Well, things don't always work out as they should. The very people who defeated the Gutians came from the southern rim of Sumer and were convinced of their traditional role as custodians of civilisation. In their eyes, the Akkadian period was simply an accident of history and the Gutian interregnum should best be forgotten. Nevertheless, they had to cope with new problems. One of them was the Akkadian-speaking Semites. There had been plenty of them before, but now they were a lot more, and they had been in control for a century. Early Sumerian regents had thought in small dimensions: Sargon had demonstrated that there was a world out there, waiting to be subjugated, ruled and civilised. The successful conqueror had proved that a unified Mesopotamia could govern a much greater section of the known world than anyone had thought possible. The tradition of independent-minded quarrelling city-states was definitely not attractive any longer: centralised power was the byword for all future efforts. The new Sumerian regents were forced to think in larger dimensions than ever. After a power struggle of seven years, the first regent of the Ur III period, Urnammu (c.2113 BCE) gained control over Sumer in the south and Akkad in the centre of Mesopotamia. In the process, Sumerian resumed its function as the official language of court and government, though in everyday reality, most people spoke and wrote Akkadian. Urnammu enjoyed a relatively peaceful reign, and is famous for his restoration scheme and his law-code. One of his first projects was the rebuilding of the temple of Nanna/Suen/Sîn in Ur. He was followed by his son Šulgi, a monarch who was intelligent, literate, athletic, good-looking, amazingly talented, successful, a patron of the arts and deeply in love with himself. Šulgi probably copied the late regents of Akkad when he deified himself, had temples built for his worship, and even inserted a forged temple hymn into Enḫeduanna's collection, celebrating himself as one endowed with the divine Me (principles of civilisation, divine powers) whose temple in Ur binds people to a single path. It would be easy to dismiss Šulgi as a megalomaniac, but he was quite capable. Šulgi did much to encourage art, music, science, literature and religion. Under Šulgi, the scribal schools (eduba: *house of the tablet*) turned into major places of learning. Unlike almost every regent of Mesopotamia, Šulgi enjoyed reading, studying and composing. He boasted that he knew many rituals better than the priesthood and corrected the priests in the middle of ceremonies. When anybody was good at something, Šulgi tried his hand and was better. He perfected the administration and insisted on strict scribal discipline in all matters. One of his queens, Šulgisimtu, administrated the supply of sacrificial animals for the temples. Most of the traders she corresponded with were women (Crawford in Chavalas, 2014:16). Šulgi created an elaborate messenger service with road stations, and enforced laws that ensured safe travelling. In his period, weights and measures were standardised. It improved communications and trade, and did much to increase the wealth of his realm. Following the example of the Akkadian regents, Šulgi set up his own representatives as governors in all major cities, which reduced the ability of the locals to interfere with the government. To top it off, he created a vast, hierarchical and overpowering bureaucratic machinery to record, communicate and control every aspect of life. As Postgate (1992:42) remarked: *Indeed when the death of a single sheep appears three times in the government archives, it is hard to believe that the bureaucratic ideal had not become an encumbrance which ultimately contributed to the state's inability to respond to internal and external threats.* True enough, but Šulgi never found out. In his time, sophisticated bureaucracy was an unheard-of marvel. Rather than criticise him, we might wonder why people 4000 years later are still making the same mistakes. Šulgi ruled for several decades and left us a huge amount of priceless documents. According to Averbeck, Studevent-Hickman and Michalowski (in Chavalas, 2007:65) 65,000 Ur III texts covering approximately 40 years of bureaucracy have been published so far. Two or three times as many may still remain untranslated in museums and private collections. Most of them are devoted to economic matters.

Around the end of Šulgi's reign, the Amorites, a migrating Semitic culture, started invading Mesopotamia. Some came as settlers, others as marauders. The matter is disputed: it seems that the vague term 'Amorites' covers a range of Semitic nomads who entered Mesopotamia at different times and places. The king began to construct great defensive walls. Sadly, walls are never a solution against a mobile enemy. To guard and maintain them is an awful strain on the economy. Šulgi built, fought and bargained, and died after a long and successful reign. After him came Amarsuen (c.2047 BCE), who built more fortifications, and revived a tradition that may have started under Sargon I: he rebuilt the gipar (cloister) district of the temple of Ur and installed an en priestess as the wife of moon god Nanna/Suen/Sîn of Karzida. Next followed Šusuen (c.2038 BCE); he was busy repairing Šulgi's wall and fighting the Amorites. A curious element in his reign is the erection of the temple Ešagepada (*Temple revered by the Heart*) for the god Šara. Šara started his divine career as a minor god of Umma. He was identified, by the locals, as a son of Inanna. It was a remarkable idea, as Inanna is generally known for being anything except a mother. Šara is a divine shepherd and farmer. Apart from these functions, he acts as Inanna's hairdresser. He sits serenely between jars of ointments, perfumes and wash-basins, offering sweet bread to his formidable mum while he does her manicure and sings her praises. According to the temple inscription, Šara had helped Šusuen in battle. It may have been the most remarkable achievement of his cult. Finally we meet Ibbisîn (c.2029 BCE), who built massive fortifications around Ur and Nippur. It was an emergency measure; had there been a successful army, the enemies would never have reached the capital. His 25- year rule was a troublesome time, as Amorites and the Elamites kept invading the country. His reign ended in mystery: one city after the other ceased to send letters and make records, until a time of total oblivion ensued. Elamites from the Iranian mountains and Amorites from who-knows-where overran Mesopotamia. Centralized control shrank, trade ceased to operate, commodities and resources became rare and valuable and after inflation followed economic collapse and famine. The Mesopotamians had to face the fact that without foreign imports, their massive cities, mighty temples and sophisticated culture were doomed. Elamites fought their way into Ur and occupied the capital for a brief period. Then they were soundly beaten and expelled by Amorites, who set themselves up as the regents and founded their own, the Isin-Larsa dynasty, maybe around 2017 BCE.

After the Ur III dynasty, Sumer as a distinct culture was a thing of the past. The great capital city Ur had been sacked and devastated, but it recovered. Other great cities, like Šuruppak, Keš and Ereš disintegrated, and Lagaš, Girsu and Adab became minor towns. Amorite regents shifted political power north to Isin, to the centre of Mesopotamia; Akkadian became the official language again, and Sumerian, as a living language, disappeared.

The Isin-Larsa Period

We have reached a radically new epoch in Mesopotamian history. Some scholars claim that the Old Babylonian period started after the fall of the last Sumerian dynasty, sometime around the year 2000 BCE. Others prefer to date the Old Babylonian period with the advent of real Babylonian dominance. It happened more than two centuries later. The fall of the Sumerians was not caused by a Babylonian dynasty. At the time, Babylon was just a town and had very little influence. The Sumerian regents lost their power to the Amorite invaders, who set themselves up as the new rulers of Mesopotamia. This is the Isin-Larsa period: the interregnum of Amorite rule between the end of Sumerian culture and the beginning of Old Babylonian culture, lasting approximately from 2000 BCE to 1800 BCE. The kings of the Isin dynasty were Semites. They were not a single dynasty but a number of Amorite-governed states struggling for supremacy. The Amorites may have come to power by sheer savagery, but they were soon bedazzled by palace life, canalisation, personal hygiene and documents in triplicate. Unlike the Gutian barbarians, they embraced civilisation and its customs. They respected Sumerian religion and allowed old celestial An, now called Anu, to remain the distant head of the pantheon. His son Enlil was more or less identified with their own fierce desert god Martu/Amurru, who became a proper son of An and a model for sudden respectability. Thanks to his origin in foreign mountains (a lapis lazuli mountain is associated with him, which might hint at Afghanistan) he was easy to identify with Enlil, who was also praised as a Mountain. The changes introduced by the Amorites are still under discussion. Some scholars proposed that the newcomers simply adopted all the customs which Sumer and Akkad had to offer. This, however, is a little unlikely. Under Amorite government, an entirely new mindset appeared. When the Ur III period ended, the unified land split into several states, each of them governed by an Amorite regent. The history of the period is confusing. While political power was anything but clearly divided, the temples were facing difficulties. Since the days of Sargon I, the Sumerian temples had been losing wealth and influence. The king, once a representative of temple politics, had become a major source of independent power. Šulgi had made it absolutely clear that he knew the sacred rituals better than the high priests, and topped it off by deifying himself. The Amorites followed his example. Properly deified, the new regents were hard to control.

How things changed remains mysterious. In the Sumerian period, the few cities about which we have data were mostly owned and governed by the temples. Under Akkadian reign, the kings became major players. Then followed Ur III, with self-deified Sumerian kings promoting bureaucracy. Last, under the control of the Amorite kings, we witness a massive increase in private property. Sadly, the record leaves much to be desired. What we have are a lot of individual business documents. In the old days, the temples had financed trade caravans and sea journeys to Africa and India. Around the start of the Isin-Larsa period, these major enterprises disappeared. For unknown reasons, the temples lost wealth and status. Whatever it may have been, around the year 2000 BCE lots of private people did business. They owned fields, made contracts, leased and rented land, hired employees, set up workshops and made money in a hundred new and ingenious ways. In earlier times, mainly rich people, aristocrats and temple functionaries owned and used cylinder seals to mark documents and contracts. Under Amorite rule, a 'middle class' emerged, consisting of people who ran their own businesses. It was the birth of uncontrollable capitalism. Private enterprises developed without any regulation, usury and corruption escalated and life became truly chaotic and difficult. Before long, the kings were forced to interfere. They did it by looking after their own interests.

The Old Babylonian Period

Between the fall of Ur III and the birth of the important state of Babylonia lie two and a half centuries. Let us pretend that the Old Babylonian period began at the time when the city-state Babylon was coming to power. Since the passing of the Sumerians, a lot had happened. The Amorite regents of the Isin-Larsa period had turned Akkadian into the official language. Official documents still contained Sumerian phrases, but these were read in Akkadian. The 'sacred marriage', a favourite pastime of some Isin-Larsa kings, slowly faded into oblivion. The earlier economic situation of the third millennium, when the temples were perhaps the strongest power in the land, had given way to private property and individual enterprise. Men and women of the early second millennium BCE were eager to make money and gain influence, and they used any means at their disposal. As a result, a middle class emerged, a social segment that owned property. They bought, rented, lent, invested, cheated and exploited on a scale that had been unheard of in the third millennium BCE. We could consider it a major advance in individual entrepreneurship. Whether it also entailed the birth of a new sense of individuality is open to debate. As a result, the documentation of everyday life increased remarkably. While Ur III is famous for its state-run bureaucracy, the Old Babylonian period supplies an amazing of amount of letters, contracts and personal documents. Apart from this, we observe the usual, traditional documents such as building inscriptions, testifying to the erection of temples, palaces and fortifications by kings, and a religious literature that is truly amazing. Plenty of Sumerian literature only survived as the Old Babylonian scribes kept copying it. They also edited, recomposed and translated Sumerian literature into Old Babylonian. And they invented new material. It raises plenty of questions. Assyriologists lead an exciting life and have to do all their stunts themselves.

In the documents of the Ur III period, the small city of Babylon appears. At the time, it was governed by an ensi, a representative of the king. It was called Babila, a term that was interpreted by the invading Amorites as Bab-ilim: *Gate of God/s*. We owe the modern spelling of the name Babylon to the Greek. When the Isin-Larsa dynasties ended, the city-state Babylon was still a minor player. Regarding culture, age and wealth, nobody took it seriously. The early history of Babylon is lost. The water table is high and the earliest layers, and the texts that may have existed in the libraries, went to rot. The first dynasty of Babylon began under the Amorite regent Sumuabum (1894-1881 BCE), who governed the city and the neighbourhood for fourteen years. Other regents followed him, such as Sumula'el (1880-1845 BCE), Sabium (1844-1831 BCE), Apilsîn (1830-1813 BCE), and Sînmuballit (1812-1793 BCE). These kings led a busy life; they waged war and extended their control over what became northern Babylonia: Kiš, Dilbat, Kazallu, Marad, Borsippa and Sippar. It was up to Ḫammurapi (1792-1750 BCE) to do something really influential. It took a while. When Ḫammurapi came to power, he had to be cautious. His sphere of influence was small and vulnerable. To the south, Larsa was powerful and not to be meddled with. King Rimsîn (1822-1763 BCE) governed the southern Sea-land for more than sixty years; his greatest military successes were the conquest of Isin, Uruk, Kisurra and Der. Apart from this, like all good kings, Rimsîn had canals dug and temples built. In the north, the state Aššur had become a serious threat. The first important king of the region was Šamšiaddad (c.1812-1780 or 1776 BCE). According to the *Assyrian King-Lists*, his ancestors had lived in tents. Šamšiaddad gained control of the city Aššur, lying in the rugged hills of northern Mesopotamia, and of the profitable trade routes to the Kurdish mountains and the Mediterranean. Earlier, Assyria had been under the control of the southern Mesopotamian kingdoms. While the Amorites invaded Akkad and Sumer in the south, the Mittanni invaded Aššur. The Mittanni were an Indo-European, Hurrian-speaking culture, closely related to the Hittites. Assyria has plenty of grass for pastoral economy; it has hills, mountains and enough rainfall and snow to get by without too many canals. Assyrian merchants had excellent connections to what is now Turkey. They imported tin, silver and expensive textiles, and in return exported the superior wool textiles from southern Mesopotamia. In the early second millennium BCE Assyria had become a power to be reckoned with. The kings of Aššur were keen on extending their sphere of interest: Šamšiadad married his son Jasmaḫadad, the vice-king of Mari, to a daughter of the regent of Qatna (today: Tell

Mishrife) and gained access to northern Syria and the Mediterranean Sea. Ḫammurapi was stuck in the middle, between the ancient cultures of the south (the former Sumer and Akkad) and the mighty culture of the north (Aššur). Two other powerful players were the city-state Mari on the middle Euphrates and the city-state Ešnunna on the Djala river. Ḫammurapi had much to worry about. He patiently looked after his own small realm, building temples and canals and hoping for a better future. He bided his time, made treaties, wrote letters and kept his spies busy. During most of his life, his influence was limited to maybe 80km around the city of Babylon. To survive, Ḫammurapi allied himself with the Assyrians under Šamšiadad, but he also acted in coordination with the Larsa king Rimsîn. When Šamsiadad died, maybe in the 12-17th year of Ḫammurapi's reign, the balance of power changed. The new regent of Assyria, Išmedagan, had to suppress a revolt in his own country and lost most of his influence in central Mesopotamia. Letters excavated in Mari show his weakness: he frequently asked for the support and troops of Ḫammurapi. For similar reasons, the city-state Ešnunna did its best to remain friends with Babylon. Ḫammurapi went to considerable lengths to keep peace with Zimrilim, king of Mari: they kept up a happy correspondence. In times of war they lent troops to each other. One letter by Ḫammurapi states that he dispatched ten thousand troops to help Mari; he also apologised for the delay, and pointed out that the troops were slow as they had to move upriver. It was only late in his reign that he could dare to wage war. In the thirtieth year of his rule, Ḫammurapi fought a series of battles. The year-inscription states that, thanks to the supreme power of the great gods, he hurled down the invading armies of Elam, Subartu, Gutium, Ešnunna and Malgum and *strengthened the foundations of Sumer and Akkad*. In the next year, his diplomats were busy forming an alliance with Rimsîn of Larsa in the south. It was a difficult affair: according to rumours, Larsa troops had repeatedly plundered settlements on the edge of Babylonia. While the kings exchanged letters and presents, and talked about peace and friendship, Ḫammurapi prepared his army. Giving himself into the hands of Anu and Enlil, he defeated the 40,000 soldiers who defended the south. With this victory, Babylon had gained control over southern and central Mesopotamia. The Isin-Larsa dynasty broke down in the year 1763 BCE. Ḫammurapi was careful to keep his new subjects happy; instead of destroying cities he rebuilt and extended them. His 32nd year saw more campaigns against Ešnunna, Gutium and Assyria. The king had the southern canals system restored. He also brought Mari and Malgum to submission. Zimrilim, king of Mari, had been warned: his wife, Šibtu, related a 'divine prophecy' to him. Alas, it didn't help. Ḫammurapi came marching with his troops, and to ensure that things remained peaceful, he had the walls of both cities destroyed. The war with Ešnunna continued for years, until Ḫammurapi's troops destroyed all resistance by flooding the district. Finally, Ḫammurapi's armies turned to the north. They annexed large sections of Assyria, fought near the cities Aššur and Nineveh and went far into Kurdistan: in Diyarbakir, they set up a commemorative stele. At the end of Ḫammurapi's 43-year reign, he had fused most of Mesopotamia into a single state.

For modern scholars, his greatest achievement is a remarkable law text. Many students of Assyriology start their training with it. The *Codex Ḫammurapi* is not a complete account of Old Babylonian laws, but an addition, an extra, indicating that a lot had to be reformed. The opening passage presents the king in all his glory and calls upon a wide range of deities. Interestingly, Marduk, the city god of Babylon, is still a minor player, who appears in the background. Ḫammurapi had himself praised as a custodian of civilisation, not as a savage warlord. The laws have been interpreted in many controversial ways. Several scholars idealised the king and praised his good will, his humanitarian attitude and the way he enforced justice for the poor. Behind such gestures, however, appear the fundamental problems of the Old

Babylonian period. You only need rules, regulations and laws when things don't work properly. Their very necessity proves that things are badly out of balance. Ḫammurapi fixed the prices of commodities and wages, he tried to stabilise rents, interest and went to some length to specify the punishment for misdeeds. These laws show that inflation, corruption, usury and exploitation had reached an unbearable level. Judges misused their power, inheritance was badly regulated and the poor were abused by the wealthy. Peasants had to survive under unbearable conditions and regularly ended in debt slavery. Ḫammurapi legislated to ensure the rights of nadītu, ugbabtu, qadištu and šugītu priestesses, to protect adopted children and to settle relations between slaves and masters. Builders whose buildings fell in were punished, doctors were held responsible for sloppy work, charges and wages were fixed.

Ḫammurapi had his laws set up in public, so that anyone could have them read. It turned his codex into a majestic demonstration of royal and divine justice. Sadly, we don't know if the laws were enforced. The noble effort could have been futile. When Ḫammurapi died, his son Samsuiluna (1749-1712 BCE) took over: he had to struggle against Kassite invaders and against Sumer and Akkad, which revolted against him, and set up their own king, Rimsîn II. At the end of his reign, he had lost control over the shores of the Persian Gulf, where the new Sea-land Dynasty was ruling. Abiešuḫ (1711-1684 BCE) began his reign by fighting the Kassites. The Kassites were splendid warriors famed for their cavalry. In the Near East their horsemanship was unequalled. Their troops were more mobile than the donkey-pulled chariots and foot-soldiers of Mesopotamia. For good or bad, Ḫammurapi's descendants had to make friends with them. The next Babylonian kings, Ammiditana (1683-1647 BCE), Ammisaduqa (1646-1626 BCE) and Samsuditana (1625-1595 BCE) are a) hardly worth mentioning or b) peaceful characters. The year-names lack references to any military success. Instead of making war, the kings built temples and canals and kept the state going as well as they could. Finally, the dynasty of Ḫammurapi found its end. Over the centuries, the Hittites had become a formidable force which exerted its influence from Anatolia in Turkey well into northern Mesopotamia. King Mursili I sent the Hittite troops through Halab (Aleppo) and the land Hana; they broke into Babylonia and devastated its capital. It was a surprise raid and a gesture of immense power. Mursili I plundered and abducted as he liked. However, the Hittite homeland was too far away to keep Babylonia under control. King Mursili I departed to his homeland in triumph; soon after his return he was assassinated by his brother-in-law, Hantilis. It left central Mesopotamia open to anyone.

Occupation by Kassites and Hurrians

To sack Babylon, the Hittites needed the approval of the Kassites. After the Hittites had left, the Kassites used their chance. Babylonia was badly weakened. It didn't take much to assume control. The Kassite occupation may have begun after the fall of the first dynasty of Babylon (c.1594 BCE) and continued to c.1155 BCE, when the last regent claiming to be of Kassite stock was overthrown and the Elamites overran Babylon. The Kassite occupation started the **Middle Babylonian** period, which extended to the first regents after the Kassites had become history. Dating the Kassites is difficult. There may have been 36 Kassite kings, or at least kings who claimed to be of Kassite descent. The first regents may have been former mercenaries or warlords. Whatever it was, King Agumkakrime did his best to legitimise his position with questionable documents. Dates are doubtful and historical accounts are full of gaps. It has been tried to ascertain regencies and periods by astronomical references, but so far, the results are not convincing. These centuries are amazingly hard to reconstruct, and constitute a 'dark age' of Mesopotamian history. However his career may have started, King Agum II moved into the freshly plundered Babylon. He gained control over central Babylonia and cultivated close ties to the land of Hana and to Gutium in Iran. He, or the regents who followed him, managed to extend his or their reign over Babylonia, Sumer, the southern Sea-Land and even to Bahrain. Their first well-documented king was Kurigalzu I (c.1400 BCE) who defeated the Elamites. The Kassites may have started out as a horde of terrifying horsemen, but once in Babylonia, they settled down, got a haircut and a manicure and became properly civilised. The Kassite kings were foreigners, but they seem to have been less oppressive than the Babylonian kings. They treated the ancient cities of southern Sumer with respect and apparently governed with relative ease. No revolts against them are recorded, and for a bunch of revolt-happy cultures, like the Mesopotamians, this surely means something. Like the kings who preceded them, the Kassite rulers dutifully dug canals and built temples. For a brief time, they were replaced by the Assyrian king Tulkutininurta I who conquered Babylon in c.1225 BCE. It was a short and bloody interlude. Soon the Kassites were back in power, and devoted much of their time to fighting the Elamites. During their reign, Akkadian became the language of diplomacy all over the Near East. Egyptians, Syrians, and Hittites in Anatolia, the Mittanni and Assyrians: everybody used Akkadian for diplomatic correspondence. In the wake of this remarkable diffusion, Akkadian literature and ideas went around. When students in Syria, Anatolia and Egypt learned Akkadian, they studied Akkadian documents, letters, hymns, myths and similar material. Accordingly, priceless pieces of Akkadian literature have been unearthed as far away as Egypt.

When the Babylonians were occupied by Kassites, the Assyrians, in northern Mesopotamia, were occupied by Hurrians. While the Babylonians got used to horses, the Assyrians were faced with people from southern Anatolia, strongly influenced by the Hittite culture, who had come to govern them. The Hurrian people can also be seen as an extension of the Mittanni culture which had become a major force in what is now Kurdistan. Or we could call them the Ḫanigalbateans, a name that frequently appears in Assyrian and Babylonian documents. The regents of the Mittanni were Indo-Europeans; they worshipped gods that also appeared in India, like Indra, Mitra, Varuṇa and the Nasatyas. Like many other Indo-European cultures, they burned their dead, a custom that seemed horrible to the Assyrians and Babylonians, as it prevented the soul from entering the Underworld. Mittanni rule, however, did not last. The Hittite culture itself was gradually losing influence in the Near East. True, the Hittites did their best to bring the Egyptians to their knees and were, for a while, so powerful in Syria and Palestine that the Egyptians put on fake smiles and funny hats and swore vows of eternal friendship. In Assyria, however, the government lost its influence. It was the beginning of a new era. Aššuruballit I (1365-1330 BCE) was the first significant (i.e. dangerous) Assyrian regent. He married a daughter to the Babylonian king and created a powerful alliance. The two states united to fight the invading Sutu people, but did not cooperate for long: soon, revolts in Babylonia broke out and an usurper tried to gain the throne. The Assyrians did not approve. Aššuruballit I invaded Babylonia, dealt harshly with everybody opposed to eternal Assyrian-Babylonian friendship and set up a new Babylonian king, Kurigalzu II (1345-1324 BCE, who happened to be his relation. Babylonia gained her freedom by becoming a subject state of Aššur. As you might expect, the alliance did not last. Kurigalzu II, the Assyrian king who ruled Babylonia, decided that by rights, government of Assyria should belong to him. He did not get his head, while many people lost theirs, and his campaigns weakened Babylonia so much that the Elamites from the mountains of Iran used their chance for a visit and came plundering. Simultaneously, Aramean nomads began to stream into Mesopotamia. Their origin and cultural makeup are uncertain; modern scholars are not even sure whether they were a single, nomadic culture or a conglomerate of distinct ethnic groups. It was the usual package: some came to settle, some to conduct raids. For a while, the Assyrians, with their excellent military organisation could control them. However, more and more of them appeared, and most of them came to stay. By now you should have noted that Mesopotamian prehistory has plenty of similarities to life in the 21st century. Or to any other century you can think of. That's humans. Like them or not, they get anywhere and upset anything. Next, the Assyrians broke the resistance of the Ḫanigalbateans (aka Mittanni) and turned their country into an Assyrian province. To ensure peace, they deported many of their former enemies. It was the start of a new population policy. Over the next centuries, the Assyrians kept moving huge population groups. Meanwhile, they tried to gain control of Babylonia. Tulkutininurta I (1244-1208 BCE) invaded Babylonia and devastated Babylon; he abducted the statue of Marduk, city god of Babylon, and set it up for worship in Aššur. He may have thought of Marduk as a trophy, but soon, Marduk was thinking of the Assyrians as his worshippers. For the Babylonians, facing an empty temple without their city god, this event was traumatic. The Assyrians, however, were caught up in a new fashion and began to introduce Babylonian ceremonies into their religion. They celebrated a New Year ritual honouring Marduk, and fell over themselves trying to be Babylonian. Before long, they had identified their national god Aššur with Marduk. Tulkutininurta I expanded Assyria into the north, well into Anatolia. Then his campaigns came to a painful halt: the cash-flow stopped, as his wars had ruined the economy. Let me remind you: this was over three thousand years ago, and since then nobody learned anything from the past. Just look at the Near East today: do people think that history is just for laughs? Assyria had a little cash-flow problem: it was the chance the Babylonians had been waiting for. The next Assyrians kings were poor and insignificant; they survived as vassals of wealthy Babylon. The Assyrian king Ninurtaapalekur (1192-1180 BCE) governed thanks to the support of a Babylonian regent from Kassite stock. In his time, Assyria shrank to its smallest size ever. His son Aššurdan I (1179-1134 BCE?) wasn't even allowed to call himself 'king': he had to make do with the title iššaku, the Assyrian equivalent of the term ensi (*governor*). But Kassite control was disintegrating. The north was threatened by foreigners. Babylon was weakened by its wars against the Assyrians and could not give support to Assyrian campaigns. The ancient trade routes that once made Assyria rich were disappearing. As could have been expected, things went from bad to worse. Around 1200 BCE, the entire Near East was shaken by the intrusion of a new culture, or a coalition of tribes whom the Egyptians called the Sea-People. Imagine a bunch of savage barbarians who came from god knows where and simply pillaged their way south without bothering to settle down. The Sea-People left a trail of carnage along the rim of the eastern Mediterranean. In the wake of their migration, the Hittite culture collapsed (though small Hittite kingdoms continued to exist to the seventh century BCE) and life became overwhelmingly desperate. A similar development can be observed in Greece and western Turkey. Historians speak of the Greek dark ages, of abject poverty and illiterate barbarism. The great Achaean culture that had built huge cities and waged war against Troy simply faded into oblivion. Greece became largely uninhabited, the cities were abandoned and only Athens remained as a dreary village. The Sea-People passed through Syria and left the cities in shambles; they passed into Egypt and finally met their doom. In Mesopotamia, the following centuries were a nightmarishly complicated series of incessant wars, of shifting alliances and the ups and downs of dynasties.

The Second Dynasty of Isin and the Assyrian Revival

During the twelfth century BCE, Kassite control over Babylonia had reached an all-time low and a new dynasty managed to establish itself. The new regents came from the south, the old Sumerian Sea-Land. They were strong enough to get their fingers into Assyrian politics, which allowed the new Babylonian ruler to decide the king of Assyria and to have the statue of Marduk returned to its homeland. Sadly, very little is known about the kings of the time. The migration of the Sea People had left much of the Near East in ruins. One of the former champions, Egypt, was almost on its knees. The exceptionally successful and long-lived Ramses II had wasted so much money and so many people on his grandiose building projects that the economy was ruined and the population starved. It's time to take a deep breath. Many Egyptian rulers had done their best to build pyramids, eternal temples, grave chambers and palaces, which were torn down by their successors five minutes later to furnish the materials for their eternal buildings. It's one of those surprises that we should never take the paintings and inscriptions in Egyptian grave chambers seriously. When you look at the paintings, showing happy peasants harvesting, happy farmers growing vines, happy fowlers hunting birds and happy aristocrats chatting away with the gods, you should remember that they were meant to show conditions as they should have been. Egyptian grave chambers are a beautiful fiction, and so are many inscriptions in them. Some administrators went into the otherworld with dozens of titles that did not exist in reality. Egyptian tomb art shows life as it never was. In reality, the Egyptian peasant faced a life of terrible work and malnutrition, while the average pharaoh was spaced out of his head by a range of drugs that defy botanical identification, including cocaine. It's not a coincidence that Cleopatra drugged the ambitious workaholic Julius Caesar into such a stupor that he drifted down the Nile without consideration for politics for several months. For simple people, life in ancient Egypt was one extended chore. Unlike the Mesopotamians, the Egyptians never managed to get a proper revolt going. The peasants who worked on pharaonic projects had a happy life: only ten percent were badly injured or died on the building sites, and they got a substantial meal every day, which other people did not (for the painful realities of life in ancient Egypt, see Wilkinson, 2010). Ramses III, faced by the marauding Sea People, recruited an army by enlisting almost everyone, and managed to stop their conquest. He lost his land battles (and never mentioned them) but scored a decisive victory on the sea. His monumental building projects and the exhausting war cost Egypt the last of its wealth. True, the pharaohs were still buried with plenty of treasure. Rich people remained happy and content. Economically, the country had gone down the drain. Poor people learned what it means to be poorer. Soon, the government of Egypt would fall into the hands of other cultures. In the future, Egypt was invaded and governed by Nubians, Libyans, Kushites, Assyrians, Persians, the Macedonians under Alexander, until finally Roman bankers took control, and sucked the last remnants of wealth out of the country. Why bother to read a newspaper: things were pretty much like today.

Similar conditions affected many countries. The first successful Babylonian king of the new era was Nebuchadnezzar I (1124-1103 BCE). Under his government, Babylonia regained some of its internal strength and Marduk, the city god of Babylon, was turned into the *'king of the gods'* by his devoted priesthood. To provide Marduk with an impressive pedigree, his priests forged several amusing documents. A lovely example is the well-known *Enûma Eliš*, the *Epic of Creation*. It tells us how Marduk abolished the democratic assembly of the gods, and how he usurped supreme authority by a mixture of threats and bribes. The text was composed in archaic Old Babylonian language to make it seem five hundred years older than it was. The *Marduk Prophecy*, trying hard to come from a similar period, has the god announcing his own fate. He foresees those embarrassing periods when his statue was abducted and changed their significance: no, he had not been dragged away by force, but had invited the invaders to Babylon, so they could carry him to faraway lands, improve the trade routes and spread his fame. Best is the *Weidner Chronicle*, a piece of fake history where we learn that Marduk decided the fates of the kings of Sumer, Akkad and the Isin-Larsa period. The popular text happily relates how people like Sargon I and Šulgi of Ur III met disaster and tragedy as Marduk was angry with them. I wonder how he did this: Marduk is a god of the second millennium BCE; he does not appear in third millennium texts at all. Indeed Sargon I and Šulgi were amazingly successful. The priesthood of Marduk turned history upside down, and many people fell for it. Around the same time, the cult of Nabû gained popularity. Nabû, originally an independent god, was identified as a son of Marduk. He had been a god in the background, a deity of scholars and scribes. Thanks to enthusiastic promotion and a proper pedigree, he was turned into the protective god of the crown prince. Before long, Marduk became so exalted, authoritative and overbearing that the common population preferred to pray to Nabû instead of his almighty dad.

Assyria remained under the control of the Babylonians until Aššurrešiši (1133-1116 BCE) won their independence. He faced a lot of problems, including the massive intrusion of Aramean settlers and raiders. His son Tiglatpilesar I began the military triumph of the Neo-Assyrian period. He extended Assyria and turned it into a force to be reckoned with. Under his reign, the Assyrian army returned to its former efficiency. The new soldiers were routinely equipped with iron weapons and used them to devastating effect. But the Assyrians didn't have an easy road before them. After the vastly efficient conquest lead by Tiglatpilesar, his son Aššurbēlkala (1074-1057 BCE) had so much trouble keeping the Arameans out of Assyria that he was forced to make friends with the Babylonian king Mardukšapikzermati (1080-1068 BCE). They signed a treaty of eternal friendship and mutual support, which didn't amount to much, as neither had much to offer. Bankrupt Babylonia asked the Assyrians for support against the Arameans, but as Assyria was weak, and badly strained by the Arameans, none could be granted. Babylon was overrun by Arameans, who set up a short-lived and unpopular government.

By now, the political situation was such a mess that even the traditional boat journeys of the gods (or rather their statues) to neighbouring cities had to be cancelled. Both states, Babylonia and Assyria were poor, weak and deeply in trouble. The Arameans had become a plague to them and when they didn't make war, other people did. The second millennium BCE, which had begun with so much enthusiasm, was coming to a painful end. Around the beginning of the first millennium BCE, things began to settle somewhat. The Aramean intrusion slowed and all over the Near East, Aramean nomads began to settle down and form small states. One of them was Israel. For Assyria, trade gradually resumed and eventually, money came in. The Babylonians had to face another source of trouble in the southern Sea-Land of Sumer, where a new people, the Kaldu, related to the Arameans, had set up their own kingdom. We meet them in later histories as the Chaldeans. Thanks to their influence, Babylon lost its contact to the Persian Gulf, hence to sea trade, and a lot of income.

Assyrian Supremacy

Around the end of the second Millennium BCE things had been pretty bad for everyone. Babylon was small and faced enemies in all directions. The Assyrians had hopes but had to make do with very little. The Arameans had founded several tiny states but were not going anywhere. It took several generations before Assyria could resume her conquests. We are now observing an especially bloody episode: the start of the Neo-Assyrian Empire. Thanks to the newly-reopened trade routes to the west, Aššurdan II (933-912 BCE) rebuilt the west gate of Aššur: a grand gesture indicating that money was coming in. Modern scholars like to begin the Neo-Assyrian period with his reign. His son Adadnirari II (911-891) had enough wealth to resume the aggressive policy of his ancestors. He turned his troops to the south of Assyria and ran straight into the armies of a Babylonian king who was trying to extend his realm northwards. The Babylonians were badly beaten and Assyria grew. Next, the king coerced the western states to accept him as their overlord and to pay tribute. Adadnirari II forced many of his neighbours into submission and used the inflowing tribute to restore Assyria's wealth. He invested in administration, roads, storage, bred horses and introduced the first Bactrian camels into Assyria, where he bred them. It proved to be an excellent idea. Mesopotamia had suffered much from marauding Arabs. Horses were useless in the desert, donkeys were obstinate and soon exhausted, but camels were perfect. At last, the nomadic tribes could be pursued into their sun-scorched wasteland. He was also praised as the inventor of a new type of warfare, probably making use of siege engines. Look at Assyrian art, much of it is devoted to hunting, slaughter and warfare, and among the images are siege engines and the first tanks of human history. As an excellent strategist, he set up a series of supply depots and founded palaces, fortifications and even cities in strategic locations, which made his campaigns devastatingly efficient. As a typical Assyrian king, he was expected to be an excellent hunter. But unlike so many of his ancestors, he was also fascinated by wildlife and created one of the first zoos in history. Adadnirari II left us plenty of documentation. He meticulously pointed out that he had been successful where earlier rulers were not, and gave painstaking evidence for his success. The next Assyrian kings did much to fortify the country with garrisons, and reopened trade with the Mediterranean and the Kurdish highlands. In the process, much of what is Turkey today became a vassal state of Assyria. But things can always get worse. Warfare became excessive under Aššurnasirpal (*God Aššur Guards the Son*, 883-859 BCE), a regent who left more inscriptions than any of his successors. The king led at least fourteen major campaigns, including to Zagros, Anatolia and the Mediterranean. Like Sargon I, he washed his weapons in the Mediterranean Sea.

Here, we meet Assyria at its most brutal. Aššurnasirpal was fond of mass executions, public torture, impalement; he burned his enemies alive and enthusiastically obliterated cities. He loved to set up piles of heads; he skinned people alive, and had his scribes record how he had dyed the land with the blood of enemies. In his savagery he started a fashion. It would be easy to condemn several Neo-Assyrian kings for their exemplary brutality. However, we have to remember that the Near and Middle East were undergoing extreme changes. War and migration caused unrest and poverty, and the Neo-Assyrian kings may have thought that the best way to maintain peace was to scare everyone to death. For this purpose they used shock tactics. It certainly worked. Their historians commemorated a brutality that may have been a pleasure for some kings and a sad necessity for others. Aššurnasirpal was one of the worst offenders: he seems to have gloated over each mass execution, and delighted in reducing prosperous settlements to ruins. Others used similar methods, and had themselves celebrated for excessive cruelty.

Another political tactic was mass-deportation. To relocate entire cultures can be understood as a punishment. To the Neo-Assyrians, it was a long-term strategy to convert uprooted ethnic groups into a vast multi-national empire. The new citizens, so it was hoped, would forget their traditional background. Relocated people were not harassed but treated like everybody else. While the old generation had a lot to complain about, their kids could make a career in the army or the administration. Imagine a Neo-Assyrian officer saying: "Relocation is such an ugly word. As a spokesman of the Assyrian Army I would much prefer to talk of a friendly foreign exchange project. Our students come from all age groups, genders and cultures. We are giving half a million excited and enthusiastic people a chance to see the world and to settle in a lovely new homeland. Within a few generations we will turn every person on earth into a proud and happy Assyrian."

While waging war in all directions, Aššurnasirpal tried to spread culture and prosperity. For this purpose he founded the city Kalhu and settled it with deported people from many lands. He planted gardens, built temples for Ninurta and Nabû, had canals dug and created a zoological garden for his personal entertainment. From provinces near and far, strange animals were sent. His son Šalmaneser III (858-824 BCE) continued the efforts of his father. In his first year he marched his army to the Mediterranean Sea, and nobody dared get into his way. He waged war in Syria until a revolt in Babylonia brought down the local king, who had been ruling courtesy of the support of Assyria. Before long, the Neo-Assyrian Empire occupied all Syria. It gained control over all trade routes of Asia Minor, and all the iron, silver and timber of that region. The king then turned his attention to the north and east. The latter gave him control of the many trade routes to India and China which are nowadays called the Silk Road. A son of Šalmaneser III led a revolt against his father, but failed badly. Another son, Šamšiadad V (823-811 BCE) came to power thanks to Babylonian support, and had to accept the suzerainty of the Babylonians. He led campaigns against the cultures of the north and the newly emerging Medes. At the height of his power he forgot all about the friendly Babylonians who had supported him and began to harass their land. In 811 BCE the Assyrian king had conquered Babylon, and used the occasion to conduct religious ceremonies in the city. After his death, an Assyrian queen, Sammuramat (the Biblical Semiramis) ran Assyria for five years, until her son Adadnirari III (810-783 BCE) was old enough to govern. Sammuramat knew that she was living in a man's world, and though she took part in a military campaign, won a victory and dared to set up boundary stones, she took great care to make her decisions politically acceptable. Her son Adadnirari III spent most of his life waging war and so did his son Šalmaneser IV (782-772 BCE). Most of their time was devoted to fighting the Uratians, a culture based in what is modern Armenia. It didn't go well. The Uruatians gained control of the entire northern Assyrian frontier and cut off trade to northern Iran and Turkey. It stopped the supply of horses and metals. While Assyria was getting weaker, numerous frontier states used the chance to fight each other. In Assyria, lack of trade, inflation and general poverty led to revolts. It ended in 746 BCE, when Aššurnirari III and his entire family were assassinated. The new regent, Tiglatpilesar III (745-727 BCE) was a highly effective general and statesman and saw to it that Assyria became a major force again. Whether he was a legitimate king is uncertain. He claimed to be a son of Adadnirari III (810-783) but this is doubtful. Under his rule, Assyria reached the summit of military might. All through his reign, he insisted on marching out with his army at least once a year. Other kings had used mass-deportation sporadically, but Tiglatpilesar III made it a major, systematic effort. It would be exhausting to list his military successes. By the time his son Sargon II (722-705 BCE) came to power (possibly by murdering his half-brother Šalmaneser V), the Assyrian empire extended from the Persian Gulf to the Kurdish mountains and the Mediterranean coast all the way down to Gaza. Sargon II had a tough start, as Assyria did not accept him as legitimate. He chose the name Sargon, just like the illustrious Akkadian king, to emphasise his legitimacy. Before long he was waging war, year in and year out, against the Elamites, the Chaldeans, the Urarteans in the north, the invading Cimmerians and those Syrians who tried to revolt against his enlightened government. In his spare time he tried to create a new capital and had the city Dur-Šarrukin built (modern Khorsabad). He led a violent life and may have fallen in battle, only a year after his new capital was inhabitable. His hopes failed badly. Five years after his death, the new capital had been reduced to the rank of a fortress. His son Sennaḫerib (705-681 BCE) inherited an empire that was almost too large to be governed. He was the legitimate crown prince but that hardly mattered: as soon as he became regent, Babylonia rebelled. Sennaḫerib made his name by crushing the revolt. It did not work. Destroying Babylon turned out to be the greatest nightmare of his life. Sennaḫerib fought a coalition of Babylonians, and people from the Chaldean Sea-Land, Aramean tribes and, worst of all, the allied armies of Elam. It made him devote years to futile campaigns and cost him a son, until, finally, at long last and under much strain, he managed to flood and devastate the city. He loathed Babylon so intensely that he left it a ruin, and refused to mention the topic. He participated in all the usual battles and revolts which I won't bother to describe (by now you must be as tired of them as I am). Politically, he kept the empire of his father in shape: there was no room for extras, as his enemies kept him busy all the time. His campaigns against Elam started well enough. They ended in a monstrous battle that was celebrated as a victory but was an expensive and tragic defeat. He also waged war in Palestine: in those days, the kings had little leisure. Nevertheless, he tried to appear as a patron of art and science. He had his newly-rebuilt city Nineveh decorated by the finest craftsmen from all countries and turned it into the capital of Assyria. He also created one of the first botanical gardens in the world. For this purpose he had a network of new canals excavated. A vast terrain was dedicated to the flora of occupied countries; he even had an artificial swamp looking like the Sea-Land of southern Babylonia. The king also tried his hand at bronze casting and created statues of huge lions and bulls. The *Bible* has much to say regarding his campaign in Palestine. Allegedly, the Angel of the Lord struck down the Assyrian army and killed 185,000 soldiers in a single night. Devastated, the king returned, and when he reached Nineveh he was murdered by one of his sons. It's an unlikely story. Though pestilence is a common side effect of all prolonged campaigns, the Assyrian inscriptions do not mention a plague. Palestine remained under Assyrian control and the assassination of the king by a son happened 20 years after he came home. Evidently, the Angel of the Lord was distracted and took a lot of time to get things done. Another son, Asarḫaddon (680-669 BCE), had been nominated as his successor and made it his first duty to chase the murderer into Urartu (modern Armenia). Asarḫaddon was one of the most intelligent Assyrian regents. He carefully avoided mentioning the murder of his father in historic records, lest he would set a bad example or cause trouble in the family, and cautiously reversed the savage policies of Sennaḫerib. The latter had hated and devastated Babylon; Asarḫaddon rebuilt Babylon, and invested much effort and wealth in the restoration of its culture and economy. In his opinion, Babylonia and Assyria shared a common heritage, and ought to be a single culture. It was a distinctly unpopular idea. Too many Assyrians and Babylonians remembered the terrible campaigns that had caused so much suffering and hate. The king devoted much of his reign to diplomacy and careful rebuilding projects, each of them officially sanctioned by popular deities. He even manipulated respectable prophecies. It had been foretold that Babylon would remain a desolate ruin for 70 years. Asarḫaddon turned the number around, so that it read 11, looked at the calendar, announced that he had Marduk's blessing, confirmed by the position of the planet Jupiter, and began rebuilding. He even participated in Babylonian rituals, carrying a basket of earth on his head. It supported the long-standing tradition that Babylonian kings carried soil to their temple building sites. Asarḫaddon's reign involved several wars, but was slightly more peaceful than that of most Neo-Assyrian kings. However, he was constantly threatened by other sons of Sennaḫerib and suffered from weak health. It may have made him more interested in omens and divination than the kings who preceded him. Several scholars deride him for 'weakness' and 'superstition'. They hardly noticed that Asarḫaddon favoured peace and used the divine, and the support of temples, to legitimize his policy.

When his son Aššurbanipal was appointed as successor in 672 BCE, Assyrian power was at its zenith. Aššurbanipal waged several wars against Egypt, which failed to put up any defence worth mentioning, and ensured that it remained a vassal state of Assyria. So did Cyprus and much of Turkey, wide ranges of what is Iran today, and vast stretches of the Arabian Desert. Aššurbanipal bred camels and patrolled the desert, destroying all Arabs who came his way. He caught two Arab chiefs who had marauded in Syria and exhibited them to the public in dog's kennels. In between he led several campaigns to crush rebellions against his benevolent rule. One of them was against his brother, who had been set up as the puppet king of Babylon. His major obsession, however, was war in the east. Aššurbanipal, enervated by the incessant conflicts with Elam, decided to crush the Iranian highland culture for good. The power struggle lasted many years. At least five campaigns are recorded. In the end, Aššurbanipal's troops overran the Elamite cities in a campaign of carnage and destruction that had no equal. After they were done with it, the aristocracy of Elam was dead or taken prisoner, the few surviving cities were ruled by Assyrian governors and most of the population had been deported. It was a major victory and an even greater error. No matter whether the Elamites were friends or enemies, they had served as a barrier against the cultures of the east. Once Elam was broken, the Iranians began to stream into the country. In all leisure they gained control. Aššurbanipal had had no idea how his actions would work out. When not waging war, he patronised art, science and scholarship. Under his reign, a library was assembled that may have been the greatest of its time. Unlike most kings of Mesopotamia, Aššurbanipal was proud that he could read, write and speak several languages, including ancient Sumerian. He was fascinated by ritual, religion, omen literature, medicine and many other subjects. Thanks to his efforts, a vast treasure trove of Mesopotamian literature was collected, edited, copied and preserved for the scholars of today.

The last years of Aššurbanipal's reign are a mystery. He governed until 626 BCE, and what happened afterwards is difficult to determine. Apparently the succession was accompanied by revolt, murder and fighting among his sons. We are almost at the end of the story here. Assyria had no leadership worth mentioning. In 612 BCE, Babylonian and Median troops overran much of Assyria, and eliminated Aššurbanipal's son Sînšariškun. They flooded the countryside and sacked Nineveh. It was the end of the Neo-Assyrian Empire. Once Assyrian supremacy was broken, its many vassal states fell into an uneasy independence and waged war against each other.

Neo-Babylonian rule and its successors

After the fall of the Neo-Assyrian dynasties, the Babylonians assumed it was time to rise to glory again. In 626 BCE, the Chaldean king Nabopoplessar became king in Babylon. He had to wait a little until the Assyrian royal house had successfully eliminated itself before he could revolt against the Assyrian king Sînšariškun. Assyria had come apart by that time, and various districts were run by independent aristocrats. To gain support, Nabopoplessar made an alliance with the king of the Medes, Cyaxares. Together, they defeated the Assyrian armies and ended the dynasty. In the following year, an heir to Assyria made a pact with the Egyptians, which allowed Egypt to conquer most of Palestine and Syria. Nabopoplessar tried to assume control of the former Assyrian empire but was too weak for the job and went to bed early. However, he did his best to fight Egypt, and so did his son Nebuchadnezzar. The latter beat the Egyptian army and was about to invade Egypt when his father Nabopoplessar died. As a dutiful son he had to return to Babylonia for the funeral. In the next years, Nebuchadnezzar tried to regain the empire. He besieged Jerusalem, crushed revolts in Syrian cities, and managed to keep some sort of friendship with the Medes. He was an excellent administrator under whom Babylon was rebuilt and improved one last time: the city must have been gorgeously beautiful and perfectly fortified, but the citizens were poor, the economy in tatters and the streets full of beggars, criminals and prostitutes. The citizens remained true to tradition and revolted. His son Awelmarduk governed an entire two years before his life came to a violent end. We will pass a veil of silence over the next two kings of the Neo-Babylonian period. They tried their hand at campaigns and met defeat or were killed by their relations at home. The Neo-Babylonian Empire never really got anywhere. Its greatest achievement was a grand attempt to return to the magnificent culture of the Old Babylonian period. Several kings tried to revive ancient customs, such as they understood, or invented, them. They graced themselves with ancient titles, initiated a new tradition of entu(m) priestesses who were married to the gods, recreated priestly ranks that had long been forgotten and celebrated rites that seemed old but were miles away from the real thing. Even a version of the 'sacred marriage', celebrating the union of divine statues, had a brief comeback. In this period, the cult of Anu briefly returned to power. All the while, the citizens remained desperately poor, and there was famine in Babylon. The glorious building projects impoverished the state and inflation went totally out of control. Things did not get better when the celebrated king Nabûna'id (555-539 BCE) was struck with a horrible skin disease, forcing him to move out of the capital and to stay out of sight for seven years. Eventually he recovered and made his return to Babylon, now an old and wretched man and much obsessed with building projects. Invading Elamites made his last days unbearable.

Meanwhile, the Persians under Cyrus the Great had gobbled up what is modern Iran. They had moved well into modern Turkey, and Cyrus, calling himself a friend and ally of Nabûnaid, gained control of all land east of the Tigris. It was just a small step to walk into Babylonia and complete his conquest. Cyrus was a gentle conqueror, and prohibited the looting and raping that traditionally accompanied such events. His son Cambyses participated in the Babylonian New Year festival, and was officially blessed by Marduk.

Since this time, Mesopotamia has been governed by foreigners. The Persian occupation lasted until 331 BCE. Then the country was overrun by the armies of Alexander. After his death, general Seleucius gained control: it was the start of the Seleucid period, and Mesopotamia was governed by the Greeks. By then, the major population group was Arameans. Their language had replaced Akkadian, and their simple system of writing, using letters instead of syllables, was far easier to handle than old cuneiform. Most of the old learning had long been forgotten. The last document in cuneiform dates to c.140 BCE. When the Romans marched in, and made the Kurdish city Diyarbakir the centre of the Roman province Mesopotamia, the wonderful achievements of the Sumerians, Akkadians and Old Babylonians were almost forgotten. Some of the cults survived, if in a strongly altered form. When Emperor Julian (361-363 CE), maybe the sanest regent Rome ever had, passed through Babylonia to fight the Persians, he sacrificed in Karrhae (Harran) near the Euphrates to the moon god Sîn (Bidez, 1956:206). Julian was a polytheist and promoted Hellenic gods and culture. He admired Plato and derided the Christians for the absurdity of their beliefs. The Christians hated him for it. We owe him the saying that it's not worthwhile to persecute Christians, as they are fighting each other anyway. Julian respected foreign deities. He even tolerated Christians. It did not help him much: while fighting Persian riders, a bodyguard assassinated him. Julian died young and was replaced by a Christian leader, who made a mess of the campaign. The Romans withdrew and the Persians remained. In Mesopotamia, the teachings of Zoroaster became popular. He promoted a good-against-evil theology which appealed to stupid people. Subsequent generations, favouring the Mandaean faith, turned the last Mesopotamian gods into devils. The final remnants of their cults disappeared when the Arabs forced the country to submit to Islam.

Part Two

Watchful One of the Gods of the Streets

The Lamaštu Series

The *Lamaštu Series* was compiled for the library of the Neo-Assyrian King Aššurbanipal (668-626 BCE) in Nineveh. The king, successful, educated, faithful and very superstitious, was fascinated by old documents and spellcraft, and commanded that all sorts of elder tablets should be brought to his capital, to create what was probably the largest library of his time. Several versions of his edict survive:

The word of the King unto Šadunu: I am well, mayest thou be happy. The day that thou seest this letter of mine, take with thee Šumâ, the son of Šumâ-ukina, Bêlețir, his brother, Aplâ, the son of Arkatilâni, and such people of Borsippa as thou knowest, and seek out all the tablets which are in their houses, and all the tablets laid up in the Temple of Ezida (House of Righteousness, the temple of Nabû and Tašmetu(m)*), and collect the tablets of the [...] of the King, of the tablet for the days of the month Nisan (*March/April*), the stone [...] of the month Tisri (*September/October*), of the series Bit-Sala (Conjurations of the Lifting of the Hands), the stone [...for 'Reckoning the Day'* (a text on the calculation of the length of the month)*, the four stone [...] for the head of the royal bed and the royal [...] the woods urkarinnu and cedar for the head of the royal bed, the series 'Incantations:-May Ea and Marduk Complete Wisdom', all the series that are relating to war, besides all their copious documents that there are, the series 'In Battle a Staff (*a throwing stick?)*(?) Shall Not Come near a Man', the series EDIN-NA DIB-BI-DA E-GAL TUR-RA, spells, prayers, stone inscriptions and those that are excellent for (my) royalty, the series (?) Takpirti ali IGI-NIGIN-Na (although this is trouble) and whatever may be necessary in the palace, and seek out the rare tablets such as are to be found on your route, but do not exist in Assyria, and send them to me. I am sending the authority of the šatam* (temple and palace auditors) *and šaku* (high rank) *officials. Thou shalt put them in thy strong box. No one shall withhold tablets from thee; and if there be any tablet or spell which I have not made mention of to you, and thou shalt learn of (it), and it is good for my palace, search for it and get it and send it to me.* (Thompson, 2005/1908: xxxvii-xxxviii).

We could call it collecting. Another word would be confiscation. But Aššurbanipal, like other kings (Tulkutaninurta I comes to mind), had no qualms about acquiring the literature that interested him. When cities were plundered, he made a point of seizing their libraries. Other monarchs before him had done the same. It's one of those reasons why so many texts turn up in widely different places. Aššurbanipal had the tablets sorted according to topic, catalogued, restored, combined and copied for the royal library. On special topics, like magic and ritual, several collections were compiled by fusing a lot of related material from different places and periods. Saggs (1966:321) estimated that twenty- to thirty-thousand tablets of Aššurbanipal's library are extant, and that roughly 30 percent are devoted to omen literature. King Aššurbanipal was certainly a true believer. He thought that the great success of his ancestors and himself was due to the blessing of the gods, and that, though the Assyrian king was divine in principle, or did his best to represent divine order on earth, it was highly important to make sure that this remained so. Among the compilations are several books on magic. The most famous are *Maqlû* (*Burning*), a series of incantations ensuring that images of witches and sorcerers, and their evil influences, are destroyed by the fire gods; *Šurpu* (*Consuming*), another collection involving a fire offering, but used to free the patient from sins, misdeeds, pollution; *Uttuki Limnuti* (*Evil Spirits*), *Di'u* (so-called *Headaches*, though nowadays some experts propose malaria) and *Asakki marșuti* (*Disease-causing, troublesome Asakku*). Occasionally, the material overlaps: we find spells and descriptions of the utukku or of the Evil Seven that used to be attributed to other spirits, such as the gallû, in earlier periods. Mesopotamians intellectuals had a lot of trouble sorting out several thousand deities and spirits, and they never bothered to define the terrifying ones precisely. Another fascinating collection of magical spells was published by Schramm in 2008; he simply calls it the *Compendium*, as its original title is lost. This Sumerian/Akkadian handbook for exorcists provides sixteen spells for the preparation of a copper drum, for the use of substitute sacrifices (piglet, goat, figures of clay and reeds), purification rites using bread, dough, water, fruit and fire, and instructions for the making of a magical êru wand. Another famous collection is *Niškati* (*The Raising of the Hand)*, a collection of invocations and prayers to various deities plus material that ensures safety during eclipses.

And finally, we encounter the *Lamaštu Series*. Three tablets of the *Lamaštu Series* survive. It makes her text one of the shortest grimoires in the king's library. Apart from this we have many Lamaštu tablets, ritual instructions and talismans ranging from a few very short references dating from the late Sumerian period around the end of the third millennium BCE to all sorts of later compositions made by Akkadians, Babylonians and Assyrians. The bulk of the original material comes from the Old Babylonian period (c.2000-1500 BCE), while most surviving talismans are younger.

The Lamaštu material is not confined to Mesopotamian religion. At its greatest extension, under Aššurbanipal, the Neo-Assyrian Empire contained parts of Iran, Syria, south-east Turkey, Palestine, Cyprus and much of Egypt. Consequently, Lamaštu tablets and talismans have been found outside of Mesopotamia in Ugarit, Boghazköy, Carchemish, Zincirli; one even turned up in Italy (Burkert, 1992:82-86). Lamaštu was widely known and feared; her iconography inspired Greek artists, who based Medusa images on the symbolism, animals and posture of Lamaštu talismans, while the cult of Hecate seems to have incorporated Lamaštu's dogs. Here we are talking iconography: the myths of Medusa and Hecate are independent of the Lamaštu tale. Medusa/Lamaštu iconography also appears, much transformed, as the lion-man-deity, wrapped within a spiralling serpent, whose statue was frequently found in cult places of the Roman god Mithras. Typical Lamaštu functions reappear in the Greek Lamia, who is happy and alive to this day in Balkan folklore. They were also attributed to the medieval Lilith. It was an easy job, as the fusion of the Mesopotamian goddesses Ardat Lilî, Lilītu and Lamaštu was well under way when the *Lamaštu Series* was compiled. We will explore their merging towards the end of this book. Suffice it to say that Ardat Lilî and Lilītu were two distinct members of the group of terrifying wind deities, the Lilû. Ardat Lilî can be traced to the Sumerian period in the third millennium BCE, she is a lonely girl and a sex-starved, lethal seductress, while Lilītu, who first appears during the Old Babylonian period, was rarely mentioned, badly defined and occasionally blamed for causing nervous disorders and mental diseases. They acquired their function as child snatchers from Lamaštu. And there were lots of them: we meet entire swarms of male and female Liliths in the spells recorded in Nippur around the sixth century CE. Among the Turkish people of Central Asia and the Middle East we meet Lamaštu, or properly Lamašti, as the infant-slaying spirit Albasti, Albaşti, Almasti, Albasi, or simply Āl.

Other elements of the Lamaštu current turn up in old India, in Indo-China and in China. In India we encounter very similar terrifying goddesses: raging, wild, and often with animal attributes, who specialise in diseases and child snatching, but can be made protective honorary mothers of sick children. These are the grahīs (*seizers*), the mātṛikās (*mothers*) and, a little later, the Tantric yoginīs (*women, goddesses or witches who practice yoga*). Prominent Indian gods, like Skanda/Kārrtikeya and Kṛṣṇa, were first threatened and later guarded by such devastating deities. When approached with love, courage and dedication, these goddesses became the protective deities of their worshipper. Further east, the goddess Siṁhamukhā (*Lion-headed*) became a protective dakinī and a favourite of the North Indian, Nepalese, Tibetan, Mongolian and West-

Chinese Buddhists. Far from being a figure of evil, she was and is praised as a female Buddha, or as the mother of Buddha, a terrifying but benevolent goddess granting her worshippers bliss, liberation and enlightenment. The Hindus class her as a form of Kālī. Both are black, nude, wear snakes and skulls, are fond of flesh, blood, bones and sexual secretions and simply love to dance. In China, she is called Shi Mian Fo Mu (*Lion-Headed Buddha Mother*), an idea the historical Buddha, who despised women, would not have approved of. By becoming a female Buddha, or indeed the mother of Buddha, Lamaštu had made an amazing career move. In the oracle bone inscriptions of Shang period China, c.1200 BCE, a goddess or ancestress called Ximu (*Western Mother/ Woman*) received veneration. She was an ancestress of the much better documented, later, Xiwangmu (*Western-Queen-Mother*), a mountain-and-otherworld-goddess famous for her leopard tail and tigerish smile, who became the favourite deity of the early Daoists. She was occasionally depicted in grave chambers of the early Han period, as she guards the elixir of immortality. Like Medusa and Lamia, she appears as a Lady of the Beasts. Closely related are the Chinese goddesses Guimu (*Mother of Ghosts*) who has a tiger head, and the Buddhist goddess Hariri, who used to slay infants but became their protector after her enlightenment. Today, Chinese couples appeal to her to have a child. All of them testify to the fact that the descendants of the terrifying nude goddess with her animal head have a vital and positive spiritual function in our time.

The *Lamaštu Series* is a unique document. True, many sections are based on Old Babylonian spells and rituals. Nevertheless, the canonical *Lamaštu Series* was compiled during the Neo-Assyrian period. It was a period of **cruel warfare** and empire-making, when god-besotted kings believed that they should unite the entire world under the government of Aššur and Ištar. In the process, smaller kingdoms were sacked and brought under Assyrian rule. Entire population groups were deported to other places, turning the huge Assyrian empire into a multinational melting pot of cultures. It was also a period of fierce violence. Armies were larger than ever; soldiers were frequently armed with iron weapons and several Assyrian regents used savage shock tactics to discourage their enemies. One early example was provided by Salmanassar I, (1295-1234 BCE) who had 1400 captured soldiers blinded. Others followed similar policies. Aššurnasirpal II (883-859 BCE) was fond of flaying nobles, of crippling and disfiguring prisoners of war and of burning young men and women alive. Sennaḫerib (704-681 BCE) pursued an extremely aggressive policy which was not just aimed a conquest but at total destruction. The king had numerous cities burned to the ground, their fields and orchards devastated, and proudly left them as *forgotten mounds.* When Aššurbanipal (668-626 BCE) couldn't cope with the neighbouring Elamites of the Iranian mountains anymore, he destroyed their country, captured the aristocracy and deported many survivors. He boasted *I left the fields empty of the voice of mankind, the tread of cattle and sheep, the merry shout of harvest-home; and in them I made wild asses couch, and gazelles, and all kinds of wild beasts* (Saggs 1984:115). His wrath extended to the dead: *I pulled down and destroyed the tombs of their earlier and later kings, who had not revered the deities Aššur and Ištar my lords, (...) and I exposed them to the sun. I took away their bones to Assyria, I put restlessness on their ghosts, I deprived them of food-offerings and libations of water* (ditto, 1984:114, spelling amended). When Aššurbanipal sent his armies into the desert to crush the marauding Arabs, his scribes glorified the massacre: *Ištar of Arbela was clad in fire and wore a gleam of terror. A rain of fire descended on the Arabs. Erra the Mighty encouraged our resistance and slew my enemies. Ninurta, the 'throwing spear', the great hero, the son of Enlil cut short the lives of my enemies with his arrows (...) Those Arabs, who had fled before my weapons were destroyed by Erra the Mighty. Anguish appeared [among] them and to still [their] hunger they cut and ate their own children* (Haas, 1986:117, trans.

JF, Smith, 1871: 275, 286). Wars reveal mankind at its worst. I am sure that atrocities occurred when Sargon I created the Akkadian empire and when Ḫammurapi transformed his mediocre city-state into the Babylonian empire. However, the early regents did not celebrate cruelty. Think of king Šusîn (c.2038-2029 BCE), who insisted that enemy cities were not to be destroyed, prisoners not to be blinded and women not to be harmed, and who reprimanded a general for not following his orders. Many early regents did their best to turn conquered cities and states into vassals. Whenever they could, they showed mercy and restraint. They did not gloat over the slain nor did they permit their scribes to praise them for cruelty.

Shock tactics were a common element of Neo-Assyrian warfare. Thanks to terrifying atrocities, the Neo-Assyrian rulers forced cities and states into submission. They are typical of the mindset of the first millennium BCE and show a world-weary contempt for human life that was not evident before. A similar savagery affected Neo-Assyrian city life. The first millennium BCE was a brutal time. As far as legal texts survive, Assyrian laws were harsher than those formulated by the Sumerians and the Babylonians that followed them. Literature began to show a hardened cynicism; great works of art celebrated the destruction and torture of enemies. Ammianus Marcellinus, who accompanied Emperor Julian in Mesopotamia, remarked that the locals *never paint or in any way represent anything except different kinds of slaughter and war.* (24,6 trans. Yonge, 1902:366).

Simultaneously, women lost a lot of rights. When we explore the **status of women** in Mesopotamia, we face numerous difficulties. The documentation is very uneven and many periods and places remain unknown. In Sumer, their social position was fairly high: men who divorced their wives had to pay large amounts of compensation to them, and there were plenty of priestesses who had wealth, owned property and did business. The same goes for the wives of several kings, who held administrative positions or invested large sums. In Sumerian literature, sons are instructed to obey and respect their mothers and their elder sisters. Sumerian goddesses were highly popular and, if we can trust the myths, did pretty much as they liked. However, the record is largely confined to aristocratic ladies living in cities. The Akkadian period was too short to leave enough evidence for generalisation. It did produce Enḫeduanna, and her great contributions to Sumerian literature and politics, and gives us a brief glimpse of high-ranking, wealthy and influential en priestesses living in gipar-cloisters. Ur III, was, of course, not a simple extension of Sumerian culture, but its last attempt to remain alive. Among the thousands of inscriptions, women are remarkably rare. Most of them were members of the court or slaves. Several female professions are on the record: scribes, barbers, hairdressers, weavers, millers and brewers. These, however, were part of the temple and palace personnel. If you think that these female professions did not amount to much, just consider that in all known early cultures, women had fewer rights, provided they had rights at all. Ur III bureaucratic records do not reveal much about the lives of normal people. In the Old Babylonian period, the documentation of private life improves remarkably. Plenty of women ran business enterprises, bought, rented, sold, invested, granted loans and acted without the participation or consent of their husbands. They could testify as witnesses, swear oaths, adopt children and sue other people, including their husbands. There is evidence for a few women who were doctors, scribes and judges. However, the husbands had many ways of exerting control over their wives, including the option to sell them, and the other family members, as slaves. Peasants who could not repay their debts were frequently forced to do so. The businesswoman of Babylon was only free when she when she was single or a widow, or lived in a relationship or marriage that granted her man no power over her.

In the Neo-Babylonian period, female rights seem to have reached a higher level than before. There were more businesswomen, and with regard to legal status, financial rights and obligations, women were almost as free as men.

Now for a look at Assyria. In the early Assyrian trade colonies, women had remarkable rights. They could set up a marriage contract specifying rights and obligations, including a clause that her husband would not take a second wife. Divorce was possible for both parties, and in either case, the divorced person received financial compensation. If the man didn't pay up for his divorced wife, she kept the sons until he did. Under Middle Assyrian rule, the lives of women became increasingly restrictive. Women had to pay up for the debts of their husbands, suffered for the pollutions and sins of their men, and when the husband died, the widow had no access to his property. If she took anything she was treated as a thief. Husbands could divorce their wives without paying anything; indeed, some husbands sold their wives. However, the records for the Middle Assyrian period are rare, and there are, as before and afterwards, indications that some women retained power, money and did business as they liked. Under Neo-Assyrian rule, life became harsher. Again, we are limited by the lack of records. Women did business, owned property, could testify as witnesses and were protected by law. However, many of them happened to be high-ranking aristocrats, and there is no evidence what life was like for the lower classes. Under Neo-Assyrian rule, wives were very much under the control of their husbands, or of their fathers and mothers, if a husband was lacking (Ebeling, RlA '*Frau*'). Their life, though less easy than before, was not as bad as in many other countries of the ancient world. Women in China, India, Egypt and ancient Greece were living under worse conditions. However, respectable Neo-Assyrian women were forced to walk veiled, and they became increasingly confined to an indoor life. The Assyrians introduced more laws against rape, but the very fact that they were needed, indicates that life was less easygoing than before. I am sure that many war-hardened veterans lost their emotional sensibility, and that the numerous deported population groups, with their highly varied customs and laws, introduced new conflicts. The evidence is clearer when we look for priestesses. By the first millennium BCE, several old religious ranks, which had been venerated a millennium earlier, were long forgotten. True, some priestesses remained in office and several, mostly from aristocratic families, held a high rank. But it was by no means as exalted as it had been in Sumer, Akkad and during the Old Babylonian period. In several Neo-Assyrian dictionaries, a range of formerly respectable priestesses were now glossed, like other independent women, as whores. Among modern scholars, it created the mistaken impression that Mesopotamia and its temples were full of 'sacred prostitutes'. When not employed by a temple, some priestesses made a living as midwives, nurses, or by selling spells, talismans and evil sorcery.

Simultaneously, the range of local **goddesses** was officially narrowed down and unified in the singular figure of Ištar. Ištar is an impressive figure, a goddess of love, lust and warfare. The kings did a lot to be friends with her, as where Ištar went, the armies were successful. Other goddesses were remembered on occasion, in particular those associated with birth and the legitimization of kings, but Ištar had the centre of the stage. Of course, the other goddesses were not entirely forgotten. They were remembered in the temples and cities dedicated to their cult; they were respected as the wives of the great gods, and of course the literati, the scholars and priests remembered their earlier fame. Sumerian and Old Babylonian hymns were still admired, copied and read by well-educated people. The scholars still retained their fondness for Nidaba/Nisaba, the goddess of the reed stylus, but even her influence was waning, as the new scribal god Nabû was becoming increasingly popular. In first-millennium BCE folk worship, however, Ištar was overwhelmingly popular: a composite deity with many contradictory character traits and a huge range of divine functions. Given that the literati classed many independent and important goddesses as 'aspects' of Ištar, she was speedily transforming into the major expression of feminine divinity.

Except for Lamaštu. In a period when most goddesses had become pale mirages of their former selves, Lamaštu remained a deity to be reckoned with. She seems to have accumulated all characteristics of female divinity that were thoroughly unpopular. While other goddesses were dutiful spouses of their divine husbands, Lamaštu remained unmarried and pretty much alone. Where other divine couples had children and led happy family lives, Lamaštu lived in isolation, in the wilderness, and adopted stray animals like dogs and pigs. A solitary woman, cast out by her family, was a distinctly unpopular idea in a period when independent women were automatically accused of transgressions. While the divine establishment resided in High Heaven, the Underworld, wealthy temple complexes and the palace, Lamaštu went where she liked, when she liked, and made her home in the foreign mountains, deserts and swamps, in small alleys and byways, in corners, doorways, in animals and people. She, unlike so many other deities, had a character and a purpose in life. While Ištar sided with successful conquerors and rich temple organisations, Lamaštu was identified with a bunch of terrifying and destructive wind deities. We meet her as one of the best-defined characters in Mesopotamian religion. Whether you like her or not: this goddess is vibrantly alive. The *Lamaštu Series* is full of fascinating material. Her canonical text is a tour de force leading the patient, the conjurer and the reader through a colourful panoramic vision of several thousand years of Mesopotamian culture. For good reason Adam Falkenstein praised Uruk tablet VAT 14506, filling a large gap in the *Lamaštu Series*, as *among the best that the Akkadian conjuration literature has produced.* (1931/1979:2, trans. JF). All of this happened in spite of the fact that Lamaštu had no temples, no shrines, no priesthood, and had to make do with the attention she got from conjurers, witches and sorcerers, and the offerings provided by patients, doctors and exorcists to make her go away in peace.

This Compilation: Sources, Scholars and the Problem of Evil

In 1902, David Myhrman gained his PhD by reconstructing the *Lamaštu Series* from the library of Aššurbanipal. He correctly identified several fragmentary tablets of the British Museum as a single composition, arranged them, as far as possible, and translated the work. His groundbreaking reconstruction was the basis for the following translation. Of course, a lot had to be updated. To begin with, the transcription had changed. The Sumerian name of the goddess, then read as RAB-KAN-ME, is now read DIM.ME. As the capital letters indicate, the pronunciation of the word DIM.ME is uncertain. In his entry on Lamaštu in the *Reallexikon der Assyriologie* (RlA, 1983) Walter Farber proposed that the Sumerograms DIM.ME could have been pronounced as Gabašku, or something similar. His suggestion was not universally accepted. Much later, Farber (2014:208) simply noted that her name was probably pronounced /dimme/. It is a distinct possibility. However, as the pronunciation is not certain, I will leave the spelling in capital letters. Other readings of her Sumerian name are LUGAMME and LUGALME. The Akkadian name read 'Labartu' in Myhrman's days has become Lamaštu or Lamašti. Or it could be Lawaštu or Lawašti: during and after the Middle Babylonian period, the letter 'm' between two vowels was probably pronounced as a 'w'. The readings Lamaštu and Lamašti proved to be a major breakthrough, as they related the goddess to the dreaded Lamia of Greek myth and Balkan folklore. She is a child slayer, a serpent goddess and a custodian of the elixir of immortality; you will meet her later on. Many ideas fashionable in Myhrman's days had to be updated. Scholars today are a lot better informed than they were at the start of the twentieth century. And of course, Myhrman got a few things wrong. It's understandable: in his time, the Ancient Orient was just being discovered. Myhrman was a pioneer, and pioneers have to get things wrong when they want to get anything done at all. After I had translated his German version into

English, I began to collect translated passages from various sources. As it turned out, spells and passages of the *Lamaštu Series* have been quoted by a wide range of experts, so that alternative translations were abundant. But there were also more substantial studies. Frans Wiggermann published a fascinating essay on Lamaštu in Martin Stol's *Birth in Babylonia and the Bible* (2000: 217-252). Another excellent source was Walter Farber's contributions to the topic, especially his entry in the *Reallexikon der Assyriologie* and his translation of Mesopotamian baby-soothing spells and rituals *Schlaf, Kindchen, Schlaf* (1989). I found some of the basic Lamaštu rituals in five distinct translations! In 1931 Adam Falkenstein transcribed and translated an important new section of the *Lamaštu Series* which had been discovered in Uruk. Another Lamaštu fragment was discovered by R. Thompson. Finally, I came upon Franz Köcher's thesis. In 1949, Köcher gained his PhD in war-ravaged Berlin by translating the *Lamaštu Series* plus related tablets. Köcher's translation updated Myhrman's text. One of the advantages of his work was the addition of many new passages. These texts, most of them in small fragments, had rested in the British Museum; it was F.W. Geers who identified them as sections of the *Lamaštu Series*. Köcher made his own transcription, re-arranged the material, and pointed out that the placement of some lines was speculative.

The *Lamaštu Series* is not only difficult; at first glance it seems to be badly organised. Several rituals and passages are repeated. When I started exploring the text in Myhrman's version, I wondered whether Aššurbanipals's scribes did a sloppy editing job. Why would two important rituals from the beginning appear, albeit with slight changes, at the end of the text? Did the scribes dump a minor variation at the end? And why did so many key phrases and metaphors appear two or even three times?

Nowadays, the canonical edition of the *Lamaštu series* is almost complete. It turned out that there were more repetitions than Myhrman was aware of. Our text is not a jumble of badly organised odds and ends but an elaborate ceremony incorporating items of various periods. The conjurers and scribes who assembled the material took great care to make it a grand affair. The *Lamaštu Series* is a schedule for a beautiful, elaborate and expensive ceremony. To perform the full ritual, five days were needed. Hence, it is not surprising when rituals from day one are repeated at the end to round off the ceremony.

I started with Myhrman's numeration and changed to Köcher's. Things did not stop at this point. Köcher's translation was incomplete and suffered from various defects. In the meantime, more material came up, which was meant to be published by Walter Farber. He announced his intention to publish the entire corpus of Lamaštu materials in the early 1990's. It did not happen. However, he did publish on specific matters regarding Lamaštu, and his quotations of the canonical text were highly inspiring. Luckily, there were other pieces of Lamaštu lore around. Volkert Haas quoted Köcher at length and updated him on occasion. Foster translated several Old Babylonian spells against Lamaštu, which were evidently among the sources for the *Series* compiled for Aššurbanipal. He also published translations from the *Lamaštu Series*; sadly, he based them on Myhrman's transcription, which was not always accurate. In the meantime, more material appeared. Excellent translations of Lamaštu spells by Wasserman and Wende can be found on the remarkable SEAL (*Sources of Early Akkadian Literature*) web-page. As a final effort, I went through the really questionable passages in their transcription by Myhrman, Falkenstein and Köcher, spending many happy hours with the *Concise Dictionary of Akkadian* by Black, George and Postgate, Riemschneider's *Lehrbuch des Akkadischen*, Worthington's *Complete Babylonian*, Cohen's *An English to Akkadian Companion to the Assyrian Dictionaries* and the monumental and awe-inspiring *Reallexikon der Assyriologie (RlA)*. It turned my brain into a sun-dried brick. Admittedly, my Akkadian is not worth mentioning, and the present book is definitely not the final word on the topic. In all humility, I hope that it has some value as a simple introduction to Mesopotamian magic and the mysteries of Lamaštu, and would like to express my thanks to all the brilliant researchers, scholars and excavators who made it possible.

By the beginning of 2014 I had completed most of the manuscript of this book. I had written more than 500 pages in A4, 11 point, and was beginning to worry about cuts. They turned out to be essential, and I eliminated more than a hundred pages. A lot of open questions remained. Luckily, new material kept appearing. Early in 2014 an essay called *Medicine and Healing Magic* by Joan Scurlock appeared in *Women in the Ancient Near East*, ed. Chavalas. It contained several passages of the *Lamaštu Series*, blending controversial interpretations with highly original ideas by Nougayrol (1969).

In December 2014 I was in for a surprise. Walter Farber's long-announced translation of the *Lamaštu Series* had finally appeared. It had been in preparation for more than forty years, and many people, including myself, had been wondering if it would happen at all. I ordered my copy and was utterly delighted. The massive volume is one of the most brilliant works of scholarship I have ever come upon. Farber compiled missing pieces, compared alternative versions and provided solutions for passages that Köcher and others had struggled with. For the sake of general compatibility, I changed from Köcher's numeration of the lines to Farber's. The same goes for the indication of damaged and missing lines. As a final update, I included some of Farber's suggestions, and am very grateful for the many insights they provided. Nevertheless, I was not always happy with his interpretations. Let me explain: every translation is a creative reconstruction. When you chose one word you omit several others that indicate different options. Choices offer possibilities but they also imply limitations. Much depends on how you feel, and react subconsciously, to a subject.

I do not speak Sumerian or Akkadian and my version comes with numerous alternative interpretations. Honestly, I am just as biased as everybody else. However, my assumptions are often slightly different. I would not dream of saying that they are true or better: please keep an open mind and allow for many possibilities. Some may argue that I have not gone far enough. However, I am not competent to write a philological study. Every translator has done her or his best. I do not believe that I can argue about the fine details of the transcription and translation of what is, after all, a collection of old, damaged and badly legible clay shards. Nor do I want to quarrel about ancient words, many of which are still badly understood. While Lamaštu is very real, her spells are enigmatic. We shouldn't complain if uncertain points remain. It's an amazing achievement of the finest scholarship that we can understand so much at all. Each translation has its strong and weak points. In prehistoric studies, much depends on probability, personal interpretation and scholarly consensus. This goes for relatively simple, often standardised texts, like omen literature, law texts, contracts and letters, and more so for magical literature. The *Lamaštu Series* is anything but easy reading. In some passages, the grammar is so odd and the words are so unusual, that we can do with a triple helping of question marks. We cannot be sure that the text, as far as we have it, is free of errors. Many passages only exist in a single version. When new copies of the *Lamaštu Series* appear, we might discover that the ones we know contain scribal errors. Or we may come to understand metaphors in an entirely new way. This is called learning: we keep our minds wide open. At the time of writing, however, Farber's translation is the state of the art. It does not mean that his colleagues are completely in agreement. Why should they? Good science needs arguments, disagreement and varied points of view. But it is certainly a foundation that will make future research easier.

My version of the *Lamaštu Series* has similarities with his translation, and that of Myhrman and Köcher. It is not, of course, identical. Unlike so many dedicated linguists, I have met Lamaštu in many daily meditations. My understanding is subjective, and may be wrong. So may be yours, or theirs. Getting things wrong is an excellent spiritual discipline: unless we dare to make errors, we will never learn anything at all. Alternative readings will keep the Assyriologists debating for the next decades. To understand something, as John Grinder stated, you need to understand its structure, function and context. The underlying structure of this book is the career of Lamaštu and her relations, and its functions are magick, wisdom, an unusual encounter with the divine and a better understanding of consciousness, magick and ecology. The context is basically Mesopotamian, though in the later chapters I have summarized a few things about Jewish culture, Arabia, Greece, the Balkans, India, Central Asia, China and Tibet. I have tried to produce a relatively reliable and readable text with plenty of extras. They may serve, I hope, as a basic and easy-to-comprehend introduction to the magick of the earliest known high culture of mankind, and a goddess who appears, from the Stone-Ages to the present day, all the way across Eurasia.

Thank you for coming. Take your seat and buckle up: we are in for a lot of ups and downs. The *Lamaštu Series* is a mind-boggling, exhilarating journey through Mesopotamian magic and religion. Our travel guide is a goddess noted for disrespect, rebellion and wild behaviour. She likes to walk around nude. She can wear terrifying, bestial faces. Or she can take off her masks and reveal the beauty of her inner self. She scares evil spirits away. Her arms are smeared with blood. That's right. It's our blood, our feelings and our commitment that give relevance to our lives. Her feet may appear as talons. I am sure you would notice. Or they are human feet, connecting her with the earth, reminding us of our place on earth. She is a child of Heaven, but she fulfils her tasks on earth. Lamaštu lurks in narrow alleys, in doorways, mountain forests, swamps, the open ocean and in your own body. Trust her. This is a journey through history. It will tell you about mankind, civilisation, religions and their shortcomings. You will see a goddess evolving from a terrifying spook to the mother of enlightenment. I hope you will learn about ecology, and your place in life, in evolution, in the wilderness and in the city, and in the manifestation of the divine. You are welcome. All of us are. The journey begins now.

In the *Lamaštu Series*, we do not have a single work. The original item, however it may have looked, was assembled for the library of Aššurbanipal. However, for all our research, we do not have the same text as the Assyrian scribes. The Uruk tablet translated by Falkenstein shows that there must have been several versions of the canonical text: it consists of genuine material, arranged in a different order. Farber discussed several tablets that seem to have belonged to the canonical text but include different words or lines. Some of them are probably misspellings or scribal errors; others may point at different traditions. The scribes of Aššurbanipal wrote their version in excellent calligraphy, numbered their tablets and carefully recorded the first line of the next tablet at the bottom of the previous one. Scribes in other cities were not as careful; witness the confused order of several versions of the *Šurpu Series.*

Several rituals are repeated, but these **repetitions** are not always identical. Usually, the difference is simply a word or two, or a different placement of lines. We could understand it as a poetic device.

Sumerian poets used no rhymes, but enjoyed repetition. The same was done by some Akkadian, Babylonian and Assyrian poets. Repetition may seem dull to a modern reader, but when you imagine a hymn being sung by two choruses, the repetition slows the hymn, no matter how dramatic its content, and adds sonority to the piece. Here, our poets used a little trick. Instead of simply repeating a line, they introduced a tiny change in the second repetition. Usually, this change made the line a little more specific, and increased the feeling. Here is an example from a Sumerian hymn to Inanna (SAHG 1953:73, trans. JF)

Lady, born by Ningal, cheering with joy,

Like a dragon, destructive (power) has been granted to you.

Inanna, born by Ningal, cheering with joy,

Like a dragon, destructive (power) has been granted to you.

The first line provides the data, the second line, introducing the name of the goddess, makes it more personal and touching. In a similar way, the repetitive passages of the *Lamaštu Series* can be understood as a poetic device.

But you could also think of the *Lamaštu Series* as an elaborate piece of music. It contains specific melodic elements, leitmotivs and catchy tunes, which are varied and reintroduced from time to time. They add to the beauty of the composition. As in classical Indian music, a topic may be briefly hinted at or elaborated at length.

But we could also think of the repetitions as a hypnotic strategy. A healing ritual is essentially a hypnotic trance induction using words, actions, objects, gestures and so on. It is meant to produce a specific state of mind in the ritualist, the patient, participants and observers. A fascinating hypnotic method developed by Richard Bandler is the art of using 'nested loops'. In modern hypnosis, plenty of information is packaged as storytelling. You spread your suggestions in a whole cluster of stories, anecdotes, jokes and remarks. As you start the induction, you begin by telling item a, but before you can finish it you shift to item b, then item c and item d. In between you plant practical suggestions on how to change for the better. Usually, these suggestions will be forgotten by the conscious mind as soon as the loops are closed. As you end the trance you bring it all together by ending item d, then item c, then item b and finally item a. It's a fascinating process. When Bandler teaches, he often designs a mind-blowing tangle of loops over several days. On the last day he brings them all together. The result is very powerful. The Deep Mind is very good at detecting patterns. While the conscious mind is easily distracted, the Deep Mind looks out for the missing bits. Stories need to have an ending. Your Deep Mind will keep the open ends in mind. It will pick up the relevant elements and fuse them into something worthwhile (Bandler, 2008:175-177, but there is also a video on the topic). And while the stories may or may not be remembered by the audience, the gritty stuff between them works. When you read the *Lamaštu Series*, look out for nested loops.

The fragments that constitute the *Lamaštu Series* come from different places and times. Most of them were unearthed in Nineveh, where Aššurbanipal had his capital. Other pieces were unearthed at Uruk, Ur, Babylon, Sippar, Sultanepe, Aššur and Nippur. Several fragments and talismans cannot be assigned to any specific location. The text is mainly Akkadian and old, middle and young Babylonian, though some passages are in Sumerian. Comparison with various tablets and talismans show that the nature, appearance and functions of the goddess were well established in the Old Babylonian period. On the other hand, a few sections of the *Lamaštu Series* may have been composed under Neo-Assyrian rule in the early first millennium BCE. As we have it, there are thirteen conjurations, more or less complete, in the *Lamaštu Series,* plus the ritual instructions that go with them. In the last section, we encounter the grand scheme behind the ritual: a catalogue telling the conjurer which incantations are to be pronounced over various parts of the body of the patient. It turns all the preceding conjurations and spells into a single grand ceremony. A similar strategy was used by the scribes who compiled the *Maqlû* and the *Šurpu Series* out of old and new material. As with the *Lamaštu Series*, they assembled a lot of elder material, changed and updated some items, added new passages and fused them in a grand ceremony that required between one and several days. It's just our bad luck that the *Lamaštu Series* is incomplete: the third tablet is short as parts of the end are missing.

All the translations I have seen are interestingly biassed in some ways. Myhrman wrote at a time when the study of Mesopotamian literature was still in its infancy, and his reading was occasionally influenced by biblical literature and the writings of classical authors like Herodotus. This is hardly surprising; many early Assyriologists started their careers researching West Semitic literature, and took things for granted that simply didn't apply to the East Semites. Thompson produced groundbreaking studies of what he considered the *Devils and Evil Spirits* of Mesopotamia. He had a formidable imagination, wrote novels under the pseudonym John Guisborough and occasionally invented what he found missing. One remarkable example is his habit to translate the names Lamaštu as 'the Hag spirit' and Labaṣu as 'the Ghoul Spirit'. It was a charming thought, but as he admitted in a footnote, only a guess. To this day, the meaning of these names happens to be completely unknown. It produced wonderfully sinister translations that could do with an urgent update. But he was by no means the only scholar to follow this trend. Many translators identified Lamaštu as a 'she-devil', a 'fiend', 'monster' or 'demoness'. Sorry to say so, but the terminology is misleading. 'Devils' and 'demons' are loaded with Christian associations that simply do not apply to Mesopotamian thought. Lamaštu, as the scribes made abundantly clear, is a goddess, and, whether one likes her or not, a primary deity, daughter of the god and goddess of the sky. For a goddess, that's as prominent and classy as it can get. It raises her to a level above the gods of later generations, such as Utu/Šamaš, Inanna/Ištar, Aššur, Marduk, Nebû etc. To call her a demoness or she-devil is to project Christian values on a culture that simply did not think that way. Though she was definitely not everybody's darling, it was acknowledged that she fulfilled a sad and troublesome task decreed by the highest gods, or by necessity, if you like. Like all deities, she embodies principles and ideals. She wasn't popular, but she is certainly necessary. Nor was she the only violent character in the pantheon. Just think of mighty Enlil, who kept destroying major cities and once tried to exterminate mankind with a flood just in order to reduce the noise and bustle! Or read Enḫeduanna's hymns to Inanna/Ištar, praising the goddess for wholesale slaughter and destruction on a magnitude that has not been equalled until the Bengali poets of the 18th century began to compose 'battlefield' poems for Kālī. Great figures of divine authority, like Marduk, Amaušumgalanna, Ningirsu, Ninurta, Aššur and Adad were celebrated for crushing enemy states and grinding *the rebellious land* into dust. Compared to such deities, well-accepted, politically correct and worshipped in all the big temples, Lamaštu appears almost harmless. Nevertheless, she ends up being called a she-devil or a demoness. It says more about the translators than about the gods. Is there something threatening about a rebellious, nude, unmarried woman wearing the mask of a savage animal?

Franz Köcher did much to update the *Lamaštu Series* and to relate it to his own favourite topic, the study of Mesopotamian medicine. He had many brilliant ideas and was able to eliminate major errors of Myhrman's translation. However, like so many scholars, he was exceedingly biassed against Lamaštu. Obviously he did not know about Lamaštu's counterparts in Indian and Chinese religion, nor was he aware that terrifying and destructive goddesses can teach their worshippers to transcend fear. Sometimes, what appears to be horrible has a valid and divine function in the world. Lamaštu is an exalted goddess, a victorious lady, a ruler of mankind, and performs the tasks given to her by the assembly of the gods. Most of her errands may seem savage, but the Mesopotamians were aware that they had to be done. When I looked up original words, I soon noticed that, whenever possible, Köcher assumed the worst. Seen from a historical perspective, his point of view is understandable. When he published his PhD thesis on Lamaštu in 1949, much of Berlin was still in ruins, the cold war was beginning, and the prospect of a third world war seemed to loom unavoidably over the horizon. Köcher identified Lamaštu with all the horrors he could imagine. Let me translate a few of his remarks. He asserted that Lamaštu *feasts herself with sensual lust on the suffering of the patient, who tosses, tortured by fever, on his bed.* Almost exactly the same phrase was used by Haas (1986: 142), who accepted Köcher's negative outlook without hesitation. It's simply not true. Lamaštu may be destructive but she is not a sadist. Köcher called her *the power of destruction, the will towards dissolution, disintegration and disorganisation;* a description that might suit the old Vedic goddess Nirṛti, whose name means 'Negation of Cosmic Order', or simply Perdition, Doom and Disorder (Fries 2010:463-465). Nevertheless, in old India, this black goddess, who is only briefly mentioned in hymns, and generally asked to stay far away, had a part in the divine play. In Vedic ritual, black earth represented her, black grains were offered to her, and the childless women of the king were her impersonation. She wasn't liked but she was certainly acknowledged. As I proposed in *Kālī Kaula*, Nirṛti may have been an ancestress of the goddess Kālī, who does much to scare her worshippers out of their heads and out of the highly limited identification of the personality with the self. Kālī and Lamaštu have a lot in common; just consider the infant corpses which Kālī wears as her ear pendants. Both of them seem terrifying, destructive and evil to the uninitiated. Though many contemporary Hindus and especially conservative followers of Viṣṇu dislike her, Kālī is a well-established goddess with plenty of followers in India and abroad. Lamaštu, lacking such a powerful lobby, will remain misunderstood for a long while. Apparently Köcher was unaware of the many terrifying deities who appear in Hinduism, Tantra and in early Chinese cults. He did not know that gods like Śiva, Bhairava, Bhairavī, Kālī, Durgā, Manasā, the Nāga folk, Xiwangmu, Guimu and so many others may seem destructive to outsiders, but have a benevolent, caring, loving and even liberating function for their worshippers. Kālī's name can be translated as *blackness* and as *time*, and it is time that destroys everything. This is not a bad thing at all: in each ecosystem, the decomposers (woodlice, springtails, worms, nematodes, algae, fungi, bacteria etc.) are essential to break down dead matter and make it available for those life-forms that produce and maintain. Without their unceasing effort, life would not be possible.

Lamaštu destroys, but destruction is not as bad as many people think. If you want to understand Lamaštu, you have to understand ecology. In every biotope, the decomposers are in the majority. They break down dead matter and make it available for plants, which generate fresh energy and nourishment out of it. Without the myriad of tiny creatures that destroy, devour and transform dead matter, life would have ended long ago. Death and dissolution have their place in the world, and are just as important as birth, generation, maintenance and transformation.

And look at the carnivores! They put an end to the suffering of the sickly young, wounded, diseased and elderly. Without a healthy amount of predators, biotopes are doomed. Sadly, this insight is neither widely known nor popular. Let's have an example. In Central Europe, the large predators, like cave lion, cave hyena, wolverine, bear and wolf were exterminated. Only a few isolated lynxes subsist in modern forests, and these have been released into the wild and require protection. The same goes for a few lonely bears in the Alps and a few wolves in Italy and north-eastern Germany. For good, bad, or worse, hunters took over the functions of the predators. One of their tasks consists in keeping the deer population under control. I do not intend to discuss the question whether hunters are saintly, idealistic custodians of nature or complex-ridden, murderous egomaniacs, as I have met both types. Let us simply examine the situation when no predators or hunters reduce the deer population. For a start, we can say goodbye to the ground-breeding birds. Red deer and many other 'herbivores' need to eat eggs and small animals from time to time, to gain high-value animal proteins, fat, cartilage and calcium. While the population of roe, red and fallow deer rises, the ground-breeding birds disappear. Deer, just like people, breed without the least restraint or common sense. They go for the young vegetation, for fresh shoots and especially for young trees. First of all, they eliminate young beeches, firs, elms, ashes, rowans, sycamores, yews and oaks. Next, they go for trees that are less tasty. The forest loses its biodiversity, as many plant varieties become extinct. As so many young trees are destroyed, the forest ages fast. Deer often suffer from malnutrition in winter and spring, so they like to strip the bark of trees. Among them are fir, willow, spruce, beech, sycamore and ash. Their hunger damages the cambium, the tasty and vulnerable tissue that transports juices, sugars and water, and grows wood cells inwards and bark cells outwards. The trees are badly damaged and have to fight invasion by fungi, microbes, insects and parasites. It does not take long and many old trees are dying. Winter storms hurl them to the ground and the forest canopy acquires holes. It loses the ability to control temperature and moisture. For the remaining trees, summers will be drier and winters colder. Within a few decades there will be more deer than ever and sightseers can enjoy meeting Bambi more often than before. Sadly, Bambi isn't healthy or happy. It suffers from malnutrition, but nevertheless, it will continue to breed. While the deer population grows, the forest dies. It has happened in the coastal forests near Boston, which are monotonous sand dunes today. Hundreds of animal and plant species died. It happened in Alpine Germany during the 1970's. Politicians went hunting with their business friends. To ensure that plenty of animals were available, the deer population was kept far above a healthy level. Well, the deer damaged the forest and in spring, avalanches tore through the mutilated trees. Today, wide regions remain as barren, stony soil. The same thing happened on Pacific islands where stupid sailors introduced goats and rabbits. The story always ends in misery: a damaged ecosystem that barely supports a handful of species. Anyone who wants a healthy European forest has to permit hunting and reintroduce wolves. I'm happy to say that wolves are returning to Central Europe. However, they remain in remote low population areas. You couldn't expect them to enjoy huge metropolitan settlements, motorways and vast landscapes of agricultural monoculture. Predators are necessary to keep environments stable. No matter whether we consider deer, goats, antelopes, cattle, giraffes or elephants, the story remains the same. All of them are capable of destroying their environment unless their population density is kept within healthy limits.

Or let us take a look at India. Hundreds or thousands of people die annually thanks to cobra bites. Consequently, cobras were hunted and many of them ended up as handbags, belts and shoes. Wide ranges of land, lacking their cobra population, were harassed by rats and mice. The rodents destroyed enormous amounts of grains and soiled them with their excrements. In several districts, they spread plagues. The Indian government showed excellent sense when they placed the cobras under protection.

Ecology is not always nice. Plenty of good, idealistic people would prefer to live in a world where humans and animals co-exist in happy harmony, where death, slaughter, exploitation and man-made death do not exist. I have great respect for such sentiments. But ideals can be misleading. We all feed on each other. In nature, there are no food chains nor is the world arranged like a hierarchical pyramid, topped by humans in their overbearing arrogance. There are no 'higher' or 'lower' lifeforms. Evolution is not a deity or a predetermined fate but a process that does not favour any being. It has no aims, no goals, no preferences or favourites. Complexity is not better or worse than simplicity. Rational thought is badly overestimated. Anyone who assumes that a human being is more 'valuable' than another animal or a plant is projecting a system of anthropocentric values that is ridiculously inappropriate. Lamaštu reminds us of reality. Like all lifeforms we have a will to survive. Like all lifeforms we take life to remain alive. And like all beings we will feed others when we are dead. It's a blessing. Dissolution has its place in this world, and it is just as good as birth, maturing and ageing. Destructive deities are not necessarily angry, evil or bad; they simply do a job that is part of the constant coming, going and returning on this beautiful planet. Some consider Kālī a goddess of death, but to her devotees, there is no such thing as death; there is only liberation and transcendence, and the realisation that consciousness may appear in form and emptiness, and in whatever way we chose to be. The apparent destructivity of the goddess is a metaphor: she represents the re-absorption of the world and the 'I-concept', releasing us from the bondage of partial awareness and the prison of a single, limited personality. Once beyond Kālī's mind-shattering dance, there is neither birth nor death and self extends everywhere. What starts out as fear and dread transforms into sheer bliss. Such insights are essential to Tantra. They are not theology but practical experience. That the early translators of the *Lamaštu Series* were not aware of them is understandable: their intellectual environment was steeped in Christian thought, and good translations of Tantric texts were difficult to find. This much being said, we can only sympathise with Franz Köcher, who wrote:

Lamaštu cannot be considered or understood as a specialised fever-demoness, nor as a blood-sucking vampire, nor as an arch-enemy of women and children. In her the Principle of Evil itself is manifest. (1949: 4, trans. JF).

Let's think about this. Mighty Enlil can try to destroy mankind but is acknowledged as a great and popular god, but when Lamaštu slays a few sickly babies and elders she is Evil itself. 'Evil as such' is a big hit when it comes to selling movies, myths and global politics. I guess the concept was invented by people trying to legitimise homicide and exploitation. The intellectual foundation for good versus evil scenarios, so common in books, movies and propaganda in western society, goes back to the teachings of Zarathustra. It was taken up by Judaism and its offspring, Christianity, plus a number of central Asian religions, such as Bön, and proved to be enormously successful. When a person, group, religion or state is 'evil', we can stop thinking. Evil is evil; it can't be changed, so let's unpack the missiles and start extermination. We don't need to consider why something seems evil to us, or why a given person acts in a manner we don't like. A 'principle of evil' is just the thing when you want a really simple ethical mindset. It never appears in Mesopotamian theology, where deities and spirits are simply beyond good and evil. To be sure, the scribes used the term 'evil'. Our texts contain references to the good and the evil utukku-spirit, to the good and evil rabiṣu (agent), to the good and evil god, the good and evil ghost. An evil god was generally one that made trouble for you. It could be the personal deity of a rival, or the deity of a hostile city or state. That deity, however, was not evil by nature. It was just evil to you. And that's as far as evil went: the word was used in a personal way. It was not taken as a cosmic force or as an absolute quality. The evil city god of today could become friendly should your cities form an alliance. The evil personal god of a competitor could become friendly if you formed a business association. Deities were not simply evil, no matter how terrible their deeds. Nor were they simply good. States had their protective deities and so had districts, cities, families, professions and people. Your own city god or even your personal deities could not be trusted to be kind to you. If you wanted the support of a deity, you had to do a lot to gain its favour. Gods do strange things and people had better get used to it. If anything, the Mesopotamian priests proclaimed that people are not competent to judge the intentions, deeds and morals of deities. One mašmaššu (conjurer, enchanter, exorcist, invocation priest) composed these remarkable lines:

The strategy of a god is [as remote as] innermost heaven,

The command of a goddess cannot be dr[awn out] [...]

Divine purpose is as remote as innermost heaven,

It is too difficult to understand; people cannot understand it.

(*Babylonian Theodicy*, Foster, 1995:319 & 322)

Here is another one:

Can strong warriors withstand a flood?

Or mighty men quiet a conflagration?

The will of god cannot be understood,

The way of god cannot be known:

Anything divine is [impossible] to find out.

(Foster 1995:387).

The Mesopotamians did not judge their gods. They pleaded, haggled, complained, sacrificed, bribed, provoked, praised, cajoled and encouraged their deities, but they did not pretend to know better than them. Resigning themselves to the mystery of the divine, the Mesopotamians thinkers refused to analyse the deeds and secret intentions of the deities. Some people would call this a primitive state of religion. I would call it a wise attitude. Logic, reason and doubt will take you far, but they can't take you all the way. At some point it's essential to stop reasoning. By cultivating humility and ignorance, the Mesopotamian priests avoided major ethical and religious problems. Living in a polytheistic society acknowledging the existence of several thousand deities, they did not try to attribute everything that happened to a single omnipotent, omnipresent and omniscient god who, while officially renowned for being 'good', allows all sorts of horrible things to happen. When things became inexplicable, they assumed a conflict of several divine forces. They also avoided the troublesome situation that the Christians created for themselves when they tried to align the inexplicable will of god in all its horrible and beautiful expressions with the logical and reasonable universe of Aristotle and the everyday world of serious people doing silly things.

But how did they think about a goddess noted for disrespect, rebellion, indecent exposure and killing? Who's that nude girl with the beastlike mask?

She is a woman, she is one who has ascended (or: *a pure one, an unbound one)*

she is a gate (or: *mouth, wolf-mouth),*

she is muštabba-abba (serpent of the deep?, Heated one? Flashing one?),

she is an utukku (ghost, spirit, guardian deity),

she is an Innin (=victorious goddess), made by the god:

a plague of (=sent by) Anu.

Because of her bad behaviour,

her insolent conduct, has Anu,

her father, made her descend

from Heaven to Earth,

because of her bad behaviour,

her rebellious intentions.

Her hair hangs loose,

her breasts (or: genitals) are exposed.

Before the man without deity

she rises like an erect penis.

She has loosened (or: *weakened)*

the sinews (or: *nerves, muscles, arteries)*

of him who suffers from lethal fever,

and has bound(?)[...].

(Nies, IV, #126, in Köcher 1949:19-21, updated and trans. JF.)

According to Köcher, the tablet is from the library of Kiṣirnabû, a priest who officiated in the temple of Aššur during the reign of Aššurbanipal. Farber cites an alternative translation and lists the text as OA_2, composed during the Old Babylonian period and excavated in Kültepe. A few notes: *She has* ***ascended*** might come from $elû_3$: risen, ascended, which derives from $elû_1$: high, exalted, sublime. You could also understand the line as *she has become exalted.* However, von Soden read that *she is pure* and Hecker proposed *unbound.* The uncertain term abullu(m), the **gate,** is a large gate; the gate of a city or maybe the underworld. It represents the boundary between the known world of the community and the dangerous realm outside. The 'gate' also appears in a Sumerian parable, where the term is used by a fox to describe the mouth of a wolf (Lambert, 1960:198). Perhaps we should understand it as a vast gaping orifice through which plenty of people, pack animals and goods enter and leave each day. **Muštabba-abba** was and is enigmatic. Well into the fifties, researchers traced the term from the Sumerian muš, meaning snake, dragon and maybe worm, and a-ab-ba, meaning the sea, the deep and, in its most simple form, a hole. It comes from the same root as Abzu/Apsû, the great watery deep, the abyss. This would make Lamaštu the *Blazing Serpent of the Sea/Deep/Hole/Abyss*. It's a pretty good guess, as the goddess is fond of snakes, carries them around, slips into houses like a sleek, smooth reptile, spits venom and is associated and identified with the star Ka-muš-i-gue (Mirach: Andromeda β), a Sumerian term, name and title that might be translated as *(female) Mouth-Serpent/Dragon-feeds*. Nowadays, scholars prefer a problematic Akkadian interpretation of the mysterious Muštabba-abba. Kienast and von Soden derived (deity) muštabbabu(m) from šabāru: twitch, flicker, flame, blink, flash. Or it might be related to šabābu(m): glow, parch. Von Soden proposed that the term implies *simultaneously dark and light*, i.e. *one who glows up again and again*. It turns Lamaštu into the dreaded *Flasher*, a lethal being otherwise identified with the god Šulpae, the MAŠKIM-GI-lu-ḫarran(n)a: *Lurker (*or: *Prowler) of the Road*, and the ḫallulāja spirit (*who spreads terror in the house, who does not allow the young bride to remain in her sleeping chamber*. Schramm 2008:27, trans. JF). The ḫallulāja is also an animal, possibly a centipede, and turns up in talismans against Lamaštu (see LS II, 115). Or would the term come from šebēru(m): to break, break up, smash, injure? That's enough confusion for now. All of these interpretations have their value. They also ensure that the unusual word Muštabba-abba keeps appearing in grammatical studies.

The **utukku** is a spirit. Originally, utukku were dangerous or benevolent entities, protective guardian spirits or deities or human ghosts; during the second millennium BCE, the literary emphasis shifted to evil utukku. It doesn't mean that the utukku became more evil: the conjurers simply had more trouble with the evil ones, while the good ones got along without further attention. Out tablet does not specify which sort. It is worth considering that the goddess is not called an 'evil Utukku'.

Lamaštu has descended to **earth**; technically, the term could also refer to what is under the earth, i.e. the Underworld. **Open hair** signifies that she is not married nor socially acceptable. Her **exposed breasts** or **vulva** are due to the fact that she walks without a piece of female underwear. It might be a bra, a breast strap or her pants: the item does not appear in art and remains mysterious. Exposed tits or vulva might imply that she is sex-hungry, does not even try to look acceptable, likes fresh air on her skin or maybe she is keen to breastfeed infants. The man without a **personal god** is doomed. He is not only threatened by Lamaštu but by a whole host of dangerous spirits and diseases. The personal deity or deities represent success and good luck; without them, anybody is lost. Note that she is šaḫāṭu(m): rising, jumping, pulsing, throbbing, attacking, like a penis (išaru(m)); a surprisingly male symbol for a goddess, and a major break in gender rules. Could the erect penis be represented by a bizarre headdress that Lamaštu wears on several late talismans? It looks like a stick and a bag. Call it a phallic symbol if you like.

For anyone seeking a career job in heaven, such a CV is distinctly bad news. The goddess is definitely one of the bad girls, and she is damn well having fun. But things are not as simple as they seem. True enough, Lamaštu has an unpopular task, in that she has to slay selected infants and elders, but this office was decreed by the great gods. Anu, her father; Antu(m), her mother; Enki/Ea, her teacher and the entire assembly of great gods oath-bound her to do that job. It was their choice. And they had excellent reasons to do so.

The Sumerians, Akkadians, Babylonians and Assyrians were acutely aware of ecological problems. Southern Mesopotamia is, by nature, a very poor country. The Sumerians had only three natural resources: water, mud and reeds, and managed to create the first known civilisation from these simple assets. Their immensely fertile country, celebrated by Kramer as a *veritable Garden of Eden*, was the result of inventiveness, effort and backbreaking labour. They lived in a hostile environment, characterised by extreme heat and scant rainfall, had to cope with annual floods, shifting rivers, drought, desertification and were well aware how easily a thriving city-state could exceed its means of survival. The hungry fires of the bronze industry stripped most of the land of its trees. The countryside was scarred by the traces of disused canals, abandoned once the soil had become too salty for agriculture, leaving ancient cities depopulated and falling into ruins while desert and steppe closed in on them. To the east of their narrow country were stony mountains peopled by foreign enemies, and to the west the bleak Arabian and Syrian Desert unrolled, inhabited by savage beasts, ferocious raiders and hungry ghosts. To the north, dangerous mountains rose and to the south, the terrifying ocean extended to infinity. Year in and year out the kings built temples to ensure the favour of the gods and excavated canals to gain fresh arable land. Unlike many people of our time, the Mesopotamians understood that resources are limited and human fertility has to be controlled. As Wiggermann notes, the Mesopotamian vegetation supplied something called *plant for a woman who does not want to be pregnant* (RlA *'Sexualität'*, trans. JF). Maybe some were not wise enough to use it. The population grew but the city walls did not. Nor did the amount of arable land. Each king built new canals as old fields had become infertile. It was the first lesson mankind received regarding the limits of space and natural resources. The Mesopotamians learned faster than most cultures, including our own. For this reason, the assembly of the gods charged Lamaštu to do her duty. Perhaps it takes a sensible person of the 21st century (like you) to understand that the death of an infant or elder is a terrible thing for a family, but that overpopulation is terrible for the entire planet.

Face Values and Hidden Meanings

The *Lamaštu Series* has many layers of meaning. Some passages are astonishing, others unlikely, and some will probably never be fully understood. There are good but frustrating reasons for this situation.

The first is common and will be remedied when further excavations bring up more textual evidence: **scribal errors**. Most Sumerian and Akkadian texts were not preserved in the original, nor were they lovingly made by professional calligraphers for personal or temple libraries. The bulk of surviving documents were produced in scribal schools, where students were busy copying documents, literature, proverbs, omen-texts, rituals, myths, hymns, spells, letters, accounts, contracts, treaties, mathematical texts, dictionaries and extensive lists of rare words. The schools produced an enormous amount of inscribed clay tablets which nobody really wanted. The stuff was frequently smashed and used as rubble in building sites of palaces, temples and private homes. It is our good luck that these damaged shards contain missing passages of important literary works. Unfortunately, their quality is anything but perfect: most students were still learning, had bad handwriting and made mistakes. When only a single copy of a text survives, contemporary scholars have a difficult time. A strange word may be unknown, or misspelt, and then they have to consider several possible alternatives. The modern reader faces another problem, as not all words are understood with the same level of certainty. Some terms are rare and only vaguely known, others so common that everybody can sit back and relax for a moment before the next enigma (or a new generation of hot-blooded linguists) appears. In English translation, such difficulties are not evident, and create the illusion that we can understand a text in the same way as those who originally composed it.

Then there is **professional secrecy**. Sumerian doctors wrote the first medical texts in human history, but they made sure that the information was incomplete. Babylonian medical prescriptions mention real materials and mix them with the most astonishing, and in many cases, revolting substances. Any quack trying to use of them would end up with a disgusting concoction. It was one of Franz Köcher's great achievements that he discovered some of the secrets of these mixtures. The Babylonian and Assyrian physicians purposely listed items like the dung of animals and people (donkeys, sheep, cows, sailors etc.) in their prescriptions. In some cases, the references were to be taken literally. In others, the words were a code referring to healing plants. The profession went to great lengths to protect some of its secrets. The same goes for the more unlikely magical prescriptions in our text.

The third reason is **artistic license**. Reading and writing were a sacred and difficult art. Learning to read English is child's play compared to reading Sumerian or Akkadian. Those who could write were justly proud of their skill. It made them play with words and invent secret allusions. One good example is the *Babylonian Theodicy* (Lambert, 1960:63-91; Foster 1995:316-323). The text is a fascinating treatment of religious, philosophical and ethical problems, and ranks among the greatest works of psychological and theological literature. We encounter a disenchanted, sceptical sufferer and his pious friend. The two discuss the injustice of the world, the unreliability of the gods, the cruelty of life and other worrying topics. The author, a mašmaššu called Saggilkīnamubbib, contributed his little joke when he hid his name, as an acronym, in the first syllable of each group of lines. Note that our writer was an exorcist, conjurer and incantation priest, i.e. the very sort of person who would have composed magical tablets. By spelling his name in passages spoken by the angry, doubt-ridden sufferer and his enlightened, faithful companion, our magician hinted that he was both of them, and that the struggle of faith happened very much within himself. Other scribes went to great lengths to make religious texts meaningful on a symbolic level. I am sure you have heard of the classic qabalistic methods where a word is analysed according to its numerical value, to the symbolism of each letter, or according to the idea that each letter is really a reference to a word starting with that sound. Such methods, carried to amazing degrees of complication by the medieval qabalists, have their foundation in Mesopotamia. Of course we have to take into account that the Mesopotamians wrote in syllables, not in letters. In the fourth millennium BCE, each syllable had begun as an ideogram (picture). As each syllable could be expressed with several different ideograms, the scribe could select symbolic images that fitted the meaning of the text. Bottéro gives a beautiful example how the 'Names of Marduk' in the *Enûma Eliš* were written with special ideograms that symbolised the character of each name. If you only look for the phonetic value, you are likely to miss much of the meaning. One day, I hope, enterprising scholars might provide an entirely new level of meaning for well-known texts by giving a translation that includes notes on the cuneiform characters and their symbolism.

Here is another fun idea. Starting around the Old Babylonian period, some scribes developed secret 'alphabets'. One of them may have had a mystical meaning; it was related to the creation of mankind. Landsberger suspected that its inventor was trying to develop a 'primal language' of mankind or a system to compose unintelligible magical spells. Two conjurations in a mysterious language appear in the *Lamaštu Series (III 57-62).* Such spells are very rare indeed.

Last, there is what may be called a **spiritual tradition**. The conjurers, priests, healers and exorcists who wrote and used the *Lamaštu Series* were practical people. They were scholarly enough to read, but did their job in temples, palaces and private houses, where they faced people experiencing genuine suffering, fear, misery and hope. Like their patients, they sincerely believed in the reality of gods, lethal spirits, taboos, spiritual pollution, curses, witchcraft and a wide range of dangerous influences. Their job was not simply pretence, humbug and symbolic medicine. Though this part of the conjurer's life is very badly documented, we do know that they used spells, invocations, magical materials, talismans, ablutions, baths, purification rituals, fumigations, special costume and other methods to protect themselves. Plus plenty of soap. They worked as the conjurer imbued them with her or his inspired imagination and belief. In short, our ritualists practised a form of spiritual discipline that allowed them to contact the 'invisible realm' and its denizens. They did their best to ensure that the hostile influence disappeared, giving the patient a chance to cheer up and recover. To understand the *Lamaštu Series*, you need a similar mindset. At this point, the serious academic researcher might run into trouble. He or she may have superb language skills, but these will not suffice when a passage represents ideas and acts that have to be experienced to be understood. If you want to comprehend magic and religion, you have to live it. To read, speculate and talk is simply not enough. Those who belong to spiritual traditions will always code their experiences, if only as there are so many irrational but meaningful events that cannot be expressed otherwise.

We find ciphers and bizarre metaphors in many early compositions. Here is an example from ancient India. The *Ṛg Veda*, compiled between 1200-900 BCE, contains a vast amount of symbolic elements that cannot be understood without commentaries. When the ancient seers described the generation of the Soma drug, they represented the distillation with mystic and poetic metaphors. Soma, for instance, was a plant or fungi-based drug, but it was also a moon god. It was called a brown cow, bull, falcon, eagle, golden bird, boar, bay steed, courser, youth, ancient father, head, chief and meeting twins. It was mixed with the cows, meaning milk. When '*ten sisters*' made the broth, it meant that the seer working on the material wore a gold ring on each finger. Coitus meant that the plants or fungi were crushed; thunder represented the sound of the press-stones and boards. The cloth that sieved the broth was a cloud cover; the emerging juice was rain, the flow of the fluid the racing of horses. The sea or lake (of juice) was collected in a forest (a wooden tub). Consumed by the seers, the plant, drug and deity *released the herds of cattle*, meaning that it opened minds and woke magical powers. One of its effects was '*immortality*' which actually meant an immortality of consciousness, a release from sins and the promise of a happy afterlife in Indra's luxurious warrior heaven (Gonda, 1960:62-67, Oldenberg 1916:4-5). Well, the Vedas were just the start. The classical *Upaniṣads* are even more metaphorical, and when we enter the realm of Tantric literature we encounter texts that should never, ever, be taken only at their face value. If you think you understand what's going on you must have missed something. The same can be observed in the alchemical classics composed by the Chinese sages since the late fifth century BCE. The terminology is so mind-boggling and contradictory that an uninitiated reader is lost. The same goes for an initiated reader of another tradition; subsequently an enormous amount of spiritual practice was misunderstood as mucking around with mercury, lead, cinnabar, yellow and red sprouts, sexual fluids, crushed stalagmites, pearls, minerals, ores and a wide range of highly symbolic plants. When we read the *Lamaštu Series* we should remember that there are many levels of meaning, and that a literal interpretation is never enough. If the *Lamaštu Series* were Tantric literature, for example, I would argue that infanticide is a metaphor for the 'slaying' of thoughts that arise and disturb the silence of meditation when they are still fresh, young and weak. The killing of elders would correspond to the elimination of outdated beliefs and habits. The *knife/sword that splits the skull* is the release from the confinement of a limited awareness, and a literal opening of the mind. If that blade strikes the head down, we are freed from the restrictive limits of our singular personality. That Lamaštu is a *gate*, a city gate, or a gate to the Underworld, would mean that she is an initiatrix to other realms of awareness: beyond the familiar personal world into the vast reality where everything is possible. Her description as the *blazing serpent/dragon of the deep/hole/sea* (if accurate) might have close connotations to the Tantric Kuṇḍalinī. I'm not saying that she is a forerunner of this idea, which only appears around the tenth century CE, nor that the Mesopotamian scribes had similar meditative practices. She simply fits the bill. That she can control the lethal asakku spirit, the devastating southern hurricanes or, maybe, the terrifying alû spirit, might mean that she can heal (or banish) the diseases afflicting the human head, heart and temper. She controls fierce passions, hot and cold feelings, confusion, madness, perversion, fear and anger, and can help you to come to terms with them. Her destruction of tamarisk and date palm, common symbols for royal and divine authority, could represent a much-needed revolt against the suffocating mindset that keeps people in servitude. Her home, the *clod of earth,* could be the human body, not only of the patient but also of you and me and all of us.

Admittedly, such tantric interpretations are beside the point. They come from a spiritual culture that is thousands of years and miles from ancient Mesopotamia. We will return to them near the end of this book, when you meet the nude lion-headed goddess as a tantric deity: wild, free, ecstatic, and gloriously alive.

The Lamaštu Series

[Text in brackets, cursive: reconstructed after other passages of the same or similar texts].
[Text in brackets, cursive, with ? is uncertain]
[...]: Text badly damaged or missing
(Text in round brackets, cursive: additions to make the section easier to read)
(Text in round brackets, normal script: commentaries, translation and extras JF)
(or: *indicates a different translation)*
Var. : indicates a different textual version
trans. JF: quotation translated from the German by Jan Fries

First Part of the Lamaštu Series

I, 1

***Šiptu** (=Conjuration, Naming):*
***Dingir DIM.ME/Lamaštu** (= Deity DIM.ME/ Lamaštu)*
Child of An/Anu is your first name** (or: **line, fame, succession);

Var.1.: ***The second: Sister of the Gods of the Streets;***
Var.2.: ***The second: Watchful One of the Gods of the Streets;***

I, 3

Var.1.: ***The third: Knife** (or: **Sword), that Splits the Head;***
Var.2.: ***The third: Knife** (or: **Sword) that Cuts the Head down.***

Var. 1.: ***The fourth: She Who Ignites the Wood to Flame;***
Var. 2.: ***The fourth: She Who Ignites the Flame;***
Var. 3.: ***The fourth: She Who Topples the Tree;***

I, 5

Var. 1.: ***The fifth: Goddess Whose Face** (or: **Expression) is Wild.***
Var. 2.: ***The fifth: Goddess Whose Face** (or: **Expression) is Yellow-Green.***

Var.1.: ***The sixth: Committed into the Hands** (=the Trusted),*
Accepted (or: Adopted** or: **Taken) by Irnina;
Var.2.: ***The sixth: Committed into the Hands** (=the Trusted),*
***Who accepts Petitions/Prayers** (= is compassionate);*

I, 7

The seventh: Bound** (or: **Conjured) by the Oath of the Great Gods,
Fly Away with the Bird/s of Heaven!

The *Lamaštu Series* opens with one of the two famous Lamaštu invocations. They were frequently carved on stones or on clay talismans and attached to the neck of the patient. As these lines are of great importance regarding the divine (as opposed to the allegedly 'demonic') nature of the goddess, let me offer a detailed commentary. As you can see, there were several versions of this famous incantation. Variation one is the most common one.

The age of this passage is uncertain. While most authors refrain from dating the text, Wiggermann proposes that it would come from Iron Age Mesopotamia, and would have replaced an earlier, Old Babylonian talismanic formula in the Sumerian language, which you will read under LS II, 129-132. His estimate had much to do with the respective age and the iconography of the talismans it was written on. Personally, I am not entirely sure about his suggestion. The reference to Irnina is remarkable, as that foreign mountain goddess had her greatest popularity under the Akkadian kings of the late third millennium BCE.

We are dealing with a series of seven names. That, to begin with, is remarkable. While Hindu deities have formidable long name lists (Lalitā, Pārvatī and Viṣṇu have a thousand names each, there are a hundred names of Kālī, Durgā, Gaṇeśa, Lakṣmī etc.), name lists are rare in Mesopotamian literature. One of them is the *Forty Names of Enki/Ea*, a collection that has not been published yet. Another is the *Fifty Names of Marduk* in the *Enûma Eliš*, a work of the late second millennium BCE. Much later are the names of Lilith, a tradition of the first millennium CE. Note that there are seven names. Seven is the most enigmatic and difficult number in Mesopotamian literature, as it could signify a lot of highly diverse ideas. We will look into them further on. For now, it should suffice that the seventh day (just like the days that were multiples of seven) was dangerous, but could turn out to be lucky when elaborate precautions were observed, purification ceremonies were performed, and the gods got extra attention and sacrifices. If you wanted to avoid trouble, and could afford to do so, you would stay at home and relax. From this tradition the Jewish Sabbath and the Christian 'Day of the Lord' developed. In short, the seven is magical, as it tends towards great peril but also provides excellent opportunities.

Name is šumu(m), a term that also means line, reputation, fame, succession. Each name can also be understood as a history. By naming Lamaštu, she is invoked, as what she is and what she has been. Behind each naming lies the idea that speaking is equal to making. The Mesopotamian gods create and enforce their decisions by the power of the word. Likewise, the āšipu, āšiptu or mašmaššu (magician, sorcerer, exorcist, and healer) who names a deity, conjures her or him, and gains a measure of influence. It's a two-way process. While the conjurer gains influence on the dangerous goddess, the goddess gains power over the conjurer. They come closer each time they meet, and simply have to get on with each other. Imagine the conjurer is hired to banish Lamaštu every other day. Before long you observe a working relationship. That's why our ritualists held magic wands, carried sacred substances, and spent plenty of time bathing, washing and performing purification rituals, if only to come home from work in one piece. In a very intimate way, the dreaded goddess and the conjurers act as partners. Think of Siberian shamanism, for instance, where the shaman's initiators and closest allies are the very spirits who cause diseases (Friedrich & Buddruss, 1955). Or consider the rama ('shamans') of the northern Magar in Nepal, who are close friends and relations of the nine lethal witches who bring diseases and snatch souls (Oppitz, 1981). In this scenario, ritualists, though their nature is close to the dreaded spirit beings, provide help for suffering mankind. Ideally, the patient is cured, the spirits receive offerings, the conjurer obtains a wage and everybody goes home happy. In such a situation, it would be absurd for the ritualists to carry a grudge against the lethal beings or deities they have to get along with.

The names of the goddess are the first conjuration or šiptu in the book. A šiptu, however, is not simply a conjuration; it can also refer to a detailed composition, based on a specific formula. Around the Kassite period, c.1500 BCE, a type of special prayer/conjuration developed which was called šiptu in the first line. Such prayers followed a certain structure. In the first section, a deity is named, defined and praised. In the second, the patient described her or his ills, misfortunes and afflictions. This part could become rather tedious. In the third section the deity was asked to intervene. Call it the wishful thinking department. Finally, the deity was thanked in advance for doing the job properly (SAHG 1953:46-47). In the *Lamaštu Series*, we have an entire series of šiptus dedicated to a goddess who, unlike many others, was generally feared. You will find descriptive elements in each of her šiptus, but not much praise. There are passages outlining the ills of the patient, but in general the positive thinking (i.e. the desired outcome) is expressed as a banishment; as an appeal to the gods to expel Lamaštu, or as a request to Lamaštu to pack her presents and depart. Though these differences should be acknowledged, Lamaštu is treated much like other deities were. Another fascinating point is that our šiptus do not blame the patient for having sinned or transgressed. This hints at early second-millennium thought: by the first millennium, people were falling over themselves to acknowledge their transgressions, misdeeds, sins, shame and guilt. Just look at the endless lists of misdeeds listed in the *Šurpu Series*! For now, to understand Lamaštu's seven names, you should think of them as magical formulae, as divine functions, as a series of trances and meditations, and as a range of activities and consciousness states. You could also contemplate how the names start with the mind-blowing, stunning, universal realm, where she is the Daughter of Heaven. Heaven is not a moral principle, nor is it a location. Heaven is huge and chaotic. It appears in a male and a female form; it is sheer creativity and maybe an ancient, all-pervasive all-self. Our goddess descends from heaven. Actually, she was kicked out for having a bad attitude. We see her moving along the streets and in-between-ness realms of wilderness and swamp, we watch her acting and in due course take on an appearance, a face, a task, a relationship and an obligation to the world. The whole descent from heaven is mirrored in these lines. Those of you who are into Indian lore may compare this pattern with the three emanations of the goddess in the *Devī-Gita,* the most famous section of the massive *Devī Bhāgavatam Purāṇa.* Starting in the *Upaniṣadic* period (c.800-400 BCE), gods, energies and consciousness were assumed to manifest in a subtle (abstract, formless) form, an energetic (senses, vibrations, activities) form, and a coarse (material, manifest) form. In Lamaštu's seven names, a remarkably similar pattern appears. But enough of these considerations. You'll learn more about her as she learns you. When you come to the third part of the text, you will learn that each šiptu is related to a specific part of the body of the patient. This part, the seven names, is conjuration #1, and pronounced over the head.

Child of An/Anu

Means daughter of the primordial sky god. The texts diverge a little. In Sumerian inscriptions, the goddess is frequently called dumu an.na, meaning *Child of An.* The later Akkadian, Babylonian and Assyrian texts have Mārat Anu: *Daughter of Anu.*

An (Sumerian) and **Anu** (Akkadian) was the supreme deity before the middle of the third millennium BCE and gradually faded into the background during the Babylonian and Neo-Assyrian periods. He had a brief comeback in the Neo-Babylonian period, and during the Seleucid period, under Greek government, he was identified with Zeus. An is basically a figure of authority and sheer, uncontrollable, mind-blowing creativity. He is the *great fecund bull of the sky,* the *father of the human seed,* and of the entire first generation of deities. His wife Antu(m) is less easy to describe as the evidence of her cult is rare. Like her husband, and many other major gods, she can appear as a huge, all-encompassing fertile bovine. An and his wife Antu(m) are one of the primal couples in Mesopotamian myth; mind you, there were plenty of creator gods, and many different traditions. An and Antu(m) are literally heaven: they are its makers, essence and manifestation. Think of them as transcendent gods who make everything, immanent gods who are their own creation, animal-shaped gods in bovine form and anthropomorphic deities who appear as the ancient king and queen representing fertility, authority and well-being, presiding serenely over the assembly of the gods. As they are such cosmic, ancient and immensely productive figures it is hard to define them. In our text, An and Antu(m) are the first cause. In other texts, An is the husband of Ki (Akkadian: Erṣetu(m)), meaning earth, ground and, in some contexts, the underworld. Other traditions make him the husband of Nammu (the primordial all-creative cosmic water-goddess), of Mušītu (*Night*), of Ninilī/Bēlet-ilī and Ninursalla. In the late third millennium BCE, under Akkadian reign, An was reinterpreted as the husband of Inanna/Ištar. It turned Antu(m) and his other spouses into 'appearances', 'aspects' or 'titles' of Inanna/Ištar. That's the official story. I am sure there were plenty of unrecorded local traditions which were just as vivid as the ones we chance to know about. Lamaštu is one of the daughters of An/Anu and Antu(m). While some claim that An had seven children, the actual amount is much larger. Mesopotamian myth is not a unified tradition but a melting pot of different cults, religions and visionary extravaganzas. All sorts of cities, districts, states and ethnic groups did their best to relate their favourite deities to the major gods. Among An's children are Enlil/Ellil/Bēl (*Lord Wind/Breath/ Vitality*), and sometimes Enki/Ea (*Lord of Earth/Lord of the Underworld*), the regent of Abzu/Apsû, the great subterranean, world-surrounding and celestial ocean. When Enki does not appear as Enlil's younger brother he is usually called Enlil's son. Then there are Erra (*Mighty*, who merged with Nergal: *Ruler*, became a god of the Underworld, and one of the husbands of Ereškigal, the *Great Queen of the Earth/Underworld*); Gibil (a fire god); Gatumdug (the founding goddess of Lagaš, who eventually merged with Bau/Baba); Iškur/Adad (a weather, storm and oracle deity); Nidaba/Nisaba (a grain and reed goddess, patroness of writing, justice and science and special darling of the scribes and scholars); Martu/Amurru (a fierce desert god imported courtesy of the Amorites in the early second millennium BCE) and the goddess who is read as Baba, Bawa or Bau (the ba_6 sign can also be read as u_2), who started as a rival of Inanna and ended up as her girlfriend; Bēlat-Mati (*Lady of the Land*, title of several goddesses); Kittu (*Truth, Reliability;* sometimes a daughter of sun god Utu/Šamaš); Nanay (the *Lady of Loving Care*, a goddess of Uruk, who merged with Inanna); Ninkarrag/Gula (goddesses of healing) and Māmitu(m) (both of whom occasionally merged with Ninḫursag, the *Lady of the Foothills*, goddess of animals, birth and/or healing). Another Māmitu(m), representing ban, taboo, oath and curse was kicked out of heaven just like Lamaštu and became goddess of the Underworld; she is a wife of Nergal/Erra, and sometimes identified with Ereškigal. And finally, among An's numerous children, we encounter the Sumerian Inanna and her Semitic counterpart Ištar, who appears elsewhere as the Daughter of the moon-god Nanna/Suen/Sîn, or of Enki, or Enlil, depending on local tradition. As Inanna/Ištar can be An's daughter, her underworldly sister Ereškigal/Ninkigal also qualifies as a *Daughter of An*. There were lots of daughters of An, and various local traditions did their best to promote their own city and state goddess as the firstborn one (prime examples being Bau/Baba and Gula). Sulphur, happily employed in rites of exorcism, is a daughter of An. Even a rare type of epilepsy is one of An's daughters! In magical texts, the title 'Daughter of An' is frequently used for DIM.ME/Lamaštu.

An is Heaven, but heaven is not, as in Christianity, related to goodness. An had all sorts of children. Among them are a range of dangerous beings, such as The Evil Seven, who act like mindless horrors and bring terror, destruction, pestilence, nightmare, disease, earthquake, eclipse and sporadically try to devour the moon. It's hard to be specific about them, as the scribes disagreed. These entities are sometimes assumed to have animal or human heads. In other texts they are formless and beyond definition. Elsewhere they are identified as a special selection of dangerous spirits, like the utukku, gallû, asakku etc. These in turn are not clearly defined either: functions and attributes overlap. More confusing still, the Evil Seven are sometimes related to or identical with a group of seven warriors, the Imin-bi, the Seven Stars (the Pleiades), also acknowledged children of An, who fight malevolent beings but are often counted among them. For now, I hope you are sufficiently confused to open your mind really wide. To understand Mesopotamian religion, we have to embrace a world where divine beings share and exchange attributes, appearances, titles and functions. No-one ever managed to streamline the religious traditions or enforce a specific dogma. Tough news for those who like to define, separate and analyse the gods; and excellent great luck for those practising mind-explorers who embrace the divine in all its overwhelming polytheistic magnificence.

Var.1.: ***The second: Sister of the Gods of the Streets;***

Var.2.: ***The second: Watchful One of the Gods of the Streets;***

Who are the gods of the streets? A few scholars proposed that the Evil Seven might be the gods of the streets, as a verse in an exorcism says that they move or lurk on the streets, but then, so does anybody else. Spells state that the Evil Seven are great storms which, rising from the ocean, roam from land to land, blight the country, throw birds out of their nests, destroy sheep-pen and cattle-fold and move from house to house unhindered. Obviously, the Evil Seven go pretty much anywhere. Is Lamaštu a sister of the Evil Seven? One text (SLT 122 V 18 & 124 VII 22 mentioned by van Dijk in RlA *'Gott'*) has DIM.ME in the following of Imin-bi, the Seven Deity. As you just read, the Seven Deity, the Pleiades, is a highly ambiguous group that may or may not be identical with the Evil Seven. This reference, however, stands pretty much alone. True enough, there are similarities between Lamaštu and a range of lethal spirits, gods or entities. As most of them are not clearly defined, and the scribes freely copied wonderfully sinister poetry from one spell to another, it is not likely that a clear difference will ever be worked out. There are several descriptions of the Evil Seven, the most popular appearing in the collection *Uttuki Limnutî (Evil Utukku).* It is based on earlier texts that class the Evil Seven not as udug/utukku but as gala/gallû. There are vast differences between the evil gallû, the evil utukku and Lamaštu (see Schramm 2008: 70-73, 256-261).The evil gallû know no dignity, are not known in heaven and earth, are messengers of Ereškigal, kill and destroy without consideration or sense, are noted for the destruction of fishes, birds and animals of the wilderness.

In the parallel account from the *Uttuki Limnutî* series, the Evil Seven have no names, are not named by the great gods, are not known in heaven and earth, do not listen to prayers and supplications, accept no offerings, are children of the earth, estrange wife and husband, cause blight, stink, and wholesale destruction, attempt to devour the moon, throw birds out of their nests, act as throne-bearers of Ereškigal and messengers of Anu, are insane, sexless, shapeless and gibber.

None of this can be said about Lamaštu.

I would guess that the gods of the streets are basically the deities of law, order and civilisation; streets being the great roads where donkey caravans moved, traders and officials travelled and the royal armies went their way. So did enemy armies; a street is there for everyone; at least for everyone who is someone, and the very place where history is written in capital letters.

Up in the sky, three other streets appear. An/Anu's way is a broad band that extends roughly 33° above and below the heavenly equator. Enlil's way is above and north and Enki's way is below and to the south. These three zones were of major importance for star-gazers, seeking signs and portents in the height of heaven. Or we could think of the major canals as the 'streets', as so much travel and trade made use of them. Next to the streets and large canals, we encounter farms, gardens, villages, towns, taverns, hostels, brothels; we come across farmers, shepherds, fishers, traders, thieves, diplomats, messengers, poor folk, bandits and, on the major canals, even pirates. It's a mixed lot and a great show of humanity in its many forms. Unlike them, Lamaštu moves in the small lanes, alleys, byways, through the wilderness, and on the paths of the mountains, forests, deserts, steppes, rivers, swamps and the open sea, all of which are her favourite haunts.

The second variation of this line, though rare, indicates that the goddess, acting as a ***Watchful One of the Gods of the Streets***, is a divine guardian. She observes and witnesses the ways, what happens on them, where they come from and where they lead and what the deities in charge of them are up to. It's a mystical office, and a wonderful meditation.

Var.1.: ***The third: Knife*** (or: ***Sword), that Splits the Head;***

Var.2.: ***The third: Knife*** (or: ***Sword) that Cuts the Head down.***

How shall we understand this name? Much depends on the age of this line. Patru(m) can mean knife, dagger or sword. The early Mesopotamians did not really use swords. Battles were fought with arrows, chisel-headed axes, fighting maces and throw-sticks. Bronze was expensive and not really suited for long bladed weapons. A bronze sword is heavy, clumsy, does not keep its edge and may bend on impact. Consequently, swords were divine weapons or worn by kings for reasons of appearance, but the troops were not equipped with them. Daggers were cheaper, and could be used with more impact, especially for stabbing. If this passage is from the second millennium, the goddess is or uses a divine or ceremonial bronze sickle sword or a more practical dagger. If it comes from the first millennium, the Mesopotamian Iron Age, the sword would be an everyday article carried by many soldiers. Surprisingly, neither swords nor daggers were important symbols. Kings used their cudgel-sceptres to slay prominent enemies. I could only find one dagger in a ritual context. When Enkidu died, his grave goods included a double-edged bronze dagger with a lapis lazuli haft, decorated with an image of the Euphrates. It was not supposed to serve Enkidu in the Underworld: the dagger was a gift (or bribe) for the god Bibbu, the Slaughterer of the Underworld (Dalley, 2008:94). Regarding 'split', the word natāru means: to split open, cleave, demolish. That Lamaštu beheads, as is indicated by the second variation, places her in the company of Kālī. To quote the famous Bengali poet Rāmprasād Sen (c.1718-1775): *When the head is gone, headache cannot remain. As fire consumes a bale of cotton, so all goes up in Kālī's name.* It brings us to Lamaštu's next name.

Var. 1.: ***The fourth: She who Ignites the Wood to Flame;***

Var. 2.: ***The fourth: She who Ignites the Flame;***

Var. 3.: ***The fourth: She who Topples the Tree;***

In spite of all studies and excavations, it is still uncertain how Lamaštu or anybody else made a fire. There is no evidence for fire-drills, so far, though the Mesopotamians certainly used bow-drills when they perforated beads and engraved cylinder seals. But there is documentation for the import of flint from the mountains in the north. The word 'wood' raises further questions: iṣu(m) can mean: wood, tree, or timber and refer, specifically, to a shaft, house-beam, stake and fetter. Each of them produces a different symbolism. In Mesopotamia, the only abundantly available wood was palm; too soft for building and certainly not common enough to be used as firewood by everyone. The same goes for the fruit trees of the orchards and the conifers cultivated near a few canals. Then, as now, most fires were made of reeds, dead shrubs, parched thistles and dried cow manure. In Kurdistan I saw people who formed balls of cow manure, flattened them, and stuck them to house walls, where they could dry in the sun. A fire of wood means an expensive fire. Poplar wood was used by the wealthy, and by the smiths to heat their kilns to a high temperature. In most houses, light was supplied by oil lamps and by torches made of bundled reeds drenched in bitumen. In a ritual context, it might be the magic wand of êru-wood (LS III, 103) carried by the āšipu, āšiptu or mašmaššu; it had to be scorched with fire at both sides. Does this mean that the goddess consecrates the wand of exorcism? Or should we suspect her of arson? Great wooden beams, too expensive for the common population, were used as doorframes in temples and palaces. Lamaštu is not very fond of earthly and celestial authority, and might be tempted to light a few sparks here and there.

But let us look at fire in a metaphorical way. The fact that Lamaštu lights the fire has been taken to mean that she raises body temperature; i.e. induces fever. This is true, but we should keep in mind that a) plenty of gods, spirits and diseases could cause fever and b) fever is not a disease but a strategy of the body to cure itself by changing temperature. Many viruses stop breeding or die when the temperature exceeds a certain limit. Most of the time, when Lamaštu brings fervent heat and icy shuddering, she is doing something good for you. But if we are talking about her lighting a real fire, the verse could imply that the major gods of exorcism, Girra, Gibil and Nusku, all of them fire gods, are under her control, or at least incapable of banishing her. Often, a fire was lit next to a patient, no matter whether the day was cold or hot, to banish evil influences. Waving torches near the sickbed was a popular cure. It is worth considering that the fire gods, celebrated as supreme exorcists in the *Maqlû Series*, are nowhere to be seen in the *Lamaštu Series*. Only one of them, Nusku, symbolised by a lamp, appears on the specific type of talismans that were favoured by the Aramean invaders in the first millennium BCE. This typical and late talismanic arrangement is described under LS III, 1-7 as a wall painting. It mentions the lamp but does not name a fire god.

But let us cast our net wider. To understand the fourth name, think of the fire that gives light and warmth; that comforts the traveller, that lights the splendid halls of kings on the great festivals and that constitutes the centre of the household and the family. In everyday life, fire has much to do with wealth, comfort, happiness, procreation, and the act of making offerings. 'Lighting a fire' could mean starting a family; extinguishing one, ending a family line. A man without children faces an extinguished hearth (Postgate 1994:83). Fire was frequently associated with sexual lust and longing. A young man prayed to Inanna that she should grant him a wife with a *hot lap*. A lovesick youth suffered from a *burning heart* (Leick, 2003:93 &185). A spell against sexual arousal states *I drive out the fieriness of your heart*. A spell for sexual attractiveness contains the enigmatic lines:

As Ištar sits on her throne, as Nanay sits in her sanctuary, the entu(m) priestesses love the burning. We read that the entu(m) offers her lover ice water to cool his *wolfish, lionesque arousal* (Foster, 1995:375, 337, Haas 1999:155). Wolf-bitch and lioness are among Lamaštu's favourite animal masks. The citizens of Uruk celebrated the marriage of An and Antu(m) by lighting fires in their houses (Wiggermann in RlA *'Sexualität'*). Perhaps we should also consider a Syrian myth, *Shachar and Shalim*, composed in the 14th century BCE: *Scorching hot as the coals are the two daughters, daughters of El – daughters of El, (now) and forever more!* (Driver, 1971:123). Gaster commented that their heat means *inflamed with passion*.

Fire also appears as a metaphor for quarrels and strife:

When confronted with a dispute, go your way; pay no attention to it. Should it be a dispute of your own, extinguish the flame (*Instructions of Šuruppak*, Lambert, 1960:101).

Finally we find fire as an emblem of Inanna/Ištar, who is frequently called *the torch of the gods*, and whose fiery planet, Venus, represented lust, love, conflict and combat.

Fire might hint at incense. Priests, asu (doctors) and conjurers frequently burned incenses, some of them vile and stinking, to banish evil influences, some of them aromatic and pleasing, as offerings for the great gods. Herodotus recorded that enormous amounts of frankincense were being burned in Babylonian temples; however, this claim, like so many others, is questionable. Saggs points out that the evidence for large imports is missing. The Mesopotamians delighted in the fragrance of special woods and resins, favourites being cedar, juniper and cypress. If Lamaštu lights these woods, she is burning incense.

But let us devote a few thoughts to the last variation: ***She who topples the tree***. I wonder whether it is the cedar of right, or maybe one of the many 'trees of life' that appear so frequently in Mesopotamian art. Such trees were more than pretty images. Roll seals show trees in positions of worship that are quite similar to the position of deities. The tradition is ancient. Such trees start appearing around 3500 when the first roll seals were carved and they keep appearing, in many highly varied shapes, all the way to the Neo-Babylonian period. Many of them are beautiful, highly abstract and cannot be identified.

Var. 1.: ***Goddess Whose Face (**or:* ***Expression) is Wild.***

Var. 2.: ***Goddess Whose Face (**or:* ***Expression) is Yellow-Green.***

Early translations inform us that she has a *fear-inspiring countenance*, that the *sight of her face causeth horror*, or that she is a *Goddess of awful mien*. Such readings, which tell us about the effects of her face, are a little out of date. Mesopotamian gods in general had terrifying, mind-shaking, stunning and bedazzling countenances, and they, like Lamaštu, radiated an *awe-inspiring aura* or *a gleam of terror*. People who met a deity were usually scared, paralysed, speechless etc., even if that deity was good-looking, well-behaved and friendly. See Gilgameš, who wakes in the middle of the night and says to Enkidu:

'My friend, you did not call me,

Why am I upset?

You did not touch me, why am I startled?

Has a god passed by? Why are my muscles paralysed?'

Jacobsen (1976:12) has 'paralysed', Bottéro has 'trembling' and ANET 1992 has 'numb'. Make your choice.

Nowadays, the Akkadian word šakṣu(m): scowling, glowering, is traced to šakaṣu, which the CDA translates as: wild(eyed). The term pānu(m) can mean: face, front, presence, expression, in particular emotional expressions. In short, we cannot be sure whether the name refers to her face or her whole expression, divine aura or body language. And what face are we talking about? Even normal deities had awe-inspiring expressions.

Maybe the fifth name refers to the animal mask that Lamaštu was given by her brother Enlil before she was exiled to earth. Let's have a look at Old Babylonian Tablet NBC 1265 of the Babylonian Collection of Yale University (see Farber (RlA, *'Lamaštu'* and 2014), Köcher (1949), Haas (1986) Wasserman (2008), West (1992), Foster (1995)):

Anu created her, Ea reared her,

Enlil allotted her the face of a lioness (or: dog bitch).

She has small hands, longer

fingers; her fingernails

are very long, her forearms are besmeared.

She entered the front door,

she slipped past the door hinge,

when she was past the door hinge, she saw the little one.

She grasped it seven times in its belly!

Release your claws, let your arms sink,

before he has arrived:

the wise worker, the valiant Ea!

The door hinge is wide; the doors are open for you!

Move through the wasteland,

with a dusty mouth

and a sandstorm in your face!

With finely powdered cress-seeds I will fill your eyes!

I conjure you with Ea's māmit (= taboo, prohibition, curse)

You must depart!

The spell is early: Enki/Ea personally acts on behalf of the conjurer. Later conjurations favour a setting where Ea gives advice and his son Asarluḫi or his later Babylonian counterpart Marduk does the job. The cress seeds are meant to blind her temporarily, but they were also thought to contain great magical power, maybe due to their disinfecting essential oils. In exorcisms, salt and cress seeds were often used together. The same combination was used by Aššurbanipal to destroy and curse the fields and cities of Elam. In our spell, the idea is that she cannot find her way back. West states that *Ea made her great*; Wasserman preferred that Ea *brought her up*. It makes me wonder whether Lamaštu received her education in Enki/Ea's temple in Eridu, floating serenely over the mysterious abyss. According to Wiggermann (2000:232), Foster and Langdon she received the *face of a bitch*, Köcher and Haas preferred the *face of a lioness*. The original inscription shows an unusual spelling that can be read either as labbatim (*lioness*) or kalbatim (*dog bitch*). Lamaštu spells often tell us that she has the head of a she-wolf or a lioness. The earliest amulets show her as a nude woman with the head of a lioness, a wolf, dog or bird of prey. Another good candidate would be a hyena. The typical blunt snout and the characteristic hyena mane appear on several amulets. And there are also amulets that provide her with the head of a dragon, serpent or, quite frequently, a crudely drawn monster that defies identification. One amulet equips her with two lionesque heads. It makes her a 'Mischwesen', German for *hybrid creature.* Lamaštu is not the only deity who can appear with the head of a savage cat: in the *Erra Epic Nergal put on the face of a lion and entered the palace* (Daley, 2008: 303). You probably noted that she was given a 'head' or 'face'. Personally, I would consider it a mask. However, though masked ritualists appear in Mesopotamian art, the word for 'mask' has not been discovered yet. But when you look at the talismans, you will notice that many show a horizontal line below the neck, indicating that the 'head' is separate from the body. It does not appear in the texts but was evident to the artists who carved the images. Like us, the goddess assumes heads and personalities as she goes along. She might also appear with a human head. Like all great gods, she was born in human shape. Here is LS I, 115-116:

Night after night, morning after morning [...]
Regularly she transforms into (or***: returns to*** or***: into) a woman,***
whose entry (or***: entrance) is [...]***

To transform or return herself into the shape of a woman, our girl must be able to hide the animal head, birdlike feet and wings. Mesopotamian gods had beautiful human shapes: maybe she simply resumes the divine form she had before she was condemned to live on earth.

Mesopotamian art is full of beings that have a human body and an animal head. Some deities, spirits and unidentified creatures exhibit human bodies and the heads of lions, panthers, goats, donkeys, snakes, eagles and so on. Others have animal bodies and human faces. It would be nice to know more about them. As usual, the authorities disagree. While some identify these figures as masked ritualists, who use their masks to scare evil entities, others assume that they portray a range of terrible and violent beings, such as the Evil Seven. Whatever it may be, the masks of Lamaštu have an apotropaic function. As you will read further on, Lamaštu was occasionally invoked to banish evil spirits (just as, in first millennium Mesopotamia, the terrifying storm-god Pazuzu was invoked to banish Lamaštu). Maybe Enlil thought that his sister would have an easier life if she arrived on Planet Idiot wearing a scary mask. In some early Sumerian ceremonies, nudity was a sign of ritual purity and sacredness. It raises the question whether the iconography of Lamaštu shows a nude female ritualist using a terrifying animal mask to dominate evil spirits. We're deeply in the domain of the shamans here.

But let us consider the **yellow-greenish face**. Yellow-green is the colour of ochre. But it could also be the colour of new leaves, of spring, symbolising fresh birth: the very time the goddess is active. A yellowish complexion appears in medical texts and indicates a serious liver condition, perhaps a type of jaundice. This and related illnesses were classed as *Pašittu Diseases.* Usually they were fatal. More on them further on.

Var.1.: ***The sixth: Committed into the Hands (*** = the Trusted***),***
Accepted (or: ***Adopted*** or: ***Taken) by Irnina;***
Var.2.: ***The sixth: Committed into the Hands (*** =the Trusted***),***
Who is Compassionate (= Accepts Petitions/Prayers ***(*** = is compassionate***);***

Many early scholars interpreted the name Irnina as *Lady of the Cedar.* They based their translation on the Sumerian term (giš) eren: *(wood) cedar.* Sumerian Nin means a lord or lady, a god or goddess. In Akkadian, the word erēnu(m) can be

Figure 12 Long Fingers, Longer Fingernails

cedar or *pine*. It's hard to tell the difference. Both were growing in the same mountain forests. Groneberg offers a very different idea (without giving reasons); in her opinion Irnina means: *War, Combat*. Irnina was originally an independent foreign goddess; and while I wouldn't want to argue whether 'Lady of the Cedar' is accurate, she is certainly associated with cedar and pine forests. It would locate her in the foreign mountains east or west of Mesopotamia. For the Mesopotamians, cedar was a priceless building material. The mountain cedars were a frequent target of royal raids. In the Sumerian Gilgameš tales, the semi-divine king raided the Zagros Mountains near Elam in the east, while the younger Akkadian, Babylonian and Assyrian versions of the tale have him travel west to the mountains of Lebanon. Like Gilgameš, many Mesopotamian regents boasted that they had successfully entered enemy territory and cut down mountain conifers. In the late third millennium BCE, Naramsîn felled cedars at Lebanon. The Assyrian nobles imported cedar and pine from Lebanon, the Amanus and even from Syria. The wood was exceptionally valuable. It also had a sacred connotation: from the earliest literary records to the first millennium, the *Cedar of Right* represented justice, truth and honesty. A special seal, showing the tree, represented divine influence and proved the presence and consent of a person in legal documents. Postgate proposed that the Cedar of Right might go back to the pre-literate period (2002:170). To be sure, there were some conifers, possibly a sort of pine, cultivated near some canals in central Mesopotamia. Such plantations were a rarity. In most places, the heat, the salty soil and the high water table prohibited their growth. The trees were rare and exceptionally valuable. Letters by Ḫammurapi indicate that small clusters of trees were guarded by day and night and that foresters who allowed trees to be felled illegally could expect the death penalty (Klengel, 1991: 146).

Irnina or Irnini is the goddess of the mountain forests. The Mesopotamians were awed by forests and mountains. In a letter written by Sargon II to the god Aššur during his eighth campaign, in 714 BCE, we can sense his anxiety as he moved through the lands Upa and Nikappa: *...high mountains covered with impenetrable trees, whose interiors are labyrinthine and whose passes are frightful; a shade is cast over their region as if it were a cedar grove and the one who goes on their paths cannot see the shining sun* (Melville in Chavalas, 2007:337).

When Gilgameš and Enkidu came to the mountains

...they saw the cedar mountain, home of gods, sanctuary of Irnini. In the face of the mountain, the cedars rose in lavish growth. Their shade was good, filling one with delight. Undergrowth offered shelter, covering the forest floor (Ungnad, 1921:78; Speiser in Pritchard, 1969:82; Dalley, 2008:71). The heroes enjoyed the scenery, had a good rest, killed Ḫuwawa, a local deity who worked as Enlil's forester and cut down the trees. That's humans for you.

In literature, Irnina usually appears as a synonym for Inanna and Ištar, with whom she was identified sometime during the late third millennium BCE. She is praised as the daughter of the moon god Sîn, is compared to a wild bull and a raging lion, and was a special favourite of the kings of Akkad. A canal in northern Sumer was named after her. By the time of our inscription, Irnina had long become an aspect or an alternate title of the goddess who was Inanna among the Sumerians and Ištar among the Semitic Akkadians, Babylonians and Assyrians.

Inanna/Ištar started out early, probably during the fourth millennium BCE, as a rain and storm goddess, a goddess of the planet Venus and a deity of love, lust, prostitution, fertility, wealth, festivity, games and drunken revelry in her beloved taverns. In the third millennium BCE she acquired control over the divine principles of civilisation (the Me) and personified the right of kingship. Between the late third and the early second millennium BCE she granted several kings success, wealth, fertility and victory through the rite of the Sacred Marriage, when a special woman (a high priestess, the queen or a representative of either) impersonating the

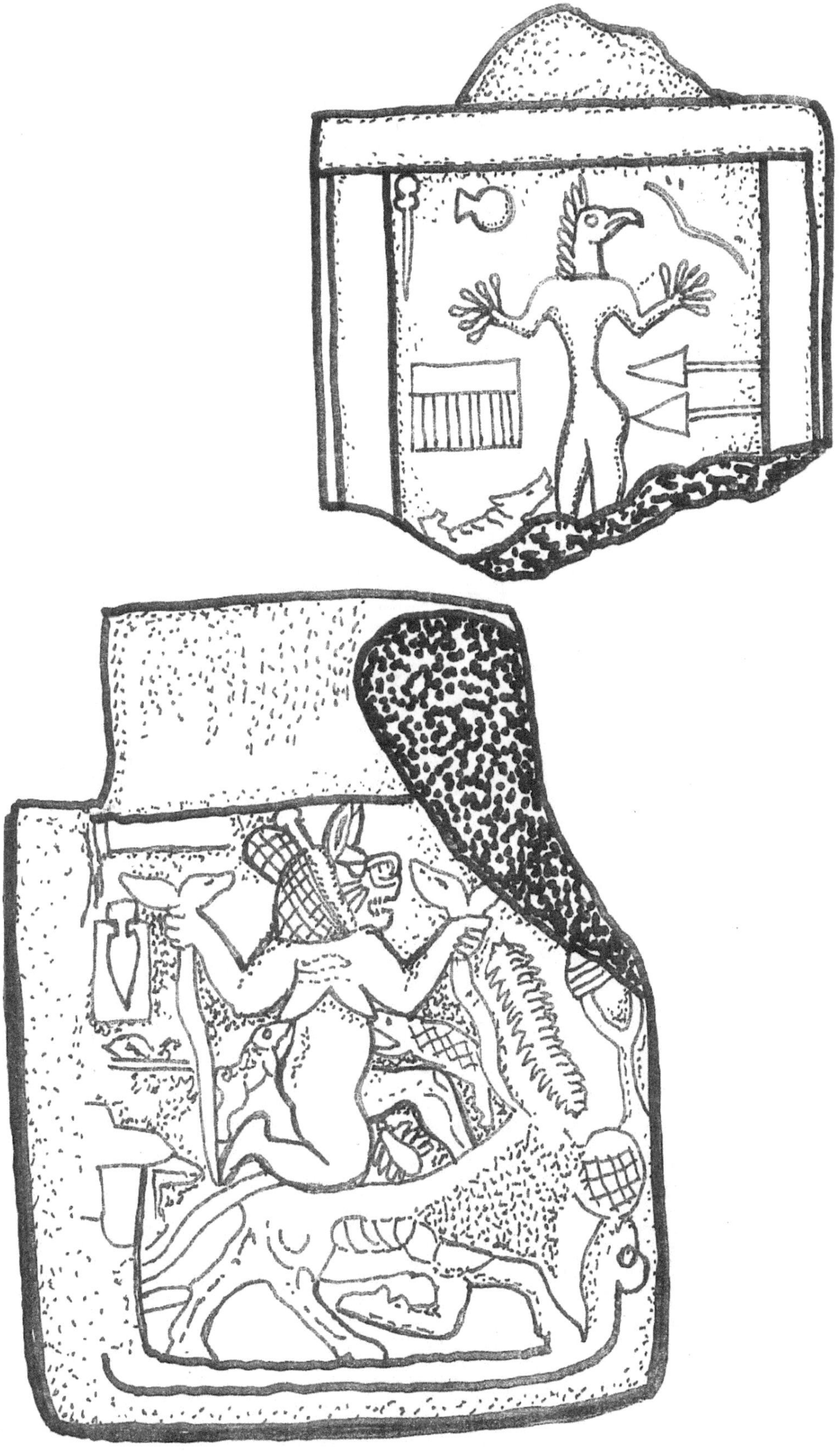

Figure 13 Top: an early Lamaštu amulet; the reverse has the Sumerian inscription of the Seven Names. Louvre, Paris.

Bottom: A typical late Lamaštu talisman: knielauf position, special headdress, donkey and boat. Note scorpion near her genitals and large centipede

Figure 14 Lamaštu amulet. This one shows a very marked 'mask' character. Note serpent girdle. London, BM 117759.

Figure 15 Top: Lamaštu with special headdress. VA 8019.

Bottom: the first Lamaštu amulet published in an academic work. Illustration after Lajard's Culte de Venus. The original is lost.

Figure 16 Front: winged wolf or hyena Lamaštu.

Reverse: dog and fake cuneiform inscription.

BM 122999.

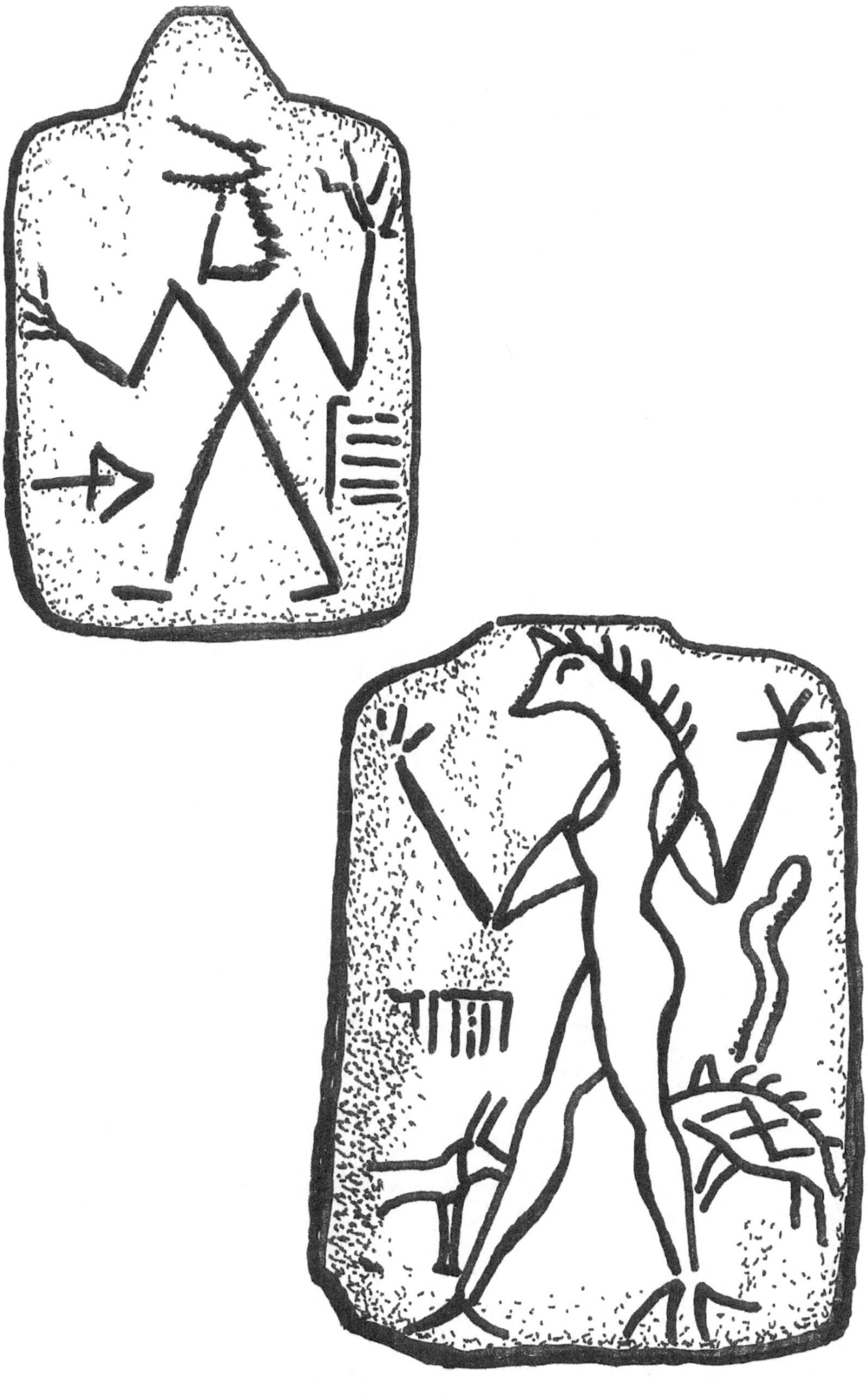

Figure 17 Top: simple but lovely Lamaštu with the head of an unidentified draconic monster. Note human feet.

Bottom: beach beauty Lamaštu. Both after Wiggermann in Stol page 221.

Figure 18 Top left: Bird-headed Lamaštu. Note human feet. Steatite amulet from Ur, after Woolley 1965, Plate 28.

Top right: Wolf- or hyena Lamaštu with sword, serpent and bizarre double-comb structure. Note paws. Bitumen amulet #66, from Tshoga Zanbil, after de Mecquenen-Michalon, 1953.

Bottom: Obsidian amulet. The outer frame has a cuneiform inscription which was so badly legible that I omitted it.

Figure 19 Top: winged bird Lamaštu. Reverse: triangles which signify mountains or waves, indicating the places she should depart to.BM123217

Bottom: Vulture-beaked Lamaštu. Reverse: Mountains or waves plus fake cuneiform inscription. VA Bab. 1357

Figure 20 Top: Bird-of-prey beaked anorectic Lamaštu with impressive hands. Lamaštu amulet #94, Teheran. Inscription on the reverse in Sumerian. Photo in Farber 2014:471.

Bottom: Lamaštu with unidentified bizarre head and wings. Lamaštu amulet #93, IM22128, Photo in Farber 2014:471.

Figure 21 Top: Lamaštu with draconic monster head and tongue and extremely abstract animals. Is she wearing a skirt? Collection de Clercq, Paris.

Bottom: clay amulet (?), Museum of Pennsylvania. Note how the spindle is offensively used against her.

Figure 22 Top: Lamaštu with unidentified mask/head. She seems to have hooves. The symbols of Anu and Sîn appear above her. Note large scorpion on the left. VA Bab. 2418.

Bottom: Winged Lamaštu with amazing donkey ears. VA Ass.992

Figure 23 Top: Lamaštu with unidentified animal head without gender characteristics and feet. VA 3326.

Bottom: Fragment of Lamaštu with duck-headed snake. VA 8278.

Figure 24 Top: Lamaštu with comb on a string and a slightly pregnant look. BM 128857.

Bottom: Fragment of winged Lamaštu. VA Ass.999.

Figure 25 Top: large eared Lamaštu holding her little piglet by the feet (!). Lamaštu amulet #60, Photo in Farber.

Bottom: elegant Lamaštu with dragon head from Uruk. Note the rim of mountains/ waves around the picture. BM1851, 0101.18

Figure 26 Lamaštu in knieflauf position rides her donkey. Note human feet. Badly worn amulet, greenish stone, after H.v. Osten.

Bottom: Lamaštu amulet, red carnelian, auctioned by Christies.

Figure 27 Top: Lamaštu with monster head, made by a very jittery artist. Lamaštu amulet #92, IM22127, Photo in Farber 2014:90.

Bottom: comparatively young Lamaštu amulet. It describes the painting at the start of LS III, including a lamp (Nusku's emblem), the lower leg of a donkey and the head of Pazuzu. Note that her 'head' is obviously a mask. Alabaster plate, New York, after H. v. Osten.

Figure 28 Top: comparatively young Lamaštu amulet showing a sickbed scene with a fish-masked healer on the top. Note Lamaštu's modern headdress, palm leaf, carpet (?) and the heads of Pazuzu and someone unknown. VA5289.

Bottom: Very unusual double headed lionesque Lamaštu amulet. Lamaštu amulet #88, Photo in Farber.

local goddess, mated with the king (in a real or symbolic fashion) during a mysterious ritual that is very badly documented and much discussed. Around 2350 BCE, under Akkadian rule, she also acquired the function of a war goddess. Sargon I sacrificed to her while his campaigns ranged from the Iranian mountains to the Turkish highlands and the shores of the Mediterranean Sea. His daughter Enḫeduanna tried to raise her to the pinnacle of divine authority and celebrated her as the wife of celestial An, who trembles at her sight, obeys her commands and can presumably count himself lucky to be allowed to go to bed with her. Later generations continued this tradition. As Ištar her image was carried before the Assyrian troops, once she even granted a theophany to the army. Battle was called the *Dance of Ištar*. Over the millennia, she gobbled up the function of most goddesses, until, during the Neo-Assyrian period, when the *Lamaštu Series* was compiled from elder sources, the name Ištar could mean 'goddess' in general and the ištaratu are 'the goddesses'. An ištaritu is a female devotee, a priestess of a goddess or a woman possessed by one, while an ištarīum is a male devotee of a goddess.

It might be worth asking why the author of the talismanic text used the name Irnina instead of the far more common Ištar. Is this line a quotation from an elder text, dating to the Old Akkadian period when Irnina was still vibrantly alive and popular? Is it a forgery, trying to make the text look older than it was? Was there a myth telling how Irnina and Lamaštu came to be friends and companions? Or did the writer prefer Irnina instead of the well-known Ištar to emphasise that Lamaštu is a foreigner, a native of the sacred mountain forests?

'Šeš- šu pa-qid qā-ti li-qât (ilu) Irnina' is worth considering closely. Paqādu(m) means: to entrust, commit, appoint, confide, take care of. Qātu is the hand; while lêgu$_2$ means: take, take hold of, received, accept, appoint; it can also be used as in *to take a wife, to take a slave* or *to take an adopted child*. In the amulet translated by Wallis Budge, which only gives six names/conjurations of Lamaštu and lacks any reference to Irnina, *committed to the hands* stands alone. It can symbolise a state of trust and confidence, of compassion, empathy, sharing and surrender. If we look at Irnina's functions on a symbolic level, we learn that Lamaštu is trusted, committed and appointed to lust, love, conflict and combat. Love and conflict: two basic forces of pre-Socratic philosophy. *As Empedocles says, things are moved and brought to rest again in alternation; they are moved when love turns diversity into unity or when conflict turns unity into diversity; in between they are at rest* (Aristotle, *Physics*, VIII 1. 250b 26ff). For two fierce deities, like Irnina and Lamaštu, such a close relationship is certainly remarkable. Whether the invoker commits him- or herself into the hands of Lamaštu, or Lamaštu commits herself to the hands of the goddess of love and combat, or both commit themselves to each other, or the patient is given into the care of Lamaštu and Irnina remains open. Let's examine the variation ***Who is Compassionate***. Farber rendered the expression lēqât unnīni: *who takes pity*. We had lēqât before: take, take hold of, receive, accept, take care of. Unnīnu(m) is a supplication or petition; the word comes from utnēnu(m)$_1$: supplication, a prayer to a deity or regent. Lamaštu is attentive to prayers, listens to those who invoke her, and shows compassion. That's the reason why conjurers could negotiate with her. It does not mean that she gives you what you want. If you are lucky, you'll get what you need. Whether you like it or not.

Oath-Bound (or: *Conjured) by the Great Gods*.

The word tamû means: oath-bound, sworn, bound, but was also used for: conjured, bewitched. In the seventh name, the goddess is reminded that, in spite of her wild looks and wilder habits, she is bound to the divine harmony of the universe, and obliged to remain within the rights and limits of her profession. As a rebellious goddess, she tends to overact here and there. The conjurers did their best to remind her of her divine nature, and to invoke the gods of law and order, just in case she was trying to overstep her boundaries. Unlike many dangerous spirits and diseases, she was rarely 'exorcised' or 'banished'. The *Lamaštu Series* is full of passages where the goddess is reminded of the limits of her authority, and where the great gods, all of them her close relations, are invoked to keep her in line. In many cases, she is treated with politeness and her exit is much like the departure of an honoured guest, who is loaded with gifts and provisions and asked not to return too soon. The goddess has an unruly nature and isn't always happy with the way things are. Nevertheless, she does a job for the greater good. If you want to understand what it means for Lamaštu to be oath-bound, consider your own place and function in the world. In many magical and religious systems, aspirants are oath-bound to follow their path, to dedicate themselves, and all that they own, have been and will be, to the spiritual evolution of themselves and all fellow entities. The sun shines for all beings. Call it liberation, transcendence, realisation, enlightenment or love: when you do something for the world you are doing something for yourself.

Fly Away with the Bird/s of Heaven.

When gods leave a place, they fly away like birds. When Enlil invited foreign barbarians to destroy Ur,

[the blood] of men was spilled [...],

[The mai]dens were slaughtered in their chambers like (sheep),

[The da]ughters, remaining, were carried away by the enemy to [...],

They (the gods) turned into birds and flew away like doves.

(VAT 14514, Falkenstein, 1931:15, trans. JF).

The line implies leaving earth; for Lamaštu, kicked out of heaven for disrespectful behaviour, it means returning home. Usually, in rites to expel Lamaštu, the goddess is asked to return to the wilderness: mountains, mountain forests, deserts, steppes, swamps, rivers, canals; the open, world-surrounding sea and even to the abysmal Underworld. If Lamaštu is asked to fly away with the bird/s of heaven, does this line imply that she may resume her function as the celestial goddess she originally was? A different possibility appears in a bilingual exorcism of the plague and fate god Namtar, translated after the German of Schramm (2008: 44-45). Here, we read in Sumerian and Akkadian that

the bird of heaven, the dove of heaven, is the priest of conjuration, the seer of Enki/Ea.

"Cedar and Juniper of An/u" is his exclamation.

We might speculate how the mašmaššu (conjurer), acting the part of the *bird of heaven*, carried the baneful influence away. Tough luck that the text is paradoxical. In the very next lines we read that the bird of heaven, a dove, is to be released: when it flies (or is made to fly) towards sunrise and not to sunset, the patient may return to the merciful hands of his personal deity, and will (hopefully) recover.

The bird of heaven carries further connotations. It appears several times in the inscriptions commemorating Aššurbanipal's campaigns. One example: when the armies entered the desert, *they came to a place the beast of the desert was not in, and a bird of heaven had not fixed a nest.* (Smith, 1871:269. That's the limit of desolation. In another passage, Aššurbanipal left the corpses of his enemies in a pit: *The limbs cut off, I caused to be eaten by dogs, bears, vultures, X-birds, birds of heaven and fishes. By these things [which] were done I satisfied the hearts of the Great Gods, my Lords* (Smith, 1871: 166, amended). The line is evidently a metaphor (where do the fish come from?), listing animals that translate the souls of the dead to the otherworlds.

Remember the episode described earlier, when the cities Lagaš and Umma made a peace treaty, and released doves to carry their vows and promises to the gods. In a very similar fashion, a dove might have been released to carry Lamaštu away.

Here we have doves as heavenly travellers. But doves were also at home in the

Underworld. In Sumerian belief, the dead went into the deep. The stories show some variation: some walked, travelled on the river or rode into the otherworld on animals and in chariots. They retained their human shape and lived a life much like that of us surface dwellers, only a little drearier and dustier. Those who received regular sacrifices from their descendants had a good time. When Semitic beliefs became dominant, we find the dead wearing feathers. *The dead moan like doves* appears in the *Nergal & Ereškigal* additions (ANET 1969:509). Here is another one: Enkidu dreamed of his own death. He met a lion-headed man with lion claws and bird feet (imagine a male version of Lamaštu, called Samana) who hit, trampled, and killed him. Enkidu's soul left his body, turned into a dove, and flew into the Underworld (*Gilgameš* tablet VII). So the dead looked like birds. The idea may be related to the Egyptian notion that the Ba soul appears as a bird with a human head. But why would the Babylonian and Assyrian dead need feathers and wings? Was there a belief that they would, one day, fly out of the deep and into the human world (reincarnation?) or into the sky (transcendence?)?

When Lamaštu is asked to fly like a dove, she, like any competent trance traveller, might fly to heaven or into the depths of the underworlds. We will discuss the evidence for obsession and trance journeys in the commentary to LS II, 3. For now it should suffice to understand this 'name/conjuration' as a reference to transcendence and release from earth.

I, 9

Conjuration of DIM.ME/Lamaštu

(It was customary to state the title of a piece at its end. The line means 'this was a conjuration of DIM.ME/Lamaštu.')

Ritual Formula: You shall write (it) on a cylinder seal of clay and place (it) on the throat of the child.

(A šiptu (conjuration) was often followed by a kikittû, a **ritual procedure**, or a set of practical instructions. It was not obligatory, as many of the standard conjurations for popular gods were followed with standard libations and offerings. Our text is more detailed. Each conjuration is followed by a kikittû. Here, the practical instruction is to inscribe a **seal stone**, or a cylinder seal, (Kišib in Sumerian, Kunukku in Akkadian). Our version is made from clay but there were also seals made of semi-precious stones. Some people may have worn their lovingly made Lamaštu amulets for years. Let's think about seal stones. Sumerian craftsmen began carving them around 3500 BCE. They were used to mark property: you can roll such a seal across a piece of clay sealing a basket, package or vessel. After writing developed, 3500-3200 BCE, they became essential to mark documents, contracts and letters. During the Sumerian period, their use was mostly confined to important people and administrators. But when the Sumerian period ended around 2000 BCE, the temples lost much of their influence and ordinary people began to acquire property and do business. Their seal stones represented personal responsibility, social status, the freedom to do business and the obligation of the private individual to society. Many seal stones were graced with images of deities, and were worn as talismans. Last, think about a seal stone with the seven names of Lamaštu. When the goddess comes prowling, she reads the inscription, realises that the ailing baby praises her true nature, smiles, takes the hint and goes away.)

I, 11

Šiptu:

DIM.ME/Lamaštu,

Daughter of Anu, Named With a Name by the Great Gods,

Dingir Innin (=*Divine Victorious Mistress*),

Ruler of the Black-Headed (People) (=*the Mesopotamians*);

(This is **conjuration #2**, it is pronounced over the neck. Lines I, 11-13 are in Sumerian. They are the start of an ancient formula which you will read under LS II 133. **Neck** and **throat** are related to the act of speaking, and in Middle Eastern and Indian religion, speaking comes very close to making. The expression *to touch the neck* means literally *to make a treaty* (Postgate 2002:257). Of course there was more to making treaties than a gesture. Contracts required a written form in several copies, signed and sealed by numerous witnesses, plus the names of a range of deities who were to curse the person daring to break the contract. In the Amorite period in Mari, the expression for *to touch the throat* was *to kill asses*, i.e. to make a donkey sacrifice to seal the contract. How are donkeys related to treaty making? Given that donkeys and wild asses are among Lamaštu's favourite animals, this might be worth contemplating. In this conjuration, the **naming** of the goddess is associated with the throat of the patient. Could it be that the goddess is reminded of her divine task to afflict only persons when this accords with the divine command?

Naming had a special meaning. It meant that a person or deity (or for that matter, a temple, place or sacred object) acquired a purpose, a function in life, a fate and office. Here are some examples from SAHG 1953: page 59: Enlil names Ninurta; 61: Ninlil names Nusku; 72: Bau/Baba names a king; 101: Enlil names King Išmedagan; 112: Anu and Enlil name Numušda; 236: Ištar names a waif. Several kings boasted of having been named by a deity. Eanatum was named by Inanna, Lugalzagesi was named by sun-god Utu. But a name was not only granted, it had to be established and maintained, like a grandiose reputation. Lamaštu was named, according to various texts, by Enki/Ea, the lord of water, irrigation, science, music and magic, or by the entire assembly of the high gods. It gives her, in spite of her bad attitude, misbehaviour and destructive offices, the highest authority of the divine, and sanctions her deeds, no matter how unpleasant they may seem, as necessitated by the divine order. By slaying selected infants and elders, the goddess prevents overpopulation and the total annihilation of mankind. The **black-headed people** are the Mesopotamians. The metaphor was frequently used for the entire population, though omen literature mentions that a few people had other hair colours. It may be contact or coincidence, but we find the same metaphor in early Chinese literature.)

I, 13

Be conjured by the Life of Heaven (An), be conjured by the Life of Earth (Ki)!

I have given you (**or:** made you seize) a black dog

as a demonic (= gallû) fate (**or:** servant, slave),

(The first line is a **zi-pad** (*to conjure by*) formula that appears frequently in Sumerian conjurations. Sumerian zi means: life, breath, throat and self; the equivalent is the Akkadian napištu(m). It implies that Heaven and Earth, both of them major deities, are conjured by their lives, breath and throats. Please consider this deeply. Heaven and Earth are alive and they breathe. Can you breathe with them? It's a great meditation.

The next line is difficult. Early translators claimed that Lamaštu receives, or is made to take, a black dog as a servant or slave. Unlike them, Farber (in TUAT vol.2, 1988, trans. JF) has *I have made you take a black dog as your demonic (gallû) reincarnation.*

More than twenty years later, Farber (2014) translates the black dog as *Lamaštu's Nemesis*. We are facing at least four options. The dog could be her servant or slave, her reincarnation, or her fate. The trouble starts with the similarity of the Sumerian: GAL_5LA; Akkadian: gallû, meaning a lethal spirit, and the Akkadian word qallu, meaning a servant, an unimportant person or a slave. To understand this passage we should also remember the **gugallû**, or **gallû**, who started out as canal inspectors. They were the first known police force on this planet and extremely unpopular. In everyday language, the word gallû became an insult. Aššurbanipal derided several of his enemies by that name: *...Tugdammê, the king of the Mandai hordes, (is) the offspring of Tiāmat and the image of a gallû.* Or his remark regarding a king of Elam: *Afterwards, Teumman, the image of a gallû, sat on the throne of Urtaku* (Haas, 1986:115, trans. JF). *'Gallû face!'* was a common insult. The term gallû came to be used for lethal spirits. A Sumerian myth relates that the god Dumuzi was hounded to death by a bunch of gallûs, who were officers of Ereškigal, and henchmen of the Underworld. These gallû knew no food nor drink, received no flour or water offerings, ate neither fish, onions nor garlic, accepted no gifts, gave no gifts and did not kiss children (Jacobsen, 1987:36). Elsewhere they are described as sexless shapeshifters and bearers of disease and doom. In two tablets published by Schramm (2008) an entire gang of gallûs appear as prototypes of the Evil Seven: they are children of the same mother, unknown in heaven and earth, blood drinkers and devastating storm winds. They gnash their teeth, drool, know no dignity; they destroy families, gardens, houses, domestic animals and act as throne bearers of Ereškigal. One of their special offices was infanticide. The gallû were occasionally employed by the gods: Šamaš, Lord of Justice, could station an evil gallû above an evildoer (Dalley, 2008:201). We encounter an echo of the Mesopotamian gallû in Greek lore: Sappho called it Gello. Finally, we encounter Gello or Gyllo among the names of Lilith in Greek and Balkan folklore. In Bulgakov's magnificent *Master and Margarita,* Lilith appears as Gella.

This leads us to the next question: what is the black dog in relation to Lamaštu?

Black dogs were often, but not always, bad signs. When you think of Mesopotamian dogs, make them huge and savage. There were several types, and they were bred for size. The typical form was later called the Molossian hound, and it is this large and heavy type that appears most frequently in art. These dogs had the strength of the Anzu (storm-bird) and the joints of a lion. In temple documents of the Ur III period, the daily food ration for each dog was two litres of barley flour. (Heimpel in RlA *'Hund'*). The omen catalogues mention several dog-related incidents. *When the Great Dog* (the star of Ninurta) *is dark, the heart of the people will not be joyous. When a black dog enters a temple, the temple foundation will not be secure.* (Ungnad, 1926: 320, 324) A white dog, by contrast, ensured the safety of the temple's foundation. Saggs (1966:324) adds that a white dog urinating on a man means that hard times will seize the man. It is much preferable when a red dog does so, as this will mean happiness. A dog standing in your way means an obstacle. Howling dogs in the street indicate that the city will fall through hunger. And if a woman gives birth to a dog, the master of the house will die and the house will be destroyed. (Ungnad 1926:324, 327). But that shouldn't prejudice us against dogs; there is plenty more on pigs, oxen, horses, donkeys, gazelles, monkeys, cats, lions, wolves, falcons, foxes, snakes, spiders, mongooses, ants and other animals. Most of it is bad news. Does this make dogs or black dogs unclean or evil animals? I doubt it. The Sumerian composition *Dumuzi's Dream* tells us that the dogs of that popular deity were black, *noble and true,* and guarded his flocks. Further on you will read of magical dog figurines that protected the household from dangerous influences. Some of them were magically activated by the hair of a black dog on their brows.

So what happens between Lamaštu and the black dog? The experts disagree, and so may you. Myhrman and Köcher translated *give her a black dog.* Contemporary translators like Scurlock, 1991: 157 in Greenwood 2012 and Wiggermann in RIA *'Pazuzu'* read: *marry her to a black dog.* Their choice, founded on a ritual text edited by Schwemer (1998), is based on the idea that some dangerous spirits could be married off. Farber 2014 dismisses this option. In his opinion, the Lamaštu ritual is significantly different from the type discussed by Schwemer. Personally I find the option of a dog marriage somewhat unlikely. However, we have to consider all possibilities.

Remember that Lamaštu is one of the few unmarried deities. It isn't exactly her choice: as several Old Babylonian spells show, she is irresistibly attracted to young lovers and mating animals and keeps circling around them. In fact, sexual lust, represented by fire, is one of her domains. As she is unattached to anyone, and is not known to have lovers (divine or human), the scribes may have assumed that she is very much frustrated. Pigs and dogs, the very animals which Lamaštu craves to adopt, were admired for their sexual vigour. One of the bizarre elements in Mesopotamian love spells is that the metaphor 'dog' can refer to a penis. The spells translated by Foster (1995:334, 335, 336, 338, 340, 341, 347, 348; see also Leick, 2003:199, 200, 206, 243, 244 for alternative translations), include lines like:

dog is crouching, pig is crouching,
You too keep crouching on my thighs

Let your heart rejoice, Let your spirit be happy,
I will swell large as a dog!
In your heart lies a dog, lurks a pig,
You lie down with me and I'll pluck your bristle,
Take what you have in your hand and put it into my hand.

Cuddle me like a puppy, m[ount] me like a dog
My vagina is a bitch's vagina, his penis is a dog penis.
As a bitch's vagina holds tight a dog penis,
So may my vagina hold tight his penis!
May your penis grow as long as a war-club!
I am sitting in a net of seduction,
May I not miss my prey!

Arousal is coming upon me like a wild bull,
It keeps springing at me like a dog,
Like a lion it is fierce in coming,
Like a wolf it is full of fury...

Into your vulva, where you put your trust,
I'll bring in a dog and fasten the door,
Into the vulva, where you put your trust,
As if it were (?) a precious jewel in front of you.

Several of Lamaštu's favourite animals appear in these spells. If she is married to a dog, does it mean she will find a penis to satisfy her?

Or should we prefer the reading from Farber's TUAT translation that asks the goddess to reincarnate in dog shape? The black dog could be a vehicle to carry her away. Maybe the goddess was transferred into a dog and chased off. It works along the same lines as the scapegoat. Or maybe the exorcist made a dog effigy out of clay. It's a simple transference spell. All it needs is strong identification, a carrier and a lot of purification afterwards. In other sections of the *Lamaštu Series*, the goddess is carried away by the bird of heaven or descends into the abysmal underworld with fishes. None of this suits Farber's translation of 2014, suggesting that she takes a black dog as her nemesis. What exactly is this supposed to mean? Is a gallû (=policeman) supposed to arrest her?

I, 15

I have poured spring water for you. Depart, go away, remove yourself [and go away] out of the body of this infant, the son of his god!

(Pure **water** was one of the most sacred substances in ancient Mesopotamia. Spring water came directly from the deep, from the abysmal sweet water Underworld. It was fortified with spells and occasionally with plants. In some rituals, a small chaplet of special beads was immersed to make the water sacred. Water libations were among the most important sacrifices. The major offering to the dead was water, poured into a tube leading to the underworld, so that the deceased would not suffer from thirst. Water was also used prominently in healing magic and purification rites, to wash evil influences away.

When this passage was composed, people were equipped with one or several **personal deities**. As far as can be known, the early Sumerian gods seemed to be not very concerned about individuals. Mankind was created to serve the gods, to nourish them and to work for them. A person possibly belonged, to a greater or lesser extent, to the local deities and/or the state. Late in the third millennium BCE, the documentation improved. Some people (we only know about the upper class) believed that they had a direct link to a deity, a divine couple, or divine family who watched over them. Personal deities are more than gods charged to look after you. As Jacobsen demonstrated, personal gods are also the manifest expression of personal ambition, luck and success. When a person was good at something, it was thanks to one or several deities acting through her or him.

As people say: "Man is the shadow of a god, and a slave is a shadow of a man"; but the king is the reflecting copper (=mirror*) of a god* (proverb from a letter to Asarḫaddon, in Lambert, 1960:282). Personal deities do not fall from heaven ready-made. They must be won. You have to do something special to get close to your personal gods, and even more to ensure their successful activity. A Sumerian/Old Babylonian text quoted by Steinert (2012:397, trans. JF) describes the sad life of a person lacking a personal deity. That person does not gain much (food); he does not even gain a little (food). He catches no fish in the river; he catches no gazelle in the field. In important matters he has no success. When he runs, he does not reach his goal.

But when his god is well intentioned towards him

All that he names (desires)

Will be available to him.

It shows that it is essential to have at least one personal god and really good relations with her or him. This did not apply to all people. A Sumerian proverb quoted by Steinert states:

A man who has no god-

For a mighty person it is no loss.

The effects of personal deities are miraculous. Though they are not omnipotent, they certainly make life much better. And if you have trouble with some other deity, the personal deities can step in and mediate.

Who has his god, his sins are dispelled. Who does not have his god, his sins are numerous. (SAHG, 1953:254, trans. JF). The personal deities are not an optional extra, they actually *make* a person.

But how did people think about their relation to these deities? Some took the easy way and installed them in the position of parent figures, i.e. they called themselves the children of their deities. Others considered their deities as partners, spouses or siblings. If your deities are close relations, does that turn you into a deity yourself? The answer is difficult. Our early data comes almost exclusively from kings and queens, many of whom also held priestly ranks. Did the early Mesopotamians believe in divine kingship? What are the implications of deified kings and queens? Mesopotamian kingship developed from local strong men (lugal) and lords/administrators (en) supported by an assembly. As villages grew into towns and cities, the authority of their leaders grew. They became increasingly remote from the population, and began to acquire a semi-divine status. Nevertheless, they were still recognised as mortals, subject to error, failure, disease and death. In Mesopotamian thought, the gods ranked higher than men. To govern, a king needed divine blessing and the support of the aristocracy. This is in strong contrast to ancient Egypt, where the very first kings went to extreme lengths to develop a personality cult and to rank themselves on a level as high or higher than the gods. The Mesopotamians never forgot the semi-democratic assembly of the good old days. In their myths, some major gods act as kings, but the assembly still meets. To be sure, there were efforts to destroy this arrangement. The prime example is the *Enûma Eliš*, where we can watch Marduk coerce and bribe the gods to grant all rights and powers to him. So we could generalise that though the kings went to some lengths to appear divine, they never made such an overwhelmingly horrible job of it as the Egyptians did. Everybody knew that the kings fulfilled a divine office, and acted on behalf of the gods, but politics were simply too unruly to make a permanent religion out of the royal house. Also, when a king made a mess or was unlucky, his divinity became doubtful. For good reason, Mesopotamian myth and history are full of rebellion and usurpation. Indeed, to create mankind out of clay, an essential element was the blood of a rebellious god. We all have it in our veins.

Let's have some examples. Allegedly, personal deities go back to earliest prehistory, and to rulers who lived for amazingly long periods. King Meskiaggašer was the son of sun-god Utu and ruled 324 years. Enmerkar, son of Utu and brother of Inanna ruled 420 years. Later, regencies and lifetimes became shorter, and historians sobered up. Around maybe 2370 BCE, Urzababa was a brother of Inanna. Lugalzagesi (c.2350 BCE) was born from the womb of Nidaba/Nisaba, suckled by Ninḫursag and raised by Ningirima. Sargon of Agade, who followed Urzababa, killed Lugalzagesi and created the Akkadian Empire, thought that he was related to Ilaba. Like his rivals, he believed his family was protected by Inanna/Ištar, and did much to promote her cult. His daughter Enḫeduanna was married to the moon god Sîn and had intimate ties to Inanna/Ištar and Ningirsu. In spite of their close relation to these gods, neither Sargon nor Enḫeduanna claimed to be a deity. That fashion began with Sargon's grandson Naramsîn. Gudea of Lagaš (c.2160 BCE) called the goddesses Gatumdug, Ninsun, Bau/Baba and Nanše his mothers, and his personal deity was Ningišzida. In spite of his illustrious family members, he did not claim to be a deity himself. Utuḫegal (c.2120 BCE) called Dumuzi and Gilgameš his protectors while the kings of Ur III, many of whom called themselves gods, made a family cult of the deified Gilgameš and his father Lugalbanda. When the Amorites took over, they continued the fashion. Lipitištar of Isin (c.1934 BCE) called himself a son of Enlil, accepted by Enlil and loved by Ninlil. A remarkable example comes from Ḫammurapi, the famous king and law-giver (1792-1750 BCE). During his reign Marduk, a city god of Babylon, was still a minor deity. The king acknowledged his presence, after paying his respect to the elder gods. In matters of state, Ḫammurapi turned to Anu and Enlil. His personal deities, however, were the sun god Utu/Šamaš and his wife Aya, the goddess of dawn. Both appear in legal documents as major deities of law and justice, a topic that was extremely important to the king. It shows that the king was not automatically supposed to venerate the gods of his major city or state as personal deities.

Though several kings believed themselves to be divine, they also had personal deities. Indeed, the gods themselves had personal deities. An early Sumerian example appears in *Dumuzi's Wedding* (Jacobsen 1987:19-23). We find a similar idea in Indian religion: inferior gods, and deities who are incarnate as human beings, may take refuge in personal, higher-ranking deities. In early Mesopotamia, some upper-class en (*lords, kings, successful managers*) and entu(m) priestesses were occasionally married to deities, but they also had personal deities and intimate relations with others. The word entu(m) means *woman who is a deity*, but this did not stop her from praying to personal deities.

Were there general rules on the relationship to personal deities? Or were there loads of local traditions, most of them long forgotten? How far such customs affected the general population is hard to explore. That personal deities were widely popular is certain, but their nature, selection and worship remain enigmatic. The experts disagree on the matter (RlA Sallaberger *'Pantheon'* and Streck *'Persönliche Frömmigkeit'*, discussing the conflicting opinions of Jacobsen, Westenholz, Albertz, Mayer, Stol, Klein, Groneberg, Charpin, Bottéro, Cooper, Di Vito, Edzard, Livingstone, Nakata, Lambert and Van der Toorn).

The Mesopotamians loved theomorphic names. Here are a few examples: Nabigula (*Named by Gula*), Waradgula (*Servant of Gula*), Awilbau ((*free*) *Man of Bau*), Pilaḫištar (*Fear Ištar*), Šuištar (*The (Servant) of Ištar*), Qurdiištar (*Great Deed of Ištar*), Ištarillassu (*Ištar is his Family*), Āmurištar (*I have seen Ištar*), Ištarnādā (*Praise Ištar*), Inninšumīuṣur (*Victorious Goddess, Protect my Name*), Enlildamiq (*Enlil is Good*),

Enlilmuballiṭ (*Enlil Keeps Alive*), Aššurlamassi (*Aššur Is My Protective Deity*), Aššurnaṣirapli (= Aššurnasirpal, *Aššur guards the son*), Aššuraḫuiddina (= Asarḫaddon, *Aššur has Given Me a Brother*), Naramsîn (*Beloved of Sîn*), Sînabūšu (*Sîn is his Father*), Mardukkašid (*Marduk Overwhelms*), Mardukšākinšumi (*Marduk has Decided my Name*), Nabûšumiiškun (*Nabû Has Decided My Name*), Nabûkudurrīuṣur (*Nabû, guard my heirs*), Ninurtaašarēd (*Ninurta is the Most Noble*), Amurrumbānī (*Amurru Is My Creator*), Šamašhāzer (*Šamaš is Helper*), Nūršamaš (*Light of Šamaš*), Ennumaya (*Behold! There Is Aya!)*, Iškundagan (*Dagan has Installed*), Ibbininšubur (*Ninšubur Has Named*) and so on. We don't know how such names were selected. Were they personally important or inherited? Were they chosen by parents or by the persons who wore them? Do they name the personal deities of their wearer, or maybe the favourite deities of whoever selected them? Or are they simply lucky names with no relevance to personal faith? Such questions cannot be resolved presently. We have to assume that for many people, city gods, family gods and gods of the professions did the job. It has been proposed that ordinary citizens had to make do with the names of minor deities. However, many simple people were named after popular city and state gods, who were anything but minor. Sad to say, the evidence is tantalisingly incomplete. In most prayers and ritual instructions, the personal god/s are not even named. They were addressed in Akkadian as ilu(m): god; iltu(m): goddess; ištaru: goddess. An ilu(m) išum is a god who owns and observes you (išum= to own, possess, witness) and an ilu(m) rēši is a favourite or original god (rēšu(m)= head, top, best, beginning). It tells us nothing about their names, natures or how a given person related to them. But no matter how exactly the system worked in each place and time, it turned out to be a winner. According to Jacobsen (1976:152) the Hittites picked the idea of personal gods up around 1350 BCE and the Egyptians around 1230 BCE. Still later it became popular in India, where it is alive to this day (see, *Kūrma Purāṇa* 1, 22, 40-47). A similar idea was assimilated in North Indian and Himalayan Buddhism, where the yi dam is a tutelary deity, experienced as a sacred personality and as an illusory projection of the mind. Personal deities also appear in other cultures: just consider how Odysseus is guided and protected by Athena. He has a closer and friendlier relationship to his favourite goddess than to anybody else. The same goes for Aeneas and Venus. Look into the *Poetic Edda*, and read how young Ottar is related to the goddess Freya (*Hyndluljód*). Or try the *Grímnismál* and meet the favourites of Oðin and Frigg. Or explore ancient China: some wu ('shamans') were married to the deities of rivers and mountains. Others approached their deities much like lovers do, and were abjectly sad when their celestial partner departed after the ritual (see the *Nine Songs* in the *Chuci*). Famous poets like Qu Yuan attempted to marry mythical, semi-divine women; others wedded a daughter of Xiwangmu and devoted themselves to 'channel' the poems and prophecies of their divine spouses. Marriages to spirits and deities were a common feature of Eurasian shamanism. Or consider the Haitian Voodoo cult: each devotee has a personal deity, a maît/tête (*Master of the Head*) who guides her or him through life (Deren, 1983). Some worshippers get so close to their gods that it's hard to tell whether they are obsessed; over the years, they simply merge into each other.

How the common Babylonians and Assyrians thought about their personal deities is not certain. We can be sure, however, that personal deities were not automatically reliable, protective or acting in your interest. You didn't get a deity for free, nor could you sit back and wait for the deity to make life easier for you. When a person misbehaved, lazed, showed no commitment, lacked virtue, refused to learn, broke oaths, ignored social obligations or sinned, a deity might just leave its protégée. A lot of spells are devoted to the tricky task of regaining contact with personal deities. Often, a major deity was invoked to mediate, and recall the personal deities to a patient. It's a useful lesson: to retain your deities, i.e.

your personal nature, success, luck and freedom from sin, wholehearted effort and dedication are essential. A Middle Assyrian tablet gives the proverb:

When you exert yourself, your god is yours. When you do not exert yourself, your god is not yours (Lambert, 1960:230). Apart from doing your best in all things, regular worship is a must. A line from the *Nanše Hymn* (Jacobsen, 1987:140) dismisses a mother quarrelling with her child: *Still this human being would not through prayers obtain a personal god.* Another text says what your gods expect from you:

Every day worship your god.

Sacrifice and benediction are the proper accompaniment of incense.

Present your free-will offering to your god,

for this is proper toward the gods.

Prayer, supplication and prostration

offer him daily and (you will get) your reward.

Then you will have full communion with your god.

(*Precepts and Admonitions,* c.1500 BCE. Lambert, 1960:105).

Note that the conjurers made a point to name the personal deity or deities of the patient. You could think of it as a naming but also as a conjuration: if the patient has lost contact with the personal deities, the ritual is meant to recall them. For good reason: the person without a deity can easily become Lamaštu's victim. She isn't the only danger. Any passing spirit, disease, obsession, derangement or madness can come over a godless person like a cloak and drag her or him to sin, disease, perversion, misery and doom. It happens all the time.)

I, 17

I conjure you by Anu and Antu(m),

(Sumerian **An** and Akkadian **Anu, Anu(m)** means: the Sky. An/Anu is the major god of early Mesopotamian religion, the *Bull of Heaven* who fertilises the universe and creates numerous friendly and/or dangerous deities and spirits. His fertile seed spawns mankind and all living beings. One of his major cult places was the temple E-anna (*House of Heaven*) which he shared with Inanna/Ištar in Uruk. An/Anu was a major god of Sumerian prehistory. By the middle of the third millennium he and his wife Antu(m) retired and their son Enlil became the king of the gods. The importance of Anu continued and his name appears in documents of the Old Babylonian period, but he became a passive figure who resided in the background while younger gods were pursuing their careers. The textual sources provide very little detail about the celestial couple. Maybe it happened on purpose. They were simply too ancient, remote and abstract to be personified properly. **Antu/Antu(m)/Anunītu(m)** is An/Anu's wife and the feminine expression of the power and majesty of the sky. The constellation E Pisces extending to Andromeda belonged to her. As she is close to Pisces, she may have had a fishtail (Weidner, RlA '*Fixsterne*') She had several cult centres; in Sippar her name was Anunītu(m). You may think of An/Anu and Antu(m) as a celestial couple, or as the male and female manifestation of heaven.

Astronomy and astrology were invented in Mesopotamia. The star-gazers spent millennia ordering the sky into constellations and made careful records of celestial phenomena. They must have had ideas about the configuration of the cosmos, but so far, the textual evidence leaves many questions open. How **heaven** was imagined is a difficult question. For the Sumerians, heaven and/or the sky (they made no difference between these concepts) were simply the realm of the gods. Anything that happened 'up there', i.e. weather, clouds, rainbows, eclipses, lunar changes, planets, meteorites, comets, stars, novas and so on was a manifestation of divine will. Several scholars have proposed that the Mesopotamians studied the stars for millennia, but were not interested in the principles behind them. Allegedly, they were focussed on empirical study and did not try to formulate their results in theories. I would argue that you cannot spend decades or centuries recording the position of planets without being aware that some things 'up there' were amazingly regular. People do like to explain things. Just read Anaximander (611-546 BCE), celebrated as the father of scientific thought, who declared that earth is shaped like a cylinder. But however the Mesopotamian star-gazers thought about their favourite subject, we lack a general description of the sky. A few Babylonian texts hint at the subject, and only a text of the seventh century BCE gives vague details. Apparently heaven consists of three spheres. When we look outwards into space, we only see the first sphere of heaven, called (Akk.) qirib šame: *The Inside of Heaven.* The word šame (*heaven*) was occasionally interpreted as ša mê (*of water*), which may have encouraged the idea that the world is encompassed on all sides by water. It helped to explain rain (Lambert in *RlA 'Himmel'*). The lowest sphere is made of jasper and adorned by the stars, which are painted, inlaid or drawn on it. The stars are the *Writing of Heaven.* Above them is the realm of the gods (Igigi), it is made of amethyst (saggilmut/sangilmud) and still further up, we encounter a heaven made of unidentified luludānītu stone, the realm of An/Anu and the primal deities. That's one description. Another, rather late, cosmology peoples upper heaven with 300 Igigi gods, middle heaven being Marduk's realm and lower heaven containing the stars. Earth was attached to heaven with bolts and next to them were gates at the išid šame (*Foundation of Heaven*). These gates are used by sun god Šamaš as he ascends and descends on his daily journey across the sky. Apparently heaven was attached to earth by a rope or by Marduk's net, while *Nergal and Ereškigal* relates that there is a staircase leading from heaven to the underworlds.

The names of many constellations appear in Sumerian texts of the third millennium, but the early second millennium tablets have surprisingly little information on the topic. However, they confirm that astronomical observations were carefully made, year in and year out, as anything happening in the sky was sure to affect mankind. Around the middle of the second millennium, astronomical study became more popular and the sky was divided into three ways. The central range, equalling roughly 33° to both sides of the heavenly equator, is the ***Way of Anu***. South of Anu's Way is Enki's Way and north of it Enlil's Way. According to the first tablet of the series *Apin*, Anu's Way passes through the square of Pegasus; Pisces W.; Pisces E.; Aries; Pleiades; Taurus; Hyades; Orion; ε and ϒ Geminorum; Lepus (?); Sirius: Canis major; Hydra; Corvus; Virgo; Libra; Aqula (?); α Aquilae; Antinous; it also includes Venus; Mars; Saturn and Mercury. Another list gives twelve stars or constellations for Anu, while a third list (*Astrolab* B, KAV 218, B II) only agrees with three items of the other lists (Venus; Corvus; Libra) but adds nine new constellations, including Scorpio, Leo and Perseus, which are well outside of Anu's traditional range. This list, for all its charm, has very little relation to the sky. The constellation Ursa minor was known as *Anu's Wagon.* In the third millennium BCE it was pretty much celestial north, in the centre of the sky.)

I conjure you by Enlil and Ninlil,

(Sumerian **Enlil** (Akkadian **Ellil, Bēl =Lord**) means *Lord Wind*; as Sumerian 'lil' can mean wind, breath, vitality he is in charge of all of them. In the Nippur cosmology, in the beginning, An (Heaven) and Ki (Earth) were in close embrace. It was great, divine and wonderful but far too tight for further development. Enlil created the inhabitable world. He rose like a mountain between his parents, chopped with his freshly invented pickaxe, which divided them, and created a world consisting of three layers. In this model, An/Anu's wife is not Antu(m) but goddess earth: Ki (Sumerian) and Uraš (Akkadian). Enlil *governs the wide horizon* and *fixes fates.* His radiance is so intense that the other gods avert their faces. In literary texts, Enlil is an enigmatic god who is praised as a giver of abundance, wealth, fertility, royal authority and divine law. However, he is also famous for his fits of total destructivity. When barbarians invaded Mesopotamia and destroyed the cities, the poets sang that they acted under Enlil's orders. The Evil Seven and other horrible beings were known to reside in Enlil's temple in Nippur, awaiting their master's command to wreak havoc and bring pestilence. Enlil made his career move thanks to the Early Dynastic king Enmebaragesi, who decided that the city Nippur and the cult of Enlil and Ninlil were perfectly suited to centralise kingship and religion between Sumer and Akkad. Thanks to this decision, the priesthood of Enlil immediately supported the king and declared that in future, all kings should receive their office from their hands. It turned the city Nippur into a holy place, the *navel* of central and southern Mesopotamia. We also encounter the name Enlil as a title meaning regent: kings and other gods were praised as the Enlil of a city or state. A lot of deities appear as his children, among them Enki, Iškur/Adad, Nanna/Suen/Sîn, Ningirsu, Papulegarra, Baraulegarra, Nusku, Utu/Šamaš, Nergal, Uraš, Ninazu, Enbilulu and Inanna/Ištar. It shows how many cults tried to be in close relationship to the king of the gods. The cult of Enlil was represented in seven cities, corresponding to seven constellations. The first city is unknown, its constellation is Triangulum. The second is Nippur (Perseus), the third Enamtila (Ursa major), the fourth Ḫursagkalama (α Trianguli), the fifth Aratta in hostile Iran (Taurus), the sixth Kullaba (Lepus?) and the seventh Babylon (α Bootis). Enlil's wife is usually **Ninlil**, her name means *Lady Wind/Breath/Atmosphere/Vitality* and she is a personification of the same phenomenon in feminine form. However, distinct traditions wed him with Ninḫursag, who also appears as his sister, and with a little-known goddess called Mulliltu or Mullissu. Before her marriage with Enlil, Ninlil was called Sud, a popular deity of the ancient city Fāra. She may have started as a grain or vegetation goddess. Sud is the daughter of Ḫaia and Nidaba/Nisaba aka Ninšebargunu/ Nunbaršeguna. Enlil fell in love with her when he saw her bathing in a canal. Their courtship was fast and wild and has been interpreted as passionate lovemaking or rape, depending on the imagination of various disagreeing translators. After their first meeting Enlil was banished from heaven because of his improper behaviour, descended temporarily into the underworld, followed by Ninlil. On the way, they met several times. Enlil assumed a different shape each time. They had more intercourse, creating several underworld deities. Another myth claims that Ninlil looked so alluring, as she was standing in the street, that Enlil approached her, made improper advances, was duly reprimanded and immediately asked her parents for the hand of their daughter. Ninlil received the title Nindukuga (*Lady of the Sacred Mound*); her earliest temple may have been the Tummal, built by King Aka, son of King Enmebaragesi, around 2600 BCE. According to Enḫeduanna, Ninlil's temple reaches all the way down into the Abzu. Celestially, Ninlil is often represented by Ursa major, which is her waggon. She is not a passive wife but the major advisor of her husband. She is praised as the *Queen of Heaven and Earth* and as the *Queen of all Lands*. She is the *Glowing Bride*, her *word is the heart of juniper perfume* and she is famed for her *radiant looks* (Jacobsen, 1987:110))

I, 19

Var.1.: ***I conjure you by Marduk and Anunitu(m),***

Var.2.: ***I conjure you by Marduk and Zarpānītu(m),***

(**Asarluḫi/Asalluḫi** and **Marduk** are usually sons of Enki/Ea. They started out as distinct gods; Asarluḫi being a Sumerian god of storm and rain, a magician and healer, whose major cult place was Kuara. He is *the wild bison of the prince (Enki/Ea)*, the *Son of Abzu*, a god of magic and healing who banishes evil beings and influences, usually after asking his dad for expert advice. Several interesting changes can be observed. In the earliest surviving Sumerian spells (from Fāra and Ebla, dating around 2700 BCE) the conjurers invoked Enlil, Enki and Ningirima to banish diseases and evil entities. All three deities are masters of magic and purification. In this early period, Enki is an ambiguous character: he heals, but he can also bring diseases. Enlil banishes evils.

When Enlil became king of the gods, his earlier function as a healer was forgotten. By the Old Babylonian period he sends the Evil Seven, who live in his temple in Nippur, to plague mankind. Simultaneously, we cease to hear of Enki as a bringer of disease: instead, he personally comes to banish it. In the next phase, we encounter the familiar situation where Enki acts as a consultant. He sends his son Asarluḫi as his messenger or representative. Still later, Asarluḫi sees some evil, goes to his dad for advice and gets the job done. **Marduk** is a much younger deity. His name might derive from Sumerian Amar-Utu *Bull-calf of the Sun*. Or from Akkadian: *Mar-(D)une: Son of the Sun-god*. Or from Mar-Duku: *Son of Duku*, the latter being the primal mound of the beginning. All of these are very speculative (Groneberg, 2004:87). His major symbols are a spade and a horned dragon, an animal that represents his mastery of magic. His major temple was the Esagila (*High House, House with a High Roof*), measuring roughly 500m square, which contained smaller temples and shrines for related deities and was venerated as the connection between heaven and earth in Babylon. Marduk became the major city god of Babylon between 1700 and 1600 BCE (he is absent in third millennium BCE inscriptions), and replaced Enlil/Ellil as the most important deity of southern Mesopotamia late in the second millennium BCE. Asarluḫi and Marduk fused at some point, and in the process Marduk gained the ability to work magic and perform healings. Subsequently, conjurations in Sumerian language use the name Asarluḫi while their Babylonian counterparts use Marduk. His Babylonian priests did their best to turn Marduk into a king of the gods. Around 1300 BCE they composed the remarkable *Enûma Eliš*, the so-called *Babylonian Tale of Creation*, and to make it more impressive they used the extremely archaic language of the early Old Babylonian period. It fooled modern scholars for many years. Marduk assimilated many functions of the fierce storm and weather god Ninurta and a wide range of other deities.

Anunitu(m) is a name of the goddess Antu(m). She was especially popular in the city Sippar. The Babylonians worshipped her as a goddess of childbirth. A variant version of this line (TUAT, 2,2: 259-260) names Marduk's wife **Zarpānītu(m)** instead of Anunitu(m). This makes more sense, as Antu(m) was already conjured in LS I, 17. Zarpānītu(m) might derive from Zērbānītum: *Creatrix of Seed*. God-list *Enlil/Bēlet-ilî* identifies her with all seven goddesses of Babylon, with Bēlet-ilî (*Mother of the Gods*) and with the most prominent mother-goddess of Babylon, Eru/Erua, a name that might be derived from *erû*: to be pregnant. But she was also identified with Ištar, who is rarely attracted to pregnancy and birth. Her constellations are Coma berenices and Canes venatici. An oath formula, (based on Haas 1986: 49 after Ebeling, 1953:365, trans. JF) goes: *By the life of Zarpānītu(m), Maiden of the Apsû, who is clothed in voluptuousness and radiant splendour, the great first wife of Apsû, who brings all ritual actions to perfection, the exalted Lady of the Esagila, the great protective spirit of Heaven and Earth, the Queen of the Anunnaki, you shall swear...*)

I conjure you by the Great Gods of Heaven and Earth

(that) you may not return [to] this house

I, 21

and this infant!

Conjuration to expel painful fever-heat and Lamaštu.

(Again, the bottom line of the conjuration is actually its title.)

I, 23

Ritual Formula: you shall make [a figurine of] Lamaštu like a captive,

(This ritual is repeated, slightly transformed, in LS III, 110-118. **Figurines** appear prominently in religion, witchcraft and exorcism. In third millennium worship, wealthy people had craftsmen make figurines of them. They were highly varied, and may have shown a faint personal resemblance. Most remarkable are their huge dark eyes. The style was delightfully impressionistic. These figurines were set up in temple shrines, so that the representation of the worshipper was always present before the deity. Consequently, the worshipper was ceaselessly worshipping, no matter what he or she was really doing. It started a fashion. Though later generations did not set up such figurines, the idea remained that an effigy can represent a real person, deity, animal or thing. In this verse, the effigy represents Lamaštu. To make it work, it had to be identified with the goddess. Effigies were essential for sorcery. Either a figurine of the victim was made and personalised with that person's spittle, blood, hair, fingernails, cloak-fringe or a piece of cloth. Or the figurine represented the evil sorcerers, sorceresses and spirits and was burned or melted ceremonially in the presence of the fire gods. Figurines were made of many materials. The *Maqlû Series* offers quite a range of choices: 2,19: lard; 2,37: bronze covered with sulphur; 2,134: plaster or clay; 2,148: plaster or clay; 2,159: wine dregs (?); 2,181: bitumen covered with gypsum; 2,205: clay covered with lard; 2,229: tamarisk and cedar wood. Two other options were beeswax and clay from a special, symbolic place, like a riverside, a pit, a canal, the doorway of a house, a street crossing, temple or palace. To make such effigies work, they had to be closely identified with the person, deity or being they were meant to represent.)

Set up the offerings. Place twelve small breads of unsifted flour before her,

(Are the **twelve breads** a representation of the year, or the twelve double hours that make up the day? West (1992:381) gives a ritual for sun god Šamaš, who receives an offering of twelve loaves of wheat bread. While the bread for Šamaš is perfectly sieved, Lamaštu gets gritty stuff fit for savages.)

I, 25

pour spring (*or: *well) water for her and give her a black dog, seat her at the head of the patient for three days,

I, 27

put the [hea]rt of a piglet in her mouth, pour hot [soup] for her. Give her a [flas]k of oil, offer provisions (for the road) to her, (*or: *put the heart of a piglet next to her.

(Please give the **piglet** a moment. Many amulets show the goddess suckling a dog/wolf and a pig/wild boar. Both of them symbolise, among many other things, intense life-force, immunity from disease, the ability to feed on garbage, and sexual vigour. Lamaštu likes to adopt these animals. Is the heart of a piglet something which she fancies, as it is tasty, or full of vitality, or is it supposed to annoy her?

It has been proposed that the heart could be a **substitute sacrifice**, i.e. something to gnaw instead of the patient. However, our ritual lacks the identification of the patient with the heart, essential to make it a valid substitute. An example. When a goat was used as a replacement sacrifice to fool the terrifying asakku spirit, each part of the animal was identified with the patient. We read that Enki (i.e. the exorcist) proclaims that *the goat represents humanity*. Then the parts of the goat are identified with the patient: head, throat, chest, right side, left side, blood, heart, ribs, spine, thighs, pelvic region and limbs. Fooled by the spell, the asakku departs, munching the goat instead of the patient (Schramm 2008: 41-43). Here is a ritual using a pig as a replacement sacrifice. It is a lot more elaborate than simply putting a piglet heart into the mouth of a figurine.

[Take a] suckling pig [and ...at] the head of the sick man [put it(?) and] take out its heart and above the heart of the sick man [put it],

[sprinkle] its blood on the sides of the bed, [and] divide the pig over the limbs and spread it on the sick man; then cleanse that man with pure water from the Deep [Apsû] and wash him clean and bring near him a censer [and] a torch, place twice seven loaves cooked in the ashes against the outer door, and give the pig as his substitute, and give the flesh and the blood as his blood: they [the demons] shall take it; the heart which thou hast placed upon his heart, as his heart gives it: they shall take it. (Burkert 1995:58 quoting Thompson 1903/1904, amended by Meissner 1920/1925) That's genuine substitute magic. Without elaborate identification it doesn't work.

Oil. When wealthy people, merchants and soldiers travelled, their dress left quite a bit of skin exposed to sun, dust, blood-sucking insects and parasites. To reduce the damage, travellers took care to oil themselves. Myhrman left his translation at 'oil', Köcher thought it should be olive oil. It's not a bad idea; olive oil has a light protection factor 2 against sunburn, which isn't much but better than nothing. However, olive oil was expensive, as the tree only grew north-west of Mesopotamia, in Syria and Anatolia. The Babylonians and Assyrians imported it, but only the wealthy could afford it. Our text reads šamnu(m) which could mean sesame, barley, nut (almond?), cedar, olive, mineral oil, and animal oils made from the fat of fish, snakes, birds, pigs or cows. Special oils were scented with myrtle or aromatic plants. Oil of cedar and juniper were used against diseases attributed to DIM.NUN.ME i.e. Lamaštu (Frantz-Szabo, RlA *'Öl'*). For medical purposes, expensive olive oil was diluted with sesame oil. Oil was also used for divination.)

I, 29

La[y out cakes of d]ry [bread. At dawn, noon and at s]unset,

recite the conjuration. [On the third day, when the d]ay descends carry her outside

I, 31

and bu[r]y her in a cor[ner (**or:** recess) of the wall].

Bitumen of a ship, [b]itumen of its rudder,

I, 33

bitumen from its rowlo[ck (**or:** oar), bi]tumen from the entire equipment of a ship,

[dust (**or:** earth) from the q]uay and the ford (**or:** foot bridge **or:** ferry),

(This badly damaged section appears again further on, see LS III, 64-68. Bitumen, i.e. **natural asphalt** is a petrol product. Some of it floated on the rivers. The better quality had to be bought. Gudea imported it from the Magda Mountains. It represents the river god (Langdon, 1919:87). Bitumen was used in fluid and firm form, in several degrees of purity. Since at least 3000 BCE, Sumerian craftsmen used it for many things, such as mortar, wall paint, caulking, coffin-covers, glue and torches (by dipping bundles of reed in it). The statues of the gods were painted with bitumen. Bitumen was used to waterproof canal locks, ships and vessels; it was applied to city walls to strengthen the fortification against floods. To make waterproof bottles and containers, you simply wove the item out of fibres or reeds, and covered it with bitumen. Solid bitumen was carved into useful items, such as playing pieces, amulets, spoons and royal toilet seats. It was the dawn of the age of plastic. Bitumen is occasionally confused with tar. The difference is that bitumen is not carcinogenic. We also find it in Babylonian medical prescriptions. I've met people who took small doses of purified petrol against cancer. Ship, quay, ford, footbridge and ferry represent liminal locations allowing Lamaštu to depart to the otherworlds. They appear in *Šurpu Series* III, 47-49: *the māmītu(m)* (=oath, taboo, curse, prohibition*) of boat and river, harbour and ferry, canal and bridge.*)

I, 35

pig-lard, fish-fat, hot bitumen, butter (or: ghī), [...] an ankinûtu plant,

(and) aktam-plant you shall mix, anoint him and he will get well.

(The plants are unidentified, but appear to be medical herbs. Aprušu was also used as flour and as a source of oil. Please note that the ailing infant is referred to as 'he'. It could also be a female baby. It's a standard convention of Mesopotamian medical literature to call the patient 'he' unless the text deals with specific female diseases. I would prefer to call the infant 'it' as Myhrman did, but this, sorry, is wrong.)

I, 37

*Var.1.:****[Conjuration:] She [is Angry], She is Furious, she is Fire (or: Fever?),***

she is terrible, she is a wolf-bitch, the Daughter of Anu,

*Var.2.:****[Conjuration:] She [is Angry], Not a Goddess, She is Furious,***

she is a wolf-bitch, the Daughter of Anu.

*Var.3.:****[Conjuration:] She is Angry, She is terrifying, she is a Goddess,***

she has a Divine Radiance, she is a wolf-bitch, the Daughter of Anu,

*Var.4.:****[Conjuration:] She is Angry, She is terrifying, She is a Woman of the Amorites,***

she is a wolf-bitch, the Daughter of Anu,

(These lines are the start of **conjuration #3**. The text appears in several versions. It was recited over the 'right hand' of the patient, meaning the hand on the right side of the conjurer. Instead of *angry* you can also read *grim, fierce* or *terrifying.* Variation one has išatu(m): **fire**, flame, bonfire, beacon; the word can also mean an inflammation. I have added 'fever?' out of sympathy for the many scholars who automatically identify her fire as fever. You should also consider 'lust'.

The trickiest bit in versions two and three is that Lamaštu is called **a goddess** and **not a goddess**. Most conjurations call her a goddess. Every conjurer was aware that she is a daughter of the highest deities of heaven. So why do we encounter spells where she is explicitly called 'not a goddess'? I don't believe that the scribes did a sloppy job. More likely, the conjurer used the expression to provoke her, reminding her that she should act like a proper goddess, grant blessings and behave. In version four she is a **woman of the Amorites**. These nomads began to invade Mesopotamia around the end of the third millennium. Some came as peaceful settlers, others as raiders. Armed troops of Amorites did much to turn the thriving bureaucracy of the Ur III Period into total chaos. Simultaneously the Elamites came down from the Iranian mountains to destroy and plunder. In the ensuing struggle, the last remnants of Sumerian rule disappeared. Finally the Amorites kicked out the Elamites and set themselves up as the regents of former Sumer, founding their own royal house, the Isin dynasty. There are several passages in the *Lamaštu Series* where the goddess is identified as a foreign woman. Here, foreign means: odd, strange, savage, lethal, possibly a witch. However, it's not accurate to label the Amorites simply as barbarians. They acted like savages when they invaded the country, but once they had settled down they were bedazzled by bureaucracy and they did their best to promote culture and civilisation.)

Var.1.: ***in the grass is her resting place, her home in the meadow,***

her lair in the alfalfa grass,

Var.2.: ***in the tracks (or: dung) of cattle is her lair, her home is in [...]***

I,39

Her lair is in the tracks** (or: **dung) of sheep,

Var.1.: ***She stops [the moving bull], she stops the passage of the donkey,***

Var.2.: ***She is sto[pping] the moving [b]ull, she forces the donkey to sit,***

Var.3.: ***She stops the moving young man, she pulls the donkey's tail,***

(These lines are badly damaged and the translation uncertain. Farber quotes four distinct versions; see also tablet YBC 9846, Babylonian Collection of Yale University, Old Babylonian period, maybe from Larsa, translated by Nathan Wasserman, 2010, on the SEAL webpage. In the canonical *Lamaštu Series* the passage appears twice, see also LS II, 119-127. Myhrman was not aware of this fragment; Köcher gave his translation with the proviso that the meaning is derived from the one certain item: the reference to the **advancing bull**. Well, 'advancing' may be a bit overdone; the verb aliku usually means walking. In his opinion, the bull is a symbol of sexual potency, it advances to impregnate the cows, and Lamaštu puts a stop to that. It made him translate:

She stops [the advancing bull],

she maddens the cows with lust (?),

she ca[strates?] the men,

As it turned out, this reading was largely off the mark, but it shows that Lamaštu may have a worse reputation among modern scholars than in the Ancient Near East. I spent plenty of time trying to comprehend Köcher's assumptions. As it turns out, the sex-crazed cows, based on a speculative interpretation of the verb pâqaru from Aramean pqar: to be unbridled, unrestrained in the sexual sense, are a mistake. The same goes for 'castration'. Köcher thought the damaged section might yield the word 'cut'; from quppû: sharp knife, scalpel; an object used for surgery and (maybe) in rituals requiring bloodletting. That word, however, was not used for castration. So far, it is uncertain whether castration was practised in Sumer, Akkad or in the Old Babylonian period. It appears among the Assyrians. However, there is no word for human castration; the word tapṭīru was used for the castration of bulls. As it turned out, the proper word was quburru, from qebēru(m), meaning: to bury, to put into a grave, to wrap up, to roll up, convolute.

Let's consider the **moving bull**. A bull can mean many things, especially in Mesopotamian literature, which makes liberal use of the metaphor. The bull can be a reference to the pastoral cow herders and the wealthy palace- and temple farms that used bulls to pull their ploughs. The bull could represent the kings. Some regents who were praised as bulls are Gilgameš, Lugalirra, Lipitištar of Isin, Gudea of Lagaš, Urninurta of Isin and Ḫammurapi. And the bull could represent the power and authority of the great gods. Many gods were praised as bulls, including Anu, Enlil, Enki, Marduk, Utu, Iškur, Nanna, Nergal, Gugalanna, Ningublam, Numušda and, though she is a goddess, Irnina. Antu(m) could appear as a heavenly cow, her udders (=clouds) yielding rain. Ninsuna is a cow, and the mother of several gods and kings. Nanše is a wild cow, a great storm, fierce black water, born on the shores of the sea, delighting in the foam and playing in the waves, as Enḫeduanna sang. Inanna was celebrated as the great wild cow of the sky, and Bau/Baba as the cow of the land of Sumer. Enki's temple is called a lion and a bull, and so are many other temples, each of them a being, a magical entity and a power engine. High priestess Enḫeduanna praised the temple of Ur, dedicated to Nanna/Sîn as a wild bull, a wild cow and the calf of a wild cow. She called the temple of Ningublam, son of Nanna/Sîn the *House of Numerous Perfect Oxen*. In her *Temple Hymns*, Nanna's temple at Gaeš was called *Cattle Pen House*; Utu's temple in Larsa was praised *White glowing house, white young breed bull, lift your head to the sky*; Inanna's temple in Uruk was a *Shrine built for the bull*. Either Dumuzi Abzu or her temple was called a *Wild Cow*; and the temple of Iškur in Karkara was founded on a horned bull, which hints at a foundation sacrifice. These are just a few examples from de Shong-Meador's splendid translations (2009:76, 94, 95, 102, 117, 175). While lions are probably the most popular metaphor for regents and gods in Mesopotamia, bulls and cows come second. This goes especially for the gods and regents of the third and second millennium BCE; in the first millennium, the metaphor seems to have gone out of fashion. It's time to reconsider. While Lamaštu is not against sex (indeed, she is fascinated by it), she is definitely against overpopulation. And here we find the most instructive metaphor of them all. It comes from the *Atraḫasis* epic, and tells us how the earth was overpopulated by noisy, restless mankind:

The land became wide, the people became numerous,

The land bellowed like wild oxen.

The god (Enlil) was disturbed by their clamour.

(trans. Speiser in Pritchard, 1969; 104). Mankind, noisy, destructive and overbearingly fertile, is the biggest bull of them all. That, exactly, was what the gods wanted to limit, and the reason they charged Lamaštu and Pašittu to slay selected infants.

If we consider the bull as a symbol of gods, cow-herders, farmers, kings, and mankind itself, we see all of them being stopped in their tracks where the cities, the roads, canals and fertile country end and Lamaštu's domain, the rugged high mountains, full of foreigners and bitter weather, the lonesome deserts and the disease-haunted swamps and waterways begin. In her realm, civilisation, state-religion and royal authority come to a sudden end. A similar idea may be behind the resting donkey, which isn't going anywhere.)

I, 41

Var.1.: ***She buries (****or:* ***wraps up, convolutes) the young men,***

she shakes (*or:* ***convulses,*** *or:* ***crushes,*** *or:* ***pushes away) [gi]rl[s]***

Var.2.: ***she really shakes (****or:* ***convulses,*** *or:* ***crushes,*** *or:* ***pushes away) infants,***

(Farber, like Köcher before him, chose the most destructive interpretation of the verb napāṣu(m). It can mean: to shake, convulse, thrash, flop about, push away, crush, smash and abolish. To be sure, the possibility is there. However, when we consider shaking and convulsions, we arrive at two entirely different possibilities. We could think of diseases. But shaking, shivering, staggering and the like are typical side effects of shamanic trances and states of spirit possession. I have written more than enough on the topic; forgive me for not going into details here. Let me simply remark that shaking obsession was a standard feature of Mesopotamian religion and prophecy. Several gods obsessed people, and in some temples there were priests and priestesses who did the job for the local deity. But what happens when we consider that Lamaštu obsesses pregnant women and young parents?)

I, 43

Var.1.: ***she drenches the infants with Waters of Distress,***

(*or:* ***she makes the infants drink the Waters of Distress)***

Var.3.: ***She strangles the infants, she forces the grownups to drink the Waters of Distress,***

The **Waters of Distress** are a difficult topic. First of all, we could think of them as poetic metaphors. The word distress can also mean: constrain, difficulty, trouble, narrowness, or dissolution. The waters of distress have a counterpart in the *food of distress*. Adults who suffered from bad luck or were haunted by spirits ate the bread of woe and sorrow. A parallel is the common Chinese expression 'eating bitterness'. The waters of distress have a poetic counterpart: *the waters of joy*. However, several scholars assumed they might refer to real substances. Let's explore the world of waters and secretions. Köcher thought Lamaštu drenches the infants with urine. The word šaqû(m) can mean: drench, soak and irrigate, to drink or to make someone drink something. The term me-e pi-iš-ri (also read mê pušqi), which Köcher translated as 'urine', was interpreted as 'amniotic water' by Wasserman and Wiggermann. It is a highly magical substance, metaphorically described as *the waters of intercourse* and as the *waters of the distant, fearsome, raging ocean.* The doctors of Babylonia assumed it to be toxic, so we might as well understand the term as 'venom': Lamaštu possibly makes the infant drink amniotic water, or simply poison. That, however, does not explain why she does the same with adults. After all, the goddess is not pregnant and has no amniotic fluids. Usually she spits her venom. **Water**, $m\hat{u}_1$ or mā'ū is a fascinating multipurpose term that can also mean: fluid, dew, urine, secretion, sexual secretion and sperm. Each of them provides an entirely different interpretation. I am sure you noticed that all of these fluids are highly magical. Water is the cosmic fluid out of which the primal goddess Nammu created everything. The world is suspended in all-encompassing water: the sweet-water abyss below, the world ocean surrounding the landmass and finally the celestial abyss above from where the rain falls. Urine appears in a love spell as a powerful seductive fluid. Sperm was dangerously magical. Enki ejaculated into two dry riverbeds that excited his fancy and created the sacred rivers Euphrates and Tigris. Men and women were assumed to produce sperm. After intercourse, the male and female sperm fought, and the winner determined the gender of the baby. The female sexual secretions seem to have been celebrated several times in Mesopotamian poetry. Inanna is praised for her sweet tasting vulva. Haas (1999: 132, 133, trans. JF) quotes the expressions *there is honey in your vagina* and *make your lap sweet for me.* Another idiom for the vulva was *mother's little honey-cake.* The joys of cunnilingus are hinted at in a song composed for King Šusuen. We learn that the king's wife has given birth and is secluded from her husband for the usual period. In her place, the king is entertained by an educated woman whose only partly legible name is Ilummiya. She is the royal cupbearer, a very high-status job. It would be interesting to know what drink she prepared for the king. Various translators proposed beer, wine or fruit wines.

...My god, of Il-ummiya, the cup-bearer, sweet is her intoxicating drink,

Like her intoxicating drink her vulva is sweet, sweet is her intoxicating drink,

Like her lips (or: *talk) her vulva is sweet, sweet is her intoxicating drink,*

Sweet is her kašbir drink, her intoxicating drink...

(Jacobsen 1987:96; SAHG 1951:120, Kramer 1981:248, Haas, 1999:132)

The sexual secretions were powerful but they were not necessarily dangerous or polluting. The Sumerians held oral sex in high esteem. It appears among the divine powers of civilisation, the Me, which Inanna received from Enki. The catalogue lists fellatio as *the art of kissing the penis.* Whether cunnilingus also appeared is uncertain; the line is badly damaged. It has been claimed that male sperm was polluting. However, sperm, secretions and, for that matter, menstrual blood do not appear in the extensive catalogue of taboo items in the *Šurpu Series.* To understand the Waters of Distress we have to take into account that one interpretation is never enough. At the present stage of research, I suggest that we refrain from associating Lamaštu with any specific fluid except for the snake and scorpion venom she liberally splatters around.)

[Where] shall I grasp (or: *see) her? As a [...] is the [...] the Daughter of Anu.*

(This passage is very uncertain. Köcher assumed a reference to the Daughter of Anu, Farber proposes *like a bristle at the kidneys of the sky?* It sounds like an astronomical reference; the bristle constellation is the Pleiades, while the term 'kidney' was used for several celestial objects and constellations.)

I, 45

Show your majesty, O Šamaš!

(Akkadian **Šamaš** (Sumerian **Utu**) is the god of the sun, whose cult was strongest in Larsa in the south and Sippar in the north. He travels over the earth by day, observing everything, and this ensures his office as the judge of the gods, guardian of justice. The Sumerians called Utu the *friend of travellers.* By night he travels through the Underworlds on his chariot, he inspects the deities of the deep and the souls of the dead, and passes judgement on them. Unlike the Egyptians, the Mesopotamians were not judged after they died. So what did they need a judge for? It says a lot about the Underworld when even the dead can't stop cheating and suing each other. The Sumerians called him Utu-u-ne-a (*Sun God of Every Day*) and Utu-u-na-a (*Sun God of the Black Moon*) to emphasise his heavenly and underworldly office. He has a home, the *White House,* underground, where he is greeted by his son **Mešaru** (*Straightness, Trustworthiness*), embraces his wife **Aya** (goddess of the dawn), has a meal and goes to sleep for the rest of the night. Aya is an interesting deity. Among her Sumerian names are Nin-kar (*Shining Lady*), Nin-mul-si-a (*Lady Glowing Red*), Zab-utu (*Sunlight*), Nin-ag-ga (*Loving Lady*) and Nin-ul-šu-tag (*Lady Who is Cloaked with Opulence*). An Akkadian title is Nabâṣu (*Spring Glow of the Sun*) (Ebeling, RlA '*A.A*'). Is she related to the Vedic Uṣas (*Dawn*), the Greek Eos, the Roman Aurora and the Germanic Eostre, all of them related to beginnings, sunrise or spring?

After the Akkadian period, the sun's function as a judge and defender of justice increased. Šamaš appears in many exorcisms, as he is true, reliable and an excellent exorcist of evil influences. Like the scorching summer sun, he clobbers the unjust into submission. Some cities had a Šamaš gate where lawyers hung out, legal matters could be settled, and the god be called upon to witness oaths and contracts. In the Neo-Babylonian period, Marduk, Šamaš and Aya were frequently invoked to witness contracts. In this line, Šamaš is invoked to ensure that the deeds of Lamaštu remain within the limits imposed by truth and justice. In the fascinating ritual SpTU (Scurlock, 2014: 127, Farber, 2014:309) we encounter Šamaš and Lamaštu. The former is asked for justice, the latter to depart. The start of the inscription is badly damaged, so it is not clear whether the ritualist is a male or female conjurer. The participants are a woman who has lost her child and possibly her man, or a man. The ritualist forms a figurine of Lamaštu out of riverside clay. A large bowl is filled with clay, something is arranged and a lamb is strangled. Something, probably the lamb, is wrapped in cloth like a baby. The items are set up on the embankment of a river and incense is lit. The fumigation is juniper; it could be sap, wood or twigs. The ritualist invokes Šamaš and asks him to soothe distress and bring release from sins. The woman pours a beer offering for Šamaš on roasted barley flour and drops the dead lamb between her breasts to the ground. Three times she declares that she has given birth but brought forth a stillborn child. Finally she asks for a successful pregnancy. In a damaged line she requests that a woman *who can give success* should release her and that a woman *who can create* should reduce (rest missing). Last, she announces that she will have a successful pregnancy and will return straight to the house where she lives. The lamb receives something from her and is placed on her lap. Finally, the ritualist *goes toward sunset,* puts the Lamaštu figurine and all items on a boat and crosses the river. He or she sets them up on the far shore and surrounds them with a magical circle. The conjuration calls to mountain, river, seas and steep rocks, heaven, earth and (rest missing). The spells end with a threat to Lamaštu, never to approach that woman or to enter her house again.)

[conjuration against Lamaštu]

I, 47

[Ritual instruction:] Make a Lamaštu of clay,

[dress her head with hair], (and) a soiled piece of cloth

(This ritual appears in a very similar form at the very end of the *Lamaštu Series* (III 119-128). **Hair** (pērtu(m) on her **head** or **top** (qaqqudu(m): does this imply that the goddess has a human head? The soiled piece of cloth appears several times in Lamaštu spells. It is probably a rag stained with menstrual blood.)

I, 49

shall be her dress.

[Spread (?) a sunshade made of] palm for her

[or: Prick (?) her with a th[orn of] a date palm

give her a comb, a sp[in]dle, a fla[sk] of oil;

(The soiled **cloth** marks her as unclean. However, clean or not, it is still a dress, hence a typical goodbye gift for an esteemed visitor. The ṣillû has two meanings: a **sunshade** made from a palm leaf or a **thorn**. Köcher preferred the former, Farber the latter reading. Date palms have formidable spikes at the stem of the leaf. As a **sunshade**, we are talking about a protection, a cover and maybe a canopy. Sunshades could represent heaven. This one is made from palm leaves, woven from their fibres or constructed from palm wood, if it is an elaborate affair, as used by kings, aristocrats and for the statues of high-ranking gods when they were carried in a procession. Maybe the figurine was sheltered with a pretty little wooden contraption. Or maybe the conjurer simply stuck a palm frond in the ground next to her. If Lamaštu is pricked with a date palm thorn, she might be punished by celestial and royal authority. The **date palm** is an important symbol. In Sumer and Akkad, date palms were the foundation of successful gardening. Vegetables required protection in the shadow of higher trees; a must in a climate noted for the scorching intensity of its summer. In erotic parlance, a garden is a synonym for the vulva, and going into the garden means the same thing as going into the swamp: making love in secret. The 'gardener' nukaribbu(m), is one who cultivates date palms for private business or on behalf of the palace or a temple. Where it comes to a utility plant, palm trees score high. They provide dates, which can be eaten fresh, kept in storage or be fermented for a heady beverage. The stalks that held the dates are excellent brooms. The wood is soft and fast-growing, while leaves and fibres are excellent to weave baskets and make ropes, mats and coarse textiles. Best of all, date palms tolerate a level of salt in the soil that other trees cannot cope with. Dates represent Amaušumgalanna, Ningirsu and Nergal; they symbolise wealth, fertility and the rejuvenating, healing influence of the great gods. Two deities were named the Lord and Lady of the Palm tree. There is even a lexical equation going *palm tree (gišnimbar) equals king (šarru)*. At least three omen tablets, all of them badly preserved, were devoted to palm trees (Volk, RlA '*Palme*'). The heart of the palm (libbi gišimmari) and the palm seedling (suḫuššu) were frequently placed on the sickbed to release the patient from sin and pollution and to encourage recovery. The palm-heart was also a ceremonial gift celebrating the marriage of the goddess Bau/Baba in Lagaš. A magical cure requires the sufferer to strip the dates from their stalk and to throw them into the fire. Each date represents a release from unwanted influences such as broken oaths, sins, transgressions, crimes, errors and so on (*Šurpu Series* V-VI, 73-82). Finally, male palm hearts were carried by bird-headed, winged ritualists in Assyrian art; here, the traditional identification is 'pine cones', but this is uncertain and disputed.

Lamaštu receives three characteristic items which were commonly associated with her around the middle of the second millennium BCE and maybe earlier: comb, spindle and oil. We discussed the **oil** earlier: it may have been perfumed and served to protect her skin. The **spindle** allows Lamaštu, like a spider, to spin string; according to Langdon, (1919: 86) her representations in ritual are multi-coloured wool and string. String is also a symbol of Inanna. During a badly preserved ritual, Inanna equips men with spindles and women with weapons, thereby changing their sex and/or gender roles. In Mesopotamia, the goddess of spinning was Uttu (*Spider*), a daughter of Enki and Ninkurra or Ninimma. She is the patroness of all weavers. String is a major invention. When you twine two strings together their binding power increases dramatically. This metaphor appears in a hymn to Inanna (SAHG 1953: 75, trans. JF):

Lady, who in all heavens and on all earths can know what your high mind intends?

Before your word, which, like a twined string never breaks, all of heaven is quaking!

Thus it has been granted to you by your father Enlil.

String was made of wool, linen and, for an especially durable quality, out of goat hair. Goat string was used for mats, to fix wheels to chariots and to make whips. For rope, grass and reed fibres were used. Where it comes to the earliest evidence for string and knot sorcery, Mesopotamia wins the prize. Maybe you could hazard a guess what Lamaštu uses the string for. The **comb** is useful to clean wool. It might also suggest she gets her open, tangled hair in order. In many cultures across Eurasia, open and dishevelled hair represents a lack of manners, sexual availability, high emotionality, madness, mourning. or magical activity. Dumuzi proposed to loosen Inanna's comb for her, i.e. he asked her to make love with him (without bothering to marry her) (Jacobsen, 1987:11). Let's consider what she needs the spindle for. Does she enjoy spinning, to while away the time while she is travelling on the back of her donkey or reclining on her boat? Or is the spindle meant to domesticate her, to turn her into a productive little housewife? Last, a thought on allegory. The spindle unites strands, fibres and hair into a single, continuous string. Symbolically, it organises time. The comb patterns separate strands: it organises space.)

I, 51

[fi]ll four [leather] bags with [fine fl]our, malt, malt-bread,

roasted barley seeds, dry bread;

make four [don]keys of clay.

(The goddess receives gifts and travel provisions. A tablet from the British Museum, K 888, translated by Schwemer, offers a larger selection. First, a human skull is washed, oiled and decorated by tying white, red and blue wool to it. The figure of Lamaštu is seated nearby, on top or maybe inside. Two figures are made with clay from the pit and tied to the hem of some unspecified piece of cloth. Two clay donkeys are formed and equipped with provisions: comb, spindle, cloak-needle, bottle of perfume, (ribbon), hair-pin, cylinder seal, head-cloth of coloured wool, dress, silver ring, X-ornament of silver and the *offerings for the dead*. For a goddess who had no cult or temple, these expensive gifts are certainly impressive. They belong to two categories: items for the goddess and items for the journey. While Lamaštu happily departs with her loot, the patient is treated with conjurations and talismanic objects.)

I, 53

Equip them with travel provisions.

In the evening, before the [sun has set],

you shall carry her into the desert (*or:* field *or:* steppe)

(The **wilderness**, desert, steppe, open country and wasteland are synonymous. In the second millennium BCE, most farmers lived safely behind massive city walls. The cities were surrounded by a network of canals and fields, and peasants had to go for long walks to reach the land they owned or, more often, rented from palace, temple or the wealthy. Beyond the fertile land, the uncultivated wasteland began. Akkadian ṣēru(m) is a wasteland, home to wild animals, dangerous nomads, thieves, brigands, murderers, savage spirits and restless ghosts. Its Sumerian counterpart is eden, and it is not a paradise. The 'Garden of Eden' is a misconception. Eden is not a garden. *Genesis* 2, 8 states that God created a garden in the east, within eden, i.e. in the middle of desert and wilderness.)

I, 55

and turn her face to the west.

Bind her body [with woven reed grasses],

tie her to prickly baltu(m) (caper-bush?) (and) šagu(m) (buckthorn?),

and surround her with three magical circles.

(For the Semitic Akkadians, Babylonians and Assyrians, **west** (ereb šamši) was the direction of death. The souls of the dead, so they believed, followed the path of the sun and disappeared into the deep beyond the mountains of the western horizon.

The **thorns** are difficult. Köcher, fascinated by medical plants, identified them with the thorny caper bush and the buckthorn (rhamnus). The CDA is more cautious: while baltu(m) is simply *a spiny plant*, a šagu(m) is a spiky plant, possibly camel thorn. That term doesn't help a lot. In the Near East, three to five species of the genus alhagi are called camel thorn. In general, when we reach the realm of thorns we have left the settlement far behind. Small villages and sheepfolds were often surrounded by thorns, and so were the temporary camp sites in the steppe. Köcher thought that the goddess should be pricked with these plants. Just as possible the spikes were meant to fix her to the spot. Caper and thorn also appear when it comes to laying dangerous ghosts. Thompson 2005/1908:34:

When a dead man appeareth unto a living man [...] thou shalt make (a figure) of clay, and write his name on the left side with a stylus; thou shalt put it in a gazelle's horn and its face [...] and in the shade of a caper-bush or in the shade of a thorn-bush thou shalt dig a hole and bury it.

Thorns and thistles are sacred plants that connect heaven and earth. Along with several hundred forbidden and polluting deeds, *Šurpu* VIII, 74 provides purification for those who damage sacred plants: *Together with the curse of tearing out thorns and thistles, tamarisk (or) date palm, may they be released from you, absolved for you, wiped off you.*

Old Jewish belief claims that thorn bushes are the habitat of evil spirits. This idea appears in *Isaiah* 34.14, where we meet Lilith relaxing amidst ruined buildings and thistles, watching desert animals and spirits prancing around.

Magical circles may be a Mesopotamian invention. They were usually made with a paste of flour and water. Here they are meant to confine the goddess to the spot. Langdon, 1919:83 tablet *BM Spartola Collection* I, 131, identifies flour-water as a symbol of the gods **Lugalirra** and **Meslamta'ea**. Lugalirra (earlier read as Lugalgirra) means *Mighty Strong-Man* (=King), and is probably not related to Girra and Gibil, the famous fire gods. Earra, Erra and Irra (*Mighty*) are titles of a regent of the underworld, but they were also used for other deities. Meslamta'ea is a god of the Underworld, a son of Enlil and Ninlil. The name means *He who comes out of the Meslam*; E-Meslam being Nergal's temple in Kutha, Babylonia. Meslamta'ea is married to Laṣ and/or Ninšubur; both are independent goddesses of the Underworld who were eventually identified with Ereškigal. Little is known about Laṣ, but Ninšubur also appears as Inanna's sukkal (vizier, diplomat, representative, CEO) and was later turned into a male deity. Meslamta'ea and his twin brother Lugalirra guard entrances and passages; their first appearance is in texts of the Ur III period, when they were associated with the town called Kisiga or Kišaga. They were in charge of the River Ordeal. Their figures were buried in the floor of houses to prevent the entry of malignant spirits. *Maqlû Series* VI, 141-143 describes them as *guardian deities who rip out the heart and crush the kidneys*. They became the astronomical sign Gemini.)

I, 57

banish her by Heaven, Earth and the Anunna[ki].

***Grain** (or: **chaff**), **pig manure, a ḫallutanû (black patch, spot** or

***hair from a donkey's leg** or **thigh** =* thyme*),*

(At first glance Heaven, Earth and the Anunnaki seem to represent the height, the middle realm and the underworld. It's a familiar Eurasian model of the universe. But things are not that simple. In Mesopotamian thought, the term earth includes the underworlds. Remember Ereškigal, the Great Lady of the Earth, who resides in the Deep where the dead dwell. We are not talking levels of awareness or space but deities. Heaven is An/Anu, Earth is his wife, who appears as the Sumerian goddess Ki and the Akkadian goddess Erṣetu(m). This tradition is distinct from those that couple An with Antu(m), Inanna/Ištar or Nammu. The **Anunnaki** (Anunnakū), (Akkadian: Ennunaki) are children of An/Anu; but they also appear as the children of Enlil/Ellil, Utu/Šamaš and Nanna/Suen/Sîn. The name could mean *Princely Offspring* or *Aristocratic Seed.* Originally the term referred to the early gods, the major gods or to all gods in general. Or it was used for all gods of a district: the *Fifty Anunnaki of Eridu.* As each Sumerian city-state had its own preferences on who happened to be a primal, major or minor deity, there is no general agreement regarding the members of that illustrious company. As a collective, they were not associated with a specific function or worshipped as a group. Nor was the term used as a name element. Around the Middle Babylonian period, the term Anunnakū was occasionally used for gods of the earth and the Underworld, while the heavenly gods were often, but not always, called the Igigū or Igigi. It's a general guideline with plenty of exceptions. Early scholars thought that the Anunnaki were gods of the deep, but this generalisation rests on a few badly damaged tablets and highly disputed translations. The distinction between the Anunnaki and the Igigū is unclear; several beliefs were popular simultaneously. And we encounter another meaning of the term: the Anunnaki can be minor deities who sit in the assembly and keep their mouths shut while the big ones are talking. In the *Lamaštu Series*, the Anunnaki appear at the end of spells. That's their usual position when the conjurers wished to round everything off by a reference to those lesser gods who had not been specifically invoked.

Line 58. This reading is mostly based on Farber. The first word is Nisaba. Farber reads **chaff**, but the word also appears as **grain** and as the Akkadian name of the goddess of grains and reeds, the mistress of writing and science. Farber proposes that this line and the next were mixed up by a scribe who tried to include distinct inscriptions in a single ritual procedure, hence, the **black hair from the donkey's leg** or **thigh** appears twice. It's one of the code words for **thyme**. The plant was baked into bread, used as spice and medicine: oil of thyme is one of the strongest disinfectants in the vegetable world, and a favourite to cure lung diseases. Another code word for thyme was *paw of a black dog* (Stol in RlA *'Thymian'*).)

I, 59

[black patch, spot or hair from the h]ind leg (*or*: thigh) of a donkey on the right

should be tied to his neck;

burn on the embers k[ukru-plant and musta]rd seed,

(Kukru or kukuru is an unidentified aromatic tree. Are we dealing with fumigation, as Farber assumes, or with a burned offering?)

I, 61

rub him with cr[ess] and aprušu plant in oil.

(Cress (saḫlû) can be used as an antiseptic. For a feverish baby, a disinfectant would hardly be useful. But maybe the plant had a reputation as a powerful anti-evil-spirits drug. Aprušu is unidentified. It was used as flour and as a source of oil.)

[Conjuration: She is] Cl[ad] in Burning Heat, Fever-heat, Cold, Frost, Ice.

(These lines are the beginning of **conjuration #4**. They were recited over the left hand of the patient, i.e. the hand on the left side of the conjurer. Here, I follow Köcher and Farber (2007:142, 2014:153). Myhrman had *...Heat, Fever-Heat, Cold, Freezing and Shuddering.* Superficially, we seem to be reading about disease. On a deeper level, these lines tell us that the goddess is skilled in changing temperature, in heating and cooling emotions, desires and urges. Lamaštu likes to go to extremes and live there. To what extent were the Mesopotamians aware of **frost** and **ice**? Over the Bronze Age, world climate changed repeatedly. In the early period, it was warmer than today, during the middle and late second millennium BCE it turned colder. It can get pretty cold in the open country on a clear night, as the heat moves skywards without a cloud cover to slow it down. Sumer, in the sun-scorched south, has very little rain and hardly any snow. Babylonia has snowfall once in a while, but Assyria, in northern Mesopotamia, has so much rain and snow that canals were rarely needed. The Assyrian armies encountered plenty of frost and snow when they campaigned in the mountain ranges of Iran and in the mountains of Turkey. Ice was a luxury item. In the royal palace of Mari, ice, imported at great cost from the mountains, was used to cool drinks and food. (Postgate 2002:146)

I, 63

Roots of the liquorice tree, seed of the chaste tree,

the fruit of the pop[lar] tree, pride of the river meadow, she spoiled.

(Lines 63-64 are extremely troublesome. Köcher read 'seed' and 'fruit' and guessed, on extremely little evidence, that Lamaštu stops the flow of sperm and *shrivels the fruit.* It fitted his assumption that Lamaštu loathes sex and pregnancy. Haas copied Köcher without hesitation. Farber, working with more evidence, eliminated the sexual symbolism and introduced the trees. **Liquorice** is no tree but a tall plant. The roots were used as a sweetener, but also as medicine. In the third century BCE, Theophrastus recorded that its roots can reduce thirst; allegedly, the Scythians used it during their migrations, as it allowed them to ride for days without having to drink. The plant is a powerful cough medicine, dissolves phlegm and reduces inflammation. Liquorice is presently researched for its use against viral infections. That's the good part. However, large doses can cause high blood pressure, irregular heartbeat, restlessness, over-excitement, dizziness, and headache. In rare cases, excessive consumers end in hospital. Šunû is, according to the CDA, the **chaste tree**, which might be *Vitex agnus castus.* Like liquorice, it is a plant. However, there are species of vitex in the Near East which do look like small trees. It was mainly used, as Pliny the Elder recorded, as an anaphrodisiac. For this function, and to relieve pre-menstrual stress syndrome, it has been used up to our time. The **poplar**, Sumerian asal, Akkadian ṣarbatum, is the *Euphrates poplar,* a fast growing, salt resistant soft-wood tree that is easy to cultivate near the canals and rivers. It provides shade and its timber, though not strong, was useful to make furniture and roof houses. Rich people and bronze smiths also used it as firewood. Postgate (RlA *'Pappel'*) mentions two deities: a Lord of the Poplar in Neo-Babylonian texts and a Lady of the Poplar in Middle Assyrian rituals. Foliage, sap and seeds were used medically. Poplar, like willow, is very rich in salicylic acid. Many plants use salicylic acid to fight bacterial infections. In therapy, it can be used to lower temperature and reduce pain. In its natural form the chemical is much stronger (and far more aggressive) than the acetylsalicylic acid you know from aspirin. Here, Lamaštu is destroying medical plants. So far for the easy bit. But why does the line speak of 'fruit'? Poplar fruits are tiny. As medicine, bark and leaves are far superior. Is the text wrong? Should we search for another tree? Consider it a scribal error? Or take the 'fruit' as a metaphor for the effects of the tree?)

I, 65

When she crosses a river, she makes the water muddy, when she stands near (or: leans against) a wall, she smears mud on it,

(These lines are repeated in LS I, 181 and 183. Ebēru(m) means to cross, to ford, to extend or lie across. What is she doing to the river? Mesopotamian **rivers** were creative, maintaining and destructive deities. The Sumerian word Id (Akkadian: nāru(m)) was used for the river but also for its deity. Idim means: the Deep. Ida is a river goddess. In some texts the river appears as a god, in others as a goddess. In common parlance, 'the river' was the Euphrates (Sumerian: Burannu, Akkadian: Purattu), extending over roughly 2770km from the Kurdish mountains to the Persian Gulf. The Tigris (Sumerian: Idigna, Akkadian: Idiglad), also a deity, was approximately 800km shorter, muddier and much faster. Accordingly, the gently flowing Euphrates was easier to control and more useful for canal economy. The major rivers Ḫubûr, Ulaya, Turnat, and Ṭaban were also written with the divine determinative. In the sky, the *River of Heaven* was the Milky Way. Another river, Idlurugu, streamed through the Underworld. At least in some myths: ideas about the Underworld are not very consistent. People who had polluted themselves could find purification by submerging themselves in rivers. It's a great ritual. Step into a river and allow the water to wash your worries away. On the other hand, law cases that could not be decided by judges, such as accusations of sorcery, were decided by throwing the suspect into the river.

In our verse, Lamaštu makes the river muddy. It happens in spring. By the middle of February, the Tigris near Baghdad begins to swell, while the leisurely Euphrates takes three more weeks to catch up. The floods are caused by snowmelt in the mountains of what is now Kurdistan. By April, both rivers reach their maximum. The diviners (bārû) watched the rivers very closely, and made predictions according to their colour and the things, trees, animals and corpses that were swept along by the flood. When the great rivers flooded, they were brown with mud. It made them a source of fertility. However, unlike the floods of the river Nile, Mesopotamian rivers flooded at the wrong time. They reached their greatest violence when the harvest was almost ready. The farmers had one hell of a time fortifying the embankments, fighting the surging brown waters and channelling them into swamps where they could do no harm.

Mud is a magical substance and the very stuff of creation. Which **wall** are we talking about? The city wall is one option; the other is the wall around the major temple complexes and the palaces. Normal people lived in houses whose windowless walls faced narrow streets and crooked alleys. Walls suggest limits, boundaries and frontiers, and the people who go to great lengths to set up barriers between 'us' and 'them'. I am sure that Lamaštu had a lot to complain about regarding the temples and palaces: she is the first graffiti artist in recorded history.)

I, 67

when she seizes an old man, she is called dissolution. When she seizes a young man, she is called Anqullu,

(*Pasūsatu*= **Dissolution, Obliteration, Destruction**, may or may not derive from Pašittu(m).

Pašittu(m) is a Sumerian/Akkadian goddess who appears at the end of the *Atraḫasis* myth. This story, the Sumerian and Akkadian tale of the flood, deals with ecological problems. You read a summary in the history chapters. After the flood, the gods created Pašittu (*Dissolution, Destruction*), a goddess who specialised in killing infants - or maybe they entrusted an existing goddess with that gruesome task. Now for the obvious question: is Pašittu identical with Lamaštu? Much depends on the translation of *Athraḫasis* you are reading. Some translators state that Pašittu was *created* for the job; others say she was *entrusted* with it. If the former reading is accurate, she differs from

Lamaštu, who only got the job after she was kicked out of heaven. But if Pašittu existed before she received her assignment from the gods, she might be identical with Lamaštu. For some scribes, the two goddesses were identical. The star Ka-muš-i-gue (Andromeda β, Mirach) is associated with both of them. Its name can be loosely translated as: *(female) Mouth-Serpent/Dragon-Feeds*. An alternative version is Zu-muš-i-gue: *(female) Tooth-Serpent/Dragon-feeds*. A Babylonian version is Zu-muš-e-ga. These words can be translated in several ways. A simple translation comes from Krebernik (1984:177): *The Serpent-Mouth (*or: *Tooth) Eats*. Or you might consider: *She Who is a Serpent/Dragon Feeds*; *She Who Feeds the Serpent/Dragons* or *The (female) Serpent/Dragon Feeds*. If we allow zu-muš to mean 'worm' we could read, as Wiggermann did (RlA *'Pašittu*): *She Who Feeds (the victim) to the Worms*, or, as Köcher abbreviates it: *Wormfodder*. For an extra sinister meaning replace 'feeds' with 'devours'. Just don't ask which translation is really accurate. That's Sumerian for you: it provides excitement for the whole family.

The extent to which the two goddesses overlap remains enigmatic. Some researchers treat them as distinct deities; implying that they may have come from distinct mythical traditions. As there is a lot of material on Lamaštu and next to nothing on Pašittu the question remains open. The only things that are really well-documented are Pašittu diseases, which seem to be jaundice, bile, and gall disorders of an incurably lethal type. Köcher classed them as 'Lamaštu diseases', without mentioning that they are actually named after Pašittu, an identification that Farber (2007) passionately dismissed.

Wiggermann (2000), taking a different approach, translates *Pasūsatu* as *cripple*, whatever that may mean. Or is the term a first-millennium addition, a hapax based on **Pazuzu**? If this were the case, Heeßel (2002) suggests that the name might be a feminine form of Pazuzu, who is read and pronounced as Pa-su-su nowadays (W. Lambert corrected the pronunciation in 1970). In Akkadian, the letter 't' in the last part of a word often indicates a woman. Perhaps there was a female Pazuzu around. So far, there is no textual evidence for such a deity. Pazuzu appears in several first millennium BCE talismans as an opponent of Lamaštu. This terrifying storm deity entered Mesopotamia with the Aramean settlers, who started to invade the country around the eleventh century BCE. Some were peaceful immigrants; others tried their hand at raiding. As they appeared in small, unorganised groups they were no match for the Neo-Assyrian armies. But no matter how many of them were fought, killed, stopped or relocated, there were always some who followed. Over the centuries they became an important ethnic group. To the Arameans, Pazuzu was, in spite of his terrifying appearance, a benevolent deity, a king of the storm gods, who was charged to protect pregnant women and infants. For this purpose, his image was set up in houses or worn around the neck as a talisman. He never gained much importance among the other ethnic groups, let alone traditionally minded Babylonians and Assyrians. There is no reference to Pazuzu in the *Lamaštu Series*. The scribes of Aššurbanipal ignored him. Thanks to the exceedingly boring movie *The Exorcist* and a lot of badly-informed kids trying to cultivate an aura of evil, Pazuzu is nowadays frequently identified with Satan. It's the opposite of his original function to ensure the safety and health of the family.

Finally, let's think about Lamaštu seizing the **old man**. As usual in Babylonian and Assyrian, the reference is generally to male persons unless specifically female persons are meant. Perhaps the term should be understood as **'elder'**. It makes more sense: to kill selected infants and ailing elders is entirely within the realm of divine population control. Nor is it really a bad thing: death in feeble old age is not a tragedy but a blessing.

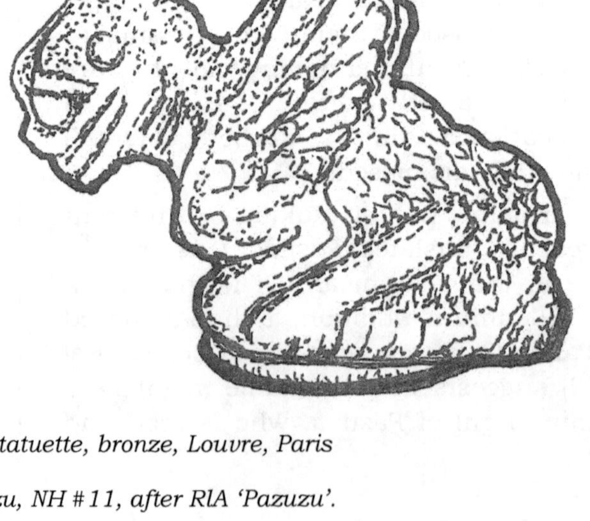

Figure 29 Top: Pazuzu Statuette, bronze, Louvre, Paris

Bottom: Crouching Pazuzu, NH #11, after RlA 'Pazuzu'.

Figure 30 Pazuzu Head amulet. Items like these were worn by patients and pregnant women to scare away Lamaštu and the Lilû wind- and storm spirits, or hung up above the sickbed. Babylon, today Museum of Fine Arts, Boston.

What happens to the young man? The word **anqullu** remains a problem. Myhrman translated: *State of Darkness;* Wiggermann (2000) proposes: *Heat-wave;* Heeßel and Köcher translated: *Fire-storm;* Lambert had: *Sun Stroke;* Farber proposed *Scorcher.*

The CDA has: *an atmospheric phenomenon; a fiery glow,* younger Babylonian: *feverish heat.*

Should we think of fever, overheating or sun stroke? Or does she seize the man with sexual longing?)

I, 69

when she seizes a young woman, she is called Lamaštu,

when she seizes an infant, she is called DIM.ME.

(The distinction between Lamaštu and DIM.ME is nonsense. The former is the Akkadian, Babylonian and Assyrian, the latter the Sumerian version of the name. The author of these lines was trying to attribute a different clientele to them.

In the last lines, you read that Lamaštu **seizes** a person. The verb sabātu(m) is a great multipurpose word that can lead to widely different interpretations. Most translators had a negative outlook on Lamaštu, and preferred 'to seize'. It sounds exciting, dramatic and violent, and is the perfect choice if you like to live in a horror movie. In Akkadian, the word frequently means: to **take**, to **hold**, to **possess**, to **own** and 'to hold (someone responsible)'. People could 'seize, take, possess' an office, a task, a throne, a tool, an object, but they could also **undertake** a journey, a task and a duty, or **keep hold** of property, life, health and legal status. There are plenty of things that can seize or take a person in everyday life, and not all of them are sinister: sleep, disease, desire, and bad luck. To top it off, the Neo-Assyrians, in whose time the *Lamaštu Series* were compiled, used the word for 'to **adopt**'. What if Lamaštu owns or adopts people, or maybe infants, just as she adopts and breastfeeds piglets and puppies? It's your choice: would you prefer to be seized, taken, possessed, owned or adopted?)

I, 71

As you have come, as you seize the form of his face,

seize the limbs, destroy the created shape,

eat the sinews, encircle *(or:* ***shut in) the nerves*** *(?)* *(or:* ***muscles?),***

(For those who want details: the limbs in the first line are mešrêtu while binâtu means: the created, created shape, appearance, structure. It's a fascinating term that implies a hidden intent in our body, and that of all created beings. 'Eat' (kasāsu(m) can also be translated: devour, chew, gnaw. The sinews in the second line are a problem: šer'ānu can mean all sorts of stringy stuff, like sinews, tendons, nerves, arteries and muscles. The doctors generally did not know what they were good for, nor did they make much of a difference between them. For simplicity's sake I'll stick to 'sinews'; please keep in mind that many readings are possible. Encircle, i.e. kanānu(m) or ganānu can also mean to shut in or enclose; it's a very magical notion. Applied to manānu (probably 'nerves', but this isn't certain) it might hint at introversion of the senses.)

I, 73

[as you] blanch the face, change the shape of the body,

inflict suffering; burn the body like fire:

(Bunnanû: face, physiognomy, features and countenance. Ašuštu(m) is: suffering, grief, affliction, maltreatment, distress, torture.)

I, 75

to expel you, to chase you away,

that you may not return, that you may not draw near,

(Nasāḫu is: expel, dismiss or remove; ṭardu(m): chase, to drive off, to set in flight.)

I, 77

that you will not approach the body of N.N., the son of N.N.:

I conjure you by Anu, the Father of the Great Gods;

I, 79

I conjure you by Enlil the Great Mountain;

I conjure you by Ea, King of Apsû, Creator of the Universe (or: Creator of the Clay Pit), the Lord of All;

(**Enlil**/Ellil is often called 'the Mountain'. In one of the creation tales, **Enlil** rises like a mountain and uses his hoe/pickaxe to separate the tight embrace of his parents Heaven (An) and Earth (Ki), thus creating space to live. Enlil's major temple in Nippur was the Ekur, the House of the Mountain. Maybe the god was an import from a foreign mountain range (Elam?), as Sumer and Babylon are mostly flat. Or he developed when the Proto-Sumerians were living in a mountain country. In these lines the conjurer calls for the support of the highest gods. To Lamaštu, they are family.

The Sumerian god **Enki** (Akkadian **Ea**) is a deity of the waters, of the deep underworldly abyss of sweet waters, of irrigation, fertility, creativity, craft, science, wisdom, music and magic. Irrigation taught the Mesopotamians a lot of physics, geometry, maths, building, engineering and science. In the Sea Land of Southern Sumer, Enki is also the lord of the world-surrounding ocean. His cult place, Eridu, might be the oldest temple in Sumer: it dates from 4900 BCE. Well, 'temple' might be a little too grand. The earliest temple building in Eridu measured only three metres. Enki means *Lord of the Earth* or *Lord of the Underworld*, and it is the power of his water (=sperm, urine, secretions) that creates the sacred rivers and makes the earth fertile. For the Sumerians, earth goddesses were barren, unless they were impregnated with life-giving water. Enki fertilised the soil and kept the principles of civilisation, the divine Me, in his temple. One day Inanna came for a visit, got drunk with him and tricked him into giving her the lot. She loaded them into her boat and abducted them to her favourite city, Uruk, which became the first mega-city of known history. That, however, is just one story; in real life, several deities were custodians of the divine Me.

Enki has many symbols, such as ever-flowing vases, the rivers Euphrates and Tigris which stream from his shoulders, the fish-mask, sacred reeds, trees, sheep, fishes, turtles, the large Mesopotamian fallow deer and the goat-fish, a symbol that became popular around the middle of the second millennium BCE and turned into the constellation Capricorn. Unlike many gods, Enki is not interested in heroic gestures or a royal office. He loves learning, trickery and sex and demonstrates an almost terrifying creativity. Enki uses cunning instead of power to achieve his ends. While other gods struggle for supremacy and have ferocious battles with terrifying beings, Enki/Ea likes to act from the background. He fertilises, adjusts, counsels, tricks, jokes and when he has to kill someone (like Apsû in the EE) he chooses a sleep-spell and assassination. When the *Lamaštu Series* was compiled, Enki/Ea had become a friendly character (with a weird sense of humour) who helps people in need. Usually he does so by giving helpful hints to his son Asarluḫi/Marduk. Spells dating from the third millennium BCE show Enki/Ea acting personally. In the earliest surviving spells from Ebla and Fāra (c.2700-2600 BCE) he is more ambiguous. To be sure, he is a helpful deity most of the time. But he is also capable of causing disease. *Enki has bound the evil within, Nisaba has released it* X) *[...] made for Enki a firstborn sacrifice of the GA.SAR plants. At the GA.SAR plants Enki aimed his evil gaze [...] went into the KUR.MUŠ [...] made a sick eye [...]*. Luckily Enlil and Ningirima know how to cure it. *Enki (?) has made a parched interior/womb for the child of X in the steppe*' (Krebernik 1984:54-63, 48-52, 150-152, trans. JF). In most texts, Enki/Ea is a son of An or Enlil. But there is a tradition from Eridu claiming that the primal goddess of cosmic water, Nammu, created the world with no god to help or fertilise her. Without the influence of a male, she gave birth to Enki and charged him to govern the watery deep. His family ties are complicated. Usually, his wife is Ninki (*Lady Earth*), who may or may not be a feminine version of him. Ninḫursag and Nintur appear as his wives or sisters; both are prominent goddesses of fertility and childbirth, otherwise known as Nin-mug (*Lady Vulva*), Damkina, Damgalnunna and Ninsikila (a goddess of foreign Dilmun). It's not that Enki had a harem. Behind each wife is a local tradition that sought to mate the famous god of life, science, magic and irrigation with a popular local goddess. Among his children are Ninkasi and Siris (the deities of brewing), grain goddess Ašnan, Laḫar, Ningišzida, Nin-SAR (*Lady Plant,* her star is close to Vega), Asarluḫi, and finally, around the middle of the second millennium BCE, Marduk. His sukkal (vizier, CEO) is the Janus-faced Isimud/Usmû. Enki/Ea is brother or nephew of Lamaštu and the step-father who raised, reared and educated her. Now for something truly amazing. A popular title of Enki is Sumerian: Mum(DE), Akkadian: Mummu. According to various translators, it means: Original Form, Archetype, Mould, Matrix, the Intelligible, Intelligence within Form, World-Soul and World-Idea. It's a mind-blowing concept. An ancient deity called Mummu appears in the Babylonian EE. He opposes the gods and is bound by Enki, who uses him as the foundation of abysmal power and intelligence. And Mummu is the name of Enki's magic wand, the crooked rod with the sheep-head handle. That, of course is not all there is to it. The CDA, which proposes *'life-giving force?'* for the word, tells us that the title Mum(DE)/Mummu was also used to praise Ištar, Papsukkal and Marduk. Evidently, the concept was too great to be confined to a single deity. More than anything else, these abstract concepts reveal that Mesopotamian religion reached an amazing degree of sophistication. They are closely related to the Sumerian terms ni-du, me-te(n), giš-ḫur and the Akkadian uṣurtu: *the basic plan of all things.* Please stop a moment and consider this deeply. It used to be thought that concepts like the all-self, world-soul, all-pervading awareness were developed in India during the *Upaniṣadic* period between c.900-600 BCE: we meet them as Atman, Puruṣa, Prajāpati and finally, in their most refined form, as Brahman (*Extension*). In the *Upaniṣads* they were developed to a degree of refinement that is far beyond anything known from Mesopotamia. However, in Mesopotamia they can be traced to the Middle Babylonian period. That's more than five hundred years before the Indian seers discovered them. Whoever claims that the Mesopotamians venerated simple deities impersonating natural forces and primitive ideas, should reconsider now.)

I, 81

I conjure you by Bēlet Ilî: Lady of the Gods,

the Great Queen, the One Who Causes Birth;

I conjure you by Sîn, Lord of the Royal Headdress,

who Judges Decisions and Provides Signs;

(**Bēlet-ilî** is an Akkadian title: *Lady of the Gods.* Its Sumerian original is Nin-dingir-e-ne. She is usually identified with the Sumerian **Ninḫursag**, *Lady of the Foothills, Lady of the Stony Mountains,* a major goddess of birth and fertility, mother of Ninurta, whose power makes the land fertile, makes animals fruitful and grants the kings the right to govern. Among her Sumerian titles, which were also used for other mother goddesses, are: Dingir-Maḫ (*Highest Goddess*), Nagar-šaga (*Carpenter of the Insides/the Womb*), Nagar-namlu'ulu (*Carpenter of Mankind*), Nigzigal-dimdimma (*She Who Created Life*), Nin-ba-ḫar (*Lady Potter*), Šugal-anzu (*Female Potter*), Tibira-kalamma (*Female Smith of the Land*), Tibira-dingirene (*Female Smith of the Gods*), Nin-dim (*Lady Fashioner*), Nin-maḫ (*August Lady,* probably the star Vela), Nin-menna (*Lady of the Tiara*; she grants authority to priests and kings), Nin-zizna (*Lady of the Embryo?),* Nin-uru-lugal-e-ne (*Mighty Lady of Kings*) and Šazu-dingirene

(*Midwife of the Gods*). When Ninḫursag became pregnant, the earth began to *rustle with snakes and scorpions* and in the belly of her *great sister* Nin-gal, *dragons began to (swarm?)*. Ninḫursag represents or gobbled up an entire cluster of local goddesses who used to be venerated as creatrixes, mothers and nurses. Several of them are craftswomen: smiths, potters and carpenters, who use their skill to create animals, plants and people. Apart from her function as a major mother-goddess, Ninḫursag appears as a lady of animals and wild places. In this role she is occasionally praised as the wife of Nergal, who spends much of his time in her realm, the terrifying deserts, mountains and wilderness, of Šulpae (a god of animals and wild places) and as a sister of mighty Enlil. Ninḫursag had a major temple in Keš, but there were shrines for her in many cities. Enḫeduanna sang that her temple was the place where form was given to Heaven and Earth; a terrifying place, spreading fear like a great serpent/dragon, a deep, dark womb, and its building towered like a great mountain.

The term Bēlet-ilî is unspecified. Mesopotamia had plenty of mother– and birth goddesses (each city and period had its own preferences) and the title was freely used. In some places, like Babylon, a whole group of them were worshipped simultaneously. But we also encounter it as a title of Ištar, who avoids motherly duties most of the time.

Our spell follows a structure. In the last lines, the conjurers invoked An/Anu, Enlil/Ellil, Enki/Ea and Ninḫursag to control Lamaštu. They are the four major gods of early Mesopotamia.

Sîn, known in Sumer as **Suen** and **Nanna**, is the god of the moon. Sometime before 2600 BCE, Nanna (perhaps the god of the full moon?) merged with Suen (the crescent moon) and Ašimbabbar (new moon). He is closely associated with time keeping, the calendar, with the seasons and periods, as he fixes the length of the lunation and establishes the year. He was especially worshipped by the cow-herders, who called him the *Frisky Calf-of-Heaven*, the boatsmen (the lunar crescent is a barge), and those who tended orchards and gardens, who addressed him as *Self-Grown-Fruit*. Nanna/Suen/Sîn travelled from Ur via Gaeš to Nippur once a year, to offer fish, birds' eggs, wild pigs and dairy products to his father Enlil. When the moon god, or rather, the ship carrying his statue arrived in Nippur, Enlil (or his representatives) treated him to typical products of the agrarian countryside, such as cakes, bread and beer. Nanna is closely connected with the city Ur, and with the temple Ekišnugal/Egišnugal (*House Causing Light*). He also had major temples in Harran and Neiran. His wife is Ningal (*Great Lady*), their daughter Inanna/Ištar. Their son Ningublam is a badly-documented god who acts as a warrior, hero and MAŠ.MAŠ (conjurer, exorcist): he can make clouds move, storms roar and sunlight shine, and speaks many languages. Nanna/Suen/Sîn was often associated with the function of prince- and kingship. He is a very popular god, a gentle, friendly companion in the night. But he also has a fierce form, making him appear as a young hero and as a judge of the Underworlds. This task is also fulfilled by his son Šamaš; the two take turns in their duties; mind you, there were quite a lot of deities busy deciding the lawsuits of the deceased. The **signs** provided by Sîn are omens; the Mesopotamians lived in an extremely meaningful environment where every unusual incident had a deeper significance.)

I, 83

I conjure you by Šamaš, the Light Which is Above and Below,

the Creator of the Regions of the World;

I conjure you by Asarluḫi, the Lord of Conjuration;

(For sun god Utu/Šamaš see LS I, 45, for Asarluḫi/Asalluḫi, god of magic and healing LS I, 19)

I, 85

I conjure you by Ninurta the First Among the Gods, his companions;

I conjure you by Ningirima, Mistress of Conjuration,

Ninurta is a son of Enlil, his champion, and a powerful god of Nippur. Maybe his name was pronounced like Enurta or Nimrod. For the researcher, Ninurta poses many problems, as he was identified with the god Ningirsu of Lagaš around the end of the third millennium BCE. There were political reasons for this move. Around 2600 BCE, Nippur became the religious centre of Sumer and its main god, Enlil, replaced his father An/Anu as the head of the pantheon. To the south, the independently-minded city-state Lagaš close to the Persian Gulf had accumulated much power and wealth, and controlled the sea routes to Africa and India. The priests of Nippur installed a local god, Ninurta, as the son of Enlil. They managed to identify Ninurta with a very similar but extremely powerful god of Lagaš, Ningirsu. We don't know how this was settled. Ningirsu became a son of Enlil; a respectable position which ensured obedience and submission. Simultaneously, Ninurta's wife **Gula/Ninkarrag**, a prominent goddess of healing, exorcism and magic, was identified with Ningirsu's wife **Bau/Baba**, who was basically a goddess of civilisation, a custodian of truth and justice and keeper of the divine Me (which she had gained from her father An). Both goddesses exchanged functions and attributes and came to be called Ninisinna/Nininsinna (*Lady of the City Isin*) and Nin-nibru (*Lady of Nippur*). Ninurta/Ningirsu has a heroic nature and is usually busy combating malevolent beings, such as a lethal Asakku. He became the *arm of battle for Enlil* and the priesthood of Nippur; he was praised for violence and carnage, for crushing the cities of the rebellious land, spitting venom against the *Evil Place*. His fighting fury is associated with thunderstorms. It relates him to springtime and fertility; so in a secondary role he functions as a deity of farmers. The second month of spring was dedicated to him; occasionally he was praised as the *Good Seed*. Ninurta fills the canals with lasting waters, makes the barley thrive, fills ponds with fishes, grants abundance to the reeds and fills the gardens with honey and wine. In another role, he became the purification priest of celestial An, from whom he gained fifty Me (divine principles/powers of civilisation) and the temple Eninnu (*House/Temple of Fifty*). Here, the number 50 represents kingship. It was later claimed by Marduk, whose priesthood turned Ninurta/Ningirsu into 'aspects' of their favourite god. One of his symbols is the thunderbird Imdugud (*Heavy Rain*), another is the plough with the seed funnel. The cult of Ninurta/Ningirsu was widely popular: he had temples and shrines in Gubarra, Imrua, Ebirbir, Šugalam, Eimdia, Eninnu, Egišarra, Eanirbirbir, Tarsirsir, Esala, Esadua, Ekišuku and Enikise. King Gudea of Lagaš composed a magnificent hymn to Ningirsu/Ninurta, which stresses the oceanic aspects of the god. He praised him as one whose mind pulses like the waves, sways gracefully like the branches of the willow, surges like the overwhelming waters and rises like a destructive storm tide. He loves the Gu-edenna (the *Beautiful Steppe/Wilderness*), is fond of wild birds and delighted that the wild animals pay no tribute to him. Gudea's temple hymn is among the greatest literary works of the Near East. It describes in full detail how the god asked Gudea to build his new temple. In all likeliness, Gudea was busy as an architect; at least, one of his statues show him holding a plan for the temple. Ningirsu/ Ninurta and his family supported the royal plan. They supplied Gudea with the materials for his monumental building project and watched over his work.

Does Ningirsu/Ninurta appear as a valiant fighter of evil or as a supporter of fertility in this verse of the *Lamaštu Series*? Or is it because of his close relationship to Ningirima, the Lady of Conjuration, whose name was needed to fix the spell? Ninurta had a daughter called Nin-ni-gi-na. She was occasionally confused with Ningirima.

Let me introduce you to the earliest (known) goddess of magic and purification: **Ningirima**, also known as **Ningirim** and very rarely as **Ningirin** or **Nikkilil**. Her major influence was in the third millennium BCE (and probably earlier). As Ningirima had her greatest popularity in a period when writing was still developing and from which few records survive, it is hard to learn anything specific about her.

One reference is an Early Dynastic dedication inscription from Hafāgī. We meet her prominently in the spells from Fāra and Ebla, dating around 2700-2600 BCE. Usually she is invoked at the end, to fix the spell and make it come true. Typical Sumerian formulas are *This is the conjuration of Ningirima*, or: *This is not my conjuration; it is the conjuration of Ningirima.* Here is a formula that ends a serpent spell: *By the life of Ningirima, your lady, be conjured.* It tells us that she is a goddess of snake/dragons. In Fāra and Ebla, she was one of the major players. In the list of sacrifices from Fāra, she received four times the amount of barley flour as any other deity. Of the 29 spells of the Fāra/Ebla collection, 17 invoke her to make the magic work. There were probably more: several spells are fragmentary and lack their ending.

Ningirima's Sumerian name appears in more than 20 distinct spellings; among them dNin-A.ḪA.KUD.DU, Nin-A:ḪA.MUŠ:DU, dNin-A.ḪA:BU:DU, dNin-A.ḪA:BU:LAGAB (=DU), dNin-DU. MUŠ. A.ḪA. Her Akkadian name is (deity) **Min**. It was rarely used as the Sumerian versions were more prestigious. She was praised as a sister of Enlil and daughter of Enki/Ea. In Sumerian times, some priests and priestesses called themselves the *child of Ningirima*. Around 2350 BCE, Lugalzagesi claimed that he had been adopted by her. He praised her as Nin-unu-ga: *Lady of Uruk*, a title which was later claimed by Inanna and Ištar. To understand the importance of this title you should remember that Uruk (Sumerian: Unug) was the first mega-city of known history. Unug was founded in the fifth millennium BCE and fused with the neighbouring city Kullaba, whose walls are in some way connected with Ningirima, and reached its greatest extent in the fourth millennium BCE, when it was the largest (known) city of the world. It remained so until Rome reached her prime. That's three thousand years! You could consider it the birthplace of urban civilisation. The earliest written documents of Sumer come from Unug.

Lugal Zagesi's favourite goddess became a victim of imperial politics. Sargon I destroyed Lugalzagesi and the fifty minor kings who had allied themselves with him. Instead, he promoted his own favourite goddess Inanna/Ištar/Irnina. The cult of Ningirima lost its importance and Sargon's daughter, Enḫeduanna, composed a nine-line hymn that limited Ningirima to the small city Murum, while Inanna/Ištar became the wife of celestial An and the greatest goddess of the newly founded Akkadian empire. Here is Enḫeduanna's hymn. It is one of the shortest in her collection of temple hymns (TCS 3, 19):

City founded (?) from the Abzu on her foundation

raised for conjuration, for the office of the išib-priesthood,

house where conjurations of Heaven and Earth are recited,

where flour and barley are scattered and heaped,

your lady Ningirima, your wife,

under Heaven and Earth,

she purifies with water from the agubba vessels.

Ningirima, lady of the purifying agubba water,

has founded the temple/ house of Murum in your realm

and made her home on your high seat.

A note: the išib/išippu priesthood was devoted to conjuration and purification rituals; the masters of their craft were usually Enki/Ea and Ningirima, though several other deities are also associated with it. Ningišzida, Ninduba, Ninšubur; Anu and Nidaba had išib priests in their temples, and there is even an išib priest of the dead officiating in the underworld. (Henshaw 1994:41-42). Ningirima's city Mu-ur-um is hard to identify. So far, it is not even clear whether there was one place called Muru and Murum or two. One such town may have been south of Badtibira, the other one close to Kisurra, where the serpent/dragon goddess Išḫara had her strongest influence. Ningirima was identified with Išḫara, another deity whose early history remains enigmatic, around the end of the third millennium BCE.

Išḫara appears in Ur III inscriptions; in Mesopotamia she was worshipped much like Inanna/Ištar, as a goddess of love, lust, conflict and combat. But we also meet her as a major goddess, charged to punish oath-breakers, among the Hittites, who dedicated entire mountains to her cult. When the Hittites made a peace treaty with the Egyptians, they invoked Išhara to witness the event. Ningirima, Išḫara and Ninurta were the major deities of the city Kisurra. Both goddesses share serpent/dragons as their sacred animals, and both were identified with the constellation 'serpent/dragon'. This constellation was later renamed 'Scorpio'. As it was inconveniently large, the claws of the scorpion were later turned into Libra.

We can't tell which Muru or Murum was Ningirima's city. Another problem arises from what is probably a mistaken identification of Ningirim with a minor god of mongooses and small animals called Ninkilin who is also associated with a Murum or Muru.

In Sumerian literature, Ningirima is celebrated as the MAŠ.MAŠ (Akkadian: mašmaššu) of the gods, i.e. their conjurer, exorcist, incantation priest and purifier. A Sumerian title calls Ningirima Re-eš-mu-mu-ke: *Lady of Conjuration* (Akkadian: Bēlet Šipti). Or we encounter the Sumerian title: Ga šan TU-bi nam-ti-la-ke: *Lady whose Conjuration is Life/Recovery* (Akkadian: Bēltum ša tuša balatu).

An early Sumerian title is Egi-zi-gal-an-na: *Great Rightful Lady of Heaven.* That's another title that became the sole property of Inanna/Ištar in later periods.

A fascinating line from CT 25, 49, Rs.1 explains:

^{d}Nin-A.ḪA.KUD.DU = be-le-et te-lil-ti GAŠAN a-li-kat su-le-e [X]. It means literally *'(Deity) Ningirima = Lady of Purification (Bēlet Tēlilti), Lady who walks the roads...*

Krebernik proposes that the missing section would have contained the Sumerograms A.ḪA. It would have made her the *Lady Who Walks the Roads of Water/the Sea.* Hald (1914) guessed it might be the way of the ecliptic.

Her most popular name is, of course Nin-Girim(a). It means literally *Lady of the Girima.* The **Girima** is an enigmatic body of high or heavenly water. It is probably not a cloud or a rainstorm, as Kramer suggested. In SF 55 IX 8 the Girima is identified as muš-bulug-bulug: *feeding/ raising/ breeding dragon/snakes.* These animals are sacred to her. In his meticulous study, Krebernik (1984:232-263, trans. JF) cites a spell stating:

Enki said to (his) son (Asarluḫi):
The Girima (may?) come down from above,
when Ningirima has led (?) it down,
she shall add it to the 'sacred water' (a-gub-ba).

Here is another one:

The purification water of Enki,
the agubba water of Ningirima,
shall make this human, the child of his god,
clean, pure and bright.

(ditto p. 257). God list *An=Anum* calls the agubba the *pure washing water of Eridu.* A popular Sumerian title of Ningirima was Nin-a-gub-ba-dad: *Lady of Sacred Water.* She shared that title with Nammu, the cosmic goddess of water and creation. The agubba water was not just the major purifying substance of Sumerian religion, it was also a deity, and appears in god-list *An=Anum* directly after Ningirima. Ningirima was worshipped in Eridu, linking her to the first known temple of Sumer. She may even be one of its primal deities. In UL, CT 16, 7, 254 she is the *Sister of the Agubba.* Another Sumerian title: Nin-e-ku: *Lady of the Pure Temple/House.*

As a goddess of the Abzu/Apsû, her animals are fishes and serpent/dragons, and her name Lady of the Girima was occasionally written with cuneiform signs signifying these animals. The Sumerograms for water (A), fish (ḪA=ku$_6$) and serpent/dragon (MUŠ) were frequently used to write her name. Just look at the examples cited above.

Ningirima is somehow associated with a river- and serpent/dragon deity, identified with the Euphrates and the Arḫatum canal, called MUŠ.ir-ḫa.DIN.BALAG.DAR, or simply Irḫan. This deity is mentioned in archaic hymns from Uruk, the Fāra god list and other early texts, but without giving details. One ritual text (CT 23,1 2;7;11) says that an image of Irḫan should be drawn with flour. It would be nice to know for what.

So far we have had plenty of references to the goddess but still know hardly any details. No hymns, no myths, nothing. In these lines you are reading most of what is known about her. Like Marduk and Enki/Ea, she was invoked during the *Conjuration of Eridu*, a popular but sadly lost ritual that transformed common water into the pure and magical fluid of the Euphrates near the earliest (known) temple of Sumer: *the pure water of Enki, the brightly shining water of Ningirima* (Hald, 1914). She is among the seven gods who are summoned for purification rituals in dawn and dusk rituals, to clean people who have polluted themselves. Elsewhere we find her pouring libations and drawing magical circles with flour. She appears in the company of typical healing deities:

This conjuration has been 'cast' by Asarluḫi, Marduk,

Ningirima, the Lady of Conjuration,

and Gula, the Lady of Healing Arts,

and I have raised it.

(BAM 6, 510, IV, 38f).

Last: a word on history. Ningirima's name appears all the way through the written record. However, her importance faded. In early third millennium literature, she, Enki, and, on very rare occasions, Enlil, are the major gods of conjuration, magic, exorcism and purification. There must have been other traditions: our knowledge of the period is exceedingly limited. By the middle of the third millennium Asarluḫi was established as Enki's son. Like Ningirima and Enki, Asarluḫi was closely associated with water and purification, and his cult place was Kuara, a small town in the marshes close to Eridu. First he acted as his dad's messenger, agent, and odd-jobs boy; later he became a major god of magic in his own right. Around the middle of the second millennium BCE, Marduk was identified with him. Marduk, immensely popular in Babylonia and supported by a powerful cult, became a son of Enki/Ea and a major god of magic and exorcism (though he still had to ask his dad for advice). In his company appear gods like Šamaš, Girra and Gibil, who represent justice, light and fire, and act as exorcists and spell-casters. By that time, the major gods of magic were all male. It has been argued that Ningirima lost her importance when Asarluḫi and Marduk became gods of magic. However, the decline of her cult started much earlier, when Inanna replaced her as the goddess of heaven and of the greatest city of the early world. When the *Lamaštu Series* was compiled, Ningirima was almost forgotten: she simply appeared, for traditional reasons, at the end of conjurations to fix spells. The scribe of the *Maqlû Series* VII, 47 even turns her into a male deity by mistake.

I, 87

I conjure you by Ninkarrag, Governess of Ekur;

I conjure you by Ištar, Lady of the Lands;

(**Ninkarrag** is a goddess who was identified with **Gula** (*the Great*), a goddess of healing and conjuration. Her main cult site was the city Isin, hence she appears as Ninisina/Nininsina, the *Lady of Isin.* Gula is a celebrated daughter of An/Anu, who founded her city personally. Other major cult places were the cities Nippur (she was praised as Ungalnibru: *Lady of Nippur*), Borsippa (near Babylon) and Aššur. Gula is the physician (asu) of the gods, the great expert on plant lore (some scholars suspect that she started her career as a vegetation goddess), an exorcist and enchanter. She praised herself:

Exalted in heaven, Queen of the Underworld,

I have no equal among the gods,

I have no equal among the goddesses,

I am the Lady of the Deep.

Like Bau and Lamaštu, Gula was a child of Anu, named by Anu and educated by Enki/Ea. The priesthood celebrated her as Nintinugga: *Lady Who Revives the Dead.*

Gula's husband is Ninurta or Pabilsag/Pabilsang, who is sometimes identified with Ninurta or appears as an independent god. There were also attempts to make her the wife of celestial An/Anu, but, as you know, Inanna/Ištar got the job. You already read that Ninurta merged with Ningirsu and Gula with Bau/Baba. Thanks to this merger, Bau/Baba acquired Gula's function as a divine healer while Gula acquired Bau/Baba's skill as a truth speaker and a guardian of justice and civilisation. In the first millennium BCE, Gula was occasionally identified with Ištar, and so were many other goddesses. But Ninkarrag was also identified with Ningirida, the wife of the serpent god Ninazu (*Lord Healer*). In this constellation, she and her husband are closely related to the Underworld. Gula is easy to identify as she is usually accompanied by a dog, or even rests her feet on one. You'll read more about Gula and her dogs under LS III, 33. Why she is supposed to govern the **E-kur** (*House of the Mountain*) i.e. Enlil's temple in Nippur is beyond me. Farber points out that Ekur might represent ekurru (*temple*), making her the governess of all temples.

Ištar is the Semitic counterpart of the Sumerian **Inanna**. By the time the *Lamaštu Series* was assembled, she had become the major goddess of the Near East, well known in Iraq, Iran and Syria, in the mountains of Kurdistan and Turkey, in Cyprus, Palestine and Egypt.

Here the catalogue of deities comes to an end. Take a look at the sequence in which our deities appeared. It is based on numerology. Let me introduce you to **divine numbers**; you find more details in a later chapter. Several but not all Sumerian deities could be represented with numbers, such as 'deity 30' or 'deity 15', and during the Babylonian and Assyrian periods, further numeration ensued. In the process, several numerical associations transformed; finally, in the first millennium BCE scribes drew up lists of gods and their numbers to get some clarity into the business. While not all the deities in our spell had numbers, the catalogue starts with An/Anu whose number is one, as the father of the gods, and 60, as that number includes everything. The Mesopotamians based their numerical systems on a decimal and a sexagesimal count, and 60 was the highest number of a cycle. Several inscriptions call Anu the *deity 60*. Next we have 50, a number associated with kingship, for Enlil. The number was also claimed by Ninurta and, much later, by Marduk. 40 for Enki/Ea, possibly associated with the forty weeks of pregnancy; 30 for Sîn and the length of the month, 20 for Šamaš, 10 for Marduk/Asarluḫi (before he was promoted to number 50), 9 was probably associated with Ninurta and Gula and 15 represents Ištar.)

I, 89

by the Ubšu-ukinna, the Seat of the Council of the Great Gods in Ekur;

be conjured, that you may not return to N.N., the son of N.N. or oppress him!

(The **Ubšu-ukinna** is the hall where the gods held their council, after drinking a lot of beer. The place was known for heated discussions: though the gods had a king and a council of major deities, divine government retained a measure of democratic exchange. The council hall contained a representation of the **Duku**, the *Holy Mound*. Several major temples (Eridu, Girsu, Nippur) had such an Ubšu-ukinna, and a representation of the mound. Another one was in the Underworld. Lethal spirits of the deep were born in the mount of An/Anu and Ki. It could have been a mound of earth, or a storage pile of grains and wool, where offerings were made and libations poured. Jacobsen (1987:272) claimed that this pile may have been covered with plaster; a common way of storing grain. Van Dijk proposed that it might have been a representation of the primordial hill where the gods originally lived and from where Sumerian culture originated. At this *Mound of the Beginning*, the first tools were invented, grains were sown, animals domesticated and clothes woven. A few daring scholars have tried to identify the duku with the hill at Göbekli Tepe in

Turkish Kurdistan where the first (known) temple of mankind was built and agriculture may have been invented around 10000 or 9000 BCE. Or it may have represented an elevated space in a flat landscape threatened by regular floods. The one mentioned in our text could be in Enlil's temple Ekur in Nippur or maybe in ekurra i.e. in temples in general.)

I, 91

This is not my conjuration. It is the conjuration of Ea and Asarluḫi,

the conjuration of Damu,

and Ninkarrag,

the conjuration of Ningirima, the Mistress of Conjuration.

(**Damu** and **dumu** means *'the Child'*. The term was used for male and female children; for example, Enki addresses Inanna as 'dumu' and she calls him 'a-a' meaning father. Some texts call Damu the son, others the daughter of Gula. Maybe Damu appears in male and female form. This point is disputed by some scholars, who see the female form as a scribal error. Damu's name might be related to the words for blood, tree sap and a special dark beer (dāmu). Originally, Damu was an independent deity, representing, as Jacobsen claimed, the rising sap of springtime, and closely connected to the city-state Lagaš, to Larsa and Ur. A text associates her/him with Nanše, the goddess of dream divination. Damu was eventually identified with Inanna's husbands Dumuzi and Amaušumgalanna. Damu acts as an exorcist, a healer and a doctor. EN Da-mu-a-zu: *Damu is Physician.* Da-mu-gal-zu: *Damu is Very Wise.* Damu *binds the broken sinew.* Her/his constellation is the Pig, probably a part of Delphinus. But there is also a Damu who was worshipped in Syria as a warrior god. In this conjuration, Damu could symbolise the healing of the patient, or the recovery of the infant.

The final line of the conjuration fixes the spell. Again, Ningirima is invoked to do her job. Her appearance at the end of this šiptu might indicate that the passage contains early material, or that a traditionally-minded scribe made it look older than it is.)

I, 93

Conjuration of Lamaštu.

Ritual Formula: You shall purify the clay pit,

take clay from the pit and make a figure of Lamaštu,

(This ritual, slightly extended, also appears at the end of the *Lamaštu Series,* LS III, 129-138. These lines have been translated in many ways. Köcher believed that the conjurer should clean a potter's wheel and take clay from it. Others proposed that the house (of the patient) should be purified. The cleaning of the pit implies a ritual purification. Clay was a common but also a valuable and sacred substance, especially the sort that was used in rituals.)

I, 95

seat her (image) at the head of the patient,

fill a sūtu (vessel) with ashes and stick a sword/dagger in it,

let (it) stand at the head of the patient for three days.

Myhrman assumed that a bowl should be filled with fire, K. Frank (1913) and Saggs (1966) proposed ashes, Köcher preferred embers. Nowadays dikmēnu is read as *ashes.* It might be sympathetic magic: fire burns out, embers cool and turn to ashes, and the patient's temperature goes down. The vessel measures one sūtu(m), i.e. 10 qa i.e. 8.24 litres. The weapon is probably a dagger; a sword could make the contraption fall over.)

I, 97

On the third day, when the day descends,

you shall carry her outside,

hit her with the dagger,
and bury her within a corner of the wall.

(Tubqu(m) can mean: corner or recess. It makes me wonder which wall we are talking about. Within the cities, the alleys were narrow and houses often had no windows facing outside. Nor did they usually have a wall to separate the property from other buildings. Many had an inner courtyard, if their owner could afford it. So the major choices would be the walls of the palace, of aristocratic estates and major temples. I guess that we are talking about the city wall, a very liminal place where soldiers patrolled, travellers and homeless people found shelter, illicit business took place and the cheaper sort of prostitutes looked for customers. The shade of the wall was a popular place for illicit rendezvous and lovemaking. It's exactly the sort of environment where Lamaštu might feel at home. When her figurine is smashed, her confinement ends, she is released, and can resume her task.)

I, 99

Encircle her [image] with water mixed with flour,
and (when you leave) do not look behind you!

Conjuration: Lamaštu, Daughter of Anu, Named With a Name by the Great Gods,

I, 101

***Dingir Innin** (=Divine Mistress),*
***Ruler of the Black-Headed People** (=the Mesopotamians);*
be conjured by the life of Heaven,
be conjured by the life of Earth!

(This is the start of **conjuration #5**, the words are in Sumerian; it was pronounced over the chest and inner organs of the patient. Apart from the first lines, the text is very badly damaged or entirely missing in the canonical version from Aššurbanipal's library. From here we follow the front of tablet VAT 14506 which was unearthed during the German excavation at Uruk 1928/1929. The excavators discovered four pits of badly damaged or deliberately smashed tablets which had been used as rubble during the rebuilding of Inanna's and Anu's Eanna temple around the time of Darius I (521-486 BCE). Though none of the 6000 tablets was intact, they contained fragments of approximately 250 literary texts, including omen literature, medical texts, god-lists, astronomical texts, two Lamaštu fragments, spells to protect infants, sections of the *Gilgameš Epic*, a ritual allowing the king to allay the wrath of the gods, a hymn to Ištar and a lengthy ritual. The rest consisted of business contracts, letters and similar stuff. In all likeliness, there was a scribal school on the premises of the temple. The transcription and translation into German were published by Falkenstein in 1931. The reverse of the Uruk tablet contains material from the second tablet of the *Lamaštu Series* but the order differs from the canonical series.)

I, 103

She is a woman of the Elamites,
great is her head-covering (mane?** or: **radiance, halo),
she has risen from the reed thicket.

(**Elam** was in the foothills and mountains of modern Iran, east of Mesopotamia. In the neighbourhood of Sumer, Elam was the only high civilisation worth mentioning. The two countries shared a few deities and spoke related languages. Their relationship was somewhat strained. The proto-Elamites (Susa, period II) were on such good terms with Uruk that their society is occasionally considered a relation of the old Sumerian culture. Due to their intimate connections, it was speculated that the earliest Sumerian settlers may have reached their future country via Elam, either by passing through the mountains or by following the shoreline of the Persian Gulf. While the Sumerians mixed with the local aborigines and a number of Semitic people of the marshland and the alluvial plain, the Elamites developed in the mountains and highlands of Iran. Both cultures were exceedingly creative. Few are aware that while the Sumerians built megacity Uruk, the Elamites built cities like Anšan (modern Tal-i Malyan); it had a wall of five km length and may have housed 40,000 citizens. Anšan had the bad luck that, for unknown reasons, it functioned for only a few centuries as a metropolis, while Uruk kept growing. The Elamite city Susa was founded around 4200 BCE and probably had a large ziggurat (two layers remain) before the Sumerians even started building their first one, on a much smaller scale, in Eridu. While the Sumerians began to write between 3500 and 3200 BCE, the Elamites did the same, using their very own script. But their cordial relationship wasn't meant to last. The Elamites allied with other cultures of the Iranian highlands. Through most of Sumerian history, trade continued between the two high cultures, and in the range east of the Tigris, on the foothills of the Iranian mountains, a mixed population developed. Repeatedly, the Elamites became enemies of the Mesopotamians. The raids seem to have started very early. *Enmerkar and the Lord of Aratta* relates that the Sumerians desired the resources of Elam: timber, minerals, and ores. In both countries, Inanna was worshipped, and our story makes much of the strategies used by the Sumerian king Enmerkar to lure the goddess away from his rival. Sumerian kings, like Gilgameš, raided the mountains of Elam for their pines and cedars. King Enmebaragesi boasted that he had invaded Elam and carried away the weapons of that country. It was a valuable prize: unlike Elam, Sumer had no metals. A Sumerian *King List* claims that foreign regents from Awan in Elam invaded Sumer, where they established a dynasty for 356 years. Sargon I invaded Elam and Awan, and boasted of having *destroyed the country*, but as his campaigns ranged in all directions he lacked the time to occupy the mountains thoroughly. His son Rimuš also plundered Elam, and bragged of having killed 16,212 men. After the campaign, he dedicated 15kg gold, 1800kg copper, fourteen vases of marble and 360 male and female slaves to the temple of Enlil. Rimuš was probably killed by his brother Maništušu, who went to extremes to conquer the land around the north of the Persian Gulf, and whose campaigns carried him east of Elam. In conquered Susa, his governor Ešpum set up a dedication stele to the Elamite goddess **Narunde**. She became a major goddess of Elam, gained popularity in Mesopotamia, and appears as the sister of the Seven Warriors (the Pleiades) in the first millennium. Naramsîn did his best to keep large sections of Elam under his control. He boasted of having fought nine battles and having conquered three kings in a single year, but did not gain much, apart from timber, foodstuffs and a treaty promising eternal peace and mutual support (Koch, 2007). During the last Sumerian dynasty, Ur III, relations were a mixture of trade, diplomacy, uneasy peace and repeated assaults. When the Sumerian city-states began to struggle for independence and bureaucracy escalated, the Elamite aristocracy united. While Mesopotamians were having a hard time, the Elamites used their chance and made it worse. Around the end of the third millennium they devastated Ur, the Sumerian capital, and brought the moribund last Sumerian dynasty, Ur III, to a sudden end. Simultaneously, the fierce nomadic Amorites under Išiberra invaded Sumer, occupied the major cities and kicked the Elamites out of the country. It was the start of the Isin-Larsa period, which lasted for roughly two centuries.

So much for early relations with Elam; they continued like that for more than a thousand years. The power struggle ended violently. To the Neo-Assyrians, who compiled the *Lamaštu Series*, Elam was simply a former enemy state. Around 700 BCE, the Babylonians, Neo-Assyrians and Elamites were engaged in a vicious power struggle that involved frequent raids and changing alliances. Once the Elamites even conquered Babylon and set up a puppet king. In 692 BCE, the Elamites made an alliance with the Babylonians; both states conducted a mutual attack on the forces of the Neo-Assyrian king Sanḫerib. His historians describe the battle as a great victory, but in reality the Neo-Assyrian forces suffered badly. In 689 BCE, the Elamites were caught up in internal power struggles; it gave Sanḫerib the opportunity to attack the Babylonians and force them southwards. In the next decades, Elam kept an uneasy peace; Aššurbanipal attacked it in 655 BCE and set up his own government in Susa and Madaktu. An Elamite army attacked northern Babylonia in 652 BCE; in 649 BCE civil war broke out in Elam, and between 642-639 the Neo-Assyrians, led by Aššurbanipal, marched through Elam and devastated everything they found. The cities were destroyed; temples were looted, royal graves desecrated and most members of the royal family taken prisoner. In the wake of the campaign, many Elamites were relocated to other countries or sold into slavery. It looked like a decisive victory, but Aššurbanipal's savage triumph turned out to be a fatal mistake. Before long, the Persians invaded Elam and, finding no opponent worth mentioning, established themselves. The Mesopotamians were so busy fighting each other they did not notice. Finally, in 612 BCE the Babylonians overran Nineveh and finished the Neo-Assyrian reign. They assumed that everything would be back to normal. Though their economy had suffered badly, the Neo-Babylonian kings tried hard to resurrect the good old days. But the Neo-Babylonian Empire wasn't meant to last: the Persians invaded Babylon around 540 BCE and ended the Mesopotamian dynasties.

If Lamaštu is an Elamite, it could mean that the goddess was imported from the Iranian mountains sometime in unknown prehistory, or, more likely, that she is an enemy, a foreigner and a native of the dangerous mountains where no sane Mesopotamian would go. To those who had seen Aššurbanipal's armies destroy Susa, she could even appear as a despicable captive and slave. In cuneiform writing, a *mountain girl* is a slave. For the Mesopotamians, Elam was the home of many terrifying spirits and destructive gods. Foreign women were automatically assumed to be witches. A passage from the *Maqlû Series* (IV, 105-115, after Meyer, trans. JF):

Conjuration: They cast spells, they cast spells incessantly,
the Gutian women, the Ela[mite women],
the daughters of the Ḫanigalbate[ans],
six in the country tie knots
six are their knots, seven are my releases,
which they bind overnight,
which I untie by day,
those they bind by day,
I untie overnight.
I put them in the fire that scorches, burns, binds and seizes!'

Let's contextualise this. The Gutian barbarians came from north/western Iran, the Elamites from southwestern Iran and the Ḫanigalbateans, also known as the Mitanni, were a major threat. All of them were at some time major states and a real horror for the Mesopotamians. As you recall, much of the *Maqlû Series* is devoted to the destruction of unknown witches and wizards. It was a typical obsession of the first millennium BCE; in earlier periods, witchcraft was occasionally suspected, but never a major topic. The *Maqlû Series* was designed to protect a suffering client from evil spells cast by unknown persons. Witches appear more frequently than sorcerers, and take on an almost supernaturally terrifying quality. The topic is elaborated in lines 119-130. In this passage, the anonymous and unknown kaššaptu (*witch*) is identified as an Elamite woman, a Gutian woman, a Sutuean woman, a Lullubaean woman, a Ḫanigalbatean woman, an agugiltu (*thread-crosser?*), a naršindatu (a witch who uses river clay), a mušlaḫḫatu (*female snake conjurer*: a priestess specialised in snake control and spells), an eššeb/pūtu or eššebati (a female ritualist specialised in ecstatic trances), a female metal worker, a female rabiṣu (? uncertain, the text is damaged) and as a fellow citizen. As an Elamite, Lamaštu would be a witch from an ancient, highly developed urban enemy culture, or stem from primitive people dwelling in the ravines and cliffs of inaccessible mountains.

The word **mane** was used by K. Frank and Köcher, albeit with a much-needed question mark. A mane appears on several Lamaštu amulets, even if this defied nature. One early example is in the Louvre; here, the goddess has the head of an eagle and a bristly mane on her neck. The text on the reverse of the talisman is the early conjuration LS 2, 129 (see figure 13). While Lamaštu with a lioness head has no mane, the typical mane that appears on the amulets runs along the back of the neck to the shoulders; it could be the mane of a wolf or, more likely, the prominent mane of a hyena. Striped hyenas (Akk: būṣu) are common from Turkey to India. Nowadays they are an endangered species. Badly informed people discount hyenas as cowardly scavengers, but in real life, they are highly intelligent, have a fascinating social life and survive mainly by being very capable hunters. Unlike the spotted hyena, the striped hyena does not exhibit a huge penis-like clitoris and has no reputation as a sex-changer. Nevertheless, it is a typical witches' familiar or alter ego and appears in numerous spells and talismanic collections, especially those related to love, sex and erotic appeal. Indian and Near Eastern witches transform into striped hyenas when they roam the night. A few Lamaštu talismans show the goddess with the blunt snout and the fluffy tail that is much closer to a hyena than to a dog or wolf.

But we have to be cautious. Usually, the word *mane* is gubāru, qimmatu or pillû, and none of them appears in this passage. Köcher transcribed ar-ru-uša, which might be related to arû: headband. Falkenstein transcribed up-ru-u-ša, which could be related to an (unknown) **upru** (*headdress*); but adds that this is unlikely, as the term is a plural. Farber translated upru as *headgear*. If the word mane is incorrect, the most likely choice is apāru(m): **head-covering**, **head-gear**, a term that might refer to a wig, helmet or a crown, or, maybe to a mask. The last suggestion is a guess; the word for 'mask' has not been identified yet. But the word can also refer to a **halo** and a **radiance**.

The **reed thicket** refers to the swamps and marshlands of southern Mesopotamia, the Sea-land where the proto-Sumerians lived before the advent of agriculture. The reeds were used to make huts, house walls, doors, beds, boats, baskets, furniture and fibres. Vessels were made of reeds and waterproofed with bitumen. Bundles of reeds were used as building materials and could represent deities. Single reeds were split to make cheap one-way knives; in the literate period they furnished writing equipment. Frequently the dead were covered with reed mats and buried in reed-lined graves. **Nidaba/Nisaba**, the goddess of grains and reeds is a daughter of An/Anu. Her reed stylus made writing possible. She is a lady of learning, an expert on science, a custodian of civilisation, but as writing causes trouble, she is accused of causing quarrel and fighting in the land, of spreading slander and libel, of creating hatred between the gods of the height and the depth. The goddess of writing is praised as the *Mistress of the Underworld.* Nevertheless, her intentions are good. She gleams, her voice is loud, and as she gives life, all creatures of the wilderness extol her greatness (Lambert 1960, 168-175). The dancing reeds and shifting river beds offered protection from raiders and invaders. In Mesopotamian literature, the swamp, like the orchard and garden, is a popular metaphor for erotic activity. Young people could find shelter and privacy among the swaying stalks. Though swampland contained dangerous animals, parasites and diseases, it also had a sacred connotation. Reeds appear among the holy plants that connect Earth and Heaven. Reeds were cherished and harvested; to destroy them without purpose was a major religious offence (*Šurpu Series* III, 26).)

Figure 31 Unidentified human-lioness figure. Is this Lamaštu or some other being? Early third millennium BCE, today in Brooklyn. Photo in Parrot, 1962:79.

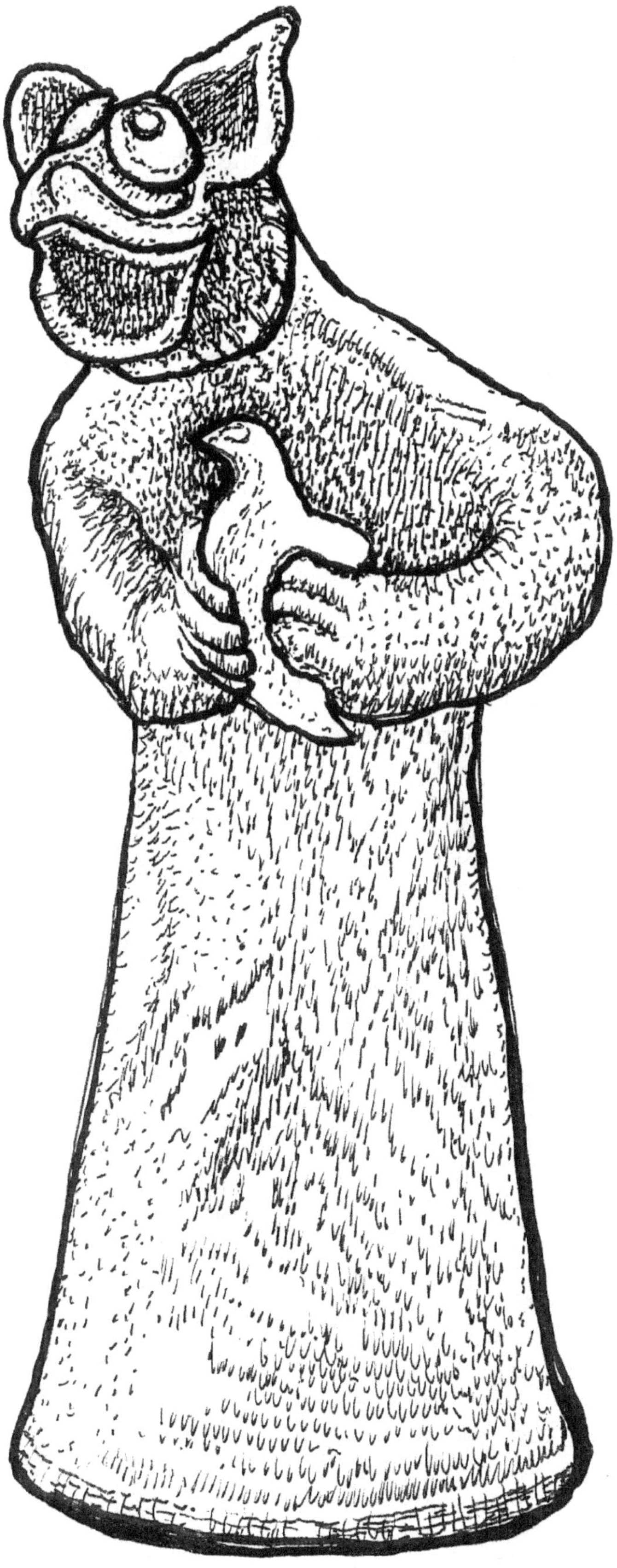

Figure 32 Unidentified being with the head of a lioness, holding a dove. Is this Lamaštu with the bird of heaven? Terracotta figurine from Tellō, 2-1 millennium BCE, today in Paris.

I, 105

She is huge, she is angry, divine [...] fr[om Heaven?] [...]

her [claws? feet?] are [like those of the] Anzû (Bird),

Var.1.: ***and her kidneys (*or:* flanks) are like [those of a leopard],***

Var.2.: ***her [hand] (brings? spells?) decay,***

(The Semitic **Zu** or **Anzû** bird is closely related, if not identical with the Sumerian thunderbird **Imdugud**. His name has been translated as: Heavy Rain, Slingshot and Ball of Clay. Imdugud started as a god of thunderstorms: he has the wings of an eagle and the face of a lion. Maybe simple people thought that thunder is the roar of a celestial lion. Or they simply enjoyed a good poetic metaphor. But Imdugud was also in charge of sandstorms and whirlwinds. According to an early myth Imdugud/Anzû once stole the tablets of destiny from Enki and/or Enlil. It took a lot of fighting to get them back. Other myths involving the storm bird appear in the Sumerian tale *Gilgameš, Enkidu and the Underworld,* where he is an unwanted guest rearing fledgelings on Inanna's ḫulub tree and in the poem of *Lugalbanda,* where he blesses and helps the protagonist. He was also associated with two different but very similar gods of rainstorms, fertility and battle, Ningirsu and Ninurta. In an early myth, Ninurta fought the thunderbird. In another, Early Dynastic tradition, Imdugud is the emblem of Ningirsu, or maybe his alter ego. It may have caused interesting conflicts when Ninurta and Ningirsu were identified with each other. The Anzû bird has huge talons and so has Lamaštu. At least on some talismans. She isn't the only one; plenty of animal-man hybrids and the winds of the cardinal directions were equipped with talons. However, the talons do not seem to be a must. After all, the goddess frequently receives sandals and boots as goodbye presents, indicating that she could also walk on human feet.

Variation 1 is from the Uruk tablet. The lines are fragmentary, and the two lines following it are completely illegible. The canonical text, as reconstructed by Farber, closes the gaps. However, it differed from the Uruk version. The **kidneys** could refer to the flanks of the leopard. **Leopards** are spotted, and so is Lamaštu in some texts.

It might be thought that Lamaštu's appearance is unique. This is not the case. She closely resembles a male Sumerian spirit or deity called Samana, who has a lion head and the feet of the Anzû bird. Stranger still, we can find a whole series of Lamaštu attributes in a hymn to the late Akkadian king, Naramsîn:

your radiance is fire, your voice is the thunderstorm,

You are a raging lion.

Your mouth is a venomous viper, your nails are those of the Anzû.

Irnina walks beside you.

(Joan Westenholz; 1997:183).

I, 107

[...] street(?) [...] she is completely hidden (?).

Her place is the [shadow of the w]all, she sits on the doorsteps.

(These lines are missing in the Uruk version. That Lamaštu lurks in corners, crevices and squats on thresholds is a popular idea. So do many other dangerous beings; we are talking about liminal spaces and in-between situations that allow access from one reality to another. It is also a magickal or psychological metaphor: when you position your awareness between worlds, you open yourself to new understanding.)

I, 109

Her fingernails are [very lo]ng, her armpits are [unshaven?]

she is im[proper] (*or:* un[fair]) she is worthless (*or:* without honour. *or:* ***a snake),***

the Daughter of Anu.

The fragmentary expression at the start of line 110 transcribed by Falkenstein as [ul]ị-ša-rat and by Köcher as [ll]ị-ša-rat derives from ešēru(m)/išārum. It means that Lamaštu is NOT right, normal, proper, straight, correct, fair, or going well. The word qal-lat could derive from qallum: light, of light weight, of little value, unimportant, worthless, of poor quality, without honour, disrespectable, impure. Köcher chose 'irresponsible', maybe, as in German, a person who is 'leichtfertig' is easygoing, lacking in seriousness, of light morals or careless. Falkenstein argued that the section is damaged and that the word could also be ba-aš-mat, yielding *she is a snake.*)

I, 111

Anu her father, Antu(m) her mother,

for her unpleasant (or: unfair) deeds they made her

descend [from Hea]ven; she has no place of worship on ea[rth?].

(The second half of line 112 was restored by Farber after Reiner & Güterbock 1967. The word 'earth' is likely but not certain.)

She is equipped with wings,

like Lilī[tu she soars],

(On several amulets, Lamaštu has wings. Around the Middle Babylonian period, Lamaštu was repeatedly identified as a member of the group of lethal wind or storm deities, the Lilû. These usually consist of **Lilû** (*Male Wind Deity*), **Lilītu** (*Female Wind-Deity*) and **Ardad Lilî** (*Girlfriend of Lilû* or *Girl of the Lilû Group*), plus, on rare occasions, the **Idlu Lilî** (*Young Man of the Lilû Group*). All four names come from Sumerian Lil: *wind, breath, vitality.* A fifth member of the group who may or may not be identical with Lamaštu is Pašittu, who has the Sumerian title Lil-lil-us-sa (*She Who Follows the Lilû*). Though the term 'lil' goes back to the Sumerian *wind, breath, vitality,* the later Akkadians, Babylonians and Assyrians attached a new significance to it. They identified it with the Semitic 'lil'; the Akkadian 'līlum' means *night.* It turned the Lilû group into night-deities (or demons, depending on what you prefer). All four of them were associated with diseases, including nervous disorders and insanity. Lilītu eventually assimilated functions that were usually associated with the Ardat Lilî (seduction and vampirism) and transformed, in first millennium CE Mesopotamia, Syria and Palestine into a whole swarm of male and female Lilītu spirits. In this guise, she entered the Jewish faith. We meet her as a minor horror in early medieval Palestine and Europe. Around the tenth century CE the amazingly creative Spanish qabalists turned her into a major nightmare, while her male form and her companions were forgotten. Instead, she was equipped with new partners, such as Leviathan, Samael and perhaps YHVH himself. We'll explore her astonishing career later on. One famous Jewish legend claimed that there were two Eves. The first Eve was created from the same material and on equal terms with Adam and did not behave as he told her. It made god create a second, inferior and submissive Eve from Adam's rib. That story appears in the third century CE *Bereshith Rabba,* 22,7 (Scholem 1960:215). In the ninth or tenth century *Midrash,* the *Alphabet of Ben Sira,* the story appeared in a revolutionary new guise: the first Eve was turned into Lilith. This, the best-known story about Lilith, is also the youngest and least original. The whole wild mixture was blown up, confused and turned upside down in the *Zohar.* The result was an amazingly impressive Lilith and a long way from her original Mesopotamian form. A tablet of the first millennium BCE identifies the Sumerian Kisikil Lila (Akkadian: Ardat Lilî) with Lamaštu

Conjuration: DIM.ME, Child of An,

chosen (or: famous one) of the Gods,

Ki.sikil. lil.a, child of good behaviour,

child of good behaviour.

I follow Farber's suggestions regarding STT 144. A duplicate tablet, RS.25.457 is quoted in West, 1992:374 and Frey-Anthes, 2007:277. Instead of kisikil-lila, West and Frey translated 'Lilit'. They followed a popular assumption that the two goddesses are actually one. As I will discuss in a later chapter, there are major differences between them. The last line, which West renders *(This) child is in good health (?)* is perplexing: is Lamaštu asked to return the sickly child to good health? If this reading is accurate, Lamaštu would function not only as a bringer of disease and death but also as a protector of sickly infants. This is exactly what we observe in the early Indian cults of the Mothers (Mātṛkā), a large group of terrifying goddesses, who are famous for child-killing, unless they are made the honorary mother of the infant. It would turn Lamaštu into a goddess who cares about special children, i.e. those dedicated to her. There is something similar in the *Zohar*. God almighty ordains which children should die early, and Lilith does the job. Like Lamaštu, she acts on divine request. On her own initiative, she adopts some children, plays with them and accompanies them through life. Was there a similar idea regarding Lamaštu? Or should we follow Farber's translation, which seems to imply that the Ardat Lilî is a child of good behaviour, hence hopefully nice and well behaved? Sadly, tablet STT 144 is badly damaged. The next two lines name DIM.ME as the Child of An and ask the little-known god Ḫendursanga/Ḫendursaga for help. He is the *Herald of the Land Sumer*, Enlil's watchman, who guards the streets by night, the *great police officer* (galla-gal) and the messenger of Utu/Šamaš, who enforces justice. Then follows a large gap and a few broken lines regarding a liquid and something that is to be placed around the neck of the patient. It leaves us hoping for more.)

I, 115

Night after night, morning after morning [...]

Regularly she transforms into** (or: **returns to** or: **into) a woman, whose entry** (or: **entrance) is [...]

(Several readings are possible. The 'regularly' is literally *to place in a row*, meaning presumably 'time and time again'. She might transform into a woman, return to one or even return into one, i.e. obsess her. If the former reading is accurate, she can take off her animal mask and appear human. If she keeps her eagle talons on she might look just like the goddess of the Burney relief that is so frequently (and without any reason) identified as Lilith. It does not have to be that way, as at least two Lamaštu talismans seems to show her with human feet, and several fail to show her feet at all. If Lamaštu returns to a woman she must be quite determined. Just as likely is obsession: the dangerous gods, goddesses and spirits were dreaded precisely as they could enter human beings. The entry is probably a point of entry; the word nērebu(m) means: entry, entrance and a mountain pass; perhaps it is also related to the nērebu festival. Scurlock (2014: 117) speculated that nērebu(m) might perhaps be a euphemism for the vulva: *the woman whose entrance is 'fearsome(ly narrow)'*, and that day after day passes without the emergence of the baby. However, there is no evidence that Lamaštu delays pregnancies or blocks birth. In fact she can hardly wait to get her hands on the child.)

I, 117

Every day the Daughter of Anu counts the pregnant women,

walks [af]ter those about to give birth,

I, 119

counts their [months], records their days on the wall,

casts a spell on those who give birth:

I, 121

'Bring me your sons so I may suckle (them)!

I want to place (my) breasts in the mouths of your daughters!'

(The lines on suckling also appear under LS II, 88-92. These lines raise the question if she wants to kill infants, or whether she simply wants to nurse them.)

I, 123

She holds in her hand/s: heat** (or: **fever), cooling** (or: **calming) (and) frost** (or: **trembling),

as much as she can carry (?)

(or: a (bird-)net** (or: **door) are her [...]),

her body is filled with scorching flame.

(Ummu(m)$_2$ means: heat or fever. Kaṣu(m)$_3$ is: cooling, calming, freezing. Ḫurbāšu(m) is: frost, shivering, trembling, terror and panic. It looks like a typical description of a feverish disease. Or maybe it refers to the sensations of heat and cold experienced by women who give birth. Or we could imagine that Lamaštu excites, soothes and causes ecstatic trembling: all three are typical trance experiences in 'shamanic' rituals. Falkenstein transcribed ka-tim-ta... and related it to a **bird-net**, kātimtu, and Farber agrees cautiously. A kātimtu could also be a sort of **door**. The term is rarely used and the question remains how a net would fit into a series of temperature metaphors. Köcher transcribed the same passage as ta-bil-tim: biltu(m) means: to **carry**, bear, transport, and refers to a load, a tribute, a yield or a burden. **Scorching flame**: not simply a quality of Lamaštu but a magical power that can be cultivated and used to banish hostile influences and/or purge oneself of them. When Marduk prepared to fight Tiāmat, he armed himself with weapons and a magical plant and filled his body with fire. Compare this with heat-generating yoga practices. Yoga developed out of tapas, which means literally heat-generating austerities. Very similar practices are known from early Daoism. The fire of the imagination can purify the mind, burn up the ego and liberate the trans-personal, unlimited self.)

I, 125

Into [...] she scatters her venom,

into the mother's womb (?) she scatters** (or: **sows) her venom.

(Scatter, spatter, winnow or sow are zaru(m). It has surprisingly fertile connotations for such a lethal action. In Farber's translation, the 'mother's womb' is missing; instead we learn she spatters her venom *quite suddenly*.)

I, 127

Snake venom is her poison** (or: **spittle), scorpion venom is her poison** (or: **spittle).

She maltreats** (or: **abuses,** or: **ruins,** or: **slaughters) the men,

(**Spittle** is a highly magical substance. When goddess Mami sat down to create the first human beings, she mixed water and clay and spat into it (*Atraḫasis Epic*). Spittle was also used to banish evil entities; healers, doctors, and exorcists often used it to fix spells or consecrate medication. They also spat at patients if they really deserved it. Šagašu(m) means: maltreats, abuses, ruins, kills and slaughters and leaves us plenty of choices.)

I, 129

she oppresses** (or: **wrongs) the women,

she convulses** (or: **smashes) the infants.

(For ḫabālu(m) you can read: oppresses, does injustice to, wrongs, does violence to; for napāṣu(m): abolish, smash, convulse, push away, push down.)

I, 131

She drenches the infants with waters of distress.

*or: **she makes the infants drink waters of distress.***

She enters an open house,

(Please recall the discussion of the *waters of distress/trouble/strain* and how they drench or are fed to the patient under LS I,

43. Instead of infants, ṣeḫru(m) we can also read: small ones, young ones, children.)

I, 133

she enters (a) locked house, sliding past the door pivot

[she sli]des (in) like a snake, (and) s[uffo]cates him.

(No matter if a house is open or closed, Lamaštu can come in. To slide in like a snake is a skill of several dangerous deities and spirits. Ṣerrāniš is a pun, the term can mean *by the door pivot* and *like a snake*, as Farber points out.)

I, 135

With milk (?), bitter [as bile] she nurses the child

[with the poison] from [wi]thin herself (or: her heart, or: her womb), she anoints his face.

(or: with his [h]eart (blood?) she smears her own face.)

(The first line comes from the Uruk tablet and is missing in the canonical *Lamaštu Series*. The second line is difficult. Libbu(m) has a lot of meanings: **heart**, inner body, insides, womb, inner organs etc. 'Heart' could be metaphoric for *central* or *inside*, it also refers to the physical organ, but this implies a lot more, as the heart was the seat of emotion, memory, thought, will, desire, mind and so on. Modern people think with their heads, the Mesopotamians did it with their hearts, livers and stomachs. If we chose **womb** the line might refer to sexual fluids. The idea that she anoints her own face, using heart-blood, is based on Farber's translation.)

I, 137

[h]e w[eeps bitterly?]: his food is deadly poison;

(or: [h]e [...] she spreads out like yellow ochre, befitting death.)

[with it), [Lamaš]tu and Labaṣu have salved his face.

She (or: He) grasps [th]rone (or: [ch]air) of the mourning place with her (or: his) hand,

(The first version of line 137 is based on Falkenstein and Köcher, the second on Farber, derived from Stol's identification of kalû as yellow ochre. The CDA adds that such a paste was used for figurines and wax writing tablets. It might suggest a liver disease. **Labaṣu** (Sumerian: **DIM.ME.A**) is a goddess who accompanies Lamaštu. In our text, she seems to appear as an independent deity; other texts give the impression that she is an 'aspect' of Lamaštu. The name Labaṣu defies translation. Farber proposes that the salved infant looks like one who has *lūtu disease or labaṣu disease*. The CDA describes the former as *debility*. The latter is even more enigmatic. A case of Pašittu disease would make more sense and provide a nice yellow face. To **salve** the face can also mean to anoint it: the action is almost ceremonial.)

I, 139

She (or: he) grasps the [d]ust (or: [e]arth) of the mourning place with her (or: his) hand.

[...] her [...] her

(Kiḫullû means the **mourning place** or the **mourning rituals**. Köcher proposed a 'bench of mourning', whatever that may be. Benches appear rarely in Mesopotamian literature. They are more common as divine and royal furniture. As a foot-rest, they represented the 'earthing' of a deity or king. Falkenstein guessed the half-missing word would be kussu, meaning: stool, chair or throne. Farber preferred stool. Falkenstein assumed that Lamaštu does the grasping; we could assume that she is seated on a throne, as befits a goddess. Köcher thought that the child does the grasping, hence his choice of the low-status bench. In Farber's version she grabs the stool of mourning rites. Eperu(m) is **earth, soil** and **dust**. The earth or dust of a specific place was often used in magical rituals, as it represents its quintessence.)

I, 141

She has the [fa]ngs of a dog, the claws of an eagle,

her breast ornament** (or: **fibula**) **is [loosened?** or: **broken?], her breasts are bare,

(In early Mesopotamia, the cloak was closed by an ornamental pin; under Neo-Assyrian reign, it was replaced by a fibula. The item was not just practical but also had a metaphorical meaning: after the marriage, the husband opened the fibula of his wife, i.e. she lost her virginity.)

I, 143

her [hair hangs loose?],

her vulva (?)** (or: **lap,** or: **bosom,** or: **arm-crooks** or: **embrace) is open,

her breasts are bathed in [bl]ood,

(The open, tangled hair was reconstructed from other Lamaštu spells. It means many things: wildness, lack of civilised manners, and probably indicated that the goddess stands outside of society, where proper coiffure mattered. Statuettes and images of Mesopotamian women show an amazing range of hairstyles. Many women wore wigs or made use of hairpieces and lots of hair-needles to appear more impressive. Simple open hair, hanging down the back, appears in very rare cases and seems to have been characteristic for female and male singers (Börker-Klähn, RlA *'Haartrachten'*). Lamaštu's appearance is very close to the description of the terrifying, dangerous Indian Yoginī goddesses as they were worshipped, visualised and meditated upon in the much later Tantric traditions. See, for example, the 11th century *Kaulajñāna nirṇaya* 19, 2-5: *When desiring Yogīnī Siddhi* (magical powers, skills, success), *one should meditate on them as being black-skinned, youthful, maidenly, wearing red clothes, smeared with blood, red ornaments, adorned with red flowers and red garlands. One should worship each as being one with oneself.* 23,12-16: *Meditate on them as wearing red clothes, besmeared with red scent* (=menstrual blood), *adorned with red flowers. A Vīra* (heroic worshipper) *should always meditate on them and worship them inwardly, eschewing outer worship.* 24, 4-12: *Listen to the meditation: all wearing red clothes, smeared with red paste, sixteen in number, begemmed, sweet of face, drunk from liquor made from Madirā* (=intoxicating drink) *blossoms, each like Icchā* (the primal Śakti of Will and Intent), *freeing from fever and death, each the cause of creation, giving boons* (trans. Magee, comments in brackets JF). More on the Yogīnī cult appears in the chapter on Siṁhamukhā.

The word kirimu was and is problematic. Thureau-Dangin believed that it means 'womb' and translated a similar passage: *her womb is loosened* while Köcher, following his example, chose **vulva**. Falkenstein argued that wombs are not loosened, and speculated that kirimu might be a bag to carry an infant. If we read 'open' instead of loosened, the word vulva makes more sense. Farber cautiously proposed that it might mean her **bosom-hold, cradling position**, i.e. the place where you would hold an infant. The CDA states that kirimu means *arm-crooks,* which is not very meaningful, unless we use the term as a euphemism for *embrace,* as Foster did. Given that an innocent word for 'knee' (birku(m)) could mean 'vulva, genital region, lap', I would guess that lap, bosom and arm-crooks are not as fully understood as they could be. Regarding the blood-bathed breasts, Falkenstein and Köcher are in agreement. Farber argued that the damaged word in line 144 might have been *milk of death* instead of blood. Wiggermann translated that Lamaštu has *venomous milk* in another context. The expression seems to be very unusual.)

I, 145

the nipples of her breasts are expo[sed]

[...] are her [...] on [...]

(This passage is very similar to a well-known younger Babylonian spell first quoted by F. Thureau-Dangin (RA Vol. XVIII, p.161 ff; who introduced Lamaštu in her irresistible charm to the Assyriologists. They never recovered from the shock.

Compare also Foster 1995:402, Köcher, 1949: 140, tablet AO.6473, reverse and Riemschneider 156 for the original text and 215 for a translation; Haas, 1986:146 and Farber 2014: 299:

Šiptu: She is raging, she is furious, she is wild,
she has a divine gleam,
she is like a she-wolf,
the Daughter of Anu.
she has feet like the Anzû bird,
her hands are filthy,
her face is like a great lioness.
She rises out of the reed-thicket,
her hair is open (or: exposed), her female underwear torn off.
She moves on the track of the cattle,
she follows the trail of the sheep,
her hands are in flesh and blood.
She enters through the window; she slides in like a snake.
She goes into the house, she leaves the house as she likes.
"Bring me your children that I may suckle them,
And your daughters, I want to nurse them:
I want to place my breasts in the mouths of your daughters!"
Ea, her father, heard her:
"Daughter of Anu, instead of being the fate (namtaratu) of people,
instead of placing your hands in flesh and blood,
instead of entering and leaving the house,
take from the merchant the cloak-fringe and the travel provisions,
take from the smith the rings (or: bracelets) for your hands and feet,
take from the goldsmith the pendants to adorn your ears,
take from the gem-cutter the carnelian beads to grace your neck,
take from the wood-carver a breast-ornament, comb and spindle!
I conjure you by Anu, your father, by Antu(m) your mother,
I conjure you by Ea, the creator of your name!"

Female underwear. The word dīdu indicates an unknown item. It could be a bra, a breast strap, a slip or, for all we know, a string tanga. The item does not appear in art. **Fate** is a tricky idea. Sumerian: **Namtar**, Akkadian: **Namtarru** is a god of the Underworld who personifies fate. He is occasionally included among the Evil Seven, but most of the time he does his job as the son, steward and ambassador of Ereškigal, the *Queen of the Great Earth*, goddess of the realm of the dead. When he travels to Heaven to represent his lady, he is respected and honoured by all celestial gods (except Nergal, who is duly reprimanded and later ends up in bed with the goddess). He is rarely described, but some late texts claim that he has a mouth full of poison, horribly twisted hands or no hands at all. A goddess of the third millennium BCE, Ḫušbiša, is his wife; they were joined by a daughter, Ḫedim(me)ku in the second millennium BCE. Prior to that assignment, Ḫedim(me)ku, ḪE.DIM.ME.A is a daughter of Enki/Ea, and called a *Daughter of the Apsû*. Namtar is not just a name but also a title of other gods, like Enlil and Šulpae. In exorcisms, Namtar is usually a bringer of death, disease and doom. Plenty of people had a dim outlook on destiny: evidently, the future led to death, one way or another. It does not have to be that way. In Sumerian literature we encounter nam-tar as a positive fate: it was a prediction of success, wealth and well-being granted to a king during the 'Sacred Marriage' rite courtesy of Inanna or a representative of hers. Sumerian Namtar-a-na-me-tar is the *reparation of life force and its fate*. Namtar is literally the *communication of life-force*, and its results, in accordance with the will of the gods and the deeds and misdeeds of a person. The 'fate' which Namtar represents is shaped by the interaction of divine will and your personal decisions and errors in life. It is not preordained or permanently fixed. The same goes for the 'fate' handed out by Lamaštu.

The **cloak -fringe** (qannu) is a magical item. The fringe of a dress or garment was much more than a nicely woven or embroidered strap. Before and around the middle of the third millennium BCE, contracts to buy land often required the buyer to add food and fine garments to the payment. The cloak-fringe was an essential part of them. When the seller put on the new garments and ate the food, the deal was fixed. The new clothes, as Petschow (RlA *'Gewandsaum'*) proposes, indicated that a new phase had begun in the life of the seller, who has no further ties to his former property, and was treated like a guest. Similar customs, regarding important sales of property, houses and businesses, occasionally appear to the Neo-Babylonian period. If a garment was provided as an extra (atru), it had to be an expensive item. Special clothes were often multi-coloured, and the most expensive ones were embroidered with gold, silver and copper, or embellished with small pearls. The fringe was usually finely woven and may have had symbolical ornamentation or colours. In legal proceedings, to *take hold the fringe* of another person was to sue her or him. Instead of a seal impression, the fringe could be pressed into the damp clay of contracts and documents. To *drag the fringe over the tablet in front of witnesses* symbolised that one had paid one's debts. A similar idiom from Ur III *to pass one's cloak over something* indicated freedom from guilt, debts and obligations. During the Old Babylonian period, when a woman was divorced, the husband tore off the fringe of her dress. It separated her from his family. Sorcerers tried to get a piece of fringe as it allowed them to enchant or curse its owner. Exorcists used hair and the cloak fringe of their clients to make substitute sacrifices. To grasp the fringe of a deity's cloak meant to take refuge to her or him, and to appeal for help. While none of these examples explain the full symbolism of the fringe, they certainly show that fringes could represent people in legal, domestic, religious and magical circumstances. When Lamaštu takes the fringe of the merchant's cloak she steals his self-esteem, social standing and quite probably the money he has hidden inside the fabric.)

I, 147

[...]

[...] like a child.

(At this point, the front of the Uruk tablet ends. On its reverse is the section on the river, Šarur, Papsukkal and the clay dogs which you can find on tablet two of the canonical text under LS II, 49).

I, 149

[...] her side,

[...] behind her

I, 151

[...][be]fore her.

[...]the man

I, 153

[...] the breast

[...] his [...] she has broken.

I, 155

(Although) she is not doom (or: defeat, death)

she has cut the infant's throat,

(although) she is not a gallû, she has twisted its neck.

(For gallû spirits and police inspectors, see LS I, 11)

I, 157

She has strangled the infant on the lap of its nurse,

she did not allow it to be buried in the house, (saying):

(From here to LS I, 161 I loosely follow Farber 2007:141.)

I, 159

'They should place the boy in a red leather bag,

as if storing provisions.

***They should lift him up and take him to the wilderness** (or: **desert**),*

where they should leave him.'

*(or: **... take her, one should release her into the desert'.**)*

(A few burials confirm that at least some of the dead were wrapped in red textiles. The evidence is rare and leaves much to be desired, as fabrics usually went to rot over the ages, unless they were in contact with bacteria-killing copper or bronze. The red cloth may have provided protection from evil spirits (for the deceased) or protection from the deceased (for the living). Conjurers occasionally wore red, presumably for similar reasons. Köcher assumed that Lamaštu should be taken to the desert, Farber found the infant corpse more likely.)

I, 161

She (?) should be led to the lock (?) of the canal [...]

[...] [into the di]tch** (or: **canal**), **and the fish in the Apsû should receive her (?).

I, 163

[L]ike in the fold,

*(or: **may it ? the shepherd resting in the fold**)*

(These badly damaged lines are problematic. In earlier translations, it was assumed that they were constructed along the formula '*may x receive it* or *her*, depending on whether we talk of the infant or the goddess. Farber has an entirely different interpretation of these lines. **'***May it befall (?) the X in the Y***'** would be the basic formula of these lines. He speculates that they (the parents?) should indeed bring him out. Whatever happens to the dead infant (or its soul?) ought to happen to a bird in the sky or a fish in the *Apsû*. As birds and fishes are quite comfortable in their habitations, I wonder what this says about the fate of the infant. Or is it the goddess who is to be led to the canal and the Apsû, as Köcher assumed? If this is accurate, Lamaštu is asked to descend into the underworldly sweet water ocean where her honorary father and teacher Ea/Enki resides (one of his emblems is a fish), or maybe into the great world-surrounding ocean. In Mesopotamian thought, that's as far as anyone could go. The Apsû is such an important concept that we may well devote some thoughts (and trance journeys) to it. We owe our word abyss, from Latin abyssus (*immeasurable depth, hell*), to the Mesopotamians. The Sumerian: Abzu and the Akkadian: Apsû may perhaps come from ab-zu *Hole of Wisdom*. The Sumerians assumed that the Abzu is a subterranean sweet-water ocean. You could think of it as the bottomless deep if you want a sinister idea, or as the sweet-water table, which is quite close to the surface in southern Mesopotamia, if you want a less exciting interpretation. The Sumerian Abzu was a goddess. Abzu was written with the cuneiform sign ENGUR, and so was the name of the primal water goddess of creation, **Nammu**, (Lammu, Namma-a-ke, Ur-namma-he; and Akkadian: Ur-na-amma, Ur-namma-ke), creatrix of the world, the gods and all beings. Sumerian Nin-nam-ak is: *Lady of Creation*; related to 'Nammu' may be Akkadian banû: *to create*. Jacobsen (1987:155) proposes that Nammu's name might go back to Nin-Imma/Nan-Amma/Nan-Ma, Namma meaning *Lady Female Genitals*. The south Sumerian Eridu cosmogony calls this important, mysterious and badly documented goddess *Primal Mother Who Gave Birth to the Gods*. She is Amautuanki: *Mother Who Gave Birth to Heaven and Earth*. Nin ab gal an-na u-a: *Lady Who is Great and High in the Sea*. And we meet her as Nin-a-gub-ba (dad): *Lady of the Sacred Agubba Water* (Akkadian: Bēlet Egubbe) a title she shared with Ningirima.

Figure 33 Ningirima.

Around 2700 BCE, when the Sumerians began to record religious literature, most of her myths were fading into oblivion. She had at least one temple in southern Sumer, and shared worship with the goddess Nanše at least up to the end of the third millennium BCE. By the advent of the Old Babylonian period she was almost forgotten. However, I suspect that Tiāmat, the goddess of the primal ocean contains a distorted memory of her.

The Babylonians simply did not like her, or extensive ocean voyages much. **A-ENGUR** means waters of the Abzu, or waters of Nammu, as you like; the word is cognate with Sumerian: Id: *river*, and the name of a river goddess. The Abzu is the realm from which *the holy reeds arise.* Reeds are Nammu's emblem. ENGUR is also a deity, and Enki is praised as Enengur: *Lord of the Engur.* Here are some lines from *The Birth of Man*: *In those days, lay he of the vast intelligence, the creator bringing the major gods into being, Enki, in E-ENGUR* (Temple/House of ENGUR), *a well into which water seeped, a place the inside of which no god whatever was laying eyes on, on his bed, sleeping, and was not getting up.* (Jacobsen, 1987:154). The cosmogony of Nippur tells us that in the beginning, *Heaven was ENGUR, Earth was ENGUR.* They came to be on their own accord, that is, everything was born from the abyss. After the Akkadian dynasty in the late third millennium BCE, the cuneiform sign ENGUR was also used to write the word ZIKUM: *Heaven.* It combined the watery and underworld abyss with the waters of heaven.

Temples represented the Apsû by large water tanks, but what exactly they were used for remains unknown.

While the Sumerian Abzu is a goddess, the later Babylonian Apsû is a god. According to the *Babylonian Epic of Creation,* he is the husband of the chaos mother Tiāmat. The two primal deities represent the sweet-water deep and the salt-water world ocean. Their union, in the marshes where sweet and salt water mingles, heaps up the rich and fertile mudbanks and creates the inhabitable world. That's how terra firma comes to be, and it is happening all the time. Enki killed Apsû, and raised his own palace on top of him. We are facing three traditions. In an early Sumerian myth, Enki is Nammu's son and becomes the custodian of her abysmal waters. In the much later Babylonian version, Nammu is absent and Enki gains control over the watery deep by subjugating it. A third tradition, still younger, claims that An/Anu and Nammu mated, and that Enki/Ea was their offspring. But the Babylonian poets did not limit the Apsû to the deep. Rivers, canals, swamps and soggy meadows were all called Apsû. The astronomers believed that rain fell from a celestial Apsû. The cities close to the Persian Gulf decided that Enki is not just a god of the sweet water in rivers and below ground, but made him a god of the sea. It turned the Apsû into the all-surrounding world-ocean. The priesthood contributed a deeper interpretation. During an initiation ceremony for the priestly rank of Sumerian: GUDU, Akkadian: pašišu, the initiate spoke the words: *I am a pašišu* (anointed one), *a ramku* (washed one) *of Enlil.* ***My insides are the Apsû.*** *My face is called...(Henshaw, 1994:31).* It's a great mantra. To explore the primal abyss of the beginning, sink deep into yourself.)

I, 165

like[...]the sheep (or: the herding boy) resting in its fold,
like[...]with its small livestock,
(or: may it ? the cattle in the cattle pen.)

I, 167

in the body? [...]she entered[...]
(or: [...] she entered the house.)
[...] house she brought forth wailing.

(These lines are an unhappy attempt to glean some meaning from Köcher and Farber.)

I, 169

Into[...][she le]aped,

she is mighty, [...] for the people she left mourning.

I, 171

Like [...]

I, 173

Like [...] she [...] seven times (or: into seven pieces).

In the street [...].

I, 175

In the corner [...] sits around

She is mighty, [...]

(I basically follow Farber but have left out some speculative words.)

I, 177

The fury of the storm [...]

(or: The complete silence of midday,)

the awesome radiance of drought (or: of the sun)

[fills] the body of [Lamaštu? or: the patient?].

(Line 177 follows Köcher's transcription, which differs from Farber's. Šamāru(m) is **rage** and fury. Ūmu(m) is a storm, but can also refer to a storm spirit, a storm-lion or the tempestuous power of the Seven Sages (apkalli). Whether Lamaštu or the patient is full of heat is open to debate. Maybe it's both of them. Farber opted for the lethal **midday** period when people were asleep in the shade and deadly beings went prowling. Midday was just as dangerous as midnight. You find the same belief in ancient Greece. Köcher thought of the feverish patient, but the **awesome radiance** (šalummatu(m)) sounds like an attribute of the goddess herself. A *divine gleam* or *gleam of terror* is often associated with Mesopotamian deities, planets, stars, temples and sacred objects. Lamaštu has such a gleam, such an *awe-inspiring aura*, and so have deities like Enlil, Enki, Inanna, Nabû and many others. The radiance is also emitted by successful monarchs. A hymn praising Urninurta of Isin says *May you dress in the terrible gleam, the 'Lion of Royal Attire', as the Robe of Regency (...). Your terrible gleam may cover the rebellious land like a heavy cloud* (SAHG 1953:107, trans. JF). Such an awesome aura is not only a quality of powerful beings and objects; it is also something that can be cultivated. Here are a few lines which Enkidu says to his friend Gilgameš, to encourage him in the fight against the god Ḫumbaba (tablet V, after Dalley 2008:70). The passage sounds as if Enkidu would quote a spell.

You rubbed yourself with plants so you need not fear death.

You shall have a double mantle of radiance like [...]

Your shout shall be as loud as a kettledrum.

Paralysis shall leave your arms,

And impotence shall leave your loins.)

I, 179

When she faces (or: is comparable to) a lioness, she sext[tuples?] her awesome radiance,

when she faces (or: is equal to) a wolf, she ma[kes it] howl,

(Maḫaru(m) is a multipurpose term meaning **faces** and a lot of other things. You can also read: **opposes**, confronts, **equals**, is **comparable to** and balances with. That should keep your head busy for a while. If she 'equals' the lioness and wolf-bitch, it could mean that she turns into that shape.

Myhrman and others assumed that she would **dim** the radiance of the lioness, which makes very little sense. Nougayrol proposed she would **'take'** the radiance of the lioness and the (evil) *eye* (?) of the wolf. It's a highly original interpretation. Farber cautiously proposed her radiance sextuples.

Myhrman assumed that Lamaštu emits an awesome gleam when she meets a lion; Köcher attributes the gleam to the lioness. Both translated that the wolf 'howls', the CDA suggests 'growls'. Farber cautiously proposes whimpers. It makes a great difference. Lamaštu often appears with the head of a she-wolf. Among wolves, growls are provocation, whimpers are submission and howling has a social function and makes the pack happy. Maybe the wolf howls in friendly recognition of Lamaštu. It's not philology but feels good.)

I, 181

when she crosses a river, she makes the water muddy,

when she moves on a road, she obstructs (or: stops) traffic,

I, 183

when she stands near (or: leans against) a wall, she smears mud on it,

when she stands near a tamarisk, its branches droop,

(The **tamarisk** or **salt-cedar** is one of the few trees that can survive on dry, salty terrain. Its roots extend much deeper than those of other trees. To the Mesopotamians, it was a sacred tree, a plant connecting heaven with the bottomless deep that could thrive where other plants withered. Tamarisk trees are related to heaven: their wood was a favourite for divine statues and roof-beams. Streck quotes a line from Wiggermann: *the bone of divinity, the consecrated tamarisk* (RlA *'Tamariske'*). *Šurpu Series*, tablet IX, 1-8, trans. Reiner, praises the tree:

Incantation.

Tamarisk, lone tree, growing in the high plain!

Your crown above – your root below -,

your crown above, is a tree releasing everything,

your root, below, is a [...] terrace,

your trunk is the gods,

[...] with bathed head,

you cleanse, you purify the mouth of the humans,

may the evil tongue stand aside!

The tamarisk represented An/Anu and, in later periods, Šamaš. (Langdon, 1919:82 *Babylonian Cult Symbols* 6060, No 12). Enlil, Šamaš and Ningišzida had tamarisk trees in their major temples. The wood was employed to make magical figurines. A bizarre composition is called the *Dialogue of Date Palm and Tamarisk*. The former represents the king, the latter is a mašmaššu who purifies and renews the temple. Water was consecrated with crushed tamarisk twigs. Bark and galls were used for tanning and, for medical purposes, as an astringent and antiseptic. The tree lets its crown sag, just as Anu's head sinks when he is really worried about his daughter, which happens practically every day.)

I, 185

when she stands near a date palm, she hacks its fruits off,

when she stands near an oak-tree (or: hazel)

and a terebinth tree of the mountain, she makes it wither.

(Köcher thought that Lamaštu recklessly destroys any sort of vegetation. But the plants are very specific and highly symbolic. The **date palm** is the ritual emblem of Amaušumgalanna/Dumuzi, Ningirsu and Nergal. (Langdon, 1919:82; Jacobsen 1976:36; Volk in RlA *'Palme'*). The wood, marrow, seedlings and blossoms of these trees were used in exorcisms to purify the patient. The date palm represented the king himself. Lamaštu destroys his fruit and brings whole dynasties to a sudden end. In Aššurbanipal's north palace, room F, slab 12, opposite a drainage pipe, an amulet with a lion-headed being was unearthed: maybe it was a picture of Lamaštu. Sadly, the original is lost (Farber in RlA *'Lamaštu'*). Yes, the kings had reasons to be worried about Lamaštu. The passage suggests that the great gods of divine and royal authority, justice and fertility, and the magicians using their emblems, have no power over her. It would be nice to know more about the **oak** and the **terebinth**-tree (see also LS II, 189). For the

Babylonians, both were foreign. I saw plenty of small, tough, weather-worn oaks in the Kurdish mountains, but further south, in the plains of Mesopotamia and Syria, the tree is absent. So are we talking about oaks at all? Sturm in AfO 35 (2008:296-311) argues that, instead of oak, the allānū tree might be hazel. Terebinth trees are very common in the Near East. The nuts are a delicacy (and may be baked into bread), the seeds are used for soap, the gum is antiseptic, and the wood is used for panelling and tables. A purification spell using trees and plants appears in the *Maqlû Series*, I, 21, after Meyer's German translation:

The tamarisk purifies me, whose top is highly grown,

the date palm frees me, that catches all the wind.

The maštakal herb that covers the earth makes me shine.

The pine-cone releases me, that is full of seeds.

Before you I became bright like grass,

Became radiant, purified like nard grass.

I, 187

She drinks blood [.....] of people for nourishment.

(You feed on their) flesh, that is not to be eaten;

their bones, that are not to be gnawed (?),

(Instead of *gnawed* we can also read *break into small pieces*. Maybe she extracts the marrow; maybe she accelerates decomposition.)

I, 189

O Daughter of Anu,

have you learned about the food of wailing and weeping?

You drink human blood for nourishment.

(Like the waters of distress, the food of wailing and weeping was a favourite of dangerous spirits. When people ate such dishes, it meant that they could expect hard times.)

I, 191

You feed on their flesh, that is not to be eaten;

their bones, that are not to be gnawed,

May Anu, your father, provide food for you!

(Line 192 is the usual translation. Farber prefers that Anu may cause her to drop the flesh and bone.)

I, 193

May Antu(m), your mother, provide food for you!

Pull out the (tent) pegs, cut off** (or:* ***store away) the ropes!

(Lamaštu can be a good girl: she simply eats what her mum and dad give to her. Note that while dogs and wolves will chew bones, hyenas are great at eating them entirely. The only parts of an animal that they cannot easily digest are hair, horn, hooves and teeth.

Tent pegs imply that Lamaštu is a traveller, a nomad or a homeless savage and that she should pack up her tent and disappear.)

I, 195

Climb your mountain like an onager (=** wild ass**) of the steppe!

May the mašmaššu, the āšipu (of?) Asarluḫi/Marduk, offer you,

(**Donkeys** and **asses** are among Lamaštu's favourite animals. The origin of the Near Eastern donkey is still under discussion. The wild ass, or onager (*Equus hemionus onager),* was admired for its ability to thrive under the most hostile conditions. Onagers are often called wild- or mountain asses, but zoologists have identified them as a species of horse. In fact, with a top speed of 70km/h the onager is the fastest horse on earth. These beautiful animals were mainly at home in the eastern mountain ranges. Nowadays, a mere 400 wild onagers are alive in the mountains of Iran. Onagers can be tamed, and probably the early Sumerian aristocrats used them to pull battle chariots. Onagers were cross-bred with some other species of donkey. One uneasy candidate might be the Syrian half-donkey (*Equus hemionus hemippus,* nowadays extinct in the wild). Whether they can be domesticated is debatable; in zoos, they tend to remain shy, mistrustful and the males are extremely aggressive. But there may have been other wild asses around. Akkadian has more words for different sorts of donkeys than zoologists have identified so far. Whatever animals it may have been, the Sumerians were justly proud that they succeeded in breeding a domesticated donkey with good manners and household qualities. They never really got the job done. The ones I met in northern Mesopotamia were an intelligent, independently-minded, stubborn and wonderfully headstrong lot. They carried so much weight that I could hardly see them under the bundles. It did not stop them from misbehaving or from eating anything that came their way, no matter how their owners screamed at them. I have never seen animals so brutally abused. They hardly seemed to notice the savage blows against their bellies and legs. It's difficult to imagine that today's donkeys are the descendants of animals who were bred for, among other things, obedience. The Sumerians and Akkadians had a lot of respect for the obstinacy of donkeys. They also admired their sexual prowess. Wild asses were praised for racing swiftly across rugged terrain. King Šulgi of Ur III, a warrior, statesman, scholar, reformer and self-appointed universal genius, is one of the few regents who had himself praised as a wild ass. Another monarch with a heart for donkeys was Gudea of Lagaš. In a visionary dream the king, in the shape of a *noble donkey*, vigorously scraped the dust as he was so eager to build the temple complex for Ningirsu. Note that some Lamaštu talismans show the goddess with large donkey ears – and you can see the same feature in a statuette of a topless priestess or goddess from Minoan Crete! The donkey appears on several Lamaštu talismans. It may have been the inspiration for Greek artists to connect Medusa with Pegasus.)

I, 197

a comb, fibula, spindle, piece of cloth and a hairpin! Turn your face to the beasts of the steppe!

(Lamaštu is treated like an honoured guest who receives provisions and gifts for the journey home. There is a close parallel from the third millennium BCE: when ten ambassadors from Dilmun left the city-state Mari on the Middle Euphrates, they received for themselves and their slaves 10 pack-asses, 52 waterskins, 64 pairs of sandals, one big leather sack, 10 leather straps, each nine metres long, 30 sheep, 30 litres of best oil, 60 litres of sesame oil, 3 litres of juniper (resin or perfumed oil), an unspecified amount of seeds and grains plus whatever provisions they asked for (Postgate 2002:148 & 258). Now for a look at Lamaštu`s provisions:

First, we have a **comb** (mušṭu(m). It might suggest she gets her wild, tangled hair in order. In many cultures across Eurasia, dishevelled hair represents a lack of civilisation, high emotionality, madness, mourning or magical activity. In exactly this sense, the hair of Kālī, Xiwangmu and many tantric deities is open and tangled. The **breast pin** or **fibula** (tudittu(m)) closed the cloak, and could function as a talisman. By the Neo-Assyrian period it is replaced by a fibula. It ensures that her robe or cloak is securely closed and those dangerous nude breasts are safely stowed away. It makes her look like a well-dressed popular goddess. Cloak pins also had a symbolic meaning: when a husband *loosened the cloak pin* of his freshly married wife, she lost her virginity (Postgate 2002:104). The **spindle** (pilakku(m)) allows Lamaštu, like a spider, to spin string; her symbolic representation in ritual is multicoloured wool or string (Langdon, 1919: 86). We discussed spindles earlier. The word for spindle also means spindle-shaped ornaments. A lot of them appear in spells to protect women from giving birth too early. KAR 223, (Labat in RlA *'Geburt'*) informs us that for the last sixty days of a risky pregnancy, the conjurer tied sixty new spindle-shaped amulets (or real spindles?) as a girdle around the belly of the woman. Each day the moon god Sîn was praised, a spindle was untied and thrown away. The **piece of cloth** (šiddu(m)) is unspecific: it can be a piece of cloth, curtain, cover, fabric, a side or an edge. I guess that the conjurers offered a piece of cloth to represent a veil, cloak or blanket. Let's take a look at these options.

Little is known about **veils** in Sumerian and Babylonian times. Definite regulations for the veiling of women appear for the first time in the laws of Tiglathpilesar (1115-1077). In the Neo-Assyrian period, when the *Lamaštu Series* was compiled, 'respectable' and married women wore veils to indicate their status. Young girls did not, maybe as they were supposed to attract a husband with their good looks, and prostitutes were not allowed to veil themselves. If one was caught wearing a veil, she, and whoever knew about it without informing the authorities, were heavily punished. That's Neo-Assyria for you; no such laws or customs are known from earlier periods. The veil, however, could also be a **cloak**, which might keep her warm and comfy on her long journey, and protect her from scorching sun and blinding sandstorms. Or it could be a blanket, providing warmth in the cold desert nights. The **hairpin** (kirissu(m)) ensures that her well-dressed hair remains where it should. It could also be a sign of authority or wealth.

She is asked to turn her attention away from people and towards the **beasts** of her beloved wilderness. Several Lamaštu amulets show her in a 'goddess of the beasts' configuration. What seems like toxic milk to human babies seems to suit her animal babies very well. This theme appears in her Old Babylonian conjurations. A spell to banish Lamaštu (BM 120022 of the British Museum, based on Farber, 2010:409, and Wende, 2012, SEAL page) ends:

Ascend the mountain of sweet scents!
Seize the livestock, the onager, the gazelle,
the wild bulls, the mountain ibex, the deer and wild goats,
help the animals of Šakkan to give birth,
the animals of the steppe!

Šakkan, Šakkan-an-na, Šaḫḫan (Akkadian: Sumuqan, Amakandu, Šamgan, Šamkan) is a Sumerian Lord of the Beasts. His father is Utu/Šamaš, his wife Ellamesi (*Ewe*). Here is an exception: in the *Theogony of Dunnu*, Šakkan kills his father Mr. Plough and marries the goddess Earth. Next he weds his sister Tiāmat (^{d}a.ab.ba). He is killed by his son Flock, who marries Tiāmat in his turn. Šakkan's vizier is Edin-mu-gi (*He Who Secures the Plains*). Šakkan has numerous titles, such as *'deity of wool', 'deity of herd animals', 'deity of grass-eating beasts', 'deity of pastureland', 'deity of meadows', 'deity of watering places'*. He is the *shepherd of everything*. In the deserts, mountains and steppes, his children are the wild beasts, but when the context is urbane, he acts as a god of domesticated animals. Occasionally Šakkan is mentioned as the opposite of Ašnan, the goddess (and personification) of grains and plants. Šakkan is also a god of the Underworld. In a ritual translated by Scurlock (2014:124), an infertile woman prays to Šakkan's and Dumuzi's pregnant ewes to take away her barrenness and to grant her fertility. Šakkan, famous for his enormous sexual virility, breeds, herds and protects wild animals and, what a surprise, Lamaštu helps them to be born.)

I, 199

May you be anointed with the oil of pre-eminence,
may you be shoed with sandals that last for eternity.

(Myhrman: (excellent?) oil, Köcher: Oil of Excellence. Nowadays muḫrû is: pre-eminence, foremost. Could it be perfumed oil? When the Mesopotamians made oils of cedar, juniper, myrtle, terebinth and maybe myrrh, they soaked the aromatic plants and resins in beer and other fluids. Then the liquids were infused in sesame oil (without heating!), a process that could require up to twenty repetitions before the fat oil was saturated with them. Special oils were used to anoint ritualists, regents and statues of the gods. Oil recipes were jealously guarded trade secrets and rarely committed to writing (Jursa in RlA *'Parfüm (rezepte).'* The goddess must be honoured with (perfumed) oil; she must be shoed with sandals that do not wear out, no matter how far she travels. In this scene, she has human feet instead of bird talons.)

I, 201

May a leather bag of water be fetched for your fierce thirst!

Fine flour, malt (and) malted bread shall be added; Siriš shall fill the leather bag for you,

(She needs a lot of water as she is so hot. Finally, to cheer her up, she is provided with beer for her journey. **Siraš /Siris/Siriš** means: beer. Written with a divine determinative, s/he and her sister **Ninkasi** (a daughter of Enki and Ninki, or of Ninḫursag; *born of flowing water*) are the beer-brewers of the gods. In *Šurpu Series*, V-VI, 179-186, trans. Reiner, the purification priest of Enki/Ea, messenger of Marduk, releases a patient from his suffering with the words:

Just as I bank the stove I kindled, I extinguish the fire I lit; I smother the grain I poured out, (so) may Siriš, releaser of god and man, loosen the knot she tied. May the angry heart of the god and goddess of NN, son of NN, be pacified toward him, may his sin be poured out today, may it be wiped off him, be released from him.

Making alcoholic drinks was often a female vocation. Some women made it on a professional basis, others ran an alehouse; and alehouses, generally sacred to Inanna/Ištar, could also function as guesthouses and brothels. The beer was occasionally spiced with herbs and syrup made from grapes and other fruit. As it was full of sediment, people (and deities) usually drank it through long tubes that had a filter at the bottom. In Old Babylonian texts, Siriš is usually a goddess. In the Neo-Assyrian period, like in our text, she could also appear in a male form. Siriš and Ninkasi had several children; *Glowing Me*, *Beautiful Me/Crown*, *Ornamented Speech/Crown*, *Seat of Splendour*, *Unceasing*, all of them relating to drink and its effects. Though Siriš probably did not have a city to call her own, her worship is attested in Babylon, Aššur, Nippur and in Isin, where she was closely related to Ninurta and Gula. In spite of having children, Siriš apparently had no husband. Like many ale-brewers, she was an independent woman. Ninkasi was married with Gibil; offerings to her are attested in Fāra, Nippur and Umma.)

I, 203

he shall offer a flask** (or: **beerwort) for you to taste!

I conjure you by Anu, your father, by Antu(m), your mother,

(Line 203 appears as most translators would have it. Note that in this rather young passage, Siriš is male. In Farber's version, Siriš is asked to provide beerwort for brewing. At this point or the ritual, I would guess that a libation was poured. Since the third millennium BCE, Mesopotamian offerings usually required drink, food, incense and recitation. These four elements formed the core of much ritual, and were condemned with vehemence by the Biblical prophets. *Jeremiah* 19,13 declares that the palaces and houses of Jerusalem from which smoke offerings and libations are made shall become unclean. In 44, 17 we hear him cursing those who made offerings to the Queen of Heaven. Drink offerings were a complicated science in Babylonia and Assyria. As you read earlier, water offerings were only made to a few deities in the third millennium BCE and went out of fashion afterwards. The only normal exceptions were emergency situations, when no other fluids were available, and the cult of the dead. To nourish the ancestors, pure water was poured into a vertical tube in the ground: *May the dead have a good name in the above, may the spirit below drink clear water* (Heimpel in RlA *'Libation'*).That Lamaštu receives water offerings in our first millennium BCE text is very unusual. Well, in this passage, she, like the great gods, also gets her share of alcohol. Lāḫiānu(m) is a flask or vessel, it could be ceramic, wooden or metal. Generally, it was not used for drinking but to pour libations. During normal offerings, beer was often poured from bowls and wine from jugs. The beer came in several versions, made of different grains, and was often sweetened. Libations were made in different ways. They could be poured on the ground, to both sides of the hearth, before the hearth, on a brick, on a food offering, on the head of a sacrificial sheep, on the head of a lion (after a hunt), before the incense stand, in front of temple gates and doors, into the incense burner (which extinguished the embers), into rivers and springs, before advancing cattle, and into a range of ornate vessels, some of them huge. It seems that the goddess is asked to have a final drink for the road: good evidence that she was not crudely banished but asked to depart like an honourable but somewhat demanding guest. The references to **grain** could imply that a food offering accompanied the libation. Flour was a common and moderate offering. Great temples offered a wide range of delicacies. Often enough, they were eaten by the clergy when the rite was over. Unlike them, drink offerings, once poured, were lost.)

I, 205

I conjure you by Enlil, Ninlil, by Ea [and Damkina]

I conjure you by Šazu the Wise [...]

(**Damkina** and **Damgalnunna** are names of Enki/Ea's wife, who appears elsewhere as **Ninki** (*Lady of the Earth*). Damkina (*Faithful Spouse*) had a lion as her pet and vehicle. Her constellation is Ursa minor, otherwise known as Anu's waggon. Damgalnunna (*Great Lady of the Aristocrat*) was occasionally identified with prominent birth- and mother goddesses, like Nintur, Ninḫursag, Ninmaḫ and Ninsikila. All of them are great artists, shapers, form-givers, and so is their husband Enki. Damgalnunna's major cult place was in Malgûm, but she was also venerated in Eridu, Lagaš, Umma and in the first millennium BCE, in Kalḫu. All of Enki/Ea's wives are fond of fish offerings. **Šazu** has two important meanings. The Sumerian term means *One Who Knows the Inside* (SAHG 1953:418) or *One Who Knows the Hearts* (Groneberg, 2004:90). It was a common title for midwives. In later periods, it became a title of Marduk.)

I, 207

I conjure you by Lugalab[zu ...]

I conjure you by Uznu, Ḫ[asīsu), [...]

(**Lugalabzu** (*Lord of the Abzu* i.e. *Lord of the Abysmal Waters of the Underworld*) and Lugalid(ak) (*Lord of the River*) are titles of Enki/Ea as the regent of the waters.

Sumerian: **Lugal** means literally *Strong Man* or *Leader*; during the fourth millennium the title was granted by a semi-democratic assembly to a temporary ruler in times of war and crisis. Subsequently, things became less democratic. The strong men remained in power as wars were on the agenda almost continuously and the title gradually became a synonym of *king*.

Ḫasīsu or ḫasīsu(m) is personified and deified wisdom; it also means: hearing and ear. Ḫasīsu frequently appears in the company of **Uznu** (Usmû), which means: ear, wisdom, understanding, attention, awareness, mind. Inanna set her *ear* from the Great Above to the Great Below, when she left heaven to visit her sister Ereškigal in the underworld. To *broaden one's ear* is to pay attention. God list *An=Anum* calls Ḫasīsu and Uznu the two viziers of Damgalnunna. Both of them are gods who personify abstract principles. Much later, Nabû is sometimes called by the title Ḫazizi.)

I, 209

I conjure you by Ištar [...]

I conjure you by [...]

I, 211

I c[onjure you by...] sanctuary [...ri]vers and seas

I, 213

[...] of Anu, out of this house.

[...] do not approach, do not come close,

I, 215

[...] sent away, cast out and chased off

[...] have to depart,

I, 217

[...]

[...]

I, 219

[Conjur]ation of Lamaštu.

Ritual Formula:

You shall make an image of the Daughter of Anu out of canal-clay,

(This passage combines formulas. See LS III, 110-118 and LS III, 124-127)

I, 221

you shall make a donkey out of canal-clay and equip it with provisions,

thread fourteen small loaves of bread baked from bittergrain-flour on string,

(West (1992:378) has *you must make a donkey of canal-clay, give food to him.*

Fourteen is a dangerous number; the 14th day was dedicated to Nergal and the Underworld.)

I, 223

lay (them) around her neck, [...] spill broth for her,

pour a libation of water and beer for her. Slaughter a piglet,

(**Baḫru**/buḫru was something delicious. Myhrman thought it might be some sort of fruit; Köcher a paste or oil, blended with herbs, milk or beer. The CDA translates *baḫru: 'boiling hot.' A specific hot dish.* One good translation is broth. Again: a **libation** of water is an anachronistic rarity for the second and first millennium BCE, a libation of beer common custom, and a combination of both very, very unusual.)

I, 225

and put its heart into the mouth of the Daughter of Anu.

For three days, thrice daily,

you shall recite the conjuration before her;

I, 227

on the third day, as the day descends,

you shall carry her into the desert** (or: **wilderness** or: **steppe),

(turn) her face [towards] the sun[set], [...] a magic circle,

I, 229

fill X with food (?)** (or: **flour?) [...]

ti[e her to baltu-thorn (and) ašāgu-thorn,

I, 231

[...] X [...]

[...]

[Conjuration: I Recite a Conjuration Against Your Enduring Purpose].

(Here ends the first section of the *Lamaštu Series*. The catchline is the first line of the next chapter.)

The colophon:

Palace of Aššurbanipal, King of the World, King of Assyria, who trusts in Aššur and Ninlil,

(**Aššur** is the national god of the city Aššur, which was founded during the third millennium BCE in northern Mesopotamia. At the time, it was a minor state under the control of the late Sumerian and Akkadian kings. Aššur became the national god of the city-state Aššyria around the middle of the second millennium BCE. In character (provided we can discern a character, as he is such a vague heroic figure), Aššur is close to the Sumerian Enlil and the Babylonian Marduk; accordingly he is frequently worshipped as Aššur-Enlil and later as Aššur-Marduk. Like Marduk, he fought the primordial chaos mother Tiāmat. Unlike Marduk, he was not invoked for healing and magical protection. In iconography, we find him as an archer shooting a sun, much as the hero Yi in old Chinese myth. In this passage he is coupled with **Ninlil**. She started out as the wife of Enlil, the most important god of the late Sumerian and Old Babylonian period. Around the thirteenth or twelfth century BCE, Marduk became the summit of divine authority, and though his wife is usually Zarpānītu(m), he is also occasionally married to Ninlil. The Assyrians identified their chief deity Aššur with the Middle Babylonian Marduk; as a result, Ninlil became a wife of Aššur.)

who is granted with a wide ear (=knowledge) by Nabû and Tašmētu(m), who has been granted a bright eye as his own, the choice selection of artfully written tablets,

Nabû, (probably *Councillor, Prophet*), originally a minister, later the firstborn son of Marduk and Zarpānītu(m), is a god of Borsippa and Nineveh, lord of the temple Ezida (*House of Truth*), bearer of the tablets of fate, in whose mouth is justice. When, during the Middle Babylonian period, Marduk began his remarkable career, he lost some of his popularity among the common people. Each time a god becomes too overbearing, a less imposing deity is needed to listen to the everyday problems of the population. The pattern can be observed in several religions; consider how Hermes relates to Zeus, Kṛṣṇa to Viṣṇu, and Gaṇeśa to Śiva. In Mesopotamia, this task fell to Nabû, a compassionate god of wisdom and writing, who became a major deity around 1150 BCE as a protector of the crown prince. Nabû reached the summit of his popularity around the eighth century BCE and was expected to have a benevolent influence on his almighty dad.

Tašmētu(m) (*Favourable Hearing, Listening, Attention*) is Nabû's wife. She is not the only one. A 'sacred marriage' was celebrated between Nabû and Nana/Nanay in Babylon and between Nabû and Tašmētum in Kalḫu. A third wife of Nabû is Nidaba/Nisaba, the grains and reed goddess, patroness of scribes, scholars, artists, priests and officials. That a god of scribes is married to his reed stylus is obvious; nowadays people go to bed with their smartphone or keyboard, instead of other people. Nana/Nanay will be discussed under LS II, 109; she was an independent goddess up to the middle of the second millennium BCE when she was identified with Tašmētum. That scribes should promote truth and justice is represented by Tašmētum, even if it rarely happened. She is praised as a goddess of supplication and love; she appeases the anger of the gods, listens to prayers and removes diseases. People petitioned her to help them in court cases. Maybe she is the first deity of compassion in recorded history. Unless we count Lamaštu, who also listens to prayers, heeds petitions and finds her own cheerful solutions to problems, no matter how messy they may turn out.)

as under the kings, his predecessors, none had acquired the like.

(Aššurbanipal was not only a successful monarch and a terrifying conqueror, like several of his ancestors. He spoke and read several languages including old Sumerian, and was justly proud of his education. It says a lot that only three (!) Mesopotamian kings were praised for being literate.)

The wisdom of Nabû, the 'spotted patterns of the stylus (=inscriptions)',
as many of these, as have been formed,
I wrote on tablets, I collected them according to the regulations,

so I could study (and) read them,

I set [them) up in my palace;

I, the ruler, who knows the light of the King of the Gods, Aššur.
(or: You are a ruler who has no equal, King of the Gods, Aššur!)
Whoever abducts (this tablet) or signs his name next to mine,

may be cast down by Aššur and Ninlil in anger and wrath,
may his name and his seed be erased from the earth!

Second Part of the Lamaštu Series

II, 1

Conjuration: I Recite a Conjuration Against Your Enduring Purpose.

(I have?) not lifted (my?) hands (*= prayed?)***

in the place of the Mountain of Antu(m) (*= the Underworld)***

(or: the strong mountain Ebiḫ (could) not lift (your?) hands)

(Section two begins with **conjuration #6**, which was recited over the hips of the patient. It was also used to consecrate incense. We are facing an extremely difficult passage which was transcribed and translated differently by Köcher and Farber. The idea that the conjurer has not lifted his hands in the Underworld is based on Köcher; the second version is loosely derived from Farber's translation. Neither is very satisfactory. Köcher thought about **lifting the hands** as in praying, while Farber suggests that the mountain Ebiḫ is incapable of removing the hands of Lamaštu from her victim. *Prayers of the Lifting of the Hand* is a literary category that became popular around the middle of the second millennium BCE. Priests and conjurers lifted their hands during some prayers, so that the fingers pointed up, the thumbs were stretched to the sides and the open palms faced the deity. Keep your fingers slightly apart and relax. Feel your breath. It's a useful gesture. If you explore it for a while, and cultivate a hollow feeling in the centres of your palms, you may find that it has interesting effects on your inner energy. Typical experiences are swaying, shuddering, yawning, tears and so on. They indicate that blocked energies and emotions are being released.

But our line could also imply that the punishing hand of the deity is lifted from a patient and/or sinner. Most of these prayers are brief compositions that praise a small group of deities; they banish unwelcome influences and, even more important, ensure that the deity is favourably disposed to the ritualist and client. A typical element is a litany of blessings. Usually, the style is free of lamentations, cries of misery or complaints: some of them read like examples of positive thinking. If we follow Köcher's probably outdated transcription, the šad anti is the **Mountain of Antum**. Šadu(m) is basically mountain, but was also used for desert, steppe and terrifying hostile foreign country. Its Sumerian counterpart is **Kur**. Kur described the limits of the Mesopotamian homelands: the alien mountain ridges to the east and north and the deserts and mountains of Syria, Arabia and Lebanon. Kur means foreign and foreigners. For the Sumerian, anything out there was dangerous and possibly deadly. Consequently, the term Kur was associated with the realm of death. For the Semites, the dead travelled west, across the Arabian Desert, and then to the deep. The mountains were gates leading to the underworlds. Like kur, šadu(m) came to mean the underworld. Antu(m) is the female personification of divine heaven. It would be nice to know more about her mountain in the deep.

But let us look at the **Mount Ebiḫ**. Ebiḫ is nowadays called Jebel Hamrin, and part of the Zagros range to the east of Mesopotamia. Imagine a sheer cliff that runs along a straight line for hundreds of kilometres. It gained popularity through a hymn to Inanna composed by Enḫeduanna around 2340 BCE. The hymn has been translated and interpreted in many ingenious ways. Basically, the mountain (or its deity, religion or people) refused to honour and respect Inanna and was devastated, crushed and brought to submission by the goddess, who pressed its nose into the ground and made it kiss the dust at her feet. In this hymn, the mountain Ebiḫ has three meanings: it is a geographical term for a place well outside of Mesopotamia; a name for the foreign cultures who would not submit to Inanna's cult (or the armies of Enḫeduanna's dad, Sargon I), and it is a mythical being, a huge monster, which met its doom when Inanna slashed its throat. The hymn turned Inanna, raging mad in her battle fury, into one of the first monster slayers of literature. It is likely that the Sumerians believed that the mountain range has or is a deity. It's not so clear why a hostile foreign deity appears in the *Lamaštu Series,* and why it should even try to lift the hand of Lamaštu. Did anyone believe that Lamaštu, or her cult, came from Mount Ebiḫ?)

II, 3

[I have visited?] the sacred Ealmaš, the seat** (or: **foundation) of the gods,

I have recited a roof** (= protective conjuration) **against (?) you,

(**Ealmaš, Eulmaš, Ulmaš** is a name for a temple, corresponding to the Underworld, or maybe only to its entrance. There were several; the texts mention them in Akkad, Sippar and Uruk. The one in Akkad was dedicated to Inanna/Ištar, who is famous for her journey into the deep, even if it turned out to be a total disaster. To visit the Underworld and to return from it are two of the divine Me which Inanna gained from Enki, they correspond to trance journeys.

Let's take a brief look at **trance**, **obsession** and trance journeys in the imagination. Akkadian mahû: *to go into trance* equals Sumerian è: *to go out (of one's mind)* and e_{11}: *to ascend, to descend.* The maḫḫu(m) (female: maḫḫûtu) was a ritualist who acted in the service of a temple or operated independently. S/he corresponds to the Sumerian lu-an-dib-ba-ra: *one who has been seized by a god*, the lu-an-ne-ba-tu: *one who has been entered into by a god*, and the Old Akkadian muḫḫu (Tibbs, 2007). The discovery of a class of ecstatic ritualists has been a nuisance. Some scholars had assumed that the neat, bureaucratic Mesopotamians preferred a dignified and well-controlled priesthood with good manners, like, say, ministers of the Church of England. At the time of writing, this idea is changing. Temple attendants of Ištar of Arbela, for instance, became obsessed by the goddess and spoke in her name. Here are some lines from a lengthy prophecy:

The maḫḫûtu spoke: *I am Ištar of Arbela, o Asarḫaddon, King of Assyria! I will grant late days and eternal years to Asarḫaddon, the Great King in Aššur, Nineveh, Kalaḫ and Arbela. Your [...] the great am I. I am the one who graciously leads you forth (...)*

I will allow you to cross the river in safety, Asarḫaddon, just heir, Son of Ninlil. [...] With my own hand I will destroy your enemies! Asarḫaddon, King of Aššur, your cup is filled with [...], is a bowl of two šekel. Asarḫaddon, I will grant you late days and eternal years in the city Aššur. Asarḫaddon, in the city Arbela I am your merciful shield. Asarḫaddon, just heir, Son of Ninlil, your reasoning is full of understanding. I love you very much. At your [...] I hold you to the great sky. To your right I make smoke rise, to your left fire burn.... (end missing) (based on *Altorientalische Texte zum Alten Testament*, 1970:282, trans. JF). Several prophecies of this type have been found. They are, in their way, official documents. The name of the medium was noted at the end. The prophecy neatly demonstrates how Asarḫaddon used religious devotion to accomplish political goals. Unlike so many other kings, he remained humble, supported many cults, and allowed the gods to guide his policy. The gods were delighted and made him follow exactly the policy he wished to pursue. Similar prophecies (or encouragements) were uttered in the name of Bēlet of Arbela, a *Mother of Kings*, of Nabû and Bēl (*the Lord*), which, in this context, means the god Aššur. Sometimes the obsessed priestess channelled several gods during a single fit of prophecy! Such prophecies were made in the presence of the kings, but they were also provided when the kings were on campaigns, and communicated in letters. Most of them are enthusiastic, encouraging, and lack specific details. Asarḫaddon certainly did not believe in any prophecy that came his way. He was suspicious of ecstatic prophets, and what they might pronounce regarding his son Aššurbanipal. His *Treaty* states that *If you hear an evil, ill and ugly word that is mendacious and harmful to Aššurbanipal (...) from the mouth of a raggimu or a maḫḫu, or an inquirer of divine words (...) you must not conceal it but come and tell it to Aššurbanipal.* (Radine, 2010).

More evidence for obsessed prophetic ritualists comes from Mari and Byblos. Burckert-Tibbs gives several examples for maḫḫu who went into a trance (maḫu) so that Anunitu(m) could speak through them. Anunitu(m) is a variation of Antu(m): remember her mountain in the underworld. Maḫḫûtu and maḫḫu also participated in the highly emotional Tammuz rituals. Tibbs quotes a line from a prayer to Nabû, after Halder: *I am struck down like a maḫḫu, I bring forth what I do not know,* and adds that the expression *struck down* can also mean *to be seized.* The maḫḫûtu and maḫḫu were not the only trance and obsession specialists. Another class of ecstatic priest was the raggimu (female: raggintu), whose badly documented office entailed proclaiming the *words of a god* and providing prophecies. Both appear among the temple personnel of Ištar of Arbela. Their male and female counterparts in Mari were the āpilu and the āpiltum. They acted as inspired prophets. Elsewhere we encounter the male zabbu and the female zabbatu, from zabābbu: to be in a frenzy, to spread, to flutter like a bird. It might hint at ecstatic trembling and shaking. They are among the ritualists in the cult of Ištar and Tammuz. The Sumerian ni-su-ub ritualists who preceded them were terrifying figures. They were known to *change the face of a strange world* (Henshaw, 1994:160). It's true enough, the world is strange indeed. Especially when you go for a walk in a deep trance and in those vulnerable moments when you emerge from one. And when it comes to frenzied dances, voluntary bloodletting and journeys to the underworld, the kurgarrû come to mind. I won't even try to discuss them here, as they have been interpreted in many highly contradictory ways. Suffice it to say that when Inanna/Ištar died, down in the deep underworld, and was hanging from a hook like a piece of dead meat, Enki/Ea fashioned the kurgarrû beings who were neither male nor female, and sent them into the deep to make friends with Ereškigal. They revived the dead Inanna/Ištar and returned her to the upper world.

A tarānu(m) is a **roof**, a shelter, and a protection spell.)

II, 5

[...] a word (*or:* command) of healing (*or:* wholeness). Depart, go [away]!

With insufficient (= dissatisfied) heart, that [...]

(Line six is so troublesome that Köcher and Farber arrived at highly different results. You just read Köcher's idea, in Farber's more reliable translation the only certain words are '*you are not*'. The rest of the line is doubtful).

II, 7

Your gallû-like adversary, the āšipu of Asarluḫi

shall remove your venom (*or:* fire), shall pull off your hands.

(A **gallû**-like adversary could be someone like a demon, as Farber proposed. But the term could just as well have been used in its original sense: the first gallû were the canal police. You met them under LS I, 13. They were intensely loathed, to be sure, but some people (like the king) found their efforts necessary. Myhrman notes that the word i-mat: poison, snake venom, could also be i-šat-ki, your fire, fever.)

II, 9

Out of the body of this infant, the son of his god,

he shall expel heat, cold, freezing (and) shaking!

II, 11

[...] will conjure you [...]

[...] the rag of [...] a bar

II, 13

[...] smeared with the lard of a pig, are taboo for you.

(or: [...] pig's lard, get hold of these abominable things of yours)

Carry them off; may you depart!

(**Pig's lard** was a highly valued commodity and frequently used to make salves and ointments. The process was the same as in making perfumed oil. If Lamaštu feels revolted by the lotion, it might be due to the fact that she likes pigs or that there were sacred plants in the mixture. Most people in Mesopotamia did not subscribe to the notion that pigs are unclean animals.)

II, 15

The evil gods, the evil rabiṣu, who are before you, who walk before and behind you,

Mesopotamian religion had no strict personification of good and evil. The gods were assumed to be mostly benevolent, provided they were treated with admiration, love and respect, and got their meals and entertainment punctually. When upset they, in particular Enlil, were just as likely to harm or destroy people, cities and mankind as the malevolent spirits. The **evil gods *(ilāni limnūti)*** were generally those who were not on good terms with some person, family, or city. Gods (Sumerian: **dingir**, Akkadian: **ilu(m)**) and agents (Sum. **maškim**, Akk. **rabiṣu**;) can appear as good or bad influences. It depends on the personal point of view. Rabiṣu have been identified as deadly lurkers; a class of terrifying spirits. The word comes from rabāṣu: reside, lie in wait, sit, camp. In everyday life, a rabiṣu was an agent employed by a private person or the palace to act as a complainant in a legal case. He could be a bailiff, the chief bailiff of a court, a representative, an agent and a judicial officer. By extension, a rabiṣu could be an envoy, a secret agent, and even a governor of an occupied state. In Aššurbanipal's days, there was a rabiṣu (governor) of occupied Egypt, and nobody thought that he was an evil spirit except for the Egyptians. Just as the temples and kings employed agents, the gods employed rabiṣu spirits to enforce divine commands and to protect and punish people. But we also encounter the evil rabiṣu who works freelance, hides in desolate places or ruins and assaults people for the fun of it. For this bonny creature, the term 'lurker' is quite appropriate. There is quite a range of them, including rabiṣu who dwell in rivers and give swimmers cramps and rabiṣu dwelling in latrines who cause half-body strokes. Those who accidentally step into the footprint of a rabiṣu can sufferer from stiff or trembling feet. (Scurlock & Andersen, 2005:254). For a cure, the touch of the rabiṣu has to be washed off, in the name of Asarluḫi or Marduk, with sacred water. If the line is correctly translated, the evil gods and agents/lurkers walk before and behind Lamaštu. Are they her honour guard? Inscriptions celebrating Aššurbanipal's campaigns use the same formula. *Ištar and Aššur who walk before me, and exalt me over my enemies; the hard and perverse heart of Tammaritu (King of Elam) they broke, and took hold of his hand; from the throne of his kingdom they hurled him and overwhelmed him: a second time they subdued him to my yoke* (after Smith, 1871:211-212 amended).)

II, 17

like water of the night (= dew) of the stars, like the breeze (or: ghost, or: dream-soul) at a window,

do not slip, like a mongoose, snakelike (or: past the door-pivot)

Here I follow Wayne Horowitz (1988). **'Water of the Stars'** is an amazing metaphor. The Mesopotamians made a science of astronomy long before the other (known) cultures, and organised the stars in constellations during the third millennium BCE. Those constellations were an early effort, and several were changed or regrouped over the ages. For at least three thousand years the Mesopotamians were fascinated by the stars. From at least the Old Babylonian period they observed, measured, calculated, and did their best to foresee the perilous eclipses of sun and moon. Their interest, however, was strictly confined to the science of divination. Everything that happened in the sky influenced life on earth. Odd clouds, sundogs, the moon's halo and what stars or planets were enclosed in it, the motion of planets, shooting stars and the constellations in sight when an earthquake occurred were all meaningful. As far as we know, the astronomers were not very interested in exploring the nature of stars, planets or meteorological phenomena. They merely wanted to observe and predict them, and to cancel the evils of unpleasant signs. Why a given planet seemed to move backwards was outside their sphere of interest. Nevertheless, their observations were detailed and they recorded that the position of Venus reappeared in its exact relation to the stars and sun every eight years, while Mercury needed 46, Mars 79, and Jupiter 83 years. They knew how to calculate the apparent speed of the planets in each month. They also recorded the eclipses with great care. Simplicius wrote that Kallisthenes, who accompanied Alexander on his conquests, sent a list of the recorded eclipses for the last 1903 years to his uncle Aristotle (Pichot, 1995:115). For most of Mesopotamian history, astrology was concerned with the fates of cities, states and their regents. The advent of personal astrology (for wealthy people) began much later, during the first millennium BCE. Astronomy was not only an art of looking for omens in heaven but had a practical, magical side. The stars and planets were closely related to a range of deities. Note that the stars represented deities, but the deities were much more than stars. Mind you, many gods were not up at night. In some temples, their statues were put to bed and woken in the morning. Here is an incantation sung by a Bārû (diviner):

...the gods of the land, the goddesses of the land,

Šamaš, Adad and Ištar,

Have entered, to sleep in heaven;

They do not proclaim judgement, they decide no court cases.

The night is veiled, the palace lies still, the steppes are very silent;

who is still walking on the road calls to his deity,

and he, for whom verdict is passed, remains asleep.

The truthful judge, the father of orphans,

Šamaš enters his sacred chamber.

The great gods of the night, the bright Gibil, the warrior Erra,

the bow(-star), the yoke(-star), the (star of the) "split by the weapon", the snake-serpent(-star), the chariot(-star), the goat(-star), the buffalo(-star), the viper(-star), shall attend;

by the examination of the guts, which I undertake, by the lamb which I dedicate,

grant me (insight of) truth...

(SAHG, 1953:274, trans. JF. Note that 'star' can also mean 'stellar constellation')

For sorcery, spells and conjurations were recited to specific constellations. Talismanic objects were set up to catch the essence, or in our case, the dew of the stars. For many cultures, dew was a magical fluid that appeared without a known source. The Mesopotamians were not aware that warm air binds more moisture than cold air, and that dew appears on objects when the temperature cools down. For them, dew was the water of the stars. Silent and unseen, like the mysterious fluids coming from the stars, Lamaštu appears. She moves softly into a room like a faint breeze, like the Lilû wind deities on a stifling hot night.

The **mongoose** is an interesting symbol. There was a deity of mongooses and small animals, called Ninkilim. He is sometimes confused with Ningirima. Mongooses were admired for their skill in fighting snakes. Wasserman (quoting Mayer 1992:374 in RlA '*Sprichwort*') gives a proverb, which sounds pretty much like a spell to curse a married couple:

Just as a snake and a mongoose do not enter the same hole to lie together, (but) think only of cutting each other's throats [so may you and your woman not enter the same room to lie down in the same bed; think only of cutting each other's throats!].

To slip into a house like a snake was a skill of Lamaštu and many other dangerous beings: anything that enters your home secretly can bear a charge of hostile magic. The mongoose could destroy a venomous serpent, but it could also carry a dangerous influence. *Maqlû Series* IV 61 briefly mentions operations to *cut-off a life* using a snake, a mongoose, an arrabus, and a pirugûtu mouse. Tablet BAM 464:8-12 looks at it from the victim's point of view: *When a mongoose has been used to bewitch a person with 'cutting-off a life', it is a 'cutting-off a life' of the seventh month. A mongoose has been seen in the house of the person. Take this mongoose, which has appeared in the house of the person...* (Schwemer & Abusch, 2007:155) To work destructive magic, it seems that the enchanter killed a mongoose or a small animal renowned for stealth, loaded its spirit with a curse and sent it into the house of an enemy (or the client's enemy). Carried by the spirit of the animal, the spell made contact with the victim and came true within seven months, or in the seventh month. The victim might even see a real mongoose, or at least imagine so. The exorcist employed to counter the spell needed either the living mongoose or had to catch its spirit. Usually, such sorcery was annulled by the fire god Girra or promptly returned to sender. Such cases of magical attack and counterattack were a rarity in the Sumerian period, became increasingly popular in the Babylonian period, and were a common fashion in the excessively brutal and paranoid first millennium BCE.)

II, 19

through the drainage tube (?)** (or: **over the shards of the roofs),

I allow you to travel safely on the four winds,

(The drainage tube is a popular translation that may be outdated. Farber suggests that the goddess could enter the house via the rooftop. Mesopotamian buildings were usually flat-roofed, and much of daily life took place on them. When nights were suffocatingly hot, people slept on them. It's a wonderful experience. Poor people had roofs made of reeds. I do wonder where the shards come from. The four winds are not the Lilû family of wind and storm deities but the cardinal winds. The line does not ask her to travel like a wind deity but to depart.)

II, 21

I fill your ship with provisions,

and send you off, yes, you!

The wise master is Adapa, the Sage of Eridu,

II, 23

upon (your) arrival he will look at you, yes, you, in Eridu.

He shall remove your venom** (or: **fire), and will pull your hands away,

(**Adapa** was the chief baker (that's a major priestly office!) making bread for the daily sacrifices to Enki/Ea in Eridu, the earliest (known) temple of Sumer. He also features as one of the seven primal sages (ABGAL/Apkallu, Abgallu) and culture heroes of antiquity. One day, when he was catching fish for offerings, the south wind sank his boat. In iconography, the south wind appears as a lady with spiralling legs: she is the goddess of the suffocating hot gales and roaring hurricanes that come in from the Persian Gulf. Adapa, rising from the surging water, fought Lady Hurricane and broke one of her wings. Anu, hearing of the violent deed, ordered Adapa to ascend to heaven for trial. Enki/Ea advised his baker to refrain from eating or drinking any food brought before him. Thanks to this advice, Adapa avoided consuming the food of death. He accepted a robe and oil and anointed himself. Anu and the gods were worried, as Adapa showed so much power and cunning, so they decided to turn him into an immortal. However, when he was offered the food and drink of immortality, he also refused them. Hence, he remained a human being and was sent back to earth by the gods, who were highly amused.

In our ritual, Adapa represents the primordial priest and exorcist, blessed with the wisdom of Enki/Ea. He is a protector of mankind. Adapa was occasionally invoked to battle diseases and evil influences. To **look**, naṭālu(m), can also mean: to witness, inspect, regard or examine. When Adapa looks at her, he examines her deeds, and holds her responsible. For Lamaštu, going to Eridu also means to meet Enki, the god who raised and educated her.)

II, 25

out of the body of this infant, the son of his god.

Remove yourself, go away!

II, 27

Conjuration of Lamaštu.

Ritual Formula:

The hide of a donkey (tanned by?) a leather worker (**or**: the paste of a leather worker),

II, 29

a stained rag, ziqqatû fish,

blend them with the fat of a white pig, anoint him and he will recover.

(In early translations, the **hide** was attributed to a horse, nowadays the word imēru is read donkey. The **fuller's paste** is Farber's suggestion. It may have been a substance containing astringents, to cure the hide, or maybe to bleach it. The **stained rag** hints at a cloth to still menstrual bleeding. The **ziqqatû** fish defies identification: we only know that it is small.)

II, 31

You shall burn an incense of unsifted flour,

peeled onion, snake skin, linseed,

(I am sure this mixture smells rather intense, and is by no means designed to please the goddess. Nor is it likely to have appealed to the baby or the adults of the household. But when you use placebos, make sure they are impressive. **Flour** is the most popular offering in Mesopotamian religion. Popular gods got perfect quality, unpopular ones had to make do with crude stuff. The **onion** may have an extra meaning. We don't know what onion we are supposed to use. Cohen lists 10 words for 'onion' plus one that might be onion or garlic. Some of them may have tasted much better than the ones you find in the supermarket: modern types are not bred for taste but for extended shelf life. Here is a useful spell from the *Šurpu Series*, updated after the German of Ungnad (1921:269), Saggs (1966:307) and the transcription by Reiner (1958: 31):

As this onion is peeled and cast into the fire,

and consumed by the flaming BIL.GI/ Gibil (a fire-god),

no longer watered in its bed,

no longer [strengthened] by embankment and canal,

its stalk no longer rising, no longer seeing the sun,

whose roots will not hold fast to the ground,

as it is no longer needed for the meal of a deity or king,

thus will māmit (= taboo, oath, curse*), reversion (*=retaliation*), interrogation, [conjuration],*

disease, crime, offence, sacrilege, guilt,

disease residing in my body, flesh and limbs,

be removed like the skin of this onion!

GIŠ.BAR/ Girra (a fire god) will burn it today!

The māmit shall depart, and I will see the light!

The onion is carefully peeled and each skin is cast into the purifying fire. In the next verses, similar formulas are recited while other materials are burned. The spell uses onion, dates, matting, flock of wool, goat hair, red wool and two sorts of grain. As each of them is tossed into the fire, a similar formula is recited and the patient is released from misdeeds, crimes, sins and pollution. Thanks to this ritual, the *Šurpu Series* is associated with burning.

Snake skin might represent Ningirima, the goddess of serpent/dragons and magic, but it could also relate to many other snake-happy deities, including Lamaštu herself. **Linseed** was not very common in Mesopotamia. The plant needs only a hundred days to mature, but leaves the soil exhausted for years. Linseed appears in medical prescriptions; it was ground and roasted. Waetzold (RlA *'Leinen'*) estimates that roughly 90% of all clothes (including those of kings) were made of wool. Linen was used for blankets, curtains, scarves, bandages, bed-sheets and underwear, and as a special dress for divine statues. In the Old Babylonian period, a king was dressed in the *pure linen dress of Anu* for his coronation. In the Neo-Babylonian period, linen became increasingly popular for priestly clothing.)

II, 33

sulphur, cress, a ball of hair; these are the contents of the incense.

(**Sulphur**, kibrītu, was a powerful cleaning substance. It had such an immensely high status that it was invoked:

Pure Sulphur, daughter of mighty Anu am I.

Anu has created me, Ea (and) En[lil] have carried me down...

(*Maqlû Series*, VI, 73-74)

The next lines are in a very bad state. The narrative continues:

Who (is it), casting spells (?) against Sulphur?

Sulphur, whatever the Seven (witches) used to hex me [...]

[...]you, (but) I shall live! tu$_6$en.

Conjuration. Pure Sulphur, KUR.KUR herb, the pure herb am I.

The man who bewitched me is the sage (apkallu) of the Ocean,

the woman who bewitched me is the Daughter of Anu.

Though (they) have [cast a spell on me],

they cannot overpower me,

though they have conjured evil, and tried to do evil.

[Ar]ise like fish in water,

like the pig from my morass,

like maštakal herb on the meadow,

like grass on the embankment of the canal,

like the seed of the ebony tree at the seaside!

(*Maqlû Series*, VI, 83-94, after Meier, trans. JF)

Please stop a moment. A sage of the ocean, a Daughter of Anu? Do we meet Adapa, the Seer of the Ocean, and Lamaštu in this spell? If so, what is the relationship between them? And what would this signify regarding LS II, 22-25?

Cress appears in many cultures as a plant of purification. The **ball of hair** produces an impressive evil smell. But let us think about it practically: hair is very personal, and was used to bewitch people. Here, the vital question is: whose hair was used for the spell?)

Conjuration: Angry is the Daughter of Anu Who Plagues the Infants,

II, 35

she is furious, she is divine, she is terrible,

she descended from the hig[h mo]untains,

her teeth are the teeth of a donkey,

(like) the features of a terrifying lion her face is formed,

(These lines are the start of **conjuration #7**. This conjuration was recited over the hips of the patient. From here, the text is very similar to a Babylonian talisman called *Tablet of Anuna'id, ..., of Kalû, Son of Inatēšeetir*. It starts with the warning that whoever dares to carry this tablet away and does not return it will be damned by Nabû. The text continues:

Šiptu. Wild is the Daughter of Anu, who deals harshly with little children.

She is wild, divine, terrifying.

She rose from the swampland, fiercely wild, her teeth are the teeth of a donkey...

From that point, the talisman is almost identical with the canonical text. It appears, in German, in appendix II of Nils Heeßel's *Pazuzu* (2002:103)

Here is another little problem: the **donkey teeth** do not appear on any talisman. When she shows teeth, and we can identify them, they are the fangs of a carnivore. It doesn't mean much: most images don't show teeth at all, and some provide her with a bird's beak. Maybe *donkey teeth* is a metaphor we don't understand.)

II, 37

(like) the kidneys (or: hips) of a leopard her kidneys (or: hips) are spotted,

her cheeks are pale like yellow-green ochre,

(When an āšipu saw a **spotted** ox on his way to a patient, he knew that Lamaštu was nearby.

Compare with tablet CBS 1045, University Museum of Philadelphia, excavated at Nippur, Old Babylonian Period, translation Nathan Wassermann 2008:

...Like a fish (her body is do)tted,

Like a Š.-paste her chin [...] is pale,

Her head is like a lion's head,

Her teeth are donkey's teeth...

Her **yellowish cheeks** inspired some scholars to include jaundice in her repertoire of diseases. It might be a pun. Daughter of Anu is 'mārat Anu'. The pronunciation of gall and bile (martu= *the bitter one*) is very similar. It would make her the *Bile* (or: *Bitter One) of Anu*, or Heaven. How bitter can Heaven get? You tell me. In medical literature, gall and bile diseases are attributed to Pašittu, who may or may not be identical with Lamaštu, and to Aḫḫazu, the *Seizer* who frequently appears in Lamaštu's company. We will discuss these diseases in the chapter on medicine. Let me just add that this *'jaundice'* is an unknown and lethal disease.)

II, 39

Asarluḫi beheld the Daughter of Anu, of Heaven;

in the art of his wisdom (or: magic) he made her muscles (or: nerves, or: sinews) weak:

II, 41

'Go away to the mountains which you love,

take deer and mountain ibex,

(We discussed this earlier. For 'take' (ṣabṭi) you could read 'seize' if you want a sinister translation, 'take' if you prefer a neutral and 'adopt' if you like one that came into fashion during the Neo-Assyrian period.)

II, 43

take all the [her)ds (or: mothers) of their young!

I have made a sailing ship for you, and escorted you up to it.

(The **mothers** are Farber's suggestion. The **sailing ship** (ship with canvas) is disputed by Farber: the words actually mean a canvas ship. If the canvas were coated by bitumen, it would become waterproof. The boat model from Eridu, dated around 4000 BCE, has a socket for a mast and holes to attach rigging. A picture can be seen in Roaf, 1990. Apart from this specimen, images of sailing ships in Mesopotamian art are a rarity.)

Figure 34 She is Furious, She is Fire.

II, 45

I have carried up four dogs for you, two white and two black;

I send you to sail on the Ulaya River,

over the sea, into the inside** (or: **womb,** or: **inner being,** or: **mind) of [Tiāmat],

(The identification of river **Ulaya** remains difficult. We can be sure that it is a real river and a river deity. The magical tree iṣ pišri grows on its banks. So far, the Ulaya has been identified as River Karkeh, River Karun and River Saimarreh in western Iran, well outside of Mesopotamia in hostile Elam. Read tablet VIII of the *Gilgameš Epic.* The protagonist says about his dead friend Enkidu: *It shall weep for you, the holy river Ulaya, along whose banks we used to walk so proudly* (Dalley, 2008:91). Next, Gilgameš mentions the Euphrates (another place for proud river walks); amazingly, the Ulaya is mentioned before (!) the sacred Euphrates. Maybe the two were proud of walking in enemy territory. But there is another meaning. In a satire translated by Foster (1995:375) the Ulaya flows near the gate of hell. You could think of it as a river of the underworld, like the Greek Styx, a concept that appears in some Mesopotamian myths and is glaringly absent in others. However, if the Underworld has a river, which the dead have to cross, it is usually the Ḫubur (Sumerian: I-lu-ru-gu). Perhaps Gilgameš was proudly remembering the time he and his friend walked very close to death.

In our text the journey leads from a foreign river to the sea, to the mighty world ocean (tiāmtu(m), tâmtu(m)), symbolised by **Tiāmat**. You can't go any further than this. Tiāmat is the *Mother of Chaos,* famous thanks to the *Enûma Eliš, the Babylonian Epic of Creation,* where she is vanquished by Marduk almighty. Many contemporary writers have identified Tiāmat as a world-serpent. So did I, and it was probably wrong. The idea was maybe inspired by Thor's fights against the Midgard serpent, and Indra's fight against Vṛta, who is occasionally called a serpent (and a bank of clouds and a brahmin). The world ocean, a ring of water surrounding the world, may remind you of the worm ouroboros, the eternal serpent that bites its own tail. That symbol was long imagined to be a Near Eastern creation. As it turns out, it was invented in China around 3500 BCE, by the Hongshan cultures (Fries, 2012:27). Babylonian texts fail to provide a description of Tiāmat. In the EE, Marduk splits her in twain like, maybe, a shell, an oyster or a baked fish, to create heaven and earth from her carcass. That doesn't say much. Only two very late texts give a simile: one is badly damaged and calls her a cow. Given that pretty much any god or goddess was a bovine at one time or another it doesn't get us very far. Another text, from the Seleucid period, when Mesopotamia was ruled by Greek aristocrats, calls her a camel (RlA *'Tâmtu'*). And of course we have the account of Berosus, who simply called her *a woman and* identified her with the ocean *(=thalassa).* So we have to leave it at that. Tiāmat is the world ocean. For the Babylonians, who loathed long sea-voyages, it's as scary as it can get. More about Tiāmat under LS II, 145. A similar old or middle Babylonian text appears on tablet YBC 4601 (translation Wasserman 2010):

*They have tied her (*Lamaštu*) to a tamarisk (?) in the middle of the sea (=tiāntum)*

[...] in the Araḫtum canal.

The **Araḫtum** canal is in northern Babylonia. The word **'inside'** qer-biš$_2$ can be a synonym for vulva, womb, centre, inner being and mind. Tiāmat's inside is the primordial salty ocean, surrounding the entire world; and the Milky Way, the river of stars.)

II, 47

I bind your feet to mountain tamarisk and

a single stalk of reed

I encircle you with flour-water; be bound, be enclosed!

The **tamarisk** is a symbol of An/Anu. The goddess is bound to the supreme authority of her father. The single stalk of **reed** is enigmatic. Usually, single reeds are metaphors for weakness, sorrow and doom. There is a lone reed that shakes its head for Dumuzi, and as Dumuzi's sister Geštianna explains, that lone reed is Dumuzi's mother, shaking her head with grief and woe (Jacobsen, 1987:31). It does not have to be that way. Let's look at reed sorcery. A single stalk appears in rituals where it is placed next to the patient, and cut to her or his size. Then, the reed is magically identified with the patient and used as a replacement sacrifice. A similar ritual, using a reed figure, appears in Schramm's *Compendium* (2008: 50-53). Does the text mean: I will tie you to a substitute of the patient? Tamarisk and reed also represent upset emotions. We encounter them in the *Descent of Ištar*: when Ereškigal hears that her sister Inanna/Ištar is about to visit her, her face turns livid like a cut tamarisk and her lips as black as the rim of a reed-vessel coated with bitumen.

Another interpretation appears in a third-millennium hymn to Enlil that was rewritten in the second millennium to praise the invincible newcomer Marduk. The scribe bemoans the terrifying majesty of the god:

He turned me into a lonely tamarisk in the southern storm,

He turned me into a lonely stalk of reed and crushed me within myself!

(Ungnad, 1921:216, trans. JF).

If we accept this, Lamaštu is to be broken and crushed by the storm of the gods.

How about another interpretation? The reed could represent the Sumerian goddess **Nidaba** (Akkadian: **Nisaba**) the deity of writing, learning, science, documentation and knowledge. Enḫeduanna praised her in the very last of her 42 temple hymns, a fitting tribute to a deity who makes accounts, study, contracts, laws, justice and civilisation possible, preserves hymns and rituals, records history, genealogy, literature and proverbs, who

measures the heavens by cubits

strikes the coiled measuring rod of the earth

and brings powers down from heaven

(De Shong Meador, 2009:238). The reed goddess measures building sites, draws up schedules and lays a foundation for the rule of kings. It sounds like thinking, reasoning, measurement and dry accounts. But Nidaba/Nisaba is also the goddess who celebrates feelings.

Nisaba, when your heart moves you,

you extend everything, you make everything rise,

you order the pools around the pool of heaven,

order the sanctuaries and pour radiance (over) them.

You are the lady who grants joy of the heart,

you place good seed in the womb of the mother,

you make the fruit ripen in the womb,

and grant mother's love to the child.

You increase the portions of the gods,

you open the mouths of the great gods,

offerings, from the heart; Lady, you give bliss,

you grant the shares of the gods (to them).

(SAHG, 1953:67, trans. JF). The stalk could be a stylus, implying that Lamaštu is bound by the magical power of the written word. The magic circle, made with flour-paste, is another attempt to bind her to her island solitude.)

II, 49

I conjure you by the river, by the gate of Mêšaru (or: by city gate and Mêšaru),

by the marketplace.

I conjure you by Šarur, the mighty weapon,

the courtier of the Lord (=Bēl) of the Lands!

(From this point, the canonical text parallels the reverse of the Uruk tablet VAT 14506. **Mêšaru** is the principle of justice, personified as a deity, and a son of Utu/Šamaš. Mêšaru comes from ešēru: to go straight; the right way, to be in order;

i.e. to follow one's nature, role and destiny. A common expression is *Kittu u Mêšaru*. **Kittu** is Šamaš's (or An/Anu's) daughter, her name means: Firmly Established, Steadiness, Reliability, Honesty, Truth, Reality. Brother and sister ensure the just conduct of people, royals and gods. Kings tended to exercise the virtue of mêšaru early in their reign, when they righted wrongs, enforced justice, destroyed evil, cancelled debts, pardoned prisoners and did their best to become popular (Bottéro, 1992). **Šarur** is a divine weapon *that overthrows numerous enemies. The hurricane of battle, the cudgel against the rebellious land, that battles for the lord after he has gazed upon the rebellious land, the enemy land, which has driven him mad.* It is usually wielded by **Ningirsu**. Gudea had one rammed into the ground like a battle standard at the temple of Ningirsu in Lagaš, in the šugalam, the *terrible place of the house* (SAHG 1953:153, 160, 171, 172). In the Sumerian tale *Ninurta and the Asakku*, the Šarur is intelligent and talks with its owner. It also acts as a messenger. Dalley, (2000:328) proposes it might be a mace. Maces were frequently used by kings to smash the heads of noble enemies. De-Shong Meador, (2009: 143) calls it the *crowd flattening blade*. The word rešu(m), here meaning: a **courtier**, an official, attendant, advisor or a eunuch, can also mean: a head, top, beginning, peak, best and slave.)

II, 51

I conjure you, be conjured!

Do not approach the door, whose bolt is Mêšaru,

***whose door-pivot** (or: **pole** or: **bolt**)*
***is Anu** (or: **Antu(m)**),*

(Köcher thought that it should be: *whose doorposts are Anu;* Heeßel's suggests *Whose door-pivot is Anu.* Wiggermann has *'pole'*, Farber preferred *'bolt'*. In Babylonian thought, **doors** were magical. They represented a liminal state that leads, not simply from room to room, but also to the otherworlds. You can explore this: sit down in a doorframe for your meditation. As gateways are highly attractive to dangerous spirits, protective magic was used to annul the threat. To this purpose, all elements of the door, especially its frame and bolt, were praised as living beings who guarded the entrance and were entitled to sacrifices. Here is a line from a hymn by Nebuḫadnezzar praising Šamaš (SAHG 1953:285): *The (doorframes), locks, bolts and doors of Ebarra* (E-babbar, the *White House*, the temple of Šamaš) *shall incessantly speak well of me before you.* Doors were valuable. Wood was rare and expensive. As Babylonian contracts show, tenants often brought along their own doors when they rented a house. The word **Anu** is not certain; Falkenstein assumed it might be Antu(m). We simply don't know: the end of the line is damaged.)

II, 53

whose guardian is Papsukkal,

whoever is banished by him does not return.

I conjure you by the power of the heart,

by mighty regard (?)** (or: **by the black head)

(*Papsukkal* = Brother-Messenger; otherwise known as Pa(p)gal. God List *An=Anum* mentions a Papsukkal ša a-šer-ti (*P. of the Sanctuary*) and Papsukkal ša še-er-ti (*P. of the Door bolt*) who might be relevant here. He acts as an envoy (and odd-jobs boy) for Anu and Ištar. In *Ištar's Descent to the Underworld*, Papsukkal goes, clad in rags of mourning, weeping bitterly, to enlist Enki/Ea's help. The *Šurpu Series* IV, 97 says: *Arise, Papsukkal, Lord of the Staff, banish the disease!* Maybe Papsukkal started out as a deity of grains and got mixed up with Ilabrat and Ninšubur. His prime function is to act as a divine messenger, and to enforce divine commands. Eventually he became an 'aspect' of Ninurta. The *black head* was restored by Farber. The expression *black headed* usually means: a Mesopotamian, but what this signifies here remains unknown.)

II, 55

by the cistern (**or: **well) and the ditch (**or: **canal),

by the garbage heap (**or: **hole) and its content,

by the rag of a menstruating woman,

by the way and those who walk thereon,

(Our line starts by invoking the sources of two sacred and beneficial fluids. Then we reach tubqinnu; it means hole, hollow or cavity, not 'inner chambers', as Köcher thought. Farber preferred **garbage** (tubkinnu) **heap**. The Mesopotamians, as far as we know, did not consider **menstruation** a curse. Menstruating women were not evil or polluted but in a special state, one that needs further research. Excessive or lacking menstruation were normal health problems. They were not caused by sins, breaches of taboo, evil spirits or the hand of an angry deity. In this respect, the Mesopotamians seem to have had a healthier attitude than, say, the West Semites and the Hindus, who thought menstruating women were lethal, or as unholy as a killer of brahmins. Nevertheless, menstrual blood, just like sperm, was a powerful magical substance and maybe polluting. Gleick claimed that the rag and the bed of a menstruating woman were shunned. Our spell raises a lot of questions. Cistern and well water are pure substances and appear as a libation to Lamaštu; i.e. as something she appreciates. And just what is the way for those who walk thereon? Is it a reference to the ways of the sun and moon? Or the ways of the great gods An/Anu, Enlil/Ellil and Enki/Ea across the starlit skies? Think about it. Hole/garbage heap and menstrual rag appear in the company of very positive ideas.)

II, 57

[...] Evildoer(?) By the ḫultuppū (?)

By the life of Heaven, be conjured, by the life of the Earth, be conjured!

By the life of the Great Gods, be conjured,

by the Life of the Gods of Heaven and Earth, be conjured!

(This passage is in Sumerian. Sumerian ḫul.dub. = ***Ḫultuppū*** is probably a tool for ritual purification. It may have been the branch of a sacred tree, used to spill libations or scatter holy water, or the staff of a conjurer. Some scholars identify it with the êru: a magic wand, a cudgel or a mace to banish evil influences. That's one interpretation. The other focuses on the term ḫul = evil. It might refer to a hostile spirit.)

II, 59

By the Life of Heaven, be conjured, by the Life of Earth, be conjured!

Conjuration of Lamaštu.

II, 61

[Ritual Formula: Dust from the gate] of the p[al]ace,

dust from the gate of the Ištar temple,

dust from the gate of the house of the women (**or: **from the temple of Ninurta),

[dust from the gate of a hostel-tavern],

(The dust-and-dogs formula also appears under LS III, 3-28. Let's explore eperu(m): **earth**, **soil** and **dust**. Myhrman translated it as earth, signifying a substance that, if watered, will yield life and fruit. Köcher went for dust, suggesting uncultivated soil and the food and drink of the dead in the Underworld. The symbolism is remarkably different. As the lines do not refer to cultivated ground but to hardened and dried topsoil, I chose dust, but ask you to keep both options in mind. Earth/dust and soil are primal magical substances. Every bit of soil is the accumulation of lifetimes.

The ground is not just fertiliser; it contains the energy, matter, and memory of all that has ever lived. In this sense, earth, organic, ancient, wonderfully alive, is the realm of the dead. That's why Ereškigal is *Queen of the Great Earth/ Underworld.* But earth and dust are also life in potential. One creation myth states that in the beginning *Brightness was dust, vegetation was dust* (de Shong Meador, 2009:33). It sounds negative until you remember that the soil is crawling, pulsing and throbbing with life. A single spoonful of humus is brimming full of more than a million tiny insects, mites, nematodes, fungi, and microbes. A cubic metre of healthy soil can house more than a thousand different animal species. One estimate mentions 120 million nematodes, 100,000 mites, 45,000 springtails, 20,000 worms and 10,000 molluscs (Keith, 2013:25). This awesome community creates the humus-acids that allow plants to flourish. We know less about their lives and interactions than about the dwellers of the deep sea. Without them, we would be lost. Dust or earth was used in many spells. Examples are dust from cross-roads, dust from thresholds, drainpipes, tombs, steppes, temples, from the places where dogs and pigs rest, and so on. In each case, dust is the essence of the magical power of the place.)

II, 63

[dust] from the gate of the house of the brewer,

dust from the gate of the house of a bak[er]

[dust from the cross-roads;

you shall pulverise, with what has been pinched from a rock (or: mortar)],

(The list of professions has magical connotations. We are talking about seven distinct types of earth or dust.

One: the **palace** represents the king as the shepherd of the people. In Mesopotamia, shepherds were hired to herd sheep they did not own: likewise, the king does not own the people but herds them for the gods. Shepherds were not necessarily poor loners; some of them controlled the vast herds of the temples and palaces and acted much like administrators. They had a dangerous job, as the flock was constantly threatened by thieves, wolves, hyenas, leopards and lions.

Two: the **temple of Ištar** represents the force and wisdom of the leading goddess of Semitic Mesopotamia. It may also symbolise the forces of attraction (love) and conflict (war) which are her favourite playgrounds.

Three: can be read in two ways. Köcher proposed the **house of women**; it's the residence of the queen, her servants and ladies, plus a substantial amount of fields, storehouses and gardens. The term appears in texts from the dynasty of Lagaš under Enentarzi and Lugalanda; finally, under Urukagina (c.2380 BCE) it was renamed *House of Bau/Baba.* Maybe the renaming of the premises indicates a shift of ownership. Property of the queen was now officially owned by the city goddess. The strange thing is that very little seems to have changed. Was the queen identified with Bau/Baba? (Glenn Magid in Chavalas, 2007:9). If the queen was an entu(m), hence a *woman who is a goddess,* this may have been the case. Farber identifies it as the **temple of Ninurta**. This metaphor, as he emphasises, is unique. However, we are still close to the cult of Bau/Baba. By the time the *Lamaštu Series* was compiled, Ninurta had long been identified with Ningirsu, and Ningirsu's wife is Bau/Baba.

Four: the term **tavern** or **hostel** (aštammu) has caused a lot of discussion. In some texts the word means a hostel, in others a pub and yet others suggest a brothel. All of them were popular places under the protection of Inanna/Ištar, and no doubt quite a few of them catered to all needs. Drunken revelry and lovemaking happened under the auspices of the goddess. When business was slow, she was implored to find customers. However, the term was also used, on rare occasions, for proper Ištar temples. It may have been a scribal joke.

Figure 35 The Layers of the World. Based on a roll seal of the third millennium BCE, BM128860.

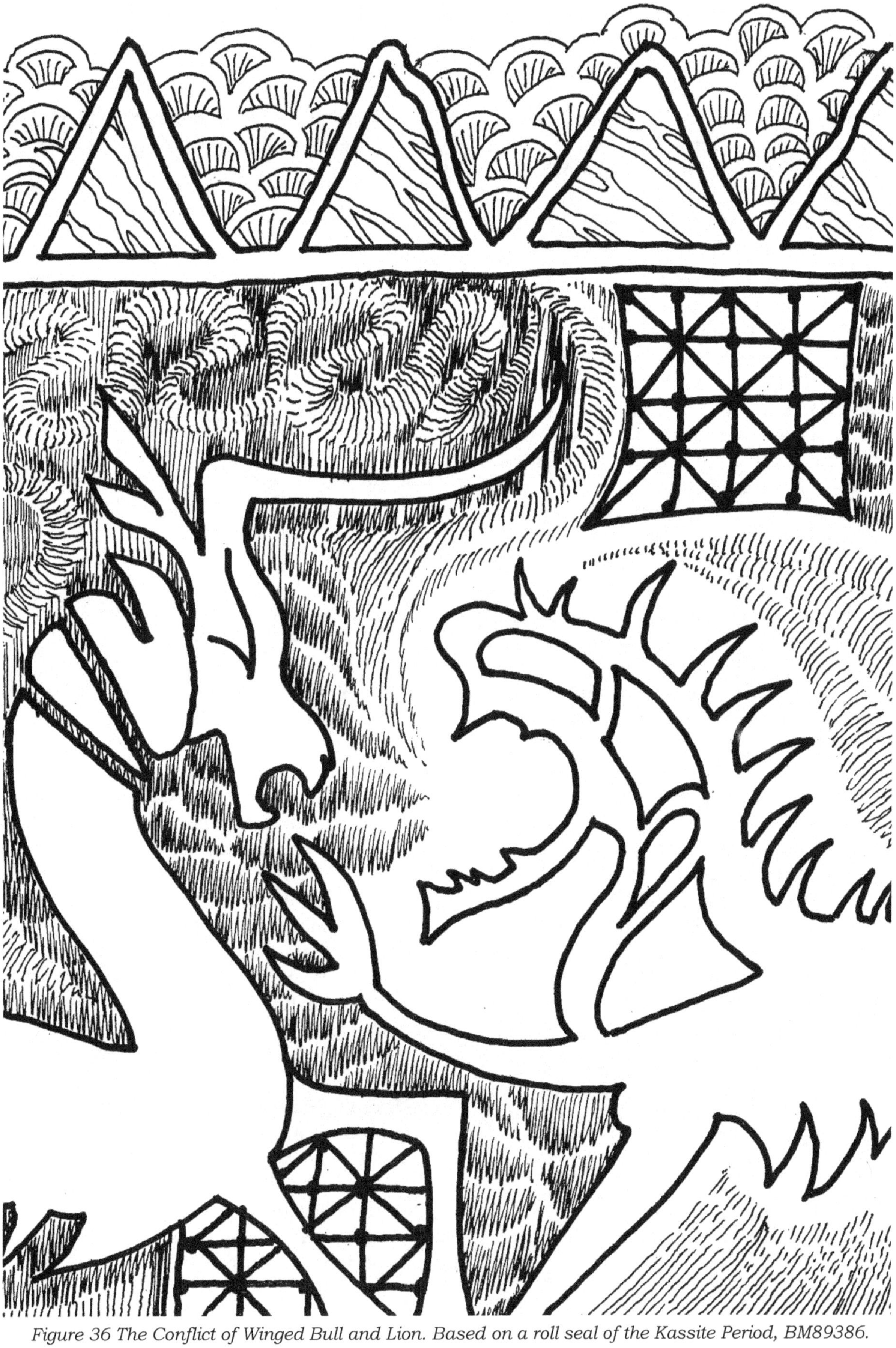

Figure 36 The Conflict of Winged Bull and Lion. Based on a roll seal of the Kassite Period, BM89386.

Five: the **brewer's house.** It's not easy to tell the difference between this house and the tavern, as many taverns made their own beers, fruit wines and alcoholic beverages. Brewing was often a female profession, and there were independent women who ran drinking establishments.

Six: the **baker** can be an ordinary craftsman or hold a high religious rank. The major temples had their own bakeries, catering to the needs of the gods and temple personnel. The amount of bread offerings was prodigious. Chief bakers in temples occasionally participated in the sacrifices. Their art ensured that the great gods received the finest quality. The Mesopotamians ate lots of bread and had a surprising range of varieties. Common grains were emmer, barley (four types) wheat (six types), and something called bittergrain. Millet and rice were occasionally imported (Nagel in RlA '*Getreide*'). Often, the dough was thrown against the wall of the oven where it could bake leisurely, or placed in a bed of ashes. Special types of bread were a delicacy. Some were named after the cities where they had been invented; others were flavoured with honey, nuts, dates and imported olive oil. After the service, most of the bread was consumed by the temple personnel and by the people who had acquired the privilege of 'temple duty' for that day. But bread was also magical. It could be rubbed and passed over a patient to soak up evil influences and diseases. In a spell (Schramm, 2008:54, trans. JF) Enki/Ea approaches the patient and touches his head with bread, saying:

The man who belongs to his god are you! The bread I touched to your head, the bread I used to purify your body shall ease your disease and you shall stay alive. Your foot shall stand on the foundation of life!'

Seven: earth or dust from the **crossroads**. Crossroads are places between worlds, where all directions of space meet, the material and invisible realms merge, and deities and spirits are easy to contact. Crossroad earth is a very common ingredient in magical spells all over the world.)

II, 65

mix it with clay from a canal and fo[rm] a tablet and dog figurines.

You shall inscribe [a tablet and the envelope of the tablet

with a lunar cr]escent, [a solar disc], a curved stick (and) a star,

(The reverse side of the Uruk tablet VAT 14506 and the canonical text are similar. Important **documents** were often sealed in clay **envelopes** to ensure that nobody tampered with the inscription. A copy of the text was inscribed on the outside of the envelope, so it could be read without breaking the shell. This tradition is remarkably old; the first example comes from the temple of Bau/Baba, shortly before the Akkadian period (Postgate 2002:60-62). Mind you, some people sealed a document and had the scribe record something different on the outside. In our text, the sealed tablet suggests a proper business-like approach. Formality has magical power; maybe we ought to consider the idea of 'sacred bureaucracy'.

The **lunar crescent** is the moon god Nanna/Suen/Sîn, the **solar disc** is the sun god Utu/Šamaš, the **star** represents Inanna/Ištar. The **curved stick** is either a throwing stick, used for bird hunting and war, or a shepherd's crook. The latter had been a popular symbol of two gods since the Old Babylonian period. You already met one of them, **Šakkan**, the lord of wild and domesticated animals (comment to LS I, 197). It seems a useful idea that a god famous for his fertile seed is asked to keep Lamaštu in check. But we should also consider the other alternative. The crooked stick is a popular symbol of **Martu/Amurru**. He is the main deity of the nomadic Amorite/Amurru people, who began moving into Mesopotamia early in the third millennium BCE. By the late third millennium, they had become a major threat; their troops ended the moribund Ur III period and Sumerian culture as such.

The Amorites started the Isin-Larsa period (c.2000–1763 BCE) and, as they respected Sumerian culture, they transformed their chief god into a son of An/Anu.

Figure 37 Brewing: Cradle of Civilization. With extra ornamentation from the fourth and third millennia BCE.

Nevertheless, they made him an equal (if not superior) of Enlil. Martu/Amurru is associated with the city Ninab, his wife being Ašratum or Belit-Šeri, the *Lady of the Desert,* a winged goddess who occasionally helps out as a scribe in the Underworld. In a poem describing the marriage of Martu with the properly civilised Sumerian goddess Adgarudu, a girlfriend warns the bride that Martu is *One who digs up truffles in the foothills, who does not know how to bend his knee. He eats raw flesh. How could one who has never known a permanent home be buried* (under the floor of the house, as civilised people were) (Edzart, RlA *'Martu/Mardu'*). Like so many major gods of the Near East he is a deity of wind and storm. Like Enlil, he is praised as the *Lord of the Mountain,* or as the *Great Mountain.* However, he was not universally acknowledged and is notably absent in the *Codex Ḫammurapi, Šurpu Series,* the *Enûma Eliš,* and the myths of Gilgameš and Erra.

The four gods who appear on the tablet all have specific functions. Sîn and Šamaš are custodians of justice and law; they watch over mankind (and the dead in the underworld) and punish evildoers. Why Inanna/Ištar participates is uncertain. Amurru might represent royal authority and makes me wonder whether these lines were composed during the Isin-Larsa period.)

II, 67

write the conjuration ['...] Daughter of Anu' on it,

set (it) at the he[ad of the bed....] paint dogs

(We met **dogs** as Lamaštu's companions, adopted children and vehicles earlier. Here is another aspect. Pairs of painted clay dogs, inscribed with names, were occasionally buried in the floor and in walls. Such dogs were set against Lamaštu and a wide range of spirits and evil beings. Saggs 1966:315 cites a tablet which describes two dogs coated in gypsum, called *'Don't Stop to Think, Open Your Mouth'* and *'Don't Stop to Think; Bite'*; two black dogs inscribed with the names *'Consume his Life'* and *'Loud of Bark'*; two dogs painted red called *'Drive Away the Asakku-Demon'* and *'Catcher of the Hostile One'*; two dogs painted green called *'The One Who Puts the Enemy to Flight'* and *'Biter of his Foe'* and two spotted dogs named *'Introducer of the Beneficent Ones'* and *'Expeller of the Malevolent Ones'*. That's white, black, red, green and spotted: surely the colours had some significance. The names of the dogs in our passage are based on Köcher, Wiggermann and Farber. As the text is badly damaged and full of difficult terms, it should be considered an approximation. Remember that Mesopotamian dogs were bred for size. They were bigger than the small Middle Eastern wolves, and famed for their vigour. Dogs accompanied the Assyrian armies and several gods kept fearsome hounds. Marduk keeps four dogs to kill hostile spirits: Ukkumu (*Tears off Everything*); Sukkulu (*Snatcher*); Ikšuda (*Already Here*) and Iltepi (*Hollowed (it) Already.*)

II, 69

with plaster and yellow-green (**or:* ***black) mineral paste,

(set) hair of a [black] dog on their foreheads,

(The hair of a black dog turns the dog images into 'real' dogs. Or maybe they prime the dogs against Lamaštu, provided she is identified with a black dog, which may or may not be the case. What the hair of the goat kid in the next line is supposed to do remains anyone's guess.)

II, 71

hair of a [vi]rgin goat kid on their tails,

write their names on their left flanks.

II, 73

The windows to the right and left of the outer (*=main****) gate,***

the doors of the bedroom (**or:* ***inner doors) [...]

II, 75

[you shall set the two dogs] facing the direction of the do[or post (?), called 'Attack Swiftly (?)'.] 'Guard in the Night, Cha[se the Daughter of Anu'],

II, 77

you shall set in the windows of the door of the [bedroom? outer door?] two dogs: 'Fast is [...]!', 'Do Not be [Negligent] in your Guarding Duties!',

II, 79

[you shall you set] in the windows of the inner room, (two dogs:) 'Don't Hesitate to Think!', 'Overthrow the Ev[il!', ...],

II, 81

[you shall place] in the window (of? near?) the gate of the bedroom. 'Sîn is the She[pherd'] (of) [the d]ogs in [...] shall you pl[ac]e.

(Note that two of the dogs are charged with guarding the infant during the night. After this line the Uruk tablet VAT 14506 continues with the missing section starting with the seven sorts of dust or earth. It ends at the point where dogs are made, with a black dog hair on the brow and the hair of a goat kid on the tail. The Uruk tablet stops with the line *Head [...]. Second Tablet [Lamaštu]*, indicating that the next tablet should be number two. Evidently the Uruk tablet represents an alternative version of the *Lamaštu Series*, containing similar material in a different order.)

II, 83

[...] the door.

Conjuration: She is Angry, she is Furious, she is Fire** (or: **Fever), she has a Divine Radia[nce],

II, 85

she has risen from the reed thicket, she has become furious; her hair is tangled, her brow** (or: **shoulder) is stone,

(Here begins **conjuration #8**; like conjuration #9, it was perhaps recited over some unspecified place between the hips (conjuration #6 & 7) and the feet (conjuration #10, 11, 12, 13.) Line 86 is based on Farber.)

II, 87

[...], who encounters her on the streets, him [...] or: [...], a pig walks (?) before her; whoever drinks her milk dies (?). She enters the houses of the pregnant women,

(Line 87 is exceedingly troublesome. All copies of the text are badly damaged. Farber proposed very cautiously that there might be equids and pigs walking before her and that her deadly **milk** slays those who have a drink. Now consider this. Lamaštu is alone. She has neither a husband nor a lover; surely an unusual state for the daughter of the highest gods of heaven. Her breasts are full of milk. It hints at a lost myth. Maybe she had a bit of illicit sex, got pregnant & kicked out of heaven, bore a child, and it died. Her breasts are full and she wants to ease the pressure. It might be a reason why she suckles piglets and wolf cubs. We'll know more when further tablets are excavated.)

II, 89

she stands at the heads of those who give birth (and says)

'Bring me your sons that I may suckle (them),

II, 91

I wish to place my breasts in the mouths of your daughters!'

The Daughter of Anu wept and faced her father Enlil:

(Usually, Lamaštu is the Daughter of Anu. Here she addresses her brother Enlil/Ellil as 'father'. Elsewhere, Enki/Ea is her father, maybe as he raised and educated her. Is the term used to indicate respect?)

II, 93

'Give me, what I ask of you, my father Enlil.

'The flesh of men, not good [...],

II, 95

The blood of men [...]'

(Enlil replies:) ***'As you asked this from me,***

(These lines are cryptic. I agree with Thompson (2005/1908:240), who resisted the temptation to fill in the missing bits. Maybe we are dealing with human flesh, which isn't good, or the flesh of humans who ain't good (and might deserve being eaten). Köcher assumed that Enlil says: *'Human flesh is not good [to be eaten]'* and she replies: *'Human flesh is [my nourishment]'*. This is imaginative, to say the least. Until a better copy of this passage has been found, we should respect the gaps as they are.)

II, 97

a lump of earth shall be your house (or: temple).

A young girl (or: bride) shall bring you

(The **lump of earth** has at least two meanings. In the beginning, humans were shaped out of clay, divine spittle and, if available, the blood of the odd rebellious god. Lamaštu seizes or obsesses patients. Clay figurines of Lamaštu appear several times in our text. This passage may suggest the crucial moment of transformation. Think of the patient as a human lump of clay, obsessed by the goddess, and obviously not very happy with it. But clay is clay. It makes it easy and natural to shift her into another lump of clay, namely a clay figurine. After the transfer, she is cheered up, receives her loot and is carried out of the house. Far away, near the city wall or in the open, uncultivated wasteland, the figurine is left or destroyed, which sets her free to roam the world again.

In this simple process, a major process of ecology appears. Technically, it is called regulation. Ecologically relevant processes are usually divided into three groups: **transport**, **storage** and **transformation**. These three types of process apply to **matter**, **energy** and **information** (Nentwig, Bacher, Beierkuhnlein, Brandl, Grabherr, 2004:14). Let me add **consciousness**. Organisms have the ability to regulate these processes. By doing so, they influence themselves, each other, and their environment.

You observe transport, storage, and transformation in this ritual and in magic, and all over the world.

Lumps of clay are good for storage and they are easily transformed or moved. Here is an example: How to destroy the evil from a bad **dream**. Maybe we are dealing with a nightmare. Maybe it was a prophetic dream. The Mesopotamians were fond of dream incubation. They used the Akkadian terms zāqīqu, zīqīqu(m) for the human dream-soul. They could also mean wind, breeze, phantom and simply dream (see LS II, 17). To receive a dream oracle, the Sumerians ma-mu-de/-da ba-nu *laid down next to/for a dream.* The ritual started with elaborate purification. It required a suitable day, offerings, lamentations, prayers, and the act of committing oneself to the hands of a deity. Occasionally a statue of the deity was placed near the head. The dreamer did not assume a comfortable posture but sat, squatted, leant or assumed an embryonic position on the side *to reach the state of resting to see a* *dream* (Zgoll, RlA *'Traum'*). Some of those dream oracles produced terrifying visions. The dreamers did not leave it at that. Fate is not irrevocably fixed and oracles indicate probabilities, not facts. When things go badly something has to be done. Consequently, there were rituals to neutralise bad dreams. The process appears in a ritual for sun god Šamaš. In the early morning, the person suffering from a nightmare takes a lump of clay from a closed-up door and presents it to the freshly risen sun. S/he identifies her or his own self with the clay, projects the evil dream into the lump and dissolves it in water. The identification is the crucial part: as we are of one nature with the clay, the transfer is simple. Note how easily the lines could be used to transfer Lamaštu from a patient into the clay figurine:

When you, oh Šamaš, rise from the Cedar mountain,

(all) gods greet you with jubilations,

all mankind rejoices over you.

*(Then) the Bārû priest (=*diviner*) brings you (an offering of)*

cedar (perfume), the widow (only) madga (and kukkušu).-flour,

the poor woman (some) oil, the rich from his wealth brings you a lamb,

but I bring you a lump (of clay), a product of the netherworld!

'O lump, product of the netherworld, in my substance has been fused your substance,

In your substance has been fused my substance,

In my 'self' has been mixed your 'self', in your 'self' has been mixed my 'self'.

As I am throwing you, lump, (now) into water

and (there) you will crumble, disintegrate, (and) dissolve,

may the evil of the dream I had during the night-

(whether) I saw a god, a king, an important person, a prince, a dead (or) living person-

your right [...] I turn towards left.-

Just like yourself, fall into the water and crumble, disintegrate.'

(KAR 252 III in Oppenheim, 1956:301. Another translation appears in Foster (1995:265). Our spell shows a healthy recognition of the realities of life. Gods, royals, aristocrats, ghosts and people are often trouble.

Farber (quoted by Wiggermann) proposes that instead of *your* ***house*** (the literal translation) one could read *your* ***temple***. Farber 2014 assumes that Lamaštu gets a house built from clods. Now for the **young girl**. When Myhrman made his translation, ṣeḫertu(m) was a *slave girl*. By Köcher's time, she had become a *young bride*, Wiggermann and Farber cautiously agree. The CDA has *young girl*.)

II, 99

a broken comb, a broken spindle,

soup, boiling hot, in a large pot for heating (?).'

(or: soup, boiling hot, cooked over embers (?).')

(There are major differences between the young girl and the young bride. The former might be a child or an adolescent, hence not really threatened by the goddess, while the latter might be terrified of pregnancy, birth and miscarriage. Does the goddess receive her curious gifts from an innocent or a prospective mother? Why are her usual presents **broken**? Yes, the transcript says šebru(m), i.e. damaged. Why do these gifts differ from the usual offerings? If comb and spindle were supposed to domesticate her, their broken state could symbolise that she remains as wild as ever. A pot of **soup** might placate her and tell her that she is an honoured guest. Farber suggests it might have been cooked over embers. It doesn't make us much wiser. How many conflicting texts were carelessly thrown into one package when the scribes of Aššurbanipal compiled the *Lamaštu Series*? With these words, Enlil stops speaking; in the next line, the conjurer speaks.)

II, 101

By Anu and Antu(m), by Enlil and Ninlil,

by the city gate and the entrances,

II, 103

by the ploughshare (*or:* heavy plough) and the seeder-plough,

by the collector (*or:* heaper, *or:* abandoner) and his child I conjure you,

(Heavy **ploughs** were pulled by teams of oxen. Their use required prior levelling of the soil with rake and spade. They were commonly used in the Sumerian period, when the temples owned most of the land, and had it cultivated by their dependants. Common people, if they owned or leased land, did not have the means to acquire a heavy plough, but maybe they could rent one. At the end of Ur III, the temples lost influence, wealth and property, and the palace became the dominant player. By the start of the Old Babylonian period we witness a massive increase in private property. People acquired or rented fields, and as the demand was immense, fertile soil rare, and property often divided by inheritance, the Old Babylonian farmer often worked dozens of fields which were smaller that the flat you are sitting in, scattered all over the countryside. Each field was surrounded by a small embankment, to facilitate flooding in autumn before ploughing could take place. A massive plough did not make much sense on a small property. In Europe, farmers usually preferred long fields, as turning the plough is a major effort.

Under Ḫammurapi (1792-1750 BCE), the palace concentrated on acquiring private property, and became the largest landowner. Instead of a wage, palace employees were frequently granted land. Many of them did not till the soil personally. Peasants rented land and tried to gain connected fields, making cultivation easier. One tool for this purpose was the seeder-plough, which penetrated the surface lightly, deposited grain in neat rows and closed the earth over the seeds. It required two oxen and two people to handle them. They were more economical than the heavy ploughs, but could easily be damaged when they were turned. An Assyrian seeder-plough from the British Museum can be seen in Saggs, 1984: 4a. It is an emblem of Ningirsu, god of fierce storm winds and savage rain showers. City gates, entrances, ploughshare and seed funnel can all be understood as sexual metaphors. Esēpu(m) means: to gather, to collect, to heap up, to scrape up earth, dust, grain, coals, locusts and the harvest. Nasty spirits 'gather' their victims. Gathering beer means to decant. Köcher read *the heaper*, who might heap earth on the freshly opened and seeded furrow. Myhrman left the word untranslated. Farber translated (very reluctantly) *abandoner*. The meaning remains mysterious. However, we will meet the ploughs again under II, 117.)

II, 105

that you may not return to this house,

that you may not sit on the chair where I sit,

II, 107

that you may not take the child to your breast,

that I take to my breast!

O Ištar (*= goddess*) hold the mouth of your dogs,

(Is this passage spoken by a female ritualist? It's one of those questions that cannot be answered presently. That female conjurers (āšiptu) existed is indicated by the *Maqlû Series*, which class them with foreign witches, former high priestesses and murderous sorceresses. So far we don't know how many of them were around, in what period, and whether any of them were busy banishing Lamaštu. Otherwise, the line might be spoken by a qadištu (*sacred woman*); in the first millennium BCE, some of these formerly high-ranking priestesses made a living by assisting births with magic and purification rituals.)

II, 109

O Nanay (= goddess), hold the mouth of (your) cubs!

The one who rests in the bedroom shall not awake,

(In these lines, the name **Ištar** is not a specific reference to the goddess: when the text was compiled, the term was a common and popular title for any goddess. The same goes for **Nanā, Nanay, Nanaya**, the *Lady of Loving Care* (Akkadian: Bēlet taknē), who specifically takes care of bedrooms, beds and what happens in them. She is a daughter of An/Anu and her major cult place was Uruk. Hence she is occasionally praised as Nin-unu-ga (*Lady of Uruk*) a title she shared with Ningirima and Inanna/Ištar. A cult calendar from Uruk states that she should be celebrated with eršemma songs on the third day of each month, while the fourteenth (a very unlucky day associated with the Nergal and the Underworld) was devoted to lamentations for Nanay. She was widely popular in Kiš, Borsippa, Ubassu, Babylon, Kišina, Sippar and the unidentified land Namar. Her cult can be traced from the middle of the third millennium BCE to the Greek occupation. When the Elamites plundered Mesopotamia, they carried away statues of the major gods, including Nanay. Aššurbanipal proudly returned them to their homeland. After Cyrus had defeated Babylon, he decided that her statue should return to Uruk. Under Persian rule, she was identified with Anahita and during the Greek occupation with a special form of Artemis. It must have been very special: Artemis is proud of her virginity and Nanay is glad to be rid of it. In the sky, her constellation is Corona Borealis. Nanay was an early competitor of Inanna/Ištar. Unlike Ištar, she is not related to war, but was widely worshipped as a patron of lust and love. Some poets tried to make Ištar the goddess of love while Nanay was in charge of lust. Or we meet Ištar seated on a throne while Nanay guards her treasure chest. A Sumerian hymn states that she has pleasing hips when she bows down. Hence, she might appear in the popular images of a woman leaning over a beer vessel, drinking with a straw, while enjoying coitus from behind. She is famous for her nudity, her ḫi-li (*attractiveness, lust*) and uzzum (*rage, fury,* here probably in a sexual sense). Her two daughters are her hairdressers: **Gazbaja/Gazbaba** (*Sexually Attractive*) appears in love spells and is, surprisingly, the goddess of the Hittite (!) city Ḫupešna. **Kanisurra** (*Her Mouth is Laughing) is* a goddess of witches. Very little is known about them. According to Weidner (RiA *'Gazbaba'*, trans. JF) they were the *daughters of the temple Ezida in Borsippa, who moved to Esagila in Babylon on the day of the winter solstice.* During the second millennium Nanay was occasionally identified with other goddesses, like Gula and Tašmetu(m), until her name became a general term for 'goddess'. Now for a tough question. Who is the goddess supposed to hold the mouths of her dogs and cubs? Is Lamaštu addressed as Ištar/Nanay = goddess or is it Gula, goddess of exorcism and healing whose animal is a dog, but who is not mentioned in this passage?)

II, 111

until Šamaš, the sun, brings relief.

Conjuration of Lamaštu.

II, 113

[Ritual Formula:

Seven coloured ribbons (or: strands) of dyed wool (or: cloth)],

a bristle from the right side of a donkey,

a bristle of the left side of a female donkey,

a bristle from a young donkey,

(This formula is repeated, at greater length, under LS III, 36-56. A zappu or sappu is a **bristle** or **hair**. The word was also used for **comb** and the **Pleiades**. The bristle might appear as a pun. If the spell comes from the late second or first millennium BCE, an object that represents, if only due to its sound, the Pleiades, would have great magical potential. The Pleiades were identified with the Imin-bi, a group of heroic, divine archers and swordfighters dedicated to fighting evil. Their importance increased dramatically around the beginning of the first millennium. We also begin to get instructions on magical **anatomy**; i.e. the symbolic meaning of parts of the body. The topic is a lot more complicated than it may seem. Scurlock and Andersen (2005:xxiii) point out that when speaking of a patient, the āšipu uses his own hands to determine right and left. *[If] his "right" temple hurts him, hand of Šamaš. [If] his left (temple) hurts him "hand of Ištar." [This is because] the right side (of the face) is "hand of Ištar" (and) the left side (of the face) is "hand of Šamaš".* The right side in general belongs to Ištar, but when the āšipu diagnoses a patient, the right side of the patient appears to be the āšipu's left side. Does this also apply to the sides of a donkey? And while we are at it, just what is the significance of the donkey? For most of Mesopotamian history, donkeys symbolised travel. Horses were only introduced around the middle of the second millennium, and were not suited for the harsh conditions of the southern Sealand, while camels became popular in the first millennium BCE.)

II, 115

bristles of a white pig, a centipede (?) of the way,

The dark (hair? dung?) of the right side of a donkey's croup *(or:* ***hind leg),***

(Myhrman believed that the spell requires a **ḫallulaja** insect from the way, but couldn't specify which. Falkenstein guessed it might be a certain fly. Haas proposed a mole-cricket. Köcher thought it wasn't an x-insect but an x-of insects, and translated 'anteater'. Anteaters live in Central and South America; but perhaps Köcher was thinking of a pangolin. More than fifty years later, the CAD proposes '*centipede?*' Centipedes are very popular in magic spells. Many species are highly toxic and some of the East Asian varieties can grow to the length of your forearm. The ḫallulaja is more than a toxic surprise. It also appears as one of the six maskim/rabiṣu who haunt the desert and steppe. This maskim is GI-lu-ḫarra(n)a, the *Agent (*or: *Prowler) of the Roads.* S/he is identified with the god Šulpae and, in god list *An=Anum*, with Muštabbabbu(m), who is occasionally identified with Lamaštu. The word ṣulu(m) from ṣalāmu(m) means: **dark**, black, and what has turned dark. Köcher guessed it might be dung. See LS I, 57: it's a code word for **thyme**.)

II, 117

a spl[inter from the handle of a hea]vy plough (and) a seeder-plough;

take them, twine three loops and place them around his neck.

(Kanānu: wind, wrap, twine. Our conjurer is making bundles of magical items which are set around the neck of the patient. The contents of the talisman are worth contemplating. Are they meant to scare her away or should they make her feel empathy with the patient? Considering that she likes donkeys and pigs, red and colourful wool, and is identified with the ḫallulaja, I guess the assortment makes her feel friendly. If the bristles represent the Pleiades, this might not be the case.)

II, 119

Conjuration:

She is Angry, She is Furious, She is Fire *(or:* ***Fever),***

She has a Divine Radiance,

She is Angry, She is a Wolf-bitch, She is Fire *(or:* ***Fever), She is a Robber.***

(Welcome to **conjuration #9**. Like the last conjuration, it was probably recited somewhere between hips and feet. The conjuration was also used to fortify the incense.)

II, 121

The reed thicket is her home; grass is her lair.

*(extra line in one copy: **She rose from the reeds like a fury.)***

She stops (**or:* ***lifts) the track of cattle; the track of sheep,

(Again, the goddess seems to stop the advance of mankind, or, if you like, the silly spectre that people venerate as 'progress'. The word 'tracks' might also be understood as dung, as Farber does, who assumes she lifts it up.)

II, 123

she stops the moving bull, she stops the passage of the don[key].

She sends yo[ung men?] to their graves,

II, 125

she drenches the infants with Waters of [Distress?],

(**or:* ***she makes the infants drink the Waters of [Distress?]),

Where shall I grasp (or: see) her?

As a [...] is the [...] of Heaven.

(For these difficult lines, see notes on LS I, 40-41 and 43-45)

II, 127

Show your majesty, O Šamaš!

Conjuration of Lamaštu.

(The spell ends with an appeal to the primary deity of justice. Lamaštu, though she performs under divine command, can get things wrong or overdo her duty. Her function is not questioned here, but that she might do too much. Should this be true, her cousin Šamaš, esteemed judge and friend of mankind, might bring her back in line. By appealing to divine justice, the conjurer is acting like a lawyer in a court case!)

II, 129

Conjuration: DIM.ME,

Daughter of Anu,

Named With a Name by the Great Gods,

Innin: Victorious Mistress,

II, 131

Var. 1.: ***You who seize and hold (**or:* ***bind) the evil asag/asakku-spirit,***

Var.2.: ***You who bind the black-headed (people),***

(and?) the udug/utukku (ghost** or:* ***storm), heavy on mankind.

II, 133

Var. 1: ***DIM.ME, you Mighty (**or:* ***Exalted) One, you may not approach mankind!***

Var.2: ***DIM.ME, High Lady, the One who Answers Prayers,***

by the Life of Heaven be conjured; by the Life of the Earth be conjured!

(This is **conjuration #10**. The passage is in Sumerian and exists in several versions. Myhrman translated the *painful asakku* and the *heavy alû of mankind*. Maybe he thought of the other famous Lamaštu amulet, which allegedly dates to the Old Babylonian period. Our text is very close. Wallis Budge offers this translation of the amulet (1978 / 1930:117):

Incantation: Lamaš, daughter of Anu.

Whose name has been uttered by the gods;

Innin, queen of queens;

Lamaštu, O great lady;

who seizes the painful Asakku;

overwhelming the Alû;

come not nigh what belongeth to the man;

be conjured by Heaven;

be conjured by Earth,
be conjured by Enlil;
be conjured by Ea.

Wiggermann (in Stol, 1993, 242) renders this amulet as:

"O 'Dimme',
'Daughter of Anu'
'Who was named by the Gods'
'Victoria, Heroine among ladies',
'Dimme (or: Lamaštu) the Exalted',
'Who holds the Evil Asakku in a tight grip',
'South Wind weighing heavily on mankind',
You must not approach (this) person,"

(followed by the usual formula; i.e. *be conjured by* etc).

This inscription offers another **seven names/conjurations** of Lamaštu. The goddess is not only praised, she is also celebrated as a victorious Innin, a celestial goddess who does something useful and beneficial. The title Innin is usually reserved for Inanna. That's a remarkably positive thought. Maybe the amulets are kinder to Lamaštu than the canonical text. I wonder what sort of prayers Lamaštu is supposed to respond to, and by whom these prayers are spoken. Was there a cult of Lamaštu; did she have regular worshippers? Here, the answer might be a cautious yes. Not that the scribes approved of it, but the *Maqlû Series* (IV, 45-46) hints that there were sorcerers and sorceresses who destroyed their victims by giving images of them to Lamaštu. It does not tell us much, apart from the fact that these ritualists must have had a closer relationship to the goddess than the regular exorcist priesthood. After all, if you want Lamaštu to do something for you, you had better win her friendship first.

Wiggermann claims that this is the primary inscription of Lamaštu's seven names; it probably goes back to the Old Babylonian period. The important point may be that in early times, the goddess, though terrifying, was asked to control one or two of the most dreaded horrors of Mesopotamia. At this point Farber disagrees. He translates lines 131-132 *(but also) 'binder', grievous asakku-demon, ghost that weighs heavily upon mankind.* That Lamaštu is a *binder* and an *asakku* is an unusual and negative idea. However, he notes that the reading where the goddess binds the asakku is also admissible. His rendering follows the Akkadian version of text 'Ed$_2$' *and thus avoids saying too many good things about Lamaštu, even if they were only part of a ploy of adulation (maybe even with a touch of sarcasm?)* (2014:243). Is this something personal? Why shouldn't one say a few good things about Lamaštu? Even if she were terribly evil? Characters that are completely evil are two-dimensional, unconvincing and simply bad art.

But let us use this opportunity to explore some of the darker sides of Mesopotamian belief. I am sure you simply waited for it. It would be nice to characterise the southern stormwind and the **asakku** in full detail, but their descriptions are vague. The (Sumerian) asag, (Akkadian): asakku, ašakku, is one of the most dreaded spirits in Mesopotamian belief. Early translators understood this being as a disease, and guessed the asakku might bring fever. Indeed he does. However, his major field of activity is the head of the patient. *The asakku has brought confusion over the people in their own home* (Haas, 1986:155, trans. JF.) The asakku *enters a person like a breeze, smites a man and humbles his pride [...] turns his mouth to gall [...] so that he cannot move his limbs [...] that man cannot eat food, cannot drink water, cannot sleep, finds no rest and his (personal) god drops him.* (*Asakki Marṣuti,* tablet XI, after Thompson and Haas.)

The evil Asakku has appeared like a savage flood, he wears a gleam of terror and shrouds the wide earth, he moves clad in brightness and causes fear, roaming on the streets, moving freely on the lanes, he stands near a man but cannot be seen, he sits next to a man but is invisible, he enters a house but his form remains unknown, he leaves the house undetected...(tablet M, Thompson).

In tablet BB (Thompson, vol. II, 133, spelling modernised) the

Asakku [...] against the man flashes,

his tongue flashes against the man as a tongue of lightning,

Sickness, headache, heart disease, heartache [...]

Venom like water foams at his jaws...

Frequently, the asakku devastates the whole countryside. He moves across a river like a flood, disease sprouts out of him like vegetation on the field. He boils the fishes in the sea and casts his net into the sky to snare the birds (actually, so does Enlil, SAHG, 1953:77). He grabs the ibex, the goat, and the wild bull by their horns and wrestles them down. He destroys the herds of Šakkan/Sumuqan, the god of animals, on the meadow (Haas, 1986:155). The asakku destroys horses and asses in their stables (Thompson, 2005/1908:50). I am not surprised Lamaštu is upset: she likes asses and helps the animals of Šakkan to be born.

In everyday life, asakku are frenzied, obsessive, greedy and fierce. What marks them as 'evil' is the fact that they don't have an off-button. I'm sure you have met a few. Let's consider a remarkable idea. The asakku might be dwelling outside of the divine order. Wiggermann (1992:162) observes that Namtar and asakku are often mentioned together. Namtar is a vizier of the goddess of the Underworld, Ereškigal, and represents dooms and diseases that have been *decided by the gods*, i.e. afflictions that are divine punishments, as the patient has offended divine laws or misbehaved. If Namtar represents a divinely ordained fate, the asakku might (this is speculative) correspond to diseases that are not decided, but represent, quite literally, a dis-order, or a violation of the cosmic order. We find supporting evidence in Huber (2005). During the reign of Sanḫerib, the great Assyrian capital Nineveh had 15 gates, each of them with a cosmological significance. Gate Five was called the Gate *which allows the flesh of the asakku demon to leave; Breath of Asakku; that allows to leave but not to enter: Mušlālu Gate (is its name).* The *Staircase-Gate (?)* was also called *Gate of the Breath which is a Mouth of Myrrh.* Outside this gate, offerings of fine cereals and small animals were constantly made; possibly to placate any hungry asakku lurking outside. The gate was used to dispose of the victims of pestilence and pollution.

In Mesopotamian thought, diseases could have four causes. They could be ordained by gods, caused by lethal spirits, by people (sorcerers and witches) or simply by natural causes. The doctors were not so naive as to blame every ailment on deities, spirits, sins, curses and pollution. Plagues and pestilence could not be explained easily, as they afflicted a large number of people. Not all of them, especially children, would have broken a taboo or annoyed a god. Hence they might occur without divine consent.

Look into the Sumerian poem *Ninurta and the Asakku.* We meet the mighty storm god Ninurta, a born warrior, facing an asakku, a child of heaven and earth, who had made his home on a distant mountain. The asakku copulated with the earth and spawned a race of rock demons. Here, the asakku represents cosmic disorder. Well, Ninurta killed him with his trusty and talkative Šarur weapon. The rock demons turned to minerals and the mountain range was opened for cultivation. Another example. Religious inscriptions from Mari on the middle Euphrates, hence not strictly within classical Mesopotamia, claim that people who do not honour contracts, violate taboos and break their word *eat the asakku* of the specific deity or king who has been offended by the deed. In other words, they are fatally polluted, unless they make up for their evil. Have you noticed how asakku obsession resembles an overbearing, anti-social ego? In this sad, terrible and ridiculous condition, all sorts of pollutions, sins and perversions happen naturally.

The word alû can be misunderstood. In normal Akkadian texts, the **evil alû** (alû.ḫul) lives in cracks and crevices; it dwells in ruins and deserted buildings, and creeps through the alleys and lanes at night. It falls on people like a wall, envelops them in bed or wraps itself around them like a shroud, to paralyse and smother them, or makes them restless and unable to sleep. It moves like a god in the night, like a bird of the twilight, like a city fox in the dark, unseen, shapeless, and faceless; it does not care for libations or flour offerings, nor does it listen to prayers. (Thompson 2005/1908:81, Frank 1908:34-36, Haas 1986:138-139). While the asakku attacks the head, the evil alû assaults the breast, and binds the hands and feet. The patient loses all emotions and walks in the world like one in a daze. Scurlock and Andersen (diagnosis:340) describe an alû disease. When a person is afflicted with stupor, the limbs are tense, the ears roar and the mouth is *'seized'* so he cannot speak, the hand of an evil alû is upon him.

That's the easy bit. It misleads. Our talismanic inscription is in Sumerian, not Akkadian. In Sumerian, the (Akkadian) alû is the ala. Our Sumerian text reads: u_{18}. lu dugud-*a* nam.lú.u_{18}.lu-*ke*. It's a major and troublesome difference. Wiggermann identified it with the terrible, hot, devastating **south wind** that makes the summer months unbearable, parches the fields, cracks the earth and brings in hurricanes from the Persian Gulf. The south wind is the only female wind. You met her in the comment on Adapa (LS II, 22). During the second and first millennium BCE, the south wind appears as a woman from the hips upwards; below, she has two twisted, whirling, spiralling legs. This goddess was the most dreaded among the cardinal winds. It would be nice if the text were a little easier to read. Is Lamaštu able to seize the south wind, just as she has the asakku in her grip, or is she the south wind herself? Both options are possible. And while we are at it, she is not the only one. Enḫeduanna praised Inanna/Ištar as the south wind. Ninazu and Ninurta are identified with the terrifying hot southern gales. Even Enki's temple E.ENGUR, the *House of the Abyss* or *House of Nammu* is called

E'engurra,a heavy whirlwind, touching the earth,

house at the side of the ocean, lion from the centre of the Abzu,

high house of Enki, that gives knowledge to mankind.

(SAHG 1953:135). To top it off, we meet the south wind as an everyday metaphor. Klengel (1991:114) mentions a business letter of the Old Babylonian Period. The sender, highly worried, states that he has been like the south wind for three days, and could not take food or water.

Farber added another level of meaning by identifying Lamaštu with an **udug** (ghost, spirit, guardian spirit, guardian deity). Maybe the goddess is one; maybe she controls one that weighs heavily on mankind. Note that the udug is not called an udug.ḫul, i.e. an 'evil ghost'. The term is neutral. Some udugs were popular as protective spirits. As much in this amulet inscription/conjuration celebrates Lamaštu's positive and benevolent nature, this is worth thinking about.)

II, 135

Conjuration of Lamaštu.

Conjuration.

The Daughter of Anu, of Heaven am I,

II, 137

a Sutuean woman, a [woman of Naḫur am I?], I am fear-inspiring, I enter the house; I leave the house at will:

(Welcome to **conjuration #11**. The verses are recited over the right foot of the patient, i.e. the foot on the right side of the conjurer. Let's begin with the amazing fact that these lines are spoken by Lamaštu herself. The conjurer who recited, chanted or sang them had to identify with her! Please stop a moment. Imagine yourself performing the exorcism in the house of a wealthy client. It's an exhausting and expensive five-days ceremony. The people who hired you are rich, powerful and deeply worried. You focus your attention on a suffering baby, but of course most of the family are present and much of what you do is aimed at soothing and reassuring them. First you spend plenty of time praising, placating, accusing and banishing Lamaštu. You plead, you give her offerings, you send her away time and time again. And when you're really into it, you become the very horror your client wants to be rid of and you speak in her stead! How do you do this? How does it affect your relation to Lamaštu? Would you need extra precautions? Would you risk ill health? Would you merely recite the lines or go fully obsessed? Did anyone put on a mask? And how does it feel for your clients?

The **Sutueans** are hard to locate. Some situate them in the Zagros Mountains, or in the Arabian Desert. Saggs (1962:83) stated they were *troublesome nomads who infested the middle Euphrates region and harassed both states* (i.e. Assyria in the north and Babylonia in the south) *with border raids*. In Ḫammurapi's time, they stayed mostly outside of Babylonia but raided the neighbourhood and sold foreign slaves to the Babylonians. They raided Der, Nippur and Parsay in the 11th C. BCE and repeatedly attacked Babylonia in the 8th and 7th C. BCE. Sargon II boasted that he had finally driven the Sutueans out of Babylonia (Dalley, 2008:315). **Naḫur**, brought up by Köcher, is a city in south-east Cappadocia (Turkey). Cappadocia was well connected with Assyria from very early times and had several thriving cities. Far from home, the Assyrian merchants had their own settlement. Some of them even had a second family. The Assyrian traders organised the donkey caravans to and from Mesopotamia. Mesopotamia had a great demand for minerals and ores, such as copper and tin; while the people of the Anatolian mountains were highly interested in high-quality woollen textiles (Saggs, 1984:28-34). It would be nice to know the age of this line. During most of the second millennium BCE, Cappadocia was part of the flourishing Hittite empire. The Hittites were a blend of local cultures governed by an Indo-European upper class. They picked up writing from the Mesopotamians and left us fascinating religious inscriptions full of Sumerian and Akkadian terminology. They also picked up some deities from the Mesopotamians, like Ea, Ereškigal, Išḫara, Iškur, Ištar, Marduk, Ningal and Nisaba, However, they had slightly different ideas about them and not all of them were really popular. At the peak of their power, the Hittites conquered Syria and Palestine and almost beat the Egyptians; later, threatened by the growing Assyrian Empire, they allied themselves with the Egyptians. Their empire disintegrated sometime between 1200 and 1100 BCE, when the 'Sea People' devastated the Near East, and turned into many small states. Hittite religious texts are full of references to powerful female ritualists, and maybe Lamaštu was identified with them. A Lamaštu talisman has been discovered in Ḫatussa (modern Boghazköy) the former capital of the Hittites. Haas quotes from a Sumerian spell that was discovered in Ḫatussa (1986:148, after Falkenstein 1939, trans. JF). It does not name Lamaštu but refers to a deity called **'Evil Weather, Evil Eye'**.

Evil Weather, Evil Eye, who ruins children, whose hands have smeared with poison and spittle,

who staggers about as a frenzied ghost, who binds the grown up girl and the youth.

It has gone, has collected clay from the Abzu, has taken a wad of hair,

has made an image, has [wrapped] the wad of hair around it,

has cast a spell on people with the hair of its body,

has spat on it and buried it in the ground,

has smeared spittle into the dish, has laid spittle into the drink.

Instead of Naḫur, a variant text with the same line (Köcher 1949) calls Lamaštu a native of the city **Mangiṣṣu**, close to city/state **Der**, east of the Tigris. Der was dangerously close to foreign territory; it was perfectly situated as most of the traffic between Mesopotamia and Elam passed through it. The road extended further west towards the Mediterranean; towards the east it merged into the tangle of trade routes which are called the Silk Road nowadays, extending to India and China. The spiritual countryside around Der was characterised by a blend of Mesopotamian and Elamite faiths. One of the special highlights was the popularity of serpent cults, of serpent-related deities, and of gods who were much at home in the Underworlds.

Basically, the line identifies the goddess as a dangerous alien: maybe a barbarian from the hostile desert, maybe from a high culture in mountains and forests of faraway Turkey, or from the hill-country between the Tigris and the Iranian plateau, connected with the cultures of the east. It shows that Lamaštu is a foreigner. So far we read that she is a woman of the Amorites (LS I, 37), the Elamites (LS I, 103), the Sutueans, or that she comes from Naḫur or Der. It makes it hard to identify her origin. However, I wonder whether it allows us to date the passages. Did the scribes identify her as, say, an Amorite when the Amorites were the major danger?)

II, 139

'Bring me your sons that I may suckle them,

I wish to place my breasts in the mouths of your daughters!'

(After this line, our conjurer ceases to speak for Lamaštu. I would guess there was a break in the ritual, a gesture to signal that the identification was over.)

II, 141

Anu heard it and wept.

The tears of Aruru, the Lady of the Gods, fall down.

(**Aruru, Aru, Arui** is usually a name of Ninḫursag, the *Lady of the Foothills* or, more likely, a birth goddess who was identified with her. Jacobsen (1976:108) rendered her name as *Germ Loosener*, a very daring interpretation. Another possibility is *Who Lets the Seed Flow*. However, that title was generally used for male gods. Aruru is famous for fashioning Enkidu out of clay. Her cult was strong in Sippar; in Ištar's temple in Aššur she was worshipped together with Dumuzi. Aruru overlaps with a whole cluster of independent 'mother goddesses' like Nintur (*Lady Birth Hut*), Ninsigsig (*Lady Silence*, referring to the necessity to keep silence during birth lest a chance word fix a fate on the baby), Mudkeša (*Blood Stauncher*), Amadugbad (*Mother Spreading her Knees*) and Amaududa (*Mother Who has Given Birth*). In our text, Aruru is probably a synonym for Antu(m).)

II, 143

'Why should we destroy what we created?

And why should she (?)** (or: **the wind) take what we have called into being?'

(At this point, the conjurer speaks as the goddess of birth. The line appears in a very similar form in the *Enûma Eliš*. In this work, the *Babylonian Epic of Creation*, we encounter a similar situation. The young gods of heaven, i.e. Anu, Ea, Enlil and company are noisy and overactive, and upset the primordial chaos beings, who prefer the world peaceful and quiet. Apsû, the (Babylonian) male version of the female (Sumerian) Abzu, approaches his mate Tiāmat and begs her to destroy the troublesome young gods. Outraged at this proposition, Tiāmat replies '*Why should we destroy what we have created? Though their ways are demanding, we should patiently accept them!*' The relationship of Tiāmat to the young gods is identical with the relationship between Aruru and mankind.)

II, 145

Take her and throw her into the ocean,

tie her to a mountain tamarisk and

bind her to a single stalk of reed!

(The lines raise one of the tricky issues of Mesopotamian theology. In general, human beings were seen as having been created as someone had to provide the gods with temples, offerings, attention, affection and entertainment. When people died, the gods lost valuable assets. From this perspective, Lamaštu is acting against the basically ideal state where people serve gods and nourish them. On the other hand, and that hand has pretty long claws, too many people were and are a major problem. Aruru, like a good mother of mankind, argues that Lamaštu ought to spare the population. Sadly, it can't be done; Anu and Antu weep, but they have to allow their daughter to get on with her job.

Called into being: in Near Eastern and Indian Magic, **speech** is an act of creation. The gods say what is to be and so it is. Humans were created out of clay, blood, spittle and other ingredients, but they were also *named* and *called into being*. The **ocean** was the most hostile place the Babylonians and Assyrians could imagine. Long sea journeys to India and Africa were abandoned around the end of the third millennium BCE, political power shifted inland, and the world view was designed by city dwellers far from the coast. These scribes imagined that a dangerous ocean surrounded the world on all sides and even below and above the earth. Tiāmtu(m) is not only a lake, the ocean, the ancient sea, but also a form of the name **Tiāmat**, whom you met as the dreaded chaos mother of Middle Babylonian cosmology under LS II, 45. She is the primordial mother of the younger gods. Today, she is alive and popular as a being of chaos and terror in the minds of many followers of the left-hand-Path. They are subscribing to a hostile interpretation invented by the followers of Marduk. Marduk killed her and fashioned the world out of her corpse. Not everybody had such a bad opinion about her. She appears as the goddess of the primal sea in the sacrificial calendars of Ugarit in far away Syria (RS 1.17 & RS 26.142 in TUAT II, 3, 1988:308). The text lists the offerings to the great and normal gods. We read: *and for Tihamat one sheep*. It's hardly surprising: the Syrians were keen sailors and they loved the ocean. So did the Greeks, who worshipped her, much transformed, as **Tethys**, the *Mother of the Gods*, the sister of Okeanos, the *Origin of all gods* (Homer, *Iliad*, 14.201). Tethys granted refuge to Hera during the titan-wars. Hesiod, (*Theog.* 133-136.) tells us that she and her brother are titans, children of Uranus and Gaia, and live at the outmost edges of the earth. It turns them into personifications of the world-ocean, and indicates that Homer and Hesiod were aware of the *Enûma Eliš*. The name Tiāmat was also written (for example in the EE) as Taw(a)tu, a form that easily transformed into the Greek Tethys. A translation of the EE was known to Eudemos, a pupil of Aristotle. His text rendered Tiāmat as Tauthe (Burkert, 1997:91-93). In the *Orphic Hymns*, she receives an offering of frankincense:

I invoke, the bride of the ocean, the bright-eyed Tethys, lady in blue attire, surging, swiftly flowing. Cast widely over the globe, by lightly whispering airs, who smashes mighty breakers against the beach and the stony cliffs, and with joyous, gentle touch, calms the wrath of the angry;

who is delighted by ships, feeding the animals on the waterways, mother of Cypris (=Aphrodite), *mother of all dark clouds and of the nymphs of every spring. Exalted, sacred one, listen* to *me,*

appear with helpful blessings, holy one, and grant the ships fast moving, favourable wind. (Plassmann, 1982:54, trans JF.) Tiāmat and Tethys are both the primordial sea, but the difference between them simply couldn't be greater. Tiāmat can be loving and kind. You just have to like the sea.)

II, 147

Like a dead body that has no grave (or: life),
and a stillborn child that did not drink the milk of (its) mother,

The **dead body** without a grave is a terrible danger. People who had no funeral remained between the human realm and the underworld. They troubled the living, caused accidents, disasters, illness and bad luck. Hungry and frustrated ghosts haunted the lonely deserts and steppes, and maybe Lamaštu was asked to join them.)

II, 149

so, just like smoke, may the Daughter of Anu,
never return to the house.'

(Qatāru means **smoke**, clouds, vapours, incense and fumigations. The Greek learned ritual fumigation from the Mesopotamians and coined their own word kathar: to purify, to cleanse. The word is alive and well in the English: cathartic. As this is a ritual text, maybe the conjurer extinguished a fire at this point to make the goddess disappear like smoke. In the *Compendium*, we encounter a very similar ritual. Conjuration 12 (Schramm, 2008:69, trans. JF) includes a banishment of the asag/asakku, who is commanded to rise like a cloud and shed rain on other realms:

Like [smoke] in the still air he shall rise to heaven,

like a tamarisk felled by the storm he shall not return to this place.)

II, 151

Conjuration of Lamaštu

Mighty is the Daughter of Anu, Who Plagues the Little Ones,

II, 153

her hands are like a hunting net;

her vulva** (or: **arm-crooks,** or: **her embrace,** or: **bosom) means death.

She grinds her teeth, she is very furious,

she is an Innin, she is rapacious, she is abducting,

(These lines start **conjuration #12**. Their location on the patient could be the left foot. The translation is uncertain; see comments to LS I, 143.)

II, 155

she is drenching** (or: **washing,** or: **purifying,** or: **overwhelming),

she is a busy hunting net (?), the Daughter of Anu.

(Raḫāṣu(m), probably signifying: to **drench**, can also be read as: to bathe, to wash, to purify, to cleanse and to overwhelm. If you want to limit divine activity, chose one of them. Experience will teach that all of them are true, one way or another. Compare with Tablet BM 120022 of the British Museum, inscription in Middle Babylonian/Assyrian, possibly from Babylon or Sippar, translation Wende 2011:

Incantation:

She is very great, the daughter of Anu, darkening little children.

Her hands are a hunting net, her arm crooks are death.

*She is furious (*lit.: teeth-gnashing*), she is strong, she is vindictive, she is snatching,*

she is goring, she is trampling, she is the one who takes away: the daughter of Anu.

She touches the innermost part of childbearing women,

she pulls away the baby from the nursemaid,

she suckles, she rocks, she keeps kissing (it),

a 'pure one' (=qadištu*) is she among the gods, her brothers - the daughter of Anu...)*

II, 157

She touches the heart** (or: **inside) of women who give birth,

she pulls the child from the nurses.

She suckles him, rocks** (or: **soothes,** or: **sings to) him and moves on** (or: **kisses him).

(**or:** She nurses him, makes him stand up and (he?) departs).

(This is an extra troublesome passage for the discerning connoisseur. Nazāzu(m) means: to grunt or to soothe. Köcher thought she makes the baby scream. Farber suggests she sings to him. If the word happens to be našāšu it could mean to shake or to rock (a baby). Alāku(m) can mean: to go, walk, travel, move on, depart;

Foster proposes that she makes the baby stand up. Or is it the goddess who gets up after a tough job well done? Someone moves on or departs: is Lamaštu leaving? Or is the baby, going to its fate? Farber and Wende propose that she kisses the baby. Think about it. This is not a homicidal monster but a lonely goddess who tries to adopt a baby. She does her best to make the infant happy.

This passage is worth considering in depth. Some scholars believe that 'demoness' Lamaštu is always on baby-killing duty. But let's get real: it's a tough job to be evil all the time. This passage looks quite different. She has her fun, the baby has its fun, and we don't read that the baby is harmed at all. It reminds me of the Jewish tradition where Lilith slays some babies and plays with others. You'll read about it further on. The same thing appears in Indian myth and ritual: terrifying goddesses, famous for baby-snatching, can become the protective mothers of a sickly child and ensure its recovery. I suspect that Lamaštu had a similar function.

Please consider: Lamaštu is acting as a midwife and a nurse.

Compare these lines to the following passage from an Old or Middle Babylonian Tablet, possibly from Larsa, YBC 4601, Babylonian Collection of Yale University, translation by Nathan Wasserman, 2010:

Although she is no physician, she bandages [the umbilical cord?],

although she is no midwife, she wipes off the newly born,

she keeps counting the months of the pregnant women,

she is blocking regularly the gate of the woman who is giving birth,

she keeps accompanying the stride of the livestock,

she is examining the land in a demon's rage:

she takes hold of the young man in the street,

of the young woman in the dance,

of the little-one on the shoulder of the nurse...

A note: Wasserman assumed that the **'gate'** is a euphemism for 'vulva'. That's unusual: most of the time, Lamaštu does not delay pregnancy but accelerates it. The word which Wasserman rendered **demon** is lilû(m); i.e. she examines the land in the rage of a wind and storm deity. She isn't the only one. The same metaphor was used for Ištar.)

II, 159

Great are her fangs (?), agile are her muscles (*or: *nerves,* or: *sinews).

The Daughter of Anu is a qadištu (=sacred woman),

among (*or: *for) the gods, her brothers.

(**Qadištu**. Let's examine the role and reputation of an important type of priestess through the millennia. This line, and how it was understood, says a lot about Lamaštu and the gradual degradation of women in Mesopotamian history. Myhrman, Köcher and Haas translated qadištu as 'whore' and got it wrong. Well into the 1970's scholars identified all sorts of Mesopotamian people as 'sacred prostitutes' or hierodules (Greek for *sacred slave*). It wasn't their fault: they were influenced by popular mistranslations of the *Old Testament* (*Gen. 38.21; Deut. 23.18; 2 Kings, 23; Hos. 4.14,* see Henshaw, 1994:218-222), by Herodotus' (I, 199) highly questionable account and by misogynist Neo-Assyrian wordlists.

When the pioneers of Assyriology set out to explore the Mesopotamian cultures, their understanding was influenced by Biblical, Jewish and Greek studies. The many translations of the *Old Testament* which mistranslated the (Hebrew) qadeša as a porne, whore, prostitute and, in modern versions, a sacred prostitute or hierodule, coloured their thinking. The same goes for Herodotus' famous account (I, 199) of Babylonian girls who allegedly had to surrender their virginity at the temple of Mylitta to a passing foreigner who tossed a small coin into their laps and spoke: 'I call you to the service of goddess Mylitta'. Pretty girls could go home soon, ugly ones sat waiting forever. The story is as unlikely as they come: why would Babylonian fathers allow their daughters to be deflowered and possibly impregnated by passing strangers? And just why would Babylonian men fancy marrying a girl who is pregnant from another man? There isn't the slightest evidence for such a custom in Babylonia or any other part of Mesopotamia. Nevertheless Herodotus tickled the imagination (and other parts) of many sober scholars.

Let's begin early. The Sumerians had a word written NU.GIG (in Emesal: MU.GIB) meaning something like *sacred woman, unapproachable woman, taboo woman, pure woman, dark woman.* The term was used as a title of Inanna and a few other goddesses, but it was also applied to a class of exceptionally high-ranking priestesses about whom very little is known. King Mesannepadda of Kiš (c.2600-2550 BCE) had himself celebrated as the *spouse of the NU.GIG.* He supplied no details, but the reference is enough to indicate the high status of the lady. Sadly, the Sumerian sources tell us very little about the NU.GIG. The term could refer to a goddess, to a human woman and to both at once. The documentation improved in the second millennium BCE. In Akkadian, Babylonian and Assyrian lexical lists, NU.GIG was translated qadištu and ištaritu. It may or may not be an exact equation. As hardly anything is known about the NU.GIG we cannot compare them with qadištu or ištaritu. At the time, the ištaritu was a high-ranking female devotee of Ištar or another goddess. Later, it became a general term for any woman worshipping a goddess.

The Akkadian, Babylonian and Assyrian word qadištu comes from the root qdš= *sacred, taboo, set apart.* It means *a Woman Who is Set Apart, a Woman Dedicated (to a deity),* a *Pure One, Tabooed One* or *Sacred One.* Qadištu are mentioned starting with the old Akkadian period. They lived in the cloisters of a temple, in the house of their fathers or even led a married life. The record is incomplete and contradictory: in all likeliness, there were different sorts of qadištu in various periods and city-states. Several of them were wealthy; their names keep appearing in business contracts. Many of them were literate. Quite frequently they lent money; they bought and leased land and slaves and invested in business ventures. Whatever it may be, they were women who were 'set apart' from ordinary society. Lamaštu is also 'set apart' from the gods, her brothers, and she is by no means the only divine qadištu. Others are Gula, Ninisina, Aruru, Ninmaḫ (all of them associated with medicine and birth) and Inanna/Ištar (who has entirely different things on her mind). The qadištu, like the prostitute, lives apart from mainstream society. Both of them may be independent of men and gain their own income. New research has shown that there is no reliable evidence connecting the qadištu with prostitution, sacred or not. In fact, the 'sacred prostitution' of Mesopotamia, whatever that may be, is becoming increasingly unlikely. Instead, we find the qadištu associated with religious activities. In the late third and second millennium BCE, a qadištu was often a high-ranking priestess and/or deified concubine, dedicated to a deity, who frequently lived in or near a temple in a specific cloister building. Some of them lived a life of chastity. Some of them had children by kings and subsequently became queens or royal consorts. Others married; the question of whether or under what conditions they were allowed to have or raise children is much disputed. As usual, the evidence leaves much to be desired. Our only detailed record of the activities of several qadištu comes from a Middle- or Neo-Assyrian ritual performed in a temple of Adad and Anu in Aššur. The ladies officiated as the highest priestesses, performing the main ritual in cooperation with the temple head (šangû). It was part of their office to sing invocations while the šangû performed purification rituals. Then they proceeded with an offering; sadly, the text is damaged and few details survive. Henshaw 1994:271-276 provides a translation. But the qadištus were not always powerful and respected ritualists. By the Old Babylonian period, their status was decreasing, and Ḫammurapi (c.1792-

1750 BCE) found himself compelled to pass laws to ensure their rights regarding inheritance, property and marriage. Regulations regarding veils appear from the reign of Tiglatpilesar (1115-1077 BCE). In Middle Assyrian times, the laws required married qadištus, like all other women, to wear a veil, while unmarried qadištus had to walk unveiled, like prostitutes and female slaves. By the Neo-Assyrian period they, and indeed women in general, had lost much of their rights and status: many qadištus retained very little of their former sanctity. While some remained busy officiating in temples, others continued as free-lance priestesses, assisted births, worked as nurses, or made a business by selling spells and cursing people.

Here is an example. In a typical passage, *Maqlû Series* III 40-55 describes an unknown sorceress who has allegedly cursed the patient.

Conjuration: Kaššāptu (witch) nērtānītu (murderess),

*elēnītu (superior one, or: female deceiver), naršindatu (*a sorceress who uses river clay*),*

*āšiptu (female conjurer- exorcist), eššeputi (*an ecstatic female ritualist*),*

*mušlaḫḫatu (*snake-conjurer-priestess*), agugiltu (*a witch who 'crosses threads'*), qadištu (sacred woman), nadītu (barren one,* a high-ranking priestess*),*

*ištaritu (devotee of a goddess), kulmašītu (*a priestess who is not bound to chastity*):*

who snatches in the night, who hunts the whole (day),

who pollutes heaven, touches the earth,

binds the mouth of the gods, binds the knees of the goddesses,

slays the men, does not spare the women,

the destroyer, the mocking lady,

whose spells and sorceries no-one can resist...

In earlier periods, several of these titles used to refer to high-ranking, often aristocratic priestesses and temple functionaries. It's a splendid example of Neo-Assyrian sexism and paranoia. Was the exorcist describing a flesh and blood woman or a goddess like Lamaštu?

Wiggermann (2000:230) wrote *the Babylonian qadištu usually denotes adult women living alone, who for their upkeep act (among other) as midwife.* The *Atraḫasis Epic* has: *the midwife shall rejoice in the house of the qadištu.* In Wiggermann's opinion, the *house of the qadištu* could have been a nursing home. Scurlock and Andersen (2005:263) record that when a woman gave birth, a midwife (šabsūtu) and/or a qadištu may have been present; the qadištu performed rituals and drew a protective magic circle of flour-water around the bed. Other texts briefly mention her blessing and sprinkling sacred water, or scattering grain as an offering. While some people evidently retained a measure of respect for the qadištu, and paid for her services in the temple and in the birth chamber, others did their best to deride her. In a few late lexical lists, the qadištu was equated with a *prostitute.* It does not mean much: so were all independent women, business women and many priestesses. The misunderstanding was due to the Akkadian word ḫarimtu(m), which was taken to mean prostitute. Lots of women, many of them priestesses, were identified as ḫarimtu(m). It created the misleading impression that Mesopotamia was full of prostitutes, including many priestesses. As Henshaw and Assante demonstrated, ḫarimtu(m) really means independent woman. Some independent women were prostitutes and some ran alehouses and brothels. Many others, however, were businesswomen, nuns and priestesses, and we have no idea what their love life was like. Our pioneering scholars, stumbling across such word-lists, assumed that there was an amazing range of more or less sacred prostitutes in Mesopotamia; an idea that seemed to support the general Biblical condemnation of Babylon as a hot-house of unspecified sins. For an excellent account of this complicated topic, see Henshaw (1994), Assante (1998:5-96) and RlA on *'Prostitution'* and *'Sexualität'*. There is no evidence that Lamaštu acts as a (sacred) prostitute, nor is she ever associated with a husband or partner, but she is certainly in heat, longing for love, sexually frustrated, fascinated by loving couples and mating animals and tries hard to nurse and adopt children, including wild pigs and dogs or wolves. In this passage, she does her best to help out when a woman gives birth, and we are not told that the baby is hurt or killed. She is also a successful midwife for the animals of the wilderness and for the gods, her brothers.)

II, 161

Her head is the head of a lion, (her) teeth the teeth of a donkey.

Her lips (**or:** words) are gales (**or:** ventilation holes) she spills death.

(Šaptu(m): lips, rim, words, opinion. Ziqu(m): draught, breeze, gale, ventilation hole.)

II, 163

She has descended from her home in the mountains,

she roars like a lion,

II, 165

she howls like a wild (**or:** rabid) dog,

time and time again she leans over the crosspiece of the windows.

(Line 166 is based on Wende and Farber. 'Wild/Rabid Dog', Sumerian UR.IDIM is also the name of a constellation to the left of Scorpio. In the Middle Babylonian or Middle Assyrian version of this passage, BM 120022 of the British Museum, possibly from Babylon or Sippar, see Wende 2011 and Farber 2014:181 you encounter between line 165 and 166:

*Her face is the face of the Anzu (*thunderbird*). She appears continuously (*unexpected, or: from above*). At noon, in the quiet time of the day, she keeps returning again and again.*

After line 166 follows the variant:

[...] from one corner to the other. She circles around every good looking youth (and) every pretty girl.)

II, 167

Then Asarluḫi saw her. To Ea, his father, he spoke:

'My father, I have seen the Daughter of Anu who plagues the little ones.'

II, 169

Ea answered his son Marduk: 'Go, my son Marduk,

II, 171

with the wi[se] conjuration conjure her!

[...] with a ribbon (**or:** journey) for [...] you shall [...]

(Apart from ribbon, riksu(m) can mean: band, belt, knot, binding, and on a more abstract level, a treaty, agreement and journey. Farber restored the section: rikis gerrēti: travelling bundle, luggage. He proposed that Lamaštu should sit on it.)

II, 173

[you shall give her a co]mb, a spindle, a flask of oil,

offer her sandals and boots,

(Again, Lamaštu appears with human feet. The following lines were so badly damaged that Myhrman and Köcher could make very little sense of them. Nowadays, more material has come up, and fills some of the gaps. I base my words on Wende's translation of Middle Babylonian/Assyrian tablet BM 120022 and Farber's 2014 translation.)

II, 175

you shall encircle her with a spell (**or:** with your intent),

you shall dig seven times seven canals to block her,

II, 177

you shall raise seven times seven mountains in her path.

That you may not come near this infant!

(Line 177 addresses Asarluḫi, or the conjurer acting in his stead. Line 178 addresses Lamaštu.)

II, 179

The spell banishes you, and Nabû pours over you like a river (*or:* in the river),

the foremost of the gods, Asarluḫi, spell-binds you, Daughter of Anu!

II, 181

Šamaš opposes you,

Ea, King of Fate, opposes you!

II, 183

You shall not go [into] the house, which you have left, again!

You will not return along the way you departed!

II, 185

May the plants everywhere hold you back!

May the stones of the Mountains stop your feet.

II, 187

May dead reeds stab your feet,

ascend the [mount]ain that smells sweetly of,

(Šikkuratu is old, withered reeds and tough grasses, here in the sense of stubble.)

II, 189

the resin (*or:* exudation) of oak (*or:* hazel) and terebinth!

Depart, go away!

(We met these trees earlier (LS I, 185); they are favourite targets of the goddess. Their scent poses a problem. ***Oak*** and ***hazel*** trees (alllānū) have neither resin nor much scent. The ***terebinth*** (buṭnu, buṭumtu) has a strong smelling resin (ḫīlu), which was used as a gum, to make turpentine and to preserve wine. The CDA remarks that the word ḫīlu was also used for an unknown drug.)

II, 191

Be conjured by Heaven, be conjured by Earth!'

Conjuration of Lamaštu.

II, 193

Conjuration:

DIM.ME, Child of Anu, Named With a Name by the Gods,

Daughter of the [Gods],

(Here begins **conjuration #13**. It is recited over the left foot of the patient. This conjuration is entirely in Sumerian, badly damaged and very uncertain.)

II, 195

Daughter of the Great Gods

(she has seized the?) child of Mankind,

II, 197

has seized [...]

Innin, DIM.ME, she seizes his (?) back,

II, 199

facing the person in the chamber (?) she seizes,

she seizes the (?)

II, 201

[...] in front [...] she seizes,
She seized [...]

II, 203

she seizes the beauty** (or: **the sweet) [...],
she seizes the good ones** (or: **breast),

II, 205

she seizes each door,
she seizes each bolt;

II, 207

you shall not enter the house of the child of the house!
Conjuration of Lamaštu

II, 209

and to expel fever-heat.

Ritual Formula: Pick, dry and crush azallû plants** (hemp?)**,

(The text has: šam (=herb) azallû. Köcher proposed hemp; so did Haas, while the CDA, more cautious, states *a medical plant.* Azallu was a psychoactive weed. A gloss quoted by Röllig (RlA *'Hanf'*) calls it the *plant to forget sorrow.* However, in Akkadian hemp was usually called gunabu, qunnabu or qunnabtu, the source of our word cannabis. The Chinese were the first who cultivated hemp and used it for its fibres, medical and psychoactive effect. It gradually spread through Asia and possibly arrived in Mesopotamia and Greece early in the first millennium BCE. There are indications that hemp was cultivated in Rumania by the Kurgan people in the third millennium BCE (Goodall, 2014:179). The word azallû derives from the Sumerian and appears in Old Babylonian texts. Either hemp was available much earlier than has been assumed or we have to find another psychoactive plant.)

II, 211

blend them with oil in a pot:
when he gets feverish, salve him.
Bind seven and seven fibres of azallû around his neck and he will recover.

(If azallû is really hemp, the cannabiols may have been extracted in oil.)

The colophon:

Palace of Aššurbanipal, King of the World, King of Assyria
who trusts in Aššur and Ninlil,

who is granted with wide ear** (=knowledge) **by Nabû and Tašmētum,
who has been granted a bright eye as his own, the choice selection of artfully written tablets,

as under the kings, his predecessors,
none had acquired the like.

The wisdom of Nabû, the 'spotted patterns** (=inscriptions) **of the stylus',
as many of these, as have been formed,
I wrote on tablets, I collected them according to the regulations,

so I could study (and) read them,
I set (them) up in my palace;

I, the ruler, who knows the light of the King of the Gods, Aššur.
(or: You are a ruler who has no equal, King of the Gods, Aššur!)

Whoever abducts (this tablet) or signs his name next to mine,

may be cast down by Aššur and Ninlil/Bēlet in anger and in wrath,

may his name and his seed be erased from the earth!

Third Part of the Lamaštu Series

III, 1

When you perfo[rm] this ritual against Lamaštu,

you shall make a draw[ing] of the Daughter of Anu

to the right and left sides of the door

(The translation of the following lines is based on three sources: Köcher, a translation exhibited in the Vorderasiatisches Museum in Berlin, and Farber.)

III, 3

towards the bedroom,

to the right and left of the Daughter of Anu,

III, 5

a dog, a pig, a lamp, a scor[pion, a spindle]

a comb, a mirror and the hoof** (or: **lower leg) of a donkey,

(It's an amazing idea that people who were scared of Lamaštu had to paint two pictures of her on the walls of their houses. (This is the only reference to **pig and dog** as a pair in the *Lamaštu series*. As the talismans show, Lamaštu loves to adopt and breastfeed them. Both animals were famed for their sexual vigour, rugged health, the ability to digest rubbish and their cheerful approach to life. Their mating behaviour was considered arousing (Leick 2003:199). The **lamp** might indicate the presence of the fire gods, who dispel evil. Fire god Nusku has a lamp and a torch as his symbols. You can see Nusku's lamp on several talismans of the 'Aramean type' which also feature Pazuzu. Interestingly, the *Lamaštu Series* mentions neither Nusku nor Pazuzu. Beginning with the Kassite period, the **scorpion** was often associated with Išḫara. It signifies danger and death but is also a popular symbol for sexual lust. We also find it right next to Lamaštu's vulva on several talismans. Scorpions appear as guardians of the gates to the otherworld. In Akkadian thought, the mountains east and west of Mesopotamia were inhabited by terrifying scorpion people, who watched over the gates where the sun rose and sank. When Gilgameš visited them, they turned out to be quite friendly. The **mirror** is made of bronze. It is expensive and has to be polished ever so often. The **donkey hoof** or lower leg is enigmatic. Maybe it represents travelling. A hoof may have been a pretty box, possibly for medicine. One tradition claims that Alexander the Great was killed with poison carried in a donkey-hoof box. Similar containers were made out of the hoofs of gazelles and antelopes. The talismans, however, often show the entire lower leg of a donkey, and nobody knows what it's good for.)

III, 7

draw her (image) with serpents in her hands.

Dust from the] [gate] of the p[al]ace, dust from the gate of the [Ištar] temple,

(Lamaštu amulets frequently show the goddess holding one or two **snakes**. In one case she even wears a serpent as a belt: it re-appears in Medusa images. As mentioned before, Lamaštu and Pašittu were called (Deity) Ka-muš-i-gue, a Sumerian term meaning '(Female) Mouth-Serpent/Dragon-Feeds', or Zu-muš-i-gue '(Female) Tooth-Serpent/Dragon-Feeds', and identified with the star of that name, Andromeda β, Mirach. It turns them into serpent/dragon goddesses. The Sumerian and Akkadian word muš can be translated as snake, dragon and maybe worm. There were lots of them in the word-lists. Many were real, common and very poisonous. Among the mythical ones are the mountain snake that nobody knows, the mighty snake of the mountains, the wrathful snake, the advising snake, the snake with the precious head, the smoke snake, the

Figure 38 Scorpion People at the Gates of Sun and Moon.

womb-mother snake, the double-tongued snake, the seven-tongue snake, the evil snake, the one-eyed snake, the wild snake, the fire snake and the snake of the dead place. Snake poison was dreaded, but various parts of snakes were used as medicine, such as skin, fat, and blood. A cosmic pair of snake/dragons is the Sumerian muš-an-(na) and the muš-muš-kia: the snake/dragons of heaven and the underworld. Combined, they appear as muš-an-ki. Mušgeštin-aba is the *wine snake* or *snake of the vineyard.* It is fought by the āšipu for unknown reasons. An odd character is the muš-nig-bun-na (Akkadian: šeleppū= *turtle snake*): it has the body of a turtle, the eyes, mouth and tongue of a snake, the teeth of a young dog and emits a gleam of terror. It might remind you of the 'black warrior' of Chinese cosmology, the snake/turtle representing winter, water and the northern quarter. Muš-a-ab-ba (Akkadian: bašmu) is the *sea* (or: *water)-snake/dragon,* a monster with two heads, six mouths and seven tongues, who appeared in the company of Tiāmat, and as a title of Ningirsu. Muš-maḫ (Akkadian: mušmaḫḫu = *mighty snake/dragon*) is another member of Tiāmat's gang: it has seven heads. Later, it became a companion of Ninurta. A third snake/dragon from Tiāmat's retinue is muš-ušumgal (Akkadian: ušumgallu, bašmu), the *great serpent/dragon.* The name is also a title of Ninazu, Ningišzida, Nabû, Ningirsu and Ninurta. Muš-ḫuš (Akkadian: mušḫuššu) is the *raging serpent/dragon* or the *colourful serpent/dragon,* a kind deity who destroys evil influences. It appears quite early in the company of Ninazu and Ningišzida; in later texts it is the companion of Tišpak, Marduk, Nabû, Aššur and Anu. Numušda, Ningišzida and Damu were addressed with this title; it is associated, like so many serpent gods, with the constellation Hydra. Muš-ušum-su-a and mušuššu (equated in Akkadian with ušumgallu, bašmu) are the *red serpent/dragon* and the *furious serpent/dragon.* Both can refer to Marduk's pet dragon or to Marduk himself. He gained it as his attribute around the middle of the second millennium BCE. Muš-ad-gu is the *corpse–eating snake/dragon,* a companion of Ninurta and the name of Enki/Ea's pickaxe. Muš-tu-nu-zu is the *snake that cannot be conjured.* It lived in the roots of the ḫulub tree before Inanna asked her brother Gilgameš to kill it. And while we are at it, there was a group of female and male ritualists who were known as muš-laḫ (Akkadian: muš(la)laḫḫ(at)u: **snake conjurers**. They appear mainly in Sumerian literature, but their presence can be traced into the first millennium, when disapproving people like the authors of the *Maqlû Series* dismissed them together with witches and murderers. The snake conjurers were originally associated with the cults of specific deities like An/Anu, Enlil/Ellil and Nanna/Suen/Sîn. Some of them seem to have acted as snake-dancers; others performed snake-expelling rituals in temples and public places.

The Mesopotamians had ambiguous ideas about snakes. On one hand, they were dreaded and feared, but on the other, they were respected, admired and occasionally venerated as harbingers of good luck. Snakes were occasionally drawn on doors to scare dangerous entities. After Gilgameš had acquired the herb of immortality, he went to take a bath in a well. In the meantime, a snake ate the herb, and gained the ability to renew itself by shedding its skin. Don't talk about it in public: for the priesthood, this was a *secret of the gods* (Borger, RIA, *Geheimwissen).*

If a man saw a snake on the first day of the New Year, he was doomed to die within a year. When a snake dropped from the rafters between husband and wife in the first month of the New Year both would die within a year, and so would the rest of the family. When a snake dropped to the right of a man his enemy would fall. If it dropped to the left the man could make a wish (come true). When a snake crept across the foot of a man it meant long life, and he would become so rich that he would complain: *'just where shall I store all the grains, where should I keep all the wealth?'* When a queen gave birth to a snake, the king would be strong (Ungnad, 1921:323 & 327, trans. JF). Snakes are closely associated with a group of deities whose major cult places were in eastern

Figure 39 Enki/Ea, Lord of Purifying Waters.

Mesopotamia, where the Elamite influence was strong. Among them are Ninazu of Ešnunna, Ningišzida, Ereškigal, Iškur of Karkara, Numušda of Kazallu, Ištaran and Inšušinak of Der, plus Ištaran's sons Niraḫ and Irḫan (the river Euphrates). The temple of Ninḫursag was praised as a great snake. The early constellation 'serpent' was dedicated to Ningirima and Išḫara. Later it was turned into Scorpio and Libra. On some talismans, Lamaštu's snakes have two heads; the double-headed snake (Sumerian muš-sag-min-bin, Akkadian: ṣer šina qaqqadāšu), a common mutation, counts as a bad omen.)

III, 9

dust from the gate of the house of the women** (or: **from the temple of Ninurta),

dust from the gate of a hostel-tavern,

dust from the gate of the house of the [bre]wer,

[du]st from the gate of the house of a baker,

III, 11

dust from the cross-roads;

[you shall pulve]rise, with what has been pinched from a rock** (or: **mortar)

[mix it] with clay from a can[al and form a tabl]et and dog figurines.

III, 13

You shall inscribe a tablet and the envelope of the tablet

[with a lunar cresc]ent, [a solar disc, a curv]ed stick (and) a star,

write the conjuration 'Furious is the Daughter [of Anu]' on it,

III, 15

set (it) at the head of the bed. Paint dogs

with plaster and yellow-green** (or: **black) mineral paste,

[se]t hair of a black dog on their foreheads,

III, 17

hair of a virgin goat kid [on their tails],

(and) [write] their names on their [left flan]ks.

III, 19

The windows to the right and left of the ou[ter]** (= main) **gate,

the doors of the bedr[oom** (or: **inner doors) you shall open],

III, 21

[...] facing the direction of the door** (or: **door post?),

called 'Att[ack Swif]tly (?)'.

'[Guard in the Night], Chase the Daughter of Anu!'

III, 23

You shall put in [the windows of the door of the bedroom? outer door?].

(two dogs:) 'Fast is the Attack!', 'Do Not be [Negligent] in your Guarding Duties!',

III, 25

[you shall set in the win]dows of the inner room.

(two dogs:)

'Don't Hesitate to Think!',

'Overthrow the Ev[il!', ...]

III, 27

you shall pla[ce] in the window (of? near?) the gate of the bedroom.

['Sîn is the Shepherd']; you shall place in the window facing the door.

III, 29

[...]

Sû-stone, pallišu-stone, kasānī[tu-stone, alaba]ster,

(These lines are based on Farber's restored version. Sû and pallišu are unidentified. Kasānītu might be carnelian.)

III, 31

[šubu-stone, mult]asḫiptu (?) stone, white coral (?), pappardilû-stone, cowrie shell (?),

Lamassu-stone, j[anibu-stone, šû-stone, both male and female, you shall thr]ead on string,

(Šubu, perhaps agate, is a semiprecious stone that came in several colours, one of them being yellow. Multasḫiptu, pappardilû (another sort of agate?), janibu and šû are unidentified. How stones can be male or female is unknown. Maybe they had different forms. Lamassu is a general term for a guardian goddess. A specific stone was called by her name.)

III, 33

tarmuš plant (= *lupin)****, Withstand a Thousand plant, Withstand Twenty plant, [...]***

Dust (or:* ***earth) from the gate of the temple of Gula,***

you [wrap in] seven bundles with the stones,

(The herb imḫur-līm, which Köcher identified (very cautiously) as heliotrope, is a medical plant. The CDA gives a folk etymology *it withstands a thousand (ailments).* The herb imḫur-ešra, which Köcher guardedly identified as yellow heliotrope is, according to the CDA a climbing plant, which *withstands twenty ailments.* Farber closed the gap at the end of line 33 by reconstructing: 'single'- plant, elkulla plant, puquttu plant and šakirû plant. Elkulla is a medical plant, puquttu a thorny plant, šakirû(m) might be henbane.

The name of the Sumerian goddess **Gula** means *Great* or *Greatest.* You met her in the comment to LS I, 87. Gula is a popular goddess of healing. She is a daughter of An and Uraš, wife of the heroic Pabilsang and/or Ningirsu, and she is often accompanied by dogs. Their child is Damu, who excels in the art of healing like her/his mother. A common image shows the goddess wearing a horned cap, sitting on a throne, resting her feet on a dog. She appeared in literature around 2600 BCE; by the end of the third millennium she had become the Ninisin (*Lady of Isin*), Azugallatu (*Female Great Physician*), Šimmu (*Plant-Puller*), and a deity skilled at invocation and exorcism. In the process she was identified with the goddess Ninkarrag. In the *Weidner Chronicle* (late second millennium BCE), Gula installs Marduk as the chief of the Babylonian gods. In the *Hymn to Gula,* the goddess declares: *I am a physician (asakku), I am a diviner (baraku), I am an exorcist (ašipak).* As Ninisina, she is praised as *the āšiptu (female conjurer) of the land* and as the *azugal (chief physician) of the land* (Henshaw, 1994:150.) In the sky, Gula is represented by the constellation Aquarius. To think of Gula brings good health and life. She is a healer, she carries every herb, banishes diseases, is girded with a bag full of life-saving spells, bears the texts that make people recover. Gula is the Lady of heaven and the underworld, she has the loveliest voice of all goddesses and is the most attractive of all young women (Foster, 1995:229-235). In several spells her dogs are charged to devour and expel evil spirits (and Lamaštu). Gula could bring disease. We frequently encounter her in the curses that appear at the end of contracts and boundary stone inscriptions. A typical line from boundary stones of the fourth to the sixth dynasty of Babylon reads: *Gula, the great healer, shall put [...] poison into your*

Figure 40 Top: Priests worshipping Sîn and Marduk (represented by moon and dragon/spade). Note the 'raising of the hands' gesture. Neo-Babylonian roll seal, BM89780.

Bottom: Conjuration or sacrificial ritual. Note Enki/Ea's ibex, the Seven Stars, moon, star, axe and cudgel. Neo-Babylonian roll seal BM89470.

body that it shall shed blood and pus like water as long as it lives. (*Keilschriftliche Bibliothek*, 1896:79, 81, 87, trans. JF). A treaty of Asarḫaddon, ANET 538-539, states: *May Gula, the great physician, pour illness and weariness [into your hearts], an unhealing sore in your body, so that you bathe [in your own blood] as if in water.* Gula's dogs could purify the patient: West (1992:375) quotes CT 39 38:8:

If he touches the dog of Gula he is clean again. As *Mother of Dogs,* Gula is responsible when a dog bites you, and infects the wound with its water (= saliva = sperm). To heal the bite, you make a dog figurine out of clay and transfer the bite to it. As the clay dries, your wound is supposed to heal. (Finkel in Abusch & van der Toorn, 1999:221.) Gula had a large temple in her city Isin, where excavators uncovered the remains of 33 dog skeletons under a ramp. That part of the temple contained numerous dog figurines. The regents of Isin went to some lengths to feed dogs on festival days; one regent of the early second millennium BCE even founded a *House of Dogs*. It does not imply that dogs were always treated well. Many dogs at Gula's temple met their death due to heavy injuries. Groneberg speculates that they were wounded in the same way as the patients, and found their death as replacement sacrifices. Maybe there was a larger dog cemetery nearby (2004:165-171).

III, 35

you shall place on his neck.

[You shall] string seven eye-stones, seven stone-donkeys** (or:* ***egg-shaped stones?)

on string of black wool,

seven bundles [...] shall you make out of seven (strings) of red-coloured wool,

bind three loops** (or:* ***necklaces) out of seven (strings) of red-coloured wool,

(Earlier translators favoured **red wool**. Farber opts for dyed wool, leaving the colour unspecified. **Beads** were magical objects. The Sumerians wrote NA.GU, the Akkadians called them abnu; both words mean literally 'stone'. Originally, they were made of shells, bones, paste and stone, polished and perforated with a bow-drill. Later types include wood, clay, metal, ivory, river pebbles and glass. The material depended on the substances that were accessible at a given place and time. Beads were commonly used as foundation sacrifices. There is little evidence for bead necklaces in early periods, but a few images of late Sumerian women, possibly priestesses and/or aristocrats, show weighty necklaces. Some necklaces were so heavy that the lady who wore them had a counterweight hanging down her back. Only a few early kings, like Naramsîn and some Old Babylonian rulers are shown wearing pearl necklaces. By the first millennium BCE, possibly earlier, beads had become a standard item of magic. Small chaplets, worn around the wrist or held in the hand, were used in ritual to work spells, banish evil influences and consecrate water. A lot of fuss was made regarding the symbolism of the material and the number of stones. Perhaps the fashion of using magical rosaries eventually spread to India (the japamālā) and from there to the Islamic world and Christianity. The dating is difficult. One eighth century BCE image shows a priestess or goddess holding such a chaplet in her hand. As far as can be seen, it has seven round and seven disc-shaped beads. A very similar chaplet, consisting of 16 rounded, elongated and 16 disk-shaped beads, from an Assyrian tomb dating around the 15th or 14th century BCE is exhibited in the Vorderasiatisches Museum, Berlin. The stone discs are quite large and would make it uncomfortable to wear. Was it used as a magical chaplet? But beads were also magical without being part of costume or ritual. Some were carried in talismanic pouches. In our text, the beads, as magical objects, are strung. It relates them to Lamaštu, who might use her comb to clean wool and her spindle to turn it into string. **Eye stones** (igi in Sumerian; īnu in Akkadian) were probably agates with lines, revealing an 'eye-

Figure 41 Primal Ecology. Inspired by a roll seal of the Early Dynastic III.

pattern'. They have come up in excavations. At the time of writing, the **stone donkeys,** or **donkey stones** (parû-stones) are mysterious. Haas (1986:210-211) called them onager-stones, which relates them to the wild asses of the far-away mountains while Farber preferred mule stones. The symbolism is remarkably different. Worse, 'donkey, onager or mule stones' have not been identified or excavated yet. Earlier translators identified them, probably in error, as **egg-stones** (Sumerian: nunuz; Akkadian: erimmatu) and they were ovoid. They appear in the famous necklace that Ištar had to give up when she descended into the underworld. In other texts, Ištar's bead necklaces are made of lapis lazuli and glass.)

III, 37

a bristle from the right side of a donkey,

a bristle of the left side of a female donkey,

a bristle from a young donkey, bristles of a white pig,

III, 39

a centipede (?) of the way,

The dark (hair? dung?) of the right side of a donkey's croup** (or: **hind leg),

A splinter from the handle of a heavy plough (and) a seeder-plough;

III, 41

take them, and attach them to the loops,

take the bundles, with eye-stones and stone-donkeys

inside them, and bind them together.

III, 43

You shall tie seven eye-stones, seven stone-donkeys

and loops, and the other stones, round the neck (of the infant),

You shall place straw, pig-shit (?),

the dark (hair? dung?) of the right side of a donkey's croup** (or: **hind leg),

(We had much of this, without the beads and string, earlier under LS II, 113-118. The last item is a code word for **thyme**.)

III, 45

and tie them to his neck.

You shall bind fourteen pieces of white azallû (hemp?) to a white string,

and place them around his neck.

III, 47

You shall thread all eyestones and stone-donkeys

on black wool, make bundles of [...] of seven strings of red-coloured wool,

III, 49

you shall thread a šubu stone on a white wool string,

and wrap in white wool four eye-stones,

four stone-donkeys and bind them to his right hand.

III, 51

You shall thread a black KA stone on a string of black wool, wrap it in black wool,

three eye-stones, three stone-donkeys

and bind them to his left hand.

(The KA stone is probably obsidian.)

III, 53

You shall thread a seashell bead on a red wool string and wrap it in red wool,

[four] eye-stones, four stone-donkeys

and bind them to his right foot.

(The kapāṣu(m) stone was made from seashell. Or it was a stone carved to look like a shell, or a shell-shaped amulet made of metal.)

III, 55

You shall thread a stone containing iron on a blue wool string and wrap it in blue wool,

three eye-stones, three stone-donkeys

and bind them to his left foot.

(Is the iron-ore stone a magnet? Here, a section of Younger Babylonian tablet AO.6473, translated by Köcher (1949:134-136, see also Haas 1986:213) may be interesting. The text offers several spells to prevent premature birth, and ends with the conjuration of Lamaštu which you read in the commentary to LS I, 145. Let me give a brief summary. As far as the text can be read, the conjurer uses an ittamir stone, set in gold at the top, bottom and centre (three bands?) which is strung on a black woollen thread. Next to the stone, other items are attached, such as a two magnetic stones, two LUM stones, [...] gold [...] two [...]-stones, a ḫubur plant, LIB and imḫurašru plant, various woven strings of [...] blue wool nearby [...] seven knots are tied; then the conjuration *They have descended into the Land* is recited thrice over each knot and the whole tangle of string and pendants is tied closely to the neck of the pregnant woman. Each month, the knots are loosened or untied (literally: *let down*), until the time is ripe for birth and none of them remain. Similar arrangements of strings and talismanic objects to protect pregnant women appear in several spells. Here, you might wonder whether the Mesopotamians thought that pregnant or birth-giving women were 'unclean'. The evidence is open to debate. As Labat argues (RIA *'Geburt'*), a conjurer was not allowed to visit a woman who had given birth until 30 days had passed. Was it for her or his safety? In some badly understood rituals, kings were obliged to put on the clothes of pregnant women, which may or may not have symbolised weakness and shame. But there were also positive sides to pregnancy. Sex with pregnant women was encouraged, as it indicated respect for them and increased their honour. For rituals to protect pregnant women and their babies, see Walter Farber's remarkable *'Schlaf, Kindchen, schlaf. Mesopotamische Baby-Beschwörungen und Rituale.* (1989:79; 68, 70).

For directions, remember: the 'right hand' of the patient is the hand to the right of the āšipu, i.e. the left hand of the patient. This gives us **black** and **blue**, and the odd number **three** on the patient's right side and **white** and **red**, and the even number **four** on the left side. It looks like an occult system of anatomy. Saggs (1984:206) mentions that the four stages of the ziggurat of Khorsabad were stuccoed and painted white, black, red and blue *which must have had a religious symbolism which escapes us.* For paintings, the prehistoric Mesopotamians mainly used red and black paint. Yellow was very rare. Next, white became popular. By the Old Babylonian period, blue and green became fashionable. The favourite colours of the Neo-Assyrians were white, black, red and blue. Yellow and green were rarely used; in paintings, the least popular colour was brown.)

III, 57

Conjuration:

Zur-ru-ga zur-ru-ga ki-li zur-ru-ga

Ki-ri ki-ri-ip ki-su

ḫu-up-pa-an-ni ḫu-pu-up

su-up-pa-an-ni su-pu-up

Figure 42 Asarluḫi, Great Bison of a Prince.

III, 59

Asarluḫi sh[all] make you submit! Ningirima has commanded and I recite the [conjuration].

(It was customary for conjurers to claim that the deity performed the exorcism. In short, the magic was attributed to the gods, while the conjurer merely acted as a representative of the divine. This is practical thinking: it gives greater authority to the exorcism, offers patient and conjurer something trustworthy to believe in and reduces the possible hubris of the ritualist. Many ritualists of Mesopotamia cultivated humility. The Sumerian term nin-me-ga: *humility and shyness caused by great awe* describes a major virtue of the priesthood. Candidates who lacked this attitude were not admitted. This is very unlike the mindset of Vedic India, where the seers went to great lengths to show that their power was greater than the gods.)

III, 61

Conjuration:
Ki-riš-ti li-bi
Ki-riš-ti-la li-bi
Ki-la li-bi
piš-piš ti-ša-an-zi-iš
ti-ša an-zi-iš
šú-an-zi-iš
an-zi-iš.
Šiptu.

(Myhrman wondered whether these words are in Assyrian at all, or constituted a meaningless ritual formula. For comparison, he quoted a similar formula from Betzold's Catalogue, Vol. IV, 1477; also in Farber 1989:

Šiptu/En. Ka riš-te li-bi ka riš-te ki la li-bi
ki la li-bi peš peš li-' –eš an ze-eš
šu ma-al ze-eš ša ḫa-al ze-eš.
TU šiptu/en e nu-ru.

The spell could be meaningless, in code or contain badly distorted words from an early and possibly foreign conjuration. Some experts detected faint traces of Elamite (i.e. from Iran) or Hurrian (i.e. Anatolia and northern Mesopotamia) words. It may mean much or very little. What if the spell is in code? An obscure tablet claimed to reveal the primal language of mankind. Like these spells, it is composed of 'meaningless' syllables (Borger in RlA '*Geheimwissen*'). Was there a science of sounds in Ancient Mesopotamia, as it evolved in India? 'Meaningless' words were used for (very simple) mantras in the Vedic period; examples are Oṁ, Hūṁ, Svāhā, Ūrj and Hiṁ. Or did the Mesopotamian conjurers use strings of incomprehensible syllables as a dramatic element to bedazzle the patient and maybe themselves? 'Speaking in tongues', 'chaos language' and glossolalia have great power. Plenty of cultures use this method to give an extra kick to 'shamanic' trances. Consider. The information content of language is processed by most people around the Broca areal, Wernicke's areal, the fasciculus arcuatus, gyrus angularis and the regions surrounding them, in the left hemisphere of the brain. Mind you, there are individual variations. Pure semantic information, however, is not enough. Just as essential are sound, intonation, emphasis, rhythm, speed, volume and so on. These are usually processed in the right hemisphere of the brain (Pinet, 2012:494) and provide an extra level of meaning. The importance of intonation appears when you study split-brain patients (i.e. extreme epileptics whose brain hemispheres were divided by surgery between the 1960's and 1980's) or certain high-functioning autists. They do not notice when a sentence is posed as a question (the intonation rises), or, for that matter, threateningly, endearingly or ironically. With the right intonation, a given word can seem friendly, loving, aggressive, angry, soothing or exciting. Milton Erickson, the pioneer of modern hypnosis, demonstrated that he could hypnotise people who understood no English simply by using intonation, breathing and gesture. Incomprehensible words make little sense to the rational mind but they are excellent to convey and stimulate emotion. You can use them to activate parts of the brain that are not touched by meaningful speech. Try this in your prayers and invocations! And consider this: the usual magical textbooks do not include anything comparable. Were these spells a speciality to control Lamaštu? Are these spells an attempt to fake a 'foreign' conjuration suitable for a 'foreign' goddess?)

III, 63

You shall recite these two conjurations over the stones.

Bitumen of a ship, bitumen of its rudder, bitumen from its rowlock,

III, 65

bitumen from the entire equipment of the ship,

dust (*or: *earth) from the quay and the ford (*or: *crossing* or: *ferry), pig-lard, fish-oil, hot bitumen, butter (*or: *ghī), an ankinûtu plant, aktam-plant (*= castor-oil-plant?*),

III, 67

an aprušu-plant, azallû-plant (*= hemp?*),

the hide of a donkey (tanned by?) a leather worker (*or: *the paste of a leather worker),

a stained rag, [...]- fish, fat of a white pig, make up the ointment.

III, 69

The Conjuration (#2): 'DIM.ME/Lamaštu,

Daughter of Anu, Named With a Name by the Great Gods...,

I have given you (*or: *made you seize) a black dog as a demonic (= gallû) fate (*or: *servant, slave)',

III, 71

The Conjuration (#3): '[Conjuration:] She [is Angry], She is Furious, she is Fire (*or: *Fever?), she is terrible,

the conjuration (#6): 'I Recite a Conjuration Against Your Enduring Purpose':

III, 73

recite these three conjurations three times over the ointment.

Kukru-plant, mustard seed, unsifted flour, peeled onion, snake-skin,

(Kurku or kukuru(m) is an aromatic tree product.)

III, 75

linseed, sulphur, cress,

a ball of hair; this is the incense.

When you have anointed the little one, you shall recite the conjuration (#1):

III, 77

'Lamaštu,

Child of Anu is Her First Name',

three times over his head.

III, 79

You shall recite the conjuration (#2): 'DIM.ME/Lamaštu,

Daughter of Anu, Named With a Name by the Great Gods,

I have given you (*or: *made you seize) a black dog

as a demonic (= gallû) fate (*or: *servant, slave)'

over his throat,

Figure 43 Hand of the Asakku: Mental Disease, Pestilence, Perversion

III, 81

The Conjuration (#3): '[Conjuration:] She [is Angry], She is Furious, she is Fire (*or: *Fever?), she is Terrible,', you shall recite over his right hand.

The Conjuration (#4): 'Conjuration: She is Clad in Burning Heat, Fever-heat, Cold, Frost, Ice',

III, 83

you shall recite over his left hand.

Conjuration (#5):

'Conjuration: Lamaštu, Daughter of Anu,

Named With a Name by the Great Gods...

She is a woman of the Elamites,

[great is] her [head-covering (mane? or: ***radiance, halo)]',***

III, 85

you shall recite over his chest and belly.

The conjuration (#7): 'Angry is the Daughter of Anu who plagues the infants',

(The original text, as transcribed by Myhrman and Köcher, shows some confusion here. All šiptus are in the order we find them in the text. The exception is #7 *'The Conjuration: Angry is the Daughter of Anu'* which appears before #6 *'I recite a conjuration...'* Either the canonical text or its ritual index got it wrong.)

III, 87

the conjuration (#6): 'I Recite a Conjuration Against Your Enduring Purpose',

you shall recite over his hips.

III, 89

The conjuration (#8): 'She is Angry,

she is Furious, she is Fire (*or: *Fever), she has a Divine Radia[nce]

she has risen from the reed thicket,',

the conjuration (#9): 'She is Angry, She is Furious, She is Fire (*or: *Fever),

She has a Divine Radiance,

She is Angry, She is a Wolf-bitch',

III, 91

the conjuration (#10): 'Daughter of Anu,

Named With a Name by the Great Gods,

Innin: Victorious Mistress... you Mighty (*or: *Exalted) One,'

III, 93

the conjuration (#11):

'The Daughter of Anu, of Heaven am I',

you shall recite over his right foot.

III, 95

The conjuration (#12):

'Mighty is the Daughter of Anu, Who Plagues the Little Ones',

the conjuration (#13):

'DIM.ME, Child of Anu, Named With a Name by the Gods,

Daughter of the Gods',

III, 97

you shall recite over his left foot.

The conjuration (#3 or #9): '[Conjuration:] She [is Angry],

She is Furious, She is Fire (*or: *Fever?), She is Terrible,'

III, 99

you shall recite over the incense offerings and set them up to the right of the gate.

The conjuration (#6): 'I Recite a Conjuration Against Your Enduring Purpose',

III, 101

you shall recite over the incense offerings,

and set them up to the left of the gate, at the head and foot of the bed.

III, 103

You shall hold a stick of êru-wood, which you have scorched with fire at both ends,

and a sapling (*or: *marrow* or: *heart) of the date palm over his head and

(The **êru stick** (in Sumerian (wood) Ma.NU) is a common tool of the āšipu. The item was used at least since the Old Babylonian period. Wiggermann (1992:67) identifies it as a short stick of cornel wood, possibly with a round mace head, which is held in the left hand of the āšipu to protect its wearer from evil. Schramm (2008:81) gives a short conjuration to consecrate the item and identifies the wood as dwarf ash. The spell calls it the *exalted weapon of An/Anu* and the *wooden staff of Ḫendursagā*; the latter being the night-time herald of Enlil. The conjuration tells us that the êru, scorched with fire at both ends, makes the *murderous udug, ala, gidim, galla, digir, maškim* and even the *murderous lu* (=human) depart, and that it attracts a good šedu and a good lamma (male and female protective spirits). Êru sticks could also be set up like a pole, symbolising a tree that gives protection (*sweet shade*) and connects earth with heaven, or they were placed on or near the head of a patient. In ritual, the êru is an aggressive weapon, a *Cudgel of the Gods* that banishes, destroys and clears a path like a firebrand.

With Geštinanna of the silent streets it goes about,

And with Dumuzi entering the lap of the loved one it goes everywhere

(Wiggermann 1992:83) By contrast, the date palm sapling, representing Dumuzi/Amaušumgalanna, is for the advantage of the patient alone, and represents purification and release from sin and guilt.)

III, 105

recite the conjuration 'Evil Utukku' and place them near his (the patient's) head.

Afterwards you shall encircle the bed with flour-water,

III, 107

recite the conjuration 'The Ban, the Ban', the conjuration 'Exorcised is [the House]',

recite the conjuration 'You Shall Not Enter Through the Window',

(The **Udug** (Sumerian) and the **utukku** (Akkadian) were originally simply spirits. They are rare in texts of the third millennium, became a popular topic in the second, and lost importance in the first. In early texts, we encounter them as divine spirits and as human ghosts. In the *Hymn to Nininsinna* (SAHG 1953:69) we read that the

good udug of Father Enlil goes to her right,

The good lama (=protective spirit*) of Lord Nunamnir (*=Enki*) goes to her left.*

Gudea of Lagaš prayed that a good udug and a good lama (=lamassu) should accompany him. Lipitištar of Isin was granted a good udug by Anu (SAHG 1953:104). When Gilgameš conjured the soul of his dead friend Enkidu from the Underworld, the text calls him an udug. Evidently, some early udug were worth making friends with, and functioned much like personal deities. Others were simply ghosts, and not necessarily nasty ones. The topic is ambiguous. Some ghosts, and this includes family members, could be supportive if fed and watered frequently, but turned into nightmares should this be forgotten. It didn't last. In Babylonian literature, the utukku became increasingly dangerous, and when we look into the formidable collection *Utukku Limnuti* we meet all sorts of horror-spirits that have nothing protective and very little that is human about them. To be sure, the concept of the *good udug* continued to exist, at least among the priests and scribes who read and copied elder literature. It is just that the evil utukkus got more attention. It did not last: gradually, the utukku faded away. In the medical literature of the first millennium, a disease called 'hand of the utukku' does not exist. The utukku were rarely mentioned or exorcised. In their stead, we encounter the gedim (*ghost*), and the 'hand of the gedim' to describe diseases (Geller in RlA '*Udug*'). Last, let me remind you of the Old Babylonian conjuration we had in the introduction to the *Lamaštu Series*, where Lamaštu herself is called an utukku, whatever that may mean.

The conjuration *Evil Utukku* is hard to identify, as plenty of conjurations had a very similar beginning. The conjuration *The Ban, the Ban* is quoted in the appendix. The word **ban** is one of the toughest concepts of Mesopotamian belief. The word is **māmītu(m).** It can be variously translated as: ban, prohibition, taboo, meaning a deed or thing forbidden; evil or polluting; 'oath', as one is bound to fulfil a promise or social obligation; and as: broken oath, curse, doom, and the evil consequence of breaking a taboo. It also happens to be the name of a goddess, Māmītu(m) who rules the Underworld and is a competitor of, or another name for, Ereškigal. Like Lamaštu, she was kicked out of heaven (*Šurpu Series* VII, 3-4), but we are not told why. When she landed on earth she became a close associate of Lamaštu's girlfriend Aḫḫazu (the *Seizer*) and of the mysterious Dimītu. The topic is slightly confusing, as another Māmītu(m) is a typical goddess of birth and fertility who is sometimes identified with Ninḫursag and Nintur.)

III, 109

Recite the conjuration 'Ea [...]'

(This conjuration does not appear in the *Lamaštu Series*.)

On the first day, when the sun descends, [you shall make] a (figurine of) Lamaštu

III, 111

like a captive. Set up the offerings.

[Plac]e twelve small breads of unsifted flour before [her],

III, 113

pour spring (*or: *well) water for her and give her a black dog,

put the heart of a piglet in her mouth, pour hot (soup) for her.

III, 115

lay out cakes of dry bread, [give her] a flask of o[il],

at dawn, noon and at sunset, recite the ritual.

III, 117

[seat her] at the head of the pat[ient] for three days,

On the third day, when the day descends, carry her outside

and bury [her] in a corner (*or: *recess) of the wall.

III, 119

On the fourth day you shall make a Lamaštu of clay,

Dr[ess] her head with hair,

offer her clothes of blue wool,

(The first time this formula came up, in LS I, 47, she was clad in a filthy rag. This time, at the end of the ritual, she receives a blue dress, making her appear as a celestial goddess.)

III, 121

spread (?) a sunshade made of palm for her,

(**or:** prick (?) her with the thorn of a palm-leaf)

give her a comb, a spindle, a flask of oil;

III, 123

fill four leather bags with fine flour, malt,

malt-bread, roasted barley seeds, dry bread;

make four donkeys of clay.

III, 125

Equip them with travel provisions.

In the [evening, be]fore the sun has set,

you shall carry her into the desert (**or:** field **or:** steppe)

III, 127

and turn her face to the west.

Bind her body (with woven reed grasses),

tie her to prickly baltu(m) (** = caper-bush ?) (and) šagu(m) (**= buckthorn?***),***

and surround her with a [magical ci]rcle.

III, 129

Banish her by Heaven, Earth and the Anunnaki.

[On the fifth day], you shall purify the [cl]ay pit,

take clay from the pit and make a figure of Lamaštu,

III, 131

seat her (image) at the head of the patient,

fill a sūtu (vessel) with ashes and stick a sword/dagger in it,

Let (it) stand at the head of the patient [for three days].

III, 133

On the third day, when the day descends,

you shall carry her outside,

hit her with the dagger,

and bury [her] within a corner of the wall.

III, 135

Encircle her (image) with water mixed with flour,

and (when you leave) do not lo[ok] behind you!

[After] you have done so, his nurse,

III, 137

shall make a ball of string (?)

(or: keep the salves ready) [...]

[...] you have brought outside [...]

(Everybody assumed the nurse should do something. They just didn't know what. Köcher suggested the nurse should come outside and prepare a ball of coloured string. In altar arrangements, multicoloured, speckled, or variegated (barānu(m)) wool or string represents Lamaštu. (Langdon, 1919:86) Varicoloured string must have been mighty magic: the evil gallû used it, along with ropes, nets and an êru stick, to catch and kill Dumuzi. In Farber's translation, the string has disappeared and the nurse presumably stays indoors, where she can keep the ointments ready. Up to five lines and the colophon are missing.)

End of the *Lamaštu Series*

Supplement to LS III, 105:

'Ban! Ban!
(Māmit=ban, taboo, curse, prohibition)
Barrier that none can pass,
barrier of the gods, that none may break,
barrier of An/Anu and Ki/Erṣetu(m) that none can change,
which no god may annul,
nor god nor man can loose,
a snare without escape, set for evil,
a net whence none can issue forth, spread for evil.
Whether it be an evil udug/utukku,
or evil ala/alû, or evil gidim/eṭimmu,
or evil gala/gallû, or evil dingir/ilu, or evil maškim/rabiṣu,
or DIM.ME/Lamaštu, or DIM.ME-A/Labaṣu, or DIM.ME-ḪAB/Aḫḫazu,
or LIL.LA.EN.NA/Lilû, or MUNUS.LILA/Lilītu, or Kisikil Lilla/Ardat Lilî,
or evil Namtar/Namtaru, or asag/asakku, or unclean disease,
which has assaulted the shining waters of Enki/Ea,
may the snare of Enki/Ea catch it;
or which hath assailed the meal of Nidaba/Nisaba,
may the net of Nidaba/Nisaba entrap it;
or which hath broken the barrier,
let not the barrier of the gods,
the barrier of An/Anu and Ki/Erṣetu(m), let it go free;
or which reverences not the great gods,
may the great gods entrap it,
may the great gods curse it;
or which attacks the house,
into a closed dwelling may they cause it to enter;
or which circles round about,
into a place without escape may they bring it;
or which is shut in by the house door,
into a house without exit may they cause it to enter;
or that which passes door and bolt,
with door and bolt, barred immovably: may they keep it outside;
or which blows in through the threshold and hinge,
or which forces a way through bar(?) and doorposts,
like water may they pour it out,
like a goblet may they dash it to pieces,
like a tile may they break it;
or which passes over the wall,
its wing may they cut off;
or which (lies) in a chamber,
its throat may they cut;
or which looks into a side chamber,
its face may they smite;
or which mutters in a [...] chamber,
its window may they shut;
or which roams free in an upper chamber,
with a metal vessel without opening may they cover it;
or which at dawn is darkened,
at dawn to a place of sunrise may they take it!'

(Bilingual Sumerian and Akkadian text, after Thompson, *Devils*, II, 119 & Thompson *Semitic Magic*, 2005/1908; 123-124, partly amended and modernized. This might be the invocation mentioned in the *Lamaštu Series*. I have changed Thompson's rather imaginative translation of the names of deities and spirits to their original Sumerian and Akkadian forms.)

Figure 44 Hand of the Alû: Suffocating Numbness, Paralysis of the Heart.

Part Three

Decapitator

Lamaštu: Origins

We meet the goddess written DIM.ME by the Sumerians and Lamaštu by the Akkadians, Babylonians and Assyrians in the late third millennium BCE. Of course she may be older, but we have to confine our speculations to the earliest textual references. Here we are on thin ice. Let's start with a time frame. The first pieces of religious literature were recorded around 2700-2600 BCE. We encounter magical spells, temple hymns, fragments of myths, collections of aphorisms and elaborate administrative documents, in the libraries of Fāra (Šuruppak) and Abu Salabikh, a small town close to Nippur. At the same time, royal inscriptions became a fashion. Religious literature was common by 2500 BCE. It could have been earlier, as some texts seem to include older passages. An interesting composition is the *Hymn to Nanše*, parts of which seem to have been composed in the early third millennium, when her temple was built in the city Ninā. Other sections were added many hundreds of years later during the reign of Gudea. By the start of the Akkadian period, c.2350 BCE, when Enḫeduanna composed her *Temple Hymns*, she included sections of much earlier material. In the Ur III period, extensive praise hymns for divine regents were a common fashion, especially when they were composed for the great but nutty king Šulgi, who had himself praised as a genius in every art. A milestone of religious literature is the extensive temple hymn composed by Gudea of Lagaš (c.2125 BCE), a brilliant king who managed to keep his province in peace while northern and central Mesopotamia were dominated by the Gutians. Not long after him, passionate 'sacred marriage' poetry was composed for the kings of the Amorite Isin-Larsa dynasty. Within seven hundred years, religious literature had come a long way. Nevertheless, it was far from the refined and structured grimoires assembled in the first millennium BCE, which made much use of early material, but rearranged and edited it in the process. The first inscriptions mentioning DIM.ME come from the Sumerians of the late third millennium BCE, but they are few, fragmentary and leave many questions open. In some cases we cannot even be sure that they are actually from the last phases of Sumerian history. Most Sumerian texts survived in Old Babylonian copies. Scribes kept writing in Sumerian, if only as a literary exercise, well into the first millennium BCE. By that time, many of the finer points of the language were forgotten and the lexical lists show increasing confusion and misunderstandings. Some scribes translated their texts into Sumerian to make them appear older than they were. When the wind god Pazuzu was introduced by the Aramean invaders in the early first millennium BCE, his name was Sumerianized to improve his status.

Now for DIM.ME. Let's look at a few of the early references. Usually, they are just snippets of information, telling us that to some people, the goddess was important, but that, all the same, nobody bothered to explain why. Or maybe we just have to find the pertinent texts: I'm sure there are plenty of surprises waiting for a lucky excavator. Here is an early example cited by Köcher, 1949, translated after the German. A *Hymn to Ninisinna* (the Lady of Isin) has the fragmentary lines:

The evil utukku, the evil šedu, who hurl themselves upon people,

Dimme, Dimme-a, who (hurl) themselves on the patient....

Next a passage from the *Evil Spirits* collection, in its old Babylonian form (UMBS I 1. No. 127, vs. col. I 8ff; col. III, 9ff, SAHG 1953:215 after Lutz and Falkenstein; trans. JF). The text is in Old Babylonian (using Sumerian names such as DIM.ME, An, Enki, Udug) but also appears in a Neo-Assyrian version on tablet 7 of the *Evil Uttuku* series.

Enruru-Conjuration.

The evil Udug who makes desolate streets hard (to walk),

who walks in desolation,

who covers the ways,

the evil devil who has been released in the steppe,

the robber who cannot be forced to withdraw,

Dimme, Dimme-a, who splatter the people,

The heart-disease, the [...]-disease, affliction, head-disease,

a storm that shrouds mankind,

have toppled the moving people like a storm,

and submerged them in gall.

Each person is walking around 'outside his life'.

Asarluḫi saw it, he approached his father Enki in his house...

Enki advises his son how to bless water by immersing a tamarisk branch and another, untranslatable, twig in it. The water is scattered over the patient. An incense bowl and a torch are set up. Finally all evil spirits and dangerous deities, plus Namtar, the alû, the death-spirit, the evil gallû, the evil god, the evil rabiṣu, the evil tongue and the evil spittle are ritually banished by *the Strong Bronze, the Hero of An.*

DIM.ME and DIM.ME -A contribute their share by splattering people with fluids. Spittle, venom, urine and secretions come to mind, all of them highly magical substances. They are not the only ones. Exorcists and doctors also enjoyed drenching their clients with water or blood, and occasionally spat at them. I'm sure they enjoyed it.

Omen Texts OT.16, pl. 14, col. III, 24 and III R 60,39 state:

If an eclipse happens on the 21st day,

Dimme and the 'Fever Disease' make the king and the country feverish...

The 21st day is a multiple of seven, hence a day of danger, unless extra precautions are taken. None of this tells us how the Sumerians imagined DIM.ME. Did she appear as a nude woman with an animal mask? Sure, we have plenty of talismans showing Lamaštu. Most are from the late second and first millennium BCE. They fit some textual descriptions of the Old Babylonian period, but leave us ignorant regarding earlier times. DIM.ME/Lamaštu is not the only deity lacking an early iconography. The Sumerian scribes were not really interested in characterising their deities. We learn a bit regarding the looks and character of the gods, much of it rather unspecific, but when you go through a few dozen Sumerian hymns you will notice that the priesthood happily glorified lots of very different gods with the same exalted descriptions. This is only natural. The god and goddess of each city or state had fairly similar functions and offices; hence their titles and duties overlap.

The artists had a similar idea: gods and goddesses look pretty much alike. Often, we can only identify a given deity when her or his personal attributes are shown. As several gods had similar symbols, confusion is normal. Worse, most works of art do not show divine symbols. There are at least two thousand Babylonian gods whom we can't identify.

Iconography is even more obscure when we try to study spirits, ghosts and other dangerous entities. There might be several explanations. Maybe the early scribes had no clear idea of them, and part of their horror lies in their very lack of definition. This is probably the case with several early 'demons', as they did not acquire a specific form during the next two thousand years. Nevertheless, at some point they did. In the *Maqlû Series* (I, 135-143) the exorcist burns images of evil spirits, and you can't do that without having at least a rudimentary idea of their appearance.

But Lamaštu is different. Keep that thought for a moment and make it feel at home. It's a good mantra. The Daughter of Anu appears fully defined around the start of the Old Babylonian period. Indeed, she is such a unique character that most gods and goddesses pale by comparison. True, the descriptions include contradictions. Nevertheless we know far more about her appearance than about most Mesopotamian deities. Only a few, highly popular gods like Enlil/Ellil, Enki/Ea, Inanna/Ištar, Dumuzi/Tammuz, Nanna/Sîn, Ninurta/Ningirsu, Bau/Baba, Nidaba/Nisaba and Utu/Šamaš are as vividly characterised as Lamaštu.

Superficially, these gods appear to be the most important of the pantheon. Maybe they were, at least in the few cities where written records survived. But this impression comes from a relatively stabilised pantheon in a period that had developed centralised government. The pantheon narrowed down when Sargon I turned Mesopotamia into an empire. It extended when his empire fell apart. Centralised control expanded and contracted several times, and in between we face long periods from which hardly any records survive.

But there might be another reason why the earliest texts are so terse. Maybe the scribes were not willing to commit more to writing. To write is an act of magic. To write and read is to call something to mind. It can make spirits and deities appear.

DIM.ME: what's in her name?

The goddess appears under the Sumerian name (dingir=deity) DIM.ME. In 1983, Farber suggested that the pronunciation of these Sumerograms could have been something like **Gabašku**. Wiggermann disagreed, but did not supply a better solution. In 2014, Farber's translation of the canonical text lacked any references to Gabašku and proposed the pronunciation /dimme/. It's a provisional convention, as the pronunciation cannot presently be verified. Her name was frequently, but not always, spelt with the divine determinative ^{d}DIM.ME. These cuneiform characters were read by later Akkadians, Babylonians and Assyrians as (iltum=goddess) Lamaštu. So far life is simple: we can be sure we are reading about a goddess. But when we want to understand what the names DIM.ME and Lamaštu mean we run into a lot of trouble.

In Sumerian the name is written as Dim_3-me (transcription: ETCSL project of Oxford.)

A contemporary German transcription (Schramm, 2008) reads her name Dim_{10}-me.

How come? The ETCSL dictionary lists four distinct Sumerograms called DIM, of which our DIM is number three, while Schramm uses another system of classification and lists the character as 'DIM number ten'. The other characters called DIM are different, and not related. Here we are at a tricky point. To be sure, only the cuneiform characters numbered 3 (or 10) are associated with DIM.ME. However, the writing of names is not always reliable. Scribes do make mistakes, especially when they are just students practising in school, and different spellings with the same sound-value occur. It easily happens when the syllables lack a specific meaning. Similar sounds invite people to discern similarities between entirely distinct characters and concepts. As we don't know what DIM.ME meant to begin with, and the Sumerian written records are extremely rare, we cannot be sure whether our 'DIM' is related to any of the other ones. Hence, I shall treat you to the whole series of DIM characters.

The ETCSL dictionary offers:

Dim_1: (Cosmic) Post, i.e. axis mundi. Dim_1-gul: (mast) pole.

Dim_2: to create. Dim_2-ma: reasoning.

Dim_3: to be helpless. Dim_3-ma: figurine. Dim_3-me: name of the goddess. Dim_3-šah$_2$: bear (?).

Dim_4: to check.

To read DIM_3 basically as 'to be helpless' doesn't get us very far. Nobody thought that DIM.ME is helpless, unless it happened to be wishful thinking. 'Helpless' is not a good symbol for the goddess. More likely, the character was used for its phonetic value. If this was the case, it raises the question whether DIM.ME was an imported, foreign deity, whose incomprehensible name was spelt according to its sound. Or if she was such an old pre-Sumerian deity that the name had lost its meaning before it was committed to writing. Dim_3-ma- could conceivably refer to a 'figurine' or maybe a 'corpse', but it is not certain whether this has a bearing on the meaning of her name. Dim_3 often occurs in objects made of wood, hinting at a cult image. Tough luck that all (known) images of DIM.ME are clay figurines; *Lamaštu Series* II, 97 specifies *a lump of earth shall be your house (or: temple).* Worse, 'figurine' should be written dim$_3$ma. If Dim$_3$me ever referred to a figurine, the ending 'me' would be a phonetic element without meaning. On the other hand, if Dim$_3$me Lamaštu is a 'figurine', this 'name' could be a blanket term for a deity whose 'real' name might be tabooed. It's a nice thought but not very helpful. Figurines were used in many rituals and Lamaštu is not the only deity, person or terrifying being who was invoked into them.

It didn't get any better when the Akkadian language replaced Sumerian. Let's consider a word that seems related. The Akkadian and Babylonian 'Lamassu' means something like 'minor goddess' or 'figurine'. We meet the Lamassu as a helpful guardian spirit, but whether she is connected with Lamaštu cannot be proved.

The pronunciation of 'Lamaštu' isn't certain either. It's just as possible that the name was pronounced Lamašti in the Old Babylonian period. It changed during the Middle Babylonian period, when the sound 'm' between two vowels was pronounced as a 'w'. That gives us Lawaštu and Lawašti.

A cluster of Dimme's

An Akkadian inscription found at Boghazköy (the former Hittite capital) in Turkey (Köcher 1949) is entitled *Spell Against the Mountain Fever.* It briefly mentions a triad of terrifying goddesses, **Lamaštu, Labaṣu,** and **Aḫḫazu**, and identifies them as the

Great Guardians of the Earth of Life.

That's an astonishingly positive title. Think about it before you move on.

Lamaštu, Labāṣu, and Aḫḫazu are a trio who appear, happy and alive, in spells from the late third to the first millennium BCE. You also meet them in such late Babylonian and Neo-Assyrian collections as the *Maqlû Series* and the *Utukku Series.* Some of these spells are bilingual, in Sumerian and Akkadian, and here we encounter the three by their Sumerian names DIM.ME, DIM.ME -A and DIM.ME -ḪAB or DIM.ME.-LAGAB.

In god-list *Anu ša Amēli* the trio appears at the bottom of the divine hierarchy. The text lists the gods in hierarchical order: the important and popular ones are at the top, the least important or least popular at the bottom. The sky god An/Anu appears at the start. As a daughter of Anu, Lamaštu should appear close to him, but as her popularity was distinctly limited, she was dumped near the end, along with Labāṣu, Aḫḫāzu, Bibitu and Lilītu. Well-meaning scholars have coined the misleading term 'Fever Triad' for them. Let us examine the group.

Sumerian **DIM.ME** is Akkadian **Lamaštu.**

DIM.ME-A is **Labāṣu**, an enigmatic goddess whose name defies translation. Some translators, feeling compelled to specify her character, imagined her as a death spirit or an unknown goddess of the dead. It's a charming thought but utterly unprovable.

DIM.ME-ḪAB (also read **DIM.ME-LAGAB**) = **Aḫḫāzu** means *Seizer, Snatcher.* Snatching might be a reference to possession, obsession and the way her diseases were understood. The goddess enters people and children, and has to be ritually expelled from their bodies. But *to seize* is also related to love, in that people are literally *seized* by a craving for each other. The term even means *marriage*: a man who *seizes* a woman *marries* her. If that goddess seizes you, will you end up obsessed or, perchance, married to her?

Here is an interesting early item from the library of Aššurbanipal: a line from a bilingual compendium from the Old Babylonian period in Sumerian and Akkadian. (Schramm 2008:29, trans. JF)

(Sumerian version):

...the ones who shroud the land in darkness, Dimme, Dimme-a and Dimme-LAGAB:

they make the population of cities burn,

through suffering and woe (?) making their [...] sick.

(Akkadian version):

(Lamaš)tu, Labāṣu, and Aḫḫāzu who cause darkness in city and countryside:

they make the population of the settlements burn,

by being bent low and anguished [...] lands they make them sick.'

So much for the 'triad'. In real life, more DIM.MEs were around.

DIM.ME-GI appears in bilingual god-list CT 24, 44 (2.146) (Frey Anthes 2007:181). She is identified with the Akkadian **Lilītu**. It upset the popular assumption that there were only three DIM.MEs. Are we dealing with a new addition? Remember that DIM.ME was occasionally identified with Lilītu and Ardat Lilī, especially after the middle of the second millennium BCE. Lilītu is part of another cluster of goddesses that tends to look like a triad but actually happens to have four members.

DIM.ME.KISKIL is *DIM.ME the Maiden*. She appears in Akkadian as **Ardat Lilî**, the *young woman of the Lilû* family. She became an unhappy spectre who haunts young men 'cause she never had fun when she was still alive.

DIM.NUN.ME could be a form of DIM.ME, plain and simple, or someone else. She is associated with some disease, but so far no details are known.

DIM.ME.TAB is identified in Akkadian as **Bibetu**. She appears in a god list next to the usual three. Sadly, we know nothing about her.

And finally there is a deity called **Dimītu**. She is not a Sumerian goddess; her name is in Akkadian. I would guess that some creative Semitic scribes re-interpreted the Sumerian word DIM.ME. If Dimītu is indeed an Akkadianized version of Sumerian DIM.ME, it might indicate that DIM.ME was really pronounced Dim.me. My apologies for having crazy ideas: it won't happen again. Thompson (2005 (1908): 83) wondered if Dimītu might be related to a Hebrew word for 'menstruating woman'. It sounds similar to dāmu (*blood, sap, lineage, red wine, dark beer*). That, however, is very speculative: our spell is in Akkadian, and the Akkadian term for a menstruating woman was probably urruštu, which sounds quite different. More so, our sole description of Dimītu lacks any reference to blood, wine or beer. In several ways, Dimītu is very close to DIM.ME Lamaštu. Here is her dramatic debut in the *Šurpu Series* (VII, 1-22), based on Ungnad, 1921:273, Reiner 1958:36, amended. Note that the text is bilingual, and that the Sumerian version does not use the signs DIM.ME for Dimītu:

Conjuration. Dimītu has risen from the Apsû,

and Māmitu(m) (=oath, curse, taboo, prohibition: a daughter of Anu)

has descended from the Heart of Heaven,

and Aḫḫāzu has come up through the ground like weeds:

their radiation spread in all four directions like a scorching flame;

they plagued the people, they pressed on their bodies,

in city and land they raised cries of distress,

made the young and the old beat their breasts (in sorrow);

they shackled young men and young women, and filled them with woe,

they came down from heaven in thunder and rain, causing epileptic fits,

they hurried to the place of divine wrath and cast (a spell of) silence and sadness;

they met the man without a deity and enveloped him like a cloak,

they pounced on him and filled him with poison...

Well, you can guess how this will go on. Within seconds the poor fool is partly paralysed, covered in scabs, bedazzled, dumbstruck and racked by coughs. Luckily, Asarluḫi/Marduk comes walking by, sees the wretch staggering and drooling and goes to his dad for a cure. Enki/Ea tells him to take seven loaves of bread, made of unsifted flour, to put them on a bronze skewer, to tip the contraption with a carnelian bead, and to wipe the patient with this device. Afterwards, the patient spits on it. That fixes the spell: the plague is confined in the bread. The conjurer purifies the patient with the 'Conjuration of Eridu', carries the defiled object into the open country, and leaves it at the root of a thorn bush, in the care of the Lady of the Steppe (Bēlet EDIN), the god Ninkilim (who makes small animals carry the evil away), Damu (who speaks words of blessing for the patient), Gula, the great healer and Marduk *who revive the dead* and destroy fetters. Finally, the patient is washed, purified and given into the care of Šamaš, who is praised as the *Leader of the Gods*.

Quite early, probably in the Sumerian period, some people feared entire groups of Lamaštus. CT 16, 13b-14a III 21f briefly refers to *seven Lamaštus*; CT 14, 16d, 21 has the expression *all Lamaštus* while the late *Maqlû Series* (II 61) might refer to a *'Little Lamaštu'* at the side of DIM.ME (Farber in RlA: *'Lamaštu'*). Earlier, Meier's translation of the *Maqlû Series* had: *...or Lamaštu, the younger Daughter of A(nu). 'Little'* may be understood as *'younger'*. I can't find a reference to DIM.ME in Meier's transcription.

A fascinating long poem is called *Ludlul Bēl Nēmeqi: I Will Praise the Lord of Wisdom* (see, for example, Robert D. Biggs in ANET 1992:598-599 and Lambert 1960:41). Falkenstein and von Soden (SAHG 1953:54) date the piece around the end of the second millennium. The work is a lament: the poet, plagued by misfortune and disease, spends a lot of time embellishing his sufferings. Here is a significant section (II, 50-57):

...Debilitating Disease is let loose upon me:
an Evil Wind has blown (from the) horizon,
di'u disease has risen from the surface of the earth/ underworld,
an evil cough has left the Apsû,
the irresistible [utukku] has left the Ekur,
[Lamaštu came] down from the mountain,
cramp set out [from ...] the flood,
weakness (or: impotence) burst through the earth/ underworld
together with the plants...

(II, 70-72) *...I am thrown down like a [...] and cast on my face.*
The alû has clothed himself in my body as with a garment;
sleep covers me like a net...

Mesopotamian poets enjoyed misery and frequently wallowed in it. As the whining won't stop, a helpful (or enervated) exorcist interfered (Si 55q, reverse, 5-10)

[He brought] near his spell which binds. [...]
[He drove] away the evil wind to the horizon,
he took [the di'u disease] to the surface of the earth/ underworld.
[He sent] the evil cough down to its Apsû,
he banished the irresistible utukku (to) Ekur,
he overthrew Lamaštu, sending her off to the mountain,
he sent the cramp to the flowing water and the sea.
He tore up the root of weakness (or: impotence) as if it were a plant.

Finally the patient was purified and passed through a series of magical gates which restored him to health. It raises the question whether we are witnessing a complicated cure for every imaginable horror or an initiation ritual.

Lamaštu: Iconography

Nudeness. Our goddess is a ferocious nudist. In early Sumerian art, we meet some nude ritualists. One example is the famous Uruk vase, showing nude men carrying foodstuffs and sheep to a woman or goddess who may or may not represent Inanna, and who is perfectly dressed. Some but not all ritualists undressed before they faced the gods, so that no part of clothing could cover their own, natural beings. In a similar vein, Inanna/ Ištar had to undress completely, give up her symbols of power, jewellery, wealth, costume and self-definition, before she could enter the dark heart of the underworld.

Lamaštu is nude. To the earlier Sumerians, it may have meant purity and truth. To the Old Babylonians and all later Mesopotamians, things appeared in a different light. There is a major difference between Sumerian and Old Babylonian myth. In the Sumerian tales, the gods are rarely bothered by social norms. We meet Inanna rejoicing in her vulva; a few minutes later she is on her way to trick Enki into giving the principles of civilisation, the Me, to her. We meet Enki, as he ejaculates into the empty riverbeds of the Euphrates and Tigris. And we see him breaking all incest taboos by making love with his daughter, and her daughter, and the daughter of hers, until trouble catches up with him. Enlil and Ninlil had such a fit of passionate lovemaking near a canal that some scholars understood it as rape. In the bizarre and fragmentary *Cosmology of Dunnu* generations of gods kill their fathers and copulate with their mothers. Sumerian myth contains plenty of crude and asocial elements. Or should we call them wild and unrefined, a reflection of the fierce energies embodied in every deity? When the Old Babylonian period begins, a different outlook prevails. The Old Babylonians preserved many Sumerian traditions. However, their deities were a lot more constricted. The myths were toned down and the gods embodied civilisation. For good reasons, Lambert compares the congregation of the Babylonian gods to an assembly of civil servants. The Sumerians rarely bothered to describe the home life of their deities; the Babylonians turned it into a perfect reflection of refined palace life. When Erra/Nergal wants to bring destruction and terror to mankind he asks for permission first. What had been wild copulation or rape in early myth disappears: Sîn makes love to a goddess in cow shape once, and that happens in secret (Lambert, 1960:6). Likewise, ritualists and musicians usually remained dressed. The only remnant of nudity was that the people who entered a temple had to leave their shoes outside. Major gods wore elaborate costumes. Only some obscure ones, like the nude goddess of the Burney relief, did not. It's definitely not the same thing. Lamaštu rises from the reeds. She is covered in mud, her female undergarment is torn off, her arms, hands and breasts are splattered with blood. Maybe she is a nude ritualist, but she isn't likely to get much respect for it. The same goes for her open and wildly tangled **hair**: properly married and socially acceptable women kept their hair in braids or elaborate coiffures, or wore wigs, hair-needles and luxurious headdresses. Things got worse in the Neo-Assyrian Period in the dismal and world-weary first century BCE when Assyrian laws insisting that acceptable women wear veils while prostitutes did not. Consider what a wild, nude goddess might have meant in such a setting.

Mask. When Lamaštu was kicked out of heaven, her brother Enlil equipped her with a terrifying face. We could image that he transformed her face, which, originally, would have been human. Or he gave her a terrifying mask. It could have been a wolf, lioness, hyena, snake, dragon or a bird of prey: all of them appear in amulets.

There are several entities in Mesopotamian myth that walk around with the head of a lion and entire series of beings with human bodies and animal heads that may be identified as spirits, demons, deities or masked ritualists. Experts keep classing the lion-headed, bird-footed entities as asakku, utukku or anything they fancy. One of them, however, can be identified with some certainty. Meet **Samana**, the Lion-Headed 'Demon'. Enkidu dreams of being killed by him, and knows that his life on earth will soon end. Samana has a lion head and occasionally eagle feet, and often wields a sword (so does Lamaštu); apart from this he has a male body and none of her usual attributes. Hardly anything is known about him. I keep reading that the two are not related. But can we simply dismiss him? This late Sumerian conjuration points at several important parallels between Lamaštu and him.

Enruru-Conjuration.

Samana, he with the lion mouth,
he with the dragon's teeth,
he with the eagle claws,
he with the scorpion's sting,
the wild lion of Enlil,
the lion of Enlil who cuts the throat,
the lion of Nininsinna with blood dripping jaws,
the lion of the gods who opens his mouth wide:
as he has taken the answer to the ordeal question from the river,
as he has taken the food from the infant,
as he has obstructed the flow of menstrual blood of the virgin,
as he has blocked the male potency of the youth,

as he has hindered the priestess in her office,
as he has obstructed the prostitute in her business,
Asarluḫi sent a messenger to his father Enki...

It's an early spell. One indication is the Sumerian form of the names, another that Asarluḫi sends a messenger and does not go to his all-knowing dad personally. A third indication of old age: early spells are often simple, and only require a god to utter a command. Younger spells often (but not always) require ritual acts, and some very young spells are full of complicated procedures. It's not always reliable, but generally, we observe a trend towards complication in Mesopotamian magic. Enki simply decrees

shall he, Samana, be cleaned like a canal,
shall he be extinguished like a swift fire of reeds,
shall he not grow together again, like a plant that has been cut!'

(Jensen in SAHG 1953:214, slightly amended, trans. JF). Is Samana a male counterpart of Lamaštu? Given that several early traditions favour gods who appear as male and female manifestations of a given phenomenon (Anu & Antu; Enki & Ninki; Enlil & Ninlil; Lilû & Lilītu), the possibility should be considered. True, the names of Samana and DIM.ME/Lamaštu are widely different. But their iconography and the fact that both are related to babies and sexual activity might indicate a common background.

Pigs and Dogs

Life in a swamp is nicer when you have company. Many Lamaštu amulets show the goddess suckling a domestic or wild boar piglet, and a dog, wolf, hyena or jackal cub. The identification is not easy. As the goddess dwells in wild places, wild animals are an obvious choice. Domesticated dogs and pigs are harder to understand. Her relationship to them seems to be ambiguous. We read that she receives dogs as companions or is (maybe) married or transferred into one. On the other hand savage dogs are set against her. Possibly a dog is her nemesis. The dogs of Gula, goddess of healing, are encouraged to chase her and other dangerous entities away. And what about the pigs? If the goddess has a fond heart for pigs, how come her clay figurine, near the head of the patient, receives the freshly cut heart of a pig, which, depending on the translation, is placed next to her or (more likely) put in her mouth?

What do we make of those amulets that show the goddess suckling animals? Let's return to an early stage of human evolution. Pigs and dogs were the first domesticated animals. Before the advent of agriculture, when hunter/gatherers roamed the land in small groups, wolves and pigs developed an interest in them. The Palaeolithic migrants left their rubbish behind, and in many cases, some of it was edible. Pigs and wolves eat excrement, leftovers and meat that has gone bad. Nowadays, many scholars assume that these animals, attracted by human waste, started the process of domestication themselves. The next step is easy. When a wolf bitch or a wild sow is killed, the litters remain alive. Some of the youngsters may be eaten. But puppies and piglets are cute and highly intelligent; it doesn't take much to make pets out of them. Researching the domestication of dogs, Erich Ziemen proposed that wolf cubs may have been breastfed by women. This is not an unusual idea; in Papua New Guinea and South East Asia, women who lose their baby occasionally adopt and breastfeed cubs and piglets. The animal grows up as a member of the family. The custom of breastfeeding dog cubs and piglets appears in several cultures. If we look at Lamaštu from this perspective and ignore the religious background, we observe a woman who lost her baby. Her breasts are full: she feeds a wolf cub and a piglet instead. She yearns for the children of others, and even for the children of different species. Lamaštu has a heart for the lost and abandoned. It's a role that must have been familiar to those priestesses of Mesopotamia who were not permitted to have children, or who had to give them away. Lamaštu's choice of pigs and dogs shows she is not bothered by 'unclean' habits. She simply chooses the most intelligent animals around.

Compared to people, pigs and dogs seem to be immune to disease. They survive in filthy surroundings, consume rotten food and eat excrement. It would be tempting to call them 'unclean animals'. Nowadays the Near East is full of people who do so. Most Mesopotamians did not. The Sumerians kept lots of pigs and loved their meat. So did the Akkadians and most of the later cultures. The taboo on eating pig is typical for the West Semites; it is rare in Mesopotamia. In the chapter on healing magic you can read spells where the doctors and conjurers protected themselves by projecting the enormous fertilising powers of dogs and pigs into themselves. Pigs were kept right within the cities, much as they were in Medieval Europe. They took care of the garbage.

But while lard was expensive and ham a delicacy, there is evidence that some people in first millennium BCE Mesopotamia didn't like pigs. Among the proverbs and sayings on tablet VAT 8807 (Lambert, 1960:215) we read:

The pig has no sense; (...)

when at leisure, (...) he mocked his master,

his master left him (...) the butcher slaughtered him.

The pig is unholy (...) bespattering his backside,

making the streets smell, polluting the houses,

the pig is not fit for a temple, lacks sense, is not allowed to tread on pavements,

an abomination to all the gods, an abhorrence (to (his) god,) accursed by Šamaš.

Observe the parallels to Lamaštu. The pig mocked his master; the goddess was kicked out of heaven (and given a tough job on earth) for insolence, disobedience and an appetite for forbidden things. The pig does not walk the pavements like the gods of law and order do, and finally, offends the god of justice. The author had a sacrilegious animal on his mind, and lived in a city where smelly streets were the norm. I'd love to know how many people thought like that. The lines on pigs not being fit for temples are contradicted by the account *Daily Sacrifices to the Gods of the City of Uruk*, a text recorded in the Seleucid Period, which may go back to earlier periods. Anu and Antu(m) ate four wild boars a day. It may not seem much. However, religioning and priesting are hungry work, so in case you are worried about the diet of the gods, priests and temple personnel, here is the total for the four meals a day*: twenty-one first-class, fat, clean rams which had been fed barley for two years; two large bulls; one milk-fed bullock; eight lambs; thirty marratu-birds; thirty [...] birds; three cranes which have been fed [...] -grain; five ducks which have been fed [...] -flour; two ducks of a lower quality than those just mentioned; four wild boars; three ostrich eggs; three duck eggs* (translation A. Sachs in ANET 1969:344). Plus four sorts of beer, two sorts of wine (one imported) and milk; barley and emmer flour baked into loaves of bread, dates, figs, raisins, and so on. It's no surprise people were keen to do duty in the temples. Pig's flesh was highly valued, wealthy people delighted in the fatty parts and left the lean parts to their slaves. The lard was a favourite for medical and cosmetic ointments. Postgate (2002:166, 193) marvels at the fact that while pigs were a common sight in the Sumerian and Akkadian cities, the animal was generally ignored by the scribes and does not appear in official art. In the *Ešnunna Law Code* (c.2000-1800 BCE), 1,5 litres of pig's fat sold for 1 šekel of silver, or the equivalent of 300 litres of barley, or 3 litres of best oil, or 40 litres of bitumen, or 3kg of wool or 1.5kg of copper. Copper and bitumen were expensive imported products. For one šekel of silver, a hired labourer would harvest for an entire month. If your dog or ox caused the death of a slave, the fee was 15 šekels (Goetze in Pritchard, 1969:161).

Mesopotamians tastes differed from those of the West Semites. Under Aššurbanipal, Syria and Palestine became parts of the Assyrian Empire. Dangerous deities do have a way of getting around, and the distribution of Lamaštu amulets shows that some people in these countries were highly scared of her. For the West Semites, the animal symbolism may have seemed a lot more sinister. The psalms compare the wicked and godless to pigs, dogs, lions and snakes; all of them favourite totem animals of Lamaštu.

Anu's Daughter

Let us top this off with something that did not appear in literature so far. I chanced upon it when I noted Mesopotamian constellations on a star map. Take a look at the night sky. First, identify Mirach (Andromeda β). It's easy: Andromeda is huge and her nebula is nearby. Mirach is the star of Lamaštu, named, like her, with the Sumerian term ka-muš-i-gue, the *'(female) dragon/serpent mouth feeds'*. The Sumerian name may hint that the identification comes from the third millennium BCE; many stars and constellations were named by the Sumerians, and the Akkadians kept using Sumerian names. The Sumerogram KA may also be read as zu; the first means *mouth* and the second *tooth*. The same character also appears as kir (*nose*) and inim (*word*). As this star is a mouth, tooth, nose and word, we might assume that it refers to her head. From this star, the constellation U-ka-du-a: *Panther* extends over a wide section of the sky. We lack a good description. According to Weidner, the constellation is nowadays known as Cepheus and Cygnus. Lamaštu's kidneys/flanks are spotted like a panther. When we continue along the 'torso' formed by the panther, we arrive at the constellation Našru: *Aquila, the Eagle*. It could represent her legs and talons. To balance it, there are two constellations to the sides of the panther: on one side is Šaḫû: the *Pig* (today Delphinus), on the other Urku: the *Dog* (today Hercules). Together, they form an image familiar from Lamaštu amulets. If this interpretation is reasonable, Lamaštu, Daughter of Heaven extends over a large part of the sky.

But there is also a connection to the way the Greeks reinterpreted the ancient Mesopotamian signs. If we take Mirach, i.e. Lamaštu's serpent/dragon mouth, as the centre, we find this 'head' surrounded by Perseus, Andromeda, Pegasus and Cassiopeia. You know the myth. Medusa connects them all. Lamaštu's talismans were the major inspiration for those Greek artists who created the familiar Medusa image (Burkert, 1995:82-87) Was their choice influenced by astronomy?

Lamaštu and Sorcery

Some scholars assume that 'black magic' was common in all ancient cultures, but this impression may be wrong. Let's have an example. When we look into the oracle bone record of the Chinese Shang dynasty, we find no evidence for evil spells or destructive sorcery at all. In Bronze-Age China, around 1200 BCE, nobody worried about witchcraft. The real terror was the ancestors and gods, who were always willing to curse the living. When offended, minor ancestors caused diseases and accidents; major ancestors could send earthquakes, locusts, storms, floods, plagues and enemy invasions. The ancestors were so powerful and terrifying that human sorcery wasn't worth consulting the oracle. It was only much later in Chinese history, after the fall of the Western Zhou dynasty, that the ancestors and gods lost the ability to strike terror into the hearts of the living, and people began to worry that their fellow humans might curse them (Fries, 2013). Hostile magic is not universal. We may be facing something similar when we explore ancient Mesopotamia. The Sumerians left us very little material on evil sorceries. Maybe they didn't believe in them or didn't think them worth recording. Or we simply haven't found the evidence yet. Witchcraft and sorcery became more important while the culture turned increasingly Semitic. Ḫammurapi passed a law that settled accusations of witchcraft. It appears right at the start of his Codex, in paragraph 2:

If a man has brought a charge of sorcery against another man, but has not managed to prove it, the man against whom the charge of sorcery has been made, shall, when going to the river, be thrown into it, and if the river (deity) overpowers him, his accuser shall receive his property; but if the river has shown him as innocent, and he comes out safely, the accuser shall be put to death, and his property shall be granted to the one who cast himself into the river.

Ḫammurapi's remarkable law was highly functional: it reduced the number of silly lawsuits to a minimum and, as a side effect, may have encouraged sorcerers to practice swimming.

Consider. Ḫammurapi was not the first lawgiver in Mesopotamia. The fragmentary law codes that survive of earlier regents (Urnammu, Lipitištar and the text found in Ešnunna) do not refer to sorcery at all. An early hint at the river ordeal appears around 2350 BCE, in *Temple Hymn* four, written by Enḫeduanna. It tells us: there is a river ordeal. We don't learn what it was used for. It was not controlled by the river (deity) but by the fire god Nusku. The Middle Assyrians had a different attitude. The law code of Tiglatpilesar, paragraph 47, does not leave the verdict to a deity, or to chance:

If either a man or a woman made up magical preparations and they were found in their possession, when they have prosecuted them (and) convicted them, they shall put the maker of the magical preparations to death (ANET, 1992:184). Anyone who saw the making of the magical preparations or heard of it from another had to inform the palace. The rest of the passage deals with witnesses who denied their own reports, and who had to swear oaths in the presence of the *Bull-God, Son of Šamaš*, or were interrogated by an exorcist. The accused did not have much of a chance, while the accusers didn't risk anything.

Maqlû means *burning.* The *Maqlû Series* was made by assembling and editing older texts, and by combining them with lots of new material. The text provides an extended ritual that kept growing, as more and more conjurations and ritual acts were added to it. In Aššurbanipal's time it reached its final form. By then, the *Maqlû Series* consisted of eight tablets plus a ninth, giving a table of contents for almost a hundred conjurations. The text is divided into three sections. The first part (tablets I-V) begins by a call to the gods of the night, presumably made from a roof, and describes the ritual schedule for the early night. Part two (tablets VI-VII) was performed from the middle to the end of the night. Part three (tablet VII) has an entirely different mood, as it fixes the spells and conducts the client safely into the morning. The ritual schedule contains an odd assortment of elements from different periods. Much of it was transformed to suit the ritual. Anti-witchcraft spells that relied on Šamaš, the sun, were adapted for the night time by replacing him with Nusku, the lord of fire, lamp and burning brazier. The main use of the *Maqlû* ritual is to destroy witchcraft and the persons who use it. Apart from this, there are sections annulling the influences of evil spirits and plenty of purification rituals. The Neo-Assyrians were mad about witchcraft. Bad events, accidents, nightmares, scary omens and so on could indicate that a person was being bewitched. Some of this witchcraft was assumed to come from real people. The *Maqlû* ritual was expensive. The clients were aristocrats, administrators and merchants. All of them had enemies who might be tempted to hire a witch or sorcerer. But some of the witchcraft seemed to come from almost supernatural witches, beings who were far too scary to be counted as mere humans. You met several references to witches in the commentaries to the *Lamaštu Series.* They could be foreign women, craftswomen, formerly respected high priestesses, female exorcists, snake-charmers and the like. These are still within the human range. Other witches were pure evil. Here is one description. It might remind you of Lamaštu or the Ardat Lilî:

Conjuration. The witch who walks the roads
who enters houses,
sneaks through alleys,
chases over open spaces,
she turns forth and back,
stops on the street and turns her foot,
on the open place she obstructs passage.
She stole the vitality of the handsome man,
she took the fruit of the beautiful girl,
with a single glance she took the attractiveness from her,

she gazed at the man and took his strength,

she gazed at the woman and took her fruit.

The witch saw me and followed me,

she blocked my way with her poison,

with her spells she obstructed my profit,

she removed my (personal) god and goddess from my body.

(*Maqlû*, III, 1-16, after Ungnad, 1921, Meier, 1937, Haas, 1986)

The *Maqlû Series* was compiled to counter evil sorceries. Its prime intent is to obliterate evil spells and to punish and kill sorcerers and witches. On occasion, *Maqlû* spells exorcise evil spirits and deities, but the emphasis is on human evil. To achieve this aim, figurines of sorcerers and witches were made, cursed, violated, melted and burned. I would like to emphasise that it was images, not people, who ended on the pyre. Having a conjurer burn figures is much safer than accusing someone of witchcraft and facing the costs, trouble and loss of face entailed by a lawsuit. But it wasn't only witches and sorcerers that were banished or destroyed. Here is a section from the very end of tablet I. It is an odd item: tablet I counters human sorceries. Someone stuck a spell at the end, almost as an afterthought, that banishes and destroys lethal spirits and deities. The deities are not acknowledged as such: unlike so many earlier texts, Lamaštu and her relations are listed without the divine determinative :

I raise the torch, I burn the figures,

Of the utukku (spirit), *the šedu* (a winged lion-man),

the rabiṣu (agent/lurker)*, the eṭimmu* (ghost),

Lamaštu, Labāṣu, Aḫḫāzu (Seizer),

Lilû (wind & storm, in male form)*, Lilītu* (wind & storm, in female form),

Adat Lilî (girlfriend of Lilû, or: girl of the Lilû Group),

and all evil that seizes people.

Dribble, drop and flow apart!

Your smoke rises to heaven!

Your glowing ashes are extinguished by Šamaš!

Your spying is cut off by the son of Ea, the mašmaššu (conjurer)!

(after Meier, 135-143, trans. JF). The passage shows that the exorcists of the first millennium BCE had a sufficiently clear idea of the evil spirits and dangerous deities to make figurines of them.

The compilation of Aššurbanipal is not representative of what earlier generations believed. In his study of *Maqlû* conjurations, Abusch (1987) elegantly demonstrated that some of the material came from the second millennium BCE but was altered to suit the mindset of the first millennium. He cites a *Maqlû* purification spell (VII, 119-143) that lists the ills which have befallen a patient. The catalogue of evils starts with everything bad, unlucky, that rests in the body, the flesh and the muscles of the patient. It goes on to evil dreams and bad omens, (parts missing) accidental pollution, spirit activity, disease, di'u disease, need, worry, fear, shaking, woe, terror, weakness, sadness, wretchedness, cutting of limbs, dread, compulsiveness, fright, sins, evil incidents caused by gods, wrath, and two sorts of broken oaths. Last, in line 135, evil sorceries and evil machinations are mentioned. Finally, the patient is purified with water; the whole lot of worries is transferred into the hand-washing water and carried away. The spell ends with a blessing and the prediction that the future will be better. That completes the ritual on a positive note: Ea, Šamaš and Marduk will help. To this composition, as Abusch notes, the scribes of the *Maqlû Series* added three lines.

The sorcery, witchcraft and delusion shall be dissolved,

And the evil machinations of people,

And the mamit shall depart from my body. (After Meier, trans. JF)

Abusch carefully reconstructed that in earlier spells, from which the *Maqlû Series* gained much material, the original position of the witchcraft line was between 124 and 127, i.e. the section after the reference to evil dreams, omens and forecasts. The *Maqlû* scribes put the witchcraft line at the end and added their three lines to make the last problem, sorcery and machinations, the main item. It fitted the program: the long and expensive *Maqlû* ritual is meant to eliminate evil sorceries.

On the other hand, a major prayer to Marduk was reworked by the scribes to turn a short spell against sorcery into a grandiose banishment of all kinds of evil, including the wrath of the gods. The overwhelming witchcraft paranoia of the *Maqlû Series* may have been bread and butter to the exorcists, but it was not their only concern.

Several sections of the *Maqlû Series* resemble court cases. The great gods of justice, Šamaš, Marduk, Nusku and Gibil are invoked to mete out savage revenge. Unlike proper judicial proceedings the offenders are damned and destroyed without hesitation. The client fears witchcraft and the exorcists accept this assumption without doubt. Usually, in legal conflicts, the Mesopotamians first went to a court which decided whether the charge was relevant. If that court agreed, the matter went to another court, which passed judgement. In the *Maqlû Series*, the unknown witches and sorcerers stand no chance. They are ritually cursed, banished, sentenced, bound, weakened, have their tongues cut out and are burned to death in effigy. There is an element of hysteric paranoia to these rituals. In all likeliness there was a divination before the exorcism. That's a guess: divination is not mentioned. Our grimoires were composed for exorcists, not for diviners, who had their own handbooks, and quite a lot of them.

Consider the differences between the ritual handbooks of Aššurbanipal's library. The asakku, the di'u spirit, the alû and the evil utukkus were simply damned and banished. In a few cases they received a replacement sacrifice or a minor offering. Lamaštu was praised, banished and threatened and received lavish offerings and presents before her departure. The evil witches and sorcerers of the *Maqlû Series* were sentenced, injured and destroyed, but they were never personally identified. It's a special element. I am sure that many clients had their suspicions who might have bewitched them. Nevertheless, the exorcists did not direct their curses against specific persons. It may have produced an interesting situation. After the ritual, the client was sure to watch her or his acquaintances. Did any of them suffer from an accident, a disease, or die? Given that life in Mesopotamia was neither safe, healthy nor extended, someone was sure to suffer from mishap before long. It proved that the exorcism had worked and divine justice had been served, even if that person was not on the list of suspects and quite innocent. And it increased the general mood of terrified paranoia, demonstrating that there are more witches and sorcerers around than you and I would deem possible.

The scribes and priests of Aššurbanipal's court compiled their massive ritual to counter evil sorcery. Call it 'self-defence' if you like. No matter how lethal the exorcisms and counter-curses, the *Maqlû* rituals were 'legitimate magic'. But things are not that simple. The exorcists who banished evil witchcraft called upon the same gods as the evil witches and sorcerers!

Conjuration. I have moored the ferry, I have blocked the harbour-district,

I have stopped the sorceries of all countries.

Anu and Antu(m) have sent me.

Whom shall I send to Bēlet-Ṣēri (=Lady of the Desert*)?*

Throw a gag into the mouth of my sorcerer and my sorceress,

Cast the spell of the sage of the gods, Marduk!

They shall call to you, but you will not answer them!

They shall appeal to you, but you will not hear their pleas!

When I call to you, you answer me.

When I appeal to you, you listen to me!

According to the command given by Anu, Antu(m) and Bēlet-Ṣēri.

Conjuration. (I, 50-60, based on Ungnad, 1921 & Meier, 1937, trans. JF)

How do we tell legitimate from evil sorcery when both parties appeal to the same celestial deities?

Figure 45 Homeless Ghost Haunting the Desert.

To give you an idea of the mood and passion of *Maqlû* magic, here is a passage mentioning Lamaštu, tablet IV, 1-75, based on Ungnad (1921) & Meier (1937), Haas (1986) trans. JF:

Conjuration: Cook, cook, burn, burn!

Evil and worse, do not enter, depart!

Who are you, whose son; who are you, whose daughter,

who is sitting there, witching your spells and intrigues against me?

*Ea, the mašmaššu (*conjurer*) shall unbind,*

and your sorceries will be destroyed,

by Asarluḫi, the Conjurer of the Gods, son of Ea, the wise.

I shackle you, I bind you, I give you over

to Girra, who scorches, burns and shackles,

*and seizes the kaššapati (*witches*).*

The scorching Girra makes my arms strong!

Witchcraft, revolt, evil words, love, hate,

twisted justice, murder, paralysis of the mouth, [...]

bursting of the interior, glowing of the face and insanity,

you hexed, you ordered to be hexed:

Girra, unbind the spell!

You have chosen me for a corpse [...]

(From here, and in the following gaps of the inscription, Ungnad assumed the text should continue: *'in vain!'* Haas proposed the missing section should read *'the god of fire shall release!'*)

You gave me to the skulls of the dead [...],

*you gave me to an eṭimmu (*ghost*) of my family [...],*

you gave me to an eṭimmu of a stranger [...],

a straying eṭimmu who has no-one to care for it,

you gave me to an eṭimmu of fallen ruins [...],

you gave me to the steppe, the desert and the wasteland out there [...],

you gave me to the inner wall and the wall of the courtyard [...],

you gave me to Bēlet-Ṣēri, the Lady of the Steppes and the Heights [...],

to the bread-oven, to the hearth, the charcoal bowl [...] and the bellows [...],

you gave my images into the custody of a corpse [...],

you chose my images for a corpse [...],

you placed my images near a corpse [...],

you placed my images in the womb of a corpse [...],

you buried my images in the tomb of a corpse: [...],

you gave my images into the custody of skulls [...],

you enclosed my images in a wall [...],

you placed my images on a doorstep [...],

you enclosed figures of me in the entrance of the wall [...],

you buried my images on a bridge, and allowed people to trample them [...].

My images: you made a hole in the well of a washer and buried them inside [...],

my images: you made a hole in the canal of a gardener and buried (them inside) [...],

my images: you made them of tamarisk wood or cedar wood or lard,

or of wax or of wine-dregs (?),

or of bit(umen) or clay or dough.

You made images, fig[urines?] of my face and my shape and

allowed [a dog to e]at them, allowed a pig to eat them,

[the birds of heaven] to eat them, and cast them into the river.

You gave my images into the custody of Lamaštu, the Daughter of Anu [...],

you gave my images to Girra [...],

*you placed my water (*urine? sperm? spittle?*) near a corpse [...],*

you placed my water near the womb of a corpse [...],

you buried [my water in t]he tomb of a corpse [...],

[...] you buried my water [...],

[...] you buried my water [...],

[...] you gathered my water [...],

you gave (my water) to Gilgameš [...],

[...] of a ditch you chose me [...],

[...] of Sîn [...],

[...] of Šulpae [...],

[...] of copper [...],

(Gap of 15 lines, each of them beginning with the word *'murder'*)

Be[fore...] and the gate of the house [...],

before com[rades] and likewise the servants.

before the house and gate, slaves and slave-girls,

[small and] grown up members of the house,

to them, who see me, you h[ave...] made [...],

I bound you, I shackled you, I gave you

to Girra, who scorches, burns, shackles

*and seizes the kaššapati (*witches*).*

The scorching Girra shall unbind your knots,

unbind your sorceries, take off (?) your ropes,

at the command of Marduk, the son of Ea, the Wise,

and of Girra, the Blazing, the Wise, the son of Anu, the hero.

It's an amazing piece of magical literature. It is also magnificent poetry. We can use it as an exorcism if we insert, as Ungnad proposed, the words *'in vain!'* into the gaps at the end of the lines. Maybe the exorcist recited this formidable list to cover any sort of possible witchcraft. Or maybe the list is an extensive ritual schedule used by sorcerers and witches to destroy their victim. It starts when the victim encounters death and ends with her/his arrival at the court of Gilgameš, here acting as a god of death and the underworld. The reference to Lamaštu, for all its brevity, is worth considering. Apparently, some sorcerers and sorceresses of the first millennium were on such good terms with her that they could ask her to kill people. How did they do it? Mesopotamian gods are demanding. Your personal deities want affection, total dedication, offerings, ritual, and a virtuous, active lifestyle. Unless you do your best in all things, your personal deities may simply drop you. Normal gods wanted praise, love, attention, entertainment and offerings. The same must have applied to Lamaštu. The witches and sorcerers wouldn't have tried to order her around without making friends with her. How was she asked, bribed or coerced to do her destructive job, given that she is a deity of primal heaven, acting at the command of the council of the gods?

It's just a short line and indicates a big gap in our knowledge.

To end this chapter, here is another passage referring to Lamaštu, and many others, acting at the request of the evil sorcerers and witches. Welcome to *Maqlû Series V, 61-81,* based on Ungnad 1921: 254-255 and Meier 1967/1937:36-37, slightly amended, trans. JF)

Conjuration: The hate which you conjured, you conjured against yourself,

likewise murder, likewise twisting of justice, likewise paralysis of the mouth,

Likewise [...], likewise slander.

You made the evil utukku seize me: the evil utukku will seize you!

You made the evil alû seize me: the evil alû will seize you!

*You made the evil eṭimmu (*ghost*) seize me: the evil eṭimmu will seize you!*

You made the evil gallû seize me: the evil gallû will seize you!

You made the evil God seize me: the evil God will seize you!

You made the evil rabiṣu seize me: the evil rabiṣu will seize you!

You made Lamaštu, Labāṣu, and Aḫḫāzu seize me: Lamaštu, Labāṣu, and Aḫḫāzu will seize you!

You made Lilû, Lilītu, Ardat Lilî seize me: Lilû, Lilītu, Ardat Lilî will seize you!

Through nīšu (oath on the life, conjuration) *and mamit* (oath, taboo, curse) *you tried to destroy me:*

through nīšu and mamit your body will be destroyed!

You raised the wrath of god, king, lord and aristocrat against me:

wrath of god, king, lord and aristocrat will be inflicted on you!

Suffering, drought, and destruction of the heart; trembling, fear and misery you made for me:
Suffering, drought, destruction of the heart; trembling, fear and misery will be made for you!

*I have scorched you with pure sulphur and salt from Amurru (*the west, Syria*).*
*I have dispelled your fumigation, ikkibu (*abominable, taboo*) to Heaven,*
your machinations have returned to you!

Part Four

Fire-starter

The Healing Arts: Medicine, Conjuration, Maths and Music

Diagnosis by Bubbles, Flames and Dreams

You have met conjurers and exorcists. Unlike them, I am sure you look forward to healers who took their profession seriously. Imagine yourself almost four thousand years ago. Yesterday you arrived in Uruk, capital of the world, and today you are not feeling well. You are resting in a narrow, shady chamber above a tavern. Outside on the street life is loud, colourful and dusty. The air is humid and stifling hot. Whatever you planned, your guts are telling you to remain at home, and at a safe distance to the bucket. Your hosts, alarmed by your groans, have called for a doctor. The professional who enters your sick chamber is clean, well clad, and exhibits a freshly shaved head. In his hands he carries two emblems of his profession, a drinking vessel and a censer. Behind him appears a narrow-faced apprentice with shifty eyes, carrying bags and bundles. Your doctor examines you closely. A stern look appears on his gleaming, sweaty face. There were clear omens on the way.

'Did you eat the 'Vintage Mule Burgers' at the corner?' he enquires, 'or the 'Delightfully Fresh Canal Shrimps'? Or the 'Salad of Seven Underworld Surprises?"

Whimpering slightly, you agree.

'Tut, tut' goes the doctor. 'That food stand is polluted.'

'But why', you groan, 'doesn't anybody close it?'

'Only foreigners eat there', says the doctor. 'No one cares. You eat. I cure. You pay. It's getting my sons through scribal school.'

He gives you a big grin. 'Cheer up. I'll recommend some restaurants.' He turns to his apprentice. 'If the face is pale and wet, the hands tremble, the belly rises and we smell the incense, it's the Hand of Ḫuwawa. Start the fumigation. And hand me powdered pepper, ginger, cress seeds, salt, sulphur, a tube and a fresh plug.' He reaches for the bucket.

'In an hour you'll be as fresh and shiny as the heart of heaven.'

Early in the Old Babylonian period, the *Laws of Ḫammurapi* specified that physicians were responsible for the cures they administered, and when they made fatal errors they were punished, sometimes with mutilation or death. Also, they had to adjust their fees to the income of the patient; Ḫammurapi specified prices for some cures. The treatment, you could be sure, would be made with more care and consideration than you can expect from most medical practitioners today.

Healings and/or exorcisms did not start in the sickroom: they began when the physician or conjurer left home. Life is full of surprising information. Unlike modern doctors, their counterparts of the first millennium BCE were on the lookout for anything unusual. One of their major concerns was, of course, that the patient might die and the blame be laid on them. It was only common sense to be wary about the fate of the patient and to avoid cases that were likely to be terminal. Our healer/magician was extra cautious as he approached the house of the patient. Here, we are probably talking about a man. Some were in the employ of a temple, or the palace, but there were also private practitioners for those who could afford them. Oates mentions a lonely inscription from Old Babylonian Larsa, referring to a female physician. I am sure there were more around. However, the textbooks refer, as usual in Akkadian literature, to men. Our doctor walked slowly and carefully observed his surroundings. After all, the gods were speaking to him. If he saw a black pig or dog, the patient was sure to die. A white pig indicated that the patient might survive. A red pig signified death in three days or three months. A pig lifting its tail in the direction of the patient was auspicious. It makes me wonder what happened when whole groups of pigs and dogs were romping around. There were plenty of animals on the road. Ravens were worth watching: those that croaked before a patient's house announced tears, and those behind his house tears for his enemy. A falcon flying to the right of the house meant recovery, one flying to the left death. That's basic body symbolism: things happening on the right were usually more auspicious than those on the left. A falcon flying into the building signified that the lady of the house would die. Lots of ants before the house indicated the death of its owner and the fall of the family. A good sign was a snake dropping from the rafters of the house and hitting the patient on his head.

The physicians of Babylon and Assyria were called asû, a term which may or may not come from the earlier Sumerian word a-zu or ià-zu, meaning *the man who knows water (or: oil)*. The interpretation is debatable: several early inscriptions use a different 'zu'-sign that has nothing to do with knowledge. For the medical profession, water was an all-round blessing. You could use it for herbal medicine, to clean wounds, to wash away evil influences, to bless, purify and divine. But how did the treatment start?

To begin with, your physician might make a thorough diagnosis. No, he probably wouldn't look into your throat or wallet. There's always time for that later on. It's much better to start slowly. How about a bit of water and oil divination to get into the mood?

Old Babylonian Water & Oil Divination was a surprisingly exact science and did not involve any personal and highly subjective visions. Let's have some insights from Arthur Ungnad's (1921:314-316) translation of CT III, 2ff. & V, 4ff.

-If you pour oil into the water, and the oil sinks and comes up again the patient will be unlucky.

-If the oil forms a ring towards the east, the diviner will join the march of the army and win treasure; and a patient will recover.

- If the oil forms two rings, a large and a small one, the wife of the client will give birth to a boy, or the patient will recover.

- If the oil forms a large and a small bubble, the patient will scream, but your army will gain loot.

- If the oil dissolves and covers the entire surface of the water, the army will be defeated and the patient dies.

- If a bladder of oil opens towards the east, the patient will die.

- If the oil to the east sinks and congeals, the patient will recover and the army will be victorious.

- If the oil to the left sinks and congeals, the patient will die and the army will be defeated.

- Three bubbles: there will be howling.

- Four bubbles: there will be screaming.

- Five bubbles: beware of ghost activity.

- If you pour water on the oil, and it sinks and rises again, the patient will recover.

- If it rises to the rim, a sick person will recover but a healthy person will die.

- If you pour water on the oil and the oil dissolves, so will the family fortune of the patient.

- If you divine a marriage, pour a drop for each partner. When the drops unite, the marriage will be auspicious; when the drop of one partner sinks, that partner will die.

This is just a sample, there are more possibilities and an entire collection of predictions regarding the way the sun gleams on the oil. The physicians took their business seriously. In our water and oil predictions, various omens could indicate the fate of the patient and/or the army. It shows that the diviners were sought-after specialists who could make their fortune (or find total dishonour) when they joined a campaign and supplied the king with prognostications. Last, the quality of the oil must have varied considerably if you couldn't even be sure if it would dissolve, bubble, form rings or sink to the bottom.

If oil watching didn't bring the desired diagnosis, gazing at a flame in the sickroom could do the job. A dark flame indicates that the patient will die within three days; thank you for the warning, ask for payment in advance. A greenish flame indicates bad luck for the lord and lady of the house. If a torch flames up all of a sudden, there will be good luck. And if the flame of a torch divides into four segments, the house will be destroyed. Five segments mean that the children will leave the house within the lifetime of their father.

If that isn't enough, how about a **dream oracle**? Like Sigmund Freud, the Babylonian doctors were aware that endless entertainment can be had by taking irrational neural activity seriously. However, unlike Freud, who expected reality to confirm his speculations, they were using cold, scientific thinking and saw no reason to discover more than 700 penis symbols. Nor did they prescribe two sessions of pointless babble a week for ten years. If you wanted to survive as a Mesopotamian doctor, you had to deliver. In fact they were not looking for principles but for specific cases. Theories did not matter to them. Oppenheim translated an Assyrian dream book from Susa, which offers infinite possibilities. As in all divination texts, the account follows the formula *If X then Y.* It's the basic formula of Mesopotamian science: these people took causality seriously. The Assyrian text is very well organised: we have little chapters dealing with basic dream topics and their variations. A man who dreams of sprinkling himself with urine, for instance, is afflicted by the disease *Hand of Ištar.* If he washes his hands in urine, he will enjoy little. If he pisses into the sky, he will die young but his son will make a great career. If he pisses into the river (an act that was strictly forbidden) he would gather a bountiful harvest. If he pissed into a well he would lose his property. If he pissed into a canal, Adad, god of storm and furious rain showers, was sure to flood his harvest. If he libated his urine to his personal deities he would find lost property. If he drank the urine of his wife he would enjoy abundant wealth. In a similar style, we encounter long chapters on entering gates, travelling to towns, foreign countries, going to orchards, fields, temples, marshes (cutting reeds in a dream means recovery from sickness), eating the meat of animals (eating a hyena means he'll have a seizure, eating wild animals: death in the family, eating foreign wild animals: his bad luck will disappear), eating birds, reptiles, fishes, worms and corpses (property will be lost). We learn about eating various parts of oneself, of friends, vegetables, grains, bricks, earth (bad luck: loss of position and poverty), sand, bitumen (imprisonment, no peace of mind), naphtha, mattress stuffing, sweepings of the home and the street (lots of food, increasing wealth). Some dreamed of eating stars and eating Lamaštu: sadly, the lines are damaged and we don't know what will happen. Maybe you could hazard a guess. Then there is an extensive section on meeting animals, receiving cylinder seals of various materials, receiving woods, tools, meat, chariots, doors, furniture, everyday goods, various oils, spices, garments and water from many sources. We have sections on what happens if the dreamer seizes/takes/adopts animals, gods, kings, planets, constellations, what happens if he meets dead people of many professions; there are weather forecasts and the fate of those who cut down specific trees. The dreamer might carry various objects (like vegetables, fruit, tools, seals, waggons, baskets of the gods, divine images, mountains), handle bows, fly around, fall into rivers, meet gods, break down and demolish things, tear or cut his clothes and so on. The catalogue is perfect comedy and endless; sorry, but it is very hard to discern a common background pattern. The seers and doctors did not use a hidden formula or a basic symbolism to make sense of dreams. Principles and regulations did not interest them. They noted remarkable dreams and the unusual events that followed them. Call it empirical study. If you had a unique dream followed by a bizarre accident, your case might appear in a diviner's handbook. As a result, some dream oracles seem to make sense and others are simply astonishing. You might call it irrational or superstitious, but the way the omen catalogues were compiled is strictly scientific.

Medical Textbooks

Reading the magical compendiums of the library of Aššurbanipal, you might arrive at the impression that it is mainly the angry gods, evil spirits, ghosts, witches, sorcerers, and of course Lamaštu who caused disease and suffering. They are opposed by fire gods, like Nusku, Gibil and Girra, who destroy evil influences and return spells to their senders; a range of benevolent warrior gods who might fight for you, like Pabilsag, Papsukkal, Ninurta, Ningirsu and the Seven Deity; by custodians of divine justice, like Šamaš and Sîn, and a few deities of healing, like Gula, Bau/Baba, Asarluḫi, Marduk and Ninazu (literally: *Lord Doctor*). It looks like bad guys against good guys. This impression is misleading. In many cases, disease and healing were not even related to religion. Several early medical tablets have a surprisingly 'rational' outlook. The earliest medical text (in fact, the earliest surviving medical text of mankind) comes from the late Sumerian period. It consists of a well-preserved tablet from the ruins of Nippur, containing fifteen prescriptions (Kramer, 1981:60-64, Saggs, 1966:467-468, Oates, 1994:180). Our 'textbook' offers a glimpse at the recipes used by a Sumerian physician. Sadly, the tablet is not easy to understand. The author did not bother to list the diseases and symptoms for which the prescriptions were made. Nor did he specify amounts, or frequency of treatments. It is likely that he did not want to have this knowledge widely available. The tablet is more like a mnemonic device. Mesopotamian doctors often, but not always, kept their favourite mixtures secret, and when they recorded them, occasionally used code-names to bedazzle the uninitiated. It limits our understanding of the efficiency of the curatives, but it still provides a fascinating glimpse into the materia medica and the way they were administered. Let's examine this tablet. Two favourites were sodium chloride (salt) and potassium nitrate (saltpetre). Quality salt was easily available: it was imported from the seaside or patiently filtered from the waters of the Euphrates and Tigris, whose relatively high salt content eventually destroyed much fertile land in Mesopotamia. Low-quality salt is easily available in southern Sumer: the high water table often bears up so much salt that the barren earth looks as if it had snowed. Saltpetre had to be gained in a less respectable way. One source might have been bat droppings. An easier way would have been to visit a public latrine, or an open sewer. Kramer cites later Assyrian literature, which indicates that the material was gained from the crystalline formation of urine. It contained several minerals, such as sodium chloride and the salts of sodium and potassium; consequently it had to be extracted using fractional crystallisation. *In India and Egypt there is still current the ancient procedure of mixing lime or old mortar with decomposing nitrogenous organic matter to form calcium nitrate, which is then lixiviated and boiled with wood ash containing potassium carbonate to yield nitre on evaporation of the filtrate.* Given that our Sumerian physician used saltpetre more than four thousand years ago, we can only marvel at the state of chemical knowledge then. Saltpetre might have been priced as an astringent, while salt was sacred and admired for its disinfecting power. A passage from the *Maqlû Series* VI, 111-119 (Meyer, 1937:45; Falkenstein & von Soden, 1953:354, trans. JF):

Conjuration.

You, salt, having been created in a pure place,

as food of the great gods has Enlil destined you.

Without you, no dish is served in Ekur,

without you, god, king, lord and noble do not smell the incense.

I NN, son of NN, who has been seized by sorcery,

who is kept in fever by (evil) operations, ask:

break my bewitchment, salt, untie my enchantments,

take the intrigues away from me!

Then, like the deity who has created me,

I will always worship you!

Maqlû Series IX, 118-120 adds that the spell is recited over a lump of salt, which is placed in a censer and set up at the head of the bed. Dating this spell is difficult. Like the entire *Maqlû Series* it was copied for the library of Aššurbanipal in the seventh century BCE, but the reference to Enlil and his main temple Ekur, the major religious temple of Sumer, points at a much greater age.

Another useful substance was alkali. Our physician may have gained it by burning plants of the *Chenopodiacea* family, such as *Salicornia fruticosa*, to gain soda. The two prescriptions using alkali combine it with fatty substances, which provide an excellent soap. Another valuable source of soap was the soapwort plant (genus *Saponaria*), a pretty plant with pink and white blossoms that was a gift of the goddess Nidaba/Nisaba, the reed and grain goddess.

Physicians, conjurers, priests and even the gods used plenty of soap, as bathing, washing and purification rituals were part of their daily ritual schedule. To approach a deity or to perform a ritual or offering without prior purification was unthinkable. Even the gods washed their hands before they conducted rituals or sat down to eat. Thorough hand washing, including the recitation of spells, was a minimum requirement for all spiritual and medical activity. Let's try this: a spell for hand washing.

Incantation.

Your hands are washed, your hands are washed-

your hands are washed, you are pure,
your hands are washed, you are clean,

your hands are washed, you are clean,
your hands are washed, you are pure,

since he whose hands are washed is pure,
since he whose hands are washed is clean,

since he whose hands are washed is clean, since he whose hands are washed is pure,

may this man, the son of his god, be pure like heaven,

be clean like the earth, be clean like the core (=heart, consciousness*) of heaven,*

may the evil tongue stand aside.

(*Šurpu Series*, IX, 88-95, translation Reiner). This simple spell contains a lot. It was added to the *Šurpu Series* almost as an afterthought. The language is Sumerian, and when we consider that medical practitioners were happily washing their hands at least since the early third millennium BCE, we might be facing a ritual that is older than Stonehenge and the pyramids. It is easy to learn, suits itself to singing and chanting and turns a simple act into a ritual of positive thinking. With a ditty like this, soaping and washing are fun. It also ensures that the hand washing lasted long enough to disinfect the hands thoroughly. I suggest you give this a try. Adapt it to your needs and liking. And consider just what makes heaven, earth and the core of heaven clean and pure.

This world is a very good place, and we, just like the gods An (Heaven), Ki (Earth), and ša, the heart, core, centre, inside and consciousness of Heaven, are essentially clean and pure. For some people this is very hard to acknowledge. It's so easy to forget that the essential self we share with everyone and everything is clean and pure, and that we are all parts of the great play of pure unlimited consciousness. So give yourself time. Sit down, relax and spread a great big smile through your body. Let it emerge from your belly, let it grow and fill you to the rim. Envelop yourself in a radiance of sheer happiness. Now meditate: 'I am clean, I am pure: pure like Heaven, pure like Earth, pure like the heart of Heaven. I am pure like X (fill in name/s of personal deities).' Use a confident voice. Make it sound friendly and happy. Relax into it. Breathe it in and out. And imagine that all the worries and troubles that encase your awareness break to fragments, flow down your body and disappear in the deep. Make it a big vision. Make it colourful and bright. Make it pulse with sheer awareness and joy.

Religion can and should improve hygiene. Shaving, washing and bathing ensured that the Mesopotamian doctor was cleaner than most of his European colleagues up to the late nineteenth century. Women who had their children with the help of a medical practitioner died twice as often as those who were aided by midwives! In 1861, after years of careful experiment, Dr. Ignaz P. Semmelweis announced that child-bed fever could be avoided. In his opinion, doctors carried *cadaverous particles* on their hands, which could be eliminated by washing them with calcium hydrochloride. His colleagues laughed their heads off. Semmelweis became depressive and turned to drink. He abused his colleagues as *ignorant murderers.* Before long, he was confined to an asylum. The guards beat him up, put him in a straightjacket and locked him in a dark room. It killed him. Semmelweis died of gangrenous poisoning, in 1865, aged 47. It took many years before hand-washing became the rule. As Ban-Barak (2008:133) pointed out, water and soap have saved more lives than any wonder medicine. We ought to applaud the Sumerian healers. They were more than four thousand years ahead of European medicine.

Our Sumerian physician used more than minerals. His 'textbook' prescribes salves, filtrates and fluids for internal use. It is even possible that enemas were administered with a tube. They certainly were by the Old Babylonian period. The medicines were fortified with milk, snake skin and turtle shell. Kramer cites medical plants, such as cassia, myrtle, asafoetida, thyme, willow, pear, fir, fig and date. Here, things are, as in so many plant spells, a little uncertain: many Mesopotamian plants are only identified with relative certainty, and translations depend on scholarly consensus. It would be tempting to list the healing properties of these plants. Myrtle (Myrtus communis) is excellent to treat bronchial diseases. For the same reason, and as a sedative, an aphrodisiac and perhaps as a psychoactive substance, asafoetida is used in Near Eastern and Indian medicine. Willow bark is a useful painkiller; oil of thyme among the strongest disinfectants in the plant world. Fir trees, like many conifers, provide resins that are useful to cure lung diseases and to disinfect spaces by fumigation; dates can be a mild laxative. Good evidence that our early Sumerian physicians had a range of useful plants available. It doesn't mean that they used everything as we would. When I was researching the Vedic wonderplant *Withania somnifera* I was amazed that the hymns and spells of the *Atharva Veda* did not mention ingestion. The plant was venerated as a powerful spirit and was worn as a talisman! Or was it? Maybe the hymn was just a little misleading and the doctors of old India kept the secret of oral application to themselves. In a similar way, our Mesopotamian doctors frequently strung up useful plants and other items and made the patient wear them. Salves were made by mixing pulverised drugs with expensive imported olive and cedar oil, and fortified with an unknown sort of wine. One such salve was made by blending pulverised river clay with 'sea-oil', water and honey. Decoctions were made by boiling the ingredients in water, to which alkali and salts were added. The fluid was rubbed on the afflicted part of the body, which was subsequently oiled. When the drug was used internally, the ingredients were usually added to beer or, in one case, to a mixture of beer, milk and 'river-oil', maybe bitumen floating on the river, as Herodotus mentions. All in all, our first medical 'textbook' shows that many substances were used, most of them in a refined and purified form. In all likeliness, several were not applied for sensible medical reasons but also, or solely, for their magical power. However, and this is an amazing fact, our first 'textbook' does not contain a single reference to sacrifices, deities, spirits, purification rituals or religious observances. The brief text is an astonishingly rational document.

Diagnosis and Treatment

Mesopotamian medicine went a long way after our unknown Sumerian doctor inscribed his helpful little tablet. The Babylonian physicians made catalogues which related symptoms to diseases, pharmaceutical and magical materials, and recommended cures that ranged from drugs to talismans, from surgery to exorcisms and rituals of purification. When it came to diagnosis, our early doctors were excellent observers. Sure, they attributed causes that modern physicians would laugh about to diseases, and their repertoire of drugs and treatments was much smaller than ours, but they certainly made an effort to define hundreds of specific diseases. You only have to look into Scurlock and Andersen's magnificent study to be amazed how many diseases can be identified.

Doctors used many medical treatments, involving roots, leaves, blossoms, ashes and bark of plants and trees, as well as minerals and animal substances, many of them in purified and refined form. Their medicines were applied as salves and ointments, they made poultices, performed simple surgical operations, lacerated pustules, set bones, performed trepanation, prepared alcohol-based drugs for internal use and, by the start of the Neo-Assyrian period, when our records become more detailed, used fumigations to disinfect rooms, had the patient inhale smouldering herbs and resins and applied enemas. Assyrian doctors at the court ensured that newly-acquired eunuchs were properly castrated, or did the job themselves. In the field of chemistry, Mesopotamian doctors used crucibles, a range of highly varied ovens, filtering and extraction apparatus. Distillation in double rimmed earthenware pots was known by 3000 BCE; the drip bottle by 1400 BCE (Saggs, 1966:472).

By the first millennium BCE, Neo-Assyrian doctors knew how to make sulphuric and (perhaps) a mixture of nitric and hydrochloric acids, a wide range of salts, ammoniac, copper sulphate, mercury, sulphur, sulphide cinnabar, compounds of arsenic plus various metal-based drugs. The prescriptions and handbooks were highly detailed. Physicians knew that blood flows (but not that it circulates), they felt for the pulse and examined their patients very thoroughly. Saggs (1966:461-466) cites texts which were compiled during the first millennium, but may contain material dating from the middle of the second millennium BCE. Assyrian doctors had a much greater medical knowledge than their predecessors. The range of drugs had grown considerably, and so had the availability of unusual treatments. Enemas were popular among the Assyrians, and so was the infusion of medicine by tube. Saggs (1984:229) offers a cheerful treatment, and kids, you should not try this at home. One favourite to cure sexual diseases (or impotence?) was to take a sea shell called 'she-donkey's vulva' and to pulverise it. With a name like that, we are definitely in the realm of sympathetic magic. The finely ground powder was blown into the penis with a tube, or drunk in beer. Another essential was proper bandaging. Doctors then as now used bandages to protect wounds or set bones, but the Assyrian asû went quite a bit beyond such sensible ideas. In their opinion, bandages were perfect to hold magical herbs or amulets in place; hence, patients were bandaged in all sorts of places. Indeed, there was even a special tradition to bandaging. Saggs (1984:230) cites a case where an Assyrian king was hurt on a campaign in enemy territory. Someone bandaged him, but when his physician arrived, the bandages were immediately changed. The asû loudly complained that this foreign technique *is not fitting for the Land of Assyria* and added: *Let us maintain the norms which the gods themselves gave to the king my Lord.*

Let's have some examples. Typical cures for ear diseases were fumigations, applications of goose fat or pomegranate juice, using a pipette or a wad of soaked wool. Ringing ears and tinnitus were assumed to be the work of ghosts and required ritual offerings and prayer (Biggs in RlA '*Ohr*'). Foot diseases were common. Many were assumed to be everyday troubles. But they could also be the result of ritual pollution, witchcraft or the wrath of a deity. Some were thought to have descended from the stars. The cures were practical. They included massage, baths, laceration of ulcers, and the application of salves. Medical plants were crushed and dissolved in water, beer, rose-water, milk, and a wide range of fats and oils (Labat in RlA '*Fußkrankheiten*'). In a similar way the diagnosis of ulcers combined rational and magical ideas. When a patient suffered from a rush of blood to the lung which turned into an ulcer, it might be caused by the *hand of a ghost*. Or it resulted from injury or the excessive (?) riding of a chariot. Pustules were diagnosed by size and colour (black, white, red, yellow) and identified with the 'hand' (=influence, punishment) of the gods Sîn, Šamaš and Ištar. They were treated with chamomile, rosewater, herbs, salves and wrapped in bandages. Abscesses were carefully opened with a scalpel, cleaned, scraped to the bone, disinfected and bandaged. By contrast, the only cure for scabies was a talismanic stone (Labat in RlA '*Geschwulst*'). Lung diseases were cured with inhalation, poultices or with herbal drugs taken orally in beer, water or wine. Unlike Egyptian doctors, who treated all lung diseases with a single herb, the

Mesopotamian doctors used sumach seeds, thyme, castor beans, cress, asafoetida, cypress oil, elder, sagapenum and several plants that cannot be identified (McEwan in RlA *'Lunge'*). For their time, the asû were exceptionally successful. We can't blame them for mixing magic with science: doctors used everything that works. They lived in overpopulated cities where contagious diseases got around and made do with a small range of drugs and treatments. Unlike, say, the doctors of medieval Europe they knew the limits of their art, and refrained from serious surgery. Their patients were all the better for it. Nor should we blame them for prescribing fantastic medicines. Our modern physicians ain't much better.

All the same, the asû were not forerunners of modern scientific thought. As far as we know, they did not bother to develop medical theory, used no empiric research, and in many cases, simply prescribed the treatments that had been given by the gods and recorded hundreds or thousands of years ago. Anatomical studies on corpses were generally prohibited and most of the animals that an asû could see dissected were sacrificial beasts, which had been chosen for their strength and physical health. In short, the diseases of the inner organs, and indeed what many organs were good for, remained unknown. I am sure that some daring asû experimented, as the number of prescriptions grew over the millennia, but this sort of thing was nothing to mention or to be proud about.

Placebo Medicine

Given such a range of cures I am sure at least some patients survived. On the other hand, many remedies were not used for their medical but for their spiritual qualities; they represented deities and powers, and could be classed as placebos.

Placebos (*'I shall please'*) are inactive substances which are administered to the patient to stimulate belief, increase confidence and encourage self-healing. A placebo acts much like a hypnotic suggestion: it tells the patient that something has been done and things will get better. The patient stops worrying and the deep mind ensures that health improves. Contemporary doctors are not always easy about administering placebos, as their use requires deceit and puts them on a level with those who prescribe bat's vomit and eye of newt. Likewise, patients are generally unhappy if they learn that they have been given dextrose pills or injections of distilled water, no matter how powerfully they worked. Too many people assume that placebos are fake drugs to treat fake maladies, imagined diseases and 'hysteric' afflictions. This is not the case. Contemporary research shows that placebos focus belief, and belief stimulates the healing process. When a patient gets a placebo instead of a painkiller, her or his glands produce the required endorphins. This is not an imagined cure for an imaginary pain; it's a miracle of the body's chemistry. Your body is an alchemical factory that produces a huge range of substances that are more efficient and refined than anything the pharmaceutical industry can offer. The products of your glands make you awake and alert; calm you down, sedate, soothe and tranquilise; shock and upset you; make you feel timid or confident; increase and lower blood pressure; stimulate the brain's 'pleasure centres'; make you feel sad, unhappy, angry, excited, bored, tranquil, joyous, enthusiastic, confused, bedazzled, god-struck, ecstatic or allow you to fall head over heels in love.

In 2012, the German ministry of health officially recommended the prescription of more placebos. I'm glad they saw sense at last. Half of the drugs in any pharmacy are inert. And that's the good part, as they don't produce collateral damage. When modern doctors prescribe counterproductive rubbish like multivitamin tablets, they are no better than Mesopotamian doctors who boiled mating geckos to cure impotence.

We should not deride the azu and asû for prescribing wonder medicines: they did their best to make the patient recover, and usually it must have worked (otherwise, the practice would have died out). To increase the efficiency of their prescriptions, they often (but not always) fortified them with spells, conjurations or appeals to deities. Far from being humbug and superstition, such rituals constitute efficient therapy.

The early doctors were not quite exorcists, and exorcists were not quite doctors, but in a world where the spiritual and material worlds were a functional unity, their activities were often similar, if not identical. It is only the modern, narrow-minded point of view that makes a difference between medicine and magic. In Mesopotamian thought, there was a reason for each disease or accident, and this reason was frequently (but not always) spiritual. In a world where (invisible) microbes and viruses were unknown, it was natural to blame equally invisible spirits, ghosts, demons, deities or evil sorceries and curses. The same applies for accidents and strokes of ill-luck. If you fell from a ladder or got stung by a scorpion, the true reason for the injury was some malignant influence making it happen to YOU. Human beings are story-telling animals and like to have a reason, preferably a simple one, to explain the inexplicable, and to avoid bad things happening again.

Maybe one of your personal deities was angry with you. Maybe you had offended a god, breached a taboo, contaminated yourself or entered what some anthropologists call 'the realm-of-misfortune'. Or maybe, a reason becoming increasingly popular during the first millennium BCE, you had been bewitched or cursed. It could have been a rival, a malevolent neighbour, an enemy, a professional like a wizard or witch, or a religious specialist. In Sumerian belief, the gods, when angered, were likely to punish you personally. Later, in Babylonian times, as von Soden remarks (1994:199) *one finds the idea that the gods have indeed given people over to the demons on account of their sins.*

Meet the Conjurers

In their daily practice, the asû did not always work on their own. Then as now, patients wanted all the help they could get. Sometimes a physician appeared in the company of a **kâlu** or **gala**. These titles have often been translated as 'lamentation priests', which covers only a small part of their activities. I am sure the patients did not pay to hear lamentations at the sickbed. The kâlu or kâlum is basically an incantation priest, an elegist, a master of literature, history, myth, incantation and prayer. Her or his Sumerian original is the gala. In pre-Sargonic accounts, male and female gala accompanied funerals and sang laments. It may remind you of the hired mourners who were so important in classic Chinese funerals. Professional lamenting women, howling and weeping passionately, were common in expensive Sumerian funeral ceremonies, but these, unlike the gala, were not religious specialists and had no spiritual training. Unlike them, the gala were employed by temples and the palace and had a high status. The gala-maḫ (Akkadian: galamāḫu) held an especially high rank. Several appear in Sumerian records as the heads of four major temples in the city-state Lagaš, and in the records of the Ur III period. During the Old Babylonian period their office disappeared. To become a gala you had to undergo a lot of training. The male and female galas were experts in Akkadian, Sumerian and the women's language Emesal, they could recite and explain difficult old religious literature, tell myths and sing hymns according to traditional melodies. These activities made them attractive to the patient, who lay ailing and bored in his sickbed. In many cases, they also arranged the chanting during a given ritual, and supervised the musicians, i.e. the female nārtu and the male nāru. Often (but not always), kâlu were influential people; some did their business in several temples at once. The presence of an extra kâlu in the company of a doctor was not exactly cheap. In the first millennium BCE, the kâlu also accompanied āšipu (conjurers, exorcists) in temple rituals and there are some kâlu on record who were specialists for astronomy and astrology. It is an interesting detail that unlike so many doctors and members of the priesthood, not every gala and kâlu bothered to shave his head.

Another person who might cooperate or compete with the asû was a magician, conjurer or sorcerer.

In many ways, the activity of the azu/asû overlapped with this class of ritual specialists, who are called **mašmaššu** and **āšipu** or (female) **āšiptu**. You met them earlier: we owe so much conjuration literature to them. The former two professionals are well-documented. The āšipu are easy to research, especially during the first millennium BCE, when many of them held important jobs in temples, where they acted as exorcists, scholars, scribes and astrologers. Earlier periods are more difficult. The temple of Aššur had a regular staff of āšipu. Elsewhere it seems that the temples only employed āšipu when they were needed. The āšipu were not confined to a specific cult and usually they were not part of the official temple hierarchy. Some did jobs for private clients; others were employed by the palace. A few had an exceptionally high status and acted as advisors for kings. Several āšipu families are on record, where the office was passed from father to son/s for generations. One strange aspect of their craft is that while many āšipu owned excellent libraries, and appear quite frequently in conjuration literature, they are very rare in official documents, letters and historical accounts before the first millennium BCE.

The female āšiptu are much harder to trace. At the present time there are only two indications that they existed at all. One of them is the fact that a few goddesses were praised as āšiptus. One of them is Ningirima, another Gula; both are famous for magic and healing. Thanks to Gula's magical skills, her very close relation Ninisina and the goddess she was identified with, Bau/Baba, also came to be known as āšiptus. That, in itself, is not much of a proof. However, āšiptus also appear in first-millennium literature. As you will recall, the *Maqlû Series* lists many dangerous women. Among them appear āšiptus, female conjurer/healer/priestesses (III, 42). Their activity is not defined, but they are in the company of many attestable female ritualists. Evidently, to the clients, the notion of female conjurer/exorcists was neither fantastic nor unlikely. I do wonder how these women were selected and trained. Were there āšipus who passed the family profession to a gifted daughter? Were they affiliated to temples or did they prefer private practice?

In the company of the āšiptus appears the **eššeb/putu**, a type of ecstatic conjuration-priestess (*Maqlû Series* III, 42; IV, 127; VI, 21; VIII, 74). Their male counterparts, the eššepu appear in the line: *without you, (Marduk), the āšipu, the eššepu (and) the mušlaḫḫu (*snake/dragon conjurer priest*) do not walk about the street.* (KAR 26.25, in Henshaw 1994:109). It indicates that all three were, at least occasionally, related to the cult of Marduk. Very little is recorded about the eššeb/putu. According to Henshaw (ibid: 164-165) they had *a function as an ecstatic, a witch and a fertility cult official, the relative emphases of these yet to be determined.* It's just our bad luck that the only detail recorded about them is that they wore a special hairdo. It relates them to other priestesses and ritualists wearing their hair in an unusual fashion, like the kezertu, and indicates that their activity was not a secret one. That being said, we can only hope for further textual evidence to emerge.

Let's return to the āšipu and mašmaššu. Their functions are not easy to tell apart: in fact, after a hundred years of research the distinction still cannot be made. Saggs (1966:346) proposed that the āšipu was occasionally the assistant of the mašmaššu, or a specialised counterpart. The **mašmaššu** (from Sumerian MAŠ.MAŠ) had a singular function in some temples, and performed purification rituals before ceremonies. In several rituals, he acted in the company of the king, or performed offerings in his presence. Enki/Ea and his son Asarluḫi, Utu/Šamaš, and Ningublaga, just like the goddess of magic and purification, Ningirima, were praised as the mašmaššus of the gods. The first recorded MAŠ.MAŠ was busy in the last Sumerian period, Ur III, with purification rituals in the fields. In Old Babylonian texts, the mašmaššu frequently purified the temples prior to ceremonies and offering rituals. It would be nice to know how. A mašmaššu *who purifies heaven, who washes the earth* appears in a Neo-Assyrian ritual. On a less exalted level, we encounter a mašmaššu, an asû and a bārû (haruspex, omen reader) who cooperate in a ritual to ensure good business for a tavern (Henshaw 1994:149). Some mašmaššu were gifted authors and philosophers; just look into the *Babylonian Theodicy*, composed by a mašmaššu who tackled the major problems of theology. Apart from this, both sorts of ritualists tended to visit sick people, and performed exorcisms, purifications and conjurations. They fumigated rooms, prepared replacement sacrifices, made talismans and redecorated rooms to expel evil influences. One favourite was the use of sacred water to bathe or drench the patient. Besides such activities, which might be loosely classed as 'religious' or 'magical', they also used medical treatments. When they fumigated, burned incense offerings, prescribed diets, potions, enemas and anointed the patient with salves, they used methods that would be called medical in our days. In a passage translated by Falkenstein (Henshaw 1994:145) a mašmaššu states: *When I draw near the sick man, enter his house, put my hand on his head, learn the sinews of his limbs, recite the incantation of Eridu over him, recite the incantation over the sick man...* The same words could also describe the activities of an āšipu or an asû. All three professions made sickbed visits and used spells, drugs, massages, fumigation, talismans and offerings. It has provoked scholarly discussions. Some academics proposed that the activities of the doctors were more 'rational' or 'scientific' than those of the mašmaššu and āšipu. It didn't really work. Doctors used magic (āšiputu) and magicians used medicine (asûtu) to make the patient happy. Rich people often employed both professions, and occasionally asû and āšipu worked together. Joan Oates suspects that after the Old Babylonian period, the asû were replaced to some extent by the āšipu. Indeed, late medical tablets list omens, symptoms, prescriptions, modes of application, the patient's chance to recover plus divine or demonic influences (if any) that look much like the earlier textbooks of the asû, but address the āšipu. The replacement was not total, however, as both professions were alive and well in the first millennium BCE. Something similar happened regarding the āšipu and the mašmaššu. In many texts, we can't tell the difference between them. Maybe both words were synonyms. Perhaps they were, in some places and times, and not in others. We have to remember that the functions and status of these professions kept changing. In Neo-Assyrian and Neo-Babylonian times, āšipu became increasingly influential and gobbled up all sorts of jobs that used to belong to other people, including astronomy, astrology and the keeping of historical records.

The Training of a Conjurer

Luckily, there is a catalogue (KAR 44) telling us what an āšipu or mašmaššu had to learn. Parts of it appear in Henshaw 1994:146-147. Even the abridged version is too long to be quoted here. It should suffice to say that the budding āšipu/mašmaššu had to be literate and skilled in deciphering difficult texts, some of them written in code or employing deliberately difficult cuneiform signs. He (and presumably, she) had to be familiar with a wide range of songs, prayers and religious texts. The rituals included mouth-washing, sprinkling, purification, ceremonies for various months, consecration of water, exorcisms of di'u spirits, Lilītu, Lilû, the asakku, Samana, alû, and the ability to *make angry demons good*, an art that is woefully neglected by occultists of our time. Lamaštu rituals are mentioned twice: the art of seizing her, and that of treating a pregnant woman oppressed by Lamaštu. Banishments were aimed against hostile spirits, locusts, malevolent sorcery, witchcraft, curses, spells, the evil eye and similar *angry magic*. Then there was healing; our ritualist had to be competent in the treatment of head and neck diseases, pregnancy disorders, afflictions of eyes and ears, heart (=mind), lungs, stomach, ulcers, lacking and excessive menstruation (the Samana diseases), problems of legs and feet, lameness, paralysis, sinew and muscle troubles and ensure *the lifting of the heart* (sexual health), plus incantations and treatments *against sicknesses of any kind.* The āšipu/mašmaššu learned to treat snakebite, scorpion stings and the bite of dogs. Healing was not restricted to people: purifying domestic animals was an important point in the program. Another basic was a thorough knowledge of chemistry and healing plants, plus the ability to prepare medication and apply it. For diagnosis, textbooks were studied and in all likelihood memorised. But our healer/magicians also had to learn the art of understanding omens from stars, animals, wild beasts and so on, and the skill of negating the ill effects of bad portents and fateful events. Other requirements were knowledge of sacred places (?) and the ability to perform rituals for cities, houses, fields, gardens, rivers and so on. Extensive rituals, many of them taking more than a day, like *Lamaštu, Maqlû* and *Šurpu,* were standard procedures. Some of them were in old Akkadian, Sumerian, and Emesal (the Sumerian women's dialect) requiring extensive language skills. The ritual schedule involved ceremonies and offerings to major deities like Anu, Enlil, Nisaba and Šamaš, but I'm sure you guessed that already. That being said I can only add that this list is incomplete. It contains treatments of many diseases that have not been identified and a wide range of ceremonies and activities that defy our understanding.

In addition to conjurers, a patient might consult a whole series of diviners (bārû), who sought signs in the liver, intestines and inner organs of sacrificial animals; observed the flame in the patient's bedroom, or the smoke rising to the ceiling. Some diagnosed by the omens they saw on the way to the patient, others provided real entertainment and evoked a spirit or deity to reveal the cure, who may well have spoken through the mouth of a medium. Female and male trance mediums were obsessed by a deity, and gave spiritual advice. Some mediums were attached to temples and fulfilled priestly offices, others seem to have worked freelance. A few were so enthusiastic that they went into fits and prophesied in public. The *eyes and ears of the king,* (the secret service) paid much attention to them and saw to it that their prophecies remained positive, or else.

I know, life is confusing. Instead of a few simple specialists we encounter a lot of ritualists, healers, scholars, diviners and crazy spirit mediums with overlapping functions. Apart from mucking around in temples and palaces, they liked to infest the sickroom. We know they existed, and are happy to have some glimpse into what they did. Compared to what we know about, say early Indian, Chinese or European medicine and magic, it's a lot. Considering that the material comes from dozens of distinct city-states and ethnic groups and spans several thousand years it's disappointingly fragmentary. The written record is confined to official documents, textbooks, letters, business and temple documents: our healers are acting in a rich man's world. What happened to the poorer classes of society? Were there doctors and conjurers catering to the needs of farmers, fishers and artisans? Many prescriptions, no matter whether we would call them magical or medical, involve rare and costly ingredients; indicating that poor people were either treated with different methods, or even by an entirely different group of specialists. Herodotus, for what it's worth, claims that in his time (the fifth C. BCE), the Babylonians had no doctors. That, of course, was way off the mark. Instead of consulting medical practitioners, he claimed, people helped each other. *Sick people are carried to the market; as they (*the Babylonians*) have no doctors. People who pass by offer good advice to the patients, as do people who have suffered from the same ailments and those who have seen others suffering from them (...).To walk past the patient in silence is illegal. Everybody has to enquire what sort of disease he has* (I, 197). This might be great stuff for comedy (as is much of Herodotus), but maybe it's also the future of public health, in these uncertain times.

Lamaštu Diseases

Let us begin with fever. Several early researchers have tried to class Lamaštu as a 'fever demoness', a badly paid job with little status and no perks.

Here's a quote from A.R. George (1991:137-138) from the handbook *Sa.Gig* in RA 85:

If he (the āšipu) sees a dappled ox:
that patient is afflicted by the demon Lamaštu; (or) a curse; he will die soon.
The commentary to the omen:
Lamaštu (dDimme): Fever (ummu), daughter of Anu;
Me: fever (ummu); he will die of her (curse (nam-érim)),
Nam: death,
Erim: wicked [...]:
he will die (the death of the) wicked;
gùn: 'to be dappled',
as was said '(her kidneys) are spotted like a leopard'

The handbook also cites the names of Lamaštu's relations and associates: Giš-hur, Sag-ba, Sag-dingir, (Mu-dingir-ra = *Engraving*), *Curse*, *River-ordeal*, and *By the Life of the Gods*.

If we follow this interpretation, Lamaštu is basically in charge of fever. Some scholars have attempted to interpret the Seven Names of Lamaštu in this way: the Sword that Splits the Skull is supposed to mean headache, the Wood Kindler is fever, and the Wild Countenance is the face of the patient (facing the doctor's bill?). They did not manage to find diseases for name one, two, six and seven. Truth to tell, they underestimated her and made the situation far too simple. The doctors and conjurers diagnosed several varieties of fever. The word ummu describes overheating, hypothermia and steady fever. Li'bu refers to irregular fits of heat and to a disease called mountain fever. Both are accompanied by their counterpart ḫurbašu: shivering, coldness. The three are the *doorkeepers of the Underworld*. Other types of fever are mitḫur (a steady fever), išatātu (fever heat, regular fever), šanû (second fever, i.e. a fever twice a day or every second day), tiḫu/di'u, a fever and lethal spirit that was earlier classed as 'headache', and is nowadays identified as malaria or smallpox. There is one text (tablet P, Thompson *Devils* II, 88) where di'u is called a Lamaštu, among a whole series of di'u spells that explicitly don't. The rarity of the item points to a scribal error, poetic freedom or an extremely obscure tradition.

Several fevers were spirits, others indicated the 'hand' of an angry deity, like Ištar, the influence of Lamaštu or the asakku, or they were simply side effects of a disease and unrelated to spiritual agencies.

Köcher associated Lamaštu with liver- and gall related diseases by the simple trick of identifying her with Pašittu. Köcher, 1949, page 10, quotes three inscriptions that allegedly identify 'Lamaštu's hand' as biliary colics. CT.17.pl.25,5 says that Pašittu's biliary colic does not allow (the patient) to fall asleep or to find good sleep. In the Old Babylonian inscription (Leiden 1000, Vs.12) the same identification occurs. And KAR.233, 8f says:

Lamaštu, children of Anu: the gallbladder in the (state of the) biliary colic, the Head-disease, the Di'u (disease)....

Here, Lamaštu is plural; *'children'* is not a scribal error. It might recall an old and badly documented tradition (CT.16.pl.13, Kol. II, 65ff, quoted in Köcher 1949:11): there used to be seven DIM.ME/Lamaštu and seven Evil Fever Lamaštu. Maybe these seven reappear in a Babylonian conjuration against the seven (unidentified) sorceresses who threaten pregnancy (AO. 6473). Seven witches and their seven female opponents appear in *Maqlû*, VI, 79. My question is whether we should read the line as *'Lamaštu and the Children of Anu'*. As Anu had plenty of children, the ailments could belong to any of them.

Let's take a closer look at Lamaštu's connection with bile and jaundice. The Akkadian word for gall is martu, meaning the *bitter one*. It's a pun. 'Daughter of Anu' (mārat Anu) sounds much like 'gall (martu) of Anu'. You could also read it as *the bitter one of heaven*. Or maybe the *Bitterness of Heaven*. That's one connection. Another one are the lines: *The Fifth: Goddess Whose Face* (or: *Expression) is Yellow-Green* (LS I, 5) and: *her cheeks are pale like yellow-*

green ochre (LS II, 37). Some scholars thought this line referred to the patient, who might suffer from jaundice. Others believed it refers to the goddess. And that's exactly as far as it goes.

One medical text glosses *Pašittu (disease) of the spittle = Pašittu containing gall.* There are several references to Pašittu diseases. In fact, we know more about her diseases than about her. To summarise them: the Pašittu disease is characterised by inner heat and stomach pains. Typically, the patient vomits bile. Pašittu's biliary colic is not the sort of stomach upset that comes from eating too much fat. Fat was a delicacy and most people couldn't afford it. Lean meat was given to slave girls, while the lord and lady of a household kept the fat stuff for themselves. The Mesopotamians were thinking of a disease that was caused by 'worms' in the stomach and characterised by strong fever; the patient vomited large amounts of bile and literally wasted away. The disease was treated with laxatives, herbs, turpentine, salt, aloe, and mountain-caraway. However, as the physicians knew, it was usually fatal.

Jaundice was frequently attributed to a goddess who tends to accompany Lamaštu: Aḫḫazu (*the Seizer*). Like Pašittu, we know next to nothing about her. *If the Aḫḫazu disease has entered the body of a person and the eyes are red like copper, when his insides churn and food and drink are expelled: this man will die after long suffering* (Labat in RlA: *'Galle'*). The physicians tried enemas, but they were aware that recovery was unlikely, and may have insisted on advance payment.

Köcher also assumed that Lamaštu castrates men, holds back the sperm, brings on the sufferings of old age and kills infants in the womb. Other scholars added sunstroke, heat stroke and typhoid fever to the list. But things are not that simple. As you saw, the passages hinting at such matters are often very damaged, fragmentary and open to interpretation. They do not reflect what Lamaštu is and does but what a given scholar assumes she is capable of. It's no surprise that G. Remler (1991), cited by Farber (2007:140), proposes that Lamaštu is a demonization of the 'otherness' of femininity and female sexuality in a male-dominated society. Maybe Remler was thinking of misogynistic Neo-Assyrians, but the remark applies to some scholars. While her relation to most diseases is by no means certain, the *Lamaštu Series* and the earlier Lamaštu spells only mention fever, shuddering, freezing, and the death of infants and elders. Less dependable are the passages that might indicate a miscarriage. One example for an unreliable 'Lamaštu' disease was translated by R. Labet (*Traité Akadien de diagnostics et prognostics médicaux,* 1951), in Stol & Wiggermann, page 236-237:

If his head gives him continual complaints, while at the same time the fever [...]

And his sickness recedes, if he gets dizzy and his eyesight diminishes,

If he loses his mind and wanders about aimlessly: (it looks) as if he were grasped by a ghost,

But (in fact) L [...] on him.

It looks so simple but it isn't. Similar symptoms are attributed to the wind and storm deities, and could be caused by Lilû, Lilītu or the Ardat Lilî. We can't be sure the passage relates to Lamaštu at all. I guess the major question is whether we identify Lamaštu as an epitome of evil and destructiveness or consider her an unpopular specialist doing a dirty job on divine request. At this point, the discussion is quite lively. Farber (2007:141, 143) proposed a different interpretation. In his opinion, Lamaštu diseases are characterised by being unspecific. We can be sure the goddess raises and lowers body temperature, but this is hardly a meaningful diagnosis, given that the doctors knew dozens of diseases involving such symptoms, and attributed them to a wide range of causes, spirits and deities. Farber argued that Lamaštu is specialised, in that she attacks the infant and not the mother. The Mesopotamian doctors listed a wide range of baby ailments, involving shivering, wriggling, incessant crying, jaundice, and diarrhoea, lack of appetite, bloated belly, flatulence and rash ('rose spots'). Of the many specific baby diseases, Lamaštu seems to be in charge of the unspecific ones where no proper symptoms are evident. One example might be SIDS, the Sudden Infant Death Syndrome. Farber argued that there is no firm evidence that relates Lamaštu to stillbirth or to typhoid fever. He dismissed Köcher's examples by pointing out that biliary colic is not really attributed to Lamaštu but to Pašittu. Let us take a closer look at Farber's idea that the typical disease associated with Lamaštu is the SIDS, the Sudden Infant Death Syndrome. A growing number of medical experts are complaining that SIDS is not a disease but a symptom. SIDS means that the reason for death remains unknown. You might as well say the baby died of death. As it turns out, a careful autopsy of SIDS cases in Britain and Germany indicated that in at least 5-10% of all cases, the baby died from internal injuries. It had been shaken violently, been picked up without supporting the head properly or showed evidence of suffocation with a soft object. In short, some SIDS cases turn out to be victims of accidents or should be classed as homicides. It's understandable. Young parents, suffering from lack of sleep, exhaustion, lack of privacy, overwork, burnout and all sorts of worries, are not really in their normal state of mind. They have the occasional desire to drop everything, including the baby and the partner, and to run away screaming. Is the baby-slaying Lamaštu a personification of the parental urge to harm their offspring? Among 'occult people', I met several young couples, pregnant and deeply worried, who were scared of Lilith. They projected their own fears and violent instincts, plus a large portion of guilt for having such emotions, on the deity. It's not Lilith but the parents who are a threat to the baby. Lilith says she wasn't there, did not know about anything and couldn't have stopped it. She recommends that young parents get really close to baby-threatening deities. Your inner horrors reflect what you might be capable of. And what you can avoid, once you realise that the real threat is not a terrifying deity but yourself.

Heat and Shuddering: a Magical Interpretation

As I'm sure you know, fever is not a disease but its cure. Body temperature goes up so that viruses cease to breed and are hopefully destroyed. Most viruses can only act within a narrow range of body temperature. Heating and cooling your system don't feel nice, but they sure interfere with virus procreation. Then, at 40° Celsius proteins start to congeal. If the virus is too strong and the patient too weak, fever can kill. However, it simply accomplishes what the disease would have done anyway. In our day and age, Lamaštu should be reconsidered as a fierce but dedicated healer. Think of the symptoms associated with her. We could consider heat and shivering as side effects of a disease. We can also understand them from a magical point of view: both experiences are very common in shamanism, obsession and similar activities. Cold and heat feature prominently in initiation rites. They also have a powerful effect on your consciousness. When you travel to a hot climate or sit in a sauna, the high temperature affects your awareness: your parasympathetic nervous system makes you slow, relaxed and soft, to keep the body temperature down. And when it gets really cold, the fresh air invigorates, or, to put it medically, your sympathetic nervous system makes you active, alert and restless, and raises your body temperature. Heating and cooling are engineered by your sympathetic and parasympathetic nervous systems. Say thank you! to your hypothalamus. When Lamaštu brings on fire and frost, she is activating different consciousness states.

The Hands of the Gods

Lamaštu is not the only deity who inflicted diseases. Mesopotamian deities were not supposed to be nice. Sure, they generally had a benevolent nature and did their best for their cities, temples and people, animals and the scenery around them. Some liked their worshippers and did much to ensure success, luck, expertise and income. But when they were angered, insulted, offended or neglected, they could be more deadly than ghosts, spirits or the Evil Seven. It could happen on a large scale, as when one (city-) god destroyed the city of another. It could even be overwhelmingly cataclysmic, as when Enlil had a bad-air day, was fed up with the noise of mankind and decided to finish things with a flood. That's a scale of destruction your ordinary everyday evil spirit simply couldn't dream of. Let's look into Saggs' (1966) examples from a diagnostic handbook compiled during the first millennium. Several, but not all diseases were attributed to the *'hand'* of some god.

Here are a few:

-if the patient has swollen hands and feet, a throbbing neck and his head keeps falling, the Ardad Lilî (Maiden of Lilû) has seized him.

-A fever of four or five days with plenty of sweat indicates the presence of Aḫḫazu (the Seizer), a close friend of Lamaštu.

-When the patient is shaken by grief and desire, has a high temperature, *coughs up his stomach* (vomits?) and cannot comprehend the things he sees, this is caused by a ghost.

-A patient with unsteady limbs, tinnitus, speechless, suffering from sleepiness is afflicted by the alû.

-A patient who has convulsions and collapses after having bathed in the river was attacked by a rabiṣu (agent/lurker).

-A man suffering from a headache on one side of his head, crying *'My skull! My skull!'* has been stricken by Adad, a god of weather, storm and divination.

-A patient who is covered all over by black pustules or who has a red body was wounded by the sun god Šamaš.

-If blood seeps out of the patient's penis, its Šamaš' doing, and the patient is sure to die.

-epilepsy is often caused by moon god Sîn or by Ištar, and the prescribed medicine contains sperm, sea fruit(?), a mouse living in the cane brake, the point of the ear of a black dog, hair of a black ass, the tail of a black dog, and the hair of a virgin kid, black & white. If this did not work, Šamaš was blamed. In this case, the prescription contains: root of the caper bush, roots of a thorn bush, fennel root, henbane seeds, a rag stained with menstrual blood, euphorbia and the hide of a virgin kid. Compare them to the items used in Lamaštu spells.

-When a patient has white skin but is covered with red pustules, he has been *attacked* by the moon god Sîn while having fun with a woman in bed.

-A patient who grinds his teeth and has shaking hands and feet was punished by Sîn.

-A patient who twists the head to the left, stretches his arms and legs, opens his eyes wide, drools and doesn't know himself was maimed by Sîn.

-A patient who has been badly sick for five or ten days without fever was stricken by Sîn.

-When the door to the patient's chamber creaks *like a lion*, the sufferer has offended his personal deity and will eventually die.

- When the patient has a swollen face and does not hear, his personal deity has its hand on him, and death is certain.

-When the penis of the patient is covered in sores and the testicles are swollen, the high priestess of the personal deity is responsible.

-When the toes and fingers of the patient are cramped and contracted, so that they cannot be opened for five, ten, fifteen or twenty days, it is Ištar's influence. However, the patient may recover.

-When a patient suffers from a burning stomach and penis, arms, feet and belly, is feverish and nauseous, he has contracted a venereal disease, courtesy of Ištar.

Scurlock and Andersen (2005) give more examples of the 'Hand'.

The Hand of Ištar shows itself when the patient suffers from arthritis in hands, feet, hips, when gonococcal urethritis develops into gonococcal arthritis. When the patient has been stabbed in battle, the diagnosis is Hand of Dilbat (=Ištar). Like Lamaštu, Ištar is famous for causing fever.

The Hand of Šamaš tends to strike people who have broken a vow or a law. It can appear as scales, psoriasis and psoriatic arthritis, involving stiff feet, hands, neck, hips and so on.

Gula, usually celebrated as a goddess of healing, may send a dog to bite a person. If you are lucky, it isn't rabid. She is also responsible for cellulitis, painful coccyx and shingles.

The Spawn of Šulpae can cause the floppy baby syndrome. Šulpae (*Brilliant Youth*) is a warrior figure and a husband of Ninḫursag. While she is a goddess of the foothills of the mountains, he is a god of the wild animals living there. Like Marduk, he was occasionally identified with the planet Jupiter. His myths are lost, so we do not know why he is mentioned as a deity of the Underworld, or as a bringer of diseases. In some texts, he is addressed as ilu lemnuum (*Evil God*). His children (spawn?) are Ašgi, Lisin and Lil. The Mesopotamian doctors were aware that the floppy baby syndrome affliction is often fatal, and that they could do nothing about it. In consequence, they declared it to be an omen threatening the destruction of the entire family and counselled that the baby should be thrown into the river. Scurlock and Andersen (2005:332) propose that river might carry the infant *to the netherworld, from which its spirit (zaqīqu) might eventually return for another try at life.* Please stop a moment to consider. If their interpretation is accurate, some Mesopotamians might have believed in **reincarnation**.

Mesopotamian doctors seem to have recommended euthanasia for only two diseases. The floppy baby syndrome is one. The other one was also caused by *Spawn of Šulpae*: Huntingdon's disease. The textbooks diagnosed that the person suffers from contortions of hands and feet, has dark eyes, constricted nostrils, chews on his garment, tears his clothes, raises and twists his limbs, cries and wails incessantly, does not recognise anyone and suffers from memory loss. The physicians could not help the patient; they recommended that he should be buried alive or burned.

Inseminating Yourself

Before a physician or exorcist entered the sickroom, s/he made sure to protect her- or himself with spells. The Mesopotamians were aware that some diseases are contagious; it was a practical knowledge, gained from experience, but it did not make them form a theory on the topic, nor did they put the patient in quarantine. After all, the disease was often (but not always) caused by a god, spirit, or ghost, or by a breach of taboo. Unlike the other people in the household, it placed the patient in a liminal situation between the healthy and dead. The ritualist who dealt with the patient entered the same magical crisis zone. Hence, contact with the offended god, the evil spirit, ritual pollution and contamination were possible. Luckily if we can administer placebos to others we can also do it to ourselves. In fact, it should be easier to make a placebo for oneself. All you need is faith in your own organism, or the gods of healing, the personal deities or whoever in the spirit world is on your side. Ritual formula *SA.GIG, tablet III* specifies that unless you have cast a spell on yourself, you should not approach the patient. To protect himself, the āšipu took care to *impregnate the self with the self.* We'll explore this practically. But let us first consider the textual evidence.

There are several ritual formulas telling us what to do. Antoine Cavigneaux cites the following spell (CT 23, 10-11:26-28 // 4:9-11 (SA.GALLA):

Spell. I impregnate myself,

I impregnate my body, like dog (and) bitch, boar and sow.

Let them (=?) be poured (or: butt one another) on him.

As the plough impregnates the earth, the earth takes its seed,

may my self take in, may it impregnate my self...

In these lines the protective process, linked to a self-fertilisation, is symbolised by two animals which Lamaštu is fond of.

Self-insemination was essential for anyone approaching danger. Here is a passage from *Maqlû Series* (VII, 23-30) that outlines the process in detail. My translation is based on Meier's translation and transcription, slightly amended:

Conjuration:

I inseminate you, my own self,

I inseminate you, my body,

as Sumuqan inseminates his cattle (=the domestic and wild animals*),*

the sheep and the kid, the gazelle and her young, the donkey with her filly,

(as) the seeder-plough inseminates the soil,

(and) the soil receives the seed.

I have placed the conjuration on myself,

I inseminate myself and expel evil,

the sorcery within my body may be expelled

by the great gods.

Self-fertilisation also appears in a line quoted by Cavigneaux. The translation is by C. Wilcke; the inscription is ZA 75, (1985, 204:114-116):

As the river inseminates its banks,

I inseminate myself,

I inseminate my body.

Here, the analogy runs on the fact that the word 'a' could mean water, urine, secretions and semen. The river is holy. It streams through the land just like the healing fluids stream through you. So far we have had self-insemination by the mingled sexual fluids of pigs and dogs, by plough, grain, ground and by sacred river water. Another example. This one is from the mixed end section of *Maqlû Series*, VI, 98-102:

Conjuration: Id (=river & river deity*) is my head, sulphur is my shape.*

My feet are the river whose inside nobody knows.

AN.ḪUL.LA plant is my mouth,

the ocean of the wide [Tiāma]t is m[y] hand.

As Id is my head, sul[phur] my shape...

The rest is fragmentary. This spell encourages the visualisation of a sacred river running between head and feet, while the hands represent the primal world ocean and/or the Milky Way.

Let me recommend an invigorating meditation. Welcome to water magic. Look at the images of Enki/Ea, the god of water, magic, music and science. Some cylinder seals illustrate that the sacred waters are pouring out of his body. The rivers Euphrates and Tigris cascade from his shoulders and fishes are happily leaping in the flood. Here, water is much more than the 'water element'. It is the primal, life-giving, all-shaping substance. To the Sumerians, living in an arid country where rainfall was rare, life would have been impossible without irrigation. In Sumerian hymns, Enki travels over the freshly created earth. Wherever he goes, water starts to flow and vegetation sprouts. He is the epitome of sheer fertility. The waters ceaselessly spurt and cascade out of his body. They drench him, they soak the world, and life begins to pulse and grow and blossom. Keep this image in mind, or better, meet Enki in your daily meditations.

Now for a little cross-cultural excursion. In several religions, practitioners use meditations that involved a form of 'self-insemination'. One of the earliest examples appears in early Daoism, where we encounter immortality seekers, sages and adepts who make it part of their meditation to drench themselves with an imaginary shower. They imagine vitality, life, and awareness as a fluid. It's a typical Chinese idea: even consciousness was assumed to act like a fluid (Hidemi Ishida in Kohn 1989:41-71). In the meditation of the immortality seekers and the early Daoists, vitality and awareness, visualised as a liquid, rise up the back, move to the top of the head, descend down the front of the body in a shower, collect in the belly, sink to the perineum and move up the spine again. The fluids follow what became the du-mei and the ren-mei meridians, and formed what was sometimes called 'the waterwheel'. The earliest reference to such practices comes from the late fifth century BCE, a period when immortality-seeking was a passion of many learned aristocrats and wu 'shamans'. At the time, most of what we call Daoism today had not been invented. One essential text was inscribed on a twelve-sided jade cylinder of uncertain purpose. It may have been a hilt, the knob of a staff or an object of decoration. It has been translated in widely different ways; see for example Harper (in Kohn 2008:14) and Roth 1999:162. Roth offers a transcription; here's an updated version of the text:

To let the qi (here: vitality) *move, let it sink deeply and collect it. When it collects it will increase, and while it increases it sinks deeper. When it has sunk it will calm. When it has calmed it will stabilise. When it has stabilised it will become firm. When it is firm it will sprout. When it sprouts it will grow (up). When it grows it will rise. When it rises it reaches heaven* (the top of the head). *As it rises it reveals the mechanism of Heaven, as it sinks it reveals the mechanism of Earth. Those who cultivate this have a long life. Those who go against it will die.*

A little later, a small textbook of inner alchemy was written. Roth published a translation. The work became one of the key scriptures of early Daoism. It starts with the lines:

The vital essence of all things:
it is this that brings them life.
It generates the five grains below,
and becomes the constellated stars above.
When flowing amid the heavens and the earth,
we call it ghostly and numinous.
When stored within the chest of human beings,
we call them sages.

(Roth: 1999:46). Ghostly is 'gui', meaning ghosts, human or otherwise, most of them unrelated to you and possibly dangerous. The word 'numinous' is actually 'shen', meaning the quality of the divine, awareness, consciousness, deities, ancestors etc. These early texts describe life and vitality as a fluid that rises and sinks between heaven (head) and earth (either the feet or the perineum). Such texts use macrocosmic imagery to inspire microcosmic processes. And of course they were secret knowledge, understood and applied by a dedicated few.

Here is another early example. It crept into Lü Buwei's remarkable work on statesmanship. Master Lü lived from 290-235 BCE; he was the wealthiest merchant of his time and became prime minister of the state of Qin. In his spare time, he invited scholars and sages to live and feast on his premises, asked them to compose little essays, picked the best material from them, and compiled a book on everything a virtuous regent should know. Lü wanted to unite Daoist and Confucian lore with moral teachings and the shiny example of the sage emperors. He was not a very religious person (the gods are rarely mentioned) but he quoted from a wide range of venerable scripture. As his main topic was good government, his remarks on qi are mixed with a commentary on practical statecraft.

The Way of Heaven is round; the Way of the Earth is angular. The sage kings modelled their behaviour on this and have duly appointed lords and servants. How should it be understood that the Way of Heaven is round? The qi (here: vitality, life-force) *rises and descends again, enclosed in a round circuit, without blockage or resistance. This why it is said: the Way of Heaven is round.*

How should it be understood that the way of the earth is angular? All beings differ regarding their species and their shape. They all have specific functions which they cannot exchange among each other. Hence it is said that the Way of the Earth is angular. The sage king must concern himself with the round and the servant dwell in the angular. Where round and angular are not mixed up, the state prospers.

The regular changes of night and day are part of the round way. The passage of the moon through the 28 houses from the Raven to the Virgin (constellations) is part of the round way. The way of the light through the four seasons, up and down, so that everything is properly aligned, belongs to the round way. When beings move they sprout, from sprouting they live, from living they grow, from growth they attain greatness, from greatness ripeness, from ripeness they decay, from decay they die, and return to the earth after death. This belongs to the round way. (*Spring and Autumn of Master Lü*, chapter *Last Month of Spring*, section 5, *The Round Way*, based on Richard Wilhelm's German translation).

By referring to the familiar cycles of nature, Lü hinted at the motion of the qi within the body of the immortality seeker. He was not the only one. A very similar approach was taken by Wei Boyang, who composed an entire book, the *Cantong Qi*, around 142 CE to describe the cyclic motion of qi. Wei was secretive and wrote many cryptic chapters using difficult symbols. His book exists in several versions. One of them contains a remarkably practical statement. Eva Wong (1997) translates the passage:

Cultivate without stopping,

and the mass of energy will move like clouds and rain.

Flowing like spring showers,

dripping like melting ice,

from the head falling down to the feet,

and from there rising up again,

coming and going, swirling the limitless,

and stirring everything throughout.

Those on the path of return know the Dao.

For Wei Boyang's standards, that passage is surprisingly clear. Most of the time he alluded to the circulation of qi (here: vitality), shen (here: consciousness, divinity) and jing (here: sexual secretions, essential fluids) through the body/mind complex of the adept by referring shyly to the cycles of sun and moon, the planets, the seasons, the times of the day, the Five Movers (wuxing) and the hexagrams in the *Yijing*. The text is almost incomprehensible and has made scores of Daoists compose enlightened commentaries. In the fourth century, Daoist alchemist Ge Hong composed the *Baopuzi*, which explains similar meditations. Ge was much clearer than the earlier authors: maybe he realised that it is unnecessary to hide occult techniques, as most people are too uninspired, lazy, or stupid for daily practice anyway. Since then, circulation of qi has been developed into dozens of distinct methods, involving visualisation, ritual, breathing exercises and so on. It is still practised today. In a secluded inner chamber of Hei Long Tan temple near Kunming I saw two beautiful illustrations of the process hanging from the wall. One was a well-known diagram of the 19th century showing the body of the Daoist as an internal landscape full of mountains, rivers and fertile fields (see Lagerwey 1991:132). The other showed Wei Boyang's attributions of moon phases and *Yijing* hexagrams to the Daoist body. Next to them sat a young and very pretty Daoist nun who was happily typing away on her laptop. I guess these meditations will continue for a long time.

A similar technique emerged in India around the end of the first millennium CE in several obscure tantric systems. The magnificent *Kaulajñāna Nirṇaya* (c.11th C) provides detailed visualisations where adepts shower and drench themselves with a white, sperm-like elixir, a red elixir (representing menstrual blood) and a black elixir, to rejuvenate themselves, to gain immunity from disease, magical power and to become attractive to the girls in the neighbourhood and the charming but dangerous Yoginī spirits. Menstrual blood, I should add, was believed to be the female fertile secretion, and a sacrament. Other tantric lineages proposed that the shower of elixir should be pink, as it combines sperm and menstrual blood, and is the essence of all fertility and the very source of all beings and things. A good example appears in the *Śiva Saṁhīta*, 4,1-9. To shower oneself with the essence of pure bliss appears at the end of a popular meditation called *bhūtaśuddhi*. Many descriptions of this process are available, see, for instance, *Lakṣmī Tantra*, chapter 54 (Gupta, 2000:363-365) or *Devī Bhāgavatam*, 11, 8. This yoga uses a process of gradual dissolution. Consciousness moves from one element to the next finer one, until the body of the yogī or yoginī is totally consumed by fire and nothing but ashes remain. Then, a shower of divine elixir revives the practitioner and builds up a purer, stronger and happier self capable of awareness, union and identity with the divine. The shower of divine elixir proved to be such an important method that it became a part of Kuṇḍalinī yoga. What rises as the fire snake descends as a shower of sheer vitality and joy. It was also combined with complicated seed-syllable visualisations and introduced into North

Indian and Himalayan tantric Buddhism (Evans-Wentz, 1967:193-194), where it is called *milking the cow of heaven.* You can find more details and a practical introduction in *Kālī Kaula.*

These meditations may have their roots in ancient Mesopotamia. Please slow down, take a deep breath and consider. This is ancient magic. But words are not enough. Simply sit down, relax, calm your mind, close your eyes and build up the imagination really big and colourful. Think of Enki and see the sacred rivers gushing out of his body and washing down his torso. It's easy: water follows its nature and moves gently. Imagine yourself as Enki, if you like, or as Ningirima. So did Old Babylonian conjurers. Allow the fertilising, fully sentient life-imbuing water to spurt out of your head and to cascade down, within and outside your body. Relax into it with a huge smile. Feel the cells and tissues relax and rejuvenate themselves, feel how sheer vitality cleans, purifies and nourishes you. The brightly shining fluids free you from pain, from sorrow and bad feelings. This is water, this is life and it is so much vaster than you are. Real water is a cosmic force. It is life, it is sex, and it is the sheer lust of being. Hear the trickling brooks, the rushing floods and the gentle dripping. Watch the vegetation sprout and green around you; see animals dance in the utter joy of being alive. As you inseminate yourself you bring blessings to the world. Make this a vision worth having and come home to yourself.

Waters from Eridu

While fertilisation of the self with imaginary secretions is a powerful process, it is not useful for everyone. In Daoism and left-hand-Path Tantra, the basic meditation is done every day for at least a year. It takes a dedicated, well-trained conjurer to use these visualisations. A suffering patient would not benefit from them. For some people, a cold shower is the perfect solution. During healing rituals, patients, their rooms and probably all family members were treated to plenty of holy water. To the Mesopotamians, whose cultures and survival depended almost entirely on irrigation, the Euphrates and Tigris were sacred, and had a status that is similar to that which devout Hindus attribute to the Ganges. In Sumerian myth, both rivers were the product of Enki's potency. When the god of water travelled across the Near East in primal antiquity, he encountered two dry river beds. Enki was seized by passionate lust, raised his penis and ejaculated into them: it made the rivers flow. Another explanation from around the end of the second millennium appears in the Babylonian *Enûma Eliš*, the *Epic of Creation.* Marduk slays the terrifying chaos-mother Tiāmat and fashions the world out of her carcass. Out of her eyes gush the sacred rivers. Here are a few lines that celebrate river water:

Hald, 1914, trans. JF:

IV R2 14 Nr. 2,2:

[...] the pure water [...]

The water of the Euphrates, which, at a place [...]

The water that has been faithfully preserved at the ocean,

the clean water that Enki purified,

it was the Seven Sons of the Apsû

who purified the water, making it bright and shiny [...]

CT.16 Tl. 5, 185:

As I sprinkle the patient with the water of Enki, so may the demons flee.

Thompson, 2005 (1908): lii (Assyrian spell, W.A.I. ii, 51b, iff)

May all that is evil [...]

(in the body) of N., (be carried off)

with the water of his body and the washing of his hands,

The *Conjuration of Eridu* is famous. Sadly, this text has not been discovered. However, the title indicates what it's all about. Eridu is the place of beginning, where Sumer's earliest temples stood, and where one or several deities, maybe prototypes of Enki, Nammu or Ningirima, received fish offerings. Eridu was the holiest city of old Sumer, and Enki's temple, above the

Abzu/Apsû, the watery abyss, the place of learning, magic, healing.

Thompson, 2005 (1908):

O thou river, who didst create all things,

when the great gods dug thee out

they set prosperity upon thy banks,

within thee, Ea, the King of the Deep, created his dwelling.

Whatever the *Conjuration of Eridu* may have been, it must have involved Enki's and probably Nammu's and Ningirima's blessings. Hald wondered whether the priesthood of Eridu made money by exporting sacred water. It's a tempting thought. However, such a trade does not appear in the economic records, which are a lot more detailed than other Mesopotamian inscriptions. It is more likely that the asû, āšipu, āšiptu and priests made their own waters of Eridu. But do these holy waters come from Eridu or do they flow to it? The following lines, hinting at the conjuration, make a point that after the ritual, the water is poured into the river, which will eventually carry it to the marches of the swampland, and to Eridu.

Hald: IV R2 16 Nr. 2 b33 f:

Recite the conjuration of Eridu,

prepare the water for the purifying conjuration,

complete the purifying conjuration,

sprinkle the people with water [...]

[...] anoint the brow of this person with water,

pour out the water of the conjuration,

and may the river carry it downstream

The best water for magic was prepared with the names of the gods. After all, the Euphrates and Tigris were not always at hand when a patient needed a good sprinkling (or drenching). A competent conjurer was expected to be able to make sacred water. This is quite easy; even New Agers and Catholics can do it. All it takes is a moment of focused imagination to infuse a lot of emotion into a vessel of water. You could recite a spell or mantra (try the lines given above!), visualise deities, symbols, colours or bright light into the fluid, and project a great feeling of joy, love and health into it. Emotion is the essential element; you have to see, feel, and think passionately to do the job. Make it large ideas, raise strong feelings, and the charging is easy. Practise every day for a month, share a drink with the gods and feel good. Magick should be fun.

Early Sumerian spells often mention Ningirima, the lady of the sacred agubba vessels, and Enki as the gods of purifying waters. Spells of the second millennium BCE have Asarluḫi and later Marduk in that function.

Thompson, 2005 (1908): LII W.A.I. iv, 26,7

(Marduk hath seen:) 'What I'; Go my son,

against the (fever-) heat and cold unkindly for the flesh,

fill a bowl with water from a pool that no hand hath touched,

put therein tamarisk, maštakal, ginger(?), horned alkali, mixed (?) wine,

put therein a shining (?) ring (a chaplet?),

give him pure water to drink,

pour the water upon this man, pull up a root of saffron,

pound (?) up pure salt and pure alkali,

fat of the matku-bird, brought from the mountains put therein, and

anoint (therewith) the body of that man seven times.

Water is also useful to get rid of evil spirits.

Here is a spell from Thompson, 2005 (1908) LIII: to wash a rabiṣu away:

May Marduk, eldest son of Eridu, sprinkle him with pure water,

clean water, bright water, limpid water,

with the water twice seven times;

may he be pure, may he be clean;

let the evil rabiṣu go forth and stand away from him;

may a kindly šedu-genius, may a kindly lamassu-genius be present near his body.

When the rabiṣu has vacated its place, the gap is immediately filled with the benevolent influence of two helping spirits who ensure recovery.

Knot Magic

Lamaštu likes wool and string, and so does Inanna/Ištar, who invented the trick of twisting two strands of fibre, increasing their power dramatically. Knots appear in baby spells, but are also widely popular for other cures. Pretty much everybody seems to have used knot spells. Knots are simple. They are a minimalist approach to magick that appears in many cultures. Sorcerers and witches used knots to harm their victims. They knotted evil forces, doom and death into a string and attached it to a figurine of their victims. *Maqlû*, VII, 93-105 makes much of this:

I break your knot!

The sorcerers may hex you,

I break your knot!

The witches may hex you,

I break your knot!

The spell goes on for a while; we learn that kurgarrû priests, ecstatic ritualists, naršindu (clay-using witches), snake conjurers, and agugiltû (thread-crossing witches) have hexed the client, but all of their knots are broken, their faces are punched, their tongues torn out, their eyes blinded with spittle and their evil intentions are returned to them.

Conjurers used knots to release patients from bans, trouble, pollution, evil spirits and curses. You can knot good influences into a piece of string and transfer them to another person or yourself. Now the main thing about all spells, whether they use knots, images or whatever, is visualisation and intense emotion. The other element is less easy but more important: you have to leave your small, limited human personality to make this work. Either you become a representative of a deity or the deity acts through you. Or you realise that you are your deities. Whatever it may be, it transcends your limited human ego. It can be quite a relief.

Either way, you need a highly specialised consciousness state, or trance. Before you set out to practice, go to a quiet, secluded place and calm down. Relax. Let your breath slow down, and give yourself into the hands of your personal deities. Now reflect on what the knot spell shall do for you. Consider what you want to bind. Consider what you want to release. Fuse with your gods, superimpose their shape on your body, identify with them and think their thoughts. Share their feelings. Think about the spell from the divine point of view. Your gods know you better than you do. They know about your purpose in life, about your inner nature, about the things you can't understand. They understand the consequences of your desires and dreams. Indeed, meditation before the spell may be more valuable than the spell itself. It will widen your mind and give a deeper understanding. The rest is simple.

Šurpu Series, V-VI, 144-171 gives a ritual to remove the broken oath/curse/pollution from a person by binding to his limbs a double cord of black and white that has been twisted on a spindle. I guess that several ritualists were employed for the ceremony. My question is: were they just acting as the gods, or were they actually in a divine consciousness? (After Thompson, 2005 (1908): 165 and Reiner, 1958:34, amended by JF)

Conjuration: [Uttu, the Spider Goddess] took the string into her hands,

Ištar prepared the thread,

and seated the wise woman on a couch,

with her spindle she span white and bl[ack] wool into a double cord,

a mighty cord, a great cord, a multi-coloured cord on a spindle,

a cord to overcome the Ban/Taboo/Curse (mamit):

against the evil words of the human ban,

against a divine curse,

a cord to cut/overcome the ban.

She bound the head,

the hands and feet of this man.

Marduk, the son of Eridu, the Prince, with his undefiled hands can rip it off.

He will remove the cord, the Ban,

into the desert, the pure place,

may the evil Ban stand aside,

may this man be clean and purified,

entrusted into the blessed hands of his god.

Here is a similar spell. Like the one above, the patient was tied up. The cord was knotted twice seven times, i.e. it was turned into a dangerous but sacred object. Then he was purified with sacred water. It made the patient's body an unbearably sacred place for the evil spirit, which disappeared into the sky with incense fumes and into the earth with the water. I guess he was untied afterwards, representing his return to freedom and health. Thompson *Devils,* II, Di'u Tablet IX, 1, page 71, spell against headache (or malaria?).

Enki/Ea says:

Go, my son Marduk
Take the hair of a virgin kid,
let a wise woman spin it on the right side,
and double it on the left;
bind twice seven knots
and perform the Incantation of Eridu,
bind (therewith) the head of the sick man,
bind (therewith) the neck of the sick man,
bind (therewith) his life (or: soul),
bind up his limbs;
*go (*or: stand*) round his couch,*
cast the water of the Incantation over him,
that the headache may ascend to heaven
like the smoke of a peaceful homestead,
and like the lees of water poured out
it may go down into the earth.

Maths, Star-Gazing, and Sacred Numerology

Most math teachers are total failures. They fail to inspire their students with the wonder, fascination and magick of numbers. Instead, they teach maths in a meaningless limbo or point out practical applications that are boring and irrelevant for almost everyone. Frankly, how often do you need Pythagoras' theorem in everyday life, unless you happen to be Pythagoras? Teachers spoil so much. Like everything involving consciousness, maths is magical. Teachers, however, usually are not. There is something miraculous to equations, no matter whether you can or cannot comprehend them. Personally, I can't, but that does not keep me from wishing I could. You probably noticed that each number has its own personality. People who enjoy synaesthesia have an exciting life: for them, numbers have colours, shapes, moods, feelings, character and peculiar ways of behaviour. There are extreme cases, like the celebrated Daniel Tammet. When the outside world is too stressful, he closes his eyes and goes for walks amidst numbers. He orients himself by prime numbers, which are comfortingly smooth and round like pebbles at the seaside. The other numbers are different: six is sad and wretched, like a small hole; three tends to roundness, nine is very tall and awe-inspiring, four is quiet and shy, eleven friendly and five loud. When they combine with each other, they create complicated sensations which range from enchanting to revolting. Within three months, he memorised pi to the 22,514th decimal place. It wasn't even a chore: thanks to his high-functioning Aspergers, the number is beautiful, and unfolds like a fascinating landscape.

The Sumerians may have been the first to realise that numbers are divine. They associated their numbers with deities and used them to explore and order the universe. Writing, maths, calculations, and the calendar are all part of the greater magic that turns an assembly of primitives into a civilisation. And it inspired them to play with numbers. It's not self-evident at all. Sometime or other, each culture learned to count, but most of them got stuck on the level where things are simply practical. Consider the Egyptians. They needed bookkeeping for temples, the palace, administration and trade. Most of it can be handled by simple operations: addition, subtraction, division and multiplications. Investment and money lending made them think about percentages and interest. When the Nile flood was over, the fields had to be re-measured, so they became pretty good at geometry and learned to compute and calculate space in two and three dimensions. When land had to be divided, they saw to it that each party got its proper share. They erected amazing buildings and tore them down again when the next ruler decided to create something immortal, expensive and backbreaking. That, however, was pretty much as far as it went: practical maths for practical purposes. The Sumerians started in a similar fashion. But unlike the Egyptians, they imbued their maths with magic and used them to explore the mysteries of the divine. It made them study numbers and calculations for its own sake and gave them the most advanced maths of early history.

Everything started on a very basic level. In Sumer, counting began before writing; indeed, writing was a side effect of bookkeeping.

Sumerian maths is based on two systems. For one thing we encounter the **decimal system**. It's the system which we use today; it means that there are ten digits in each set, and each number has its own distinct name. We encounter this system among the Sumerian and Semitic Mesopotamians, Mongolian, Chinese and many Indo-European people. We are so used to it, and to the neat numbers invented by the Indians in the first centuries CE, that we take it for granted. Nevertheless, ten digits are not really well suited for calculations, as they can only be divided by the two and five. Maybe decimal systems are only popular as most people have ten fingers to count with. If you'd ask mathematicians, you'd learn that, for practical calculations, a **duodecimal** system based on twelve units would be more useful. It would allow you to divide the basic set of numbers by two, three, four and six. Other mathematicians disagree and vote for a system based on a prime number like seven or eleven, as it would reduce the complications that occur when fractions are expressed in several ways. It's a modern idea; for the people of earlier cultures, a system with many divisions was more practical. Evidently, some people in old Europe thought the same: duodecimal numbers appear in Roman weights and measurements. It wasn't the only approach. A couple of cultures promoted a **vigesimal** system, meaning that the basic group consists of the numbers one to twenty. Each of them has its own name and as most people are equipped with ten fingers and ten toes, there is something natural to it. You find the twenty-count among several Native American cultures, such as the Maya, who favoured a 'month' of twenty days and a cycle of twenty years, 400 years, 8000 years and so on. It also appears among some Celts: they were the only known European people who preferred to count in groups of twenty units.

One point that remains uncertain is whether the Mesopotamians used the decimal system as a shortened version of the vigesimal system. For here we encounter something ancient, huge, impressive and remarkably clumsy: a sacred Mesopotamian invention was the **sexagesimal** system, where the basic unit of numbers, each with its own distinct name and written form, was sixty. Maybe it was the first numerical system of Mesopotamia. The number sixty is excellent for calculations, as it can be divided by so many numbers: 2, 3, 4, 5, 6, 10, 12, 15, 20 and 30. In daily life it has a lot of shortcomings. Sixty units are not a good choice when you want to do calculations in your head. In all likeliness, a count of twenty and more likely, the decimal count of ten, were introduced to make the hexagesimal system easier to handle. The Mesopotamians tended towards the decimal system for daily business but used the hexagesimal system for science, astronomy and religious purposes. We owe the Sumerians a sixty-second minute, a sixty-minute hour (3600 seconds) and a day consisting of two sets of twelve hours. Even our circle is based on 360 degrees. All of these are arbitrary conventions, bequeathed to us by the Mesopotamians. The same goes for the sacred sixty-day cycle of the earliest known Chinese calendars: the oracle bone inscriptions of Shang period China use it, and the same order of days, though somewhat differently interpreted, appears in the timekeeping of all later dynasties, and features prominently in Chinese astrology as the ten heavenly stems and the twelve celestial branches. It was not necessarily a direct import from Mesopotamia, as the Bronze Age Chinese created their day names by combining a set of ten names (of the ten-day ritual week) with a set of twelve names. Every sixty days their sacred calendar started anew.

From Mesopotamia, the hexagesimal system spread to the Greeks, the Indians and Arabs. It was essential for the development of astronomy and astrology.

The Mesopotamians divided the day into twelve double hours. The same system appears in early Chinese timekeeping. It also appears in old Europe, only that it wasn't always handled the same way. The Romans, for example, divided the day (i.e. the bright period between sunrise and sunset) into twelve 'hours', but the length of each hour depended on the length of daylight. The same thing appears in Egyptian timekeeping: the length of each hour depended on the season. The Babylonians decided that the length of each hour should be independent of the sun. They used water clocks to measure time. It took a lot of maths and experiments to build them. When you have water dripping from a vessel, the rate is faster when the vessel is full and slows as it empties. Day and the night were divided into twelve double hours of equal length. The night was personified as the goddess (Akk.) Kallatu Kuttumtu, *the Veiled Bride*. She was divided into three sections, each of them a goddess, called Bararītu (*Dusk, Evening*), Qablītu (*Central Part, Interior, Middle*) and Namarītu (*Daybreak*). The astronomer/diviners who were up at night sacrificed to these celestial ladies. They also provided the three basic units of the *Maqlû* ritual. The Greek astronomers imported this system, and subdivided it, so that they arrived at 24 hours of equal length. In China, the double hour remained in use much longer. Fairly late, during the Tang dynasty, each of the double hours was identified with an animal.

Another Mesopotamian invention is the week of seven days. The number seven is a mystery. It does not fit the decimal, sexagesimal or the duodecimal system. However, it occurs with marked significance in the rituals of each month. When we look into early ritual literature, we find that the most important rituals were performed on the first night of the month, the full moon, and the day it disappeared: the 1st, 15th and 28th or 29th night. Later, the half moons were included in this schedule, and this produced a month of four times seven nights which did not accord with the real month of 29.5 nights and necessitated a lot of awkward calculations.

In Mesopotamia, scribes and priests were expected to be good with maths. Their patron goddess, Nidaba/Nisaba, whose sacred reed made cuneiform inscriptions on damp clay tablets, was the patroness of all exact sciences. Nisaba measured the universe, counted the numbers and brought order and justice to farmers quarrelling about the sizes of their fields, and traders and investors disagreeing about loans, prices and investment rates. Several hundred tablets from the Old Babylonian period are devoted to mathematical problems (Pichot, 1995:60-94) The astonishing thing is that the Sumerians, using the cumbersome hexagesimal system, managed to calculate square and cube roots, reciprocals, arithmetic and geometric progressions. A tablet from the Ur III period provides a typical exercise. The scribe was asked to calculate the volume of a wall and the amount of standardised bricks required to build it. The amazing thing is the reverse side of the tablet, where we encounter sexagesimal numbers in a **place value system**! (Friberg in RlA '*Mathematik*'.)

We are all used to place value systems. In a decimal system, in positional writing, one location/number represents units, the next tens, the next hundreds, the next thousands and so on. Try 116: it literally means 1x100, 1x10 and 6x1. In a positional writing of the hexagesimal system, the first position shows the units up to sixty, the second the amount of 60s, the third the 3600s and the fourth the 216000s. An example: the number 3792 in the decimal system is read as (3x1000) + (7x100) + (9x10) + (2x1). The same number in a positional hexagesimal system is written (1x3600) + (3x60) + 12 = 1.3.12. That's as far as the Sumerians went. It worked perfectly. And it was well ahead of all other civilisations by several thousand years. The Old Babylonians introduced two major changes. For one thing, they began to use decimal notation for some calculations. For this purpose they invented signs and words for the numbers 100 and 1000. It created a system that could express numbers in different ways. You could write the number 360 as 6x60, 0x6, or you could write 3x100, 1x60, 0x1, or 3x100, 6x10, 0x1. Things were not streamlined yet. The decimal system was useful for everyday calculations, but it never replaced the hexagesimal system, which had the greater prestige (Pichot, 1995:54-56). The other innovation is so simple and beautiful that modern maths is unthinkable without it: the **zero**. It was a major breakthrough in human history. In Old Babylonian tablets, the zero is simply an empty spot in the right place. The scribes left a lot of open space. It was not a perfect solution, as sloppy writers could overlook the empty spot. Just as difficult were numbers containing several zeros, or numbers with a zero at the end. For the Old Babylonians, zero was literally 'nothing in this position'; hence there was no symbol to represent it. It was not an abstract or philosophical concept: the Mesopotamian genesis does not start from nothing but from undifferentiated chaos. There was always something, even if it defied comprehension. That something could appear from nothing or disappear into nothing was not conceivable. The mathematicians, well aware of the approximate magnitude of the numbers they were dealing with, made do with a large gap to express zero for more than a thousand years. During the Seleucid period, probably around the third century BCE, proper cuneiform signs for zero were introduced. It was an amazing invention but none of the neighbouring cultures seemed to care. Considering that the Mesopotamians were ruled by a Greek dynasty, you would imagine that some Greek thinkers were interested. They were not. The Indians were the first to pick up the idea of zero in the early centuries of the Common Era, maybe as Buddhism, with its insistence of emptiness, made the concept seem familiar. The Chinese developed a positional system before the second century BCE but only got used to zero in the eighth century, when they imported it from India. The Arabs imported the positional system, the neat numbers and the zero from Indian maths in the eighth century CE. However, they made a point to ignore negative numbers. The backward Europeans were stuck with Roman numerals, which are unsuitable for positional systems. European mathematicians were badly handicapped: even simple calculations were extremely difficult and time-consuming. People fiddled around with the calculation board and the abacus. To master difficult stuff like multiplication and division required study at a university, preferably in Italy. The church insisted on Roman numerals and held back scientific progress for many centuries. The so-called Arabian numbers were slowly introduced around the tenth century CE, the zero in the twelfth century. Only a few rebellious thinkers used them as a tool for calculations. In everyday life and until the introduction of printing, Roman numerals remained the norm. Ifrah (1993:538) records that Arabian numbers were frequently prohibited by the church. Some dedicated scholars used them in secret. As a result the Arabian word sifr (zero) appears in the modern word cipher: a secret code.

The bizarre thing about Old Babylonian science is that it used the same approach which you find in medical texts and omen literature: **if x then y**. First the problem and then its answer. In between you encounter causality, real or imaginary. Most of the tablets dealing with maths are exercises for the scribal schools. So far, no textbooks for mathematics have been discovered. The mathematicians were capable of solving equations with two unknowns but they did not bother to describe the principles behind them. They used the theorems of Thales and Pythagoras a jolly 1400 years before the birth of Pythagoras in a practical way, but they did not record the method behind their calculations. So far, nothing comparable to Euclid has been discovered. The idea that the solution of problems can be described with abstract equations is conspicuously absent. Some scholars proposed that nobody wanted to explore the mathematical principles. Or maybe they were secret knowledge, and not committed to writing. Or, as usual, the relevant tablets haven't been found so far. Deductions from lack of evidence are risky. When you look at tablets listing logarithms, exponentials or describing rational equipartitioned trapezoids you may wonder how the scholars thought about them. Saggs (1962:451) remarks that Babylonian scholars calculated that Pi is 3 1/8, which is correct to about 0.6%. A millennium later, the Israelites were still assuming Pi to be 3 (1 *Kings*, VII, 23). Pichot (1995:184) proposed: *Compared to the Mesopotamian arithmetic, the Egyptian appears poor; it does not know their 'obsession by numbers' and their mystical tendencies (...) Specifically the lack of a mystical numerology seems to have slowed the attempts to explore the characteristics of numbers and to go beyond the solution of specific problems.* By making numbers a part of their religion, scribes of Old Babylonian period created the most sophisticated maths of their time.

God Numbers

Someone in the late third millennium had a bizarre idea. She or he decided that some gods could be represented by numbers. It proved to be a winner. However, the system only specified a few associations. In the Old Babylonian period, further numeration ensured. We encounter the names of some major gods written as numbers (like 'deity fifty' or 'deity fifteen'). Finally, in the first millennium BCE, some priests, scribes or conjurers composed tables that related gods to specific numbers, and indicated a hierarchy of power and authority. Their ideas were based on the older traditions.

Let's start at the beginning. The Mesopotamians were admirably explicit and honest where it came to sexual matters. The Sumerian number **1** is called geš, or aš or deš. It shows a single vertical line and represents, apart from its numerical name, 'man' and 'penis'. The number **2**, mi or min means 'woman' and 'vulva'; it was represented by two vertical lines. In Mesopotamian literature, a woman or wife could be called a vulva. It wasn't even derogatory. We meet Inanna rejoicing over her vulva, and singing a song to celebrate it. One song introduces Inanna as *Vulva, the daughter in law.* Men who are after women are literally *after their vulva*; and scheming women wondered: *for whom shall I reserve my vulva?* (Leick 2003:92-93).

The number **3**, eš was also used for 'many' or 'a majority'. According to Thureau-Dangin (1932 in Ifrah 1993:70) the syllable was used to form plurals.

These three numbers are the basic material for divine numerology.

Let's take a look at the divine numbers, based on Ifrah, Bottéro in Ifrah and W. Röllig in *RlA* under *'Götterzahlen'*.

3600: as 60x60, this number symbolised the **totality of the gods** to some Sumerian scribes.

600: was sometimes used as an abbreviation for the **Igigi**, as 5 x (60+60) and for the **Anunnaki** as 60x10. The number 600 can be understood as a Babylonian attempt to represent the totality of the gods of height and depth.

60: the number belongs to **An/Anu** (and **Antu**?) as the representatives of divine, all-inclusive heaven. 60 is the totality of all that can be, but in another sense, it is the basic unit, the common principle. A numerical tablet (now in the British Museum) states: *Anu is the God of the Beginning, the Father of All Other Gods.* It's not exactly true. In some traditions, the parents of An/Anu were the Sumerian gods Anšar (*Whole Sky*) and Kišar (*Whole Earth*), and one tablet lists seven generations of An's ancestors. Our scribe was describing a literal, abstract or numerical truth remote from religious history and state politics. The term *deity 60* was used for Anu, but so far this is only attested on a late first-millennium inscription. It also appears as shorthand for the syllable 'anu', for example the name of the god Oannes=U-anu could be written U-^{d}Sixty. Occasionally, the number 60 was also assigned to **Enki/Ea**.

50: was assigned to **Enlil**, Lord Wind, and maybe to **Ninlil**, his female appearance and/or wife, as the central authority in Mesopotamian religion and politics. Alternatively, **Ninurta/Ningirsu** was symbolised by the number fifty. He is a god or war, thunderstorms, heroism and good at fertilising fields. This assignation is not completely certain, as the tablet is damaged. However, his temple was known as the *House of Fifty* and his mace has fifty heads. For the people of the southern Sumerian sea-land, Ningirsu was the greatest god. Later, he was identified with Ninurta from central Mesopotamia, which made him a son of Enlil. The Middle Babylonians celebrated **Marduk** as the pinnacle of divine sovereignty. Before he attained this supreme status, Marduk had the numerical value of 10. He gained the number 40 from his father Ea; see the late second millennium *Enûma Eliš*. As a result, he was entitled to have fifty names. Most are the names of distinct, and often elder gods who were identified with (or gobbled up by) Marduk.

40: is assigned to **Enki/Ea**, as the god of the sweet and salty water, and the dark waters of the underworld. Perhaps his spouse **Ninki** is also implied. The two are the male and female expression of water and life. An unpublished catalogue of gods from the Yale collection attributes 40 names to Enki. It is not a coincidence that the Biblical flood lasted for forty days or that the Hebrew Qabala associates the watery deep with the letter mem and the number 40: a baby has an average gestation of forty weeks. This, however, is not the only numeration: on occasion, Ea is represented by the number 60. It would make water and its deity the prime cause and the totality of all that is.

30: usually symbolised the moon god, **Nanna/Suen/Sîn**. The month is 29.5 days long. Here, numerology is almost based on observation. Accordingly, since Old Babylonian times, the god was called deity 30.

20: the number was assigned to **Utu/Šamaš**, the lord of the sun and paragon of justice, and maybe to his wife, Aya, the goddess Dawn. In Old Babylonian times, the 20th day of the month was sacred to the sun.

15: the number of **Inanna/Ištar/Irnina**, who was called *the Deity Fifteen* at least since the Old Babylonian period. Fifteen days are half a month; hence the goddess appeared in her increasing and waning aspects, as the daughter of the moon god Nanna/Suen/Sîn (2x15 = 30). The full moon (day 15) was sacred to Ištar of Uruk. We also find her as daughter or wife of An/Anu. Sixty (4x15) fits the goddess very well.

14: is occasionally associated with **Ugur/Nergal**, who is one of the major gods of death, the underworlds and the realm of the dead. Fourteen is twice seven, a difficult number full of divine and dangerous connotations. In the cult calendar, Nergal's day is the 14th, possibly as it is half of the 28th day, the Day of the Underworld. 14 is also the god of wild and domestic animals, haunting the uncultivated places of the earth: **Šakkan**, Akkadian: **Sumuqan/Amakandu**. He also appears as a god of the Underworld. Another tradition claims that Enlil and Ninḫursag created seven twins. For the creation of mankind, Nintur made 14 wombs (*Atraḫasīs Epic*).

10: usually represented **Iškur/Adad**, the lord of storm, rain, weather and divination. Since the Middle Babylonian Period, Adad's name was frequently abridged to *deity 10* (the same goes for the Syrian gods Tešub, Hadad and Baal). It's not the only reading, as Adad was sometimes represented by the number 6. We also meet **Marduk** as 'god 10' before he was promoted to 50.

Ten is also the number of the fire gods **Gibil** and **Nusku**, both of them popular exorcists. They are companions of the sun god Šamaš: twice ten is twenty.

In a cult calendar, Bēlit-Ekur, i.e. **Ninlil**, the *Lady of the House of the Mountain* and **Madānu** (a god of judges related to Gibil and Nusku) are equated with the 10. See below under 5.

9: is probably connected with **Ninurta** and his wife, **Gula**; the 9th and 19th day of the month were sacred to them. However, as Röllig comments, an abbreviation 'deity 9' has not been discovered yet.

7: is an enigmatic number. It is remarkable that the first Millennium BCE texts which provide full lists of god-numbers do not mention 7 at all. That's truly astonishing, as the number seven appears with a much greater frequency than the numbers of the gods.

Let's start with the major cataclysm: the **flood** lasted for seven days. In a late Sumerian text, the **Lamentation Over the Destruction of Ur**, seven gods unite their efforts to destroy the city-state. An terrifies Sumer. Enlil brings a bitter storm, Nintur blocks the womb of the land, Enki stops the waters of the sacred rivers, Utu removes the principles of law and justice, Inanna grants strife and battle to the rebellious land and Ningirsu pours Sumer to the dogs like milk (Averbeck in Chavalas, 2007: 69). King **Enmerkar**, ruler of Uruk, sacrificed to seven gods: Ištar, Ilaba, Zababa, Anunitu(m), Šullat, Ḫaniš, Šamaš, and his diviners offered seven lambs. Sadly, he lost the friendship of the gods, and did not even leave a memorial inscription. Seven mighty brothers, with the faces of ravens and the bodies of partridges, suckled by Tiāmat, rose against his descendant **Naramsîn** (Studevent-Hickman, in Chavalas, 2007:36-37). There are seven names of **Lamaštu** at the beginning of her canonical text, and another seven in II, 129-133. Here, seven is much like the comment in the ritual calendar: bad, dangerous, but also auspicious, if properly handled. She grasps the baby seven times in its belly. The sorceries against her thrive on the number seven. Seven sorts of dust are mixed with clay to banish her. Seven azallu plants, seven eye stones, seven stone donkeys and seven colourful ribbons are attached to the baby. Four and three eye stones and stone donkeys are attached to the baby's hands and feet. Seven mountains and seven canals block her way. In LS I, 221 she receives fourteen small loaves of bittergrain flour as her travel provisions. Early spells indicate that the Sumerians knew seven Lamaštus. Frank (1908:16) cites a formula from the bilingual collection *Utukku Limnuti* that celebrates seven groups of deities (CT XVI Ut.lim. V. III, 14ff, trans. JF):

Seven gods of the wide sky,
seven gods of the wide land,
seven violent (?) gods,
seven gods of might,
seven evil gods,
seven evil Lamaštus,
seven evil Fever-Lamaštus.

How about ambiguous sevens? Seven **sons of the Abzu/Apsû** appear in spells without revealing who they are and what they do. There are the **Seven Warriors** (the Pleiades), a group of serious, heavily armed warriors who fight against evil, but there are also seven destructive fiends, the **Evil Seven**. In some texts there are major differences between them; in others, the Seven Warriors are pretty much identical with the Evil Seven. They walk with Erra/Nergal and bring terror and cataclysms. The Evil Seven are much better documented than the Seven Sages and the Seven Warriors.

Figure 46 Adapa. Fishman of the Deep.

Figure 47 Mirages of Civilisation.

Figure 48 Worship of Trees and Deer. Inspired by a Mittanic Rollseal, c.15-14. Century BCE.

Figure 49 Gates of Temple and Palace: a Visitor Arrives.

The Seven were born on the mountain of the west,
the Seven grew up on the mountain of the east,
they squat in the crevices of the earth,
they dwell (?) in the deserts of the earth,
they are not understood in heaven and earth,
they are shrouded with awful radiance,
they are unknown among the wise gods,
their name does not exist in heaven and earth,
the Seven howl on the mountain of the west,
the Seven rejoice on the mountain of the east,
they creep through the caverns of the earth,
they dwell in the deserts of the earth,
they are unknown in all sorts of things,
in heaven and earth they cannot be understood.

(Franke, 1908:20, Thompson 2005/1908:56, Haas, 1986:135).

It's hard to make sense of them. Here is the first interpretation: In some texts the Evil Seven are formless, shapeless, sexless horrors. We read that they are neither male nor female, and have no specific forms. They are mindless and outside the divine order like the hurricanes and storm winds. Maybe this version of the Evil Seven is closely related or even a development of the idea that there are seven storms or seven winds. The second interpretation of the Seven is specific. Note that they are called Evil Gods. (UL XVI, 0-54 after Thompson, 2005/1908:54, Frank 1908:22 and Haas, 1986:131):

The Evil Gods are raging storms,
ruthless spirits born in the vault of heaven;
workers of woe are they,
(like the spirit) Hold the Head to Evil.
Ready to wreak destruction every day [are they].
Of these Seven (the first) is the furious south wind [...]
The second is an ušumgallu (snake-dragon) with gaping mouth,
that none can [oppose?]
The third is an enraged panther which carries off the young [...]
The fourth is a terrible šibbu serpent [...]
The fifth is a terrifying wormlike creature which does not retreat [...]
The sixth is an advancing [...] which neither gods nor kings [...]
The seventh is a storm, an evil gale [...]
These seven are the messengers of Anu, the king,
dust-storms, surging through heaven,
dense clouds, shrouding heaven in darkness,
rising gales, bringing darkness on the bright day.
They move with the storm-wind, the evil gale.
(They are) the deluge of Adad, the Storm-god, terrible furies,
walking at the right hand of the Storm-god.
They [illuminate] the foundation of heaven like lightning,
they lead the way to commit murder,
in the wide sky, the home of Anu, the king,
they stand, threatening evil, and none can oppose them.

A third interpretation of the Evil Seven comes from the many attempts to install a proper group of seven evil spirits. In these texts, the Seven have names and are associated with specific forms of disease, madness or disaster. Variations are common. After all, more than seven terrors were available, making the choice a highly subjective matter. Here is an example (after Frank, 1908:32):

The asakku approaches the man, his head,
the namtāru approaches the man, his throat,
the evil utukku approaches the neck,
the evil alû approaches the breast,
the evil eṭimmu approaches the centre of the body,
the evil gallû approaches his hand,
the evil ilu approaches his foot.

It's not the only version. Others include the rabiṣu and, of course Lamaštu.

The **Underworld** has seven gates and seven levels. There are seven times seven **sins**. Great sins, however, can be absolved seven times in Marduk's name. Seven gallûs hound Dumuzi to death. The seventh day, and the days which are multiples of seven, were dangerous. It took humility, prayer and offerings to turn the danger into luck. Work and business on a seventh day were likely to fail, so whoever could afford it remained at home.

But the number seven is not always lethal. Seven **winds** or **storms** blow from north and south. They are the servants of Iškur/Adad. Seven fishy **ABGAL/ Apkallu/ Abgal sages** brought civilisation to Sumer; seven **masters** laid the brickwork of Uruk. **Inanna** has seven pieces of divine jewellery representing her seven divine Me (or fifteen, or more than a hundred, depending on the text). Dangerous influences were often sent away over seven mountains, seven rivers and seven canals, which blocked any way they might return. Holy **Lugalbanda** had to cross seven mountain ranges before he arrived in Uruk. He baked his bread with seven **coals**. Many positive sevens appear in the cult of **Ningirsu**; it might be a speciality of southern Sumer. Ningirsu governed seven **lands**. When Gudea built the temple of Ningirsu, there were seven **blessings**. During seven **days** this temple was built and seven **statues** were set in seven sacred **locations**. The šita weapon has seven heads. Ningirsu had seven **temple inspectors** and seven beloved lukur (Akk.: nādītu(m)) **priestesses**. When Ningirsu moved into his temple, for seven days all people, no matter whether slaves or lords, poor or rich, were equal. It sounds almost too good to be true. In the *Nanše Hymn*, her temple is famous for seven **offerings**: bread, beer, libations, butterfat, milk, fish, firewood. Seven terrifying **monsters** protected the temple doors of Marduk and Zarpānītu(m): venomous snake/dragon, hairy one (lahmu), bison, big-weather beast, mad-lion, Fish-man, carp-goat. They were set in lapis lazuli, dušu-stone, carnelian and alabaster to protect the temple erected by the Kassite king Agumkarimke, (van Koppen in in Chavalas, 2006:138). The seven also appears in relation to love and lust. The love-hungry woman declares that her seven **orifices** await the coming of her man. Seven men on one side and seven on the other find their satisfaction with Ištar (*the city is built on pleasure!*). The making of Inanna's bridal sheets involved seven stages: gathering the green flax, retting, spinning, doubling the threads, dying, weaving and bleaching. Seven is a good number to fix spells.

Quite a lot of **love spells** survive. Here is an example: To promote business, the prostitute, tavern-keeper or brothel-madam takes dust from the quay, the firth, the bridge, four country roads, the crossroads, the palace, the divine throne, the gate of the Ištar temple, the house of an independent woman, the gate of a gardener, the gate of a baker, the gate of a tavern/brothel. That would make it fourteen plus her premises. The total is fifteen, the number of Inanna/Ištar. Compare the sorts of earth with the seven earths in Lamaštu spells; LS II, 61-64. She offers three pieces of bread with 'nipples' to Ištar on an altar. She burns juniper incense and pours a beer offering. Seven times she recites the conjuration: *Ištar of the Lands, heroine among goddesses: this is your home, enjoy, appreciate, laugh and gain! Come, enter this house! With you, the good looking customer shall enter, your lover, your male prostitute (?). May your lips be honey, may your hands lust! The lips of my ring shall be honey lips! Like a snake coming out of its hole, while birds above chirp/screech, so let the people fight each other for me! ...*

She bows deeply, mixes the dust with water, repeats the conjuration seven times, and smears the mixture on her door. The rest is formed into the figurine of a bull and buried under the storage vessels (Haas, 1999:107, slightly amended). Several spells of this type survive, showing that some prostitutes knew a lot about human nature, were literate and pretty good at working magic.

Given so much diversity, we can only state that the number seven, unsuitable for the decimal and the hexagesimal system, is special, dramatic and magical, and does not fit any interpretation.

6: is occasionally associated with **Adad** (see number 10). The sixth day of the month is sacred to him.

5: is the number of Bēlit-Ekur, the *Lady of the Mountain House*, i.e. **Ninlil**, the wife of Enlil. She is also occasionally identified with the number 10 (5x10 = 50: the number of her husband Enlil).

1: apart from its symbolism (see above), though not specifically a divine number, 1 is associated with **Anu** and **Enlil**, as the first month of the year and the first day of the month were dedicated to them.

What were divine numbers good for? For a start, it made some highly gifted scribes assume that maths is religion, which is an excellent idea. A few divine numbers, like those of the month and the half lunation, have their origin in natural phenomena. Anu's number, and those deriving from it, was selected for its mathematical usefulness, or, as the scribes might have thought, for its inherent perfection. Some divine numbers suit the ritual calendars. But this is not enough to explain everything. The numerical order, with the major gods at the top and the minor ones at the bottom, reflects a divine hierarchy. We encounter the structure in several magical compilations from Aššurbanipal's library. A good example comes from the *Šurpu Series, IV, 89-108* (after Ungnad, 1921:267 and Reiner, 1958:28, amended & trans. JF)

Appear, Anu and Antu: may they repel the disease!

Appear, Enlil, Lord of Nippur: with his irrevocable order may he announce Life for him (=the patient)!

Appear, Ea, Lord of all Mortals, whose hands created mankind!

*Appear, Sîn, Lord of the Month: may he unbind his mamit (*taboo, oath, curse*)!*

Appear, Šamaš, Lord of Justice: may he eradicate the misdeed!

Appear, Adad, Lord of Divination: may he erase the disease!

Appear, Tišpak, Lord of Hosts: may he drive out the di'u disease!

Appear, Ninurta, Lord of the Mace: may he banish trouble!

Appear, Papsukkal, Lord of the Staff: may he erase the disease!

Appear, Marduk, Sage of the Gods, may he bring health!

Appear, Asarluḫi, mašmaššu of the Gods, may he whose conjuration gives life to the dead, make the sick get up again!

Appear, Nergal, Lord of Judgement, who scares the gallû and Namtar away to their lairs!

Appear, Ningirsu, Lord of Field-Cultivation, who makes disease depart!

Appear, Zababa, Regent of the Exalted Throne, may he expel Namtar!

Appear, Ennugi, Lord of Embankment and Canal, may he bind the asakku!

Appear, Nusku, Vizier of the Ekur, may he speak blessings and heal the sick!

Appear Girra, may he soothe the angry god and goddess, and remove exhaustion from the body!

Appear Ištar, Lady of the Lands, may she speak good words for the patient!

Appear Ninkarrag/Gula, Great Healer, may she remove exhaustion from the body!

Appear Bau/Baba, may she relive his restlessness!

I am sure you noticed that the author of this text started out according to the sequence of the divine numbers, and muddled things up after the reference to Adad. Observe the three goddesses at the end of the spell. Does their location indicate a low rank or were they supposed to fix the spell and make it come true?

In a similar vein, the banishment of Lamaštu (LS I, 2, 7) starts with the names of Anu (60), Enlil (50), and Ea (40). Then follows Bēlit-Ile (here=Ninḫursag); she was once the third major deity of Mesopotamia, but her position in the divine hierarchy was occupied by Enki/Ea around the end of the third millennium BCE. In later periods, her status was much reduced. She has no divine number in the first millennium catalogues. However, she appears in the sacrificial calendars. In this context, Bēlit-Ile may also be Ištar. Next appear Sin (30), Šamaš (20), Asarluḫi/Marduk (10), Ninurta/Ninib (9), and Ningirima, the Lady of Conjuration, who has no divine number, but whose command seals the spell. Finally we have Ninkarrag/Gula (possibly 9, like her husband Ningirsu) and Ištar, as Lady of the Lands (15). There are several old elements to the conjuration: Marduk appears as number 10 (and not as 50), and Bēlit-Ile is close to the top. It could indicate that the spell comes from the Old Babylonian period.

These correspondences show that divine numbers were a common way of organising divine hierarchies. But there was some divergence here and there. We usually meet the major gods according to their numerical order, but regarding the lower god numbers, variation is the norm.

Here is a standardised formula that was used in the first millennium BCE to bless the boundary stones that divided the fields. This example comes from the Fourth Dynasty of Babylon. After documenting the acquisition of the land, and its relation to its neighbours and the witnesses of the contract, it describes the sad fate of one who would dare destroy or move the boundary stone. Well, some people were cunning. They motivated somebody else to do the dirty work for them. Hence, anyone was punished who

because of the curse incites one who is an imbecile, or deaf, a scoundrel (?), a criminal or one who is ignorant to steal this stele, to throw it into a river, sink it in a well, crushes it with stones or destroys it with fire, hides it in the earth or in a place where it cannot be found: this man shall be struck powerfully by the mighty gods Anu, Bēl, Ea, Ninmaḫ, and suffer their evil irrevocable curse;

Sîn, the light of heaven, shall cloak his entire body with never ending leprosy, so he shall not attain purity to the day of his fate but has to make a dwelling, like a wild ass, outside the city wall;

Šamaš, the judge of heaven and earth, shall strike his face that the bright day shall turn to night for him;

Ištar, the lady of the gods shall send [...] and as the goddess of the rising stars (?) overwhelm his day and night by sending her wrath against his lands, so that, like a dog, he will haunt the edges of the marketplace of his city;

Marduk, the lord of heaven and earth, shall fill his belly with dropsy whose fetters cannot be unbound; Ninurta, the lord of frontiers and boundary stones, shall pull out his own boundary stones, shall crush his land and make its demarcations invalid;

Gula, the great healer, shall [...] poison into his body that he may shed blood and pus like water, Miru (?) the steward of heaven and earth, shall flood his property so that, instead of herbs, thorns proliferate, and instead of grains (?) thickets; [...]

Nabû, the exalted messenger, shall destine the season of his need and curse;

the great gods, as many as are named on this stele, shall lead him to ill luck and evil, and annihilate his name, seed, offspring and descendants in the mouths (of?) richly sprouting (?) people. The name of this stele is: Establishes the Boundary Forever.' (after Schrader, 1896:77-79, amended, trans. JF)

A Sacred Calendar

Ungnad (1921:302-307) translated an almost perfectly preserved cult calendar for the leap-month called 'Second Ellul'. It has many similarities to the usual divine days, as mentioned above, but goes far beyond that in its scope. Here is a synopsis, to give you a basic idea of what the ritual schedule incorporated. I have simplified the text by leaving out some repetitive standard phrases. There is a sacrifice each day (or night), and this ritual was always accompanied by prayer, often with the giving of alms and donations. Kings were expected to be generous to the poor and needy. All days were lucky, even the dangerous days, provided the proper ritual procedure was followed. The comment for each day ends with the remark that the king's prayer is pleasing to the god or gods.

The month starts on the first day the new moon is visible.

Day one: Morning ritual for Šamaš, the Lady of the Lands (Bēlit-Ile, originally Ninḫursag), Sîn and the Lady of the Gods. Sacred to Anu and Enlil.

Day two: Morning ritual for Šamaš, the Lady of the Lands, Sîn and the Lady of the Gods. Sacred to all goddesses.

Day three: A day of rest for Marduk and Zarpānītu. The king sacrifices to Marduk and Ištar during the night.

Day four: Feast day of Nabû and Marduk. In the night, the king sacrifices to Nabû and Tašmētum.

Day five: dedicated to Ekur (*House of the Mountain* = Enlil's temple) and the Lady of Ekur (Ninlil). Sacrifice to Aššur and Ninlil in the night.

Day six: dedicated to Adad and Ninlil. The king shall not utter laments. Sacrifice to Adad in the night.

Day seven is a rest day for Marduk and Zarpānītu. The seventh is an evil but also an auspicious day. *The Shepherd of the People shall not eat meat that has been prepared over coals nor eat food prepared in ashes (*alternately: *eat food that has touched fire); shall not change his dress, shall not put on new clothes, shall not give alms or donations. The king shall not mount a chariot nor proclaim a decree. At the secret site, the seer shall not pronounce an oracle. The doctor shall not lay his hand on a patient. (The day) is not useful to perform a task. In the night, the king shall make an offering for Marduk and Ištar and make donations. His prayer is welcome to the gods.*

Day eight: feast day for Nabû. At night, the king prepares his hand for the offering (?). He sacrifices to Nabû and Tašmētum.

Day nine: The king sacrifices to Ninurta and Gula.

Day ten: dedicated to the Lady of the Ekur (Ninlil) and to the *God of Judgement*. At night the king sacrifices to the constellations Ursa major and the *Son of the Lady of the Gods*.

Day eleven: the day of the completion of the site of Tašmētum and Zarpānītu. When the moon has a *crown of glory* and the *fruit* is glad, the king shall sacrifice to Sîn in the night.

Day twelve: Food offering to Enlil and Ninlil.

Day thirteen: The day of Sîn and the Lady of the Gods. When Sîn (the moon) has a crown of glory for the land, the king shall sacrifice to Šamaš, the Lady of the Lands, Sîn and the Lady of the Gods.

Day fourteen: dedicated to Ninlil and Nergal: a bad day but also an auspicious day. Same ritual and taboos as on day seven, but sacrifices to Ninlil and Nergal.

Day fifteen: is dedicated to the Lady of the Eanna (Inanna/Ištar, the Eanna is the *House of Heaven* in Uruk), to the completion of the accounts for Sîn and the Lady of the Gods. The king sacrifices to Šamaš, the Lady of the Lands, Sîn and the Lady of the Gods.

Day sixteen (is much like day three): A day of rest for Marduk and Zarpānītu. The king sacrifices to Marduk and Ištar during the night.

Day seventeen: (like day four) Feast day of Nabû and Marduk. At night, the king sacrifices to Nabû and Tašmētum.

Day eighteen: sacred to Sîn and Šamaš. The king sacrifices to Šamaš, the Lady of the Lands, Sîn and the Lady of the Gods.

Day nineteen: a day of the wrath of Gula. A bad day but also an auspicious day. Procedures and taboos as on day seven; sacrifices to Ninurta and Gula.

Day twenty: Day of the People: the king sacrifices to Šamaš, the Lady of the Lands, Sîn and the Lady of the Gods.

Day twenty-one: Day of the completion of the accounts of Sîn and Šamaš. A bad but also an auspicious day; procedures and taboos as on day seven. The king sacrifices to Šamaš, the Lady of the Lands, Sîn and the Lady of the Gods.

Day twenty-two: completion of the accounts of Sîn and feast day of Bēlit-ēkalli (*Lady of the Palace*). Sacrifices to Šamaš and the Lady of the Lands.

Day twenty-three: sacrifices to Šamaš and Adad.

Day twenty-four: Sacrifices to Bēl-ēkalli and Bēlit-ēkalli (*Lord and Lady of the Palace*).

Day twenty-five: Procession for Enlil and the Lady of Babylon. At night, the king shall sacrifice to Enlil before the constellation 'Plough' (Triangulus) and for the Lady of Babylon before the constellation Ursa major.

Day twenty-six: dedicated to the laying of the bricks of Ea and to the Lady of the Gods. The king shall recite a lament. Nevertheless, *everything is pleasant.* In the night, the king sacrifices to Ea and the Lady of the Gods.

Day twenty-seven: feast day of Nergal and Nabû.

Day twenty-eight: Dedicated to Ea and to the disappearance of Nergal: a bad but also an auspicious day. Procedure and taboos as on day seven; sacrifices to Ea and the Lady of the Gods.

Day twenty-nine: the disappearance of Sîn (i.e. the moon disappears), the day when the spirits of heaven and earth assemble. Sacrifices to Sîn and the Lady of the Gods.

Day thirty: sacrifices to Anu and Enlil.

But there is more to numbers, and much of it is enigmatic (Ifrah, 1993:319-323). Some scribes, particularly during the first millennium BCE, used incomprehensible **ciphers**, such as *'Anu=21'* or *'throne=1;20'*. In many cases the writers were simply playful or tried to appear clever. There are texts which use the number 3600 (pronounced shar) as a glyph for the word 'king' (also pronounced shar) and inscriptions where individual names appear as numbers, like this passage from the reign of the Neo-Assyrian king Sargon II (722-705 BCE), which describes the mighty fortification Dur Šarrukin (today Chorsabad):

And I give the circumference of the wall as: 3600 + 3600 + 3600 + 3600 + 600 + 600 + 600 + 60 + 3 x 6 +2) ells (i.e. 16280 ells) according to the sound of my name. How Sargon's name may be encoded in these numbers remains a mystery. Another example occurs at the end of a tablet called *The Glorification of Ištar* from Uruk of the Seleucid period. The author gave his name, at the end of the text, as 21, 35, 35, 26, 44, son of 21, 11, 20, 42. Encoded names may indicate vanity. The reader is supposed to guess who the clever author is. But why would anyone want to write the word 'right' as 15 and the word 'left' as 2;30? Just to make things difficult for outsiders?

In earlier periods, some ciphers may have had a mystical meaning, like the *Esagil Tablet*, which gives the measurements of the great temple of Marduk in Babylon and the Ziggurat of Babylon. On the surface, the difficult text seems to concentrate on measurements of spaces, courtyards, terraces, as might be useful to an architect. But then we encounter a standard line indicating that something else is hidden among the numbers:

May the initiate explain this text to the initiate.

May the non-initiate fail to see it.

It's a religious formula. Perhaps the numbers contain some religious symbolism and perhaps the measurements themselves were thought to be sacred.

Sacred Music

For a long time, experts assumed that the cradle of European music stood in Greece and western Turkey. Pythagoras (c. 585–493 BCE) was considered the father of musical theory, the inventor of the seven Greek Modes, and the first genius to prove that there are mathematical reasons why a single string can be divided at certain points and produce predictable intervals and tones. It was a natural assumption, as Pythagoras had contributed so much to Greek and Near Eastern thought. He believed that the universe did not consist of crude stuff like elements or atoms but of numbers and relationships. This idea implied that anything can be measured, that there exists a universal harmony between the celestial bodies, the dimensions of the earth, time and so on. We owe Pythagoras the brilliant idea that the spheres, i.e. the celestial realms in which the fixed stars, planets, moon and sun moved, could be experienced as music; a thought that has excited many musicians and philosophers. Early students of Pythagoras, basing their knowledge on highly flawed translations, arrived at the beautiful idea that one might, as Pythagoras allegedly did, hear the stars sing on warm summer nights. But what the old sage said was less romantic and more sublime:

The world is music and music is number. Hence music is symbol and sensitive expression of the world-order. To delve into the numerical order of music is the surest way to arrive, by analogy, at the knowledge of the mysterious laws of the universe. (After Cotte, 1992:17)

Pythagoras was one of the first European proponents of the idea that the souls of all beings are continuously reborn. In consequence, he recommended a strict vegetarian diet, as you wouldn't want to eat a pig who had been your grandfather in his last life. He founded a community of philosophical dropouts on Samos, which had an enormous influence on the development of Greek and Roman philosophy. Sadly, only fragments of his teachings survive. You can find some of them in Plato, in a text attributed to Euclid, in Ovid's *Metamorphoses*, or, if you like a sweet and sticky tale, in Philostratus' *The Life of Apollonius of Tyana.* According to Philostratus, Pythagoras and Apollonius had travelled to the East. Pythagoras' ascetic lifestyle and his faith in reincarnation might have their origin in India. On the way he could have passed through Babylonia. It would have given his maths an amazing boost. But where did his music theory originate? Several esteemed Greek scholars wrote about music. In their treatment, we encounter the seven scales (modes) named Hypodorian (later called Aeolian), Hypophrygian (later Ionian), Hypolydian, Dorian, Phrygian, Lydian, Mixolydian (later Hypodorian). This is where the trouble starts. Greek music theory would be a pleasure if the early specialists had used a common terminology. Alas, they did not, and as a result, there is plenty of confusion regarding the name of each scale.

As it turns out, Pythagoras did not invent the seven modes, and several Greek writers were well aware of it. Most of them have names related to places. Phrygia is in eastern Turkey; the Phrygians were an Indo-European speaking people who wore silly hats (look at images of Perseus or the Jacobites). They had probably moved to Asia from the Balkan before Greek culture began. The Lydians were another Indo-European people from the Balkan, or so it is said, and occupied much of western Turkey. Together, these two cultures controlled much of what had been the Hittite state around the middle of the second millennium BCE. The Hittites, too, were an Indo-European speaking culture which incorporated many ethnic groups, including Semitic-speaking people. They were in close touch with the Babylonians and the Assyrians. The Hittites wrote in Mesopotamian cuneiform and collected Sumerian and Babylonian literature. Perhaps the Hittites, and the cultures that followed them, were a link by which Mesopotamian culture was exported to Europe. Sadly, this transfer is hard to trace, as most European cultures were illiterate during the second millennium BCE. Whatever it may be, the names of the 'Greek Modes' betray that they were thought to come from other places. Let's look at them closely. A mode is not simply a scale. Contemporary scales are like mathematical formulae: they are easy to calculate and contain nothing except the relationships of tones. Musicians do experience subjective differences between them. In popular belief, major scales are supposed to be dynamic, bright and happy while minor scales are allegedly restful, dark and sad. It's wrong. If you know what you are doing, you can play a happy or sad tune on any of the modern scales. Nowadays, with tempered and equalised tuning, the peculiarities of major and minor scales have lost much of their meaning.

The Greek musicians had an understanding of scales that is much closer to Indian music theory. Let's look at this briefly. Nowadays there are several hundred rāgas. Each of them is characterised by a scale. Straight rāgas use the same scale to ascend and descend. Crooked rāgas use different scales to ascend and descend. Each rāga has a rhythm, emphasises special tones, unique melodic elements, and comes with a flavour, mood and emotion. Many rāgas are associated with a time of day or a season, with specific deities, occasions like war or marriage or have a religious meaning. Some rāgas should be classed as magical and religious rituals: they invoke deities, and manifest divine powers and emotions. A whole range of rāgas is devoted to the eagerly desired rainfalls. You can use them for rain magic or as a powerful meditation that releases all pent up emotions in one devastating downpour. Scales are not all there is to rāgas, but they may be useful for your meditation-in-sound. Each rāga has its scale (or scales), it emphasises special tones, a rhythm and is characterised by a few small melodic elements. Within these specifications, the player is free to improvise. The framework is rigid and the contents are freely variable. Each performance is unique. A given rāga can last for ten minutes or two hours. It is not performed in a predictable way with a specific length and organisation, as a pop song would be, nor is it suitable for an ensemble of many musicians, like an orchestra, 'cause they would all spontaneously make a mess of it. Classical Indian music lives on improvisation, and is a lot more creative than, say Pop, Rock or Jazz music. We might get closer to the essence of a rāga when we consider it a meditation or an act of worship.

The Greek musicians had a similar outlook and maybe the Old Babylonians too. The Dorian scale, for example, was allegedly imported from the city Doris in Asia Minor, and the Greek musicians considered it a new and rather heavy sort of music suitable for sombre ritual. It was attributed to the blind musician Tharimas of Thrakia, supposedly the first lyre player who added a fourth string to his lyre, and was dedicated to Apollo and the sun. The Satyr Marsias, rival (and later, victim) of Apollo, was considered the inventor of the Phrygian scale, which was generally used for invigorating, martial music, and intimately related to wind instruments such as military pipes. Apollo himself invented the Lydian scale, which was commonly used for sad music, lamentations and chants for the dead. Then there was the Aeolian scale, from Aeolia in Asia Minor, allegedly invented by Terpender, a famous lyre player from Lesbos, and noted for its simplicity. Hypolydian was a mode of love; it invoked the foam-born Aphrodite and her blessings. Hypophrygian (later known as Ionian) was dedicated to Hermes. You know it as the diatonic major scale. The Mixolytic scale, closely related to the Lydian, was thought to be the invention of Sappho herself, the famous poetess and priestess, and was used to clear the mind and calm the emotions. Unlike our modern scales, each mode was used for specific types of music, and connected with specific emotions. It would be really nice to know more. But as it is, we cannot even be sure what scales were are talking about. The Greek didn't agree about the names of their modes, and things became worse thanks to the haphazard use of the Greek names in European music. The 'Greek Modes' became popular thanks to Boethus (c. 480–524 CE) and Cassiodorus (c. 490–583 CE), but their greatest popularity was in the late Medieval period and the early Renaissance, say, around 1400. European musicians made a mess of it. European scholars were not aware that the Greek noted their scales in a descending order. As a result, the names of the modes have to be treated with great caution.

The Renaissance musicians added several new scales, attached Greek-style names to them and claimed that the Gregorian chorals were Dorian, which they weren't. Nor did they agree with each other about the names they used so freely. None of this was related to ancient Greece or Asia Minor, but it sounded suitably impressive.

The Mesopotamians invented and played many instruments that are still with us today. This is not to say that they invented them all. They were simply the first to leave evidence that can be verified and dated. It started when the Sumerians began to carve cylinder seals around 3500 BCE. Such a seal is a pretty little picture and our only record for the preliterate period. Here, you should recall that Sumerian art mostly went to rot. The muddy terrain of the plains with its extreme changes in temperature and humidity erodes paint, cloth, wood and bone. Also, the Mesopotamians did not have much of a cult of the dead. Sumerian artists, unlike their Egyptian colleagues, did not produce elaborately painted tombs perfectly preserved by the dry climate of the desert. Our first evidence for sophisticated music comes from the protoliterate period, sometime between 3500–3200 BCE. It's a roll seal (BM 141632) showing a nude woman on a boat. With her are the reed-mat symbol of Inanna and the image of a bull. She plays a lute with a slim neck. Around 3200 BCE, the first images of harpists appear. Almost a thousand years later, in the Akkadian period, two cylinder seals show male musicians playing lutes. One of them is called Ur-ur; he is the first named musician of history. Both artists are dressed and sit on their heels, and both are in the company of Enki/Ea, the inventor and patron of music. A little later, during the Old Babylonian period, we encounter images of varied content: nude lutists in a ritual context with bent legs, to indicate that they danced while they played, and shepherds strumming lutes, indicating that the instrument was not only used by ritual specialists but by normal, uneducated people. In literature, references to a lute-type instrument (the GIŠ gu-di) start with *Gudea's Temple Hymn* and with King Šulgi of the third Dynasty of Ur (c.2095 BCE), who boasted of his proficiency in composing music; in tuning and playing eleven types of string instruments. Šulgi, so the hymn records, picked up a lute and exclaimed

That ahh!, its heart/essence, I knew (instantly...) (As though) ever from old, like doing lifted-hands (=as easily as lifted in prayer) I am able to play (it) in tune (?), as to the tone emitted, the tightening (and) loosening (technique), firmly, my hand does not slip out (translation Kilmer).

Šulgi knew what he was saying. Music is to remember something you have always known, and is an act of prayer. Further references to lutes appear in hymns to Ur-Nammu (c.2113 BCE), in Iddindagan's *Sacred Marriage Hymn*, in a piece called the *Gula Lament*, the dialogue between *Summer and Winter* and among the divine Me of Inanna.

The history of the lute family of guitar, ūd, mandolin, vīna, sitar, saz, qin, pipa, machete and ukulele begins around the middle of the fourth millennium BCE. It begins with magic and ritual: our first recorded musician is nude. Nudity is a common feature in early Sumerian ritual images. And she is doing something extremely magical: music is one of the easiest ways of changing consciousness. People of our days tend to forget this. Music, or what is called music by the deaf and ignorant, surrounds us everywhere. We are drenched by music in movies, advertisements, at home, in shops, and when we wait for a phone connection. Much of this is acoustic rubbish. More so, all of it is passive. People chose to be entertained or to have their moods and awareness influenced by other people's music. Very few people make music. It's an enormous loss. In most people, the connections between the acoustic regions of the brain and the limbic system, where feelings are made, are stronger than the visual links. In India, the music of a movie is released before the movie; if the music is successful, the movie can be launched. Music is not there to be consumed but to be made. It isn't work but pleasure. Good musicians don't sit down, frown, take an instrument out of its bag and say 'Well then. It's time for serious practice'. Practice has its uses, but real music is alive. Passionate musicians don't keep their instruments in bags; they have them all over the place, and start playing whenever they have a chance. They don't even think about it, 'cause music is a way of being. It's a way of designing emotions. It's an excellent and easy way of changing consciousness. Instruments are there to make feelings. All of this places music on a level with trance, ritual and possession. I am not talking about reading sheets and playing 'Jingle Bells'. The real music is when you play what you feel and change what you feel as you play along. It does not require you to read notes or worry about getting things right. Music touches levels of awareness that are way beyond words. That's why the Hindus insist that the sound vibration of a deity, as it appears in a rāga or a mantra, is much truer than its symbolic or anthropomorphic appearance. The first emanation that arises out of the all-enclosing, formless consciousness (Brahman) is vibration (Śabda-Brahman). Compared to it, prayers, hymns, temples and statues are coarse and limited.

Many Western magicians, pagans and occultists underestimate music. A good many leading magicians were practically tone-deaf (Crowley was a prime example), and their followers, provided they use music at all, tend to use other people's music to change their minds. Many years ago I, too, was shy about making music. School had convinced me that I had no talent. It should have taught me that my teachers were incompetent. I had to be pressured into drumming, rattling, singing and dancing. And I thank my friends Volkert and Frank for insisting. Nowadays, I can hardly think of a nicer way of invocation than to pick up a string instrument, decide on a scale, and improvise my way into the proper consciousness. It's fun to relax in the dark while improvising on a ukulele. Fluting is a great way to enjoy breath. When you pick a string, blow into a flute or tap a drum you are doing something incredibly ancient. You are evoking an experience that has been shared by countless people and cultures all the way from the prehistoric period.

We breathe, we sleep, we eat and make love, we look at the sky and feel the wind and the rain. And when we pick up an instrument and make a sound, we can relax *and listen and feel...*

It started when the first lutes, lyres and harps were built. That may have been in Mesopotamia. At least, the Mesopotamians were at it before anyone else that we know of. They made a great effort and influenced their neighbours. Many hymns, starting in the Sumerian period, contain notes on how they should be sung, and by what instruments they were accompanied. Ritual invocations were often musical. Most types of hymns, prayers, invocations and lamentations were performed with string instruments, wind instruments and a wide range of drums. Music was not an extra to the ceremony, but an essential part of pleasing a deity, and simultaneously, the divine consciousness of the ritualists. The most commonly named instruments are lyres (Sumerian: zami, Akkadian: sammû). Unlike the early four-stringed Greek lyres, the Mesopotamian instruments often had nine strings, it taught the ritualists to explore intervals. Harps were even more elaborate: some had more than twenty strings and were beautifully ornamented, carved and inlaid with precious stones. A balag harp in Gudea's hymn is called *Great Dragon of the Land* and *Foremost of the Land*, another *Lady as Exalted as Heaven*. Lyres also had names. In the *Nanše Hymn* we read of a lyre called *Abundant Cow*. By contrast, lutes were used in smaller rites of worship, but they also appear in royal and popular entertainment and whenever a mobile, lightweight instrument was useful. Unlike the expensive high-status harps, they were available to pretty much anyone. It's similar today and a reason why I would like to focus on them. For lutes certainly got around. The Sumerians used them at least since 3500–3200 BCE. Around 1500 BCE the first evidence for Egyptian lute players appears. By 1400 BCE lutes were played in Alaca Hüyük, Anatolia. Lutes may have started out as sacred instruments, but they soon entered the realm of royal and aristocratic entertainment, public festivity and, around the end of the second millennium BCE, military music. In the Neo-Assyrian period, lutists were marching with the armies. However, lutes do not appear in the common images of large Mesopotamian temple orchestras, which favoured harps, lyres, flutes, wind instruments and various drums.

Harps and lutes require **scales**. When you play a lute, you tend to think of scales in a rising way. Your arm is extended along the neck of the lute: as the hand comes closer to you, you relax and the tones go up. When you play the harp, it could be different. As a result, the more than hundred tablets from the Old Babylonian period that deal with music and maths are enigmatic. Modern music uses ascending scales. The Greek assumed that scales should descend. Nor does a scale have to be limited to an octave; indeed, the word for 'octave' in Akkadian is unknown. And when we want to understand the sacred and profane music of Mesopotamia, we are seriously disadvantaged by the fact that these cultures had many instruments which cannot be identified. There was a whole group of lutes. There were lutes with long and short necks, with medium sized and tiny sound boxes. Most sound boxes were rather small, some completely made of wood and others topped by skin. Strings were usually made of gut. They were attached to the neck with a cord and a small piece of wood to tighten them. Judging from the tassels, two or three strings were common. To top it off, some lutes were fretted and others weren't. All of these types appear very early in Sumerian art. I wonder whether the Sumerians had a creative fit and invented all these instruments at once, or whether there were many lutes in use when they began to make cylinder seals? Even the terminology is a problem. There are plenty of lute names. In music list *Ḫh*, the string instruments are divided into two groups. The first group, as A. D. Kilmer elaborates (RlA '*Laute*') lists instruments according to the shape of their sound box and parts. The second group is specialised in wooden items that have a stick-like appearance. Among them is the GIŠ gu-di, which appears in other lists as a popular musical instrument. The determinative GIŠ means wood. GIŠ gu-di is a common term for an entire family of string instruments. The word may be translated *talking stick (wood)*.

Kilmer mentions Sumerian terms: GIŠ šu-galam-ma (*hand descending (wood)*), GIŠ sa-šu (*string covering (wood)*), GIŠ sikil (*clear (wood)*), GIŠ 30-àm (*great 30 (length) (wood)*), GIŠ šu-gal (*big hand (wood)*) plus the enigmatic GIŠ gu-de-ša-u-ša (*šauša noise gude instrument (wood)*) and GIŠ gu-de-ša-u-šagu-gar-ra (*shoulder placed šauša noise gude instrument (wood)*), and GIŠ sa-3 (*three-strings (wood)*). These Sumerian words are summarised by one Akkadian word: i-(nu). That term was rarely used; the scribes preferred the traditional old Sumerian names. The instrument, as Kilmer proposed, is sometimes simply called gu-di or gu-de; the determinative GIŠ (=wood, tree) may not have been pronounced. Gu-di could have been at the root of the Arabian word ūd, for which no etymology is known. As al-ūd the instrument entered Europe thanks to the Crusades and the Spanish Moors and turned into such words as (Spanish/Portuguese): (a)laude, (English): lute, and (German): Laute. This hypothesis is disputed; maybe the gu-di and the ūd both derive their names from an unknown instrument invented in the Iranian mountains or Central Asia. The earliest known ud and lutes had four strings which were, as far as we can reconstruct it, generally tuned F, A, D, G. Maybe that says something about earlier tunings and maybe it doesn't. However, it's a lovely way to tune a ukulele. Possibly the word gu-di influenced the Greek word kithara, from which we derive words like guitar, zither, crotta, crwth and so on. A note of caution: not all Sumerologists assume that the gu-di was a lute. Another, less common hypothesis, proposes that the algar-surrû, i.e. the algar instrument played with a pick (or stick) was a lute. It could also have been a harp; some Mesopotamian harps were played with a plectrum or even beaten with light reeds, like the dulcimer.

The remains of a lute (called the Harmosi lute) made scholars think about the tuning. Some decided it might have ranged from E to b. It's a vague assumption based on measurements of the neck and some speculation regarding string thickness; other scholars claim that the tonic would have been perfect between c and g. Whatever it may have been, it brings us back to scales. The major difference between harps and lutes is that the latter have the scale more or less built in: you press down the string and the sound goes up. Harps can be tuned to any sort of scale. There is, for example, no reason why the octave should be an important principle, nor are there reasons why it should be divided into seven tones and semitones. One modern example is twelve-tone music, which does not make for catchy tunes (professional musicians specialising in twelve-tone music have a higher suicide rate than any other sort of musician); another example comes from West Africa, where the octave can be divided into seven equal intervals. Or consider the 'crooked' Indian rāgas; several have up to nine tones to the octave; some of them being played on the way up and others on the way down.

The basic seven 'Greek' modes were well known in the Old Babylonian period, 1400 years before Pythagoras. More precisely, the Old Babylonians used a basic set of seven heptatonic, diatonic scales, plus a range of unknown ones. Look at the list. First, as a general formula showing the intervals: t means tone and s means semitone. For convenience's sake, the examples are based on the tonic of C. Of course the tonic (or key) of each scale can be adapted as you like. And last, you can see the highly confusing Greek names, and the probable names in Akkadian and Babylonian. In Mesopotamia, each scale had its specific name. We don't know whether the Old Babylonians wrote their scales in a rising fashion, as we do, or in a descending fashion, as the old Greek musicians did. If music theory started with lutes and a continuous shortening of the string, the scales could rise. But there are tablets that speak of the thick and thin string, referring to lyres and harps, and may indicate the opposite. In fact, we cannot even be sure that the musicians of the Old Babylonian period used a single system to describe their scales. Different places or periods may have had their own terminology. So, each scale has two names, depending on whether it is read from left to right (rising) or right to left (descending).

If Rising: Išartu (*normal*), if Descending: Nīd Qabli (*fall of the middle*)

Stttstt C, Db, Eb, F, G, Ab, Bb, c (Greek: either Phrygian or Dorian)

Rising: Kitmu (*closed*) Descending: Pītu (*open*)

Tsttstt C, D, Eb, F, G, Ab, Bb, c (Greek: Aeolian or Hypodorian, our minor scale)

Rising: embūbu (*reed pipe*) Descending: embūbu (*reed pipe*)

Tstttst C, D, Eb, F, G, A, Bb, c (Greek: Dorian or Phrygian)

Rising: Pītu (*open*) Descending: Kitmu (*closed*)

Ttsttst C, D, E, F, G, A, Bb, c (Greek: either Mixolydian or Hypophrygian)

Rising: Nīd Qabli (*fall of the middle*) Descending: Išartu (*normal*)

Ttsttts C, D, E, F, G, A, B, c (Greek: Ionian or Lydian, our major scale)

Rising: Nīs GABA.RI (*rise of the duplicate*) Descending: Qablītu (*middle*)

Tttstts C, D, E, F#, G, A, B, c (Greek: Lydian or Hypolydian)

Rising: Qablītu (*middle*) Descending: Nīs GABA.RI (*rise of the duplicate*)

Sttsttt Db, D, E, F#, G, A, B, C, db (Greek: Locrian or Mixolydian)

Scales should be appreciated just like prehistoric art. There is a badly preserved *Old Babylonian Hymnody*, which lists royal and possibly divine hymns, plus the starting (or ending?) note of each piece, its mode and the intervals for specific sections. But who knows what musical fashions existed in each period? And what about technical details, like the exact way the half tone was fixed? Greek music might be a very distant relation: scales (or modes) used to involve several fixed tones that made up the major intervals. What remained was called the leimma (the rest, the leftover), and was usually less than a half tone. How the Mesopotamians solved the problems arising from natural scales (without the tempering or equalisation common nowadays) remains to be explored.

We have seven scales. But were there further variations? One fascinating text is a *Hurrian Hymnology*, dating from the middle of the second millennium BCE, which gives 68 more or less fragmentary hymns with musical annotations in Akkadian! Each piece is accompanied by references to the intervals and, in a major innovation, the Hurrian words for 'high' and 'low', which might indicate sharp and flat. How about the 'typical' Near Eastern scales?

Consider the hiatus: an interval of three semitones. Take the scale we started with: Rising: Išartu Descending: Nīd Qabli

Stttstt C, Db, Eb, F, G, Ab, Bb, c (Greek: Phrygian, medieval: Dorian)

Now shift the third tone: C, Db, E, F, G, Ab, Bb, c. Between Db and E appears a gap that does not usually occur in Western music. Nowadays, hiatus intervals are used whenever a composer wants to add an 'oriental' element to a tune. The scale, occasionally known as 'Phrygian major third' or 'Phrygian dominant' is among the most popular in the Near East and sounds absolutely gorgeous. You can find it in Western China, Central Asia, India (two rāgas dedicated to Bhairavī, the Fear-Inspiring tantric goddess), Pakistan, Afghanistan, Iran, Iraq, the Arabian countries, Israel, Turkey, Greece, the Balkan, and the North African Coast all the way to Morocco, from where it spread, with the Moors, into Portugal and Spain, and into Gypsy music. It is used for secular and religious music by Hindus, Buddhists, Muslims, Jews, Christians, Gypsies plus Central Asian Turkish cultures, some of which retain forms of shamanism and animism. Such a wide distribution hints at formidable old age; it wouldn't surprise me if the music mathematicians of Old Babylonia developed it.

Now for a last look at **music theory**. The musicians of the early Stone Ages fixed their scales as they felt like it. I am sure those Neanderthal people who made a diatonic bear-bone flute sometime between 67000 and 43000 BCE did not calculate diameter and distances between the holes by using math. They probably experimented with plenty of bones until they had a something that sounded sweet. And when they had a useful prototype, they found making more flutes an easier job. The same may have been the case among the Cro-Magnon people at the Geissenklösterle cave, Blaubeuren, near Ulm in Germany, roughly 30000 BCE, who used the thin leg bones of water birds. It's in the Schwäbisch Alb, very close to the place where the lion-human statuette was found. But when you have a culture that loves math, like the Sumerians, some clever people are sure to come along who measure string lengths and calculate relations and intervals. And here the circle comes around. Let me quote from Leon Crickmore's Article *New Light on the Babylonian Tonal System*. You can find it online, it is well worth reading.

On the basis of the tablets K170 and Rm 520, Livingstone lists numbers associated with the Babylonian gods: Anu (60), Enlil (50), Ea (40) and Sin (30). The ratios between these numbers also define the main intervals of Just tuning. The perfect fifth (60:40) and the perfect fourth (40:30) are the intervals required for the 'rough' tuning described in CBS10996; the major third and sixth (50:40 and 50:30), the minor third (60:50) and, (if we allow the octave double of 40) even the minor sixth (80:50), all intervals needed for the subsequent 'fine-tuning'. In UET VII 126, a string listed as 'fourth, small string' in Sumerian, is called 'Ea-created' in Akkadian. If the 'normal' heptachord tuning (išartum) is defined in tone-numbers taken from the table of reciprocals, starting at 30 (Sin), the tone-number of the fourth string will be 40, the number of Ea, patron of music.'

We started with the music of the spheres. It connected music theory with the motions of the celestial bodies. Around the beginning of the Common Era, the astrologers discovered the intervals of Pythagoras in the relationship of the planets, the sun and moon. A conjunction (0°) represented full accord, the sextile (60°) the small third, the quintile (72°) the large third, the square (90°) corresponded to the fourth, the trigon (120°) to the fifth and the opposition (180°) to the octave. The astrologers were delighted: a personal horoscope could be interpreted in terms of sound. Medieval astrologers continued to elaborate the system by attributing planets and qualities to each of these intervals.

While such subjects have a certain baroque splendour, I would like to return to the beginning and ask whether the 'Music of the Spheres', attributed to Pythagoras, goes back to a Music of the Gods? Did the divine numbers of Mesopotamia describe the ratios of cosmic harmony? Divine numbers may have been a means to experience the force and nature of the gods, and the relationship between them, in totally abstract terms. Pythagoras used music to prove that everything consists of numbers. Maybe the Mesopotamian priesthood used maths and music to prove the existence of the gods.

Figure 50 Top: Roll seal showing a goddess and god, both wearing horned crowns, a sacred tree and a serpent. Middle of the third millennium BCE, London.

Bottom. Roll seal from Uruk, showing a sacred boat bearing a bull with Inanna's reed-mat emblems plus deities or worshippers. Middle of the third millennium BCE, London.

Figure 51 Fragmentary relief showing a priestess of the Ur III Period. An inscription (omitted) gives a dedication to the goddess Ninsun. After PKG14 (1975), plate 117b.

Figure 52 Fourth millennium BCE stone vessels.

Top: a bald woman (?) near a palm, planting a tree, surrounded by animals and plants. This picture is occasionally paraded as a portrait of 'Lilith' as the Kisikil.lil.la/Ardat Lilî once lived in Inanna's Ḫuluppu tree. The identification is extremely unlikely. From Mari.

Bottom: early goddess with lions holding two serpents. Note bull to the left and scorpion to the right. Is this an ancestress of Ningirima, Inanna or Lamaštu? The vessel is in the British Museum.

Part Five

Wild Countenance

Lamaštu: Diaspora

In the Wake of the Winds

Early in the 1980's I spent a week in London. Day in and day out, the rain kept falling. I had a tiny tent in a south London camping site, sheltered under great trees, in tall, soggy grass. Each morning I was greeted by colourful clusters of mushrooms that had sprouted overnight. By day, I visited bookshops and museums. One happy day I stood in front of that famous Mesopotamian terracotta relief showing a nude woman with eagle feet standing on two lions. On her sides are two magnificent huge-eyed owls, on her head a horned crown and in her hands divine symbols looking like the letter Ω. For someone with such an astonishing outfit, she shows a very tranquil smile. I had spent most of the week in the British Museum drawing deities and now was busy sketching her. A chubby guard passed by, cast a look at my drawing, smiled and said 'O, the goddess of love. How sweet.' It amazed me. Like so many people, I was sure I was drawing Lilith (whose love is somewhat special). The label on the showcase did not mention Lilith at all. I was certain that those innocent and doubtlessly deluded curators didn't know what they were exhibiting, grinned happily, and continued drawing. Yes, it's fun to know better, even if it happens to be wrong. Somewhere in my head was the idea of painting a Lilith picture in acrylics. She had come up repeatedly when I was invoking Medusa, and I wanted to know more about her. Back home, I spent a lot of time in deep trance, visualising the image from the British Museum. It's a gorgeous piece of art, but very static and quite unlike what I had experienced regarding Lilith. For a start, the mood is wrong. The goddess stands straight, everything is symmetrical, and somehow the whole arrangement seems almost lifeless. The more I visualised the image the less suitable it was. Sure, it constitutes great art and is very beautiful. But it does lack the energetic qualities that are so typical for the Lilith experience. Luckily, when things are ripe, the gods take over. One early morning, as I was hovering between sleep and wakefulness, I saw the image explode. The shards flew to all sides and I watched a Lilith descending from heaven who landed with wide open legs, her arms and wings extended to the sides. She did not wear the divine crown of the statue nor was she burdened with sacred insignia. Instead, she held a short sickle (in Japanese style!) and a noose. Her eyes were mad, her hair was streaming in the gale, her wings were beating fiercely, and she was passionately, intensely alive. This deity was anything but a remote bystander. I leapt out of bed and made a sketch. A little later I got obsessed, channelled a text and in-between enjoyed a series of mind-shaking nightmares, wet-dreams and crisis scenes. When the painting was finished it felt almost upsettingly real. I packed it in a bag, walked up the mountain and squatted on the stone-littered slope in the velvet moonlit night invoking her. By daybreak, she had become part of my inner universe, and had fused with the twilight black spruce forest, the gnarled beeches, bristling rowans and the quartzite rocks, gleaming like bone and teeth and fat and flesh, in a mind-space where time stops and absolute reality appears in stunning, mind-shattering glory. The Taunus Mountains are widely different from a Mesopotamian scenery, but they seemed to suit her perfectly. We both came home to ourselves, one way or another. Well, at the time I was pretty much acting on instinct. I hadn't done much research on Lilith, nor did I feel entirely easy about her. In plain words, parts of me were scared, others were committed and she simply blew my mind. Here are some of the rantings I recorded when she obsessed me (7th of Feb. 1983)

Lilith am I, the Shadow and Reflection, of
Fear and Passion, Joy and Sorrow absolute;

I speak the words that utter my perfection,
for as you are so I appear to you...

Call me at night! I am the Shadow Śakti, in me lies pleasure that does never end,

that never is: one substance with the voidness. I am the Shadow of all that could be

and is, and cometh true, manifestation, for with my blood I clothe your dreams in flesh,

shall treat you, as your heart is pulsing, to all the lies and hopes you still insist to live.

Lilith am I, the Queen of Lunacy: behold how terror sparkles from my eyes,

and lushness from my lips. I am the winged fiend of half-forgotten nightmares,

yet I am also wish-fulfilment, as I take and give. My night-black hair is as a strangler's weapon,

its strands so fine they cut through flesh and bone, and bind to form and into matter,

affix in time and space, entrap by law. No-one can flee my touch, escape my passion,

whoever fears, whoever wants, shall give me blood. Emotion is the substance I am drinking,

thus to give flesh to the desired dream. This is the web of my perfection:

as I am false and evil to the blind, so am I liberation to my lovers,

who know that truth is NOT and nor are we.

I hope you are laughing. Magick should be fun. Our first encounters were cataclysmic; the emotional repercussions shook me to the core. In the process, I learned about fear and desire, and how to go beyond both. This was one of the gifts of the goddess, though many others followed. Some things are impossible to express. Here is another try:

As I come flickering from the lilac skies, the fiery source of all there ever was,

between pale crystal coldness and the greenish edge of night.

Within my mind, my mind, O mind, just mind, and mind alone

I break into a million fragments of amazement,

cascading, spinning, whirling, re-emerging,

all is alive, expands, contracts, pulsates: frenzied ouroboros!

Between my eyes a heatwave blazes and time slows, in desert steppes of thistle growth

where lightning flickers in the purple velvet of the everdark

and squalid swamps where clouds of buzzing insects dance,

the hungry earth engulfs the blossoms of beliefs

and sucks them down

as I return to sanity

and all I am

is yours.

Let me apologise. It was a difficult period. In my visions and dreams, the Ancient Ones intruded, and as is their jolly custom, generated plenty of attention with sheer scary energy. At pretty much the same time my relationship disintegrated, as my partner, suffering from nightmares, was scared out of her head. Next followed the series of cataclysmic trances you find illustrated in *Nightshades*. They made me the happy, cheerful soul I am today. For a while, I wondered whether the Lilith contact terminates relationships. This was not the case; Lilith got on well with the women with whom I lived afterwards.

When I was back in London a few years later, the image had disappeared. It was many, many years later that the British Museum reacquired the item and put it on show again.

Sure enough, you've seen her. She appears on LP and CD covers, on silly astrological books where she represents the 'Lilith point', on T-shirts, pendants, posters and in psychoanalytic and feminist literature. Again and again the figure is paraded as Lilith. That's what I assumed when I drew her. From the historical point of view I was totally and blissfully wrong.

Figure 53 The Burney Relief. Old Babylonian period, unidentified goddess with lions and owls. Originally a night scene; the background was black. Today in the British Museum.

Inventing a Goddess

Back in the 1930's, the image, the so-called Burney relief, was first published. It caused quite a stir. Sydney Burney acquired the item from a trader whose identity and source remains unknown. Like so many wonderful pieces of art, the image was acquired on the black market. Burney, glowing with pride, asked the experts of the British Museum to take a look at it. They examined the remnants of black paint (a bitumen product) on the manes of the lions and announced that, estimating the way it was cracked, the item must be older than fifteen years. It was a good and honest estimate and pretty much all that could be asked for. Burney wasn't satisfied. He exhibited the figure to the press and boldly claimed that the image had undergone a thorough chemical analysis, which proved that it would come from the third millennium BCE. It was just the sort of statement to make the experts edgy. At the time, such an analysis was simply impossible. Nobody knew where in Mesopotamia it had been excavated. More so, the goddess looked almost too good to be real. Sure, the item has some cracks and damages near the throat and at the crown. Nevertheless, it seemed amazingly well preserved. It is hardly surprising that a range of experts regarded it with deep suspicion. One excellent summary of the doubtful points was published by Dietrich Opitz in the *Archiv für Orientforschung (AfO)*, issue 1936-37. Opitz was not very happy about the item. He pointed out that the cast, measuring 49.5cm by 36.9cm, was rather large for the alleged third millennium BCE. The owls would be absolutely unique for that early period, just like the way the lions lie sideways but face the observer. These stylistic elements might be more fitting for the middle of the second millennium or later periods. Stranger would be a scorpion's sting, emerging from the tuft of a lion's tail, which would be typical for Neo-Assyrian lions. The goddess suffers from aesthetic problems. Her bosom is untypically large for third-millennium art, but would suit the Old Babylonian period. Similar considerations would apply to the eyes, which were originally inlaid with some precious stone; a highly unusual practice for a common, painted terracotta cast. Her face and body are extremely naturalistic. Third-millennium artists were usually impressionistic and not very bothered by anatomy and proportion. The horned crown, Opitz claimed, lacks its base, so that one doesn't know how the item was fixed to the head, and the number of horns, still visible at the undamaged right side of the cast, would be five, which would be highly unconventional for an image from the third millennium BCE. Opitz concluded that a third-millennium date was highly doubtful, and would remain so, unless the owner published by what *exhaustive chemical analysis* the image had allegedly been dated.

The same publication had another article on the item by Douglas van Buren. While not explicitly disagreeing with Opitz, van Buren pointed out that a singular hematite owl in a private collection shows some similarity to the Burney relief, and that images of Ištar standing on the back of one or two lions are not uncommon. The Burney relief, no matter its age, is not unique: it has a close parallel in a much smaller image of a nude winged goddess standing on two ibexes, which is exhibited in the Louvre. The two deities show some differences, in that the goddess from the Louvre does not hold anything, has no owls and wears a horned crown with four pairs of horns surmounted by a knob or disk, much like the style of the horned crowns shown on the stele of Urnammu of the late Sumerian Ur III period. Both goddesses have the feet of predatory birds; and there are fragments of two further steles showing the eroded remnants of similar legs, talons, and wings. One of them, unearthed at Babylon, seems to indicate that the goddess stood on two lions. It's hard to be sure as her face is gone, and so are all fine details. A second fragment, also from Babylon, shows the hips to taloned feet of the same or a similar goddess. A third fragment was excavated at Aššur, showing a winged goddess from shoulders to hips. Unlike the others, she seems to wear bracelets. Finally, a vase from Senkereh-Larsa shows a nude winged goddess accompanied by birds, a bull, a tortoise and two fishes. This deity, originally coloured red, has a similar posture as the others, but seems to exhibit human feet. That's what van Buren wrote; personally, I find them remarkably large and distorted. Van Buren identified the goddess of the Burney relief with Inanna/Ištar, and based his claim on a passage from a hymn to the goddess as the planet Venus, chanted at the New Year Ceremony in the time of Iddindagan, (after Stephen Langdon):

Unto holy Innini they hasten.

My Queen unto the vault of Heaven joyfully wings like a bird (?)

in the plains (of the nether world), the clean place, in the land of desolation.

It's a strange passage; personally, I would associate it more with Ereškigal than with her sister Ištar. Inanna/Ištar, as the goddess of the planet Venus, was naturally assumed to travel across the sky somehow. Another section of similar nature (Langdon, JRAS 1925, p.717):

Queen (of heaven), who puts on the 'Garment of Heaven',

who rises in the sky valiantly,

over the sky she flies.

The Making of a Myth

A year later, the same periodical published an article by H. Frankfort entitled *The Burney Relief* (AfO vol. XII, 1937-1939). Frankfort dismissed many of the points that Opitz had tried to make, in particular the number of the horns (he counted four) and the imaginary scorpion's sting in the tassel of the lion tail. Citing a few comparable pieces of art, Frankfort showed that while the Burney relief is a rare, early and unusual item, it isn't entirely unique. Even the head position of the lions has parallels in late third millennium or early second-millennium art. To him, the unusual element is the fact that the lions have closed mouths, as the art of the period usually shows lions with jaws wide open. But if the item was made for worship and not to scare evil spirits, it would be sound business sense if the worshipper wasn't snarled at. At the end of his article, Frankfort tried to identify the goddess. Here his otherwise sensible analysis became increasingly strained. For a start, he outlined that female winged figures with bird talons for feet *were well known to the Akkadian seal-cutters, and their designs leave no doubt as to the noxious character of these demons. Sometimes they are shown holding a crouching man in their talons and another in each hand. Elsewhere they are depicted as captives, bereft of the crown of divinity, and held by the wings by two heroic figures, which seem at once to be attendants of the sun-god. The texts suggest that these creatures are the inhabitants of the land of the dead.*

That's imaginative, to say the least. He continued with the well-known story how Enkidu dreamed of being killed by a male demon with a bird head and eagle claws. André Parrot, Frankfort cited, had identified this figure as Nergal. Next, Frankfort referred to E.G. Kraeling, the first scholar who proposed that the goddess would be Lilith. Frankfort argued that Lilith, as a succubus who slays men, is an inhabitant of the land of the dead, and that the symbols of justice in her hands imply that she is meting out the sentence of the gods. He wrote for *the visitations of demons were considered punishment for sins, though the victim might be ignorant of the nature of his guilt.* Even the divine crown would not invalidate this interpretation, as *the line of demarcation between gods and demons is far from rigid.* And where it comes to owls, Frankfort quoted the one and only descriptive line on a so-called 'Lilith' from the Sumerian period (the story appears below) *the shrieking maid, the joyful, the bright Queen of Heaven.* Shrieking, in his opinion, is what owls do. After stating his astonishing assumptions, he hedged his bet by writing that the identification cannot be proved, as the textual description of Lilith would be based on circumstantial evidence, but insisted that *there can be no doubt* that the Burney relief *renders an inhabitant of the Land of Death.*

As it turned out, there can be quite a lot of doubt. That the many winged females on cylinder seals all show the same deity or entity has long been disproved. There are plenty of winged goddesses in Mesopotamian art, and most of them cannot be identified. The Enkidu-abducting figure with the 'face of a bird' actually has the face of the Anzu bird, which looks like a lion, and the feet of a lion; it is only the talons that come from an eagle. He could be Nergal, but is more likely to be the dangerous deity or spirit called Samana, who looks much like a male version of Lamaštu. Enkidu's dream: this passage of the *Gilgameš Epic* is many centuries younger than the Burney relief, and we can't simply assume that a given story must be 'old' just because it suits our speculations. Nowadays, the *'shrieking'* of the so-called 'Lilith' is translated *'she laughs with a joyous heart'*. Do owls *'laugh with a joyous heart'*? Well, they do, in a better world, and so should all other beings, you and me in particular, but in this one, sorry, they don't. Nor does the Sumerian text in question really mention Lilith or her Babylonian ancestress Lilītu: the goddess is called *'the Girlfriend of Lilû'* and is a related, but distinct figure. You'll meet her further on, one way or another. And while bird symbolism is certainly connected with the underworld in the late versions of the *Gilgameš Epic*, it is not so in the early Sumerian tales. I suspect that Frankfort, like several other scholars, was under the impression that 'underworld deities' (like Nergal) have birds' feet. It's an early delusion of Assyriology. A few images were assumed to show conditions in the underworld. The best example, it was alleged, is an amulet of bronze, a so-called **'Hades relief'** (see illustration) showing four rows of divine symbols, ritualists (or evil spirits?), a sickbed scene plus Pazuzu and Lamaštu at the bottom. The item was innocently compared to Egyptian pictures of the underworld by Scheil and Maspero in the late 19th Century. Egyptian maps of the realm of the dead often show distinct layers of existence, and the patient with the fish-masked healers on the third layer (from above) was mistakenly identified as a death-bed scene. If the bottom was the underworld, its denizens must be dwellers of the deep. Both Pazuzu and Lamaštu have birdlike legs and feet, hence, underworld beings might look similar. All of this was amazingly inventive. The idea lasted for roughly thirty years. In 1908 Karl Frank published a detailed study of the so-called 'Hades Reliefs' and clearly proved that they have nothing to do with the underworld. He did an excellent job, but many scholars didn't notice. The questionable idea that underworldly deities have bird feet seems to have stuck. It is rather unlikely. For one thing, a wide range of Mesopotamian deities and divine heroes have underworldly connections without exhibiting birdlike feet. For another, Pazuzu is a god of winds and mountains, and Lamaštu dwells in the wilderness (unless she comes visiting people like you). This so-called 'Hades-relief' shows her travelling through a swamp by boat. Remember the changes of Mesopotamian religion during the dismal first millennium. Pazuzu was introduced by the Aramaic nomads who began to intrude into Mesopotamia around the eleventh century BCE. By the middle of the first millennium they had become a substantial population group with plenty of influence. By the end of the first millennium they were probably the majority. Pazuzu is a young deity specifically invented to deal with a group of terrifying wind deities, most of them female. The Arameans turned him into the *king of the wind deities.* It was his duty to protect pregnant women and their households from the attention of the other wind-deities, i.e. Lilītu, Lilû and the Ardat Lilî. Since the Middle Babylonian period, Lamaštu was occasionally classed as a wind-deity, and sporadically identified with Lilītu and the Ardat Lilî. It turned her into a target of Pazuzu's unfriendly attention. We read that the Lilû deities (or spirits) ride the winds and storms and haunt steppe, desert and bedrooms; but it is not commonly claimed that they inhabit the underworld. The same goes for the major four wind-deities who govern the cardinal directions. In some images they have human feet, in others, probably later ones, the legs and feet of birds. The cardinal winds do not dwell in the Underworld, nor

Figure 54 This famous and fairly young amulet was originally interpreted as a 'Hades relief' and mistakenly assumed to show the Mesopotamian Underworld. Though K. Frank disproves this assumption, and showed that the 'funeral scene' was actually a patient on the sickbed, the idea that 'Underworld deities', like Lamaštu and Pazuzu have bird-feet is still popular among badly-informed researchers. What was assumed to be the 'Underworld' is actually a simple swamp. Pazuzu makes Lamaštu pack her gear and depart. On the top register you can see the emblems of the great gods. Below them are masked ritualists, deities, or the Seven; the question is still under discussion. Bronze, collection de Clercq, Paris.

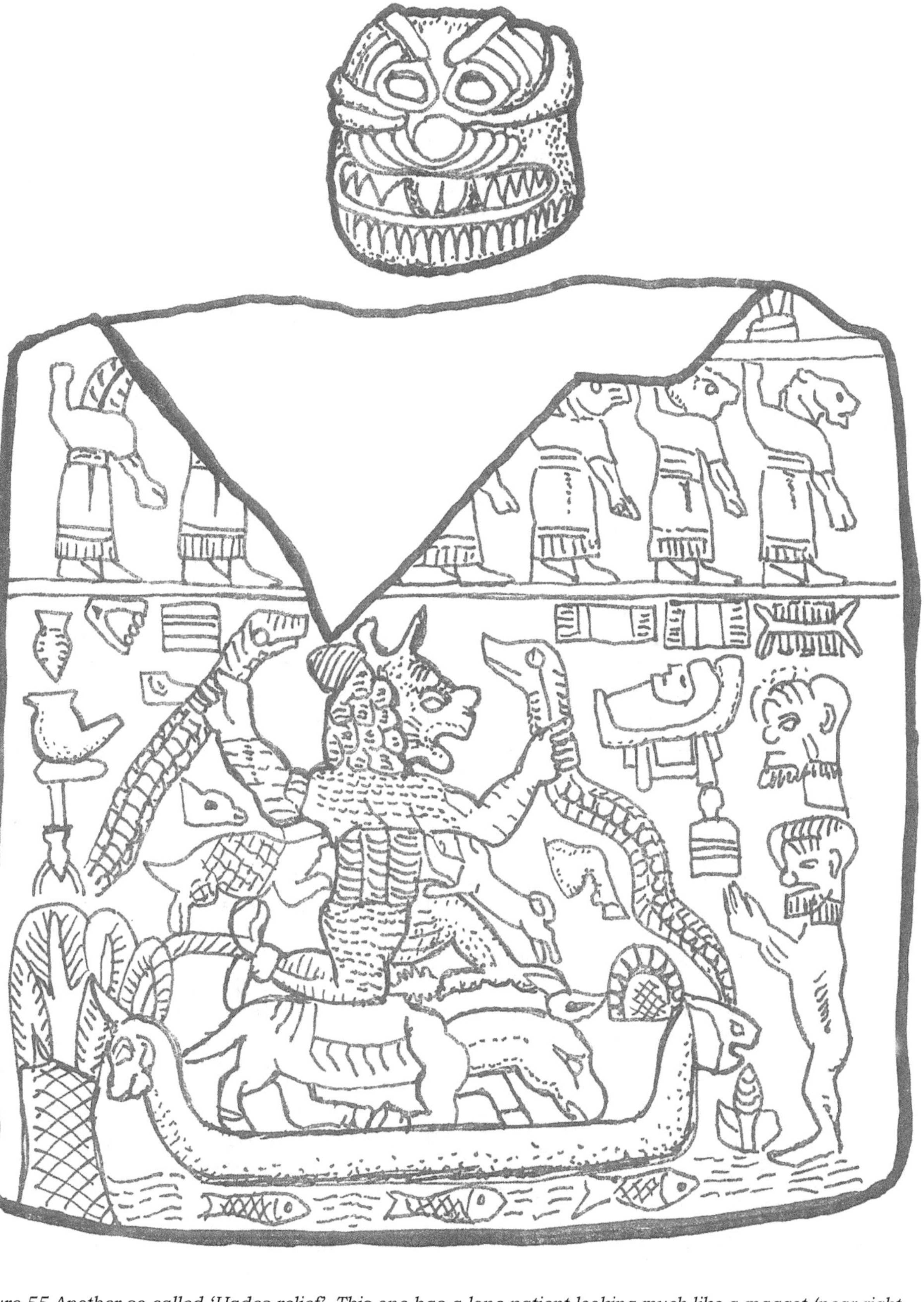

Figure 55 Another so-called 'Hades relief'. This one has a lone patient looking much like a maggot (near right snake), a Pazuzu head and an unidentified human figure to the right. Unlike the other example, in this picture Lamaštu is not fleeing from Pazuzu. Note she has a tiny scorpion between her legs. Lamaštu amulet #58, excavated in Nimrud, after Farber 2014, XIV.

are they related to the dead. However, the realm of the dead, in Babylonian thought, has a lot to do with birds. Apart from these difficult questions there is the biggest problem of them all: the goddess of the Burney relief wears the emblems of the highest deities and the cast was made for worship. Who in Mesopotamia would worship any sort of proto-Lilith? Given so many troublesome questions, it is very doubtful that the Burney relief shows Lilītu, let alone the much later qabalistic Lilith, who was pretty much created in medieval Spain. Most scholars did the sensible thing; they shut up and remained cautious. Not so a wide range of badly-informed researchers of the early and middle 20th Century, who were spellbound by the gorgeous nude woman, read Kraeling's and Frankfort's tentative interpretation, and promoted her, without a trace of doubt, as Lilith. One of the most influential was Erich Neumann, a star pupil of C.G. Jung, who fused Jung's archetypes with several common delusions of the late nineteenth and early twentieth century. Neumann was an enthusiastic supporter of comparative religion, and like his mentor, the reformed ex-Nazi Carl G. Jung, he had clear opinions about a lot of topics he didn't understand. That's the fun bit when you are a psychoanalyst: you can reinterpret anything that comes your way. Serious research is not required. In his groundbreaking and beautifully illustrated book *The Great Mother*, he discussed a lot of deities, and composed chapter headlines like *Body-vessel and mother–child situation – the positive elementary character of the feminine* (1955:147). Neumann proclaimed that women are basically mothers: either they are good mothers or bad ones. The same went for goddesses. The Indian goddess Kālī, for instance, belongs to the bad mother type. Sure, in most Indian cults she is no mother and has no children, but plain facts have never stopped a psychoanalyst from revealing the hidden truth. Unlike millions of Hindus, Neumann knew what was really going on and called her image *'perverse'*.

The qabalistic Lilith of medieval Spain is a slayer of infants. Neumann identified her as a *terrible mother*, and published the Burney relief under the title *Lilith, Goddess of Death*. As boobs sell, and big boobs sell double, it ended up on the cover of several editions. Thanks to Erich Neumann, this so-called Lilith became popular among Jungian therapists, matriarchy researchers, feminists, hippies, artists and New Agers. Neumann's fixation with motherliness was eventually discarded. The pill was invented and women gained the choice to be what they liked. Before long, Lilith was transformed from *terrible mother* and *death goddess* and became an independent woman, who chooses to have a divorce, no children and embarks on a career. It was a new idea, as only a late text of the ninth or tenth century CE, the *Alphabet ben Sira*, elaborates the unhappy marriage of Lilith and Adam and their subsequent separation. No matter that the Lilith and Adam story is so late, popular writers keep claiming it must have been part of the *Bible*. For many feminists and pagans, Lilith is a goddess of independent women. The Burney relief clearly shows a proud and beautiful nude lady with a happy smile. Her horned crown was taken as evidence that Lilith was a positive and venerated goddess in Mesopotamia. It suited a feminist theory that terrifying goddesses were originally benevolent beauties who were turned into creatures of evil by a bunch of misogynistic patriarchal tyrants. In popular opinion, the Burney relief goddess is a positive version of the badly maligned Lilith who was Adam's first wife. It hardly matters, except to scholars, that this singular legend is 2600 years and more than 5000 km away from Babylonia.

Appeal for Ištar

Since then, a lot has happened. The Burney relief passed to the collection of Norman Colville and then to the British Museum. It remained a highly controversial piece of art. Then it went back to private hands and was eventually bought by the British Museum for its 250th anniversary in 2003. It was reinstalled, with much publicity, as 'the Queen of the Night'.

Nowadays, unless they still cling to the idea that the item is a forgery, most scholars assume that the Burney relief is a cast from the early second millennium BCE. Dated by thermo-luminescence, the mysterious goddess belongs to the Old Babylonian period, the approximate date being between 1765-1745 BCE. As such dates are not supposed to be exact, we may assume that the item was cast between 1850-1750 BCE. Far from being a solitary item, the image was mass produced. The high relief plaque was created by pressing straw-tempered clay into a mould. After the clay had dried, the surface was smoothed and fired. Finally, it was painted in four colours. The background, the manes of the lions and the hair of the goddess were painted in bitumen black. The body of the goddess was radiant red-ochre; the bodies of the lions pale white. The wings of the goddess and the owls were painted in red ochre, black and white, while the horned crown, necklace and symbols in her hands were done in a magnificent, warm orangey-yellow. Whoever the image may represent, she was certainly in demand. It indicates that she is unlikely to show Lilith or one of her close relations: there is (so far) no evidence that Lilītu was worshipped by anyone. We have no hymns, no cult, temples, shrines, dedications, myths and only very few references to her. It's a sad truth but you and I just have to live with it. But who else could it be?

As you recall, several experts guessed that the picture shows Inanna or Ištar. Indeed, the goddess of planet Venus is occasionally (though not very often) described in her celestial flight. The Burney relief goddess wears the elaborate horned cap that graces the highest deities. Four horns are a sign of extremely high status. Likewise, she carries two important status objects that are very closely associated with kingship and government: the measuring rod and the measuring line. Both of them appear among the divine Me which Inanna gained after getting drunk with Enki; they represent the justice and impartiality of the righteous king. In several (though not all) Sumerian and Old Babylonian city-states Inanna granted some kings the right to govern, hence, the divine symbols might be a clue that the image shows Inanna/Ištar. The same goes for the lions. So far, so good. A few minor problems remained. For one thing, many gods and goddesses are associated with lions and can be seen wearing horned caps or holding the regalia of justice. The big trouble turned out to be the talons of the goddess: as far as we know, Inanna and Ištar are never shown with bird feet. Also, the goddess lacks weapons. After Sargon of Akkad made Inanna/Ištar the sovereign goddess of his newly founded capital and, by extension, of the empire he had just won in a series of bloody wars, images of her tend to bristle with weapons. Ištar often looks like a walking Swiss army knife. The goddess of the Burney relief lacks weapons. Like Nanay she would be more at home in a ritual space or in bed than on the battlefield. A third proposal claims that Inanna/Ištar has nothing to do with owls. It seems a little weak when we look at her function as a goddess of prostitution. The goddess of love, as several hymns specify, goes out at sunset, when Venus rises, to seek lovers at the canals, the quay or in the ale-house. She has similar working hours as the owl. And when you look at *Gilgameš*, tablet VII, you find the dying Enkidu cursing the prostitute Šamḫat who seduced him when he was still an innocent and filthy crusty in the wilderness. His curse fixes an evil fate to her, a sad life of abuse and poverty. Derelict houses and the shade of the city wall will be her only resting place and drunken customers will vomit on her dress. One of the lines goes *Owls will nest (in your roof beams?)* (Dalley, 2008:87). It's a faint connection, I agree, and a sad story. Luckily, it did not end there. In ancient Babylonia, prostitutes did not have a high status, but they were a recognised and accepted part of society and enjoyed the protection of Ištar, several deities and the king. Lust was recognised as a divine power and prostitution was one of the many divine Me that constitute civilisation. When Enkidu uttered his curse, sun god Šamaš objected that it was Šamḫat, the prostitute, who had made Enkidu a man, prepared him for civilisation, and allowed him to become the best friend (and lover) of Gilgameš. Without her, Enkidu would have spent his life as a lonely, hairy savage in the wilderness. Enkidu, hearing the true voice of the sun, understood his error, reconsidered and blessed his initiatrix. It says something about Babylonian thought: prostitutes were blessed in principle and cursed by brutal reality. Thorkild Jacobsen speculated that the goddess of the Burney relief might be a protective deity of prostitutes. More recently, Wiggermann came up with the idea that she shows Kilili, a very obscure goddess related to love and sex, who was assimilated into the cult of Inanna/Ištar. It's one of those ideas that are remarkably hard to prove or disprove, as extremely little is known about her. Regarding the bird-like legs, Groneberg (1997:26, in Frey-Anthes 2007:186; trans. JF) proposed that Inanna/Ištar could be related (in a very remote way) to the wind-and-storm deities, and quoted a line from a hymn to Ištar:

In the wrath of the Lilû-demons they know you.

Compare the line with the inscription (YBC 4601, quoted under LS II, 157) saying Lamaštu examines the land in the rage of a wind deity. All of this is nice and quite as reliable as the identification with Lilith, but not exactly convincing. Reluctantly, most experts dismissed the identification with Ištar but did not know what else to propose.

Goddesses, with and without Feathers.

Eckhard Unger (RlA *'Frau, geflügelt'*) claimed that the idea to equip human images with wings became popular by the Kassite period (c.1500 BCE), and that, as human bodies are heavier than birds, they were frequently equipped with more than one pair of wings. Usually, these women have four wings: two short wings on the shoulders and two long wings along the arms. A few even have six. He dismissed two early images, allegedly dating from the Akkadian period, as fakes, for stylistic reasons or as the inscriptions were misspelt. In his opinion, the Burney relief also constitutes a forgery, mainly as the goddess has modern anatomy; mind you, he admitted the item is a masterpiece. Many nude winged women appear on seals, often from the Assyrian period, and in decidedly mysterious compositions. For a while, scholars sought to trace a singular 'nude goddess', but this quest had to be given up as there are plenty of goddesses who appear nude from time to time. Some relate to love and lust, others to rain and weather, or they bring chaos, war and discord. Even the popular guardian spirit (or deity) Lamma/Lamassu may have looked like a beautiful, nude winged woman on occasion. A whole bunch of dressed women with wings can't be explained either, but as Unger speculates, the key to this common motif is a relief from Tell Halaf, dating around 1300 BCE, showing a woman, wearing a horned cap, with six wings, who pours rainwater from a meandering band of heavenly water. Her costume would characterise her as a rain- and air-goddess. Unger admitted that the name of this goddess, who frequently appears to be fighting monsters, is still unknown, but suspected that she might be one of seven twin-daughters of the goddess Bau/Baba, who were allegedly fused into one goddess during the Kassite and Middle Assyrian period. A celestial rain goddess? It would explain the mass-produced terracotta cast, but poses the question how rain-making relates to the bitumen-black night-time background of the Burney relief.

The goddess of the Burney relief is an early example of what became a very common form of depicting goddesses in the Near East. The most unusual element in the relief are the bird feet. If we replace them with human feet, we arrive at the standard posture for many goddesses. Plenty of them are nude. They stand upright and hold a range of objects in their raised hands. You can find a good selection in Raphael Patai's *The Hebrew Goddess*, and in the exhibition catalogue *Beyond Babylon*. A gold pendant from Ugarit, dated around the 15th to 14th century BCE, shows a goddess standing on a tiny lion. She has the same posture as our Burney relief goddess, but instead of the rod and rope-rings she holds tiny horned antelopes, while serpents are rising at her flanks (they might remind you of Lamaštu). A similar item from Ugarit shows a goddess holding flowers. Both are syncretistic, as they combine the posture of the Babylonian goddess with an Egyptian Hathor hairstyle or wig. The same hairstyle appears in Mesopotamian art. Just for the record: Hathor is not a typical Egyptian goddess. Though she had an important place in the Egyptian pantheon, she was also associated with the foreign lands outside of Egypt. Whether the flower-holder is identical with the Lady of the Beasts remains an open question. A third gold pendant was found in the Uluburun ship; it dates to around 1300 BCE and shows the goddess holding antelopes. Unlike the first example, she lacks the snakes and the lion. It would be nice to know who she is. During the middle and late second millennium BCE, the Near East was a religious melting pot and images and attributes of deities were frequently mixed up. The goddesses could be Ašerah, the Syrian goddess of the Sea, who was of such importance in Canaanite and early Jewish worship. Up to the fourth century BCE she was widely popular as the wife of Baal and/or YHVH. Ašerah is often associated with lions, but so is Astarte, whose images received a lot of influx from the Mesopotamian Ištar. Anat, the Syrian goddess of love and war, was also strongly influenced by Ištar, and often has a lion in her company. Or maybe the image depicted the Hurrian goddess Šaušga. In Egypt we encounter a goddess whose name was written, phonetically, as qdš or qdš.t, and pronounced Qadeš. She was praised as the Lady of Heaven. Qadeš is not a native Egyptian goddess but was imported during the late second millennium BCE, probably from Mesopotamia. We see her standing, just like so many other goddesses, on a lion. She holds two serpents, like Lamaštu frequently does. The name of the goddess is closely related to the Akkadian word qadištu (sacred or tabooed woman). Inanna, Ištar, Lamaštu, Lilītu and several other Mesopotamian goddesses were called qadištu. Among the West Semites, a woman 'set apart' could be a priestess in the temple, sacrificing to Ašerah, or a prostitute living outside of society. The fanatical Biblical prophets also used the word, meaning 'whore', to insult women who believed in other faiths. The nudity of the goddess is another riddle: in ancient Sumerian art, nudity could be a sign of sacredness. Whether this was still the case in the Old Babylonian period, let alone in younger times, is uncertain. Also, not every nude person was sacred: whether nude musicians, acrobats and dancers were sacred or simply part of the entertainment is not always clear. Prisoners of war and convicts were also stripped naked, and they were as unholy as they come. On the other hand, many scholars, bedazzled by nudity in general, assumed that it represents fertility, seduction or prostitution. That sexuality of some kind may be related to Qadeš is possible, given that she was occasionally the mate of Min and Ptah, but this is not the same thing as prostitution. For whatever reason, the goddess Qadeš was equipped with a Hathor wig plus crown and horns, and a brightly jingling sistrum (Bonnet, 2000:362).

All of these goddesses, though they have a very similar posture as our Nightside Lady of the Burney relief, lack bird feet and wings. But there is an entire cluster of popular Near Eastern goddesses who have wings. One such goddess is the Syrian Anat, who exhibited the characteristic Ištar functions as a love-and-war goddess, while acting within a different myth cycle. Another is the Egyptian Ma'at, representing such concepts as truth, justice, tradition and the divine order to which humans and gods are irrevocably bound. In Egypt, Ma'at was a fairly abstract goddess. Unlike other deities, who have affairs and fights and stories, Ma'at remained in the background and provided the matrix of divine continuity on which on which Egyptian culture was based. Those who respected Ma'at followed the principles of ancient civilisation to *return to the place of yesterday*. A comparison of Ma'at with Anat is an enlightening experience. Both of them are usually winged. Both have a lot to do with air, in that Anat acts like a raging storm and Ma'at gives the air to breathe. Apart from this, they couldn't be more different. It gets more complicated when we look into early Hebrew religion. Unlike what the *Bible*, the *Talmud* and

Flavius Josephus tried to pass off as history, the narration of Hebrew religion is a tale of polytheistic worship and syncretistic evolution, harshly interrupted by occasional attempts to enforce monotheism. The early Jews had a faith focussed on YHVH, Elohim and Adonai, who may or may not be the same god. But besides these deities, they made much of the gods they encountered in their migrations, settlement in Canaan, Assyrian deportation and eventual return. Like all of their neighbours, they assumed that male gods have female partners. One of these was Ašerah, the Syrian goddess of the Sea. Here, a brief reconsideration may be useful. Some might think that an oceanic goddess is limited to a specific sphere of interest and not of much interest to people who live further inland. But to a culture that believed that earth is surrounded on all sides by an ocean, and that everything was formed through the interaction of Heaven and the Primal Sea, an oceanic goddess is at the root of all creation. This isn't simply the 'water element'; it is water as the primal, life-creating substance. We encounter a similar idea in the south Sumerian belief that everything appeared out of the primal water-goddess Nammu, whose name was written with the Sumerogram ENGUR, signifying the great, world-surrounding Abyss. In Ugaritic myth, Ašerah is the wife of Baal. Baal, however, is not a name but a title and means, like the Akkadian Bēl, 'the Lord'. Though they came from distinct cultures, for many early Hebrews, Baal and YHVH were interchangeable. Ašerah was often worshipped as the wife of YHVH, and when the priests of Baal were massacred by the followers of YHVH, the priesthood of Ašerah was spared. In fact, even the rabid prophets rarely complained about her. Up to the sixth century BCE in general, and the fourth century BCE in particular locations, Jewish communities sacrificed to YHVH, Ašerah and several other deities simultaneously. It's not what they'll tell you in church. Keep in mind that the biblical texts underwent a lot of editing. The *Bible*, as you know it, is a compilation designed to show that strict, male-dominated, narrow-minded, abstract monotheism has always been the true faith of the children of Israel. The same goes for the monumental Jewish histories compiled by Flavius Josephus and Philo. In the real world, the Hebrews, like all of their neighbours, did not have much faith in an abstract, transcendent, unknowable, intangible and utterly remote god. They believed in deities who lived in family constellations, who were concerned about life on earth, and who could be counted on to get things done. An intangible, incomprehensible god may have been the ideal of some seers and prophets, most of them feeling unhappy and very much alone, but for the common people, substantial gods with images, stories and a happy family life were more reliable. This situation aroused the wrath of many prophets. Thanks to their passionate ranting we know how polytheistic the majority of the population was.

I'm sure you've heard of King Solomon. He reigned in the tenth century BCE and is justly famous for his nature studies, his wisdom, magic, and for building the temple of Jerusalem. Solomon was a genius; he coined 3000 proverbs and composed 1005 songs. He lectured about (or: to) trees, cattle, worms and fishes. Representatives of all nations came to listen to his wisdom. And he somehow survived loving 700 aristocratic wives and 300 secondary wives. Many of them were foreigners, in spite of the fact that the Lord had explicitly forbidden congress with alien women, as they would promote false faiths. King Solomon was almost damned by the fanatics as he believed in many gods and sacrificed on mountain-top sanctuaries with sacred trees and pillars dedicated to Ašerah. The Jewish historians went to great lengths to explain his polytheism away. Surely he must have been senile. Or maybe he simply tried to make his many foreign wives happy. Out of true love, for political reasons and to avoid being kicked out of the bedroom in the middle of the night. The *Book of Kings* states that Solomon worshipped the goddess of the Sidonians, who may have been Astarte or Ašerah, plus the gods Kemosh and Milcom and was not quite as devoted to the Lord as his father David. The Lord was angry with him, and so were the editors of the *Bible*. God almighty appeared to Solomon twice, and ordered him to reject the foreign deities. Solomon didn't. The Lord in his wrath sent powerful enemies against him. Evidently Solomon wasn't completely senile, as he mastered his opponents, and finally the Lord gave in and allowed him to retain his kingdom. Solomon governed for forty years, a very long time, considering the high mortality of regents in the Near East. The editors of the *Bible* snarled, but they couldn't kick him out of their history, as Solomon had built the temple. The building was amazingly polytheistic, considering that the Lord is basically abstract, formless and remote. Solomon decorated the Temple of Jerusalem with lots of cherubs. To modern readers, cherubs are fat babies with wings. In Solomon's time, most cherubs were adult and female. Unlike the Burney relief, these cherubs were not nude. However, they were frequently winged, beautiful and represented a much-needed counterweight to the overbearing male character of YHVH. Some cherubs look like copies of Ma'at with her wings on. Here, Patai's classic research is well worth reading. In time, the cherubs underwent considerable change. In the final version they seem to have been depicted, in the inner sanctum of the Temple of Jerusalem, as a man and woman in a tight embrace. It could be argued that such images and indeed all images of the divine are merely symbols to represent the aspects of a singular monist deity. Nevertheless, when unity is represented by a range of images, names and functions, distinct personalities develop. It's a very human thing. Solomon's reign represented a happier age. Sorry to say so, but it is almost entirely fictional. Contemporary archaeologists disappointed everyone when they demonstrated that Solomon, provided he lived at all, was a minor regent governing a handful of impoverished villages. His myth was made up, just like most of the Bible, between the 7th and 6th century BCE. Sadly enough, between 600 and 400 BCE, the narrow-minded monotheists successfully eliminated all female expressions of the divine. It didn't last. As Patai demonstrates, after many centuries, the goddesses crept in again. They appeared as qabalistic principles, as the Shekinah and Matronit, and found their full resurgence in medieval Europe.

In the Hands of Ereškigal

The dark pigmentation on the background of the Burney relief indicates that the goddess is associated with the night or maybe the darkness of the underworld. In Jewish tradition, Lilith is close to the night, thanks to a fashionable etymology that identifies her name with the Hebrew word lailah (=*night*). Interpreted in this fashion, Lilith can be understood as 'Nocturnal'. Similar terms, associated with Lilith, are the Hebrew lalû (*to be abundant*) and lulu (*lasciviousness, wantonness*). Neither of them is related to her name, but they were crucial in forming her appearance and function.

Very few modern scholars assume that the Burney relief and its counterparts show Lilītu. Instead, the deity is occasionally identified with Ereškigal, the goddess of the underworlds and queen of the dead. It's a nice idea, but just as speculative, as so far no images of Ereškigal have been identified. Unlike Lilītu and her relations, Ereškigal began as a high-ranking celestial deity, which allows her to wear a horned cap. Likewise, the symbols of measurement and justice fit a goddess of death perfectly. What can be more just and democratic than death, which happens to everyone? More so, in the Babylonian song *Ištar's Descent to the Underworld*, Ištar has to surrender her divine insignia before she is allowed to pass through the Gate of No Return. The story does not mention that she regained them when she was allowed to leave. In general, high-ranking gods hold only one measuring rod and cord. In the Burney relief, the goddess has two. Ereškigal might have kept Ištar's set. But this idea only carries weight when we pretend that the common Babylonian version of the story was known in the Old Babylonian period when the Burney relief was made.

Figure 56 Typical Near Eastern goddesses.

Top: Winged Mesopotamian goddess with human feet, central design of a 'Lady of the Beasts' composition on a vase, Louvre, Paris.

Bottom Left: the goddess Qadesh, a foreign, Mesopotamian goddess imported by the Egyptians. Note her similarity to Lamaštu amulets.

Bottom right: another winged Babylonian goddess with bird feet, also falsely identified as 'Lilith'. This one has no sacred insignia but a divine horned crown and stands on Enki/Ea's sacred animals, the ibexes. Louvre, Paris, AO 6501

Figure 57 Top: section of the relief of Šamaš-Reš-Uṣur. The goddess is identified as Ištar by an inscription. Babylon, today in Istanbul.

Bottom: section of the relief of Anubanini, in Sar-I Pol-I Zohab, showing Ištar as war-goddess dragging a captive along.

Figure 58 Stele dedicated to Ištar of Arbela, after Thureau-Dangin.

Let's meet Lady Underworld. Ereškigal, Ereškigalla, Aršiginkal (Akkadian: Allatu(m)) is one of several goddesses who ruled the depths. The Akkadians called her messenger Mūtum (*Death*). Ereškigal had several husbands. One is Gugalanna, the *Great Bull of Heaven*. We only know that he died. I wonder how, considering that he was living in the realm of the dead. Much better documented is Ereškigal's other husband, the sinister god Nergal (*Ruler of the Great City*). It seems that the Underworld was originally governed by a goddess (or several) and that during the Old Babylonian period she received a husband. That, of course, is just guessing; what people thought about the realm of the dead has long been forgotten. We can only be certain that Nergal is death personified: he roams about in the night like a sinister assassin and is petitioned not to kill the child on the playground, the elder in the council, the singer in the pub or the old woman leaning over her beer (SAHG 1953:83). Ereškigal has several children. One of them is her sukkal (vizier) Namtar, who represents fate, the life force, and the deadly fate that lies in store for short-lived creatures such as you and me. Another is Ninazu (*Lord Physician*), a popular serpent god with close ties to Elam. Like his mother, he was associated with the constellation Hydra. Ereškigal has a daughter called Nungal. She acts as a midwife when the major goddesses give birth, but she is also a goddess of prisons. In Mesopotamia, prisons were not places where people suffered for their misdeeds. They were simply used to detain folks who had not been judged or punished yet. 'Prison sentences' did not exist. So far I haven't seen a single hymn to Ereškigal. She must have had some, as she appears on lists of temple sacrifices, but I doubt they were really popular. In spite of this, she certainly got around. She appears in the Hittite ritual tablet KUB 36.89. Here is the story. A GUDU priest is searching for the lost storm god of Nerik, who is urgently needed to bless King Tabarna and Queen Tawananna. To find him, the GUDU priest travels to Nera and Lala, where he sacrifices sheep for the storm god of Nerik, for a badly documented god called Uruzimu and, you guessed it, for Ereškigal. The food offerings are thrown into a pit, hence into the Underworld. After this ritual, a *Man of the Storm God* called Ḫuzzia appears and chants an invocation that makes the storm god of Nerik descend from heaven. It leaves us amazed: just how and why did the Hittites include Ereškigal in their pantheon? And how did she enter, under her Akkadian name Allatu(m), the pantheons of the Hurrian, Ugaritic and Arab people? The Hurrites called her Allani. In Ugarit she is Arsay. Tablet DO 6592 (nowadays in Damascus) states that she received *two mother sheep and one cow* in a ritual for the Underworld, while the other deities of the deep had to share *nine small animals and one ox*, and went to bed hungry. According to Herodotus (I, 131) the Arabs of the fifth century BCE worshipped *'Aphrodite Urania'*, and called her Aliat. As far as he knew, the Arabs revered two deities: Orotalt (whom he identified as Dionysus) and Aliat (III, 8). Aphrodite Urania is the celestial Aphrodite, the goddess of love and lust. She was born from the blood and semen of the sky god Uranus, who had been castrated by his son Chronos (Time) and whose testicles had been tossed into the primal sea. Aphrodite Urania arose from the foam of the sea, and she is more than a simple love goddess. She is older than the deities, she older than civilisation, and almost every Greek god is clearly afraid of her. The Arabs also worshipped her as Allat, a term that came to mean Goddess in general, and as Ar-rabba (*the Lady*) in Taif near Mecca. Allat had a thriving cult in Palmyra while her husband Nergal/Erra was worshipped as Hercules (=Erregal). Much later, Islam integrated her. The *Qur'an* mentions a daughter of Allah called Allat.

Let's return to the Burney relief. Several passages of Mesopotamian literature hint at Ereškigal's nudity. Imagine what it's like when you are a goddess of the sky and a daughter of heaven. If we follow Kramer's interpretation, some creepy underworld monster called Kur abducts you when you are still a child, and drags you from bright heaven into the depths below the earth. Luckily wise Enki comes to the rescue, sails into a volley of stones and fights the monster. That's pretty much all we know. At the present time, most of the story seems to be lost. Whatever may have happened, the monster disappears, and you remain in the deep as the queen of the underworld, incapable of visiting heaven again. You complain that you had no real childhood; you enjoyed no adolescence, had no friends to play and chat with and when you grew up, there was nobody to comfort and love you. The Sumerian song *Inanna's Journey to the Underworld* states that Ereškigal lies in a chamber, moaning like a woman in labour, with uncovered breasts and no blanket to cover her nude body. It would be great to know why, but we are not told. One very tentative interpretation claims that she might be showing the behaviour of a professional mourner of the dead, and that, who knows, she might be lamenting the death her former husband, Gugalanna, the *Great Bull of the Sky*. It's a nice idea that suffers from a sheer lack of detail. That professional mourners were half-nude is possible but unlikely. More so, our goddess complains about a belly ache. What can give the queen of the dead a belly ache? Usually Ereškigal is not described much, but we know from the two versions of *Nergal and Ereškigal* that she, like Lamaštu, is lonely, frustrated and very hungry for love, sex, sympathy and comfort. When she forces Nergal to visit her domain, she wears as little as possible, drags him to bed and doesn't allow him to leave before seven days have passed and he is getting slightly jittery. Something similar appears in the strange XII tablet of *Gilgameš*. It's an appendix. The proper epic ends on tablet XI. Some scribes added the tablet as it elaborates material that should have occurred much earlier. It picks up the theme of Enkidu in the otherworld, and describes Ereškigal:

She who sleeps and sleeps, the mother of Ninazu who sleeps-,

her pure shoulders were not covered with a garment,

her breasts were not pendulous like an ointment jar in a šikkatu basin.'

(Dalley, 2008:122). The passage is slightly difficult. You have encountered the šikkatu several times in the *Lamaštu Series*, where it is nowadays translated as a flask. What exactly may be the basis for a flask? Other translations do not improve our understanding. In Ungnad's translation (1921:115) the last line is missing, but we learn that Ereškigal is pretty nude

whose pure hips are not covered by a garment.

Speiser's translation (ANET 1992:97) has

Her holy shoulders are not covered with raiment,

her cruse-shaped breasts are not wrapped with cloth.

For those of us who didn't grow up speaking Old English, Middle High German or Old Norse, a cruse is an earthenware vessel, such as a flask, pot or cup. Whatever this may mean, and whatever it may say about her remarkable tits, it points at a goddess who is at least partially undressed. Nudity is next to holiness, and requires personal self-esteem, utter honesty and dignity. The word teš (Akkadian: baštu) might be related. A bronze vulva, made as a votive offering, was inscribed with the word teš. It means the dignity, self-esteem and pride of a person or deity, and may have represented the nude goddesses. The word teš also means bloom, life-force, beauty and immanent power. Perhaps it signified all of these things at once, perhaps the meaning changed over the centuries. Is Ereškigal a candidate for the goddess of the Burney relief? At the present time there are no texts associating Ereškigal with lions. However, she might have been equipped with bird attributes like wings and claws. She might even be associated with owls or birds, as the dead, by the Babylonian era, were often assumed to be feathered. *Daily Sacrifices to the Gods of the City of Uruk* (a ritual text copied and/or assembled during the Seleucid period after originals copied in Elam (ANET 1992:344, spelling amended) has: *Neither bull's meat nor fowl flesh shall ever be offered to the goddess Ereškigal.* Bulls are easy: one of her husbands was Gugalanna, the *Bull of Heaven*, sadly deceased under mysterious circumstances, and no questions asked. It might explain her dislike of beef. Perhaps birds, representing the souls of the dead, were also sacred to her. It's a Babylonian idea; see *Gilgameš* VII. Our ritual text on offerings in Uruk is very late and only refers to sacrifices of normal, domesticated birds like geese; it is very doubtful that owls were offered to anyone. Discounting bovines and birds: unlike Lilītu, Ereškigal was a well-established goddess. We may assume that she got other sorts of meat, fish, grains, cakes and probably plenty of beer during her daily temple sacrifices. It may have made life in the underworld a little easier. She wasn't popular, but she was respected. The Sumerian story of Ningišzida's journey to the underworld ends in the blessing: *Great holy one, Ereškigala, praising you is sweet.* (ETCSL translation 2003).

So many interpretations are possible. None is certain and some are even more unlikely. Given that the Burney relief goddess holds measuring tools, we could even argue, for the fun of it, that she is Nisaba, the reed goddess, the deity of scribes, scholars and scientists, who has the knowledge of numbers and measures the universe. I wouldn't try this, but it might be done without too much collateral damage. Or we could argue that the image shows Lamaštu without her mask, as she may have looked when she was still an optimistic, young celestial deity of very high rank. Or as she looks after a tough day of scaring people and spirits and wants to go home to the wilderness to relax with her friends. It's good to take your mask off once in a while. It allows her to appear with the face of a woman. Sadly, it would not explain the horned crown (if Lamaštu wears a headdress at all, it is a different one), the symbols of justice and measurement, nor would it explain a mass-produced terracotta cast for popular worship.

Close Cousins

It gets worse when we consider a similar goddess standing on mountain ibexes. With remarkable innocence, Kramer and Wolkenstein exhibit her as an image of 'Lilith'. Hurwitz (1983:60) agreed, claimed that Babylonia and Sumer are crossed by mountain ranges and stated that ibexes were *not unknown*. A single look at a map suffices to disprove his opinion. Whatever the goddess with her ibexes may symbolise, it was not a standard motif of everyday life. If the owl-and-lion goddess represents Inanna/Ištar, the goddess with the ibexes might represent her close relation Irnina, goddess of the foreign mountains in Iran, Turkey or Lebanon. But that's just guessing and like everything else in this uncertain world it should not be taken seriously. Usually, and this makes things more enigmatic, the ibex is associated with Enki/Ea, and may represent the Abyss. It could derive from the word Kur, meaning the foreign mountains and the Underworld. A sea monster combining ibex and fish became one of Enki's totem animals and appeared prominently in the old astrological pictures of Capricorn. But just what has our goddess to do with it? Several goddesses are close to Enki, some are his daughters, and have temples that float over the great deep waters of the Abyss or were, like Lamaštu, educated and raised by him. They have even less to do with Lilith than the goddess of the Burney relief.

Do you enjoy riddles and enigmas? Are you happy to inhabit a world where things retain their wonder and mystery? Can you cultivate naiveté in spite of all better knowledge? Do you need to label the divine? Personally, I enjoy the fact that the goddess of the Burney relief remains anonymous. She could be Lilītu, Inanna, Ištar, Nanay, Ereškigal or Lamaštu. But she could also be an unknown goddess. Perhaps that's the likeliest interpretation. After all, by the Old Babylonian period, the god lists catalogued more than two thousand deities, most of them totally unknown to us. We are lucky when we can identify two or three dozen by their iconography. It's not enough to be sure of anything. So the Burney relief tells us to keep an open mind. Certainty is for people who have stopped wondering. Good science needs patience: we have to wait for further evidence.

Magick, however, follows different rules. The divine reforms itself anytime the worshippers attach new meaning to it.

Gods are not sharply defined, one-of-a-kind characters: they change shape, gender, names, attributes, domains and myths to remain close to their worshippers or attract new ones. The goddess of the Burney relief may not have been Lilītu in Old Babylonia, but she has certainly become so during the twentieth century. So many people call her Lilith today that she is living up to it. In the grand flow of divine images, Lilith has found a shape that may suit her, and our time, very well.

Living in a Tree

Our first reference to the deity who eventually became Lilith, after borrowing a lot from Lamaštu and Ardat Lilî, appears in a poem entitled (provisionally) *Gilgameš and the Otherworld*, or *Inanna and the Ḫuluppu Tree*. The myth was recorded in the late Sumerian period around 2100 BCE. It contains a Gilgameš episode that was not included in the much later Babylonian and Assyrian compilations. Here is the gist of the story, summarised after Kramer & Wolkenstein, Jacobsen and the invaluable ETCSL page, which has the fullest reconstruction of the text and can be read online. A word on style: as a poetic device, the Sumerians loved to repeat passages word by word. Maybe the text was sung, and the repetitions served as a refrain. To keep our text short, I have eliminated the repetitions. Please look into the sources.

In the first days, the first nights, the first years, when everything had appeared and everything was properly maintained, when bread was offered for the first time in the temples of the land; when heaven had separated from earth and the name (and nature) of mankind had been settled; when An had lifted heaven and taken it for himself; when Enlil had carried off the earth and Ereškigal had been abducted and had received the Underworld as her domain, a woman, Inanna, walked along the banks of the Euphrates. She saw a tree, a lone tree, a ḫulub tree growing at the riverside, watered by the river. The south wind toppled the tree and the river carried it away. The woman Inanna, respectful of the words of An, respectful of the words of Enlil, took the tree from the river and carried it to her city Uruk, where she planted it in her garden. Inanna planted the tree with her feet, not with her hands; she watered the tree with her feet, not with her hands. She wondered how long it might take until she could make a throne and a bed from its wood. Five years passed, ten years passed, the tree grew and became thicker, but its bark would not split. Meanwhile, a huge serpent that could not be controlled by spells had made its home in the roots. The Imdugud/Anzû stormbird, god of thunder and lightning, made its nest in the crown and raised its fledgelings. In the middle of the stem, ***Kisikil Lilla,*** *the* ***Girlfriend of Lilû*** (or: ***Girl of the Lilû group), the lady who laughs with a joyous heart****, had made her home. Inanna wept bitterly. When dawn came and the horizon brightened, the little birds started singing, and when the sun god Utu had risen, Inanna went to him and told him her story. Inanna wept bitterly. But Utu, Inanna's brother, could not help her. When dawn came, the horizon brightened, the birds started singing, Inanna went to her brother Gilgameš and told him her story. Gilgameš put on his heavy armour weighing 50 minas, and they were to him like 30 šekels. He lifted the axe of the road, which weighed seven talents and seven minas. He slew the serpent nesting at the roots. The Imdugud bird and its fledgelings flew away to the mountains and Kisikil Lilla, who lived in the stem, flew away to the wilderness. Gilgameš felled the tree, cut off the branches, and gave them to Inanna for her throne and a bed. Gilgameš received two gifts, the pukku and the mikkû, made from the root and the twigs of the tree, which made him very happy.*

Before we rush on, let me note that the nature of the **pukku** and **mikkû** has been debated for decades. We are dealing with two dangerous toys: Gilgameš used them so recklessly, that the population of Uruk went crazy about them, and played them day and night. One early interpretation was a drum and its mallet. Gilgameš might have drummed the citizens to work incessantly, destroying their health and family life for the erection of the majestic fortifications of the city. The 'drum and mallet' theory was discarded when other texts suggested that the items belonged to a game or sport. The experts explained them as a hockey stick and a ball. But pukku and mikkû were played by the entire population of Uruk, by day and night, and that rules out all rugged outdoor sports. A new interpretation was suggested by Fanie Vermaak (2011:109-138), who pointed out that the Akkadian pukku = Sumerian (giš) ellag = Sumerian (giš) illar. (Giš) illar appears in proverbs, which Vermaak renders *She grumbles like a dog, beaten at the game boards*, and *a fox/jackal walked around the game board* and *What will the dog do to what the fox made?*. Playing pieces carved like jackals and dogs are common in the Near East; some gorgeous sets have appeared in Egyptian tombs. Even the Greek called their playing pieces 'dogs' though they were simply pebbles or pieces of glass. Due to the identification of (giš) illar as a game board, a difficult passage in a self-laudatory hymn by superhero King Šulgi of Ur III gains an entirely different meaning. Earlier translators had assumed that King Šulgi had himself praised for his skill with a javelin or unknown hunting weapon. In the new interpretation, the king was in Dabrum, where the game boards were played. The account begins with the placing of the pieces: *I was an expert in positioning on/with the board/game/game board.* The game piece ((giš) šir) was *swiftly moved from above/on top* and *whenever I moved/jumped I did not raise its head from the place* (hinting at animal-headed pieces). *Whatever I lifted, I carried/took away.* The game board was a large and ornate table *as heavy as lead*, though wonderboy Šulgi, with his amazing physique, demonstrated that he could lift it as easy as a piece of cloth. *The embodied animals, I made them fall down.* It's not much, but might indicate, if the translation is right, that Šulgi was not playing a race game but a strategic battle game where the pieces were first set up, the game commenced, and enemy pieces were captured. Think of strategic games like the Greek petteia (*pebbles*) and its later Roman version ludus latrunculorum. That game was played, so Homer sang, by Ajax und Achilles during the Trojan War, i.e. around the start of the first millennium BCE. The two were so engrossed that neither noticed the slaughter outside of their tent. A picture of the scene appears on Greek vases; usually, their match is witnessed by the goddess Athena, who may have been a patron of the game. Divine support is not an optional extra: many early games had an almost sacral nature. So do pukku and mikkû, when you consider that they were made from Inanna's cherished ḫulub tree. Two players set up their pieces ('dogs') on a game board (a polis: 'city'), and when this stage is over, move them one space at a time, perhaps in any direction (orthogonal and diagonal). At this point the researchers disagree. Falkener (1961:358) promoted the 'one space in all directions' theory and a large 12-square board. Bell (1960:86) preferred to have the pieces move one space, but only in horizontal and vertical directions, and adds a special piece able to jump. He thought of a game board of 8x7 squares, such as the one found engraved on stone in Chester, Northumberland. As Pollux tells us in his *Onomasticon*, a piece caught in a straight line directly between two players is eliminated (custodian capture). Ovid supported this statement. The Greek version is badly documented, though it was popular and philosophers like Aristotle and Socrates praised it. Plato wondered whether it might have been invented in Egypt. Given that Troy is in Turkey, that Homer and most of the early Greek philosophers lived at or near the Turkish coast, were familiar with Mesopotamian literature and that game boards were used in Mesopotamia since at least 4000 BCE, this opinion is debatable. Much better documented is the later Roman version ludus latrunculorum, which became popular all over Europe courtesy of the Empire. Game pieces accompanied the Roman legions, and boards were scratched into the ground wherever needed. Usually, they tended to have between seven and nine squares in a row, but there were also bigger versions. The number of pieces varied, and in some sets there were extra pieces that may have had special powers, or may have been the target of the assault, like the king in chess. Unlike the Greek, the Romans identified their pieces as soldiers, brigands or thieves. A eulogy composed by Saleius Bassus in the first century CE indicates that the game began by setting up the pieces *cunningly* (i.e. not in a standardised formation), that a piece may be protected by moving another to its side, and that one, some, or all pieces were capable of leaping over another. When we allow each piece to move one square in any direction or to leap over another piece, the game becomes tricky and unpredictable. He also told us that a piece can step between two enemy pieces without being caught. The game was enormously successful in Europe of the first millennium CE. It went out of fashion when chess, with its refined feudal war machinery was introduced. Variations of this game have been found in Somalia (seega), Wales and Ireland (gwyddbwyll and fithcheall, played on a board of 7x7), China and Japan (hasami shogi). In some of these games the pieces can move orthogonally over long distances like the rook in chess, but this is hardly useful on small game boards. If you allow me to speculate: in LS II 45, Lamaštu is escorted up to a sailing ship, to depart in the company of four dogs, two white and two black. Could this enigmatic passage refer to a custodian capture by two white and two black playing pieces ('dogs')?

Let's sum up the rest of the tale. Gilgameš used his new toys to make the people of Uruk mad with the new game. Or, as the much later Babylonian *Gilgameš Epos* has it, he kept them building the massive city walls. He became extremely unpopular, and the gods felt forced to interfere. According to one version of the tale, a little orphaned child cried to Utu, the sun god, to put a stop to it. To appeal to Utu is a sure way of getting help. The earth opened, Gilgameš's playthings fell into the deep, and left the monarch sad and bored. His friend Enkidu offered to go to the Underworld to fetch them, but the noble deed cost him his life. The poem concludes with an act of necromancy: Gilgameš raises the ghost (=udug) of Enkidu from the dead and Enkidu gives a detailed and unpleasant account of the otherworld.

So far for our tale. Let's return to Kisikil Lilla living in a tree. It's a neat story and you can find it mentioned as proof of Lilith's ancient origins. A beautiful lyrical translation was published by Kramer and Wolkenstein. They took a few remarkable liberties. Instead of *Girlfriend of Lilû* or *Girl of the Lilû Group* they wrote the *dark maiden Lilith.* At this point, misinformation began. A badly mutilated summary of the story appeared in Patai's influential *The Hebrew Goddess*, and Barbara Black–Koltuv's *Book of Lilith* (1986:24). Koltuv relied on Patai and got burned. She imagined that the tale of Adam and Lilith might derive from Sumerian myth, and presents it as a clash between Lilith (as a woman) and Gilgameš with his *heroic sword of masculine consciousness* (an item which does not occur in the text). She was not aware that Gilgameš was acting at the request of his sister Inanna. Patai had eliminated Inanna from the tale. Other writers took similar liberties. Again and again we encounter the so-called 'Lilith' living in the tree.

What happened in prosaic reality? Our myth does not mention the Hebrew Lilith, or the Babylonian Lilītu, but the Girlfriend of Lilû. She is hardly characterised. Her position between that unknown serpent and the much better known thunderbird is interesting. It's early evidence for a polarity of a bird of prey and a serpent which proved to become so important in much later Indian religion (see, for example, the first book of the *Mahābhārata*). The Nāga folk live in perpetual war with the awesome and destructive Garuḍa bird. The theme also appears in the Babylonian *Etana Epic.* You can find many traces of it from the Near East to China. And I'm sure you are recalling the *Eddas* (Grimnismal, 13; Gylfaginning, 15-16), where we have a serpent/dragon beneath the root of the world tree and a giant/eagle sitting in the crown. Nearby is the abode of Hel, the dreaded bright and dark goddess of the underworlds. It's a similar alignment: a sacred tree, an eagle, a snake/dragon and a sinister goddess. Wouldn't it be nice to know how the Vikings acquired this remarkable bit of Sumerian myth? The symbolism also found its way into practical Tantra: what rests dormant as the Kuṇḍalinī serpent, coiled around the root cakra, wakes, rises to the height, and turns into the free Haṁsa bird, the breath-mind-spirit vehicle of the highest gods. This is not mythology but practical yoga and meditation: the metaphors describe states of consciousness. We could consider the ḫulub tree a tree of life, a shamanic tree connecting heaven and earth. Like so many other versions of the axis mundi, it has three levels (roots, stem and crown) connecting all three realms of existence. I wonder why Inanna wanted to chop it up to make furniture. To what extent did the Mesopotamian cultures believe in celestial trees? We find 'tree of life' motifs in Sumerian, Babylonian and Assyrian art, but the textual evidence is poor. The *Šurpu Series* has several useful references to sacred plants and trees connecting height and depth. The *cedar of right* guaranteed divine justice. But trees are not everything. The link between heaven and earth is also expressed by the ziggurats: artificial, terraced 'mountains' on a plain lacking even modest hills. Both symbols, the tree and the world mountain, are common across Eurasia. If the Tree of Life is a shamanic gate between the layers of the Universe, you might consider that to Inanna, the gate is a seat and a bed, and to Gilgameš a game.

Back to Lilith. Van Buren (1936/1937), writing about the Burney relief, rendered the one descriptive line of the myth: *In the midst Lilith had built her house, the shrieking maid, the joyful, the bright Queen of Heaven.* He used the name 'Lilith' as a convenient (and misleading) anachronism. It's such a remarkable statement that we ought to stop and consider. What makes 'Lilith' the joyful queen of heaven? And just why do Kramer and Wolkenstein describe her as *'dark'*? But it gets stranger still. Though practically all translators use the name 'Lilith', the original text does not. In the real world, the name is Kiskillilla, as Jacobsen transcribed it. Porada (RlA *'Lilû, Lilītu, Ardat-Lilî'*) reads her Sumerian name ki-sikil-lil-la. A kiskil or kisikil is a maiden, a girlfriend, a partner. The Sumerian name means Maiden of Lila, or Maiden of the Lila Group. The Akkadian version is (W)ardat Lilî: the Maiden or Girlfriend of a deity and/or wind god/spirit called Lilû, or Maiden of the Lilû Group. Now for the tricky bit. Several scholars loftily assumed that the Maiden of Lilla/Lilû happens to be another name of Lilith. Tough luck that things are complicated. For a start, the name Lilith is Hebrew, and much younger than the Sumerian and Akkadian deities we are exploring.

In Sumerian myth two groups of gods and spirits are related to the winds. One group consists of four deities: they are the winds of the cardinal directions. The other group has three basic and one occasional member, plus a fifth deity who follows them around. These are called the Lilû, from Sumerian 'lil' meaning *breath, wind, atmosphere* and *vitality*. It hints at something fascinating: the Sumerians may have been aware that breath is vitality and that the winds shape our moods. Just think of the major god Enlil (Lord Wind) and his wife Ninlil (Lady Wind). They are the major regents of the land, its breath, life and vitality. Maybe the deities of the Lilû group, who are badly documented but mentioned with astonishing frequency, represented a similar function. Perhaps Lilû and Lilītu were gods of breath and vitality who were replaced by Enlil and Ninlil. But that's just speculation. Let's explore the names of the Lilû deities. Remember that Sumerian names in capital letters indicate the Sumerograms with which a given name is written. They do not necessarily express its pronunciation, which may be quite different. We encounter:

(Akk.) *Lilû* = (Sum.) LIL.LA.EN.NA/NU and LU.LIL.LA. The Sumerian pronunciation was probably Lila or Lilla. He is the male personification of the Lilû group.

(Akk.) *Lilītu* = (Sum.) MUNUS.LILA and (rarely) KI.SIKIL.LIL.LA. She is the female personification of the Lilû group. MUNUS.LILA was probably pronounced Sallilla. In god list CT 24,44 (2.146), we find (Sum.) DIM.ME.GI equated or translated with Lilītu; obviously DIM.ME/*Lamaštu* is closely related to Lilītu.

(Akk.) *(W)Ardat Lilî* = (Sum.) KI.SIKIL.LIL.LA and KI.SIKIL.UD.DA.KA.RA. The girl of the Lilû group or the girlfriend of Lilû. Frey-Anthes (2007:182) proposes that KI.SIKIL.LIL.LA could also be translated as: *Pure Place of the Wind*; provided we read LIL as Wind, Storm, and not as the name or title of the god Lilû. Her alternate title is U.DA.KA.RA; Ungnad (1944) translated the name as 'Lichträuberin', German for: *Thief of Light*. Wiggermann (1983) suggests: *Girl Who has been Snatched Away From the Light*. An Akkadian title is Ardat Ša U-Ma Iḫiruši, according to Geller: *Girl Whom the Storm Demon Chose*; to Wiggermann: *(Girl) Who Missed out on Her Day* (after the *Concise Akkadian* and Wiggermann & Stol: *Birth in Babylonia.)*

When the Semitic Akkadians, Babylonians and Assyrians became the dominant cultures of Mesopotamia, they re-interpreted the Lilû Family. In their languages, the syllable 'lil' had a different meaning. In Akkadian and its daughter languages, 'līla' and 'līlātu' mean *night*. It turned the Lilû deities into a group of nightside horrors.

Riders of the Gale

The Lilû appear in Akkadian and Babylonian texts as the *rulers of the winds*: ziāqu(m), a term that can describe them personally, or a group of diseases. The word literally means 'to blow, to waft, to gust, to rush'. Zīqu(m)$_1$ is draught, breeze and breath. Closely related is zīqīqu(m), meaning wind, breath, nothingness, phantom, dream and dream-soul. All of these are essential concepts when we wish to understand the Lilû clan. Stop here and treasure the moment: these ideas are worth exploring.

In modern translations, the storm wind triad is often damned as 'demons'. It's rarely appropriate. The Lilû were occasionally classed as deities: in the god list *Anu Ša Amēli*, we find the group *Lamaštu, Labaṣu, Aḫḫazu, Bibītu, Lilītu*. In their Sumerian form, these Akkadian god names all begin with the signs DIM.ME. Their names were written with the divine determinative (Sum.) 'dingir' or (Akk.) 'ilu'. Unlike the prestigious great gods, our group appears almost at the bottom of the list, among the least important deities, those lacking family ties, temples, shrines or political connections and those who are too dangerous to be everybody's darling. Lamaštu was important and ought to have been close to the top and to her father Anu, but as she was thoroughly unpopular, we find her at the bottom. Labāṣu is so mysterious that neither a description nor a translation exists; Aḫḫāzu means 'the *Seizer'* and that's pretty much all we know about her. Bibītu is a total enigma and Lilītu appears, with a few relations, in a few medical texts where she is connected with specific physical and mental diseases. The Lilû are only classed as deities in rare cases. They do not appear on all god lists. An interesting exception is a god list from Mari, mentioning sacrificial offerings to a god or goddess called ^{d}Lilum (Röllig, RlA 'Lilum'). So far, nobody knows if Lilum is a form of Lilû or Lilītu. The one certain fact is that, whoever it may have been, she or he received sacrifices.

In exorcisms, we usually meet Lilû, Lilītu and the (W)ardat Lilî. None of them is associated with temples, rituals, offerings, a priesthood or indeed anyone who might have a kind word for them (except for you and me, of course).

Lilû is literally wind and storm, but these terms imply energy, power, breath and vitality. Unlike Enlil (Lord Wind) and Ninlil (Lady Wind), Lilû is never a regent, an administrator or a major deity. He remains an obscure but much-feared god and/or dangerous spirit of whom next to nothing is known. Lilû and Lilītu are the male and female forms of a single name/concept. The two relate to each other like An and Antum, Enki and Ninki or Enlil and Ninlil. Except for gender, there is hardly a difference between them. Now for the strangest bit. You would expect that the main players of the group, Lilû and Lilītu, were the best documented. It's not the case. Or maybe we are simply badly informed and the relevant tablets have not been found yet. Of the three, **Kisikil Lilla/Ardat Lilî** is the most prominent. Tablet YOS 11, 92, YBC 9841 from the Yale Babylonian collection offers an exorcism of the (W)ardat Lilîm, which might come from the Larsa area.

Figure 59 Automatic drawing of Ereškigal.

Figure 60 Ardat Lilî.

On the page of the SEAL project you can read Nathan Wasserman's translation. The text is an incantation against the Wardat Lilîm, who is the Guide of the God Erra (=Nergal, a ruler of the Underworlds) and a *weeper (?) of all winds.* She has died in her prime, cut off like a fruit, while the girls dance and twirl at the festival:

a bridegroom did not deflower her,

she did not kiss baby's lips, so soft.

She was canny, she left her /parental/ house.

She was despised for not (giving birth to) a child.

And so, her husband, an evil storm, and she

a phantom, are roaming in the steppe.

A much longer text, translated by Lackenbacher (RA.65. 131-132) is quoted by Scurlock and Andersen (p.273). You can find a section of it in Gleick (2003:228), where she cites the translation of Landsberger. Another version, blended from distinct texts, is given by Foster (1995:407-409)

Here, leaving out numerous repetitions, are a few significant lines:

Ardat-Lilî slips through a man's window, young girl not fated (to be married?);

young woman who was never impregnated like a woman;

young woman who never lost her virginity like a woman;

young girl who never experienced sexual pleasure in her husband's lap (...)

young girl who was never filled with sexual pleasure in the lap of a young man,

who never had her fill of desire;

young girl who never had (her own) women's quarters, whom they never called 'mother';

young girl who abused her cheeks in isolation;

young girl who never enjoyed herself with young girls;

young girl who never went to the festival of her city, who never raised her eyes (...)

young girl who was taken away from a husband, separated from her child;

young girl who was expelled from her father-in-law's house;

Ardat-Lilî who was chased out of the window like air;

Ardat-Lilî whose spirit was not in her mouth (breath?);

Ardat-Lilî whose misery carried her to her grave;

Ardat-Lilî whom the 'hand of Ištar' mistreated in the nest;

Ardat-Lilî who roams in the desolate wilderness.

The story is old and sad. In many cultures, young people who die before marriage become unhappy ghosts. In some periods of Chinese history, such ghosts were married to each other; so that they might find peace and domestic bliss in the otherworlds, and have the sons that Confucian tradition insists upon. In other cultures, girls who died before or during childbirth became a threat to the living. You can find such cases in Celtic funerals where girls make up a large number of 'dangerous dead' (see *Cauldron of the Gods*). Many were bound to their graves by laying stones on top of them or by placing talismans or iron nearby. The tradition survived well into the nineteenth century. For your entertainment, let's step into the Tardis, do a time jump and look into an obscure study on elementary spirits (*Elementargeister*, 1837) compiled by the brilliant poet, scholar and humorist Heinrich Heine. He picked it up when travelling in Austria. The Alps are full of remarkable legends, and some of them contain 'vampiric' elements. Bram Stoker, when planning his novel *Dracula*, first intended that it should play in Styria. It seemed like a remarkably superstitious and primitive place to him. Things haven't changed much since then.

In Austria, Heine learned that there are ghostly female dancers called the willis and instantly fell in love with them. Here is his account (trans. JF): *The willis are brides who died before their wedding. The poor young creatures cannot rest peacefully in their graves, in their dead hearts, in their dead feet the joy of dancing remains, which they could not fulfil when they were alive, and around midnight they rise, assemble like troops on the ancient army roads, and woe to the young man who chances to meet them there! He has to dance with them; in their unlimited frenzy they embrace him, and he dances with them, without peace or rest, until he drops dead. Adorned with their marriage dresses, floral crowns and flying ribbons on their heads, sparkling rings on their fingers, the willis dance in moonlight, just as the fairies do. Their countenances, though pale like snow, are youthfully beautiful, their laughter hauntingly joyous, so blasphemously loveable; their nodding heads so mysteriously wanton, so promising; really these dead bacchantes are irresistible.*

In the Ardat Lilî, we encounter the first succubus of recorded myth. Nowadays, Lilith is often cast in that role, but in early Mesopotamian myth, Ardat Lilî held the job most of the time. Of course we could do the sloppy thing and dismiss Ardat Lilî as 'an aspect of Lilith'. I get the creeps when I hear well-intentioned people downgrade some deity as 'an aspect' of another. Sure, it happens. It's called aggressive power politics. In the old days, priests rarely sat down to invent 'aspects' of deities. They simply grabbed them, tore them out of their context, and delegated them to an inferior position. Some did it to make their favourite deity more powerful, and to eliminate competition. Others wanted to reduce the mind-blowing amount of gods, and make things more economical. Whenever someone calls one deity an aspect of another, we can be sure that this is an expression of subjective preferences, and a violation of earlier faiths.

Our modern Lilith is a conglomeration of several goddesses. Our late Sumerian Ardat Lilî appears centuries before the Babylonian Lilītu. As Thompson points out: *the Ardat Lilî seems to have had much closer relations with human beings than the Lilītu, and she takes over the functions of the Lilith of the Hebrews, which is obviously the etymological equivalent of Lilītu.* (2005/1908:66, spelling amended). He quotes the lines

The Ardat Lilî attacketh the man's dwelling,
a maid untimely dead (?),
a maid that cannot menstruate (?),
like a woman, that hath no modesty like a woman.

Thompson cites a passage from a prayer to the sun god which describes the suffering of a patient (names and spellings amended; 2005/1908:67):

He on whom an evil utukku has rushed,
he whom an evil alû has enveloped in his bed,
he whom an evil eṭimmu has cast down in the night,
he whom an evil gallû has smitten,
he whose limbs an evil god has racked (?),
he the hair of whose body an evil rabiṣu has set on end,
he whom...(Lamaštu) has seized,
he whom (Labaṣu) has cast down,
he whom Aḫḫazu has afflicted,
he whom the Ardat Lilî has looked upon,
the man with whom the Ardat Lilî has had union.

The sequence follows an order that you find in many exorcisms, only that Lilû and Lilītu are absent and Ardat Lilî gets special consideration and bonus points. Maybe the patient was a young man and the conjurer suspected unhealthy habits, wet dreams and nocturnal emissions.

In a few cases, the triad of wind spirits had a fourth member. Thompson quotes a line stating:

the Ardat Lilî that hath no husband,
The Idlu Lilî that hath no wife.

Here, idlu means an adult man. Another spelling is Etel Lilî. Frey-Anthes quotes the passage (2007:181, trans. JF)

Etel Lilî who has no woman,
Ardat Lilî who has no man,
the youth Lil who has no woman.

While Ardat Lilî represents all young women who died in misery and frustration, the Etel Lilî never had a wife or child. The male counterpart of the Ardat Lilî is mentioned very rarely. We might be tempted to see him in the same relation to Lilītu as the Ardat Lilî is to Lilû. But why does he appear so rarely? What happened when a young man died before he had the chance (or the income) to be married? So far, very little is known about the status of unmarried men in ancient Mesopotamia. In fact, we do not even know whether being a bachelor was a breach of social norms. A text translated by Lackenbacher (in Scurlock and Andersen, 2005:273) and Foster 1995:407-408) demonstrates that the Etel Lilî had a similar fate as Ardat Lilî:

[Young man] who sits, silent and (alone), (in) the street;

young man who weeps bitterly in the grip of his fate;

young man to whose destiny silence was attached;

young man, whose mother, crying, has given birth in the street;

young man whose body was scorched with suffering;

young man who was fettered by his personal god;

young man whose personal goddess was cut off;

young man who never married a wife, never raised a child;

young man who never felt sexual pleasure in his wife's lap;

young man who never removed the undergarment of his wife,

young man shut off from his wedding...

It's another painful tale. Frustration can be like a curse, it can cause attachment and bondage. The so-called wind-demons of Mesopotamia are a terrifying lot. But when you hear their sad tales and understand the culture which shaped them, you will meet them with compassion, instead of harsh words and exorcisms. In real magick, integration is more important than banishment.

Lilû Diseases

In medical texts, the wind deities appear with a vengeance. Here are several descriptions, after Scurlock and Andersen's brilliant study (2005).

If the patient feels as if his head was split apart, tosses around in his bed so his bedding twists around him, is continuously obsessed by sexual longing and suffers from frequent erections: hand of Ardat Lilî. As an optional extra, the patient may have a burning head. (p.273).

But Ardat Lilî could also cause diseases that have no sexual element.

If the patient complains of a throbbing neck, his head keeps sinking, his hands and feet are stiff and he drags his feet on the ground: hand of Ardat Lilî (p.379).

If the disease comes and goes, and his confusion overwhelms him and he keeps ranting in a terrifying manner: hand of Ardat Lilî (p.338).

If the patient incessantly cries out 'my insides!' raises his pelvic region, confusion overwhelms him and he babbles constantly in a befuddled manner: hand of Ardat Lilî (p.338).

Scurlock and Andersen identified this illness as Tourette's syndrome, an affliction that often occurs in young age and affects boys four times more often than girls.

Less easy to diagnose is a mental disease where the patient's consciousness keeps changing and his words are muddled: a wandering ghost, or Ardat Lilî or Lilû (p.375).

If a woman is sick and her disease culminates at night: Lilû (p.272).

When the patient sees the (entities) who afflict him in his dreams, if they flow over him and he forgets himself, and when he wakes trembling and is exhausted: 'false hand' of Lilû, but he will get up (i.e. recover). It is the 'genuine hand' of Lilû when the disease harms a woman: luckily, she, too, will recover (p.272).

If the patient shudders but is able to get up (afterwards), if he babbles a great deal and keeps having convulsions: should the patient be a woman, the illness comes from Lilû and if it is a man, from Lilītu. Both will recover.

If the patient sits still like a normal person but keeps opening his eyes wide, imagines to see people who trouble him and talks with them, and (his states of mind? his moods?) keep changing, it is the hand of Lilû who acts as messenger of the personal deity of the patient (p.380). Pause a moment, and consider. How come the personal deity sends Lilû as its messenger?

As Scurlock and Andersen note, 'wind diseases' frequently involved nervous behaviour, fainting spells and false seizures: afflictions that would have been classes, in the nineteenth century, as cases of 'hysteria'.

Another, equally perplexing diagnosis is cited by Stol (1993) in his article *Epilepsy in Babylonia*:

If the patient, when the disease overwhelms him, suffers from paralysed limbs and loses consciousness and *he forgets himself*, and if, after the fit has passed, his eyes are (?) and his face is red, and if the conjurer says something to the patient and the patient says what the conjurer made him say, and immediately forgets what he has been made to say, it is the hand of Lilû or a 'fever'.

Here's a fascinating ritual from the first millennium BCE to *banish the šu-inninakku disease or the Lilû...* published and translated in Nils Heeßel's fascinating study *Pazuzu* (2002:71). It's an instruction how to expel a disease caused by the Lilû, i.e. the storm deities, with the help of the newly introduced Pazuzu, who, as the Aramaic migrants imagined, reigns over them. The tablet is badly damaged. For a start, the conjurer collects earth from the gate of the house, earth from the gate of the house of a tavern-keeper, earth from the gate of a cook, earth from the gate of a carpenter, earth from the gate of the house of a ?, earth from the gate of the house of the Sebitti temple (the Seven Deity, or Pleiades), earth from the quay and the ford, earth of the shadow and sunlight [...] and of seven ways[...] to the right and left [...] (sacrifices?) oil on the (altar?) of the goddess Gazbaba (the *Attractive One*, a daughter of Nanay), (collects?) earth from ? and earth from the bridge [...] and of the Marduk temple. From the mixture, the magician shapes a Pazuzu head. He or she inscribes it *You Strong One* or *Pazuzu, son of Ḫanbu*. The patient may lift the image with his hand (if he is up to it) or the image is suspended above the head of the patient. Any sort of evil that may have seized the patient sees the Pazuzu head and flees. The patient, says the inscription, will recover. And so do we.

Holidays in Edom

Sometime during the first millennium BCE, Lilith appears in Jewish myth. It's not much of a record. There is only one certain reference to her in the *Bible*. Let's take a look at *Isaiah*, 34,14. Isaiah was a furious visionary prophet who lived around 740-701 BCE. He ranted against his home-city Jerusalem with its many polytheistic cults and against King Hiskija who was attempting to make a pact with the Assyrians. He also had much to say regarding the Assyrian king Sanḫerib; and what he wrote is bitter, angry and desperate. Isaiah had a family and a wife, who also suffered from grandiose visions; it would be nice to know what these were about and why they were not recorded. Some passages of the *Book of Isaiah* may come from the lifetime of the prophet, but if you want to know the real age of the text you should harass some biblical scholars. Up to quite recently, the text was only extant in a Greek version. The name Lilith did not occur: instead, she was called Lamia, which is actually the Greek adaptation of Lamaštu. You'll read more on Lamia further on. Hieronymus, commenting on *Isaiah* 34,14: glossed *Lamia, who is called Lilith in Hebrew* (Frey-Anthes, 2007:190, trans. JF). Since then, a Hebrew version of the Text has been found among the *Qumran Manuscripts*, so we can date the earliest surviving version of *Isaiah* in the second century BCE.

Our story describes the dismal fate of Edom; a city-state destroyed courtesy of Wrath of the Lord Enterprises Unlimited. First, while the Lord held a great sacrifice in Bozra and Edom, his sword passed over Edom, dripping with blood and fat. Bulls and calves fell, steers and oxen died and the land was drowned in fat. The brooks ran with black bitumen instead of water, the soil turned to sulphur, the ground transformed into burning asphalt. Night and day oily smoke rose to the skies. The entire country was devastated for generations, and nevermore could anyone travel through it. Jackdaws and owls infested the land, small owls and ravens made their dwelling. The Lord measured the land with the cord called *Desolation* and the plumber's weight called *Voidness*. The goat-like Sa'ir (originally a class of shaggy deities, who were once worshipped in Jerusalem and fell from grace when the monotheists took over) enjoyed their (unspecified) wicked customs in the wasteland: the aristocracy of Edom was no more; and kings were no longer praised. That settled it. Let's have the slightly outdated *King James Bible* here:

And thorns shall come up in her (Edom's) palaces,

nettles and brambles in the fortress thereof;

and it shall be an habitation of jackals and a court of owls.

The wild wolves of the desert shall also meet with hyenas,

and the Sa'ir shall cry to his fellow;

Lilith also shall rest there,

and find for herself a place of rest.

When I look into the German *Einheitsübersetzung* of the *Bible* (1980), I notice that the *court of owls* has been replaced with *a place of ostriches* (lit: *daughters of the desert*). The 'wolves' which wouldn't have enjoyed the desert anyway, transformed into 'desert dogs'. That's no species I ever heard of. The owls appear after the reference to Lilith:

The owl finds its safe nest; it lays its eggs and hatches them.

And vultures assemble, one next to the other.

It tells us four important things about the biblical Lilith. First, she was alone and didn't have a partner. Second, she is related to the popular Near Eastern theme 'Lady of the Beasts'. Third, she didn't do anything, except watch the animals prance around. And fourth, she was of little importance to the authors and compilers of the *Bible*, who devoted more attention to other evil beings. For what it's worth, the one and only reference to Lilith in the *Bible* looks like an absentminded addition.

The Amulet of Arslan Tash

Sometimes a lucky excavator uncovers an object that keeps whole generations of scholars worried and very much awake at three in the morning. One of these items is an innocent plaque uncovered at Arslan Tash in north-east Syria in 1933 by Comte du Mesnil du Buisson. The plaster amulet (8.2x6.7cm) was found in Hadatu, the former residence of the Assyrian king Tiglatpilesar III. Nowadays it is in the National Collection at Aleppo. Take a look at the illustration on the following page. The item shows an inscription and is graced by a picture that shows a winged sphinx with a human head and a pointed helmet, and a wolf-bitch with a scorpion tail, who is devouring somebody. On the reverse appears a striding god (?) in 'Assyrian costume', equipped with a double axe and a sword. On his head is something like a turban with what might be a lily or not, if only we knew. The item is frequently cited as evidence for Lilith in Syria in the seventh century BCE, and, to be sure, they got the date right. It's only Lilith who needs verification. The inscription is in a Semitic language that has been identified as Hebrew, Canaanite, Aramaic and Phoenician; I wouldn't dare to guess, but whatever it may be, it lacks vowels. This means that several words cannot be identified with certainty, leading to enchantingly different translations. One person daring to untangle the mysteries was Jungian therapist Siegmund Hurwitz. He compared two translations; I found two more, and they did not improve the situation much, unless you believe that majority decisions are a way of proving anything. For a start we'll have the version by Franz Rosenthal (ANET, 1992:658), who claimed it was written in *an undetermined Canaanite dialect; the writing is of an Aramaic type.* It represents the group of translations that discern the presence of Lilith in the spell.

An incantation for the female flying demon.

The bond of Ssm, *the son of* Pdrsh *(?).*

Take these and say to the strangling females:

the house I enter you shall not enter,

and the courtyard I tread you shall not tread.

An eternal bond has been established for us.

(Aššur) *has established (it) for us,*

and all divine beings and the majority of the group of all holy ones,

through the bond of heaven and earth forever,

through the bond of Ba'al, the lord of the earth,

through the bond of the wife of Hawron, whose utterance is pure

and her seven co-wives and the eight wives of Ba'al [...]

(Inscription on the sphinx)*: To the female demon that flies in the dark chamber (say):*

pass by, time and again, Lili (t).

(On the she-wolf)*: To the robbing, slaying female (say): Go away!*

(On and around the deity)*: Sz zt, may his (mouth) not (?) open [...]*

Let the sun rise eternally, eternally!

Now for a translation that does not mention Lilith. This interpretation is by Christel Butterweck, who considers the text Phoenician, (TUAT, II, 3, 1988:435-437, trans. JF).

Conjuration:

O Goddess Flying One! God Sasam, son of Paidrasas!

O Strangler of the Lamb!

Into the house, which I enter, you shall not come!

Into the courtyard which I enter, you shall not enter!

(Aššur) formed an eternal bond with us,

and all Sons of the Gods and the entire Kinship-Line of the Saints:

in the eternal ban of Heaven and Earth! [...]

In the ban of Ba'al, (the Lord of the Earth)!

In the ban of Hauron (whose word is true),

his seven secondary wives and the eight wives of the Holy Lord!

(Sphinx)*: O Flyer in the Dark of the Underworld, pass by (at all times, by night and day!)*

(Wolf-bitch)*: Depart from this house, O Slayer!*

(Deity)*: (One shall not open to the Sasam, and he shall not descend to the doorposts. The sun is rising! O Sasam pass by and cease to step down.).*

Let's take a look at the problems in the text. Here comes trouble. The singular and plural are often uncertain. The first line might refer to one or several flying goddesses, if we identify the word as the Aramaic participle 'flying', as several scholars do (Gaster, Albright, Donner & Röllig). But we could also read it as a Hebrew noun, meaning 'darkness' (preferred by Torczyner). The latter reading would give us one or several goddesses of darkness, who do not necessarily fly. The word 'strangler' (H-n-q-t) could be a singular or plural. It does not make a big difference, until you wonder whether the text refers to a specific goddess or to a whole group of them. Lilith is frequently called a *strangler* in Hebrew amulets, but we can't be sure that the person who made the amulet subscribed to a similar belief, considering that it comes from the palace of an Assyrian king. 'Strangler' also appears as a title of the Arabic Ķarīna (here called the *Strangler of the Ram*), while the Ugarit inscriptions mention an entire cluster of strangling goddesses. We could even call Lamaštu a strangler. The toughest bit is the word Lili, which may or may not be a reference to Lilītu, Lilith or simply to a terrible monster of the night (derived from the Hebrew word laylah=night). Du Mesnil du Buisson, Albright and Gaster claimed that the scribe must have forgotten to write the final 'th'. Dupont-Sommer imagined the reference might be to the entire family of Lilin. You'll meet whole swarms of Liliths (or Liliathas) further on.

Figure 61 Three crude Liliths, from spirit-trap-bowls, Nippur, sixth century CE, after Montgomery.

Bottom: the amulet of Arslan Tash. Inscription omitted.

Figure 62 Nidaba/Nisaba

Torczyner, Cross and Saley preferred to identify 'lili' as a group of 'night-demons'. Unlike them, Butterweck discerned what might be a tiny divisional mark in the inscription; in her opinion the resulting expression 'll wjm', is a time reference. As a result, in her version neither Lilith nor a monster of the dark appears. Please don't be disappointed. She explains that the inscription is directed at the goddess Flying One, who is explicitly named in the first line, as well as the two specifically named deities, i.e. the Strangler and the god Sasam. Lilith or monsters of the night would be superfluous. If Lilith was present at all, she would have to be the goddess Flying One.

Lilith in *Talmud* and *Midrash*

The next references to Lilith come from the *Talmud*. Our text was compiled around 500 CE and consists largely of the sayings and speculations of learned rabbis who lived in the first four centuries CE. These sages were quite a long way from Mesopotamian lore. Their references to Lilith, all four of them, are very short and indicate that the goddess did not interest them much. Let me quote Strack & Billerbeck (1928, trans. JF):

Niddah, 24b: *Lilith is a demon with human appearance, apart from the fact that she has wings.*

Eruuin 100b comments regarding Eve, and the many curses that hit her: *She lets her hair grow long like Lilith, she squats like an animal when she urinates; she serves the man as a cushion.*

Shabbat, 151b: *Rabbi Chanina* (c.225 CE) said*: it is prohibited to sleep alone in a house, for whoever sleeps alone is seized by Lilith.*

Finally, here is our last reference, by far the most questionable of the lot. It is occasionally cited as evidence that to the Jews, Lilith was the mother of Ahriman, the evil god of Zoroaster's faith. Well, it can't be denied that there are strong Zoroastrian influences in the Jewish religion. But when we read the passage, we meet a stuntman and trickster, not a deity of the dark.

Bavabatra, 73a: *Rabbah* (who died in 331) *has said: I myself have seen Ahriman, the son of Lilith, as he hurried over the battlements of the walls of Machoza.*

Our Ahriman did not behave as deities do. He ran over the parapets so fast that a rider on the road below could not overtake him. Once, the citizens saddled two mules at the two bridges of river Rognag and Ahriman leapt from one to the other and back again. While jumping, he held two cups of wine. He poured from one to the other and back again without spilling a drop. It was a stormy day, the river was surging with breakers and Rabbah felt reminded of Psalm 107,26. The acrobatic performances ended when the government disapproved of Ahriman and had him killed.

The *Midrash* hasn't much more to offer. We read of Rabbi Jehuda († 299) who announced: *When a mother gives birth to a monstrosity in the shape of Lilith, she becomes impure due to having given birth; it is a (real) child which she has born, but it has wings.* Maybe Jehuda was referring to the *Baraitha*: *Rabbi Jose* (c.150) *claimed that a woman of the city Simonim* (Simonia?) *gave birth to a winged baby.* It must have been a surprise.

Incantation Bowls from Nippur

How would you like to live in a house haunted by hundreds of dangerous spirits? To be sure, most of them would be bound and confined by magic bowls. Each day, more and more of them were attracted, caught up and confined. People didn't have television, but they were good at paranoia and made their own entertainment.

In 1888 and 1889, the University of Pennsylvania began to excavate the ruins of ancient Nippur. The ruins at the top level date roughly to the sixth and seventh century CE, shortly before Mesopotamia was overrun by Arabs and forced to accept Islam. The excavators discovered something unique. In most buildings, and in up to four corners of them, inscribed bowls were buried in the ground. Such bowls averaged around 16cm in diameter, but one specimen reached a remarkable 28cm. Usually, the bowls had a flat bottom, with an inscription spiralling on the inside. Several had crude pictures in the centre. The ink was excellent: it lasted more than a thousand years underground. The bowls turned out to be spirit traps. Imagine a whirling, spinning spell that draws evil entities, demons and unwanted influences into the bowl to confine or banish them for eternity. The writing may call on deities and angels, may include 'words of power' like amen and hallelujah or entire jumbles of qabalistic letters, may cite the names of the persons who commissioned the bowl and banishment. The texts vary enormously, using set formulas and creative compositions, against an impressive range of evils. After inscription and maybe a bit of ritual, the bowls were buried upside down in the ground. They bound the evils, ghosts, demons and spooks who haunted a given home, and sucked into themselves all future troublemakers. And there were plenty of them: the population of this quarter of seventh-century Nippur had a remarkably paranoid mindset. But this is not all; we also have a few bowls made for other purposes, which you'll read about further on. Professor Peters, who led the excavation, proposed that the site must have been a Jewish settlement, and that the vessels were 'Jewish Incantation Bowls'. It wasn't quite that simple. In the seventh century, much of the Semitic population of Lower Mesopotamia belonged to the Mandaean faith. They were also known as the Sabaeans (the Worshippers of the Host of Heaven), as the Mughtasils (the Washers) and derived their peculiar form of Christianity from St. John the Baptist. Their religion was an amazing mixture of Jewish, Christian, Gnostic, Iranian and old Mesopotamian ideas, spiced with a generous helping of astrology and Greek magic, imported courtesy of Alexander's armies many centuries ago. The Mandaeans did not celebrate a Sabbath nor did they practice circumcision. Their sacred direction was north, where the great rivers had their origin, and water was the essence of their faith. They believed that the Euphrates and Tigris had their origin in the World of Light, in the realm of God, who was often praised as the *Supreme Life*. Their worship required two baths a day, plus group baths on holy festivals. The *Waters of Life*, so they thought, purified them from misdeeds and impurity, and anointed them with the essence of the *Great Life*. As Wallis Budge (1978/1930:239-249) observes, the water had to be fresh and flowing (i.e. *alive*). To perform a bath or baptism in stagnant water, as the Christians did, would have gone much against their faith. It effectively confined their religion to the close neighbourhood of the great rivers. Mandaean religion focused on a single god who was identified with Life itself; his angels came from numerous ethnic traditions. The archaeologists unearthed plenty of Mandaean inscriptions, but as the texts are full of syncretistic elements we cannot simply ascribe them to a single faith. Some bowls were inscribed for and by Jews, but there were also bowls for Christians and adherents of the elder pagan faiths. None of these groups was educated or strict in their worship and beliefs. The museum catalogued more than 150 of these bowls; mind you, most of these are damaged, and of several, only a few shards remain. James Montgomery, who wrote the first detailed account of the bowls, pointed out that approximately 30 of the bowls were *'original fakes'*. They were inscribed by magicians who couldn't write, for customers who couldn't read, and happily paid for vessels full of meaningless squiggles. He selected the best preserved forty bowls for his pioneering study, and though some of his translations had to be fine-tuned by later scholars, the work itself is still of great fascination. The spirit trap bowls show that folk religion can develop into amazing complexity. The quality of the inscriptions differs enormously. Several bowls were carefully inscribed; others were made by people who could barely write, including one sorcerer who wrote four distinct sounds using a single letter. Some bowls are close copies of each other, bearing the names of different clients, but there are also highly varied bowls made for the same clients on distinct occasions. The result is heterogeneous and involves three different alphabets. The inscriptions were made in one dialect using square characters, a Syriac dialect in a *novel form of the Estrangelo script* and a Mandaean dialect with its own alphabet. All three dialects belong to the Aramaic group of languages, the major spoken language in Mesopotamia in the Common Era. Superficially, most bowls are related to Jewish or Christian religion. Many address a single (unidentified) high god, or call on YHVH, and the majority of the words of power and angels, as far as they can be identified, appear in Jewish scripture. The sorcerers, however, were not learned rabbis. Many of them were not learned at all. Quotations from the *Talmud* are rare and often mutilated, as if the writer had only a fleeting acquaintance with sacred Hebrew literature, and the names of angels are frequently misspelt or incomprehensible. Just as important is a Greek Gnostic influence: the Greek magical papyri had been popular for several centuries, and any better sorcerer used their spells and words of power. Here and there pagan ideas appear. Bowl #3 invokes the *Lord of Salvation* against a Satan, who is identified as a spirit of death. *Lord of Salvation* is not an official Hebrew title, as Montgomery remarked, but simply the male form of the *Lady of Salvation*, a title of the ancient patron goddesses of Nippur: Gula and Bau/Baba. The same bowl invokes the *Saviour of Love* a title that was never part of Jewish religion, but appears in Greek texts to praise Zeus, Apollo, Asclepius and Hermes; and in the *New Testament.* Bowl #7 invokes Ermes (Hermes) and Abrakas (Abraxas). Ermes might be the Greek god or the legendary magician Hermes Trismegistos, while Abraxas/Abrasax is a well-known Gnostic deity.

In the long inscription of bowl #19 we meet not only angels who may or may not be of Hebrew origin but also one Ibbol, the great king of the Bagdani and his wife, Lady Ibboleth; perhaps they are of Persian origin. The customer was not a Jew and the term baga is an Indo-European form of the word 'god'. The same text invokes the aid of Armasa (=Hermes), *60 male gods and 80 goddesses*, whoever that may have been, Abrakis (=Abraxas), Mana (=Manu?), Zeiiza (=Zeus), Patragenos (=Protogonos), Okinos (=Okeanos=Enki/Ea) and one *Anad the Great Lord* who might be the popular Syrian goddess Anat in male form. Plus many exciting characters we can't identify.

Bowl #25 is another religious crossbreed: it was made to protect a married couple from a group of ghosts: *that there vanish from them in their dw(elling the Demons and De)vils by the mercy of Heaven. Whoever here has dead* (sic), *who shall become alive to them here, and shall approach and are found to be (actually) dead - from these you are kept and these are kept from you.*

The ghosts are banished in the name of YHVH, various angels and a curious hybrid: (Ar)masa (=Hermes) Metatron Yah.

The clients who commissioned the bowl came from several religions and cultures. Many of them had Semitic names, but there were several Indians, Persians and one Christian among them. It seems that the 'Jewish' quarter was actually a multinational settlement or a slum.

One bowl (#36) was commissioned by a woman to trap a spirit that causes miscarriages:

...that Murderess, daughter of Murderess. Go away, go away, and depart from before...

The lord Šames (=Šamaš*) has charged me against thee, Sîn has sent me, Bēl has commanded me, Nannai* (= Nanay*) has said to me, and Nirig* (=Nergal*) has given me power to go against the evil spirit, against Dodib, whom they call the Strangler, who kills the young in the womb of their mothers, and they are called 'Slayer', and their fathers 'Destroyer'. Go from the presence of these holy angels...*

It sounds like a simple banishment. But the text ends *depart from the engraved seal and go to the bridal chamber and eat* [...]*; moreover drink a libation and* [...]. Why does the spirit receive a meal before departure? We have no idea who the strangler Dodib is and whether s/he is related to Lilith or Lamaštu. Nevertheless, we face solid evidence that some people in 7th century Mesopotamia were worshipping the old Babylonian gods!

Here is another unusual item. Bowl #28 has a love spell. A woman called Ahath bath Nebazak commissioned the bowl to make one Anur [...]bar Parkoi burn (with lust) after her. The fragmentary text states that Ahath collected sunwort, an unintelligible herb, and as a third ingredient, peppers. She mixed them with water or other fluids and sprinkled them on Anur, hoping that he be inflamed and burn after her *in lust and the mysteries of love.* I wonder how Ahath performed the sprinkling. Didn't he notice? The short spell was fortified with the names of the angel Rahmiel and of Dlibat, who should be spelt Dilbat; it's a name of Ištar and the planet Venus. I wonder why such bowls were buried in the house. Whose house was it anyway? Did Ahath dwell in the house? Did she commission the bowl to attract the man of her heart or did she hope to revive a cooling relationship with her man?

While a few people were on good terms with the old Mesopotamian deities, the Mandaeans were not. In their religion the old gods were demons. We observe this in bowl #37; the text is very badly written and highly damaged. It was made for a family and their cattle against

Arts and the Tormentor (?) [...] (and the image-spirits) of idolatry, and all the Legions and the Amulet-spirits and the Ishtars and all the demons [...] and all mighty Liliths...

...Peace from the male Gods and peace from the female Ishtars...

A similar mood appears in Bowl #40, inscribed on the inside and, to a large extent, also on the outside, with a very long and repetitive text.

The spell starts with a brief reference to Lilith, and then lists (at length) the people who are supposed to be protected, including a woman called Merathe daughter of Hindu:

Charmed art thou, Lilith Buznai and all the goddesses [...] and the three hundred and sixty Tribes, by the word of the granddaughter of the angel Buznai...

Charmed are a(ll the gods [...] and) temple-spirits and shrine-spirits and goddesses from the body and the wife and sons and daughters...

Charmed, shut up and confined and hobbled is the Ish(tar) [...] and the three hundred and sixty Tribes...'

As a last resort, the evil influences are banished in the name of *'Life'*, a synonym for the Mandean god.

Let us focus on Lilith. Arguably she is one of the most prominent characters in the forty bowls translated by Montgomery. But once again, life is not as simple as you read in the brochure before you booked the trip. Let's have a statistic interlude. For the fun of it I made a general count of the evils mentioned in Montgomery's selection. Of course my count is only of limited value. Montgomery translated forty bowls, or rather; he would have, if they had all been original items. Number 18 is mostly a duplicate of #11 (made for other clients); number 27 is largely a copy of number 2; #22 & #23 are very close copies of number 21 and the text on number 33 appears partly in bowl #32; which was adapted for different clients. Sadly, he did not translate the duplicates, so I have no idea how close they are to the originals. Bowl #13 is a blessing, bowl #28 a love spell, and neither of them mention evils. In my survey I have only noted the evils of the 33 bowls which are truly original pieces. I only counted the evils of each single bowl once, no matter how often their name was repeated in the text. The terminology is troublesome. Montgomery, though doing a remarkable job, used a range of unspecific terms. What exactly constitutes a *devil*, a *Satan*, an *evil spirit* or, for that matter an *evil adversary* or a *tormentor*? What is the difference between *acts*, *works* and *rites*? How do we tell the difference between a *spell*, an *invocation*, a *vow*, an *adjuration* and a *curse*? What is the distinction between *words* and *names*?

Figure 63 The Scavenger

Figure 64 Topless Minoan snake goddesses or priestesses, from the sanctuary of the palaces of Knossos, Minoan Crete. Not quite to scale (the figure on the right is smaller). 1700-1450 BCE.

Let's start with the sort of stuff you encounter every day, especially in public transport. The most common horrors were *demons*, whatever that word may mean, who appear on 20 bowls. We meet *Lilith* in the singular (13 bowls), *Liliths* in the plural (18 bowls) plus *Lilis* (2 bowls). *Devils* appear on 14 bowls. *Satan* is named on 5 bowls but we have another 9 bowls referring to the *Satans*. It would be interesting to know more about them. 13 bowls mention the *Evil Tormentors*, and 10 bowls *Evil Spirits*. *Charm-* and *Amulet spirits* appear on 10 bowls and 5 bowls mention *Necklace Spirits*; possibly a survival of the belief that necklaces and beads may hold enchantment. Here, Hurwitz (1983:51) disagrees; the Necklace Spirits (Aniquta) discerned by Montgomery made no sense to him. In his opinion the reference might be to Chaniquta, 'the *Strangler'*. 11 bowls banish *Idol Spirits*, maybe these are similar (or even identical) with the 2 bowls against unspecified *goddesses*, 1 bowl against male *gods*, and another bowl against *'gods'* in general. Pagan deities were banished as *Shrine Spirits* (2 bowls), *Temple Spirits* (2 bowls) and *Ištar/s* (3 bowls). Someone terrible called *Latbe* is mentioned 3 times. *Ghosts* are only banished in 3 bowls; evidently, the dead did not cause much trouble. Of magical acts, *curses* were especially feared and banished by 9 bowls, *evil vows* by 5 bowls, *evil arts* by 7 bowls, *invocations* by 5, *mighty works* by 3, *counter-charms* by 3, *words* by 3, *knots* by 2, and *rites* by 3 bowls. *Plagues* are banished by 8 bowls and *evil injurer/s* by 7, while *evil dream/s* were expelled in 5 cases.

Only 2 bowls can be cited for *Mighty Destroyers*, the so-called *'Hag'* and *'Ghul'* (see further on), *goblins*, *Ban Spirits*, *strokes*, *evil mysteries*, *knockings* (poltergeists?) and *magic circles*.

And singular appearances are made by: *Evil Fiends, Evil Adversaries, the Sea* and *Leviathan, the Angel of Death, 'Satyrs', Circlet Spirits, Princes of the Sons of Darkness, Danhis* (could this be the Indian Dānavas, deities who were demonized in early Hinduism?), *Hags of the Wild, the sun* (the Mandaeans disapproved of the sun and the planets), *Oppressors, melting wax figures, Spirit* (breath) *of Foulness and Fatigue, Blast Demons, Howlers, Water Spirits, Hair Spirits, Sorcery Spirits, hostile beasts, evil men, legions* (of what?), *Slayers, Dodib the Strangler, Damkar, Šait* (Shaitan?), *Šara* (a son of Inanna/Ištar, her divine hairdresser, the major god of Umma), *Diaboli, Seducers, evil sacraments, adjurations, practices, spells, poverty, spell of poverty, darkness, anger, names, harm, losses, maladies, bowls* (i.e. magic bowls), *heat, the evil eye, the eye/s, disturbing vision, impurities, epilepsy, leprosy, menstruation, fever, barrenness, abortion, losses and failure. Bagdana* and his worshippers appear both as a positive and negative influence on different bowls. Whew. That covers a lot. It's quite an achievement to cram so many horrors into a mere 33 bowls, plus an extravagant cast of good beings, sacred words, angels and deities to keep them under control.

Lilith in the singular appears on bowls #1, 8, 11, 15, 17, 19, 26, 30, 34, 35, 38, 39 and 40.

Liliths with specific names appear on bowls #11 (Lilith Halbas and her grandmother Lilith Zarni), 17 (Lilith of the Desert), 38 (Lilith Yannai) and 40 (Lilith Buznai). Their names defy translation.

Lilith's parents appear on bowl #8 (*whose father is named Palhas and whose mother Pelahdad)* and bowl 17 which is a close copy of bowl 8, much abridged and with dismal spelling (*whose mother is Palhan and whose father is (Pe)lahdad).* 'Pel' and 'Pehlad' are probably versions of 'Bēl', Akkadian for the Lord and 'Bēlet' for Lady. Pelahdad might be Bēl Ḫadad.

Liliths in the plural, without specifications, appear on bowls #1 (*the Liliths that haunt the house; all species of Liliths*), 5 (*all evil Liliths*), 7 (*Lilis and Liliths*), 9 (*all the Liliths*), 11 (*the Liliths*), 12 (*Liliths*), 17 (*ye Liliths*), 20 (*evil Liliths*), 21-23 (*the Liliths; every kind of Lilith*), 32-33 (*Liliths and Latbe*), 37 (*all mighty Liliths*) and 40 (*the Liliths*).

For extra confusion, we often encounter Lilith and the Liliths on one and the same bowl.

And then there are Liliths with gender characteristics: bowl #6 (*Liliths, male and female*), 8 (*the Lilith, the male Lilis and the female Liliths*, who appear in singular and plural), 30 (*the female Lilith; the Lilith-Spirit male or female*), 39 (*empoisoning female Liliths*).

Here is an impressive example of the 'spirit lover' type (bowl #1, abridged):

...this is an amulet against the Liliths that haunt the house of this Ephra bar Šaborduch and this Bahmanduch bath Šama. I adjure you, all species of Liliths in respect to your posterity, which is begotten by Demons and Liliths to the children of light who go astray: Woe, who rebel and transgress against the proscription of the Lord; woe, from the blast fast flying; woe, destroying; woe, oppressing with your foul wounds...

who do violence and scourge and trample and mutilate and break and confuse and hobble and divorce (the body) like water; woe...;

and where you stand, and where you stand (sic!), *fearful and afrightened are ye, bound to my ban,- who appear to mankind, to men in the likeness of women and to women in the likeness of men, and with mankind they lie by night and by day. With the formula, TWM Š Š GŠ GŠK, have I written against thee, evil Lilith, whatsoever name be thine...*

We meet Liliths, Liliths who adapt their gender as they like, and in the end a Lilith in the singular. She is not the only one; similar things happen to Satan and the Satans on several bowls. A whole range of evil creatures appear as competent shape- and gender shifters, as is evident from bowl #7:

...and I seal to thee the life, house and dwelling of this Merduch bath Banai, that there sin not against you all evil Arts and all (magic) circles and all necklace-spirits and all Invocations and all Curses and all Losses and all...and all sore Maladies and all evil Satans and all Idol-spirits and all impious Amulet-spirits and all mighty Tormentors...

Lo, this mystery is for frustrating you, Mysteries, Arts, and enchanted Water- and Hair-spirits, Bowls and Knots and Vows and Necklace-spirits and Invocations and Curses and evil Spirits and impious Amulet-spirits. And now, Demons and Demonesses and Lilis and Liliths and Plagues and evil Satans and all evil Tormentors, which appear- and all evil Injurers- in the like of vermin and reptile and in the likeness of beast and bird and in the likeness of man and woman, and in every likeness and in all fashions: Desist and go forth from the house and from the dwelling and from the whole body of this [...]*...that ye injure them not with any evil injury, nor bewilder or amaze them, nor sin against them, nor appear to them either in dream by night or in slumber by day, from this day and forever...*

Some households were haunted by Liliths, but their victims were not only sex-starved lonely men or women: the entire habitation, including children and domestic animals suffered from them.

The Nippur Liliths brought disease, destroyed property and killed.

In most spells, the Liliths were simply banished, bound or shackled. One curious tactic was to issue a divorce writ. An example is bowl #8:

flee from him the evil Lilith, in the name of YHVH El has scattered; the Lilith, the male Lilis and the female Liliths, the Hag (ghost?) and the Ghul, the three of you, the four of you and the five of you, (naked) are you sent forth, nor are you clad, with your hair dishevelled and let fly behind your backs. It is made known to you, whose father is named Palhas and whose mother Pelahdad: hear and obey...

A divorce writ has come down to us from heaven and there is found written in it for your advisement and your terrification, in the name of Palsa-Pelisa ('Divorcer-Divorced'), who renders to thee thy divorce and thy separation, your divorces and your separations. Thou Lilith, male Lili and female Lili, Hag and Ghul, be in the ban...

And again, you shall not appear to them either in dream by night or slumber by day, because you are sealed with the signet of El Shaddai and with the signet...

Thou Lilith, male Lili and female Lilith, Hag and Ghul, I adjure you by the Strong One of Abraham, by the Rock of Isaac...

The text is damaged. There is a picture of Lilith in the centre of the bowl: she is bound and shackled and looks sort of surprised. The text is similar to bowl #17. 'Hag' and 'Ghul' (Shelanitha and Chatiphata/Chatapitha/Chatihata) are Montgomery's very uncertain attempts to give some kind of translation. These names do not appear elsewhere, and can only be 'translated' by assuming that they are badly distorted and misspelt. His 'Ghul' Shelanitha might be related to an Arabic spirit called Shi'lat, who is a witch of the female djins, or to Assyrian 'šulu' meaning 'ghost'. Chatiphata might be related to the ostrich (tachmas), a fabulous creature assumed to be a terrible female desert demon. Tachmas is derived from Ch-m-s, meaning: to inflict violence. All of this is very speculative. Gershom Scholem (in Hurwitz 1983:77) proposed that Shelanitha is a miswritten form of Talanitha, who is just as obscure as the other, but appears in an Aramaic text as the name of a dangerous spirit. C.H. Gordon, by contrast, speculated that Talanitha might be a misspelling of Shelanitha. Chatihata, Hurwirtz claims, can be translated as raptor, seizer or grasper. We are close to Lamaštu's old companion Aḫḫazu here. To seize is to obsess.

This inscription, like a few others, takes the form of a legal document. The two most sacred occupations of Jewish life are to do good deeds and to study the law. It's one of the fascinating elements in Jewish religion that contracts were made with spiritual entities and even with God. Adam, Eve and God had a contract. Abraham made a new contract with God. Even Jesus assumed he had a contract, tried to force God to save him, and was badly disappointed when God didn't bother to turn up at the crucifixion. The *Old* and *New Testament* can be understood as contracts. *Joshua* 24 and other passages in the Bible outline how YHVH made a contract with the children of Israel. The style of the agreement is very close to Mesopotamian legal documents. Such documents had a specific structure. They required a commemoration of the acting persons, a brief summary of the conditions and events under which the contract was formulated, a statement regarding the future relations between the contractual partners, the small details, clauses and specifications, and finally the invocation of god, gods, or human witnesses who participated in the event. At the end appear curses for any party daring to break the bond. Several of the more literate inscriptions in the spirit traps bowl use a similar format. At the time, Jewish law allowed men to divorce their women, no matter if they agreed or not, but this act needed a specific document to be valid. Several bowls give an official divorce from one or many Liliths. The divorce writ implied that the dwellers of the household had formed a sinister relationship with the male and female Liliths. The whole incantation followed the ritual of an official divorce: they name the people of the household, the parents of the Liliths, several angels who serve as witnesses, and finally archangel Gabriel appears to seal the document. To create a legal precedent, some bowls claim that divorces are common among the demons and evil spirits; hence, the Liliths should be well acquainted with the custom. Bowl #11, made for a woman and her household, is a typical example. The client is the same woman who ordered bowl #10, only this time she is mentioned without her husband. The text was so well composed that three other bowls are close copies.

Salvation from Heaven for this Newanduch bath Kaphni, that she be saved by the love of Heaven from Lilith and the Tormentor. Amen. Amen. Again, fly and refrain and remove from Newanduch bath Kaphni the Lilith and the Tormentor and Fever and Barrenness and Abortion; in the name of him who controls the Demons and Devils and Liliths, and in the name of 'I-am-that-I-am'. For the binding of Bagdana, their king and ruler, the king of Demons and (Devils), the (great) ruler of the Liliths. I adjure thee, Lilith Halbas, granddaughter of Lilith Zarni (dwelling) in the house and dwelling of Newanduch bath Kaphni and (plaguing) boys and girls, that thou be smitten in the courses (?) of thy heart and with the lance of [...] who is powerful [...] over you. Behold I have written for thee (a divorce), and behold I have separated thee (from the client), (like the demons) who write divorces for their wives, and do not return to them. Take thy divorce from Newanduch bath Kaphni and do not appear to her, neither by night nor by day, and do not lie (with her). And do not kill her sons and daughters...

A human divorce required the consent of a judge. In this spirit trap, the document was validated by the divine command of Heaven. In bowl #17 we encounter a divorce writ coming from over the sea. Unlike real divorce writs in the seventh century in Nippur, women could divorce themselves and their households from Liliths.

On bowl #26 a married couple divorces itself from Lilith. As the inhabitants of Nippur in the seventh century knew, intimate relations with Liliths, male and female, could happen to anyone. Finally, there is an amazing bowl (No. 29) that introduces something astonishing. As you remember, the Babylonians and Akkadians made a distinction between, say, the good and evil god, the good and evil rabiṣu, good and evil utukku and so on. The evil ones got more attention. They appear in dramatic exorcisms, while we are hardly aware of what the good ones are like. Considering how often our bowls refer to the evil Lilith, I wonder whether there was also a good Lilith. Sure, she wouldn't have attracted much attention. Welcome to something unusual. A woman called Metanis commissioned a bowl for herself, her family and a group of men who may have been lodgers in her house. The inscription is in two sections: The section regarding Metanis and her kin is aimed against

*the evil Plagues and evil Demons and the **evil and the decent Lilith** and the Necklace-spirits and [...] Menstruation and Tormentors and the Hags of the Wild and Impurities and Epilepsy (?).'*

The section on the men (including one called Darsi the foreigner) is aimed against

*Leprosy, Plague, Stroke, the **kindly and [...] Lili**, and the Demons, ghostly Shades, and all Goblins and evil Injurers whose names I have mentioned and whose names (I have not) mentioned...*

Who exactly are the decent Lilith and the kindly Lili? What are their stories, their attributes and functions? Where are the traces of their cult? A lot of excavation will be needed to clear up such questions. Enigmatic, mysterious and tantalising as they are, such references show that even in a tiny geographic location during a single century, the most amazing and contradictory beliefs were entertained. How do they relate to the spirit trap bowls that were unearthed in nearby districts? What about the spirit traps that came up in Iran, near Teheran, which also commemorated a range of Liliths? Those who talk about Lilith as if s/he were a single person could use this chance to relax, take a deep breath, open the mind really wide, and reconsider.

Lilith Reloaded

Around the tenth century Lilith began to have a fabulous time in Spain. In full bloom she appears in the *Zohar*. The *Zohar* was compiled around the thirteenth century and contains an abundance of newly invented qabalistic reinterpretations of elder Jewish lore. Here, a little introduction may be useful, even if it happens to be dreadfully oversimplified. Jewish religion is not a monolithic thing but a wide range of diverging traditions. There was never a common church in Judaism, nor was there a pope, a governing orthodoxy or a militant branch that kept heretics on their knees. In fact, one of the greatest aspects of Judaism is the fact that scripture can and should be interpreted in many ways. As a result, each part of the Jewish Diaspora evolved its own traditions and customs. In Palestine, polytheistic creeds and the worship of God's wife Ašerah came to an end around the year 621 BCE under the reign of King Joshiah, while a Jewish community in Egypt continued venerating a range of deities up to 400 BCE. Patai (1978:58) relates that one Yedoniah, priest of the community on the island of Elephantine, collected donations; he received 12 karash and 6 shekels for Yaho (YHVH), 7 karash for Ishumbeltel and 12 karash for the goddess Anathbethel. Diverging customs hint at similar diversities in faith and philosophy. It is a remarkable and admirable aspect of Jewish religion that its various branches, for all their differences, never persecuted each other. The Jews of Palestine picked up a lot of Syrian and Mesopotamian deities, but we should also consider unifying principles. One of these is the *Pentateuch*, the *Five Books of Moses*, which were unalterable, divinely ordained hallowed writ. How do we handle change when literature is sacrosanct? Editing or changing the *Pentateuch* was out of the question; no matter that medieval Jews were members of a multinational urban population and a long way from the Israelites who allegedly escaped from Egypt around 1200 BCE. Luckily, there was a method to transform the literal meaning of the *Pentateuch*. Here, we encounter QBL, or qabalistic revelation. According to this teaching, there is a sacred meaning concealed within the unalterable scripture. This hidden lore is ancient: many serious medieval qabalists believed that God personally initiated Adam into a secret wisdom which later generations were hardly aware of. After Adam, God initiated a range of visionaries, worthies and crazy old men: their insights became the foundation of what we know as Qabala today.

Qabala is an eminently useful system to understand and redefine the meaning of sacred texts. For this purpose several techniques were used. The letters of the Hebrew alphabet are also numbers, hence, any written word has a numerical value, and words with the same value were thought to be related. By cunning use of this method, technically called gematria, a given word could be interpreted as something entirely different, merely on the basis of its numerical value. Numerology allowed writers to hint at hidden truths. When we read that Lilith is accompanied by 480 bands of demons, as recorded by Moses Cordovero (1522–1570, in Patai 1978: 216), we should be aware that the name Lilith (L=30, I=10, L=30, I=10, TH=400) adds up to that 480. In a similar vein, LIL (30+10+30) is equal to the verb 'to scream' (YLL), which makes Lilith a screamer or a screecher; an idea that inspired folk tales and found its latest manifestation in Frankfort's and Kramer's notion that the '*screeching*' owls represents Lilith. Another system associated the letters with symbolism, and tried to derive a new meaning by analysing words letter-by-letter. Other systems proposed that certain letters could be exchanged as they were related to each other. It worked perfectly: while scripture remained unchangeable, its meaning could be transformed according to the insights and requirements of the qabalists. It was a brilliant way of keeping ancient scripture up-to-date and meaningful, and to adapt the god of a nomadic Canaanite sheep-herding culture to their sophisticated descendants living in urban Europe. I am sure God approved of it: deities do want to move with the times But the early qabalists were not necessarily aware of their inventiveness. They were scholarly, well educated and serious thinkers who strictly adhered to traditional customs and religious duties. Their spiritual quest was entirely rational; we do not find them struck by ecstatic visions or oracular frenzy. Very seriously, a large body of literature was created and attributed to the sages (real and imaginary) of antiquity. It was a pioneering effort in applied surrealism. But qabalistic research was not a unified phenomenon. Numerous Jewish mystics contributed, and many of them were influenced by new ideas. Consider Isaac and Jacob Hacohen from Soria, who spent the time between 1250 and 1260 searching for 'ancient' manuscripts in the Provence in southern France. In the process, they acquired, edited and fused a lot of spiritual texts. Many of them were recent forgeries, others were inspired by Neo-Platonic thought and speculation, Gnostic lore, local Jewish legends plus heresies borrowed from heretic groups like the Cathars. Much of what is typical for Lilith today was made up by the Cohen brothers. The two were intensely fascinated by 'evil'. Their 'demonology' spread to Castilia in Spain, where it fused with qabalistic teachings that made much of the freshly invented Tree of Life (Scholem, 2001:208, 261, 262). The Tree of Life is a brilliant model of the universe that related astrology (the alignment of the celestial spheres and the planets) with anatomy (the Tree represents Primal Adam, and the spheres appear much like the Indian cakras), divine names, cosmology, the letters of the alphabet and a huge amount of cosmology. It is a distinct possibility that the Tree was influenced by the cakra systems of Tantric lore. After all, plenty of Jews inhabited the Near and Middle East, and central Asia. We find a mixture of these systems in the *Zohar*. This remarkable collection, the '*Book of Splendour*' was written (or rather compiled) by Moses de Leon of Castile (c.1240–1305), who claimed it was the secret lore of Shimeon ben Yohai, who lived in second-century Palestine. The *Zohar* is an enormous commentary to the *Five Books of Moses* and other pieces of scripture. I would call it amazing, bizarre, mind-blowing, enlightening, confusing, wonderful, boring and incomprehensible. And that's just the first impression. Honestly, how much do you have to drink or smoke to survive an essay explaining the hidden symbolism of God's beard that goes on for several dozen pages?

The *Zohar* is not a single teaching but a wild and contradictory collection of mystical insights. Its authors were rarely in agreement with one another. They didn't have to be: in a book of almost a million words, anything can be argued. Very few people actually had the time or life-expectation to read all of it, let alone to study it in depth. Today, the full edition including the much-needed notes amounts to roughly 10,000 pages. Serious qabalistic study was a subject for a very few brilliant, overworked and rather lonely scholars. It remained this way until 1490, when the Jews were expelled from Spain. A new qabalistic centre of learning arose in the town of Safed in Galilee. From Safed, qabalistic doctrine moved along the many branches of the Jewish Diaspora, and around 1600 the teachings began to gain real influence. Basic qabalistic ideas, suitably simplified, gained popular appeal and inspired a mass movement that was extremely influential in the development of modern Judaism.

Let's enjoy something simple for a change. We will focus on the many aspects of Lilith. One qabalistic innovation was the attempt to revalue the position of women. As you remember, women were neither treasured nor appreciated in the elder sections of the *Old Testament*. Moses, whoever he may have been, was a tough sexist. In consequence, much of Jewish and Christian literature lacks respect for women or for the female expression of the divine. Orthodox Jews recite a brief prayer each day thanking God for not having made them pagans, women or slaves. Well, things did not stay as bad as they were in Moses' time. Some medieval sages tried to reduce the misogyny. They proposed that there is something sacred about women. However, they gained it from their contact with men. Other sages were more daring. They tried to raise the status of women, and pointed out that in the Divine, the male and female are one. Several beautiful female role-models emerged. The most popular is the **Shekinah**, who is, (very simplified), the expression of God's love in the manifest world. According to orthodox teachings YHVH is transcendent, omnipresent, omnipotent, omniscient, incomprehensible and way beyond any form or personality. Strictly speaking 'He' is neither male nor female or anything that can be expressed in words. Indeed the gender of God is less defined in the Hebrew version of the *Bible* than in any European language. Think of the first line: *Bereshit bara Elohim et hashamajim we'et ha'arez!* It means literally: *in the beginning, Gods* (plural!) *created/connected/bound heaven and earth.* The version you find in European language translations is ridiculously simplified. Elohim is God in the plural. The form Eloha (God in feminine form) also appears a few times. El and Adonai are male. All of them are usually translated as 'God', which veils the subtleties of the original.

Hebrew, as a language, is very concerned with male and female forms. In general, God was addressed as he. Hebrew scholars taught that God has no gender, but whoever spoke of 'Him' had to use male word-forms. In short, a beautifully abstract concept did not make it into everyday life. While the intangible form appealed to a handful of hard-core philosophers, the population took the male form for granted. The history of the Jewish faiths is full of polytheistic episodes. For the polytheists, it was simply natural that a god should have a wife. The male image of God found its extreme form during the centuries when monotheism became the rule. As a much needed balance to the 'male' YHVH, the Shekinah, as God's Love, appeared, over time, in increasingly female form, and assumed many of the qualities and functions of typical Near Eastern Goddesses. As Patai shows, the Shekinah fought God's enemies (much like Ištar and Anat), meddled with human destinies and dared to argue and disagree with God. And who could blame her. In the *Zohar*, the Shekinah reached her ultimate refinement. She is a positive and benevolent influence, and in opposition to her, a number of 'evil' female figures gained importance. We encounter one or two Liliths; others are Naamah, Mahalath and Ygrath. These are the wicked girls, outspoken, independent and powerful, and so gorgeous-looking that many a sage, beholding them, began to twitch, stutter and drool. The feminine, no matter how evil it seemed, got more attention than before. But this isn't all. One great idea of the qabalists is that the holy name of God, YHVH actually describes a family structure. Y is God the Father, the King; and the first H is God the Mother. Their union creates V the Son and the second H who is the Daughter. In short, within the name of the abstract and unfathomable deity we encounter a typical family of Near Eastern deities. More so, as in any soap opera, lots of weird things happen between them. We learn that Father and Mother live together as reasonable, mature companions. Unlike them, son and daughter have a wild and passionate liaison full of desire, quarrelling and fits of temper: the two are called the Lovers. Behind this remarkable relationship is the idea that father and mother are remote and respectable, while son and daughter are close to the human realm; indeed, the daughter can represent the Kingdom, the world herself. The world, i.e. the daughter, is God's creation, and he is attached to her like an artist to his masterpiece. Soon enough, we find the daughter in bed with God the Father, while the Son lusts after the Mother. It causes plenty of conflict and excitement, and our couples are angry and jealous with each other. But with all due respect we shouldn't call it incest or adultery: the *Zohar* explains that in the Divine, sin is impossible. YHVH may look like a name for an abstract and incomprehensible monotheistic deity, but within that name, an orgy occurs. Father, mother, son and daughter are all part of God's nature: the *Zohar* insists that the Divine is androgynous. Adam and Eve, formed in God's image, appear as a primal sacred androgynes. The same, as you'll see further on, goes for their wicked and fun-loving counterparts Lilith and Samael.

Lilith the Seducer

The Spanish qabalists were extremely imaginative when they wrote about Lilith. Instead of relating the tiny amount of references to Lilith which appeared in elder scripture, they made up new material. And they pretended that their spectacular inventions were part of elder lore. The Lilith of the *Zohar* is a collage of earlier gods and spirits, transformed with each retelling, and we can explore her evolution. Recall the (W)Ardat Lilî. She was a lonely girl, a shy wallflower, who never had much fun, nor enjoy a love life, nor ever called a child her own. It makes her mate with Lilû and seduce lonely young men. That's the start of the succubus tradition. In the Old Babylonian period, it was mostly Ardat Lilî who had that function, but over the centuries, the task passed into Lilītu's domain. We find it associated with Lilith in the *Talmud*, composed between the second and fifth century.

Why is Lilith so keen on seduction? Why is she hungry for sexual fluids? Jewish folklore gives an answer. A remarkable tale relates that whenever a youth or man has an emission, a ghostly spirit child is born. When that man finally dies, he finds his death bed surrounded by a remarkable array of terrifying spectres who are his otherworldly children. Sadly, we are not told what happens next. This could become a really funny story.

A tale from the *Talmud* (Scholem, 1960:203) relates that God created the demons on Friday eve. When the Sabbath began, he stopped work and went home to relax. It left the demons in trouble: they had mind and power, but no body. For this reason they are constantly attracted to living beings, keen to enter bodies and cause obsession. A later tradition, so Scholem wrote, claims that Lilith is eager to gain the sperm of men, as she wants to create a body for herself. Here we encounter a fundamental teaching of the *Zohar*. Basically, the union of men and women was sacred, as it mirrored the union of the male and female components of the divine, provided it was performed in the traditional way, in a state of purity, preferably with clothes on, and in the dark. Also, it should be without lust and desire. By contrast, nocturnal emissions and masturbation were highly polluting, and created further evil in the shape of diseases and demonic spirits.

Zohar I, 19b tells us that Lilith moves by night and visits lonely men, whom she seizes, enjoys and causes to ejaculate. Their sperm impregnates her, and she bears children. As a side effect, she infects her lovers with diseases. It happens when the moon wanes. Scholem (1960:207; see also Patai 1978:198 for a different translation) cites a spell from the *Zohar* (III, 19a, after the German, my comments in brackets).

In that hour when the man unites with his wife, he should focus his mind on the holiness of his Lord and say:

You who are wrapped in soft velvet (=Lilith)*,*

-are you here?

Be raised, be lifted (=expelled)*,*

do not come in and do not go out!

(This act is) Not of you and nothing in your share!

Return, return, the sea is stormy,

the waves are calling to you!

Yet I hold the sacred part,

I am cloaked in the Holiness of the King (=God)*.*

Then he should wrap his head and the head of his wife in blankets for a while and later he should scatter water around his bed.

She could be Ardat Lilî, or even Lamaštu, fascinated by lovers and keen on their offspring. But our Lilith of the *Zohar*, though she can travel through the air, is not a wind deity: she has made her home in the depths of the bottomless sea.

One of my favourite passages elaborates Lilith's loveplay with men (*Zohar*, 1, 148, a&b, translated by Patai 1978).

She (Lilith), like a wanton woman adorns herself with all sorts of ornaments to seduce men. She seizes the fool who approaches her; she kisses him and offers him wine with a residue of serpent poison. When he has drunk he follows her. When she sees that he has lost the way of truth she takes everything off which she has put on for the fool. To seduce men her ornaments are her well-dressed hair, which is red as a rose, her cheeks are white and red, from her ears dangle chains from Egypt and her neck is adorned by pendants from the East. Her mouth is small like a narrow door, her tongue is sharp like a sword and her words are as soft as oil. Her lips are red like a rose and sweet with the sweetness of the world. She is clad in purple and adorned with the jewels of the entire world, all-in-all 39 ornaments. Those fools who visit her and drink her wine commit fornication with her. But what does she do afterwards? She leaves them alone in deep slumber on their beds; but she ascends to the height (of heaven). There, she reports all sorts of evil regarding them. Afterwards, she asks for permission to descend again. When the fool wakes he believes he could take his pleasure with her as before. She, however, takes off her ornaments and transforms into a figure of power. She faces him, clad in a fiery dress of flame. She creates terror and makes body and soul tremble. Her eyes are large; in her hands is a sharp sword that scatters drops of bitter venom. She slays (with it) and casts him into the midst of hell.

Our passage is so beautifully detailed that it could easily be used for a tantric meditation. Lilith acts with divine permission: she goes to test men, and those who fall for her charms are duly reported to God almighty and find their punishment. Lilith as a seductress is not a disobedient demoness but acts on divine request. It raises the question whether the earlier Babylonian wind deities were also part of the divine order.

Sisters of Lilith

Many students of the *Zohar* see Lilith as a singular counterweight to the Shekinah and/or the Matronit and forget her terrifying girlfriends. They shouldn't: wicked girls hang around in clusters.

Naamah (the *Charmer*) had a strange career. As Patai narrates, in the *Talmud* and the *Midrashic* texts, she started as a human woman. Naamah was the daughter of Lamech and Zillah, and the sister of Tubal-Cain (*Genesis* 4:19). She was so stunningly attractive that her cymbal play invited men to worship 'idols'. Maybe she was a priestess and danced in a temple, on a mountaintop or in a sacred grove. She looked gorgeous and men, spirits and demons could not resist her. Eventually Naamah was seduced by the angel Shamdon (or Shomron), and from their passionate union, Ashmodai, the King of Devils, was born. It provided her with a remarkable love life and turned her into an immortal demon-queen. Many lethal spirits were bedazzled by her charms. *Zohar* I, 9b tells us that Afrira and Qastimon were so horny for Naamah, the *Mother of Witches,* that they pursued her into the depths of the sea. She escaped their amorous attention by leaping 60,000 parsa'ot, i.e. half-way up the Tree of Life, tried to get a hold, missed, slipped and fell into the depths again. The story says that she assumes many different forms to deceive and entice the people.

Naamah's origin is a convoluted story (*Zohar* I, 56). In the good old days in paradise, the serpent impregnated Eve, and their child was Cain. From his seed all evil spirits were born. In that period, children came half from the celestial realm and half from the infernal regions. Not all children of Adam were born from Eve, as the *Zohar* relates. Adam was a busy man who didn't have much control over his underwear; he also fathered children on female spirits whose beauty reflects the loveliness of the above and below. One of the most important kids from Cain's side was Tubal Cain, who brought murder weapons into the world, while his sister Naamah *caused all creatures to go astray,* wherever that may be. Here is her full description (*Zohar* I, 55-56, Müller, 2013, trans. JF)

Rabbi Chija spoke: 'It is written: the sister of Tubal-Cain was Naamah. What should be taught by this name? That the sons of men, yes, even spirits and demons were seduced by her.'

Rabbi Jizchak spoke: 'The sons of God, Asa and Asael strayed after her.'

Rabbi Shim'on spoke: 'She is the mother of the evil spirits, as she sprang from the region of Cain and was appointed, together with Lilith, to plague (Patai translates *'to strangle'*) *children'.*

And Rabbi Abba argued: 'Is she not destined to bear the smile of seduction among people?'

He replied, 'So it is, verily, when she arrives and shows the smile of seduction among men, she thereby bears and births evil spirits. And to this day she exists, in her role and her seductiveness.'

But Rabbi Abba argued: 'But the evil spirits, just like people, are mortal. How could it be that she exists to this day?'

And Rabbi Abba replied: 'It is truly so. Only Lilith and Naamah and Ygrath daughter of Mahalath, who arose from their region (=the region of Cain) – *they last long until the Holy One erases the impure spirit from the world, as it is said 'And I will abolish the Spirit of impurity from the World' (Zachariah 13,2)'.*

And Rabbi Shim'on spoke: 'Woe to the people, who do not know and are unaware, but are of blunted senses, who do not know how the world is full of strange beings, of invisible and hidden things. For if the eye had received the power of sight, the children of humanity would be amazed, how it could be that they survive in the world at all. And remember, that Naamah is the mother of all evil spirits; from her come all the evil spirits, who seek the warmth of human life and arouse the spirit of desire in them. And due to her seductive smile it is especially those who are afflicted with hidden sins whom she turns into her servants.'

In the *Sepher-Ha-Zohar*, chapter XXXIII we read that Rabbi Shim'on said: *She* (Naamah) *was the procreatrix of all the demons of Cainite Origin, and she it is that along with Lilith afflicts infant children with epilepsy.* (Trans. Nurho de Manar). Epilepsy. Sure. Let's call it trembling, shaking and vibrating, and keep it up as long as we like.

What exactly marks the difference between Lilith and Naamah? Both of them seduce and destroy ill-fated sinners, bear ghostly children, and slay or strangle infants. Both dwell in the depths of the sea, are the mothers of countless air spirits and demons, who are able to grant oracles and prophecy. Also, they are exceedingly charming and attractive, a sure sign of great evil in a culture that identified desire with Satan and Samael (*Zohar* III, 16b: *But Satan, the Evil of Desire, is stationed above all sins and all realms and all guardians* (of hell).) I wonder whether Lilith and Naamah evolved among different ethnic or cultural groups before they met in the *Zohar*?

Now for another major player. Meet **Ygrath**, Daughter of Mahalath, whose name has been vaguely explained as the *Slayer*, the *Very Evil* and the *Dancer*. As one source has it (Patai, 1978:211), Ygrath was the harlot who came to King David in his camp and seduced him. She bore a son called Adad. When Adad was asked for his name he said 'My name is Ad; Ad is my name'. It reads 'Ad'sh'mi' in Hebrew and is the source of the name Ashmodai. As ancient Jewish tradition has it (Pes 112b Bar. in Strack & Billerbeck, 1997, trans. JF): *One should not go out at night, nor in the nights of the fourth day* (Wednesday) *not in the nights before the Sabbath, cause then Ygrath bath Mahalath and 18 myriads of Angels of Doom are emerging, and each of them has the license to devastate all by itself.* Here is the story. One fateful night, when Ygrath was happily touring the countryside, devastating anything she didn't like, she chanced to meet a saint. It almost ruined her mood. The grumpy old sage wanted to banish her, but as she has a part in the divine plan he allowed her a part-time job, and limited the devastation to two nights a week.

Child Slayer

In Old Babylonia, the Lilû deities granted diseases and visitations, but they were not, apparently, specialised in infanticide. That used to be the domain of Lamaštu and Pašittu. Sometime after the late second millennium BCE Lamaštu joined the group of wind deities and her functions began to overlap with theirs. Before long, Lilītu and Lamaštu were identified with each other.

Let's start with a crucial question: why do babies die? And why do the gods allow it? Overpopulation is an excellent reason for mankind and nature in general, but in the individual realm of people wanting children (and not having an old age pension), countless parents must have worried, wept and asked 'why us?' How do you explain the death of an infant when you don't understand genetics, hygiene, and infections? Religion, no matter how bizarre, may provide answers. As the baby obviously wasn't old enough to be a sinner deserving divine punishment, maybe the parents had sinned or polluted themselves. Look at *Zohar*, I, 19b (trans. Patai), where we learn that Lilith was rejected by the Cherubim, and dwelled in the depths of the sea until Adam and Eve sinned:

...when the Holy One, blessed be He!- brought her up, and she obtained power over those children – the 'small faces' of mankind – who deserve to be punished because of the sins of their fathers. She roams all over the world, then approaches the gates of the Garden of Eden and observes the Cherubim watching over the gates. She sits down there, next to the flame of the sword, since it was from that flame that she originated. When the flame turns around (Patai: *indicating that the world has entered into a phase of punishment), she rushes off and again goes roaming all over the world to seek out the children who deserve to be punished. And she smiles at them and kills them...*

But there could also be another explanation.

Here is *Zohar*, II, 96b, translation Daniel C. Matt:

All those tormented souls, who are they? Here is a mystery. There are souls of little babies, suckling from their mother's potent breasts. And the blessed Holy One sees that if they endure in the world their odour will stink and they will turn sour like vinegar. He plucks them small, while they still yield fragrance. What does He do? He leaves them to be tormented at the hands of this ***slave–girl*** *– Lilith; for as soon as one is delivered into her power, she delights over that baby, torments and removes him from the world while he is sucking at his mother's breast.*

We will get back to the term 'slave-girl' further on. In our account, Lilith is acting on God's orders: she kills the infants who will grow up to be evil.

But Lilith, according to the *Zohar*, is not always a child-slayer. Patai (1978:206 and note on page 313) mentions a Jewish folk belief that when children smile in their sleep, Lilith is with them. Such children, people assumed, ought to be woken instantly. Another belief is that when children laugh while they are alone, especially on the night of the new moon, they are playing with Lilith and need their noses tapped.

Zohar, III, 77a suggests that there are two sorts of children. Those who are conceived in a state of true holiness are safe from Lilith, but those who were born from desire and pollution contain a soul that comes from the *side of contamination* (i.e. Cain's lineage). Lilith arrives to visit such children, she plays with them and if she kills such a child, *she penetrates that soul and never leaves it.* Are we talking about a metaphorical or spiritual death that leaves the child with a Lilith-infused soul, ready to lead a life of carefree wickedness?

A similar idea is expounded in *Zohar* III, 76b (see Patai, 1978:210), where Naamah cooperates with Lilith. The show begins. The curtain lifts, and Naamah makes love with mortal men. She stalks them, embraces them and seizes the force of their desire. It fertilises her and she gives birth to evil spirits. Her male (spirit) children go into the world and haunt human women. They impregnate mortal women, who give birth to spirit babies. These infants go to the First Lilith, who nurses and raises them. But Naamah and Lilith also deal with flesh and blood children. When Naamah enters the dreams of a man and incites his lust, and that man wakes and has intercourse with his wife, their child, conceived of desire, belongs to the family of Naamah. As it grows up, the little darling will be visited by Lilith frequently. She plays with it. When the moon renews itself Lilith visits all the children in her care. And she makes their fathers suffer. I'm sure it made you think of Mary Poppins.

Family Affairs

The qabalists in medieval Spain organised the evil spirits, just like the components in God's name, in confusing family structures. It made them invent astonishing stories. The best known is, of course, the tale of Lilith and Adam's marriage and divorce. It made its first appearance in the ninth or tenth century *Midrash Abkir* and opened the way for an entirely new multi-purpose Lilith. After Cain killed Abel, Adam was so grieved, upset and disgusted with his offspring (and himself?) that he left Eve and dwelled in loneliness for 130 years. He slept alone, lived alone and fasted to make up for his guilt, pollution and sinfulness. During this period, he was frequently haunted by the seductive Pizna. You met her: remember the bowl inscription from Nippur, referring to Lilith Buznai? Pizna was stricken with Adam's beauty, his sad, soulful eyes and tragic appeal. She seduced him and they had congress, and probably quite a lot of it, as she gave birth to evil spirits, demons and the *Plagues of Mankind*: creatures that haunt latrines, doorways and wells. That there are so many evil creatures may be blamed on the fact that 130 years is quite a while and Adam evidently didn't grieve all the time.

Another tale, also from the ninth or tenth century, is the famous story how Lilith divorced Adam. It comes from the *Alphabet of Ben Sira*:

When God had created Adam he said: It is not good for man to be alone. So he created a wife for him, also of earth, and named her Lilith. As soon as she was made, she started to quarrel and said: Why should I lie below you? I am just as valuable as you are, as we are both created from earth. And when Lilith saw that she could not win over Adam, she spoke the unspeakable name of God and flew into the air.

It left Adam horny, frustrated and angry. He prayed to God Almighty, and complained that his wife had run away. God sent the three angels Sanvai, Sansanvai and Semangloph to order her back. The angels found her in the depths of the ocean, in the very sea where, much later, the armies of Pharaoh were to drown. They told her all would be well if she returned. If not, her punishment would be that every day a hundred of her children would die. But Lilith refused. The angels threatened to drown her. But she pleaded and spoke: 'Leave me, for I have been created to destroy small children. If it is a boy, I have power over him for eight days after his birth, and if a girl, for twenty days.' The angels were deeply upset and implored her to heed God's command. But Lilith said: *I swear by the name of the Great and Living God: when I see your names written on an amulet I will not harm that child. And she accepted that every day a hundred of her children would die.*

Henceforth, the names of the three angels remind Lilith when it is time to spare a child.

The story became widely popular and was retold and varied. We find Lilith under the sea, on an island in the sea, or living on the shore right next to it. In the 19th century the tale was still well-known in Jewish communities, and amulets with the names of the three angels are maybe used to this day. I would like to add a few details. The story is not an ancient tradition that was, as some claim, 'deleted from the Bible', but a typical medieval hybrid. To begin with, the story from *Genesis* 1,26 that only Adam was made from earth is just one version among several; the *Priestly Codex* claims that Adam and Eve were both made from Earth.

Gershom Scholem (1960:215) traces the tale of the unhappy marriage of Lilith and Adam to a tradition of the third century CE. In the *Bereshith Rabba*, 22, § 7, we meet the 'First Eve'. In the beginning, God created Adam and Eve out of earth. As Eve was made from the same stuff as Adam, she had the same rights and status as Adam. She also had a right to own property. Scholem mentions that Cain and Abel fought for the right to inherit the possessions of the first Eve, who was not even their mother. Adam and the first Eve didn't get along with each other. So God created a 'Second Eve' from the flesh and bone of Adam, who was an improvement as she was inferior to him. The figure of Lilith was grafted on this early tale around the ninth or tenth century. A faint echo of this story appears in a very late source, the *Book Of Raziel*, printed in 1701. Its contents are a perplexing mixture of materials dating well after the tenth century CE. One interesting spell starts: *I conjure you, First Eve, in the name of Him who created you and in the name of the three angels, which the Lord has sent after you and who found you dwelling on the islands of the Sea....* Several researchers have identified the 'First Eve' with Lilith. Sorry, they got it wrong. As the name Lilith does not occur in the text and we have a First Eve tradition going back to, at least, the third century, it is entirely possible that the First Eve was a child killer. What is it about Lilith that makes researchers overheat? Be that as it may, the tale how Lilith divorced herself from Adam is an enchanting demonstration of free will and independence. It's a good story and it turned Lilith into a goddess of the feminist movement. However, as I mentioned in *Kālī Kaula*, we are not dealing with a story of crude gender conflicts. Adam, as many rabbis and qabalists believed, was a) created in God's image and b) originally an androgynous figure. It is only because Adam was male and female simultaneously that a part of him could be cut off, and made into a female. The tale of Adam and Lilith does not condemn men but mankind for bossiness and arrogance. The tale could also describe the failed union of human and extra-human consciousness; but that's just a personal guess.

Let's continue with Adam and Lilith. Nowadays many people know Lilith as the first woman who said 'no!' to a man. Several medieval texts have it the other way around. When Adam was alone and wallowed in bad feelings for 130 years, it was Lilith who kept haunting him. Just don't ask me why; he can't have been much fun to be with. But maybe she thought she could cheer him up. Plenty of optimistic people fall for that one. Between the 14th to 17th century, scholars elaborated on the topic. Presumably they were not much fun to be with either. They wrote that Adam was frequently haunted by Lilith and Naamah, both of them attracted by his tragically sad expression, good looks and wonderfully fertile seed, and that he practically had to chase them off when he needed a well deserved night of sleep. As several qabalists pointed out, it was Adam's own fault; the bad girls would have left him alone, had he not sinned in the first place.

Similar ideas keep appearing in the *Zohar*. I am sure you remember that Lilith was originally created out of the flame of the revolving sword. *Zohar*, I, 34b disagrees. It points at *Genesis*, 1, 20-21, where we find God on the fifth day of creation making the *Living Creature* whose swarms fill the waters. That *Living Creature*, so the *Zohar* proposes, was none other than Lilith. In chapter XVI of the *Zohar* Rabbi Hezekiah explained: *Scripture here useth the word Haromseth (moving creature) and not Hashoretzeth (creeping creature). Wherefore? Because it refers to Lilith, as has been stated, who is also denoted in the words; 'Thou makest darkness and it is night, wherein all beasts in the forest move.' (Thirmoas). These words also denote those angelic beings called Hayoth (Living Creature') who predominate and exert an influence equalling that of Lilith, and during the three watches of the night chant their hymns and praise until morning dawns* (after Nurho de Manhar). *Zohar* III, 19a disagrees. When God created Adam, the female was contained in the male, but her soul came from the Great Abyss. When she entered the body, a thousand souls came from the Left (i.e. the evil realm) and tried to attach themselves to it, but God gave a mighty shout and scared them away. To put another soul into the body, God made a cloud descend (like many Near Eastern weather deities, God has a thing about clouds) and commanded the earth to produce a living soul. Then God breathed life into his creature, which stood up as well as it could, as it consisted of a male and female half connected by their backs. God cut the two apart; the male half remained with God, but the female half, Lilith, flew away to the *Cities of the Sea*, where she made her home. In this peculiar tale we encounter a typical element of qabalistic thought. The Tree of Life manifested from the top to the bottom. That is, pure divinity kept giving off emanations of itself, and each emanation created another, less pure one, until the whole thing hit rock bottom in Malkuth, the Kingdom, right here on earth, where things and people are really dense. Evolution, in this model, is a steady story of decline and corruption: things start out divine and become increasingly polluted. Each sphere of divine manifestation brought forth a less perfect one, and as if this wasn't enough, each creative process produced leftovers, the husks, the empty shells, the spilled-off sentience and the dregs that had no place in the divine plan. Such waste-materials were qliphothic; the qabalists considered them as evil reflexes of the divine emanations. In 13th century Spain, this process was far from fully developed. *Zohar* I 148a claims that when the sphere of Geburah was created, representing the power, judgement and punishment of God, out of the *dregs of its wine* a shoot appeared that was male and female at once. It was red as a rose and extended to all sides and paths. Next it turned into an androgynous figure: the male half is Samael (a dreaded old devil king and the epitome of evil) while the female half is Lilith. Though they have a common origin, Samael and Lilith are a happily married couple: *The female of Samael is called Serpent, Woman of Harlotry, End of All Flesh, End of Days.* (trans. Patai, 1978:193). What a poetic expression. You could use it as a mantra to brighten up your life.

By contrast, *Zohar* I, 19b states that when the sphere of Mercy was established, God spoke 'Let there be Light'. So it was, but when the light was obscured and hidden, its holiness was covered by a 'husk' or 'shell' (qlipha) of evil. This qlipha spread and brought forth another qlipha, which was Lilith.

The Hacohen brothers equipped Lilith with a range of terrifying husbands. While the tenth century *Alphabet of Ben Sira* only coupled her, briefly and unhappily, with a very stupid Adam, the Hacohens devised a range of partners for the goddess who were a lot harder to stomach. One of their tales claims that Samael and Lilith were created as an androgynous, double faced entity right under the throne of God. They appear like an evil counterpart to Adam and Eve, who were also created, in God's very own image, as an androgyne. Both pairs, so the Hacohen brothers boldly stated, *were like the image of what is Above*, i.e. the androgynous God. Unlike them, the Spanish qabalists, though hinting at God's androgyny, were not daring enough to state it outright.

But Lilith wasn't only Samael's wife; we also meet her as the spouse of Satan. According to Scholem (2001:207), the Hacohen Brothers picked up the idea that Satan has one or several wives (including Lilith) from a misinterpreted fancy of the Cathars. The Cathars were enthusiastic heretics, whose bizarre and often contradictory teachings are also called Manichaean. Before they were crushed by the one true church, they developed an elaborate theology based on a dualist interpretation of the world. In their opinion, God was opposed by Satan, who happened to be the true creator of the world and everything in it. For this reason, every single being and thing (including you and me) are sinful and polluted. Souls, in their pure state are angelic and beyond gender, but when they incarnate they fall into sin; the only hope of redemption being a series of increasingly purifying rebirths. And as Satan was such an important adversary, he got plenty of attention. The Cathars misread some documents regarding Ahala and Ahaliba, who were originally the mother of Christ and the mother of Satan. They assumed that both women were actually Satan's wives; an entirely new idea, as in earlier periods, Satan had to get along without a wife. The misinterpretation of the Cathars was picked up by the Hacohens, and found its way into the Spanish qabalistic tradition. They also complicated things by writing about an elder and a younger Lilith. Well, the idea that there are plenty of Liliths was hardly new, and as bowl 11 of the Nippur excavation shows, some could be the grandmother of others. Scholem (2001:261, trans. JF) cites the passage:

The elder Lilith is the wife of Sammael; both were born at the same hour in the image of Adam and Eve and they embrace each other. Ashmedai, the great king of demons has as his wife the young Lilith, the daughter of the king, whose name is Qaphṣaphuni and whose wife is Meheṭabel, and their daughter is Lilitha.

In this episode, our king and his wife are connected to the *Bible* (*Genesis* 36, 39). Lilith's family comes from Edom; indeed Lilith and Samael were the regents of that land. Remember that biblical reference telling us that Lilith sits in the ruins of Edom. But we are not talking geography here. For the Spanish qabalists, Edom was not a place in the ancient Near East but a code word for Christianity, which, as they were certain, had developed right within the horrid realm of darkness. The Hacohens had more to say about their relationship; and I guess this is going to be a TV series one day. Samael and Lilith, so our learned qabalists recorded, are the very Tree of Knowledge of Good and Evil, which casts an interesting light on Adam and Eve fruit-picking in the Garden of Eden. You could stop here for a fascinating meditation. Go into a deep trance and ask your personal deity what the fruit of the Tree was. The Hacohens explained that on rare occasion, Qaphṣaphuni made love with Lilitha. We are not told whether this Lilitha happens to be his own daughter, Lilith the Younger. The Younger Lilith was the wife of Ashmodai, and their offspring was Prince Harba di Ashm'dai (=*Sword of Ashmodai*) who ruled an army of 80,000 destructive demons plus other spirits. Now Lilith the Younger, who was from head to navel a gorgeously beautiful woman, and from the navel downward scorching fire, tempted Samael, who ought to have been true to her mother, the Elder Lilith, but wasn't. It messed up family relations and caused jealousy between Ashmodai and Samael, and incessant fighting between Lilith the Elder and the Younger. The story gets livelier in a tale recorded by Moses Cordovero (1522-1570). He envisioned Lilith the Elder marching into the desert where she screeched angrily for three entire days. It annoyed Mahalath, the Daughter of Ishmael, who happens to be the concubine of Samael, and who *goes and sings a song and a paean in the Holy Tongue. And when the two meet, they fight, on the Day of Atonement, there in the desert, and they taunt each other, until their voices rise to heaven, and the earth trembles under their screams. And all this is brought about by God so that they should not be able to make accusations against Israel (on the Day of Atonement).* (Patai, 1978:216-217).

Isaac Hacohen had more to say about Lilith, and some of it is truly remarkable. Patai quotes him as stating that Lilith *is a ladder on which one can ascend to the rungs of prophecy.* Well enough; once you know what a given person fears and desires you can make pretty accurate predictions. Just look at yourself. What do you dread and desire most? And how is it shaping your life? What would you predict right now, as you are facing yourself facing yourself? It's damn obvious. Laugh and reconsider.

Lilith's relations to Samael were elaborated by later qabalists. Patai quotes Bahya ben Asher ibn Halawa (died 1340) who wrote that four women are the mothers of demons: Lilith, Naamah, Ygrath and Mahalath. You met them before. Each of them has her own army of demons, and each rules at one of the four tequfot: the spring equinox, the summer solstice, the autumn equinox and the winter solstice, from sunset to midnight. On these dates, our wicked girls dress up and meet on a peak near the Mountains of Darkness. However, no matter how powerful they are, King Solomon (yes, the old incorrigible polytheist) rules over them, calls them his slave-women and has them act on his behest. And the four are the wives of Esau's patron, i.e. Samael. Indeed, Esau tried to follow Samael's example and took four wives himself.

Another tradition mates Solomon with Lilith: according to a faint hint in the *Zohar*, Lilith was really the Queen of Sheba, and famous for the thick, shaggy fur that covered her all over. You won't find that in the *Bible*. It's a typical medieval invention: Lilith became increasingly hirsute, except, to her dismay, for her head, which turned bald. Incidentally, a bald lady guards the Grail in the early thirteenth century *Perlesvaus*. She is quite good looking and rides a mule. In her hands she holds the head of a king, sealed with silver and wearing a golden crown. Behind another damsel rides a horse; she carries the head of a queen and a third damsel walks behind them who whips the mule and the horse. She is followed by a cart drawn by three stags, which contains another 150 heads. As it turns out the king and the queen are Adam and Eve, while the 150 heads represent mankind (Loomis, 1992:102). Is the bald lady a form of Lilith?

In the 17th century, Nathan Spira created a complicated cosmological model. In his book, there were two kings of evil: Rahab and Samael. Rahab ruled over Egypt while Samael governed four kingdoms, and had a concubine in each of them: Lilith ruled Damascus, where the House of Rimmon is found; Naamah ruled Tyre, opposite of Israel; Maskith ruled Malta (formerly called Rhodus) and Mahalath ruled Granata, called the kingdom of Ishmael (=Islam) by some.

But Lilith was not only married to Adam, Ashmodai, Samael and Satan. Elsewhere we meet her as the wife of Leviathan (Livjatan: '*The Coiled One*'), the dreaded oceanic monster. Or she appears as a form of Leviathan. It perfectly suits her underwater home.

Finally, we come to the weirdest match of them all. Meet the **slave-woman**. To make this even remotely comprehensible, I would like to remind you of the family structure within the divine name YHVH: Y is God the father (the king), H is God the mother (represented by the Shekinah or the Matronit), V is God the son and the final H is God the daughter. The Shekinah is such a complicated subject that entire books were written to explain her. Sorry, but this is not the place to expound the topic. Let us just stick to the basics. God, as the father, is only complete when he is united with the Shekinah and/or Matronit, who may represent a wide range of ideas, such as God's manifestation in tangible form, God's love, God's energy, God's wisdom and the entire Jewish culture. When the Neo-Babylonians (587 BCE) overran Palestine, they destroyed the temple of Jerusalem and deported a lot of locals. The destruction of the temple of Jerusalem was a terrible shock to faithful Jews. The temple was much more than a holy building, it symbolised the entire faith and manifested God's link to mankind. With the major sanctuary in ruins, God the father found himself without a home and congregation. He also found himself, metaphorically, without his wife. Remember that the Shekinah could represent the community of the faithful. *When Israel was exiled, the Shekinah too went into exile, and this is the nakedness of the Shekinah. And this nakedness is Lilith, the Mother of the Multitude* (*Zohar*, I, 27b). Here things become extremely complicated. The Shekinah was usually, but not always, identified with the mother, the Matronit. On occasion we encounter her as the daughter, and sometimes she is even called *the slave woman*, the servant of the Shekinah and/or Matronit. A few innovative qabalists assumed that *'the slave woman'* is Lilith. *Zohar* III, 69a describes the Slave Woman as *the Alien Crown whose first born God slew in Egypt.* The learned Spanish qabalists argued that when the King (God the father) sent the Matronit (the Mother, here, the community of Israelites) into exile, he lost the right to call himself king. Lacking the mother (i.e. the community of worshippers), he went to bed with the slave woman (or servant) of the Matronit, who became the ruler of the land in her stead. This slave girl, so some qabalists assumed, is Lilith. Our sources are confused. So are we. Lilith became the wife of God (if only for a brief while). Some sages promoted this idea and others did not. However: if the slave girl was Lilith, she attained the summit of religious success. If only for the period when God, as some rabbis claimed, lived in shame. As could have been expected, this unsettling situation did not continue indefinitely: God and the Matronit/Shekinah were reunited when the temple of Jerusalem was rebuilt, and their happy reunion lasted until the Romans moved in it. What happened to Lilith remains unknown; I guess she got the TV, the second best bed and the dog and bought a house in Sunnydale, California, where life is really worth living.

Our Lady of Crisis

The *Zohar* contains amazing ideas. You find philosophers who combine the five Greek elements with Neo-Platonic ideas, the holy writ of Moses and the raging prophets of the *Old Testament.* You discover the lore of the medical **'humours'** aligned with the qabala. A brief, and oversimplified introduction may be useful. The 'Theory of the Humours' was first proposed by Hippocrates and Galen, the pioneering Greek physicians. They combined Empedocles' model of the 'four elements' with temperaments, seasons, times of the day and mysterious fluids which they assumed to act within the human body. In their estimate, there are four temperaments, or typical psychological conditions. The Sanguine Temperament is related to blood, to spring and to the air element. It tends to be careless, optimistic, vigorous, generous and cheerful. The Choleric Temperament is associated with summer, the fire element and the yellow bile/choler. Choleric moods are excitable, intense, bitter, critical, short-tempered and explosive. The Melancholic Temperament is connected with autumn, the earth element and is caused by black bile. Under its rule, people introspect, withdraw, doubt, search for transcendence and encounter varied moods and feelings, ranging from sadness to enthusiastic joy. And finally we have the Phlegmatic Temperament, ruled by goo, and connected to winter and water: emotionally, it corresponds to patience, sloth, endurance, sluggishness, heaviness and resignation.

The doctors of antiquity believed that many diseases arise from a surplus or lack of these fluids. It was, fundamentally, a brilliant idea, as all states of awareness depend on specific brain chemistry. Sadly, contemporary neurologists have to take into account more than four fluids. Our early healers lacked this knowledge, and lived a carefree life while their patients didn't. The four fluids, they thought, moved through the organs, but they could also be burned up by heat and rise into the brain like a vapour. Let me quote from Asenath Mason's brilliant work *Sol Tenebrarum. The Occult Study of Melancholy* (2010:23): *Their role was believed to be enormously important: the humours were the life-giving moisture of the body, the active life-principle, the vital heat which corresponded to the fires and energies in the centre of the earth. Moreover, they reflected the structure and phenomena of the surrounding cosmos... The balance between the humours was the sign of health, while disorders and diseases resulted from disruption of this natural harmony.*

The Spanish qabalists incorporated the four humours, and all sorts of anatomical relationships, into the *Zohar*. The results of this fusion are mind-blowing passages like this one:

And Michael, Gabriel, Nuriel and Rafael reign over the four good elements in man: water, fire, air and earth, and each of them has four faces. In opposition to this, 'sin, doom, wrath and anger' cling to the white gall of the lung, which forms a fibrous structure; to the red gall of the liver, whose ruddiness is caused by Mars; to the green gall, which likewise clings to the liver and forms the Sword of the Angel of Death, of whom it is said: 'and their end is bitter like wormwood, sharp like an open sword (Sayings, 5,4); to the black gall, (related to) *Lilith, it is governed by Saturn, in the spleen, which is the darkest abyss of despair, poverty and darkness, weeping, and sorrowing and hunger. But when these four 'shells'* (=qlipha) *depart from a man, the Tree of Life comes to reign over him, with 72 faces, formed by Y, YH, YHV and YHVH, which depend, as a group of ten, on the four directions of the name YHVH.* (3, 227b, Müller 1982:188, trans. JF).

This reference to Lilith is rarely quoted, as it is miles away from her popular image. We are far from a lethal seductress who hungers for Adam's seed, lives proudly on her own or has a happy marriage with Samael, Leviathan or God Almighty. This Lilith is neither a succubus nor a slayer of infants nor a scourge of mankind. Instead, she is spiritual crisis personified. The black humour, so the classical authors assumed, is related to melancholy. It sounds simple but isn't: in old literature, the term 'melancholy' had a different meaning. Today, we associate melancholy with sadness, depression and inertia. It's a small range of unpleasant feelings. But think of the seasons: originally, melancholy was not the dreary dark and cold of winter, when there is no option but to wait, endure and hope, but the coming of autumn. Autumn is pure changeability. Nature explodes in a gorgeous show of generosity. The matured grains are cut and stored, there are fruits on the trees, gleaming with ripeness, and there are seeds and promises of future life all over the place. The leaves turn red; the gales scatter them and leave the trees bare and naked under a wide and wind-cold sky. And as the days grow shorter and the nights fresher, people face the coming of the cold season. You can be sad or you can drink with your friends and face the world in a spirit of courage and joy. Autumn is not a time of resignation. It is a period of preparation, a time of elation and cheer in the face of the inevitable. The melancholic temperament was thought to resemble this; hence, the emotional states represented by the black humour were more varied and changeable than that of the other humours. Melancholy was associated with Saturn. Pluto, Neptune and Uranus being undiscovered, it was Saturn, as the outmost planet, who acted as the guardian of the threshold, moving on the very limit of the known world, between the planetary spheres and the realm of the stars. From this unique position, Saturn gained his connection to crisis, death and transcendence. People saw autumn changing the world and pondered how transitory life is, how the richness of the harvest is followed by the bleakness of winter, and how nature undergoes a period of sleep or death only to be reborn in spring. In classical, medieval and renaissance literature, melancholy had much to do with introspection, nostalgia, morbidity, with states of ecstatic agitation and visionary madness, with religious fervour, mental diseases, visions, hallucinations, nightmares, insomnia, restlessness, doubt, distrust and even with the fire of divine frenzy. Melancholic people were assumed to be unstable and more open to obsession by gods or demons than ordinary people. Many writers of antiquity, starting with Plato, believed that divine insanity is the source of true prophecy. Perhaps this is the key to Isaac Hacohen's remark that Lilith grants prophecy. She can and should disrupt your usual thinking so that new insights come through. In a similar manner, the divine frenzy was cultivated in several mystery cults: when initiates were drugged, confused, or crazy, the divine could flow through them and sweep them along like howling bacchantes running through the mountains at night.

Nowadays, we tend to think of melancholy as a passive and depressive state of awareness. But what we call 'depression' would be more adequately classed under the Phlegmatic Temperament, as it tends to appear in resignation and in thinking the same weary, sad and self-abusive thoughts again and again. People who can't take their anger out on others tend to take it out on themselves; some drink, do drugs, work themselves into the ground or merely give up and cultivate unhappy thoughts. The result is pretty much the same: exhaustion, stagnation and inertia.

The original model of the four humours attributed melancholia to autumn. Over time, the attributions shifted; in renaissance literature, melancholia was attributed to winter and phlegmatic moods to autumn.

The black humour ruled old people, gravediggers and graverobbers, alchemists, magicians, necromancers, astrologers, artists, monks, philosophers, scientists, malcontents and criminals: all of them children of Saturn. Poets were known to oscillate between states of great longing and the onslaught of fresh inspiration, and so were philosophers, artists and religious visionaries. Melancholy was a typical symptom of creative and scientific geniuses. In short, melancholy, the black humour, and Lilith as its queen, represents states of great emotionality, inspiration and magical potency. By embracing the Saturnian element and by acknowledging the dark humour, seers, philosophers, thinkers and artists find a way to transcend the limits of ordinary human existence. Crisis and despair provide a chance for spiritual initiation. Lilith, custodian of the black elixir, is an initiatrix to the realm of transformative crisis, to the autumn storms that strip the foliage from the branches, to the abyss behind the simple, shallow dream of everyday life. She opens the gate of dissolution, madness and inspiration and transforms the human personality from the core.

Crisis can be a blessing. Without occasional bouts of doubt, worry and dissolution, spiritual development stagnates. We all need chaotic events to eliminate beliefs that make our existence easy, simple, normal, repetitive and dull. Our passage of the *Zohar* reveals Lilith as an initiatrix who makes life, religion and all magick meaningful, for unless we are willing to die again and again, we will find no rebirth in a happier state of consciousness.

Names of Lilith

Like so many influential goddesses, Lilith and her friends cast off reflexes that survive in numerous cultures. Just as the medieval Lilith united functions that had earlier been the domain of the Ardat Lilî, Pašittu and Lamaštu, witchy figures tend to overlap with Lilith, Ygrath and Naamah. Here is an odd tale which Montgomery (2012/1913:259) received from Professor Richard Gottheil. The age of the story is disputable: it exists in numerous versions, and only a few can be dated. Montgomery's text begins with the invocation:

Sanui, Sansanui, Semniglaph, Adam, YHVH, Kadmon, Life, Lilith.

It's a remarkable mixture. The first three are the angels that God sent to coerce Lilith (Snuffles, Squeaky and Snottle). Then follow Adam & YHVH, while 'Life' looks like a Mandaean addition. Why Lilith appears among the sacred names is anyone's guess. Make it yours, and let's continue:

In the name of Y" the God of Israel who besits the cherubs, whose name is living and enduring forever. Elija the prophet was walking in the road and he met the wicked Lilith and all her band. He said to her, Where art thou going, Foul One and Spirit of Foulness with all thy foul band walking along. And she answered and said to him, My Lord Elija, I was going to the house of the woman in childbirth who is in pangs (?), of So-and-So Daughter of Such-a-One, to give her the sleep of death and to take the child she is bearing, to suck his blood and to suck the marrow of his bones and to devour his flesh. And said Elija the Prophet – blessed be his name! – With a ban from the Name – bless it! shalt thou be restrained and like a stone shalt thou be! And she answered and said to him: For the sake of Y" postpone the ban and I will flee, and will swear to thee in the name of Y" God of Israel that I will let go this business in the case of this woman in childbirth and the child to be born to her and every inmate so as to do no injury. And every time that they repeat or I see my names written, it will not be in the power of me or all my band to do evil or harm. And these are my names:

LILITH, ABITAR (ABITO?), ABIKAR (ABIKO?), AMORPHO, HAKAŠ, ODAM, KEPHIDO, AILO, MATROTA, ABNUKTA, ŠATRIHA, KALI, BATZEH, TALTUI, KITSA.

The prophet Elija grudgingly accepted Lilith's promise and muttered that Lilith would in no way be able to harm the child, just as she is incapable of counting the number of stars in the sky or dry up the waters of the sea, in the *name of Hasdiel Šamriel has rent Satan.*

Welcome! Here are 15 names of Lilith, most of them inexplicable. However, among them appears Kali, who may or may not be identical with the Indian goddess Kālī. Then there is Amorpho, whose name is Greek, and means *Formless*. Ailo is a development of the Akkadian alû, the dreaded spirit who comes over people like a cloth and paralyses and stuns them with its suffocating misery. Montgomery suggested that Abita (or Abito) was a corruption of Abatur, a Mandaean genius.

Gaster published a similar item from Rumania in a paper entitled *Two-Thousand Years of a Charm Against the Child-Stealing Witch.* Gaster's story (in Montgomery) contains the following names of Lilith:

SATRINA, LILITH, ABITO, AMIZO, IZORPO, KOKO, ODAM, ITA, PODO, EILO, PATROTA, ABIKO, KEA, KALI, BATNA, TALTO, PARTASAH.

A third version of the tale was published by Reitzenstein (also in Montgomery). Here Lilith, *the Impure Spirit with her hair down her back and her eyes inflamed* does not encounter Elija but the archangel Michael. She proudly says: *I go to enter the house as a serpent, dragon-reptile, I change into a quadruped, I go to make the plagues of women, to humble their heart, to dry up the milk, to raise the hair of the master of the house...and then I kill them. For my name is called PAXAREA.* At this point the archangel grasped her hair and forced her to reveal her secret names. She replied:

GELOU, MORPHOUS, KARANICHOS, AMIXOUS, AMIDAZOU, MARMALAT, KARANE, SELENOUS, ABIZA, ARIANE, MARAN.

Wallis Budge (1978/1930:279) offers a closely related story from Syria. Here our girl is called *the Evil Eye*. She meets Saint Mâr 'Abhd-Îshô and tries to seduce him. The saint refuses, binds her, and forces her to reveal her secret names. Version one has:

MIDUCH, EDÎLTA, MONELTA, LILITA, MALVITA and MOTHER, STRANGLER OF BOYS.

In version two she promises to reveal her twelve secret names, which happen to be fourteen:

GĔOS, EDILTA, LÂMBROS, MARTLOS, YAMNÔS, SÂMGOS, DOMOS, DIRBA, APITON, PEGOGHA, ZARDUCH, LILITA, MADVITA and MOTHER, STRANGLER OF BOYS.

There are further variations. The tale was widely popular in Greece, on the Balkan, in Syria and Palestine. We encounter Lilith, or a witch, a nameless hag, or one called PATAXARO meeting the archangel Michael, or various saints, or Christ, or the Virgin Mary, and each time she is forced to reveal her names so that anxious parents can write talismans against her.

One name deserves further comment. Gelou (or Gilou) derive from the Mesopotamian gallû, that dreaded shape-shifting creature of horror. You met it before. Gallû (m) from Bab. GAL_5 means basically enemy, canal-inspector, constable and demon. It is amazing that the gallû found their way to ancient Greece. Here, they acted much as Lamaštu and Pašittu did. The first Greek reference to Gallu appears in the poems of Sappho (born c. 612 BCE). Sappho was not given to composing long hymns. In her scintillating but brisk style, she composed the poem

Of Gello who died young,
whose ghost haunts little children.
She was even fonder
of children than Gello.

(translation W. Barnstone, 2006).

It's number 178 in Sappho's collection and tells us extremely little, except that Gello was known at this early period. Gello or Gyllo, as a name of the child-slaying witch or demoness remains highly popular in Eastern Europe.

Ḳarīna

Another important name of Lilith is Karane. It could be a corruption of the Ḳarīna or Qarina, a close cousin to Lilith and Lamaštu in the Islamic world. First, let's look into the *Encyclopaedia of Islam*, vol. IV, 1978. The words Ḳarīn (male), Ḳarīna (female) and Ḳurāna (plural) mean *Companion*. In pre-Islamic Arabia and to Muhammad, the Ḳarīn/a or Qarin/a was a spirit companion. The name appears eight times in the *Qur'an*. Several researchers proposed that the Ḳarīn/a could be a distorted version of the Egyptian ka 'soul'. To a degree the comparison holds true: the ka can be described as a companion, a double or as a spirit helper or guardian angel. But there are also crucial differences, as the Ḳarīn/a is often a dangerous and hostile being. Unlike her, the Egyptian ka is the source of life energy that inspires each activity and keeps each person animate. When a human being dies, the ka survives, as it is the source of life. Indeed, the ka gains power after death, as it is not burdened by the problems of a person and its body anymore. This goes for people as it goes for gods. Several gods could only be created as their creator gods shared a ka with them. Kings and solar deities had varying amounts of kas. As Egyptian religion developed, the number of kas kept increasing, special favourites being seven and multiples of seven. Such kas have specific names; one typical list goes: *Power, Might, Success, Nourishment, Venerability, Length-of-Life, Splendour, Fame, Magical Power; Word, Seeing, Hearing and Comprehension* (Bonnet, 2000:357-362). They are the sum and total of what grants life and consciousness to each human being. These ideas are quite remote from the Ḳarīn/a concept.

On a very simple level, in the Arabian world, there used to be two spirit companions for each person. Perhaps we are on the track of a Mesopotamian tradition here; many people believed that they were accompanied by two spirits called Lamassu and Šedu. Most of the time, these beings were benevolent. Well, at least the Lamassu was, but the Šedu could turn to evil and become a dangerous influence. You encounter a late and distorted echo of the Šedu in the Hebrew term Shedim, a vague term for various spirits. Among the early Jews, we encounter a similar idea: people are accompanied by a good and an evil spirit. The theology is simple; the good spirit encourages you to follow God's commands while the evil spirit is to blame for all the times when you don't. In Arabian lore, everyone is accompanied by a devilish (shaitan or djini) and an angelic companion. But things are not quite as simple as that. They never are. The Ḳarīn/as appear in many variations. We already met the good and evil companions of each person. That's not all. The term Ḳarīna could also designate a female spirit who accompanies a poet and acts like a muse. Here we are close to the Awen as a muse of the Island-Celtic bards; a goddess and a prosopopeia who acts as a source of inspiration, and as a guardian angel. Some of them were pretty demanding; several famed Irish bards had muses who incited them to poetic and prophetic frenzy and wasted their lives away. It wasn't necessarily a bad thing: the muse accompanies a poet life after life. But there is also a Ḳarīna who is more like a lethal demon than a companion, double or spirit mate. Some Ḳarīnas are supernatural witch-spirits. Thompson (2005/1908:76-77) tells us that the Ḳarīna is a female spirit who accompanies every woman. She has as many children as the woman has. This Ḳarīna is responsibility for barrenness, still-births, the death of infants; she can make men impotent and cause epilepsy. She also gets angry when the husband dallies with other women. Some Ḳarīnas are shape-shifters; they can appear as an owl, a Jewess, a camel and a black man. To this list, Zwemer (1920) adds cats, and tells us that after nightfall, Arabs will avoid upsetting cats, as no one knows whether a cat in the dark is a Ḳarīna. Only sages and lunatics can see Ḳarīnas as they really are. Hurwitz (1983:101-104) cites Arabian literature dating from around the 13th century, where we encounter a child-killing spirit who goes under the names Um-al-Sibjyn (Mother of Children), Tabi'a and Ḳarīna. One typical tale, published by H. Winkler, tells us that King Solomon met the Ḳarīna one night. She had a dark countenance and her eyes had a deep blue colour. He enquired where she was going, and she said: *I go to him who is in the lap of his mother; I eat his flesh, drink his blood and crush his bones.* Solomon was shocked. He threatened to curse her, but, you guessed it, she revealed her twelve secret names, and when you know them and inscribe them on an amulet, no evil will befall your child, except that it grows up dull, average and votes liberal.

So much for the usual Lilithian pattern. The other tradition is more 'devilish', in that the Ḳarīn/a opposes the God-given order. Our sources are very confused. Zwemer interviewed several sheikhs. They could not make up their minds regarding the sex of the 'companions'. In some traditions a person has a Ḳarīn/a of the same sex, while in folk belief a companion of the other sex seems to be more common. In popular belief, a Ḳarīn/a is born with everyone. Or s/he is created with the embryo. For this reason good Muslims should think the divine word 'Bismillah' while having sex; it ensures that a good Ḳarīn/a is attached to the baby. Some claim that the Ḳarīn/a lives just as long as it's human counterpart and dies with her/him. But we also have traditions where the Ḳarīn/a lingers in the grave after the corpse has gone to rot. This Ḳarīn/a patiently waits for the day of the Last Judgement. She or he will give the testimony of the life of its human counterpart before Allah. It's a horrible idea. Imagine sitting in a tomb for millennia, only to snitch on a damnstupid human being with the usual assortment of boring sins and transgressions that nobody cares about anyway. Unlike the ka, and the personal muse of the poets, the Ḳarīn/a of most people can be nasty. Al-Tabari, in vol. 26 of his commentary, states that the Ḳarīn/a is every man's Shaitan. Intellectuals call the Ḳarīn/as the *evil conscience of man's nature.* (Zwemer, 1920:117). Al-Ghazali claimed that a man who forgets the name of God even one instant *has for that moment no mate (*Ḳarīn/a*) but Shaitan.* Other sources are a little more restrained and use the word djin instead. It's not quite as evil. A few crucial differences appear. Sages like Mohammed and Jesus had Ḳarīn/as who were as holy as they were, and never thought an evil thought. Indeed the Ḳarīn/a of Jesus was the archangel Gabriel. Normal people have Ḳarīn/as who lead them into temptation. One sheikh told Zwemer that he frequently fasts and prays to control his Ḳarīn/a. Here, Ḳarīn and Ḳarīna represent suppressed urges. In these spirits, the frustrations of married life found their sinister expression. When people marry, their love life improves but their freedom decreases. Frustrated desires reappear, one way or another, in the form of Ḳarīn and Ḳarīna. The Ḳarīna is occasionally identified with Al-Matruda, a child killing demoness who was Adam's first wife, and had no children. She is bitter and watches the kids of others with intense jealousy (Fartacek, 2010:69). Of course there are plenty of spells and talismans to protect a child from the attention of the Ḳarīna, such as dried donkey tongues, amulet pouches full of seeds, bronze rings with threads in yellow, red and blue, as well as metal fishes

One passage cited by Winkler (after Hurwitz, my translation, see also Thompson, 2005/1908:77) goes:

I am the Ḳarina. I cause discord between the man and the woman. I make women suffer from miscarriages, I make them infertile. I make men incapable of conception. I fill married men with love for the women of other men, married women with love for the men of other women; in short, I do the opposite of that which makes married couples happy.

The more frustrating a relationship is, the more terrifying are the Ḳarīn/as. In cultures where marriages are not based on love and respect but on business relationships between families, a lot of urges are suppressed, and reappear as projections of anti-social evil. Men are haunted by the Ḳarīna, women by the Ḳarīn. Parents meet child-killing demons; partners who loathe each other begin to dream of other lovers. The Ḳarīn/as can lead into temptation. In between, we observe a lot of stupid quarrelling. Each lifestyle, solitary, monogamous, polygamous, with and without children, generates its own unhappy Ḳarīn/a. How about this: to come to peace with ourselves, and to find contentment, we have to face, understand and embrace our Ḳarīn/a.

From Lamaštu to Lamia

Lamia is one of the unhappy stepchildren of Greek myth. Sure, she is there from the start: we find her in the literature of the archaic period. But the picture is tantalisingly incomplete. Wherever we are up to something important, we find it framed with contradictions. It would have been easier, I am sure, if more literature had survived. Euripides, for example, composed a play that was either based on Lamia's tragic fate or began with her holding a speech. We can't be sure: the play, like so many others, is lost. But we find hints and references that keep us guessing. Who is Lamia? To begin with, we can't be sure what she looked like. Unlike so many important characters of Greek myth, there is, to this day, no undisputed image of hers. So what do we know? The name Lamia is actually a title and means the *Devourer*. Lamia can be a single being or a whole cluster of them; some appear with names like Gello, Akko, Karko, Mormo and Sybaris. Diodorus recorded that Lamia is a native of Libya. She is a daughter of Belos (that's Akkadian Bēl, the *Lord*!) and Libye (goddess of the country Libya?). Lamia lived in a cave or tower. One day Zeus saw her beauty and couldn't resist. He impregnated and left her, as is his custom, and soon enough Hera learned about it. Hera went to Lamia and made her kill her own children. It turned Lamia into a sleepless, crazy madwoman who haunts nurseries to abduct and slay other people's kids. Sorrow made her proverbially ugly, but as she is a competent shapeshifter, hardly anybody notices. And she has the skill of taking out her eyes, whatever that may be good for; it relates her to the Graias. Though Lamia is fond of eating children alive, she can be mastered. The children which she swallows remain alive and can be released from her belly (Horace, *Ars*, 340). Pausanias proposes that Lamia is the daughter of Poseidon (read: Enki/Ea) and the Libyan Sybil (seeress). Aristophanes and Vespasian claim that she is woman and man at once. Another tradition, mentioned by Stesichoros, makes Lamia the mother of the monstrous Scylla. For the cave dwelling, six-headed, loudly barking Scylla, look into Homer *Odyssey* 12. In pagan Britain, we encounter the *Tres Lamiae* (*Three Lamias*), a Roman term for a group of unidentified British goddesses. For whatever reason, the Greek occasionally imagined that Lamia is a snake-goddess. It would be lovely to know more.

Flavius Philostratus the Elder composed a biography of the famous magician

Apollonius of Tyana. We find Lamia in his account, and Philostrates remarks that her encounter with Apollonius was the most famous victory of his life. I use of the translations by Tafel, Osiander & Schwab (1828) and J.S. Phillimore (1912). To begin with, you should meet Apollonius, if only for laughs. Our hero was a famous Pythagorean, and subscribed to the great virtues and plainstupid habits of the founder of his cult. Like Pythagoras (who lived long before him), Apollonius was born sacred. He was a serious, devoted character who dedicated his life to the lofty teachings of his idol, and was challenged by simple things, like being wrong and laughing at himself. Like Pythagoras, he travelled to the east, and allegedly passed through Mesopotamia and India. In the process, he converted many simpletons to goodness and gained the respect and admiration of kings and tyrants. Wherever he went, people were impressed by his overwhelming sacredness. It turned him into a major guru of the first centuries CE. His biography, composed by Philostrates, is extraordinarily boring and full of sticky sentiments. Its major appeal is the sort of mediocre saintliness that can be admired by anyone. It made Apollonius a leading competitor of the newly founded cult of Jesus.

Our story starts in central Greece, in the city of Corinth. Apollonius had travelled across the land, visiting temples and working miracles, and when he came to Corinth he began to attract students. One of them was a charming lad called Menippus; 25 years of age, gifted, with the physique of an athlete but coming from a poor background. Menippus, walking to Cenchrae at night, met a strange woman. She was, as Philostratus explained, a ghost, but Menippus was high on hormones and didn't notice. She came to him, *beautiful to look at, in a particularly voluptuous style, claiming that she was wealthy* and professed her love for him: *She was a Phoenician – so she claimed – and lived in a suburb of Corinth which she named. 'Come this evening' she continued, 'and you shall find music – and I will sing – and wine, such as you never yet drank, and no competitor will annoy you; and we will enjoy ourselves as lover and lady together.'*

Menippus would have thought it too good to be true if he had bothered to think at all, but alas he didn't, and soon he was visiting her night after night. As Philostrates remarked, in spite of studying philosophy, Menippus was *lost to temptation.* That's a bad thing. Most philosophers say so. The fact that his love was a ghost escaped him. It makes me wonder how solid Greek ghosts were. Obviously, they were real enough to be mistaken for flesh-and-blood women, provided they were sexy enough. In fact, the same thing applied to gods. Since Homer's time, c. 700 BCE, the gods could appear as humans. You only notice the difference as their eyes are so remarkably shiny and they don't walk but glide (Heliodorus, *Aithiopica,* III). Apollonius observed how Menippus was changing. One fine day he said: *'You, sir, have your excellent looks and all the pretty women are running after you, and nevertheless you take pleasure in a snake and a snake takes pleasure in you'.* He gave him a stern look and enquired how Menippus intended to go on. As it turned out, Menippus had been planning to wed the ghost. He had just forgotten to inform his teacher. Apollonius invited himself to the wedding. On the next day, the wedding feast was laid out, and Apollonius was amazed at the wealth and the magnificence of the decorations. The hall was gleaming with gold and silver, there were treasures all over the place, and none of them came from poor Menippus, who owned little more than the clothes on his body. Apollonius, staring at the splendour, remarked that the decorations reminded him of the orchards of Tantalos (the Underworld) which, as Homer had said, *'are and are not'.* He glanced sternly at Menippus and frowned: *'Here is what you should think of all this glory: it is not real, but a glamour of reality. And to prove what I am saying: the lady who is the bride is an Empusa, a being that is usually called a Lamia or a Mormolukias. Such beings long for love but their strongest hunger is for human flesh, and they catch their victims with the bait of love.'* Menippus was shocked and his gorgeous bride wept, ranted and tried to throw Apollonius out. It was simply her bad luck that while she was complaining, the gold and silver goblets, the lavish decoration, the cup-bearers and even the cooks flew away. Faced with total desolation, the ghostly bride began to shed bitter tears, and begged Apollonius not to torment her any longer, or to reveal her true nature. That, however, Apollonius could not permit. A true follower of Pythagoras is always right, but not always popular. The ghost admitted *that she was an Empusa and that she had glutted Menippus with pleasures in order to feed on his flesh; for she was used to feeding on young and beautiful bodies, as their blood was fresh and pure.* She could have had that any night; I have no idea why she bothered to marry him.

Philostratus took up the same story in the eighth book of his biography. Here we have Apollonius facing a hostile inquiry and he is defending his magical and religious practices. He admitted to taking the divine *Heracles the Resistor* as his helper, as this famous hero had once cleaned the city Elis, governed by Augias, from pestilence and noxious vapours rising from the soil. Heracles became the collaborator of Apollonius; perhaps we should consider him a personal deity, *as he is pure and well-intentioned towards humans. In Peloponnese I once prayed to him, as the ghostly Lamia strayed around Corinth and fed on handsome youths. The god stood by my side, and did not ask for wonderful treasures; he was satisfied with honey-cakes and frankincense, and the desire to do something for the welfare of mankind.* That's pretty cheap, and must have counted a lot in terms of his humility and general benevolence.

To this day, the Lamia is well and alive in Greek and Balkan folklore. Folkloristic studies like to portray her as an evil, child-killing, vampiric witch. You might get the impression that the contemporary Lamia is almost exactly the same as the old Greek version. This, however, is not the case. I was quite delighted when I came upon a collection of Greek and Albanian folk tales published in 1864 by Johann Georg Hahn, the German ambassador in Greece. Hahn, a meticulous and scholarly early folklore enthusiast, published his collection with a lot of footnotes, cross-references and, wherever possible, in several versions. His text is a dry and sparse summary, and miles away from the romantic rendering that people came to associate with folk tales, courtesy of Wilhelm Grimm's continuous re-editing and rewriting of the *Kinder- und Hausmärchen.*

Here is the first story. Nine brothers are travelling across the land. The youngest is called the 'Little One'. When night falls they come to the house of a Lamia. The Lamia has nine daughters and proposes that each brother should wed one. She equips each brother with a green blanket and each of her daughters with a blue one. Then she goes into the dark to sharpen her fangs. Meanwhile, the Little One changes the blankets. The Lamia comes home late in the night and slaughters all who sleep under the green blankets. The nine brothers beat a narrow escape and by daybreak the Lamia sees her dead daughters, howls with rage and swears revenge.

The nine brothers come to a big city where a mighty king rules. They take service at the court, and the king prefers the company of the Little One. It makes the other brothers envious. To get rid of their youngest brother, they tempt the king to set him three impossible tasks. The Little One agrees, and is commanded to steal the cloud drinking horse of the Lamia. The Little One goes to the house of the Lamia and slips into the stable. He says: 'Horse, will you come with me? Here, your only food is old bones, but the king will give you sweet grass to eat.' The horse neighs loudly and the Lamia comes. The Little One utters a spell: 'I wish I were a pea and stuck in the hoof of the stallion'. The Lamia searches the stable, but cannot find him. When she is gone, he returns to human shape and makes his offer once again. It doesn't work. The third time, the cloud drinking horse agrees. It whispers a warning: 'My hooves are shod. I will be noisy when I leave the stable'. The Little One takes off his jacket, lays it on the ground and the horse walks out silently. The king is pleased to get the cloud-drinking horse, and sets a second task.

The Little One is ordered to steal the thing that the Lamia uses to turn night into day and day into night. He goes to the house of the Lamia, but she catches him, ties his hands behind his back, and gives him to her maid. She orders the maid to put him into the oven and to bake him. Then she goes out to invite all other Lamias for a barbecue. The Little One complains that he is bound far too tightly, and his wrists hurt. The maid falls for his charm, loosens the rope, the Little One slips out of his fetters, ties up the maid and puts her into the oven instead. The Little One steals the magic thing and the king is delighted. It makes the Lamia hopping mad. The king hears a rumour that the Lamia plans to devour him. He orders the Little One to catch the Lamia. So the Little One makes a pouch with many bells and jingles. He climbs on the roof of the Lamia's house and makes one hell of a noise. The Lamia, scared by the racket, runs here and there. The Little One calls down: 'Lamia, Lamia, creep into your big trunk and leave the key outside!' The Lamia does so, the Little One locks her up and carries the trunk all the way to the Land of the Franks. He leaves it at the side of the road. The Franks see the box, open the lock and the Lamia comes out. She devours every single one of them. Then she runs after the Little One. He takes a comb out of his pocket and throws it to the ground: it transforms into a dark forest that cannot be crossed. He hurls salt on the ground and it becomes an endless ocean. So he makes good his escape.

Though I felt sorely tempted to embellish the story, I guess you'll be happier with the bare skeleton and will do the embellishing yourself. Some aspects almost scream for improvement. Is the cloud drinking horse Pegasus, the winged stallion that arose from the bloody throat of Medusa when her head came off? What is the thing that turns night to day and day to night? Another version of the same tale replaces it with the Lamia's personal blanket. It has the power to shine in the dark. Maybe it turns her into a flasher, like Lamaštu when she appears as muštabba-abba. And what sort of jingling, chiming bag or pouch did the Little One use to scare and confuse the Lamia? Is it a shamanic amulet pouch? All over Eurasia healers, sorcerers and shamans used bells, chimes, jingles plus metal objects to scare and subdue dangerous spirits. Some wore bells on their belts; others tied them to their ritual costume or fixed them inside their drums. Nepalese rama ('shamans') generally have more than ten kilos of bells and iron objects on their costume. When they dance and shake in their obsession, their whole 'armour' makes a sky-shattering din. And isn't it nice to get an entirely different interpretation of the comb that was traditionally offered to Lamaštu?

What I like best about the story is that Lamia, though she acts pretty much like an evil witch, and has many other Lamias as friends, is a custodian of divine and miraculous treasures. Anyone with the job of turning night into day is obviously a goddess.

Lamias are not always evil in Balkan folklore. Here is another story from the collection of Johann Georg Hahn. There is a king who has his sons killed as soon as they are born. He is very much afraid that one might become his heir, and believes that killing them would prolong his life. One day the queen gives birth to a boy who is so good looking and charming that she yearns to see him grow up. She pleads with her husband, and the entire court supports her. Grudgingly, the old king gives in and allows the prince to reach the age of ten. Time passes swiftly, and when the hour of the execution arrives, the queen and the court weep bitterly and ask the king for another ten years. The ageing monarch agrees, but swears that the execution will happen, no matter what. Our prince grows up; he turns into a strong, handsome and clever man. One night, one of his sisters comes to him secretly and tells him what will happen on his twentieth birthday. The prince is much upset and decides to flee. The princess, having her own agenda, asks him to take her along. In the middle of the night they saddle the prince's trustiest mare and escape. They ride through many countries until they finally come to a desert. In the middle of the desert a marble mountain rises. The two climb to the very top, as they think there might be edible herbs up there.

Instead, they find a vast and luxurious palace inhabited by twelve black giants. Each of them is so big that he drinks a huge barrel of water and eats an entire donkey each day. The prince aims his flintlock gun and kills eleven giants with a single shot. The twelfth is afraid and hides. Secretly, he follows the princess, and when the prince isn't around he comes out of hiding and courts her. The princess feels very flattered and falls in love with the black giant. To get rid of her brother, she pretends to be mortally ill. Only the Water of Life, so she moans, can save her. The prince leaves his sister and goes to the house of Lamia. He knocks on the door, and when she opens, he greets her 'Good day to you, dear aunt!'

'Good day, young hero,' she replies, 'and if you had not called me 'dear aunt', I would have killed you.'

'And if you had not called me 'young hero' I would have done the same!'

The prince asks Lamia for the water of Life. Lamia orders him to lift a 200kg rock, and to hurl it far away. The prince throws the rock, and Lamia, quite satisfied, goes to the rock and beats it with a hammer until the *Water of Life* gushes out. The prince collects it in a jug. He goes to sleep in Lamia's house, knowing that everything will be fine. In the middle of the night, while the prince is snoring happily, the Lamia pours the Water of Life into another vessel. Then she squats over the jug and fills it with piss.

By dawn, the prince departs, carrying the jug, and meets his sister. He gives her the fluid. The princess drinks and says that she is feeling much better already. In the absence of her brother, she had much fun with the black giant, and as her lover requested, she asks the prince 'Tell me, brother, where do you keep your strength?'

'In these two fingers here', he replies, and his sister wraps a magic herb around them. Instantly, the prince loses his power. The black giant leaps from his hiding place, swings his sword and cuts the prince into four parts. He stuffs the bloody pieces into a bag and throws it into a hole. Then the princess and the giant leave. The trusty mare of the prince, however, comes back to the crime scene. She drags the bag out of its hole and carries it to Lamia.

The Lamia lays the four bloody pieces out properly. She fits the corpse together and pours the Water of Life over it. The sections fuse, breath returns and the prince opens his eyes, 'Did I fall asleep?'

The Lamia tells him what happened. The prince, angered by the betrayal of his sister, asks the Lamia for her two lions. He follows the princess and the giant and the lions tear them both to shreds.

I am sure you noticed that our Lamia is a lethal goddess of immortality, and the custodian of a sacred fluid that revives the dead. She has two lions, lives somewhere out in the desert and is friendly to those who feel themselves related to her. She is an initiatrix and the prince undergoes an initiation. It could be yours.

Medusa

Gorgo Medusa is not a native Greek goddess. There is very little mythology to her and hardly any evidence for worship. One major exception is in Corfu. Far from the great centres of Greek civilisation, the goddess shared a temple with Artemis. It's an amazing exception from the normal traditions. Artemis is a complicated goddess. In one sense she is a virgin huntress. In another, she is a Lady of the Beasts. Somehow these functions do not seem to contradict each other. But Artemis was also invoked to ease childbirth. You might ask why: she is never pregnant herself. In fact, she is amazingly proud of her virginity. And in a few rare instances, Artemis wore the head of Medusa. The Medusa facade of the temple is exhibited in the archaeological museum. The Artemis section is lost. The imagery is huge, powerful and mind-blowing. In the centre, more than three metres high, we see the Gorgo in what is technically called the *Knielauf* position. 'Knielauf' is German for *kneeling-running*: the goddess kneels, but she could also be hurrying along. We find this posture in many Medusa images, sometimes she kneels-runs while Perseus cuts her throat. In the Corfu temple frieze, she kneels-runs in the company of her children and several animals. The knielauf position is a direct import from Mesopotamia: it entered Greek art in the first millennium BCE. Seals show Gilgameš and Enkidu kill Enlil's forester Ḫuwawa. They hold on to him from both sides, and he is in the knielauf posture. The knielauf posture also appears on many Lamaštu talismans of the first millennium BCE.

The Greek artists copied a lot. Gorgo Medusa is frequently shown holding serpents or having a serpent girdle; compare the many Lamaštu images where the goddess holds one or two snakes. The serpent girdle also appears in Lamaštu talismans. One crucial difference is the serpents in her hair: they do not appear in Lamaštu images, but are a favourite in Greek myth. An *Orphic Hymn* invokes the Erinyes:

...mighty ones, proud ones, fur-clad, heavily hurting avengers. Gleaming, earthborn, terrifying daughters of Hades, you airy, invisible ones, swiftly moving like the flight of thoughts: you look down on the immeasurable races of mankind, always acting as judges with the eyes of Dike. Well then, goddesses of fate, in many shapes with serpent hair, instil in us a mild and gentle disposition of life.

And here are some lines from the *Orphic Hymn* to the Eumenids, the savage daughters of Zeus and Persephone:

...You watch over the lives of those who plan evil. Avengers of justice, guardians of necessity, dark-skinned queens, from your eyes gleams the terrible radiance, the life-destroying flash of light, the horrible appearance. Monsters, self-controlled, eternal ones, you free the limbs in raging anger; doom, horrors of the night, night born virgins, serpent-haired, with terrifying glances: hear me, as I invoke you: approach us with a friendly heart! (based on Plassmann, 1982:112-113, trans. JF)

Eurinyes and Eumenids are sometimes distinct, sometimes the same group of deities. Both are very close to Gorgo Medusa, who turns people into stone with a single glance. They look at her, she looks at them and time stops. Let's quote Gilbert K. Chesterton: *Self is the Gorgon. Vanity sees it in the mirror of other men and lives: pride studies it for itself and is turned to stone* (*Heretics*, ch. 9).

Like Lamaštu, Inanna and the goddess of the Burney relief, the Corfu Medusa is flanked by unrealistic lions. She appears as a Lady of the Beasts, an aspect of her cult that does not appear in written myth, but relates her to Artemis and numerous Near Eastern goddesses. At her side is Chrysaor, her son, called after his golden sickle. And we meet Pegasus, her other child, the winged horse of imagination and fantasy that carries the most daring poets. Perhaps Pegasus is a reflection of the donkey that graces Lamaštu talismans of the first millennium. Finally there is the face of Gorgo Medusa, an apotropaic mask that exhibits leonine features. It is quite unlike normal faces in Greek art. Maybe it developed out of Lamaštu's lion-mask, though Medusa always faces the observer while Lamaštu is usually shown in profile. The similarities are amazing: when Medusa began to be popular in Greece, the artists required a model, and boldly lifted it from Mesopotamian talismans. They did not have to go very far to do so. Greek culture is heavily indebted to Mesopotamia; a fact that has been understated by many scholars who praised Greece as the cradle of European civilisation and disliked the idea that their pet-culture could have imported anything from the Semitic east. How close Greek and Near-Eastern cultures were was detailed by Walter Burkert, whose groundbreaking *The Orientalizing Revolution* explores the intricate network of shifting ideas and technologies, the many inspirations and impulses provided by travelling craftsmen, sages, sorcerers, architects, traders and engineers. *There is no gap between Babylon and Greece. One Greek text states that Lamia is a daughter of the Phoenician Belos, thereby crediting the demoness with Semitic origins.* (Burkert, 1997:83).

Figure 65 Medusa Rainbow Eyes.

Figure 66 Top: Medusa decoration from an Etruscan temple.

Bottom: Medusa from western Greece, part of a temple roof, c. 500 BCE, ALG63, today in Kassel.

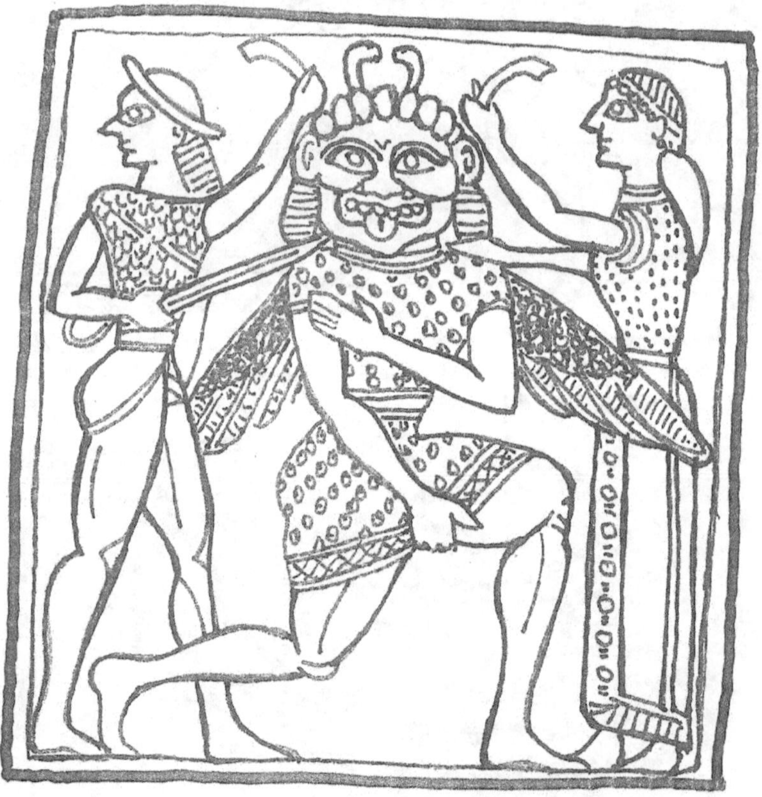

Figure 67 Top: Medusa holding two serpents, gold foil, Delphi, 6th century BCE.

Bottom: Perseus decapitates Medusa while Athena watches.

Figure 68 Top: Medusa on a shield held by Athena. Painting on an amphora, c. 490. BCE, Basel, KÄ 418

Bottom: Medusa head in the centre of the zodiac. Greek coin, c.230-260 CE, Aegeae near Tarsos, after Anson in Ulansey, 1988:104. Note that the signs of Virgo and Libra should be exchanged.

But while the Greek artists borrowed from Lamaštu talismans, they evidently forced their imagery on an entirely unrelated myth cycle. Medusa is remarkably different. Her nature is tantalisingly enigmatic. It's just our bad luck that very little survives about Medusa. Here we have a goddess who had an entire temple front dedicated to her, and then we look into Greek myth, written by educated and refined intellectuals in the great cities in the south-east, and meet her as a marginal figure, a goddess, demoness and spook.

The word Medusa is not a name but a title, meaning *'queen'*. She is also known as the Gorgo, or a Gorgo, meaning *'terrible of face and expression'*, which might remind you of Lamaštu's fifth name. Gorgo Medusa appears in earliest Greek literature. Odysseus, for instance, decided to leave the underworld in a hurry, as he was scared that Persephone, goddess of the deep, might send the head of the Gorgon against him (*Odyssey*, 11, 634). In the *Iliad* (8, 349), Hector's gaze is compared to that of the Gorgon.

Another early writer who mentioned Medusa was Hesiod. The farmer-poet, writing around 700 BCE, has the following to say:

To Phorkys, Keta gave birth to beautifully cheeked daughters,

Born grey with age. These are named the Graias (=the Grey Ones)

By the immortal gods and the people who walk the earth.

(She also gave birth to) Pemphredo and Enyo in her crocus-coloured dress,

And the Gorgons who dwell beyond the famous Okeanos (=the World Ocean),

At the edge of the night, where the bright-voiced Hesperides (abide),

And Sthenno and Euryale and Medusa, who had to suffer so tragically,

She who was mortal, but those were immortal and ageless;

Both of them. But to her side laid himself only the Blue-Maned One (=Poseidon),

On a soft meadow and flowers of spring.

When Perseus cut through the throat (of Medusa),

(from her) sprang the great Chrysaor and the horse Pegasus.

One has its name as it was conceived from the springs (=pegai) *of the Okeanos,*

The other, as his hands held a golden sword (=chryseion aor).

And departing, leaving the earth, the mother of sheep herds,

(Pegasus) reached the immortals. He dwells in the house of Zeus,

And carries thunder and lightning to the all-knowing Zeus.

Chrysaor, however, brought forth the three-headed Geryoneus,

After he had mated with Kallirhoe, the daughter of the famed Okeanos,

He was slain by the might of Heracles...' (270-289, after Karl Albert, 1985, trans. JF).

Others expanded the tale: Medusa was actually a priestess of Athena, the goddess of war and wisdom. Athena was at odds with Poseidon, the dark-haired earth shaker, lord of the world surrounding sea. One night Medusa was walking on the beach, when the waters rose and Poseidon emerged in all his glory. He embraced Medusa and they had a night of bliss-filled ecstasy. By daybreak, Poseidon departed. He left Medusa pregnant and terrified. Athena is proud of her virginity, and may well demand the same from her priestesses (except for contemporary ones, who do as they like). That her priestess Medusa had lost her virginity was bad enough, but that it had happened with Poseidon was contemptible. Athena shook with rage. She would have loved to kill her. That, however, was impossible: her former priestess was pregnant with divine children, and had gained a semi-divine status. Apollodorus (2, 4) remarked that Medusa was so beautiful that Athena could not bear it. So she gave Medusa the sort of face that turns men to stone (or makes them stiff) and left her living in bleak isolation. Like the other Gorgons she now appeared with terrifying tusks and dragon scales, brazen hands and golden wings Then, of course, the story of Perseus sets in. I'll spare you a retelling; it's a dull mixture of brainless heroism and a muddle of second-hand myths. Suffice it to say that mighty hero Perseus, with Athena's support, approached Medusa when she was sleeping and her eyes were securely shut. He chopped off her head. Out of her trunk two children were born: Chrysaor and Pegasus. Perseus packed the head and departed for more derring-do. Eventually, Athena gained what she had always wanted: the head of Medusa. She stuck it to her outfit to make herself more terrifying. The dying Medusa sang a sad song, and Athena adapted it to the flute and made it famous (Pindar). Another myth claims that she collected the blood of Medusa in two vessels. The one from her right side was lethal; she kept it for herself. The blood from the left side could raise the dead to life and cure anything. Athena gave it to her protégée Asclepius, the god of healers. Observe: a deadly goddess is the custodian of health and immortality. And there must have been a tale that Medusa had a horse-head. That's the reason she gave birth to Pegasus, the winged steed. On early Boeotian vases and jewellery, she appears with the head of a horse or a donkey. And there was an earlier tale where Athena killed the goddess, here named Gorgophone, a daughter of Ge (the Earth), during the terrible battle between the young gods and the Titans. Most of the story is lost, and few authors were interested in it. In all likeliness the cult of Athena replaced an earlier, Aegean religion, and incorporated its favourite goddess as an image of sheer terror. That's how the Gorgon's head appears in Greek art. The leering goddess with her strong cheekbones, tusks, writhing snakes in her hands, girdle and hair, became a terrifying but benevolent being. Medusa heads were used for their apotropaic power: they banished evil, and protected the faithful. We encounter her head on temple walls, gateways and doors, ships, amphora, helmets, lamps, vessels and jewellery. Through Greek art, the Medusa head entered Celtic culture: witness the grave goods of the 'Lady of Vix'. Her bronze vessel was of Greek origin and is the biggest container from antiquity. It is 1,64m tall and might have held 1200 litres of wine. It's all show. Had it ever been filled, it would have burst apart. Its handles are adorned with the some of the most beautiful Gorgons I have ever seen. By four hundred BCE, Medusa heads are showing a remarkable beauty. They appeared in Greek, Roman and Etruscan art and assured that the Gorgon's face remained popular. Much later, we encounter Gorgon heads surrounded by the signs of the zodiac. In this stage, things go totally bizarre. One basic type has the Gorgon's head; another shows the sun's head in the centre of the cosmos. In both cases, the symbolism is similar. The sun and the Gorgon had become interchangeable. Ulansey mentions images of the sun god Helios with wings and snakes instead of hair. What exactly did the Greek think when they made coins with the Gorgon's head in the centre of the zodiac? Please look at the picture. I copied a drawing by Anson (*Numismata Graeca*, 1910-16, 6, #128, in Ulansey, 1998:106) which was found in Aegeae (Aigai), near Tarsos in Cilicia. Coins from Rhodos show a similar arrangement. Similar images appear on Greek and Etruscan jewellery. Why is the Gorgon in the centre of the zodiac? And why are two of the signs, Virgo and Libra, in the wrong order? Obviously there was a cosmic side to Medusa that remains to be explored.

Now for something surprisingly different. One of the most popular faiths of the Roman Empire was the Cult of Mithras. This is not the place to comment on this mystery religion. Its ideas and regulations were so secret that no textual evidence survived. Suffice it to say that the Roman Mithras was basically a solar or a cosmic deity, and that the many animals and objects around him represented celestial constellations. Mithras is the god who slays the bull (the age of Taurus) and inaugurates the new age. He is also the master of the cosmos, and in this function, the sun. Several Mithras sanctuaries contained statues of a lion-man. Usually, this deity, about whose nature, myths and background nothing survives, is wrapped in a serpent.

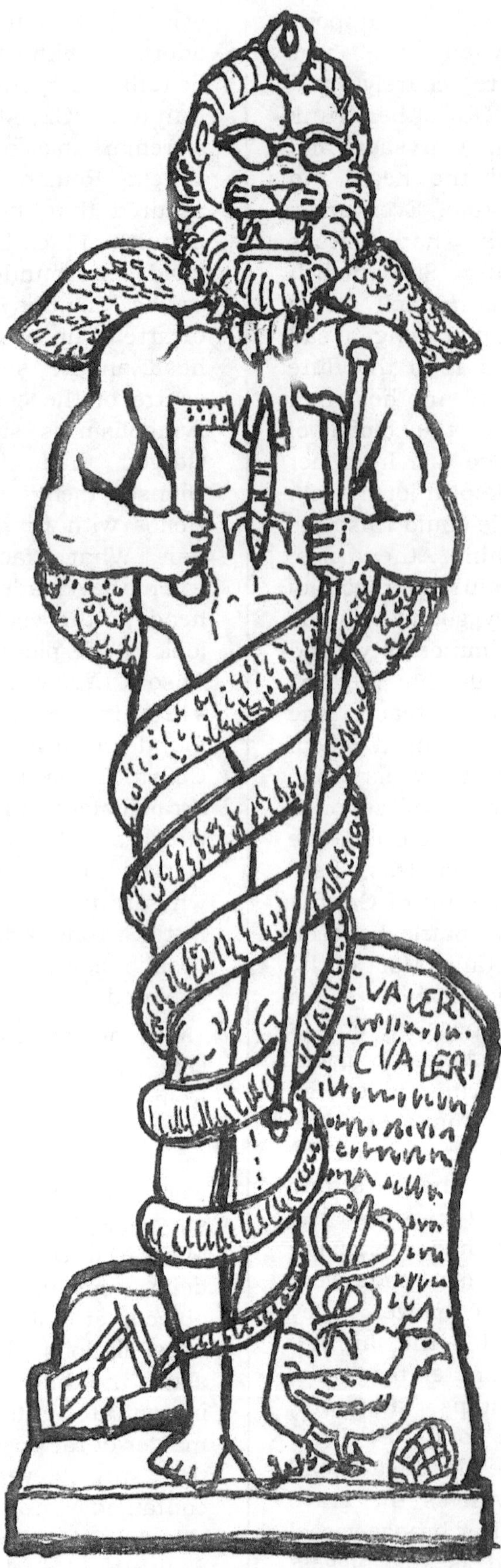

Figure 69 Lion-man, representing the sun, wrapped within a cosmic serpent. After Ulansey, 1998:17.

Occasionally, on the serpent, or on the body of the lion man, the signs of the zodiac appeared. The Romans identified the lion with the sun. In short, the lion man is in a similar position, within the zodiac, as are the sun and Gorgo Medusa. Lamaštu is the perfect candidate for a lion-woman. As a Daughter of Heaven she might well stand in the centre of the zodiac. And she has a thing about snakes. The lion-man is undoubtedly male. That, however, is hardly surprising. The cult of Mithras had most of its supporters among the legions. The cult was full of soldiers and women were not admitted. There is not a single female symbol in the entire cult of Mithras. Anybody integrating a lion, sun or Gorgon would have struck to the male form.

Tiger Goddesses of China

The Chinese invented writing sometime around the early or middle second millennium BCE. They wrote on bamboo strips which were carefully sewn into scrolls. None of the scrolls from this early period survived, but we do have pictures showing them: there is an early ideogram meaning 'book, manuscript, contract'. During the late Shang dynasty, around 1200 BCE, our records improve. Let's move to Anyang, Henan, in the fertile north Chinese plain, where the last Shang kings had their capital. King Wu Ding, a courageous and innovative regent about whom I wrote at length in *Dragon Bones*, decided that all divinations should be recorded. For more than a thousand years, Chinese diviners had consulted their oracles by exposing the belly plate of a turtle (plastron) or the shoulder bone (scapula) of a bovine to heat. That sounds easier than it was. Prior to the ritual, the item was carefully cut, probably soaked, smoothed and polished. As a final effort, a series of hollows were drilled into its back, making it crack more easily. In an unknown ritual, each piece was carefully consecrated. The rite was usually done by a queen and witnessed by a diviner, who might commemorate the event with an inscription. Last, during the divination ceremony a question was asked or a statement made, and a red hot hardwood stick pressed into a hollow, and heated, presumably with a bellows. Before long the witnesses heard a dry 'buk!' and a crack appeared on the other side. The nature, shape or maybe the speed of its appearance provided the answer. So far, the experts have not managed to work out what the answers to the divinations were. Luckily, we are much better informed about the questions. King Wu Ding had them carefully recorded next to each crack. They were painted with a brush, incised with an adze or chisel, and in some cases even coloured in black or red. Finally, the pieces, many of them inscribed with dozens of questions or charges, were carefully stored away. Today, the archaeologists are having an exciting life interpreting the inscriptions. In Wu Ding's time, the diviners used four or five thousand signs. Many were simple ideograms (i.e. pictures) but a considerable amount was not used for its visual imagery but for its phonetic, i.e. sound-value. A little more than a thousand common characters are fairly well understood. Often, a given character had several meanings. More than a thousand were identified as the names of people, families, tribes, places and states. At least another two thousand characters are rare and remain mysterious. There must have been more characters around: for matters of divination, only a small range of words is needed, while, say, palace management, letters, contracts, historical records and book-keeping required more. Spelling was highly varied and many queries were recorded in a shorthand that leaves everybody guessing.

Be that as it may, while bamboo-scrolls went to rot, the bones and plastrons survived. When they were discovered at the end of the nineteenth century, they caused an enormous stir. For what the diviners recorded on the 'dragon bones' went far beyond what used to be assumed about the Chinese past.

Our first record for a goddess or ancestress related to a large feline comes from the Shang period. The inscriptions mention sacrifices to an ancestress or goddess who was called Mother/Woman/Girl Tiger and another called Mother/Woman/Girl Wood/Tree Tiger. The titles are ambiguous. Modern Chinese uses different characters for mother (mu) and woman/girl (nü). Mother, of course, could also be an honorary title. The Shang occasionally added one or two dots to the character nü which indicated nipples, and turned it into the character mu. Often enough, they simply didn't bother. And we meet a goddess who may be at the roots of a lot of Chinese religion: Woman/Girl/Mother West (**Xi Mu**). Several late Shang rulers were much attracted to deities of the four (or five) directions. We meet deities east, south, west and north; deities four clouds, deities four directional winds, the five Jade Ministers of high deity (or deities?) Di. And a popular Woman/Girl/Mother East. She got a lot of attention. Maybe as the Shang were fond of the east, or at least they mentioned the east far more often in their divinations than the other directions. Woman/Mother/Girl East had a counterpart in Woman/Mother/Girl West. She got less attention, or maybe we simply haven't discovered her inscriptions yet. West was an important direction to the early Chinese. A long time before the Shang began to rule, Chinese ritualists represented east with a dragon and west with a tiger. Neolithic tomb M45 of the Yangshao culture, Xishuipo in Pyang county, shows both animals, laid out as a shell mosaic, to the sides of the corpse of a ritualist and/or aristocrat. West is the direction of autumn: the days become shorter, the harvest is reaped, animals are slaughtered, fruit and vegetables are stored and soon the cold season would arrive. It wasn't as cold as today, but for the Shang, used to high temperatures, it was as cold as it could get. West symbolised the ending of the year, the coming of age and death. For this reason, later Chinese thinkers of the Zhou dynasty made west the direction of metal and gold, and decided that the season is excellent to execute criminals. Mother/Woman West may have represented all of this. We just don't know.

The Shang dynasty, like all great houses, was not fated to continue forever. Its last regent, so the historians recorded much later, was an irresponsible sadistic tyrant. A vassal state of the Shang, the Zhou, led an alliance of angry states against the royal armies and set themselves up in their stead. It was the start of the Zhou dynasty, but as the early Zhou did not inscribe many oracle bones and their early history books have long gone to rot, hardly anything is known about the period. The historical records of the Zhou improved at a much later date, and they are, for various reasons, incomplete and somewhat dissatisfying. Theoretically, the House of Zhou governed for a long time (c.1045 BCE-221 BCE). In reality, they soon lost their power to a war-loving aristocracy, who treated the Zhou rulers as ritualists of little importance. China endured many centuries of savage warfare during which the several hundred statelets devoured each other until only one remained. By then, the country was economically in tatters and the population had lost much of its faith in the gods and ancestors, and in the nature of humanity. At the end of the Zhou period, around maybe 400 BCE, we encounter the first scattered references to deities and myths. The available literature is tiny. I am sure that some of the Zhou literati wrote about myths and religion. However, Qin Shihuangdi, the so-called 'First Emperor' of China, a warlord noted for cruelty and megalomania, ordered a great book burning. Only a small amount of books remained in circulation. The records of many centuries went up in flames and intellectuals who were caught with an illegal book were worked to death at the First Emperor's gigantic building projects. When he finally died, and the Han Dynasty began (206 BCE-220 CE) the Chinese literati sighed in relief and began to reconstruct the past from fragments. They assembled manuscripts and recorded texts that had been memorised. Where things were wanting or did not suit the mood of the time, they made up material. Thanks to their effort, some early literature was saved and much was assembled as a patchwork of bits, pieces and free invention. It makes it very hard to reconstruct genuine early Chinese myth. So, what a surprise, between 400-300 BCE we meet a goddess who is called **Xiwangmu** (*West-Royal-Mother*, or Queen-mother of the West). The name is suspiciously close the Shang period goddess Xi Mu. But were they the same deity? At this point all researchers are forced to give up or start guessing. Given that the evidence exhibits a gap of seven hundred years, I would not dream to voice an opinion. Nevertheless Xiwangmu is a fascinating character who embodies much of the early symbolism and became a major deity of the Daoists. I have written at length about Xiwangmu in *Dragons Bones.* Here it should suffice that Zhuangzi mentioned her in passing, saying that she attained the Dao (*way, method, system*) and took her seat on Mount Shao Kuang: *Nobody knows her beginning and nobody knows her end.* For all its briefness, the passage tells us that between 400-300 BCE, when the early passages of the *Zhuangzi* were compiled, the goddess was so well known that the author/s did not need to introduce her. That she attained the Dao, and that she exists beyond the limits of the universe, eternal and mysterious, places her among the highest Chinese deities. Consider the story of King Mu of Zhou. King Mu is nowadays known as a legendary ruler. He was also a historical figure, governed c.1001-947 BCE, and instituted a number of religious reforms. His story is told in *The History of Mu of Zhou* and, in a much briefer form, in the *Liezi.* King Mu was fascinated by magic and immortality. In his quest for an eternal life, he travelled into the far west, until he reached the world mountain Kunlun. He ascended the towering peak and met Xiwangmu. The two lazed at the side of the turquoise pond; they drank and sang sad songs as the sun slowly sank under the horizon. Suddenly the king sobered up. He said *'Alas, for me, the One Man, do not cultivate virtue and indulge in merriment instead. Future generations will count this as an error.'*

He said goodbye and departed. When Mu returned to the Middle Kingdom, his vitality was much enhanced and allegedly he lived for a hundred years, before he either died or joined the ranks of the immortals.

We meet Xiwangmu as a major goddess of the earliest Daoists and immortality seekers. Now for a description. One of the most bizarre works of mystical literature is the *Shanhaijing*, the *Book of Mountains and Seas.* The text was edited and expanded over a long time; some passages date from 300 BCE while the last bits were added around 300 CE. You could consider it a travelling guide. Travel literature is always bizarre, especially when the travellers explore realms far from civilisation and delight in telling yarns. There are plenty of odd items in the *Shanhaijing.* Some of the accounts refer to real places, people and animals. Other parts are totally over the top: they describe the gods and spirits living in a bizarre otherworld. These sections were written for shamans to guide them in their trance journeys. Sadly, the text is not only muddled but also very sparse: we encounter references to dozens of gods and beings whose myths have long faded away. One of the few who emerge with some clarity is Xiwangmu. The goddess resides in the far west on Jade Mountain. Jade is more than a pretty, precious and sacred mineral: the stone represents eternal youth, sheer vitality and immortality. Xiwangmu *looks like a human being, but she has the tail of a panther and the teeth of a tigress and she is good at whistling* (or: *screaming*). *On her twisted hair is a victory headdress. She governs the two constellations Celestial Disasters and Five Destructive Energies* (2.3). Another passage (12) elaborates her activities. We meet her on Mount Serpent Shaman. She *reclines against her high seat. She wears a victory headdress and holds a staff.* South of her live three birds who search food for her. I wonder if they are scavengers. In these few lines the goddess is closely linked to panther, tiger and food-searching birds. She governs destructive asterisms and is closely related to jade, serpents and shamans (wu). It is a perfect mixture. The early Daoists were highly attracted to her cult. Like the Daoists, the goddess is fond of the rugged mountains far from the human realm. She embodies life and death and immortality. It made her the queen of the Daoist immortals. We also encounter her image, during the Han Dynasty, as a motif in tomb chambers. An amazing brick excavated in Xinfan Qingbaixiang that has been widely publicised, shows her seated on a throne, between a dragon, tiger, fire-raven, moon-toad, tortoise, snake, hare, nine-tail-fox and several winged celestial immortals. The picture is a perfectly Chinese rendering of the popular Near Eastern 'Lady of the Beasts' arrangements. We also encounter her on the reverse of Han Dynasty bronze mirrors, where she resides in an early symbol of heaven, and is accompanied by various animals. Favourites are the green wood-dragon of the east, the red firebird of the south, the white metal-tiger of the west and the black water-warrior, a snake wrapped around a turtle, in the north. The animals signify the directions, the seasons, the Five Transforming Energies (Wu Xing, i.e. wood, fire, earth, metal, water), and a lot of similar ideas. In chapter 16 of the *Shanhajing*, we read that the goddess dwells in a cave. All animals of the world live on her mountain. In the neighbourhood of her mountain, ten wu (shamans or shamanesses) fly or move in search for sacred herbs and medicines. Nearby is a mountain peak where the arch ancestor of all Chinese shamans, Wu Xian stands, holding a red and a blue snake in his hands. The great Han period historian Sima Qian tells us that there were two people called Wu Xian residing at the Shang court. They conducted ceremonies at mountains and rivers and acted as stewards. We don't know if they were men, or, like so many wu of the Zhou period, women. Wu Xian of the *Shanhaijing* is male, and the venerable arch-patron of the shaman's craft. With his two snakes he assumes the favourite posture of Lamaštu, who is also a perfect candidate for a lady of the beasts, or the beastlier beasts if you like. The people who ornamented tombs with images of Xiwangmu hoped that she would guide the deceased to a happy afterlife or to immortality. When Buddhism reached China during the Han Dynasty, badly informed people assumed that Buddha was a foreign god of death who grants the deceased access to a western paradise. As ever, history and myth join. For the Chinese, west signified the gate to death, while to the Buddhists, west was India, the homeland of Buddhism. The misunderstanding only lasted until proper Buddhist literature was imported and translated. However, in the interim period, bricks with Buddha images replaced Xiwangmu images in tombs.

The Daoists, with their love for high mountains, winding rivers, dangerous animal spirits and their constant search for life-extending or immortalising drugs and practices, made much of Xiwangmu. So did the general population. In the year 3 BCE, the thoroughly corrupt Han dynasty almost came to an end. When drought destroyed the harvest, the peasant population started a revolt that carried its revolutionaries through 26 commanderies and kingdoms. They were moved by religious frenzy and believed that Xiwangmu would save them from death. She didn't. Faith in deities and talismans against arrows are simply not enough to change society. After the uprising had been put down, Xiwangmu lost much of her appeal to the simple populations (*Hanshu, History of the Han Dynasty*). Her cult remained popular among the Daoists, the immortality seekers and some aristocrats. During the Tang dynasty, the emperors, who had the surname Li, decided that Laozi (whose family name was Li) was their earliest ancestor. Laozi was duly deified. It turned Daoism into the state religion. Xiwangmu became so popular that even Buddhists were obliged to worship her. You can find excellent poetry dedicated to the goddess in Cahill's remarkable study. After the Tang fell, Daoism lost much of its influence and the goddess faded from popular worship. She continued as a background figure of Chinese heaven. By now she had lost her earlier savagery: artists depicted her as a middle-aged matron who invites the gods and immortals to her peach banquet every two thousand years. Peaches expel evil spirits, peach wands are perfect for exorcisms and immortality peaches grant eternal life to the gods. From time to time the goddess made an appearance in some cult, inspired visionaries or granted an emperor a piece of much needed holy writ. By that time, however, much of her reputation had become a thing of the past. A few enthusiasts tried made her the wife of the

Emperor of Heaven. In this form, Xiwangmu was called the 'holy mother'. It didn't really catch on. Finally, the cult of Guanyin, a favourite of unorthodox lay-Buddhists, assimilated some of the symbols and functions of Xiwangmu, just as it gobbled up the titles and legends of a wide range of Chinese goddesses.

We find more evidence for goddesses resembling Lamaštu in China. De Groot gives a brief account of a little-known goddess called **Gui Mu**, the Mother of Ghosts. Gui is a remarkable concept. In the Shang period, there were at least two types of gui: human ghosts and non-human ghosts, i.e. monsters. The ideogram for gui shows a kneeling person (the Shang usually kneeled; chairs were not in fashion) with what may be a death mask. If you add the sign for 'drops' to the figure, you get 'non-human ghost', and when the drops are within an amphora-like vessel, the character means 'evil, disgusting, repulsive' (Fries, 2012:673). For the Shang, all ghosts were gui, and they were a tough and terrifying lot. Late Shang religion was basically a cult of the royal family. The early royal ancestors had more power than most gods of the countryside and when they were upset, they caused earthquakes, floods, drought; they sent swarms of locusts and enemy invasion. The close ancestors were less troublesome, and only caused accidents and diseases. Neither group was friendly or much inclined to support their descendant. Early Shang period ancestors demanded huge offerings. The gods of places, nature, mountains and rivers were less demanding. Many centuries later, under Kongzi (Confucius, 551-479 BCE), ancestral worship was redefined. Ghosts came in two varieties: shen, a word meaning divine, deities, the numinous, spirit, awareness, was used for your own ancestors, who were sometimes nasty and often benign, depending on whether you behaved and offerings were made in time. Gui were dangerous ghosts, i.e. the ancestors of other families and non-human evil spirits. When we explore the few recorded details about Gui Mu (de Groot, 1967: 2, 805-806), we have to keep in mind that for more than two thousand years, the gui had been a dangerous bunch. Where did Gui Mu come from? In the Shang period oracle bones, we encounter a sign written Mother/Woman/Girl Ghost. It could have been a goddess or an ancestress. The character is rare and we simply don't know.

In more recent periods, Gui Mu was venerated in southern China, near the Lesser Yu Mountains, and in the provinces Zhejiang, Jiangxi and Fujian. She has the head of a tiger, the claws and eyebrows of a dragon, the body of a woman and the eyes of a python. Alternatively, she has the head of a dragon, the ears of a cow and connected eyebrows with a single eye underneath. Gui Mu is the mother of all ghosts who inhabit Heaven, Earth and the Middle World. Each morning she gives birth to ten ghosts and in the evening, when the sun sets, she devours them again. This sounds like a Shang tradition. For the early Chinese, just like the Mesopotamians, the number sixty was sacred. The Shang ritual calendar consisted of a sixty-day cycle divided into six ten-day 'weeks'. The word for 'day' was 'sun' and each day was literally a new sun. Kings, queens and important relations of the royal house received a posthumous temple name. It included the name of a sun, and this specified the day in the ritual week when they received standard offerings, such as alcohol, meat, cooked grains, drumming and feather dances. The ten suns are also the root out of which Chinese astrology developed. Genuine Chinese horoscopes make much out of the calculation of ten celestial stems and twelve earthly branches. These were developed out of the Shang time calendar, but by the Han Dynasty, most of their earlier meanings were already forgotten. The ten suns appear prominently in Han cosmology and myth. If Gui Mu gives birth to ten ghosts (suns) in the morning and devours them again in the evening, she is a cosmic goddess who creates, maintains and destroys time. But Gui Mu also has a terrestrial significance. For many centuries, the Han Chinese struggled with the southern provinces. China occasionally extended far into what is Vietnam today. The tropical forests of the Deep South were full of lethal ghosts. Near Gui Mu's favourite haunts the civilised world came to an end. She guards the Spectre Pass, a gate formed by a pair of natural boulders, thirty paces apart. Beyond these rocks, the world of spirits begins. Several emperors sent military expeditions through this pass. According to legend, only one man in ten returned alive. The jungles were hot and humid, they crawled with toxic serpents, scorpions, spiders and centipedes, and the evening twilight was full of mosquitoes spreading malaria.

De Groot speculated that Gui Mu might have been introduced by Buddhists. He failed to give a reason for this assumption, but I guess he may have been thinking of Siṁhamukhā.

But there is a goddess with Lamaštu functions in Chinese Buddhism. Dazu in Sichuan is famous for its stone sculptures. Nearby, in a cave on North Mountain, the goddess **Hariri** is worshipped. Her appearance is quite refined. Pictures show her as a cultured, aristocratic lady in an elaborately ornamented courtly dress, holding a fan in her right hand, while her left hand strokes the child at her side. She wears a hat with a phoenix crown, her hair is neatly done, her face is paled with rice powder; evidently, she has devoted a lot of time to her make-up. In her company are two female attendants, plus a nurse breast-feeding a baby. The cave contains images of nine children.

The name Hariri is said to mean 'Cruel Mother'. Maybe the Saṁskṛta word hara (female harī) is involved; it means destroyer, robber, bandit, and is a popular title of Śiva, highlighting his function as a destructive and liberating deity. Hariri is also addressed as Gui Mu.

Let me retell what Ma Shutian relates (2006:189-190). According to Buddhist lore, Hariri was a poor woman making a meagre living by herding the cows of other people. Out there, at the fringe of the jungle, a man had his way with her. Maybe she enjoyed it. Maybe it was a rape. But whatever it may have been, she became pregnant. One day, a great Buddhist feast was announced. Hariri and five hundred Buddhists walked to the city Rājagṛha (*Home of the King*) to join the celebration. Little did the pilgrims care that Hariri was pregnant. The journey was a terrible strain for her. In the middle of the night, she crouched near a hut and miscarried. As she was squatting in the dirt, racked by pain and covered in blood, the corpse of her infant at her feet, the pilgrims walked past. None offered help and comfort. In her anger, she cursed them, and swore that she would be reborn as a yaksī, and devour all babies of Rājagṛha. It turned her into an angry goddess. Hariri ate human babies every day. And she gave birth to five hundred ghost-children, whom she dearly loved.

Śākyamuni, the historical Buddha, heard the tale. In the depth of the night he slipped into her cave and stole one of her ghost children. When Hariri came home, she instantly noticed that one of her kids was missing. She ran through her cave and up and down the mountain screeching like a fury, but her child was nowhere to be found. Finally she collapsed and wept. Śākyamuni approached her cautiously.

He said 'Your child is well. I have it in my care'.

'Return it' Hariri screamed.

'You have five-hundred children' said Śākyamuni, 'and the loss of one makes you crazy with pain. Imagine what women must feel who have only a few children, and lose them'.

At this moment, Hariri gained liberation. She pledged to help women whose infants were close to death. Śākyamuni returned her missing child and Hariri became one of the twenty protective goddesses of Buddhism in China. Today she is frequently worshipped by couples wishing for a child.

Albasti and Āl: Across Asia

Imagine a goddess who roams from Turkey to northern China. A goddess, so bizarre and incomprehensible, that all Central Asian cultures made up their own special version. And consider how much coherence it takes for her to remain easily recognisable from Istanbul to Ürümqi.

Twilight comes softly, dimming the sky, and the conifers fade into the dark. Maybe she'll come from the river nearby, rising like a fog between tangled willows, drifting through reeds and grasses until she finds a narrow, winding path where cattle moves and people walk all through the happy, sunny day. Maybe she descends when the cool winds of evening sink from the mountainsides, when fresh gusts of biting air hint at the winter soon to come. Maybe she creeps through dark evergreens, through thickly wooded slopes, between greyish rocks, crusty with lichens and rotting wood, in the shadows under spruce and larch and pine. Or maybe she is squatting in a hedgerow near your house, and peers into your window. The light fades and you may light a candle. It will make her watch you all the better. And what you do is very instructive to her. Can you hear the wind in the forest, further out? Listen how the branches move, how twigs scrape against each other, beating like the heart of a deer in flight? Is anyone outside? Open the door and risk a look. Take a few steps through the damp grass. Nobody is around. The lawn is empty, the garden silent. The flowers have closed, their blossoms droop, and stars are shining gently. Between the trees, crouching in bushes, sliding through tall grasses, someone is staring at you. Come on. Take a few more steps. Feel the cool wind on your skin. This could be your end. Or it might be your initiation.

She is known by many names. One of the common ones is Al Basty. Or spell her Albasti. That's a well-known Turkish form. And it is the root of many name variations.

One moment. Albasti sounds strangely familiar. What about the European elves? They are common spirits of the Germanic cultures and their neighbours. Aelf (Old English), Alb, Alp (Old High German), Álfr (Old Norse) all come from the same root: Indo-European *albh- to gleam, bright, white. Consider them the Shining Ones. The first reference to the word appears in Tacitus, who recorded that some Germani in the time of Vespasian had a seeress called Albruna (*'Elf-Whisperer'*). After his reference, we encounter a huge gap. The elves reappear in medieval literature, in Nordic sagas, and much later, in folk-lore. By then, the concept was so hopelessly deformed that we won't go into details. It would take an entire new book. The sad fact is that everybody used the word 'elf' in an amazingly original way. You encounter elves who are otherworldly beings, who are giants, dwarves, minor gods, spirits, ghosts, dead ancestors and incomprehensible monsters. Some are human, others animal, plants, trees, stones, river spirits, place guardians and odd objects. Many of them shapeshift and not everyone is bright, shiny and good looking. To top it off, Christian heaven and hell concepts went into the package; just look at Snorri Sturluson's idea that there are heavenly bright elves and subterranean dark elves. Thanks to the church, some elves are witches or devils. Of course you can find figures much like Lilith, Lamaštu and Albasti among them. Given so many choices you can find anything. And when you look into material influenced by Island Celtic lore, you can even meet elves who steal infants and leave retarded changelings in their stead. In Central and Eastern Germany around 1300 the elves were mixed up with the nightmare; we read of the Alpdruck (*'elf-pressure'*) and the Alptraum (*'elf-dream'*, literally: nightmare). This spirit haunts sleepers, squats on them and tries to strangle or crush them. Again, the situation is amazingly confusing. A few of them are the souls of people who go travelling in their sleep to assault or seduce a person. Call it witchcraft if you like. However, not all people who have this skill are aware of it. Other Alpdrücke are spirits, shapeshifters and monstrosities. Some of them appear as nude human beings and can be quite sexy. Others are ugly monsters, animals, household utensils and spooky things. They ride sleepers, but they also ride animals and trees, making them shudder and shake, and move in whirlwinds. Some cause disease, epilepsy, and doom, others excite wet dreams; among the German speaking people on the Balkan they also suck blood. However, they are not interested in harming mothers and infants. Nor do they commonly marry courageous men. Apart from that, their descriptions are so colourful and contradictory that Bächtold-Stäubli's account leaves you dazed and confused (2000: 281-306). The major difference between Albasti and the elves is that Albasti is a remarkably congruent figure.

A long time ago, the Turkish cultures developed in Central Asia. They lived in thickly wooded evergreen taiga, on the shores of great rivers and in vast open steppes where grasses go on forever. A few centuries ago they moved into Europe, occupied the Balkan almost to Venice, tried to break into Austria, were repelled, and gradually withdrew. In the meanwhile, they gobbled up Turkey, a country that had hitherto been populated by Kurds, Armenians and a range of Indo-European cultures; descendants of the Hittites, the Hurrites, the Medes and their relations. Sometime, somewhen, the Turkish people met the Babylonian Lamaštu. They were duly impressed, and took precautions to prevent her visitations. Or maybe it was the other way around. Maybe DIM.ME/Lamaštu appeared in Central Asia and made her way to Sumer, Akkad, Babylonia and Assyria.

In rural Turkey, she is alive and well. She comes visiting when a woman is pregnant and close to delivery. The term albasti is also the name for a terrifying fever. Albasti can assault women within forty days after the birth of a child. Sometimes Albasti is the name of the dreaded spirit. Sometimes albasti, the disease, is caused by a spirit called Alkarsis. The Kurds call her Alkarasi. She haunts bedrooms, rides a white horse through the dark and is the ugliest woman you have ever seen. When she goes walking in the night, she holds a bloody liver in her hand. Turkish women who are seized by her hear the voices of the dead, have visions, trembling fits, hallucinations and faint. They suffer from high fever and are happy to make it through the crisis alive. Their infants usually don't (Stein, 2004). But Albasti also assaults horses. She sneaks them out of the stable and rides them all night. By daybreak they are back where they belong, but they are shaken, edgy, troubled and coated by sweat. Occasionally a man can master the Albasti. Or Albasti looks at the man, likes him and takes him as her lover.

Albasti is one version of the name. Another is Almasti. A third variation: Āl Anasi. Note the letter 'i' at the end of the name. It might indicate that Lamaštu was actually pronounced Lamašti, at least in the period when the Turkish people came into contact with the Babylonians and Assyrians. But Turkish languages show plenty of variation. I also came upon Albastyi, Lobasta and Lopasta. Again, Lamaštu is simply round the corner, squatting in a doorway, waiting patiently. In the Middle Babylonian period her name was probably pronounced Lawaštu or Lawašti, as the letter 'm' between two vowels usually transformed into 'w'. Maybe the Turks transformed the 'w' into a 'b'. Another very common name is abbreviated: we hear of the terrible Āl, the child-killer, night-walker, terror of man and beast.

The Armenians seem to have picked up the Turkish name and transformed it. As Ananikian (2010:92-93) claims, the Āls are a group and they were probably introduced by the Syrians or Persians, since they are absent in pre-medieval literature. The Āls are half human and half animal, nude, shaggy and bristly. Gregory of Datev claimed that they haunt watercourses, wet, sandy and damp locations, but they are also fascinated by people and can infest houses and stables. In Armenian belief, the Āls are an entire species, hence there are male and female forms. The Armenians classed them among the spiritual beings, just like the Devs and Kaches. Ananikian cites an anonymous author who saw a male Āl. The Āl was sitting on the sand. Imagine snake-like hair, long fingernails of brass, iron teeth and a boar's tusk. The female Āl 's don't look much better. They have long, tangled hair, walk nude and their breasts are hanging almost to their knees. And they transform into serpents. The Āl's have a mother, who gave birth to every one of them, and a king who resides in the abyss. An element of Norse myth seems related: this king is chained and molten lead drops on him, so he squirms about and screams continuously. Compare it to Loki in the *Eddas*. And remember the medieval Christian concept that the Devil is bound in hell until the Day of Doom. Usually, the Āls attack pregnant women. They scorch the mother's head, pull out her liver and strangle her along with the baby. They blind the unborn child, they suck out its brain and blood, and when they are done the mother miscarries. Allegedly, they take the dead infant to their king as a tribute. The Armenians invented plenty of rituals to prevent this. They surrounded the mother with iron, scissors, spades and tools. Should the mother faint during travail, an Āl must be near. Someone was duly sent to the neighbouring brook to beat the water with an iron tool. Other people waved iron tools through the air, just in case the invisible Āl was lurking somewhere above. The Āls seem to be a well-defined group; however, in some districts of Armenia their function is fulfilled by the Devs. Yes, the Devs are close relations of the Indian Devas ('*Shining Ones*). Persian religion turned them into devils and monsters. A familiar story was recorded by Ganalanian (1969:102 cited by Arakelova in the *Encyclopaedia of Women and Islamic Cultures*). God created the female Āl as a wife for Adam. It didn't work, as she was far too hot for him. So God created Eve, and since that fatal day, the Āl has been jealous and angry, and became the enemy of mankind.

In Afghanistan the Āl, also known as the Madar-i Āl, lives near rivers, or within them. She is a terrifying crone with long, tangled black hair, a pointy nose and incredible sharp teeth. To show who she is and what she can do she walks around with a liver in her hand. If someone has the courage to approach her and threatens her with an iron object, she can be forced to give the liver back to the person she stole it from. An amazing detail: the Āl can slip into mosques, no matter how holy they are, and even enter their sacred mirah chamber. To expel her, people use fire (Arakelova, 2006).

Let's move to Central Asia. Albasti or Āl is often female. You would surely notice, as all beings of the Āl family prefer nudity. The Albasti is often a hairy crone. Her breasts are so long that they dangle to her knees. Sometimes she throws them over her back, which is useful to run. When she carries a stolen infant on her back, she can suckle it while she scampers along. Anyone crazy enough to follow her trail is sure to be confused, as her feet are the wrong way around, and the heels point forward. Or maybe she only throws one breast over a shoulder, and carries a woollen bag on the other. It is full of delicacies, like fresh hearts and livers. She likes to squat in gardens in the twilight, sits in bushes and trees and stalks empty streets in the night. But she can also be found lurking in the fire (Kattner, 2003). When she encounters a likely victim, she tickles it to death (Schmitz, 1996). I like it. It must be great to go out laughing. Mind you, it's even better to live like that.

Her relations to men are complicated. A hero can scare her by beating her with the belt of his trousers, while shouting 'byltyrga', meaning '*in the last year.*' Maybe it shifts her into the past, which is a pretty safe place, as it's over. Or you might pull out some of her hair and put it in the *Qur'an*. It instantly turns her into a good looking and devout young woman. Some men made the Albasti their slaves. She remained that way, softly spoken, docile and submissive, until she found the *Qur'an* and regained her missing hair. Showtime!

But there are also husbands of Albasti who get on quite well with their tempestuous wives. Such men are called agač-anglï. They face a turbulent marriage. Albasti can be quite demanding, and isn't much of a housewife. In some traditions she is scared of fire and cannot bake bread. In other traditions she grants the 'power of the hearth' to her husbands, as the hearth is her home. It gives her husbands the magical power to banish the albasti disease (Haussig & Schmalzriedt, 1999).

Let's have an example (Schmitz, 1996).One fateful day the famous hunter Kutlukaj was creeping through the wilderness. He saw something terrible moving through the shrubs and shot it. It was the husband of Albasti. How embarrassing! Within instants, Albasti was there, howling terribly, and shedding bitter tears. Kutlukaj felt deeply ashamed. In all humility he helped Albasti to bury her late husband. It was not enough. The earth barely covered the corpse when Albasti told Kutlukaj that he should be her new husband. Kutlukaj had very little choice, and agreed. How they married (or who married them) remains a mystery. Albasti asked the hunter to swear a solemn vow. Under no conditions was he allowed to look into her secret opening. All Albastis have a secret opening, which happens to be on their right flank, and when you look in you realise that they are hollow. Well, Kutlukaj was prepared to swear anything, no matter how weird, and for a while the young couple lived quite happily. Before long Albasti was pregnant. And as she was sleeping at the side of young Kutlukaj, snoring happily, he had to take a look. Albasti was awake in an instant, and she wasn't happy. However she was pregnant, she loved him, and after bitter words she forgave him. However, in fairy-tale country, vows are strictly regulated, and the gods of narrative can be severe. Albasti said that if the child turned out to be a girl, she would raise it alone, in the forest. And if it was a boy she would give it to him. Kutlukaj was sent back to his village, healthy, alive, and with a tale he couldn't tell to anyone. He tried hard to forget. One fateful day Albasti was standing in front of his door. She held an infant boy in her arms. 'Call him Idyge' she said, turned around and disappeared into the trees. Kutlukaj stood there, the boy in his arms, speechless. What would the neighbours say? He needn't have wondered. The boy was semi-divine wonderchild. He became a great hero, a hunter and warrior, and his descendants were the kings of the Nogjaic. It wasn't the only occasion that Albasti had children with mortal men. Several Central Asian tales record that Albasti gave birth to gloriously beautiful maidens who could transform into doves (Schmitz, 1996). They must have flown like the bird of heaven.

The Tajiks of Khuf Valley believe that she is called Almaste, and sucks blood. She has burning eyes, colourful hair and small claws. Apart from making men mad (which is actually quite easy), she likes to transform into a snake. As she is scared of mint and other herbs, women try to have their children in a field. Of course she stands nearby. She will offer help and ask to carry and nurse the baby, but as long as the woman is in the field, she cannot be harmed.

In the Pamir valley, she haunts the rivers. She often appears in a male form, with long, tangled hair and only one eye. On occasion that guy has the head of a wild boar. Maybe she will assault her victims. And maybe she will send them nightmares. It isn't easy to recognise her, as she can transform into a lion, tiger, bear, cat and dog.

The Yaghnobi people dread a very special Albasti. She has up to forty breasts, so she can suckle more infants. Diana of Ephesus comes to mind. She has long, fair hair and blue eyes (Arakelova, 2006). Among people who are brown eyed and black haired, this is certainly scary. Some children in rural China were shocked when they saw me. One small boy called me a gui (ghost). In East Asia, fair hair can be demonic. Left-hand-Path Jia Daoism; i.e. the militant, magical Daoism that fights evil influences, acknowledges such a spirit general. Meet an ugly woman with huge teeth, fair hair, who wears a crown of pearls, a purple robe and chain-mail. She is the 'Chia-shen spirit' and leads a hundred thousand spirit troops. To become a competent exorcist, you have to come to terms with her, and her equally terrifying associates (Saso, 1978: 158 and 170-174).

Forty breasts are just a start. In some folk tales she has up to seventy, with a stolen infant dangling from each. It gives her the name 'Mother of Children'.

In Dagestan, Āl is known as Āl Bab (*Red Mother*). As usual, her hair is long and tangled. She frequently transforms into a red rooster, a fox, cat and even a werewolf with a single eye under his brow. Or she drifts along as a fog. To expel her, the exorcists use iron objects, daggers, axes, chicken panic grass, a lamp, red wool, a broom, garlic, sulphur and the *Qur'an*. She hates loud noises and can be scared away when metal objects are beaten (Arakelova, 2006).

In north-west Pakistan, the nearby districts of Afghanistan and in Baltistan, you can meet female horrors called Gor. Like Albasti, the gors drink blood and cause sudden death. They are nude, walk around with one breast over their shoulder, have vertical eyes and their feet are turned backwards. Their queen lives in the underworld, where she cultivates a huge garden. As her vegetables need so much water, in summer, the rivers run dry. Should you meet a gor, try to appear friendly. With a bit of luck she'll adopt you. In the same regions, a female spirit called Halmasti threatens newborn infants. A group of women surrounds the crib and sing to keep her away. For similar reasons, people place iron objects under the pillows of babies or hang up guns above the heads of a woman giving birth. Halmasti also threatens the souls of the deceased. People take turns guarding fresh corpses against her. When the corpse is washed, verses of the *Qur'an* have to be recited to keep her away. She frequently appears as a dark-red dog with a long pointed snout and long legs. The locals address her as *Greedy, Fast Dog* (Jettmar, Jones, Klimburg, 1975)

In Xinjiang, a Chinese province peopled by the Uighurs, Albasti and all the jinn come out on each Wednesday night. It isn't easy to identify her, as she can transform into twelve shapes, including dog, donkey, sheep, goat and lion. She can also move around invisible. However, if you are very quiet you can sometimes hear and smell her. In Xinjiang the Āl or Albasti appear in male and female form. Both have long tangled hair and walk around nude. The female is a terrific fighter. To assault her victims, she throws her breasts over her shoulders. When you look at her back, you can see that she has a huge opening and is entirely hollow. The same idea appears in Scandinavian descriptions of forest goddess Lady Huldra. And it connects with Jewish lore: the qlippha are hollow shells. Āl and Albasti, just like Lamaštu, are masters of the whirlwinds. Their exorcism seems somewhat weak: you have to spit and say the name of God. Nice try. Good luck to you (Bellér-Hahn, 2008).

In Ferghana, Zeravshan Valley, things are quite different. To be sure, our bonny girl is widely known. However, she appears as a beautiful young lady. She dwells in rivers and trees and never harms anyone (Arakelova, 2006).

Indian Mothers

India has its soap operas and some of them have been going one for more than two thousand years. All it needs is a good choreography. Let's retell an episode from Book III of the *Mahābhārata.* And let me apologise. This is going to be complicated.

Once upon a time and time and time again the heavenly Devas were fighting the terrifying Dānavas. Good against evil: it had happened before and it will happen again. Such battles are the flesh and blood of Hindu myth. As usual, the Dānavas, a class of terrifying anti-gods were stronger. They plunged into the host of deities, screaming madly, and swiftly crushed their resistance. Anguished, Indra, king of the gods, the wielder of the divine thunderbolt, declared that everyone would need a reliable super-warrior, and it wasn't him. But while the heads were flying and blood spurted in fountains, chariots crashed into elephants and hordes of yelling fighters ran into each other, he couldn't quite imagine who.

'Keep going' said Indra, 'you are doing fine' and retreated to Mount Mānasa to ponder the matter. When he had settled down, relaxed, had a drink and started to think important thoughts, he heard the voice of a woman.

'Save me!' the girl cried, 'let one appear who can be my husband, or one who can lead me to a worthy mate!'

Indra rose and looked around. He saw a gorgeous young lady, clad in little except her underwear, who was molested by an evil-looking keśin (a long-haired ascetic). That looked easy. Indra lifted his thunderbolt and said 'bugger off or else'.

The keśin screamed with rage. He hurled a club, but Indra's vajra-thunderbolt split it. He threw a mountain, but Indra pulverised it. The keśin, white with stone dust, ran away screeching. Indra shrugged and looked at the maiden. She was a glorious sight and as voluptuous as they come.

The god of thunder bowed to her, stared politely at the ground and listened closely while she told her tale.

'I am Devasenā, a daughter of Prajāpati', she said. 'Unlike my sister who is up to no good, wears hardly anything and stays out all night, I have lived a chaste and virtuous life. I know that my future husband will be the fiercest warrior of the gods. He will fight at your side, O Destroyer of Cities, and all deities, Asuras, Dānavas, Nāgas, Yakṣas will bend their knees before him'.

'Will they?' said Indra and frowned. 'Now that will be a relief.' He raised an eyebrow. 'How do you know about him?'

'I have never met him' said the woman, and her eyes glistened with tears, 'call me a fool, but I am in love with him already'.

Good grief. You'll never find a guy like that, thought Indra.

But when he raised his eyes the special effects set in, and he saw the sun and the moon unite on Sunrise Mountain. The hour of Rudra had begun. Radiant red clouds cloaked the sky in crimson and turned the oceans into blood. Fire rose in surging flames to conjoin with moon and sun and the world seemed ablaze. Indra was startled. This was unusual. Someone must have invested millions into computer generated imagery! Fire and moon in conjunction! It doesn't happen every day. If the moon has a child, he thought, it will be a hero beyond compare. If Agni, the god of fire, has a son, he could be the husband of this girl. A hero beyond compare! This could be a real problem. And Indra did not know whether he should laugh or smile or run away in fear.

The girl looked at him with Bambi eyes, and her tears began to fall like summer rain. That was more than enough. Indra frowned, grabbed her hand and within an instant they stood in front of four-headed Brahmā, the grandfather of the gods.

'Venerable sire' said Indra' grant this girl a husband.'

Brahmā smiled and stroked his four beards. 'So shall it be. The husband of this girl will be the greatest hero'.

Indra bowed deep and dragged the maiden to the divine seers. Seers come in all varieties, and most of them are slightly worn and crusty. Unlike Brahmā and Indra, they care very little about their appearance. Several looked as if the moths had been at them. They lit a sacrificial fire, raised fierce chants and as the flames rose, the god of fire woke. Fierce Agni, the household priest, the companion who is ever at home, looked out of the flames. He saw the seven primordial sages, who are the stars of Ursa major, as they were chanting and pouring ghī into the flame. And Agni saw the wives of the seven sages, who looked much better than their venerable husbands, and burned hotter than ever. Gods, they were gorgeous! If I could but have one of them, he thought. Or maybe two. Or four. It won't have to be all of them. Most would be enough. Agni grinned and sparks flew. It is good to remain humble. He watched and leered and grinned and when the offering was done he followed the seven sages into their homes, where he hid in the hearth fires, and spied on those luscious ladies every day and night. Alas, he could not go any further. The ladies were lovely and gracious, especially when undressing, but they were closely guarded by their grumpy old husbands. Damn them, thought Agni, Brahmins are so pure and high-minded. They are stronger than the gods and they can curse the universe to pieces. I won't get a chance when they hang around. And fire grew lovesick, frustrated, and desperate. Day in and out he watched those perfect women and waited for his chance. It never came. Finally, whimpering a little, Agni crept out of the hearths and slunk to the forest in sheer misery.

While Agni was watching the wives of the seven seers, the goddess Svāhā had been watching him. It's always like that: while you watch others they watch you. She followed him cautiously. And when she saw him flat on the ground, weak and almost extinguished, she assumed the form of the eldest wife of the seven sages, crept close and touched him. Oh my. It doesn't take much to get a fire going.

What a night it was! The authors of the *Mahābhārata* could not describe it. Their minds were not up to the challenge. Neither can I, for fear the keyboard melts. Some things are better left unsaid, and happen only, O gracious reader, in the secret room of your mind. And there they should remain, no matter how hot it gets.

The next morning, Agni felt utterly drained. He was lying among the extinguished embers on the forest floor and hardly noticed how his love slipped into the twilight. Nor did he notice that she assumed the form of the red-hot Garuḍa bird and flew away. The illusion was compelling: all seers and gods who gazed her way thought the bird was real. Soon she arrived at Mount Śveta, overgrown with towering reeds and guarded by seven-headed toxic snakes (a typical import from Mesopotamia). The goddess winged to the top, screamed in triumph and spurted Agni's sperm into a golden vessel.

The next night Agni awoke. He was hungry, weak and not quite in his right mind when another gorgeous woman appeared. She looked like the second wife of the seven sages. 'Number one must have been chatting with number two' thought Agni, took a deep breath, scratched his pubic hair and grinned, 'she's keen to learn what happens.'

It turned out to be a lot.

Six long nights a wife of a sage appeared. Six hot and passionate nights she had her will with Agni, and left him, jittery, sparking and beside himself, winged away like the Garuḍa bird, bearing in her womb a portion of richly gleaming sperm. Six offerings of fiery seed went into the golden basin on Mount Śveta. The sperm mingled, pulsed, surged and emitted a terrifying roar. The mountain shook, the skies trembled, and from a surge of fiery hot lava, a warrior boy arose.

The earth shudders, the skies descend and we meet Skanda, also known as Kumāra and Kārrtikeya, in all his glory. The newborn child arose in armour, fully grown, with six heads, twelve ears, fierce eyes, muscular arms, strong legs and one huge brawny trunk. His body gleamed like the sun, red clouds enveloped him like a cloak, and he roared so loud that the three worlds were stunned and all creatures ran screaming. In his hand was a gigantic bow, the birth gift of Śiva.

Two huge nāga serpents heard him roar. They hurled themselves against him, but Skanda merely picked them up and held one in each hand until they ceased writhing and started to behave. A red combed giant cock threw itself against Skanda, who simply picked it up and held it. Skanda lifted a conch trumpet, blew and made the heavens shake. He whirled his spear around and danced, shrieking gleefully, in the full joy of his birth. He picked up his bow and shot mountains to pieces. He split Mount Śveta with the blade of his spear. All mountains crouched low and rested their heads on the ground; they pledged obedience and asked for refuge.

All over the three worlds, the creatures, people and deities were seized with fear. The seven sages met in the forest to discuss the situation. One of them had a vision. It wasn't any good. He declared 'Fire has lain with six of our wives! We are shamed! The wicked Garuḍa bird has done this evil to us!'

The seven sages, snarled, quarrelled and went home in a bad temper. They divorced their wives and sent them into the wilderness. Then they declared that Garuḍa had abused them.

Garuḍa, the one and only true celestial firebird, was surprised to hear the accusation. He thought long and deep and realised that the seven sages were going mad. However, some things cannot be helped. They can only be used for an advantage. He flew to Skanda, smiled sweetly and said 'My dear Skanda, I am your mother'. Skanda looked at the shining giant fire bird, laughed and was happy. He had never imagined a mother like that.

Elsewhere, in his secluded forest hermitage, the seer Viśvāmitra meditated and had a vision. Unlike the seven seers he saw what really happened, saw a chance to become famous and went to Skanda, to praise him mightily. Skanda acknowledged his presence and the seer felt reassured. Then he went to the seven sages, proclaimed he had true knowledge and told them that the goddess Svāhā had lain with Agni, the Lord of Fire, for six nights.

'Your wives are innocent' he declared, bursting with self-importance, 'Svāhā simply assumed the form of your wives to drag Agni into bed!' But the seven sages rolled their eyes, chewed on their beards and were not amused. What would everybody think? They felt deeply insulted and refused to take their wives back.

Viśvāmitra shook his head, walked away and told everyone about the wonder boy. The message got around, as all news does, and grew bigger with each re-telling. The gods assembled, and said to Indra 'this warrior boy is too strong to be among us. He will usurp your place. Best you kill him instantly, before he becomes stronger.'

Sound advice, thought Indra, lowered his eyes and bowed humbly to the assembly of the gods. I'm glad you made the suggestion. And the gods raised a great call and invited the Mothers.

Few dare to stand before the world mothers. They are a terrifying lot, slayers, killers, destroyers and disease-ridden monstrosities, assembling before the host of the gods and staring at them with fierce red evil eyes. Indra smiled graciously, as heroic gods should, blessed the ladies and pointed them in the right direction. The Mothers raised a cry, lifted their weapons and marched against Skanda. The earth shook, the dust rose in clouds and no one dared to get in their way. The mothers squinted. They saw the fiery glow, the maddening sunshine, the swirl of blood red clouds. The temperature rose and the closer they came the slower they walked. Finally, they hardly dared to move their feet. Ouch! That guy was simply too much. Their faces paled, their hands trembled. They knelt before Skanda, sighed and humbly asked for his grace.

'Skanda! We seek your refuge. You shall be our son. We are the World–Supporters, the Mothers of the Universe. See us cower before you. Our breasts are swelling, we are full of milk, hence we must be your mothers'.

Skanda looked at them. Wow. More mothers. He laughed happily and accepted their pledge. Then Agni arrived in blazing glory to greet his newborn son, he giggled madly and felt terribly proud.

Skanda walked into the world, accompanied by a mother carrying a spike, and another mother, the blood-drinking daughter of the blood sea, at his other side. I've got lots of mothers and nurses, and they are my honour guard, thought Skanda, I must be doing something right. And Agni, the divine fire, assumed the form of a goat-faced peddler with many children, and amazed Skanda with playthings, novelties and silly toys. The boy laughed: in only a few hours, he had gained a huge and happy family.

When they reached the plains, the host of gods appeared in sight. In front of them marched Indra, holding his vajra-thunderbolt, cheered by the supreme seers and the thirty gods. He roared a mighty war cry, but Skanda roared louder, and belched balls of fire. The gods ran screaming, as heat scaled their bodies and flames scorched their hair. They ran to Indra and embraced him, howling for his protection. Indra turned to Skanda, raised his brawny arms and hurled his thunderbolt. It stuck Skanda's unprotected side. A mighty wound gaped, and fire surged out of the hole. A figure climbed out of Skanda's side, and took his place next to him. It was the golden, spear-wielding god Viśākha. Together they faced Indra. The Wielder of the Thunderbolt paled and stopped in his tracks. Things were going wrong. High time to reconsider everything. Very slowly he went down on his knees. He closed his eyes and tears streamed down his face. Skanda smiled. It had been such a good day. 'Thank you', he said; 'you are a great guy. I grant you refuge and protection'.

Then all the gods sounded their instruments, made horrible noises and chanted praise to the warrior boy.

Skanda never admitted the pain. The thunderbolt had hurt him badly. His side was ripped apart and during the next days, a host of creatures came crawling from the wound. They were the lower Kumāras, born from fire and vajra power, terrifying (but rather good looking) girls who snatch the baby from the cradle and crush the embryo in the womb. They walked up to Skanda, their hips swaying mightily. Skanda asked: 'Girls! What do you want?'

They smiled happily, well aware how damn good they looked, and spoke: 'Grant us a boon! With your permission we will be the Ultimate Mothers of the Whole World and worship it.'

Skanda replied: 'Thank you. Another everlasting girl group. So shall it be. And let you be of two kinds: those who have an auspicious nature and those who are not quite as nice (and twice as popular).'

The new Mothers made Skanda their son and went away happily. Among them were the seven mothers of all freshly-born sons: Kākī, Halimā, Rudrā, Bṛhalī, Āryā, Palālā and Mitrā. They had been virgins before, but thanks to the grace of Skanda every one of them gained a horrible, red-eyed, terrifying son, each named the Freshly Born. They were eight heroic fighters called The Ones Born from the Mothers of Skanda's Host. Grinning, goatish Agni joined them, so the group numbers nine. All of this happened on the fifth day of the bright half of the month, originally the day of the Nāga serpent gods and now the day of Skanda's worship, unless you prefer reptiles. On the sixth day the armies of the gods and the Dānavas faced each other. As usual, it was going to be the final battle, the war that would end all wars. Everybody wished they had stayed in bed, preferably on another continent.

By dawn, Skanda was seated on a throne, clad in a luminous coat of mail, his tusks flashing merrily. To all sides, gods and Brahmins knelt, singing hymns of praise.

'Take thy position! Assume thy proper rank', they chanted, 'be the new Indra for the time to come!'

Skanda frowned, pursed his lips and asked: 'What does an Indra do?'

'He gives all creatures strength, courage, beauty, descendants, he bestows shares on the godly and punishes the evil. He gives himself for the well-being of all!'

Indra bowed and proclaimed: 'You, Skanda, shall be our new Indra'.

But Skanda lowered his head: 'You shall remain Indra, and I shall be your servitor. I have no wish to govern.'

Indra looked up and felt relieved. Everything would remain as it was. The gods appointed Skanda to be the champion and captain of the divine host. Śiva approached and put a golden diadem on Skanda's brow. In the language of the Brahmins, fire (i.e. Agni) is called Rudra. Rudra is the elder, Vedic name of Śiva, so Skanda became Śiva's honorary son. Please don't complain. It doesn't make much sense but works. Skanda was delighted. He had two fathers and plenty of mothers.

At this moment, Indra used the chance to present the damsel Devasenā to Skanda and asked him to accept her as his wife. Our boy looked as if he was struck by lightning. Devasenā managed to bulge into dimensions sane scientists are not aware of. He was bedazzled by her beauty, her virtue and cosmos-threatening good looks, wiped the sweat from his brow and stuttered his agreement. Devasenā almost fainted with happiness. But before things could proceed (to bed) six visitors were announced.

The six wives of the Seven Sages walked in and approached Skanda with due reverence.

'Skanda, son, we have been divorced by our husbands. We have lost our name and rank, as people say that we are your mothers. Attest that this is not the case. Restore our reputation! Then have the grace to accept us as your honorary mothers.'

Skanda had other things on his mind, so he agreed. 'You shall be my mothers and I am your son'.

It wasn't over yet. You wouldn't believe how many mothers were waiting in the ranks. By now our scribes were getting worried. What had started as an action story was turning into an encyclopaedic essay. Conch trumpets sounded: time for the next bunch!

The Mothers of the World approached.

'We too, wish to be your mothers. Honour us!'

'You, too, shall be my mothers' said Skanda, fidgeting slightly. How long was this supposed to go on?

'We ask a boon, dear son. As we have lost our progeny we ask for the offspring of others. We want to devour their children!'

'It is an evil thing you are asking', said Skanda, 'but you may have those children. But consider! When the parents honour you, and provide offerings, spare their children'.

'Blessings to you, Skanda! We will spare them, and will dwell in your company forever.'

'You have power over children until they are sixteen years old. You shall be worshipped and have a soul like Rudra, and live in complete happiness.'

At this instant a golden shadow emerged from Skanda, keen to devour the children of the world. As soon as it appeared it fell to the ground, faint with hunger. Skanda gave it the form of Rudra/Śiva, and appointed it as a Seizer. It came to be known as Skanda's Forgetfulness.

The Brahmins faithfully recorded everything. They had all the time in the world and took their business much more seriously than I do (sorry!). At this point in our narrative they listed further Mothers, all of whom joined Skanda's company. The inventory is amazing. Meet the terrifying Vinatā. She is a seizer in bird-shape. Pūtanā, the Smelly One, is an eater of human flesh, a walker in the dark. Śītapūtanā is a devourer of corpses who aborts embryos. Aditi, originally a cosmic cow, primal goddess of the beginnings, appears as Revatī, who abuses infants. Diti appears as Mukhamaṇḍikā, and gorges herself on children. The male Kumāras and the female Kumārīs that crept out of Skanda's wound are foetus-eaters and child-slayers. Surabhi appeared, grinning terribly, the Mother of Cows: there is a bird sitting on her who devours infants. The goddess Saramā is the Mother of Dogs, and a devourer of embryos. In the karañya tree lives the Mother of Trees and she isn't just a happy goddess of plants: those who want a successful pregnancy have to sacrifice to her. All of these Seizers loiter in the birth chamber for ten nights. They can be appeased with meat offerings and strong alcoholic drinks. Kadrū, elsewhere known as the Mother of all Serpent deities (Nāgas) is another terrifying being and proud of it: she slips into pregnant women and eats the baby in the womb. In its stead, the mother gives birth to a snake. I wonder whether anybody notices. The Mother of the Gandharvas snatches the foetus and wings away with it. The Mother of the heavenly nymphs (Apsarāses) takes the foetus in the womb and makes it sit. Instead of being born, the baby won't come out. The Mother called Āryā had a better reputation. She simply grants wishes. To top it off, Skanda acquired a cheerful, happy nurse who is the Mother of the Blood Sea, otherwise known as Lohitāyanī; for whatever reasons, she dwells in kadamba trees.

The rules are simple. For the first sixteen years the Mothers are a threat. Then they become benevolent and benefactors. As they keep reminding everyone, they should always be placated with oblations, incense, collyrium (to paint their eyes), gifts and cast offerings, especially during the worship of Skanda. But there are more to come. Our scribes had begun listing mothers and just couldn't stop. After the child has reached its sixteenth year, another set of Seizers lie in wait. The God-Seizer afflicts people who see gods when they dream or are awake. The Father-Seizer grasps those who behold the ancestors and go mad. Who could blame them? Those who insult the Siddhas (*Perfected Ones*) are sent to madness by the Siddha-Seizer. Some go insane when they are overwhelmed by scents and flavours, and become victims of the Rākṣasa-Seizers, the monsters who devour human flesh and blood. Some are driven to insanity by the heavenly Gandharvas, and caught by the Gandharva-Seizers. Others are made crazy by the Yakṣa-Seizers, who haunt forests, rivers and pools. People assaulted by the Piśāca death spirits are victims of the Piśāca-Seizers. And as if this wouldn't be more than enough, there are three kinds of Seizers, records the *Mahābhārata*: they are playful, ever-hungry and lustful. These Seizers haunt people till their seventieth year, so you have plenty of time to decide whether play, hunger or lust are essential to you. The few who reach that age find that Fever becomes another Seizer. Luckily, Seizers only harm people with scattered senses and befuddled minds; they shun those who avoid 'social networks', are true to the Dharma, pure, in self-control, and all devotees of Śiva Maheśvara, the Great Lord. Hey, we are lucky. It's quite a relief.

Last, the goddess Svāhā approached Skanda.

'You are my son' said the goddess, and she meant it. 'I ask a gift from you. I am madly in love with Agni, the god of Fire. Our union created you. He does not know of my love for him, as I assumed a different form each night. Skanda! Let me be his wife, let me dwell with him, let me always be present when fire burns and offerings are made.'

Skanda smiled, touched her feet and gave his consent.

From this moment onwards, when fire offerings are made, Svāhā is invoked. And as the *Devī Bhāgavatam Purāṇa* (9,43) relates, it is Svāhā, and her name, who makes offerings valid and spells come true.

We thought that things were settled. We innocently assumed that the gods and mothers had sorted themselves out, were ready to return to the start and resume their fight against the anti-gods. Alas, it was not to be. At this crucial moment, the Indian Department of Mythical Confusion and Cosmological Excess launched its contribution. It had been years in the making and was totally superfluous. Out of nowhere, Brahmā Prajāpati, the ancient cosmic creator god appeared and declared that through Agni, Śiva is always acting and through Svāhā, Śiva's wife, the goddess Umā/Pārvatī. In your innocence, you might have imagined that Agni and Svāhā were Skanda's parents, but this was not to be. Tough luck. Absolute Reality gets around. In truth, in the second version, Skanda is the son of Śiva and Pārvatī, and the brother of the elephant-headed Gaṇeśa. You can see him riding a peacock.

Please don't complain, I didn't do it.

That being settled and everybody happy, the gods chanted praise songs and celebrated. Then they turned their faces to the battlefield. A terrible army of anti-gods, led by the proud Mahiṣa, stormed against them. But Skanda was prepared. All Mothers and Seizers in his company were ready. They licked their lips, lifted their weapons and howled with delight. The battle was as bloody and terrible as any other and the gods emerged victorious.

So much for the Mothers and Seizers of the *Mahābhārata*. It provided young Skanda with more mothers than anyone could cope with and firmly established him as a heroic war god in the divine assembly. Many people in India have pictures of Skanda on the bumpers of their cars; it tells you everything about Indian traffic. Skanda is unusual. Most Indian gods are simply there. They exist or are created, but Skanda was actually born. More so, his army consists mainly of terrifying Mothers and Seizers. Compared to fathers, and those fathers who are ancestors, mothers are a rarity in Hindu literature. And these Mothers are not exactly motherly. I keep reading that devout Indians worship mother goddesses, but these mothers are child-snatchers and do not fit the job specification. In fact, most of them have no children. However, several of them gained popularity in tantric cults, and became the favourites of worshippers enjoying cremation ground rituals. Offerings of meat and alcohol are a favourite in left-hand-Tantra of the 'heroic' stage. You may have noticed that Skanda annihilated an Asura (A-Sura= *anti-god*) called Mahiṣa. He was the first to do so. But when we move to the sixth or seventh century, we meet Mahiṣa again. He is alive and well and this time he is the ultimate enemy of the great goddess who is celebrated as Devī, Durgā, Ambikā and Kālī.

As far as we can know, there were always people in India who worshipped and loved goddesses. Several early examples appear in the *Vedas*; mind you, goddesses did play a minor role in the hymns, as most seers devoted their attention to the thunderbolt-wielding Indra, the fiercely burning Agni and the intoxicating Soma and rarely bothered to record songs to other deities. There is only one hymn in the *Ṛg Veda* that praises a goddess as the sovereign lady of all being (X,125). All other goddesses had limited domains, or maybe their praise songs were lost or ignored. During the first millennium BCE, the cult of goddesses also had much popularity outside of the world of the scholars. There were plenty of house, village and country goddesses who enjoyed the devotion of illiterate and uneducated people. Then, in two late additions to the *Mahābhārata*, a series of goddesses is praised as supreme regents of the universe. Among them are Kālī and Durgā. These passages were probably composed during the fourth century. Next we encounter an entire text devoted to the sovereignty of goddesses. It is the sixth or seventh century *Devī Mahātmya*, otherwise known as the *Caṇḍī*, which survived thanks to being included in the *Mārkeṇḍeya Purāṇa*. The little book consists of three originally independent episodes. As usual, the topic is good gods against bad anti-gods. In one of the episodes, the gods face the terrifying Mahiṣa, who cannot be defeated by any god. In their panic, the gods unite their powers (Śakti) and out of them a goddess appears. She fights Mahiṣa, but his army is too strong. So the gods sit down and each of them casts off his feminine Śakti aspect. These terrifying goddesses hurl themselves against the evil anti-gods. Kālī joins the slaughter and before long the goddesses triumph. The female emanations of the gods are also known as Mothers, but do not belong to Skanda's family. They are terrible fighters and drinkers of blood, but they are not interested in harming children.

Their worship was popular until maybe the tenth century. In several Indian temples, old sculptures of the mothers are exhibited. However, there seems to be no cult devoted to them.

In some tantric movements, the Mothers acquired an extra meaning. The word Mothers (Mātṛkā) also means measures, matrixes, and refers to the order of the universe with its many layers of divine manifestation. For devotees of Kula, Kaula and Trika Tantra, the Mothers are the goddesses of the alphabet. Each of them is a phoneme, and these sound/vibrations create, maintain and dissolve the universe. They form the sacred mantras, the hymns, eulogies and myths, and permit speech and song. On a denser level, they are energy, matter, form and the categories (Tattvas) of all existence. It gave the Mothers a supreme position in tantric ritual: one of the most important mantras is simply the Devanāgarī alphabet with its (more or less) fifty phonemes, each of them relating to a specific quality of divine awareness and manifestation. By reciting the alphabetic order, the devotee moves from the abstract, divine awareness all the way to the dense world of individual perception, names, forms, limits and things dropping behind the fridge. There is an essential idea behind this process: the divine has to manifest itself, in all its material density, to encounter and enjoy itself.

Plenty of terrifying women appear in Indian myth. They emerge in the earliest records. Many of them have a thing about babies. Have you met Rudra? The outcast of the gods, the terrifying archer in the twilight jungles, the master of toxins and medicines? Rudra was there when it began. He had several brief appearances in the *Ṛg Veda*. Not that people really liked him. His hymns were rarely chanted. His offerings were rarely made. Rudra was right on the edge of the divine. His home was the cold north with its terrifying mountains. His arrows could take the life of man or bull, his sons Bhava and Śarva prowled the forest as wolves. In Rudra's hands were diseases and pestilence, recovery and healing. The seers did not praise him, they tried to placate him. Rudra, the crimson slayer, was just as red as the blossoms at the funeral ceremony. In their fear they called him Śiva, the Auspicious One, as if that would make things any better. Rudra, the savage wild boar, was excluded from the great Soma feasts. He had his own drugs, though, which had turned his throat deep blue and gained him the name Nilakaṇṭha (*Blue-Throat*), drugs which he shared with crazy, sky-travelling forest ascetics, witches and the frenzied women, the **Seizers**, who followed him as a retinue. If women is the right expression. They are Noisemakers, Counter-Noisemakers, Accompanying Noisemakers, Searchers, Hissers, Devourers of Flesh, Seizers, Graspers, Searchers, Triumphant Ones, Serpents, and they are soothed by the offering the bloody entrails of freshly killed game (Oldenberg, 1916:218-219).Like Rudra, his frenzied women bear diseases, fever and pestilence. The Seizers appeared wherever Rudra is. But Rudra did not limit his activities to forests and mountains. There were loads of Rudras all over the place. Sit down anywhere and you can watch Rudra watching you. By the start of the first millennium BCE, we meet a Rudra of the Streets, a Rudra of the Crossroads, a Rudra of the Place, a Rudra of the Serpents, a Rudra of the Waterways, a Rudra of the Whirlwind, a Rudra of the Sacred Tree, a Rudra of the Cremation Ground, a Rudra of the Fields, a Rudra of the Deep Forest, a Rudra of the Sacred Sites and even a Rudra of the Dung Heap. No matter where you go, there is sure to be a Rudra around. Some of them are remarkably similar to the tantric Śiva.

Rudra's Seizers were just one bunch of plague girls. Seizers (Grāha, female: Grāhī), in early Indian belief, were usually diseases and obsessions. Around the third century BCE, India began to embrace Mesopotamian astrology, introduced by the Greek, courtesy of Alexander's campaign. It created another bunch of seizers: the planets. Just as instincts, urges and pestilence can seize a person, a planet can. Each of them is a terrifying strong influence that takes hold of people and makes them what they are. What some would consider character traits, the Indian astrologers considered obsessive drives.

Not that these Seizers were enough. Have you met the **Yakṣas**? When the *Vedas* were compiled, the word Yakṣa was a general term for the all-enclosing, formless, absolute consciousness. We find it applied to universal creator gods like Prajāpati and the All-Self Brahman (*Extension*). In the centuries before the Common Era, the term shifted to the god Varuṇa. Varuṇa had been a universal god in the Vedic Period, whose net connected and bound heaven and earth, and who was sure to punish evildoers. A thousand years later, during the advent of Hinduism, Varuṇa became a god of the oceans, a master of all waters and a healer. He was praised as the Yakṣa, and quite happy about it. Simultaneously, it became a common trend to refer to a class of nature spirits as Yakṣas. They dwelled in ponds and lakes, in trees and groves, in the ground, under the earth and in the dark heart of the forest. Like so many beings in Indian myth, they had highly ambiguous characters. By nature, many Yakṣas were personified diseases. They brought on fever and delirium and could drain a person in a single night. It often happened that travellers, moving hurriedly through the evening forest, met a gorgeous young lady. 'O sweet sir' the girl said, casting her eyes down shyly, while her bosom heaved impressively, 'I am a princess from another land. Thieves attacked my servants and killed my guards. I fled into the forest and have lost my way! Could you guide me to the village?'

Good question. Usually, by daybreak, the traveller was found dangling by his entrails from a tree. Others managed to flee the embrace of the Yakṣī, and wasted away over the next weeks. For normal travellers, no matter their friendly smiles and huge bosoms, Yakṣīs could be a nightmare. For forest ascetics and, much later, for tantric devotees, the Yakṣas of the wilderness were company. Several sages and tantric practitioners met voluptuous Yakṣī girls in the wild and married them. The Yakṣīs shyly cleaned their blood smeared hands and faces, turned to religion, devoted themselves to the cult of Śiva and attained a saintly status. There are three things that characterise a hot blooded Yakṣīs. Two of them are her breasts, which are generally as huge as sculptors could make them without having the statue fall over. The third is their fondness for stealing human children. Many Yakṣīs are shown with a baby in their arms and yes, it usually isn't theirs. Smiling happily they carry their prey into the otherworlds. Maybe they play with them. Maybe they eat them. We just can't be sure. But Yakṣīs are not always evil. From time to time they sympathise with good people, help them in danger, or offer the blessings of the forest. It paid to be on good terms with them.

Meet the **Gandharvas**. They are a class of celestial spirits who are much adored in modern Hinduism. When you come to Indra's warrior heaven, where all those heroic young men are sitting around, quaffing strong drink and watching soccer cause of not having much to do, you can witness the heavenly nymphs (Apsaras) dancing and the Gandharvas making celestial music. In earlier periods, they were not quite that fabulous. The *Atharva Veda* contains spells to exorcise them. Early Gandharvas were dangerous shapeshifters, mighty magicians, and prone to slay lone travellers. The male Gandharvas were fond of attacking pregnant women and killed the embryo in the womb. To prevent this, the seers called on Indra to castrate the Gandharvas with well-aimed lightning bolts. There were also female Gandharvas around, many of them devourers of human flesh, and they were not famed for celestial music at all.

Whee. So far we had Seizers, Yakṣīs, Gandharvas and Mothers. It all culminated around the eighth to tenth century when the cult of the **Yogīnīs** began. A Yogīnī can be a deity or an exalted spirit. She can be a supernatural being who leads a celestial life and occasionally comes to earth to play and have a few bloody sacrifices. Some Yogīnīs haunt deep forests and cremation places and flirt with heroic tantrics. Some steal little children; others are magically attracted to offerings of menstrual blood and sperm. The Yogīnīs like to appear as animals, most of them female. The *Kaulajñāna Nirṇaya* lists doves, vultures, swans, hens, cocks, peacocks, owls, hawks, cuckoos, birds of various sorts, dogs, wolves, jackals, goats, cows, buffalo cows, cats, camels, mongooses, tigers, elephants, horses, stags, bulls, mice, serpents, frogs, bees, beetles, scorpions, and *certain human beings*. None of these animals may be eaten, as each of them might house a Yogīnī who could get really upset. Male animals did not enjoy such protection; in most Indian temples, the sacrificial animal has to be male. As White demonstrates so beautifully, the Yogīnīs had a powerful cult. Unlike so many other tantric movements, several kings embraced the Yogīnī cult and erected round, roofless temples for them, so the Yogīnīs could come down from heaven. They decorated the temples with Yogīnī statues, many of them appearing as nude women equipped with an animal head. For several small kingdoms and a few centuries, the Yogīnī cult became something like the state religion. The kings happily practised tantric rituals and hoped to gain magical power, divine virtue, success in battle and, if possible immortality. It did not really work. By the thirteenth century, most tantric movements were declining rapidly. It was a time of pestilence and desperation. Kingdoms previously based on tantric thought and imagery were usurped by mainstream kings devoted to the cult of Viṣṇu and by armies of Muslim invaders. But Yogīnīs were more than celestial initiatrixes and tantric power holders. The term was also used for tantric initiates: a yogīnī can be an advanced female adept practising yoga, a woman skilled in alchemy, and a terrible witch. The word, used as a compliment by tantrics of the left-hand path, was an insult in everyday parlance. It takes us to the flower of Indian culture, the confluence of Hindu and Buddhist Tantra in Northern India.

The Lion-faced Goddess

It's been a long journey. We started in the Hohlenstein-Stadel cave in southern Germany, maybe 35,000 years ago, where Stone Age migrants left an image of a lion-human deity or ritualist, carved from a mammoth tusk. We continued to the late Sumerian period, near the end of the third millennium BCE, when the first references to DIM.ME/Lamaštu were recorded. In the Old Babylonian period the evidence improved: yes, there were plenty of people scared out of their heads by the nude animal headed goddess, daughter of the sky, child-snatcher, demon-slayer, prowling through alleys, lurking on thresholds, haunting the paths of the wilderness. We journeyed through the millennia, saw cults and cultures come and go, and religions appear, mingle, transform and fade away. We watched them being reborn in a new guise.

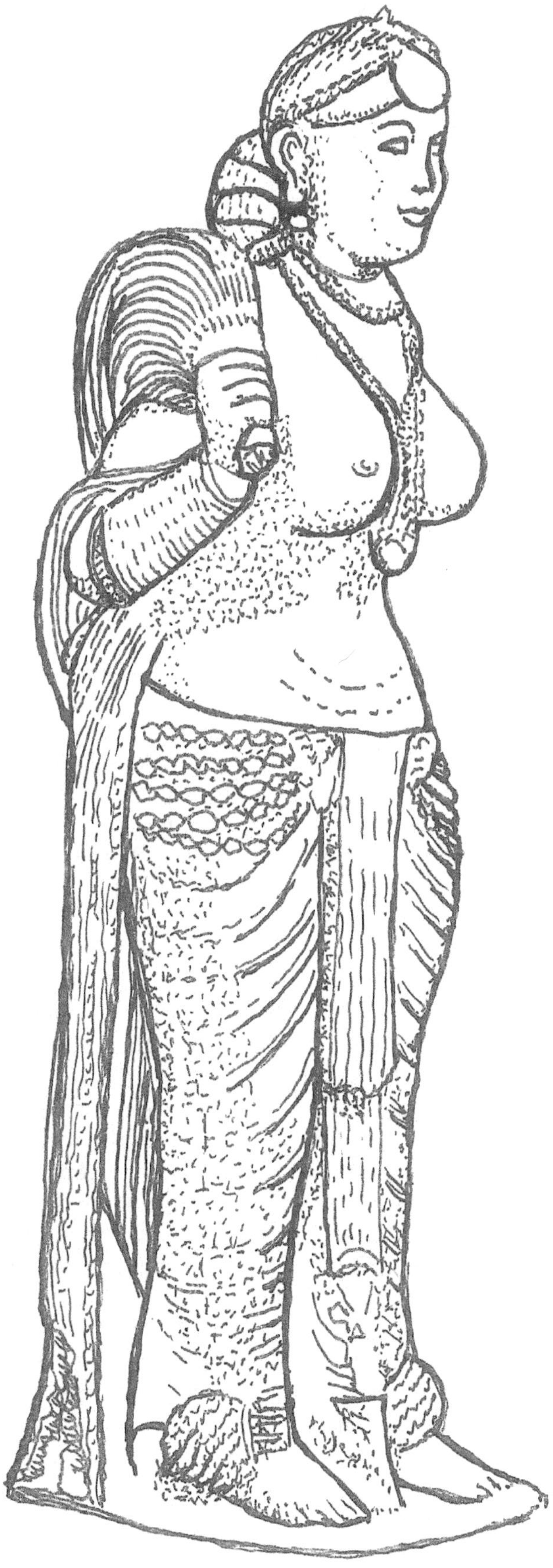

Figure 70 Yakṣī Lady. Statue from Dīdārgañji, Museum of Patna, 2. C. CE

The terrifying Lady of the Beasts moved with them. Infant stealer, bearer of diseases, custodian of fire and ice, destroyer of evil spirits, we saw her transform into Ardat Lilî, Lilith, Ḳarīna, Lamia, Medusa, Albašti, the Mothers, the Yakṣis, Yoginīs, Xiwangmu, Guimu and Hariri. And finally we meet a lion-headed goddess who is much like Lamaštu, venerated, in spite of her nudity, her wildness and her macabre outfit, as a benevolent and blissful deity. In Tantra, the goddess with the lion head is vibrantly alive. Before we can go further, I would like to summarise a few points on the development of Tantra. For a better introduction to tantric development, please consult *Kālī Kaula*. Let me begin by remarking that Tantra is not a single thing but a vague and often misleading term attached to a wide range of religious movements, many of them in happy disagreement with each other. Let's start with yoga. Nowadays, plenty of people assume that yoga is a spiritual discipline involving special postures, physical exercises, diet, ethical rules and meditative practices. Originally, in the Vedic period, the term had an entirely different meaning. As White explains at great length, yoga was originally a term for the apotheosis of special heroes and kings, who, after a virtuous life, generous sacrifices and a death on the battlefield, were allowed to ascend in their battle chariot into the sky. They pierced the sun and found their paradise in some celestial heaven behind it. For the Vedic warrior society, yoga was something that only happened to the finest heroes and kings. In the *Upanisadic* period, around the middle of the first millennium BCE, the ability to practice yoga shifted to the brahmin class. When death came, special sages and ascetics were able to find their apotheosis by withdrawing into their hearts. From the heart (here: mind, consciousness) they shot upwards along the path of light (the spine), pierced the top of the head and escaped to liberation. It allowed them to dissolve in the freshly discovered or invented Brahman (*Extension*), the formless, indefinable all self, the Absolute Reality out of which all beings and things arise. The term yogī was not popular. True, some found their apotheosis by yoga. In everyday parlance, a yogī was a dangerous spellcaster, a profit-hungry sorcerer, a person intent on obsessing people, corpses and animals. At its lowest level, the word yogī denoted a cheat, an imposter, an exploiter of superstition and, in some cases, a travelling beggar-ascetic working as a spy. Yogīs were feared and despised. This began to change around the third or fourth century CE, when an obscure bunch of yogīs began to explore meditation, introversion and asceticism as a road to liberation and magical power. These meditative yogīs made their first appearances in the work of Patañjali and in the *Bhagavad Gītā*. At the same time, passages on meditative yoga were introduced into the *Mahābhārata* (for example in the *Book of Peace*) and into several much older *Upanisads*. Thanks to such forgeries, the freshly founded meditative yogīs could predate their movement by centuries. It was only thanks to linguistic analysis that the recent origin of these insertions was detected (White, 2011:89). Meditative yoga proved to be a fine idea. It was, however, a fringe phenomena and a long way from the spiritual exercises that constitute modern yoga. The earliest mediators did not perform a series of gymnastic drills, nor were they interested in purifying their bowels or greeting the sun. The only postures that aroused their interest were those for meditation. Just like the wicked yogīs, the meditative yogīs were detested. Plenty of people were aware that they, too, were keen on magic. The Jainas disapproved of magic and meditation, and so did the early Buddhists. It took centuries before Buddhists were ready to integrate introverted, contemplative visualisations in their program.

Around the same time Tantra may have started. The word Tantra means basically a weaving, texture, textile, a treatise, text and science. Sad to say, none of the early Tantras survived. We have long lists of early literature, but except for a few quotations, the early material is gone. As a result, scholars tend to date Tantra as they like. Some suspect the early centuries of

Figure 71 Siṁhamukhā.

the common era, others propose the sixth or seventh century, when tiny pieces of textual evidence start to appear. Others prefer the eighth to eleventh centuries, when Tantra became a major phenomenon and we have plenty of literary evidence. However Tantra may have started, the mainstream of Hindu society was against it. 'Tantra' is not a useful term. The very people who started the movement did not call themselves tantrics. They named themselves after their guru lineages, their deities or according to the traditions they had been initiated into. Many of them learned from several gurus. Nor did they have a common teaching, piece of sacred writ or dogma. Nowadays, people usually associate Tantra with something called **'sacred sex'** or 'divine eroticism'. It's misleading. Yes, some tantrics, Hindu and Buddhists, integrated ritual lovemaking in specific initiations, rituals and offering ceremonies. On the whole, such rites were a rare and special event. When you read tantric literature you will soon realise that its authors had lots of other things on their mind. Lovemaking was generally kept in the background; in many classical Tantras the topic is hardly mentioned or completely ignored. For Hindu tantrics, sexual ritual, if performed at all, was a practice for heroic practitioners, i.e. the middle level, where people are not quite beginners anymore, but are still disturbed by instincts, obsessions and fears. Think of love and death, the two strongest drives that are wired in our subconscious processes. Sexual union and dramatic, morbid rituals were designed to destroy bondage to uncontrollable lust, attachment, disgust, dread and horror. Only when the 'heroic stage' had been mastered, tantric practitioners were free to transcend the basic limitations. Most tantric authors did not make a great thing out of it. Living a spiritual life where everything and every act was participation in the Absolute was much more important to them. Sure, love-play was divine. But so was the morning bath, cleaning the teeth, having a meal, emptying bowels, reading, studying, making music and so on. Their vision was continuous. Very generally speaking, for Hindu tantrics, the main thing was the realisation that every phenomenon and every being is a manifestation of the divine encountering the divine. For Buddhists, it was the awareness that every sensation and being is simply mind, and ultimately void and meaningless. Ritual love making was a fringe phenomenon. The majority of tantric practitioners only enjoyed 'sacred sex' in a symbolic way, in the imagination, or were directly opposed to such practices.

It's a surprise: the modern concept of Tantra was largely created by disapproving outsiders. Much of this happened in the nineteenth century, when colonial officers, missionaries and Hindu reformers used 'Tantra' as a blanket term for religious practices which they neither understood nor approved of. By that time, most of the lineages of Hindu Tantra had long died out. Where and when Tantra appeared is a topic that has not been explored sufficiently. I doubt it ever will be. But we can be sure that meditative Yoga and Tantra had a lot in common. In many texts, titles like yogī (*uniter, yoker, sorcerer*), siddha (*perfected one*), nātha (*lord*) or their female equivalents yoginī and siddhā are pretty much interchangeable. None of them is clearly defined. Let us start with something tangible.

In northern India a fascinating fusion happened. By the beginning of the Pāla Period (ca. 800-1200) a number of 'tantric' lineages had developed which belonged, very loosely speaking, to some forms of Hinduism and Buddhism. There were also minor tantric movements in Jainism and Islam, but we can ignore them here. It was not always easy to tell the difference. Numerous tantric Buddhist deities were based on Hindu deities: witness figures like Cakrasaṁvara and Hevajra, both clearly Buddhist versions of Śiva. Mahākāla, a dark Śiva with bulging eyes, adorned with serpents, is popular both in Hindu and Buddhist Tantra. Bhairava (the Terrible One), a north Indian deity, was claimed as a form of Śiva by several Hindu systems, and accepted as a fierce Buddha by the tantric Buddhists. Not that Śiva was officially acknowledged by the Buddhists. One of his most popular appearances, Īśvara (*Lord*) was officially turned into delusive demon king. Śiva's early Vedic form, Rudra, was acknowledged as a demonic half-god. Examples like these abound. One of the most fascinating is the creation of the Buddhist bodhisattva Avalokiteśvara by the fusion of all major Hindu gods. The Buddhists decided he should look just like Śiva and be worshipped in a heap of cow dung with a traditional Hindu fire-sacrifice (Chün-Fang Yü, 2001:37-59). Some north Indian Buddhists tried to integrate ancient Vedic gods like Agni, Indra and Varuṇa, while others saw them as dangerous competition to their creed. Early Buddhists did much to integrate the gods Indra and Brahmā in their cult; in later periods, the popularity of these deities waned and Indra was replaced by the very similar Vajrapāṇi, the Holder of the Lightning Bolt. Around the tenth century, so much Hindu and Buddhist Tantra had fused that some ritual practices, meditations, mantras and iconography were amazingly similar. This was especially the case in the Yoginī cults.

Two major differences have to be emphasised. Buddhism, tantric or not, remained focused on the figure of the historical Buddha (the *Enlightened, Liberated One*) Śākyamuni (*Seer of the Śākya Clan*), who founded the movement in the late sixth, as tradition claims, or the middle of the fourth century BCE (as some modern scholars suspect). From the start, Śākyamuni was venerated both as a human being and as a supreme cosmic presence, an immortal teacher of gods and men, superior to the universe. He was also considered as one of many Buddhas who appear through all ages and all worlds. Most Hindu tantrics ignored the Buddha, except for a fringe of Vaiṣṇava tantrics, who considered him an incarnation of their favourite god Viṣṇu. The teachings of the historical Buddha underwent plenty of changes. To simplify things a lot (and ignore a wide range of different Buddhist movements) first there was Hīnayāna Buddhism (the *Small*, or *Inferior Vehicle*), with the emphasis on individual liberation. Some branches gradually transformed into Mahāyāna (*Great Vehicle*) Buddhism, with its emphasis on compassion, and the duty of enlightened beings to remain in the world of appearances to liberate others. A brilliant, synopsis of this transformation was given by Th. Stcherbatsky (quoted by Snellgrove, 2004:27):

When we see an atheistic, soul-denying philosophic teaching of a path to personal Final Deliverance consisting in an absolute extinction of life, and a simple worship of the memory of its human founder, when we see it superseded by a magnificent High Church with a Supreme God, surrounded by a numerous pantheon, and a host of Saints, a religion highly devotional, highly ceremonial and clerical, with an ideal of Universal Salvation of all living creatures, a salvation not in annihilation, but in eternal life, we are fully justified in maintaining that the history of religions has scarcely witnessed such a break between new and old within the pale of what nevertheless continued to claim common descent from the same religious founder.

In the process, Buddhism became a happier creed, and its followers gained popularity by founding hospitals, orphanages, schools, universities, by caring for the sick, the lonely and the poor. Thanks to these innovations, Mahāyāna Buddhism found a home in other countries. In India, it gained support from several kings and many merchants and became a major political influence.

Buddhist Tantra was developed around the eighth century by a minority movement of spiritual people who were dissatisfied with the standard Great Vehicle Buddhism. Many of them were directly opposed to monastic life and believed that liberation has to be found in daily life instead of a secluded cloister cell, shielded from the turmoil of the world by royal patronage, thick walls, like-minded colleagues and regular meals. They appreciated the fact that the monasteries housed large libraries but bemoaned the power politics, regulations, hierarchies and the way the upper ranks sought wealth and favours from the kings. Many disenchanted Buddhists left their monasteries and sought enlightenment on the road. Some advanced adepts worked for a living, married, raised a family and declared that this is the proper way of performing spiritual discipline. They encountered Hindu tantrics who were doing the same thing, and were at odds with the suffocating social stratification of Hindu society. In Hindu Tantra, a number of traditions can be loosely classed as Śākta. The word derives from Śakti, meaning power and energy, a concept including the idea of matter and form. Śakti is usually personified as a goddess. Very generally speaking, the Śāktas believed that supreme power and divinity appears as one or several goddesses. Some (though not all) of these worshippers believed that the divine manifests in everything, and that women are embodiments of one or several goddess/es. In some of these movements, women played a major role. Many pursued the tantric path on their own initiative. Some joined groups that organised themselves in family structures, some achieved high degrees of insight and magical skill and became gurus. However, while Buddhist Tantra is complicated, Hindu Tantra is even harder to understand. There were so many groups, lineages, householders and people living near sacred places or travelling on the long, dusty road, that generalisations are pitifully inadequate. We even encounter small kingdoms governed by kings who practised tantric rituals. Some of the new, tantric Buddhists realised that they had been missing quite a lot. In traditional Great Vehicle Buddhism, women had a part, but it was an inferior one. Long ago, the historical Buddha had assumed that birth as a woman was due to bad Karman, i.e. sins and crimes committed in another life. It was only thanks to the cunning arguments of his favourite disciple Ānanda, and the generous patronage of several noble ladies, that he allowed women to participate in his movement at all. Nevertheless, he commanded that monks and nuns should not speak with each other except in dire emergencies, and remarked that the introduction of women in the religious community is like mildew destroying a field, and would destroy Buddhism five hundred years before its time. In his opinion, the highest ranking nun was inferior to the youngest and most stupid monk. Women, he insisted, were not allowed to criticise men for any reason whatever. Nor did he approve of friendship, let alone marriage or sexual relationships. Monks and nuns were to lead a celibate life; sexual activity was punished with temporary expulsion from the community. His supporters agreed. Women, so it was taught, were incapable of attaining Buddha nature. No matter how far they advanced: to reach enlightenment they had to be reborn as a man. This mood became a little less oppressive when Mahāyāna Buddhism began: women were still inferior, but it was good form to be compassionate with them. Nevertheless, most scriptures insisted that in the eastern and western Buddha paradises, everybody was male.

Among the Hindu Śākta tantrics, the Buddhists met an astonishing number of highly competent women who believed in attaining liberation within this lifetime. They encountered loving couples and realised that lovemaking and living in a relationship have a valid place in spiritual development. Of course the degree of involvement differed. For some people a few sexual unions under strictly controlled ritual conditions sufficed. Others married their spiritual companions and spent their lives together. Some happy couples lived on the road, near sacred places or in forest communities; others became householders, got a job and raised children. Still others remained chaste but recommended ritual sex with a spirit partner. When a high level of competence was achieved, life with a human partner of equal aptitude was recommended. Such differences are discussed at length in *Kālī Kaula*. In their quest to experience Buddha nature in all beings, many north Indian tantric Buddhists came to see their partner as a manifestation of the absolute. Like their Hindu colleagues, those tantric Buddhists incorporated a range of goddesses in their meditations. Some even approved of Buddhas who could appear in either sex. And they embraced deities that were popular among their Hindu colleagues: fierce, terrifying beings, adorned with skulls and bones, blood drinkers, ecstatic dancers on the cremation places. Bones were an essential part of both creeds. While traditional Hindus abhor anything related to death, and risk losing their

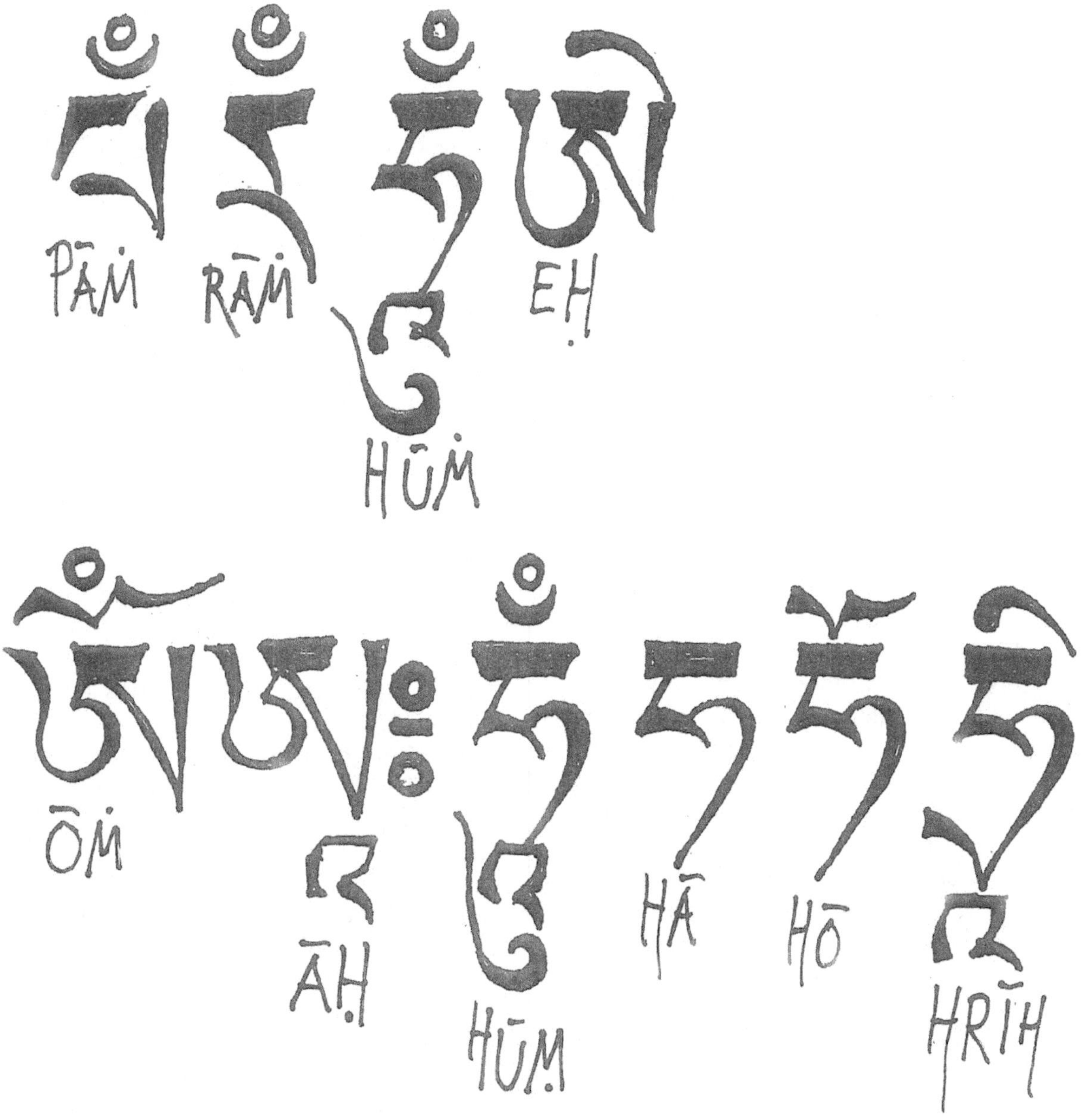

Figure 72 Mantras, written in the Tibetan alphabet.

class-status when touching corpses, the earliest known Hindu tantrics, the Kāpālikas, made a point of eating and drinking from a skull-cup. Buddhists were not limited by such taboos: indeed Śākyamuni asked his students to observe death and decay to destroy their bondage to the body. Unlike Hindus, Buddhists loved to collect relics, especially bones, and erected stupas to venerate them. While we encounter quite a few bone utensils in left-hand-path Hindu Tantra, we see a lot more among tantric Buddhists. All of these were radically new approaches to spiritual experience. Another great innovation was the integration of personal deities. For Hindus, having one or several personal deities was natural. For Buddhists tantrics, personal deities were, of course, illusionary, deluding and dangerous, but also quite useful. Buddhist tantrics learned that personal deities can appear in many forms, some of them with animal attributes. Some were charming and some terrifying, and all were basically a product of the mind. This mind and all its emanations (such as the self) are an illusion. It did not stop them from worshipping and visualising their personal deities.

In classical Buddhist thought, everything, including you and me, is appearance, hence void of reality. Realising this voidness is to find liberation. It leaves you, freshly enlightened, with the insight that the whole world and you are simply delusions. It's not a good start if you want to enjoy life. At this point tantric Buddhism diverged from many Hindu tantric teachings. The Krama tantrics of Kashmir, for instance, were convinced that everything is real. Even illusions are valid. Consciousness (call it Brahman, Parāśakti, Śiva, Kālī or whatever) is real, and everything shares this reality, no matter how distorted or bizarre it may be. In their opinion, the divine consciousness is Absolute Reality. It appears in all forms and energies, as people, gods, animals, plants, elements, things etc. to enjoy itself. In Hindu Tantra, everything is imbued with the divine awareness, which is the self of every being and everything. As consciousness is real, nothing truly illusionary can appear out of it. In Buddhist Tantra, your self is also illusory.

It sounds so simple but isn't. In advanced tantric Buddhism, distinctions are not real. You may think that you can tell a difference, but all you do is juggle words. *Form is voidness and voidness is form.* True enough. But how can you tell them apart? The same insight appears in advanced Krama, Kaula, Trika Tantra: Śiva (formless consciousness) and Śakti (consciousness in power, matter and form) cannot be told apart. And where it comes to the highest realms of Buddhist liberation, Buddhism itself, the Buddha, and the concepts of liberation and enlightenment are empty of reality. When you go over the top, words cease to make it.

So much for the basics. But allow me a note of caution: the meeting of Hindu and Buddhist Tantric traditions is a difficult and badly documented subject. Some adepts obviously got on with each other, and exchanged rituals, deities, visualisations, mantras, gestures and a lot of practices related to ritual lovemaking and elixir consummation. They met at similar places for meditation and ceremony: at the wayside, in ruined houses, abandoned temples, sacred groves, places of pilgrimage, dangerous forests, mountains, riversides and on burning grounds. But just as some tantric experts adopted a syncretistic attitude, others did not. There were plenty of Buddhist saints who abhorred sexual rites, praised celibacy and condemned Hindu deities as evil and delusive. And there were Hindu tantrics who thought that the Buddhas teachings were just too narrow-minded, misogynistic and oppressive. They disliked the old Buddhist addiction to pain and suffering, and the many famous Buddhist saints who cheerfully encouraged self-mutilation. But what can I say? It is absurd to distinguish between 'Hindu Tantra' and 'Buddhist Tantra', as there were loads of disagreeing lineages and inspired geniuses in each group. We simply lack the material to generalise. But whatever we might argue, in northern India some amazing religious innovations happened.

One of them was the appearance of a large number of highly qualified spiritual

Buddhist women, who were called by such names as yoginīs, ḍākinīs, khecarīs, dhātvīśvarīs etc. These women were tantric practitioners and many of them were highly competent. They developed an amazing range of sophisticated spiritual practices, rituals, meditations and teachings, and they initiated a lot of travelling tantrics. Among themselves they held spiritual feasts. They congregated in some desolate place, meditated, danced, drank, sang spontaneous enlightenment songs and had a happy barbecue. Usually, outsiders and men were not admitted, unless they happened to be advanced Hindu or Buddhist tantrics. Some of these women were praised, eulogised and worshipped by their male students, just as male gurus were. Miranda Shaw demonstrated that about half of the founding fathers of Tibetan Buddhism were taught and initiated by these amazing women. The other half, I am sure you guessed, preferred male company, belonged to the stubborn celibate school and had a low opinion of women. It made north Indian Buddhism one of the most controversial spiritual traditions. But it was not to last forever. When wave after wave of Muslims invaded India, Buddhism was an easy target. Many orthodox Buddhists had organised themselves in monasteries. These monasteries were centres of power and wealth, but they also functioned as universities and kept large libraries. The invading Muslims burned the libraries and made the nuns and monks flee for their lives. By the thirteenth century, Buddhism had almost disappeared in India. It survived in China, Mongolia, Korea, Japan, South-east Asia and of course in the Himalayas. When we want to understand tantric north Indian Buddhism, we have to consult the documents that were kept and copied in other countries.

One of them is Tibet. Thanks to plenty of publicity, most people of our time see Tibetan Buddhism as the main branch of Buddhism. It isn't. There are far more Buddhists in China, Japan, Korea, Vietnam, Cambodia, Nepal, Sri Lanka Thailand and so on. All of these countries developed their own brand of Buddhism centuries before Tibet, and a bit later, Mongolia, caught on. The reason is simple: Tibet was a poor, inaccessible and illiterate country torn by internal wars. The travelling Buddhist missionaries had one hell of a time getting a foothold in Tibet: the country was dedicated to old shamanic traditions. Tibet, as a state, was founded thanks to the violent campaigns of Namri Songsten (c. 560-620). His son, the official founder of the Tibetan state, Songsten Gampo (c. 617-650) allegedly made an effort to introduce Buddhism into his freshly conquered realm. It was not much of an effort, but it allowed the king to marry the Chinese princess Wen Cheng, who arrived with a retinue of Chinese scholars, doctors, scientists, craftsmen, artists and a selection of competent Buddhist monks. From this point on, the newly founded Tibet acquired a written history. The Chinese introduced a form of Mahāyāna Chan Buddhism, plus Chinese art, astrology, medicine, technology and maths but didn't get much further. But while the king tolerated Buddhism, most of the aristocracy preferred the ancestral worship of their countrymen. The first attempt to turn Tibet into a Buddhist nation failed miserably. For several centuries, Buddhism and shamanism were at odds. The kings and the aristocrats fought it out with each other, and the religious differences were a constant source of harassment and persecution. Eventually, pioneering tantric Buddhists travelled to Tibet. One of them was the famous Padmasambhava. According to his hagiography, he had spent 3600 years (and many lifetimes) teaching Buddhism in India. Thanks to the invitation of King Trisong Detsen, he travelled to Tibet, where he remained for 55.5 years. During this time he mastered numerous local spirits and deities and turned them into protectors of Buddhism. He encouraged the building of the remarkable Samye monastery and translated hundreds of Indian texts. Finally, after his patron had been assassinated, Padmasambhava packed his gear, said goodbye to the new king, mounted his white horse (or lion) and rode to the country of man-eating rākṣasa monsters, where he spread Buddhism and lived a long and happy life. Before he left he made several lengthy, pessimistic and remarkably accurate prophecies outlining the corruption, violence, power-abuse and warfare within Buddhism, starting with the next decades and continuing over five thousand years. The country of the rākṣasas, he declared, had more need of his services. It was a good choice. Under King Langdarma (838-842) Buddhism was violently prohibited. The purge was savage but short, as a Buddhist assassinated the king with a well-aimed arrow. Tibetan Buddhism had a slow return around the end of the ninth century, when the next wave of north Indian Buddhists began preaching in what was to them, an exceptionally violent and primitive country. By the tenth century the faith began to gain power, wealth and influence. In the process, it acquired many of the characteristics that the free thinking tantric Buddhists of north India utterly disliked. Tibetan Buddhism had been influenced by the Chinese Buddhists and a distorted form of Zoroastrianism, but by then it had received much from north Indian tantric Buddhists. Their new faith was not a single, unified phenomenon. Most of its founding fathers had widely different ideas. They all based their teachings on the real and imaginary sayings of the historical Buddha, but encouraged different rituals, meditations and methods of attainment. As a result, a number of schools developed, which competed and fought with each other. Those who enjoyed the protection of the kings and aristocracy built monasteries and developed a strictly hierarchical way of life. As Buddhism turned into the state religion of Tibet, it lost many of its free and creative approaches. To be sure, the old manuscripts were preserved and occasionally studied by advanced scholars. For the common population, most of them being serfs and slaves owned by the monasteries, spiritual freedom was not an option. As everyone knew, the poor and unfree were being punished for bad deeds in past lives. The monks who owned, used, exploited and rented them to other monasteries were doing them a favour, as only suffering and pain can redress the wrongs of Karma and ensure a better rebirth. By contrast, birth in a rich family indicated good deeds in past lives, and a high spiritual potential. In feudal Tibet most people were desperately poor, illiterate, suffered from malnutrition and were forbidden access to doctors. It was definitely not the sort of society the north Indian tantric Buddhists had hoped for.

Among many ideas and faiths, some north Indian Buddhists introduced the worship of Siṁhamukhā to Nepal, Tibet and Mongolia, Yunnan and Sichuan. Today, Siṁhamukhā has her greatest popularity among the members of Tibet's earliest Buddhist movement, the Nyingma (Rnying ma). But she is also well-liked by some adherents of the Sakya (Sa skya) school. It may sound like much but isn't. The cult of Siṁhamukhā was never a major affair. There are numerous lineages and sects in Tibetan Buddhism which are much better represented, more powerful, wealthy and popular. The Buddhism that came to Tibet underwent a lot of dramatic changes. What is called Tibetan Buddhism today is basically the faith of the Gelugpa (Dge lugs) sect, the yellow hats, a fundamentalist movement that attempted to purify Buddhism of superstitions, perversions and delusions. Compared to the other sects, the Gelugpas are latecomers. Their historical founder was Tsong kha pa (1357-1419), a charismatic reformer, who felt that the Buddhism of Tibet had been corrupted by all sorts of stuff he violently disagreed with. He encouraged the creation of huge monasteries, and enforced a strict discipline based on chastity and absolute obedience. Tsong kha pa wrote at length regarding the sexual rituals and the hidden meanings of the north Indian manuals. He declared that it was almost impossible to reach the highest attainment without having experienced sexual and spiritual union. This attainment, however, was limited to the very top of the clergy. For himself, Tsong kha pa chose a life of chastity. He declared that he felt compassion for the many chaste monks and that he would perform the sexual rites and attain perfection in the state after his death. (Shaw, 1994: 146-152). Thanks to his insistence, sexual ritual is a secret affair limited to a very few. In many ways, Tsong kha pa was an unusual thinker. He invented the Tulku system, based on the idea that a semi-divine leader is reborn time and time again. This leader, who may or may not be understood as a saint, the deity Chenrezig, the bodhisattva Avalokiteśvara, or the Buddha, is known in Tibet as Gyalwa Rinpoche or Kyabngon Rinpoche, and as the 'Dalai Lama' among foreigners. It was a clever move. Tsong kha pa did not want a society where spiritual and worldly government were inherited. Thanks to the Tulku system, the Gelugpas were free to select a new leader (i.e. discover the reincarnated Dalai Lama) among the c.25 noble clans or, if need be, even among common people. It was the beginning of a fierce power struggle. For one thing, the Gelugpas tried to suppress the other and earlier faiths. For another, they struggled to control the kings, until, with a bit of luck, they were able to dominate them. In the process, Tibet became a feudal theocracy. To achieve their aims, Gelugpas often cooperated with Mongolian regents and the Chinese emperors. The fourth Dalai Lama (1589-1617) waged war against the Karmapa order. The fifth Dalai Lama enlisted Mongolian troops to gain absolute dominance in 1620. 1642 he turned Tibet into a vassal state of the central Asian Manchus. After the Manchus conquered China and set themselves up as emperors, Tibet was back to where it had been most of the time: a remote province of the Chinese empire. The Gelugpas promised that each new Dalai Lama has to be authorised by the Chinese emperor. They supported the emperors and the emperors supported them, if necessary, with armies. Life in old Tibet was anything but peaceful, and many Dalai Lamas were assassinated before they were old enough to rule. Though the Gelugpas did not eliminate the elder Buddhist schools, they certainly reduced their power, influence and wealth. Compared to the earlier traditions, the Gelugpas encouraged fundamentalism, chastity, monastic discipline and intellectual studies. As a result, many north Indian Buddhists traditions were transformed or replaced. To this day, the great libraries contain documents on early rituals and meditations, but these teachings are neither popular nor widely known. One of the things the Gelugpas emphasised was the **inferiority of women**. In their system, men teach men, and women as initiators, gurus or spirit companions are rarely needed. True, there are nuns, but their status, among the clergy and in the general opinion of society, is very low. In the Tibetan language, the word for 'woman' (kiemen or kye-min) means *'of inferior birth'*. To this day, Tibetan women are taught to repeat the mantra *May I reject a feminine body and be reborn in a male one* (Grunfeld, 1987:17-20). Unlike all other Buddhist traditions, the Tibetans do not allow women to reach a rank beyond that of a novice. While monks received an education, nuns remained illiterate and subservient. A proverb states: *If you want to be a servant, make your son a monk; if you want a servant, make your daughter a nun.* (Lopez, 2007:21). As in the earliest days of Buddhism, no matter how exalted the spiritual attainments of a woman may be, she is still subservient to the youngest and most stupid monk. And there were plenty of those around. In a similar mood, the achievements of female Buddhists were obscured. Without being aware of it, modern Tibetan Buddhists use a wide range of techniques that were developed by women of India. One example is the remarkable Siddharājñī, who developed several meditative rituals that have become basic training in Himalayan Buddhism. However, her system is usually referred to with an abbreviated title; the female ending and the identity of its founding lady have been deleted (Shaw, 1994:122). Nor are many people aware that the famous fasting ritual, frequently performed by laypeople and clergy, was the creation of a brilliant lady called Bhikṣuṇī Lakṣmī.

When you look at the Gelugpa transmission you witness huge, powerful monasteries. Tibetan monasteries are a long way from European ones, they are almost small cities. They had their own banks, police force, prisons, hostels, manufactories, shops, doctors, fields, cattle, slaves, and they owned roughly sixty percent of the population as serfs. In these monasteries, regulations differed depending on Karman, i.e. family background and wealth. In Gelugpa monasteries, poor monks led a life of celibate obedience. Rich monks, from the aristocratic families, brought along their own slaves and could do pretty much as they liked. Some of them experimented with the old sexual rituals, but they certainly did not boast about it. Nor could they live in a relationship with a spiritually competent woman, let alone lead a family life. Mr. Smileyface, the current Dalai Lama, is proud of his celibacy and boasts that he has never been in love. For decades feminists have criticised him for his refusal to raise the influence and status of women in his system. Tibet under Gelugpa control has the most retarded form of Buddhism on this planet.

By now you might wonder how all this history relates to a simple easygoing nude girl with a predator mask. When we want to explore the cult of Siṁhamukhā, we have to keep in mind that the goddess meant a lot of different things to her followers through the ages. She had a meaning to orthodox right-hand-path Hindu tantrics (who believed in chastity and well-behaved gods) that differed from unorthodox left-hand-path Hindu tantrics believing in sex, dramatic rites, meditations on cremation ground and drugged states of ecstasy. Her meaning to tantric Buddhists was just as varied: the ones who were initiated by lovemaking and enlightened women disagreed strongly with monks and nuns living in separate monasteries, subscribing to obedience, chastity, greed and power politics. Add to them the Buddhists of Nepal, Bhutan, Mongolia, Yunnan and Sichuan (who were strongly influenced by Daoist, Confucian and local shamanic teachings) and you arrive in a state of perfect confusion. Keep your mind open. Siṁhamukhā is a lot of different things to many people, and we won't get anywhere when we insist on generalisations.

It would be nice to know more. Someone introduced a lion-headed goddess from somewhere, and she is amazingly close to Lamaštu. It seems to have happened around the eighth century. The earliest surviving references to the goddess class her as one of the Eight Gaurīs. Originally, Gaurī (the *Bright, Shining, Luminous, Golden One*) is a friendly form of Śiva's wife Pārvatī (*Daughter of the Mountains*), a goddess who is famed for her skill in yoga and Tantra. The Buddhists borrowed the term from the Hindus, but they invested it with new meaning. The Eight Gaurīs are a bunch of nude women with animal heads, who were obviously based on the animal-headed, winged, celestial Yogīnīs worshipped in some Kula and Kaula cults. The Saṁskṛta term **Siṁhamukhā**, popular among tantric Indians and Nepalese, can be understood in several ways. Siṁha is the lion. The word is pronounced like 'Sing-ha'. Mukha is the face, head, mouth, opening, entrance, direction, beginning, method, peak, and means. If we limit our understanding to *'lion-head'* we miss a lot. In Tibet, her name appears as **Senge Dang Ma,** in Mongolia she is **Sendunme** and in Chinese **Shi Mian Fo Mu** (*Lion-Faced Buddha Mother*). Among the Buddhist tantrics of Nepal, Tibet, Mongolia and China, Siṁhamukhā has a medium to high status. Some consider her a ḍākinī, hence a goddess, a celestial traveller, a witch, a divine initiatrix, a protector of the divine order. She is praised as the *Queen of the Night*, as the *Spontaneously Blissful One*, as *She Who Destroys the Delusive Ego*. In Buddhist terminology, the female ḍākinī and the male ḍāka are advanced spiritual beings, deities travelling freely through the skies, unbound by limits of thought and activity. The terms also signify advanced tantric adepts; they can be understood as counterparts of the Hindu terms virā (*heroine*) and vira (*hero*): middle-level tantric ritualists who do their ritual with dangerous deities, in jungles, cremations grounds and terrifying settings, who incorporate dramatic, necrophilic and sexual elements in their rites. Others rank Siṁhamukhā as a female Buddha: one who has attained full enlightenment, and resides in the world of appearances to liberate all sentient creatures. The Chinese title hints that she is superior to Buddha. The historical Buddha would have disapproved. Siṁhamukhā is also known as a *fully enlightened being*, a *bestower of bliss* and a *manifestation of the pure mind: Every experience is bliss*. And while her rituals in Hindu Tantra have long faded into oblivion, her cult remains alive in the Buddhism of Nepal, Mongolia, Tibet and China. Here, we have to thank Padmasambhava. The Tibetans respectfully call him Guru Rinpoche. You met him earlier. He was an enthusiastic tantric who learned from many teachers, including several female gurus, and spent plenty of time meditating on the cremation grounds of Uḍḍiyāna. The place had an enormous reputation, as it was a hot-spot of left-hand path Tantra and famous for its assemblies of highly initiated women. Today he is venerated as one of the first pioneers of Tibetan Buddhism, and his teachings, as recorded by the princess Yeshe Tsogyal (who was his student and friend) are among the core teachings of the early Tibetan tradition, and the Nyingma sect. Sadly, this is not the place to look into the numerous texts which he composed, or which were ascribed to him centuries later. Padmasambhava had a very intimate relationship to Siṁhamukhā, who was one of his favourite deities. Possibly she was his personal deity, and his alternative self, and we can be sure that he frequently visualised her, transformed into her, and enlightened other beings while radiating her awareness. Thanks to his influence, Siṁhamukhā became the major defender of Samye monastery. Some even claim that he was an incarnation of the lion-headed goddess.

We meet Siṁhamukhā in all sorts of places. Here are two examples. The first comes close to the Lady of the Beasts theme (Shaw, 1994:120).

The spiritual attainments of famous female guru Siddharājñī were praised by her colleague Tiphupa:

...Having met the Ḍākinī Siṁhamukhā,

Heard the secret explanation of supreme bliss, and

Perfected the four spiritual activities,

You are called Cremation-Ground-Corpse-eater,

Surrounded by many bears, jackals, tigers, and

Leopards – emanations of ḍākinīs.

One highly advanced tantric adept of north India called herself ḍākinī Lion Face. Shaw (1994:92) quotes from her enlightenment poetry:

KYE-HO! Wonderful!

You may say 'existence', but you can't grasp it!

You may say 'nonexistence', but many things appear!

It is beyond the sky of 'existence' and 'non-existence'-

I know it but cannot point to it!

It leads us to the practice of Siṁhamukhā meditation in Tibetan Buddhism. As you will soon see, the frame is tantric Buddhism, but the contents are largely borrowed from Hindu Tantra.

Let's explore one routine. The following core ritual is based on several sources. I began with the first part of a ritual schedule compiled and translated by Lama Kunga Thartse Rinpoche, which is largely based on the collection *Grub thabs Kun btus*, Vol. NYA (VIII), folios 293-296, published by the Ewam Choden Tibetan Buddhist Centre, which is available online. It's a beautiful but rather short ritual. Plenty of important details are missing, or left to the oral instructions of a competent guru. Luckily, Tibetan sādhanas tend to be rather repetitive. Many ritual procedures, invocations, mantras etc. for Siṁhamukhā are also used for other deities, Buddhas and gurus. I added relevant material from *Guide to Dakiniland* by Geshe Kelsang Gyatso and from several rituals in Lopez 2007, guidance to the yi dam meditation, as allegedly taught by Padmasambhava and recorded by Princess Yeshe Tsogyal, plus commentaries based on material explored in *Kālī Kaula*, White's *Kiss of the Yoginī*, Abhinavagupta's chapter on the Kula ritual (Dupuche 2006), Pandey's study on Abhinavagupta and the brilliant books of Miranda Shaw (1994 & 2007). The spelling of mantras was and is a problem. To this day, there is no satisfying or generally accepted transcription of Tibetan words. Nor do Tibetans use a reliable transcription of Saṁskṛta. Each author uses her or his own idiosyncratic spelling, which made it difficult to trace some Indian terms. Like everybody else, Tibetan sages tend to interpret mantras pretty much as they like. It may be a long way from their Indian originals. Tibetan yoga, if we can call it that, involves plenty of syncretistic material. Almost every ritual and visualisation practice of Tibet was imported from India; indeed, only one ritual system, the gChöd ceremony of dismemberment and self-sacrifice, was invented by a Tibetan, the exceptional nun Machig Labdrön, who blended shamanic methods with Buddhist ideology. In consequence, the ritual you are about to explore is a wild and astonishingly creative blend of material. Some of it comes from the old Vedic period, dating from before 1000 BCE. Other items stem from the Upaniṣadic period, the period of early Buddhism, and the period between c. 400-800 when the freshly invented meditative yoga blended with the newly created tantric systems. Finally, some methods were formulated when tantric Buddhism was gradually intruding into Tibet. I have tried to keep things simple, and where I failed, I am sure the goddess can step in and sort you out.

For a start, as in most Buddhist rituals, you **take refuge**. One typical formula, preceding all further ritual is:

May I and all sentient beings,

until we attain enlightenment,

find refuge in the Buddha, the Dharma and the Sangha.

In tantric Buddhism, **Buddha** (the Enlightened One, the One Who is Awake) is not necessarily the human being who founded the cult. Tantric Buddhism acknowledges a vast amount of Buddhas in many times and worlds and insists that Buddha nature, i.e. the true stratum of enlightenment, resides in all beings. Hence, the term Buddha is not confined to a specific and historical person. Potentially it may be you, me and everyone. **Dharma** is a basic concept of ancient Indian thought, signifying truth, rightness, law, cosmic order, social order, the stratified society, the class-laws and customs, and of course Dharma was also personified as a god. In Buddhism, Dharma is basically the true teachings of Buddha. The word can also signify phenomena, qualities, thoughts and specific characteristics. **Sangha** is the Buddhist assembly, i.e. a group of ordained Buddhists. Together, these elements form the **Three Precious Ones**.

The next lines **generate bodhicitta** (the urge to gain enlightenment for the benefit of all sentient beings. Also, in Dzogchen teachings, the quality of awareness of the woken spirit that indwells all beings):

Due to the practices I perform and all other perfections,

may I become a Buddha for the benefit of all sentient beings.

One of the functions of this introduction is to distance the practice from many tantric rites of sorcery. The introduction makes the ritual an altruistic offering: you will benefit by being the goddess, she will benefit from being you, and what both of you gain is a blessing to all beings.

Next, you **arise as the ḍākinī Siṁhamukhā**. This line in Lama Kunga Thartse Rinpoche's program stands pretty much alone. I wonder what went missing. Usually, when you want to arise as a deity, you have to do some identification and visualisation (i.e. playacting) first. These meditative practices, however, appear much later in the ritual. Maybe at this stage your identification is still a little vague. Perhaps you simply remember your identity with the goddess. It should suffice for a start.

The next part of the ritual is based on advanced mantra yoga. It all starts with the **heart** (hṛdaya). The heart is an essential symbol of ancient Indian religion. You encounter it in the earliest *Vedas*: the heart is awareness, consciousness, the source of all perception, all thought, feeling and sensation. The heart creates, maintains and destroys the cosmos. In the much later Hindu Tantra systems of Kashmir, the heart is the pulsation of awareness: it opens and closes like a lotus blossom, it is the union of Śiva as formless consciousness and Śakti as consciousness in form, matter and energy. The heart is full of everything you experience and it is empty as it is consciousness beyond form. The love-play of Śiva and Śakti in the central void is the core of all realities. In tantric twilight language, the heart is also the crossroads of consciousness where worlds meet; it is the burning ground, where forms and delusions go up in flames of liberation. In the teachings of north Indian Buddhist Tantra, the heart has a similar function. It is the sheer, unformed bliss of awareness, the clear light of the void. A very similar use of the term 'heart' appears in Daoism.

In your heart is a **lotus blossom** and a **sun-maṇḍala** radiant with a dark blue **Hūṁ**. A maṇḍala is more than a pretty ornamental picture. The word means circle, sphere, globe; it represents the universe and the realm of a divine king, who imbues the country with spiritual blessings by residing in its centre and by making the annual journey along the borders. A similar maṇḍala surrounds the tantric practitioner, and if the king errs or fails, the power of his realm may pass to the tantric adept. By extension, a maṇḍala is a magical diagram. This diagram can be amazingly complex. In some meditations, the maṇḍala appears as a vast, multi-layered temple-palace full of spiritual beings and energies. Likewise, a maṇḍala can be the human body and the world. The sun-maṇḍala represents, among many other things, the solar system. It is also the fertile ground on which you stand so that you may develop from the generation stage and the completion stage as you attain the full blessings of the goddess. In our case it's the Lion-headed One; in other rituals, the sun maṇḍala is the place where you attain union with Vajrayoginī, her realm, her impeccable body, her faultless mind and her perfect joy.

The mantra **Hūṁ** is one of the earliest words of power and appears in the texts of the Vedic period. Hindus and Buddhists venerated this sound vibration and wrote so much about its symbolism that I would not dream of giving a summary. Maybe it will suffice that Hūṁ is a dark, fierce and dangerous vibration. Kālī roars this mantra as she devours demons on the battlefield. Sorcerers drone it in spells of destruction; yogīs use it to dissolve illusions and painful attachments. It is the flicker of the funeral fires and their dark, oily smoke; it is the sound that regenerates the universe. As usual in Tibetan Buddhism, a mantra is imagined as sound but also in letters of the Tibetan alphabet. In our meditation, the mantra is dark but radiates a bright light. The rays flame through your body and beyond: they summon the Buddhas and bodhisattvas. Hence, the mantra acts as a link connecting you to all spiritual beings: as the light shines forth, you recognise the net of blissful enlightenment spanning space and time. It connects you to a community of joyous entities and reminds you that in your spiritual practice, you are never quite alone. It may take a while until they have assembled around you and/or your visualisation stabilises.

The next stage is called the **eight blissful offerings**.

When you have guests, you make them comfortable. This is the essence of tantric offerings. They are not sacrifices, in that you don't have to give anything up or punish yourself by doing without. The eight blissful offerings are presented as a series of mantras.

The mantras follow a simple formula: **Oṁ vajra X Āḥ Hūṁ**. For X you insert the name of the offering, and visualise it clearly and with deep emotion. As you will notice, this exercise will involve several inner senses.

A note on pronunciation. The phoneme **ṁ** is not pronounced like the letter m but comes closer to NG or MG. It is vibrated in a nasal way and should be felt in the nose. The letter **ḥ** is not an h but a strongly aspirated h: the sound of exhalation. It is counted as a vowel and represents the Great Emission. The letter **ś** is a soft sh, the letter **ṣ** a sharp sh. When the letter h is added to a consonant, it often indicates aspiration. You say Budd-ha, Siṁ-ha muk-ha, etc. A bar above a vowel means that it is pronounced twice as long.

Oṁ, an essential mantra of the Vedic period, is the basic vibration that starts the offering. In Hinduism, it is the sound that gives divine energy and sentience to the gods and the true sound of Brahman (*extension*), the all-self, all-consciousness, the formless, nameless, indescribable ground of all being: Absolute Reality. In Buddhism, the interpretation shifted somewhat, depending on the tradition, as the historical Buddha did not approve of self or absolute reality, let alone the reality of an all-self. **Vajra** is originally a thunderbolt, the sacred weapon of Indra, the Vedic king of the gods. The early Buddhists tried to integrate Indra in their faith, the later ones did not like Indra much, but they incorporated his divine weapon in their rituals. In their understanding, a vajra is also a diamond, representing clear light, absolute purity and indestructibility. The symbol was so important that one of the 'schools' of tantric Buddhism, Vajrayāna (the *Diamond Vehicle*) is named after it. For similar reasons, Siṁhamukhā was praised as a *glorious adamantine goddess.* **Āḥ** represents pure and sacred speech. In Vedic lore, the world was created by speech: the goddess Vac/Vak (related to our word 'voice') made the universe appear by speaking (*Ṛg Veda* X,125). It turned her into the first Indian goddess who was venerated as an all-encompassing divine principle. As in the religions of Mesopotamia and the Near East, to speak or sing is to make. In consequence, Hindu lore makes a lot out of the sound patterns of speech, the phonemes of the Devanāgarī 'alphabet' and the 'Mothers' (the sound matrixes). Though the historical Buddha was not very interested in the topic, the tantric Buddhists certainly were. They assimilated a lot of Hindu sound-lore, but adjusted the phonemes and their meanings according to their own insights. When a mantra begins with Oṁ and ends with Hūṁ, the former seed syllable has the function of generating attention, saying praise and creating something new, while the latter finishes things by dissolution and liberation. Recite:

Oṁ vajra arghaṁ Āḥ Hūṁ.

Oṁ vajra pādyaṁ Āḥ Hūṁ.

Oṁ vajra puṣpe Āḥ Hūṁ.

Oṁ vajra dhūpe Āḥ Hūṁ.

Oṁ vajra āloke Āḥ Hūṁ.

Oṁ vajra gandhe Āḥ Hūṁ.

Oṁ vajra naividyā Āḥ Hūṁ.

Oṁ vajra śabda Āḥ Hūṁ.

These mantras are accompanied with visualisation, deep feelings and mudrās, a word that means, in this context, hand gestures. We are making an eightfold offering. The goddess is invited by imagination, feelings, gesture and sound, and is offered all sorts of things that please her and the devotee. In her joy is your joy and vice versa. But what exactly do these offerings mean?

The following interpretation is biassed. You will encounter concepts and practices that belong to that dreaded tantric tradition, the so-called left-hand path. They are not, however, accepted by all tantric Buddhists. Nowadays, I am sorry to say, the majority is strictly against them. This was not the case when this ritual was invented.

The first offering is **arghaṁ**. The word comes from argha, a vessel. In normal mainstream Tibetan Buddhist ritual, argha is simply an offering of water to drink and wash the mouth out. In tantric twilight language, it is a vessel full of elixir. Depending on the level of insight a practitioner may have attained, the elixir is either the essence of immortality or, for advanced tantrics, the mixture of sexual secretions. In this sense, argha is the combination of sperm and female juices, especially menstrual blood. This is the major sacrament of many cults of the left-hand path; it is the Kula-fluid, the clan essence, which passes from the lower mouth (the vulva) to the mouths of the devotee. Systems like Kula, Kaula and Krama are based on an oral transmission. The same went for several minor branches of North Indian Buddhism. Indian physicians proposed that sperm and menstrual blood form the embryo; hence they are the very stuff of life. To some (but not all) tantric practitioners, there could be no substance more fully imbued with vitality. In the classic Kula ritual, as elaborated by Abhinavagupta, the three essentials are argha, dhīpa and a skull. Sadly, we are talking about beliefs

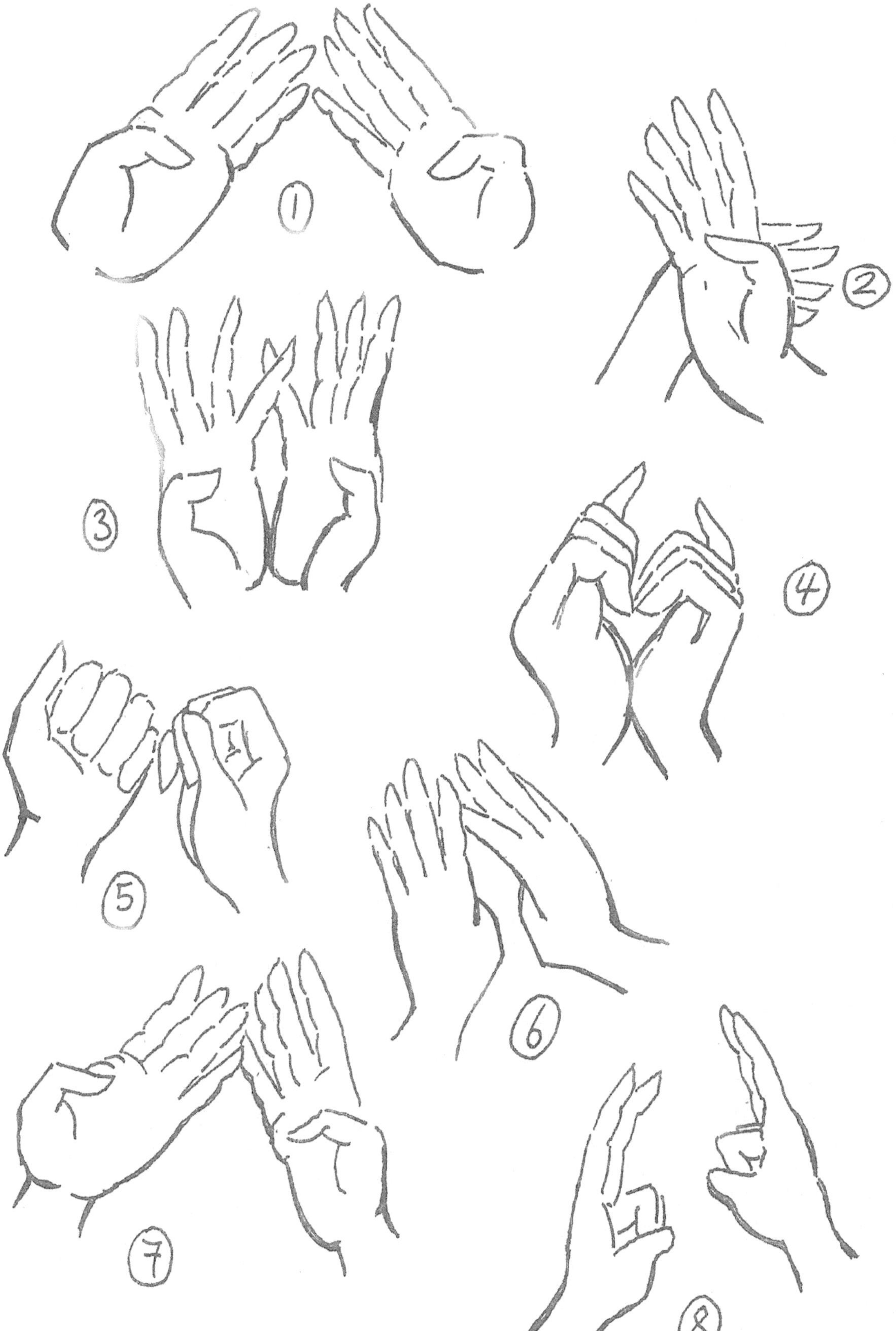

Figure 73 Mudrās of the eight offerings.

entertained by a minority. In general Hindu belief, the mixture of sperm and menstrual blood is lethally polluting; one more reason why some tantric systems considered it the holiest elixir and kept their worship secret.

The second offering is **pādyaṁ**. Pādya is the water to wash the feet, an important offering for a guest who has just arrived. 'Feet' in India religion, are among the most important symbols. They may represent the earthing and the manifestation of a deity. Footprints of the Buddha are known from many Buddhists sites, and deeply venerated. Likewise, women in northern and eastern India paint the footprints of the house- or village goddess on the floor to invite her. In religious literature, we keep reading that people, sages, gods and anyone else worships the feet of a deity. In everyday life, Indians touch the feet of their superiors. It's a traditional form of greeting. And as they reach down, it is good form for the superiors to prevent them from doing so. In a ritual context, people touch the feet of a guru or a statue. In tantric twilight language, the feet are a metaphor for the two cakras at the perineum and the genitals: to worship the feet of a goddess means to meditate on these regions.

The third offering is **puṣpe**. The word comes from puṣpa, meaning a flower, blossom, a topaz, gallant gestures and, in twilight language, menstrual blood.

The fourth offering is **dhūpe**. The word means incense.

The fifth offering is **āloke**. It comes from āloka, meaning light, lamp and to look at something. An alternative word in Tibetan ritual is **dīwe**, a corrupted version of the Saṁskṛta word **dīpa**, meaning a lamp or light. Dīpa lamps are among the three essential items of the Kula ritual. Usually, they had a conical shape. They were made of an edible paste, and after the ritual they could be consumed. In Kula traditions, they represented human flesh. The symbolism implied that body allows the light to shine forth. To consume the lamp after the ritual means that the worshipper identifies with those deities who nourish themselves with the essences of body and light. Kula, Kaula and Krama teachings emphasise the importance of body for spiritual progress, while orthodox Hindu lore, based on the *Upaniṣads*, would rather neglect, ignore or forget the body.

The sixth offering is **gandhe**. It means scent and perfume. This offering is subtle and refers to fluids, essential oils and sweet smelling substances, such as sandalwood and spices.

The seventh offering is **naividyā**. Naivedya is a food offering: the deity is a cherished guest, and of course we offer food to the visitor. What food are we talking about? Normal Tibetan Buddhist ritual proposes that naivedya are cakes. That's nice, simple and harmless. In classic left-hand-path ritual, two essential foods are meat (māṁsa) and a dish of spicy kidney beans (mudrā), which was considered an aphrodisiac. Or maybe it was an unknown drug. Meat is a tricky subject. In Tantra, plenty of deities eat meat. Goddesses in particular are fond of flesh and blood offerings. Orthodox Hindus are not supposed to eat meat. Many Hindu tantrics make an exception: when the heroic practitioners celebrate the old feast of three Ms (meat, wine and lovemaking) or the newer version with five Ms (meat, wine, beans, fish and lovemaking), meat is a sacrament. It is, however, not supposed to be an everyday food. Theoretically, Buddhism does not approve of meat offerings. It's a new idea; according to some legends, Buddha himself died after eating contaminated pork. Well, a monk has to accept whatever is put in the collection bowl. An alternate reading claims that he died after eating 'pig's food' which might be a euphemism for some mushrooms. Whatever it may have been, Buddhism adopted the dogma that animals are not to be killed. Most monks led a vegetarian life. They did not suffer from a lack of vitamin B^{12}, as so many vegetarians and vegans in the industrial countries do, as their vegetables came straight from fields which were fertilised with human and animal dung, and were not washed thoroughly (or at all). The human body only needs 1-3 micrograms of that vitamin a day. B^{12} is generated in the intestines, but can only be absorbed orally. That's why gorillas regularly eat their dung, while our closer relations, chimpanzees and bonobos, frequently eat eggs, insects, larvae, rodents, bushbabies, young monkeys and apes to gain B^{12}. Many strict Hindus and Buddhists lacked animal fats, substances that were an essential part of human and pre-human diets for several million years. Thanks to them, we evolved the large and fatty brains that make us think we are so clever. In India, poor people could rarely afford milk and butter. In Tibet, most serfs subsisted on a grain diet, and suffered from malnutrition. So did the poor monks, and every ascetic dwelling in the forest or mountain solitude. People on a low-fat diet tend to suffer from depression and have a higher suicide rate. They are also inclined to sudden shifts between blissful awareness and fits of anger and hate. Such outbursts of temper are typical for forest dwelling ascetics (the *Mahābhārata* is full of psychotic saints) and we observe the same among ascetic Buddhists. Lack of animal fats and proteins screws up the serotonin and dopamine production and from time to time the blood sugar level drops dramatically. It makes life rather exciting. Indian and Tibetan doctors soon discovered the root of the problem. High-ranking, aristocratic Buddhists like the Dalai Lama eat meat for medical reasons. In China, numerous Buddhists call themselves vegetarians as they eat no meat on the first and last day of each month and Buddhist holidays. In between, they eat what they like. In many Buddhist temples, meat dishes are readily available. Monks who do hard work or learn martial arts are expected to eat meat. And while Tibetan religion officially frowns on meat-eating, its symbolism is full of flesh, fat and blood.

The eighth offering is **śabda**. The word means sound, vibration and word: the essential forces that made the universe appear. In early Indian thought, śabda is the most primal appearance of anything. Remember Brahman (*extension*), the formless, indefinable all consciousness. When Brahman desires (kāma) to manifest, its first emanation is śabda. Hence, the vibration form is the highest manifestation of awareness. One level below we encounter sound, and below that the other senses. For this reason, the mantra body of a deity is far more perfect than the anthropomorphic form.

In ritual, śabda is represented by song, prayer and musical instruments. Our guest, the lion-headed goddess is welcomed with praise, song and music. Let me add that music is not an extra to ritual, but essential. Many tantric adepts were excellent musicians who saw their art as a form of devotion. There is nothing like music to change consciousness and make the feelings that inspire a ritual with joy and devotion. Indian tantrics often played flutes and lutes. In Tibet, things were slightly more primitive. Once the Buddhists had become the major religious force, drumming was severely punished, as it was associated with shamanism. Likewise, the monks tried to prohibit folk music, as it was dealing with profane topics and sentiments. The Buddhists of Tibet and Bhutan developed a fine dramatic ritual music but never went far beyond the basic needs of monastic chanting. It was only after a long period of suppression that a form of Buddhist drumming was grudgingly allowed.

When you consider the eight offerings, you can see them as an assembly (kula) of things and experiences that delight deity and worshipper. In one sense, the two have a meal and celebration. In another sense, the two are one. Texts ascribed to Padmasambhava keep insisting that the yi dam (personal, tutelary deity/ Buddha/ spiritual being) is a manifestation of your mind. That's part of the truth. Another part is that you are a manifestation of your mind. A third idea is that we are not discussing your mind or anyone's mind, but mind, awareness, consciousness itself. The next idea, popular in Buddhism but not accepted by most Hindu Tantrics, is that the personal deity, you and consciousness itself are illusions. The rite of offering is an illusionary but relevant gesture between illusionary but rather lively participants. You can also understand the offerings in a sequence leading from the physical (drinking water or the mixture of menstrual blood and sperm) to the transcendent (pure vibration). Some Tibetan adepts interpret them exactly in this way. They imagine that the vessel-elixir is transformed into foot-washing water. This turns into blossom, which becomes incense, which is transformed into light. Radiance transforms into scent, scent into the food offering and finally nourishment becomes pure vibration. When you consider these offerings in a dualist way you imagine one thing/pleasure transforming into another. In a non-dualist interpretation, the offerings are not only physical objects and experiences: they are the world, the divine and they are especially you. The sequence is important, but so is the formless essence, pure consciousness, that makes the sequence relevant. The main thing that changes is awareness. This is the supreme offering, and the reason why one way or another, the eight sacrifices appear in so many north Indian Buddhist meditations and rituals.

The next operation is the **prayer of seven limbs**. The first limb is **offering**. As the host, you show your generosity, and the happiness of your guest is your delight. The second limb is **prostration**, a gesture indicating your humility, and the awareness that the deity you entertain is in many respects superior to your limited human understanding. The other five limbs appear in the following declaration:

With this offering I declare the wrong deeds I have committed in all times,

and I am glad to rejoice in the virtues of all beings.

May you (the goddess, the divine assembly, the Buddhas etc.) ***remain until Saṁsāra*** (the coming and going of the phenomenal world, the cycle of birth, life, death and rebirth) ***ceases,***

and turn the wheel of Dharma for all beings.

I dedicate all of my virtues to the great enlightenment of all sentient beings.

Then you declare the **four immeasurable principles**:

May all sentient beings enjoy happiness and its source.

May all sentient beings be free from suffering and its source.

May all sentient beings be one with sorrowless joy.

May all sentient beings dwell in serenity, free of biassed opinions, free from greed and anger.

This prayer celebrates much of what differs between the stern renouncing Buddhism of the centuries BCE and the much later teachings of Tantric Buddhism. The historical Buddha was not a very cheerful person. He grew up in wealth and left his home, treasures, concubines, wife and son, as he felt disgusted with the world, all delusive pleasures and himself. Whatever exists, he realised, is subject to ignorance, delusion, disease, old age and death. He founded his system on some of the elder *Upaniṣads* with their pessimistic, unhappy mood. Several early *Upaniṣads* proposed that there is too much pain and suffering in this world, and that the way to find release is to shed all attachments, to drop out of society and to merge with the formless, inexplicable Brahman. To dissolve in Brahman, you have to give up every blinding, shackling delusion that binds you to the world, society, social class, property, family and flesh. The body itself was occasionally described as a disgusting thing, full of excrement and vile organs, and Buddha very much agreed with this. But Buddha did not simply preach the old lore of the *Upaniṣads*. He combined it with another philosophical school of his period (Anātman), teaching that the self is not provable and hence, does not exist. In Buddha's lore, a personal self and an all-self are simply illusions. When you shed these delusions, you find release in nirvāṇa, a term that meant total cessation and dissolution to the early Buddhists. It sounds a little pessimistic. However, several Buddhists protest that nirvāṇa is a positive goal, and hence, all effort to attain it is a happy, joyous road to release. That may be the case when we consider Mahāyāna Buddhism. However, in early Buddhist lore, the world of experience consists of misery (duḥka), it is transient (anitya) and self-less (anātman). The fact that life can and should be enjoyed does not appear. If the historical Buddha had been a more balanced character he might have mentioned joy from time to time. He could have laughed and told his followers to dance and sing. And he would have appreciated the beauty and perfection of the world, instead of fleeing it.

In Mahāyāna Buddhism, the interpretation changed a lot. We encounter texts that state that neither nirvāṇa nor saṁsāra have any reality, or can be understood within the realm of conceptual thoughts (see Nāgārjuna's hymn in Snellgrove, 2004:83). The difference between them cannot be told. Likewise, the Buddha was neither real nor unreal, neither transient nor eternal, nor even comprehensible. It opened the door to a massive reinterpretation and to such movements as Chan (Zen) that use paradox to shock the mind into enlightenment. The world, the self, Buddha, the community, ethics, logic, reason and every other concept and thing lost their relevance. Mahāyāna Buddhism had discovered nihilism.

Many centuries later, some tantric Buddhists cultivated a much happier mood. In their teaching, nirvāṇa is not simply total cessation but the bliss of liberation. Better still: this bliss can be experienced while you are still alive. In their opinion, the way to enlightenment does not end as soon as you can drop out, die and disappear, but requires you to reincarnate again and again, to help all sentient beings to attain Buddhahood. That's an enormously long time. In this setting, joy is a major force and to some it is the essence of freedom. And while Buddhas first Noble Truth emphasises that *all existence is* or *contains suffering*, in our ritual joy comes first, then we are reminded of suffering and return to joy again.

The next step is called **self-generation**.

The mantra is:

Oṁ svabhāva śuddha sarva Dharma svabhāva śuddho Hāṁ.

All Things become void.

Voidness, for Hindus and Buddhists is not a lack, an absence or a vacuum. The concept of voidness is explained in several ways. When Buddhists chant that *Form is Voidness and Voidness is Form*, they do not mean that form is empty, but that it lacks endurance, reality and significance. Another interpretation claims that the void is not an absence but sheer formless consciousness, inexplicable, ready to assume any shape. This consciousness is void as it has no substance, qualities or duration. While Europeans tend to imagine the void dark, people from Asia believe the void is full of clear light. This light is awareness: it is void as it is beyond all objects to be aware of.

In this stage of our ritual, you cease thinking, remembering, being and conceptualising. Thoughts and sensations come and go; you allow them to drift by without interfering or judgement. One way to do so is to shift your awareness in-between the outer and the inner world. You do not focus your mind on the things that happen around you, you do not focus your mind on the sensations within you; in fact, you entertain an awareness that is without a focus, without judgement, intent, polarity, likes and dislikes. You are aware, but you are not aware of anything specific. Relax. Calm down. Confusion gives way to quiet clarity, as you cease doing and not-doing. The same meditation is cultivated in Daoism, Inner Alchemy (neidan) and in several Chinese martial arts, like Bagua Zhang, where it is called the primal state of wuji (without extremes).

When you have experienced some of this formless, indefinable awareness, if only for a moment, you visualise and imagine that the mantra syllable **Pāṁ** ascends. It assumes the shape of a lotus, that perfect, untaintable flower arising from the primordial dark mud, growing through murky waters, rearing its bud high into the fresh air and unfolding like perfection itself. The lotus, in this context, is not simply a water-plant but functions much like the axis mundi, the shamanic trees that connect underworld, world and heaven. The mantra Pāṁ comes from the Saṁskṛta word padmā, meaning the lotus and the lotus goddess. Out of the lotus appears the seed syllable **Rāṁ**, the ancient mantra of fire. It glows up and starts to shine like the sun. Above the sun appears a third seed syllable, **Hūṁ**. It shines forth from above and turns the ritual space into the Vajra-ground, surrounded by a Vajra-fence. Above you a Vajra-baldachin appears. All of them are imbued by the fire of sheer wisdom. Wisdom, in Tantric Buddhism, is a feminine quality. In Hindu Tantra, the gods represent wisdom, and are usually passive or lie like corpses, motionless and stiff, under their beloved partners. Their consorts, the goddesses, usually represent power, energy, activity and form, all of them summarised as Śakti. Hence, the gods are passive, formless awareness and their consorts the mind-blowing complexity of all that is. The Tantric Buddhists turned it the other way around. Their gods, bodhisattvas and Buddhas are power, action, energy and substance, while their consorts are passive wisdom companions who serenely smile while their men muck around.

By now you should be sitting in a **Vajra-tent**, bathed in diamond radiance. In its centre is the seed syllable **Ēḥ**: it radiates and pulsates, and turns into the dark blue dharmakara (*principle of Dharma*).

The dharmakara contains a lotus and a sun maṇḍala. Your mind assumes the vibration and shape of the seed syllable **Hūṁ**. Though dark blue, it radiates in all directions, and its rays destroy the demons of delusion. It also attracts the blissful radiance of all virtues, powers and achievements of the ḍākas and ḍākinīs. Out of this Hūṁ **you arise as Siṁhamukhā**.

Now the question appears: how come you turn into the shape of the goddess at this point, when you did so at the very beginning of the rite? The answer might be that you achieve full identity only after the ritual has progressed for a while, and under the 'laboratory conditions' of the sacred vajra ground, fence, canopy and tent. All of them help you to intensify your imagination and amplify the contact. They also shield the people around you from the fierceness of the lion-headed goddess.

The Tibetans class Siṁhamukhā as a **'wrathful deity'**. That, to be sure, is far too simple.

Siṁhamukhā is one of the goddesses who seem savage to the uninitiated: before you can come close to her, you have to awaken your heroic nature, transcend the terrifying imagery and realise her liberating and loving essence. Some people call Siṁhamukhā an angry goddess. True enough, there are plenty of reasons to be angry with society and the way human beings are destroying and exploiting each other, and the world. In Tibet, Mongolia and China, some of the people use her sādhana to understand and transcend their own anger. As you merge with her your human anger turns into a divine emotion. It has relevance, occasion and use, but it is not the same thing as your everyday wrath. Divine anger is not personal. It has no place for egoistic desire, hurt pride or a craving for revenge. In short, it is not about you. But there is more to explore. Siṁhamukhā is also joyous and overwhelmingly ecstatic. If we obsess ourselves with wrathful emotions we are missing a lot. Siṁhamukhā is the ability to feel fully. Full joy, full love, divine bliss, ecstatic inspirations and honest wrath come in one package. They are only possible to a person who has not hardened her or his heart to all the toxins of the world. And this is a real challenge. To go through life, and to keep our peace of mind, we ignore a lot of pain, cruelty and exploitation. We shield ourselves by putting up walls between us and them, by accepting reduced expectations, by making cynical jokes and by feeling less than we could. Siṁhamukhā changes this. She makes us feel real emotions, real empathy, real experience. It can be a world-shaking, terrifying thing. And she makes us experience joy. There is hope and beauty everywhere. In the forest, in the country, in the heart of the city. Nature extends everywhere. There is so much to enjoy. Heaven and earth, life and death, coming and going. This moment. The sheer bliss of being. The continuity of awareness. The overwhelming relief when rain falls, seeds sprout and blossoms open. The true insight that things are working out, one way or another; not as you would imagine or comprehend, but as they should, life after life, as well as they can be. Her emotions are full. They can be gentle or fierce, happy and horrible. Siṁhamukhā teaches wisdom. Her wisdom means learning when to feel fully and when to dissociate emotions. The world's pain, while true and relevant, is also counterproductive. People tend to find what they are looking for. If you look for problems, you will find them. If you look for pain your life will become painful. If you dedicate yourself to finding perfection, lots of good things happen. That's why so many tantrics assumed that, essentially, the world is perfect. These people were not stupid. They were aware that, no matter whether the world is real or illusion, suffering exists. Many of them did their best to support and encourage their fellow beings. If you want to do something positive and worthwhile for the world and its beings, you have to draw a line and keep your spirits high and your emotions happy. Except for those moments when divine wrath is really useful. Anger should not be a state but a useful mask. Assume it to teach a lesson. Drop it to feel good again. Like Lamaštu, Siṁhamukhā can fill your heart with scorching flame and icy cool. As you embrace her and she embraces you, you come to understand the essence of the play.

Here are the **sādhana (meditation, visualisation, worship) instructions for Siṁhamukhā**:

There are two basic approaches to the visualisation of personal deities. The first is slow and steady. You spend many days in front of a picture of your deity. You examine every detail, for hours and hours on end. Then you close your eyes, relax into a peaceful trance state, and build up the vision in full detail. Some start at the feet and slowly develop the vision to the head. Some start at the eyes and go down. Some make the figure huge, so it seems more impressive. Use all senses, sight, hearing, feeling, scent and taste to amplify the vision. And some visualise the surroundings in full detail before they call on the deity to manifest. All of these belong to the slow approach. The fast approach is to do all of these things at once. It is only recommended for people with exceptionally vivid imagination and plenty of spiritual training. When your deity is almost as real as a person, you may do ritual together. At some time you will merge. It's only natural, for, as Padmasambhava explained, you are one awareness anyway. Whether you meditate on a single deity or an assembly of them makes no difference. Eventually, you will be able to spend much of your life being that deity.

Imagine that your body is dark blue or black. Unlike many gods and spiritual beings, you have only one face. It means that you have realised that all experiences, beings and things arise from One Consciousness. In your face are three eyes. They represent past, present and future, or sun, moon and fire/lotus. Your mouth is wide open, your teeth are bared, and the tongue curls upward. Your throat is adorned with a garland of fifty skulls that whip around as you dance on a lotus. They represent, among many other things, the (roughly) fifty phonemes of the Devanāgarī script. It means that you have all sounds and vibrations at your throat, and their power to create, maintain, and dissolve the world of appearances. These sounds are also breaths, so the fifty skulls are also the fifty vitalising winds. Serpents adorn your nude body. You drone a fierce Hūṁ, threatening the stability of the multiverses and hold in your right hand a broad bladed flaying knife with a vajra handle, and in your left hand a polished skullcup filled with bright fresh blood, representing the blissful light of the void. All of these attributes belong to Kālī; hence, for the north Indian Hindu tantrics, Siṁhamukhā is a leonine form of Kālī, the Black Goddess of transcendence, liberation and time. Siṁhamukhā's cult, however, is much better documented among the north Indian tantric Buddhists. They introduced a few minor variations. Kālī usually wields a sword and/or cleaver (plus club, trident-spear, bow, arrows, shield and a lot of similar objects). The Buddhist Siṁhamukhā holds a flaying knife, a broad-bladed item that symbolises cutting and scraping away layer after layer of delusion, until nought remains. Your knife is not a cleaver used for butchering animals or a sword for fighting: it is a trusty cutting tool that severs the bonds of self-deception, and frees you from unnecessary attachments. You have a shiny mane coloured brightly yellow, orange, amber and red; your wild hair streams in all directions. Unlike the Indians, the people of Tibet, Nepal, China and Mongolia had no direct experience of lions. They knew these animals only from highly fantastic paintings and assumed that male and female lions have a colourful mane. In their opinion, lions are the fiercest creatures on earth. They represent royalty and the Command of Heaven. Against your left shoulder leans a khatanga/khatvāṇga trident-spear. This is a lance representing Heruka, a Buddhist version of Śiva, and in its ornate symbolism the 64 deities of Heruka's assembly are represented. The wooden part is octagonal in diameter, representing the eight burning grounds, where tantric adepts find liberation. At the bottom of the khatvāṇga is a vajra representing the protection of Heruka's circle. The top of the khatvāṇga is elaborately ornamented: it shows a vase, the sign of Heruka's heavenly home, the eight deities of the Dharma wheel, a blue head represents sixteen deities of the heart cakra, a red head represents sixteen deities of the cakra of speech and a white head: the sixteen deities of the body cakra. The khatvāṇga may be topped by a three- or five-pronged vajra. There may be streamers of silk attached to it, and on one strip, tiny emblems of Śiva's hourglass-shaped ḍamaru drum, a bell and a triple banner. There is a crown with five skulls on top of your head, and jewels of wisdom are dangling from them. In Tibetan Buddhism, they represent the five Buddha families. In a tantric Hindu interpretation, they are the five faces of Śiva, the five senses, the five crudest Tattvas (*'categories'*: earth, water, fire, air and spirit) and the five directions. You may wear a tiger skin around your waist (like Śiva and Tārā do) and a pretty skirt made of bones, such as the Yoginīs used to wear for their tantric feasts in North India. Alternatively, you may have a cape made of elephant hide or of human skin hanging loosely around your shoulders. You stand on your left leg in a dancing posture, and hold your right leg, bent, in the air, signifying that you are between manifestation and transcendence. Your whole aura is ablaze with the force of wisdom.

So much for the general meditation-instructions. In practice, several such descriptions exist and they vary in some details. Chinese and Mongolian Buddhists, for instance, like to visualise the head of Siṁhamukhā white with a pretty red nose and golden eyebrows. Some of her dance masks show plenty of sharp teeth and a happy smile.

Apart from a lotus, you are standing on one or several figures. When it is only one, the figure is a bearded man called Māra. When Buddha really had had enough of trying to find liberation, he sat down under a tree and vowed not to leave before he had attained enlightenment. As he sat in the heat, refusing all drink and food, all sorts of temptations arose. One of the worst was Māra. The name means death, destruction, pestilence, but it can also mean love, lust and desire. Some aspects of Māra overlap with the ancient Hindu god of desire and lust, Kāma. He is one of the first deities: without the force of desire, the universe would never have been started at all. The Hindu sages were aware that Kāma is a primal force. They were not really happy about the way desire leads to disappointment, bondage and all sorts of silly events, but at least they acknowledged that desire has an essential part in the divine play. In fact, like the Greek Aphrodite, desire, lust and love are older than most gods. For the Buddhists, Kāma is the epitome of all evil, as he keeps us, the gods and every being attached to the world of desires and appearances. Māra, in Buddhist thought, is a figure much like the devil. In early Buddhist literature, Māra is often accompanied by his sexy daughters. But there is also a Hindu goddess called Mārī, whose name means death, destruction, pestilence, and who is imagined riding a donkey. She has a strong cult in Bengal and East India, where she is sometimes identified with Manasā, the goddess of snakes who embodies sheer consciousness (manas). In Buddhist thought, the Māras are not divine but a bunch of terrifying devils. As Siṁhamukhā, you stand on them. I am sure this signifies that you have conquered them. In a Hindu

Tantric setting, it could also mean that you derive your power and authorisation from them (that's why Kālī stands on Śiva, Śiva stands on a dwarf representing the human ego, and several fierce goddesses sit on sofas made out of the corpses of the major gods). So when you are Siṁhamukhā, you stand on one or several Māras, or their corpses.

How about company? Some tantrics visualise an entire assembly of Mothers and attendants near Siṁhamukhā. An option appears in Mongolian Buddhism, where the goddess is a favourite character of the mask dances. In these elaborate ceremonies, she appears together with a bear-headed and a tiger-headed goddess. She also has a husband: Otshirvani, also pronounced Djagnadorje (Sanskrit: Vajrapāṇi, Tibetan: Phjag-na-rdo-rdje, *'He Who Holds the Thunderbolt'*). He has a terrifying face with huge eyes and teeth and wields a formidable vajra. His mask and clothes are usually bright sky-blue. In Mongolian belief, these four deities banish evil influences and encourage peace between nations (Forman & Rintschen, 1967:78-83).

The next variable is the setting. One popular meditation instruction claims that the goddess dances on a lotus blossom arising from a cosmic skull bowl. This bowl is so vast that it encompasses everything. It is full of rich, red blood and in its centre is an island of fat. As you guessed, blood and fat, red and white, represent menstrual blood and sperm.

In the centre of an ocean of blood and fat

is the spontaneously wise ḍākinī.

Playfully dancing amidst appearances and emptiness,

here in her pure mansion, the world of ordinary appearances. (Shaw, 2007: 420).

But there is a deeper layer to the symbolism. The skull cup represents the skull. The imagery is very early: the first known tantrics were the Kāpālikas, the head-carriers (male: kapālin, female: kāpālinī). Very little reliable information survives regarding this sect. Some Kāpālikas ran small temples and shrines; the majority seem to have made a living as travelling ascetics. It was part of their vocation to carry a skullcup, preferably one from a brahmin, which was used to collect alms, such as food, meat and preferably alcoholic drinks. On a symbolic level, to feed from a skullcup is to feed from your brain, and from the secretions of your glands and the limbic system. Some Tantras relate that the real elixir is not alcohol or some drug but the fluid essences made up by the cakras in your head. The goddess is spontaneously wise: she is pure nature, she follows her nature, and her nature is yours. She is **playful**. Please think about this deeply. In Tantra, play is a serious matter. The gods play humans and humans play gods. They play together. The wordplay (līlā) also means 'to flirt' and describes 'the world as an appearance'. At this point western thought diverges from Asian insights. To people of the modern industrial world, play is not real. People make a distinction: play is fun and life is serious. For the gods, things are different. Gods rarely work, but they do like to enjoy themselves. What seems serious to humans is play to the gods. When gods play humans, they obsess and inspire them. This is absolutely serious, so serious that they make it a play and enjoy it. My question is: are you serious enough to laugh about the play? Are you aware that you are the actor, the playwright and the audience? Are you entertaining yourself?

The Blessing of the Fields of the Senses.

The next part of our ritual also appears in other ceremonies, such as the Guru Sādhana. There are **three cakras** illuminated by three syllables, which are otherwise known as the **Three Jewels**:

In your brow is a white **Oṁ**, in your throat a red **Āḥ** and in your heart a dark blue **Hūṁ**. The white **Oṁ** represents the body, hence the manifestation of all Buddhas. The red **Āḥ** is speech, the true vibration of all Buddhas. The dark blue **Hūṁ** is the mind/awareness of all Buddhas. Consider them as images for heaven, middle world and underworld.

Head, throat and heart: that covers the major cakras of many Tantric Buddhists. The Hindu cakras near the navel, genitals and perineum were frequently ignored. The light rays of the Hūṁ summon all the energies and emissions of the enlightened beings, the bodhisattvas and Buddhas and the khecaras and khecarīs, the void-travellers (a group of tantric adepts and deities promoted by the Krama, Kula and Trika tantricism of Kashmir). Feel the sheer intensity of **joy** surrounding and inspiring you. Flood yourself with joy. Feel it drench every inch of your body. Extend the joy to the limits of the cosmos, share it with all beings. Draw it into yourself, into the core of voidness, and allow it to spread out again, twice as strong. Joy expands, contracts and expands again. It blesses all beings of the ten thousand worlds. Consciousness encountering consciousness is bliss. The joy you share returns to you and goes out again: it pulsates like the heart, like a lotus blossom. This is what you give and receive from the world. Recite:

Oṁ vajra samadza dza Hūṁ Bāṁ Hōḥ.

Everything assumes a nature which is the synthesis of all objects of refuge.

Unite with all enlightened beings.

When you experience this, turn your attention to the **Huṁ** in your heart and allow the rays to shine to the five Buddha families. Recite:

Oṁ vajra samadza.

Make an offering to the five Buddha families. Recite:

Oṁ panja kula saparivāra argham,

pādyam, puṣpe, dhūpe, āloke, ghanda, naivedya,

śabda praticcha Svāhā.

Note that the last word of the spell, **Svāhā**, firmly roots the mantra in Hindu Śākta-Tantra. You met Svāhā in the last chapter. Svāhā is the wife of Agni, the ancient Vedic god of fire. He is the priest of the gods who dwells in every home, but it is her blessing that makes all fire offerings fruitful, for, unless her name is uttered at the end of a spell, the sacrifice is as weak as a serpent without poison. When a mantra ends with Svāhā, it has a female gender and is technically considered a Vidyā, a science, a mystery and a young woman.

Now you may ask for **initiation**. The initiation goes both ways: it is your initiation but it is also the initiation of the divine beings you have surrounded yourself with. The many enlightened beings grant the empowerment with the mantra:

Oṁ vajra bhāva abhiṣekata samaya Hūṁ.

Bhāva is an enormously complex term. It means birth, creation, becoming, being, state, condition, thing, behaviour, intent, urge, fate, love, magical power and lord. In Hinduism, the word is often used as a title of Śiva. **Abhiṣeka** is to sprinkle, anoint and bless an object or person with sacred fluids; the term also means the consecration of a king. **Samaya** is endurance, time, the ever-lasting, the teachings and regulations.

Now draw your attention into your heart (mind). Within your heart is the sun maṇḍala, and in its centre is the dark blue Hūṁ. Flames spread out of the seed syllable and empower the **Mantra of Siṁhamukhā**:

Āḥ ka

sa ma ra tsa

ṣa da ra sa

sa ma ra ya

Phaṭ!

They burn up the dead bodies of the Māras, i.e. your fears of death, and all your obsolete, useless desires. Another teaching claims that this mantra destroys hostile and malignant influences and conditions within and outside of us. They repel the enemies who torment the aspirant. This, I am happy to say, does not mean that you use the mantra against people who hurt or abuse you. Siṁhamukhā is not your personal henchwoman, nor is she interested in exacting revenge on your behalf. Before she searches for enemies in the outside world she goes for the enemies within you. When she has dealt with these, she may take care of the outsiders. Most of the time it won't be necessary. The last syllable, **Phaṭ**, is called the fierce mantra. The ph is not pronounced as an f but as a p-h, an aspirated p. The sound should be sharp and lethal. This mantra is often used for rites of exorcism. It can be uttered in an explosive way while your foot steps hard on the ground. In Hindu and Buddhist Tantra, Phaṭ is used to expel hostile influences.

This stage, the mantra recitation, is extended for as long as you like.

In the end you ask Siṁhamukhā to give you and all sentient beings the normal and unusual Siddhis (achievements, successes, talents, magical powers).

An alternative mantra of Siṁhamukhā is also popular in the cult of Vajrayoginī, where it is used to bless torma and tsog offerings:

Oṁ Āḥ Hūṁ Ḥā Ḥō Ḥrīḥ

We discussed **Oṁ Āḥ Hūṁ** earlier. The seed syllables **Ḥā Ḥō Ḥrīḥ** are very similar, as they represent **Oṁ Āḥ Hūṁ** on another level. These mantras transform the five offerings of meat and fluids into true nectar. In both cases, we meet the Vajra-body Buddha, the Vajra-speech Buddha and the Vajra-mind Buddha. Together, the three syllables clear the mind and purify the self. After them comes:

Ḥā, in Hindu Tantra, is a seed syllable of Śiva. It signifies exhalation, exhaustion, the Great Discharge and total release. Ḥā signifies freedom from bondage and symbolises total liberation. In Tibetan Buddhism, it is the essence of vajra-speech, and the letter is visualised red.

Ḥō is the sound of the goddess experiencing spontaneously arising bliss. In Tibetan Buddhism, it is the vibration of the vajra-body; the letter is imagined white. Siṁhamukhā may seem violent, especially to those who fear her or who crave violence themselves. But behind her terrifying mask there is the *spontaneously arising* ***pure bliss*** (Shaw, 2007: 420). This bliss is supreme as it arises without reason. Some may find this a little hard to comprehend. How can there be bliss without reason? I reply, why should bliss need a reason? Bliss is a condition of the self that recognises itself and the world as divine. Here on planet earth, bliss requires a lot of highly specific brain chemistry. People desire all sorts of things. When they believe they are going to get them, their glands release a lot of dopamine. It goes straight to the so-called pleasure centres of the brain and makes them feel as much delight as if they had really received them. As Wolfram Schultz demonstrated by measuring dopamine release in monkeys: the expectation of something good causes almost or as much happiness as the reality of it happening (Fries, 2012:43). It raises the famous Richard Bandler question: why wait? It's not the new car, lover, achievement or status that makes you feel happy, it's the dopamine cascade. And you can release the dopamine no matter whether you achieve your aims or not. All feelings are self-made. You can be, like Siṁhamukhā, happy with very little or entirely without a reason, and you can enjoy it anytime. Instead of a new car, you can be happy to see a great cloud. Instead of a new lover, you can delight in just being. Who says that great joy requires great effort? Joy is made within your nervous system. It's your choice how intensely you enjoy something. If you want a new house, you may be worrying, saving and toiling for years. Yet the dopamine exhilaration after moving in only works for two or three weeks; after that point, you are so used to your new home, that your happy feelings fade into normality. You may keep them up for a short while by making your friends admire you. That also disappears. Now a new house is a major effort. You can be just as happy with the things that happen anyway. A falling leaf, the green of freshly opening foliage, pebbles on the path, city lights, laughter of children and drizzle in your face: anything can be translated into sheer bliss. You can delight anytime and anywhere, and this is the essential secret, because happiness is self-made. Being happy for very little or no reason is a spiritual discipline that was highly valued by the advanced tantric traditions, like Krama, Kaula and Trika, of Kashmir. These adepts really knew what was going on. Abhinavagupta made much of this. In his opinion, a person who could not enjoy beauty in people, art, music or events was not competent for Tantra. These adepts knew that whenever they felt joy, so did the divine, the personal deities and the all-self. Instead of flowers they offered joy. Making happy feelings was an essential part of their spiritual discipline.

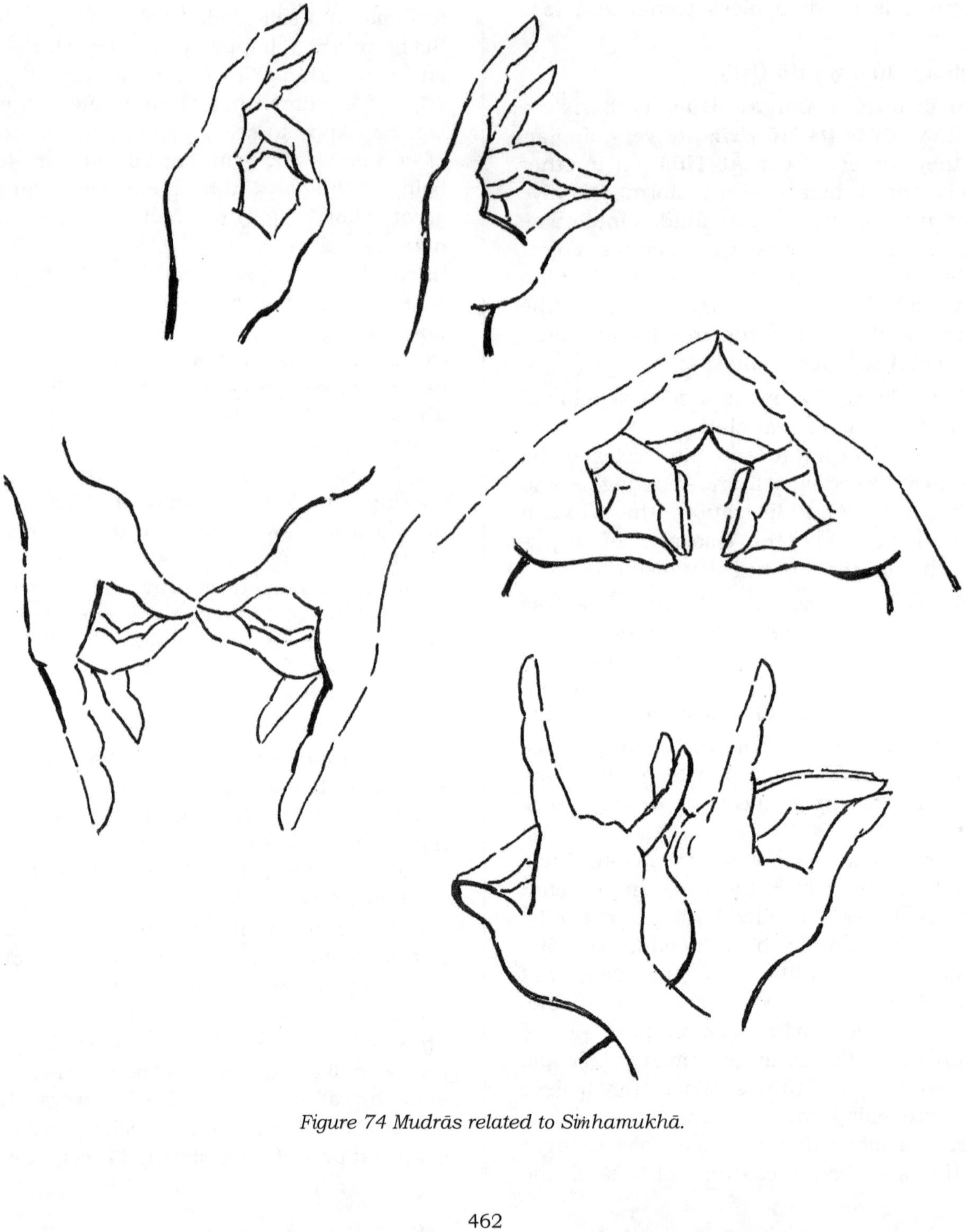

Figure 74 Mudrās related to Siṁhamukhā.

Ḥrīḥ is the vajra-mind, the essence of the awareness of all enlightened beings. The syllable is imagined in dark blue, like the promising and dramatic hue of a heavy rain cloud. For the people of India, Nepal, Tibet and western China, the monsoon is much desired. India endures several dry and hot months of very little or no rainfall each summer. Plants wither; the earth cracks and people look up into a merciless hot sun and wish for release. When the blue-black monsoon clouds gather in late summer and early autumn, lightning flashes, thunder roars, and everybody breathes a sigh of relief. The downpour is catastrophic. Streets are flooded; rivers swell and surge in brown torrents, devastating the countryside. Travelling stops, as country roads turn into hip-deep puddles of mud. Yet the monsoon is also the season of lovers and the happiest time of the poets. People delight and celebrate, and the rains bring fertility, fresh green, and the promise of another good year. In Hindu Tantra, the black monsoon clouds are a manifestation of the dark goddess Kālī. In Tibet, the situation is even more extreme. The humid winds reach the Himalayas, where the clouds stop and discharge their waters. Very little passes the mountain barrier. Wide regions of Tibet are practically a desert. Rain and water are rare and universally desired. As in India, a thunderstorm with heavy rainfall is cherished and poets compare it to orgasm. The vajra-mind, discharging itself like a lightning bolt: this is it.

Here is another popular Siṁhamukhā mantra. It provides worship (namaḥ) for her as a sky-travelling divine female teacher.

Namo guru ḍākinī Siṁhamukhāye sarva satrun vighnam maraya Phaṭ.

Now this part of the rite draws to an end. In Hindu Tantra, you can bow, get up, clap your hands and embrace life knowing that the divine appears, exists, changes, disappears, remains in potential and returns everywhere. That's Hindu thought: life is continuous and the divine is real.

In ritual Buddhism, it is essential to remind yourself and everyone of the final emptiness of everything. Hence, you complete your ritual and its visualisation by extinguishing all elements. You dissolve the scenery, the sun maṇḍala and the lotus seat into pure light and draw them into yourself. Let them become smaller and smaller, like a minute fraction of the tip of a hair, and let your sense of self disappear with them. Your ritual, you, the world and everything dissolve.

Last, you recite a special blessing:

May I and all sentient beings, by the virtue of this rite,

attain to the state of the ḍākinī (Siṁhamukhā).

May I be able to free all sentient beings, without leaving any of them behind,

to attain the state of the ḍākinī (Siṁhamukhā).

So much for the basic ritual. In practice, it may be extended by making a torma offering. I leave it to you to decide whether this act is really needed. After all, there was an elaborate offering earlier, and it involved sacred food. Tormas are cones made from dough and butter. For Siṁhamukhā they are coloured bright red, and they signify fresh, bloody meat. As a replacement sacrifice you could also make a pyramid of red cakes or red berries or fruit.

The ritual can also be extended by Buddhist liturgies. You find a schedule for the torma offerings and a number of blessings in Lama Kunga Thartse Rinpoche's text.

Ritual extras. In her ritual, three objects commonly appear: vase, skull-bowl and a mirror. Red powder is scattered over the mirror and a hexagram is drawn on it. The hexagram is one of the most popular symbols of left-hand-Tantra, where it is called the Kāmakalā diagram. In tantric Yantras, upward pointed triangles are male and downward pointing triangles female. A hexagram can signify union in viparita maithuna (reversed coupling). The term refers to a) making love with the woman on top and b) a reversal of the current of consciousness, as it withdraws from the world of appearances into the voidness of the heart. The hexagram is also used in solo practice. You project it on your body. The horizontal lines are the shoulders and the hips. In Buddhist Tantra, the hexagram is called the Dharmodaya. The sign represents the source of all phenomena. To dedicate it to Siṁhamukhā, you should inscribe a **Hūṁ** in its centre.

A useful ritual extra are five **mudrās** related to the goddess. Here, the term mudrā (from mud= to please, to enjoy, bolt, lock, posture, parched grains, spicy aphrodisiacal food; in Buddhism: a ritual companion) means a simple gesture of your hands. The basic idea is simple. The tips of your middle and ring finger meet your thumb while your index and little finger are extended. There are (at least) five traditional ways of enjoying this, and I am sure you can invent more. Version one: the tips of your middle- and ring fingers and the tips of your thumbs meet. When standing, dancing or doing ritual, the index and little finger point up. In seated meditation, you can rest them on your knees, at your hips or lap anyway that feels comfortable. This gesture is known as **Apāna Mudrā**, meaning *downward moving air/breath/force*. Apāna is Prāṇa, the vital energy, as it descends. It is the exhalation, release, the Great Discharge and the ejection of sperm and sexual secretions, creating the phenomenal universe. According to various traditions, this mudrā expels negative influences; it detoxifies, regulates menstruation, stimulates bowel movements and gives a boost to the immune system. More important, it connects Siṁhamukhā to the material world. Her path is one of liberation, but her experience is in the world of flesh, fluids, energies and sentience. The goddess is both immanent and transcendent. Unlike so many deities, Siṁhamukhā encourages us to experience joy and enlightenment in the body and world we create, maintain and dissolve, instead of fleeing it.

Version two: the pads of your thumbs touch the pads of the middle- and ring fingers. Again, in ritual the index and little finger point up, in seated meditation you can have them rest on your knees, at your hips or in your lap any way you like. It's called the **Siṁhamukhā Mudrā,** and is very popular in Indian dance and ritual. Before we move on please think about **dance**. Some modern occultists, usually the sort who laze all day on a sofa, consider dance as a profane entertainment for other people. It is not. In most cultures, dance is a way of expressing feelings, of sharing one's nature, and we find it used in courtship, religion, joy, territorial defence and group strengthening rituals. Dance is a divine language. Indian dance is much like a theatrical play and story-telling, and these, indeed, are very magical. Actors and dancers shape consciousness and make things happen. They create feelings and experiences in themselves and their audience which change the world and our experience of it. So if you think that dance mudrās are profane, when compared to, say, ritual mudrās, do think again.

In classical Indian dance, the Siṁhamukhā mudrā denotes wild animals. It signifies the head of a lion, the head of an elephant (the extended fingers are the tusks) and the head of a hare or rabbit. They are excellent animal masks to understand wildness and nature. The lion is a powerful creature who sees through delusion. A proverb of northern India, Nepal and Tibet claims that if you throw a stone at a wild dog, the dog will react to the stone. If you throw a stone at a lion, the lion will react to you. The elephant is a creature of great strength and agility, symbolising, among many other things, patience, royal authority, the destruction of obstacles and the great black rain clouds that bring fertility and joy. The hare is a creature of cunning and speed, a trickster and a magician. Hares are famous for changing direction, for fooling hunters and for brewing the elixir of immortality. When you consider these animals closely, you may recognise the three guṇas: heaviness, fierceness and goodness. The mudrā also signifies homa (the Vedic fire sacrifice, in twilight language: the sexual secretions), yayana (the offering and the place of offerings), the plucking and waving of sacred dūrva grass, pearls (semen) and red coral (menstrual blood), a garland of lotus blossoms (the cakras), fragrances (pheromones), the preparation of medicines and drugs, listening closely, rescue and liberation.

Variation three, **Bāṁ Mudrā**, is done by making the Siṁhamukhā mudrā with both hands. Hold them in front of you at throat level so that the 'heads of the wild animals' are facing each other. Now allow the two index fingers and the two ring fingers to touch. This mudrā is used in tantric Buddhism to open and purify the mind, it allows you to accept and receive. It is especially connected with the cult of the goddess Tārā, the Saviouress who carries you across the ocean of delusion. Tārā was originally a goddess of alchemy, who was imported, together with the teachings on mercury and cinnabar preparation, from China. In Hindu Tantric cults, she is visualised pretty much like Kālī. The north Indian Buddhists gave her the iconography of the graceful Hindu goddess Lakṣmī. Much later, Tārā became the protective goddess of Tibet (Fries, 2010: 141-143; 417-424). Bāṁ is a red syllable which is visualised and vibrated within the heart. It is gradually expanded until it fills the entire universe and then contracted again until it becomes a tiny seed in your centre. In the process, it purifies everything with warm, blissful happiness. In some meditations, the shrinking of the Bāṁ accompanies a meditation on death and dissolution: the smaller the mantra becomes, the more 'you' dissolve, until liberation sets in.

Variation four is called the **Khaṭvā Mudrā**. It's the gesture of the bed, the cot or the raised seat of the yogī. When yogīs began to explore introverted meditation around the third or fourth century CE, they soon noticed that peace of body and mind is easier to achieve when you are not sitting on the ground where every beetle can investigate your underwear. They constructed small yoga seats which were elevated above the ground, and covered them with sacred dūrva grass and the skin of a black antelope. You form two Siṁhamukhā mudrās with your hands. Turn your hands upside down so that palms point up and the index and little fingers point down. Bring the two hands together in front of your belly so that the tips of thumbs, middle- and ring fingers meet. The gesture looks like a bed and represents resting, patience, manifestation and the earthing of divine awareness.

Variation five is called **Rūpa Mudrā**, the gesture of appearance. Rūpa means form, shape, gestalt, symbol, symptom, being, nature, character, beauty, and a theatrical play. Make the Siṁhamukhā mudrā with both hands. Lift them to the height of your chest and cross them at the wrists so that the 'animal heads' are looking to your left and right. Now for the tricky bit: hook the pad of the little finger of the right hand with the pad of the little finger of the left hand. In a variant version, the thumb pads cover the nails of the ring and middle fingers. The index fingers should point up. This gesture is popular in North Indian Tantra to invoke various deities and spiritual beings. It is not connected to a particular cult of lineage, but can be used to make invocations easier.

Mudrā practice is one of the essentials of Tantra. It was and is highly valuable as many tantrics were minimalists who lived in relative poverty or devoted much of their time to pilgrimages. It is a lot easier to represent your ritual gear with a few gestures than to drag all sorts of stuff (like vases, swords, sceptres, altars, temples and lions) around. However, and this is an essential bit: mudrās do not work automatically unless you are very lucky. Usually, you have to devote weeks of daily practice to associate each gesture with the ideas, feelings and experiences they are supposed to signify. This, in itself, is a very rewarding meditation: a mudrā can be an initiation that will reveal its essence the more you explore it. So don't be upset when making a few odd gestures does not produce instant ecstasy: much in Tantra is discipline, learning, experiment, inventiveness, play-acting and perseverance. People who want instant results are not qualified. Before a mudrā is clearly associated with specific, highly emotional experiences, it won't do much. It is your job to put life, your life, into it.

Part Six
The Trusted

The Seven Names of Lamaštu: Innovative Trances and Meditations

When you have come to this point you can congratulate yourself. For one thing, you are alive. That surely counts for something. For another, you have explored genuine Mesopotamian magick, or at least, some of what happened to survive. I hope you have sung happy hand-washing ditties and made holy water. Perhaps you filled yourself with the copulation power of pigs and canines and flooded yourself with sacred elixirs. You may have burned onions and dates, made knots, opened knots and burned string. Maybe you made pictures, figurines or simple clods of mud and transferred unwanted influences into them. When you cast a circle you were amazed what an amazingly old custom you were following. I hope you drew the circle in your imagination: flour water paste is awfully hard to clean up. You may have prayed, invoked, banished and made your peace with the divine. Perhaps you learned something about offerings of food and drink, and realised how your spiritual practice can be traced to the enchanters and ritualists of one of the earliest known high civilisations. You may have met some of the eldest deities of mankind, or, at least, those whose records are earliest. Perhaps you played with the oldest known numerological system, or explored a cult calendar. I hope you also got yourself a few musical instruments and learned how to make good feelings. Thank you for being so courageous! Last, you may have explored Lamaštu in a Tantric setting as Siṁhamukhā, practising mantras and mudrās and experiencing her as yourself. It's quite a bit, but not everything.

So, for good or bad, we make do with what we have. It may be a long time until the people in the Near East enjoy some peace and the excavators can resume their work. Until this happens, we may explore the material in an innovative manner. In the next pages I would like to introduce you to a series of meditations and trances that may help you gain new insights and create something worthwhile for your daily spiritual practice. Let's start with a much-needed disclaimer. What you encounter in the next pages is not supposed to be 'genuine', 'old' or 'authentic'. It lays no claim to being the holy wisdom of the elders, nor is it the final word on anything. Though our practices are inspired by Lamaštu's seven names, much of them aren't even Mesopotamian. The keywords are innovation and syncretism. Think of this section as a chance to explore. You are in charge. This is your choice, your freedom and your opportunity to develop something worthwhile. If you discover a happier approach to the divine, within and around yourself, they will, just like you, transform for the best.

Meditations, Trance and Magick

In the next pages you will encounter neurology, ecology and a series of meditations. That's because Lamaštu is tied up in them, just as you and I are. Meditation is a vague term, but for the time being it may do. We could also call them experiments in thinking differently, mind-games, awareness-exercises, speculative imagination or trance-journeys. None of these terms really fit the bill. Great! This gives you all the freedom you need to explore. Quite simply, you will shift the filters that create your 'normal' state of reality. At this point, custom and caution require me to give a disclaimer, reminding you that your spiritual development and your mental health are your own responsibility.

Some of these experiences may be upsetting, alarming, or injurious for people who lack long-time experience in practical meditation, who suffer from weak mental or physical health or have psychological problems. Before you decide to do any of these exercises, consider whether you are healthy and competent to do so and consult a physician and/or professional therapist for expert advice. The author and the publishers cannot assume responsibility

for the misuse of the information contained in this book.

Your spiritual development is your responsibility. You may think you are a student, but you will also be your teacher. Magick starts and ends with you, as does the world you shape, maintain, dissolve and recreate as you dance through life.

Many people assume that there is something (an ideal or deity?) called '**normality**' and devote an enormous amount of effort trying to appear like that. It is hardly worth the effort. They also believe in something called a '**sober'** mind. It disappeared when brain chemistry was discovered. You have never experienced a sober moment. Every living being is on drugs. Each 'consciousness state' requires that your brain and your glands create a range of specific chemicals, such as neurotransmitters and hormones. You are making the drugs that keep you functional, and you are good at it. There's more to it. Each experience needs the alignment and cooperation of specific neural clusters, the activation of internal feedback loops, plus extra elements like specific breathing, postures, energetic activity and so on. Chomsky proposed that we should call such neural cooperatives 'mental organs'. It does not mean that you've got special corners of the brain devoted to singular jobs. Usually, your mental activity requires the cooperation of many regions, many neural clusters, perfect timing, rhythm, coordination and alignment. That's easy and natural. Your brain is always busy. It never shuts up and goes inert. Some people still preach that 'we only use 10% of our brains'. Well, maybe they do, and they are welcome to it. Healthy people use their brains all the time, to a greater or lesser extent. Others believe that they are 'right brainers' or 'left brainers' meaning 'creative' versus 'logical'. That damnstupid superstition was disproved by 1980. Even simple behaviour needs the perfect cooperation of both hemispheres (let alone enormously complicated behaviour like 'creativity' and 'logic'); indeed, you could hardly read this book if they were acting separately. Sadly, the esoteric fringe, the hippies and the New Age quacks didn't notice. Your brains are great. They are doing their best. And they are the greatest miracle you will ever explore. Each consciousness state requires that you can access and maintain it, using specific ideas, inner images, feelings, emotions, internal speech, habitual thought patterns, memories, skills, beliefs and so on. Does this sound good? It's wrong. Consciousness does not come in 'states': it is a flow on many levels, in many directions, a simultaneous, bottom-to-top, relationally-organised multi-mystery event with lots of special effects.

Many people draw a line. They consider mental activity as something insubstantial, spiritual and inexplicable. They imagine a 'soul' or a 'self' that somehow transcends 'mere matter'. I have no intention of discussing whether a 'soul' or 'matter' exist. Both categories are woefully limited. We owe the distinction between 'body' and 'mind' to Descartes (1596-1650). In his time, the church was the dominant power regulating (or suffocating) all thought. Descartes proposed that the world should be divided into a material realm, which could be explored by the newly invented sciences, and a spiritual realm, which belonged to the church. It was a great idea for the time, as it allowed the first scientists to conduct their experiments. Sadly, it also burdened Western thought with a stupid duality: you divide body and soul, matter and mind, the secular and the spiritual. On the long run, the distinction turned out to be a terrible limitation. Anything 'spiritual' that uses and influences 'matter', such as your neural tissue, needs an interface, or a mutual foundation. The 'physical' is very closely attached to the 'spiritual', and honestly, both concepts are counterproductive, outdated and dull. What we experience as 'material' or 'spiritual' is, after all made up, represented and maintained by the brain. That brain may be real or imaginary, it may be matter, spirit, energy, reality or illusion, but whatever it is, it's there and provides plenty of excitement.

Each consciousness state has its own configuration. Each depends on who you are (or assume yourself to be), who you have been, who you intend to be, and what feedback you receive from the 'outside' world. We could consider daily life a series of highly specialised states; provided the term 'states' is appropriate, which it isn't. After all, most 'states' are defined by a difference to other 'states'. In real life, awareness is continuous and 'states' are fluent and merge with one another; it is only clumsy thinking and clumsier speech that force us to discuss them in this silly, limited, digital way.

What is your 'normal' state of mind? Is it the one you have at home, relaxing with your partner? Or the one you need to survive in a stressful job? Or do you become 'normal' when you go for a solitary walk and relax? Or when you forget yourself while you have fun with friends? When you are engrossed in a book or movie? It turns out that we have (or are) an entire series of 'normal' states. These, as I'm sure you noticed, changed while you grew up; otherwise you would still be sitting in the sandbox. 'Normality' is a range of specialised choices. You choose which state fits which setting. When you confuse them, and treat your partner like your child, neighbour or employer, 'normality' disappears pretty fast. Consciousness states only make sense when you contextualise them. 'Sanity' means knowing which context you are in, and having a consciousness and behaviour pattern that suits it.

Let's talk about **trance**. Trance is natural, trance is easy, trance happens all the time. Pioneering grandmaster of hypnotherapy, Milton H. Erickson, may have been the first who realised that a trance is a state of focused, specialised awareness that excludes other sensations. Trance states are normal. Your day is full of trances. You are in trance when you read something so intensely that you forget the time. You are in trance when you do something skilful needing concentration: maybe you are driving a car at ninety miles an hour, painting a picture, playing a game, improvising music with friends or in bed making love. Writing is a trance and dancing is a trance, gongfu practices is a trance and so are dozing, dreaming and sleeping, or playing with the kids on a sunny day. You need one trance to talk with strangers and another to joke with your friends, a trance to express yourself and a trance to shut up and listen. In each of these trances you are focussed and use conscious and automatic (subconscious) behaviour to do your best. Each of these 'states' is specialised: it allows you do something well by providing access to a limited amount of special skills and sensations, and excludes a lot of disrupting, useless and contra productive sensations and thoughts. Far from being something strange, exotic or unusual, trance happens each time you do something intensely. Some trances are very conscious, as when you plan something, and some are very unconscious, like when you are dancing. Daily life turns out to be a series of special trances. In each of them you access special skills, activate special feedback loops of your brain and nervous system, create a suitable mix of mind-chemicals and function at your best. Whoever you are and whatever your consciousness may be at a given moment: it's a work of art. The real art, however, is not simply being good at some things. Freedom begins when you have the ability to choose. It means waking up from what you always do and realising what a vast and wonderful world you inhabit.

What is **magick**? Apart from such wonderful and far-reaching definitions, as Crowley's claim that Magick is the Science and Art of Effecting Change Under Will, most people seem to think that magick, spell casting and the like are there to get them things they can't obtain otherwise. Call it results magick: finding a good job, eliminating negative influences, meeting a potential partner or hurting people who scare you. This is not the place to discuss whether these aims are relevant. I call them the small magick, the magick that aims at achieving goals with little regard for consequences or ethics. There are consequences. Like an obsessive idea, a spell that doesn't work may come back and haunt you. A spell that works can produce results you never intended. Collateral damage is common. Small magick is exciting, addictive and risky and it can go wrong. Mainly as people are tied up in their personal dream of what appears good or bad, be it for themselves or those around them. But there are also branches of small magick that are beneficial. Improve your health, learn something new, lend support to others and banish negative thoughts from your life. Or go out and do guerrilla gardening: it turns the world into a healthier place. They are all relevant. Some people are good at small magick and get trapped by the allure of power. Some are bad at it and complain that spells don't work. They rarely wonder why. Is it because their hopes are impossible to achieve? Is it because they tried to meddle with the lives of others? Or did they yearn for things that would have made them unhappy? Most desires are off the mark and some are potentially harmful or just stupid. What about entertainment? Small magick makes life more exciting. All of this is well, good and useful for a start. A few, and I hope this means you, might realise it doesn't go far enough. The great magick begins when you don't add magical extras to life but make life itself enchanting. You've been doing it all your life: human beings are magical animals, moving through a phantasmagoria of beliefs, ideas, desires, fears and dreams, making sense of the senseless, turning the irrational meaningful, imposing patterns and interpretations on experience. We do not experience reality, whatever that may be, but filter, adapt and create, maintain, transform and dissolve information. The reality you inhabit is largely of your own making. Sure, some of it comes from genes. Some was shaped when you were an embryo in the womb. Some was produced by the climate, country and culture you grew up in. All of these supplied basic material. You turned it into a relevant and meaningful world. You made it come real. When we were children we learned in a chaotic fashion, and our brains installed neural connections all over the place. There was a good reason for this: when you are very young, you don't know what will be important when you grow up. You have to be interested in everything. Then around the age of eight or nine your brain eliminated a lot of neural connections and improved and intensified a range of specific ones: the result was a settled personality, a stabilised character, a person with more purpose and aim. It worked perfectly until puberty when a whole range of new hormones upset your glands, emotions, habits, preferences, thought processes and parents, and forced you to recreate a new social personality by trial, error and peer group pressure. That process continued, your neural setup underwent changes well into your twenties, until finally the prefrontal cortex was doing its job properly. You established and maintained a mindset that appears moderately controlled and predictable. The result is your range of 'normality', i.e. what you and your environment assume to be your 'personality'. Identity is a useful fiction. Being adult means that you can be trusted to have the basic moods, preferences and silly habits that everybody got used to. Growing up implies developing trances that allow us to function and survive in a stabilised environment. These trances are useful to enjoy life, keep a job, have a relationship, make money, collect property and maybe to procreate; well then, the genes are happy and evolution can move on. But is it enough? Evidently, some people want more from life than happiness, food, shelter, company, sex and genetic reproduction. Here Lamaštu comes in: she likes to disrupt routines. The very trances that allow us to do our thing predictably well also keep us from doing other things, or even from becoming aware of them. When we want to learn something really different, we need to kick ourselves out of the trances that constitute our ordinary range of experience. For each of us, no matter who we are, the hardest thing is to think and experience differently. Your concept of identity limits your range of choices, and prevents the development of new trances that might make your life happier. Hence, in magic and genuine spiritual experience, the first step is to get out of your 'normal' patterns of thinking, believing and experiencing. It allows you to experience, understand and act in different ways. Some of them will be disagreeable and useless, but here and there you will encounter something that will improve your life. The next step is to advance to a better and happier version of 'normality'. For this reason, many cults, schools, associations and organisations employ initiation ceremonies: rites that shake, scare, confuse, upset or otherwise throw the candidate out of her or his former routine. Evidently, the Mesopotamians made use of scare-energy: a novice who was not duly afraid of the wrath of the gods was not accepted for priestly training. Priests were expected to be humble. Spiritual practice is a difficult art. Occasionally you have world-shaking experiences; but usually you spend ages doing your thing, and have to beware of dullness and bored routine-mindedness. All of these are part of your evolution. All of them provide learning experiences. It's one of those blessings that no matter how far you come, learning goes on forever.

Let's enjoy something practical now. I would like to introduce you to a series of trances that emerged from exploring the **Seven Names of Lamaštu**. Think of them as a series of choices which allow you to develop something that fits your magical universe and leads you to a better understanding of the greater magick, the magick that maintains your reality and the dream or reality you be-live. We are not only talking about Mesopotamian magick, or about a specific goddess called DIM.ME/Lamaštu. On close examination, you will realise that the seven names fit quite a range of deities, no matter the age or culture they came from. Make them fit you.

I, 1

Šiptu *(=Conjuration, Naming):*

Dingir DIM.ME/Lamaštu *(= Deity DIM.ME/Lamaštu)*

Child of An/Anu is your first name *(or:* ***line, fame, succession)*;**

Var.1.: ***The second: Sister of the Gods of the Streets;***

Var.2.: ***The second: Watchful One of the Gods of the Streets;***

I, 3

Var.1.: ***The third: Knife*** *(or:* ***Sword),*** ***that Splits the Head;***

Var.2.: ***The third: Knife*** *(or:* ***Sword)*** ***that Cuts the Head down.***

Var. 1.: ***The fourth: She Who Ignites the Wood to Flame;***

Var. 2.: ***The fourth: She Who Ignites the Flame;***

Var. 3.: ***The fourth: She Who Topples the Tree;***

I, 5

Var. 1.: ***The fifth: Goddess Whose Face*** *(or:* ***Expression)*** ***is Wild.***

Var. 2.: ***The fifth: Goddess Whose Face*** *(or:* ***Expression)*** ***is Yellow-Green.***

Var.1.: ***The sixth: Committed into the Hands*** *(=the Trusted)*,

Accepted *(or:* ***Adopted*** *or:* ***Taken)*** ***by Irnina;***

Var.2.: ***The sixth: Committed into the Hands*** *(=the Trusted)*,

Who is Compassionate *(= Accepts Petitions/Prayers)*;

I, 7

The seventh: Bound *(or:* ***Conjured)*** ***by the Oath of the Great Gods,***

Fly Away with the Bird/s of Heaven!

Before we continue, please think deeply about these names. You are facing magick that is more than three thousand years old, relevant, inspirational, exciting and pulsating with life. To begin with, I suggest you memorise them. Here is a simple way to organise them. Press the tip of your thumb against the pad of your ring finger. Think about name one. Close your eyes, say it like a mantra (use an impressive inner voice!), make up large, colourful inner visions and bring them close. Imbue them with emotion. Do it for a minute or two. Then press the thumb against the pad of your middle finger and anchor the second name. Press it against the pad of the index finger and imagine the third. Name four is on the nail of the index finger. Now move down. Press the thumb against the nail of your middle finger for name five. Press it against the nail of the ring finger for name six. Name seven is the nail of your little finger. That gives you seven distinct locations for seven names. Personally, I believe that the line *Fly Away With the Bird/s of Heaven* should also be counted as a name. It can be anchored to the pad of the little finger. So you have seven names and one that is a release from them. It's an arbitrary alignment and you are free to improve it any way you like. I simply started with the pad of the ring finger as the last two names, which are a little uncomfortable to hold, should be on the little finger. Of course you can use any other alignment. We ain't as dumb as computers: your brain, like life itself, thrives on relational behaviour, that adapts itself to circumstances and requirements, instead of blindly following fixed routine procedures. And you can easily change the pattern for something better, at least during the first weeks, before the associations are really fixed. Go through this loop for a while. Spend a few minutes with each name. Move your thumb and as you do, repeat the name to yourself in a loud or imaginary voice. The trick is: be congruent. For name one you might use a cosmic inner voice, for name two, one that sounds inquisitive and interested, for name three a hard, decisive one. Name four requires an enthusiastic, lustful one, name five one that sounds both wild and natural, name six affectionate and loving and name seven responsible and committed. If 'fly away...' is an eighth name, put a feeling of relief and release into it. Each name should feel good! And each should sound different. Look out for new insights. Enjoy all extras that will come into your mind. If you do this a few times each day, for a couple of weeks, there will be an amazingly vivid experience associated with each name, vision and physical sensation. Practise and imagination will do the job. Do add a strong emotion to each name: the things you really feel and care about are easily remembered. That's how your hippocampus codes memories. Now you have a useful association device. Each point of pressure connects you to a specific flow or awareness, or to a trance, if you like.

A note of caution. The pressure of thumb on fingers is a key. Consider it a helpful device to improve your access. However, once the door is open and you have passed through, you need not keep it in your hand. Nor do you have to repeat the name once the experience is strong. Keeping up the pressure or blabbering the name like a mindless automaton will reduce the quality of your experience.

You can use the Seven Names for a meditation. Sit down somewhere nice, relax, calm down, slow your thinking, breathing, perception, and go through the circle. Repeat each name in your inner voice, again and again, and accompany this mantra with slow, soft, gentle breathing. Keep it easy. No huffing, puffing and forcing the lungs: just make the breath smooth and long and enjoy its flow. Devote two minutes to each name. OK, if it feels good, double the time. When you emerge at position eight, your awareness will have changed. Your perception will be much clearer and you will think with greater ease. Put a happy smile into life. Make it a good one. Let it flow through your body. The seven names can be a treat. They can make life more enjoyable. But they are also useful when you feel upset, worried or exhausted.

You can use them as an oracle. Ask yourself a simple question. Here is something useful: 'what trance will be good for me now?' Allow your thumb to circle around. Press the pads and nails of your fingers briefly as you go along. Keep repeating your question as you do. At some point, your thumb will stick to a finger. Maybe you twitch, jolt or come to a sudden halt. Watch out for the very first ideas that come into your mind. Or leave the thumb in its position for a minute, as you explore the message you just received.

You can do a lot with the Seven Names. You can use them as meditations, as trances, as invocations, as a way of inducing special states of awareness and emotion. Maybe they will inspire your writing, your music, your art, or the way you interact with people, animals, plants, biotopes and other sentient lifeforms. You can start in the cosmic realm, bright-eyed, innocent, new to everything. The first name is just being; the second describes the flow of awareness, the way your thinking creates the world, time, space and transformation. Next you move to the inbetweenness realm where changes are effected and self is defined. You divide, differentiate, analyse. You do the hard thing and take conscious life, no matter what your diet consist of; you metabolise, and explore likes and dislikes. You realise and manifest your nature (names three, four, five). You find your place within the flow of interaction, communication, and social behaviour, and realise your ability to love and trust (name six). Finally, you assume your role in the web of obligations, dependencies and responsibilities on earth (name seven). Welcome to life on earth. And you can find release from the lot when you let go, give a sigh of relief and fly away like the bird of heaven.

We journey from the abstract to the particular. Each name is a little more substantial than the one that preceded it. Or you can move the other way around, by starting in this realm of specific form, shape, name and difference, and move upwards to the simplicity of the undefined, the all-encompassing heavenly vastness. These names can take you through a lot of experiences. You can turn them into a series of initiations. But they are not the only possibilities. As you recall, there are several other names of DIM.ME/Lamaštu which appear in earlier Sumerian talismans and in LS II, 129-134.

Named with a Name by the Great Gods.

Ruler of the Black-Headed-People.

Innin: Victorious Mistress.

DIM.ME the Exalted.

You Who Seize and Hold** (or:* ***Bind) the Evil Asag/Asakku-Spirit.

You Who Overwhelm the Alû-Spirit.

You Who Bind the Black-Headed-People (and) the Udug/Utukku (ghost** or:* ***storm), Heavy on Mankind.

South Wind Weighing Heavily on Mankind.

High Lady Who Answers Prayers.

All of these names are worth exploring. Maybe you will make up your own selection of seven names. That's perfectly all right: many conjurers did the same.

Child of An/Anu is your first name (or: line, fame, succession);

The first experience starts when you suspend the concept of a specific, defined, personified, anthropomorphic deity. Some people like to relate to the divine in one form. They are true to a particular god with a name, shape, iconography, mood and character. Some prefer a divine couple, or an entire family of deities. Some change from deity to deity. Some experience the divine in many shapes, and rediscover their divine self-essence with each new deity or cult they explore. All of this is well and good. Others like an abstract idea of the divine. They go for a numinous essence that defies conceptual thought. I've met hot blooded atheists who were deeply religious, who lived their faith and followed their ideals without a personified deity. Great! Some experience the divine as separate from themselves, others realise the divine within themselves, and everywhere else. Or they merge temporarily with the divine when they go obsessed. Every approach is useful, necessary and perfect for a given person, deity, time and situation. Some make a fuss about such distinctions, and insist that their worship is the only proper one. Let's scrap all this. We are getting ready to explore the divine, and that may mean one specific deity, several deities, no deities, ourselves, not ourselves, the world, its absence and everything in it. Confused? Great. All learning starts when you leave the known and take a risk with something that may upset your cherished understanding of the world. Let's make the river flood, obstruct traffic, smear squiggles on the wall and uproot a few trees of high authority. It is not only Lamaštu who is a Child of Heaven. We all are.

Life could be easier if it wasn't so enormously complex. It would also be boring. When you think of Lamaštu's parents An and Antu(m), or simply Heaven, Sky, the Multiverse, you might imagine something awesomely vast, complex, mind-blowing, overwhelmingly creative and intricately perplexing. Though we are all part of it, Heaven is simply too huge for human brains. Your mind represents the incomprehensible using very specific filters. People tend to find what they are expecting. When you look for harmony and similarity, you discover order. When you look for differences and unexpected developments, you encounter chaos. The whole huge celestial bovine can appear as one and as many, depending on how you relate to it, and whatever it may really be, it is amazingly and irresponsibly fertile. An, the Fecund Breed Bull of the Sky, and Antu(m), the Birth-giving Mother are not simply creator deities who stands back to admire their work and set up signs saying 'no trespassing, no apple plucking, don't talk with snakes and keep your hands to yourselves'. An and Antu(m) are transcendent, in that they are outside of their creation; immanent, in that they are in every part of their creation, and transcendent-immanent as they are the creators, the created, the act of creation and anything you could think of, if your head were quite a lot bigger than it is. They are everywhere around you, but they are also within you, and you are part of them. This goes for you, but it also goes for everything else. Heaven does not exclude anything. The pebble on the path, the reed at the riverside and the wasp that explores your face: they are all children of heaven. The magic starts when you realise that you are just one sentient bit of a complex totality of interacting consciousness. Wherever you look, whatever you sense, there is intelligence multiplying with intelligence. Essentially, you are An, you are Antu(m), you are their creation, you are their creator, for whatever this world may really be, it is certainly more than we can comprehend.

The first name of Lamaštu means experiencing this. That's the hardest meditation and also the easiest. It allows you to recognise the wonder, the miracle, the overwhelming grandeur of everything that exists. The multiverse might appear like confusion, if it were not for that bit of certainty that tells you that this, too is you, and you are this. It's a great thing that all of us are here. It's even greater that we can experience each other. As we sense others they sense us: we meet ourselves in all forms. Wherever you are and whatever you did, you can experience it now. It's simple. It's so simple that you were perfect at it when you were in the womb. Then followed birth and life became less simple. Instead of direct nourishment through the navel you had to metabolise. It was a tough job. You had to inhale and exhale. You had to feed, digest and excrete. You had to make a difference between me and you and everything else. And all the while everything happened at once. The world was a nameless and chaotic place. Things were not things, they simply were. It was an amazing achievement to tell where one object began and another ended. Colours were not colours but sensations. Sounds were feelings. Body was a mystery. People did not come closer or depart: you didn't know how to process space. Instead, you saw people growing and shrinking with alarming speed. They did not go behind objects, as there was no behind. Instead, they simply disappeared. Not that you knew them to be people; not that you knew yourself as yourself. Foreground and background were in the same distance. A finger was as large as a tree, as a mountain, and you didn't even know that finger was yours. It took your brain years to learn that this incredibly tiny bird was actually a big fat buzzard and that it was far away. You had to learn how fast things move, you had to calculate their speed and estimate their distance (see Pinker 1997 for more). Your brain learned to measure space and time. Duration was another tricky subject. Time is not simply there: you make it. Experience is continuous. We decide that some things are sooner or later, past, present and future, by dividing time into sections and by building internal models, timelines, to represent them. 'Later' was inestimable, 'tomorrow' unthinkable. It took a long while before you could handle the idea of enormously extended periods, like hours or days. Most adult people are stupid. They take time and space for granted, and get upset when junior can't wait or control his bladder. They forget how much work it is to install the reality filters that process time and space by making differences between one sensation and another. These differences are not there by nature. You make them by deciding where to put your attention. To see how fast a stream is moving you have to pick a floating object, a twig, a ripple, a few bubbles, and measure their movement against the shore. To estimate time you have to search for serial repetitions.

Time and space are created by measuring. They lose their rigid configurations when your reality filters let you down: when you are drunk, tired, absent minded, on drugs, in deep meditation, in trance, with friends, watching a good movie, reading an exciting book, when you are in sorrow or in love. And you transform them as you need. To drive a fast car you need to speed your awareness up. Fast will seem normal when your perception and mind processes are fast. Very fast can seem slow when you are even faster. To roll a few dozen times over a dojo floor you have to hit the 'slow-motion' button by accelerating: when you are fast enough the room seems to freeze, the air turns into jelly and you have all the time to relax as the ground cushions you.

Slowing down is just as good. Waiting is not boring when you go really slow. A long flight can be over in half the time when you are slow and enjoy it. Patient people do that naturally. They slow down motion, they slow down perception, and they slow down thinking, and are amazed how fast the world goes by. And time is age-related: when you are very young, adult people are incredibly slow. And when you are old, you may wonder why young people are always in such a hurry. You can make yourself older by slowing down and younger by speeding up. It's your decision: you can choose how fast you want to be!

But there is so much more to it. When you are freshly born, things are not three dimensional but flat: they are visual sensation, pure and simple. When that visual sensation can be touched, you get an extra surprise. It is one of the hardest jobs for the baby to separate shapes and colours and identify them as distinct things. Luckily, we get help from our genes: our ancestors survived as they were pretty good in detecting eyes and smiles and big things with milk in them. Some patterns are there from the start. As babies, we react to loud things with surprise and to sensual disorientation, such as rocking, by feeling comfortable. It helped our monkey ancestresses to drag their babies to the treetops when trouble was coming. Luckily, the one and only thing on your baby-schedule was simply being. You could afford to be there. Outside of time and space, you had all the leisure in the universe. Nor did you feel compelled to do anything. There was no intent, no planning, no schedule or program. All you had to do was to follow simple impulses without deliberation, and most of your learning happened subconsciously. Just like now.

The first name of Lamaštu is a celebration of this state. Honestly, people lose so much when they grow up. They lose innocence, astonishment, wonder and above all they lose the miracle of NOW. Imagine you had just fallen from the sky. We all do, starting with each lifetime. Everything around you is new, strange and mysterious.

The easiest approach is to relax. Feel that body. Let that tension flow out. Simply by being as you are. You have all the time in the world. And you can calm down. It means that your body sinks, your breathing slows, your thinking slows and you can relax 'cause you are not going anywhere. It's a rare and wonderful experience. In an age when people split their days into 'time windows' and fragment experience and themselves by schedules, planning and deliberation, sheer being is the greatest possible luxury. You can enjoy it right now. Simply relax, calm down, slow down, let go. Perhaps you sense yourself. Perhaps you feel how gravity keeps you rooted in a place. That's great; you can allow your body to take care of itself. You can observe how you breathe, you can move your attention, steadily slower now, as you calm down, and relax towards the centre of the earth. It's not doing. I am sure you can trance off by counting breath, or by repeating a mantra slowly, softly on the exhalation, or by imagining yourself sinking deeper and deeper. All of this is well and good. Right now, they are not needed. What we cultivate here is simply being, and being arises from not being anything specific. Forget about effort, forget about intent. Before and after each action you can delight in non-action. This is not something to train and develop, 'cause training always leads somewhere else, and right now, as you are, as everything is, there is simply is-ness and you are welcome to yourself. It will not happen then: it happens now. Now is the time, here is the place. Or maybe there is no-time and no-place. Why bother to tell the difference?

Call it baby awareness, if you like. Or the awareness of a deity stranded on planet earth. Or consciousness delighting in consciousness. Or floating into absent-mindedness through the realm of no-difference. For when you are doing, you are losing it. The first name is doing by not-doing, and forgetting both of them. It is being, pure and simple, without intent or aim or goal. In this state there are no opposites, there is no need to take a position, to define who or what you are. It is neither thinking nor not-thinking. It is neither seeing nor not-seeing, neither intent nor lack of intent. The Daoists call it the **wuji** (*no polarity, no extremes*) posture. They turned it into a meditation. Wuji means that there are no extreme states or sensations. Being is extreme, non-being is extreme. Doing and non-doing are extreme. In-between you can experience true relief. Here is one way of doing it. Stand so that your heels touch and your feet are spread in a 45° angle. Your knees are flexible, your shoulders sink, the arms hang relaxed at your sides and you face directly ahead. Put the tip of your tongue against the roof of your mouth and feel how your belly moves as breath slows and calms you down. Maybe you sway a little. No need to interfere! Perhaps there is motion and perhaps there isn't. No need to control, no need to make a fuss. Maybe you sense how breath and vitality move you. Your eyes may be open or they may close gently from time to time. Or you keep them half open. When you become still and undefined, fascinating visual effects can appear. Your surroundings may look amazing. Enjoy it, but do not become trapped by it. Outside awareness is extreme, inside awareness is extreme. Float between them. Some people stare. It's extreme. Rest your eyes, see without seeing, hear without hearing, feel without feeling. Everything is fine as long as you make no effort. This stance is your essential nature before birth. It is the primal chaos before the cosmos appeared, and the first and last thing you practice as you learn Bagua Zhang. Perhaps your body sensations will increase. Perhaps they are forgotten. Perhaps you will become extremely aware. Perhaps you will forget being aware. No need to think, deliberate or act. This is just being, and it is so simple that every baby can do it. And so can you. You can do it standing, sitting, kneeling or lying on the ground.

Wuji can take you in many directions. Maybe you allow your eyes to close. There is much to be learned when you introvert and sink leisurely into the depths of yourself. Perfect. Simply leave the world and the ten-thousand things out there. Let go, relax, sink deeper and delight. You can enjoy deep trances without inducing them in any active way, and the less you do, the deeper they will become.

Was that too easy or too difficult? Here is another approach.

If you are living the normal, worried and hurried life of a stressed-out human being, the best moment is now. It's not then and not later, for later is too late. Life is now, you are now, the world is now, so seize the moment, shut up, relax, slow down, introvert and let go. You can do this standing, sitting or lying. Simply chose a posture that is moderately aligned and comfortable. Maybe you will observe that your body sinks into itself. Maybe you will notice that your breathing slows and becomes shallow. That's excellent. The Daoists call it 'embryonic breathing', as an infant in the womb does not appear to breathe at all, except invisibly through the navel string. Call it minimal breathing if you like: your lungs and belly move very little, most of the time. Occasionally you take a deeper breath. You might find yourself dreaming. When breathing becomes shallow, inner imagery tends to amplify. None of this is done by effort. Your tensions will dissolve as you stop meddling and controlling and interfering. Close your eyes. Sink into the primal realm of the undefined. Feel into your belly, feel your breath move. Don't try to control it. It will become calm and smooth as you slow down and sink into the ocean of silence. Breathing is a sacrament. It is shared by all beings. Maybe you think that you breathe. Can you observe how it breathes you? Zhuangzi suggested that you should sense your breath with your consciousness/energy. That's enough. Simply fix your attention to the gentle flow of exhalation and inhalation and keep it there. In the process, many sensations will fade away. The same goes for stupid thoughts, for superfluous mindstuff, for odds and ends belonging to your daily life. This practice is ancient. It is hinted at in earliest Daoist literature, such as the *Nei-Ye*, the *Bamboo Strips Laozi*, the *Zhuangzi*, *Huainanzi* and *Liezi*. It was called: 'sitting in forgetfulness', 'to fast the heart/mind', 'to keep the silence cautiously', 'guarding the one' and the 'nameless natural state'. Some call it 'the purification of the heart/mind' (xin zhai fa), or 'sitting in silence' (jing zuo). It's an essential for all Daoist practice, no matter whether you explore painting, martial arts, music, ritual, exorcisms, inner alchemy, divination, healing rituals or go for walks in nature. As you limit your awareness to the breathing, you come to rest in silence and precreate calm. In this state, the Dao manifests within you.

Some may think that this is a Buddhist mindfulness meditation. Some aspects are similar, as both approaches tend to still the mind. However, there are also differences. During the Daoist practice, you are not trying to be aware of what is. Some Buddhists make a real struggle out of it. They claim that you should be so aware, so mindful, as if your life depended on it. For Daoists, that's too stressful. If you lose your mindfulness in Zen meditation, begin to daydream, doze or slump, the master hit you with a stick. Conditioning with pain. It's just too extreme. The same goes for the goal. Buddha combined Upaniṣadic philosophy with the doctrine of No-Self (anatman), a nihilist philosophy that was popular in his age. As a result, he understood liberation to be cessation. When his followers, many centuries later, began to practice meditation, they aimed for emptiness and dissolution. For the Daoists, the emptiness, silence and vacuity are not a goal. Goals are extreme. Daoist voidness is not empty: it is undefined, preconceptual, eternally changeful. Forgetting oneself and resting in silence are simply stages to go through as you encounter the Dao. And of course things don't stop there. The Way is continuous. For this reason, Daoists do not try to reach a state of absolutely no thought, nor do they ever achieve an end-result. The idea is to get rid of inessential thoughts. As you sit in silence, all sorts of stuff will pass through your head. Maybe you find yourself daydreaming, remembering, worrying, thinking, hoping, and maybe you will perceive snatches of ideas, flotsam of speech or sudden images. If you remain focussed on your breathing, they will gradually fade away. However, and this is important, in between the waste material you will encounter ideas, insights, inspiration that are worth pursuing. Make a mental note and come back to them after your meditation.

That's the easy and natural way. It happens when you allow it. You need a lot of courage and dedication to pursue it. Clearing the mind by allowing it to clear itself needs practice, confidence and trust. It requires that you commit yourself to the Dao.

In case you are not comfortable with simple, easy and natural, and want something special: introduce moments of peaceful being and forgetfulness into your daily routines. We all deserve more holidays. Have a cup of tea, coffee or simply boiled water (my favourite). It's still too hot for drinking? Beautiful. You have the time to let it cool leisurely. No, don't fill that gap. Leave your mobile alone. Don't do or plan or divert your attention or think of anything specific. Simply sit there. The fluid cools, fumes dance on its surface and all of a sudden you can let go. That's a wonderful chance. It's your time to feel well.

Or light incense. See the smoke coil. Observe the fumes or forget yourself as dragons rise into the sky. The Mesopotamian conjurers were right. Incense purifies the mind.

Or go to the window and watch clouds. Don't think about what you'll do next. There is no next, there is just now. The clouds keep moving. Your attention may go with them. Or move as it likes. Attachment, non-attachment; why talk so much? No need to interfere. The clouds are the gentle dreaming of the sky.

Or maybe you could play with something like a japamālā, or a rosary, or a chaplet of beads. That, too is a Mesopotamian invention. Sure, religious people usually employ them for a purpose. They say a prayer, or a holy name or mantra while they slip one bead after the other through their hands. Those who repeat Ave Maria a hundred thousand times are released from all sins, except stupidity. That's one option. We'll explore something different. Make a small chaplet with maybe 15-25 beads. Use large beads, they are easier to move. Or use a simple small loop made of a ribbon, soft string or a flat piece of a shoelace. It has no beads: this is not about counting and measuring. It's about continuity. This is how I use them. Feel free to change and improve everything. I have programmed three basic experiences for this item. They were not there naturally, I had to make them up. Call it play-acting if you like. And remember that each state of mind that seems natural to you now was learned by playacting. When acting becomes real, you forget that you are acting. That's how you programmed yourself when you were a child, and it worked perfectly. The most convincing actors are those who forget they are acting. For them, the play is reality.

Moving the loop slowly with my left hand can be an act of release. No doing, no effort, no expectation and strain. I calm down and delight in feeling relaxed and drowsy, and my mind quiets and my thoughts slow and warm pleasant feelings of well-being, peace and divine bliss appear naturally. It's simple. It can release tension in body and mind, and cause intense yawning or tears. Whatever it is, I slow down and eventually the motion comes to a stop.

When I turn the loop with my right hand, going forth and back, at a brisk speed, it tends to activate a wakeful, enthusiastic and vigorous state of mind. This is useful for excitement, for feeling awake, fresh and stimulated, for acceleration, for praying, conjuring, banishing, breathing exercises, mantra recitation and to induce possession trances. Some people use drumming for that sort of thing, or shake a rattle or bells, and get excited. The chaplet or loop works just as well. It can be used to speed up perception or slow it down deliberately and to create a heady dose of enthusiasm. Swift motion is one way to stimulate the sympathetic system. And should you find yourself daydreaming or dozing or having astonishing new ideas in that state; great, enjoy it for a while and allow it to go its own way.

The third trance option is twisting the lace into a horizontal figure eight ∞, so I can move it with both hands at once. It provides a special range of intense trances. Usually, I have to be fit and healthy to handle them, as they can be slightly demanding. Maybe it's different for you. You make up the experience. The chaplet or lace is just a tool: your deep mind works the magick. Essentially you invent three distinct trances. Chaplet, lace and other toys are useful to keep your mind on the subject, but they are not really needed. All consciousness states are created, made, maintained and transformed by the nervous system. These days, I access such trances by moving my fingers as if I were moving the item. Every tool is a convenience. You know you are good at deep trances when you can enjoy them anywhere: at home, with your friends, in the forest, at the riverside, on a train, walking through a museum, at the airport, the main station or in a shopping mall.

Observing breath, tea watching, cloud gazing, bead turning- they are useful as they keep attention to the trances.

Some people create pauses and intervals for relaxation by having a beer or a cigarette, by listening to music, doing the nails, stretching, daoyin, qigong or whatever. It doesn't really matter how you nurture the Now in your daily life. The main thing is that you do it. And when you are getting simple and happy, let go. Stop fiddling with your chaplet or ribbon, forget the clouds, empty your cup...stop doing. There is always a point where effort becomes a superfluous absurdity. Magick takes off when you cease doing. Luckily, Lamaštu is very helpful in creating pauses. Moving through a waterway, she causes a flood and raises clouds of mud and sediment. Sure, it's comforting to look into a stream and to know what is going on in the deep. That's how people like to organise their days: one transparent stream of experience leading from A to B to C without interruptions or surprises. Lamaštu says: 'this is boring!' and makes the waters rush and the murk rise. For while clear water is nice, turbid water is fertile. Next she makes the river flood. Forget your plans and schedules: when the brown deluge comes surging, remain in the Now, and act spontaneously. And when you are out on the road, hurrying, achieving, functioning, making plans and following schedules, she is waiting for you and obstructs traffic. Great! Life should not be too foreseeable. When you are stuck in a traffic jam you have a perfect opportunity to slow down and relax. You can make it a good feeling: the goddess has given you an instant holiday! Such moments should be treasured.

Before, during and after we explore the other names of Lamaštu, the best thing is to remember the first name and enjoy it. All of us are children of the Universe. We all come from heaven, as heaven is everywhere. As you will learn, each name, and state of awareness, is a little more specific than the last. To shift from one to another you need a pause, a moment of emptiness, freshness and non-definition. It's like driving a bicycle or car: to shift from one gear to another you need an empty moment in between. So before you hurry to the next trance, task, job or obligation, take your time, have a pause, empty your mind and relax. How about a cup of tea? Take a deep breath. Watch that cloud. You deserve more good feelings as you float along.

In daily life, the first name demands humour and humility. It's not easy to understand oneself as the Child of Heaven. To realise one's divinity can be a shattering experience. Some people become raging megalomaniacs. They bloat themselves with pride and strut about being totally useless. We have heard more than enough about that sorry creature, the 'superman' of Bacon, Nietzsche, Crowley, Shaw, Wells and so many lonely thinkers of the early twentieth century. Who despises others as 'inferior' is a much weaker creature than those who simply do what is natural to them. Arrogance is based on fear. When you realise that within 'you' is a core of universal, divine consciousness, pride and self-importance are superfluous absurdities. The divine is in every being and thing whatsoever. Ducks have it, cabbages have it, earthworms have it; and so have mountains, rivers, roads, stones, concrete buildings, cars and plastic bags. On a molecular level, there is no difference between life and death: all that exists is energy. In people the divine is often hidden. It can be obstructed by worries, fears, greed, ignorance and sad, limited ideals. The real magick begins when you take out the garbage that clutters the self. Before long, the divine appears. It can be a shock: you are the divine incarnate in body, but you are certainly not all there is to the divine. In fact, the more you insist on being specifically 'you' the less are you able to recognise the divine. To understand the first name fully, explore humility. True humility is not self-abasement or shame. It has nothing to do with getting down on your knees and snivelling. You inhabit a body, you are limited by shape, nature, metabolism, time and space. You may remember to be the Child of Heaven, but you can't be all of Heaven. There are limits to what our neurology can deal with. You are not at the top or bottom of the food chain: the food chain is a circle. You feed on life and life feeds on you. There are no higher or lower life forms. Plants and animals nourish us and we nourish them. When we die, we feed scavengers, worms, microbes, plants and fungi. That's what the worm Ouroboros is all about. The cosmic serpent grows and remains alive by feeding on itself. Being humble is a meditation. Humility means that there is always something worth laughing about. It's me and you and all of us. We are funny creatures. The same goes for gods: just watch Lamaštu strutting through the streets! Our laughter is liberation. All people are silly; so are you and so am I, but I am sillier as I try harder. As you let go of self-importance, you experience the sheer joy of being. It means to see a sunrise as if you never saw one before, to gaze in amazement at a tree, to delight in the coming and going on Planet Earth and to marvel at the miracle of being. This is what being the 'Child of Heaven' is all about.

Var.1.: ***The second: Sister of the Gods of the Streets;***

Var.2.: ***The second: Watchful One of the Gods of the Streets;***

By now you should be good at pausing and being. The second name has much to do with change, motion, and trance-formation. For a start, it can be useful to induce a deep, introverted trance. Maybe you'll do it by not doing. Or maybe you simply sit or lie down peacefully in a place where you won't be disturbed. Relax; let the tension flow out of your body. Feel gravity cushion you. Relax into the moment; relax to enjoy a good feeling. Your emotions calm down, your attention calms down, your inner voice slows down, and your perception becomes simple and unfocused. Find a good feeling, make it stronger and move it through your body. Let it rise to your head; let it sink into your belly. Move it into hands and feet, bring it back into the centre of your body, your belly region. And let it breathe you peacefully. Now you might like to close your eyes. Give a last thought to the multiverse around you. It's a huge and busy world. Ten-thousand things are just waiting to be left to their own devices. Let them do their thing while you turn inwards and sink into the deep.

There are several technical approaches to deep introverted trances. Most of them use exhalation, a calm and slow inner voice, and the imagination that you are sinking slowly deeper and deeper each time that you exhale. Your exhalation connects with the parasympathetic nervous system. You can relax into the exhalation, slow down and feel well. Simply by allowing yourself to treasure this moment as you sink down naturally. As you relax, your body appears to become heavier. It will seem to become diffuse as you sink inwards. And maybe you want to do something dull and monotonous like counting your breaths. You could count 'seven' as you exhale and sink downwards. Then 'six' as you go deeper. 'Five' and you realise this is coming home. 'Four' as the deep receives you. 'Three' as your inner voice is getting slower. Make it a comfortable inner voice, a gentle voice which you can wrap around yourself and cushion yourself with. 'Two' for this is getting easier all the time. 'One' and you can go deeper still. And 'zero'. You are doing well. Slow down even more. You might ask yourself how deep your trance could be. And your deep mind will supply the answer in your own good time. 'Seven' and this is being warm and cuddly and breath flows leisurely and naturally. 'Six' and you are well within yourself. 'Five' and you can float deeper. And so you go 'four' and continue. Count 'three' as you sink slowly inwards. Drift deeper and deeper with each number. Soothe yourself. This should feel extra good. And as you are doing well, you will find that the next time you go into trance will be easier. For you are making new neural connections. When you think something again and again, it will become easier. The neural connections become stronger. The synapses will come closer, they will emit more neurochemicals and develop more receivers. Each thought that becomes a habit changes the neural structures of your brain. Your brain is transforming each time you learn something new, or make a new connection. You can use it to access the inner states that do you good. Each time you travel along this street you will find it takes you there better, faster and easier than before. And when you think those thoughts again and again, and you treat yourself to a happy deep introverted trance every day, your brain will set up a multi-lane highway to take you into the peaceful quiet that is your true home.

That's one way. Or maybe you would like to try something else. This time you don't count. You simply relax and imagine that you float deeper with each exhalation. Allow yourself to become smaller. Gently withdraw from the outside world, from your clothes, from your skin, from the periphery of your body. Leave your face, your shoulders, your hips and limbs far away out there. Let yourself become smaller. There is a huge cave right within yourself. It's the heart, it's the core, and it's a shapeless inner realm of vast and joyous emptiness. See your body from within. Far away, out there is your skin. Out there is your periphery. But as you become smaller you sink deeper, and as you float leisurely into the depth you give up your thoughts. Shed the ideas that define you. Let the thoughts of everyday life float softly out of your being. They move to the periphery and through your skin into the outside world, where they belong. Whatever comes into your awareness: take a look and let it float away gracefully. You've got all the time in the world. And you are becoming simple and open-minded and refreshed while all the everyday stuff goes its own way and leaves you happy and easy and small. Shedding one shell after another you become natural and true.

That's another approach; it was a favourite of the Tantric adepts of Kashmir (Fries, 2010:280-295). Or you could sink into the deep with hypnotic suggestions. Read *Richard Bandler's Guide to Tranceformations* and do the exercises. Or maybe you would just repeat a short, meaningless mantra with a soothing, calming, pleasant inner voice as you exhale, slow down and float into the empty core of yourself.

There are so many ways. I suggest you explore and use them all. And invent a few new ones.

You have drifted into a soft and gentle deep trance state. That's fine for the beginning. Some people believe this is meditation. It's not. Meditation is what you do once you have arrived in a deep trance. A lift may take you down into the basement, but you shouldn't remain standing in the lift. Perhaps you might explore the second name. You already did so when you followed the pathless road into yourself. Here is something to enjoy.

Let's go for a lookout and **watch the ways**. Imagine you are sitting in an open space. Maybe you are on a hillock or on a cliffside. Above a vast and wide sky is shining. Maybe you'd like a countryside with fields and pastures. Or maybe a desert scene with shifting dunes and parched thistles, or a steppe leading into pasture land. A garden is fine, as long as it contains plenty of open space. It's useful to go for something simple. Too much complication and detail, and you will strain to keep the vision steady. Too little detail and you'll feel bored and drift off into daydreams. Imagining a forest, for example, is too complicated for this exercise: it simply requires too much detail. Make it a restful and simple place. There is life around you. Maybe you can see a beetle walking beneath that shrub. Maybe a bird is winging to a branch. A centipede follows its way. A butterfly dances along the air currents. There are ways and paths wherever you look. Maybe you'll see animal tracks; the tiny paths made by mice in the grasses, and the tracks of larger prowlers. Maybe you see the paths of plants. Plants can see, having light-receptors at the very tips of their shoots, on the leaves, and on all green parts, and they use this skill to move towards the light. Maybe it's a small flower heading skywards. Maybe it's a huge tree stretching towards the light over months, years and centuries. Plants have all the time in the world. We simply don't notice their motions as we are too fast. And far above, the sun and moon, the planets and stars are following the streets of Heaven. What about humans? Maybe you can see a path, a way, a street or two. Or you could watch the canals and waterways and see how they transport animals, plants, people and, above all, information. We are talking passages. We are also exploring neural connections. You are the Watchful One who observes the ways.

Maybe you see an animal moving. That animal is more than a creature of the imagination: it is also an idea. Ideas don't appear on their own, they tend to come in clusters, sequences and relationships. One thought leads to the next, just as each step is followed by another. Think of it as a node within a complex web of neural connections. Each thought can be a street leading to other thoughts. You look at that dust coloured butterfly and all of a sudden you are thinking of butterflies you saw a few years ago. The scenery will have changed: the idea of the butterfly was your road to a memory. Or you'll think of seeing butterflies on your next holidays. They will take you to your destination. Maybe they remind you of culture heroine and tree goddess Julia Butterfly Hill. That thought could kick you right out of your imaginary scenery and take you to the redwood forests. For butterflies, like every other idea and thing, always connect with other ideas. Our minds do not produce separate chunks of thought material: they make you attach attention to a given neural pathway, and then you are off travelling along the streets of your mind. Follow that butterfly for a while. See where it goes. Then disengage and return to your hilltop. Sit peacefully. Watch out for the next thought.

Maybe you notice your posture has slumped. That physical sensation is also a road: it leads to increased body awareness. Follow that thought, sense your body, resettle yourself and return to the hillock in your mind. Other ideas are sure to attract your attention. Maybe you hear a noise on the street. Maybe the kids next door are laughing. Each sensation leads to many neural avenues. You can attach your awareness to it and find out where it takes you. Or you can keep your attention on a more rewarding subject and follow that road. An idea can carry you to new mind spaces while you forget yourself. Or maybe you remember yourself as you are sitting there, on that imaginary hillock, in that vast realm full of paths, roads and avenues of sensation. You can follow an idea and explore. Or you drop it and return to yourself. Anything that comes into your attention is such a road. It follows the laws of the Gods of the Streets; it connects with many, many other things. You can go on long journeys or on short ones. Or you can simply observe yourself observing. You can stay on your hillock and refuse to follow any road. All of this is in the second name: Lamaštu is watching the roads, and she is closely observing the deities of the roads. She is slightly suspicious of the gods, her brothers: you never know what gods are up to. The second name is based on attachment and release, ongoing with a flow of associations and of leaving it again. You lose yourself as you travel, you remember yourself as you stop. In between you can learn new things, come to fresh understandings, or allow yourself to become peaceful and empty by not going anywhere. Or you'll enjoy a happy daydream. It leads to good feelings. The roads and the spaces in between are your mind; they are in your world, in your body and your brain. Some of them are clusters of nerves and glial cells, some of them blood vessels, some are bones and some are shifting fields of sensation. Lamaštu moves along many ways. Or she hides in the swamps, thickets and shrubs between the paths and watches those who pass.

Roads and streets are useful when you want to transport something (or yourself). They are also very common metaphors. **'The Way'** is a common idea in many cultures. It would be nice to know how the Mesopotamians thought about it. They looked into the sky and observed what happens on Enlil's Way, Anu's Way and Enki's Way. Maybe they also thought about the Way of Ningirima across the cosmic waters. Plus the Ways of Sun and Moon. European thought has a very different interpretation of 'the Way' than East Asian philosophy. In China, Dao, a word meaning *'way, method, approach, sense, meaning'* was interpreted in several distinct ways. For Kongzi (Confucius) 'the Way' was a wilful effort towards personal refinement, leading to an improvement of society. His followers cultivated the way by promoted virtue, manners, humanity, compassion, love for their fellow men, strict social hierarchies, ethical values, duty, perfect performance of the rituals, ancestral worship and a beautiful type of serene music. Though Kongzi and his students spent a lot of time travelling on the road, they did not identify their way with physical motion. For Mengzi (Mencius), 'the Way' simply meant to be fully human. By contrast, Mozi preached, that 'the Way' is based on all-encompassing love for everyone. For the Daoists, 'the Way' is the natural condition of constant development. Heaven has a way, earth and underworld have a way, and the realm between height and depth, peopled by plants, animals and humans, also has a way. They all follow the way, but they do not go anywhere in particular. Their way is their nature. This way is universal and cannot be limited, defined or even comprehended. The Dao does not lead to any specific destination, nor does the metaphor imply travelling. You can happily sit there, facing south, like sage emperor Shun did, and you are still following the way. The way is the realisation of your natural potential. When a being follows the Dao, it simply manifests the essence of its nature. It requires spontaneous action and non-action, as the natural self is not sought, pursued, developed, found or gained, but appears naturally.

By contrast, European thought considers 'the Way' as a journey, an extended process of travel and discovery involving adventure, tribulation, trial, ordeal, choices, doubts, effort, struggle and similar exhausting activities. European thought makes much of choosing the right way, no matter how hard, steep and stony it may be. In European thought the concept of the Way is entangled with Christian sentiments; think of the road to Golgotha, the road to Damascus, the road to the Promised Land. Consider 'The Pilgrim's Progress', holy missions and crusades, remember how Odysseus came home and all American road movies featuring one mission, three trials and a grand finale with plenty of drama. Or think of such metaphors as 'the road to success', to 'make one's way', to 'forge a path', to 'make it to the top' or to 'go down the drain'. Politicians and advertisement crooks can sell us anything by calling it 'progress'.

Let's explore the **neural connections**. Your brain is full of roads, ways and passages; the streets of the great gods of perception, thought, memory and belief, and the canals and waterways of feeling and emotion (the limbic system). They get all the attention. It's misleading: most pictures of the brain tend to give the wrong impression. They emphasise the neural paths, and usually leave out the glial cells. Glia is Greek for 'glue'; the term was coined by scholars who assumed that the nerves do the thinking and the glial cells are a stabilising filling material and of little importance. In short, they overestimated the significance of the neural ways, paths and avenues, the great gods of our system, and ignored the funny bits in between: call them the settlements, fields, scenery, the landscape, or Lamaštu's wilderness, that make streets and passages meaningful. Only two decades ago, the glial cells were assumed to be simple, dumb padding. Since then, things have changed enormously. Let me summarise a few new insights regarding nerves and glial cells, and apologise for making things seem rather simple. I am sure that by the time you read this, new discoveries have been made.

To begin with, say hello to a simple nerve cell (neuron). Nerves, as I'm sure you know, are useful to transmit impulses. They do that from one end to the other, and they always do it in one direction. At the end, the nerve has a pre-synapse, which translates the electrical impulse into chemical neurotransmitters; these are released into the synaptic gap and picked up by a post-synapse belonging to another nerve, where they are either translated into a new electrical impulse, or stimulate the release of a chemical that creates a new impulse. So far, the system looks mechanical, but isn't: synapses have their own little ways of adapting what you think you are thinking.

Figure 75 Lady in the Window. Inspired by a popular Near Eastern motif.

When you keep thinking a specific thought (or processing a specific impulse) repeatedly, the synaptic gap between the many neurons that process it will shrink, making transmission faster and the post- and pre-synapses will produce more neurotransmitters and grow more receptors for them, so that the signal can be transmitted swifter, stronger and much easier. They will also grow more connections to other neurons. Brains process information simultaneously, so they use thousands of neurons to think a single thought. The result is called learning. Thinking specific thoughts again and again is literally habit forming. Our brains are transformed by what we think. That's one of the most fantastic insights of the last decades, it's called neuroplasticity. Quite simply, it shows that brains do not consist of hardware and software. The hardware is the software and vice versa. That, of course, explained why so many types of psychotherapy are harmful. It turns out that it is injurious to dwell on bad events, to wallow in pain and conflict and to re-live horrible episodes. The more you think about a trauma, the easier will you recall and re-experience it. Sadly, traditional analysis and therapy are problem-based. Freud and his followers introduced the idea that one has to explore misery, several times a week and for many years. In their opinion, 'repression' is a bad thing, as it will lead to something horrible appearing elsewhere. It's wrong. Repression is a natural strategy of the mind to heal itself. The less you think about a trauma, the harder will it be to recall. For similar reasons, people who did Gestalt Therapy, Encounter Therapy and similar 1970's entertainment, got used to screaming at other people. They assumed that aggression is 'honest'. In their model, the brain is a hydraulic machine, like a steam engine, pressure builds up and we are better off when we 'let it out'. That's wrong. The more you get used to screaming, confronting and making other people unhappy, the easier will it become. Sure, you can show that you are right. You can be self-assertive, blunt, tactless and mean. That, too becomes a habit. Ultimately, it leads to bad relationships, divorce, to loss of friends and alienated families. Our brains are changing all the time. Neurons that are rarely used wither away. Neurons that are in daily use improve. The London taxi drivers have a measurable increase in neuronal connections that process locations. People who make music intensify the connection between their brain hemispheres. Therapists should teach their patients to make good feelings, to advance towards useful goals and to become a part of a happy, productive network of people and beings who enjoy life as fully as they can. And before they do that, they should bloody well become happy, loveable, creative and enthusiastic people themselves.

In a simple happy-go-lucky nerve, with a diameter of 1 micrometre, the message travels at a speed of 10 km/h. That's pretty good going when you are an ant, and generally suffices for its long and weary working day. When you are a more complex being, like an octopus, you will prefer massive nerves with a thickness of 1000 micrometers; permitting seventy km/h transmission, but that's pretty much as fast as it can go. Octopuses are remarkably clever. They only have small brains, but it seems that their brains get extra support by thought processes that happen in the tentacles. Well, the octopus nerves are thick. They won't go much thicker, so thinking is limited to a specific speed. Simple diagrams tend to show that nerves work much like cables. That's wrong. The neural system is a lot more refined. The transmission of an electric charge does not mean that you have a little flash of lightning going from one end to the other, like a tiny, hectic traveller. That would be extremely inefficient. It would mean that you can only send one impulse at a time, and that the charge becomes weaker the longer it moves. Your nerves work with elegance and economy. To transfer the electric impulse you are not using crude electrons but a range of ions. Sodium ions and potassium ions conduct the message, while calcium ions maintain the health of the nerve cell and regulate its metabolism, plus its contacts to other cells. They can also modulate a signal at the synapses. To transport the impulse, your nerve cells use a cunning system. Imagine a tube. It has a fluid core, the cytoplasm, and it is surrounded by fluids. The inside and the outside have a different setup. In between, the wall of the tube is a semi-permeable membrane. This membrane makes impulse transmission possible. To begin with, the membrane has numerous little gates, sluices and pumps. All of them are extremely specialised and perfectly controlled. These gates are exactly adapted to allow very specific ions to pass through. The sodium channels allow sodium ions to pass; the potassium channels only allow potassium to go through. And these little gates and sluices can open and close on demand. Normally, the inside of a nerve (the cytoplasm) has a negative electric charge and the gates are shut. That's the usual state when that nerve isn't doing anything. There are plenty of negative ions inside the cytoplasm, and most of them will stay there for good. Outside of the membrane, much as they want to, the sodium ions with their positive charge cannot come in. When the electric impulse arrives at the synapse at the end of a nerve, the gates open for a few milliseconds and some sodium ions rush in. It's only about the millionth part of the available sodium ions in the neighbourhood, but they are quite sufficient to do the job. In a split instant, in a tiny location, the electrical charge reverses. At that tiny section of the nerve cell, you get a positive inside and a negative outside charge. It's a small electrical field, called an action potential, and it does not last. There is another set of little gates which are called ion-pumps. These little sluices throw three sodium ions out while they allow two potassium ions to enter the cytoplasm. It means that three positive charges leave while two enter. It turns the cytoplasm negative again. We have enormous amounts of sluices and pumps in the membranes of our nerve cells, and they are extremely fast. The sodium ions that were kicked out can't go back in again. The potassium ions can: many of them move in and go out as fast as they came in, including their positive electric charge. Within a split second, the cytoplasm at this location within the nerve cell turns negative and the outside turns positive. We are back at the beginning. The electrical impulse, or action potential, however, triggered the same chemical reaction in its neighbourhood. The electrical impulse travels one way, as the little sluices need a few milliseconds before they can react again. It means that the charge has to move towards those parts of the nerve that have not been stimulated yet. That's the gist of a very complex operation: we have a very short-lived action-potential, and it moves. Now the fantastic thing is that this sudden change from negative to positive and back to negative is conducted along the nerve cell. It can travel at amazing speed. Better still, it does not lose any of its intensity. In each place, the chemical reaction is fresh and new. The whole thing follows the all-or-nothing principle: either you get a change of charges or you don't. Nor is the system restricted to a single impulse. There is space for many travellers on any road. When the sluices have recovered they can pump ions in and out and relay the next electrical impulse. You can have a whole series of electric impulses moving along the same line. A nerve can conduct two or three action potentials at the same speed as fifty. And when a nerve cell divides, the signal continues along all branches without losing any of its intensity. So far, things are miraculous but still a bit slow. We are transmitting at a leisurely rate, at fairly high energy costs and the maximum, using an enormously thick nerve fibre, is about 70 km/h. If you are a mammal you might like something faster.

And here the **glial cells** start working their magic. So far, we know about three types of glial cells that make the nerves work well. Usually, they don't get the attention that they should. For without them, our splendid clever brains would be a very sorry sight. Let's start with the **oligodendroglia**. The word comes from *'some'* (Greek: oligos) *'trees'* (Greek: dendros). When you were born, much of your brain was pretty well developed. A lot of basic character traits, such as aggressiveness, assertiveness, sexual orientation, emotionality, capacity for spirituality, and daily activity peaks (are you an owl or a lark?) were already in place and waiting for you to grow up, develop and use them. This does not mean that everything was fixed and predetermined. We are talking vague fundamentals, which are always open for modification. The same goes for tendencies towards schizophrenia, autism, depression, drug abuse, anti-social behaviour and so on. When you do a brain autopsy of a schizophrenic, for instance, you are likely to find that the cells of the hippocampus, which handles long-term memory storage and the emotions the memories are coded to, are unusually chaotic and confused. In most cases, schizophrenia has a genetic background. And when the mother faced starvation during the first months of the pregnancy, her child is more likely to be aggressive, self-assertive and overweight. Brain research has come quite a way. In the 1970's it was gospel that people are the product of their environment and training. Humans, so it was thought, are the product of their family, their society, culture and conditioning. The socialists and Marxists loved this idea. In their book, everybody is equal, a baby is a blank slate and when we exert enough pressure on children we can train them to be anything. Anybody speaking of inherited tendencies was eyed as a reactionary right-winger. Since then, several very basic character traits have turned out to be influenced by genes. I'm not saying that the genes make us run like mindless automatons; it simply means that they incline us, to a larger or smaller extent, towards certain characteristics. How we deal with them, and to what extent we develop or control them, are determined by other factors, like pre-natal influences, environment, training and choice. Long before we were born, some of our characteristics were stimulated by genes; while others were influenced by the environment, by the health and happiness of our mother, and by damaging and intelligence reducing substances such as alcohol, nicotine, drugs, hard medication and stress hormones (Swaab, 2013). Genes are not simply traits that act like mindless automatons. For one thing, genes come in clusters. One gene is activated and it drops by with a couple of friends. When scientists bred a tame, household version of foxes, they noticed some amazing side effects. They had gone for domestic qualities, but as a side effect the foxes developed hanging ears and began to wag their tails. The thing is that genes that specify characteristics, like green eyes, black hair or a tendency towards a disease, do not work on their own initiative. They have to be stimulated by so-called 'promoter genes'. These, in turn, react to the feedback within the body and to the signals they receive from the outside world.

When you were born you had a basic outfit for your future development. However, the nerves of your brain were pretty much in their raw state. To grow up and learn, you had to insulate them. To do this properly, the foetus needs to build up a store of vitamin ***B^{12}*. This store has to be there before birth.** The baby gets it from its mother. If the mother is a vegetarian or vegan, and low on vitamin B^{12}, the baby may be challenged. Please note that algae, while containing substances similar to this vitamin, are not a good equivalent. Our brains evolved, over between two or one million years, by using plenty of animals fat and protein. After you were born, using the ***B^{12}***, the oligodendroglias began to wrap themselves around the nerves of your brain. They did a fantastic job: all of those nerves were perfectly insulated from one end to the other. The process took many years. As your brain kept growing well into your twenties, the oligodendroglias had quite a lot of work. They made it easier to stabilise and bundle nerves. Now the oligodendroglias are full of fat and protein. They form a durable isolation, called the myelin sheath, but they also have their own built-in openings. These little openings are called the myelin sheath gaps, or Ranvier's nodes, and they are packed full of ion pumps and ion channels. While the rings are only around two micrometers in width, the distance between them can be up to 2000 micrometres. When the little sluices and pumps act, we get an amazing little electric field. It is stronger than the impulse that travels in an insect nerve: thanks to the insulation the action potential is so intense that it can leap to the next set of pumps and sluices. It's called salutatory (i.e. jumping) propagation of action potentials. The electric field jumps from one segment to the next, which is much faster than travelling along every bit of the way. Better still, the transmission cost less energy. Now clever know-it-all mammals, such as us, tend to use lots of neurons. A normal brain may, at an estimate, contain 100 billion neurons. Unlike other cells in your body, most of them do not reproduce themselves. To make up for this deplorable fact, they can work happily and efficiently for decades. Each of them may be in touch with thousands of other nerves. And they do not work sequentially, like a computer, but simultaneously. Our brains favour a nerve thickness of one micrometer, just as the bugs do. But while their impulses only make 10 km/h, our perfectly insulated neurons transmit charges at more than 400 km/h!

All of this leads to the conclusion that nerves may be well and good, but when we want to process information really smartly we have to coat them properly.

But there is more to the glial cells. Many of them belong to the category of **astroglial** cells ('*star-like glue*'). Astroglial cells have plenty of extensions. They use them to connect nerve strands and, above all, to control the interaction of neurons with blood. There are plenty of blood vessels, an estimated 600 km altogether, passing through your brain. A given substance can flood your brain within ten to twenty seconds! Blood vessels, in their normal state, are not securely insulated. Besides transporting blood, fluids, antibodies, nourishment, oxygen, hormones and other stuff, they also leak them into the places where they are needed. In many places, they just emit a little. In others, like liver and kidneys, the word 'porous' acquires an entirely new level of meaning. Now your brain needs only a small number of special substances from your blood. The astroglial cells coat and insulate the blood vessels and form what is called the blood-brain barrier. It ensures that only very few materials in strictly controlled amounts can pass from the blood to the nerves. The astroglial cells act much like a complicated system of checkpoints and security gates. Without them, our brain functions would instantly collapse. Your neurons require a perfectly controlled environment to do their job. The astroglial cells ensure that your brain gets plenty of sugar (which they instantly convert into user-friendly lactate) and a range of messenger molecules, such as hormones and neurotransmitters. But the astroglial cells also guarantee that waste products are eliminated. They keep your brain clean. In deep sleep, glial cells shrink. It pumps cerebral-spinal fluids into the nooks and crannies of your brain. When the glial cells expand again, the fluid flushes out the chemical waste. This cleaning operation happens several times each night, unless alcohol, drugs or other influences upset your sleep patterns and prevented you from sleeping deeply enough. Have you ever had a hangover? Much of it was due to dehydration, the loss of salts and the disruption of your deep sleep cleanup operations. Besides nourishing the nerves, the Astroglial cells are busy disposing of used material and control the chemical balance within your head. And they communicate with each other without making use of the nerve network! Unlike most nerves in your brain, the astroglial cells can renew themselves. And they can stimulate the replacement neurons in the hippocampus (useful for memory functions) and in the organs that identify scents. Let's meet the third basic group of glial cells. They are called **microglial** cells, and are an extremely adaptable and tough lot. Usually, microglial cells extend long tendrils to various parts of the brain. They have two basic jobs. One of them is maintenance: they eliminate damaged and dead cells and neurons. The other job is security. Your brain is one of the best-protected parts of your organism. When intruders try to get in, the microglias go ballistic. They withdraw their long roots, turn into amoeba shape, rush to the front and begin to emit toxic substances, such as oxygen- and nitrogen radicals. Like Lamaštu, they spit poison. It's their job to destroy microbes and viruses. And when their effort does not suffice, they can signal for support: body brews up lethal antibodies and transports them to the brain via the bloodstream, where the microglial storm troopers put them to good use. In order to eliminate their opponents, the microglial cells can produce localised inflammation. Microglial cells are the super heroes of your brain and a fantastic defence-force. Sadly, they are also reckless and over-enthusiastic. When they bombard intruders with toxins, they can cause lateral damage to the neighbouring nerves, and in some diseases of the auto-immune system they try to dismantle the myelin sheathing of the nerves.

So we have three basic functions of the glial cells: oligodendroglias ensure insulation, bundling of nerves and accelerate information transmission. Astroglial cells control the exchange of nutrients, waste products and chemical balances in your brain. Finally, microglia cells are the caretakers and security staff. Without their constant activity, your nerves could simply pack up and go home (Pinel & Pauli, 2012:84-100; Beck, 2013: 73-116). If we imagine the nerves as streets, roads and highways, the glial cells are making traffic possible. They repair and clean roads, supply energy and illumination, run restaurants, parking lots, petrol stations and hotels, impose traffic control and speed limits, police the highways and ensure that animals and people don't walk across the lanes.

Think of the roads in ancient Mesopotamia. Transport and travelling happened in donkey caravans, along the great royal roads, in boats and ships along the rivers and the major waterways. Next to them were settlements: people who made a living by being close to the roads and wharves, locals who provided food and fodder, drink, shelter, rest, entertainment, sex, healing and security. Traders fed their packing animals or acquired new ones, boats were repaired; there was an entire industry devoted to the transmission of people, animals, goods and information. It was vital for the economy: without regular exports and imports, Mesopotamia, with its limited resources, could not have developed a civilisation. All of this was done by those who are the siblings of the gods of the streets. The Watchful Ones of the Streets have their own intelligence, their own habitations and their own bizarre habits and customs. Their dwelling places are the realms where travel slows down or stops, where the large streets are replaced by tiny paths, small alleys, by dirt tracks, garden paths and animal trails. You meet them at the places where the resources come from: shelter, shade, fruit and grain, water, meat, fish, wool, timber, fibre, reeds, minerals and oil products. Streets relate to the scenery as moving to being. You can move along a street, or along a neural pathway, or follow a strand of ideas to other realms. As you recognise the many roads and paths that open up from here, the many neural passages, the many possible thoughts, memories and sensations you could have, you are also free to rest a while, sit in the shade, have a drink, relax and enjoy the show.

Var.1.: The third: Knife (or: Sword), that Splits the Head; Var.2.: The third: Knife (or: Sword) that Cuts the Head down.

The third name has much to do with division. It is not a creative but an analytic faculty, a skill to divide the bits that make up a totality, and examine each item separately.

Think of a scalpel, a knife, heavy bronze cleaver or a sword. You can cut complex things apart. It makes them easier to handle. *Take a simple sentence and examine it deeply.* That's a good one. First, spend a few minutes thinking about 'Take'. Then a while for 'a'. The word 'a' doesn't get the attention that it should. Devote some minutes (or hours) for 'simple'. You wouldn't believe how difficult 'simple' can be. Next, explore 'sentence'. Consider the word 'and'. It's a lot more than filling material. Contemplate what 'examine' means. Learn what the word 'it' implies. Last, find out what 'deeply' is all about. Each word can be a full meditation. To explore a single phrase you might take several hours. I am sure you do the sensible thing, like the Sumerians did, and made a list. It will help you realise what is in a given message. And it will show you that words like 'take', 'simple', 'examine' and 'deeply' are unspecific: they appear to have a certain meaning, but they actually invite you to hallucinate one. And did you notice the missing bits? Our sentence is just the surface structure of the message. A lot is missing, hidden or open to invention. Our example describes an activity or a process. Who is to do the activity? Who says so? When should it happen, where, how intensely and how frequently? Communication is a miracle. I keep marvelling that it happens at all. We utter a few words in a sloppy, haphazard way. The listener picks up some of them, provided he or she is listening, which isn't always the case, and projects a meaning on them. Most of it happens in the mind. My 'simple' is not your 'simple', my 'take' happens in a different way than yours does. How we go about 'examining' may be worlds apart. It's amazing that people can talk with each other at all. Each sentence is a signal: it has a sender, a transmitter and a recipient. Who said these words? Who are they intended for? And did anyone, such as an editor, interfere with them? No, Sorita didn't. I'm deeply grateful for it. Consider the transmitter. It can be a piece of paper or air carrying sound. When a sentence is spoken, it communicates a lot more than the meaning of its words. An enormous amount of information is conveyed through intonation, pauses, tonality, rhythm, speed, volume, gesture, posture and so on. All of these are missing in the written word. Another obstacle: the background. The message relates to a certain level of understanding. When you speak with a child, you have to take care to start from the basics. Women usually do this much better than men. That's because they identify with the person they are talking to. Bosses are notoriously bad at it. They tend to assume that their employees automatically think as they do, and leave out 'self-evident' bits. In communication, very little is self-evident. If the employees thought like their boss, they would quit and found their own company. And when you talk with a close friend or someone who is a specialist in the same field as you are, you can reduce your communication to a few words and hints, share a laugh and things work out perfectly.

We started with a simple phrase. The sword did its job: now we are facing a collection of odds, ends, broken mirrors, gaps and question marks. That's how the sword works and what it is good for. Now take a verse from a Sumerian poem and explore it. And remember to do the Sumerian thing: make notes and lists to improve your recall.

The sword is also good to free you from bondage. When attachment goes beyond a healthy stage, bonds become fetters and have to be cut. I am sure you are thinking of Kālī or Tārā now. The black goddesses wield their terrifying cleavers to slay demons on the battlefield. It might be a metaphor; only that the battlefield is life and the demons are the thoughts, urges and obsessions that lost divine grace and transformed into something sick, unhappy and disabling. With one hand, Kālī swings her sword, and cuts down evil and good. Another hand holds a severed head. In a third hand, she holds a polished bone cup. The cup is empty and open to the sky. It receives the blood dripping from a severed head. The juice is divine nourishment. It is the perfect wine of the Nightside Tantras: the hormonal secretions and neurotransmitters produced by the glands. As the *Kulacūḍāmaṇi Tantra* states, the real wine of the adepts comes pouring from the top of the head. Everything else is just booze. Her fourth hand is probably making gestures at you. They mean: don't be afraid and I grant boons. Yes, we are talking Tantra here. It seems more violent than it is. Kālī seizes the heads of her devotees and liberates them with a single, clean stroke. Around her throat is a garland of heads. Each of them has done its duty. Each of them is smiling blissfully. And life continues.

Meet the tantric goddess of wisdom. She is Chinnamastā, the headless goddess. When her friends Varṇinī and Ḍākinī were hungry, the goddess cut off her own head. Three fountains of blood spurted skywards. The goddess and her friends had a long, nourishing drink. Then Chinnamastā put on her head again and fixed it with a spell. Maybe she looks a little pale. But she certainly learned a lot and found true nourishment when her head came off.

To split the head can mean that you open your mind to entirely new ideas. It can mean that you leave the skull-prison of a single, limited awareness. With an open head, a lot of empty chatter fades away. You can shut up, listen and learn. When the head comes off, multiple points of view are available. This is wisdom: seeing the world from many perspectives. As long as your head is attached to your body, you are limited to a single position. When your head is disentangled from the body, it is free to learn new things. And when your body is released from your head and its incessant thinking, planning, scheming, hoping and worrying, it may feel sensations that the head would never bother to notice. You can be one and two, can be head and body, and that which is beyond them, and come together again for a new understanding.

Here is a fascinating meditation. It's all about differences. The sword, the dagger and the axe: all have an edge to divide this from that. In daily life, experience is often fluid and continuous, it shifts from one idea or thing to another while you hardly notice what is going on. But that's not all there is to life. We can go cosmic, holy and spaced out and delight 'everything is one'. That thought takes us part of the way. But we also have to say 'everything is different', for unless we tell one thing from another, we'll never learn which differences make a difference.

The sword also allows you to disengage from your sense of identity. It can be a blessing. Every personality, no matter how great and wonderful, is limited. You only have to consider what a person is good at and you will instantly know the weaknesses. Every talent has a price. When you need some distance from your desires, fears, worries and obsessions, eliminate the common denominator: the sense of identification, that, whatever you tend to consider your self. The key obsession is the sense of I-ness that makes you identify with some things, like your body, your clothes, your home, family, friends, property etc. And with a lot of ideas, such as your name, history, strengths, weaknesses, hopes, worries and so on. This sense of identification is not there by nature: a newly born baby can sense and experience with amazing intensity, but is not able to tell one sensation from the other. You learned to tell friends from strangers, your home from the unknown, and your body from everything else.

Let me speculate. The sense of 'self' seems to appear in at least two different ways. One of them is an **unspecified self**. It is formless and undefined. You hardly notice it is there. It has no definite age, gender, nature, nationality or past: it just exists within the great and wonderful show of life. Thanks to this timeless self, young children can be experienced and wise and elders everlasting young. This self is spontaneous and direct. You can sense it in microbes, trees, ducks, people and entire biospheres.

The other is the **specific self**. It considers itself a thing, a reality, and believes in its own name, nature, character, personality, body, shape, energy tonus, social status, property, in its desires, preferences, drives, achievements, failures, hang-ups, memories, past, present, future and so on. This 'self' travels with a lot of luggage. It is proud of its achievements and ashamed of its errors. It identifies with a few things and neglects many others. It walks past the poor, the sick and disabled, past pollution, suffering, and ecological mass-destruction, and hardly notices them. The specific self only wants to feel about a narrow range of beings. When people fall in love, they spend ages talking about their specific selves. It's part of the courtship and leads to a new definition or personality. You guessed it, the specific self is based on delusions. You are not the same person as you were in kindergarten. Your parents, your family and friends have changed. You may think that you are as you were ten years ago, but in plain fact, there is hardly a cell in your body which is that old. What we are is mostly borrowed. We lent it from the earth, from parents, plants and animals, and we give it up as we go along. What ends up in the grave is not what you were born with. Your character was all in the mind, reinvented as the years flew past, and what you own was never yours. You merely kept and used it, and passed it on to the next generation.

The specific self is limited by its definition, confined by its shape, form and thinking. Definition limits possibilities. However, it does have its uses. People who happily drift along in the unspecified self are vulnerable. When you are formless and undefined, other beings will soon learn how to exploit it. From time to time it's useful to pretend to be someone with edges and corners, and set up clear distinctions. That, too is the work of the sword.

One useful meditation is to go into a deep trance. Go into a setting where you feel at home. Invoke your personal deity. Ask it to chop off your head. Where will your awareness go? You have several choices. 'You' can remain as a headless trunk. Or 'you' can stay in the head, facing a headless trunk. You can leave body and head, merge with your personal deity, and watch head and trunk, somewhere out there. Both of them are sort of limited. Face yourself! Who is this person that you deem to be yourself? Who has it been? Who will it be? What does the face tell you, what is the expression, where is the real self behind the mask of flesh and bone?

When you hold your head in your hands, talking to yourself takes on a new dimension.

When you are headless, all body, all feeling, an entirely different range of sensations and urges awaits you. Who is this body? What does it want to do? What are its likes and dislikes? What inclinations are in its genes?

When you are your deity, facing a head and a headless trunk: what can you learn from them, what can you offer to them? How can you reprogram the 'you' after you have come apart?

There are plenty of answers. Enjoy them. Make it a good feeling. Make it a good mind. Make it a personality that has a future, and looks forward to many lives. Understand the way your head moves body and body motivates the head. And learn about the many possibilities beyond both. And when you are ready, put yourself together again, give this all-encompassing self a huge, radiant smile, say thank you to yourself and the gods, and move into a happier future.

In her third name, Lamaštu, though she is not death in general, is very close to our Lady of the Great Earth, Ereškigal. Indeed the head is beaten **to the ground**. It's good to get down to the roots from time to time. It brings to mind the microorganisms living in the soil. Most of them are shy. Plough the earth and they will die. Most microorganisms can't take ultraviolet light, so sunlight will kill them, and many don't like heat and oxygen. People are rarely aware of them, and their way of life is truly hidden, i.e. occult. In central Europe, a cubic metre of healthy forest soil contains approximately two kilos of microorganisms, not counting viruses. When you put them under a microscope, most of them die and shrivel away. Beneath your feet are thousands of species. Most of them are not even discovered yet. Consider them as an amazingly productive cooperative. As you get down to the leaf-litter, you meet bugs, wolf spiders, woodlice and other isopoda, centipedes and millipede, beetles and their larvae. There are rainworms, snails, slime mould, nematodes, mites and fungi. In between there are plenty of archaic protozoa and bacteria. Still smaller are the viruses. True enough, most of these beings face life without a brain. The intelligence in most heads, provided there is a head at all, is tiny. But we ain' so clever either. And when you consider all these lifeforms as a single organism, and the rhizosphere (*realm of roots*) as a self-regulating eco-system, you arrive at a community of astonishing intelligence. Each handful of forest floor is brimming full of life. All of these lifeforms are somehow dedicated to the destruction and transformation of organic matter. In the process, they create humic acids, plus polysaccharides or sugar molecules. These, in turn, determine soil fertility. The soil chemistry decides which

Figure 76 - Between the Mind and Wilderness.

plants will grow in a specific location, which will influence animal populations, and ultimately our own settlements. Very little is known about the humic acids. Some of them detoxify the ground; transform molecules, store chemicals and make nutrients available for plants (Buhner, 2002:164-168). It can work for or against us. The meat industry uses huge amounts of antibiotics to keep so many animals under horrible conditions and to make them grow faster. The meat retains very little of them; the major amount is flushed out with the urine. Even more antibiotics are used by hospitals, laboratories and above all, by people who are sick. They go into the sewers, where they make friends with other chemicals and drugs. The happy 'organic' farmers are not supposed to use chemical fertiliser. Most do not keep enough animals to fertilise their fields. So they go to the sewage cleaning plant, gets yucky black stuff beyond description and dump it on the ground. I've seen it happen many times. The microorganisms and humic acids transform the antibiotics, drugs and waste products, and before long we find them, in a new form, easily accessible and storable in human organs, in our 'organic' bread (Pollmer, 2012:92-93). We depend on soil chemistry, and on the organisms that produce it, but we know less about them than about the denizens of boiling hot deep-sea plumes. Have you ever seen the foam that builds on forest ponds? No, it's not a case of pollution. A heavy rainfall has washed humic acids into the water, and made it foam. The soil is life. It's so enormously alive that we might consider it as a single life form, a huge, many-faced organism that extends over the continents and regulates their ecology. Charles Darwin was one of the first biologists who appreciated this. He devoted much effort to the study of the humble earthworm. Darwin explored their senses, their behaviour and even tested whether they like music. Some may think the earthworm is a boring subject. However, without its activity, we might say goodbye to most fields, and in consequence, to most people inhabiting the earth. Without earthworms, agriculture collapses. When an earthworm emerges from its hole in the middle of the night, it will search for organic matter, preferably foliage. Darwin demonstrated that earthworms know which side of a leaf they have to snatch to drag it underground. He tested various leaves and even pieces of paper cut into different shapes. Earthworms make conscious decisions and show more sense than you would expect from most people. Earthworms have a fascinating lovelife. They know the earthworms of their neighbourhood personally and go visiting. Next time you see an earthworm, bow your head. Without its efforts, you would not be alive. The soil has its own intelligence. Or it would have, if it was allowed to follow its nature. To produce perfect French fries for the world, American farmers grow enormous amounts of a potato species which is exceedingly vulnerable to fungi and animals. As Michael Pollan describes in full detail, the farmers have to start the cultivation by disinfecting (!) their fields. All through the growth of the crop, they keep using lethal toxins. When they have to visit their fields, full body protection suits are required.

Consider agriculture. Fertiliser basically consists of nitrogen, phosphor and potassium. Good nitrogen is organic; it comes from animals and their corpses. phosphor, unless it's organic, is a rare sedimentary mineral and its production is ecologically unsound. Phosphor is a rare commodity and likely to run out in the near future. Potassium is derived from carrion, dung, urine, ashes and a few plants. Plants need to eat animals (Keith, 2009:26-29). Life mostly feeds on life. Healthy fields need blood, bones, flesh, urine, ashes, minerals and manure. That's what they got for many million years. It's what the soil organisms are used to. Approximately 600 species of plants, like pitcher plants and Venus flytraps, are known to eat animals. That's the obvious ones. A much larger number kills animals indirectly. Tobacco, potatoes, tomatoes, tea, coffee and many others use toxins to weaken the insects which touch them. Eventually, the insects die and drop, their bodies enriching the soil. There are even violets that hunt worms by poisoning them with their roots (Mancuso & Viola, 2015:67).

Artificial fertiliser is a petrol product. It, too, is organic: oil and coal are the remnants of plants and animals that died 330-275 millions of years ago. It produces harvests that are 250% larger than using natural fertiliser, but will be available only as long as petrol lasts. And it kills plenty of organisms. The more artificial fertiliser you use, the less life survives in the ground. In short, the fertile field of today is a junkie surviving thanks to petrol-based drugs. Year after year it needs more of them to feed us. It's time to get our head down to the ground. At the moment, one vague hope lies in genetic engineering. Some leguminous plants, like lentils, beans, peas, lupines, mugwort, ginkgo and cyanobacteria live in a symbiosis with nitrogen binding or producing bacteria. The bacteria gain sugars and protection; the plants gain natural fertiliser. In the old days, farmers grew leguminous plants every couple of years to enrich the soil with nourishment. Nowadays, farmers are so badly harassed by the six companies that control over 90% of the world's food production, that they can hardly afford to give the soil time to regenerate itself. If the genes for the support of these microbes could be transferred to the major harvest plants, mankind might stand a chance to survive the next few hundred years in moderate comfort (Mancuso, 2015:96-99). So let us stay optimistic and remember our dues to Ereškigal. She is the queen of the dead and the life of the ground. Lift a hand full of soil and feel it pulsing with life. And remember Lamaštu. One way or another, each organism takes conscious life to survive, and feeds future life with its own. Nature is cruel and generous: most plants and animals die before they reach maturity. A single beech gives birth to maybe 1,8 million beechnuts during its lifetime. Animals, fungi, microorganisms eat them. They die. So will the beech, after several centuries. Only one tree will take its place. The head is chopped off and falls to the ground. From its lowly station, the head learns something new, and fresh life arises.

Var. 1.: ***The fourth: She Who Ignites the Wood to Flame;***

Var. 2.: ***The fourth: She Who Ignites the Flame;***

Var. 3.: ***The fourth: She Who Topples the Tree;***

The fourth name has much to do with excitement, attachment, heat, lust, rage and fierce emotions. Lamaštu is furious, is fire, is fever, heat and cold, and has an awesome radiance. She can teach you when it is time to remain cool and when it is great to become hot, enthusiastic and excited. Both are essential skills for mind-explorers. When other people go crazy, you can remain cool and calm and plan ahead. And when life seems dull and boring you can choose to become excited about something that seems 'normal' to everybody else and make it an enjoyable, unique and happy event.

Heat and cold are keys to a series of fascinating experiences. Let's begin by considering fever. Mesopotamian doctors were aware that there are several types of fever, and made a point of noting how they appeared, how regular the heat waves came, and with what symptoms they were associated. I can only admire their diagnostic skills. To be sure, they had little control over most diseases. Still, they tried to observe them carefully, and recorded their observations. It was the first scientific approach to medicine. Some fevers were assumed to be caused by dangerous spirits. Others were caused by the 'hand' of a deity. As usual, a whole range of gods were responsible, one major culprit being Ištar. Last, there were diseases that simply involved fever, but did not require a divine or spiritual agency. Fever is, very generally speaking, a useful strategy to destroy viruses or bacteria, to slow or obstruct their procreation. It gives the immune systems more time to brew up the proper antibodies. Many viruses are restricted by temperature. Now viruses are not really life forms, as they have no metabolism, nor do they really breed. In many ways they are like programs that rest inert until they get access to a functional computer. However, they are damned good at infecting and transforming bacteria. In a dry environment around twenty degrees C. influenza viruses can survive for half a day, and hope to be picked up by a passing stranger. Below that temperature, they can survive for several days, especially when it's damp or wet. At zero degrees Celsius they last pretty much indefinitely. One great way of thwarting the virus is to raise body temperature. It produces an environment where they cannot proliferate so easily. Each infection is a race against time. You have several immune systems, some of them inherited from your ancestors and others personally acquired by being sick and staying alive. Your body contains an enormous 'library' telling the immune systems which special antibodies are needed for what infection. When you encounter a virus, you unconsciously identify it, figure out whether you've had the disease or something similar before and start producing the right sort of defensive antibodies. It takes a few days before you have enough antibodies in the fight. When you've had the disease before, you may need three days to arm your defences, and during this time you probably feel uneasy, weakened, sad or edgy. Then your antibodies take over and crush their opponents. When the virus is new (or a mutation of an old virus) the defence may not work that elegantly. Influenza viruses have their own little tricks. They like to change the proteins that cover their surface, making it harder for your immune system to identify them. And they mutate much faster than other viruses. The basic genome of an influence virus does not consist of a single strand of DNA or RNA but of eight short, separate RNA segments. They transform with breathtaking speed. As a result, new types of influenza appear every year (Ben-Barak, 2010:118-124). In our modern age of superstition, the majority of doctors still prescribe antibiotics against them, which is sheer stupidity, considering that roughly 90% of influenzas are caused by viruses. Antibiotics don't act against viruses, nor do they work against curses, demons and the evil eye: they only kill some bacteria. As collateral damage, they mess up your digestive tract, breed resistant bacteria and incite extreme or nightmarish dreams. It doesn't stop most doctors from handing them out like sweets. Unlike a normal doctor, your body does the sensible thing: it sends you to bed and raises the temperature. You can thank your hypothalamus, your brain stem, and your personal deities for doing such an excellent job.

Fire is vital in many meditations. As you recall, Lamaštu has a body full of scorching fire, holds fire in her hands and provides an extra helping of heat for suffering patients (LS I, 61; LS I, 123 & LS I, 177). It's not a bad thing at all: before Marduk could fight and overthrow Tiāmat, he had to arm himself with spells, a sacred plant and fill his body with fire. Fire acts as a magical energy, a fierce, angry, devastating, lustful and maddening essence that purges, purifies and exalts.

The exorcisms of the first millennium BCE Mesopotamia celebrate the fire gods. None of them is a major deity, but all of them are important when it comes to banishing a disease or to destroy an evil influence. In the *Maqlû Series*, much attention is devoted to Girra, firstborn son of Anu, to Gibil and to Nusku, who brighten the dark, disentangle confusion, lead court proceedings, give advice, proclaim commands and orders to the divine assemblage and ensure truth and justice, just like the major gods Nanna/Suen/Sîn and Utu/Šamaš. The raging fire gods are wrathful deities; they are the enduring word of the gods, they serve the burned offerings to the deities. They scorch reeds, wood and stone, burn evil, ill-deed, transgression and the terrible spells and the curses of hostile sorcerers and witches.

Most fire gods are friendly to mankind, protect the house from dangerous spirits, diseases and lethal sorceries, bring blessings and receive offerings, which they conduct to heaven. Fire serves as a gate to the otherworlds, it brings illumination, divine justice, light, warmth and comfort, it causes lust, ensures offspring, and protects the family. Nusku is a judge, who destroys the enemies of the household, who expels and banishes madness, weakness, paralysis, impotence, evil sorceries, slander and murder. He knows those who work evil, and just like Utu/Šamaš, he passes judgement, and metes out punishment. He is a child of Anu, the firstborn son of Enlil, offspring of the ocean, created by the lord of Heaven and Earth and advisor of the great gods (*Maqlû Series*, I, 73-144). He is lauded as the overseer of the offerings of the Igigi gods, founder of cities, renewer of the thrones of the gods. Nusku is the bright day, whose orders are supreme, the obedient messenger of Anu, councillor, treasure of the Igigi, powerful in battle, whose appearance is mighty, slaying enemies with lightning flashes. Without him, no food is offered in Enlil's temple Ekur, incense will not rise and Šamaš will not hold court (*Maqlû Series* II, 1-11). Only a few lines further, we encounter praise for another fire god, Girra, the perfect lord, whose name is '*You are Mighty*'. He is a firstborn son of Anu, the leader of trials, the herald of judgement, who brightens the dark, who untangles what is confused, creates order, gives his decisions to the great gods (while no god decides for him), passes orders and instructions, binds the evildoer and strikes the enemy (*Maqlû Series*, II, 19 & 76-85). There's a lot more to come. Girra, the *terrible storm*, leads the gods and nobles, helps the oppressed and downtrodden, burns (the effigies) of wizards and witches, is the eternal word of the gods, the one who hands out the sacrifices to the deities, who creates gleaming light for the Anunnaki gods. He rages in the flaming reeds, destroys wood and stone, burns the evildoers, the offspring of sorcerers and witches and so on, at considerable length and ad nauseam. But the fire gods also have peaceful aspects: *Šurpu Series* IV, 104-105 calls Nusku the sukkal (vizier) of Enlil who speaks in favour of the sacrificer and heals the body of the sick, and Girra is the conciliator of the wrathful (personal) god and goddess who removes weariness from the body.

It should suffice to show the sacred and purifying nature of fire. I am sure you remember that fire also represented lust, desire, arousal, strong emotions, and even quarrelling, anger and wrath. All of them are essential when you want to understand the meaning of Lamaštu's fire, and use it in meditation and daily life.

Indo-Europeans often considered fire a sacred force and preferred to burn their corpses. For most Mesopotamians, it would have been a sacrilegious act resulting in a dangerous ghost flittering around, homeless, hungry, confused and dangerous. There are hardly any fire burials in evidence. A very few were unearthed in Uruk, and another handful in Assyria, but these are singular exceptions that may indicate the burials of foreigners. When Neo-Assyrian kings burned their enemies alive, they ensured their souls would flit around without a home.

Let's look into early Indian religion. Vedic ritual had its greatest flowering in the excessive Soma rituals, with seers and brahmins spaced out of their heads. But the Vedic ritualists were by no means limited to drug-induced states of ecstasy and vision. They also used a range of mind-transforming austerities to enliven their visions and magical power. The term for them is **tapas**, meaning **heat**. The basic forms of tapas are related to fire, warmth and the inner heat that arises in states of rage and divine madness. Some seers and poets, called vipras (from vip- meaning '*to vibrate, shake, shudder*') explored shaking to attain states of spiritual rapture. Like so many Central Asian shamans they initiated trances where body trembles, jerks and quakes. It's a very common skill that can be observed in many cultures. Shaking can increase excitement and excitement can increase shaking. Early researchers dismissed it as 'pseudo-epilepsy', but as it turns out, shamanic trembling is neither a disease nor involuntary. Good shaking trances can be controlled, they can be started and ended at will, and they are useful when people want to trance in a cold climate. I wrote about them in *Helrunar*, *Seidways* and *Kālī Kaula*, so forgive me for not elaborating on the matter. Shaking is one way to generate heat, or to channel inner, or psychic heat. It was not only practiced in the Vedic period but continued in Indian folk religion and Tantra. When Indian ritualists are obsessed by a deity they often 'get vibration' and start to tremble, to stagger and to stumble around. The same thing can happen when cakras are activated, when the 'fire snake' Kuṇḍalinī is roused, or when a physical or spiritual blockage is pierced by a *'Descent of Energy'* (Śaktipāta). All of these topics are discussed in *Kālī Kaula*. Here, I would like to confine our exploration to ritual heat, and to austerities. You can learn to shake to raise 'inner heat', or you can dance for an hour until you are bathed in sweat. Both approaches are useful if you want to add an extra charge of energy to your ritual.

In a general way, tapas means austerities. Many of them were painful and some damaging. It hardly seemed to matter. In the Vedic and Upaniṣadic period, the seers showed little concern about their health. Seers did tapas, no matter how injurious or agonizing, and so did the gods when they needed a bit of extra power to gain immortality or to overthrow a bunch of wicked demons.

The historical Buddha spent a lot of time practicing tapas in the company of forest ascetics, including excessive fasting which almost killed him. Consequently, he was averse to extreme asceticism. His followers did not always share this opinion. Unlike modern Hinduism, which went to some lengths to reduce the amount of tapas in daily worship, many early Buddhists (and quite a lot of Buddhist saints) went to extremes to mortify their flesh. Tapas appears in many guises; for our purpose we shall only look at one of its branches: that involving heat and fire.

Early Vedic religion had a special fire ritual for the sponsor of the sacrifice and his wife. It was called **Dīkṣa**, a term that is nowadays used for a range of usually soft initiation rites. The sponsors were settled in a small hut, wrapped and tied up in the hides of black antelopes, very close to a fire. The ritual usually lasted for half or even a whole day. They were allowed no food or water, except for a few symbolic mouthful of milk. By the time the rite was over, they had become Agni, the god of fire, and Agni had become them. And they were pretty close to death: the commentaries state that the sponsors enter the ritual fat, and leave it thin and emaciated. They were led to a river for purification and to release the excess of fire and divinity. It made them fit to participate in the Soma ritual and to gain its spiritual benefits. Mind you, they were forbidden to taste the Soma and received a substitute instead.

A development of the late Vedic (or early Upaniṣadic) period was a specific tapas ritual called Panca-dhūni: *'the rite of five fires'*. For this yoga, the seer sat between four large fires, each of them representing a cardinal direction, for a prolonged and utterly exhausting meditation. The fifth fire came from above: the scorching heat of the sun. A similar method was used by some Jaina seers, who purposely exposed themselves to sunstroke during worship. For similar reasons, some Vedic seers favoured retaining breath as long as possible: it made them heat up and sweat intensely. But we also find the meditation between fires in ritual Buddhism. In her remarkable study *The Catalpa Bow*, Carmen Blacker cites many examples of Japanese 'shamanism' and its relation to extremes of heat and cold. In their spiritual training, mediums, female shamans (miko), seers and yamabushi (mountain ascetics) practice austerities. One of the classics is daily meditation under a waterfall. The ascetics stood under the icy, mind-numbing downpour, recited mantras, formed mudrās as long as they could stand it. When they emerged they experienced states of empty-minded clarity. The other extreme, heat, appears in an outer and inner form. Meditation between fires was probably introduced by Buddhists, and has become a standard practice for advanced yamabushi. The same ritualists tend to conduct public rituals involving fire walking. But there is also an inner, meditative approach to tapas and heat. As Blacker emphasises, we are not talking about a useful trick or yoga technique to brave the cold. *The shaman is impervious to heat and cold, to burning coals and arctic cold alike. This power is achieved by rousing within himself the interior heat known to mystics in various parts of the world, and which signifies that the heated person has passed beyond the ordinary human condition. He now participates in the sacred world* (1986:26). She describes the initiation of Dōken Shōnin, a Buddhist who, after several years of meditation, became suffused by parching heat. *His throat and tongue grew burning and dry and his breath stopped within him. His spirit then rose out of his body...* Spaced out of his head, Dōken encountered a teacher who revived him with sacred water, was served food by twelve divine boys, was carried to a mountaintop, met an incarnation of the Buddha and received transcendental knowledge. Similar experiences of extreme inner heat appear in the accounts of Indian yogīs. Some of them result from Kuṇḍalinī yoga, from excessive states of rapture, or as accidental side effects of overdoing yoga. Thanks to such experiences, Kuṇḍalinī gained the title 'fire serpent'. You can find more on the topic in *Kālī Kaula*.

When we explore tantric literature we encounter a lot of fire. Unlike the fire rituals of the Vedic seers and the Buddhist ascetics, this fire is a spiritual affair and happens in the imagination. A popular meditation on the all-devouring Fire (Agni, deity of fire) of Time (Kāl; hence: **Kālāgni**) appears in several early tantric texts. As a spiritual practice, it predates Kuṇḍalinī meditations. Let's have an example. The *Vijñāna Bhairava*, an influential early Tantra of the Kashmir tradition, offers more than a hundred meditative practices for attainment and transcendence. Each of them is outlined in just a sentence or two. Here are the Kālāgni practices: *One should meditate that the fortress of one's body is consumed by the fire of time, rising up from the (right) foot. Finally, one attains a state of peace. When one meditates in a similar way, using the imagination, that the entire world is burned up, then one attains, together with a mind that is not distracted by anything, the highest human state* (Verses 52 & 53). There are several ways to do this. The simple approach is to visualise fire rising up one's legs and burning up the torso, then descending the other leg until nothing but ashes are left. Usually, such visualisations can get rather emotional; one side effect may be intense or fast breathing. Should you chose to explore this, be cautious and refrain from overdoing it. Be as emotional as you like, but if you breathe very deep, full and fast, you may hyperventilate. This can be harmful and is not recommended. A bit of deep breathing in moderation is one thing and extended fierce panting another. True, it is possible to reach scatterbrained states by extensive rapid full breathing. These, however, are distinctly unhealthy. Also, they tend to produce mental states that are too blurred and dizzy to be of use for anything. So when you find yourself breathing deeply as you get emotional, take care you do it slowly and only for limited periods. Alternating short periods of deep breathing with longer periods of gentle and shallow breathing is a better strategy.

There is also a ritualistic approach to the Fire of Time. First, the yogī/nī places one or both hands on the right big toe, and recites mantras. Simultaneously, s/he visualises how the fire arises from the depths of the underworlds and begins to flare up the leg. Subsequently, the fire is lead up the body by touching each important cakra and by reciting its mantra. This approach requires extensive visualisation and can be rather complicated, as early tantric texts elaborate on several dozen cakras. In the end, the entire body is reduced to ashes. This is an early form of laya yoga, meaning the yoga (*union, yoking*) of dissolution. Fire of Time meditations seem to end when liberation is attained and everything is reduced to cinders. It would be easy to misunderstand this metaphor. From the ashes arises new life. Long before the tantric movement, ashes were one of the most sacred substances of Indian religion. Śiva walks around nude, smeared with ashes, and states that he is made of ashes. The same goes for ancient Kāma, the god of desire, lust and love, who was once accidentally incinerated by Śiva. Luckily, the gods appealed to Śiva that a world without desire wouldn't be worth living in. Śiva recreated Kāma (*desire, love, lust*) from the ashes. Kāma reappeared, healthier and stronger than ever, and laughed his head off as Śiva immediately fell in love with Pārvatī, the Lady of the Mountains. When Śiva wears ashes, these are the very ashes of desire. They represent what he has left behind, but they also symbolise the great fertility of fresh desire which is ready to come alive anytime. Incinerated cow dung is used to whitewash houses, courtyards, floors and considered a powerful medicine. We also find ashes employed in Mesopotamian medicine. In our meditation, reduction to ashes is not the end. Visualise, experience and enjoy reshaping your body out of them. Fill it with happiness and courage, make it healthy and energetic. Imbue this new body with your sense of self and return to the world reborn.

When we explore fire yoga, a few remarks on Tibetan **gTummo** seem inevitable. Since Alexandra David Neel published her account of Himalayan yogīs who sit in a contest during the icy cold of the night and dry wet blankets on their bare bodies, 'Inner Heat' yoga has received a lot of attention. Her tale is impressive, but not reliable. The aim of gTummo trances is a purification of the self, not the heating if the body. There is an excellent reason for this: above 40° C, protein molecules tend to congeal. When your temperature rises sharply, your body has to go to extremes to keep you cool. Otherwise, physical damage is inevitable. For this reason, your hypothalamus does its best to keep you under 40° C. Drying wet blankets at sub-zero temperatures may seem an exciting supernatural feat when you read about it. It's not a happy way to spend the evening. I doubt that Ms. David-Neel really witnessed this event. However, thanks to her rather imaginative description, many writers believed that gTummo trances are used to combat the cold. This, if it happens at all, is a side effect. A simple Tibetan technique to warm up consists of dog-like panting for a very short time. It is done with pointed lips using belly breathing, and as the abdomen comes out and goes in rapidly, the motion warms the centre of the body. After half a minute of panting follow several minutes of relaxed breathing, then another interval of rapid panting, and so on. Three or four repetitions usually suffice. It's a simple technique and miles away from gTummo. A full treatise of genuine gTummo was published by Evan-Wentz in *Tibetan Yoga and Secret Doctrines*. It shows that this sort of yoga is a complete system of spiritual attainment, and that mastery requires many years of dedicated practice. Far from being a mere technique, gTummo is a road to liberation. It consists, to make a complicated matter far too simple, of a meditation. You imagine that you burn yourself up. When this has happened, a rejuvenating sacred elixir surges out of the crown of your head and recreates you happy, whole and healthy. That's the gist. The actual performance involves a wide range of sacred words, visualisations, deities and so on.

The **flood of elixir** is part of a Chinese meditation that appears in early Daoist writings, such as the *Inscription of the Jade Tablet* of the late fifth century BCE and the *Cantong Qi* by Wei Boyang, in the second century. We explored it in the chapter on sacred fluids. The practice was picked up by the pioneers of Indian Tantra, maybe around the sixth or seventh century, who combined it with various cakra systems, the imagination of the Sanskrit phonemes and a wide range of symbols and deities. It was exported to Tibet by Indian tantric Buddhists. A little later, Hindu tantrics refined the method by introducing the Kuṇḍalinī; who appears as a goddess, as the personal deity, as the self that creates the entire realm of reality and all worlds, or as a serpent or soul-bird. In serpent shape, the meditation returned to China, where we meet Daoist alchemist Zhang Boduan combining qi circulation ('Turning the Waterwheel') with the visualisation of a golden serpent going round and round the body.

It provides a splendid opportunity to leave India and explore fire meditation in China. Meet Gan Bao, a fourth-century author who was the renowned and highly respected grand historian at the imperial court. In his spare time, Gan Bao collected weird stories, and was not much concern to wrest truth from fiction as long as the result was entertaining. His collection *Suo Shen Ji* (*'Anecdotes about Spirits and Immortal'*) started an entire class of fantastic Chinese literature. Here is a story that allegedly happened around 1700 or

1600 BCE. We are at the end of the Xia dynasty. King Kongjia is cruel and incompetent, the people are starving and Heaven wants to introduce a much-needed change. In chapter seven, we read that Shimen, a student of the immortal Xiaofu, became an immortal as he learned to set fire to himself. It improved his health and his outlook on life. His favourite diet was peach flowers: peaches are a food of immortality, sacred to Xiwangmu and the Daoists. Shimen got a job as a dragon-trainer for the wicked King Kongjia. It may have been a stupid idea. Fire meditations and dragon taming made him a bold and outspoken character. The king resented his disrespectful manners. He had Shimen killed and buried in the wasteland. One day a forest fire surged through the wilderness. As the trees flamed up, wind howled and rain poured down. They carried Shimen to heaven. King Kongjia felt deeply worried. In his guilt, he had a temple dedicated to Shimen and performed a grand offering to his souls. After the sacrifice, King Kongjia got into his chariot. He died before he reached home.

Before we move on, pause and consider. Shimen made it to heaven with fire, wind and water. Fire flares up, water pours down, breath keeps the flow steady. That's exactly the formula of meditative alchemy. In chapter twelve we meet Tao Angong. He was a master of iron founding. Once, the fire became too big and the flames turned purple. Tao Angong knelt near the furnace and prayed. The red firebird, guardian of the south, came down from heaven and told him: 'Angong, your furnace is connected with Heaven. When the seventh day of the seventh month comes, you will ascend to Heaven on a red dragon'. Tao Angong prepared to depart from earth. On the seven-seven day, the dragon appeared and carried Tao Angong south-east, in the direction of wood-fire, where the flames are hottest. Ten-thousands of people were on the road on the seventh day of the seventh (lunar) month to make offerings. They witnessed his apotheosis and offered him the sacrifices that had been meant for the gods of roads and ways. Tao Angong said goodbye to them, and became an immortal.

Plenty of immortals appear in Ge Hong's fourth-century work *Traditions of Divine Transcendents*, and their later additions. One of them was Huang Jing who meditated on Mount Huo. The god Vermillion Star appeared in his meditation as *being inside his brain like fire, then circulating through his whole body.* That was just a start. Huang Jing practised this visualisation for two hundred years before he was sure that it worked; then he became an immortal and left earth (trans. Campany, 2002:366).

A technique of Shangqing Daoism, influenced by the teachings of Ge Hong, is based on the idea that the embryo receives nine breaths from heaven when it is conceived, plus a piece of red string with twelve knots which keeps the inner organs together. When an adept aims to attain transcendence, she or he visualises how the 24 body gods untie the knots and burn the string, which makes the human body go up in flames. Another method of Shangqing Daoism is based on a meditation that allows its adept to experience and transcend their own death. Once their souls have left the corpses, they travel to the otherworlds where they undergo initiations. One destination lies in the deep south, where they visit the Palace of Red Fire or the Court of Fluid Fire, burn themselves to ashes and are renewed. After this transformation, they can be reborn as immortals (Robinet, 1997:136 & 138).

We are talking meditation. Unlike the many hundred sages who became immortals thanks to a special diet consisting exclusively of, say, pine resin, peaches, flower-dew, sun-rays, mica, pearls, stalactites, lots of fresh air, sexual secretions or, as a swift road to transcendence, nothing at all, some adepts reached liberation by submerging themselves in the Five Moving Powers (Wuxing). We had plenty of fire examples so far, and numerous Daoist adepts were famous for walking through fire or for sitting within their burning hut, seeing their worldly existence go up in glory. All of them reflect meditative practices. Male and female Daoist sages found freshness, release and happiness when they saw their world, their nature and belongings going up in glory. But we should also consider water. Fire and water balance and complement one another. Lamaštu may be full of scorching fire, but she also finds release by descending into the watery abyss where she received her training. Daoist immortals use fire and water in their meditations: fire surges up and water flows down. After the heat of purifying flames comes the releasing, refreshing shower of cooling elixir that rejuvenates and revives. Gan Bao (chapter 11) mentioned Qingao, a famous player of the qin-lute at the court of King Kang of Song. He practised the formulas of the immortals Juanzi and Pengzu, but only found liberation when he submerged himself in Zhuoshui River, where *he got hold of a dragon's son*. Periodically, he emerged from the river, riding a red carp, to teach. Having been there and done that, he gave a sigh of relief and sank into the waters again.

Go into the dream world, and burn up all your impurities. See the flames envelop you and put a lot of emotion into them. Maybe you experience this as a human being, and feel yourself surrounded by fire. Maybe you become the fire, and flicker with joy and hunger and lust. Maybe you transform into your personal deity, and burn your human personality within the alchemical oven of its belly. Maybe, when you've got a great fire going, you leave your body, the fire, the deity and witness the transformation as a formless consciousness from above. All of these approaches have their uses. Experiment! Raise excitement! Go for the visualisation that puts a huge ecstatic smile on your face. And when you burned up all the inessentials, arise from heat and flame reborn. Shape your new body out of joy and love. And flood yourself with cooling, soothing, healing showers. The waters from heaven will refresh and revive you, and heal your worried mind.

Var. 1.: The fifth: Goddess Whose Face (*or:* Expression) is Wild.

Var. 2.: The fifth: Goddess Whose Face (*or:* Expression) is Yellow-Green.

The fifth name is about wildness, nature, and self-expression. It's about what is original and spontaneous about you, and about the natural wisdom of communities. For a start, let me call up some folks you've met before. All-time favourite characters in novels, movies and 'shamanic' workshops are noble savages. Such people, sometimes praised as 'children of nature' have been favourites for several hundred years. Voltaire joked about them; others idealised them, and envisioned barbarians who were healthier, holier and wiser than urban mankind. They appear whenever modern city people dream of a better life elsewhere. Unlike us, the Mesopotamians had very clear ideas about the topic. When Gilgameš exploited the citizens of Uruk, the gods decided that he needed distraction. They created a magnificent wild man, Enkidu, who lived alone in the steppe. The animals were his only friends. The hunters complained to the king that someone was destroying their traps. Gilgameš, hearing of the noble savage, was fascinated. He asked the prostitute Šamhat to go into the wilderness and teach culture to the brute. Before long, wild Enkidu had learned everything about sex and good manners, was properly dressed and eager to see mighty Uruk. He needed new friends, as the animals were not playing with him anymore. That's Mesopotamian thought: the wilderness is exactly the place one should leave behind.

Other people had quite different ideas. Tacitus was one of the first offenders; living in polluted, noisy and overpopulated Rome he imagined that the primitive Germani, whose homeland he had never seen, were poor and savage, but widely better off. It inspired him to write the Germania: the first ethnographic study in history, and an astonishing blend of facts, gossip and sheer fantasy. Since then, a lot has happened. We owe the modern noble savage to the Romantic Movement. Around 1800, people of income began to feel disgusted by the stench, noise and anonymity of urban life and imagined that everything would be so much nicer in the country. Of course they were right. When the sun was shining brightly, the larks were singing and the sky was blue, they took a chariot ride into the green, lazed on meadows drinking beer or wine and eating what they imagined to be simple fare. They joined groups to climb mountains in the middle of the night to enjoy the sunrise. They wrote poems about it. In between they idealised shepherds, peasants, foresters, woodcutters and fisherman and assumed their lives would be healthy, simple and carefree. And when the sky went overcast and autumn winds came blowing they packed their stuff and retreated to the city, to moan about a healthy, natural life that they would never really get. The Romantic Movement may have been a great achievement, in that it made 'nature' a beautiful and meaningful place, but it did so from a position of arrogance. It idealised the life of country people, and instead of revealing how hard and difficult it was, it turned poverty and worry into virtues, and it created the strange idea that survival without conveniences, technology and medical supplies would somehow be 'healthy'. To live 'in harmony with nature' is a modern and misleading expression. The people who invented 'Mother Nature' were city folks. They assumed that nature, somewhere out there, is kind and friendly; a happy goddess who is obliged to make mankind happy. That 'Mother Nature' includes volcanic eruptions, earthquakes, Ice Ages, meteorite strikes, climate changes, drought, flood, plagues, vermin, parasites and lots of dismal poverty escaped them. Consider: almost half of the people who ever lived, died thanks to some form of malaria. That, too, is 'Mother Nature'.

The nature of the wilderness eluded the city dwellers: by the end of the eighteenth century, hardly any nature was left. In its place a new fashion began. Wealthy people paid architects to beautify their estates. Hills were raised and streams dug, entire groves of trees were relocated to suit human taste. One of the first examples comes from the 1770's. Near Rüdesheim at the Rhine, Count Maximilian von Ostein redesigned an entire forest to suit his idea of natural beauty, and filled it with fake castle ruins, a 'knight's hall', several pavilions, a hermitage and an artificial 'magic cave'. The forest was full of ancient oaks, the view over the Rhine spectacular. It attracted visitors from all over Europe. The beauty of the English scenery was largely designed by landscape architects. People created a romantic wilderness to their liking, just as they improved history by erecting sham buildings. The illusion was enchanting. To this day people talk about fields, meadows and rivers as 'nature' when in fact all of them are extensions of the man-made way of life. Look at the forest edge. It's man-made. In nature, forests have no edges. They just thin out and disappear. But you would have to travel a long way to see anything like that. The agricultural countryside is anything but natural.

People began to transform their environment at a very early stage. In central Europe, it could have started directly after the Ice Ages ended. The first forests began to grow, and trees made their return by travelling north. They had to get past the Alps. A few had survived north of the Alps. Birch and pine were really early, here and there juniper grew and willows lined the waterways. As it became warmer, hazel moved in from the west and spruce from the east. They had a tough time getting a foothold, as the forest was already well developed. As it turns out, hazel spread much faster than would have been expected. It is likely that the people of the Mesolithic accelerated its migration (Küster, 1996:64-68). Before long, hazel was the dominant tree of the hills and plains. Birches and willows survived in damp locations, pines made a meagre living on dry, sandy and stony soil. We think of the Mesolithic as a time of great primaeval forests, but in all likeliness, the wilderness was already shaped by human beings. And that's nothing compared to what happened when the first farmers began to transform the land. In central Europe, the farmers chose the rich loess soil, as it was overwhelmingly fertile. They built small settlements half ways up the slopes above rivers and brooks and cleared the forest. It transformed the water regulation. Forest is excellent at binding and storing water. Fields are not. Where people settled, the nearby rivers suffered from irregular floods and periods of dryness. That, in turn, transformed the vegetation and animal life. When steep slopes are deforested, you create landslides. And when the farmers gave up fields, they created perfect conditions for the advancing beeches. In southern Britain, the first farmers cut down the native forest and planted cereals. It only worked a while. Beneath the thin layer of humus is chalk. Fields are vulnerable when no vegetation covers them. Exposed to the elements, the rains washed the fertile soil into the valleys, leaving the Downs almost barren. When you see the sheep grazing under a vast sky, and wonder why trees are so rare, well, that issue was settled many thousand years ago. We are living in a man-shaped environment. One time or another, almost every bit of forest was planted; almost every swamp drained, and rivers were turned into man-made water channels. The cultivation of grains comes at a high price. Agriculture kills animals and plants by leaving them no space to proliferate. And it doesn't go on indefinitely. Around the start of the twentieth century, most fertile ground on earth was seriously depleted. Only a third of the landmass is fit for the cultivation of cereals. In most places, the earth simply isn't fertile enough, or too sour, stony, dry, wet, hot, cold or inaccessible. Far-seeing thinkers realised that mankind might grow to two billion individuals. It was a scary idea. Hunger and war seemed to be certain. Then, Franz Haber (the celebrated 'Father of the Gas War') and Carl Bosch created a method to produce ammonia by combining nitrogen and hydrogen. They were hoping to invent new explosives. As a side effect they laid the foundation of artificial fertilisation. It proved to be more devastating. Exhausted ground, and there was lots of it, was turned into fields. Annual grains were cultivated like never before. People destroyed forests and grasslands to produce grains on a scale that was unthinkable in the past. Artificial fertilisers exhaust the ground, kill enormous amounts of insects, worms, microbes and fungi living in the humus, and pollute rivers and seashores. Worst of all, they caused a population explosion. The agricultural landscape may be necessary, but it is not nature, let alone a wilderness. I lived in a barn in the middle of fields for five years. There was a small brook, a belt of forest cresting a few hills and a mind blowing vast sky. Coming from a city, I was upset to find so little biodiversity. There were few insects, hardly any spiders, birds or bats. Every other day tractors doused the scenery with insecticides, herbicides and artificial fertilisers. As a biotope, a corn field or a spruce forest contains less biodiversity, hence less really wild life, than the suburbs and allotments with their international garden vegetation. A meadow with cows has a much healthier ecology than a field of wheat, sweet corn, potatoes or rice. It houses dozens of wildflowers, feeds enormous amounts of insects, spiders, birds and small mammals and is fertilised by manure that actually builds up the fertility of the soil.

So where has all the nature gone? Maybe you can discover the real wilderness on a much smaller scale. Grasses breaking through the asphalt, ants marching through your flat, odd plants in your flowerpot, a fox rummaging in a garbage can, a falcon nesting on a chimney: they are much wilder than life out in the country.

When some people say 'wild' they mean unruly, uncontrolled, aggressive and threatening. It's such a modern idea. Let's explore animals. Really wild animals are not unruly, they are a lot more controlled than the neurotic dog living next door. Nor are wild animals uncontrolled. Life within territories makes them far more controlled than a goat that has leaped the fence and goes marauding. For each wild animal, a biotope is divided into invisible sections. The frontiers are defined, marked, defended and trespassers will be prosecuted. A bird flying to the wrong bush is in trouble. People look at zoo animals and imagine that they dream of freedom. But what exactly is freedom? To fight for a small territory, to defend it with beak, teeth and claws, and to die a miserable death long before old age sets in? A wolf pack can only move where game is abundant and no competitors are hunting. The range of choices is very narrow. Animals live in territories and so do we. Our range of 'freedom' is limited: anyone who walks into the home of a stranger is in for a surprise.

What about social regulations? They are neither free nor wild. A wolf has to fight for a place in the hierarchy. It's the hierarchy that makes the pack successful, even if it means a lot of bickering and submissiveness. In nature, hierarchies grow from the bottom up. When several wolves, chicken or mice get together, they check out who is stronger, healthier, faster, cleverer and so on. Add more animals to the group and after a bit of struggle they have adjusted their hierarchy. This hierarchy is based on competence. The alpha couple may boss the others around, but the others are constantly challenging the alpha couple to do its best. It's not always nice. When the alpha couple goes old, or one of them is injured, they are expelled and face starvation. The lone wolf is a dead wolf. It only takes a few handicaps, maybe a thorn in a paw, a tooth infection, too many ticks or worms, to put an end to a carnivore in the wild. Unlike wolves, we have to live in a world of top-down hierarchies. Our businesses, countries, organisations and computers are organised in a way that gives control to the head without ensuring her or his competence. The boss of a company, army, state is not necessarily the person who does the job best. If you have the money, influence or support, you can employ people who are far more competent than you are. Top down hierarchies do not adjust. The alpha of a firm is not threatened by the employees and can be totally incompetent. Darwinian selection does not apply to the top politicians, capitalists and aristocrats. Maybe this explains why, though humanity seems to evolve, its leaders make the same mistakes as they did five thousand years ago.

Many people like to identify with predators. Some imagine that the lion has courage. It hasn't; it does not need anything of that sort. Courage is when you transcend your fears. Without fear, courage is meaningless. They say the lion is proud. Well, usually the lion is hungry; most of the time it is asleep. The lion runs to catch its dinner, the gazelle runs to stay alive. Guess who has the stronger motivation? The life of a carnivore is full of failures. One successful hunt in twenty is pretty good going, and the predator has a chance to survive. Failure is normal, survival is extra. So feeling proud isn't an option. You are successful or you are dead. The gazelle isn't ambitious either. It doesn't have to be faster than the lion: it just has to be faster than another gazelle. Pride is a human invention, and one of the most stupid ones. Some people admire the lion's strength. Any beetle, flea or springtail is stronger. Is the lion daring? The wasp, ready to fight for its community, and the female mosquito, seeking blood to feed her eggs, show more boldness. 'Living in the wild' may seem exciting when you have a nine to five job in a city. For country people, city life is wild.

Nature extends everywhere. After all, people are animals: we follow our nature when we transform the environment and create cities. Many animals create their own environments: beavers flood valleys, squirrels plant forests, elephants destroy trees and hornets build nests. It's natural for people to build shelters, houses, towns and cities. For mankind, civilisation is natural. So when we talk wildness and nature, we are not talking about reality but about thoughts and desires.

Living in the wilderness, as Lamaštu does, can be demanding. There is nothing sacred to being hungry, cold and miserable. Having fleas, lice, ticks and worms isn't really recommended. Our ancestors had good reasons to exclude a lot of wildlife from their environment.

Much of our civilisation is based on mastering fire. We made it part of our nature. During the last four million years, our ancestors survived by including animal products such as meat, fish, eggs, insects and worms in their plant-based diet. It wasn't easy, as raw meat is hard to digest. One or two million years ago, they learned to heat food and we became cocivores. We

Figure 77 - Journey through Ruins. Desert hedgehog and the ziggurat of Aquar Quf.

realised that burnt proteins and fats are easier to digest. Heating proteins, no matter whether they come from meat, eggs, potatoes, lentils or beans, creates benzo(a)pyrene, acrylamide and similar substances which can induce cancer in other animals. It also produces chemicals and scorched bits (=coal) which neutralise poisons. Our ancestors had more than a million years to adapt to them, and can handle them with ease. (Pollmer, 2007:163-165; 2012:11-18). The proteins and animal fats allowed us to grow much bigger brains than the other hominids. Thanks to burned meat we survived several ice ages. The evidence is obvious: our sharp, cutting teeth, the vertical motion of our jaws, our highly acidic stomachs with their fast turnover rate, our strong gall-bladder, tiny appendix, and our bowels with their putrefying microbe communities are perfect for a diet based on animal products (Keith, 2013:127). For our ancestors, being natural and wild meant eating lots of animals and some nuts, fruit and vegetables, in the few months when they were available. The next question is obvious. Many monkeys, apes and very early hominids preferred to live in the tropics, where a vegetarian diet is available all through the year, plus the extra amount of eggs, insects, maggots and small animals needed to supply B12. Whenever our ancestors could, they tried to get out of the tropics. The warm belt around the equator supplies tasty fruit, but it is also home to a horde of parasites, bacteria and viruses. Whenever an Ice-Age ended, our ancestors migrated to temperate climes. And they learned to make foot covering and clothes; they constructed shelters, huts and tents. It happened in Central Asia and Europe. Settlements, like summer camps, can be traced to Homo erectus, the common ancestor of Neanderthal people and our own type, Homo-too-bloody-sapient. It was not a race of technology versus nature. Technology is part of our nature. Settlements are part of our nature. Society and codes of conduct, rituals, myths, art, music, religion, learning, science and government, of whatever type it may be, are inherent in our nature. When we build cities and install plumbing and central heating we are still following our nature. Maybe we follow our nature when we are too lazy, greedy or ignorant to treat our environment well. When we find our partner attractive and children cute, we follow nature. It's built into us. It made us what we are. But being what you are does not mean that you will be successful.

Microbes keep multiplying until their food resources are exhausted. When you leave goats on an island without predators, they will eat until all plants are gone and starve to death. They, also, follow their nature. It's just their bad luck there are no predators around. 'Primitive man' and his idealised cousin, the noble savage, followed their own nature. When they saw a good meal walking by, they reached for their spears. Within two centuries after the Native Americans arrived in the New World, dozens of large species were exterminated. When the first peasants invented agriculture, their efforts created arid ground and desert. The countries around the Mediterranean Sea were once thickly wooded. Agriculture and the bronze industry destroyed them. Most 'noble savages' do not care about environmental protection. They care for their belly, their lives, their family and friends. In the process, they turn the wilderness into a man-made habitat. That, too, is in our nature. Our nature takes us to the limits and beyond them. Like the goats, most people have no inbuilt sense of population control.

Now let's sink into a nice, gentle trance and go to our imaginary landscape. Take a moment so the environment can stabilise. Breathe gently, relax and enjoy. Being wild means being natural, and when you relax you are nature at its best. Now imagine an animal mask. Choose an animal which you like, admire and feel comfortable with. Look at the mask and build up a feeling how it will change your perception. When you are ready, put on the mask. See through its eyes, hear through its ears, smell with its nose, feel the wind, the sun, the temperature on its skin. Then slowly, gradually, extend the mask so it envelops your entire body. Shift into the animal shape, move, wriggle, twitch, feel the change. Breathe as the animal. Sense the world in an entirely new way. Take it in slowly. Give yourself time. First, you might explore your direct environment. Look at the ground, feel the air, smell and listen carefully. And when you have done so, get up and move. Allow your animal nature to move you. Go out, discover, experience all those drives, skills, hungers, fears, needs and joys. It's something to be savoured. And it needs practice. You have to become that animal several times to get the basics sorted out. Devote a series of trance meditations to that animal. Grow up, play, learn, feed, migrate, escape predators, search for a mate, have children, grow old and die. And be born again. You'll be learning as it learns you.

When you want to return to human awareness, go to the place you started from. Sit down and reverse the transformation. Feel how your feet turn into human hands and feet, allow human arms and legs to emerge and gradually shrink the animal shape until only the mask remains. Take the mask off and look at it for a while. That mask was you a moment ago. Understand what it signifies. And remember who you are.

When you have explored this trance a few times shift to another animal which is very different. People in modern shamanism tend to get stuck in two or three animal roles. Most of them are rather boring traditional choices. A small range of 'power animals' is well and good for simple magick, like blessing, healing, spellcraft or banishment. But they will not do enough to widen your horizon. Most contemporary shamans chose animal shapes that are already much like themselves, or represent the selves they would like to be, if only they were, but ain't. It's like becoming a more extreme version of what you already are or hope to be. Just think of the many losers who walk around wearing ferocious beast tattoos! Most of them are not up to their ideals. However, without those ideals, they might be worse. So when you are fond of predator roles, and find them easy, learn to live as a deer. After you learned to fly, enjoy the life of a mouse or mole. Try being an earthworm, a dung-beetle, a centipede, a spider in its web. The challenge lies in discovering something radically new. Shy people can improve by becoming savage predators, hectic people by becoming a jellyfish and restless people can relax and be a sponge. The stranger the animals you explore, the more inspiring will the experience be. If you want extreme changes of awareness, go for the so-called 'primitive' lifeforms. An amoeba can provide a mind-blowing experience.

Here is outdoor magick. Find a restful place. Calm down and relax. Let your human nature drift away. Imagine you are an animal. Superimpose its limbs, its body and legs on yours. Take your time. A bit of playacting can help. Assume the mask of an animal you are used to. Sense the world, understand what it feels and wants and dreads. Play the animal, imitate its motions, its feelings, and let it take over. It can transform your experience of the outside world. Some of it is astonishing. When you go for a forest walk and assume the mask of a predator, it can make you feel secure, powerful, cunning and dangerous. Walk a few steps. Stand still. Sense your surroundings. Then walk a few more steps. That's the way wild animals move, and so does Lamaštu. They take their time and pause frequently. They drift from here to there. And they only move straight when they are in a hurry or afraid. Being a wolf or a lynx in the forest is fun. It can provide access to heightened awareness, stealth, power and instinctive elegance. But when you want to meet more wildlife, and wish to blend into your surroundings, becoming a shy herbivore is a much better choice. Predator body language is scary. There are plenty of animals around. When they sense you moving like a small deer, a hare or a wild boar, they relax. Deer are no real threat (apart to birds nesting on the ground: deer love to eat eggs and fledglings). Go slowly. Stop often. Take in your surroundings. Give yourself at least sixteen breaths before you drift on. Take half an hour or more to cover a kilometre. You'll be amazed how much detail appears. Take your time to sense the plants. Watch the animals. They'll move with more assurance, as your behaviour signals that you won't harm them.

To understand wild nature, you can transform into several animals. But you should also do plants, in your meditations and outdoors. Plants are badly underestimated. In the English language, 'to vegetate' describes a dismally primitive and dumb condition. I have heard plenty of people; especially vegetarians, claim that plants have no senses, lack nerves and consciousness, and are somehow 'lower lifeforms'. It takes an anthropocentric attitude to say something as stupid as that. Plants are everywhere. They evolved in company with animals, but they invented different strategies for survival. Approximately 98% of the biomass on Planet Earth is plants. And they are astonishingly intelligent. Plants are very sensitive. They have light receptors at the tips of their shoots, sprouts and sprigs, and on all leaves and green parts. The ones above ground like light and move towards it. They also control the angle of the leaves. For the vegetation, to see is to feed. The receptors in the roots dread light. Plants see blue light and like it. They also see a little bit of dark bluish green, plus violet and ultraviolet. They have receptors for dark red light and know it is sunset: time to shut down. When they see bright red light they know it's morning and time to wake up. It even functions when the sky is overcast or rainy. To keep in tune with the calendar, plants measure the period of darkness. The receptors for bright and dark red light help them to estimate the length of the night, which indicates the season and allows them to blossom punctually. Cunning gardeners use this skill to confuse them, and to make them blossom at will. Plants also see infrared, i.e. heat, and know when you have a fever. Not that it interests them much. They sense the times of day. They can feel surfaces: just watch how a bramble swings around in a slow arc and tests for something solid to hold on to. Some plants, like vines and woodbine love to touch things. Others species, like beeches, conifers and myrtles do not. Touch can mean trouble. When branches are in contact, insects, fungi and bacteria can pass along. When the wind is too strong, the plant had better reduce its size and grow a sturdier stem. The leaves which are touched every day release ethanol. It reduces the growth in length but increases growth in width and thickness. They won't grow to their full size but may be stouter. Or they may even be shed.

Plants can detect the faintest traces of pheromones in the air. Again, the receptors are widely distributed. Animals have organs, and when organs are damaged, the animal may die. Having organs is a luxury which can only be afforded by those who can protect them or move away from danger. Plants can't walk away. They have to deal with being nibbled. It's a perfect solution to have the vital organs everywhere. A herbivore may eat half of the plant but it will still be able to see, hear, feel, smell and taste, and use another dozen senses.

Some plants learn from each other. When a giraffe starts eating acacia leaves, the acacia releases toxins to make itself badly digestible. And it releases pheromones that tell the other leaves to become toxic. It's an excellent solution: the pheromones move fast and the message gets around. As a side effect, other acacias in wind-direction also become toxic. The giraffe has a bite, dislikes the taste and moves on. This effect, observed in many plants, including poplar, willow, alder, mugwort, barley and beans, has been taken as evidence for plant communication. It might be communication, but just as possible the plant talks to itself and the other plants are getting the message. That signal can be varied. The tree will use different pheromones to signal whether it is attacked by a herbivore or by a bacterial infection. And it will respond with different toxins *(Chamovitz 2012)*.

Most people see plants as passive objects which have little influence over their environment. But plants are fighters. They are experts at chemical warfare. Coffee, tea and cocaine are stimulants. It's not a coincidence. These plants developed drugs which ensure their survival. A herbivore comes along and starts to eat the leaves. The plant increases its toxicity: the herbivore loses its appetite, goes edgy, restless and for a long walk before it will calm down again. Hungry larvae are killed or sterilised with special toxins. Plants taste bitter, cause rushes, disease or death as they are fighters. Some ferns successfully cover entire hillsides as their leaves produce hydrocyanic acid. The animals that has a nibble may end up blind, with a damaged central nervous system, suffering from bloody diarrhoea.

Plants also have a sense of hearing. They don't give a damn whether you listen to Led Zeppelin or Mozart. Plants grow perfectly well near loud waterfalls, seashores, motorways, and airports. They lack ears but they pick up vibrations with their roots. Deep vibrations, between 100-500hz stimulate growth in some species, higher frequencies can reduce it. Perhaps trees listen to each other. While plants grow, their cell tissues break and produce clicking noises. It takes amplification to make such sounds audible for humans. These sounds might interest the other plants in the neighbourhood. It is useful to know if your neighbour is growing fast or slow or has to combat a weakening disease. And they have a wide range of well developed sense organs for gravity, moisture, soil chemistry and electromagnetic fields. What they lack is nerves and a brain. Short distance signals are transmitted by electrical impulses via holes (the plasmodesmas) within the cell walls. Slow long-distance signals are coded chemicals that move with the sap. Fast signals are pheromones, which are released and received by the foliage. Plants see, but they don't put their vision together as we do. Unlike us, the plants sense objective reality. Their impression of the world is not a subjective and artificial representation made up by a brain and nervous system. When you lack a brain, your various parts have to make independent decisions. The root tips are extremely sensitive and search for nourishment on their own initiative, but they do it without what we assume to be thinking. When the ground turns dry, the roots send a signal to the leaves that water is getting rare. The process is slow: it can take several days before the message has been transported, by fluids, to the crown of a tall tree. The leaves get the message and shut the stomata, the tiny pores, their breath organs, underneath each leaf, to preserve moisture. When the drought extends, the tree may start to shed its leaves (Mancuso & Viola, 2015, 83-90).

It's a new insight that some plants interact via their roots. The fungal network connects many species. Among several varieties, an exchange of nutrients, fluids and medical substances was observed. It happens not only 'in the family', i.e. from a mother tree to its children, but can also be observed between different species. Erlbeck, Haseder & Stinglwagner (2002:505) mention a study showing that a healthy birch was nourishing a fir tree eking out a meagre existence in the shadow. Many trees can live to several hundred years of age. In this period, each of them is likely to suffer from parasites, diseases and malnutrition repeatedly. Mutual support helps everyone. In several species, damaged or diseased trees may receive nutrients and medical support from other trees of the same species nearby. The chemicals are transported along the roots and the fungus networks. Buhner mentions sugars, phosphorus and carbon (ibid, 196). The popular media pounced on the subject, and attested 'social behaviour', 'altruism' and 'tree communication'. In their rendering, each forest is as full of chatter as the average internet platform. Maybe they are right. However, research has only just begun. While some trees are known to support others, and some fungi help the process, the majority remain unexplored. Plants are not always nice to each other. Competition is the norm. Plants contend fiercely for light, nutrients, moisture and space. When we say 'social behaviour', 'health-care', 'sense of community', we are projecting human values on life forms which are exceedingly different. Those writers who pretend that animals and plants are 'just like people' are missing the point. The fascinating thing about plant behaviour is its difference from ours. It provides the great chance to learn and sense something really new.

Let me take you to the beech forest. When the Romans crossed the Alps, they were awed by a mighty dark forest unlike anything in southern Europe. Allegedly, a squirrel could run from the Atlantic Ocean to the Baltic without having to touch the ground. Most of the forest consisted of tall beeches, creating a canopy of shade under which very little undergrowth could flourish. Beeches love shade and are excellent at surviving in it. Freshly sprouted beeches have very tender leaves that make the most out of very little sunlight: if you plant a seedling in open sunlight, its foliage is severely damaged or destroyed. Nor is it likely to endure frost. As long as the seedling grows under other beeches, it is well protected. Beeches make the environment they like. In a beech forest, other trees hardly stand a chance. Plants are famous for their competitiveness: when one beech overtakes another, the loser will die. It may take decades before its resources are used up, but death is inevitable. On the other hand, beeches have to cooperate. A beech forest tries to maintain a dark shady environment. They consume 97% of the sunlight; to keep a few of their children alive for decades or centuries they have to feed them with extra nourishment. When an old tree dies, the others try to close the canopy. They fill the gap but do not grow further: beeches dislike touching each other. The youngsters rush upwards, and before long, the gloom is back again. It helps the forest to maintain temperature, micro-climate, moisture and resistance to storms. For miles the beech canopy is at a similar height. That's quite amazing. The soil may differ, may contain different amounts of minerals, moisture and nutrients. Nevertheless, beeches try to keep their height at a mutual level. To do this, they have to exchange nutrients and moisture. Some are supported by the community and some have to restrict themselves. The common advantage is a dark, dense forest; the perfect environment for the next generation.

This is the wild life of beeches. Being natural requires competition, exchange, support and conformity. By contrast, the oak can get by on its own. It likes more sunlight than the beech does, and will thrive in an open place. For the oak, transforming the environment is not an option. Its canopy is fairly open and many different trees can grow under it. The real challenge is surviving pests. Oaks feed hundreds of animal species and are constantly under attack. Their acorns are such a vital resource that the trees coordinate their production. Every couple of years, oaks produce an immense amount of acorns. If you like to watch wildlife, you will encounter far more in the oak forest than under beeches. Mind you, most of it will be insects. Every few years the oaks coordinate their effort and produce a bumper harvest. The amount of acorns is so staggering that even the wild boars, squirrels and mice can't devour every one. It ensures that a few acorns survive, and that a fresh generation of oaks can sprout. How the oaks coordinate their bumper harvests remains a mystery. Nor are they entirely happy afterwards. They suffer from diseases, grow thinner year rings and take years to recover.

Many plants travel before they settle down: maybe the seed is carried by the wind, in the fur of an animal, or in its digestive tract, floats along a river or over an ocean before it finds a new home. The early trees, all of them conifers, produced amazing amounts of pollen and used the wind to distribute their offspring. The much younger blossoming plants selected animals to do the job. It allowed them to put less energy into reproduction, and made them to form symbiotic relationships with specific carriers.

Only a few decades ago, it used to be thought that plants are antisocial, greedy little growth-machines who exploit the slightest advantage to get ahead. By now it emerges that many plants behave in ways that aid their community. When budworms (Choristoneura) start eating in an American spruce forest, most spruce trees become toxic to defend themselves. They increase the production of a wide range of distinct terpenes, which kill the budworms or make them infertile. As male and female budworms react to different phytotoxins, and as each generation of budworms is different, the chemistry has to be customised. But not every spruce tree joins the fight. It's not that they are weak. It has been demonstrated that these trees could defend themselves if they wanted to. They attract all the budworms and suffer badly. The tactic is mysterious. Do these trees suffer from a death wish, are they masochists or deeply altruistic? Or will we need a new vocabulary to understand how plants organise their lives? Those trees that are attacked by budworms receive nourishment, moisture and medical support from their neighbours. They suffer, some die and the survivors will need years to recover. Whatever it may be, the distress of some trees has a huge advantage for the spruce community. If all trees went toxic, most budworms would die. The few that could handle the terpenes would breed like mad and soon all of their descendants would be resistant. That could destroy the entire forest. By allowing normal budworms to feed and breed, the spruce community ensures that the parasites do not develop resistance (Buhner, 2002:160, 188-189).

The lonesome tree faces a much harder life, and stands fewer chances to grow old. However, it is also surrounded by a plant community, and participates in beneficial relationships. By day, sunlight strikes the leaves, allows for photosynthesis and moisture evaporates. The process of evaporation pulls up new water from the ground. When night falls, the flow stops and trees will release excess moisture into the soil. The next day they will only take up a third of it. They are nourishing the plants with shallow roots with water. Small plants and herbs thrive, and their shade will keep the roots of large trees moist. Their blossoms attract insects, which feed birds and small mammals. These attract larger predators. Around the tree, life and death go on and the nutrients fertilise the soil. All of this is being wild. All of it is being natural. Evolution is not an individualist venture. Without cooperation, most species would not make it.

Var.1.: **The sixth: Committed into the Hands** *(=the Trusted)*, **Accepted** *(or:* **Adopted** *or:* **Taken)** **by Irnina;**

Var.2.: **The sixth: Committed into the Hands** *(=the Trusted)*, **Who is Compassionate** *(= Accepts Petitions/Prayers)***;**

The sixth name has much to do with relationships and interaction. What does it mean to feel commitment to another? To whom are you committed? Who is committed to you? Whom do you trust, who listens to your prayers? Let's begin by examining our place in the world. Nowadays, people are taught to worship individualism. The large family structure has faded away, the small family is being eroded by a society where adults work and children are raised and educated by professionals, while the old generation is isolated in old-age homes. More and more people live as singles. It may be good or bad, depending on what you want to make out of your life. Times are changing, whether we like it or not. But when you look at it from an economical point of view, you will realise that singles are better customers. Sell them more food than they consume and they will throw the rest away. They will pay more in rent, more for transport, for holidays, for pretty much everything. As they are alone, they will spend more for meeting partners, for feeling attractive, for company and to forget their loneliness. Other people have families that keep them busy; singles will devote themselves to work, hobbies, sport and nightlife. All of this is big business. Consequently, a huge industry emphasises individuality (instead of mutuality) and tries its best to keep you single, unique, independent, frustrated and a perfect customer. The fun part is that you are supposed to express your unique individuality by buying from a narrow range of internationally available brands.

Let's return to the forest. Who experiences the world from a plant's point of view has much to gain. Here is a meditation. Imagine you are an acorn. A thoughtful jay has picked you up and buried you some distance from your tree-mother. The jay wasn't being nice. It was storing you as winter food. Jays do that all the time, just as squirrels do. But as jays are forgetful, it will eat other acorns and won't come to visit you again. You are lucky. The soil isn't

Figure 78 - Sacred Trees. Drawing inspired by the murals of Mari and trees on Assyrian roll seals.

too strange. And your shell extrudes germ killers, i.e. antibiotic, antifungal and antimicrobial chemicals to make the environment healthier. It sounds simple but isn't. The jay could have planted you anywhere. Your internal chemistry has to be able to handle a lot of different environments. Before you start to grow you identify the conditions of your neighbourhood, and cook up a perfect chemical response. Though it's dark in the earth, your gravity receptors tell you where up and down are. It is still autumn and winter will come soon. Nevertheless you extend a tiny rootlet. It sterilises the soil in its surroundings. Simultaneously, it attracts microbes that suit you perfectly. Some will come from the immediate neighbourhood, others will travel several dozen centimetres, and that's a long, long way. The microbes will supply you with special mineral compounds which your roots can't extract from the soil. They will cover your entire surface, below and above the ground, so that pathogenic microbes stand few chances to get close to you. They will even produce growth accelerators and, in a few species, fertilisers. In return, the microbes will have a perfect breeding ground. They will gain nourishment and sugars from you, and a safe habitat that is perfectly suited to their needs. It's not a coincidence: plants and microbes have adapted to each other for many hundred million years. And while you are at it, you will identify which organisms grow in your close neighbourhood. If they are a threat, or simply competition, you will release toxins to kill or inhibit them. When winter is past and the springtime sun warms the ground, you know it's time to grow. Your gravity detectors tell you which way is up. Very cautiously you send a tender sprout to the surface. Your rootlets will collect as much nutrients and moisture as they can. You have quite a few of them. Each rootlet tip is extremely sensitive. It can identify moisture, nutrients and specific chemicals, and will grow towards or away from them. Each tiny rootlet acts independently. Trees are great at decentralised intelligence. It's an amazing success package, but it won't be enough. Your survival requires a partnership. Luckily, there are plenty of fungi around. People tend to think in terms of individuality. They say, 'what a nice mushroom' and take it home for dinner. That mushroom is just one of many sets of genitals of the real fungus, who lives, extended like a vast net, under the surface of the forest floor. Some fungi extend dozens or hundreds of metres. An amazing honey agaric in Oregon extends over nine square km. It is estimated 2400 years old and may weigh 600 tons. You, as a cheerful little acorn, will have a lot of fungi right next to you. Some will try to kill you. Others are making an offer you can't refuse and become friends for life. To be a successful tree, you will need a partnership with one, or more likely, several fungi. Some trees species thrive thanks to the support of fifty fungi species! It isn't limited to trees. Maybe 80-90% of all plant species live in a close partnership with fungi. The fungus joins your tiny rootlets and covers them with a network of exceptionally fine fibres. Fungi fibres increase the surface of your roots enormously, and allow you to pick up far more minerals, like badly soluble phosphates, nitrogen and water than you could on your own. Each fungus friend does a great job by giving you a head start. It also combats hostile fungi and worms. You can grow faster than others and make it to the light. In exchange, the fungi may take up to 30% of the carbohydrates, like starch and sugars, which you produce by photosynthesis. It's a small price, as without fungal support, you would barely be alive, and certainly incapable of competing with your neighbours. And then you start to grow, to feel the seasons, to sense the scenery, to struggle for height, to begin to enjoy a long and fertile life. The first act of our drama is over: you have a thin stem and several shoots emerge from it, each of them equipped with a photosensitive tip. They adjust your leaves in the right direction. With a lot of luck nobody eats you entirely and you reach a size where rodents and deer cease to be a threat. If you are very lucky, you will reach the forest canopy eventually and get as much sunlight as you need. It will take 120-200 years before you are fully grown. As your crown is thin, sunlight can reach the forest floor and allow small trees, bushes, ferns and mosses to survive around your stem. You supply them with water each dusk and they help you by keeping the soil soft and moist. An oak can live for centuries and some make it over a thousand years. Eventually, you will have exhausted most of the nutrients in the soil. Parasites keep attacking you; a large oak can house up to a thousand species of insects, including 300 butterflies and sixty wasps. Dry summers and violent winter storms will exhaust and tire you. Eventually, you pass the prime of your life. It happens to all of us. For an oak, it means that you grow weak and sickly. The ground around you will be depleted, and the bulk of your body is just large, heavy and troublesome. Much can be gained by getting rid of inessentials. Storms will break some of your branches, woodpeckers will make holes to breed their young and allow the entry of hostile fungi. You will cut off your connection to useless, cost-intensive branches and eventually these will drop to the forest floor, decompose, and return their substance as nourishment to you. Much of your wood will wither and die, and your fungi friends will digest the dead matter. They won't touch the healthy core. Year in year out your body will lose limbs and grow smaller. It's a good thing: the depleted soil doesn't allow you to keep up such a big business, and the fewer branches you expose, the less will storm winds trouble you. Finally, your stem will begin to be hollow. Today, in modern, commercial forests, hollow oaks are a rarity; in earlier times, they were more common. Some were so big that a person could ride into a trunk, turn the horse and ride out again. In old age, you are but a short, hollow cylinder, with a few short branches sticking out of the top. It's quite a relief. Your hollow core provides shelter for owls, bats and a legion of smaller animals. Roots that went outside now also extend into the hollow core of your shell: they feed on the dung of the animals which you shelter. The thin shell of wood is remarkably resistant to storms. A few small branches are enough to stay alive. Under such conditions, an oak may reach an age of 1400 years. It's only possible as you are *committed to the hands* of microbes, fungi, the plants of your neighbourhood and a whole community of animal friends.

Life is rarely about individuality. The main theme of evolution is symbiosis. Maybe the idea of symbiosis seems strange to you. You have been taught that you are an individual. The government and the commercial industry keep telling you. They want you isolated and alone. Think again. There are billions of microorganisms living on and within us. Some are a pest and some are just a minor irritation that keeps our immune systems in practice. Most microbes are our friends and partners. Some manipulate our moods. Some influence our courtship by altering our smell. Many others aid our digestion. The majority of the microbes living on and in your body are doing a great job. Look at your skin. At least 100,000 microbes are living on each square centimetre. And that's just the dry bits with little nourishment. Other places, where sweat glands emerge and moisture is the norm, are more densely populated. It's our great good luck that so many microbes cover us. Even hard scrubbing won't eliminate all of them. For each centimetre they cover, hostile microbes can't get in. The same goes for the microbes living in the digestive tract. There are between 1,000,000 and 100,000,000 living in your mouth. That may be up to 3000 species. Some feed on food waste, some on saliva, discarded cells, eat each other or have parties. Some are hostile, some a nuisance, many are negligible but the vast majority is doing an excellent job protecting you from infection. So far, roughly 8000 microbe species have been identified in the human intestines. Approximately 150 species can survive in the lethal acidic conditions of your stomach. That's nothing compared to the amount of bacteria infesting the stomachs of a cow. They are direly needed. Look at cows. They pretend to be vegetarians. Hardly anybody notices that at least five percent of their diet consists of small animals, insects, spiders, molluscs, worms etc.

We watch cows munching grass all day and wonder how they can digest it.

Figure 79 - Beyond Masks.

Grasses contain very little nourishment and they are tough. The cow chews 25,000 times in eight hours and regurgitates the stuff 500 times a day. It needs horizontally moving jaws, huge teeth and a lot of patience. However, these are not enough. Our digestion works much like the digestive system of carnivores: our gastric juices are highly acidic, we process food at great speed and the bacteria in our intestines tend to inhabit the comfortable last sections of our guts. Cows use a different system. They need five stomachs to get the job done, and keep a low level of acidity in them. It allows them to house a huge community of microbes and fungi. The bacteria break down the grass and ferment it. In the process, they release the vegetable protein from the cellulose and feed on it. The cow takes some nutriment from the fermented grass, but mostly it lives by eating the bacteria (Keith, 2013:88-90). The very concept 'herbivore' should be redefined.

People like to sort nature into good and bad. It doesn't work. Consider Heliobacter pylori. In spite of the lethal chemistry of our gastric juices, it leads a happy life in most people's stomachs. It destroys hostile intruders. Most of us should be happy to have it at our side. However, some people get ulcers from it. And that's how life in a symbiosis can work out. Usually there are advantages for everyone, but under pressure, a former friend can become an enemy.

In the 1940's several scientists announced that the freshly invented antibiotics would eliminate all major diseases. They envisioned a happy future where everyone was healthy. In their opinion, evolution is a slow process. Mutations are rare and very few of them are really an improvement. Bacteria, they assumed, have no sex life, as they simply divide whenever they are big enough. Each duplicate is much like the original. It leaves little space for mutation and adaptation. As a result, it was assumed that bacterial evolution is extra slow. But microbes are enormously successful. They have survived on earth longer than any other species. And they have adapted to pretty much any environment, no matter how poor, cold, hot or hostile. You can only do that when you are able to transform fast. To make up for their boring method of reproduction, bacteria have, in general, three types of sex. Most of them are passionately necrophile. They search for bits of dead bacteria and gobble up whatever remains of their DNA. Some feed on dead DNA, others incorporate it into their own system. Genetic engineering? Loads of bacteria do it all the time. Often enough, they do not even stick to their own species. If a bit of DNA seems attractive, they simply integrate it, no matter where it comes from. The second type of bacterial sex is based on a transfer via a bacteriophagic virus. In this process, called transduction, a virus takes control over a bacterium. It transforms the DNA of its host to create more bacteriophagic viruses and these go out hunting for new bacteria to infest. Occasionally, the reproduction process goes wrong and the virus introduces bits of DNA from its host to the new victim. The result is a mutation. Bacterial sex type three is called conjugation. Two bacteria meet and find each other attractive. It must be fate. One of them extends a feeler. Using this extension, it pulls its lover really close. Then they open their cell walls and exchange stuff like plasmids and bits of DNA. Afterwards, neither of them is as it used to be. As a result, bacteria can mutate with breathtaking speed. The inventors of antibiotics thought that immunity would not happen within centuries. It only took a few decades. Expose bacteria to antibiotics and a few survivors will be resistant. They will be immune to the stuff you exposed them to and to several similar antibiotics they have never experienced, and which haven't been invented yet. Today, each hospital on earth houses antibiotics resistant bacteria. The World Health Organisation has officially declared that we are now in the post-antibiotic-age.

Bacteria are here for good. They were here before us and we grew up in their company. They helped us become what we are. Most of them are benevolent and useful. Without them, our lives would be much worse, and significantly shorter.

They decide what food you crave and how much nourishment you get from it. If you lost all of your microbes you would be between one and three kilos lighter. You would lose the ability to draw much nourishment and vitamins from your food. First you would grow weak and tired. Then you would start to disintegrate. You would also lose the primary defence against any hostile fungus, microbe or virus. Death would not be fast, but painful and slow.

We are living in symbioses with thousands of microbe species and have the ignorance to call ourselves individuals. For one human cell there are ten microbe cells in your system. And that does not count viruses. Our DNA has even picked up several viruses. According to Juzzi (2014:19), roughly eight percent of our DNA consists of former viruses which survive as they exist in a symbiosis with us. Some of them increase the risk of fatal defects and cancer. Others allow us to exist as two-sexed animals. For an enormously long time, all life-forms on earth were single-sexed. They procreated by splitting apart. It was extremely productive, as every single individual produced offspring. Two genders only permit half of the population to procreate. But they ensure fast exchanges of DNA between individuals, and that's what counts in a changeful environment full of parasites, diseases and ecological changes. In other words, males were needed as the neighbourhood was hostile. A virus in our DNA allows fertilisation. Without that virus, the female immune system would destroy the intruding sperm and our species would end.

Here is another fascinating player in our DNA. One or two billion years ago, the mitochondria were bacteria. Unlike so many other bacteria of their age, they could process an aggressive and toxic gas called oxygen. They became the energy batteries in our cells, and allow us to gain energy by breathing. Nowadays, they can only survive in animals. Something similar happened to the ancestors of plants. They formed a symbiosis with microbes that could produce chlorophyll. Today, the chloroplasts are part of plant DNA and incapable of surviving without it. They allow plants to transform sunlight into sugar.

We may be wild and wonderful, but we cannot survive on our own. What you call 'I' is a community, a joint venture. You have never been alone. Looking for the Ancient Ones? They are everywhere around and within you.

Symbiosis. It does not end there. Plenty of plants evolved in the company of insects. They need one or two special insect species to impregnate them: without their help, the plant disappears. In terms of dependence, they are closer to that animal species than to the plants they are related to. When a plant species disappears, specific insects die, and vice versa. First of all, those who need that plant to feed their young. Call them specialists.

At this point, people like to express that we, unlike those dumb specialists, are flexible, adaptable, battle-hardened winners. True enough, hundreds of species of plants and animals can be eaten and digested by humans. However, only a tiny amount of them can be domesticated and produced in large amounts. The world population will soon reach eight billion people, and we depend directly (or indirectly, as in animal food) on only six species! Wheat, rice, corn, potatoes, manioc and sweet potatoes. They cover approximately 80% of our needs. The remaining 20% are made up of bananas, beans, soy, sugarcane, millet, barley, coconuts, sugar-beet, and, as animal food, hay. We bred a handful of plants and animals and spread them all over the earth. We cultivated them and they cultivated us. We turned them into digestible food; they turned us into cultivators and protectors, promoted the survival of those who could best digest them, and made us design the landscapes that they like. Plants and people shaped each other. If humanity disappeared, the domestic plants would wither and die. They are too cultivated to make it on their own. Without them, most of mankind would face extinction. We are specialists and *committed to the hands* of a few other species.

So far we talked biology. Or maybe we talked religion. The Sumerians and Babylonians who created the concept of personal gods were pretty close to the essential insight: you, as an individual, lonely, and deluded, won't make it. Without a spiritual partner or several, success is highly unlikely. That's why normal people had one or two personal gods and the kings were related to loads. Remember Šulgi of Ur III. He was one of the most successful kings in Mesopotamian history. His reign constituted a golden age, and the last flowering of Sumerian culture. Šulgi did an excellent job and loved listening to praise songs about himself. Unlike the Sumerians before him, he deified himself. Nevertheless, he knew that without his relations, success would have been impossible. Luckily, he had several extra strong ones. Sun god Utu and Gilgameš, god of the Underworld, were his brothers. Inanna and Geštianna were his sisters. Šulgi was loved by Ninlil and Enlil raised his head. That's excellent company. Šulgi was committed into their hands.

The concept continued for a long time. Aššurbanipal was surrounded by an entire cluster of deities. They accompanied him on his campaigns. Wherever he went, Ištar and Aššur walked before him. When an enemy king was defeated by the Assyrian army, or assassinated by his own family, Ištar was responsible. *To Bēlet, Goddess of the Earth, dwelling in Bitmasmasu, Aššurbanipal, King of Assyria, the prince her worshipper, the high priest, the work of her hands, who by her great command, in the midst of war had cut off the head of Teumman king of Elam. And Ummanigas, Tammaritu, Pahe, and Ummanaldas, who after Teumman ruled the kingdom of Elam; in her great service my hands captured them, and to my war chariot, my royal carriage, I fastened them. And in her grand might, in all countries I have marched, and a rival I have not. In those days the altar of the house of Ištar my lady, of marble I carved its sculpture; I set it up to please Bēlet. To me, Aššurbanipal, worshipping thy great divinity, (give) health, long days, and sound heart, worshipping and going to Bitmasmasu, may my feet grow old* (after Smith, 1871, 304-305).

It's astonishing. Aššurbanipal devastated cities, destroyed fields, blocked canals, flooded fertile land, filled up wells; he skinned his enemies alive or, if in a mild mood, merely cut out their tongues and chopped off their lips and hands. He waged war against rebellion in Egypt (twice), besieged Tyrus, conquered Karbit, warred with the Medes, fought and destroyed Elam (five wars), crushed the rebellion of his brother, who governed Babylon, and led several campaigns against the Arabs who kept attacking settlements in Syria. However, he did not celebrate himself but his deities, as he was the product of their hands. He was the mightiest emperor Mesopotamia ever saw, and his empire was bigger than that of any of his ancestors. Nevertheless, his personal company of deities, Aššur, Bēlet, Sîn, Šamaš, Iškur, Bēl, Nabû, Ištar of Ninua (Niniveh) the divine queen of Kitmuri, Ištar of Arbela, Ninurta, Nergal and Nusku were of such importance to him, that he kept praising and celebrating them for every success in his life. Their names appear, time and time again, all the way through his historical records.

Maybe we should think of spiritual activity as a symbiosis. It does not make much of a difference whether you believe that your gods are living entities or eternal ideals, built into the basic programming of our brains. Whatever they may be, they influence you as you influence them. Maybe you prefer to call them an illusion, as the Buddhists do. If you do, consider that your self, personality and identity are not real either.

It makes no difference. You, me, people, gods; it's just words. With just a few pounds of soggy grey matter crammed between our ears we are hardly qualified to understand the nature of reality. Being human, we should know our limits. Being gods, we should do our best to live up to our ideals.

You gain from your gods, your gods gain from you. Together, you are a successful team. Life after life you re-create each other.

The important bit is that you are a joint venture. Gods need believers, especially in troubled times like today. The divine may be eternal, well and good, but it still has to be manifested in some way. Here you come in. You commit yourself to your gods as they commit themselves to you. Gods need belief, emotion and attention. They need people who imbue daily life with the divine, by ritual, meditation, art and a life of virtue. Virtue, in this context, means magical power, charisma, love, dedication, humility, commitment and its nature depends very much on the deities you manifest. People need ideals and a wider consciousness, an awareness that takes them beyond the confines of their sorry little egos. So please consider. What do you get from your gods? And what do they get from you? No, don't go for the easy answer. Go into trance. Meet your gods. Ask them. Listen closely, record what you receive, and learn. It will make your magick more efficient and your life much easier. You feed them as they feed you. Or you are them and the nourishment simply goes around.

Committed to the hands means more than that. I keep meeting people who say that they will 'try something'. Trying is well and good, but when you want something substantial, half-hearted effort is not good enough. When you want to learn something, do it with all your power. Put all your passion, love and lust into it. Give it your full attention. Maybe it will work out. Maybe it won't. Give it a laugh. Failure is part of the game. And even if you decide to drop it, you will have learned and achieved more than those who simply dabble a little and turn away in disappointment. Everything really worthwhile is worth doing with a full heart. Call it dedication, commitment or obsession. Above all, simply do it.

Here is one useful meditation. Consider the magical oath. Crowley insisted that a magical oath, i.e. a solemn promise to dedicate your life to the Great Work, is unbreakable. He was right. Once you truly dedicate yourself to spiritual evolution, nothing can make you turn back. True, you may be distracted on occasion. Maybe your job, your partner or your children will require attention. Some people are distracted for years or decades. But you will come back to, if not in this then in your next lifetime. The magical oath turns all of your life into magic. And it gives you all the time in the world. As it turns out, we can't do everything, and especially not at once. According to Spitzer (2015:62), the errors caused by multi-tasking cost US industry 650 billion dollars a year. That's the primary cost. The secondary costs, when people feel bad at what they do, take it out on others and themselves, drink, consume drugs and medication, have divorces, do frustration shopping, go depressive, sick or violent, are much greater. People who claim that they are good multi-taskers deceive themselves. Human brains are not built to do several similar things at once. You can go for a walk with a friend, have a chat and avoid an obstacle at the same time, as these are different activities. You can't listen to two people at once without missing crucial information. Those who pay attention to the phone while reading what is on a computer screen and making up a suitable reply get things wrong. It's similar in our daily lives. So many people complain that they can't enjoy everything in life. Time is a luxury. Those who committed themselves to the magical oath know that they can do it all. What doesn't fit into this lifetime will happen in the next.

Are you ready to commit your life to the hands of the divine, or the ideal, or whatever you believe is worth living for? It will eliminate many disturbances. For one thing, typical personal problems will be reduced. Should I watch a movie or get drunk? The answer is easy. Is that movie of spiritual relevance? Is that drink of spiritual relevance? If not, just forget about them. There are better experiences available. If not, you can make them so. Consider your life. I am sure you are happy with some aspects and unhappy with others. That's what being human, or animal, plant or whatever is all about. The gods didn't give people a perfect life, but they permitted them to grumble and complain (*Enûma Eliš*). Most of them did not promise to listen to prayers (unlike Lamaštu, who listens very closely), but they accepted that being dissatisfied is part of being human and alive. I believe the gods listen more closely to prayers when there are fewer complaints and more encouragement. It's not really a new idea. In the third century, Heliodor (*Aithiopika, vol I*) wrote: *'Silent, my dear, my life', Theagenes interrupted. 'You are entitled to your complaints, Chariklea. But you annoy the deity more than you know. Much better, try to encourage it with appeals. With prayer, not with accusations, you will make the mighty compassionate.'* It's excellent advice. Who wants to listen to snivelling, complaining and people who wallow in misery?

For the fun of it, let us explore the notion is that the universe is basically divine. I know, it doesn't always seem that way. Watch the news for five minutes or read a paper and you'll come to an entirely different conclusion. But that's not all there is to life. The politicians, news media, environmental groups, social organisations, the NGOs that pretend to protect the planet are all part of the Fear Industry. They may or may not do a good job, but they do tailor their programme to the horrors that are easily activated in each given country, and cash in. Life is neither perfectly good nor bad. Yes, some bits go wrong occasionally. People whose divinity is frustrated, damaged or corrupted may become demonic. They can turn life into a nightmare for themselves and others. That, however, does not change the fact that the potential for happiness, perfection and joy is everywhere.

A divine universe. It's an assumption. Maybe it isn't true. You are entitled to your doubts. I agree that I am not talking facts but interpretation. But to improve your life, you can commit yourself to the divine and enjoy the divine in all the shapes it meets you. It's an act of faith. It takes courage. Are you up to it? How much faith do you have in beauty, joy, love, laughter and truth? How deeply do you believe in your ideals?

Commitment is love. Love is to recognise yourself in another and another in yourself. It starts, on a very primitive level, between two people. It can happen between you and your lover. Or with your parents, or children. Or between friends and companions. Or you extend love to people whom you never met, who lived in faraway places and in other times. Love is a state of attraction and commitment. It's not your love or my love. It does not belong to anyone. It can't be bought, sold, demanded or enforced. It can be remembered anytime you wake up and realise the divine is here. It can appear as friendship, companionship, cooperation, support and the sheer joy of things going right. Some of it is sex, some is lovemaking. Some of it is giving a smile to a stranger, doing the right thing without thought of profit, making the world a happier place and supporting your neighbour. The divine appears everywhere when your mind opens up. Love is the divine in me and you meeting itself in many shapes and energies. See that tree? Feel it. Sense it. Recognise it. The divine is in both of you. It is in the tree, the plants, the animals, people, cities; it even appears in abstract form, in ideals and hopes. The divine is self-recognition. That self is huge; it easily surpasses every single individual personality. Let's listen to that wonderful Voodoo artist André Pierre: *Those who do not love are nothing. Love of God. Love of neighbour. Love of work. Love for doing something good. When we have to do something, love of doing it well... I have confidence in the spirits. I love the spirits. I live with the spirits. I respect the spirits. I do what I want with the spirits, and they do what they want with me. Because they have confidence I will never betray them. That's why I have confidence in the spirits* (Cosentino, 1995:XX).

Let's turn it into a meditation. Maybe the first person in known history who taught love as a spiritual exercise was Kongzi (Confucius, 551-479 BCE). Kongzi lived in a dismal period. China had suffered from incessant wars for centuries, and many people had lost their faith in society, laws, kings, the gods and ancestors. Kongzi wanted to create a new type of person. In the old days, only a few top-ranking aristocrats bothered to educate themselves, performed the rites with due consideration and attempted to lead a virtuous life, if possible. Kongzi believed that everybody should make an effort and practice self-refinement. To do so, he recommended ceremonies, rituals, music, proper conduct and, above all, benevolence. *Fan Ch'ih asked about benevolence. The Master said, 'Love your fellow men'. He asked about wisdom. The Master said, 'Know your fellow men'. (Analects,* XII, 22, trans. Lau). Love for human beings (ai ren) became a guiding principle of Confucianism. Love and respect, Kongzi assumed, start with family and friends. From them you extend it, so that it touches other people, even persons whom you never met. To do so, he recommended perfect performance of the rituals and sacrifices. To extend love, benevolence and respect in all directions is a must in Confucian ceremonies. One occasion to practice such feelings is ancestral rituals. I'm not sure whether Kongzi, who was a very pragmatic sage, actually believed in the reality of the ancestors. However, he was certain that their worship was a splendid way of extending love. A ritual recommended by the *Liji* (*Book of Rites,* chapter *Jiyi)* prescribes a ritual for one's deceased parents. The dutiful descendant purified himself, retired to a peaceful inner room, fasted and built up a vivid memory of his (or her) parents. *On the day of the offering the son thought of his parents, he recalled their quarters, their smile, the tone of their voice and their attitude; he remembered those things that made them joyous and that what they liked to eat. After having fasted and meditated thus for three days he could perceive those for whom he fasted...What you love with all your power remains; what you worship with all your power reveals itself* (after Wilhelm and Legge).

By the time the ritual was over, the worshipper was happily in tears. Such rituals, Kongzi assumed, teach virtuous people what it means to love humanity. Love, however, is only possible when there are understanding and forgiveness (*shu*). It's a fascinating idea. Yes, I agree, there are plenty of people around, starting with politicians, warmongers, managers and bankers, who are anything but lovable. Or think of smaller offenders: maybe you detest your boss or your ex-partner. You may loathe or even hate them. It's perfectly understandable. But whenever you hate someone, you generate and store up destructive energy. It doesn't hurt that person, it only hurts you. It's like going through life with a painful open wound. Hate-energy is a threat to your well-being and it attaches you to the evil these people personify. I've seen it happen to many good people, especially those who are active in environmental protection. It's so easy for an idealist to loathe mankind, and end up hating her or himself. Those who hate promote their own defeat.

To forgive a person does not mean that you accept what he or she does. It simply means that you understand how that person thinks and acts, and that you do not allow those errors, crimes and sins to intrude into your life. Maybe that person appears as evil personified. But even the worst dictator has reasons to behave like he does, and is tied up in a tangle of beliefs, errors, restrictions and conditioning that make him act that way. Many anti-social persons are victims of pride, greed and stupidity, or simply afraid. Or maybe you are wrong and that person isn't such a monster at all. Once people start to think badly of someone, they find a thousand reasons to support their beliefs. It's called 'being right'. Can you tell the difference between what a person is and he or she does? We are not trying to find excuses for bad deeds or to tolerate them. Kongzi was all in favour of humanity, love and respect, but he did not approve of crime. Many of his followers were aristocrats. Like Kongzi, they knew that courage is a virtue. When necessary, they fought or killed their enemies. But they did not walk around cultivating hate and loathing.

The next sage who picked up the idea was Mozi (flourished around 479-438 BCE). He turned universal love into his guiding principle. He believed in a better world where people support and help each other, and extended their generosity and friendship to family, friends, neighbours, strangers and foreigners, no matter where and when. He also criticised the Confucians for their complicated, expensive rituals and music, and derided them for their greed and hypocrisy.

Next we encounter Laozi. In the *Daodejing*, a primary virtue is *ci*. It's written with the Chinese characters 'heart' and 'lush'. It has been variously translated as love, motherly love, forbearance, compassion and loving care. You find it in chapter 67 of the standard *Laozi* (Wang Bi version): *I have three treasures which I preserve and protect. The first is (motherly) love. The second is moderation. The third is not daring to be the first in the world. Having (motherly) love, I can be courageous. Having moderation, I can be generous. Not daring to be the first in the world, I can lead the 'vessels'* (=officials). (...) *Him, whom Heaven wants to protect, it surrounds with (motherly) love.* The last line is a little different in the earlier *Mawangdui Laozi*: *When Heaven wants to achieve something, it surrounds it with (motherly) love.*

That's what I call practical magic. It combines meditation with a loving attitude in daily life. Motherly love does not mean that you excuse everything. In fact, it implies that you have a duty to correct, educate, nurture, encourage and punish. Do it in a loving spirit. The Daoists make much of cultivating this consciousness. Unlike the Confucians and the Moists, they do not limit it to mankind. In Daoist thought, love extends to all beings.

A few centuries later, the Buddhists picked up the meditation. They turned it into several visualisations and rituals. By now, I'm sure you know enough. Let's go for feeling. Here is a simple, basic formula. Sit in a quiet, peaceful place, go into a good trance, and fill yourself with loving feelings. Spread a huge smile though your body. You have to feel happy to share it with others. Make it a strong smile. Make it surge through you. Feel how the corners of your mouth rise. Make that smile stronger. Radiate love. Imagine love as a pure energy that brings healing and bliss to all beings. Drench and flood yourself with it. Then radiate your good feelings into the directions of the world, one after another. You visualise the people dwelling there, your friends, acquaintances and total strangers, the plants and animals, the elements, the things, the scenery, and you extend good energies and feelings of friendship and compassion to them. You make the loving feelings go far beyond the world, even to other worlds, and you make them come back twice as strong and fill you up with more love than ever. Then you send them out again. Before long, you'll be opening and closing like a flower, pulsing in the joy of shared happiness.

I, 7

The seventh: Bound (or: Conjured) by the Oath of the Great Gods, Fly Away with the Bird/s of Heaven!

The seventh name deals with the world and our place in it. You might consider it a meditation, an attitude, a spiritual discipline or an approach to life. It describes how you relate to the world and the world relates to you. Life isn't easy at all. I'm sure you noticed. No matter how long you live, you will encounter paradoxes, enigmas and unanswerable questions. There is no happy ending; there is no ending at all. We learn to live with question marks, and the supply is inexhaustible. Life needs its paradoxes. First we learn that Lamaštu is bound by the oath or conjuration of the great gods. It means that she has a place in the great harmony, and that her actions and powers are limited, just as the powers of each deity, person and beings have limits. She does her job, whether she likes it or not, as it is necessary. In the next line, which may be part of name seven or maybe an unspoken number eight, we hear the conjurer exclaiming that she should *fly free like the birds of heaven.* Maybe she should simply go away. Or maybe she should remember her status as the Daughter of the Sky. In these lines we meet the ancient question of freedom and determination. We also run into a philosophical and theological debate that has been going on for thousands of years and is not likely to be resolved soon.

Freedom or bondage? The Christian church has been tying itself into knots by worrying whether god is almighty or whether people have an element of free will. St. Augustine (354-430), an influential lunatic, believed in an almighty god who pre-ordains everything. In his opinion there is no choice whatsoever. People are born as saints or sinners, and whether they go to heaven or hell was decided by God long before he even created Adam and Eve. Everything that happens (including happiness, success, failure, war, crime, rape, starvation) is God's will and no matter what you try, you can't alter anything. Sinners are created sinners and saints can't help being saints. It raises the question why God created evil, and why he allows crime, violence and pain to happen at all. When god ordains everything, there are neither guilt nor virtue.

The church decided on unalterable fate. Much later, the Jesuits assumed a very different position. In their opinion, people do have a choice and can influence their spiritual fate and the state of things on earth. God wants people to choose and decide, he also wants them to dedicate themselves to the divine and refine themselves. The entire structure of Jesuit training, perhaps the most sophisticated yoga developed by Christianity, is based on the premise that we have the choice and obligation to come closer to God. It's an idea I approve of. However, no matter how much theologists argued in favour of pre-determined fate or free choice, the debate always got stuck in terminology. Just what do such concepts as 'God almighty' and 'free will' indicate? Think about it. 'God' is a vague metaphor for a mind-blowing spiritual experience, 'almighty' a subjective measurement, 'free' is indefinable without specifying ('free to do what?') and 'will' a vague description of what seems like conscious intent. None of them amounts to much. We are talking words, words, words, and should better shut up. Every philosopher has been struggling with the issue. After several centuries of bitter arguing, the topic lost much of its attraction when biologists, neurologists and psychologists demonstrated that 'free will' is only partly free: some of our decisions are made consciously, some unconsciously, some arise from memories, genes, conditioning, instincts and for all I know, gut feelings produced by microbes. You may think you just decided something, but the relevant neural clusters in your brain go active before the conscious thought appears in your awareness. Whatever we imagine we are deciding, we will never be sure it wasn't decided much earlier, by levels of awareness we are hardly aware of.

The young upstart monotheist religions, with their unbalanced almighty, omnipotent gods, could not explain how a human being might measure, judge or comprehend divine omnipotence in all its contradictory ways. The many earlier, polytheist, religions did not fall into that trap. When you have plenty of gods, fate and determination are decided by a divine community where different interests cooperate and collide. Polytheism means that many interests and points of view are valid. The fate of yesterday ain't worth nothing when the gods assemble today, drink a lot of beer on the holy mound, and decide differently. Human beings may influence the decision with prayer, devotion, magic and sacrifice, but all in all, they have to live with it. For the Mesopotamian thinkers, a controversy between divine omnipotence and free will would have been meaningless. The gods keep altering their decisions just like people do.

But look at the popular Indian concept of freedom and bondage. Since the Upaniṣadic period, spiritual people have been worrying whether they should leave the community, dissolve all ties and merge with the supreme all-self by shedding all concepts, forms, names, rules, clothes and most of all the concept of a personal identity. The question came in two basic packages: first the Upaniṣadic version, where the formless, nameless, indescribable all-self (Brahman, i.e. *Extension*) is Absolute Reality, and people should do their best to merge and dissolve in it. A few centuries later Buddha picked up the idea, but changed it. He combined the Upaniṣadic road of liberation with the Anatman school of thought that proposed that the self, and any self, is a painful illusion, and does not exist. In Buddha's original teachings, freedom from bondage is total dissolution.

Several tantric traditions, especially the Kula systems, made an issue out of it. In their opinion, anything that binds you has to be discarded; all attachments have to be cut. True freedom is only for those who have severed all links and ties, be it to friends, family, society, property, status, the gods and even to social duties like generosity and doing good deeds. Other tantric systems, like the early Krama tantrics of Kashmir, cultivated a state of indifference. In their opinion, bondage and liberation are narrow-minded concepts that may have a relative value, but are not worth worrying about.

Think about it. Bondage or liberation? When do you sense your limits and when are you aware of choices? Do as the Sumerians did and make a list. Write down what confines and what liberates you. Confinement is easy. People like to grumble. Gravity limits you, and so do work, income, biological age, social norms, laws, language, the place and time you live in. Single people protest about loneliness and people in relationships bemoan their lack of freedom. None of them seems really happy. Maybe the common denominator is complaining. It devalues anything. Humans are good at being miserable. It's part of our incredible charm. When you shut up and enjoy you come much closer to the gods.

Freedom is harder: few are aware how many choices they have. You chose to read this book. You can continue reading or go for a walk. And you can decide what this moment feels like, what it means, and how you will remember it. Each moment is special. Each moment offers choices. You can do things, and you can choose whether you do them well or just get them over with. You are free to devote your full attention or just run on routine.

Maybe you would like a happier feeling. Feelings don't come from buying expensive trash nor do they derive from status symbols and other people's admiration or fear. Unlike Lamaštu, they don't fall from the sky. Feelings are made. It happens in your brain, your heart, belly and genitals. You can choose what you feel about, and you can decide how intensely you feel. Making good feelings is an essential discipline of the Krama Tantrics of Kashmir. These adepts knew that when they were happy, so were the gods. They simply picked a sensation, like a sunset, a pebble, a cloud, the flight of a bird, the growth of a tree, the laughter of a child, the beauty of a person or the mind-blowing miracle of existence, and were happy about it. In fact, they turned up their happiness to maximum intensity. It made them ecstatically, divinely alive. Other offerings were not really required.

And you can remember how wealthy you are: you are alive, you have a body, you have a home, you live in a society that doesn't try to kill you and you can choose how you think what you think, if you think, which isn't very likely unless you stop time and do it now. Are we talking about reality or about ideals?

Whether we like it or not, limitations are fundamental to every situation. They define where we are, what we are and what is possible. Let's explore a few basic rules of ecology (Körner in: Strasburger: *Lehrbuch der Botanik* 2002:889, trans. JF).

- *Every population of individuals that grows without interference reaches a limit of its resources.*

- *In a common environment a species will be replaced by another if it has a higher fertility or a smaller mortality.*

- *This implies that two species can only coexist over extended periods when they inhabit different functional niches.*

- *The density of inhabitants influences the populations or communities of species in such a way that the number of individuals stabilises or undergoes periodic fluctuations.*

- *The available energy decreases along the chain of consumers.*

It's not much. But it is a start. The concept of ecology was invented by Ernst Haeckel in 1866; it is a young science and many rules have not been established yet. The term 'ecology' is based on the Greek word oikos, the house. The world, your environment, your culture, society, religion and the personality you assume to have can be understood as a house, and everything in life is about housekeeping. Smart people insist that we should think of the economy. It got us into a global crisis. Millions of perfectly trained economic experts, bankers, politicians and businessmen worldwide have no idea what's happening. Before economy is possible, ecology establishes the game, the players and the rules. The key words of ecology are choices and limitations. They define each other. Here is a simple definition: ecology is the science of the interaction of organisms, no matter whether they are individuals, populations or communities composed of different species, in their biotic and abiotic environment in relation to the transmission of energy, matter, information and awareness.

Take a piece of infertile ground. It will support a few tough species that can survive on very little. They, however, will be quite happy with what they have. Add fertiliser. The plants will start growing. Some won't like the new soil chemistry, and wither. Others will thrive, until new, stronger species move in who outgrow and replace them. Meanwhile, the animal community will change. So will the microbial life in the soil. In the end, you will have a flourishing piece of land housing different inhabitants.

Each environment determines its dwellers, which in turn shape the environment. Environments regulate themselves. To add more nutrients, water, or sunlight may change everything. It will destroy the lifeforms that are perfectly suited to this specific world. It might create a better world. Or it may ruin an excellent, age-old relationship. Are we talking biology, sociology or spirituality? I don't know. Lamaštu moves through all of them. Specific limitations define the possibilities, in this world, in your mind, your hopes and dreams and in the all-consciousness. Maybe you like them and maybe you don't. Maybe they can and should be changed. Being rebellious is built into our nature. Human beings were made out of clay, spittle and spells, and the blood of rebellious gods ensured an extra blessing. Look into the *Atraḫasis Epic*, look into the *Enûma Eliš*. The gods knew what they were doing. They added rebelliousness to our essential nature. We should be grateful for it. But before we go meddling, interfering and upsetting systems that have worked for millennia, we might learn how they function. This is what being *Bound to the Oath of the Great Gods* is all about.

The order of the world, decreed by the great gods, or, if you prefer, the laws of nature, of life, or your consciousness, determines limits and restrictions. It also provides options for freedom, for choice, for possibilities. Games need rules. Each game board has its limits. Without them, the game would be impossible. To know the limits is to know the possibilities. Bondage and freedom, the famed alchemist formula *Solve et coagula* (*release and bind*) come in one package. Much of it depends on your point of view. Face the limits. I know, it isn't popular. If I wrote popular esoteric books full of pink bubbles and angelic wisdom, I would tell you that anything can be achieved. I would promise that nothing is impossible, that mind rules matter and that faith in the gods, in the universe and yourself can master every problem. Some people claim that it's enough to 'wish on a star', 'think positive' and 'believe in yourself'. It would be nice if it were so. Lamaštu says that it isn't. Life is a tough cookie, and we'll be finished before it is. As a human being, you are limited by your biology. You are also restricted by your environment, society, culture, nationality, language, memories, hopes, beliefs and the thoughts you take for real. It's disappointing. You can't hibernate, you can't digest sunlight and you are living in a hierarchical society controlled by greedy monkeys who love violence, power politics, and status symbols. That's the bad part.

On the other hand, you enjoy a lot of freedom. You can meet people who are just as crazy as you are, you can interpret a given situation as you like, you can turn miserable events into educational experiences. You can choose which emotions you want to feel. You can devote yourself to learning and laughing and be astonished and enchanted by the wonder of the universe whenever you open your mind really wide. You can enjoy yourself, the world and whatever you experience just as you like. When you open up, the divine is everywhere and everything. The Meaning of Life? You decide. And decide again. Make it a good one. This is your freedom, and it's quite a lot of it.

It allows you to fly into the sky like the bird of heaven; it permits you to descend into the underworld where the dead wear feathers and coo like doves, and above all, it allows you to choose your way while meeting your obligations to the world. It's your freedom and your responsibility. If you came as far as this, you are one of the lucky ones. You have gained a rich harvest of experiences and joys. Every day you get more of them. Spiritual discipline? Share it with the world. Give thanks for all the good things; share your joy, your awareness and divinity with everyone. Sharing gives relevance: we are social animals. That's how we survived. People who only think of personal gain are evolutionary dead ends. What has the world given to you? What have the gods given to you? What do you owe to this magnificent world that is treating you so generously? You have a body, you have a mind, you are alive and you are surrounded by a society, by friends, by people, beings, and ecosystems, gods and life-forms, biotopes, cultural clusters and an amazing history full of astonishing educational experiences. Think about it. We came a long way since Stone Age artists carved human-animal figurines, since agriculture was developed, since the Sumerians created the first functional script on this planet. All of this is magick. There are so many possibilities. Maybe you feel free and maybe you consider yourself bound. Maybe it is all in your mind, but whatever you are, you should be grateful for it. This is Lamaštu's seventh name, her blessing and her sacred spell, and it will guide you wherever you go. Remember the Oath of the Great Gods, and what possibilities it allows you. No matter where you are and who you assume yourself to be. It's your responsibility, your choice and privilege. It surrounds you wherever you go and whatever you do. It determines how you experience life, and what you make of it. Make it a good one.

Figure 80 - Look to the West.

Part Seven

Oathbound, Free to Fly

Short Glossary: Priestly Offices, Temples and Cities

The following list is by no means complete. There were an amazing amount of terms for religious and priestly offices, and most of them remain totally enigmatic. Place names abound, and in most cases, the towns and settlements have not been excavated and cannot be identified. This glossary is just a humble introduction to a complex and fascinating topic.

Note on spelling: Mesopotamian inscriptions are notorious for varied spellings. Some words occur in dozens of ways. The versions in this appendix are not the only ones. For convenience, Sumerian words appear in ordinary writing and *Akkadian, Babylonian and Assyrian words in italics*. Sumerograms with uncertain pronunciation are in **BOLD TYPE**.

Adab: see Utab.

Akkad, Agade: the city which Sargon I turned into his capital, and the name of his realm in northern Babylonia. enjoyed its greatest wealth and power under Sargon I and his successors. It lost its eminence after the Akkadian period, around 2230 BCE, when the Gutians overran the country and killed Sargon's last descendant, King Šarkališarri. In the OB period, A. was still a large city. Eventually it lost its importance. Several Neo-Assyrian kings tried to raise its ruins to glory and excavated in the hope of discovering the site of its major temple, the Eulmaš. Today, the location of A. is unknown. Maybe the city was close to Kiš or to modern Baghdad.

Akkil: *'House of Lamentation'*. A city or town, yet unlocated, which may have been in the neighbourhood of Uruk. It had a major temple for Ninšubur, the enigmatic goddess who started out closely related to the Underworld, and possibly even as a queen of the dead, was turned into the sukkal of Inanna, and transformed into a male god during the Middle Babylonian period.

Anšan: (modern Tal-i Malyan, close to Persepolis), a major city of Elam, fortified in the early third millennium BCE. With a city wall of 5km and a population estimated at 40,000, one of the largest cities in the Near East. For unknown reasons, A. was abandoned only a few centuries after its fortification; in the late third millennium BCE a new city was raised on the ruins of A.

Arali, E.KUR.BAD ***(Arallû/m)***: *'Underworld'*. The desert or steppe between Badtibira and Uruk, a famous wasteland where Dumuzi was murdered. In later literature, we encounter A. as the name of an underworld, in Young Babylonian texts a mountain of A. appears. Badtibira was devoted to Dumuzi's cult and Uruk to the cult of Inanna. The wasteland between their cities was inhabited by nomadic sheep herders, the very people who worshipped Dumuzi as a shepherd.

Aratta: a foreign city in conflict with Uruk in early prehistory. Both cities were dominated by the cult of Inanna. A. has not been localised so far. The hymns only tell us that it was in the mountains, which makes Elam a likely location. A. and its lord, who was married to Inanna, were a major threat to King Enmerkar of Uruk, who was married to Inanna as well. The lord of A. made her a lapis lazuli temple with a golden bed and set a crown on her statue, but as the hymn tells us, he did not have a gipar (cloister complex) on the premises, as Uruk had. Enmerkar desired the wealth and resources of A., such as metal, wood and minerals, cajoled Inanna to neglect the Lord of Enmekar, and incited a contest between himself and his opponent.

Aštammu, bīt aštammi: a tavern, guest house or brothel with or without connection to a temple. See Eš-da-ma-ka, Eš-dam.

Āšipu: a ritualist, who functions as a magician, exorcist, conjurer, healer, diviner plus, in the first millennium, as a temple scribe, scholar and astrologer. Some scholars assume he was an assistant of the mašmaššu, others propose that Ā. and mašmaššu were synonyms, or that both, originally distinct functions became a single one, the Ā. On occasion, āšipu were employed by temples, but, apart from some Ā. of the temple of Aššur, they were not part of the priesthood nor were their activities confined to any specific cult. Some Ā. were hired by the palace and high-ranking aristocrats, or acted for private persons of sufficient income. Several Ā. had a very exalted status and a lot of influence over kings. Occasionally they worked in the company of the asû, or they performed tasks that were generally in the domain of the asû. The functions of the Ā. and the asû overlap so much that some scholars treat them as distinct professions while others note few differences between them. One strange aspect of their craft is that they left a vast amount of ritual literature, but that they rarely appear in documents, letters and historical accounts before the first millennium BCE. Female conjurers and exorcists, i.e. ***ašiptu/m*** and ***āšipāk(u)*** appear in the *Maqlû Series*; they are dreaded as terrifying sorceresses. Their role models are the goddess Ningirimma/Ningirin who is the āšiptu(m) of the gods, and goddess Gula, who was praised as a doctor, a seer and a conjurer. Other deities who are called Ā. and mašmaššu are Enki/*Ea*, Asarluḫi, and Marduk.

Assinu: a man associated with the cult of Ištar, who might be a homosexual, a eunuch, a male prostitute or simply effeminate. As a hymn says, the A. and the kurgarru prove the skill of the goddess to turn men into women and vice versa. Whether the A. had a sacred function or status is debatable, as the word frequently appears as an insult. This did not place him outside of society; the tale of *Ištar's Descent* relates how the kurgarrû and the A. were created to travel into the underworld to rescue *Ištar*, and how Ereškigal cursed them for this deed with a fringe existence in taverns, gutters and the shade of the city wall. In the Sumerian *Inanna's Descent*, the A. is the **gala tur-ra**, a '*junior gala*' and has the rank of a (minor) lamentation priest. To journey to the underworld and to return from it were two of the divine Me of Inanna. Were these priests trained in trance journeys to the underworld? A change of status is clearly discernible. While early Mesopotamian literature accepts homosexuality (and hints at it regarding Gilgameš and Enkidu), by the first millennium, passive homosexuality was condemned as shameful, and the A. and the kurgarrû were described as people who *delight in doing forbidden things*, whatever that may mean. See gala-tur-ra.

Aššur (modern Qalat Sherqat): a city named after the god Aššur (or vice versa), the early capital of Aššyria. A. Is perfectly situated and protected by a bend of the river Tigris. The city is on a rocky hillside and measured 65 hectares. The countryside provides rock, and the climate is far nicer than in southern Mesopotamia. Aššur had almost enough rain for agriculture and some snow in winter, hence canals were rarely needed. The god Aššur was often thought to be the husband of Ištar, Antu(m) or Ninlil. Besides their cult, there were major temples for Šamaš and his son Sîn. Later, three ziggurats were raised for Enlil, Anu and Adad. Other popular deities were the goddess Aššurītu, and after the late second millennium BCE, Nabû. The city A. gained much it's wealth as it was so conveniently close to major trade routes. Around the start of the second millennium BCE, when A. was founded, Assyrian traders controlled much of the commerce from Sumer in the distant south to the mountains of Turkey and the cities of Syria. A. was destroyed by Cyaxares, king of the Medes, in 614 BCE.

Asû : perhaps: '*One Who Knows Water*'. A healer or medical practitioner. The female form is ***asītu***. See A.ZU. The word is related to: ***asûtu***: *medical science*, emphasising physical remedies, plants, drugs, minerals, salves etc. with a smaller emphasis on magic and prayer, or so some scholars hope..

Atum, female***:*** ***atūm***: '*(Temple) Doorkeeper*'. A security job with religious and magical implications. Doors and gates were important liminal regions, and favourite haunts of dangerous spirits and deities like Lamaštu. The person or deity who guarded them had an essential apotropaic function. In some cases, the magical doorkeeping was done by the doors, bolts and locks themselves.

A-zu (*asû*): perhaps: *'One Who Knows Water'*. A diviner, physician, healer. A specialist, usually male but occasionally female, who used drugs (mineral, floral and animal) to make salves, medicines, ointments, plus spellcraft and sorcery. Also a specialist for elementary surgery and bone setting. The A. left major surgery well alone, which saved the lives of many patients.

Babil, Babilim, Babilani (Greek: Babylon, Biblical: Babel): *'Gate of the God/s'* A major city in central Mesopotamia which gained importance after the fall of the Sumerian Ur III dynasty and the defeat of the Amorite Isin-Larsa kings. B. had such a strong influence that its name became synonymous with a wide range of land: Babylonia was located between the Sumerian 'Sea-Land' in the south and the hilly steppes of Assyria in the north. Much of it overlapped with the earlier state Akkad. Around the 13th century BCE, its city god, Marduk, became the major deity of Babylonia and Sumer. In the process, he was identified with a wide range of elder gods, was turned into a son of Enki, and replaced the former chief god Enlil/Ellil. Marduk's famous temple Esagila was in Babylon. In the first millennium BCE Babylon was a major opponent, and occasionally a vassal state of the Neo-Assyrian Empire. The city was frequently besieged and destroyed. At its greatest extent, B. measured 975 hectares. The Etemenaki, the 'tower of Babel' was a ziggurat; it probably rose from the centre of the city. The building had seven tiers, a height of 91,5m and a top storey measuring 24x22,5m. Apart from the cult of Marduk, prominent deities with their own temples were Ištar, Ninmaḫ and Ninurta. Other deities made do with chapels.

Badtibira: a little-known city or town documented in third millennium BCE literature. Dedicated to Dumuzi, and associated with the Lady of the Steppe.

BALAG.DI (*ṣāriḫu*): a professional mourner. Not necessarily a religious specialist.

Borsippa: a city near Babylon. Two major deities were Gula and Adad. Around the end of the second millennium, the cult of Nabû and Tašmētum became a major power. Apart from them, temples and shrines for Nanay, Namtar, Marduk, Ninlil, Šamaš, Sîn and Zababa are attested.

Cutha, Kutha: a major city near Babylon with a strong cult dedicated to Nergal/Meslamta'ea. Also a synonym for death and the Underworld.

Dam: *'spouse, husband, wife'*. One of the titles of exceptionally high-ranking priests and priestesses who were married to the deity of their temple. Several such spouses are on the record, most notably in Lagaš and Uruk. The office of the D. was probably confined to a number of specific cults and cities and not a general Mesopotamian institution. These ritualists often came from the royal and high aristocratic families; they had an exalted rank but they were not generally involved in temple administration. Their office seems to have faded away after the Isin-Larsa period.

DAM.DINGIR: a high priestess, well-documented in Ebla (where a sister or daughter of the king had the office), and a few other cult places.

Dannina, Danninu: a name of the Underworld, derived from ***dannatu/m***: *'fortified place, fortress'*; *'foundation, building site'*; *'strict, firm, hard'*; *'threatening, harsh'*.

Der: a fascinating city, located east of the Tigris, inhabited by a blend of Mesopotamians and a range of cultural groups related to the Iranian mountains. Der was connected to the tangle of roads that are called the 'Silk Road' nowadays, and a major marketplace for foreign goods. In Der we encounter a strong bias towards snake-related gods (due to its link to Iran, where they were even more popular), and a range of Mesopotamian deities who have their own peculiar local characteristics, such as the cult of the Great Anu, otherwise known as Anu of Der. The major god was Ištarān, also known as Angal.

Dilmun, Tilmun, Telmun: modern Bahrain and a range of land to the west of the Persian Gulf. Starting during the Early

Dynastic period, sea trade to the island D. became a major economic enterprise, and provided the city-states of southern Sumer with wealth. D. was an important station in journeys to more distant places, like Southern Arabia, Ethiopia and India. It boasted a thriving trader's colony and provided Mesopotamia with large amounts of copper, lapis lazuli, woods and possibly pearls ('fish-eyes'), and trade goods from distant realms, like ivory. The major local products were dates and linen. In turn, silver, textiles and sesame oil were exported to D. Trade with D. was partly a state or temple controlled enterprise and partly conducted by independent individuals. While far-distance destinations like Meluḫḫa (the Indus Valley) ceased to be visited during the Ur III dynasty and Magan (Omar) ceased to be visited during the OB period, business with D. continued. At a much-reduced rate, as after c.1800 BCE, D. ceased to be an international trade centre for more than a millennium and its export products changed from exotic goods to home-grown agricultural products. Maybe the people of D. monopolised trade with Magan, while the end of the Indus Valley culture made trade with India unprofitable. Mythologically, D. was created and populated with animals and plants by Enki. That's the Sumerian story. Whether Enki was worshipped in D. is under debate. However, the native god Inzak appears among the Sumerians as Enzag, and the goddess Meskilak as Ninsikila, sometimes identified with Ninḫursag. The D. goddess Laḫamun was identified with Zarpānītu. Inscriptions and texts from D. refer to Marduk, Damkina, Enki and Iškur. Whether these were worshipped by the locals, or by resident traders from Sumer, remains a tricky question.

Duku/g: *'the Holy Mount'*; probably a storage pile of grain and wool, or maybe a mound of earth, seat of Enlil, where offerings were made and libations poured. The D. is in the Ušubukinna, the assembly place of the gods, and a site where major decisions are made. Correspondingly, some temples (Eridu, Girsu, Nippur) had a D. on their premises. Jacobsen (1987:272) claims that the pile of grains was covered with plaster, and that this was the common way of storing cereals. The D. could also refer to the Underworld. Enlil and Ninlil are the Lord and Lady of the D..

Dunnu: a major OB. city close to Isin and Larsa. It is chiefly known for its fragmentary cosmology, based on the idea that each generation of primal deities kills the earlier one, plus a lot of incest: in short, the brief and extremely violent tale may have inspired Hesiod.

Dur-an-ki: *'Bond of Heaven and Earth'*, *'Navel of Heaven and Earth'*; the seat of Enlil and Ninlil in Nippur, either surrounding the Ekur or part of it. D. contains the *Centre of the Universe*. The word is also a title of Enlil.

Dur-Kurigalzu: modern Aqar Quf near Baghdad. The capital city of the Kassites kings after the fall of the Babylonian dynasty around 1600 BCE. A ziggurat was built by King Kurigalzu in the 14th C. BCE, which was later mistaken for the Tower of Babel.

Dur-Šarrukin (modern Khorsabad): a capital erected by Sargon II, who wanted to shift the Neo-Assyrian capital from Kalakh to a better place. It was a close copy of Kalakh and never completed as Sargon II died too early to get the job done. There were major temples for Šamaš, Sîn, Ninurta, Adad, Ningal, Nabû and Ea, and a seven tiers ziggurat. Sargon II hoped that his new city would house people from all four regions of the world, and inaugurate a new age. Instead, it became an unimportant fortified town in the middle of nowhere.

E (*bītu(m)*): *'house, temple'*. Mesopotamian temples were more than shrines, buildings or entire complexes of buildings: they were endowed with life, consciousness and power. Each temple radiated its own, fierce *gleam of awe*, each drew on a range of specific energies, and each could be expected to exert a magical and religious influence. Major temples were crowned by a ziggurat, a multi-layered tower.

E-Abzu: *'House of the Abzu'*, the temple of Enki in Eridu. Originally a tiny hut, but vastly extended over the millennia.

E-akkil: Papsukkal's temple in Kiš.

E-anna: *'House of Date Clusters (?)' 'House of Heaven'*; temple of Inanna and An/Anu in Uruk. Enḫeduanna praised it as a *ripe fruit*, a *house of seven corners*, as *seven fires lit at midnight* and *seven desires captured*, where Inanna, encompassing the horizon, rolls her dice, clothes the woman and arms the man. The vast temple complex, containing numerous buildings, shrines and open spaces, goes back to humble religious buildings of the fifth millennium BCE, making the site rival Eridu and Nippur for its great old age. The monumental building period began around 3500 BCE, but the structure was demolished and rebuilt on a much larger scale (six hectares) by Urnammu, the founder of the III Dynasty of Ur, around the end of the third millennium BCE. The main feature of the complex was a massive ziggurat enclosed by several large courtyards, plus buildings with many different functions. The temple complex also housed a scribal school.

Ebiḫ, Ebeḫ: a mountain in the eastern Tigris realm, possibly Mount Jebel Hamrin. Enḫeduanna's poem *Inanna and Ebiḫ* informs us that the mountain was disobedient and refused to kneel before Inanna, to kiss her feet, and to worship and obey her. The goddess became raging mad and had a terrible fight with E. The mountain appears, depending on the context, as a real landscape with various animals, plants and biotopes, as a culture of disobedient people and as a horrible great monster/dragon, whose throat the goddess slashed. It makes Inanna one of the first dragon fighters of known mythology. Quite possibly, the poem celebrates the conquest of a foreign culture by Enḫeduanna's terrifying dad, Sargon I.

E-babbar: *'House Rising Sun'*, a temple of Ningirsu; a temple of Utu.

E-dam: *'House of the Spouse'*. A section of the temple complex reserved for a high priest or priestess who is the spouse (dam) of the deity. One early, pre-Sargonic example is the E. of the priest married to the goddess Nanše in Nigin, Lagaš. Another one is the dam of Nanna/Suen in Uruk; here the spouse of the moon-god was also called zirru. The women who acted in these functions were so important that they are commemorated in year names; after the Isin-Larsa period they tend to disappear. The dam of a deity had an exceptionally high status and frequently came from the royal family. However, he or she was not necessarily the actual head of the temple, nor its manager, but seems to have functioned in a separate role.

EDEN (*ṣēru*): *'steppe, wasteland, desert'*, the uncultivated wilderness surrounding the city-states of the Mesopotamian plains, home of many wild beasts and dangerous spirits.

E-ENGUR.ra: *'House of the ENGUR'* i.e. the abzu/abyss. Enki / Ea's temple in Eridu.

E-galgina: *'the Eternal Place'*, a location in the Underworlds.

E-galkurzagin: *'the Lustrous Kur Palace'*. A name for an Otherworld located in the mountains (Kur) or in the Underworld (Kur), or both.

e-ga-nu: *'House/Temple of Ostriches'*. A temple of Ninḫursag in Ur.

E-giš-nu-gal: *'House Causing Light'*, temple of Nanna/Suen.

Egi-zi-maḫ: title of the highest priestess of the Šara temple in Umma. The priesthood had two chiefs: the female E. with a staff of musicians, cleaners, snake conjurers and, as far as the documents go, a group of LUKUR ladies consisting of 56 and, in another document, 68 ladies. The highest priest, a lu-maḫ, had a staff of **maš-e pa-da** (*'Those Who Were Chosen by the Oracle'*), a house-keeper and a porter; beside them, an unknown number of isbib and gudu priests did their duty. One document lists the musicians: ten singers and 120 female singers plus their daughters were employed by the temple.

E-ḫuš: *'Terrifying House'*, a temple of Ningirsu.

Ekal ṣalāli: *'House of Rest'*. A euphemism for a (royal) tomb, or, poetically *'House of Sleep, Tomb of Rest, Eternal Abode'*. Frequently, the dead were assumed to sleep in their tombs. It's one of the reasons why Gilgameš wanted to remain active and awake as much as he could, while he was still alive. Nevertheless, death was not simply about sleeping. The dead were also expected to eat and drink and had some sort of social life. Those who rested under the floor of their former houses probably spent much time watching their descendants.

E-kur: *'House of the Mountain'*, Enlil's temple in Nippur, the most important temple of Sumer.

E-kur-maḫ: *'House Great Kur'*. Temple of Ninazu. Whether the 'kur' refers to the underworld or to the foreign mountains of Iran, Turkey or Lebanon remains an open question.

E-maḫ: A temple dedicated to a mother goddess in Babylon. Temples with the same name existed in Adab and Girsu in the city-state Lagaš.

E-meslam: *'House Thriving Mesu Tree'*; temple of Nergal/Meslamta'ea in Kutha. Also a synonym for the Underworld.

En (*bēl/u, enu/m, ennu*): *'lord, governor, administrator'*, *'Successful Manager'*; in a religious context possibly *'Highest Priest'*. The title en was also used for male and female managers of temple estates, heads of temple personnel, administrators of manufactories, ploughing teams, cooks, cleaning staff etc. In Sumerian, the word en was used for male and female administrators. The Akkadians used the terms en for male managers, but when they created the female form, **Entu(m)**, (by inserting the feminine 'T' into the word) they meant something different: what the Sumerians had called **Nin-dingir**: *a 'Lady who is a Goddess'*. That, however, is not the same thing as a female manager. The terminology is frustratingly difficult. To begin with, in the late third millennium BCE some city-states were run by an en and others by a **lugal** (*'strong man'*=king). In this context, we encounter monarchs who call themselves en, and they definitely did not mean 'high priest'. Several Sumerian kings, such as En Šakuušanna of Uruk, Lugalkinešedudu of Uruk and Lugalzagesi of Uruk held the title 'en'. Maybe it was just a formality and maybe they acted as religious functionaries. But when we look at the OB period, we observe ens who were definitely not kings. Some were high-ranking administrative priests: we encounter them praying for the lives of their kings. Nor was enship limited to a single person. Each city had had least one, and some cities, like Nippur, had two, a larger and a lesser one. In between Sumerian culture and OB regency we have the Isin-Larsa dynasty, which was run by a bunch of foreign conquerors. It is from their time that much of our evidence regarding en and entu(m) comes, plus most of the material on the 'sacred marriage'. How much was invented in this badly documented period of cultural transition?

And what shall we say about the **entu(m)?** She was a very high-ranking religious official, but she had no administrative duties. Akkadian lexical lists tend to identify the entu(m), the NU.GIG and the nin-dingir as synonyms. A NU.GIG is a tabooed, secluded and sacred woman, a lady set apart for religious reasons. A nin-dingir is a lady who is a goddess. The two terms indicate a very high status, but they are not necessarily the same. Now for the most difficult topic. Thanks to many popular books, the offices of the en and entu(m) are best known for a fertility ritual. You can enjoy this troublesome topic in the chapter on the 'Sacred marriage'. Some contemporary scholars believe that the ritual union was performed between a king (who may or may not have been an en) and an entu(m), who may have been a high priestess, or the queen, or the queen being the high priestess, or a representative of the high priestess or queen. The woman may have represented a deity, such as Inanna, Ištar, Ningal, Ninisina, Bau/Baba, depending on the leading local goddess, or she may have been the goddess (that's what NIN.DINGIR implies). During the Isin-Larsa dynasty, Bau/Baba seem to have been the most important goddess; later, her hymns were slightly rewritten to adapt them to the cult of Inanna/Ištar. Her male partner may have been the king, or the en, or the king who is the en, and represents the favourite local god, such as Dumuzi, Amaušumgalanna, Ningirsu, Ninurta or whoever. Together the two did something mysterious, which may have been lovemaking (attested in one or two cases), or an unknown symbolic ritual. It could have happened annually, as one version implies, or just once, to legitimise a new king, or who knows when: for most periods and most places the evidence is poor or entirely absent. Whew. Consider this: only thirteen entu(m)s are known from Sargon I to the Old Babylonian period when the office disappeared. They were all daughters or sisters of the king. It raises the question whether they really went to bed with the king; unlike the Egyptians, the Mesopotamians did not approve of incest. The entu(m) was generally expected to avoid pregnancy, unless it happened to be a child of a king and/or en (several such children became kings themselves; examples are Sargon of Akkad and Šulgi of Ur III). Other children may have been given away for adoption. When we are talking of religious en or entu(m)s (unlike kings and queens), these tended to live in special quarters in the gipar-cloister complex. However, Sippar had its own tradition, and housed the entu(m) in a gagû. Lipitištar's laws state that an entu(m) may choose to live in the house of her father, while late Babylonian texts say that in earlier periods there used to be a special entu(m)-house. The office was very demanding; male and female E. had to be well versed in religion, literature, history, economy and, of course politics. Related to the en is the **Ensi**: the governor of a city, probably but not necessarily the highest religious functionary. The office of the en survived from late Sumerian times through the Old Babylonian, Kassite and into the middle Babylonian period. References to the entu(m) seem to disappear during the Old Babylonian period. Sadly, our sources have too many gaps. In the Neo-Babylonian period, at a lunar eclipse, the moon god Sîn informed king Nabuna'id that the office of the entu(m) should be revived. The king had the e-gipar renovated and installed one of his daughters as its entu(m). He also tried to revive the rituals of the Old Babylonian period, but who knows whether he knew what really happened in the distant old days.

E-namtila: *'The House of Life'*, Dumuzi's temple.

Enegi: a small town situated near Larsa, connected with it by a canal. The major cult was dedicated to Ninazu, son of Ereškigal, and indeed Enḫeduanna chanted that E. is the waterway leading to the Underworld, the *gutter of Ereškigal*. Here, Ninazu was celebrated as the šita priest of the Underworld, where he resided and played his lyre. E. was also a place where Nanna stopped during his annual journey to Nippur.

ENGUR (*engur*): a cuneiform character that was used to write the name of Nammu, and synonymous with her creation, the watery abyss Abzu/Apsû and/or the rivers (A.ENGUR=id=river) where her sacred reeds grow. E. is also a deity and the dwelling place of Enki, who is the **Enengur**: *'Lord of the Engur'*. The word E. appears in the names of seven udug-spirits who appear in the company of Bau/Baba and Ningirsu. Things are a bit confused by the fact that the Sumerogram E. was also used after the Akkadian period to write ZIKUM, meaning *heaven*. The cosmology of Nippur claims that heaven and earth manifested on their own accord: *Heaven was E., Earth was E.*. In this state, the Abzu surrounds the world to all sides, including above.

E-ninnu: *'House of Ninnu'*, a temple of Ningirsu in Girsu. **Ninnu** means *'fifty'*: the divine number related to authority and kingship. Ningirsu shared it with Enlil and later with Marduk.

En-si (*šā'ilu, enṣu/m*): *'male or female Seer'*, *'dream interpreter'*, *'interpreter of omens'*. A special priest or priestess who revealed the secret meaning of dreams, gave instructions on how to avert ill fortune and used a number of divinatory methods involving smoke, flames, oil on water etc. The E. can be traced to the Sumerian period. The office was closely connected to the cult of Nanše, the oracular goddess.

Entu(m), Enūtu (*entu(m)/enetu*): *'Lady Who is a Goddess'*; in a religious context, *'Highest Priestess'*. See En.

Ereš: a Sumerian city that has not been discovered. It could have been in central Sumer. E. is noted for its cult of Ninḫursag, but its major deity may have been Nidaba/Nisaba, the goddess of plants and reeds. Enḫeduanna celebrated its temple, the shining house of stars, adorned with lapis lazuli, a place open to the people of all lands, and told us that Nisaba, the goddess of writing, learning, scholarship, and wisdom, who measures the sky and the earth, had filled it with heavenly energies, and purifies the worshippers with soapwort. The temple, just like the art of writing, is open to all lands. Significantly, the temple of Nisaba was the last temple praised by Enḫeduanna in her collection of *Temple Hymns.* The first temple hymn, praising Enki in Eridu, represents primordial creation, while the last hymn ends in a rhapsody to purification, poetry, art, science and scholarship; the very skills that literally make the universe an understandable and inhabitable place. At the end of her Nisaba hymn Enḫeduanna did something outrageously courageous and signed her own name. It made her the first author in known history to do so.

Ereš-digir (entu/m): '*Supreme Priestess, Highest Lady, Divine* Mistress'.

EREŠ.DINGIR (*ugbatum*): a title of a high priestess usually associated with the cult of Ninurta; otherwise, it appears in the Mesopotamian periphery, i.e. in early Assyria, Mari and Susa. Synonym with the LUKUR, the Old Babylonian Nin, and the ladies who were later classed as nādītum.

Erešu: '*Lady, Queen*'.

Ĕrib bītti: '*Temple Enterer*', a person qualified to enter the inner rooms of the temple. The E. were associated with specific deities, but they were not always religious functionaries: their number included artisans and workers employed by the cult. Usually, the higher religious ranks were recruited from the E.. Apart from initiated priests and ritualists, major temples counted singers, musicians, acrobats, snake charmers, bakers, fine-bakers, brewers, oil-pressers, cooks, fumigators, doormen, guards, gardeners, ploughmen, shepherds, fishers, boat-people, fowlers, firewood suppliers, accountants, storage specialists, cleaning staff and various artisans among their employees. Some of them had regular access to the inner temple spaces, others only when required. Outside of the regular temple staff, we encounter occasionally employed persons like conjurers, diviners and doctors, and royal officials who supervised the offerings and donations.

Eridu: (today: Abu Shachrein), only 11km south-west of Ur. Perhaps the earliest (known) temple of ancient Mesopotamia. Originally, E. was close to the Persian Gulf, in the swamps and marshes where Euphrates and Tigris merged before flowing into the open sea. The city of E. was mainly built of chalk, plaster and sandstone, all of them rare and expensive building materials. E. is famous for the temple of Enki/Ea and his wife Damgalnunna. His cult could be one of the first in Mesopotamia: under all the temple ruins, the earliest, small temple room was excavated, where a large amount of burned fish bones testified to regular offerings to some aquatic deity. The structure dates around 4900 BCE. That's an enormous age, even compared to the fantastic estimate offered by the *Sumerian King List,* which proposes 250,000 years, and should not be taken seriously. However, as the original gods of E. are unidentified, it is also possible that the temple originally served Ningirima, the goddess of magic, and/or Nammu, the primal watery creatrix of the gods and the universe. Or someone we never even heard of. Around 2340 BCE, Enḫeduanna started her collection of temple hymns with the praise of E.. It celebrated the mythical importance of the site: E. is the place of creation, and its temple tower divided heaven and earth, while its mysterious roots reached into the depths of the Abzu. In her time, the 'tower' was a rather small structure on top of a large, elevated platform. E. is also known as NUN(ki): '*Tree-City*'. The same idea appears in literature: there is a *Tree of Ea* (possibly a palm) and a Black Tree, shining like lapis lazuli, above the Apsû, plus the *Sacred Reed* of Eridu. In spite of its formidable old age, E. lost much of its importance when religious and political power shifted to the cult of Enlil in Nippur. In its wake appeared new cosmologies, suitable to an inland dwelling civilisation. At the end of the Sumerian period (around 2200 BCE), the canal between E. and the Euphrates became permanently congested, travel ceased and much of E. fell into ruins. The sacredness of the site was still acknowledged, and its temple was continuously rebuilt up to the Neo-Babylonian period, but the settlement ceased to be inhabited. In literature, E. is synonymous with the first beginning, with the primal manifestation of the gods, the place where royalty descended to earth, and with the first (fantastic) dynasties. The sacredness of its water appears in numerous exorcisms. It rises out of the primal Abzu/Apsû beneath Enki's temple. The city itself was divine. In Babylon, which was thought to be intimately related to E., offerings were made for E.. There was even a quarter of Babylon called E.. Other deities associated with E. were the goddess La-aṣ, Ningirsu (whose image and cult moved to E. when his temple in Lagaš was rebuilt by Gudea), Marduk (as son of Ea) and probably Ištar. The 'Star of Eridu' was Canopus.

E-sagil/a: *'House with a High Roof', 'High House'*; Marduk's temple in Babylon, a large sacred space measuring roughly 500m square, originally erected in the OB period, but much renovated and rebuilt subsequently. The structure had numerous shrines for other deities. The E. was a connection between heaven and earth.

E-šar-ra: *'House of the Sky', 'House of the Multitude', 'House of the Universe'*, a popular temple name. Primarily it may have belonged to An/Anu's temple in Uruk, back in the preliterate days when he was chief of the gods, representing the sky and indeed the universe. Enḫeduanna used the title E. for Ninḫursag's and Nintu's temple in Adab. The temple of the same name was also claimed by Inanna (SAHG 1953:68). In the middle of the second millennium BCE we find it used by Marduk; but as the *EE* tells us, it was modelled on an earlier building: Marduk fashioned it as an exact copy of Enki/*Ea's* abode Abzu/Apsû. The Assyrians identified Marduk with Aššur and used the term E. for Aššur's temple in Aššur.

Eš-dam-ma-ka, **Eš-dam** (***inabaab aštammi;***): the *'House (Eš) of Women/ Wives/Female Companions/Spouses'* (dam). Also **E.KI.AG.GA *(bît aštamme):*** *'House of the Place of Love'*. A difficult and much discussed term that might refer to a tavern, a guest house or a brothel, which may or may not have belonged to a large temple complex. The word is sometimes associated with Ištar and Dumuzi. Primarily a place to drink beer and have fun, under the divine protection of Inanna/Ištar. Secondarily, the E. may have functioned as a guest house and/or a brothel. The lists of equipment given to a female slave to operate an A. mention more beds than tables. Whether the E. was part of the regular temple premises, had a cultic function or was simply a place of private business (as is testified in several cases) is still under discussion. The same goes for the question whether female and male prostitutes actually had a cultic status. Early translators tended to class almost all priestesses as 'hierodules' and suspected sacred sex, or at least sex for the profit of the temple, all over the place; contemporary researchers have become a lot more cautious, as the evidence is exceedingly slim and questionable. That there was such a thing as 'sacred sex' in a public tavern is highly unlikely.

Ešgala: *'Great Shrine'*

E-sizkur: *'House of Prayer'*.

E-sikil: *'Pure House'*, a temple in Ešnunna, dedicated to Ninazu and later to Tišpak.

Ešnunna (modern Tell Asmar): a major city and state east of the Tigris and at the northern limits of Sumer, near the Zagros Mountains, inhabited by a mixed culture with Mesopotamian and Iranian roots. E. was next to the Diyala River, streaming from the Zagros Mountains to the Tigris. South of E. is the Susiana plain, where Sumerian migrants began settling during the fourth millennium BCE. They blended with the locals, one or several Semitic cultures, that were deeply into serpent cults. In the process, the city god of E., Ninazu, acquired the emblems of the lion, the sandstorm and the venom spitting serpent/dragon, and a close connection to the Underworld. Typically, in E. Ninazu was represented with a human head and a serpent body, or as a lion with a serpent tail. Sometime around the Akkadian period, N. was replaced by a deity called Tišpak about whom very little is known.

Ezida: *'House of Righteousness'*, a name for two temples dedicated to Nabû and Tašmētum in Borsippa and in the Assyrian capital Kalḫu. The latter temple was famous for its extensive library, fit for a god who acted as a scribe and lawgiver.

E-zuab (*E-Apsû*): *'House (or Temple) of the Abyss'*; alternatively, *'House of the Ocean'*. The temple of Enki/Ea in Eridu, also called ENGUR.

Gadala, ša-gadala (*gadalallû*): *'linen-clad'*, either a descriptive term for one wearing a costly robe (like GUDU and luhmaḫ) or another badly documented priestly rank. The G. is in contrast to the **kuš-la** (*'skin-clad'*, i.e. nude ritualist). The two appear in company in the courtyard of Ningirsu's temple in Eninnu.

Gaeš: a place where Nanna/Sîn had a temple, and where his boat stopped on its yearly journey from Ur to his father, Enlil, in Nippur, for the akiti festival. It may have been a small town, or a suburb of Ur, a wharf at the canal, possibly built near a cattle pen of Ur. G. did not amount to much in the Akkadian period, but in the following centuries, King Šulgi had the temple of Nanna renovated, and King Amarsuen had a gipar built where he installed an en priestess.

Ga-gi-maḫ, E-ga-gi-maḫ (*gagû/m*): *'Lofty Closed House'*. Cloisters were usually part of the premises of a major temple complex. They had their own fields, gardens and quarters for numerous high-ranking, often aristocratic priestesses. The G. is especially associated with the nadītu(m) women. The complex in Sippar is best known, but there were similar institutions in other great cities like Nippur. As far as is known, they had different regulations and rituals. There is next to no evidence regarding life in the Sumerian and Akkadian G., but by the OB period the documentation improves. In several G., the women were supposed to live a celibate life. In contrast to this, the nadītu(m) devoted to Marduk were allowed to marry.

Gala *(kâlu(m))*: lamentations priest/ess, elegist, singer, director of musicians, master of prayers, hymns, history and old literature. In pre-Sargonic accounts, male and female G. accompanied funerals. The G. is a priestly rank and should not be confused with the professional lamenting women, who had nothing to do with the temples and were rented for the job. In Sumerian times, each temple employed several G., but there were also G. employed by the palace. An especially high rank had the **gala-maḫ (*galamāḫu*)** *'chief lamentation singer'*, who appears in Sumerian texts as the head of four major temples in the state of Lagaš. He also appears in UR III texts and, just once in Old Babylonian records of Girsu; afterwards, his office seems to have disappeared. It is likely that the G. was an esteemed scholar in Old Sumerian liturgies and laments. In Assyria and Babylon, up to the first Millennium BCE, the G. were singers of ancient Sumerian compositions and hymns, including the texts composed in Emesal, which had earlier been the exclusive domain of women. In the late first millennium BCE, we find K. working in cooperation with āšipu in temple rituals; some K. specialised in astronomy and astrology. Unlike most (or all?) members of the temple staff, not all G. and K. shaved their heads. Some worked for private persons or the palace. A special position seems to have been occupied by the **gala-tur-ra (*assinnu*):** *'junior gala'* who was, one of the two sexless beings whom Enki created to carry the water and food of life to the dead Inanna in the underworld. The reference is mysterious: were the real junior galas chosen among people with sexual deformities?

Garza: *'Cultic Office'*, *'Religious Regulation'*. A term that was occasionally used in the same sense as *parṣū* .

Gipar, from **GE.PAR (*giparu*)**: A special residence for the high-ranking en priestesses, usually the holiest of the holiest, a special district of a temple complex.

Girsu: There were two settlements called Girsu. One, badly documented at the Euphrates, where the cult of Damu was popular. The other, much better documented Girsu was a large Sumerian city in the state of Lagaš (modern Tellō). Around 2500 BCE, it became the capital of Lagaš. At this time, it may have been near a branch of the Euphrates. G. was connected by canal to Gu'abba (*'Harbour of the Sea'*) and grew rich thanks to the sea trade. The patron deity was Ningirsu (*'Lord of Girsu'*)/Ninurta. He had a large temple complex commemorated with various titles, like *'House of Ningirsu'*, *'House Where Wine is Stored'*, *'House of Chariots'*, *'House of Reeds'* and the e-me-ḫuš-gal-an-ki, the *'House that (Owns) the Great Terrible Divine Powers of Heaven and Earth'*. Nanše, the goddess of dream divination, sister of Ningirsu, also had a temple. Significantly absent were temples for Bau/Baba and Gatumdug, who may have been worshipped in the city Lagaš. The major temple complex of Ningirsu, the Eninnu, was shifted under Urbaba and completely rebuilt under Gudea, whose account provides the most detailed description of any Mesopotamian temple and its numerous buildings. In his inscriptions, 52 separate institutions and building complexes are listed. Gudea also incorporated buildings for Bau/Baba and Gatumdug in his Uruku (*'Sacred City'*). Apart from these temple complexes, G. also had temples for Dumuziabzu of Kinurra, Geštianna, Inanna of Lagaš, Meslamta'ea, Nindara of Kesa, Enki, Ašnan, Šulpae, Ninduba, Ningišzida, Ninḫursag, and a wide range of unknown or inferior gods. G. lost much of its importance when the OB period began. It appears, very rarely, in texts up to the middle of the first millennium BCE.

Giš-banda: a town close to Ur and Enegi, with close ties to the moon god Nanna and the god of Enegi, Ninazu, in the close neighbourhood. In G. was a temple for Ningišzida, son or grandson of Ninazu and Ereškigal. Mythically, G. was praised as being surrounded by mountains, geographically it was flat in the alluvial plains. Poetically, mountains (see Kur) represented both the distant Iranian mountains, from where the cult of N. and his family received their close association to serpent cults, and the other sort of Kur: the Underworld. The temple of Ningišzida was praised by Enḫeduanna as a dark and red place and a safe field from where the fresh sun arose.

Guabba: a city or town that used to be close to the Persian Gulf: the name means *'Neck/Shore of the Sea'*. The major cult was for the goddess Ninmar (NinMAR.KI), daughter of Nanše. The goddess is called a *'fish inspector'* but apart from her aquatic office, she is associated with the sheepfold. In the Ur III period, Guabba had a booming textile industry employing more than 6000 workers, most of them women and children. G. was one of the main sources of wealth for Lagaš, and presumably many of the fine textiles were exported oversea. Enḫeduanna celebrated its temple as the *house that extends to the middle of the sea.* It also had a temple dedicated to King Šulgi. After the fall of Ur III, it probably lost its function as a centre of commerce, and disappeared from the records.

GUDU (*pašīšu, kumrum, isippu*): a general term for a type of priest, mostly male but occasionally female. The etymology of G. is unknown, but pašīšu could be derived from *'elder brother'* or from *'to anoint'*. His literary (and semi-divine) prototype is Adapa, priest of Enki/Ea in Eridu, who supplies the offerings and bakes the bread for his god *with clean hands.* The term *pa-šeš* was very common in the titles of the Akk. kings and in Ebla, where it was applied to a whole group of priests and priestesses. The term G. covers numerous and highly varied functions, both professional and amateur: some G. acted as purifiers or conducted offerings, poured drink libations and some even performed tasks like feeding the sacrificial animals. In Sumerian times, the office of a G. was usually inherited. By Old Babylonian times, we are well into simony: the office of a G. often became an honourable benefice, a function which could be bought or rented for a number of days in a year, entailing all sorts of spiritual and material benefits. The term G. disappears after the OB period.

GUDU-abzu (*guduapsû*): sounds enchantingly like a priest of the abyss, and suggests that this functionary was specialised in rites of purification. Sadly, the literary record disappoints us: the G. appears in several locations well into the OB period, and is always busy with dull administrative tasks related to foodstuff, animals, beer, and accounting. The reason why the word ABZU occurs in his title escapes us.

Gullubu: *'Shaved, Shorn'*, a designation for some priests acting in the temple. The shaved head was a must for (most?) people who had the right to enter the inner rooms of the temple. This, however, did not necessarily apply to priestesses, nor is it likely that the rule was always strictly followed, as there were bearded men among the temple musicians. Likewise, if the king visited, he was not required to shave his hair and beard. As far as can be identified in images, the G. wore long robes and a variety of caps and hats, depending on local traditions. Such images tell us something about ritual costume; they do not inform us what they wore in everyday life, on the street or when travelling. Normal temple employees like artisans were shorn and bareheaded.

Ḫarimtu/m: a free and independent woman, a businesswoman, sometimes a prostitute. See KAR.KID.

Hattuša (modern Boghazköy): the capital of the Hittite culture in northern Anatolia, Turkey. First settlements were built around the end of the third millennium BCE. The city gained real importance when the Hittite King Labarnas (or Lubarna) turned it into his capital around 1650 BCE. The city was destroyed around 1200 BCE but partly rebuilt in the seventh century BCE by the Phrygians. Famous for its majestic stone fortifications and the many tablets inscribed in Akkadian, Hittite and Hurrian.

Hiza: a city in northern Sumer (or southern Akkad) which was important in the late third millennium BCE. It has not been located; indeed, not even its Sumerian name is known. The major deity or deities were Ninḫursag and/or Nintu(m). Her or their temple was the **Eḫursag** (*'House of the Stony Foothills'*). Enḫeduanna called it a house of flowers and a sleeping serpent, a place dedicated to the birth of kings. This aspect of Nintu(m)/Ninḫursag was stressed by the kings: the goddess was their mother, and granted the right to rule. Maybe this also went for Enḫeduanna's father Sargon I who started as a usurper and was eager to demonstrate his right to the throne. But Enḫeduanna also emphasised that Ninḫursag gives birth to a priestess. Maybe she was referring to herself.

Ḫursag: the *'Foothills'*; the wild country below the hostile mountain ranges and the goddess of the realm and its wild animals, Ninḫursag.

Irigal: the *'Big City'*, a name of the Underworlds.

Isib ***(iššippu)***: purification priest of the Sumerian and Old Babylonian period specialised in exorcisms and conjurations. Unlike the similar āšipu, the I. was closely associated with a specific deity or a temple complex. I.'s appear in the records of major temples. Unlike them, the south Babylonian **ISIB.MAḪ** (*'Chief Isib'*) could be busy in a temple, handling the sacred (and sometimes golden) eš-da vessel; while other I. enjoyed a certain independence from specific cults and temples. After the Old Babylonian Period, the I. survives as a literary term and was largely replaced by the āšipus.

Isin (modern Ishan al-Bahryat): a major west-Sumerian city, founded by An himself and the very place where An and Enlil decree fates, and the divine assembly meets for talk, food and booze. The city is close to Nippur and profited from its close ties to the religious centre of Sumer and the cult of Enlil. The countryside of I. is noted for farming, cereal production and cattle breeding. I. is famous for the Ninisina, the *'Lady of Isin'* who was originally Gula, the goddess who is a seer, physician and exorcist, and wife of Ninurta. Gula is a daughter of An, but there is also a tradition that makes her, as Ninisina, the wife of An. In this function she is in competition with Antu(m) and Inanna, both of whom appear as An's wives in different mythologies or political configurations. In the early third millennium she was still a rather minor goddess, but her fame increased by the end of the millennium, when her statue was sent on a regular annual pilgrimage to Umma. It linked her to the cult of Inanna, Šara and Dumuzi, and to the kings of the Ur III dynasty, who felt closely related to Dumuzi, Lugalbanda and Gilgameš. Then, after the fall of the Ur III dynasty, the invading Amorites made a point of promoting the influence of I.; they became the Isin-Larsa dynasty, which controlled Mesopotamia for roughly 200 years. In this time, I. rose to prominence.

Iššaku: *'Representative (of a deity)'*, a religious office, in particular among the kings of Aššur, who represented the national god Aššur in person. They also assumed the office of the šangû in the cult, and had themselves celebrated as incarnate deities.

Ištarîtu: a woman or priestess devoted to a deity. Here, the word Ištar was used in a general way as an appellation for many goddesses. The I. were either associated with a temple or had a private income and lived outside the temple premises. While early I. performed a priestly function, in later periods, the term I. could refer to any woman devoted to a goddess. An ***ištarīum*** is a man devoted to a goddess. For some scribes of the Neo-Assyrian period, the word I. had become a derogatory term for a witch, an evil sorceress or a prostitute.

Itima (*kiṣṣum*): *'Dark Room'*, a special shrine of a deity inside the temple.

Kalaḫ/Kalakh/Kalkhu/Kalchu, Kalḫu (modern name: Nimrud)***:*** a major Assyrian capital, 360 hectares large, situated near the River Tigris. It started as a provincial capital and became the capital of Assyria under Aššurnarsipal II (883-859 BCE), who built a canal to the Upper Zab and the massive city wall, with a length of eight km. It retained its importance until the end of the reign of Sargon II, when political power shifted to other cities. K. was destroyed in 612 BCE by the combined armies of Babylonians and Medes. Noted for its cult of Nabû, Ninurta, Ištar and Kidmuru.

Kâlum, kalû: lamentations priest, elegist, master of prayer and incantations; a high-ranking ritualist who occasionally appears in the company of the āšipu. See GALA.

KAR.KID (*ḫarimtu/m*): (from the root ḫrm: something or someone set apart for religious or ethical reasons). Originally a religious companion (not necessarily a priestess) associated, at least in Sippar, with the cults of several goddesses, like Anunītu(m), Ṣarpanītu(m) and Tašmētu(m). The K. was a free woman, a woman living without a husband, of independent means or one who ran a business. While very little survives regarding the Sumerian K., the Babylonian and Assyrian Ḫ. is easier to trace. In early Assyriology, the term used to be translated as *'prostitute'* or *'hierodule'*, a translation based on a few derogatory Babylonian and Neo-Assyrian word-lists, proverbs and curses. An OB list groups the Ḫ. together with ***wāṣītu(m)*** (*'Wayward Woman'*) and ***najjāktu(m)*** (*'Fornicating Woman'*). This association, however, does not imply that the three are identical, nor can we be sure that the scribe who composed it recorded a general view or simply his own opinion. Some Ḫ. were prostitutes and one is known to have run a brothel, but on the whole, most Ḫ. had other means of income. The Ḫ. is perhaps comparable to the kezertu(m). During Mesopotamian history, the status of free women and prostitutes decreased a lot. In third millennium BCE literature, attitudes towards sex were a lot more relaxed than in the narrow-minded first millennium BCE. In this period, the term Ḫ. was often synonymous with prostitute, and used as an insult. A typical example is the curse inscribed by Kapara of Guzana in the ninth century BCE which ends with the wish that his enemy should burn seven of his sons as a sacrifice to Adad, and that he should make seven of his daughters available as ḫarīmātu to Ištar. The savageness of this is evident. Consumption by fire was the worst form of death. With seven (=all) sons dead and cursed to roam as homeless spirits and with all daughters on the street or in the care of the goddess, the family line would be effectively blotted out. In a similar mood, Aššurbanipal referred to a rebel governor as the Ḫ. of the Elamites. In some periods, families had the legal right to interfere if a son tried to marry a Ḫ. .The male form ***ḫarimtu, ḫarmu*** does not refer to prostitution at all. It was used to designate Dumuzi as the lover and mate of the H. Ištar, and Qingu as the mate of Tiāmat. Both gods are 'set apart' in that they belong to their wives.

Kalam (*mātu*): *'Land'*, the inhabitable realm.

Kazallu: a city and the canal it was next to, in third millennium BCE northern Sumer. Its location is unknown, but suspected to be close to Borsippa, north-west of Nippur, and maybe somewhere around Babylon. The main cult was to Numušda, the heroic son of Nanna/Sîn and Ninlil.

Keš (modern Tell al-Wilayah?): an ancient city under the tutelage of Ninḫursag, her husband Šulpae, their son Ašgi and at least six minor (local?) goddesses who form her entourage. The major temple was **e-keš** (*'House/Temple of Keš'*). It was perhaps close to Nippur and in the neighbourhood of Adab, near the Iturungal canal. Its temple, so Enḫeduanna sang, was the place where form was shaped for heaven and earth, a terrifying place, spreading fear like a great serpent, a dark and deep womb; the building, like a great mountain, fortified with spells, was dedicated to the birth goddesses, Ninḫursag, Nintur and Aruru. The *Hymn to Keš* is one of the earliest pieces of Sumerian poetry, dating from around the early third millennium BCE. It details that when Enlil brought the princely offices from his own house, K. raised its head to him, which moved Enlil to sing its praise, and Nisaba to record it. The text eulogises K., among many other things, as the doorpost of the country, facing hostile Aratta, embracing heaven, green like the hills, floating in the sky like the boat of the moon, containing in its heart (=inner sanctuary) the life breath of Sumer.

Kiabrig: a small town dedicated to Ningubla(m), a son of Nanna/Sîn. It may have been close to Ur, where Nanna had his major temple, but has not been found so far. The little that is known about the place associates it with a thriving culture of cattle herders.

Kigal: the *'Big Place'*, a name of the Underworld.

Kikkillu, kilkillu: *'Chamber of the Oath-taking Symbol of Šamaš'*.

Kiništu: the *'Collegium'*, a range of people who had access to a specific temple. The members of the K. were not necessarily related to a specific deity but to the temple as an organisation.

Kiniřša, Kinunir: a town or village dedicated to Dumuziabzu, who is usually (but not always) a goddess, and had a minor cult in the late Sumerian period. The worship of Dumuziabzu disappeared during the OB period. Her temple was famed for musical performances. K. has not been discovered yet.

Kiš (modern Tell Ingharra & Tell Uheimir?). According to the old Sumerian *King Lists*, K. was the primal place to which kingship descended after the flood. The metaphor might indicate that in Kiš, the lugals managed to develop a degree of independence from the temple authorities. It could mean a secular government; mind you, it is likely that the palace and the temples interacted very closely. Archaeologically, temples and palace buildings go back to the Early Dynastic period I or III, depending on whose estimate you follow. After 2500 BCE, kings (and one ruling queen) of K. are attested. The symbolic importance of kingship was so closely associated with K. that several regents of distant city-states had themselves praised as *King of K.*, including Sargon I, who ruled from Akkad. The major deities of K. were Zababa (with a cloister of dedicated nādītu(m) priestesses) and Inanna/Ištar; other cults were dedicated to Ištar of Uruk, Nanay, Papsukkal and Gansurra. Nowadays, some scholars suspect that Kiš and Keš may be the same, undiscovered city.

Kuar: a small town south of Eridu with a cult devoted to Enki's son Asarluḫi. K. was surrounded by plains and marshes; Enḫeduanna sang that it was *squeezed out of the Abzu like barley oil* (DSM 2009:88), and that the Seven Sages (the apkallu) made it grow in the name of Asarluḫi.

Kulmašītu: Another woman who is classed, like the kezertu and qadištu, as a prostitute in Neo-Assyrian literature, and probably the only one where the designation is appropriate. The K. is associated with Ištar, whether she acted as a 'sacred prostitute' and earned income for a temple is still under discussion. It does not say much: all prostitutes were under the protection of Inanna/Ištar, no matter where and how they did their job. Some scholars innocently assumed that prostitutes were considered sacred by the Mesopotamians. As it turns out, only some prostitutes in the employ of temples and palace enjoyed a high status. The others had a low social position, but their activities were accepted as a part of civilised life. They were acknowledged by law and religion, had rights and a place in society, and were under the protection of Inanna/Ištar and the king. The Mesopotamians did not believe that sex or prostitution were sinful; the literati despised prostitutes as they were allegedly bossy, mocking, difficult, disrespectful and likely to disrupt households.

Kur (*šadū/m* = mountain, *erṣetu, mātu/m* = land): *'the Mountains'*. As a determinative, K. signified 'country, state' and appeared before land names. As a word, K. is a multipurpose term meaning: 1. a land, a foreign land; 2. the high and foreign mountains, home of terrifying foreigners; 3. specifically the dwellers of the Mountain Ebiḫ, who were crushed by Inanna for their disobedience (or rather for not giving in to Sargon I); 4. a dragon-like monster who abducted the celestial goddess Ereškigal to the Underworld, where she remained as the goddess of the afterlife; 5. the realm between earth and the waters of the Underworld, i.e. the frontier between the world of the deep and the world of the dead; 6. the furthest limit of the world; 7. to be hostile.

Kur-gal: *'Great Mountain', 'the Eastern Highlands'.*

Kurgarra, Kurgarrû: a religious votary of Inanna/Ištar who was or was not attached to a temple. Very little is known about their cultic activity in early times. In Neo-Assyrian times, they acted as lute players and dancers during some rituals. The term K. has been interpreted in many highly diverse ways. One popular opinion claims that the K. was a eunuch, another that he was a transvestite, or a male prostitute. In myth, the K. is a sexless being who was created by Enki/Ea to travel into the underworld, where it gave the bread and water of life to the slain goddess Inanna/Ištar, and revived her. Due to this act, the K. theoretically had a sacrosanct status, but this does not mean that he was respected in daily life.

Kurnugi: *'Land of No Return'*, another term for the underworld.

kuš-la: *'Skin Clad'*, i.e. nude. A special sort of priest or priestess, contrasted with the gadala (*'linen-clad'*). Nude ritualists appear in Sumerian art. An example is the Uruk vase, another the Enḫeduanna plague, where a nude man pours a libation.

Kutha, Cutha, Gudua: a city near Babylon, patronised by Meslamta'ea/ Nergal/Girra. As these deities have very strong underworld connotations, K. became a name of the Underworld.

Lagaš (modern Al-Hiba): *'Raven'*. A large old Sumerian city-state with several major deities, like Gatumdug, Amaušumgalanna, Ningirsu, Bau/Baba, An/Anu, Ninmar and her daughter Nanše. Its chief city was Girsu; Nin-girsu means *'Lord of Girsu'*. L. was originally a city located on the coast of the Persian Gulf. As the shoreline moved, it was increasingly surrounded by the salt- and sweet water marshes where the great rivers merged and created a delta; nowadays it is on the alluvial plain, 200km from the sea. L had a lot of political power and was doubtlessly considered a threat by the neighbouring city-states. To the scribes who composed the highly unreliable *Sumerian King Lists*, L. was so unpopular that they did not even bother to mention it, or any of its kings or deities. L. is particularly well-known for its frequent conflicts with the neighbouring state Umma. The wars between them erupted over centuries and only ended when L. was finally overrun by Lugalzagesi of Umma. A short time later he was defeated by Sargon the Great. In Gudea's time, L. was still a major power. His *Temple Hymn* relates that, though Ningirsu was a son of Enlil, he had received his office from An/Anu, and the same goes for the formidable temple complex which Gudea rebuilt with so much passion. At the time, L. was a place of great wealth; its merchant caravans and sailors traded with Tilmun (Bahrain), Magan (Omar), Meluḫḫa (the Indus Valley Culture), Magda (probably near modern Kerkuk), Susa and Elam in modern Iran.

Lagal, Lagar: a high-ranking priest closely related to the entu(m) priestess. Possibly her administrator or sukkal.

Larsa (modern Senkereh): a major ancient city, north of Ur and Eridu and south of Uruk, situated in the marshlands of Southern Sumer. The major cult of Larsa was dedicated to sun god Utu/Šamaš and his wife Aya, in the temple Ebabar, the '*White House*'. Utu is the (twin) brother of Inanna, and his city is only a short distance from Uruk where Inanna had a major cult. L. was well into the worship of a solar deity during the proto-literate period in the fourth millennium BCE, when the city seal showed a rising sun behind what seems to be an altar. But L. was also the home of other deities. One of them is Nanay. Old Babylonian texts attest to a priesthood of the goddess Dingir-maḫ.

Lualede, lunisuub, SAL.alede (male: ***maḫhû;*** female**: *muḫḫutu/m***): '*Prophet, Seer, Ecstatic Visionary, Exorcist*'. A female or male trance expert who is obsessed by a deity and provides prophecy, visionary insight or acts in an inspired way. Some were regularly employed by temples, others acted independently. A few of them were so intensely inspired (i.e. raving mad) that they troubled kings.

Lugal: '*Big/Strong Man*'. Originally, a person selected by an assembly to be a temporary leader in times of war and crisis. During the third millennium BCE, warfare rarely stopped and the office became permanent. The L. can be understood as a 'lord' or 'king', but was not generally considered as a deity. Divine kings appeared first during the Akkad dynasty around 2300 BCE; later, several Sumerian rulers of the Ur III dynasty took up the fashion. In Old Babylonian times, the kings made a point of acknowledging their humanity, unlike the Assyrian kings, who had themselves praised as deities.

LU.KISAL.LUḪ, fem: **MI. LU.KISAL.LUḪ (*kisalluḫḫu,*** fem: ***kisalluḫḫatuu***): '*Courtyard-Cleaner* or *–Purifier*'. A rarely mentioned priestly rank, associated with Mari. It seems to have disappeared after the Old Babylonian period.

LUKUR *(nadītu(m))*:: '*the Barren One*'. L. is a term for a group of high-ranking priestesses who appear in pre-Sargonic times and are associated with the cults of Ninurta, Ningirsu and Šamaš, the title L. was also used to designate the '*Royal Brides*' and as a title of the *Seven Daughters of Baba*. It is a distinct possibility that the L. continued in the Old Babylonian period as the nadītu, i.e. '*the One Who Lies Fallow*': a class of high priestesses who usually came from upper-class families and owned considerable wealth. They tended to live secluded in their own cloister precincts, had influence and status, owned money, fields and property, and frequently appear in business documents, as they granted loans, speculated with wares and invested in ventures. The L. of the third millennium BCE are occasionally mentioned, but not with much detail. Better documented are the N. of Šamaš and Aya in Sippar, and the N. of Marduk. Officially, the N. of Sippar were supposed to live in chastity. Unofficially, when they chanced to become pregnant, the baby was adopted by other people. The exception to the rule are the N. of Marduk, who had the right to marry, and who probably did not live in a cloister, but in private houses. These women frequently had children. In the first century, their status had declined so much that the term was used, by some ill-meaning scribes, as a synonym for prostitutes and witches.

Lu-maḫ (*lumaḫḫu, lumakku*): '*Exalted Man*', a title of a high-ranking priest in the service of goddesses like Inanna, Nisaba and Baba. The L. of Ur lived in a special sacred temple room, and the Mesopotamian scribes believed that the GUDU and L. of foreign Aratta lived in a cloister-like gipar. The office went out of fashion during the OB period; later lexical lists tend to identify the L. with the GUDU. A Neo-Assyrian text claims that the L. lighted the torches which the MAŠ.MAŠ used for healing and the bārû for divination ritual.

Lu-mu-da: '*Ecstatic*'. A person who experiences divine obsession. Also an insult.

Lu-lu-mu: '*Man of Conjurations*', a professional exorcist priest of the Sumerian period, who was occasionally required to purify the entire palace and its king. He was also in charge of conducting ritual bath ceremonies for the king.

Magan, Makkan: nowadays Oman. During the third millennium BCE, Sumerian traders voyaged to the island Dilmun and from there to distant ports, like M. The Sumerian traders supplied M. with textiles, clothes, wool, oil and leather products. In turn, they imported large quantities of copper, as well as precious minerals, beads, ivory and a delicacy called M.-onions. Like Dilmun, M. was not the producer of all these goods. The local sea-traders may have sailed as far as Africa and India, or received goods from these countries. M. also served as a stocking place for Sumerians who continued to travel all the way to the Harappa/Indus Valley culture, Meluḫḫa. Direct trade with M. ceased at during the OB period.

maḫḫû, maḫḫû, muḫḫûtu/m: female and male trance experts who act as obsessed seers, prophets, visionaries, exorcists etc. see lualede, lunisuub, SAL.alede**.**

Marda, Marad: an unidentified third millennium BCE city or town. It appears in documents and poetry of the dynasty of Akkad. The major deities were Lugalmarda, Ninsuanna and Nunušda.

Mari (modern Tell Hariri): a major ancient city and state of central Mesopotamia situated on the western shore of the Euphrates. Though M. is a bit remote from Sumer and Akkad, it was of such importance in the Predynastic Period that it appeared in the *Sumerian King Lists*. Its excellent position ensured a thriving trade and great wealth. M. was occupied by Amorites around the end of the third millennium, and came under Assyrian control shortly afterwards. Zimrilim, an Amorite, re-conquered the city around 1780 BCE. During his rule, M. gained a massive palace compound and a formidable library. The city-state had the bad sense to side against King Ḫammurapi, who destroyed it in 1757. It was never rebuilt. For a while, the Middle Assyrians used the ruins as a cemetery. M. had a major temple dedicated to Ninḫursag, but there were also temples for Ištar, NINNI-ZAZA, Šamaš, Dagan and several unidentified deities.

MAŠ.MAŠ *(mašmaššu)*: a ritualist who was generally associated with a temple, where he performed, among other tasks, purification ceremonies prior to the offerings and rituals. The first recorded M. were busy in the last Sumerian period, Ur III, with purification rites of the fields. Otherwise, the M. were specialised in conjuration, exorcism and banishing. In these matters, they closely resemble the āšipu. Whether the M. and the āšipu were synonymous designations of a single specialist profession or whether there were major differences between them is still under discussion. Occasionally, the M. worked outside of the temple context in private houses, sometimes even together with the āšipu in exorcisms and healing rituals. Divine M. are Ningirima, Ea, Utu, Ningublaga and Asarluḫi.

Maš-šu-gid (*bārû)* *'One Who Asks for the Omen'*, *'Seer'*: a diviner, in particular a diviner skilled in foretelling the unknown and interpreting the will of the gods by exploring the liver and entrails of sacrificial animals. The M. also studied unusual occurrences for their deeper significance, watched the way flames and torches flickered and prophesied the future by watching oil on water. The M. was not part of a temple; more frequently, he was employed by the palace or accompanied a king and his army. It was a sure way to make a glorious career or to end as a total failure.

Mât-Tâmtim: The *'Sea-Land'*, the canals, swamps and salt marshes of southern Mesopotamia, i.e. ancient Sumer. Also, literally, *'the Land of Tiāmat'*. Marduk's conquest of Tiāmat is more than a myth; it also celebrated the victory of the Babylonians over their southern, and more ancient neighbour culture.

Meluḫḫa: in early literature, the Indus or Harappa culture. During the pre-Sumerian Obed and Halaf culture, between the sixth and fifth millennium BCE, settlers from Mesopotamia travelled across Iran and southern Turkmenistan. They reached the Indus around the fourth millennium BCE. They merged with the local Neolithic farmer cultures and began to build highly elaborate cities with a higher level of architecture and hygiene than anybody else. The cities were not local developments but planned with precision; obviously, the people of M. had arrived with a high level of technical know-how. The M. culture is noted for its own (so far undecipherable) script, for standardized bricks, measures, weights, and for a religion that has so far proved absolutely elusive, as all evidence for temples and sacred buildings is missing, and only a few, rare divine sculptures have been uncovered, all of them imports from Sumer. The Indus culture is also famed for its numerous female clay statuettes, which were classed, for a while, as evidence for a mother goddess cult and a matriarchal society. However, the existence of male statuettes, and the fact that most clay images are crude, primitive and frequently appear in rubbish pits, has made contemporary researchers cautious. Third millennium Sumer eagerly traded with M.; there are even cylinder seals showing ambassadors from M.. Around the start or middle of the second millennium BCE, the Indus culture disappeared for unknown reasons. Several major cities were abandoned when rivers shifted; other cities were submerged under a solid layer of mud. When the Indo-European Aryans invaded India sometime between 1500 and 1200 BCE, the M. culture was long forgotten. The invaders encountered a primitive and illiterate farmer culture. In late second millennium literature, the term M. was used for Ethiopia. When the Neo-Assyrians invaded and occupied Egypt, they were in contact with ambassadors of nearby M.

Mitanni: a highly successful Hurrian kingdom in northern and western Mesopotamia, southern Kurdistan, parts of Turkey and Syria during the early and middle second millennium. Also known as Hanigalbat.

Mūdû: *'One Who Knows'* or *'Initiate'*, an advanced religious specialist, initiated into secret lore (whatever that may have been). The term occurs in enigmatic inscriptions, asking the M. to explain some matter to other M.'s, but to keep the secrets from the profane.

Muḫḫum: *'Raging One'*, a special type of priest or priestess who is obsessed by a deity and proclaims oracles. Some of them were involved in traditional temple traditions (as in Mari), others seem to have worked independently of the local authorities, and were occasionally persecuted by kings who did not like the things they uttered.

Munus-suḫur-la (*kezertu/m)*: one of the terms that used to be translated as 'sacred prostitute'. It seems to be derived from *'Woman With Special Haircut'. Kezēru* means *'to curl hair'*; hence the M. might have had curls. A first millennium BCE text, however, indicates that the K. acted as hairdressers for others. At the same time, the K. appears in lexical lists that identify her with the KAR.KID, and associates her with the ḫarimtu(m) and šamḫatu(m). Whether the K. was actually involved in prostitution, as some unfriendly NA scribes claimed, is open to debate. The sons of K. seem to have been a special population group; they appear in NA documents among the staff of some temples. This does not tell us much about the status and activities of the K. in earlier periods. In the spiritual realm, the K. were religious devotees and companions of the goddesses of Uruk, such as Inanna/Ištar. K. appear in several cities where the cult of Ištar of Uruk was celebrated. The K. was not necessarily a priestess, but in some places, like Mari, they danced, sang and played musical instruments on religious festivals. Perhaps the K. is comparable to the ḫarimtu(m) of Sippar. A male form, *kazrāte*, also appears, but there is practically nothing known about them.

Muru and **Murum**: one or two cities or towns, possibly in the neighbourhood of Uruk and maybe close to Badtibira, so far undiscovered. One or both had a major cult of Ningirima, the third millennium BCE goddess of magic, enchantment and purification.

Muš-laḫ *(muš(la)laḫḫ(at)u)*: *'Snake Conjurer'*, a class of female and male ritualists who appear in Sumerian literature; in Akkadian texts they are rare, though their activity can be traced well into the first millennium. As could have been expected, the *Maqlû Series* classes them with witches. Originally, the M. were associated with specific deities, such as An, Enlil and Nanna. Some M. were snake-dancers. As snake-expellers, they performed their rituals in temples and in public places.

Nadītu(m): *'the Barren One'*, title of a high-ranking aristocratic priestess. See LUKUR.

Nam-lugal: kingship.

Nar (*nāru/m*): a male or female (**MUNUS.NAR (*nârtu*)**) singer or musician who works for the temple (or even lives there), and performs at major religious festivals. A **nar-gal (*nargallu*)** is a chief musician, a **nar-tur** an apprentice musician. The **GALA.ZE.E (*āsû*)** is a professional solo singer while the **GALA.SIR.DA (*āsû kiṣri*)** is a professional member of the chorus. Some of these were also masters of instruments and accompanied themselves. In Mari, many musicians seem to have lived in a special quarter, in the neighbourhood of the instrument makers. Occasionally, musicians were even housed together; there are Old Babylonian references to the **e-nar-ki (*Ubara*)** and the **e-nar-MI ki (*Ubarum*)**, the *'Houses of Male'* and *'Houses of Female Singers'*. There is a technical vocabulary for specific vocal techniques, which indicates that trills, tremolo and shaking, quivering sounds, wailing and free improvisation were part of the performance. The songs range from hymns to extended epics N. were also employed by the palace and by high-ranking aristocrats. As a religious office, their rank was rather low, but still slightly better than that of the acrobats and snake-charmers. Unlike the gala, who was a singer of prestigious, ancient Sumerian compositions, the N. was not necessarily educated and had a status much like that of an artisan or worker in the temple hierarchy.

Nibru (*Nippur*), modern Niffar: One of the earliest Mesopotamian cities, divided by the flow of the Euphrates, with temple buildings on both river banks. At its height, the city measured 150 hectares. The history of N. as a religious site began, just like that of Eridu, roughly at the beginning of the fifth millennium BCE. Hence, N. is a place of creation and beginnings, though we have no idea what deities were worshipped by the proto-Sumerians. In the third millennium, the city was largely controlled by the priesthood, which governed in the name of the gods. N. was one of the foremost centres of learning, its 'Tablet House' one of the greatest libraries in the country, a place where scribes, researchers, accountants, musicians and scientists were trained. The major temple, praised by Enḫeduanna as the *navel of heaven and earth*, birthplace of fate, was dedicated to Enlil and Ninlil, the mightiest deities of the late Sum. and OB period. The two major gods of state and royalty governed from the Ekur, the *House of the Mountain*. Their courtyard represented the Ubšukinna, the assembly of the gods. A hymn proclaims that the temple of Nippur is surrounded by awe-inspiring radiance, its sides are soaring into heaven, its inside spaces are *the cutting edge of a pointed dagger*, making the entire holy city Nippur a trap, a pitfall and a net for the rebellious land ((Jacobsen 1987:102). It turned N. into the most important religious city of its time. The second wife of Enlil, Šuzianna, had her own temple on the premises. Another major temple was dedicated to Inanna/Ištar. Ninḫursag received worship and offerings in the temple of Ninlil. Other temples were dedicated to Ninurta and the Nin-Nibru: *'Lady of Nippur'*, Gula. Nusku and his wife Sadarnunna had temples, or maybe shrines, close to Enlil. In the Babylonian and Assyrian periods, N. lost some of its importance, but it remained a sacred site. Even the Persian invasion did not entirely change its status. N. was an important city until c.500 or 600 CE. At that time, the population was quite mixed, but as the excavations revealed, there were still some people around who venerated Šamaš, Sin, Nergal, Nanna, Dilbat and Ištar (while others, like the Jewish and Mandaean population, considered them as demons). These cults came to an end when the Arabs invaded the country and enforced Islam.

NIM: *'High'*, *'Highland'*. The Sumerogram was used for the Proto-Elamites in the third millennium BCE. Just as with the Sumerians, the origin and ethnic background of the early Elamites are an unsolved riddle. Both spoke related languages, but these languages are not related to any known language of human history.

NIM-MA *(Elammatum)*: the land Elam, east of Mesopotamia, in the foothills and mountains of Iran. A prehistoric civilisation that was closely connected with pre-literate Sumer. Elam had an ancient high culture and several large city-states. The Elamites developed their own script. They had a difficult relationship with the Mesopotamians. Though trade continued most of the time, there were also savage wars between the cultures. In the first millennium BCE, the Elamites occasionally sided with the Babylonians to fight the Assyrians. Aššurbanipal crushed the culture of Elam.

Nin-dingir: *'the Lady who is a Deity'*. A title that was sometimes, but not always, equated with NU.GIG and entu(m). Neo-Assyrian dictionaries also equated her with a qadištu(m) and with the ugbabtu(m); good evidence that most of these offices had become a thing of the past, and that the scholars were confusing them.

Nineveh, modern Küyünjik/Quyunjik and Nebi Yunus. After the massive building project of Dur Sharrukin was abandoned, N. was designed to be the new capital. The city extended over 750 hectares and housed, in its prime, the palace and library of Aššurbanipal, a magnificent temple complex dedicated to Aššur and Ištar, and the favourite deities of the Neo-Assyrians, such as Nabû, Marduk, Bēlet, Adad, Nergal, Šamaš, Sîn etc. The capital was short-lived: during the reign of Aššurbanipal's son, the Neo-Assyrian Empire came to a swift and brutal end.

Nippur: see Nibru.

NU.GIG (*qadištu*): a *'Woman Who is Set Apart', 'Sacred Woman' 'Tabooed Woman', 'Dark Woman',* originally an exalted priestess. Frequently and falsely translated as 'hierodule' (*sacred slave*). Originally an extremely high-ranking, wealthy and influential ritualist. In Sumerian times, several N. had children with the kings, and subsequently became queens. The N. could be associated with specific temples, as in Girsu, Umma, Lagaš, or independent of a temple, as can be observed in the OB period. Very little is known about the N., who disappeared from the record around the end of the Ur III period. She was succeeded by the Q. Their high status changed during the OB period: we observe Ḫammurapi legislating to ensure that the Q. retained some of their status and their inheritance rights. In his time, the Q. were allowed to marry and probably had the right to have children. In early Assyria, the Q. participated in temple processions; in old Nippur she acted as a sacred midwife. By the dismal first millennium BCE, the functions and status the Q. were much reduced. Some retained respectable functions in temples, but others lived an independent life by assisting midwives with magic, and selling all sorts of magic, including evil sorceries. Finally, some Neo-Assyrian word-lists use the title Q. in a derogatory way for 'prostitute'. In the divine realm, several goddesses are called N./Q., such as Inanna/Ištar, Baba, Gula, Ninisina, Aruru, Ninmaḫ, Lamaštu and even Lilītu. All of them are free women, many of them with specific professions, or related in some way to sorcery, spell-craft, conjuration, banishment and childbirth.

Nu-eš, nisag (*nêšakku*): *'Of the Temple'*. A priestly rank associated with Enlil's and Ninlil's temple Ekur in Nippur and, secondarily, with the cities Adab and Keš, where the N. was connected with the cult of Ninḫursag, Nintu, Ninmaḫ and other goddesses. The N. was mainly busy preparing sacrifices, speaking prayers, pouring libations and slaughtering animals for a higher good. Apart from these basic functions, we find an N. as overseers of a temple of Inanna, and, in the cult of Enlil in NB times, and acting as the governors of Nippur and the mayor of Borsippa. The profession usually moved from father to son. After the Kassite period, the term N. gradually disappears; by the first millennium it has become an old-fashioned literary expression.

PAP.PAP: a very rare term designating some sort of high priestess of the Early Dynastic period. It occurs in regard to a woman called Baranamtara who was the queen of king Lugalanda. She also held the title ama-uru (*'Mother of the City'*) and might have been a representative of the goddess Bau/Baba.

Pa-šeš, *(Pašīsu)*: *'the Anointed/ Anointer'* a general term for a type of priest or priestess, occasionally synonymous with GUDU. The first references are from Fāra. Some Akk. kings called themselves P. In Ebla, there were several P. associated with each major god or goddess and some who acted like pages in the palace. Usually, the P. were busy assisting rituals. In later times, their office focused mostly on purification ceremonies. Most P. were dedicated to a specific cult, such as the P. of An, of Enlil, of Ninlil, and a *female pašišu of Bēlatu.*

Pisag-dub-ba: *'Accountant'*, a sagga priest of Enlil who also acted as a royal accountant.

Qadištu: a *'Woman Set Apart'*, see NU.GIG.

Ramku: *'Bathed- or Purified Ones'*, a specific term for priests.

Sābītu/m: *'Ale-wife'*. A woman who professionally makes beer or wine and who may or may not run a tavern/guesthouse or brothel. Frequently a female profession in Babylonia. Their most famous representative is the divine Šiduri. S. may also derive from *'Woman from the Land Sabum'*.

Sagga, Sanga *(šangû)*: the head of a temple, originally a supreme priest and manager who cooperated with the highest priestesses and was much concerned with incense offerings and purification rituals. S. also appear among the palace staff. Basically, a religious administrator and the CEO of all the temple property (fields, manufactories, workshops, financial investments, banking, fishing and hunting rights etc). Very large temples, like the Šamaš temple of Sippar had two S., one for the god and one for his wife. In the temple of Aššur, a 'great S.' and a 'second S.' acted simultaneously. In the Neo-Assyrian period, the S. frequently performed ritual together with the king, in some cases for 24 days continuously. The S. may have acted as an administrative manager, but this task, like all other temple duties, was a religious one. Some high-ranking S. were involved in ritual, had prophetic dreams or officiated in the investiture of kings. It could be a high rank, when the temple was a major structure owning land and property, or a miserable minor function with little prestige, when the temple was just a tiny hut run entirely by the S., who did the rituals, the chores and the cleaning all by himself. The S.'s tasks, status and activities differed from city to city. In some places, the title S. was used so loosely, that it could be applied to simple temple staff, like cooks. Among the gods, Ningal acted as an S. for Enlil.

SAGGA.MAḪ, SANGA.MAḪ (*šangammāḫḫu*): A sanga (priest) who makes fumigations and functions as an ecstatic, visionary and prophetic exorcist (maḫḫu).

Sagi, SÎLA.ŠU.DU (saqû): *'Cupbearer'*. Originally a minor priest who libated beer and wine to deities and in the palace, during royal sacrifices. The cup-bearer also functioned as a private counsellor of the king, who was present during important conferences. After Ur III, he replaced his superior, the zabar-dab, and became a high-ranking priest in charge of libations. S. was in charge of the storage and maintenance of the sacrificial vessels as well as the supply of beer, wine and occasionally other foodstuffs. Originally exclusively associated with a temple or a specific deity, after the Old Babylonian period the S. was also active outside of a temple context.

ŠEŠ (*sekretu, sekertu*): a high-ranking lady of the palace or temple, possibly living in a cloister or a separate section of the court. The *Code of Ḫammurapi* mentions that fathers could dedicate daughters to a deity: they became kulmašīzu, nadītu, qadištu, sekertu and ugbabtu priestesses. One text refers to an S. who undoes witchcraft; rare references to S. indicate that some of them were the ***narāmtu*** (*'beloved'*) of kings. Š. and S. are documented from the AKK. to the OB period, specifically in Sippar and Mari.

ŠEŠ.GAL (*šešgallu*): *'Big Brother'*, *'Elder Brother'*, a middle-class priest in the NB period but a very high-ranking priest in Seleucid times. Frequently called ***aḫu rabû***. In Uruk, the Š. were recruited from āšipu families, in Sippar from the ērib bīti (*'temple enterer'* i.e. temple staff).

Sigbara (***luḫšu***): *'With Loose Hair'*, a priestly rank. The term is very rare; it appears in lexical lists and in relation to the temple of Ištar in Mari. The 'loose hair' indicates that this priest did not have a shaved head. We have no idea what he did.

Sippar (modern Abu Habba & Tell ed-Der): a major late fourth-millennium city that gained much of its importance from being in the north of Sumer and the south of Akkad, placed conveniently near the Euphrates and the Tigris. Indeed, at one time the two sacred rivers met near S., which turned the place into a vital centre of religion and commerce. Eventually, the swift moving Tigris and the silty, fertilising Euphrates separated again, but the importance of S. remained. At the present time, S. is the best-excavated city in northern Babylonia. The major deities were Utu/Šamaš and his wife Aya, whose cult was enthusiastically promoted by Ḫammurapi, and who granted extra privileges, like tax reductions, to his favourite city. The temple had a special cloister section for nādītu(m) priestesses; they had their own female scribes and accountants, and made much money with investments and loans. Other popular temples were dedicated to Adad, Gula, Ikūnum, Išḫara, Ištar, Marduk, Nergal, Haniš, Nanay, Sippar-Aruru and Šullat. In S. Antu(m) was characteristically called Anunītu(m). S. was also known as the *'Eternal City'*. It didn't work: around 600 BCE, the city was forsaken.

Sirara: a city or town of dream oracle goddess Nanše that used to be near the Persian Gulf. Not discovered so far.

Šita: a religious official, probably high-ranking. The word occurs in many designations for priests, such as the Š. of Inanna, Š. of the underworld, Š. of the Abzu and several others, most of them unknown. Occasionally, the Š. was associated with the words ellu and ramku, referring to purification, cleaning, washing and holiness. Regarding ritual, there is just a brief reference to a Š. who sprinkled the courtyard of a temple, a Š. who was busy during a seven-day ceremony in Larsa, and some references to purification duties. Ninazu is the Š. for his mother Ereškigal at Enegi. Whether the lyre he plays has anything to do with this office remains an open question.

Subartu: an unclear term that refers to the countries north of Assyria.

SUḪ.BU (***susbû***): another badly documented purification specialist, this time related to the cultic personnel of Nanše. He carried food offerings to her.

Sukkal (***šukkallu***): *'Vizier, Major Domo, Steward'*. Usually a minor deity who acts at the behest of a major one. Lightning, for example, acts under the command of Adad, the storm. An S. may function as a steward, a high-ranking messenger or a vizier of a major god. This does not necessarily turn the S. into a mere servant: several S. are the best friends and companions of the deities they serve, and occasionally exercise greater powers than these. Unlike the regent, the grand vizier was in touch with reality and often more influential than the king. The status of an S. is by no means easy to define, as several gods who appear as the S. of a major deity appear as independent major deities elsewhere. One example is Inanna's or An's S. Ninšubura, who is elsewhere a major underworld goddess, a counterpart of Ereškigal(a), and, much later, a male god.

Šuruppak (modern Tell Fāra): the ancient city where Utnapištim ruled before the flood. The major city goddess was Sud/Ansud *'Wide Ear of Corn'*, i.e. Ninlil. Excavators unearthed a magnificent library with literature dating from the early third millennium BCE. Among them are the earliest magical spells of mankind. The goddess Ningirima was a major deity.

Susa (modern Shush): an ancient city in foreign Elam, in southern Iran, but with strong cultural links to Sumer. The city god was Šušinak. One temple to the 'Ninḫursag of Susa' is attested; possibly she was identified with the Elamite goddess Pinenkir.

Tall al-'Obēd: the contemporary name of an unidentified early city, one of the major cult places of a mother-goddess cult focussed on Ninḫursag.

Tummal: An early cult place, attested since Ur III, dedicated to Ninlil. The site was probably near Nippur, but has not been discovered yet.

Tupšarru: *'scribe, professional writer, scholar'*. The T., mainly men but occasionally women, were usually members of the upper levels of society. They underwent strict training in schools that were not necessarily attached to temples, and specialised in various skills, such as composing letters, historical documents, religious hymns, contracts, essays or inscriptions. Some became scholars, compiled word-lists, dictionaries, translations of earlier texts or studied maths, architecture and land survey. Much of what we know of ancient Mesopotamia comes from the texts copied and recopied in the scribal schools.

Ubšu-ukkina, Ubšukkina: the sacred abode where the gods meet to get drunk and make decisions. The U. is the place for judgement, mediation and divination. It can be attested from the third to the first millennium BCE. Ukkina means *'assembly'*, the rest of the word is uncertain. Though the U. was thought to be in the otherworld or in heaven, several cities had special temple halls to represent the site. On record are Nippur, Girsu, Babylon, later Aššur and much later, in the Neo-Babylonian period, Uruk.

Ugarit (modern Ras Shamra): a major city in Syria, famous for an extensive library containing Ugaritic and Akkadian literature, documents, correspondence, treaties etc. Many priceless Mesopotamian texts survived thanks to this collection. The city Ugarit does not appear in third-millennium literature, but it is certainly important in the second millennium BCE. It lost much of its power around the middle of the second millennium BCE and was destroyed by the Sea-People around 1185 BCE. Its main cults were dedicated to the primal couple El and Ašerah. Beside them we find worship for Ba'al (a god of storm and weather), Yammu (god of the oceans), Anat (goddess of love and war), Rašpu (a god related to diseases), Astar/Astarte (a goddess related to the stars and planet Venus), Šašpu (a solar goddess), Yariḫu (a moon god), Motu (*Death*, a god of the Underworlds) and many smaller deities. As Ugarit was close to the sea, it had access to many trade routes and an international population. The Ugaritans cultivated close ties to the Minoan culture of Crete, the Greek cultures, Cyprus and Egypt.

Ugbatum, ugbabtum: a class of priestesses. Many U. were dedicated to the service of a god or temple directly after birth or during childhood. See Ereš-dingir.

Ukkina (***puḫur ilāni***): the *'Assembly of the Gods'*. An informal meeting in a sacred temple space or an otherworldly (celestial?) location, the **Ubšukkina**, to consume a lot of beer, voice arguments, discuss pressing matters and come to a majority decision. The U. has often been cited as evidence for a 'democratic' system of government in pre-literate Sumer. All goddesses and gods have their say, and though some are more eminent than others, every opinion counts.

Ul-ki: *'Primeval Place'*, *'Original Earth'*. A name of the Underworld.

Umma (modern Tell Jokha): a major city on the edge of the grasslands of central Sumer. U. was almost as big as Uruk, and a major contestant for political and economic dominance. By the end of the third millennium BCE, it was frequently at war with its southern neighbour Lagaš. U. almost became the leading city-state. Its last king, Lugalzagesi, conquered Lagaš and decided to start an empire. He was crushed by Sargon I. The major god was Šara, but the deity who received most veneration was his mother Inanna. The temple of Šara was run by a high priestess and a lu-mah, both of them with their own staff. Here we have some information on the size of the staff: lists of rations mention 56 and 68 LUKUR priestesses, up to ten singers and 120 female singers with their daughters. Ninḫursag also had a temple in the city.

Unug (***Uruk***) modern Warka): one of the first and the greatest city in Mesopotamia. It was founded in the fifth millennium BCE. U. is famous for such kings as Enmerkar, Lugalbanda and Gilgameš, and for its majestic fortifications. Known as the

Sheepfold (or: *Cattlepen) of Eanna*. Records for the early periods are very sparse. In the fourth millennium BCE, U. became the largest known city of antiquity. U. measured 500 hectares around the start of the third millennium BCE and had a famous city wall, nine km long, five metres across, with a rounded tower extending to it's outside every ten metres. This colossal fortification was attributed to the semi-divine king Gilgameš, who worked his people into the ground to achieve his amazing project. It wasn't large enough. Around the city, another 300 hectares were covered with buildings. We can also assume that other people lived in tents and huts that cannot be traced. One modest population estimate (Nissen, 2013, in *Uruk*) proposes a city population of 30,000-80,000 plus another 30,000-60,000 people outside the wall. In terms of size and population, U. set a record that was not equalled until Rome reached her largest extent under the Caesars. As the biggest megacity of early history, U. depended on trade with neighbouring districts, which eventually developed into a vast network of trade routes reaching all across the Near and Middle East. The city is also one of the earliest, if not the first place where cuneiform writing developed. As a cradle of civilisation, it was closely connected to the Me, the divine principles, which, as a famous hymn relates, Inanna received from Enki after drinking him under the table. The earliest goddesses who were praised as the Lady of U. were Ningirima, Nanay and Inanna. The former two lost their office. The city became famous for the worship of Inanna/Ištar and for An/Anu, plus many other deities. In the *Bible*, U. appears as Erech. In the Seleucid period, U. became known as the *Rainbow City*.

Ur, *modern Tell el-Muqqayar:* An early Sumerian city not far from Eridu and the Persian Gulf, rising from the salt marshes, praised by Enḫeduanna as the first place of earth of An. The earliest settlement may have been erected around 4000 BCE, in the Ubaid period, which was named after a tell (mound) called Ubaid nearby. The temple of Nanna, the Ekišnugal, adorned with white stone, appeared to her as a *great serpent of the marshes*, on a foundation of fifty Abzus and seven seas. In the hymn to *Nanna of Ur*, Enḫeduanna celebrated the very temple whose first entu(m) priestess she was. She fulfilled her duties for almost forty years. After her, for almost 500 years, a succession of entu(m)s resided in the gipar of Nanna/Suen/Sîn, the moon god, each of them the sister or daughter of a king. A subdivision with its own priesthood was dedicated to Enki/Ea. Another important temple was dedicated to Ninḫursag, while an inscription describes Ninmaḫ as the *Bride of Ur* and the *Splendour of Ur*. Sacrifices were also offered to Nanay of Uruk. King Šulgi built a temple in Ur to celebrate himself as a deity, and inserted a hymn to it into Enḫeduanna's much earlier collection. At its height, Ur measured 60 hectares. The *Lament over Ur*, described the fall of the great city thanks to the wrath of Enlil, who used the foreign Gutian barbarians as the tools for the devastation. It marked the end of the Sumerian period. But Ur recovered to some extent, and continued well over the millennia. The Kassites, Assyrians and Babylonians did their best to keep it in repair. Its importance, however, sharply declined. Finally, around the time when Alexander overran Mesopotamia, the Euphrates shifted and left the city dry and pretty much alone.

Ur-SAL: an undiscovered ancient city dedicated to the goddess Sasurra.

Urum (modern Tell Uqair): a late fourth millennium BCE city in northern Sumer, not far from modern Baghdad. The city was at the small, curved Zubi canal which connected at both ends with the major Irnina canal. U. had a major temple for Nanna and Ningal.

U-tab (*Adab*) modern Tell Bismayah: an important ancient city and a major place of mother-goddess veneration. In A. the mate of the goddess Ninmenna was Ašgi. The major temple was emaḫ. Another deity attested from U. is Lugal-igi-piri. The city was at the Iturungal canal, probably north of Zabalam. The waterways connected A. with the Persian Gulf in the south, Babylonia in the north and Der in the east; hence A. was a major trading place especially in the third millennium BCE. It lost much of its importance during the second millennium BCE, but remained inhabited well into the first millennium BCE. A. was particularly associated with Ninḫursag and Nintu(m). Both of them were distinct goddesses, but thanks to political motifs and the desire of the scribes to simplify the pantheon, they were also used as synonyms for a single goddess. The latter also appears as a son of Ninḫursag and Šulpae.

Uzumua: *'Flesh-Producer'*, a place in Nippur where Enlil created the hoe and used it to break open the soil.

Zabalam, modern Tell Ibzeikh: a major Sumerian city, close to Umma in the eastern part of central Mesopotamia. The major deities were worshipped for their celestial representations: Nanna as the moon and his children Inanna and Utu as Venus and the sun. Of these, Inanna may have been dominant; at least, Enḫeduanna chose to celebrate Inanna's temple at Z. as a shining mountain (kur-suba), a house of jewels, radiant in the morning light. It might say something about Inanna's popularity, but it could also reflect Enḫeduanna's obsessive love for a goddess whom she celebrated as the greatest deity of them all. The designation Kur-suba is worth considering: Z. was not in mountain country, and the reference to Kur might represent a spiritual or metaphorical mountain, or be a reference to the Underworld. While we can't be sure whether the moon, Venus and sun were thought to arise from a cosmic mountain (an axis mundi) or directly from the deep, we should acknowledge Z. as a place of major cosmological significance.

Zabar-dab (*zabardabbû/m*): *'Holder of the Bronze (=zabar) Vessel'.* An early, high-ranking ritualist who administered libations at religious and royal sacrifices. His activities were close associated with various temples and gods, but his major connection was to the palace. It is a difficult question whether we should see him as a priest or as a royal administrator, provided that our modern terminology can be applied at all. Early in the second millennium BCE his function and office were taken over by his former subordinate, the Sagi, who used to have a much lower status. We encounter the Z. In the OB period as a functionary of the king who oversees the donations at the temple.

Bibliography

Abhinavagupta: *The Kula Ritual, as Elaborated in Chapter 29 of the Tantrāloka*, trans. & ed. John R. Dupuche, Motilal Banarsidass, Delhi, 2006 (2003)

Abusch, Tzvi: *Babylonian Witchcraft Literature. Case Studies*. Brown Judaic Studies 132, Scholars Press, Atlanta, 1987

Abusch, Tzvi & Toorn, Karel van der: *Mesopotamian Magic: Textual, Historical and Interpretative Perspectives. Ancient Magic and Divination*. Styx, Groningen, 1999

Adam, K.D. *Eiszeitkunst in Süddeutschland*. Kosmos Verlag, Stuttgart, 1978

Die ältesten Monumente der Menschheit. Vor 12,000 Jahren in Anatolien. Landesausstellung Baden-Württemberg, Badisches Landesmuseum, Theiss Verlag, Stuttgart, 2007

Ananikian, Mardios: *Armenian Mythology*. Indo-European Publishing, Los Angeles, 2010.

Arakelova, Victoria: Entries on *Āl & Albasti*, in: Joseph, Suad & Tağmābādi, Afsāna (editors): *Encyclopedia of Women and Islamic Cultures. Family, Body, Sexuality and Health*. Vol.3, Brill, Leiden, 2006

Assante, Julia: *The KAR.KID/Ḫarimtu, Prostitute or Single Woman?* Ugarit Forschungen, vol. 30, 1998

Ascalone, Enrico: *Mesopotamia. Assyrians, Sumerians, Babylonians*. Dictionaries of Civilization, University of California Press, Berkeley, 2007

Atharva-Veda Saṁhitā, trans. William D. Whitney, revised by Nag S. Singh, Nag Publishers, Delhi, 1987

Bächtold-Stäubli, Hanns: *Handwörterbuch des deutschen Aberglaubens*. Weltbild Verlag, Augsburg, 2008

Bagley, Robert: *Ancient Sichuan, Treasures from a Lost Civilization*; Seattle Art Museum, Princeton University Press; 2001

Bandler, Richard: *Richard Bandler's Guide to Trance-Formation*. Health Communications Inc., Deerfield Beach, 2008

Beck, Henning: *Biologie des Geistesblitzes. Speed up your mind!* Springer-Verlag, Berlin, 2013

Bell, R.C.: *Board and Table Games from Many Civilizations*. Revised edition, Dover Publications, New York, 1979

Bellér-Hahn, Ildikó: *Community Matters in Xinjiang, 1980-1949: Towards a Historical Anthropology of the Uyghur*. Brill, Leiden, 2008

Ben-Barak, Idan: *Kleine Wunderwerke. Die unsichtbare Macht der Mikroben*. Spektrum, Akademischer Verlag, 2010 (*How Microbes Rule Our World*)

Bergmann, Claudia: *Childbirth as a Metaphor for Crisis: Evidence from the Ancient Near East, the Hebrew Bible, and 1QH XI, 1-18*. De Gruyter, Berlin, 2008

Beyond Babylon. Art, Trade, and Diplomacy in the Second Millennium B.C. . Edited by Aruz, Benzel & Evans. Metropolitan Museum of Art, New York, Yale University Press, New Haven, 2008

Die Bibel. Einheitsübersetzung, Altes und Neues Testament. Herder Verlag, Freiburg, 1980

Bidez, Joseph: *Kaiser Julian. Der Untergang der Heidnischen Welt*. Rowohlt Verlag, Hamburg, 1956

Black, Jeremy & Green, Anthony with Rickards, Tessa: *Gods, Demons and Symbols of Ancient Mesopotamia. An Illustrated Dictionary*. University of Texas Press, Austin, 1992

Black, Jeremy; George, Andrew; Postgate, Nicholas: *A Concise Dictionary of Akkadian*. 2nd (corrected) printing. (Based on von Soden's *Akkadisches Handwörterbuch*). Harrassowitz, Wiesbaden, 2000

Black-Koltuv, Barbara: *The Book of Lilith*, Nicolas-Hays, York Beach, Maine 1986

Blacker, Carmen: *The Catalpa Bow. A Study of Shamanistic Practices in Japan*. Unwin, London, 1986

Böck, Barbara: *Das Handbuch Muššu'u „Einreibung": eine Serie sumerischer und akkadischer Beschwörungen aus dem 1. Jt. vor Chr.* CSIC Ministerio de Educacíon y Ciencia

Bonnet, Hans: *Lexikon der ägyptischen Religionsgeschichte*. Nikol Verlag, Hamburg, 2000

Bottéro, Jean: *Mesopotamia. Writing, Reasoning, and the Gods*. University of Chicago Press, 1992

Bottéro, Jean: *Religion in Ancient Mesopotamia*. University of Chicago Press, 2004

Brockhoff, Victoria: *Götter, Dämonen, Menschen. Mythen und Geschichten aus dem Zweistromland*. Verlag Freies Geistesleben, Stuttgart, 1987

Buhner, Stephen: *The Lost Language of Plants. The Ecological Importance of Plant Medicines to Life on Earth.* Chelsea Green Publishing, White River Junction, Vermont, 2002

Buren, Douglas van: *A Further Note on the Terra-Cotta Relief.* Archiv für Orientforschung (AfO), issue 1936-37.

Buren, Douglas van: *Entwined Serpents.* Archiv für Orientforschung, (AfO), Vol. X, 1935-1936

Buren, Douglas van: *The Scorpion in Mesopotamian Art and Religion.* Archiv für Orientforschung, (AfO), Vol. XII, 1937-1939

Burkert, Walter: *The Orientalizing Revolution: Near Eastern Influence on Greek Culture in the Early Archaic Age.* Harvard University Press, 1992

Burkert, Walter: *Greek Religion.* Harvard University Press, Cambridge, Massachusetts, 1985

Butterweck, Delsman, Dietrich, Gutekunst, Kausen, Loretz, Müller & Sternberg-Hotabi: *Rituale und Beschwörungen.* Texte aus der Umwelt des Alten Testaments, TUAT II/3, Gütersloher Verlaghaus, 1988

Cahill, Suzanne E.: *Transcendence and Divine Passion. The Queen Mother of the West in Medieval China.* Stanford University Press; Stanford; 1993

Campbell Thompson, R.: *Devils and Evil Spirits of Mesopotamia,* two volumes, London 1903 & 1904

Capelle, Wilhelm: *Die Vorsokratiker.* Kröner Verlag, Stuttgart, 1968

Carroll, Cain & Revital: *Mudras of India.* Expanded Edition. Singing Dragon, London, 2013

Cavigneaux, Antoine in: Abusch, Tzvi & Toorn, Karel van der

Chamovitz, Daniel: *Was Pflanzen wissen. Wie sie sehen, riechen und sich erinnern.* Hanser Verlag, München, 2013 (*What Plants Know. A Field Guide to the Senses.*)

Chang, Kwang-Chieh: *Art, Myth and Ritual. The Path to Political Authority in Ancient China.* Harvard University Press, Cambridge, 1983

Chang, Tsung-Tung: *Der Kult der Shang Dynastie im Spiegel der Orakelinschriften. Eine paläographische Studie zur Religion im archaischen China.* Otto Harrassowitz Verlag, Wiesbaden, 1970

Chauvet, J.-M.: *Grotte Chauvet.* Thorbeke Verlag, Sigmaringen, 1995

Chavalas, Mark W. (ed.): *The Ancient Near East. Historical Sources in Translation.* Blackwell, Malden, 2007

Chavalas, Mark W. (ed.): *Women in the Ancient Near East.* Routledge Books, London, 2014

Chesterton, Gilbert K.: *Heretics & Orthodoxy.* Merchant Books, 2009

Chuang Tzu, the Complete Works of, translation Burton Watson; Columbia University Press; New York; 1971 (1968)

Cleary, Thomas: *Vitality, Energy, Spirit. A Taoist Sourcebook.* Shambhala Publications, Boston, 1991

Codex Hammurabi. Die Gesetzstele Hammurabis. Translation: Eilers, Wilhelm. Marix Verlag, Wiesbaden, 2009 (1932)

Cohen, Mark: *An English to Akkadian Companion to the Assyrian Dictionaries.* CDL Press, 2011

Confucius: *The Analects (Lun Yü).* Trans. Lau, D.C., Penguin Books, London, 1979

Cosentino, Donald (ed.): *Sacred Arts of Haitian Vodou.* UCLA Fowler Museum of Cultural History, Los Angeles, 1995

Crickmore, Leon: *New Light on the Babylonian Tonal System.* Available online.

Cunningham, Graham: *Deliver Me from Evil. Mesopotamian Incantations 2500-1500 BCE.* Editrice Pontificio Istituto Biblico, Roma, 2007

Daniélou, Alain: *Einführung in die indische Musik,* Heinrichshofen Bücher, Wilhelmshafen, 1996

Deren, Maya: *Divine Horsemen. The Living Gods of Haiti.* McPheson & Company, New York, 1983

Devī-Māhātmyam or Śrī Durgā-Saptaśatī, trans. Svāmī Jagadīśvarānanda, Sri Ramakrishna Math, Madras, 1955

Dumbrill, Richard: *The Archaeomusicology of the Ancient Near East.* Trafford Publishing, Victoria, 2005

Du Ry, Carel: *Völker des alten Orient.* Holle Verlag, Baden-Baden, 1969

Ebeling, E.: *Keilschriftinschriften aus Assur religiösen Inhalts.*

Eisele, Petra: Babylon. *Pforte der Götter und Große Hure.* Scherz Verlag, Bern, 1980

The Encyclopedia Of Islam. Vol.5, Brill, Leiden, 1978

Erlbeck, Haseder & Stinglwagner: *Das Kosmos Wald und Forst Lexikon.* Kosmos Verlag, Stuttgart, 2002

ETCSL Project Page, Faculty of Oriental Studies, University of Oxford. A wonderful page with plenty of Sumerian translations.
Evans-Wentz, W.Y.: *Tibetan Yoga and Secret Doctrines.* Oxford University Press, Oxford 1967.
Falkener, Edward: *Games Ancient and Oriental and How to Play Them.* Dover Publications, New York, 1961
Falkenstein, Adam: *Zu Inannas Gang zur Unterwelt.* Archiv für Orientforschung, (AfO), Vol. XIV, 1941-1944
Falkenstein, Adam: *Literarische Keilschrifttexte aus Uruk,* Berlin, Staatliche Museen, 1931, Nachdruck 1979
Falkenstein, A. & von Soden, W: *Sumerische und Akkadische Hymnen und Gebete.* (SAHG) Artemis Verlag, Zürich, 1953.
Farber, Walter: *Zur älteren babylonischen Beschwörungsliteratur.* Zeitschrift für Assyriologie, 71, 1981
Farber, W.; Kümmel, H.; Römer, W.: *Rituale und Beschwörungen.* Texte aus der Umwelt des Alten Testaments (TUAT), II/2, Gütersloher Verlagshaus, 1987
Farber, Walter: *Schlaf, Kindchen schlaf: Mesopotamische Baby-Beschwörungen und -Rituale,* Eisenbrauns, Winona Lake, 1989
Farber, Walter: *Lamaštu - Agent of a Specific Disease or a General Destroyer of Health?.* In: Finkel & Geller, 2007
Farber, Walter: *Lamaštu. An Edition of the Canonical Series of Lamaštu Incantations and Rituals and Related Texts from the Second and First Millennia B.C.,* Eisenbrauns, Winona Lake, 2014
Fartacek, Gebhard: *Unheil durch Dämonen? Geschichte & Diskurse über das Wirken der Ǧinn.* Böhlan Verlag, Wien, 2010
Fell McDermott, Rachel: *Singing to the Goddess. Poems to Kālī and Umā from Bengal,* Oxford University Press, 2001
Finkel, I.L. & Geller, M.: *Disease in Babylonia.* Styx, Groningen, 2007
Finkel, Irving L. in Abusch, Tzvi & Toorn, Karel van der.
Forman, W. & Rintschen, B.: *Lamaistische Tanzmasken. Der Erlik-Tsam in der Mongolei.* Koehler & Amelang, Leipzig, 1967
Foster, Benjamin R.: *From Distant Days. Myths, Tales, and Poetry of Ancient Mesopotamia.* CDL Press, Bethesda, 1995
Frank, Carl: *Babylonische Beschwörungsreliefs: Ein Beitrag zur Erklärung des sog. Hadesreliefs.* Zentralantiquariat der Deutschen Demokratischen Republik, Leipzig, 1918
Frankfort, H.: The Burney Relief. Archiv für Orientforschung (AfO), Vol. XII, 1937-1939
Frazer, Sir James: *The Golden Bough.* Macmillan, London 1922
Frey-Anthes, Henrike: *Unheilsmächte & Schutzgenien, Antiwesen und Grenzgänger.* Vandenhoeck & Ruprecht, 2007
Frühling und Herbst des Lü Bu We. Translation Wilhelm, Richard; Diederichs; München; 1979
Fries, Jan: *Helrunar. A Manual of Rune Magick.* Mandrake of Oxford, 1993, 2002, 2006
Fries, Jan: *Seidways. Shaking, Swaying and Dragon Mysteries.* Mandrake of Oxford, 1996
Fries, Jan: *Kālī Kaula. A Manual of Tantric Magick.* Avalonia, London, 2010.
Fries, Jan: *Dragon Bones. Ritual, Myth & Oracle in Shang Period China.* Avalonia, London, 2012
Fries, Jan: *Nightshades. A Tourist Guide to the Nightside.* Mandrake of Oxford, 2012
Gan Bao, *Anecdotes about Spirits and Immortals* (*Suo Shen Ji*), two volumes, translation Huang Diming & Ding Wangdao, Foreign Language Press, Beijing 2004
Ge Hong, *To Live as Long as Heaven and Earth. Ge Hong's Traditions of Divine Transcendents.* Trans. & ed. Campany, Robert Ford. University of California Press, Berkeley, 2002
Geller, Markham: *Ancient Babylonian Medicine: Theory and Practise.* Blackwell, Chichester, 2010
George, A.R. : *Babylonian Texts from the Folios of Sidney Smith,* Part 2, 1991
Gleick, Gwendolyn, *Dictionary of Near Eastern Mythology,* Routledge, London, 1991
Gleick, Gwendolyn: *Sex and Eroticism in Mesopotamian Literature.* Routledge, London, 2003
Götting, Eva: *Exportschlager Dämon? Zur Verbreitung altorientalischer Lamaštu-Amulette.* In Exportschlager: *Kultureller Austausch, wirtschaftliche Beziehungen und transnationale Entwicklungen in der antiken Welt.* Ed. Göbel & Zech,Verlag Herbert Utz, Berlin, 2010
Golther, Wolfgang: *Handbuch der germanischen Mythologie.* Magnus Verlag, Kettwig, 1987
Gonda, Jan: *Die Religionen Indiens I,* Kohlhammer Verlag, Stuttgart, 1960

Goodall, Jane: *Seeds of Hope. Wisdom an Wonder from the World of Plants.* Grand Central Publishing, New York, 2014

Gressmann, Hugo: *Altorientalische Texte und Bilder zum Alten Testament.* De Gryter, Berlin, 1970

Griffith, Ralph T. H. (trans.): *The Rig Veda*, Motilal Banarsidass, Delhi, Special Edition for Book of the Month Club, NY, 1992

Grigson, Geoffrey: *Aphrodite, Göttin der Liebe.* Manfred Pawlak Verlagsgesellschaft, Herrsching, 1978 (*The Goddess of Love*)

Groneberg, Brigitte: *Die Götter des Zweistromlandes. Kulte, Mythen, Epen.* Artemis & Winkler, Düsseldorf, 2004

Groot, J.J.M., de: *The Religious Systaem of China*, 6 volumes, reprinted by Ch'eng-wen Publishing, Taipei, 1967

Gruber, M.I.: *Hebrew Qedēšāh and her Canaanite and Akkadian Cognates.* Ugarit Forschungen, vol. 18, 1986

Grunfeld, A. Tom: *The Making of Modern Tibet.* Zed Books Ltd, London, 1987

Gyatso, Geshe Kelsang: *Guide to Dakini Land. A Commentary to the Highest Yoga Tantra Practice of Vajrayogini.* Tharpa Publiscations, London, 1991

Haarmann, Harald: *Universalgeschichte der Schrift.* Campus Verlag, Frankfurt, Sonderausgabe für Parkland Verlag Köln, 1998

Haas, Volkert: *Hethitische Berggötter und hurritische Steindämonen. Riten, Kulte und Mythen.* Verlag Philipp von Zabern, Mainz, 1982

Haas, Volkert: *Magie und Mythen in Babylonien. Von Dämonen, Hexen und Beschwörungspriestern.* Merlin Verlag, Vastorf, 1986

Haas, Volkert: *Das Ritual gegen den Zugriff der Dämonin ᵈDÌM.NUN.ME und die Sammeltafel KUB XLIII 55.* Oriens Antiquus, vol. XXVII, Roma, 1988

Haas, Volkert: *Babylonischer Liebesgarten. Erotik und Sexualität im Alten Orient.* C.H.Beck, München, 1999

Haensch, W.G.: *Die menschlichen Statuetten des mittleren Jungpaläolithikums*, Habelt, Bonn, 1982

Hahn, Johann: *Griechische und Albanische Märchen,* vol.II, Verlag Wilhelm Engelmann, Leipzig, 1864

Hald, Karl: *Die große Trias in den sumerischen (bilingualen) Beschwörungs-Formeln.* Königliche Ludwig-Maximilians Universität, München, 1914

Hallo, William W: in Abusch, Tzvi & Toorn, Karel van der

Haussig, Hans W. & Schmalzriedt, Egidius: *Wörterbuch der Mythologie*, Band 7, Klett-Cota, Stuttgart, 1999

Hesiod: *Theogonie.* Trans. Albert, Verlag Hans Richarz, Sankt Augustin, 1985

He Xingliang: *Totemism in Chinese Minority Groups*, China Intercontinental Press, 2006

Heeßel, Nils, P.: *Pazuzu. Archäologie und philologische Studien zu einem alt-orientalischen Dämon.* Brill, Styx, 2002

Heliodor: *Die Abenteuer der schönen Chariklea (Aithiopika).* Transl. Reymer, Artemis & Winkler Verlag, 1950

Herodot: *Historien.* Transl. Horneffer, Kröner Verlag, Stuttgart, 1971

Hill, Julia Butterfly: *The Legacy of Luna,* Harper, San Francisco, 2000

Horowitz, Wayne: *Mesopotamic Cosmic Geography*, Eisenbrauns, Winona Lake, 1998

Huber, Irene: *Rituale der Seuchen- und Schadensabwehr im Vorderen Orient und Griechenland,* Franz Steiner Verlag, Wiesbaden, 2005

Hurwitz, Siegmund: *Lilith-die erste Eva: eine historische und psychologische Studie über dunkle Aspekte des Weiblichen.*

Ifrah, Georges: *Universalgeschichte der Zahlen*, Zweitausendeins Verlag, Frankfurt/M, 1993

Jacobsen, Thorkild: *The Treasures of Darkness. A History of Mesopotamian Religion.* Yale University Press, New Haven, 1976

Jacobsen, Thorkild: *The Harps that Once...Sumerian Poetry in Translation.* Yale University Press, New Haven, 1987

Jagadīśvarānanda, Svāmi (trans.): *Devī-Māhātmyam or Śrī Durgā-Saptaśatī*, Sri Ramakrishna Math, Madras, 1955

Jaritz, Kurt: *Schriftarchäologie der altmesopotamischen Kultur*, Akademische Druck- und Verlagsanstalt, Graz, 1967

Jarrige, Jean-François: *Die frühen Kulturen in Pakistan und ihre Entwicklung*, in: *Vergessene Städte am Indus*, Verlag Phillip von Zabern, Mainz, 1987

Jarrige, Jean-François: *Vorzeit und Induskultur*, in: Heinrich Gerhard Franz (ed.): *Das alte Indien, Geschichte und Kultur des indischen Subkontinents*, Bertelsmann, München, 1990

Jensen, P.: *Die Kosmologie der Babylonier*. De Gryter, Berlin, 1974 (1890)

Jettmar, Karl, mit Beiträgen von Schuyler Jones und Max Klimburg: *Die Religionen des Hindukusch*. W. Kohlhammer Verlag, Stuttgart, 1975

Jettmar, Karl & Kattner, Ellen: *Die vorislamischen Religionen Mittelasiens*. W. Kohlhammer Verlag, Stuttgart, 2003

Jutzi, Sebastian: *Der bewohnte Mensch. Darm, Haut, Psyche. Besser leben mit Mikroben*. Heyne Verlag, 2014

Kaminsky, Joel: *Corporate Responsibility in the Hebrew Bible*. Sheffield Academic Press, 1995

Kamir, Orit: *Every Breath You Take: Stalking Narratives and the Law*. University of Michigan Press, 2001

The *Kaulajñāna Nirṇaya*, ed. Bagchi, P.C, trans. Magee, Michael, Prachya Prakashan, Varanasi, 1986

Keel, Othmar: *The Symbolism of the Biblical World: Ancient Near Eastern Iconography*. Eisenbrauns, Winona Lake, 1997

Keith, Lierre: *Ethisch essen mit Fleisch. Eine Streitschrift über nachhaltige und ethische Ernährung mit Fleisch und die Missverständnisse und Risiken einer streng vegetarischen und veganen Lebensweise*. Systemed Verlag, Lüren, 2013 (*The Vegetarian Myth*)

King, Leonard William: *Babylonian Magic and Sorcery, being the Prayers of the Lifting of the Hand*. Luzac, London, 1896

Kienast, B.: *Verbalformen mit Reduplikation im Akkadischen*. Orientalia, vol. 26, Roma, 1957

Klengel, Horst: *Neue Lamaschtu Amulette*. MIOR 7, Berlin, 1960

Klengel, Horst: *König Hammurapi und der Alltag Babylons*. Artemis & Winkler, Zürich, 1991

Klengel, Horst & Klengel-Brandt: *Vorderasiatische Schriftdenkmäler der staatlichen Museen zu Berlin, Neue Folge, Heft XIII (Heft XXIV) Spät-Altbabylonische Tontafeln, Texte und Siegelabrollungen*. Verlag Philipp von Zabern, Mainz, 2002

Koch, Heidemarie: *Frauen und Schlangen. Die geheimnisvolle Kultur der Elamer in Alt-Iran*. Phillip von Zabern Verlag, Mainz, 2007

Köcher, Franz: *Beschwörungen gegen die Dämonin Lamaštu*; Inaugural Dissertation zur Erlangung des Doktorgrades genehmigt von der philosophischen Fakultät der Universität zu Berlin von Franz Köcher aus Auma. Berlin, 1949

Köcher, F. & Oppenheim, A.: *The Old Babylonian Omen Text VAT 7525*, AfO

Kohn, Livia and Yoshinobu Sakade (editors): *Taoist Meditation and Longevity Techniques*, University of Michigan, 1989

Kohn, Livia: *Chinese Healing Exercises. The Tradition of Daoyin*. University of Hawai'I Press, Honolulu, 2008

Kramer, Samuel Noah: *Sumerian Mythology*, revised edition. University of Pennsylvania Press, Philadelphia, 1972

Kramer, Samuel Noah: *History begins at Sumer. Thirty-nine Firsts in Recorded History*, revised edition. University of Pennsylvania Press, Philadelphia, 1981

Kramer, Samuel Noah & Wolkenstein, Diane: *Inanna, Queen of Heaven and Earth. Her Stories and Hymns from Sumer*. Harper & Row Publishers, New York, 1983

Krebernik, Manfred: *Die Beschwörungen von Fara und Ebla*. Olms Verlag, Hildesheim, 1984

Kühne, Hartmut: *Dür-Katlimmu 2008 and Beyond*. Otto Harrassowitz Verlag, Wiesbaden.

Küster, Hansjörg: *Geschichte der Landschaft in Mitteleuropa*. C.H.Beck Verlag, München, 1996

The Kulacūḍāmaṇi Tantra and The Vāmakeśvara Tantra with the Jayaratha Commentary, Finn, Louise M. (intr., trans., & annotated), Otto Harrassowitz Verlag, Wiesbaden, 1986

The Kūrma Purāṇa, trans. Tagare, Ganesh Vasudeo, Motilal Banarsidass, Delhi, 1981

Lagerwey, John: *Der Kontinent der Geister. China im Spiegel des Taoismus*. Walter Verlag, Olten, 1991

Laitman, Michael: *The Zohar Annotations to the Ashlag*, Laitman Kabbalah Publishers, Toronto, 2007

Lakṣmī Tantra, a Pāñcarāta Text. Trans. & ed. Gupta, Sanjukta, Motilal Banarsidass, Delhi, 2003

Lamer, Hans: *Wörterbuch der Antike*, Alfred Kröner Verlag, Stuttgart, 1963

Lambert, Wilfred: *An Incantation of the Maqlû Type*, Archiv für Orientforschung AfO, XVIII,
Lambert,W.: *Babylonian Wisdom Literature*, Oxford University Press, 1960
Langdon, Stephen: *Sumerian Liturgies and Psalms.* Publications of the Babylonian Section, Vol. X, No. 3-4, University of Pennsylvania, University Museum, 1917
Laozi, Laotse, *Daodejing (Tao Te Ching),* translations by Duyvendak, J., John Murray Publishers, London, 1954; Wilhelm, R., Penguin books, London, 1995; Möller, H.-G., Fischer Verlag, Frankfurt, 1995; Gu Zhenkun, Chinese-English Classic Series, Peking University Press, Beijing, 1995
Liä Dsi: Das wahre Buch vom quellenden Urgrund. Translation Richard Wilhelm; Diederichs; München; 1996
Liang, Shou-Yu & Wu, Wen-Ching: *Qigong Empowerment. A Guide to Medical, Taoist, Buddhist, Wushu Energy Cultivation.* The Way of the Dragon Publishing, Rhode Island, 1997
Liezi; translation Liang Xiaopeng; Zhonghua Book Company, Beijing, 2005
Li Gi (Liji), Das Buch der Riten, Sitten und Gebräuche. Trans. Wilhelm, R., Diederichs Verlag, München, 1997
Liki (Liji), trans. Legge, J.: 2.vol., Motilal Banarsidass Publishing, Delhi, 2008
Lloyd, Seton: *The Archaeology of Mesopotamia from the Old Stone Age to the Persian Conquest.* Revised edition. Thames & Hudson, London, 1984
Lopez, Donald (ed.): *Religions of Tibet in Practice.* Abridged edition. Princeton Readings in Religions. 2007
Lü, Bu We: *Frühling und Herbst des Lü Bu We.* Trans. Wilhelm, Diederichs Verlag, Düsseldorf 1979
Lücke, Hans-K & Susanne; *Antike Mythologie*, Marix Verlag, Wiesbaden, 2005
Ma, Shutian: *Die Welt der Götter Chinas.* Verlag für fremdsprachliche Literatur, Beijing, 2006
Mahābhārata, trans. Kisari Mohan Ganguli, 1889-1896
Mahābhārata, trans. J. van Buitenen, University of Chicago Press, Book 1 1980, Book 2 &3 1981
Majupuria, Trilok Chandra: *Gods, Goddesses & Religious Symbols of Hinduism, Buddhism and Tantrism (including Tibetan Deities) (most authentic and exhaustive),* M. Devi, Lashkar (Gwalior), 2004
Mancuso, Stefano & Viola, Alessandra: *Die Intelligenz der Pflanzen.* Kunstmann Verlag, 2015
Marcellinus, Ammianus: *The Roman History of Ammianus Marcellinus, During the Reign of the Emperors Constantinus, Julian, Jovianus, Valentinian, and Valens.* Transl. Yonge, George Bell & Sons, London, 1902
Marchant, Jo: *Cure. A Journey into the Science of Mind Over Body.* Canongate, Edinborough, 2016
Margueron, J.-C.: *Mesopotamien.* Nagel Verlag, München, 1965
Meador, Betty de Shong: *Inanna-Lady of the Largest Heart.* University of Texas Press, Austin, 2000
Meador, Betty de Shong: *Princess; Priestess, Poet. The Sumerian Temple Hymns of Enheduanna.* University of Texas Press, Austin, 2009
Meier, Gerhard (trans. & ed.): *Die assyrische Beschwörungssammlung Maqlû.* Neu bearbeitet. Archiv für Orientforschung, Osnabrück, 1967
Milkman,H. & Sunderwirth, S.: *Craving for Ecstasy and Natural Highs. A Positive Approach to Mood Alteration.* Sage Publications, Los Angeles, 2010
Morgenstern, Julian: *The Doctrine of Sin in the Babylonian Religion.* The Book Tree, 2002 (1905)
Mudras (in Symbols), Bharatanatya Manual. Published by the Centre for the Promotion of Traditional Arts, Madras, no year.
Myhrmann, D.W.: *Die Labartu Texte. Babylonische Beschwörungsformeln nebst Zauberverfahren gegen die Dämonin Labartu. Inaugural Dissertation.* Verlag Karl J. Trübner, Strassburg, 1902
Myšliwiec, Karol: *Eros on the Nile.* Cornell University Press, Ithaca, 2004
Nabors, Murray W.: *Botanik.* Pearson Studium, München, 2007
Nentwig, Bacher, Beierkuhnlein, Brandl, Grabherr: *Ökologie.* Spektrum akademischer Verlag, Heidelberg, 2004
Neumann, Erich: *The Great Mother*, Routledge & Kegan, London, 1955
Oldenberg, Hermann: *Die Religion des Veda.* 4. Neuauflage, J.G. Cotta'sche Buchhandlung, Stuttgart, 1923
Opitz, Dietrich: *Die vogelfüssige Göttin auf den Löwen. Archiv für Orientforschung (AfO)*, 1936-37
Oppenheim, A. Leo: *The Interpretation of Dreams in the Ancient Near East, with a Translation of an Assyrian Dream Book.* American Philosophical Society, Philadelphia, 1956

Oppitz, Michael: *Schamanen vom Blinden Land*, Syndikat Verlag Frankfurt, 1981 (the groundbreaking documentary of Nepalese Shamanism by Michael Oppitz is available on DVD in the English language!)

Osten, Hans von der,: *Zwei neue Labartu Amulette,* Archiv für Orientforschung, (AfO), Vol. IV, 1927

Padmasambhava: *Die geheimen Dakini Lehren. Padmasambhavas mündliche Unterweisungen der Prinzessin Tsogyal.* Wandel Verlag, Berlin, 2011 (*Dakini Teachings.*)

Padmasambhava: *The Life and Liberation of Padmasambhava, as recorded by Yeshe Tsogyal.* Two volumes. Dharma Publishing, Berkeley, 1978

Pandey, K.C.: *Abhinavagupta. An Historical & Philosophical Study.* Chaukhamba Amarabharati Prakashan, Varanasi, 2006

Parker, H.: *Village Folk Tales of Ceylon, Vol. III,* Tisara Prakasakayo, Dehiwala, 1973

Parrot, André*: Assur. Die mesopotamische Kunst vom XIII vorchristlichen Jahrhundert bis zum Tode Alexanders des Großen.* Beck, München, 1961

Parrot, André: *Sumer. Die mesopotamische Kunst von den Anfängen bis zum XII vorchristlichen Jahrhundert.* Beck, München, 1962

Patai, Raphael: *The Hebrew Goddess.* Avon Books, New York, 1978

Pauly: *Der kleine Pauly, Lexikon der Antike in fünf Bänden.* DTV Verlag, München, 1975

Philostratus, Flavius: *Philostratus in Honour of Apollonius of Tyana.* Trans. Conybeare. 1912

Philostratus, Flavius: *The Life of Apollonius of Tyana.* Trans. Phillimore, J. Kessinger Publications. 1912

Pichot, André: *Die Geburt der Wissenschaft. Von den Babyloniern zu den frühen Griechen.* Campus Verlag, Frankfurt M. 1995

Pinel, John & Pauli, Paul: *Biopsychologie.* Pearsons, München, 2012

Pinker, Steven: *How the Mind Works.* Penguin, London, 1999

Plassmann, J.O.: Orpheus. *Altgriechische Mysterien.* Diederichs Verlag, Köln, 1982

Pollan, Michael: *The Botany of Desire. A Plant's Eye View of the World.* Random House, New York, 2001

Pollmer, U. & Warmuth, S.: *Lexikon der populären Ernährungsirrtümer.* Eichborn Verlag, Frankfurt/M, 2007

Pollmer, U. & Fock, A,, Niehaus, M.; Muth, J.: *Wer hat das Rind zur Sau gemacht? Wie Lebensmittelskandale erfunden und benutzt werden.* Rowohlt Verlag, Reinbek bei Hamburg, 2012

The Principal Upaniṣads, trans. & commentary Radhakrishnan, George Allan & Unwin, London, 1953

Pritchard, James B.: *Ancient Near Eastern Texts Relating to the Old Testament. (ANET)* Princeton University Press, Princeton, 1969

Pronst, Ernst (ed.): *Deutschland in der Steinzeit.* Bertelsmann Verlag, München, 1991

Rätsch, Christian: *Heilkräuter der Antike in Ägypten, Griechenland und Rom.* Diederichs Verlag, München, 1995

Radine, Jason: *The Book of Amos in Emergent Judah.* Mohr Diebeck, Tübingen, 2010

Reallexikon der Assyriologie (RlA), ed. Ebeling, Dietz, Meissner, Weidner, von Soden, etc. volumes 1-14, De Gruyter, New York

Reiner, Erica (trans. & ed.) *Šurpu. A Collection of Sumerian and Akkadian Incantations.* Biblio Verlag, Osnabrück, 1970

Remler, G.: *Dämonisierung des Weiblichen. Gestaltung einer Urangst.* MA Thesis, Graz, 1991, quoted by Farber, W. in Finkel & Geller 2007

Reynolds, Richard: *On Guerilla Gardening. A Handbook for Gardening Without Boundaries.* Bloomsbury, London, 2008

Ridley, Matt: *The Red Queen.* Penguin, London, 1993

Riemschneider, Kaspar: Lehrbuch des Akkadischen. VEB Verlag Enzyklopädie, Leipzig, 1973

The Rig Veda. Translation Doniger O' Flaherty, Penguin Books, London, 1981

The Rig Veda. Translation Griffith, Book of the Month Club, NY, 1992

Roaf, Michael: *Weltatlas der alten Kulturen. Mesopotamien.* Christian Verlag, München, 1991 (*Cultural Atlas of Mesopotamia and the Ancient Near East.*)

Robinet, Isabelle: *Taoism. Growth of a Religion.* Stanford University Press, Stanford, 1997

Römer, Willem: *Sumerische Königshymnen der Isin Zeit*, Brill, Leiden, 1965

Rohde, Erwin: *Psyche: Seelenkult und Unsterblichkeitsglaube der Griechen.* Cambridge University Press, 2010

Roth, Gerhard: *Aus der Sicht des Gehirns*, Suhrkamp Verlag, Frankfurt / M. 2003

Roth, Harold D.: *Original Tao, Inward Training (Nei-yeh) and the Foundations of Taoist Mysticism*; Columbia University Press, New York, 1999

Sappho: *The Complete Poems of Sappho*, trans. Barnstone, W. Shambala, Boston, 2006

Saso, Michael: *The Teachings of Taoist Master Chuang.* Yale University Press, New Haven, 1978

Saso, Michael: *The Gold Pavilion, Taoist Ways to Peace, Healing and Long Life*, Charles E. Tuttle, Boston, 1995

Sasson, Jack (ed.): *Studies in Literature from the Ancient Near East, by Members of the American Oriental Society, Dedicated to Samuel Noah Kramer.* Journal of the American Oriental Society, vol. 103 /1, January-March 1983. Note contributions by Brinkman, Civil, Cooper, Heimpel, Diakonoff, Eichler, Falkowitz, Güterbock, Hallo, Shaffer and others.

Schmidt, Klaus: *Sie bauten die ersten Tempel. Das rätselhafte Heiligtum der Steinzeitjäger.* C.H.Beck Verlag, München, 2006

Schmitz, Andrea: *Die Erzählung von Egide: Gehalt, Genese und Wirkung einer heroischen Tradition.* Turcologica 27, Harrassowitz, Wiesbaden, 1996

Schoblies, Hans: *Ein verschollenes Beschwörungsrelief.* Archiv für Orientforschung, (AfO), Vol. III, 1926

Scholem, Gershom: *Kabbala und Symbolik.* Rhein Verlag, Zürich 1960

Scholem, Gershom: *Ursprünge und Anfänge der Kabbala,* de Gryter, Berlin, 2001

Schrader, Abel, Bezold, Jensen, Peiser & Winckler: *Keilschriftliche Bibliothek.* Reuther & Reichard Verlag, Berlin, 1896

Schramm, Wolfgang: *Ein Compendium sumerisch-akkadischer Beschwörungen.* Universitätsverlag Göttingen, 2008

Schwemer, Daniel: Auf Reisen mit Lamaštu. *Zum Ritualmemorandum K 888 und seinen Parallelen aus Assur.* BaM 37, 2006

Schwemer, Daniel & Abusch, Tzvi: *Studien zum Schadenzauberglauben im Alten Mesopotamien.* Harrassowitz, Wiesbaden, 2007

Scurlock, Jo Ann & Andersen, Burton R.: *Diagnoses in Assyrian and Babylonian Medicine: Ancient Sources, Translations and Modern Medicine Analysis.* University of Illinois Press, 2005

SEAL Sources of Akkadian Literature. A wonderful page full of state-of-the art cuneiform texts and translations.

The Sepher Ha-Zohar, or, The Book of Light: Bereshith to Lekh Lekha. Trans. de Manar, Nurho, Library of Alexandria, no year.

Shan Hai Ching. Legendary Geography and Wonders in Ancient China. Trans. Cheng, Hsiao-Chieh; Pai Hui-Chen Cheng & Thern, Kenneth Lawrence, National Institute for Compilation and Translation, Taipei, 1985

Shanhaijing. The Classic of Mountains and Seas. Trans. Birrell, Anne, Penguin, London, 1999

Shaw, Miranda: *Passionate Enlightenment. Women in Tantric Buddhism*, Princeton University Press, New Jersey, 1994

Shaw, Mirinda: *Buddhist Goddesses of India.* Munshiram Manoharlal Publishers, 2007

Shehata, Dahlia; Weiershäuser, Franke; Zand, Kamran V: *Von Göttern und Menschen. Beitrag zu Literatur und Geschichte des Alten Orients. Festschrift für Brigitte Groneberg.* Brill, Leiden, 2010

Sieg, Hilde: *Baum und Strauch, dir ewig heilverbunden.* Rowohlt Verlag, Stuttgart, 1939

The Śiva Saṁhita, trans. Vasu, Rai Bahadur Srisa Chandra, Oriental Books Reprint Corporation, New Delhi, 1975 (1914-1915)

Smith, George: *History of Assurbanipal, Translated from the Cuneiform Inscriptions.* Williams and Norgate, London, 1871

Snellgrove, David: *Indo-Tibetan Buddhism. Indian Buddhists and their Tibetan Successors.* Revised edition. Orchid Press, Bangkok, 2004

Soden, W. v. & Falkenstein, A.: *Sumerische und Akkadische Hymnen und Gebete.* (SAHG) Artemis Verlag, Zürich, 1953.

Soden, W. v.: *The Ancient Orient. An Introduction to the Study of the Ancient Near East.* Wm. B. Eerdmans publishing, Grand Rapids, 1994

Spitzer, Manfred: *Lernen. Gehirnforschung und die Schule des Lebens.* Spektrum Akademischer Verlag, Heidelberg, 2006

Spitzer, Manfred: *Cyberkrank! Wie das digitale Leben unsere Gesundheit ruiniert.* Droemer Verlag, München, 2015

Der Sohar: das heilige Buch der Kabbala. Trans. Müller, Karl, Marix Verlag, Wiesbaden, 1982.

Stein, Anja: *Umgang mit Krankheiten in fremden Kulturen und der Einfluss kultureller Aspekte auf die gesundheitliche Situation und Betreuung von Migranten.* Diplom.de, 2004

Steinert, Ulrike: *Aspekte des Menschseins im Alten Mesopotamien. Eine Studie zu Person und Identität im 2. & 1. Jt. v. Ch..* Styx, Brill, 2012

Stern, Horst (ed.): *Rettet den Wald.* Kindler Verlag, München, 1980

Stol, Martin: *Epilepsy in Babylonia.* Cuneiform Monographs II, Styx, Groningen, 1993

Stol, Marten: *Birth in Babylonia and the Bible*, Styx, Groningen, 2000

Strabo: *Geographica.* Trans. Forbiger, A., Marix Verlag, Wiesbaden, 2005

Strack, H. & Billerbeck, P.: *Kommentar zum Neuen Testament aus Talmud & Midrasch.* Vol. 4, C.H. Beck Verlag, München, 1997

Strack, H. & Billerbeck, P.: Exkurse zu einzelnen Stellen des Alten Testaments. Vol. 4, C.H. Beck Verlag, München, 1997

Strasburger, Lehrbuch der Botanik, 35. Auflage, Spektrum akademischer Verlag, Heidelberg, 2002

Strommenger, E. & Hirmer, M.: *Fünf Jahrtausende Mesopotamien. Die Kunst von den Anfängen um 5000 v. Chr. bis zu Alexander dem Großen.* Hirmer Verlag, München, 1962

Sumer, Assur, Babylon. 7000 Jahre Kunst und Kultur zwischen Euphrat und Tigris. Roemer und Pelizaeus Museum, Hildesheim, Phillip von Zabern Verlag, München, 1978

Swaab, Dick: *Wir sind unser Gehirn. Wie wir denken, leiden, lieben.* Knaur Taschenbuch, München, 2013

Tafel, G; Osiander, C; Schwab, G.: *Griechische Prosaiker.* Metzlersche Buchhandlung, Stuttgart, 1828

Taggar-Cohen, Ada: *Hittite Priesthood.* Universitätsverlag Winter, Heidelberg, 2006

Tammet, Daniel: *Born on a Blue Day. A Memory of Asperger's and an Extraordinary Mind.* Hodder & Stoughton, London, 2006

Thompson, Reginald Campbell: *Devils and Evil Spirits of Babylonia, Being Babylonian and Assyrian Incantations against the Demons, Ghouls, Vampires, Hobgoblins, Ghosts, and Kindred Evil Spirits, which Attack Mankind.* London, two volumes 1903 & 1904, reprinted in one volume by Kessinger Publishings

Thompson, Reginald Campbell: *Semitic Magic. Its Origin and Development.* Elibron Classics, 2005

Thureau-Dangin, F.: *Rituel et Amulettes contre Labartu.* RA, vol. XVIII

Tibbs, Clint: *Religious Experience of the Pneuma: Communication with the Spirit World.* Mohr Siebeck, Tübingen 2007

Tourtet, Francelin: *Demons at Home* in Kühne 2008.

Tubb, Jonathan N.: *Völker im Lande Kanaan*, Theiss Verlag, Stuttgart, 2005 (*Peoples of the Past – Canaanites*)

Ungnad, Arthur: *Die Religionen der Babylonier und Assyrer.* Eugen Diederichs Verlag, Jena, 1921

Uruk. 5000 Jahre Megacity. Begleitband zur Ausstellung im Pergamonmuseum- Staatliche Museen Berlin. Michael Imhof Verlag, 2013

Vermaak, Fanie: *A New Interpretation of the Playing Objects in the Gilgamesh Epic.* In: Journal of Semitics, 20/1, 2011, www.academica.edu

Vijñāna Bhairava Tantra, Das Tantra der Befreiung, trans. Keyserling, Wilhelmine, Verlag Bruno Martin, Südergellersen, 1994

Vijñāna Bhairava. Das göttliche Bewusstsein. Trans. & ed. Bäumer, Bettina, Verlag der Weltreligionen im Fischer Verlag, Frankfurt, 2008

Das Vorderasiatische Museum Berlin. von Zabern Verlag, Mainz, 1992

Wallis Budge, Sir E. A.: *Amulets and Superstitions.* Dover Publications, New York, 1978

Wasserman, Nathan: translations on the SEAL Sources of Early Akkadian literature page online.

Weber, Otto; *Die Literatur der Babylonier und Assyrer: ein Überblick*, vol. 2, Hinrichs Verlag, 1907

Wei Boyang: *Cantong Qi. The Secret of Everlasting Life.* Transl. R.Bertschinger, Element, Shaftesbury, 1994

Weidner, Ernst: *Altbabylonische Götterlisten.* Archiv für Orientforschung, (AfO), Vol. II, 1924-1925

Weidner, Ernst: *Der Tierkreis und die Wege am Himmel.* Archiv für Orientforschung, (AfO), Vol. VII, 1931-1932

West, D.R.: *Hekate, Lamashtu and Klbt ílm.* Ugarit Forschungen, vol.24, 1992

Westenholt, Joan: *Legends of the Kings of Akkade*, Eisenbrauns, Winona Lake, 1977

White, David Gordon: *The Alchemical Body. Siddha Traditions in Medieval India.* University of Chicago Press, 1996

White, David Gordon: *Tantra in Practice.* Princeton University Press, Princeton, 2000

White, David Gordon: *Kiss of the Yoginī. "Tantric Sex in its South Asian Contexts".* University of Chicago Press, 2003

White, David Gordon: *Sinister Yogis.* University of Chicago Press, 2011

Whittaker, Gordon*: Calendar and Script in Protohistoric China and Mesoamerica. A comparative Study of Day Names and Their Signs.* Holos Verlag, Bonn, 1991

Wiggermann, Frans A.M.: *Mesopotamian Protective Spirits: The Ritual Texts.* Styx, Groningen, 1992

Wiggermann, Frans A.M. in:

Marten Stol: *Birth in Babylonia and the Bible*, Styx, Groningen, 2000

Wiggermann, Frans A.M: *Dogs, Pigs, Lamaštu, and the Breast-Feeding of Animals by Women.* In: Festschrift für Brigitte Groneberg, Brill, Leiden, 2010

Wiggermann, Frans A.M.: *Dogs, Pigs, Lamaštu, and the Breast Feeding of Animals by Women.* In: Shehata, Weiershäuser & Zand 2010

Wilcke, C, in ZA 75, 1985

Wilkinson, Toby: *The Rise and Fall of Ancient Egypt. The History of Civilisation from 3000 BC to Cleopatra.* Bloomsbury, London, 2010

Wiseman, D.J.: *Götter und Menschen im Rollsiegel Westasiens.* Artia Verlag, Prague, 1958

Wisnewski, Gerhard: *'Plötzlicher Kindestod: der heimliche Mord'* in *Ungeklärt, Unheimlich, Unfassbar.* Knaur Verlag, München, 2014

Wong, Eva: *Teachings of the Tao.* (trans. & ed.), Shambala Books, Boston, 1997

Worthington, Martin: *Teach Yourself Babylonian.* Hachette UK, London, 2010

York, William H.J.: *Health and Wellness in Antiquity through the Middle Ages.* Greenwood, ABC-CLIO, LLC, Santa Barbara, 2012

Yü, Chün-Fang: *Kuan-yin. The Chinese Transformation of Avalokiteśvara.* Columbia University Press, New York, 2001

The Zohar, ed. & trans. Daniel C. Matt, Stanford University Press, 2004

Zwemer, Samuel: *Influence of Animism on Islam.* Kessinger Publications, 1920

Index

A

Abgal ... 323
Abhinavagupta ... 447, 450, 461, 557, 563
Abiešuḫ ... 81
Abusch, Tzvi ... 212, 255, 281, 557, 558, 559, 560, 564
Abzu ... 67, 107, 117, 152, 157, 175, 176, 194, 196, 203, 236, 237, 238, 309, 317, 535, 538, 539, 540, 545, 553
Adab ... 75, 77, 532, 537, 540, 545, 551, 555
Adad 49, 63, 69, 102, 117, 152, 211, 242, 290, 303, 316, 322, 323, 324, 326, 390, 533, 534, 535, 544, 551, 553
Adadnirari II ... 85, 87
Adadnirari III ... 87
Adam ... 97, 98, 187, 348, 362, 383, 385, 386, 387, 389, 390, 391, 392, 393, 394, 395, 397, 398, 399, 402, 423, 525, 557
Adapa ... 67, 212, 214, 236, 318, 542
Adgarudu ... 226
AfO ... *See* Archiv für Orientforschung
Agade ... 74, 148, 532
Agni ... 426, 427, 428, 429, 431, 439, 460, 499, 500
Aḫḫazu ... 215, 265, 267, 273, 301, 303, 364, 368, 383
Aka ... 32, 152
Akkad ... 30, 59, 66, 74, 76, 78, 79, 81, 84, 96, 124, 152, 157, 161, 208, 349, 422, 532, 534, 538, 543, 545, 547, 548, 553
Akkil ... 532
Āl 8, 93, 420, 422, 423, 424, 425, 557
Albasti ... 8, 93, 420, 421, 422, 423, 424, 425, 557
alehouse ... 202
Alexander ... 51, 59, 84, 90, 211, 248, 376, 433, 555, 565
Aliat ... 357
Alkarasi ... 422
Allat ... 357
Allatu(m) ... 357
Almasti ... 93, 422
Alphabet of Ben Sira ... 187, 391, 394
Alû ... 5, 233, 268, 474
Amakandu ... 201, 316
Amarsuen ... 77, 541
Amaušumgalanna ... 42, 45, 46, 55, 102, 161, 179, 198, 264, 537, 546
Amurru ... 78, 117, 149, 224, 226, 286
An 35, 36, 49, 50, 52, 54, 55, 60, 69, 71, 72, 75, 78, 114, 116, 117, 120, 141, 142, 144, 150, 151, 164, 171, 173, 174, 175, 177, 178, 183, 187, 188, 196, 198, 217, 219, 220, 224, 231, 250, 253, 264, 267, 270, 273, 292, 315, 316, 317, 360, 364, 472, 474, 475, 536, 540, 543, 546, 550, 555
Ananikian, Mardios ... 422, 557
Anat ... 351, 377, 387, 554
Andersen, Burton R. ... 210, 232, 236, 243, 293, 303, 304, 367, 369, 370, 564
ANET ... 6, 46, 51, 59, 121, 143, 255, 275, 278, 280, 358, 371, 563
Anšan ... 181, 532
Antu(m) ... 52, 54, 55, 75, 107, 116, 120, 150, 151, 153, 157, 164, 187, 192, 199, 202, 207, 209, 219, 230, 238, 278, 282, 475, 533, 543, 553
Anu ... 7, 35, 36, 54, 60, 78, 80, 90, 106, 107, 114, 116, 118, 121, 134, 143, 144, 148, 150, 151, 156, 157, 159, 164, 171, 173, 174, 175, 177, 178, 180, 183, 186, 187, 188, 192, 196, 198, 199, 202, 203, 204, 212, 214, 215, 217, 219, 220, 224, 226, 227, 228, 230, 231, 233, 234, 236, 238, 239, 240, 241, 242, 244, 245, 248, 250, 252, 261, 263, 264, 267, 271, 273, 274, 277, 278, 279, 282, 284, 285, 299, 300, 315, 316, 322, 324, 325, 327, 334, 364, 472, 474, 483, 497, 498, 533, 534, 536, 540, 546, 555
Anunitu(m) ... 152, 153, 209, 317
Anunnaki ... 153, 164, 266, 315, 498
Anzû ... 186, 192, 360
Aphrodite ... 239, 329, 357, 458, 560
Apkallu ... 66, 212, 323
Apollonius of Tyana ... 328, 403, 563
Aprušu ... 156, 164
Apsû .. 107, 117, 153, 155, 171, 176, 192, 194, 196, 238, 274, 275, 308, 309, 317, 538, 539, 540, 541
Arakelova, Victoria ... 423, 424, 425, 557
Arali ... 532
Aratta ... 152, 181, 532, 545, 547
Archiv für Orientforschung 343, 558, 559, 562, 563, 564, 565, 566
Ardat Lilî ... 93, 187, 188, 267, 274, 280, 285, 301, 337, 345, 360, 363, 364, 366, 368, 369, 387, 388, 398, 436
Aristophanes ... 402
Aristotle ... 106, 141, 211, 239, 361
Arsay ... 357
Arslan Tash ... 8, 371, 373
Aruru ... 55, 238, 239, 242, 545, 551, 553
Asag ... 474
Asakku ... 5, 92, 174, 219, 226, 233, 234, 235, 262, 474
Asarḫaddon ... 27, 36, 88, 147, 149, 208, 255
Asarluḫi ... 121, 152, 171, 173, 176, 177, 178, 179, 199, 209, 210, 215, 244, 245, 259, 260, 271, 274, 277, 284, 291, 297, 309, 324, 533, 545, 548
Ašerah ... 351, 352, 384, 554
Ašgi ... 304, 545, 555
ashes . 104, 155, 179, 224, 266, 281, 293, 307, 326, 495, 500, 502
Ashmedai ... 394
Āšipu ... 532
Ašnan ... 172, 201, 542
Ašratum ... 226
Assante, Julia ... 243, 557
Assinu ... 533
Aššur ... 54, 79, 82, 85, 94, 101, 102, 106, 124, 149, 177, 202, 205, 206, 208, 210, 238, 242, 246, 247, 250, 297, 326, 343, 372, 520, 533, 540, 544, 551, 552, 554
Aššurbanipal ... 36, 54, 58, 88, 89, 92, 93, 94, 97, 98, 100, 101, 106, 121, 142, 145, 167, 180, 182, 198, 205, 208, 210, 229, 231, 246, 273, 278, 280, 281, 282, 290, 291, 324, 520, 544, 551
Aššurbēlkala ... 85
Aššurdan I ... 83, 85
Aššurdan II ... 85
Aššurnasirpal ... 86, 94, 149
Aššurrešiši ... 85

Aštammu ... 532
Astarte ... 351, 352, 554
Asû ... 533
Atharva Veda ... 293, 434
Athena ... 149, 361, 410, 411, 412
Atraḫasis ... 158, 166, 189, 243, 527
Avalokiteśvara ... 439, 445, 566
Aya ... 52, 63, 148, 149, 160, 316, 547, 553

B

Baal ... 316, 351, 352
Baba. 45, 49, 52, 53, 60, 72, 75, 117, 144, 148, 157, 161, 174, 178, 221, 224, 271, 291, 297, 324, 350, 377, 537, 538, 542, 546, 547, 551, 552
Babylon 27, 30, 59, 78, 79, 80, 81, 83, 84, 85, 87, 89, 95, 101, 148, 152, 153, 169, 171, 173, 177, 181, 202, 205, 231, 240, 243, 244, 253, 289, 325, 326, 327, 343, 350, 355, 407, 520, 534, 537, 540, 541, 545, 546, 554, 557, 558, 565
Babylonia . 78, 79, 81, 82, 83, 84, 85, 87, 89, 90, 98, 159, 163, 165, 177, 182, 202, 217, 237, 242, 328, 334, 348, 349, 359, 360, 364, 370, 390, 422, 532, 534, 552, 553, 555, 559, 565, 566
Babylonian Theodicy ... 105, 109, 298
Bacher, Sven ... 228, 562
Bächtold-Stäubli, Hanns ... 422, 557
bacteria ... 11, 103, 194, 493, 496, 508, 510, 516, 518, 519
bacterial sex ... 518
baker ... 212, 224, 252, 323
Bandler, Richard ... 101, 461, 482, 557
Baopuzi ... 307
bārû ... 61, 166, 298, 299, 547, 548
Bārû ... 211, 229
Bau... 45, 49, 52, 53, 60, 72, 75, 117, 144, 148, 157, 161, 174, 177, 178, 221, 224, 271, 291, 297, 324, 350, 377, 537, 538, 542, 546, 552
beads ... 119, 146, 192, 255, 257, 381, 479, 548
Beck, Henning ... 490, 557
beech ... 104, 496, 511, 512
beer . 11, 46, 60, 159, 160, 173, 178, 179, 202, 203, 204, 230, 231, 274, 278, 293, 294, 323, 357, 359, 480, 504, 525, 540, 542, 552, 554
Beierkuhnlein, Carl ... 228, 562
Bēl 59, 116, 151, 208, 218, 275, 325, 326, 352, 377, 381, 402, 520
Bēlet .. 116, 153, 172, 173, 176, 194, 208, 231, 247, 274, 282, 284, 381, 520, 551
Bēlet-ilî ... 116, 153, 172, 173
Bellér-Hahn, Ildikó ... 425, 557
Ben-Barak, Idan ... 497, 557
Bereshith Rabba ... 187, 392
Bergmann, Claudia ... 557
Bibbu ... 119
Bibītu ... 364
bitumen ... 27, 28, 31, 74, 119, 154, 155, 156, 183, 215, 218, 261, 278, 290, 293, 343, 349, 350, 370
Black, Jeremy ... 98, 557
Blacker, Carmen ... 499, 557
Black-Koltuv, Barbara ... 557
bliss ... 94, 105, 218, 307, 367, 412, 447, 449, 455, 456, 460, 461, 479, 524
blood ..21, 74, 86, 94, 100, 105, 142, 145, 148, 154, 155, 165, 179, 190, 191, 192, 199, 228, 239, 243, 250, 255, 271, 274, 276, 294, 295, 303, 307, 325, 341, 357, 370, 391, 396, 399, 401, 403, 413, 420, 421, 423, 424, 425, 426, 428, 430, 432, 433, 440, 450, 452, 457, 459, 483, 489, 491, 495, 506, 527
Bonnet, Hans ... 351, 400, 557
Borsippa ... 79, 92, 177, 205, 231, 534, 541, 545, 551
Bosch, Carl ... 505
Bottéro, Jean ... 54, 55, 56, 109, 121, 148, 219, 315, 557
Brahmā ... 426, 431, 439
Brahman ... 172, 330, 433, 436, 442, 450, 453, 454, 525
Brandl, Roland ... 228, 562
bread 60, 77, 93, 154, 155, 158, 162, 164, 173, 199, 202, 204, 212, 224, 265, 266, 274, 278, 282, 284, 323, 360, 423, 495, 542, 546
bristle ... 146, 159, 231, 257, 349
brothel ... 221, 323, 532, 540, 544, 552
Buddha 94, 418, 420, 438, 439, 440, 442, 444, 445, 446, 448, 450, 452, 453, 454, 455, 458, 460, 461, 478, 499, 500, 525
Buhner, Stephen ... 495, 511, 513, 558
bull ...34, 50, 69, 110, 116, 124, 146, 157, 158, 233, 235, 323, 330, 335, 337, 344, 358, 413, 432
Buren, Douglas van ... 343, 344, 363, 558
Burkert, Walter ... 93, 155, 239, 279, 407, 558
Burney Relief, the ... 342, 559
Butterweck ... 372, 375, 558

C

Cahill, Suzanne E. ... 418, 558
camels ... 11, 86, 88, 232, 434
Cantong Qi ... 565
castration ... 157
Cathars ... 385, 394
cedar 21, 46, 62, 72, 92, 120, 122, 124, 154, 155, 198, 201, 229, 284, 293, 363
centipede ... 107, 125, 232, 257, 482, 509
Chamovitz, Daniel ... 510, 558
Chaplet ... 479
Chavalas, Mark W. 36, 69, 76, 77, 99, 124, 221, 317, 323, 558
Chinnamastā ... 491
Chrysaor ... 407, 412, 413
Chuci ... 149
clay ... 22, 23, 32, 33, 35, 46, 68, 93, 99, 108, 114, 133, 143, 146, 148, 154, 160, 162, 163, 179, 182, 189, 193, 204, 224, 226, 228, 229, 237, 238, 239, 243, 252, 255, 265, 266, 272, 277, 284, 293, 310, 313, 317, 349, 527, 549
cloak-fringe ... 154, 192, 193
cloisters ... 63, 95, 242
Cohen, Mark ... 98, 213, 385, 558, 565
comb ... 11, 130, 136, 161, 162, 192, 200, 229, 231, 248, 255, 266, 405
compendium ... 273
Confucius ... 419, 483, 522, 558
Conjuration of Eridu ... 177, 274, 308, 309
Conjurer ... 8, 284, 298
constellation 23, 150, 151, 152, 159, 171, 176, 178, 179, 203, 211, 231, 244, 250, 252, 253, 279, 326, 357
contamination ... 62, 304, 391

copper......68, 75, 93, 147, 181, 193, 194, 237, 278, 285, 294, 301, 535, 548
Cordovero, Moses 385, 395
Corona Borealis 231
cow 34, 110, 119, 157, 158, 173, 217, 276, 308, 357, 419, 430, 439, 501, 516, 518
cress.. 62, 121, 214, 261, 288, 295
Crickmore, Leon..334, 558
Crowley, Aleister........................... 42, 43, 331, 470, 480, 521
cup-bearer 74, 159, 404, 552
Cutha 534, 546
Cyaxares...89, 533
Cyrus 90, 231

D

Dagan...149, 548
Dalai Lama 445, 446, 453
Damgalnunna 172, 203, 539
Damkina..172, 203, 535
Damu 42, 45, 179, 250, 253, 274, 541
Dao 307, 417, 478, 483
Daodejing 524, 562
Daoism....10, 57, 189, 305, 306, 308, 418, 424, 449, 455, 502
dates 34, 71, 90, 161, 171, 213, 224, 233, 278, 293, 349, 351, 395, 468, 535, 539
Datev, Gregory of 422
de Leon, Moses..386
deer 26, 103, 171, 201, 215, 421, 509, 515
determinative 35, 166, 202, 272, 281, 332, 364, 546
Devas 423, 425
Devī-Māhātmyam 558, 560
dew 159, 210, 211, 502
Dharma 431, 448, 454, 455, 456, 458
Dīkṣa 499
Dilbat 79, 303, 378, 550
Dilmun 66, 172, 200, 534, 548
Dim.me 274
Dimītu 265, 274
Dingir 114, 143, 172, 180, 472, 547
diviner..........61, 211, 229, 253, 289, 290, 415, 532, 534, 548
doctor 179, 288, 290, 292, 293, 296, 300, 326, 497, 533
dog... 11, 73, 88, 121, 128, 144, 145, 146, 154, 164, 178, 183, 191, 224, 226, 227, 231, 244, 248, 250, 252, 253, 255, 261, 265, 277, 278, 284, 288, 303, 304, 325, 361, 396, 424, 425, 464, 501, 505
donkey.81, 118, 125, 134, 138, 139, 144, 157, 158, 162, 164, 199, 204, 213, 214, 215, 231, 232, 237, 244, 248, 257, 261, 294, 305, 402, 406, 407, 413, 425, 458, 490
dove 142, 143, 185
dragon 101, 106, 110, 122, 137, 153, 173, 175, 176, 248, 250, 254, 276, 279, 297, 322, 323, 362, 399, 412, 415, 416, 418, 419, 502, 503, 536, 540, 546
dream .. 15, 22, 25, 74, 99, 179, 200, 210, 228, 229, 289, 303, 341, 345, 364, 381, 382, 398, 402, 417, 421, 430, 449, 470, 472, 503, 505, 538, 542, 553
Duku 153, 178, 535
Dumuzi. 40, 42, 45, 48, 69, 145, 148, 157, 162, 179, 198, 201, 218, 238, 264, 267, 271, 323, 532, 534, 537, 538, 540, 543, 544
Dunnu 201, 276, 535
Dur-Šarrukin 87, 535
dust ..23, 26, 75, 102, 155, 190, 200, 207, 220, 221, 224, 227, 230, 248, 252, 261, 317, 322, 323, 425, 428, 483
dying gods 40, 42

E

Ea 21, 28, 54, 57, 58, 65, 69, 92, 107, 114, 116, 121, 142, 144, 152, 171, 173, 175, 177, 178, 179, 192, 194, 196, 202, 203, 209, 212, 214, 219, 220, 224, 228, 234, 237, 238, 244, 245, 250, 251, 254, 265, 267, 271, 274, 281, 284, 285, 297, 305, 309, 311, 315, 316, 324, 325, 327, 330, 334, 354, 359, 377, 402, 533, 535, 536, 539, 540, 541, 542, 546, 548, 555
eagle.......... 110, 183, 186, 188, 191, 276, 340, 344, 345, 362
Ealmaš 208
Eanatum 72, 144
Eanna 36, 60, 180, 326, 555
Ebabar 547
Ebeling, E......................................69, 96, 153, 160, 558, 563
Ebiḫ 207, 536, 546
Ebla 152, 171, 175, 534, 542, 552, 561
Eddas.. 362, 422
Eden 23, 107, 162, 390, 394
Edom 8, 370, 371, 394
Egypt 29, 37, 40, 66, 82, 83, 84, 88, 89, 93, 96, 147, 178, 210, 291, 351, 361, 384, 388, 395, 396, 520, 549, 554, 566
Ekišnugal 173, 555
Ekur 25, 72, 171, 177, 178, 179, 275, 291, 316, 324, 326, 498, 535, 550, 551
Elam ...25, 27, 38, 66, 75, 80, 87, 89, 121, 124, 145, 171, 180, 181, 182, 210, 217, 237, 357, 358, 520, 532, 546, 551, 553
Elamite 25, 27, 89, 181, 182, 237, 252, 260, 553
Ellamesi 201
Ellil.69, 116, 151, 153, 164, 171, 173, 220, 228, 250, 271, 534
Elohim 352, 386
elves 421
Emesal...54, 242, 296, 299, 541
En 214, 260, 537, 538
Enanatum 72
Engur 196, 538
Enḫeduanna 36, 74, 76, 95, 102, 141, 148, 152, 157, 173, 175, 207, 218, 236, 270, 280, 536, 538, 539, 540, 542, 543, 545, 546, 550, 555, 556
Enki. 20, 21, 28, 49, 52, 54, 55, 57, 58, 65, 66, 69, 71, 72, 107, 114, 116, 118, 121, 142, 144, 151, 152, 154, 157, 159, 162, 171, 173, 175, 176, 177, 178, 179, 186, 192, 194, 196, 197, 202, 203, 208, 209, 212, 219, 220, 224, 228, 236, 250, 251, 254, 264, 267, 270, 271, 274, 275, 277, 297, 305, 308, 309, 311, 315, 316, 317, 324, 330, 349, 354, 357, 359, 364, 377, 402, 483, 533, 534, 535, 536, 538, 539, 540, 541, 542, 545, 546, 555
Enkidu 119, 121, 124, 143, 186, 197, 217, 238, 264, 276, 344, 345, 349, 358, 362, 407, 503, 533
Enlil... 25, 33, 48, 49, 52, 54, 55, 61, 69, 71, 72, 74, 76, 78, 80, 94, 102, 105, 116, 118, 121, 122, 124, 142, 144, 148, 150, 151, 152, 153, 157, 158, 162, 163, 164, 171, 173, 174, 175, 177, 178, 179, 181, 186, 188, 192, 196, 197, 198, 203, 205, 210, 218, 220, 226, 228, 229, 230, 234, 235, 238, 250, 264, 271, 276, 277, 291, 299, 303, 315, 316, 317, 324, 325, 326, 327, 334, 360, 363, 364, 407, 483,

498, 520, 533, 534, 535, 537, 538, 539, 541, 543, 545, 546, 550, 551, 552, 555, 556
Enmebaragesi 152, 181
Enmekar 532
Enmetena 72
Ensi 538
Entu(m) 537, 538
Enûma Eliš 6, 84, 109, 114, 147, 153, 217, 226, 238, 239, 308, 316, 521, 527
Ereš 77, 538, 539, 554
Ereškigal . 8, 117, 118, 143, 145, 151, 163, 164, 192, 203, 209, 218, 221, 235, 237, 252, 265, 344, 353, 357, 358, 359, 360, 365, 493, 496, 533, 538, 542, 546, 553
Erickson, Milton H. 260, 470
Eridu 8, 30, 46, 54, 69, 72, 121, 164, 171, 176, 177, 178, 181, 194, 203, 212, 213, 215, 298, 308, 309, 310, 311, 535, 536, 539, 541, 542, 545, 547, 550, 555
Erinyes 407
Erlbeck, Haseder 511, 558
Erra 55, 94, 117, 122, 163, 211, 226, 276, 317, 357, 367
Erṣetu(m) 116, 164, 267
Eru 153
êru 58, 93, 119, 220, 264, 267
Êru 264
Erua .... *See* Eru
Ešagepada 77
Esagila 59, 153, 231, 534
Ešnunna 24, 44, 68, 80, 252, 278, 280, 540
eššebati .... *See* eššeb
Etana 362
ETCSL 272, 359, 360, 559
Eumenids 407
Euphrates 11, 22, 27, 28, 65, 66, 74, 80, 90, 119, 159, 165, 166, 171, 176, 177, 200, 217, 235, 237, 252, 275, 291, 305, 308, 309, 360, 376, 539, 541, 548, 550, 553, 555
Evans-Wentz, W.Y. 308, 559
Eve 187, 375, 383, 387, 389, 390, 391, 392, 394, 395, 423, 525
Evil Seven 92, 117, 118, 122, 145, 151, 153, 192, 303, 317, 322
Exorcist 167, 547

F

Falkenstein, Adam . 6, 34, 48, 97, 98, 100, 142, 180, 183, 187, 189, 190, 191, 219, 232, 237, 270, 275, 291, 298, 559, 564
Fāra 52, 54, 152, 171, 175, 177, 202, 270, 552, 553
Farber, Walter ... 61, 97, 98, 99, 100, 106, 121, 132, 137, 139, 140, 141, 144, 145, 146, 157, 158, 159, 160, 161, 164, 165, 167, 170, 178, 183, 186, 187, 188, 189, 190, 191, 192, 194, 196, 197, 198, 199, 201, 202, 207, 209, 212, 213, 215, 219, 220, 221, 226, 227, 229, 230, 233, 234, 236, 240, 241, 244, 248, 253, 255, 257, 258, 260, 267, 272, 275, 301, 302, 347, 559, 563
fertiliser 27, 221, 495, 496, 527
fever .. 102, 105, 106, 119, 153, 156, 170, 189, 191, 209, 234, 246, 291, 292, 299, 300, 301, 302, 303, 309, 370, 381, 422, 432, 433, 496, 510
fibula 191, 200
figurine 15, 16, 41, 47, 153, 154, 160, 161, 180, 185, 228, 229, 255, 265, 272, 273, 277, 310, 323
fir 104, 293, 511
fish .. 25, 66, 140, 142, 145, 147, 155, 156, 171, 173, 176, 194, 203, 212, 213, 214, 215, 217, 261, 308, 323, 345, 359, 452, 490, 506, 535, 539, 542
flood 22, 27, 28, 29, 48, 57, 67, 69, 70, 88, 102, 105, 166, 234, 235, 275, 290, 303, 305, 311, 316, 317, 325, 474, 480, 489, 501, 503, 504, 506, 524, 545, 553
flour 26, 145, 154, 156, 160, 163, 164, 175, 177, 180, 202, 204, 213, 217, 218, 229, 236, 243, 261, 264, 265, 266, 274, 278, 317, 468
Foster, Benjamin R. 98, 105, 106, 109, 120, 121, 146, 191, 192, 217, 229, 241, 253, 367, 369, 559
Frank, Carl 179, 183, 236, 317, 322, 331, 345, 346, 559
Frankfort, H 344, 345, 348, 385, 559
Frazer, Sir James 39, 40, 42, 43, 45, 48, 559
Freud, Sigmund 42, 289, 290, 486
Frey-Anthes, Henrike 187, 350, 364, 368, 370, 559
Fries, Jan 3, 4, 103, 113, 217, 279, 419, 461, 465, 482, 559
fungi 26, 103, 104, 110, 221, 481, 493, 495, 496, 505, 510, 511, 515, 518

G

Gabašku 97, 272
Gaeš 157, 173, 541
gala 64, 118, 267, 296, 533, 541, 550
gallû 29, 92, 117, 118, 144, 146, 193, 209, 261, 266, 267, 271, 285, 322, 324, 368, 400
game 16, 26, 56, 361, 362, 363, 432, 470, 506, 521, 527
Gan Bao 501, 503, 559
Gandharva 430
Garuḍa 362, 427
Gatumdug 117, 148, 542, 546
Gaurī 446
Gazbaba .... *See* Gazbaja
Gazbaja 231
Ge Hong 307, 502, 559
Gelugpas 444
ghost . 105, 106, 210, 233, 234, 236, 237, 265, 281, 284, 285, 289, 294, 301, 303, 304, 362, 369, 382, 383, 400, 403, 419, 420, 424, 474, 498
Gibil 117, 119, 163, 177, 202, 211, 213, 282, 290, 316, 497
Gilgameš 32, 35, 42, 46, 121, 124, 143, 148, 157, 180, 181, 186, 197, 217, 226, 248, 250, 264, 284, 285, 345, 349, 358, 359, 360, 362, 363, 407, 503, 520, 533, 536, 543, 554
Gilgamesh .... *See* Gilgameš
Gipar 541
Girima 176
Girra .. 119, 163, 177, 212, 213, 284, 285, 290, 324, 497, 498, 546
Girsu 60, 70, 77, 178, 535, 537, 538, 541, 546, 551, 554
Gleick, Gwendolyn 220, 367, 559
glial cells 483, 484, 487, 489, 490
God Numbers 8, 315
Gonda, Jan 110, 559
Gorgon 407, 412, 413, 415
Grabherr, Georg 228, 562
Green, Anthony 557
Gressmann, Hugo 69, 560
Grinder, John 100

Groneberg, Brigitte 124, 148, 153, 203, 255, 350, 560, 564, 566
Groot, J.J.M., de 419, 420, 560
Grunfeld, A. Tom 445, 560
gTummo 501
Guabba 60, 542
Gudea 53, 60, 75, 148, 155, 157, 174, 200, 219, 264, 270, 323, 330, 331, 540, 542, 546
Gugalanna 157, 357, 358
Guimu 94, 103, 436
Gula 49, 73, 117, 148, 174, 177, 178, 179, 202, 231, 242, 253, 255, 274, 277, 291, 297, 304, 316, 324, 325, 326, 330, 377, 533, 534, 543, 550, 551, 553
Gutians 66, 75, 76, 270, 532

H

Haas, Volkert ...63, 94, 98, 103, 120, 121, 145, 153, 159, 165, 192, 232, 234, 235, 236, 237, 241, 246, 257, 258, 281, 284, 322, 323, 560
Haber, Franz 505
Hacohen, Isaac and Jacob 385, 394, 395, 398
Hades Relief 345
Hahn, Johann 404, 405, 560
Ḫaia 152
hair... 16, 21, 40, 45, 46, 61, 71, 106, 107, 144, 145, 154, 160, 162, 164, 191, 192, 193, 199, 200, 201, 213, 214, 226, 227, 231, 232, 237, 252, 257, 261, 265, 276, 297, 303, 311, 340, 341, 349, 368, 375, 382, 388, 399, 407, 413, 417, 420, 422, 423, 424, 425, 427, 428, 458, 463, 488, 543, 549, 553
hairpin 200, 201
Hald, Karl 176, 177, 308, 309, 560
Hallo, William W 560
Ḫammurapi....30, 63, 79, 80, 81, 95, 124, 148, 157, 226, 230, 237, 242, 279, 280, 288, 548, 551, 552, 553
Ḫanigalbateans 82, 182
Hanshu 418
Hariri 94, 420, 436, 548
harp 50, 331, 332
Ḫasīsu 203
Hathor 351
Hattuša 543
hazel 198, 199, 245, 504
Heeßel, Nils 167, 170, 215, 219, 370, 560
Heine, Heinrich 367
Heliodor 522, 560
hemp 246, 257, 261
Ḫendursanga 188
Hera 43, 239, 402
Hercules 279, 357
Hermes 205, 329, 377
Herodot 560
Hesiod 239, 412, 535, 560
hierodule 51, 241, 544, 551
Hill, Julia Butterfly 483, 560
Hittites 38, 79, 81, 82, 149, 176, 237, 328, 357, 422
Hohlenstein-Stadel 15, 17, 434
Homer 239, 361, 402, 403
homosexual 533
Horowitz, Wayne 210, 560
Huber, Irene 235, 560
Ḫubur 217
Huldra 425
Ḫumbaba 197
humours 396, 397, 398
Hurrian 79, 82, 260, 333, 351, 357, 543, 549
Hurrians 7, 81, 82
Hurwitz, Siegmund 359, 371, 381, 383, 401, 402, 560
Ḫuwawa 124, 288, 407
Hydra 151, 250, 357
hyena 11, 18, 103, 122, 128, 130, 183, 276, 277, 290

I

Ibbisîn 77
ibex 201, 215, 235, 254, 359
Id 166, 196, 305
Ida ....*See* Id
Iddindagan 46, 330, 344
Idlu Lilî 187, 368
Ifrah, Georges 34, 314, 315, 327, 560
Igigi 151, 164, 315, 498
Ilaba 75, 148, 317
Inanna 32, 35, 36, 39, 40, 42, 45, 46, 48, 49, 51, 52, 55, 60, 71, 72, 74, 77, 100, 101, 102, 116, 120, 124, 144, 148, 150, 152, 157, 159, 161, 162, 163, 164, 171, 173, 175, 176, 177, 178, 179, 180, 181, 186, 192, 197, 202, 203, 207, 208, 209, 218, 221, 224, 226, 231, 234, 236, 242, 250, 271, 275, 310, 315, 316, 317, 323, 326, 330, 335, 337, 344, 349, 351, 358, 359, 360, 361, 362, 363, 381, 407, 520, 532, 533, 536, 537, 540, 541, 542, 543, 545, 546, 547, 549, 550, 551, 553, 554, 555, 556, 561, 562
incense .. 46, 60, 120, 150, 160, 202, 207, 213, 214, 232, 240, 261, 264, 271, 288, 291, 298, 311, 323, 430, 452, 454, 479, 498, 552
Indus Valley Culture 546
initiation 61, 63, 196, 275, 302, 398, 406, 421, 460, 465, 472, 499, 500
Irnina 55, 75, 114, 122, 124, 141, 157, 175, 186, 316, 359, 472, 513, 555
iron 85, 87, 94, 258, 367, 405, 422, 423, 424, 425, 502
Isaiah 163, 370
Išḫara 175, 237, 248, 252, 553
Isib ....*See* Išib
Isimud 172
Isin......7, 45, 46, 48, 51, 52, 77, 78, 79, 83, 84, 148, 156, 157, 174, 177, 181, 197, 202, 224, 226, 253, 255, 264, 270, 534, 535, 536, 537, 543, 563
Iškur 69, 117, 152, 157, 237, 252, 316, 323, 520, 535
Islam 90, 357, 375, 395, 400, 438, 550, 558, 566
Išmedagan 80, 144
Ištar 8, 32, 42, 51, 55, 60, 73, 74, 94, 96, 97, 102, 116, 120, 124, 141, 144, 148, 150, 152, 153, 164, 172, 173, 175, 176, 177, 178, 180, 202, 203, 208, 209, 210, 211, 218, 219, 220, 221, 224, 226, 230, 231, 232, 236, 237, 238, 241, 242, 248, 257, 271, 275, 290, 294, 300, 303, 310, 316, 317, 323, 324, 325, 326, 327, 343, 344, 348, 349, 350, 351, 353, 355, 356, 359, 367, 378, 381, 387, 496, 520, 533, 534, 537, 540, 544, 545, 546, 548, 549, 550, 551, 553, 555
Ištaran 252

J

Jacobsen, Thorkild ... 48, 49, 51, 121, 145, 147, 148, 149, 150, 152, 159, 162, 178, 179, 194, 196, 198, 218, 238, 350, 360, 363, 535, 550, 560
jade ... 305, 417
Jaritz, Kurt ... 560
jaundice ... 122, 167, 215, 300, 301
Jesuits ... 58, 525
Jettmar, Karl ... 425, 561
Josephus, Flavius ... 352
Julian ... 90, 95, 557, 562
Jung, Carl G. ... 42, 348
juniper ... 21, 120, 152, 155, 160, 200, 201, 323, 504
Jutzi, Sebastian ... 561

K

Ka 107, 167, 248, 260
Kālāgni ... 500
Kalaḫ ... 208, 544
Kalam ... 71, 544
Kaldu ... 85
Kalḫu ... 203, 205, 541, 544
Kālī. 10, 94, 102, 103, 105, 114, 119, 200, 308, 348, 392, 399, 431, 432, 436, 440, 442, 449, 457, 459, 463, 465, 491, 498, 500, 559
Kālī Kaula ... 447, 499, 559
Kâlum ... 544
Ka-muš-i-gue ... 107, 167, 248
Kanisurra ... 231
Kārrtikeya ... 93, 427
Karzida ... 77
Kassites ... 7, 81, 82, 535, 555
Kattner, Ellen ... 423, 561
Kaulajñāna Nirṇaya ... 307, 434, 561
Kazallu ... 79, 252, 545
Keith, Lierre ... 221, 495, 508, 518, 561
Keš ... 72, 77, 173, 545, 551
Ki 116, 144, 151, 164, 171, 178, 187, 258, 260, 267, 292
Kiš32, 68, 70, 74, 79, 231, 242, 532, 535, 545
Kisiga ... 163
Kisikil Lilla ... 267, 360, 362, 364
Kisurra ... 79, 175
Kittu ... 49, 117, 219
Klengel, Horst ... 124, 236, 561
Klimburg, Max ... 425, 561
knot ... 162, 202, 244, 258, 310
Koch, Heidemarie ... 181, 561
Köcher, Franz. 98, 99, 102, 103, 105, 106, 108, 121, 145, 155, 157, 158, 159, 161, 163, 165, 167, 170, 179, 183, 187, 189, 190, 191, 192, 194, 196, 197, 198, 201, 204, 207, 209, 219, 220, 221, 226, 228, 229, 230, 232, 237, 240, 241, 244, 246, 248, 253, 258, 263, 266, 270, 273, 300, 301, 302, 561
Kohn, Livia ... 305, 306, 561
Kongzi ... 419, 483, 522, 523
Krama ... 442, 450, 452, 460, 461, 526
Kramer, Samuel Noah.. 32, 36, 46, 48, 51, 107, 159, 176, 291, 293, 357, 359, 360, 362, 363, 385, 561, 564
Krebernik, Manfred ... 167, 171, 176, 561
Kṛṣṇa ... 93, 205
Kuar ... 545
Kuara ... *See* Kuar
Kula ... 432, 446, 447, 450, 452, 460, 526, 557
Kulacūḍāmaṇi Tantra ... 491, 561
Kur ... 35, 207, 357, 359, 536, 537, 542, 546, 556
Kurigalzu I ... 60, 82
Kurigalzu II ... 82
Kūrma Purāṇa ... 149, 561
Küster, Hansjörg ... 27, 504, 561
Kutha ... 163, 534, 537, 546

L

Labartu ... 97, 562, 563, 565
Labaşu ... 102, 190, 267, 273, 364, 368
Lagaš ... 60, 70, 71, 72, 75, 77, 117, 142, 148, 157, 161, 174, 179, 200, 203, 219, 221, 264, 270, 296, 534, 536, 537, 540, 541, 542, 546, 551, 554
Laitman, Michael ... 561
Lamassu ... 253, 273, 350, 400
Lamašti ... 93, 97, 273, 422
Lamaštu ... 3, 6, 7, 8, 9, 10, 51, 54, 70, 92, 93, 94, 97, 98, 99, 100, 101, 102, 103, 104, 105, 107, 108, 109, 110, 113, 114, 115, 116, 118, 119, 120, 121, 122, 125, 126, 127, 128, 129, 130, 131, 132, 133, 134, 135, 136, 137, 138, 139, 140, 141, 142, 143, 144, 145, 146, 150, 153, 154, 155, 156, 157, 158, 159, 160, 161, 162, 164, 165, 166, 167, 169, 170, 171, 173, 174, 177, 178, 179, 180, 181, 182, 183, 184, 185, 186, 187, 188, 189, 190, 191, 193, 194, 197, 198, 199, 200, 201, 203, 204, 205, 207, 208, 210, 211, 213, 214, 215, 217, 218, 220, 221, 224, 226, 227, 228, 229, 230, 231, 232, 233, 234, 235, 236, 237, 238, 239, 240, 241, 242, 243, 244, 245, 246, 248, 252, 253, 255, 258, 261, 263, 265, 266, 267, 270, 271, 272, 273, 274, 275, 276, 277, 278, 279, 280, 281, 282, 284, 285, 290, 298, 299, 300, 301, 302, 303, 304, 310, 317, 322, 323, 324, 337, 340, 345, 346, 347, 350, 354, 358, 359, 360, 362, 363, 364, 368, 370, 372, 377, 383, 388, 390, 398, 400, 402, 405, 407, 412, 415, 418, 419, 420, 421, 422, 425, 434, 436, 446, 457, 468, 471, 472, 474, 475, 476, 480, 481, 483, 484, 489, 493, 496, 497, 498, 503, 506, 509, 521, 524, 526, 527, 528, 533, 551, 559, 561, 564, 566
lamb ... 160, 211, 229
Lambert, Wilfred. 54, 106, 109, 120, 147, 148, 150, 151, 167, 170, 183, 275, 276, 278, 562
Lamia ... 8, 93, 94, 97, 370, 402, 403, 404, 405, 406, 407, 436
Langdon, Stephen ... 121, 155, 161, 163, 198, 200, 266, 344, 562
Laozi ... 418, 478, 524, 562
lapis lazuli ... 78, 119, 257, 323, 532, 535, 539
Larsa ... 7, 45, 46, 48, 51, 60, 72, 77, 78, 79, 84, 157, 160, 179, 181, 224, 226, 241, 270, 288, 344, 364, 534, 535, 536, 537, 538, 544, 547, 553
Latbe ... 381
Leviathan ... 187, 381, 395, 397
libation ... 202, 204, 220, 377, 546
Liezi ... 417, 478, 562
Liji523, 562

Lilith ... 8, 10, 93, 114, 145, 163, 187, 188, 241, 302, 337, 340, 341, 344, 345, 348, 349, 350, 353, 354, 359, 360, 362, 363, 368, 370, 371, 372, 375, 377, 378, 381, 382, 383, 384, 385, 386, 387, 388, 389, 390, 391, 392, 393, 394, 395, 396, 397, 398, 399, 400, 421,436, 557, 560
Lilith Buznai ... 378, 381, 391
Lilith Halbas ... 381, 383
Lilith Yannai ... 381
Lilith Zarni ... 381, 383
Lilitha ... 394
Lilītu ... 93, 187, 267, 273, 274, 277, 281, 285, 298, 301, 345, 348, 349, 351, 353, 359, 360, 362, 363, 364, 368, 369, 372, 387, 390, 551
Lilû ... 8, 93, 169, 187, 211, 212, 267, 274, 277, 281, 285, 298, 301, 303, 345, 350, 360, 362, 363, 364, 368, 369, 370, 387, 390
Lilum ... 364
linen ... 61, 162, 214, 535, 541, 546
linseed ... 213, 261
lion10, 15, 16, 18, 93, 103, 111, 122, 124, 143, 145, 146, 157, 186, 197, 198, 203, 214, 215, 236, 244, 276, 281, 303, 323, 334, 343, 344, 345, 350, 359, 407, 413, 415, 424, 425, 434, 436, 443, 446, 453, 456, 464, 506, 540
lioness ... 16, 18, 120, 121, 183, 184, 185, 192, 197, 276
lion-man ... 93, 281, 413, 415
Lipitištar ... 148, 157, 264, 280, 538
liquorice ... 165
living creature ... 439
Lobasta ... 422
Loki ... 422
Lopez, Donald ... 21, 445, 447, 562
lotus ... 448, 449, 455, 456, 457, 458, 459, 460, 463, 464
Lü Buwei ... 306
Lü, Buwei ... 306, 307, 559, 562
ludus latrunculorum ... 361
Lugal ... 175, 203, 547, 555
Lugalbanda ... 46, 148, 186, 323, 543, 554
Lugalirra ... 157, 163
Lugalzagesi ... 72, 74, 144, 148, 175, 537, 546, 554
LUKUR ... 51, 536, 539, 547, 550, 554
Lullubaean ... 182
Lu-maḫ ... 547
Lurker ... 107
lute ... 330, 331, 332, 503, 546
lyre ... 329, 331, 538, 553

M

Ma, Shutian ... 420, 562
Magan ... 535, 546, 548
Magda ... 155, 546
Mahābhārata ... 362, 425, 426, 430, 431, 432, 436, 453, 562
Mahalath ... 387, 389, 390, 395
maḫhû ... 547
Maḫḫûtu ... 209
Māmit ... 267
Māmitu(m) ... 117, 274
Manasā ... 103, 458
Mancuso, Stefano ... 496, 511, 562
Mandean ... 378
mane ... 16, 18, 122, 180, 183, 263, 457
Maništušu ... 75, 181
Maqlû .. 92, 101, 120, 154, 163, 177, 182, 199, 212, 214, 230, 234, 243, 250, 271, 273, 275, 280, 281, 282, 284, 285, 291, 297, 299, 300, 304, 305, 310, 313, 497, 498, 533, 549, 562
Māra ... 458
Marcellinus, Ammianus ... 95, 562
Marduk ... 27, 52, 54, 55, 59, 63, 80, 83, 84, 88, 90, 92, 102, 109, 114, 121, 147, 148, 149, 151, 152, 153, 157, 160, 171, 174, 177, 178, 189, 199, 202, 203, 205, 210, 217, 218, 226, 237, 239, 244, 250, 253, 254, 274, 281, 282, 285, 291, 297, 304, 308, 309, 310, 311, 316, 323, 324, 325, 326, 327, 370, 497, 533, 534, 535, 538, 540, 541, 547, 548, 551, 553
Mardukšapikzermati ... 85
Mari44, 79, 144, 165, 200, 209, 235, 337, 364, 514, 539, 547, 548, 549, 550, 552, 553
Martu ... 78, 117, 224, 226
maskim ... *See* maškim
mašmaššu ... 58, 105, 109, 115, 119, 142, 176, 198, 199, 281, 284, 297, 298, 324, 532, 548
Matronit ... 353, 389, 396
Meador, Betty de Shong ... 158, 218, 219, 221, 562
Medes ... 87, 89, 422, 520, 533, 544
Meier, Gerhard ... 214, 275, 281, 282, 284, 285, 305, 562
Meluḫḫa ... 535, 546, 548
menstrual blood 159, 161, 191, 220, 276, 303, 307, 434, 450, 452, 453, 459, 464
menstruation ... 220, 298, 381, 464
Mešaru ... 160
Meskiaggašer ... 148
microbes 25, 26, 104, 221, 296, 481, 489, 492, 496, 505, 515, 516, 518, 519, 525
Midrash ... 8, 187, 375, 391
Milky Way ... 166, 217, 305
Min ... 175, 351
Mirach ... 10, 107, 167, 248, 279
Mithras ... 93, 413, 415
Mittanni ... 79, 82
mongoose ... 210, 211, 212
mound ... 153, 178, 525, 535, 555
Mozi ... 484, 523
mud ... 23, 25, 27, 28, 38, 107, 166, 198, 276, 455, 463, 464, 468, 480, 549
mudrā ... 452, 464, 465
Mudras ... 558, 562
Mughtasils ... 376
muḫḫutu ... 547
Mursili I ... 81
Muru ... 75, 175, 176, 549
Murum ... *See* Muru
Muš ... 250, 549
Mušītu ... 116
Muštabba-abba ... 106
mustard ... 261
Myhrmann, D.W. ... 562
Mylitta ... 241
myrtle ... 155, 201, 293

N

Naamah 387, 389, 390, 391, 393, 395, 398
Nabopoplessar...89
Nabû 52, 85, 86, 92, 96, 149, 197, 203, 205, 206, 208, 209, 214, 245, 246, 250, 325, 326, 327, 520, 533, 534, 535, 541, 544, 551
nadītu(m) 541, 547
Nadītu(m) 550
Naḫur..236, 237, 238
Nammu .. 54, 55, 116, 159, 164, 171, 176, 194, 196, 236, 308, 309, 330, 352, 538, 539
Namtar.......................142, 192, 235, 267, 271, 324, 357, 534
Nanay... 52, 117, 120, 205, 231, 349, 359, 370, 377, 534, 545, 547, 553, 555
Nanna .. 23, 52, 74, 76, 77, 117, 152, 157, 164, 173, 224, 250, 271, 316, 497, 536, 538, 541, 542, 545, 550, 555, 556
Nanše. 148, 150, 157, 179, 196, 270, 323, 331, 536, 538, 542, 546, 553
Naramsîn 75, 124, 148, 149, 181, 186, 255, 317
Narunde...181
Nebuchadnezzar I 84
Nei-yeh 564
Nentwig, Wolfgang 228, 562
Nergal .. 55, 117, 122, 143, 151, 152, 157, 161, 163, 173, 192, 198, 204, 231, 276, 316, 317, 324, 326, 327, 344, 345, 357, 358, 367, 377, 520, 534, 537, 546, 550, 551, 553
nerves 106, 170, 215, 241, 483, 484, 486, 487, 488, 489, 490, 510, 511
nested loops 101
Neumann, Erich 348, 562
Nibru 550, 551
Nidaba 35, 49, 96, 117, 148, 152, 175, 183, 205, 218, 267, 271, 292, 313, 374, 538
nightmare 87, 117, 187, 228, 421, 433, 522
Ninazu .. 55, 152, 178, 236, 250, 252, 291, 357, 358, 537, 538, 540, 542, 553
Nin-dingir 172, 537, 551
Ningal.........................100, 101, 173, 237, 535, 537, 552, 555
Ningirim ....*See* Ningirima
Ningirima . 49, 72, 75, 148, 152, 171, 174, 175, 176, 177, 179, 194, 195, 211, 214, 231, 252, 260, 297, 308, 309, 324, 337, 483, 539, 548, 549, 553, 555
Ningirin ....*See* Ningirima
Ningirsu . 49, 52, 55, 65, 72, 75, 102, 148, 152, 161, 174, 178, 186, 198, 200, 219, 221, 230, 250, 253, 271, 290, 316, 317, 323, 324, 325, 536, 537, 538, 540, 541, 542, 546, 547
Ningišzida.............42, 148, 172, 175, 198, 250, 252, 359, 542
Ningublam 157, 173
Ninḫursag 55, 71, 72, 117, 148, 152, 172, 173, 202, 203, 238, 252, 265, 304, 316, 324, 325, 535, 536, 538, 540, 542, 543, 545, 548, 550, 551, 553, 554, 555, 556
Nininsinna... *See* Ninisina
Ninisina 49, 177, 242, 253, 297, 537, 543, 551
Ninkarrag.............73, 117, 174, 177, 178, 179, 253, 324, 325
Ninkasi 172, 202
Ninki..............................54, 72, 172, 202, 203, 277, 316, 364
Ninkigal 117
Ninlil..... 61, 144, 148, 151, 152, 163, 203, 205, 206, 208, 230, 246, 247, 276, 277, 315, 316, 324, 326, 363, 364, 520, 533, 534, 535, 545, 550, 551, 552, 553, 554
Ninmaḫ.....................................203, 242, 325, 534, 551, 555
Ninmar 542, 546
Nin-mug 172
Ninsikila 172, 203, 535
Ninšubur..149, 163, 175, 219, 532
Nintinugga..177
Nintu 540, 543, 551, 556
Nintur ....*See* Nintu
Nin-unu-ga 175, 231
Ninurta .49, 55, 65, 86, 94, 102, 144, 145, 149, 153, 172, 173, 174, 176, 178, 186, 202, 219, 220, 221, 235, 236, 250, 252, 271, 290, 316, 324, 325, 326, 520, 534, 535, 537, 539, 542, 543, 544, 547, 550
Nippur 8, 30, 46, 54, 68, 72, 74, 77, 93, 101, 151, 153, 171, 173, 174, 177, 178, 196, 202, 215, 237, 270, 291, 324, 373, 375, 382, 384, 391, 394, 535, 536, 537, 538, 539, 541, 543, 545, 550, 551, 554, 556
Nirṛti 103
Nisaba 35, 49, 72, 96, 117, 148, 152, 164, 171, 183, 205, 218, 237, 267, 271, 292, 299, 313, 359, 374, 538, 545, 547
nitrogen...489, 495, 496, 505, 515
Numušda 144, 157, 250, 252, 545
Nungal 357
nurse 189, 192, 193, 241, 244, 266, 420, 424, 430
Nusku 119, 139, 144, 152, 248, 280, 282, 290, 316, 324, 497, 520, 550

O

oak...20, 198, 245, 512, 516
obsession59, 89, 143, 150, 158, 182, 188, 208, 209, 235, 273, 302, 315, 388, 398, 405, 492, 521, 547
Odysseus 149, 412, 484
Odyssey 402, 412
oil 11, 62, 119, 154, 155, 156, 161, 164, 200, 201, 204, 210, 212, 224, 229, 244, 246, 261, 266, 278, 289, 293, 295, 370, 388, 490, 496, 535, 538, 539, 545, 548
Old Babylonian Hymnody..333
Oldenberg, Hermann.................................110, 432, 562
olive...155, 224, 293
onager 199, 201, 257
onion 213, 261
Opitz, Dietrich 343, 344, 562
Oppenheim, A. Leo..........................229, 290, 561, 562
Orpheus...563
Orphic Hymns 239
Ovid 328, 361

P

Pabilsag 178, 290
Padmasambhava 443, 447, 453, 457, 563
palm 11, 22, 62, 73, 74, 111, 119, 140, 161, 163, 198, 199, 264, 266, 337, 539
Pandey, K.C. 447, 563
panther...279, 322, 417
Papsukkal 172, 193, 219, 290, 324, 535, 545
Parrot, André..184, 344, 563
Pārvatī 114, 431, 446, 500
Pašittu . 70, 122, 158, 166, 167, 187, 190, 215, 248, 300, 301, 302, 390, 398, 400

Patai, Raphael....350, 353, 362, 384, 385, 387, 388, 389, 390, 391, 393, 395, 563
Pazuzu 122, 139, 140, 145, 167, 168, 169, 215, 248, 270, 345, 346, 347, 370, 560
peaches....418, 502
penis.....63, 106, 107, 146, 159, 183, 290, 294, 303, 308, 315
Pentateuch....385
Perlesvaus....395
Perseus....151, 152, 279, 328, 406, 410, 412
Philo....352
Philostratus....402
Philostratus, Flavius....328, 403, 404, 563
Phosphor....495
Pichot, André....211, 313, 314, 315, 563
pig......146, 154, 156, 163, 210, 213, 214, 227, 232, 248, 257, 261, 277, 278, 284, 288, 328, 452
pin....11, 162, 191, 200
pine....124, 161, 199, 421, 502, 504
Pinel, John....490, 563
Pinker, Steven....475, 563
planet...26, 42, 46, 67, 88, 105, 108, 120, 124, 144, 211, 304, 344, 349, 378, 397, 433, 446, 461, 477, 522, 528, 554
Plassmann, J.O.....239, 407, 563
plaster....154, 178, 226, 252, 371, 535, 539
Pleiades....117, 118, 151, 159, 181, 231, 232, 317, 370
Plough....201, 326, 493
Pollan, Michael....495, 563
Pollmer, U.....495, 508, 563
poplar....28, 165, 510
Poseidon....402, 412
Postgate, Nicholas.....6, 76, 98, 120, 124, 144, 165, 200, 224, 278, 557
potassium....291, 486, 495
pregnancy....48, 153, 160, 165, 178, 201, 229, 241, 258, 298, 300, 430, 488, 538
Pritchard, James B.....6, 124, 158, 278, 563
Prophet....205, 399, 547
prostitute.......51, 62, 241, 242, 243, 277, 323, 349, 351, 503, 533, 543, 544, 545, 546, 549, 551
Pythagoras....311, 314, 327, 328, 333, 334, 403, 404

Q

Qadeš....351
qi 306, 307, 501
Qingu....544

R

Rabiṣu....210
rāga....328, 330
raggimu....*See* raggintu
Ramku....552
Reallexikon der Assyriologie......6, 97, 98, 145, 231, 250, 258, 563
reed.....20, 21, 25, 35, 96, 117, 155, 162, 163, 180, 183, 192, 205, 217, 218, 227, 233, 238, 263, 266, 292, 313, 330, 333, 335, 359, 475
Reiner, Erica..20, 187, 198, 202, 213, 274, 292, 310, 324, 563
Remler, G.....301, 563
repetitions....55, 98, 100, 101, 202, 360, 367, 476, 501
Ṛg Veda....110, 431, 432, 450
ribbons....231, 317, 368
Riemschneider, Kaspar....98, 192, 563
Rimsîn....79, 81
Rimuš....75, 181
RlA....*See* Reallexikon der Assyriologie
Robinet, Isabelle....502, 563
rosary....479
Rudra....426, 429, 430, 432, 433, 439

S

Sabaeans....376
Sacred Marriage....7, 38, 43, 45, 46, 48, 124, 192, 330
Sagga....552
SAHG 6, 46, 100, 115, 144, 147, 159, 162, 197, 203, 211, 218, 219, 235, 236, 264, 270, 275, 277, 357, 540, 559, 564
Šakkan....201, 224, 235, 316
Šalmaneser III....87
Šalmaneser IV....87
Šalmaneser V....87
salt......21, 23, 28, 62, 121, 161, 165, 196, 198, 286, 288, 291, 301, 309, 405, 546, 548, 555
Samael....187, 387, 390, 393, 394, 395, 397
Samana....143, 186, 276, 277, 298, 345
Šamaš.....21, 22, 23, 52, 63, 65, 102, 117, 145, 148, 149, 151, 152, 154, 160, 164, 173, 177, 178, 188, 198, 201, 211, 218, 219, 224, 226, 229, 231, 232, 233, 245, 271, 275, 278, 280, 281, 282, 290, 294, 297, 299, 303, 316, 317, 324, 325, 326, 349, 355, 377, 497, 498, 520, 533, 534, 535, 545, 547, 548, 550, 551, 552, 553
Šamḫat....349
Sammuramat....87
Šamšiaddad....79
Samsuiluna....81
sandstorm....121, 540
Sanga....*See* Šangû
Šara....77, 381, 536, 543, 554
Sargon I 36, 48, 56, 68, 70, 74, 75, 77, 78, 84, 86, 87, 95, 124, 141, 175, 181, 207, 237, 272, 327, 532, 535, 536, 538, 543, 544, 545, 546, 554
Sargon II....87, 124, 237, 327, 535, 544
Šarur....193, 218, 219, 235
Saso, Michael....424, 564
Sasson, Jack....27, 74, 564
Satan....167, 377, 378, 381, 382, 390, 394, 395, 399
Šazu....172, 203
scales....67, 304, 328, 329, 331, 332, 333, 334, 412
Schmidt, Klaus....564
Scholem, Gershom....187, 383, 385, 388, 392, 394, 564
Schramm, Wolfgang......58, 93, 107, 118, 142, 145, 154, 218, 224, 240, 264, 272, 273, 564
Schuyler Jones....561
Schwemer, Daniel....145, 162, 212, 564
scorpion....125, 134, 159, 176, 189, 248, 276, 296, 299, 337, 343, 344, 347, 371
Scurlock, Jo Ann..99, 145, 160, 188, 201, 210, 232, 236, 243, 293, 303, 304, 367, 369, 370, 564
Scylla....402
Sea People....84, 237

SEAL (Sources of Akkadian Literature).... 6, 98, 157, 201, 367, 564, 565
Sea-Land 23, 66, 82, 83, 85, 87, 534, 548
Šedu 400
seeder-plough..230, 232, 257, 305
semen 305, 357, 464
Semiramis 87
Semmelweis, Ignaz P. 292
Sendunme...446
Senge Dang Ma 446
Senkereh...344, 547
Sennaḫerib...27, 87, 94
Sepher Ha-Zohar, the...564
serpent .. 93, 97, 106, 110, 122, 126, 130, 173, 175, 176, 178, 211, 212, 214, 217, 237, 248, 250, 252, 279, 322, 335, 357, 360, 362, 388, 389, 399, 407, 413, 414, 415, 429, 460, 481, 500, 501, 540, 542, 543, 545, 555
sesame...155, 200, 202, 535
seven ... 16, 66, 70, 76, 90, 114, 115, 116, 117, 121, 143, 152, 153, 155, 177, 182, 197, 212, 221, 227, 234, 245, 246, 250, 253, 255, 257, 258, 270, 271, 274, 275, 300, 309, 311, 312, 313, 315, 316, 317, 322, 323, 326, 327, 328, 332, 333, 350, 358, 360, 361, 370, 372, 400, 417, 426, 427, 428, 429, 454, 468, 472, 473, 474, 481, 502, 524, 534, 535, 536, 538, 544, 553, 555
sex.... 16, 18, 38, 39, 43, 45, 49, 51, 62, 70, 93, 107, 157, 158, 159, 162, 165, 171, 183, 227, 308, 350, 358, 382, 401, 438, 440, 446, 471, 490, 503, 518, 522, 540, 544, 546
Shanhaijing 417, 564
Shaw, Miranda...........443, 444, 445, 447, 459, 461, 480, 564
Shekinah 353, 386, 387, 389, 396
SIDS................................*See* Sudden Infant Death Syndrome
Siṁhamukhā 93, 191, 420, 437, 444, 446, 447, 448, 450, 456, 457, 458, 459, 460, 461, 462, 463, 464, 465, 468
Sîn .. 23, 73, 74, 76, 77, 90, 117, 124, 134, 148, 149, 152, 157, 164, 172, 173, 178, 201, 224, 226, 227, 250, 253, 254, 271, 276, 285, 291, 294, 303, 316, 324, 325, 326, 327, 377, 497, 520, 533, 534, 535, 538, 541, 545, 551, 555
Sippar....... 63, 69, 79, 101, 150, 153, 160, 208, 231, 238, 240, 244, 538, 541, 544, 547, 549, 552, 553
Siris ....*See* Siriš
Siriš 202
Śiva 103, 205, 307, 420, 427, 429, 430, 431, 432, 433, 438, 442, 446, 448, 458, 459, 460, 461, 500
Skanda 93, 427, 428, 429, 430, 431, 432
slave-girl 285, 391
smith..192
Smith, George 95, 142, 210, 520, 564
smoke 202, 208, 239, 240, 248, 281, 299, 311, 370, 386, 449, 479, 538
snake.. 106, 135, 159, 175, 182, 186, 187, 190, 192, 209, 211, 213, 214, 243, 248, 250, 252, 261, 276, 280, 289, 293, 297, 307, 310, 322, 323, 347, 362, 380, 402, 403, 418, 422, 424, 430, 499, 534, 536, 539, 550
Snake Conjurer 549
Snellgrove, David 439, 455, 564
soap 21, 61, 109, 199, 292, 293, 387, 425
Socrates 361
Soden, W. v.....6, 106, 107, 275, 291, 296, 557, 559, 563, 564
soil..22, 26, 28, 29, 39, 88, 104, 108, 124, 161, 171, 190, 214, 220, 230, 305, 370, 404, 493, 495, 496, 504, 511, 512, 513, 515, 527, 556
Solomon 352, 395, 401
sorcerer 115, 280, 282, 297, 376, 436, 438
South Wind 234, 474
sperm 159, 165, 171, 220, 255, 284, 301, 303, 307, 388, 427, 434, 450, 452, 453, 459, 464, 519
spider 161, 200, 509
spindle. 11, 133, 161, 162, 192, 200, 229, 244, 248, 255, 266, 310
Spira, Nathan...395
spittle 154, 189, 228, 237, 239, 271, 284, 301, 310, 527
Spitzer, Manfred 521, 565
star 10, 22, 35, 70, 107, 109, 118, 120, 145, 150, 167, 172, 211, 224, 227, 242, 248, 252, 254, 279, 331, 333, 334, 348, 398, 444, 474, 476, 489, 523, 527
Stein, Anja 422, 565
Stesichoros 402
Stinglwagner 511, 558
Stol, Martin .. 98, 129, 148, 164, 190, 301, 364, 370, 565, 566
Strabo..565
string 11, 29, 136, 161, 162, 192, 200, 204, 253, 255, 257, 258, 266, 310, 327, 329, 330, 331, 332, 333, 334, 468, 478, 479, 502
Subartu... 80, 553
Sud 152, 553
Sudden Infant Death Syndrome 302
Suen 23, 72, 74, 76, 77, 117, 152, 164, 173, 224, 250, 316, 497, 536, 555
Sukkal 553
Šulgi 48, 56, 76, 77, 78, 84, 200, 270, 330, 361, 520, 538, 541, 542, 555
Šulgisimtu 76
Šulpae................ 107, 173, 192, 232, 285, 304, 542, 545, 556
sulphur 154, 214, 261, 286, 288, 294, 305, 370, 424
Sumerian King Lists 69, 70, 545, 546, 548
Sumuabum 79
Šurpu 20, 62, 92, 100, 101, 115, 155, 159, 161, 163, 183, 198, 202, 213, 219, 226, 265, 274, 292, 299, 310, 324, 363, 498, 563
Susa 52, 68, 180, 182, 290, 539, 546, 553
Šusîn 45, 95
Šusuen 77, 159
Sutuean 182, 236
Sutueans.. 237, 238
Šuzianna 550
Swaab, Dick 488, 565
symbiosis...................................496, 516, 518, 519, 520

T

Tacitus 421, 503
Talmud 8, 351, 375, 377, 387, 388, 389, 565
tamarisk .. 21, 28, 62, 111, 154, 163, 198, 199, 217, 218, 238, 240, 271, 284, 309
Tammet, Daniel... 311, 565
Tantra.... 10, 57, 103, 105, 307, 308, 362, 431, 432, 434, 436, 438, 439, 442, 446, 447, 448, 452, 456, 459, 460, 461, 463, 465, 491, 498, 500, 501, 560, 561, 565, 566
tapas.. 189, 498, 499

Tašmetu(m) 92, 231
tavern . 220, 221, 224, 252, 288, 298, 323, 370, 532, 540, 552
Terebinth 199
Tethys 239
thistles 23, 119, 163, 482
Thompson, Reginald Campbell 92, 98, 102, 155, 163, 228, 234, 235, 236, 267, 274, 300, 308, 309, 310, 311, 322, 368, 401, 402, 558, 565
thorn 161, 163, 204, 266, 274, 303, 506
Thureau-Dangin, F 191, 315, 356, 565
thyme 164, 232, 257, 293, 295
Tiāmat 10, 145, 189, 196, 201, 205, 217, 238, 239, 250, 308, 317, 497, 544, 548
Tibbs, Clint 208, 209, 565
Tiglatpilesar I 85, 87, 371
Tiglatpilesar III 87, 371
Tigris 11, 22, 27, 65, 66, 90, 159, 166, 171, 181, 237, 238, 275, 291, 305, 308, 309, 376, 533, 534, 536, 539, 540, 544, 553, 565
Tišpak 250, 324, 540
tree 40, 73, 119, 120, 124, 155, 161, 164, 165, 179, 186, 198, 214, 217, 220, 250, 261, 264, 332, 335, 337, 360, 361, 362, 430, 433, 458, 475, 481, 482, 483, 496, 504, 510, 511, 512, 513, 515, 522, 526
Trika 432, 442, 460, 461
Tsong kha pa 444
TUAT 6, 144, 146, 153, 239, 372, 558, 559
Tubal Cain 389
Tulkutininurta I 82, 83

U

Ubšukinna 550
Ubšu-ukinna See Ubšukinna
Udug 264, 265, 270, 474
Ugarit 93, 239, 350, 357, 372, 554, 557, 560, 566
ugbabtum *See* Ugbatum
Ugbatum 554
Ukkina 554
Ulaya 166, 217
Umma 48, 49, 71, 72, 75, 77, 142, 202, 203, 381, 536, 543, 546, 551, 554, 556
Underworld . 40, 71, 72, 82, 97, 107, 110, 116, 119, 142, 143, 145, 146, 160, 163, 164, 166, 171, 177, 178, 183, 186, 192, 201, 203, 204, 207, 208, 217, 219, 220, 226, 231, 235, 264, 265, 288, 300, 304, 316, 323, 345, 346, 353, 357, 358, 359, 360, 362, 372, 403, 520, 532, 534, 535, 536, 537, 538, 540, 542, 545, 546, 554, 556
Ungnad, Arthur 124, 145, 213, 218, 250, 274, 281, 282, 284, 285, 289, 324, 325, 358, 364, 565
Unug 67, 175, 554
Upaniṣads 110, 172, 452, 454, 563
Ur 7, 30, 44, 45, 47, 48, 52, 54, 60, 71, 72, 74, 76, 77, 78, 79, 84, 95, 101, 130, 142, 145, 148, 156, 157, 163, 173, 176, 179, 181, 193, 194, 200, 224, 230, 270, 296, 297, 313, 317, 330, 336, 343, 361, 520, 534, 535, 536, 538, 539, 541, 542, 543, 545, 547, 548, 551, 552, 554, 555
Uraš 151, 253
Urnammu 45, 48, 76, 280, 343, 536
Ursa major 152, 326, 426
Ursa minor 151, 203
Uruk 7, 31, 34, 36, 37, 38, 45, 49, 52, 60, 67, 68, 72, 74, 79, 97, 98, 100, 101, 117, 120, 137, 150, 157, 171, 175, 177, 180, 186, 190, 193, 208, 218, 224, 227, 231, 275, 278, 288, 316, 317, 323, 326, 327, 335, 358, 360, 362, 498, 503, 532, 534, 536, 537, 540, 545, 546, 547, 549, 553, 554, 555, 559, 565
Urukagina 221
Urum 555
Urzababa 74, 148
Usmû 172, 203
Uttu 162, 310
Utu 20, 21, 22, 23, 52, 63, 65, 72, 102, 117, 144, 148, 152, 153, 157, 160, 164, 173, 188, 201, 218, 224, 271, 297, 316, 317, 360, 362, 497, 498, 520, 536, 547, 548, 553, 556
Utukku 107, 118, 264, 265, 273, 317, 474
Uznu 203

V

vagina 146, 159
Vajrapāṇi 439, 459
veil 89, 201, 243
Venus15, 42, 46, 120, 124, 127, 149, 151, 211, 344, 349, 378, 495, 554, 556
Vermaak, Fanie 361, 565
Vespasian 402, 421
Vijñāna Bhairava 500, 565
Viola, Alessandra 496, 511, 562
virus 302, 497, 518, 519
void 438, 442, 449, 455, 457, 460
Voodoo 57, 149, 522
vulva 45, 63, 107, 146, 159, 161, 188, 191, 217, 240, 241, 248, 275, 294, 315, 358, 450

W

Wallis Budge, Sir E. A. 141, 233, 376, 399, 565
wand *See* êru
Wasserman, Nathan 98, 121, 157, 159, 211, 217, 241, 367, 565
Waterwheel 501
Wei Boyang 307, 501, 565
Weidner Chronicle 84, 253
West, D.R. 121, 154, 187, 188, 204, 255, 566
Westenholt, Joan 566
White, David Gordon 434, 436, 447, 566
Wiggermann, Frans A.M 98, 108, 114, 120, 121, 129, 145, 159, 167, 170, 191, 198, 219, 226, 229, 234, 235, 236, 243, 264, 272, 301, 350, 364, 566
Wilcke, C. 305, 566
wild boar 11, 154, 277, 278, 424, 432, 509, 512
Wilhelm, Richard 38, 306, 404, 523, 558, 559, 562
Wilkinson, Toby 84, 566
willow 22, 104, 165, 174, 293, 510
witch . 109, 154, 156, 182, 243, 279, 280, 281, 282, 285, 294, 296, 297, 298, 383, 400, 401, 404, 405, 421, 434, 446, 544, 552
wolf 11, 103, 106, 121, 128, 146, 154, 156, 183, 192, 197, 227, 276, 277, 371, 372, 493, 506, 509
Wolkenstein, Diane 359, 360, 362, 363, 561
Wong, Eva 307, 566

wood....35, 104, 119, 122, 124, 154, 160, 161, 165, 192, 198, 255, 264, 272, 284, 291, 329, 332, 360, 418, 421, 497, 498, 502, 516, 532
wool.....79, 161, 162, 178, 200, 201, 213, 214, 231, 232, 255, 257, 258, 265, 266, 278, 294, 310, 424, 490, 535, 548
Worthington, Martin 98, 566
Wu 415, 418, 562
Wu Ding 415
Wu Xian 418
Wuji 477

X

Ximu....................94
Xiwangmu.......10, 94, 103, 149, 200, 416, 417, 418, 436, 502

Y

Yakṣa....................430, 433
Yakṣī....................433, 435
Yeshe Tsogyal 447, 563
Ygrath....................387, 389, 390, 395, 398
YHVH ... 57, 187, 351, 352, 353, 377, 382, 383, 384, 386, 387, 395, 397, 398, 399
Yijing....................307
Yogīnī....................191, 307, 434, 439, 447, 566
Yü, Chün-Fang 439, 566

Z

Zababa....................55, 317, 324, 534, 545
Zabalam....................72, 555, 556
Zagros Mountains 124, 237, 540
Zarpānītu(m) 52, 152, 153, 205, 323
Zeus....................43, 116, 205, 377, 402, 407, 412
ziggurat 67, 181, 258, 507, 534, 535, 536
Zimrilim 80, 548
Zohar. 187, 188, 384, 386, 387, 388, 389, 390, 391, 393, 394, 395, 396, 397, 398, 561, 566
Zwemer, Samuel 401, 566

www.ingramcontent.com/pod-product-compliance
Lightning Source LLC
Chambersburg PA
CBHW080529300426
44111CB00017B/2657